ESSENTIALS *of* PSYCHOLOGY

ESSENTIALS *of* PSYCHOLOGY

***Essentials of Psychology,* Fourth Edition,** offers an **integrated pedagogical system** designed to help students get the most out of their reading. Hallmark features include an *outline, a preview statement, preview questions, instructional captions, In Review charts, and a marginal glossary.* Each chapter ends with an **Active Review** that includes a *Linkages diagram, a chapter summary, Learn by Doing* and *Step into*

Action sections, a review of key terms, and multiple-choice questions.

Two optional chapters on *Industrial/ Organizational Psychology* and *Neuropsychology* can be packaged with the text upon request. Please consult your sales representative for further details.

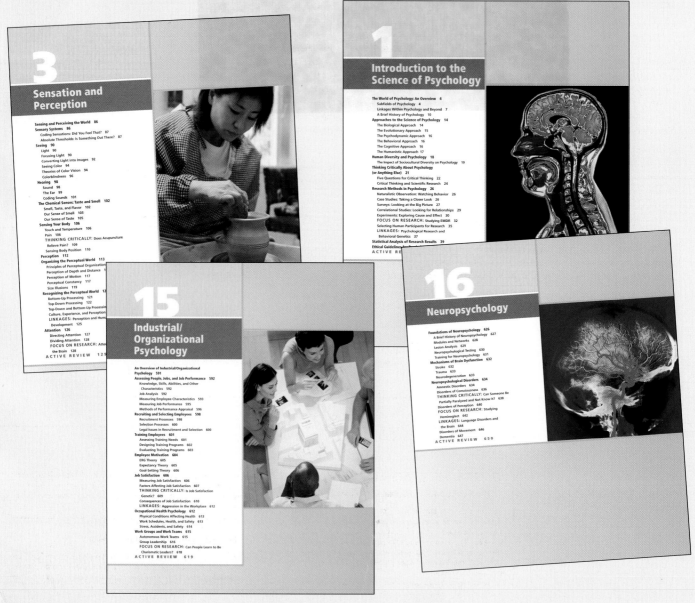

An Integrated Pedagogical System

Each chapter opens with a full **outline**, a **brief preview statement**, and a list of **preview questions** related to each main section of the chapter. These preview questions are repeated at the start of each section and within the chapter summary.

PREVIEW

Have you ever forgotten where you parked your car? Have you ever had a name on the tip of your tongue, but couldn't quite recall it? Researchers in the field of memory explore these common experiences. *Memory* is a complex process of storing and retrieving information. You use different kinds of memory for different types of information, such as personal experiences, specific skills, and abstract concepts. Once information is stored in your memory, recalling it can sometimes be difficult. In this chapter, you will learn about some techniques that can help you to retrieve memories. What psychologists have learned about memory has been used to create study techniques that really work!

← **Preview Statement**

Reading this chapter will help you to answer the following questions:

▶ How does information turn into memories? 208
▶ What am I most likely to remember? 213
▶ How do I retrieve stored memories? 218
▶ How accurate are my memories? 222
▶ What causes me to forget things? 227
▶ How does my brain change when I store a memory? 234
▶ How can I remember more information? 237

← **Preview Questions**

"'ll make him an offer he can't refuse." "I'll be back." "Trust no one." "Life is [...] ow me the money." "Is that u heard these words? They *minator, The X-Files, Forrest e a Millionaire.* Can you say d do you know which clas- k a friend who knows about tion is Rick, the café owner tually said this often-quoted

useful information from all d the nature of memory— how you forget.

Forgetting

▶ **What causes me to forget things?**

← **Preview Question**

The frustrations of forgetting—where you left your keys, the answer to a test question, an anniversary—are apparent to most people nearly every day (Neisser, 2000b). Let's look more closely at the nature of forgetting and what causes it.

The Nature of Memory

▶ How does information turn into memories?

Memory is a funny thing. You might be able to remember the name of your first-grade teacher, but not the name of someone you met five minutes ago. Mathematician John Griffith estimated that in an average lifetime, a person stores roughly five hundred

208

Summary

← **Preview Question**

THE NATURE OF MEMORY

▶ **How does information turn into memories?**

Human memory depends on a complex mental system. There are three basic memory processes. *Encoding* transforms stimulus information into some type of mental representation. Material can be encoded by *acoustic* (sound), *visual* (appearance), or *semantic* (meaning) *codes. Storage* maintains information in the memory system over time. *Retrieval* is the process of gaining access to previously stored information.

Most psychologists agree that there are at least three types of

capacity of long-term memory to store new information is extremely large and perhaps unlimited. The appearance of a *primacy effect* and a *recency effect* suggests that short-term and long-term memory may be distinct systems.

RETRIEVING MEMORIES

▶ **How do I retrieve stored memories?**

Retrieval cues help people remember things that they would otherwise not be able to recall. The effectiveness of retrieval cues follows the *encoding specificity principle:* Cues help retrieval only if they

An Integrated Pedagogical System

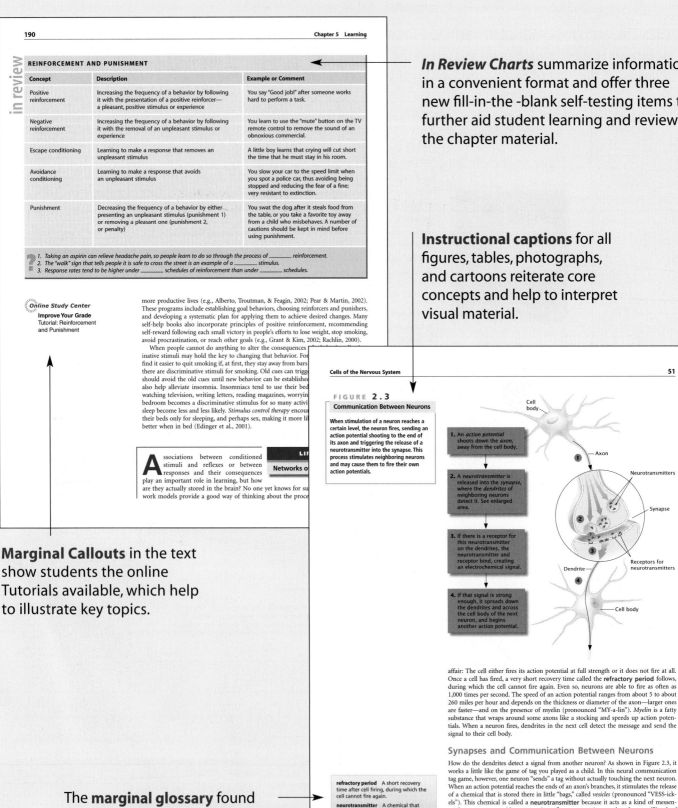

In Review Charts summarize information in a convenient format and offer three new fill-in-the -blank self-testing items to further aid student learning and review of the chapter material.

Instructional captions for all figures, tables, photographs, and cartoons reiterate core concepts and help to interpret visual material.

Marginal Callouts in the text show students the online Tutorials available, which help to illustrate key topics.

The **marginal glossary** found throughout the text defines key terms on the appropriate pages.

---

in review

REINFORCEMENT AND PUNISHMENT

Concept	Description	Example or Comment
Positive reinforcement	Increasing the frequency of a behavior by following it with the presentation of a positive reinforcer—a pleasant, positive stimulus or experience	You say "Good job!" after someone works hard to perform a task.
Negative reinforcement	Increasing the frequency of a behavior by following it with the removal of an unpleasant stimulus or experience	You learn to use the "mute" button on the TV remote control to remove the sound of an obnoxious commercial.
Escape conditioning	Learning to make a response that removes an unpleasant stimulus	A little boy learns that crying will cut short the time that he must stay in his room.
Avoidance conditioning	Learning to make a response that avoids an unpleasant stimulus	You slow your car to the speed limit when you spot a police car, thus avoiding being stopped and reducing the fear of a fine; very resistant to extinction.
Punishment	Decreasing the frequency of a behavior by either presenting an unpleasant stimulus (punishment 1) or removing a pleasant one (punishment 2, or penalty)	You swat the dog after it steals food from the table, or you take a favorite toy away from a child who misbehaves. A number of cautions should be kept in mind before using punishment.

1. Taking an aspirin can relieve headache pain, so people learn to do so through the process of _____ reinforcement.
2. The "walk" sign tells people it is safe to cross the street is an example of a _____ stimulus.
3. Response rates tend to be higher under _____ schedules of reinforcement than under _____ schedules.

Online Study Center
Improve Your Grade
Tutorial: Reinforcement and Punishment

more productive lives (e.g., Alberto, Troutman, & Feagin, 2002; Pear & Martin, 2002). These programs include establishing goal behaviors, choosing reinforcers and punishers, and developing a systematic plan for applying them to achieve desired changes. Many self-help books also incorporate principles of positive reinforcement, recommending self-reward following each small victory in people's efforts to lose weight, stop smoking, avoid procrastination, or reach other goals (e.g., Grant & Kim, 2002; Rachlin, 2000).

When people cannot do anything to alter the consequences of their behavior, dis-inative stimuli may hold the key to changing that behavior. For [example], people find it easier to quit smoking if, at first, they stay away from bars [or others where] there are discriminative stimuli for smoking. Old cues can trigger [old habits, so one] should avoid the old cues until new behavior can be established. [This principle can] also help alleviate insomnia. Insomniacs tend to use their bed[rooms] for eating, watching television, writing letters, reading magazines, worrying, [and so on. The] bedroom becomes a discriminative stimulus for so many activities [that falling] sleep become less and less likely. *Stimulus control therapy* encour[ages them to use] their beds only for sleeping, and perhaps sex, making it more li[kely that they sleep] better when in bed (Edinger et al., 2001).

Associations between conditioned stimuli and reflexes or between responses and their consequences play an important role in learning, but how are they actually stored in the brain? No one yet knows for su[re], [but net]work models provide a good way of thinking about the proce[ss].

FIGURE 2.3

Communication Between Neurons

When stimulation of a neuron reaches a certain level, the neuron fires, sending an action potential shooting to the end of its axon and triggering the release of a neurotransmitter into the synapse. This process stimulates neighboring neurons and may cause them to fire their own action potentials.

1. An *action potential* shoots down the *axon*, away from the cell body.

2. A *neurotransmitter* is released into the *synapse*, where the *dendrites* of neighboring neurons detect it. See enlarged area.

3. If there is a receptor for this neurotransmitter on the dendrites, the neurotransmitter and receptor bind, creating an electrochemical signal.

4. If that signal is strong enough, it spreads down the dendrites and across the cell body of the next neuron, and begins another action potential.

affair: The cell either fires its action potential at full strength or it does not fire at all. Once a cell has fired, a very short recovery time called the **refractory period** follows, during which the cell cannot fire again. Even so, neurons are able to fire as often as 1,000 times per second. The speed of an action potential ranges from about 5 to about 260 miles per hour and depends on the thickness or diameter of the axon—larger ones are faster—and on the presence of myelin (pronounced "MY-a-lin"). *Myelin* is a fatty substance that wraps around some axons like a stocking and speeds up action potentials. When a neuron fires, dendrites in the next cell detect the message and send the signal to their cell body.

Synapses and Communication Between Neurons

How do the dendrites detect a signal from another neuron? As shown in Figure 2.3, it works a little like the game of tag you played as a child. In this neural communication tag game, however, one neuron "sends" a tag without actually touching the next neuron. When an action potential reaches the ends of an axon's branches, it stimulates the release of a chemical that is stored there in little "bags," called *vesicles* (pronounced "VESS-ick-els"). This chemical is called a **neurotransmitter** because it acts as a kind of messenger between neurons. Neurotransmitters flow across a tiny gap, less than a millionth of an inch wide, which separates the axon of one neuron and the dendrites of another. This is the *synaptic gap*, often referred to simply as the **synapse** (see Figure 2.4) When they reach the dendrite of the next cell, neurotransmitters chemically fit, or bind, to proteins

refractory period A short recovery time after cell firing, during which the cell cannot fire again.

neurotransmitter A chemical that transfers messages across synapses.

synapse The tiny gap between the axon of one neuron and the dendrites of another.

Active Review

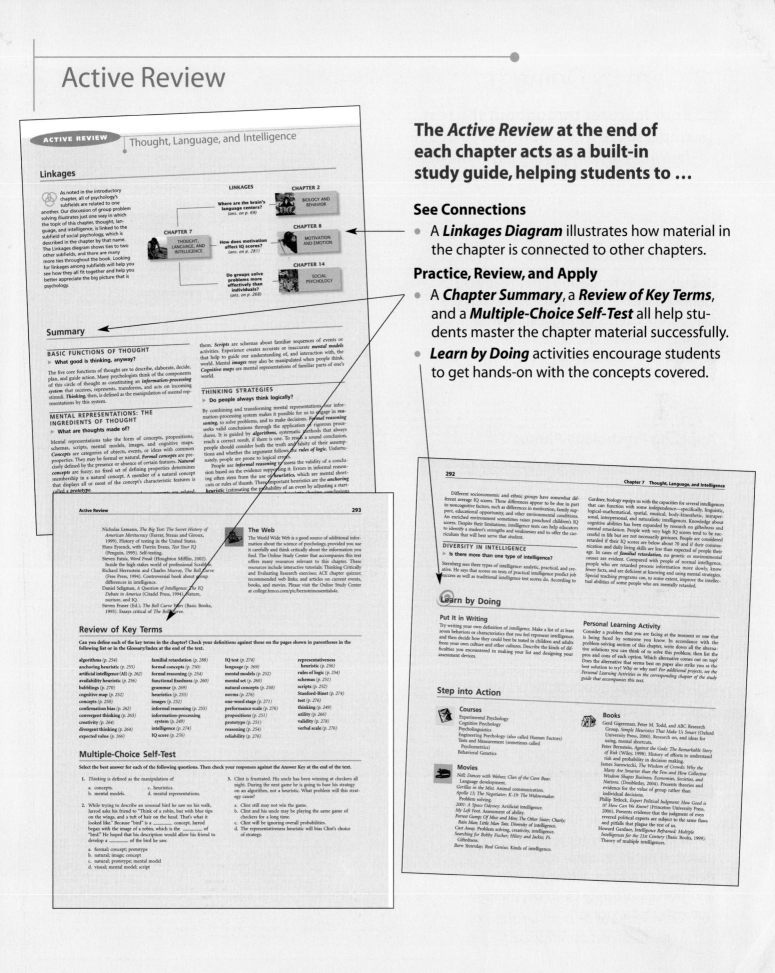

The *Active Review* at the end of each chapter acts as a built-in study guide, helping students to …

See Connections

- A *Linkages Diagram* illustrates how material in the chapter is connected to other chapters.

Practice, Review, and Apply

- A *Chapter Summary*, a *Review of Key Terms*, and a *Multiple-Choice Self-Test* all help students master the chapter material successfully.

- *Learn by Doing* activities encourage students to get hands-on with the concepts covered.

Learn by Doing

Four features throughout the text underscore a commitment to *active learning* and *applying psychology*.

Figure and Photo Captions

Dozens of new figure and photo captions identified with a "Learn by Doing" symbol reinforce concepts by suggesting ways in which students can demonstrate the concepts for themselves.

Applying Psychology Photos

These photos highlight the diversity of applied psychology.

Learn by Doing Icon

A symbol appears next to the text where active learning opportunities occur.

Put It in Writing and Personal Learning Activity

As part of the Active Review section, ***Put It in Writing*** invites readers to write about a specific chapter topic, and ***Personal Learning Activity*** provides another opportunity to do psychology—not just read about it.

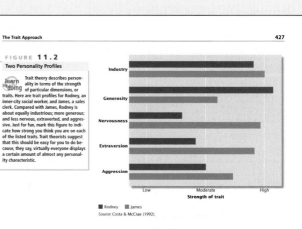

FIGURE 11.2

Two Personality Profiles

learn by doing Trait theory describes personality in terms of the strength of particular dimensions, or traits. Here are trait profiles for Rodney, an inner-city social worker, and James, a sales clerk. Compared with James, Rodney is about equally industrious; more generous; and less nervous, extraverted, and aggressive. Just for fun, mark this figure to indicate how strong you think you are on each of the listed traits. Trait theorists suggest that this should be easy for you to do because, they say, virtually everyone displays a certain amount of almost any personality characteristic.

■ Rodney ■ James
Source: Costa & McCrae (1992).

that organize and control behavior in many different situations. Central traits are roughly equivalent to the descriptive terms used in letters of recommendation (*reliable* or *distractible*, for example) that are meant to tell what can be expected from a person most of the time (Schultz & Schultz, 2005). Allport also believed that people possess *secondary traits*—those that are more specific to certain situations and control far less behavior. "Dislikes crowds" is an example of a secondary trait.

applying psychology SELECTING A JURY Some psychologists employ trait theories of personality in advising prosecution or defense attorneys about which potential jurors are most likely to be sympathetic to their side of a court case.

3. People differ in how much of a particular personality trait they possess; no two people are exactly alike on all traits. The result is an endless variety of unique personalities.

In short, psychologists who take the **trait approach** see personality as a combination of stable internal characteristics that people display consistently over time and across situations (Pervin et al., 2005). Trait theorists seek to measure the relative strength of the many personality characteristics that they believe are present in everyone (see Figure 11.2).

Early Trait Theories

Today's trait theories of personality are largely based on the work of Gordon Allport and Raymond Cattell. (The contributions of another early trait theorist, Hans Eysenck, are discussed later.) Allport spent thirty years searching for the traits that combine to form personality. When he looked at the nearly 18,000 dictionary terms that can be used to describe human behavior (Allport & Odbert, 1936), he noticed that there are clusters of terms referring refer to the same thing. For example, *hostile, nasty,* and *mean* all convey

trait approach A perspective on personality that views it as the combination of stable characteristics that people display over time and across situations.

learn by doing a similar meaning. To better understand this clustering, think of a close relative, and jot down all the personality traits that describe this person. If you are like most people, you were able to capture your relative's personality using only a few trait labels. Allport believed that the set of labels that describe a particular person reflects that person's *central traits*—those that are usually obvious to others and

---

Learn by Doing

Put It in Writing

What is stress like for you? To help you understand the role of stress in your life, write a page or two describing a stressful incident that you had to face in the recent past. Identify what the stressors were, and classify each of them as physical or psychological. List your physical, emotional, cognitive, and behavioral responses to these stressors, and how long the responses lasted. Include a brief summary of how you coped with these stressors and how successful your coping efforts were. Some research suggests that writing about stressful experiences can help people to deal with those experiences. Did this writing project have any such benefits for you? For more about writing and health, visit http://homepage.psy.utexas.edu/homepage/faculty/pennebaker/Home2000/WritingandHealth.html

Personal Learning Activity

To get an idea of the differences in people's stress-coping methods, create a one-paragraph story about a stressful situation (such as losing a job, having one's home destroyed by fire, working for an obnoxious boss, or being overburdened by schoolwork). Now show this description to ten people and ask each of them to tell you how they would cope with the situation if it happened to them. Classify each of their coping methods as problem focused or emotion focused. Did you notice any relationships between the kind of coping responses these people chose and their personal characteristics, such as age, gender, ethnicity, or experience with stress? If so, why do you think those relationships appeared? *For additional projects, see the Personal Learning Activities in the corresponding chapter of the study guide that accompanies this text.*

Thinking Critically

A dedicated section in each chapter helps improve this vital skill.

Structured around five questions, these sections encourage readers to analyze material before drawing conclusions:

- What am I being asked to believe or accept?
- Is there evidence available to support the claim?
- Can that evidence be interpreted another way?
- What evidence would help to evaluate the alternatives?
- What conclusions are most reasonable?

THINKING CRITICALLY

Is Psychological Diagnosis Biased?

Some researchers and clinicians worry that problems with the reliability and validity of the diagnostic system are due partly to bias in its construction and use. They point out, for example, that if the criteria for diagnosing a certain disorder were based on research that focused on only one gender, one ethnic group, or one age group, those criteria might not apply to other groups. Moreover, diagnosticians, like other people, hold expectations and make assumptions about males versus females and about individuals from differing cultures or ethnic groups. These cognitive biases could color their judgments and might lead them to apply diagnostic criteria in ways that are slightly but significantly different from one case to the next (Garb, 1997; Hartung & Widiger, 1998).

■ **What am I being asked to believe or accept?**

Here, we focus on ethnicity as a possible source of bias in diagnosing psychopathology. It is of special interest because there is evidence that, like social class and gender, ethnicity is an important sociocultural factor in the development of mental disorder. The assertion to be considered is that clinicians in the United States base their diagnoses partly on a client's ethnic background and, more specifically, that there is bias in diagnosing African Americans.

■ **What evidence is available to support the claim?**

Several facts suggest the possibility of ethnic bias in psychological diagnosis. For example, African Americans receive the diagnosis of schizophrenia more frequently than European Americans do (Manderscheid & Barrett, 1987; Minsky et al., 2003; Pavkov, Lewis, & Lyons, 1989). Further, relative to their presence in the general population, African Americans are overrepresented in public mental hospitals, where the most serious forms of disorder are seen, and they are underrepresented in private hospitals and outpatient

---

New! *Active Learning* and *Critical Thinking* booklets provide a wealth of thought-provoking, hands-on activities that help students to apply key concepts to their own experiences and develop important critical thinking skills. Both of these password-protected booklets may be accessed from the *Online Study Center* via a passkey packaged upon request with the text. Instructor versions of these booklets are available on the *Online Teaching Center*. Please consult your sales representative for further details.

THINKING CRITICALLY

Focus on Research

Highlighting a particular study, these sections emphasize the value of research and the creativity with which it is often conducted.

These sections are organized around five questions:

- What was the researcher's question?
- How did the researcher answer the question?
- What did the researcher find?
- What do the results mean?
- What do we still need to know?

FOCUS ON RESEARCH

Self-Esteem and the Ultimate Terror

Why is self-esteem so important to so many people? An intriguing answer to this question comes from the *terror management theory* proposed by Jeff Greenberg, Tom Pyszczynski, and Sheldon Solomon. This theory is based on the notion that humans are the only creatures capable of thinking about the future and realizing that we will all eventually die. Terror management theory suggests that humans cope with anxiety, including the terror that thoughts about death might bring, by developing a variety of self-protective psychological strategies. One of these is the effort to establish and maintain high self-esteem (Greenberg, Pyszczynski, & Solomon, 2003; Pyszczynski et al., 2004).

■ **What was the researchers' question?**

In one series of experiments, Greenberg and his colleagues (1992) asked whether high self-esteem would, in fact, serve as a buffer against anxiety—specifically, the anxiety brought on by thoughts about death and pain.

■ **How did the researchers answer the question?**

About 150 students at several North American universities participated in one of three studies, each of which followed a similar format. The first step was to temporarily alter the participants' self-esteem. To do so, the researchers gave the students feedback about a personality or intelligence test they had taken earlier in the semester. Half the participants received positive feedback designed to increase their self-esteem. The other half received feedback that was neutral—it was neither flattering nor depressing. (Measurement of the students' self-esteem showed that the positive feedback actually did create higher self-esteem than the neutral feedback.) In the next phase of each experiment, the researchers used either a film about death or the (false) threat of a mild electric shock to create some anxiety in half the participants in the positive-feedback group and half the participants in the neutral-feedback group. The amount of anxiety created was measured by the participants' self-reports or by monitoring galvanic skin resistance, a measure of perspiration in their skin that reflects anxiety-related arousal (Dawson, Schell, & Filion, 2000).

Linkages

The *Linkages* feature reflects the relationships among the subfields of psychology.

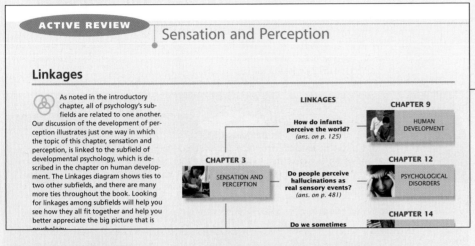

ACTIVE REVIEW   Sensation and Perception

Linkages

As noted in the introductory chapter, all of psychology's subfields are related to one another. Our discussion of the development of perception illustrates just one way in which the topic of this chapter, sensation and perception, is linked to the subfield of developmental psychology, which is described in the chapter on human development. The Linkages diagram shows ties to two other subfields, and there are many more ties throughout the book. Looking for linkages among subfields will help you see how they all fit together and help you better appreciate the big picture that is psychology.

LINKAGES

CHAPTER 3
SENSATION AND PERCEPTION

How do infants perceive the world? (ans. on p. 125)

CHAPTER 9
HUMAN DEVELOPMENT

Do people perceive hallucinations as real sensory events? (ans. on p. 481)

CHAPTER 12
PSYCHOLOGICAL DISORDERS

CHAPTER 14

Do we sometimes

Linkages Diagram

In the Active Review section at the end of each chapter, a **Linkages diagram** presents three questions to illustrate how material in the chapter is related to other chapters in the book.

Marginal Callouts

The Linkages diagram directs students to the pages that carry further discussion of each question, where a **marginal callout** appears.

LINKAGES
How do infants perceive the world? (a link to Human Development)

We have seen that perception is influenced by the knowledge and experience we gain over time, but what perceptual abilities do we start with? To learn about infants' perception, psychologists have studied two inborn patterns called *habituation* and *dishabituation*. Infants stop looking when they repeatedly see stimuli that they perceive to be the same. This is habituation. If they see a stimulus that is perceived to be new and different, they resume looking. This is dishabituation. Using the habituation/dishabituation technique, researchers have found that newborns can perceive differences in stimuli showing various amounts of black-and-white contrast but that they cannot yet distinguish differences between colors (Burr, Morrone, & Fiorentini, 1996). Other studies using the same methods have shown that newborns can perceive differences in the angles of lines (Slater et al., 1991). Taken together, these studies suggest that we are born with the basic components of feature detection.

LINKAGES

Perception and Human Development

Linkages Sections

One of the questions in the Linkages diagram is discussed at length in the chapter's special section titled **Linkages.**

LINKAGES

Media Resources for Instructors

Two powerful tools designed to enhance and maximize the teaching and learning experience:

***Psych In Film*® DVD/VHS** contains 35 clips from Universal Studios films illustrating key concepts in psychology. Clips from films like *Apollo 13*, *Schindler's List*, *Snow Falling on Cedars*, and many others are combined with commentary, discussion questions, and teaching tips to make psychology come alive for students!

Eduspace® is a powerful course management system powered by Blackboard that makes preparing, presenting, and managing courses easier. Use this distance-learning platform to manage large courses online, as well as to access, customize, create, and deliver course materials and tests online. You can easily maintain student portfolios using the gradebook where grades for all assignments are automatically scored, averaged, and saved. Our premium Eduspace content for *Essentials* Fourth Edition includes our ***Psych In Film*® video clips**, complete with **teaching tips**, **discussion questions**, and **trackable quizzing** (in addition to our computerized test bank material); self-assessment **quizzes** and interactive Tutorials for your students; as well high quality **presentation tools** such as PowerPoint slides and art from the textbook. All in one easy-to-use platform!

NEW for Instructors!

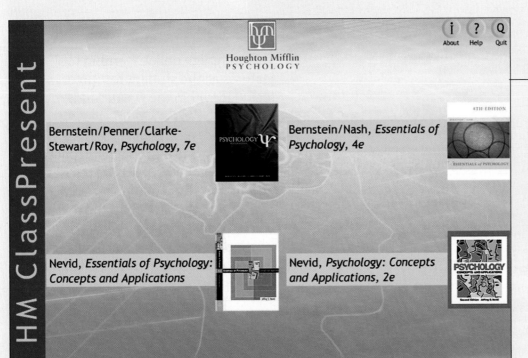

HM ClassPresent

Includes over 45 animations that project effectively in a lecture hall. Easy to navigate and searchable by thumbnail images organized by topic. Export the animations to your own computer or simply use them for presentation directly from the CD.

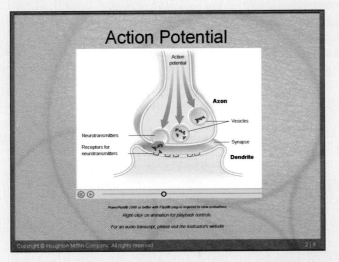

Enhanced PowerPoint® Presentations

Include lecture outlines, tables and figures from the main text, and hyperlinks to interactive tutorials that help to enliven lecture content and illuminate specific topics ranging from action potential to classical conditioning.

Classroom Response System (CRS) Content

An additional set of PowerPoint slides for use with a CRS system gives you the flexibility to perform "on-the-spot" assessments, deliver quick quizzes, gauge students' understanding of a particular question or concept, conduct anonymous polling for class discussion purposes, and take their class roster—all easily. Students receive immediate feedback on how well they understand concepts covered in the text and where they need to improve. Answer slides provide the correct answer and explanation of why the answer is correct.

HMCO Psychology Image Gallery

Includes over 150 images from the text as well as other sources, which can be downloaded for inclusion in your classroom presentations. The intuitive interface displays thumbnail images that make identifying images easy.

NEW for Students!

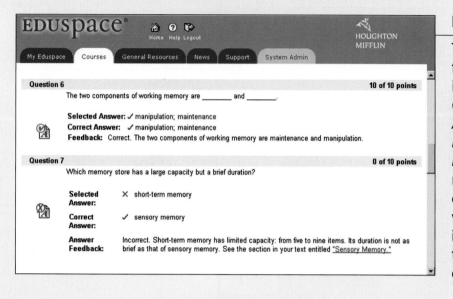

Eduspace®

This complete online learning tool features all the student resources included within the *Online Study Center*, such as *tutorials, flashcards, ACE practice tests, chapter outlines, learning objectives*, and *online concept maps*. Gradable *Homework Exercises* now include remediation from each question to the section of the text where corresponding topical coverage is found. Remediation is provided on the feedback screen upon completion of the quiz.

The **multimedia eBook**, available only within *Eduspace*, integrates an online version of the textbook with interactive media. Students can access *tutorial activities* and *Psych in Film video clips* that expand upon and reinforce main concepts in the text. Students can also link to ACE practice quizzes to test their understanding of the text material, as well as use the electronic flashcards to review key terms and concepts.

Online Study Center
Improve Your Grade
Tutorial: Immediate Memory Span

parallel distributed processing (PDP) models   Memory models in which new experiences are seen as changing one's overall knowledge base.

information-processing model   A model suggesting that information must pass through sensory memory, short-term memory, and long-term memory in order to become firmly embedded in memory.

sensory memory   A type of memory that is very brief, but lasts long enough to connect one impression to the next.

sensory registers   Memory systems that briefly hold incoming information.

Storing New Memories

▶ **What am I most likely to remember?**

The storage of information is critical to memory, because we can retrieve only information that has been stored. According to the information-processing model, sensory memory, short-term memory, and long-term memory each provide a different type of storage. Let's take a closer look at these three memory systems in order to better understand how they work—and sometimes fail.

Sensory Memory

To recognize incoming information, the brain must analyze and compare it with what is already stored in long-term memory. This process is very quick, but it still takes time. The major function of **sensory memory** is to hold information long enough for it to be processed further. This "holding" function is the job of the **sensory registers**, which act as temporary storage bins. There is a separate register for each of the five senses. Each register can store a nearly complete representation of a sensory stimulus, but only briefly, often for less than one second (Eysenck & Keane, 2005).

Sensory memory helps us experience a constant flow of information, even if that flow is interrupted. To see this for yourself, move your head and eyes slowly from left to right. It may seem as though your eyes are moving smoothly, like a movie camera scanning a scene, but that's not what is happening. Your

ESSENTIALS *of* PSYCHOLOGY

FOURTH EDITION

Douglas A. Bernstein
University of South Florida
University of Southampton

Peggy W. Nash
Broward Community College

with

Alison Clarke-Stewart
University of California, Irvine

Louis A. Penner
Wayne State University
University of Michigan

Edward J. Roy
University of Illinois at Urbana-Champaign

Houghton Mifflin Company   Boston   New York

To my friends and colleagues, who have shared my good times and stood by me in bad times.
   Doug Bernstein

To my family and sons, Rob and Jeff, with love.
   Peggy Nash

Executive Publisher: George Hoffman
Sponsoring Editor: Jane Potter
Marketing Manager: Amy Whitaker
Marketing Assistant: Samantha Abrams
Development Editor: Laura Hildebrand
Editorial Associate: Henry Cheek
Senior Project Editor: Aileen Mason
Editorial Assistant: Andrew Laskey
Senior Art and Design Coordinator: Jill Haber Atkins
Cover Design Director: Tony Saizon
Senior Photo Editor: Jennifer Meyer Dare
Composition Buyer: Chuck Dutton
New Title Manager for College & Trade: Priscilla Manchester

Cover image: © Photodisc, Ryan McVay, Getty Images

For permission to use copyrighted materials, grateful acknowledgment is made to the copyright holders listed on page A-98, which is hereby considered an extension of the copyright page.

Printed in the U.S.A.

Library of Congress Control Number: 2006934310

Instructor's exam copy:
ISBN-(10): 0-618-83396-X
ISBN-(13): 978-0-618-83396-2

For orders, use student text ISBNs:
ISBN-(10): 0-618-71312-3
ISBN-(13): 978-0-618-71312-7

2 3 4 5 6 7 8 9-VH-11 10 09 08 07

Brief Contents

Features

Contents

3 Sensation and Perception 84

4 Consciousness 135

5 Learning 169

Preface

PSYCHOLOGY IS A RICH and varied science, covering the breadth and depth of human behavior—everything from fleeting reflexes to enduring memories, from falling asleep to falling in love. In our experience, most students enter the introductory course thinking that psychology concerns itself mainly with personality, psychological testing, mental disorders, psychotherapy, and other aspects of clinical psychology. Many of these students are surprised, then, when they find themselves reading about such topics as the structure of the brain, optical illusions, the effect of jet lag on Olympic athletes, AIDS and the immune system, and prenatal risk factors, to name just a few. Yet these are all topics under the umbrella that is psychology.

For all its diversity, psychology is also a remarkably integrated discipline whose subfields are linked to one another through common interests and overarching research questions. As psychologists and scholars, we wrote this book to portray the wide range of topics that make up the science of psychology. As teachers, we focused on the essentials of the discipline, the core concepts of psychology that we hope will be especially accessible and interesting to students. We also tried to present these topics through an integrated, active pedagogical system designed to help students get the most out of the text.

In creating the fourth edition of *Essentials of Psychology*, we continued our commitment to presenting a textbook that is not only clear and enjoyable to read but that also provides features to support the learning process in all students, regardless of their academic background. Specifically, we set these goals:

- To focus on topics that represent the full range of psychology, from cell to society, without overwhelming the reader with details.

- To provide many active learning exercises that invite students to work with the text material in ways that can help them understand and remember it.

- To help students develop their ability to think critically and scientifically by examining the ways that psychologists have solved, or failed to solve, fascinating puzzles of behavior and mental processes.

- To explain the content of psychology with an emphasis on the doing of psychology, grounding all discussions in current and classic research studies. (We help students appreciate the importance of research by exploring one study in detail in a special feature in each chapter.)

Our discussion of research in psychology is also designed to remind students that although, in some ways, "people are people wherever you go," sociocultural factors—including gender, ethnicity, cultural background, and geography—often shape human behavior and mental processes. We repeatedly point out, therefore, that psychological research on the thinking styles, perceptual habits, psychological disorders, social pressures, and other phenomena seen in North America or Europe, for example, may or may not apply to other cultures—or even to subcultures within Western countries.

Rather than isolating discussion of sociocultural material in boxed features, we have woven it into every chapter so that students will encounter it repeatedly as they read. We introduce the importance of sociocultural factors in Chapter 1 and continue to reinforce it through coverage of such topics as the impact of culture and experience on perception (Chapter 3), classrooms across cultures (Chapter 5), ethnic differences in IQ (Chapter 7), social and cultural factors in sexuality (Chapter 8), gender differences in stress responses (Chapter 10), personality, culture, and human development (Chapter 11), gender and cultural differences in depression and suicide (Chapter 12), and cultural factors in aggression (Chapter 14), to cite just a few examples. Please refer to the tabbing guide on the inside front cover of this text, for a comprehensive listing of sociocultural coverage.

What's New in This Edition?

Feedback from faculty colleagues and students suggests that the changes we made in the third edition of *Essentials* were well received. Accordingly, in creating the fourth edition, we have sought to update and upgrade all the book's best features rather than change them for the sake of change. We hope that the result of our efforts is a book that offers even more of what faculty and students want and need.

Chapter Organization

Designed for presentation in a single semester, the book's fourteen-chapter organization has been retained, and the chapters appear in the same sequence as before. Have we arranged those fourteen chapters in an ideal sequence? The sequence reflects the way we teach our introductory courses, but we know that your preference for chapter sequencing may not match ours. Accordingly we have again ensured that each of the fourteen chapters appears as a freestanding unit so that you may assign the chapters in whatever order you wish. For example, many instructors prefer to teach the material on human development relatively late in the course, which is why it appears as Chapter 9. However, the chapter can be just as comfortably assigned earlier in the course.

For the third edition, we added an **optional** fifteenth chapter, on **Industrial/Organizational Psychology.** For the fourth edition, we have added an **optional** sixteenth chapter, on **Neuropsychology,** coauthored by Doug Bernstein and Joel Shenker, a diplomate of the American Board of Neurology and Psychiatry who specializes in memory loss, dementia, and neuro-cognitive behavioral impairments. Either (or both) chapter(s) may be included in the textbook upon request, and select ancillaries contain supporting material for these chapters. Note that in the end-of-book materials—such as answer keys, references, credits, and the combined glossary/index—the entries for these chapters are printed in blue.

A Continued Emphasis on Learning by Doing

Based on the continued popularity of active learning activities, we have continued to enhance this focus in the fourth edition. Three kinds of **Learn by Doing** features appear throughout the book.

- First, there are dozens of new or revised figure and photo captions that help students understand and remember a psychological principle or phenomenon by suggesting ways in which they can demonstrate it for themselves. In the memory chapter, for example, a photo caption suggests that students show the photo to a friend, and then ask questions about it to illustrate the operation of constructive memory. These captions are all identified with a Learn by Doing symbol.

- Second, we have placed Learn by Doing symbols in the pages at even more places where active learning opportunities occur in the narrative. At these points, we ask students to stop reading and try *doing something* to illustrate or highlight the psychological principle or phenomenon under discussion. For example, in the sensation and perception chapter, we ask the student to focus attention on various targets as a way of appreciating the difference between overt and covert attention shifts.

- Finally, we have carried the active learning theme through to the end of each chapter, where—as part of the built-in study guide we call **Active Review**—students will find sections called Put It in Writing and Personal Learning Activity. These sections invite students to (a) write about a specific chapter-related topic, and (b) collect, analyze, and discuss some data on a chapter-related principle or phenomenon.

Active Review

The Put It in Writing and Personal Learning Activity sections are just one part of our effort to add educational value to the built-in Active Review study guide. The Active Review's other features include

- A Linkages diagram, which helps students understand and appreciate the ways in which the chapter they have just read relates to other subfields of psychology.

- Twenty-item multiple-choice self-tests. We have revised some of the questions, and they continue to focus on the application—as well as the definition—of principles, concepts, and phenomena.

- A **Step into Action** section, which—to highlight our emphasis on active learning—lists the courses in which students can further pursue chapter-related study, and provides a newly expanded and annotated list of movies and books related to each chapter. We also refer students to Houghton Mifflin's *Online Study Center,* where—as the result of a continuous updating and upgrading process—they can easily find the latest, most interesting, and most valuable web addresses related to chapter content, as well as a range of interactive activities and practice quizzes for each chapter.

- An updated **Review of Key Terms** section, which invites students to write their own definitions of the most important terms presented in the chapter.

Applying Psychology Photos

As in the third edition, we continue to emphasize the many ways in which psychological theory and research results are being applied to benefit human welfare. We further highlight the diversity of applied psychology by including in each chapter at least one **Applying Psychology** photo that offers a memorable example. In the social psychology chapter for example, a photo illustrates the way some organizations use petitions to identify people who are likely to become supporters of that organization's goals. In the personality chapter, the Applying Psychology photo illustrates the use of personality trait theory in jury selection.

Updated Content

As in the previous editions, our goal in preparing this new edition of *Essentials* was to present the latest, as well as the most established, results of basic and applied research on topics that are both important to psychology and of high interest to students. Accordingly, we offer updated coverage of research on how drugs affect the brain (Chapter 2), the basis for optical illusions (Chapter 3), the effects of subliminal messages (Chapter 4), the importance of active learning in the classroom (Chapter 5), the accuracy of eyewitness testimony (Chapter 6), the origins of intelligence (Chapter 7), sources of sexual orientation (Chapter 8), the development of morals (Chapter 9), the effects of stress on health (Chapter 10), what determines and shapes our personalities (Chapter 11), the causes of multiple personality disorder (Chapter 12), the effects of psychotherapy (Chapter 13), and the development of ethnic prejudice (Chapter 14).

In this new edition, students will also encounter the latest evidence on topics such as

- The value of dietary supplements in improving memory and slowing memory loss (Chapter 2)

- Individual differences in taste abilities, including how to determine if one is a "supertaster" (Chapter 3)

- The role of expectations on the effects of psychoactive drugs (Chapter 4)

- The role of active learning processes in long-term retention of information (Chapter 5)

- Factors that may make people more susceptible to reporting false memories (Chapter 6)

- The process of acquiring language (Chapter 7)

- Factors that influence subjective well-being (Chapter 8)

- The origins of infantile amnesia (Chapter 9)

- The "tend and befriend" response to stressors, and its relationship to the traditional "fight-or-flight" syndrome (Chapter 10)

- Biological theories of personality (Chapter 11)

- The origins of schizophrenia, depression, and anxiety (Chapter 12)

- The current status of psychologists' efforts to gain the right to prescribe psychoactive drugs (Chapter 13)

- Social neuroscience, which lies at the interface between biological and social psychology (Chapter 14)

Special Features

The fourth edition of *Essentials of Psychology* contains improved versions of a number of special features found in its predecessor. Designed to promote efficient learning and mastery of the material, these include, in each chapter, an integrated pedagogical system, as well as sections on Thinking Critically, Focus on Research, and Linkages, along with an Active Review section.

An Integrated Pedagogical System

Our integrated pedagogical system is designed to help students get the most out of their reading. Based on the PQ4R study system (discussed in detail in Chapter 6, "Memory"), learning aids in each chapter include the following elements.

Preview Questions To help students survey and question the material, each chapter opens with a full outline, a brief preview statement, and a list of questions related to the key topic of each main section of the chapter. Those questions are repeated within the chapter at the start of each corresponding main section, and they appear again in the Active Review, where they help to organize the chapter summary.

Margin Glossary Key terms are defined in the margin of the page where they appear, reinforcing core concepts without interrupting the flow of reading. (For the fourth edition, we have revised many of our phonetic guides to make it even easier for students to correctly pronounce unfamiliar key terms—as well as other terms whose pronunciation is not immediately obvious.) In the Active Review section at the end of each chapter, a definition exercise encourages students to restate these core concepts in their own words.

Instructional Captions Captions to all figures, tables, photographs, and cartoons reiterate core concepts and help students learn to interpret visual information. And, as mentioned earlier, many of these captions prompt students to engage in various kinds of active learning experiences.

In Review Charts In Review study charts summarize information in a convenient tabular format. We have placed two or three In Review charts strategically in each chapter to help students synthesize and assimilate large chunks of information—for example, on drug effects, key elements in personality theories, and stress responses and mediators. We have added additional fill-in-the-blank self-testing items at the bottom of each In Review chart to further aid student learning and review of the chapter material. The answer key is at the back of the book; answers printed in blue indicate those for the optional Industrial/Organizational Psychology and Neuropsychology chapters.

Active Review As mentioned earlier, the built-in Active Review study guide at the end of each chapter includes

- A **Linkages diagram** containing questions that illustrate three of the ways in which material in each chapter is connected to other chapters in the book.

- A **chapter summary** organized around major topic headings and the related preview questions. The summary is presented in short, easy-to-read paragraphs that are focused on subheadings.

- A **Learn by Doing** feature that is designed to promote active learning. Here, students will find Put It in Writing and Personal Learning Activity sections that invite them to (a) write about a specific chapter-related topic, and (b) collect, analyze, and discuss some data on a chapter-related principle or phenomenon. For example, in the personality chapter, the Put It in Writing section suggests that students list a celebrity's personality traits, then summarize how various personality theories would account for the development of those traits. In the biology and behavior chapter, students are asked to write about how research on brain development might affect one's choice of an infant day care center. These Put It in Writing suggestions may be helpful as writing-across-the-curriculum assignments.

- The Personal Learning Activity section suggests ways in which students can *do* psychology as well as read about it. In the motivation and emotion chapter, for example, the Personal Learning Activity section suggests a way in which students can collect data on lie-detection skills. In the social psychology chapter, students are invited to test some assumptions of evolutionary theories of mate selection by analyzing personals ads in a local newspaper. Each Personal Learning Activity section ends by referring the student to additional projects listed in the study guide that accompanies the book.

- A **Step into Action** section, which (a) suggests courses that students can take to pursue further chapter-related study, (b) presents an annotated list of movies and books related to each chapter, and (c) encourages students to visit Houghton Mifflin's *Online Study Center* for resources related to the chapter in the form of interactive activities, self-quizzes, and web links.

- A **Review of Key Terms,** which invites students to write their own definitions of the most important terms presented in the chapter. These lists have been updated to include all the key terms discussed in the new edition.

- A twenty-item **Multiple-Choice Self-Test** designed to help students assess their understanding of the chapter's key points prior to taking quizzes and exams. As before, we provide an answer key at the back of the book that identifies and briefly explains each correct answer, and refers students to the page on which the tested material was first discussed. Note that the answers printed in blue are for the optional Industrial/Organizational Psychology and Neuropsychology chapters.

Thinking Critically

A special Thinking Critically section in each chapter helps students hone their abilities in this vital skill. Our approach to writing centers on describing research on psychological phenomena in a way that reveals the logic of the scientific method, identifies possible flaws in design or interpretation, and leaves room for more questions and further research. In other words, as author-teachers, we try to model critical thinking processes for our readers. The Thinking Critically sections are designed to make these processes more explicit and accessible by providing readers with a framework for analyzing evidence before drawing conclusions. The framework is built around five questions that the reader should find useful in analyzing not only psychological research studies, but other forms of communication as well, including political speeches, advertising claims, and appeals for contributions. These five questions first appear in Chapter 1, when we introduce the importance of critical thinking, and they are repeated in every chapter's Thinking Critically section.

1. What am I being asked to believe or accept?

2. Is there evidence available to support the claim?

3. Can that evidence be interpreted another way?

4. What evidence would help to evaluate the alternatives?

5. What conclusions are most reasonable?

Using this simple yet powerful framework, we explore issues such as subliminal persuasion, pornography and aggression, recovered memories, and memory-enhancing dietary supplements, to name just a few. Page xvi includes a complete list of the Thinking Critically features.

Focus on Research

Scientists in psychology have helped us to better understand behavior and mental processes through their commitment to empirical research. They have posed vital questions about psychological phenomena and designed research that is capable of answering, or at least illuminating, those questions. In Chapter 1 we introduce readers to the methods of scientific research and to basic research designs in psychology. Every subsequent chapter features a Focus on Research section that highlights a particular research study to help students appreciate the value of research and the creativity with which psychologists have conducted it. Like the Thinking Critically sections, the Focus on Research features are organized around five questions designed to help readers organize their thinking about research questions and research results.

1. What was the researcher's question?

2. How did the researcher answer the question?

3. What did the researcher find?

4. What do the results mean?

5. What do we still need to know?

These Focus on Research sections help students to see how psychologists have used experiments, surveys, observations, and other designs to explore phenomena such as learned helplessness, infant cognition, evolutionary theories of helping, and human sexual behavior. A full list of the Focus on Research features appears on page xvi.

Linkages

In our experience, introductory psychology students are better able to appreciate the scope of our discipline when they look at it not as a laundry list of separate topics but as an interrelated set of subfields, each of which contributes to—and benefits from—the work being done in all the others. To help students see these relationships, we have built into the book an integrating tool called Linkages. There are three elements in the Linkages program.

- *Linkages diagrams* The first element of the chapter's Active Review is a Linkages diagram, which presents a set of questions that illustrate three of the ways in which material in the chapter is related to other chapters in the book. For example, the Linkages diagram in Chapter 2, "Biology and Behavior," contains questions that show how biological psychology is related to consciousness ("Does the brain shut down when we sleep?"), human development ("How do our brains change over a lifetime?"), and treatment of psychological disorders ("How do drugs help people who suffer from schizophrenia?"). These diagrams are designed to help students keep in mind how the content of each chapter fits into psychology as a whole. To introduce the concept of Linkages, the diagram in Chapter 1 appears within the body of the chapter.

- *Cross-references* The page numbers following each question in the Linkages diagrams direct the student to pages that carry further discussion of that question. There, the linking question is repeated in the margin alongside the discussion.

- *Linkages sections* One of the questions in each chapter's Linkages diagram reminds the student of the chapter's discussion of that question in a special section titled, appropriately enough, Linkages (see page xvi for a complete list of Linkages sections).

These three elements combine with the text narrative to highlight the network of relationships among psychology's subfields. This Linkages program is designed to help students see the "big picture" that is psychology—no matter how many chapters their instructor assigns or in what sequence.

Teaching and Learning Support Package

Many useful instructional and pedagogical materials have been developed to support the *Essentials of Psychology* textbook and the introductory course. Designed to enhance and maximize the teaching and learning experience, this fourth edition focuses on greater integration of the supplemental package components with the text itself. New features of several supplements reflect the text's emphasis on active learning and writing across the curriculum.

For the Instructor

Online Instructor's Resource Manual   The *Online Instructor's Resource Manual,* by Linda Lebie, Travis Sola (both at Lakeland College), Douglas A. Bernstein, and Peggy W. Nash, contains for each chapter of the textbook a complete set of learning objectives, detailed chapter outlines, and numerous classroom supplements that include discussion and lecture suggestions, Thinking Critically and Put It in Writing activities, and related handouts. The manual also contains a video guide and a Pedagogical Strategies section that covers implementing active learning, encouraging critical thinking, using the Linkages feature and the Research Focus supplements, and writing across the curriculum, as well as suggestions on how to build a syllabus. For instructors switching from the third to the fourth edition of the text, the manual includes a detailed transition guide for each chapter, outlining the key changes between editions. Note that in addition to the **fifteenth** chapter of supporting material for the optional Industrial/Organizational Psychology chapter (offered with the third edition), this revised *Instructor's Resource Manual* comes with a **sixteenth** chapter offering supporting material on the *new* optional Neuropsychology chapter specially written for the fourth edition. As noted earlier, either—or both—of these chapters can be included in your text upon request; see your Houghton Mifflin sales representative for details.

Online Test Bank   The *Test Bank,* by Chris Armstrong (University of Illinois) and Douglas A. Bernstein, contains 125 multiple-choice items plus three essay questions per chapter. All multiple-choice items are keyed to pages in the textbook and to the learning objectives that appear in the *Instructor's Resource Manual* and *Study Guide.* Each question is identified by whether it tests simple factual recall or deeper conceptual understanding. Over **45 percent** of the items have been class-tested with between 400 and 2,500 students, and a statistical performance analysis is provided for those items. The computerized version of the *Test Bank* allows instructors to edit questions, integrate their own, and generate paper or online exams. **New** to the fourth edition *Test Bank* are an additional 100 test questions for each of the two optional chapters (the Industrial/Organizational Psychology and Neuropsychology chapters) that may be bundled with the text. The *Test Bank* is available on the *HM Testing CD-ROM.*

HM Testing CD-ROM (0-618-83497-4)   *HM Testing* (powered by Diploma) is a flexible testing program that allows instructors to create, edit, customize, and deliver multiple types of tests via print, network server, or the web on either the Mac or Windows platform. The test bank contains over 2,000 multiple-choice and essay questions, including 100 questions for each of the two optional chapters (these chapters may be packaged with your text upon request). Over **45 percent** of the multiple-choice questions have been class-tested with between 400 and 2,500 students, and the test item analysis including a quintile graph for each of these items is included within the testing program. The *Test Bank* Word files are also included on the CD-ROM for easy reference.

New! Enhanced PowerPoint® Presentations   An enhanced set of *PowerPoint Presentations* consists of lecture sequences, tables, figures, and photos from the main text. **New** to this edition are hyperlinks to interactive tutorials that enliven lecture content and illuminate specific topics ranging from action potential to classical conditioning. The slides are available on the *Online Teaching Center.*

New! Classroom Response System (CRS)   *Classroom Response System (CRS)* content, available on the *Online Teaching Center,* allows instructors to perform "on-the-spot" assessments, deliver quick quizzes, gauge students' understanding of a particular question or concept, conduct anonymous polling for class discussion purposes, and take their class roster easily. Students receive immediate feedback on how well they understand concepts covered in the text and where they need to improve. Answer slides provide the correct answer and explanation of why the answer is correct.

New! HM ClassPresent   *ClassPresent* includes over 45 newly developed animations that project effectively in a lecture hall. The CD also has an easy-to-navigate interface, with searchable thumbnail images organized by topic. These animations can be easily inserted into PowerPoint presentations or projected directly from the CD.

New! Active Learning and Critical Thinking Booklets The *Active Learning* and *Critical Thinking* booklets build on the pedagogy of the main text by offering a wealth of interesting exercises that help students apply key concepts to their own experiences and develop important critical thinking skills. The annotated instructor versions of these booklets contain additional tips for helping students derive the full benefit from these activities, and where applicable, include suggested answers to questions raised by some of the activities. Both instructor booklets are available from the *Online Teaching Center.* Students can get access to their version of these password-protected booklets via the *Online Study Center* with the **Your Guide to an A** access card, which comes packaged with all new texts (please consult your sales representative for details).

Online Teaching Center (0-618-82532-0)   The *Online Teaching Center* at **college.hmco.com/pic/bernsteinessentials4e** that accompanies the fourth edition of *Essentials* is a comprehensive gallery of online teaching resources that gives you one central place to access all of your teaching preparation tools. It includes the complete *Instructor's Resource Manual,* PowerPoint Presentations, CRS content, downloadable PDFs of the overhead transparencies, and selected art from the textbook. **New** to this edition is a comprehensive image gallery of over 150 pieces of art from the text as well as other sources. Also included are video guides, ideas for encouraging critical thinking and active learning, and tips on how to use and assign the student activities available on the *Online Study Center.* Premium content on the student *Online Study Center* is passkey-protected and may be accessed with the **Your Guide to an A** access card, which comes packaged with all new texts (please see your sales representative for details).

Eduspace®   *Eduspace* is a powerful course management system that enables instructors to create all or part of their courses online using the widely recognized tools of Blackboard™ and text-specific content from Bernstein, *Essentials of Psychology,* Fourth Edition. Instructors and students have access to automatically graded online homework, *Psych in Film* video clips with quizzes, and tutorials with accompanying pedagogy. Instructor presentation tools include PowerPoint Presentations, CRS content, downloadable PDFs of overhead transparencies and select art from the textbook. **New** content includes *self-assessment quizzes* that provide scoring, explanation of correct and incorrect answers, and remediation back to specific sections of the text; an interactive eBook; and newly added correlation from the homework exercises back to the main text.

Content for Course Management Software *Blackboard* and *WebCT* course cartridges are available with the fourth edition of *Essentials,* allowing instructors to use text-specific material to create an online course on their own campus course management system. The *Essentials* cartridges feature all of the content described in the aforementioned Eduspace course.

New! Eduspace® Online Multimedia eBook Available in an interactive PDF format, this eBook offers an online alternative to the print text, complete with embedded links to multimedia assets such as animations, video, and self-practice exercises. Students can access *tutorial activities* that expand upon and reinforce main concepts in the text. Electronic *Flashcards* provide an interactive study tool to review key terms and concepts. And students can link to *Psych in Film* videos and quizzes that engage their interest by connecting textbook material to current films that students recognize.

Houghton Mifflin Psych in Film® DVD *Houghton Mifflin's Psych in Film DVD* contains 35 clips from Universal Studios films illustrating key concepts in psychology. Clips from films like *Schindler's List, Snow Falling on Cedars,* and many others are combined with commentary and discussion questions to help bring psychology alive for students and demonstrate its relevance to contemporary life and culture. Teaching tips are correlated to specific text chapters and concepts in the *Online Teaching Center.*

Houghton Mifflin's Lecture Starter CD-ROM *Houghton Mifflin's Lecture Starter CD-ROM* contains 40 clips, with an accompanying guide available on the web site. (Note that Lecture Starter material is also available for child development, abnormal, and social psychology. Please consult your sales representative for further details.)

New! Industrial/Organizational Psychology and Neuropsychology Chapters The optional Industrial/Organizational Psychology and Neuropsychology chapters are available for inclusion in the main text, via the custom group. Supporting material for these chapters is available in all of the print supplements and in the HM Testing (computerized testing) program.

For the Student

Online Study Center (0-618-82532-0) The *Online Study Center* at **college.hmco.com/pic/bernsteinessentials4e** contains additional study aids including Ace practice tests, interactive tutorials, and flashcards—all designed to help you get a better grade. **Your Guide to an A** gives you access to premium online study tools that include the **Active Learning Booklet, Critical Thinking Booklet, Study Skills Video Modules,** and **Online Concept Maps.** Please use the code in the **Your Guide to an A** passkey that came with the new copy of your textbook. If you purchased a used textbook, the passkey is available for purchase through your bookstore or through Houghton Mifflin's eCommerce (go to **college.hmco.com/pic/bernsteinessentials4e** and click on the Purchase Product link for **Your Guide to an A**).

New! Active Learning and Critical Thinking Booklets The *Active Learning* and *Critical Thinking* booklets provide a wealth of fun and interesting exercises that help you to apply key concepts to your own experiences, and develop important critical thinking skills. Both of these password-protected booklets may be accessed from the *Online Study Center* via the access card packaged with your new text.

New! Interactive Tutorials The *Interactive Tutorials* walk you through some of the more difficult concepts in the text by bringing them to life through creative game scenarios, simulated research, and video. Accompanying quizzes test your understanding of the material. These tutorials are available within the Eduspace, WebCT, and Blackboard course cartridges and in the *Online Study Center.*

New! Online Concept Maps The *Online Concept Maps* are visual diagrams that show the relationships between concepts discussed in a given chapter. Available within Eduspace, WebCT, and Blackboard course cartridges, and in the *Online Study Center.*

Study Guide (0-618-82431-6) The *Study Guide,* written by Kelly Bouas Henry (Missouri Western State College) and Douglas A. Bernstein, augments the Active Review study materials built into every chapter of the textbook. Introductory sections in the guide provide tips on developing critical thinking skills, studying Linkages, reading a textbook, and developing writing skills. For each chapter of the text—including the optional Industrial/Organizational Psychology and Neuropsychology chapters—the guide includes learning objectives, key term hints and examples, a Concepts and Exercises section that shows you how to apply your knowledge of psychology to everyday issues and concerns, a Critical Thinking exercise, and several Personal Learning Activities of the same type as those in the text. A section of each chapter—called "What Should I Write About?"—provides advice on how to choose an appropriate term paper topic related to the chapter. Finally, each chapter concludes with two multiple-choice quizzes with wrong-answer rejoinders and a self-diagnostic quiz analysis to pinpoint weaknesses in topic and cognitive skill areas.

Introductory Psychology Readers *Psychology in Context: Voices and Perspectives*, Second Edition, by David N. Sattler and Virginia Shabatay, contains engaging first-person narratives and essays keyed to major psychological concepts. Two additional readers by Laura Freberg—*Perspectives: Introductory Psychology* and *Stand! Introductory Psychology*—contain articles that explore contending ideas and opinions relating to fundamental issues in introductory psychology courses.

Our Commitment to You

We are committed to the highest standards of customer support and service. Please don't hesitate to contact us with any questions or queries you may have.

For technical questions related to web site access, CD-ROMs, HM Testing, and HM ClassPresent, please call Houghton Mifflin's Software Support line at (800) 732-3223 (Monday through Thursday 9 A.M.–8 P.M. EST, Friday 9 A.M.–5 P.M. EST) or go to **college.hmco.com/how/how_techsupp.html** to submit an online help form. To learn more about Eduspace, please go to **www. eduspace.com.** To contact your sales representative, go to http://college.hmco.com/instructors/index.html and use our Sales Representative Locator.

Acknowledgments

Many people provided us with the help, criticism, and encouragement we needed to create *Essentials of Psychology*, and to revise it into this fourth edition. We are of course indebted to our colleagues Louis Penner, Ed Roy, and Alison Clarke-Stewart, who, as co-authors of the Bernstein, Penner, Clarke-Stewart, and Roy textbook, *Psychology*, provided invaluable assistance in reviewing the revised *Essentials* manuscript as it developed. We also offer sincere thanks to Professor Paul Spector of the University of South Florida, who took the lead in helping us to create the optional chapter on Industrial/Organizational psychology, and to Joel Shenker, M.D., Ph.D., who took the lead in helping us to create the optional chapter on Neuropsychology (both chapters are available upon request for this edition). We are indebted, too, to a number of other colleagues for their expert help and advice on the revision of various chapters in the fourth edition of *Essentials*. These colleagues include, for Chapter 3, Melody Carswell, University of Kentucky; for Chapter 4, Joel Shenker; for Chapter 5, Doug Williams, University of Winnipeg; for Chapter 6, Kathleen McDermott, Washington University; for Chapter 7, Paul Whitney, Washington State University, and Robert Thorndike, Western Washington University; for Chapter 8, Nancy Dess, Occidental College; for Chapter 10, Catherine Stoney, National Center for Complementary and Alternative Medicine; for Chapter 12, Edward Bernat, University of Minnesota; for Chapter 13, Geoff Kramer, Grand Valley State University, and for optional Chapter 15, Kim Schneider, Illinois State University.

Special thanks are also due to our dear friend and valued colleague, Sandra Goss Lucas, director of Introductory Psychology at the University of Illinois, who worked closely with us as we shaped and organized the new edition of *Essentials*, helped us to revise and improve the multiple-choice self-tests at the end of each chapter, and created the *Active Learning* booklet available with this new edition.

We also want to offer heartfelt thanks to our friends and colleagues who did such a wonderful job in creating revised versions of the ancillary materials for *Essentials*. Most of these people have worked with us for years, and many of them had been graduate student instructors in the University of Illinois introductory psychology program out of which this textbook emerged. They include Kelly Bouas Henry, Missouri Western State College; Sandra Goss Lucas, Amanda Allman, Jonathan Nall, Chris Armstong, and Valerie Werpetinski, all of the University of Illinois; Linda Lebie and Travis Sola, both of Lakeland College; Elaine Cassel, Lord Fairfax Community College; Billa R. Reiss, St. Johns University; David B. Strohmetz, Monmouth University; Terry Shapiro, College of DuPage; and Mark Laumakis, San Diego State University.

We wish to thank several of our colleagues who helped to get the fourth edition off to a good start by reviewing and commenting on the strengths and weaknesses of the third edition:

Kathleen P. Bonnelle, *Lansing Community College*

J. Peter Burton, *Santa Fe Community College*

Kevin M. Clark, *Indiana University, Kokomo*

W. Keith Douglass, *Armstrong Atlantic State University*

Lori L. Driscoll, *Colorado College*

Barry Fish, *Eastern Michigan University*

Dr. Rita Fotinatos, *Deree College, Greece*

Kevin B. Handley, *Germanna Community College*

Allen I. Huffcutt, *Bradley University*

Nancy W. Jackson, *Johnson & Wales University*

Mark Kelland, *Lansing Community College*

Eric D. Miller, *Isothermal Community College*

Bonnie Nichols, *Arkansas Northeastern College*

Art Olguin, *Santa Barbara City College*

Edward I. Pollack, *West Chester University of Pennsylvania*

Melissa Terlecki, *Villanova University*

Fernelle L. Warren, *Troy University*

We owe an enormous dept as well to the colleagues listed next for their invaluable contributions to the text over the life of many editions:

Patricia Abbot, *D'Youville College*

Gary Altmann, *York University, UK*

Robin A. Anderson, *St. Ambrose University*

Grace Auyang, *University of Cincinnati*

Alan Baxter, *Technical Career Institutes, New York*

James Bean, *Lock Haven University*

Beth Benoit, *University of Massachusetts, Lowell*, and *Middlesex Community College*

Joseph J. Benz, *University of Nebraska at Kearney*

Doris A. Bitler, *George Mason University*

Charles Blair-Broeker, *Cedar Falls High School*

Winfield Brown, *Florence Darlington Technical College*

J. Peter Burton, *Santa Fe Community College*

James F. Calhoun, *University of Georgia*

Yiwei Chen, *Bowling Green State University*

Saundra Ciccarelli, *Gulf Coast Community College*

Samuel Clay, *Heartland Community College*

Anne M. Cooper, *St. Petersburg Junior College*

Nat DeAnda, *Los Madanos College*

John R. Foust, *Parkland College*

Laura Freberg, *California Polytechnic State University, San Luis Obispo*

Grace Galliano, *Kennesaw State University*

Christopher Gilbert, *Bristol Community College*

Craig W. Gruber, *Walt Whitman High School*

Lynn Haller, *Morehead State University*

Wen Harris, *Lane Community College*

Diane Herbert, *Hofstra University*

Debra Hollister, *Valencia Community College*

Gene Indenbaum, *SUNY Farmingdale*

John S. Klein, *Castleton State College*

Ronald Kleinknecht, *Western Washington University*

Janet L. Kottke, *California State University, San Bernardino*

Jennifer M. Lancaster, *St. Francis College*

Ken LeSure, *Cuyahoga Community College*

Barbara Lusk, *Collin County Community College*

David S. Malcolm, *Fordham University*

Joseph G. Marrone, *Siena College*

Joseph A. Mayo, *Gordon College*

David Murphy, *Waubonsee College*

Sheila M. Murphy, *Mount Wachusett Community College*

Malinda Jo Muzi, *Community College of Philadelphia*

Bonnie J. Nichols, *Missouri County Community College*

Steve A. Nida, *Franklin University*

Christine Offutt Lingenfelter, *Lock Haven University*

Arthur G. Olguin, *Santa Barbara City College*

Randall E. Osborne, *Indiana University East*

Les Parrott, *Seattle Pacific University*

Ralph G. Pifer, *Sauk Valley Community College*

James S. Previte, *Victor Valley College*

Sheila O'Brien Quinn, *Salve Regina University*

Wayne J. Robinson, *Monroe Community College*

John L. Romanek, *Jefferson Community College*

Kenneth M. Rosenberg, *State University of New York, Oswego*

Elisabeth D. Sherwin, *University of Arkansas at Little Rock*

Nancy Simpson, *Trident Technical College*

Maggie Sokolik, *University of California, Berkeley*

Cynthia J. Smith, *Wheeling Jesuit University*

Jane A. Smith, *Concordia University*

Mitchell Speaks, *Keene State College*

Holly Straub, *University of South Dakota*

Linda K. Swindell, *Anderson University*

Parsram S. Thakur, *Community College of Rhode Island*

Inger Thompson, *Glendale Community College*

M. Lisa Valentino, *Seminole Community College*

Mary A. Waterstreet, *St. Ambrose University*

Michael J. Wenger, *University of Notre Dame*

Fred Whitford, *Montana State University*

Gordon Whitman, *Sandhills Community College*

Robert Wildblood, *Northern Virginia Community College*

Jean M. Wynn, *Manchester Community College*

C. Van Youngman, *Art Institute of Philadelphia*

The process of creating *Essentials of Psychology* was greatly facilitated by the work of many dedicated people in the College Division at Houghton Mifflin Company. From the sales representatives and sales managers who reinforced our colleagues' requests for the text, to the marketing staff who worked to tell our colleagues what *Essentials* has to offer, it seems everyone in the division had a hand in shaping this book, and now in revising it into its fourth edition. Several people in the editorial and production areas at Houghton Mifflin deserve special mention, however, because they did an absolutely outstanding job in helping us develop and revise the *Essentials* manuscript and turn that manuscript into the beautiful book you are now holding. Senior Development Editor Jane Knetzger was involved in the shaping and development of *Essentials* from day one; her advice and suggestions were invariably helpful. For this fourth edition, our Developmental Editors Rita Lombard and Laura Hildebrand did a great job as we worked on the new manuscript and tried to meet the goal of focusing on the essentials of psychology. Thanks to both of you for all your help. And many thanks to Aileen Mason, Senior Production Editor, for once again coordinating the myriad production tasks associated with this project and for keeping them, and us, on schedule. We appreciate it very much. We also want to thank Ann Schroeder, Charlotte Miller, Jessyca Broekman, and Karen Pugliano for their outstanding work in the creation of the art and photo program throughout the editions of *Essentials*. And many thanks, too, to Elaine Kehoe for her flawless copyediting of the final manuscript; Shelley Dickerson, who proofread the pages; Chris Arden, who created the combined glossary/index; and to Katherine Leahey and Andrew Laskey for their work as Production Assistants. Also our thanks to Editorial Assistants Liz Hogan and Chip Cheek for their assistance in managing the supplements, and to Lynn Baldridge, Digital Products Manager and Lynne Blaszak, Senior Media Producer, for helping to refine and strengthen our technology offerings for this edition. To Jane Potter, Sponsoring Editor; Laura McGinn and Amy Whitaker, Marketing Managers; and Kris Bishop and Samantha Abrams, Marketing Assistants; for their unfailing support in this project, we offer our sincere thanks. Without these people, and those who worked with them, the fourth edition of *Essentials of Psychology* would still be just an idea.

Finally, we want to express our thanks to our friends and our families who helped sustain us as we worked on this new edition. Your love and support mean more to us than we can ever express in words.

Doug Bernstein
Peggy Nash

1

Introduction to the Science of Psychology

The following people all hold truly interesting jobs. What do you think they

studied to qualify for those jobs? See if you can fill in the blank next to each job description with one of the fields of study listed in Table 1.1.

▶ **Kristen Beyer** works for the Federal Bureau of Investigation, where she develops questionnaires and conducts interviews aimed at identifying common features in the backgrounds of serial killers. _____

▶ **David Buss,** a professor at the University of Texas, conducts research and teaches courses on how evolution influences aggression, the choice of sexual partners, and other aspects of people's social behavior. _____

▶ **Anne Marie Apanovitch** is employed by a major drug company to study which of the company's marketing strategies are most effective in promoting sales. _____

▶ **Rebecca Snyder** studies the giant pandas at Zoo Atlanta in an effort to promote captive breeding and ultimately increase the wild population of this endangered species. _____

▶ **Michael Moon's** job at a software company is to find new ways to make Internet web sites easier for consumers to use. _____

▶ **Elizabeth Kolmstetter** works at the Transportation Security Administration, where, following the September 11, 2001, terrorist attacks, she took charge of a program to establish higher standards for hiring and training security screeners at U.S. airports. _____

▶ **Marissa Reddy,** codirector of the U.S. Secret Service's Safe Schools Initiative, tries to identify risk factors for violent behavior in high school students. _____

▶ **Sharon Lundgren,** founder of Lundgren Trial Consulting, Inc., helps prepare witnesses to testify in court and teaches attorneys how to present their evidence in the most convincing way. _____

▶ **Evan Byrne** works at the U.S. National Transportation Safety Board, where he investigates the role of memory lapses, disorientation, errors, and other human factors in causing airplane crashes. _____

▶ **Capt. Karen Orts,** chief of mental health services at a U.S. Air Force base, provides psychotherapy to military personnel suffering combat-related stress disorders and teaches leadership courses to commissioned and noncommissioned officers. _____

Because Captain Orts offers psychotherapy, you probably guessed that she is a psychologist, but what academic field did you associate with Rebecca Snyder, who studies giant pandas? It would have been perfectly reasonable to assume that she is a zoologist, but she, too, is a psychologist. So is Michael Moon, whose work on web site design might suggest that he was a computer science major. And although Sharon Lundgren spends her time working with witnesses and conducting mock trials, she is a psychologist, not a lawyer. The fact is that *all* these people are psychologists! They may not all fit your image of what psychologists do, but as you will see in this chapter, and throughout this book, psychology is much broader and more diverse than you might have expected. We hope that reading this book will give you a fuller picture of psychology and that you will find our field as fascinating as we do.

This chapter begins our exploration of psychology with a brief look at some of its interrelated specialty areas, or *subfields*. We then tell the story of how psychology came to be, and we review several theories and approaches that guide psychologists in their work.

We also point out how the activities of psychologists in virtually every subfield are affected by human diversity, especially by age, gender, ethnicity, and other individual characteristics encountered in today's multicultural societies. Finally, we consider how critical thinking, scientific methods, and ethical standards guide psychologists as they conduct research and evaluate the evidence they collect.

Reading this chapter will help you to answer the following questions:

▶ **What is psychology, and how did it grow? 4**

▶ **Why don't all psychologists explain behavior in the same way? 14**

▶ **How does your cultural background influence your behavior? 18**

▶ **How can critical thinking save you money? 21**

▶ **How do psychologists learn about people? 26**

▶ **What does it mean when scientists announce that a research finding is "significant"? 39**

▶ **Do psychologists deceive people when they do research? 40**

TABLE 1.1

What's My Line?

learn by doing Try matching these educational backgrounds with the people described at the beginning of the chapter by writing the correct field of study next to each person's job description.

A. Engineering	F. Advertising
B. Criminal Justice	G. Biology
C. Computer Science	H. Education
D. Law	I. Zoology
E. Psychology	J. Business Administration

The World of Psychology: An Overview

▶ **What is psychology, and how did it grow?**

Psychology is the science that seeks to understand behavior and mental processes and to apply that understanding in the service of human welfare. So, although the ten people we have just described are engaged in many different kinds of work, they are all psychologists because they are all involved in studying, predicting, improving, or explaining some aspect of behavior and mental processes. But even this wide variety of jobs fails to capture the full scope of psychologists' interests. As a group, the world's half-million psychologists are interested in all the behaviors and mental processes that make you who you are and make other people who they are in every culture around the world.

Subfields of Psychology

Source: Botwinick (1961).

FIGURE 1.1

Husband and Father-in-Law

learn by doing This figure is called "Husband and Father-in-Law" (Botwinick, 1961) because you can see it as two different people, depending on how you mentally organize the features of the drawing. The elderly "father-in-law" faces to your right and is turned slightly toward you. He has a large nose, and the dark areas represent a coat pulled up to his chin. However, the tip of his nose can also be seen as the tip of a younger man's chin. The "husband" is in profile, also looking to your right, but away from you. The old man's mouth is the young man's neck band. Both men are wearing broad-brimmed hats. Can you see them? Cognitive psychologists point out that your ability to see two different figures in the same drawing—and to choose which one to see at any given moment—means that you actively manipulate incoming information rather than just passively receiving it.

psychology The science that seeks to understand behavior and mental processes and to apply that understanding in the service of human welfare.

cognitive psychologists Psychologists whose research focus is analysis of the mental processes underlying judgment, decision making, problem solving, imagining, and other aspects of human thought or cognition.

learn by doing To appreciate how many things come under the umbrella of *behavior and mental processes,* think for a moment about how you would answer the question, Who are you? Would you describe your personality, the sharpness of your vision or hearing, your interests and goals, your job skills and accomplishments, your IQ, your cultural background, your social skills, or perhaps a physical or psychological problem that bothers you? You could list these and dozens of other things about yourself, and every one of them would reflect some aspect of what psychologists mean by *behavior and mental processes.* When psychologists focus their work on particular aspects of behavior and mental processes, they enter one of psychology's many subfields. Let's take a quick look at the typical interests and activities of psychologists in these subfields now; we will focus on many of them in more detail in later chapters.

- **Cognitive psychologists** study basic mental processes such as sensation and perception (see Figure 1.1), learning and memory (including the question of whether people can forget, and then suddenly recover, traumatic memories), and judgment, decision making, and problem solving.

- **Biological psychologists,** also called *physiological psychologists* or *neuroscientists,* study topics such as how genes and brain chemistry are related to the appearance of mental disorders, how brain cells communicate with each other in forming memories, whether certain patterns of brain activity can reveal that a person is lying, and how stress hormones weaken the body's immune system. Have you ever experienced *déjà vu,* the feeling that a new experience, such as entering an unfamiliar house, has actually happened to you before? Biological psychologists studying this illusion suggest that it may be due to a temporary malfunction in the brain's ability to combine incoming information from the senses, creating the impression of two "copies" of a single event (Brown, 2004).

- **Personality psychologists** study individuality—the unique features of each person. Your personality traits, like your fingerprints, are different from those of all other people. Some personality psychologists use tests to describe how one individual compares with others in terms of openness to experience, emotionality, reliability, agreeableness, and sociability. Others study particular combinations of personality traits that may predict particular patterns of behavior. For instance, personality psychologists interested in *positive psychology* are identifying the characteristics of people who can remain optimistic even in the face of stress or tragedy and find happiness in life (Snyder & Lopez, 2006).

- **Developmental psychologists** study and describe changes in behavior and mental processes over the life span, trying to understand their causes and effects (see Figure 1.2). They explore areas such as the development of thought, friendship patterns, and parenting styles and whether everyone must face a midlife crisis. Some of their research has been used by judges and attorneys in deciding how old a child has to be in order to serve as a reliable witness in court or to responsibly choose which divorcing parent to live with.

FIGURE **1.2**

Where Would You Put a Third Eye?

In a study of how thinking develops, children were asked to show where they would place a third eye if they could have one. Part A shows that nine-year-old children, who were still in an early stage of mental development, drew the extra eye between their existing eyes, "as a spare." Having developed more advanced thinking abilities, eleven-year-olds (Part B) drew the third eye in more creative places, such as the palm of their hand "so I can see around corners" (Shaffer, 1973).

Drawing by a nine-year-old
(A)

Drawing by an eleven-year-old
(B)

Source: Shaffer (1973), Box 4–2.

biological psychologists Psychologists who analyze the biological factors influencing behavior and mental processes.

personality psychologists Psychologists who focus on people's unique characteristics.

developmental psychologists Psychologists who seek to understand, describe, and explore how behavior and mental processes change over the course of a lifetime.

quantitative psychologists Psychologists who develop statistical methods for evaluating and analyzing data from psychological research.

clinical, counseling, and community psychologists Psychologists who seek to assess, understand, modify, and prevent behavior disorders.

educational psychologists Psychologists who study methods by which instructors teach and students learn and who apply their results to improving such methods.

school psychologists Psychologists who test IQ, diagnose students' academic problems, and set up programs to improve students' achievement.

■ **Quantitative psychologists** develop and use statistical tools to analyze vast amounts of information generated by research results from all of psychology's subfields. Later in this chapter we show how quantitative psychologists use correlation coefficients and other statistical tools to evaluate psychological tests and to estimate the relative contributions of heredity and environment in determining our intelligence. To what extent are people born smart—or not so smart—and to what extent are their mental abilities affected by their environments? This is one of the hottest topics in psychology today, and quantitative psychologists are right in the middle of it.

■ **Clinical, counseling, and community psychologists** study the causes of behavior disorders and offer services to help troubled people overcome these disorders. Generally, clinical psychologists have Ph.D. degrees in psychology; most provide therapy services, and many conduct research as well. A counseling psychologist might work as a mental health counselor, for example, and have either a Ph.D. or a master's degree in psychology. Community psychologists offer psychological services to the homeless and others who need help but tend not to seek it. By working for changes in schools and other social systems, they also try to prevent poverty and other stressful conditions that so often lead to disorder. All of these psychologists differ from *psychiatrists*, who are medical doctors with a specialty in abnormal behavior (psychiatry).

■ **Educational psychologists** conduct research and develop theories about teaching and learning. The results of their work are applied in programs designed to improve teacher training, refine school curricula, reduce dropout rates, and help students learn more efficiently. For example, they have supported the use of the "jigsaw" technique, a type of classroom activity in which children from various ethnic groups must work together to complete a task or solve a problem. These cooperative experiences appear to promote learning, generate mutual respect, and reduce intergroup prejudice (Aronson, 2004).

■ **School psychologists** have traditionally specialized in intelligence testing, diagnosing learning disabilities and other academic problems, and setting up programs to improve students' achievement and satisfaction in school. Today, however, they are also involved in early detection of students' mental health problems and in crisis intervention following school violence (Benjamin & Baker, 2004; Elliot, Reynolds, & Kratochwill, 2006).

■ **Social psychologists** study the ways that people influence one another. For example, they conduct research on social-influence strategies, such as the effectiveness of

applying
psychology

GOT A MATCH?
Some commercial dating services apply social psychologists' research on interpersonal attraction in an effort to pair up people whose characteristics are most likely to be compatible.

safe-sex advertising campaigns designed to halt the spread of AIDS. They also explore how peer pressure affects us, what determines whom we like (or even love), and why and how prejudice forms. They have found, for example, that although we may pride ourselves on not being prejudiced, we may actually hold unconscious beliefs about certain ethnic groups that negatively affect the way we relate to people from those groups (Vanman et al., 2004).

social psychologists Psychologists who study how people influence one another's behavior and attitudes, especially in groups.

industrial/organizational psychologists Psychologists who examine factors that influence people's performance in the workplace.

health psychologists Psychologists who study the effects of behavior on health and the impact of illness on behavior and emotion.

sport psychologists Psychologists whose research is aimed at maximizing athletic performance.

forensic psychologists Psychologists who are involved in many aspects of psychology and law.

engineering psychologists Psychologists who study and try to improve the relationships between human beings and the computers and other machines they use.

environmental psychologists Psychologists who study the relationship between people's physical environment and their behavior.

■ **Industrial/organizational psychologists** study leadership, stress, competition, pay, and other factors that affect the efficiency, productivity, and satisfaction of workers and the organizations that employ them. They conduct research on topics such as increasing the motivation of current employees and helping companies select the best new workers. They also explore the ways in which businesses and industrial organizations work—or fail to work—and they make recommendations to help these organizations to work better (Spector, 2003). Companies all over the world are applying research by industrial/organizational psychologists in the development of employee training programs, effective goal-setting procedures, fair and reasonable evaluation methods, and systems for motivating and rewarding outstanding employee performance.

Our list of psychology's subfields is still not complete. For example, **health psychologists** study the effects of behavior on health and the impact of illness on behavior and emotion; **sport psychologists** search for the keys to maximum athletic performance; and **forensic psychologists** assist in jury selection, evaluate defendants' sanity and mental competence to stand trial, and deal with other issues involving psychology and the law. **Engineering psychologists,** also known as *human factors psychologists,* study the relationships of human beings to the computers and other machines they use. Their research has been applied in the design of computer keyboards; Internet web sites; aircraft instrument panels; controls for hospital beds and nuclear power plants; and even on-screen programming systems for TV sets that make them more logical, easier to use, and less likely to cause errors. Finally, **environmental psychologists** study the effects of the environment on people's behavior and mental processes. The results of their research are applied by architects and interior designers as they plan or remodel residence halls, shopping malls, auditoriums, hospitals, prisons,

GETTING READY FOR SURGERY   Health psychologists have learned that when patients are mentally prepared for a surgical procedure, they are less stressed by it and recover more rapidly. Their research is now routinely applied in hospitals through programs in which children and adults are given clear information about what to expect before, during, and after their operations.

offices, and other spaces to make them more comfortable and functional for the people who will occupy them. (See Table 1.2 for a summary of the typical activities and work settings of psychologists in the United States.)

Linkages Within Psychology and Beyond

We have listed psychology's subfields as though they were separate, but they often overlap, and so do the activities of the psychologists working in them. When developmental psychologists study the growth of children's thinking skills or friendships, for example, their research is linked to that of colleagues in cognitive or social psychology. Similarly, biological psychologists have one foot in clinical psychology when they look at how

IMPROVING BAD DESIGNS   Consultation by engineering psychologists, who apply cognitive research to the design of equipment, would surely have improved the layout of these self-service fuel pumps. The system will not operate until you press the red spot (see upper right) under the yellow "push to start" label, which is difficult to locate among all the other signs and stickers. Such user-unfriendly designs are all too common these days (e.g., Cooper, 2004; visit www.baddesigns.com for some amazing examples).

Photograph courtesy of www.baddesigns.com.

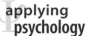

PLANNING SPACES
Environmental psychologists are often asked to consult on the design of offices. Here, the consultants suggested the use of aquariums filled with tropical fish to help reduce the stress that is created when many employees work in close quarters.

TABLE 1.2   Typical Activities and Work Settings for Psychologists

The fact that psychologists can work in such a wide variety of settings and do so many interesting—and often well-paying—jobs helps account for the popularity of psychology as an undergraduate major (Fogg, Harrington, & Harrington, 2005; National Center for Education Statistics, 2003). Psychology courses also provide excellent background for students planning to enter medicine, law, business, and many other fields.

Percentage of Psychologists	Work Setting	Typical Activities
22.8%	Colleges, universities, and professional schools	Teaching, research, and writing, often in collaboration with colleagues from other disciplines
27.5%	Mental health facilities (e.g., hospitals, clinics, counseling centers)	Testing and treatment of children and adults
31.8%	Private practice (alone or in a group of psychologists)	Testing and treatment of children and adults; consultation to business and other organizations
6.1%	Business, government, and organizations	Testing potential employees; assessing employee satisfaction; identifying and resolving conflicts; improving leadership skills; offering stress management and other employee assistance programs; improving equipment design to maximize productivity and prevent accidents
4.5%	Schools (including those for developmentally disabled and emotionally disturbed children)	Testing mental abilities and other characteristics; identifying problem children; consulting with parents; designing and implementing programs to improve academic performance
7.3%	Other	Teaching prison inmates; research in private institutes; advising legislators on educational, research, or public policy; administering research funds; research on effectiveness of military personnel; etc.

Source: Data from 1999 APA Directory Survey (APA, 2000).

FIGURE 1.3

Linkages to the Science of Psychology

The questions listed in this diagram highlight just three of the many ways in which psychology's subfields are linked to one another. Three additional linking questions appear in the Linkages diagram included in every chapter to come. Each diagram lists the page number on which each question is answered. When you turn to that page, you will find a *Linkages* symbol in the margin where the answer is discussed. Sometimes the discussion is brief, but every chapter also contains a special Linkages feature that examines linked research in more detail. By staying alert to linkages among psychology's subfields, you will come away from this course not only with threads of knowledge about each subfield but also with an appreciation of the fabric of psychology as a whole.

chemicals in the brain affect the risk of depression. And when social psychologists apply research on cooperation to promote group learning activities in the classroom, they are linking up with educational psychology. Even when psychologists work mainly in one subfield, they are still likely to draw on, and contribute to, the knowledge in other subfields.

So if you want to understand psychology as a whole, you have to understand the linkages among its subfields. To help you recognize these linkages, we highlight three of them in a diagram, similar to the one in Figure 1.3, near the end of every chapter. Each chapter's Linkages diagram contains questions that illustrate three relationships between the topics discussed in that chapter and the topics of other chapters. The page numbers after each question indicate where discussions related to them appear (look for "Linkages" symbols on those pages). There are so many linkages throughout the book that we could not include them all in our diagrams, but we hope those diagrams will remind you to look for linkages that we didn't mention. This kind of detective work can actually help you to do better on exams and quizzes, because it is often easier to remember material in one chapter by relating it to linked material in other chapters.

Psychology itself is linked to other disciplines. Some of these connections occur because of the interests that psychologists share with researchers in other fields. For example, cognitive psychologists are working with computer scientists to create artificial intelligence

applying psychology

LINKING PSYCHOLOGY AND LAW Cognitive psychologists' research on the quirks of human memory has led to revised guidelines for police and prosecutors (U.S. Department of Justice, 1999). These guidelines warn that asking witnesses leading questions (e.g., "Do you remember seeing a gun?") can distort their memories and that false accusations are less likely if witnesses are told that the real criminal might not be in a lineup or in a group of photos (Doyle, 2005).

systems that can recognize voices, solve problems, and make decisions in ways that will equal or exceed human capabilities. Other links occur when research in one discipline is applied in another. For example, physicians and economists are using research by psychologists to better understand the thought processes that influence (good and bad) decisions about caring for patients and choosing investments (Handgraaf & van Raaij, 2005; Slovic et al., 2005). In fact, psychologist Daniel Kahneman recently won a Nobel Prize in economics for his work in this area. Other psychologists' research on memory has influenced how lineups are displayed to eyewitnesses attempting to identify criminals, how attorneys question eyewitnesses in court, and how judges instruct juries (Memon, Vrij, & Bull, 2004). And psychological studies of the effect of brain disorders on elderly patients' mental abilities are shaping doctors' recommendations about when those patients should stop driving cars (Reger et al., 2004).

This book is filled with examples of other ways in which psychological theories and research have been applied to fields as diverse as health care, law, business, engineering, architecture, aviation, and sports.

A Brief History of Psychology

Psychology is a relatively new science, but its origins can be traced through centuries. Since at least the time of Socrates, Plato, and Aristotle in ancient Greece, philosophers have debated such psychological topics as where human knowledge comes from, the nature of mind and soul, the relationship of the mind to the body, and even the possibility of scientifically studying these matters (Wertheimer, 2000).

So scientific psychology has its roots in philosophy, and especially in a philosophical view called **empiricism** (pronounced "im-PEER-eh-ciz-em"). In the 1600s, empiricists such as John Locke, George Berkeley, and David Hume challenged the claim—which had been made by philosophers as far back as Plato—that some of what we know is present at birth. Empiricists argued that our minds are more like a blank slate (*tabula rasa* in Latin) on which our experiences write a lifelong story. In other words, according to empiricism, knowledge comes to us only through our experiences and observations. For nearly 130 years now, empiricism has guided psychologists in seeking knowledge about behavior and mental processes not through speculation but through observations governed by the rules of science.

Wundt and the Structuralism of Titchener   The birth date of modern scientific psychology is usually given as 1879. This is the year in which Wilhelm Wundt (pronounced "voont") established the first formal psychology research laboratory, at the University of Leipzig in Germany (Benjamin, 2000). Wundt was a physiologist, and like other physiologists of his day, he had been studying vision, hearing, and other sensory-perceptual systems. However, Wundt's more ambitious goal was to use the methods of laboratory science to study **consciousness**—the mental experience that arises from these systems. In doing so, Wundt began psychology's transformation from the *philosophy* of mental processes to the science of mental processes.

Wundt wanted to describe the basic elements of consciousness, how they are organized, and how they relate to one another (Schultz & Schultz, 2002). In an attempt to study conscious experience, Wundt used *introspection,* which means "looking inward." Edward Titchener, an American who had been a student of Wundt, later used introspection in his own laboratory at Cornell University to study sensations, feelings, and images associated with conscious experience. To understand introspection, look at the object in Figure 1.4, but try to describe not what it is but only how intensely and clearly you experience its sensations and images (such as redness, brightness, and roundness). This was the difficult task that Wundt and Titchener set for carefully trained "introspectors" in a search for the building blocks of consciousness. Titchener called his approach *structuralism* because he was trying to define the structure of consciousness. Wundt and Titchener were not the only scientific researchers in psychology, and their work was not universally accepted. Other scientific psychologists in Europe were studying sensory limits and the capability for learning and memory. They saw the structuralists' work as too simplistic.

empiricism The view that knowledge comes from experience and observation.

consciousness The awareness of external stimuli and our own mental activity.

WILHELM WUNDT (1832–1920) In an early experiment on the speed of mental processes, Wilhelm Wundt (third from left) first measured how quickly people could respond to a light by releasing a button they had been holding down. He then measured how much longer the response took when they held down one button with each hand and had to decide—based on the color of the light—which one to release. Wundt reasoned that the additional response time reflected how long it took to perceive the color and decide which hand to move. As noted in the chapter on thought, language, and intelligence, the logic behind this experiment remains a part of modern research on cognitive processes.

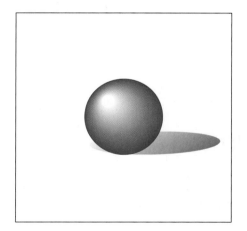

FIGURE **1.4**

A Stimulus for Introspection

learn by doing Look at this object and try to ignore what it is. Instead, try to describe only your conscious experience of it—such as redness, brightness, and roundness, and how intense and clear these sensations and images are. If you can do this, you would have been an excellent research participant in Titchener's laboratory.

Gestalt Psychology Around 1912, another group of European psychologists, led by Max Wertheimer, Kurt Koffka, and Wolfgang Köhler, argued against the value of trying to break down human experience or consciousness into its component parts. They were called *Gestalt psychologists* because they pointed out that the whole (or *Gestalt,* in German) of conscious experience is not the same as the sum of its parts. Wertheimer noted, for example, that when two lights are placed near each other in a dark room and go on and off in just the right sequence, we experience not two lights but a single light "jumping" back and forth. This is called the *phi phenomenon,* and you have probably seen it in advertising signs that create the impression of a series of lights racing around a display. Movies provide another example. Imagine how boring it would be to browse through the thousands of still images that are printed on a reel of film. Yet when those same images are projected onto a screen at just the right rate, they combine to create a rich emotional experience. In other words, said the Gestaltists, consciousness should be studied as a whole, not piece by piece.

Freud and Psychoanalysis While Wundt was conducting scientific research on consciousness in Germany, Sigmund Freud, a physician, was in Vienna, Austria, exploring the unconscious. In the late 1880s, Freud began to question the assumption that biological factors were behind all behavior and mental processes, including illnesses. Using hypnosis and other methods, Freud suggested that the cause of some people's physical ailments was not physical. The real cause, he said, was deep-seated problems that the patients had pushed out of consciousness (Friedman & Schustack, 2003). He eventually came to believe that all behavior—from everyday slips of the tongue to severe forms of mental disorder—can be traced to *psychological processes,* especially to internal conflicts that he said take place without our being aware of them. He believed that many of these unconscious *psychodynamic* conflicts are created when our sexual and aggressive instincts clash with the rules set for us by society. For nearly fifty years, Freud revised and expanded his ideas into a body of work known as *psychoanalysis.* His theory included explanations of how personality and mental disorder develop, as well as a set of treatment methods. Freud's ideas are by no means universally accepted, but he was a groundbreaker whose psychodynamic theories had a significant influence on psychology and many other fields.

William James and Functionalism Psychology took root in North America not long after Wundt began his work in Germany. In the late 1870s, William James set up the first psychology laboratory in the United States, at Harvard University. His lab was used mainly to conduct demonstrations for his students (Schultz & Schultz,

WILLIAM JAMES'S LABORATORY
William James (1842–1910) established this psychology demonstration laboratory at Harvard University in the late 1870s. Like the Gestalt psychologists, James saw the approach used by Wundt and Titchener as a scientific dead end; he said that trying to understand consciousness by studying its parts is like trying to understand a house by looking at individual bricks (James, 1884). He preferred instead to study the ways in which consciousness functions to help people adapt to their environments.

2002), but in 1883, G. Stanley Hall at Johns Hopkins University established the first psychology *research* laboratory in the United States. The first Canadian psychology research laboratory was established in 1889 at the University of Toronto by James Mark Baldwin, Canada's first modern psychologist and a pioneer in research on child development.

William James rejected both Wundt's approach and Titchener's structuralism. Influenced by Darwin's theory of evolution, James wanted to understand how sensations, memories, and all the other mental events that make up our ever-flowing "stream of consciousness" help us adapt to our changing environments (James, 1890, 1892). This idea was consistent with an approach to psychology called *functionalism*, which focused on the function of consciousness in guiding our ability to make decisions, solve problems, and the like. James's emphasis on the functions of mental processes encouraged other psychologists in North America to look at how those processes work to our advantage and also at how they differ from person to person. Some of these psychologists began to measure individual differences in learning, memory, and other aspects of intelligence and to make recommendations for improving educational practices in the schools. A few even began to work with teachers on programs for children in need of special help (Bernstein, Kramer, & Phares, in press).

John B. Watson and Behaviorism   Besides fueling James's interest in the functions of consciousness, Darwin's theory of evolution led other psychologists, especially in North America after 1900, to study animals as well as humans. If all species evolved in adaptive ways, perhaps their behavior and mental processes would follow the same, or similar, laws. Psychologists observed animal behavior in mazes and other experimental situations. From these observations, they drew conclusions about the animals' conscious experiences and about the general laws of learning, memory, problem solving, and other mental processes that might apply to people, too.

John B. Watson, a psychology professor at Johns Hopkins University, agreed that the behavior of animals and humans was the most important source of scientific information for psychology. In 1913, Watson wrote an article called "Psychology as the Behaviorist Views It." In this article, he argued that psychologists should ignore mental events and concern themselves only with *observable* behavior (Watson, 1913, 1919). His approach, known as *behaviorism*, did not address consciousness, as structuralism and functionalism did, let alone consider the unconscious, as the Freudian view did. Focusing on consciousness, said Watson, would prevent psychology from ever being a true science. Watson believed that *learning* is the most important cause of behavior. He was famous for claiming that if he had enough control over the environment, he could create learning experiences that would turn any infant into a doctor, a lawyer, or even a criminal.

American psychologist B. F. Skinner was another early champion of behaviorism. From the 1930s until his death in 1990, Skinner studied *operant conditioning,* a learning process through which rewards and punishments shape, maintain, and change behavior. Using what he called *functional analysis of behavior,* Skinner would explain, for example, how parents and teachers can unknowingly encourage children's tantrums by rewarding them with attention. He noted, too, that a virtual addiction to gambling can develop through the occasional and unpredictable rewards it brings. Skinner said that functional analysis not only reveals the learned foundations of behavior but also suggests what rewards and punishments should be changed in order to alter that behavior.

Watson's and Skinner's vision of psychology as the learning-based science of observable behavior found favor with many psychologists. Behaviorism dominated psychological research in North America from the 1920s through the 1960s. ("In Review: The Development of Psychology" summarizes behaviorism and the other schools of thought that have influenced psychologists over the years.)

Online Study Center

Improve Your Grade
Tutorial: Psychology Schools of Thought Timeline

in review

THE DEVELOPMENT OF PSYCHOLOGY

School of Thought	Founders	Goals	Methods
Structuralism	Edward Titchener, trained by Wilhelm Wundt	To study conscious experience and its structure	Experiments; introspection
Gestalt psychology	Max Wertheimer	To describe organization of mental processes: "The whole is greater than the sum of its parts."	Observation of sensory/ perceptual phenomena
Psychoanalysis	Sigmund Freud	To explain personality and behavior; to develop techniques for treating mental disorders	Study of individual cases
Functionalism	William James	To study how the mind works in allowing an organism to adapt to the environment ,	Naturalistic observation of animal and human behavior
Behaviorism	John B. Watson; B. F. Skinner	To study only observable behavior and explain behavior via learning principles	Observation of the relationship between environmental stimuli and behavioral responses

?
1. Darwin's theory of evolution had an especially strong influence on _____ ism and _____ ism.
2. Which school of psychological thought was founded by a medical doctor? _____
3. In the history of psychology, _____ was the first school of thought to appear.

FIGURE **1.5**

Visualizing Brain Activity

Magnetic resonance imaging (MRI) techniques allow biological psychologists to study the brain activity accompanying various mental processes (Poldrack & Wagner, 2004). This study found that, while reading, males (left) and females (right) show different patterns of brain activity, as indicated by the brightly colored areas (Shaywitz et al., 1995).

Psychology Today   By end of the 1960s, however, behaviorists' lack of attention to mental processes was seen by more and more psychologists as a serious limitation (e.g., Ericsson & Simon, 1994). As the computer age dawned, psychologists began to think about mental activity in a new way—as information processing. At the same time, progress in biotechnology began to offer psychologists new ways to study the biological bases of mental processes. Armed with ever more sophisticated research tools, many psychologists today are trying to do what Watson thought was impossible: to study mental processes and, as shown in Figure 1.5, even watch the brain perform them. So psychology has come full circle, once again accepting consciousness, in the form of cognitive processes, as a legitimate topic for research (Haynes & Rees, 2005; Kimble, 2000).

Approaches to the Science of Psychology

▶ **Why don't all psychologists explain behavior in the same way?**

We have seen that the history of psychology is, in part, the history of the differing ways in which psychologists have thought about, or "approached," behavior and mental processes. Today, psychologists no longer refer to themselves as structuralists or functionalists, but the psychodynamic and behavioral approaches remain, along with some newer ones known as the *biological, evolutionary, cognitive,* and *humanistic approaches.* Some psychologists adopt just one of these approaches, but most are *eclectic* (pronounced "ek-LECK-tick"). This means that they blend aspects of two or more approaches in an effort to more fully understand the behavior and mental processes in their subfield (e.g., Cacioppo et al., 2000). Some approaches to psychology are more influential than others these days, but we will review the main features of all of them so you can more easily understand why different psychologists may explain the same behavior or mental process in different ways.

The Biological Approach

biological approach   The view that behavior is the result of physical processes, especially those relating to the brain, to hormones, and to other chemicals.

As its name implies, the **biological approach** assumes that behavior and mental processes are largely shaped by biological processes. Psychologists who take this approach study the psychological effects of hormones, genes, and the activity of the nervous system, especially the brain. When studying memory, for example, these

THE BIOLOGY OF EMOTION Robert Levenson, a psychologist at the University of California at Berkeley, takes a biological approach to the study of social interactions. He measures heart rate, muscle tension, and other physical reactions as couples discuss problems in their relationships. He then looks for patterns of physiological activity in each partner, such as overreactions to criticism, that might be related to success or failure in resolving their problems.

A FATHER'S LOVE Mothers are solely responsible for the care and protection of their young in almost all species of mammals. These species survive without male parenting, so why are some human fathers so active in child rearing? Do evolutionary forces make fathering more adaptive for humans? Is it a matter of learning to care? Is it a combination of both? Psychologists who take an evolutionary approach study these questions and others relating to the origins of human social behavior.

evolutionary approach A view that emphasizes the inherited, adaptive aspects of behavior and mental processes.

researchers try to identify changes taking place in the brain as information is stored there. (Figure 6.13, in the chapter on memory, shows an example of these changes.) And when studying thinking, they might look for patterns of brain activity associated with, say, making quick decisions or reading a foreign language. Research discussed in nearly every chapter of this book reflects the enormous influence of the biological approach on psychology today.

The Evolutionary Approach

Biological processes are also highlighted in an approach to psychology that is based on Charles Darwin's 1859 book, *The Origin of Species.* Darwin had argued that the forms of life we see today are the result of *evolution*—of changes in life forms that occur over many generations. He said that evolution occurs through *natural selection,* which promotes the survival of the fittest individuals. Those whose behavior and appearance allow them to withstand the elements, to avoid predators, and to mate are able to survive and produce offspring with similar characteristics. Those less able to adjust, or *adapt,* to changing conditions are less likely to survive and reproduce. Most evolutionists today see natural selection operating at the level of genes, but the process is the same. Genes that result in characteristics and behaviors that are adaptive and useful in a certain environment will enable the creatures that inherited them to survive and reproduce, thereby passing those genes on to the next generation. According to evolutionary theory, many (but not all) of the genes that animals and humans possess today are the result of natural selection.

The **evolutionary approach** to psychology assumes that the *behavior and mental processes* of animals and humans today is largely the result of evolution through natural selection. Evolutionary psychologists see aggression, for example, as a form of territory protection, and they see gender differences in mate selection preferences as reflecting different ways of helping genes to survive in future generations. The evolutionary approach has resulted in a growing body of research (Buller, 2005; Buss, 2004a); in later chapters, you will see how it is applied in relation to topics such as mental disorders, temperament, interpersonal attraction, and helping.

The Psychodynamic Approach

The **psychodynamic approach** to psychology offers a different slant on the role of inherited characteristics in shaping behavior and mental processes. Rooted in Freud's theory of psychoanalysis, this approach assumes that our behavior and mental processes reflect the constant, and mostly unconscious, psychodynamic conflicts that are said to rage within each of us. According to Freud, these conflicts occur when the impulse to instantly satisfy our instinctive needs—such as for food, sex, or aggression—are opposed by our learned need to follow society's rules about fairness and consideration for others. So psychologists taking the psychodynamic approach might see aggression as a triumph of raw impulses over self-control. At the same time, they consider anxiety, depression, and other psychological disorders as the outward evidence of inner conflict.

Freud's original theories are not as influential today as they once were (Mischel, 2004a), but in other chapters you will see that modern versions of the psychodynamic approach still appear in various theories of personality, psychological disorders, and psychotherapy.

The Behavioral Approach

The assumptions of the **behavioral approach** to psychology contrast sharply with those of the biological, evolutionary, and psychodynamic approaches. For one thing, the behavioral approach is rooted in the behaviorism of Watson and Skinner. As we mentioned earlier, behaviorism focused entirely on observable behavior in humans and animals and on how it is learned. Accordingly, psychologists who take a strict behavioral approach concentrate only on observable behavior. They want to know how life's rewards, punishments, and other learning experiences act on the "raw materials" provided by genes and evolution to shape behavior into what it is today. So whether they are trying to understand a person's aggressiveness, fear of spiders, parenting methods, or tendency to abuse drugs, behaviorists look mainly at that person's learning history. And because they believe that behavior problems develop through learning, behaviorists seek to eliminate those problems by helping people learn new and more adaptive responses.

Recall, though, that behaviorism was criticized precisely because it ignored everything but observable behavior. That criticism has had an impact on the many behaviorists who now apply their learning-based approach in an effort to understand thoughts, or cognitions, as well as observable behavior. Those who take this *cognitive-behavioral, or social-cognitive,* approach explore such topics as the ways in which we learn our thoughts, attitudes, and beliefs and, in turn, how these learned cognitive patterns affect observable behavior.

The Cognitive Approach

The growth of the cognitive-behavioral perspective reflects the influence of a more generally cognitive view of psychology. This **cognitive approach** focuses on how our behavior is affected by the ways in which we take in, mentally represent, process, and store information. Consider how the cognitive approach might guide the analysis of an incident of aggression: A person in line for movie tickets (1) *perceived* that someone had cut into the line, (2) used information stored in memory to *judge* that this act was inappropriate, (3) *assumed* that the act was due to the other person's rudeness, (4) *considered* several possible responses and their likely consequences, (5) *decided* that punching the other person was the best response, and then (6) *executed* that response. Psychologists who take a cognitive approach suggest that mental processes like these—some of which occur outside of awareness—can help us to understand many kinds of individual and social behaviors, from decision making and problem solving to interpersonal attraction and intelligence. In the situation we just described, for example, the person's aggression would be seen as the result of poor problem solving, because there

psychodynamic approach A view developed by Freud that emphasizes unconscious mental processes in explaining human thought, feelings, and behavior.

behavioral approach A view based on the assumption that human behavior is determined mainly by what a person has learned in life, especially by rewards and punishments.

cognitive approach A view that emphasizes research on how the brain takes in information, creates perceptions, forms and retrieves memories, processes information, and generates integrated patterns of action.

WHY IS HE SO AGGRESSIVE?
Psychologists who take a cognitive-behavioral approach suggest that there are several ways in which children learn to be aggressive. Children might see others being rewarded for acting aggressively and then might be rewarded themselves for doing the same. Aggressiveness might also be made more likely if a child constantly hears that other people can be dangerous and that aggression is the only way to deal with threats, disagreements, and other conflict situations (Gifford-Smith et al., 2005).

were probably several better ways to deal with the problem of line cutting. The cognitive approach is especially important in the field of *cognitive science,* in which researchers from psychology, computer science, biology, engineering, linguistics, and philosophy study intelligent systems in humans and computers. Some of their progress in creating artificial intelligence in computers is described in the chapter on thought, language, and intelligence.

The Humanistic Approach

Mental processes play a different role in the humanistic approach to psychology (also known as the *phenomenological approach*). Psychologists who favor the **humanistic approach** see behavior as determined primarily by our capacity to choose how to think and act. They don't see these choices being guided by instincts, biological processes, or rewards and punishments but by each person's view of the world. So if you perceive the world as a friendly place, you are likely to be optimistic and secure. If you perceive it as full of hostile people, you will probably be defensive and anxious, or perhaps unfriendly and aggressive. Like their cognitively oriented colleagues, then, psychologists taking a humanistic approach would agree that the movie theater incident stemmed from someone's perception that aggression was justified. However, instead of trying to find general laws governing *all* people's thoughts and actions, humanistic psychologists try to understand how each individual's unique perceptions guide *that* person's thoughts and actions. In fact, many who prefer the humanistic approach claim that, because no two people are exactly alike, the only way to understand behavior and mental processes is to focus on how they operate in each individual. Humanistic psychologists also believe that people are essentially good, that they are in control of themselves, and that they seek to grow toward their fullest potential.

The humanistic approach began to attract attention in North America in the 1940s, mainly through the writings of Carl Rogers and Abraham Maslow. As you will see in later chapters, their views have had a major influence on the way some psychologists think about the development of personality, about how to do psychotherapy, and about the reasons people are motivated to behave as they do. Overall, however, the humanistic approach to psychology is less influential today than the biological, cognitive, behavioral, and evolutionary approaches. Many psychologists

humanistic approach   A view of behavior as controlled by the decisions that people make about their lives based on their perceptions of the world.

in review

APPROACHES TO PSYCHOLOGY

Approach	Characteristics
Biological	Emphasizes activity of the nervous system, especially of the brain; the action of hormones and other chemicals; and genetics
Evolutionary	Emphasizes the ways in which behavior and mental processes are adaptive for survival
Psychodynamic	Emphasizes internal conflicts, mostly unconscious, which usually pit sexual or aggressive instincts against environmental obstacles to their expression
Behavioral	Emphasizes learning, especially each person's experience with rewards and punishments
Cognitive	Emphasizes mechanisms through which people receive, store, retrieve, and otherwise process information
Humanistic	Emphasizes individual potential for growth and the role of unique perceptions in guiding behavior and mental processes

?
1. *Teaching people to be less afraid of heights reflects the _____ approach.*
2. *Charles Darwin was not a psychologist, but his work influenced the _____ approach to psychology.*
3. *Assuming that people inherit mental disorders suggests a _____ approach.*

find humanistic concepts and predictions too vague to be expressed and tested scientifically. (All the approaches we have described are summarized in "In Review: Approaches to Psychology.")

Human Diversity and Psychology

▶ **How does your cultural background influence your behavior?**

Today, the diversity seen in psychologists' approaches to their work is matched by the diversity in their own backgrounds. This was not always the case. In the early twentieth century, most psychologists—like most members of other academic disciplines—were white, middle-class men (Walker, 1991). Still, women and people of color had played a part in psychology almost from the beginning (Schultz & Schultz, 2002). Throughout this book you will find the work of their modern counterparts, whose contributions to research, service, and teaching have all increased in tandem with their growing representation in psychology. In the United States, women now constitute about 48 percent of all psychologists holding doctoral degrees (National Science Foundation, 2004a). Women are also earning 75.7 percent of the new master's degrees and 66.9 percent of the new doctoral degrees awarded in psychology each year (National Science Foundation, 2004b). Moreover, about 18 percent of new doctoral degrees in psychology are being earned by members of ethnic minority groups (National Science Foundation, 2004b). These numbers reflect continuing efforts by psychological organizations and governmental bodies, especially in the United States and Canada, to promote the recruitment, graduation, and employment of women and ethnic minorities in psychology (Maton et al., 2006).

MARY WHITON CALKINS (1863–1930) Mary Whiton Calkins studied psychology at Harvard University, where William James described her as "brilliant." Because she was a woman, though, Harvard refused to grant her a doctoral degree unless she received it through Radcliffe, which was then an affiliated school for women. She refused but went on to do research on memory, and in 1905 she became the first woman president of the American Psychological Association (APA). Margaret Washburn (1871–1939) encountered similar sex discrimination at Columbia University, so she transferred to Cornell University and became the first woman to earn a doctorate in psychology. In 1921, she became the second woman president of the APA.

GILBERT HAVEN JONES (1883–1966)
When Gilbert Haven Jones graduated from the University of Jena in Germany in 1909, he became one of the first African Americans to earn a doctorate in psychology. Many others were to follow, including J. Henry Alston, who was the first African American to publish research in a major U.S. psychology journal (Alston, 1920).

The Impact of Sociocultural Diversity on Psychology

As diversity among psychologists has increased, so too has their interest in the diversity of people in general. This change is significant, because psychologists once assumed that all humans were essentially alike and that whatever principles emerged from research with one group would apply to people everywhere. They were partly right, because people around the world *are* alike in many ways. They tend to live in groups; have religious beliefs; and create rules, music, dances, and games. The principles of nerve cell activity or reactions to heat or a sour taste are the same in men and women everywhere, as is their recognition of a smile. This is not true of all characteristics, however. Research has shown that people's striving for achievement, their moral values, their styles of communicating, and many other aspects of behavior and mental processes are shaped by a variety of **sociocultural variables,** including gender, ethnicity, social class, and the culture in which they grow up (Miyamoto, Nisbett, & Masuda, 2006; Shiraev & Levy, 2004).

Culture has been defined as the sum total of the values, rules of behavior, forms of expression, religious beliefs, occupational choices, and the like among a group of people who share a common language and environment (Fiske et al., 1998). Culture is an organizing and stabilizing influence. It encourages or discourages particular behaviors and ways of thinking; it also allows people to understand others in that culture and to know what to expect from them. It is a kind of group adaptation, passed on by tradition and example, rather than by genes, from one generation to the next. Culture determines, for example, whether children's education will focus on skill in hunting or in reading, how close people stand when they talk to each other, and whether or not they form lines in public places.

Cultures can differ in many ways (Abi-Hashem, 2000; Triandis, 1998). They may have strict or loose rules governing social behavior. They might place great value on achievement or on self-awareness. Some seek dominance over nature; others seek harmony with it. Time is of great importance in some cultures, but not in others. Psychologists have tended to focus on the differences between cultures that can be

sociocultural variables   Social identity and other background factors, such as gender, ethnicity, social class, and culture.

culture   The accumulation of values, rules of behavior, forms of expression, religious beliefs, and occupational choices for a group of people who share a common language and environment.

THE IMPACT OF CULTURE   Culture helps shape virtually every aspect of our behavior and mental processes, from how we dress to how we think to what we think is important. Because most people grow up immersed in a particular culture, they may not notice its influence on their thoughts and actions until—like these young women who immigrated from Africa to Denmark—they encounter people whose culture has shaped them in different ways (Nisbett & Masuda, 2003).

TABLE 1.3

Some Characteristics of Behavior and Mental Processes Typical of Individualist Versus Collectivist Cultures

Psychologists and anthropologists have noticed that cultures can create certain general tendencies in behavior and mental processes among the people living in them (Bhagat et al., 2002). As shown here, individualist cultures tend to support the idea of placing one's personal goals before the goals of the extended family or work group, whereas collectivist cultures tend to encourage putting the goals of those groups ahead of personal goals. Remember, though, that these labels represent very rough categories. Cultures cannot be pigeonholed as being either entirely individualist or entirely collectivist, and not everyone raised in a particular culture always thinks or acts in exactly the same way (Oyserman, Coon, & Kemmelmeier, 2002).

Variable	Individualist	Collectivist
Personal identity	Separate from others	Connected to others
Major goals	Self-defined; be unique; realize your personal potential; compete with others	Defined by others; belong; occupy your proper place; meet your obligations to others; be like others
Criteria for self-esteem	Ability to express unique aspects of the self; ability to be self-assured	Ability to restrain the self and be part of a social unit; ability to be self-effacing
Sources of success and failure	Success comes from personal effort; failure, from external factors	Success is due to help from others; failure is due to personal faults
Major frame of reference	Personal attitudes, traits, and goals	Family, work group

described as individualist or collectivist (Triandis & Trafimow, 2001; see Table 1.3). In *individualist* cultures, such as those typical of North America and Western Europe, people tend to focus on and value personal rather than group goals and achievement. Competitiveness to distinguish oneself from others is common, but so is a sense of isolation. By contrast, in *collectivist* cultures, such as those found in Japan and other parts of Asia, people tend to think of themselves as part of family or work groups. Cooperative effort aimed at advancing the welfare of those groups is highly valued. And although loneliness is rarely a problem, fear of rejection by the group is common. Many aspects of mainstream U.S. culture—from self-reliant movie heroes and bonuses for "top" employees to the invitation to "help yourself" at a buffet table—reflect its tendency toward an individualist orientation (see Table 1.4).

TABLE 1.4

Cultural Values as Seen in Advertising

learn by doing The statements listed here appeared in advertisements in Korea and the United States. Those from Korea reflect collectivist values, whereas those from the United States emphasize a more individualist orientation (Han & Shavitt, 1994). See if you can tell which are which; then check the bottom of the next page for the answers. You might want to follow up on this exercise by identifying the cultural values appearing in the ads you see in newspapers and magazines and on billboards and television. By surfing the Internet or scanning international newspapers, you can compare the values conveyed by ads in your culture with those in ads from other cultures.

1. "She's got a style all her own."

2. "You, only better."

3. "A more exhilarating way to provide for your family."

4. "We have a way of bringing people closer together."

5. "Celebrating a half-century of partnership."

6. "How to protect the most personal part of the environment: Your skin."

7. "Our family agrees with this selection of home furnishings."

8. "A leader among leaders."

9. "Make your way through the crowd."

10. "Your business success: Harmonizing with (company name)."

Source: Brehm, Kassin, & Fein (1999).

We often associate cultures with particular countries, but in reality, most countries are *multicultural*. In other words, they host many cultural groups within their borders. For instance, the United States encompasses African Americans, Hispanic Americans, Asian Americans, and American Indians, as well as European Americans whose families came from Italy, Germany, Britain, Greece, Poland, Sweden, Ireland, and many other places. In each of these groups, the individuals who identify with their cultural heritage tend to share behaviors, values, and beliefs based on their culture of origin. In other words, they form a *subculture*.

Most of us don't realize how strongly our culture or subculture has shaped our thoughts and actions until we come in contact with people whose culture or subculture has shaped them differently. Consider hand gestures, for example. The "thumbs-up" sign means that "everything is OK" to people in North America and Europe, but it is considered a rude gesture in Australia, Nigeria, and Bangladesh. And when, during the 2005 inauguration parade, President George W. Bush and his family greeted the University of Texas band with the "hook 'em horns" salute (a raised hand with the index and pinky fingers extended), many people watching in Norway were horrified. In their culture, this gesture is considered a salute to Satan. And though making eye contact during social introductions is usually seen as a sign of interest or sincerity in North America, it is likely to be considered rude in Japan (Axtell, 1998). Even some of the misunderstandings between people in the same culture can be traced to slight, culturally influenced differences in communication (Tannen, 2001). In the United States, for instance, women's efforts to connect with others by talking may be perceived by many men as "pointless" unless the discussion is geared to solving a particular problem. As a result, women often feel frustrated and misunderstood by men, who tend to offer well-meant, but unwanted, advice instead of conversation.

For decades, the impact of culture on behavior and mental processes was of concern mainly to a relatively small group of researchers working in *cross-cultural* psychology (Miller, 2002). As you will see in the chapters to come, however, psychologists in almost every subfield are now looking at how ethnicity, gender, age, and many other sociocultural variables can influence the behavior and mental processes of the people they serve and the people they study. In other words, psychology is striving to be the science of *all* behavior and mental processes, not just of those in the cultures in which it began.

Thinking Critically About Psychology (or Anything Else)

▶ **How can critical thinking save you money?**

In order to appreciate the effects of sociocultural variables on behavior and mental processes, psychologists had to think about their field in new ways. For one thing, they had to question the assumption that studying people of just one gender, age range, ethnic group, or culture can tell us about people in general. This kind of "thinking outside the box" can lead to new insights, but it takes effort, and it sometimes upsets those who hold more traditional views. No wonder, then, that some people prefer to simply accept what they are told, especially when it comes from a believable source (see Table 1.5). Some advertisers, politicians, TV evangelists, and social activists hope for this kind of easy acceptance when they go after your money, your vote, or your loyalty. They want you to believe their promises or claims without careful thought on your part. In other words, they don't want you to think critically.

Critical thinking is the process of assessing claims and making judgments on the basis of well-supported evidence (Wade, 1988). Let's consider some of the questions that arise from thinking critically about psychology (or anything else) and then review the scientific research methods that psychologists use to try to answer those questions.

critical thinking The process of assessing claims and making judgments on the basis of well-supported evidence.

Answer key for Table 1.4: U.S. ads are numbers 1, 2, 6, 8, and 9.

TABLE 1.5 Some Popular Myths

Ask some friends and relatives what they think about the statements listed in the left-hand column of this table. Most people will probably agree with at least one of them, even though all of them are false. Perhaps you already knew that, but don't feel too smug. At one time or another, we all accept something we are told simply because the information seems to come from a reliable source or because "everyone knows" it is true (Losh et al., 2003).

Myth	Fact
Many children are injured each year in the United States when razor blades, needles, or poison is put in Halloween candy.	Reported cases are rare, most turn out to be hoaxes, and in the only documented case of a child dying from poisoned candy, the culprit was the child's own parent (Brunvald, 1989).
If your roommate commits suicide during the school term, you automatically get A's in all your classes for that term.	No college or university anywhere has ever had such a rule.
People have been known to burst into flames and die from fire erupting within their own bodies.	In rare cases, humans have been consumed by fires that caused little or no damage to the surrounding area. However, this phenomenon has been duplicated in a laboratory, and each alleged case of "spontaneous human combustion" has been traced to an external source of ignition (Benecke, 1999; Nienhuys, 2001).
Most big-city police departments rely on the advice of psychics to help them solve murders, kidnappings, and missing persons cases.	Only about 35% of urban police departments ever seek psychics' advice, and that advice is virtually never more helpful than other means of investigation (Nickell, 1997; Wiseman, West, & Stemman, 1996).
Murders, suicides, animal bites, and episodes of mental disorder are more likely to occur when the moon is full.	Records of crimes, dog bites, and mental hospital admissions do not support this common belief (Bickis, Kelly, & Byrnes, 1995; Chapman & Morrell, 2000; Rotton & Kelly, 1985).
You can't fool a lie detector.	Lie detectors can be helpful in solving crimes, but they are not perfect; their results can free a guilty person or send an innocent person to jail (see the chapter on motivation and emotion).
Viewers never see David Letterman walking to his desk after the opening monologue because his contract prohibits him from showing his backside on TV.	When questioned about this story on the air, Letterman denied it and, to prove his point, lifted his jacket and turned a full circle in front of the cameras and studio audience (Brunvald, 1989).
Psychics have special abilities to see into the future.	Even the most famous psychics are almost always wrong, as in these predictions for the year 2002: "Satan will be discovered working in a homeless shelter, reading to the blind, and delivering Meals on Wheels," "The Super Bowl will be cancelled after the first half because team owners will refuse to cough up an extra $10,000 for each player," and "A time tunnel will be created to allow people to make a one-way trip back into time." No psychic's 2001 predictions included the September 11 terrorist attacks on New York and Washington. When psychics do appear to be correct, it is usually because their forecasts are either vague ("Hillary Clinton will be much in the headlines with a scandal") or easy to predict without special powers ("Prince Charles and Camilla Parker-Bowles will marry") (Emery, 2002).

Five Questions for Critical Thinking

Francine Shapiro, a clinical psychologist in northern California, had an odd experience while taking a walk one day in 1987. She had been thinking about some distressing events when she noticed that her emotional reaction to them was fading away. She realized that she had been moving her eyes from side to side, but had these eye movements caused the emotion-reducing effect? Perhaps, because when she made these same eye movements more deliberately, the effect was even stronger. Was this a fluke, or would the same thing happen to others? To find out, she tested the eye-movement effect in friends and colleagues, and then with clients who had suffered childhood sexual abuse, military combat, rape, or other traumas. She asked the clients to recall these traumas while keeping their eyes focused on her finger as she moved it back and forth in front of their faces. They said that their emotional reactions to the memories, like Shapiro's, faded. They also reported that trauma-related problems such as nightmares, fears, and emotional flashbacks decreased dramatically, often after only one session (Shapiro, 1989a). These successful case studies led Shapiro to develop a new treatment called *eye movement desensitization and reprocessing,* or *EMDR* (Shapiro, 1991; Shapiro & Forrest, 2004). Today, Shapiro and 30,000 other therapists in 52 countries are using EMDR to treat an ever-widening range of anxiety-related problems in children and adults, from phobias and posttraumatic stress disorder to marital conflicts and skin rashes (Beaulieu, 2003; Edmond & Rubin, 2004; Lawson, 2004; Manfield & Shapiro, 2004; Maxwell, 2003; Omaha, 2004; Russell, 2006; Silver et al., 2005).

Would the phenomenal growth of EMDR be enough to convince you to spend your own money on it? If not, what would you want to know about EMDR before deciding? As a cautious person, you would probably ask some of the same questions that have occurred to many scientists in psychology: Are the effects of EMDR caused by the treatment itself or by the faith that clients might have in any new and impressive treatment? And are EMDR's effects faster, stronger, and longer lasting than those of other treatments?

Questioning what we are told is an important part of a more general critical thinking process that can help us make informed decisions, not only about psychotherapy options but also about many other things—such as which pain reliever or Internet service to choose, which college to attend, what apartment to rent, which candidate to vote for, and whether we believe that cell phones can cause cancer or that shark cartilage can cure it. One way of applying critical thinking to EMDR or any other topic is to ask the following five questions:

■ What am I being asked to believe or accept?

In this case, you are asked to believe that EMDR reduces or eliminates anxiety-related problems.

■ Is there evidence available to support the claim?

Shapiro began her EMDR research on herself. When she found the same effects in others, coincidence became an unlikely explanation for the observed changes.

■ Can that evidence be interpreted another way?

The dramatic effects that Shapiro's friends and clients experienced might have been due to their motivation to change or to their desire to please her, not to EMDR. And who knows? They might have eventually improved on their own, without any treatment. In other words, even the most remarkable evidence cannot be accepted as confirming an assertion until all reasonable alternative explanations have been ruled out. Doing that leads to the next step in critical thinking: conducting scientific research.

■ What evidence would help to evaluate the alternatives?

The ideal method for testing the value of EMDR would be to identify three groups of people who are identical in every way except for the anxiety treatment they receive. One group receives EMDR. The second group gets an equally motivating but useless treatment. The third group gets no treatment at all. If the EMDR group improves much more than the other two, then it is less likely that the changes following EMDR can be explained entirely by client motivation or the mere passage of time.

■ What conclusions are most reasonable?

The evidence available so far has not yet ruled out alternative explanations for the effects of EMDR (e.g., Goldstein et al., 2000; Hertlein & Ricci, 2004). And although

Uncritically accepting claims for the value of astrologers' predictions, "get-rich-quick" investments, unproven therapies, or proposed government policies can be embarrassing, expensive, and sometimes dangerous. Critical thinkers carefully evaluate evidence for *and against* such claims before reaching a conclusion about them.

DOONESBURY

those effects are often greater than the effects of no treatment at all, they appear to be no stronger than those of several other kinds of treatment (Hughes, 2006; Ironson et al., 2002; Taylor, 2004; Taylor et al., 2003). Accordingly, the only reasonable conclusions to be drawn at this point are that (1) EMDR remains a controversial treatment, (2) it seems to have an impact on some clients, and (3) further research is needed in order to understand it.

Does that sound wishy-washy? Critical thinking sometimes does seem to be indecisive thinking, but the reason for that is that scientific conclusions must be guided by the evidence available. In the long run, though, critical thinking also opens the way to understanding. (To help you sharpen your critical thinking skills, we have included in every chapter to come a feature in which our five critical thinking questions are applied to a particularly interesting topic in psychology.) Let's now consider how psychologists translate critical thinking into scientific research.

Critical Thinking and Scientific Research

Scientific research often begins with curious questions, such as, Can eye movements reduce anxiety? Like many seemingly simple questions, this one is more complex than it first appears. Are we talking about horizontal, vertical, or diagonal eye movements? How long do they continue? How many treatment sessions should there be? Are we

TAKING YOUR LIFE IN YOUR HANDS?   Does exposure to microwave radiation from cell phone antennas cause brain tumors? Do the dangers outweigh the benefits of hormone replacement therapy (HRT) for postmenopausal women? What about the value of herbal remedies, dietary supplements, and other "alternative" treatments for cancer, AIDS, and depression (Specter, 2004)? These questions generate intense speculation, strong opinions, and a lot of wishful thinking, but the answers ultimately depend on scientific research based on critical thinking. So, even though there is no conclusive evidence that cell phones cause tumors (Christensen et al., 2005; Hepworth et al., 2006; Schoemaker et al., 2005), some scientists suggest there may be danger in long-term exposure (Lonn et al., 2004), and research continues. Evidence that HRT may be related to breast cancer and heart disease led to the cancellation of a large clinical trial in the United States (Kolata, 2003), and scientists are calling for new research on the safety of the testosterone replacement therapy that about 250,000 U.S. men receive each year (Groopman, 2002; Kolata, 2002).

referring to mild or severe anxiety, and how will we measure improvement? In other words, scientists must ask *specific* questions in order to get meaningful answers.

Psychologists and other scientists clarify their questions about behavior and mental processes by phrasing them in terms of a **hypothesis**—a specific, testable statement or proposition about something they want to study. In the case of EMDR, the hypothesis might be as follows: *EMDR treatment causes a significant reduction in anxiety.* To make it easier to understand and objectively evaluate their hypotheses, scientists employ **operational definitions,** which are statements describing the exact operations or methods they will use in their research. In the hypothesis we just proposed, "EMDR treatment" might be operationally defined as a certain number of back-and-forth eye movements per second for a particular period of time. "Significant reduction in anxiety" might be operationally defined as a drop of at least ten points on a test that measures anxiety. The kind of treatment a client is given (say, EMDR versus no treatment) and the results of that treatment (how much anxiety reduction occurred) are examples of research **variables,** the specific factors or characteristics that are altered and measured in research.

In addition to collecting evidence, scientists must also check on how good it is. Usually, the quality of evidence is evaluated in terms of two characteristics: reliability and validity. **Reliability** is the consistency of the evidence that is obtained. **Validity** is the degree to which the evidence accurately represents the topic being studied. For example, if Shapiro had not been able to repeat, or *replicate,* the eye movement effects with others, or if only a few clients had shown improvement, she would question the reliability of her evidence. If the clients' reports of improvement were not supported by, say, changes in their overt behavior or confirming statements by close relatives, she would doubt their validity.

The Role of Theories   After examining research evidence, scientists may begin to favor certain explanations as to why these results occurred. Sometimes they organize their explanations into a **theory,** which is a set of statements designed to explain certain phenomena. Shapiro's theory about EMDR suggests that eye movements activate parts of the brain in which information about trauma or other unpleasant experiences has been stored but never fully processed. EMDR, she says, promotes the "adaptive information processing" required for the elimination of anxiety-related emotional and behavioral problems (Shapiro & Forrest, 2004). Because they are tentative explanations, theories must be subjected to scientific evaluation based on critical thinking about the evidence for and against them. For example, Shapiro's theory about EMDR has been criticized as vague, not well supported by evidence, and less plausible than other, simpler explanations (e.g., Carpenter, 2004; Gaudiano & Dalrymple, 2005; Herbert et al., 2000; Lohr et al., 2003). So although a psychologist's theory may be based on research results, it usually also generates predictions that stimulate additional research. These predictions will be tested by many other psychologists, and the theory will be revised or even abandoned if research does not support it.

The process of creating, evaluating, and revising psychological theories does not always lead to a single "winner." You will see in later chapters that there are several possible explanations for color vision, mental disorder, prejudice, and many other aspects of behavior and mental processes. As a result, we can't offer as many final conclusions about psychology as you might want. The conclusions we do offer are always based on what is known so far, and we always cite the need for additional research. We do that because research often raises at least as many questions as it answers. For example, a certain treatment might work well for mild depression in women, but would it work as well for men, or for cases of severe depression? Answering those questions would require more research.

Keep this point in mind the next time you hear a talk show guest giving simple solutions for complex problems such as obesity or anxiety or promoting easy formulas for a happy marriage and well-behaved children. These self-proclaimed experts—called "pop" (for *popular*) psychologists by the scientific community—tend to oversimplify issues, cite evidence for their views without concern for its reliability or validity, and

hypothesis   In scientific research, a specific, testable proposition about a phenomenon.

operational definitions   Statements that define phenomena or variables by describing the exact research operations or methods used in measuring or manipulating them.

variables   Specific factors or characteristics that can take on different numerical values in research.

reliability   The degree to which test results or other research evidence occurs repeatedly.

validity   The degree to which evidence from a test or other research method measures what it is supposed to measure.

theory   An integrated set of propositions used to explain certain phenomena, including behavior and mental processes.

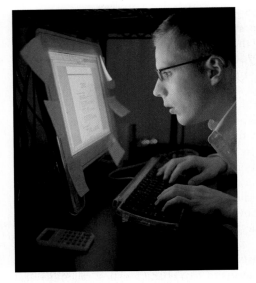

LITTLE REMINDERS   If you asked this person what he needs to use various computer programs efficiently, he might not think to mention the notes on his monitor that list all his log-in names and passwords. Accordingly, researchers in human factors and industrial/organizational psychology usually arrange to watch employees at work rather than just ask them what they do, how they do it, and how they interact with machines and fellow employees.

ignore good evidence that contradicts the pet theories that they live on. Psychological scientists must be more cautious, often delaying final judgments about behavior and mental processes until they have collected better data. Still, psychological research has created an enormous body of knowledge that is being put to good use in many ways (Zimbardo, 2004). And today's knowledge forms the foundation for future research that will further increase understanding. Let's look now at the scientific methods that psychologists use in their research and at some of the pitfalls that lie in their path.

Research Methods in Psychology

▶ **How do psychologists learn about people?**

Like other scientists, psychologists try to achieve four main goals in their research: to *describe* a phenomenon, to *make predictions* about it, and to introduce enough *control* in their research to allow them to *explain* the phenomenon with some degree of confidence. Five research methods have proven especially useful for gathering the evidence needed to reach each of these goals. They include *naturalistic observation, case studies, surveys, correlational studies,* and *experiments.*

Naturalistic Observation: Watching Behavior

Sometimes, the best way to describe behavior is through **naturalistic observation,** which is the process of watching without interfering as behavior occurs in the natural environment (Hoyle, Harris, & Judd, 2002). This method is especially valuable when more noticeable methods might alter the behavior you want to study. If you ask people to keep track of how often they exercise, they might begin to exercise more than usual, so their records would give a false impression of their typical behavior. Much of what we know about, say, gender differences in how children play and communicate with one another has come from psychologists' observations in classrooms and playgrounds. Observations of adults, too, have provided valuable insights into friendships, couple communication patterns, and even into responses to terrorism (e.g., Mehl & Pennebaker, 2003a, 2003b).

Naturalistic observation can provide a lot of good information, but it is not without its problems. For one thing, people tend to act differently when they know they are being observed (and research ethics usually requires that they do know). To combat this problem, researchers typically observe people long enough for them to get used to the situation and begin behaving more naturally. Still, observations can be incomplete or misleading if the observers are not well trained or if they report what they expect to see rather than what actually occurs. Further, even the best observational methods do not allow researchers to draw conclusions about what is causing the behavior being observed.

Case Studies: Taking a Closer Look

Observations are often an important part of **case studies,** which are intensive examinations of behavior or mental processes in a particular individual, group, or situation. Case studies can also include tests; interviews; and the analysis of letters, school transcripts, or other written records. Case studies are especially useful when studying something that is new, complex, or relatively rare (Sacks, 2002). Francine Shapiro's EMDR treatment, for example, first attracted psychologists' attention through case studies of its remarkable effects on her clients (Shapiro, 1989b).

Case studies have played a special role in *neuropsychology,* which focuses on the relationships among brain activity, thinking, and behavior. Consider the case of Dr. P., a patient described by neurologist Oliver Sacks (1985). Dr. P. was a distinguished musician who began to show odd symptoms. He could not recognize familiar people or distinguish between people and things. For instance, while he and his wife were at the neurologist's office, Dr. P. mistook his foot for his shoe. When he rose to leave, he tried

naturalistic observation   The process of watching without interfering as a phenomenon occurs in the natural environment.

case studies   Research involving the intensive examination of some phenomenon in a particular individual, group, or situation.

TRANSLATING OBSERVATIONS INTO EVIDENCE Observing people in natural settings can provide important clues to understanding social interaction and other aspects of behavior and mental processes. It is harder than it looks. Imagine you are studying these children at play, and make a list of the exact behaviors you would count as "aggressive," "shy," "fearful," "cooperative," and "competitive."

to lift off his wife's head as if it were a hat and put it on his own head. He could not name common objects, but he could describe them. When handed a glove, for example, he said, "A continuous surface, infolded on itself. It appears to have . . . five outpouchings, if this is the word . . . a container of some sort." Only later, when he put it on his hand, did he exclaim, "My God, it's a glove!" (Sacks, 1985, p. 13). Using case studies such as this one, pioneers in neuropsychology have noted the symptoms suffered by people with particular kinds of brain damage or disease (Banich, 2004). Eventually, neuropsychologists were able to tie specific disorders to certain types of injuries, poisons, and other causes. In Dr. P.'s case, it was probably a large brain tumor that caused his symptoms.

Case studies do have their limitations. They may not represent people in general, and they may contain only the evidence a particular researcher considered important (Loftus & Guyer, 2002). Nonetheless, when conducted and used with care, case studies can provide valuable raw material for further research and can serve as the testing ground for new treatments, training programs, and other applications of research (Tavris, 2004).

Surveys: Looking at the Big Picture

In contrast to the individual close-ups provided by case studies, surveys offer wide-angle views of large groups. In **surveys,** researchers use interviews or questionnaires to ask people about their behavior, attitudes, beliefs, opinions, or intentions. Just as politicians and advertisers rely on opinion polls to test the popularity of policies or products, psychologists use surveys to gather descriptive data on just about any behavior or mental process, from parenting practices to sexual behavior. However, the validity of survey data depends partly on the way the survey questions are asked (Bhopal et al., 2004). In one survey study at a health clinic, patients were asked how frequently they experienced headaches, stomachaches, and other symptoms of illness (Schwarz & Scheuring, 1992). If the wording of the question suggested that most people frequently experience such symptoms, the patients said that they frequently experienced them, too. But if the wording suggested that people rarely experience these symptoms, the

surveys Research that involves giving people questionnaires or interviews designed to describe their attitudes, beliefs, opinions, and intentions.

LEARNING FROM RARE CASES
Dustin Hoffman's character in the movie *Rain Man* was based on the case of "Joseph," an autistic man who can, for example, mentally multiply or divide six-digit numbers. Other case studies have described autistic *savants* who can correctly identify the day of the week for any date in the past or the future or tell at a glance that, say, exactly 125 paper clips are scattered on the floor. By carefully studying such rare cases, cognitive psychologists are learning more about human mental capacities and how they might be maximized in everyone.

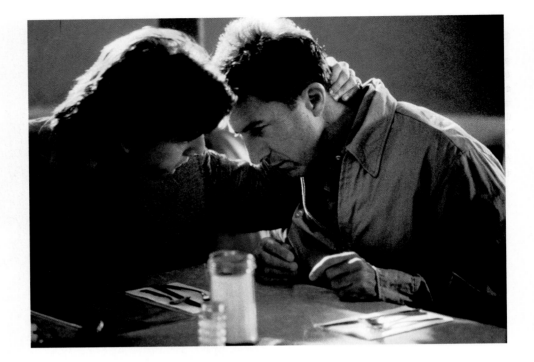

patients said that they experienced the symptoms infrequently. A survey's validity also depends on who is surveyed. If the people surveyed do not represent the views of the population you are interested in, it is easy to be misled by survey results (Gosling et al., 2004; Kraut et al., 2004). For example, if you were interested in Americans' views on how common ethnic prejudice is, you would come to the wrong conclusion if you surveyed only African Americans or only European Americans. To get a complete picture, you would have to survey people from all ethnic groups so that each group's opinions could be fairly represented.

Other limitations of the survey method are more difficult to avoid. For example, the American Society for Microbiology (ASM) found that 95 percent of the U.S. adults it surveyed said that they wash their hands after using toilet facilities. However, naturalistic observations of thousands of people in public restrooms across the United States revealed that the figure is closer to 67 percent (ASM, 2000). In other words, people may be unwilling to admit undesirable or embarrassing things about themselves, or they may say what they believe they *should* say about an issue. And sometimes those who respond to a survey hold views that differ from those who do not respond (Visser et al., 2000). Survey results—and the conclusions drawn from them—will be distorted to the extent that these tendencies distort people's responses and researchers' access to responses (Hoyle et al., 2002). Still, surveys provide an efficient way to gather large amounts of data about people's attitudes, beliefs, or other characteristics.

A SEVERELY FLAWED SURVEY
Using survey methods like this, you could probably get whatever results you want! Psychologists work hard to write questions and use methods that maximize the validity of their surveys' results.

© Scott Adams/Distributed by United Feature Syndicate, Inc.

DESIGNING SURVEY RESEARCH How do various people feel about whether gay men and lesbians should have the right to legally marry? To appreciate the difficulties of survey research, try writing a question about this issue that you think is clear enough and unbiased enough to generate a valid portrait of people's views. Then ask some friends whether or not they agree that it would be a good survey question, and why.

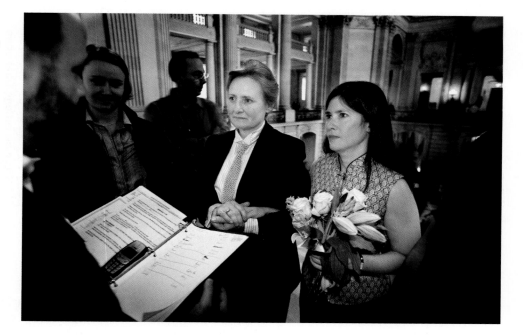

Correlational Studies: Looking for Relationships

Data collected from naturalistic observations, case studies, and surveys provide valuable descriptions of behavior and mental processes, but they can do more than that. The data can also be examined for what they reveal about the relationships between research variables. For example, fear surveys show that most people have fears, but correlational analysis of those surveys also shows that fear is related to age. Specifically, as people get older, they tend to have fewer fears (e.g., Kleinknecht, 1991). **Correlational studies** examine relationships between variables in order to describe research data more fully, to test predictions, to evaluate theories, and to suggest new hypotheses about why people think and act as they do.

Correlation refers to both the strength and the direction of the relationship between two variables. A *positive correlation* means that the two variables increase together or decrease together. A *negative correlation* means that the variables move in opposite directions. For example, James Schaefer observed 4,500 customers in 65 bars and found that the tempo of the jukebox music was negatively correlated with the rate at which the customers drank alcohol. The slower the tempo, the faster the drinking (Schaefer et al., 1988). Does this mean that Schaefer could have worn a blindfold and predicted exactly how fast people were drinking by timing the music? Could he have plugged his ears and determined the musical tempo just by watching people's sip rates? No and no, because the accuracy of predictions made about one variable from knowing the other depends on the *strength* of the correlation. Only a perfect correlation between two variables would allow you to predict the exact value of one from a knowledge of the other. The weaker the correlation, the less one variable can tell you about the other.

Psychologists describe the strength and direction of correlations with a number called a *correlation coefficient*, which can range from a high of 1.00 to a low of .00 (see the "Statistics in Psychological Research" appendix). If the correlation between two variables is *positive*—if they both move in the same direction—the correlation coefficient will have a plus sign in front of it. If there is a minus sign, the correlation is *negative*, and the two variables will move in opposite directions. The larger the correlation coefficient, the stronger the relationship between the two variables. The strongest possible relationship is indicated by either +1.00 or −1.00 (see Figure 1.6). A correlation of .00 indicates that there is virtually no relationship between variables.

Correlation coefficients can help to describe the results of correlational research and evaluate hypotheses, but psychological scientists must be extremely careful when

correlational studies Research methods that examine relationships between variables in order to analyze trends, test predictions, evaluate theories, and suggest new hypotheses.

correlation The degree to which one variable is related to another.

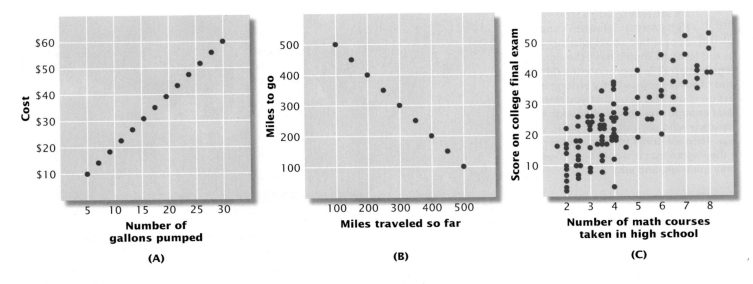

F I G U R E   1 . 6

Three Correlations

The strength and direction of the correlation between variables can be seen in a graph called a scatterplot. Here are three examples. In Part A, we have plotted the cost of a gasoline purchase against the number of gallons pumped. The number of gallons is positively and perfectly correlated with their cost, so the scatterplot appears as a straight line, and you can predict the value of either variable from a knowledge of the other. Part B shows a perfect negative correlation between the number of miles you have traveled toward a destination and the distance remaining. Again, one variable can be exactly predicted from the other. Part C illustrates a correlation of +.81 between the number of math courses students had taken in high school and their scores on a college math exam; each dot represents one student (Hays, 1981). As correlations decrease, they are represented by less and less organized scatterplots. A correlation of .00 would appear as a shapeless cloud.

experiment   A situation in which the researcher manipulates one variable and observes the effect of that manipulation on another variable, while holding all other variables constant.

independent variable   In an experiment, the variable manipulated by the researcher.

dependent variable   In an experiment, the factor affected by the independent variable.

interpreting what correlations mean. The mere fact that two variables are correlated does not guarantee that one is causing an effect on the other. And even if one variable actually does cause an effect on the other, a correlation coefficient can't tell us which variable is influencing which, or why (see Table 1.6). Consider the question of how aggression develops. Correlational studies of observational data indicate that children who are in day care for more than thirty hours a week are more aggressive than those who stay at home with a parent. Does separation from parents actually *cause* the heightened aggressiveness with which it is associated? It might, but psychologists must be careful about jumping to that conclusion. The most obvious explanation for the relationship found in a correlational study may not always be the correct one. Perhaps the aggressiveness seen among some children in day care has something to do with the children themselves or with what happens to them in day care, not just with separation from their parents.

One way psychologists evaluate such alternative hypotheses is to conduct further correlational studies to look for trends that support or conflict with those hypotheses. Further analysis of day-care research, for example, shows that the aggressiveness seen in preschoolers who spend a lot of time in day care is the exception, not the rule. Most children don't show any behavior problems, no matter how much time they have spent in day care. This more general trend suggests that whatever effects separation has, it may be different for different children in different settings, causing some to express aggressiveness, others to display fear, and still others to find enjoyment. As described in the chapter on human development, psychologists are exploring this possibility by examining correlations between children's personality traits, qualities of different day-care programs, and reactions to day care (NICHD Early Child Care Research Network, 2005). Throughout this book you will see many more examples of how correlational studies help to shed light on a wide range of topics in psychology.

Experiments: Exploring Cause and Effect

Still, to make the best choice among alternative explanations and to confirm cause-and-effect relationships between research variables, psychological scientists prefer to exert some control over those variables. This kind of controlled research usually takes the form of an experiment.

In an **experiment,** the researcher makes a change in one variable and then observes the effect of that change on another variable, while holding all the other variables constant. The variable that is changed, or manipulated, by the experimenter is called the **independent variable.** The variable that is measured following this manipulation is called the **dependent variable,** because it *depends* on the independent variable (see Table 1.7). So in an experiment on the effects of TV violence, for example, the independent variable might be the amount of violence that different groups of children

TABLE 1.6 Correlation and Causation

learn by doing

Look at the relationships described in the left-hand column, then ask yourself why the two variables in each case are correlated. Could one variable be causing an effect on the other? If so, which variable is the cause, and how might it exert its effect? Could the relationship between the two variables be caused by a third one? If so, what might that third variable be? We suggest some possible explanations in the right-hand column. Can you think of others?

Correlation	Possible Explanations
A recent survey found that the more sexual content that U.S. teenagers reported watching on television, the more likely they were to begin having sex themselves during the following year (Collins et al., 2004).	It might have been some teens' greater interest in sex that led them to watch more sexually oriented shows and also to become sexually active.
The number of drownings in the United States rises and falls during the year, along with the amount of ice cream sold each month.	This relationship probably reflects a third variable—time of year—that affects both ice cream consumption and the likelihood of swimming and boating (Brenner et al., 2001).
In places where beer prices are raised, the number of new cases of sexually transmitted disease falls among young people living in those places.	If price increases cause less beer consumption, people might stay sober enough to remember to use condoms during sexual encounters. The relationship could also reflect coincidence, because prices do not always affect alcohol use. More research is required to understand this correlation.
A recent study found that the more antibiotics a woman has taken, and the longer she has taken them, the greater is her risk of breast cancer (Velicer et al., 2004).	Long-term antibiotic use might have impaired the women's immune systems, but the cancer risk might also have been increased by the diseases that were being treated with antibiotic drugs, not the drugs themselves. Obviously, much more research would be required before condemning the use of antibiotics.
The U.S. stock market rises during years in which a team from the National Football Conference wins the Super Bowl and falls during years in which an American Conference team wins.	The so-called "Super Bowl Effect" has occurred 30 times in 37 years; striking as this might seem, coincidence seems to be the most likely explanation.

TABLE 1.7 Independent and Dependent Variables

learn by doing

Fill in the names of the independent and dependent variables in each of these experiments (the answers are listed at the bottom of page 33). Remember that the independent variable is manipulated by the experimenter. The dependent variable is measured to determine the effect of the independent variable. How did you do on this task?

1. Children's reading skill is measured after taking either a special reading class or a standard reading class.	The independent variable is _____. The dependent variable is _____.
2. College students' memory for German vocabulary words is tested after a normal night's sleep or a night of no sleep.	The independent variable is _____. The dependent variable is _____.
3. Experiment title: "The effect of a daily walking program on elderly people's lung capacity."	The independent variable is _____. The dependent variable is _____.
4. People's ability to avoid "accidents" in a driving simulator is tested before, during, and after talking on a cell phone.	The independent variable is _____. The dependent variable is _____.

are allowed to watch: a lot, a little, or none at all. The **experimental group** is the group that is exposed to an experience of interest to the experimenter (a lot of violent TV, for example). A group that receives no such exposure, or a differing amount of exposure, is called the **control group.** Control groups provide baselines against which to compare the performance of the experimental group. If everything about the groups is exactly the same except for exposure to some experience, then any differences between groups at the end of the experiment should be due to that experience.

Studying EMDR

Let's consider how Francine Shapiro used the experimental method to explore whether her EMDR treatment was actually causing the improvements she observed in her clients. (Each chapter to follow contains a Focus on Research section like this one, which presents a different example of how researchers in psychology ask and answer questions about behavior and mental processes.)

■ What was the researcher's question?

Like other scientists, Shapiro phrased her question about the value of EMDR in the form of a hypothesis, namely that *EMDR treatment causes a significant reduction in anxiety.* Does it?

■ How did the researcher answer the question?

To find out, Shapiro operationally defined "EMDR treatment" as making a certain number of back-and-forth eye movements per second for a particular period of time. And "significant reduction in anxiety" was operationally defined as a certain amount of reduction in clients' self-reported discomfort.

Shapiro then identified twenty-two people who were suffering the ill effects of traumas such as rape or military combat. These were her research participants. As shown in Figure 1.7, she assigned these participants to two groups. The experimental group received one fifty-minute session of EMDR. The control group focused on their unpleasant memories for eight minutes but without moving their eyes back and forth (Shapiro, 1989b). The experimenter controlled whether EMDR treatment was given to each participant, so the presence or absence of treatment was the independent variable. The participants' anxiety level was the dependent variable. In Shapiro's experiment, having a control group allowed her to measure how much change in anxiety might be expected from exposure to bad memories without EMDR treatment.

■ What did the researcher find?

The results of Shapiro's experiment showed that participants receiving EMDR treatment experienced a complete and nearly immediate reduction in anxiety related to their traumatic memories. Those in the control group showed no such change.

■ What do the results mean?

At this point, you might be ready to believe that the treatment caused the difference. Before coming to that conclusion, though, look again at the structure, or *design,* of the experiment. The treatment group's session lasted fifty minutes. The control group focused on their memories for only eight minutes. Would the people in the control group have improved if they, too, had spent fifty minutes focusing on their memories? We don't know, because the experiment did not compare methods of equal length.

■ What do we still need to know?

Experiments have now been conducted that introduce enough control into the treatment situation to evaluate alternative explanations for the EMDR effect. Most of the controlled

experimental group   The group that receives the experimental treatment.

control group   The group that receives no treatment or provides some other baseline against which to compare the performance or response of the experimental group.

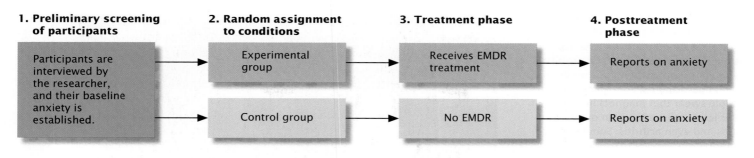

FIGURE **1.7**

A Simple Two-Group Experiment

Ideally, the only difference between the experimental and control group in experiments such as this one is whether the participants receive the treatment that the experimenter wants to evaluate. Under these ideal circumstances, at the end of the experiment any difference in the two groups' reported levels of anxiety (the dependent variable) should be attributable to whether or not they received treatment (the independent variable).

confounding variable　Any factor that affects the dependent variable along with, or instead of, the independent variable.

random variables　Uncontrolled or uncontrollable factors that affect the dependent variable along with, or instead of, the independent variable.

random assignment　A procedure through which random variables are evenly distributed in an experiment by placing participants in experimental and control groups on the basis of a coin flip or some other random process.

placebo　A treatment that contains no active ingredient but produces an effect because the person receiving it believes it will.

studies completed so far cast doubt on whether the eye movements in EMDR are causing clients' improvement (e.g., Davidson & Parker, 2001; Lazarus & Lazarus, 2002; Van Deusen, 2004), but we still don't know for sure what is producing the effects that EMDR proponents report. As the research continues, it will be important for these proponents to avoid *confirmation bias,* the human tendency to look only for evidence that supports their own hypotheses. In fact, all scientists have a responsibility to combat confirmation bias by looking for evidence *for* and *against* even their most cherished hypotheses.

Shapiro's (1989b) experiment reminds us to be on the lookout for flaws in experimental design and control that might affect the conclusions we can draw from research results. In fact, we have to consider anything that could confuse, or *confound,* our interpretation of those results. Any factor that might have affected the dependent variable, along with or instead of the independent variable, may operate as a **confounding variable.** When confounding variables are present, we can't tell whether it was the independent variable or the confounding variable that produced the results. Let's consider three sources of confounding variables: random variables, participants' expectations, and experimenter bias.

Random Variables　In an ideal research world, everything about experimental and control groups would be the same except for their exposure to the independent variable (such as whether or not they received treatment). In the real world, however, there are always other differences between the groups that reflect random variables. **Random variables** are uncontrolled, sometimes uncontrollable, factors, such as differences in the time of year when research takes place and differences in each participant's cultural background, personality, health, and sensitivity to stress. There are so many ways in which participants might vary from each other that it is usually impossible to form groups that are matched on all of them. Instead, experimenters simply flip a coin or use some other random process to assign each research participant to experimental or control groups. These procedures, called **random assignment,** tend to spread the effects of uncontrolled variables randomly (and probably about evenly) across groups. This minimizes the chance that they will distort the results of the experiment (Shadish, Cook, & Campbell, 2002).

Participants' Expectations: The Placebo Effect　Differences in what participants think about the experimental situation can act as another confounding variable. For example, if participants expect that a treatment will help them, they may try harder to improve than those in a control group who receive no treatment or a less impressive one. Improvement created by a participant's expectations is called the *placebo effect.* A **placebo** (pronounced "plah-SEE-boe") contains nothing known to be helpful, but it still produces benefits because a person believes it will do so (Stewart-Williams & Podd, 2004; Wager et al., 2004).

Answer key to Table 1.7: The independent variable (IDV) in experiment 1 is the type of reading class; the dependent variable (DV) is reading skill. In experiment 2, the IDV is the quality of sleep; the DV is the score on a memory test. In experiment 3, the IDV is amount of exercise; the DV is lung capacity. In experiment 4, the IDV is using or not using a cell phone; the DV is performance on a simulated driving task.

EVER SINCE I STARTED WEARING THESE MAGNETS . . . Placebo-controlled experiments are vital for establishing cause-effect relationships between treatments and outcomes with human participants. For example, many people swear that magnets held against their joints relieve the pain of sports injuries and even arthritis. Some research supports this view (e.g., Harlow et al., 2004), but most experiments have found magnets to be no more effective than placebo treatment with an identical, but nonmagnetic, metal object (Collacott et al., 2000; Feingold & Flamm, 2006; Winemiller et al., 2003).

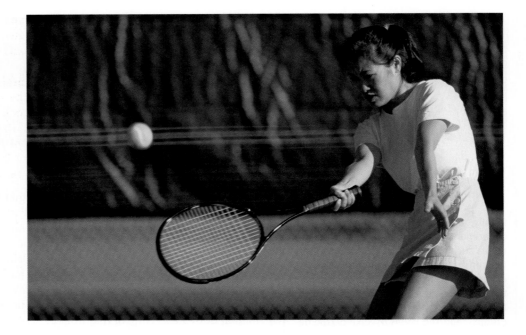

How can researchers estimate the strength of placebo effects in an experiment? The most common strategy is to include in the experimental design a special control group that receives *only* a placebo. The researchers then compare results for the experimental group, the placebo group, and a group of participants receiving no treatment. In one stop-smoking study, for example, participants in a placebo group took sugar pills that the experimenter said would help them endure the stress of giving up cigarettes (Bernstein, 1970). These participants did as well at quitting as those in the experimental group, who had received extensive treatment. This result suggested that the experimental group's success may have been due largely to the participants' expectations, not to the treatment methods. Some studies suggest the same conclusion about the effects of EMDR, because significant anxiety reduction has been observed in clients who get a version of the treatment that does not involve eye movements or even focusing on traumatic memories (Cahill, Carrigan, & Frueh, 1999; Cusack & Spates, 1999; Rosen, 1999). In fact, although EMDR appears to benefit some clients, its failure to outperform impressive placebo treatments (or other established methods for helping clients deal with unpleasant images) has led many researchers to conclude that EMDR should not be a first-choice treatment for anxiety-related disorders (Davidson & Parker, 2001; Lohr et al., 2003; Taylor, 2004; Taylor et al., 2003).

Experimenter Bias Another possible confounding variable is **experimenter bias,** the unintentional effect that researchers can exert on their own results. Robert Rosenthal (1966) was one of the first to demonstrate the power of experimenter bias. His participants were laboratory assistants who were asked to place rats in a maze. Rosenthal told some of the assistants that their rats were "maze-bright." He told the others that their rats were "maze-dull." In truth, both groups of rats were randomly drawn from the same population and had equal maze-learning capabilities. Still, the so-called maze-bright animals learned the maze significantly faster than the "maze-dull" ones. Why? Rosenthal concluded that the result had nothing to do with the rats and everything to do with the experimenters. He suggested that the assistants' expectations about their rats' supposedly superior (or inferior) capabilities caused them to slightly alter their training and handling techniques. These slight differences may have speeded (or slowed) the animals' learning. Similarly, when giving different kinds of

experimenter bias A confounding variable that occurs when an experimenter unintentionally encourages participants to respond in a way that supports the hypothesis.

anxiety treatments to different groups of people, experimenters who believe that one treatment will be the best might do a slightly better job with that treatment. When the results are in, this unintentional difference might make the favored treatment look better than the rest.

To prevent experimenter bias from confounding results, experimenters often use a **double-blind design.** In this design, the participants *and* those giving the treatments are unaware of, or "blind" to, who is receiving a placebo, and they do not know what results are to be expected of the various treatments. Only researchers who have no direct contact with participants have this information, and they do not reveal it until the end of the experiment. Double-blind studies have not yet been conducted with EMDR, which is another reason for caution in drawing conclusions about this treatment.

In summary, experiments are vital tools for examining cause-effect relationships between independent and dependent variables, but they are also vulnerable to error. To maximize the value of their experiments, scientists try to eliminate as many confounding variables as possible. They then repeat their work to ensure consistent results and adjust their interpretation of those results to take into account the limitations or problems that remain.

Selecting Human Participants for Research

Visitors from another planet would be wildly mistaken if they tried to describe the typical earthling after meeting only Arnold Schwarzenegger, Michael Jackson, Madonna, and a trained seal. Psychologists, too, can be led astray if the participants they encounter in their research are not typical of the people or animals about which they want to draw conclusions. Accordingly, one of the most vital steps in scientific research is the selection of participants, a process called **sampling.**

If they want to make accurate statements about the behavior and mental processes of any large group, psychologists must select a **representative sample** of participants whose characteristics mirror the rest of that group in terms of age, gender, ethnicity, cultural background, socioeconomic status, sexual orientation, disability, and the like. In theory, psychologists could draw representative samples—of people in general, of Canadians, of Florida college students, or of any other group—by choosing them at random from the entire population of interest. Doing this would require putting hundreds of thousands, perhaps millions, of names into a computer, running a program to randomly select participants, then tracking them down to invite them to take part in the research. This method would result in a truly **random sample,** because every member of the population to be studied would have an equal chance of being chosen. (Any selection procedure that does not offer this equal chance is said to result in a **biased sample.**)

However, random sampling is usually too expensive and time-consuming to be practical, so psychologists may have to find their participants in populations that are more conveniently available. The populations from which these *convenience samples* are drawn depend to some extent on the size of the researcher's budget. They might include, for example, the students enrolled in a particular course, the students enrolled on a local campus, the students who are willing to sign up for a study, or visitors to Internet web sites or chat rooms (e.g., Nosek, Banaji, & Greenwald, 2002; Stone & Pennebaker, 2002). Ideally, this selection process will yield a sample that fairly represents the population from which it was drawn. Still, scientific researchers are obliged to limit the conclusions they draw in light of the samples they draw (Kraut et al., 2004). Because of this obligation, psychologists often conduct additional studies to determine the extent to which their initial conclusions will apply to people who differ in important ways from their original sample (APA Office of Ethnic Minority Affairs, 2000; Case & Smith, 2000; Gray-Little & Hafdahl, 2000). For a recap of the strategies psychologists use in their research efforts, see "In Review: Methods of Psychological Research."

double-blind design A research design in which neither the experimenter nor the participants know who is in the experimental group and who is in the control group.

sampling The process of selecting participants who are members of the population that the researcher wishes to study.

representative sample A sample of research participants chosen from a larger population such that their age, gender, ethnicity, and other characteristics are typical of that larger population.

random sample A group of research participants selected from a population each of whose members had an equal chance of being chosen.

biased sample A group of research participants selected from a population each of whose members did not have an equal chance of being chosen.

learn by doing **SELECTING RESEARCH PARTICIPANTS** Suppose that you want to study people's willingness to help each other. You have developed a way of measuring helpfulness, but now you need a sample of people to test. Take a minute to think about the steps necessary to select a truly random sample; then ask yourself how you might obtain a representative sample instead. Remember that although the names are similar, *random sampling* is not the same as *random assignment*. Random sampling helps ensure that the people studied are representative of some larger group. Random assignment is used in experiments to create equivalence among various groups.

Online Study Center

Improve Your Grade
Tutorial: Research Methodologies

in review

METHODS OF PSYCHOLOGICAL RESEARCH

Method	Features	Strengths	Pitfalls
Naturalistic observation	Observation of human or animal behavior in the environment in which it typically occurs	Provides descriptive data about behavior presumably uncontaminated by outside influences	Observer bias and participant self-consciousness can distort results.
Case studies	Intensive examination of the behavior and mental processes associated with a specific person or situation	Provide detailed descriptive analyses of new, complex, or rare phenomena	May not provide representative picture of phenomena.
Surveys	Standard sets of questions asked of a large number of participants	Gather large amounts of descriptive data relatively quickly and inexpensively	Sampling errors, poorly phrased questions, and response biases can distort results.
Correlational studies	Examine relationships between research variables	Can test predictions, evaluate theories, and suggest new hypotheses	Cannot confirm causal relationships between variables.
Experiments	Manipulation of an independent variable and measurement of its effects on a dependent variable	Can establish a cause-effect relationship between independent and dependent variables	Confounding variables may prevent valid conclusions.

? 1. The _____ method is most likely to use a double-blind design.
2. Research on a new treatment method is most likely to begin with _____ .
3. Studying language by listening to people in public places is an example of _____ research.

LINKAGES

Is behavior influenced by our genes or by our environment?
(a link to Biology and Behavior)

LINKAGES

Psychological Research and Behavioral Genetics

One of the most fascinating and difficult challenges in psychology is to find research methods that can help us understand the ways in which genes and the environment—sometimes called *nature* and *nurture*—combine to influence behavior and mental processes (Moffitt, Caspi, & Rutter, 2005). Consider Mark and John, identical twins who were both adopted at birth because their parents were too poor to care for them. John grew up with a couple who made him feel secure and loved. Mark went from orphanage to foster home to hospital and, finally, back to his biological father's second wife. In other words, these genetically identical people had encountered quite different environments. Yet, when they met for the first time at the age of twenty-four, they discovered similarities that went beyond physical appearance. They used the same after-shave lotion, smoked the same brand of cigarettes, brushed with the same imported brand of toothpaste, and liked the same sports. They had joined the military within eight days of each other, and their IQ scores were nearly identical.

How had genetic influences operated in two different environments to result in such similarities? Exploring questions such as this has taken psychologists into the field of **behavioral genetics,** the study of how genes and environments work together to shape behavior and mental processes. They have already discovered that most behavioral tendencies can be influenced by many different genes but also by many environmental events and conditions, before and after birth. Accordingly, research in behavioral genetics aims to explore the relative roles of genetic and environmental factors in creating differences among people in personality, mental ability, mental disorders, and other phenomena. It also seeks to identify specific genes that contribute to hereditary influences.

Some behavioral genetics research takes the form of experiments, mainly on the selective breeding of animals (Suomi, 2004). For example, Stephen Suomi (1999) identified monkeys whose genes predisposed them to react strongly or weakly to stress. He then mated strong reactors with other strong reactors and mated weak reactors with other weak reactors. Within a few generations, descendants of the strong-reactor pairs reacted much more strongly to stressors than did the descendants of the weak-reactor pairs. Selective-breeding studies must be interpreted with caution, though, because it is not specific behaviors that are inherited. What is inherited are differing sets of physical structures and capacities that make certain behaviors more or less likely. These behavioral tendencies are often very specific, and they can be altered by the environment (Grigorenko, 2002). For example, when Suomi (1999) placed young, highly stress-reactive monkeys with unrelated "foster mothers," he discovered that the foster mothers' own stress reactivity amplified or dampened the youngsters' genetically influenced behavioral tendencies. If stress-reactive monkeys were placed with stress-reactive foster mothers, they tended to be fearful of exploring their environments and had strong reactions to stressors. But if equally stress-reactive young monkeys had calm, supportive foster mothers, they appeared eager to explore their environments and were much less upset by stressors than their peers with stress-reactive foster mothers.

Research on behavioral genetics in humans must be interpreted with even greater care. Legal, moral, and ethical considerations obviously prohibit the selective breeding of people, so most research in human behavioral genetics depends on correlational studies, not controlled experiments. These usually take the form of family studies, twin studies, and adoption studies (Plomin, DeFries, et al., 2001; Rutter et al., 2001).

In *family studies,* researchers look at whether close relatives are more likely than distant ones to show similarities in behavior and mental processes. If increasing similarity is associated with closer family ties, the similarities might be inherited.

behavioral genetics The study of how genes and environments combine to affect behavior and mental processes.

FIGURE **1.8**

Family and Twin Studies of Schizophrenia

The risk of developing schizophrenia, a severe mental disorder, is highest for the siblings and children of patients with schizophrenia and lowest for those who are not genetically related to anyone with schizophrenia. Does this mean that schizophrenia is inherited? These results are consistent with that interpretation, but the question cannot be answered through family studies alone. Environmental factors, such as stressors that close relatives share, could also play an important role. Studies comparing identical and nonidentical twins also suggest genetic influence, but even twin studies do not eliminate the role of environmental influences.

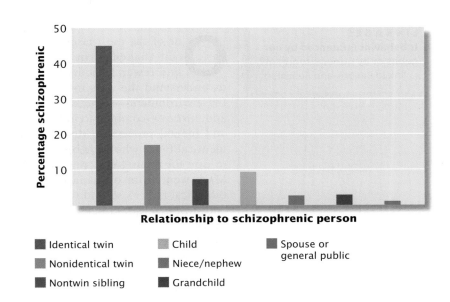

Relationship to schizophrenic person

■ Identical twin   ▢ Child   ■ Spouse or
                                                general public
■ Nonidentical twin   ▦ Niece/nephew
■ Nontwin sibling   ■ Grandchild

For example, data from family studies suggest a genetic basis for schizophrenia, as Figure 1.8 shows. Remember, though, that a correlation between variables does not guarantee that one is causing the other. The appearance of similar disorders in close relatives might be due to environmental factors instead of, or in addition to, genetic ones. After all, close relatives tend to share environments, as well as genes. So family studies alone cannot establish the role of genetic factors in mental disorders or other characteristics.

Twin studies explore the nature-nurture mix by comparing the similarities seen in identical twins with those of nonidentical twin pairs. Twins usually share the same environment and may also be treated very much the same by parents and others. So, if identical twins—whose genes are the same—are more alike on some characteristics than nonidentical twins (whose genes are no more similar than those of other siblings), those characteristics may have a significant genetic component.

TWINS AND BEHAVIORAL GENETICS
Like other identical twins, each member of this pair has identical genes. Twin studies and adoption studies help to reveal the interaction of genetic and environmental influences in human behavior and mental processes. Cases in which identical twins who have been separated at birth are found to have similar interests, personality traits, and mental abilities suggest that these characteristics are significantly influenced by genetic factors.

Adoption studies take advantage of cases in which babies are adopted very early in life. The logic of these studies is that if adopted children's characteristics are more like those of their biological parents than those of their adoptive parents, then genetics probably plays a clear role in those characteristics. In fact, the personalities of young adults who were adopted at birth do tend to be more like those of their biological parents than those of their adoptive parents. Adoption studies can be especially valuable when they focus on identical twins who, like Mark and John, were separated soon after birth. If identical twins show similar characteristics after years of living in very different environments, then the role of heredity in those characteristics is highlighted. Adoption studies of intelligence tend to support the role of genetics in variations in mental ability, but they show the impact of environmental influences, too.

Remember that family, twin, and adoption studies can tell us about the relative roles of heredity and environment in creating differences among individuals, but they cannot determine the degree to which a *particular* person's behavior or characteristics are due to heredity or environment. The two factors are too closely entwined in each of us to be separated that way. In the future, though, behavioral genetics research will be shaped by the results of the Human Genome Project, which has now unlocked the genetic code contained in the DNA that makes each human being unique (International Human Genome Sequencing Consortium, 2001; Venter et al., 2001). This achievement has allowed behavioral geneticists and other scientists to begin pinpointing some of the many genes that contribute to individual differences in disorders such as autism, learning disabilities, hyperactivity, and Alzheimer's disease, as well as to the differences in personality and mental abilities that we see all around us (Plomin et al., 2002; Saudino, Ronald, & Plomin, 2005). Finding the DNA differences responsible for certain personal attributes and behaviors will eventually make it possible to understand exactly how heredity interacts with the environment as development unfolds. Analysis of DNA— collected by rubbing a cotton swab inside an individual's cheek—may someday be used not only in behavioral genetics research but also in clinics, where it will help psychologists more precisely diagnose clients' problems and choose the most appropriate treatments (Plomin et al., 2002).

Statistical Analysis of Research Results

▶ **What does it mean when scientists announce that a research finding is "significant"?**

Naturalistic observations, case studies, surveys, correlational studies, and experiments generate mountains of numbers, known as **data,** that represent research results and provide the basis for drawing conclusions about them (Keselman et al., 2004). These data might represent scores on intelligence tests, levels of stress hormones in blood samples, tiny differences in the time required to detect various visual signals, ratings of people's personality traits, or whatever else a psychologist might be studying. Like other scientists, psychologists use descriptive and inferential *statistics* to summarize their data and interpret what they mean.

As the name implies, *descriptive statistics* are used to describe a set of data. For example, the performance of a group of students on a math test could be described statistically by the average score of the group. The difference between the performance of men and women could be described by the size of the difference between the average scores for each sex. And, as mentioned earlier, when psychologists want to describe the relationship between two variables, they use a descriptive statistic called the correlation coefficient.

Inferential statistics are mathematical procedures that help psychologists to make inferences—that is, to draw conclusions from their data and make assumptions about

data Numbers that represent research findings and provide the basis for conclusions.

the meaning of results. Suppose, for example, that a group of trauma victims scored an average of ten points lower on an anxiety test after being treated with EMDR and that the scores of victims in a no-treatment control group dropped by an average of seven points. Does the three-point difference between these two groups reflect the impact of EMDR, or could it have been caused by random factors that made EMDR appear more powerful than it actually is? Inferential statistics allow researchers to estimate the likelihood that the difference between the average scores of the two groups reflects chance factors rather than the impact of the differing treatment they received. Other inferential statistics can help psychologists to decide whether a correlation between two variables is large enough to suggest an important underlying relationship or is just a fluke.

When inferential statistics reveal that a correlation coefficient or the difference between groups is larger than what would be expected by chance alone, the results are said to be **statistically significant.** Statistical significance alone does not guarantee final "proof," but scientists do tend to pay more attention to correlations or other research findings that are statistically significant, especially when those results have been repeated, or *replicated,* in separate studies. So, when thinking critically about research, part of the process of evaluating evidence about hypotheses is to ask whether a researcher's results are statistically significant and repeatable. (For more details on descriptive and inferential statistics, see the "Statistics in Psychological Research" appendix).

Ethical Guidelines for Psychologists

▶ **Do psychologists deceive people when they do research?**

A few years ago newspaper headlines claimed that "Hair dye causes cancer." Hairdressers were alarmed at first, then angry. The information given to the public was less than accurate. Rats—not humans—had been used in the research, and the animals developed cancer only after drinking the hair dye! Later research showed that using hair dye does not significantly increase people's cancer risk (Takkouche, Etminan, & Montes-Martinez, 2005).

Splashy headlines sell newspapers, but scientific psychologists have an ethical obligation not to manipulate, distort, or sensationalize their research results. The obligation to analyze and report research fairly and accurately is just one of the ethical standards that guide psychologists. Preserving the welfare and dignity of their research participants is another. So although researchers *could* measure anxiety by putting a loaded gun to people's heads, or study marital conflicts by telling one partner that the other has been unfaithful, those methods could be harmful and are therefore unethical.

Whatever the research topic, psychologists' first priority is to investigate it in accordance with the highest ethical standards. They must find ways to protect their participants from harm while still gathering data that will have potential benefits for everyone. So to measure anxiety, for example, a psychologist might ask people to enter a situation that is anxiety provoking but not traumatic (for example, approaching a feared animal or sitting in a dark room). And research on marital conflict usually involves observing couples as they discuss controversial issues in their relationship.

Psychologists take very seriously the obligation to minimize any immediate discomfort or risk for research participants, as well as the need to protect those participants from long-term harm. They are careful to inform prospective participants about every aspect of the study that might influence their decision to participate, and they ensure that each person's involvement is voluntary. But what if the purpose of the study is to

statistically significant Referring to a correlation, or a difference between two groups, that is larger than would be expected by chance.

CARING FOR RESEARCH ANIMALS
Psychologists are careful to protect the welfare of animal participants in research. They do not wish to see animals suffer, and besides, undue stress on research animals can create reactions that can act as confounding variables. For example, in a study of how learning is affected by food rewards, the researcher could starve animals to make them hungry enough to want the rewards. But this would introduce discomfort, which would make it impossible to separate the effects of the reward from the effects of starvation.

measure people's emotional reactions to being insulted? Participants might not react normally if they know ahead of time that an "insult" will be part of the experiment. When deception is necessary to create certain experimental conditions, ethical standards require the researcher to "debrief" participants as soon as the study is over by revealing all relevant information about the research and correcting any misconceptions it created.

Government regulations in the United States, Canada, and many other countries require that any research involving human participants must be approved by an Institutional Review Board (IRB) whose members have no connection with the research. If a proposed study is likely to create risks or discomfort for participants, IRB members weigh the potential benefits of the work in terms of knowledge and human welfare against any potential harm.

The obligation to protect participants' welfare also extends to animals, which are used in a small percentage of psychological research projects (Plous, 1996). Psychologists study animals partly because their behavior is interesting and partly because research with animals can provide information that would be impossible or unethical to collect from humans. For example, researchers can randomly assign animals to live alone and then look at how these conditions affect later social interactions. The same thing could not ethically be done with people, but animal studies offer clues about how social isolation might affect humans (see the chapter on motivation and emotion).

Contrary to the claims of some animal-rights activists, animals used in psychological research are not routinely subjected to extreme pain, starvation, or other inhumane conditions. Even in the small proportion of studies that require the use of electric shock, the discomfort created is mild, brief, and not harmful. High standards for the care and treatment of animal participants are outlined in the Animal Welfare Act, the National Institutes of Health's *Guide for the Care and Use of Laboratory Animals,* the National Institute of Mental Health's *Methods and Welfare Considerations in Behavioral Research with Animals,* the American Psychological Association's *Guidelines for Ethical Conduct in the Care and Use of Animals,* and other laws and regulations. In those relatively rare studies that require animals to undergo short-lived pain or other forms of moderate stress, legal and ethical standards require that funding agencies—as well as local committees charged with monitoring animal research—first determine that the discomfort is justified by the expected benefits to human welfare.

The responsibility for conducting research in the most humane fashion is one aspect of the *Ethical Principles of Psychologists and Code of Conduct* developed by the American Psychological Association (2002b). The main purpose of these standards is to protect and promote the welfare of society and those with whom psychologists work. For example, as teachers, psychologists should strive to give students complete, accurate, and up-to-date coverage of each topic, not a narrow and biased point of view. Further, psychologists should perform only those services and use only those techniques for which they are adequately trained. Psychologists should not reveal information obtained from clients or research participants, except in the most unusual of circumstances (see the chapter on treatment of psychological disorders). Finally, they should avoid situations in which a conflict of interest might impair their judgment or harm someone else. They should not, for example, have sexual relations with their clients, students, or employees.

Despite these guidelines, doubt and controversy arise in some cases about whether a proposed experiment or a particular practice, such as deceiving participants, is ethical. The American Psychological Association has published a casebook to help psychologists resolve such issues (Nagy, 1999). The ethical principles themselves must continually be updated to deal with complex new questions—such as how to protect the confidentiality of e-mail communications—that psychologists face in their ever-expanding range of work (APA, 2002b; Pipes, Holstein, & Aguirre, 2005).

ACTIVE REVIEW | Introduction to the Science of Psychology

Summary

THE WORLD OF PSYCHOLOGY: AN OVERVIEW

▶ **What is psychology, and how did it grow?**

Psychology is the science that seeks to understand behavior and mental processes. The broad concept of "behavior and mental processes" encompasses virtually all aspects of what it means to be a human being. Psychologists study a wide variety of topics, from the activity of individual nerve cells and the way we sense and perceive things to the way we think, make decisions, and experience emotion to the way people cooperate or compete with each other.

Because the subject matter of psychology is so diverse, most psychologists work in particular subfields within the discipline. For example, *cognitive psychologists* focus on basic psychological processes such as learning, memory, and perception. *Biological psychologists* explore the influence of brain chemistry and other physiological factors on behavior and mental processes. *Personality psychologists* focus on characteristics that set people apart from one another. *Developmental psychologists* specialize in trying to understand the development of behavior and mental processes over a lifetime. *Quantitative psychologists* develop methods for statistical analysis of data. *Clinical* and *counseling psychologists* provide direct service to troubled people and conduct research on abnormal behavior. *Community psychologists* work to prevent mental disorders and extend mental health services to those who need it. *Educational psychologists* conduct and apply research on teaching and learning, whereas *school psychologists* specialize in assessing and alleviating children's academic problems. *Social psychologists* examine questions regarding how people influence one another; *industrial/ organizational psychologists* conduct research on topics such as increasing the motivation of employees and helping companies select the best new workers. *Health psychologists, sport psychologists, forensic psychologists, engineering psychologists,* and *environmental psychologists* work in some of psychology's many other subfields. Psychology's subfields often overlap, and psychologists often work in more than one subfield, sharing knowledge with colleagues in other subfields and contributing to knowledge in other disciplines.

Scientific psychology has its roots in philosophy, and especially in a philosophical view called *empiricism.* The modern science of psychology began to emerge in the late nineteenth century as scientists in Germany and North America established laboratories to conduct research in psychology. In Germany, Wundt explored the building blocks of *consciousness;* Gestalt psychologists there later studied it as a whole. In Vienna, Freud explored the unconscious. At about the same time in the United States, James was applying Darwin's theory of evolution to the exploration of human behavior. In the early twentieth century, Watson argued that to be truly scientific, psychologists should focus only on observable behavior. He founded behaviorism, which dominated psychology for decades. Today, consciousness—in the form of cognitive processes—is being intensively studied once again.

APPROACHES TO THE SCIENCE OF PSYCHOLOGY

▶ **Why don't all psychologists explain behavior in the same way?**

Psychologists differ in their approaches to psychology—that is, in the assumptions, questions, and methods they believe will be most helpful in their work. Those psychologists who adopt a *biological approach* examine how physiological factors shape behavior and mental processes. Darwin's theory helped stimulate the *evolutionary approach,* which emphasizes the inherited, adaptive aspects of behavior and mental processes. The *psychodynamic approach* sees behavior and mental processes as a struggle to resolve conflicts between impulses and the demands made by society to control those impulses. Psychologists who take the *behavioral approach* consider behavior to be determined primarily by learning based on experiences with rewards and punishments. The *cognitive approach* assumes that behavior can be understood through analysis of the mental processes that underlie it. The *humanistic approach* views behavior as controlled by the decisions that people make about their lives based on their perceptions of the world.

HUMAN DIVERSITY AND PSYCHOLOGY

▶ **How does your cultural background influence your behavior?**

Most of the prominent figures in psychology's history were white males, but women and people of color made important contributions from the start, and they continue to do so. Psychologists are increasingly taking into account the influence of *culture* and other *sociocultural variables* such as gender and ethnicity in shaping human behavior and mental processes.

THINKING CRITICALLY ABOUT PSYCHOLOGY (OR ANYTHING ELSE)

▶ **How can critical thinking save you money?**

Critical thinking is the process of assessing claims and making judgments on the basis of well-supported evidence. This process involves asking five questions: What am I being asked to believe or accept? Is there evidence available to support the claim? Can that evidence be interpreted another way? What evidence would help to evaluate the alternatives? What conclusions are most reasonable?

Often, questions about psychological phenomena are phrased in terms of *hypotheses* about *variables* that are specified by *operational definitions.* Evidence for hypotheses must be evaluated for *reliability* and *validity.* After gathering research evidence, scientists may organize their findings into a *theory,* a set of statements designed to explain certain phenomena. Theories must be subjected to careful evaluation.

RESEARCH METHODS IN PSYCHOLOGY

▶ **How do psychologists learn about people?**

Research in psychology, as in other sciences, focuses on four main goals: description, prediction, control, and explanation. Psychologists have found several research methods especially useful in gathering the evidence needed to reach each of these goals. *Naturalistic observation* entails watching without interfering as behavior occurs in the natural environment. *Case studies* are intensive examinations of a particular individual, group, or situation. *Surveys* ask questions, through interviews or questionnaires, about behavior, attitudes, beliefs, opinions, and intentions. *Correlational studies* examine the *correlation,* or relationship, between variables in order to describe research data, test predictions, evaluate theories, and suggest hypotheses. In *experiments,* researchers manipulate an *independent variable* and observe the effect of that manipulation on a *dependent variable.* Participants who receive experimental treatment are called the *experimental group.* Participants in comparison conditions are called *control groups.* Experiments can reveal cause-effect relationships between variables, but only if researchers use *random assignment* and other strategies (such as *placebo* conditions and a *double-blind design*) to avoid being misled by *random variables, experimenter bias,* and other *confounding variables.*

Psychologists' research can be limited if their *sampling* procedures do not give them a *representative sample* of the population they want to study and about which they want to draw conclusions. Anything other than a truly *random sample* is said to be a *biased sample* of participants. In most cases, psychologists try to select a *representative sample* of the populations that are available to them.

STATISTICAL ANALYSIS OF RESEARCH RESULTS

▶ **What does it mean when scientists announce that a research finding is "significant"?**

Psychologists use descriptive and inferential statistical analyses to summarize and analyze *data,* which are the numbers that represent research findings and provide the basis for conclusions. When a correlation coefficient, a difference between groups, or some other research finding is larger than would be expected by chance alone, it is said to be *statistically significant.*

ETHICAL GUIDELINES FOR PSYCHOLOGISTS

▶ **Do psychologists deceive people when they do research?**

Ethical guidelines promote the protection of human and animal participants in psychological research, and set the highest standards for behavior in all other aspects of psychologists' professional lives.

Learn by Doing

Put It in Writing

Choose one or two recent newspaper, magazine, or Internet articles describing a research study in psychology, and then, based on the article alone, try to answer the five critical thinking questions we described earlier *(What am I being asked to believe or accept?, Is there evidence available to support the claim?, Can that evidence be interpreted another way?, What evidence would help to evaluate the alternatives?,* and *What conclusions are most reasonable?).* When you have finished, write a paragraph or two describing how well you think the popular media cover the results of scientific research in psychology and how that coverage could be improved.

Personal Learning Activity

Try designing an experiment on a hypothesis of your choice. First, state your hypothesis as specifically as possible, being sure to include operational definitions of the independent and dependent variables. Then tell how and where you will get your research participants, what the experimental and control groups will experience, and what all your research procedures will be. For example, if your hypothesis is that rock music played during studying improves students' memory for the material, then you should decide what you mean by "rock music" and "improved memory," what the experimental and control groups will hear while studying, what they will study, and how you will measure the students' memory for what they learned. *For additional projects, see the Personal Learning Activities in the corresponding chapter of the study guide that accompanies this text.*

Step into Action

Courses

History and Systems of Psychology
Experimental Psychology

Movies

Me and Isaac Newton (scientific research methods)
Gorillas in the Mist; Blow-Up; Kitchen Stories (naturalistic observation)
The Joy Luck Club; Daughter from Danang (cultural influences on behavior)
Mr. Baseball (collectivist versus individualistic cultures)

Books

Ludy T. Benjamin and D. B. Baker, *From Seance to Science: A History of the Profession of Psychology in America* (Wadsworth, 2004). The development of clinical, counseling, school, and industrial/organizational psychology.

Alan M. Goldstein (Ed.), *Forensic Psychology* (Wiley, 2006). Overview of the role of psychological science in the legal system.

Paul Bell, *Environmental Psychology* (Wadsworth, 2001). Applications of psychology to solving problems in natural and artificial environments, including college campuses.

Steve Jones, *Darwin's Ghost: The Origin of Species Updated* (Random House, 2000). Evolutionary theory explained with modern examples.

F. Barbara Orlans, Tom Beauchamp, Rebecca Dresser, and John Gluck (Eds.), *The Human Use of Animals: Case Studies in Ethical Choice* (Oxford University Press, 1998). Case studies related to animal research.

Peter Gay, *Freud: A Life for Our Time* (Norton, 1998). Comprehensive biography of the founder of psychoanalysis.

Roger Hock, *Forty Studies that Changed Psychology* (Prentice Hall, 1995). Reports of famous psychological studies.

Alice Wexler, *Mapping Fate* (University of California Press, 1996). The story of Nancy Wexler's discovery of the gene for Huntington's disease.

Joel Best, *Damned lies and statistics: Untangling numbers from the media, politicians, and activists* (University of California Press, 2001). Examples of the need to think critically about statistics.

The Web

The World Wide Web is a good source of additional information about the science of psychology, provided you use it carefully and think critically about the information you find. The web site that accompanies this text offers many resources relevant to this chapter. These resources include interactive tutorials and animations; ACE chapter quizzes; recommended web links; and articles on current events, books, and movies. At http://college.hmco.com, select *Psychology* and then this textbook.

Review of Key Terms

Can you define each of the key terms in the chapter? Check your definitions against those on the pages shown in parentheses in the following list or in the Glossary/Index at the end of the text.

behavioral approach *(p. 16)*
behavioral genetics *(p. 37)*
biased sample *(p. 35)*
biological approach *(p. 14)*
biological psychologists *(p. 5)*
case studies *(p. 26)*
clinical, counseling, and community psychologists *(p. 5)*
cognitive approach *(p. 16)*
cognitive psychologists *(p. 4)*
confounding variable *(p. 33)*
consciousness *(p. 10)*
control group *(p. 32)*
correlation *(p. 29)*
correlational studies *(p. 29)*
critical thinking *(p. 21)*

culture *(p. 19)*
data *(p. 39)*
dependent variable *(p. 30)*
developmental psychologists *(p. 5)*
double-blind design *(p. 35)*
educational psychologists *(p. 5)*
empiricism *(p. 10)*
engineering psychologists *(p. 6)*
environmental psychologists *(p. 6)*
evolutionary approach *(p. 15)*
experiment *(p. 30)*
experimental group *(p. 32)*
experimenter bias *(p. 34)*

forensic psychologists *(p. 6)*
health psychologists *(p. 6)*
humanistic approach *(p. 17)*
hypothesis *(p. 25)*
independent variable *(p. 30)*
industrial/organizational psychologists *(p. 6)*
naturalistic observation *(p. 26)*
operational definitions *(p. 25)*
personality psychologists *(p. 5)*
placebo *(p. 33)*
psychodynamic approach *(p. 16)*
psychology *(p. 4)*
quantitative psychologists *(p. 5)*
random assignment *(p. 33)*
random sample *(p. 35)*

random variables *(p. 33)*
reliability *(p. 25)*
representative sample *(p. 35)*
sampling *(p. 35)*
school psychologists *(p. 5)*
social psychologists *(p. 6)*
sociocultural variables *(p. 19)*
sport psychologists *(p. 6)*
statistically significant *(p. 40)*
surveys *(p. 27)*
theory *(p. 25)*
validity *(p. 25)*
variables *(p. 25)*

Multiple-Choice Self-Test

Select the best answer for each of the following questions. Then check your responses against the Answer Key at the end of the text.

1. The first research laboratory in psychology was established to study

   a. consciousness.
   b. the unconscious.
   c. perceptual processes.
   d. the collective unconscious.

2. Dr. Gauzz believes that low-income families who live in crowded conditions are more likely to need mental health services. Therefore, he works to eliminate high-rise communities for low-income families. Dr. Gauzz is most likely a(n) _____ psychologist.

   a. developmental   c. industrial-organizational
   b. community   d. engineering

3. Dr. Hemmings believes that human behavior is influenced by genetic inheritance, unconscious motivations, and environmental influences. Dr. Hemmings uses a(n)_____approach.

    a. Evolutionary
    b. Eclectic
    c. Humanistic
    d. Behavioral

4. Dr. Foreman studies what teachers actually do when they are teaching students to read. Dr. Foreman is most likely a(n) _____ psychologist.

    a. cognitive
    b. school
    c. educational
    d. community

5. Larry says that people act the way they learned to act. He believes that if others stop rewarding a person's annoying behavior, that behavior will decrease. Larry most likely takes a(n)_____ approach to psychology.

    a. behavioral
    b. cognitive
    c. evolutionary
    d. humanistic

6. Leonard just won a college scholarship because of his outstanding grades. If he is from a collectivist culture, he is most likely to say:

    a. "I've worked very hard for this honor and I appreciate the vote of confidence."
    b. "I had some tough times when I didn't think I would succeed, but this has made it all worthwhile."
    c. "I could not have won this award without the help of my teachers and family."
    d. "I am so happy that the committee recognized my hard work and perseverance and is rewarding it with this scholarship."

7. Dr. Rose, a cross-cultural psychologist, is most likely to find which behavior to be similar in all of the groups she studies?

    a. Striving for achievement
    b. Rules governing social behavior
    c. Styles of communication
    d. Recognition of a smile

8. You are watching an "infomercial" that claims that if you drink liquefied seaweed twice a day, you will lose ten pounds a month. As a wise consumer who knows the five critical thinking questions listed in this chapter, you would FIRST say to yourself:

    a. "I don't know whether the person making the claim about the weight-loss effects of seaweed is a doctor or not."
    b. "The only evidence they present in support of their claim is one woman's personal experience."
    c. "I'll bet you also have to exercise to lose the ten pounds."
    d. "They are asking me to believe that I can lose ten pounds a month by drinking seaweed."

9. Dr. Lucas is interested in the effect of color on people's moods. She has participants complete a mood survey in either a bright red room or a stark white one. The participants' score on the mood survey is her

    a. descriptive statistic.
    b. random variable.
    c. independent variable.
    d. operational definition of mood.

10. Case studies are used to

    a. avoid a placebo effect.
    b. determine the effects of an independent variable.
    c. collect descriptive data.
    d. provide control in an experiment.

11. Before using survey results to support a hypothesis, we must be sure about which of the following?

    a. The questions are properly worded.
    b. The sample used is representative of the population of interest.
    c. The responses are not strongly biased by efforts to appear socially acceptable.
    d. All of the above.

12. When Dr. Beren compares the performance of his experimental group and his control group, he finds the difference in their scores to be statistically significant. This means that

    a. the difference is larger than would be expected by chance.
    b. he used descriptive statistics.
    c. his results were confounded by random variables.
    d. he used a double-blind method.

13. Dr. Daneli believes that memory is aided by an increase in a brain chemical called serotonin. To avoid the possibility that experimenter bias might confound the results of an experiment aimed at testing this hypothesis, he should use a(n)_____design.

    a. operational
    b. naturalistic
    c. random
    d. double-blind

14. In Dr. Daneli's experiment, Group A receives serotonin before taking a memory test, whereas Group B takes the same test without receiving serotonin. In this experiment, performance on the memory test is the _____ variable.

    a. dependent   c. control
    b. independent   d. random

15. Jeremy designed an experiment to test the effects of praise on the sharing behavior of children. Children in Group A will be praised after they share; children in Group B will only be observed. Group A is the_____ group.

    a. control   c. operational
    b. experimental   d. random

16. José wants to know whether growing up in an abusive family causes children to become physically violent. Which of the following research methods would create the greatest ethical problems in trying to scientifically study this question?

   a. case studies
   b. experiments
   c. observations
   d. surveys

17. Choose the strongest correlation coefficient.

   a. +.75
   b. −.99
   c. +.01
   d. −.01

18. A correlation coefficient can tell us all of the following *except* the _____ of a relationship between two variables.

   a. strength
   b. direction
   c. existence
   d. cause

19. Your psychology professor asks you to learn about the smoking habits of all students on your campus. The most practical yet scientific way to get participants for your study would be to find a

   a. random sample of all students.
   b. random sample of smokers.
   c. representative sample of all students.
   d. representative sample of all nonsmokers

20. Why do psychologists follow ethical guidelines?

   a. Psychologists would not want the cost of participating in an experiment to be too high in comparison with the information to be gained.
   b. The American Psychological Association has set standards for psychologists to follow when conducting research and treating clients.
   c. Stress and pain could act as confounding variables in an experiment.
   d. All of the above.

2

Biology and Behavior

Before you read the next sentence, close your eyes and touch your nose. This task

is easy, but it is not simple. To get the job done, your brain used specific nerves to tell your eyelids to close. It used other nerves to tell your hand to extend a finger and then sent a series of messages that moved your arm in just the right direction until it received a message that your finger and your nose were in contact. This example illustrates that everything you do—including how you feel and think—is based on some kind of biological activity in your body, especially in your brain. This chapter tells the story of that activity, beginning with a basic biological unit of the body, a specialized cell called the *neuron*. Collections of neurons form the systems that receive information from our senses, process that information, and biochemically translate it into behavior, thoughts, and emotions.

Reading this chapter will help you to answer the following questions:

▶ **What are neurons, and what do they do?** 49

▶ **How do sights and sounds reach my brain?** 53

▶ **How is my brain "wired"?** 54

▶ **How do biochemicals affect my mood?** 74

▶ **How can my hormones help me in a crisis?** 77

The fact is that biological factors are intimately related to *all* behavior and mental processes. The question of how they are related takes us into the realm of **biological psychology**—the study of cells, genes, and organs of the body and the physical and chemical changes involved in behavior and mental processes. As we describe the biology of behavior and mental processes, we keep in mind the role of the environment in influencing those processes. You will see later, for example, that the experiences we have in the environment can change the chemistry, and even the structure, of our brains. Let's begin to consider in more detail the relationship between your body and your mind, between your brain and your behavior.

Understanding how we think, feel, act, and react requires some knowledge of the human body and how it works. Two primary systems—the nervous system and the endocrine system—direct the activities of the body. The nervous system receives information, sends messages from one part of the body to another, and begins actions. The endocrine (pronounced "END oh-krin") system regulates internal activity of the body with glands that secrete chemicals, called *hormones*, into the bloodstream to control energy consumption, reactions to stress, sexual functioning, and the like. These are the basic pieces of the puzzle of the body. Putting the pieces together is the next step in understanding the biology of our complex behavior.

biological psychology The study of physical and chemical changes involved in behavior and mental processes.

Cells of the Nervous System

▶ **What are neurons, and what do they do?**

We begin by considering the **nervous system,** a vast network of cells that tells you what is going on inside and outside your body and allows you to make appropriate responses. For example, if you are jabbed with a pin, your nervous system gets the message and immediately causes you to flinch. But the nervous system can do far more than detect information and make responses. When information about the world reaches the brain, that information is *processed*—it is combined with information about past experiences and current wants and needs—to allow you to make a decision about how to respond (see Figure 2.1). We begin our exploration of the nervous system at the "bottom," with a description of its individual cells. Later we consider how these cells are organized to form the structures of the human nervous system.

Neurons

As Figure 2.1 shows, the nervous system is actually an information-processing system with three functions: input, processing, and output. These functions are possible partly because the nervous system is made up of cells that communicate with each other. Two major types of cells, neurons and glial cells, allow the nervous system to carry out its complex signaling tasks efficiently. The specialized cells that send and receive signals are called **neurons.**

Most of our discussion of brain cells concerns neurons, but glial cells are important, too. *Glial* means "glue," and scientists had long believed that glial cells did no more than hold neurons together. We now know, however, that **glial cells** also help neurons communicate by directing their growth, keeping their chemical environment stable, providing energy, secreting chemicals to help repair damage, and even responding to signals from neurons (Fellin et al., 2004). Without glial cells, neurons could not function, and recent research suggests that malfunctions in glial cells may play a role in problems ranging from recurring pain to depression and other mental disorders (Miller, 2005a).

FIGURE **2.1**

Three Functions of the Nervous System

The nervous system's three main functions are to receive information (input), to integrate that information with past experiences (processing), and to guide actions (output). When the alarm clock goes off, this person's nervous system, like yours, gets the message, recognizes what it means, and takes action—by getting out of bed or perhaps hitting the snooze button.

nervous system A network of billions of cells that detects what is going on inside or outside the body and guides appropriate responses.

neurons Specialized cells of the nervous system that send and receive messages.

glial cells Nervous system cells that hold neurons together and help them communicate with each other.

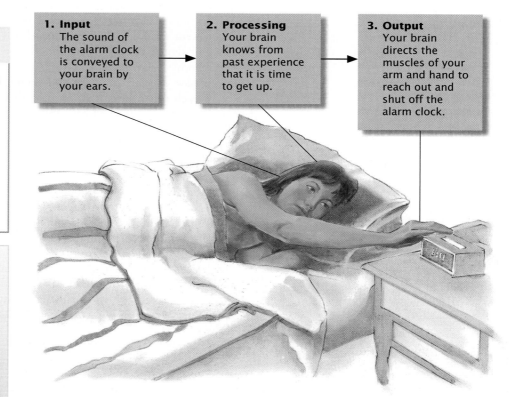

1. Input The sound of the alarm clock is conveyed to your brain by your ears.

2. Processing Your brain knows from past experience that it is time to get up.

3. Output Your brain directs the muscles of your arm and hand to reach out and shut off the alarm clock.

FIGURE **2.2**

The Neuron

Part A shows fibers extending outward from the cell body of a neuron, which is a nervous system cell. These fibers are called *axons* and *dendrites*. Part B shows an enlarged drawing of the neuron's cell body. The cell body of a neuron includes an outer membrane, a nucleus, and mitochondria.

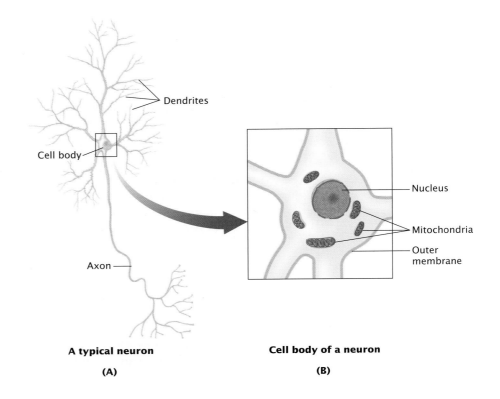

A typical neuron

(A)

Cell body of a neuron

(B)

axon   A fiber that carries signals away from the cell body.

dendrites   Fibers that receive signals from the axons of other neurons.

action potential   The electrochemical impulse or message that is sent down an axon and stimulates release of a neurotransmitter.

Every cell in the body has a skin, called an *outer membrane;* a cell body that (with the exception of red blood cells) contains a core called the *nucleus;* and tiny "engines," called *mitochondria* (pronounced "my-toh-CON-dree-uh"). Neurons are no different. A neuron's outer membrane acts like a screen, letting some substances pass in and out while blocking others. In the neuron's cell body, the nucleus (or center) carries genetic information that tells the cell what to do. And neurons' mitochondria turn oxygen and glucose into energy. This process is especially vital to brain cells, because although the brain accounts for only 2 percent of the body's weight, it uses more than 20 percent of the body's oxygen. All of this energy is required because brain cells transmit signals among themselves to an even greater extent than do cells in the rest of the body.

Neurons have special structural and chemical features that allow them to communicate with each other. Let's first examine their structure. Although neurons come in many shapes and sizes, they all have long, thin fibers that reach outward from the cell body like arms (see Part A in Figure 2.2). When these fibers get close to other neurons, communication between the cells can occur. The interweaving of these fibers with fibers from other neurons allows each neuron to be close to thousands or even hundreds of thousands of other neurons.

Fibers extending from the cell body are called axons and dendrites. As shown in Figure 2.2, each neuron generally has only one **axon,** whose function is to carry signals away from the cell body. An axon may have many branches along its stem, much like a tree. Axons can be short or long. In the brain, they may extend no more than a fraction of an inch, but the axon from your big toe to your spine is more than three feet long! **Dendrites** are the fibers that receive signals from the axons of other neurons and carry those signals to the cell body. As you can see in Figure 2.2, a neuron can have many dendrites, each of which usually has many branches. Remember that *axons* carry signals *away* from the cell body, and *dendrites detect* those signals.

Action Potentials

The communication signal between neurons begins with an electrochemical pulse called an **action potential,** which shoots down the axon. This is an "all-or-nothing"

FIGURE **2.3**

Communication Between Neurons

When stimulation of a neuron reaches a certain level, the neuron fires, sending an action potential shooting to the end of its axon and triggering the release of a neurotransmitter into the synapse. This process stimulates neighboring neurons and may cause them to fire their own action potentials.

1. An *action potential* shoots down the *axon*, away from the cell body.

2. A *neurotransmitter* is released into the *synapse*, where the *dendrites* of neighboring neurons detect it. See enlarged area.

3. If there is a receptor for this neurotransmitter on the dendrites, the neurotransmitter and receptor bind, creating an electrochemical signal.

4. If that signal is strong enough, it spreads down the dendrites and across the cell body of the next neuron, and begins another action potential.

Cell body

Axon

Neurotransmitters

Synapse

Receptors for neurotransmitters

Dendrite

Cell body

affair: The cell either fires its action potential at full strength or it does not fire at all. Once a cell has fired, a very short recovery time called the **refractory period** follows, during which the cell cannot fire again. Even so, neurons are able to fire as often as 1,000 times per second. The speed of an action potential ranges from about 5 to about 260 miles per hour and depends on the thickness or diameter of the axon—larger ones are faster—and on the presence of myelin (pronounced "MY-a-lin"). *Myelin* is a fatty substance that wraps around some axons like a stocking and speeds up action potentials. When a neuron fires, dendrites in the next cell detect the message and send the signal to their cell body.

Synapses and Communication Between Neurons

How do the dendrites detect a signal from another neuron? As shown in Figure 2.3, it works a little like the game of tag you played as a child. In this neural communication tag game, however, one neuron "sends" a tag without actually touching the next neuron. When an action potential reaches the ends of an axon's branches, it stimulates the release of a chemical that is stored there in little "bags," called *vesicles* (pronounced "VESS-ick-els"). This chemical is called a **neurotransmitter** because it acts as a kind of messenger between neurons. Neurotransmitters flow across a tiny gap, less than a millionth of an inch wide, which separates the axon of one neuron and the dendrites of another. This is the *synaptic gap*, often referred to simply as the **synapse** (see Figure 2.4) When they reach the dendrite of the next cell, neurotransmitters chemically fit, or bind, to proteins

refractory period   A short recovery time after cell firing, during which the cell cannot fire again.

neurotransmitter   A chemical that transfers messages across synapses.

synapse   The tiny gap between the axon of one neuron and the dendrites of another.

FIGURE **2.4**

A Synapse

This photograph taken with an electron microscope shows part of a synapse between neurons, magnified 50,000 times. The end of one neuron's axon is shaded green; the green ovals are mitochondria. The red spots are neurotransmitter-containing vesicles. The synapse itself appears as the narrow gap between the first cell's axon and the dendrite of the second cell, which is shaded blue.

called *receptors*. Like a key fitting into the right lock, a neurotransmitter snugly binds to its own receptors, but not to receptors for other neurotransmitters. The receptors "recognize" only one type of neurotransmitter. In the dendrite, this binding creates an electrochemical signal that is called a *postsynaptic potential* because it occurs *after* the neurotransmitter has crossed the synapse. The postsynaptic potential, in turn, passes the message to the cell body for the signaling process to continue.

Generally, more than one message must go to a cell to make it fire. Signals from groups of cells often arrive at the same postsynaptic cell at about the same time. The messages from these many cells may conflict with one another. Some messages

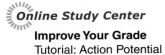
Online Study Center
Improve Your Grade
Tutorial: Action Potential

in review

NEURONS, NEUROTRANSMITTERS, AND RECEPTORS

Part	Function	Type of Signal Carried
Axon	Carries signals away from the cell body	The action potential, an all-or-nothing electrochemical signal that shoots down the axon to vesicles at the tip of the axon, releasing neurotransmitters
Dendrite	Detects and carries signals to the cell body	The postsynaptic potential, an electrochemical signal moving toward the cell body
Synapse	Provides an area for the transfer of signals between neurons, usually between axon and dendrite	Chemicals that cross the synapse and reach receptors on another cell
Neurotransmitter	A chemical released by one cell that binds to the receptors on another cell	A chemical message telling the next cell to fire or not to fire its own action potential
Receptor	Proteins on the cell membrane that receive chemical signals	Recognizes certain neurotransmitters, thus allowing it to begin a postsynaptic potential in the dendrite

1. For one neuron to communicate with another, a _____ has to cross the _____ between them.
2. The nervous system's main functions are to _____, _____, and _____ information.
3. The two main types of cells in the nervous system are _____ and _____.

FIGURE **2.5**

Organization of the Nervous System

The brain and spinal cord make up the bone-encased central nervous system (CNS), the body's central information processor, decision maker, and director of actions. The peripheral nervous system, which is not housed in bone, functions mainly to carry messages. The somatic subsystem of the peripheral nervous system transmits information to the CNS from the outside world and conveys instructions from the CNS to the muscles. The autonomic subsystem conveys messages from the CNS that alter the activity of organs and glands, and it sends information about that activity back to the brain.

tell the cell to fire, whereas others tell the cell not to fire. Whether it actually does fire depends on which kinds of signals are most numerous. So axons, neurotransmitters, synapses, and dendrites allow cells of the nervous system to communicate. If these components are damaged or disordered, however, serious problems can result. For example, spinal cord injuries may cut the neural communication lines that had once allowed victims to feel and move their bodies. And when the myelin surrounding some axons is destroyed by the brain disorder known as *multiple sclerosis (MS)*, the result can be disruption of vision, speech, balance, and other important functions.

Organization of the Nervous System

Impressive as individual neurons are (see "In Review: Neurons, Neurotransmitters, and Receptors"), we can best understand their functions by looking at how they operate in groups. The billions of neurons that make up the nervous system are organized into two main parts—the *central nervous system* and the *peripheral nervous system* (see Figure 2.5). We describe them in separate sections, but they work together closely to coordinate behavior and mental processes. The **central nervous system (CNS)** consists of the brain and spinal cord, which are encased in bone for protection. Like the chief executive officer in a company, the CNS receives information, processes it, and determines what actions should result. The **peripheral nervous system** extends throughout the body and relays information to and from the brain.

The Peripheral Nervous System: Keeping in Touch with the World

▶ **How do sights and sounds reach my brain?**

central nervous system (CNS) The brain and spinal cord.

peripheral nervous system The part of the nervous system that sends messages to and from the central nervous system.

The peripheral nervous system sends sensory information from the eyes, ears, and other sense organs to the CNS. The peripheral nervous system also carries messages from the brain and spinal cord to the muscles, glands, and other parts of the body. Unlike the CNS, it is not protected by bone. To accomplish its relay tasks, the peripheral nervous system has two subsystems—the autonomic nervous system and the somatic nervous system.

The Somatic Nervous System

Imagine that you are at the beach. It is hot, and the ocean smells salty. An attractive stranger approaches, catching your eye. The stranger smiles. You smile in return. The stranger continues walking away. In these few seconds, your nervous system has been busy. You feel the warmth of the sun and smell the ocean because your **somatic nervous system** takes in these pieces of sensory information and sends them to the central nervous system for processing. The CNS evaluates the warmth and the smells, sending messages through the somatic nervous system to the muscles that allow you to turn over, sit up, or put on more sunscreen. *Sensory neurons* bring information into the brain. *Motor neurons* carry information from the part of the brain that directs motion.

The Autonomic Nervous System

The **autonomic nervous system** carries messages back and forth between the CNS and the heart, lungs, and other organs and glands. For example, the autonomic nervous system takes that passing stranger's "attractive" rating from the CNS and translates it into an increase in heart rate, pupil dilation, and perhaps a little blushing. This system is called "autonomic" (pronounced "aw-toh-NOM-ic") because its activities, including digestion and sweating, for example, are generally autonomous, or independent of your control. With training and practice, some people can use a technique called *biofeedback* to bring some of their involuntary responses, such as heart rate, under conscious (CNS) control.

As shown in Figure 2.5, the autonomic system has two subsystems of its own—the *sympathetic nervous system* and the *parasympathetic nervous system*. These two subsystems work like a seesaw on a playground. Generally, the **sympathetic nervous system** readies your body for action in the face of stress. The **parasympathetic nervous system** calms you down once the crisis has passed. So the *sympathetic nervous system spends* energy, whereas the *parasympathetic nervous system preserves* energy.

The functions of the autonomic nervous system may not get star billing, but you would miss them if they were gone. Just as a race-car driver is nothing without a good pit crew, the somatic nervous system depends on the autonomic nervous system to get its job done. For example, when you want to move your muscles, you create a demand for energy. The autonomic nervous system fills the bill by increasing sugar fuels in the bloodstream. If you decide to stand up, you need increased blood pressure so that your blood does not flow out of your brain and settle in your legs. Again, the autonomic nervous system makes the adjustment. Disorders of the autonomic nervous system can make people sweat uncontrollably or faint whenever they stand up; they can also lead to other problems, such as an inability to have sex. We examine the autonomic nervous system in more detail in the chapter on motivation and emotion.

The Central Nervous System: Making Sense of the World

▶ **How is my brain "wired"?**

The amazing speed and efficiency of the central nervous system—the brain and spinal cord—have prompted many people to compare it to the central processor in a computer. But the CNS does not simply function as a high-powered computer. It certainly isn't laid out as neatly, either. The layout of the brain is more like the map of a college campus. There are clusters of offices for the administrators in one place, clusters of faculty offices in another place, and classrooms in yet another. Some of the sidewalks or hallways that connect these clusters are wide; others are narrow. There are many different but connected ways to get to the same place. Like a campus with its office clusters, the CNS has clusters of neuron cell bodies called **nuclei** (pronounced "NUKE-lee-eye"; *nuclei* is the

somatic nervous system   The subsystem of the peripheral nervous system that transmits information from the senses to the central nervous system and carries signals from the CNS to the muscles that move the skeleton.

autonomic nervous system   The subsystem of the peripheral nervous system that carries messages between the central nervous system and the heart, lungs, and other organs and glands in the body.

sympathetic nervous system   The subsystem of the autonomic nervous system that readies the body for vigorous activity.

parasympathetic nervous system   The subsystem of the autonomic nervous system that typically influences activity related to the protection, nourishment, and growth of the body.

nuclei   Clusters of nerve cell bodies in the central nervous system.

IS THAT YOUR FINAL ANSWER?
The geographically largest U.S. state is (a) Montana, (b) Texas, (c) Alaska, (d) Wyoming. Like contestants on shows such as *Who Wants to Be a Millionaire*, you must rely on your central nervous system, and especially on the information-processing power of your brain, to understand the question, recognize the correct option, and direct movements of your vocal muscles to make your answer heard. (The correct choice in this case is c.)

plural of *nucleus*). The sidewalks and hallways of the CNS are axons that travel together in bundles called **fiber tracts,** or *pathways.* The axon (hallway) from any given cell (office) may merge with and leave many fiber tracts (sidewalks) and send branches out to other tracts. Let's consider a practical example of nervous system functioning to begin learning our way around the "campus" of the brain.

It is 6 A.M. and your alarm clock goes off, creating the simple case of information processing illustrated in Figure 2.1. Your ears receive sensory input in the form of sound from the alarm. The sound is converted into neural signals and sent to the brain. Your brain compares these signals with previous experiences stored in memory and correctly associates the sound with "alarm clock." Your muscle-guiding output is not yet at peak performance, though, because your brain activity has not yet reached the waking state. So you fumble to turn off the alarm, shuffle to the kitchen, and accidentally touch the coffeemaker's heating element. Things get more lively now. Heat energy activates sensory neurons in your fingers, generating action potentials that speed along fiber tracts going into the spinal cord. Your motor neurons are reflexively activated by the CNS, causing muscles in your arm to contract and quickly withdraw your hand.

The Spinal Cord

The **spinal cord** receives signals such as pain and touch from the senses and passes those signals to the brain. Neuron fibers within the cord also carry signals downward from the brain to the muscles. Some cells of the spinal cord can direct simple behaviors without instructions from the brain. These behaviors are called **reflexes,** because the response to the incoming signal is directly "reflected" back out, as shown in Figure 2.6. Spinal reflexes, such as the one that pulled your hand away from the heat, are very fast because they include few time-consuming synaptic links. Reflexes are called *involuntary* because they occur without instructions from the brain. As reflexes occur, though, action potentials are also sent along fiber tracts to the brain. So you officially "know" you have been burned a fraction of a second after your reflex got you out of trouble.

The spinal cord is an example of a *feedback system.* When touching something hot sets off a simple reflex, one set of arm muscles contracts, and an opposing set of muscles relaxes. If this did not happen, the arm would go rigid. The muscles also have receptors that send information to the spinal cord to let it know how extended they are so that adjustments can be made for a smooth contracting motion. Information about the

fiber tracts Bundles of axons that travel together.

spinal cord The part of the central nervous system that receives information from the senses, passes these signals to the brain, and sends messages from the brain to the body.

reflexes Simple, involuntary, unlearned behaviors directed by the spinal cord without instructions from the brain.

FIGURE **2.6**

A Reflex Pathway

learn by **doing** Sit on a chair, cross one leg over the other, and then use the handle of a butter knife or some other solid object to gently tap your top knee, just below the joint, until you get a "knee jerk" reaction. Tapping your knee at just the right spot sets off an almost instantaneous sequence of events that begins with stimulation of sensory neurons that respond to stretch. When those neurons fire, their axons, which end within the spinal cord, cause spinal neurons to fire. This, in turn, stimulates the firing of motor neurons with axons ending in your thigh muscles. The result is a contraction of those muscles and a kicking of the lower leg and foot. Information about the knee tap and about what the leg has done also goes to your cerebral cortex, but the reflex is completed without waiting for guidance from the brain.

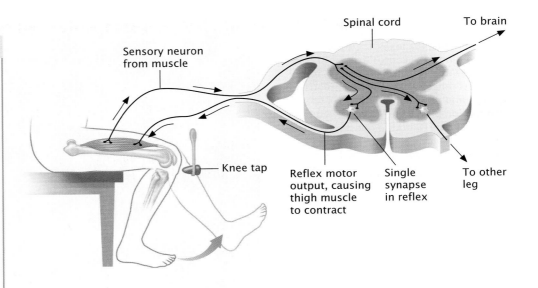

consequences of an action goes back to the source of the action for further adjustment. That is a feedback system.

The Brain

When pain messages from that hot burner reach your brain, you don't become aware just of being burned. You might also realize that you have burned yourself twice before in the past week and get annoyed at your own carelessness. The brain is the most complex element in the central nervous system, and it is your brain's astonishing capacity for information processing that allows you to have these thoughts and feelings. A variety of new brain-scanning techniques, combined with some older measures, are giving scientists ever better views of the workings of the human brain (Amaro & Barker, 2006; Miller, 2003; see Table 2.1).

Each technique can indirectly measure the activity of neurons firing, and each has different advantages and disadvantages. One of the earliest of these techniques, called the *electroencephalograph (EEG)*, measures general electrical activity of the brain. Electrodes are pasted on the scalp to detect the electrical fields resulting from the activity of billions of neurons (Figure 4.3 in the consciousness chapter shows how EEG can be used to record brain activity during sleep). Although this tool can associate rapidly changing electrical activity with changes in the activity of the brain, it cannot tell us exactly where the active cells are.

A newer technique, called the *PET scan,* can locate brain cell activity by recording where radioactive substances become concentrated when injected into the bloodstream. *PET* stands for *positron emission tomography.* It records images from the brain that indicate the location of the radioactivity as the brain performs various tasks. For instance, PET studies have revealed that specific brain regions are activated when we look at fearful facial expressions or engage in certain kinds of thoughts (Morris et al., 1998; Wharton et al., 2000). PET scans can tell us a lot about where changes in brain activity occur, but they can't reveal details of the brain's physical structure.

A detailed structural picture of the brain can be seen, however, using *magnetic resonance imaging,* or *MRI.* MRI exposes the brain to a magnetic field and measures the resulting radiofrequency waves to get amazingly clear pictures of the brain's anatomical details (see Figure 2.7). *Functional MRI,* or *fMRI,* combines the advantages of PET and MRI and is capable of detecting changes in blood flow and blood oxygen that reflect ongoing changes in the activity of neurons—providing a sort of "moving picture" of the brain (e.g., Shu et al., 2002). The newest techniques offer even deeper insight into brain activity, structure, and functioning. These techniques include a variant on fMRI called *diffusion tensor imaging (DTI),* as well as a procedure called *transcranial magnetic stimulation (TMS).*

TABLE 2.1   Techniques for Studying Human Brain Function and Structure

Technique	What It Shows	Advantages (+) and Disadvantages (−)
EEG (electroencephalograph): Multiple electrodes are pasted to the outside of the head	Lines that chart the summated electrical fields resulting from the activity of billions of neurons	+ Detects very rapid changes in electrical activity, allowing analysis of stages of cognitive processing − Provides poor spatial resolution of the source of electrical activity; EEG is sometimes combined with magnetoencephalography (MEG), which localizes electrical activity by measuring magnetic fields associated with it.
PET (positron emission tomography) and SPECT (single-photon emission computed tomography): Positrons and photons are emissions from radioactive substances	An image of the amount and localization of any molecule that can be injected in radioactive form, such as neurotransmitters, drugs, or tracers for blood flow or glucose use (which indicates specific changes in neuronal activity)	+ Allows functional and biochemical studies + Provides visual image corresponding to anatomy − Requires exposure to low levels of radioactivity − Provides spatial resolution better than that of EEG but poorer than that of MRI − Cannot follow rapid changes (faster than 30 seconds)
MRI (magnetic resonance imaging): Exposes the brain to a magnetic field and measures radiofrequency waves	Traditional MRI provides high-resolution image of brain anatomy. Functional MRI (fMRI) provides images of changes in blood flow (which indicate specific changes in neural activity). A new variant, diffusion tensor imaging (DTI), shows water flow in neural fibers, thus revealing the "wiring diagram" of neural connections in the brain.	+ Requires no exposure to radioactivity + Provides high spatial resolution of anatomical details (< 1 mm) + Provides high temporal resolution ($< \frac{1}{10}$ second)
TMS (transcranial magnetic stimulation): Temporarily disrupts electrical activity of a small region of brain by exposing it to an intense magnetic field.	Normal function of a particular brain region can be studied by observing changes after TMS is applied to a specific location.	+ Shows which brain regions are necessary for given tasks. − Long-term safety not well established.

FIGURE **2.7**

**Combining a PET Scan and
Magnetic Resonance Imaging**

Researchers have superimposed images
from PET scans and MRI to construct a
three-dimensional view of the living brain.
This figure shows the brain of a young
epileptic girl. The picture of the outer
surface of the brain is from the MRI; the
pink area is from the PET scan and shows
the source of epileptic activity. To the right
of the figure are separate MRI and PET
images taken at one plane, or "slice,"
through the brain (indicated by the line on
the brain at the left).

THINKING CRITICALLY

**What Can fMRI Tell Us About
Behavior and Mental
Processes?**

A picture may be worth a thousand words, but the pictures of brain activity offered by fMRI are generating millions of them. As of 2005, more than 4,000 scientific articles have reported the results of fMRI scans taken while people engaged in various kinds of thinking or experienced various emotions. Neuroscientists who use brain imaging techniques are now to be found in psychology departments around the world, and, as described in other chapters, their work is changing the research landscape in cognitive, social, and abnormal psychology. Excitement over fMRI is not confined to scientists, however. Popular and scientific magazines routinely carry fMRI pictures that appear to "show" people's thoughts and feelings as they happen.

■ **What am I being asked to believe or accept?**

In the early 1800s, similar excitement surrounded *phrenology,* a technique that involved feeling bumps and depressions on the skull. It was claimed that these contours reflected the size of 27 structures on the brain's surface that determine personality traits, mental abilities, talents, and other characteristics. Although wildly popular with the public (Benjamin & Baker, 2004), phrenology did not survive the critical thinking of nineteenth-century scientists, and the technique has long been discredited. Today, some scientists wonder whether fMRI is a twenty-first-century version of phrenology, at least in the sense that their colleagues might be accepting its value too readily. These scientists point out that, although fMRI images can indicate where brain activity occurs as people think and experience emotion, there is no guarantee that this activity is actually *causing* the associated thoughts and feelings (Aldridge, 2005). Questions are also being raised about the assumption that particular thought processes or emotions occur in a particular brain structure, or set of structures. It is easy to talk about "thinking" or "attention," but these psychological terms might not correspond to specific biological processes that can be isolated and located by *any* technology. In short, critics claim that the results of fMRI scans can be misleading and that they don't necessarily tell us much about how the mind works (Uttal, 2004). Perhaps it would be better to focus on *how* the brain produces thoughts and feelings instead of searching for their locations.

■ **Is there evidence available to support the claim?**

When the participant in an fRMI experiment thinks or feels something, you can actually see the colors in the brain scan change, much like the color changes you see on weather radar as a rainstorm intensifies or weakens. Looking at an fMRI scan, you get a clear impression that the brain areas that "light up" when a person experiences an emotion or performs a mental task are the ones involved in that emotion or task (see Figure 1.5).

These scans are not as precise as they seem, though, because fMRI doesn't directly measure brain cell activity. The colors seen in an fMRI scan reflect instead the flow of blood in the brain and the amount of oxygen the blood is carrying. Changes in blood flow and blood oxygen are *related* to changes in the firing rates of neurons, but the relationship is complex and not yet fully understood (Buxton et al., 2004). Further, when brain cells process information, their firing rates may either increase or decrease (Gonsalves et al., 2005). If the increases and decreases in a particular brain region happen to cancel each other out, an fMRI scan will miss the neuronal activity taking place in that region. In fact, compared with the direct measurement of brain cell activity that can be done in research with animals, fMRI technology is still rather crude. It takes coordinated changes in millions of neurons to produce a detectible change in the fMRI signal.

Critics also argue that the results of fMRI research can depend too much on how experimenters choose to interpret them. In a typical fMRI experiment, participants are shown some kind of display, such as pairs of photos, and asked to perform various tasks. One task might be to press a button if the photos are exactly the same. A second task might be to press the button if objects in the photos are arranged in the same way. In this second task, a participant should press the button if one photo shows, say, a short man standing to the left of a tall woman and the other photo shows a small dog standing to the left of a giraffe. Both versions of the task require the participant to compare two images, but only the second of them requires considering whether things that look different are actually similar in some way. The fMRI scans taken during these tasks might show certain brain areas "lighting up" only during the second task. If so, the researcher would suggest that those areas are involved in recognizing *analogies,* or the similarities between apparently different things (Wharton et al., 2000). The researcher would base this conclusion on a computer program that compares fMRI scans taken during two tasks, subtracts all the "lighted" areas that are the same in both scans, and keeps only those that are different. But what the computer classifies as "different" depends on a rule that is set by the experimenter. If the experimenter programs the computer to display only big differences between the scans, not many "lit up" areas will remain after the comparison process. But if even tiny differences are allowed to count as "different," many more "lighted" areas will remain after the subtraction process. In our example, then, there could be large or small areas apparently associated with recognizing analogies, all depending on a rule set by the researcher.

These problems aside, critics wonder what it really means when fMRI research shows that certain brain areas appear activated during certain kinds of tasks or experiences. Their concern focuses on studies such as one from the new field of *neuroeconomics* that suggests that excessive activity in a particular brain area leads to bad investment decisions (Kuhnen & Knutson, 2005). Another fMRI study claimed to show the "neural basis of romantic love." In this study, investigators scanned people's brains as they looked at pictures of their romantic partners and compared these scans to those taken while the same people viewed nonromantic friends (Bartels & Zeki, 2000). According to the "difference" rule established by the experimenters, four brain areas were more active when viewing a romantic loved one than when viewing a friend. But does this result tell us anything about how or why these areas became active or what results this activity might have? In other words, do we know more about love? Critics of fMRI would say no.

■ Can that evidence be interpreted another way?

Supporters of fMRI disagree. They believe that the colorful areas seen on fMRI scans can provide vital new information that will eventually allow scientists to answer

EXPLORING BRAIN FUNCTIONS WITH fMRI   As this participant performs a mental task, a functional magnetic resonance imaging scanner records blood flow and blood oxygen levels in her brain. The resulting computer analysis shows as "lit up" areas the parts of the brain that appear to be activated during the task, but critics doubt that fMRI scanning is as clear or accurate as its proponents suggest.

important questions about behavior and mental processes. They point, for example, to fMRI research on brain mechanisms that help us to appreciate what other people are feeling—that is, to experience empathy—and to learn by watching others.

These *mirror neuron mechanisms* were discovered accidentally by scientists who had been using surgical techniques to directly record the activity of brain cells in monkeys' brains (Rizzolatti et al., 1996). They found that neurons in an area called F5 are activated not only when a monkey plans to reach for an object, such as a peanut, but also if the monkey sees *an experimenter* reach for a peanut! After fMRI scanning became available, researchers could begin looking for mirror mechanisms in the human brain. And, in fact, some of the mirror systems they found in humans correspond to the F5 region in monkeys (Rizolatti & Arbib, 1998). One of them is called *Broca's area,* and, as described later, it is an important component of our ability to speak. It makes sense that Broca's area contains a mirror mechanism, because language is a skill that we learn partly by imitation. The new fMRI findings suggest that Broca's area may also be important for many other skills that involve imitation. One recent study found that this area "lights up" when a guitar student learns chords by watching a professional guitarist (Buccino et al., 2004). Other fMRI research has found that mirror systems in other parts of the brain become active when a person sees someone experiencing emotion. For example, the brain area that is activated when you experience disgust (from the smell of rotten eggs, for example) is also activated if you see a video in which someone else reacts to a smell with disgust (Wicker et al., 2003).

So fMRI can be uniquely useful, say its defenders. Without it, research on mirror neurons in humans could not have taken place. And because of it, we have evidence that the experience of empathy comes about because seeing the actions and emotions of others activates the same brain regions that would be active if we were doing or feeling the same things ourselves. Some fMRI studies have also found that malfunctioning mirror mechanisms are associated with the impairments in language development, in imitative skills, and in empathy seen in children diagnosed with autistic disorder (Dapretto et al., 2006; Miller, 2005b; see the chapter on psychological disorders).

■ **What evidence would help to evaluate the alternatives?**

As technology continues to be refined, the quality of fMRI scans will continue to improve, giving us ever better images of where brain activity is taking place. But the value of this scanning technology will depend on a better understanding of what it can and cannot tell us about how brain activity is related to behavior and mental processes. We also need more evidence about correlation and causation in fMRI research. For example, a recent study conducted fMRI scans on compulsive gamblers as they played a simple guessing game (Reuter et al., 2005). When they won the game, these people showed an unusually small amount of activity in a brain area that is normally activated by the experience of rewards, or pleasure. Noting the correlation between compulsive gambling and lower-than-normal activity in the reward area, the researchers suggested that an abnormality in the brain's reward mechanisms might be responsible for gambling addiction. But recent case studies also suggest that compulsive gambling appears in people taking a prescription drug that *increases* activity in reward areas—and that the gambling stops when the drug is discontinued (Dodd et al., 2005). As noted in the chapter on introducing psychology, correlation does not guarantee causation. Is the brain activity reflected in fMRI scans causing the thoughts and feelings that take place during the scanning process? Possibly, but those thoughts and feelings might themselves be caused *by* activity elsewhere in the brain that affects the areas being scanned.

Reaching an understanding about questions like these will require continuing debate and dialogue between those who dismiss fMRI and those who sing its praises. To make this interaction easier, a group of government agencies and private foundations has recently funded an fMRI Data Center (http://www.fmridc.org/f/fmridc). This facility stores information from fMRI experiments and makes it available to both critics and supporters of fMRI, who can review the research data, conduct their own analyses, and offer their own interpretations. Having access to an ever-growing database such as this will no doubt help scientists get the most out of fMRI technology while also helping each other to avoid either overstating or underestimating the meaning of fMRI research.

■ **What conclusions are most reasonable?**

When the EEG was invented nearly 100 years ago, scientists had their first glimpse of brain cell activity, as reflected in the "brain waves" traced on a long sheet of paper rolling from the EEG machine (see Figure 4.3). To many of these scientists, EEG must have seemed a golden gateway to an understanding of the brain and its relationship to behavior and mental processes. EEG has, in fact, helped to advance knowledge of the brain, but it certainly didn't solve all of its mysteries. When all is said and done, the same will probably be true of fMRI. It is an exciting new tool, and it offers previously undreamed-of images of the structure and functioning of the brain, but it is unlikely on its own to explain just how the brain creates our behavior and mental processes. It seems reasonable to conclude, then, that those who question the use of fMRI to study psychological processes are right in calling for a careful analysis of the value of this important high-tech tool.

Although the meaning of fMRI data will remain a subject for debate, there is no doubt that brain scanning techniques in general have opened new frontiers for biological psychology, neuroscience, and medicine (Goldstein & Volkow, 2002; Miller, 2003). Let's now explore some of the structures highlighted by these techniques, starting with three major subdivisions of the brain: the hindbrain, the midbrain, and the forebrain.

The Hindbrain

Figure 2.8 shows the major structures of the brain. The **hindbrain** lies just inside the skull and is actually a continuation of the spinal cord. Incoming signals from the spinal cord first reach the hindbrain. Many vital autonomic functions, such as heart rate,

hindbrain The portion of the brain that lies just inside the skull and is a continuation of the spinal cord.

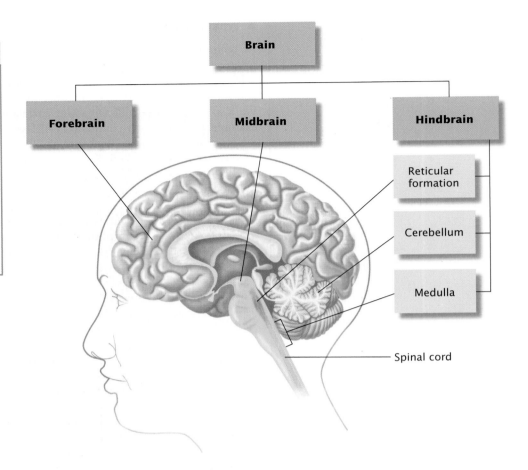

FIGURE 2.8

Major Structures of the Brain

This side view of a section cut down the middle of the brain reveals the forebrain, midbrain, hindbrain, and spinal cord. Many of these subdivisions do not have clear-cut borders, because they are all interconnected by fiber tracts. The brain's anatomy reflects its evolution over millions of years. Newer structures (such as the cerebral cortex, which is the outer surface of the forebrain) that handle higher mental functions were built on older ones (such as the medulla) that coordinate heart rate, breathing, and other more basic functions.

medulla   The area of the hindbrain that controls vital autonomic functions such as heart rate, blood pressure, and breathing.

reticular formation   A collection of cells and fibers in the hindbrain and midbrain that are involved in arousal and attention.

cerebellum   The part of the hindbrain that controls finely coordinated movements.

blood pressure, and breathing, are controlled by nuclei in the hindbrain, particularly in an area called the **medulla** (pronounced "meh-DU-lah").

Weaving throughout the hindbrain and into the midbrain is a mesh-like collection of cells called the **reticular formation** (*reticular* means "net-like"). This network is involved in arousal and attention. Cutting off fibers of the reticular system from the rest of the brain would put a person into a permanent coma. Some of the fibers that carry pain signals from the spinal cord connect in the reticular formation and immediately arouse the brain from sleep. Within seconds, the hindbrain causes your heart rate and blood pressure to increase. You are awake and aroused.

The **cerebellum** (pronounced "sair-a-BELL-um") is also part of the hindbrain. For a long time its primary function was thought to be control of finely coordinated movements, such as threading a needle. We now know that the cerebellum also allows the eyes to track a moving target accurately (Krauzlis & Lisberger, 1991) and that it may be the storehouse for well-rehearsed movements, such as those associated with dancing, playing a musical instrument, and athletics (McCormick & Thompson, 1984). The cerebellum might also be involved in the learning of these skills (Hazeltine & Ivry, 2002), as well as in more uniquely human tasks such as language and abstract thinking (Bower & Parsons, 2003). For instance, abnormalities in the cerebellum have been associated with reading disabilities (Rae et al., 2002), and surgery that affects the cerebellum sometimes results in a syndrome called *cerebellar mutism*, in which patients become unable to speak for periods ranging from a few days to several years (Gelabert-Gonzalez & Fernandez-Villa, 2001). In short, the cerebellum seems to be involved in both physical and cognitive agility.

Reflexes and feedback systems are important in the hindbrain. For example, if blood pressure drops, heart action reflexively increases to make up for that decrease. If you stand up quickly, your blood pressure can drop so suddenly that you feel lightheaded until the hindbrain reflexively "catches up." You will faint if the hindbrain does not activate the autonomic nervous system to increase your blood pressure.

A FIELD SOBRIETY TEST   The cerebellum is involved in the balance and coordination required for walking. When the cerebellum's activity is impaired by alcohol, these skills are disrupted, which is why the police ask suspected drunk drivers to walk a straight line.

A FIELD SOBRIETY TEST   The cerebellum is involved in the balance and coordination required for walking. When the cerebellum's activity is impaired by alcohol, these skills are disrupted, which is why the police ask suspected drunk drivers to walk a straight line.

The Midbrain

A small region called the **midbrain** lies above the hindbrain. If you focus your eyes on another person and then move your head, midbrain circuits allow you to move your eyes smoothly in the direction opposite from your head movement so you never lose focus. Did you ever swing a bat, swat a mosquito, or jump rope? Part of the midbrain and its connections to the forebrain allowed you to produce those movements smoothly. When a car backfires, causing you to reflexively turn your head and look in the direction of the sound, it is again the midbrain at work. Together, the midbrain and parts of the hindbrain other than the cerebellum are called the *brainstem*.

The Forebrain

In humans, the **forebrain** controls the most complex aspects of behavior and mental life. It completely covers the rest of the brain. The outer surface of the forebrain is called the *cerebral cortex*. Figure 2.9 shows some structures of the forebrain.

Two structures deep within the forebrain, the *hypothalamus* and the *thalamus*, help operate basic drives, emotion, and sensation. The **thalamus** acts as a relay station for pain and sense-organ signals (except smell) from the body to the upper levels of the brain. The thalamus also processes and makes sense of these signals. The **hypothalamus** lies under the thalamus (*hypo* means "under") and helps regulate hunger, thirst, and sex drives. The hypothalamus is well connected to the autonomic nervous system and to other parts of the brain. Damage to parts of the hypothalamus upsets normal appetite, thirst, and sexual behavior.

Can you set an "internal alarm clock" to wake up in the morning at whatever time you want? If you can, it is with the help of a remarkable part of your hypothalamus, called the *suprachiasmatic nuclei*, that contains the brain's own clock. The suprachiasmatic (pronounced "soo-pra-kye-as-MAT-ik") nuclei operate on approximately a twenty-four-hour cycle, controlling daily biological rhythms such as waking and sleeping, as well as cycles of body temperature. Studies of the suprachiasmatic nuclei in animals suggest that having different night or morning energy times is biological and stable throughout a lifetime (Cofer et al., 1992). In humans, such differences may make some of us "morning people" and others "night people."

Other parts of the forebrain, especially the *amygdala* (pronounced "ah-MIG-duh-luh") and the *hippocampus*, help to regulate memory and emotion. The **amygdala** links different kinds of sensory information in memory, such as the shape and feel of objects (Murray & Mishkin, 1985). If you close your eyes and pick up an object, your amygdala helps you recognize it. The amygdala also plays a role in fear and other emotions

midbrain   A small region between the hindbrain and the forebrain that, among other things, helps produce smooth movements.

forebrain   The part of the brain responsible for the most complex aspects of behavior and mental life.

thalamus   A forebrain structure that relays messages from most sense organs to higher brain areas.

hypothalamus   A forebrain structure that regulates hunger, thirst, and sex drives, with many connections to and from the autonomic nervous system and other parts of the brain.

amygdala   A forebrain structure that links information from various systems and plays a role in emotions.

FIGURE **2.9**

Major Structures of the Forebrain

The structures of the forebrain are covered by an outer "bark" known as the cerebral cortex. This diagram shows some of the structures that lie within the forebrain. The amygdala, the hippocampus, and portions of the cerebral cortex are part of the limbic system.

Cerebral cortex
Corpus callosum
Hypothalamus
Thalamus
Amygdala
Hippocampus

(LeDoux, 1995; Whalen, 1998), connecting emotion to sensation. People who suffer from posttraumatic stress disorder have unusual amygdala activity (Pitman, Shin, & Rauch, 2001). The amygdala, hippocampus, and some portions of the cerebral cortex are part of a group of brain structures called the *limbic system,* which is activated when emotions are being generated.

The **hippocampus** also helps you form new memories. In one case, a patient known as R.B. suffered a stroke (an interruption of blood flow to the brain) that damaged only his hippocampus. Although his intelligence remained above average and he could recall old memories, he was almost totally unable to build new memories (Squire, 1986). Damage to the hippocampus within a day of a mildly painful event seems to erase memories of the experience. However, if the damage occurs several days after the event, the memory remains. It seems that memories are not permanently stored in the hippocampus but instead are transferred from there to somewhere else in the brain.

The hippocampus becomes smaller with age, and research shows that this shrinkage relates to the declining memory function that many elderly people experience (Golomb et al., 1996). On average, the hippocampus of a person with Alzheimer's disease has been found to be 40 percent smaller than that of a person without the disease. Alzheimer's disease is a major cause of senile dementia, which involves the decay of cognitive capabilities. About 10 percent of people over age sixty-five and 47 percent of people over eighty-five suffer from this disease (Kukull et al., 2002; U.S. Department of Health and Human Services, 2001a). The financial cost of Alzheimer's disease is more than $100 billion a year in the United States alone (U.S. Department of Health and Human Services, 2001a). The cost in human suffering is incalculable.

The Cerebral Cortex

On the surface of the forebrain is the **cerebral cortex.** The total area of the cerebral cortex is one to two square feet, but it fits into the skull because it is somewhat wrinkled and folded. You can wad up a T-shirt and fit it into a small bowl in much the same way. The cerebral cortex is much larger in humans than in most other animals (dolphins are an exception). It analyzes information from all the senses and controls voluntary movement, abstract thinking, and the other most complex aspects of our behavior and mental processes. The cerebral cortex looks somewhat round, with a long groove down the middle creating two halves, called *cerebral hemispheres.* The **corpus callosum,** a massive bundle of more than a million fibers, connects the two hemispheres.

hippocampus   A forebrain structure associated with the formation of new memories.

cerebral cortex   The outer surface of the forebrain.

corpus callosum   A bundle of fibers that connects the left and right cerebral hemispheres.

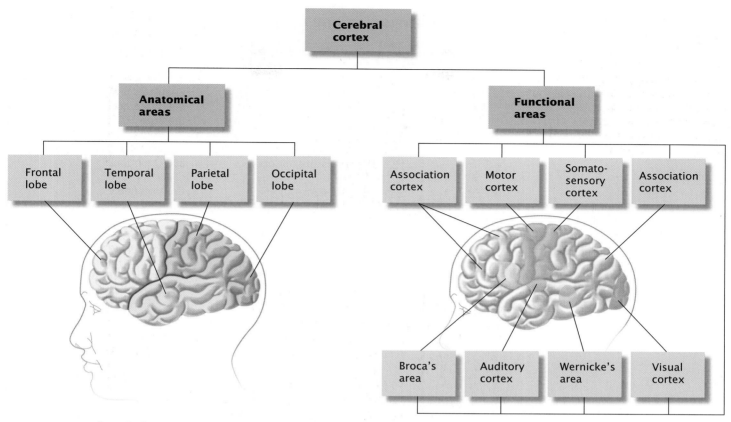

The Cerebral Cortex (viewed from the left side)

The brain's ridges (gyri) and valleys (sulci) are landmarks that divide the cortex into four lobes: the frontal, parietal, occipital, and temporal. These terms describe where the regions are (the lobes are named for the skull bones that cover them), but the cortex is also divided in terms of function. These functional areas include the motor cortex (which controls movement), sensory cortex (which receives information from various senses), and association cortex (which integrates information). Also labeled are Wernicke's area and Broca's area, two regions that are found only on the left side of the cortex and that are vital to the interpretation and production of speech (Peña et al., 2003).

The folds of the cerebral cortex give the surface of the human brain its wrinkled appearance, its ridges and valleys. The ridges are called *gyri* (pronounced "ji-rye"), and the valleys are known as *sulci* (pronounced "sulk-eye") or *fissures*. As you can see in Figure 2.10, several deep sulci divide the cortex into four areas: the frontal (front), parietal (top), occipital (back), and temporal (side) lobes. The gyri and sulci provide landmarks for describing the structure of the cortex, but the *functions* of the cortex do not follow these boundaries. When divided according to function, the cortex includes areas of sensory cortex, motor cortex, and association cortex. ("In Review: Organization of the Brain" summarizes the major structures and functions of the brain.)

Sensory and Motor Cortex

The **sensory cortex** lies in the parietal, occipital, and temporal lobes. Different regions of the sensory cortex receive information from different senses. Occipital lobe cells called the *visual cortex* receive visual information. Temporal lobe cells called the *auditory cortex* receive information from the ears. And information from the skin, such as touch, pain, and temperature, is received by cells in the parietal lobe. These skin-related areas are called the *somatosensory cortex* (*soma* is Greek for "body"). Information about skin sensations from neighboring parts of the body comes to neighboring parts of the somatosensory cortex. It is as if the outline of a tiny person, dangling upside down, determined the location of the information (see Figure 2.11). This pattern is called the *homunculus* (Latin for "little man"). The amount of sensory cortex that responds to particular sensory stimulation can be modified by experience (Candia et al., 2003). For example, if a limb is lost, sensory cortex that had been stimulated by that limb will now be stimulated by other regions of skin. Similarly, practicing the violin will increase the number of sensory neurons that respond to touch; the same thing happens when blind people learn to read Braille with their fingertips (Amedi et al., 2005; Pascual-Leone & Torres, 1993).

sensory cortex The part of the cerebral cortex located in the parietal, occipital, and temporal lobes that receives stimulus information from the skin, eyes, and ears, respectively.

ORGANIZATION OF THE BRAIN

Major Division	Some Major Structures	Some Major Functions
Hindbrain	Medulla	Regulates breathing, heart rate, and blood pressure
	Reticular formation (also extends into midbrain)	Regulates arousal and attention
	Cerebellum	Controls finely coordinated movements and certain cognitive processes
Midbrain	Various nuclei	Relays sensory signals to forebrain; creates automatic responses to certain stimuli; initiates smooth movement
Forebrain	Thalamus	Interprets and relays sensory information
	Hypothalamus	Regulates hunger, thirst, and sex drives
	Amygdala	Connects sensations and emotions
	Hippocampus	Forms new memories
	Cerebral cortex	Analyzes sensory information; controls voluntary movements, abstract thinking, and other complex cognitive activity
	Corpus callosum	Transfers information between the two cerebral hemispheres

?
1. *The oldest part of the brain is the _____.*
2. *Cells that operate as the body's twenty-four-hour "time clock" are found in the _____.*
3. *Memory problems seen in Alzheimer's disease are related to shrinkage of the _____.*

In the frontal lobe, specific neurons of the **motor cortex** control voluntary movements in specific parts of the body (Indovina & Sanes, 2001). The motor cortex's arrangement mirrors that of the somatosensory cortex. So the parts of the motor cortex that control hand movement are near parts of the sensory cortex that receive sensory information from the hands.

Seems easy, doesn't it? You have a map of your body parts in your cerebral cortex, and you activate cells in the hand region of the cortex if you want to move your hand.

motor cortex   The part of the cerebral cortex that controls voluntary movement.

Motor areas (end view)   **Sensory areas (end view)**

Note: Did you notice the error in this classic drawing? (The figure shows the right side of the body, but the left hand and left side of the face.)
Source: Penfield & Rasmussen (1968).

FIGURE 2.11

Motor and Somatosensory Cortex

The areas of cortex that move parts of the body (motor cortex) and receive sensory input from body parts (somatosensory cortex) appear in both hemispheres of the brain. Here we show cross-sections of only those on the left side, looking from the back of the brain toward the front. Areas controlling movement of neighboring parts of the body, such as the foot and leg, occupy neighboring parts of the motor cortex. Areas receiving input from neighboring body parts, such as the lips and tongue, are near one another in the sensory cortex. Notice that the size of these areas is uneven; the larger the area devoted to each body part, the larger that body part appears on the "homunculus."

In fact, the actual process is quite complex. Recall again your sleepy reach for the coffee pot. To grasp its handle, your cortex must first translate the pot's location into a position relative to your body—to your left or right, for example. Next, the cortex must determine which muscles must be contracted to produce the desired movement toward that exact position. Groups of neurons work together to produce just the right combinations of direction and force in particular muscle groups. Making these determinations involves many interconnected areas of the cortex. Computer models of neural networks are showing how these complex problem-solving processes might occur (Graziano, Taylor, & Moore, 2002; Krauzlis, 2002).

FOCUS ON RESEARCH

The Case of the Disembodied Woman

Neurologist Oliver Sacks described the case of "Christina," a woman who had somehow lost the ability to feel the position of her own body (Sacks, 1985). This case study led to important insights about biological psychology that could not be studied through controlled experiments. It showed, for example, that a sense known as *kinesthesia* (pronounced "kin-es-THEE-see-uh") not only tells us where our body parts are but also plays an important role in our sense of self.

Christina was a healthy young woman who entered a hospital in preparation for some minor surgery. Before the surgery could be performed, however, she began to have difficulty holding onto objects. Then she had trouble moving. She would rise from bed and flop onto the floor like a rag doll. Christina seemed to have "lost" her body. She felt disembodied, like a ghost. On one occasion, for example, she became annoyed at a visitor for tapping her fingers on a tabletop. But it was Christina's fingers, not the visitor's, that were tapping. Her body was acting on its own, doing things she did not know about.

■ What was the researcher's question?

Christina could not walk or use her hands and arms. Why was a seemingly normal, healthy young woman falling and dropping things?

■ How did the researcher answer the question?

A psychiatrist at the hospital thought that Christina was suffering from *conversion disorder,* a condition in which psychological problems cause physical disabilities (see the chapter on psychological disorders). Unconvinced, Sacks conducted a careful case study of Christina.

■ What did the researcher find?

It turned out that the psychiatrist was wrong. Sacks's examinations and tests revealed that Christina had lost all sensory feedback about her joints, muscle tone, and the position of her limbs. Christina had suffered a breakdown, or degeneration, of the sensory neurons that normally bring kinesthetic information to her brain. In other words, there was a biological reason that Christina could not walk or control her hands and arms.

■ What do the results mean?

In his analysis of this case, Sacks noted that the sense we have of our bodies is provided partly through our experience of seeing but also partly through *proprioception* (sensing the self). Christina herself put it this way: "Proprioception is like the eyes of the body, the way the body sees itself. And if it goes, it's like the body's blind." With great effort and determination, Christina was eventually able to regain some of her ability to move about. If she looked intently at her arms and legs, she could coordinate their movement somewhat. She was able to leave the hospital and resume many of her normal activities, but Christina never recovered her sense of self. She still feels like a stranger in her own body.

■ What do we still need to know?

Notice that Christina's case study did not confirm any hypotheses about kinesthesia in the way an experiment might. It did, however, focus attention on what it feels like to have lost this sense. It also highlighted a rare condition that, though almost unknown when Sacks reported it, has been observed more often in recent years, especially among people taking large doses of vitamin B6, also known as *pyridoxine* (Sacks, 1985). These large doses—or even smaller doses taken over a long period of time—can damage sensory neurons (Dordain & Deffond, 1994). How and why vitamin B6 does such damage still needs to be determined. Are there other causes of this kinesthetic disorder? What treatments might best combat it? These questions remain to be answered by the research of psychologists and other scientists who continue to unravel the mysteries of behavior and mental processes.

Association Cortex

Parts of the cortex that do not directly receive specific sensory information or control specific movements are referred to as **association cortex.** The term *association* describes these areas well, because they receive input from more than one sense or input that combines sensory and motor information. For instance, these areas associate words with images. Association cortex appears in all lobes of the brain and forms a large part of the cerebral cortex in humans. For this reason, damage to association areas can create serious problems in a wide range of mental abilities.

association cortex   The parts of the cerebral cortex that integrate sensory and motor information and perform complex cognitive tasks.

Consider language. Language information comes from the auditory cortex for spoken language or from the visual cortex for written language. Areas of the motor cortex produce speech. Putting it all together in the complex activity known as language involves activity in association cortex. In the 1860s, a French surgeon named Paul Broca described the effects of damage to association cortex in the frontal lobe near motor areas that control face muscles. This part of the cortex is on the left side of the brain and is called *Broca's area* (see Figure 2.10). Damage to Broca's area disrupts speech organization, a condition called *Broca's aphasia*. Victims have difficulty speaking, often making errors in grammar. Each word comes out slowly.

Other language problems result from damage to a portion of association cortex described in the 1870s by a Polish neurologist named Carl Wernicke (pronounced "VER-nick-ee"). Figure 2.10 shows that, like Broca's area, *Wernicke's area* is on the left side of the brain, but it is in the temporal lobe, near the area of the sensory cortex that receives information from the ears. Wernicke's area also receives input from the visual cortex and is involved in the interpretation of both speech and written words. Damage to Wernicke's area produces complicated symptoms. It can leave patients with the ability to speak but disrupts the ability to understand the meaning of words or to speak understandably.

Case studies illustrate the different effects of damage to each area (Lapointe, 1990). In response to the request "Tell me what you do with a cigarette," a person with Wernicke's aphasia replied, "This is a segment of a pegment. Soap a cigarette." This speech was fluent but without meaning. In response to the same request, a person with Broca's aphasia replied, "Uh . . . uh . . . cigarette [pause] smoke it." This speech was meaningful, but halting and awkwardly phrased. Surprisingly, when a person with Broca's aphasia sings, the words come easily and correctly. Apparently, words set to music are handled by one part of the brain and spoken words by another (Jeffries, Fritz, & Braun, 2003). Some speech therapists take advantage of this fact through "melodic intonation" therapy, which helps Broca's aphasia patients to gain fluency by speaking in a "singsong" manner (Lapointe, 1990).

It appears that written language and spoken language require the use of different areas of association cortex. So does language involving specific parts of speech (Shapiro, Moo, & Caramazza, 2006). For example, two women—H.W. and S.J.D—each had a stroke in 1985, causing damage to different language-related parts of their association

LINKAGES
Where are the brain's language centers? (a link to Thought, Language, and Intelligence)

learn by doing **LANGUAGE AREAS OF THE BRAIN** Have you ever tried to write notes while you were talking to someone? Like this teacher, you can probably write and talk at the same time, because each of these language functions uses different areas of association cortex. However, stop reading for a moment, and try writing one word with your left hand and a different word with your right hand. If you had trouble, it is partly because you asked the same language area of your brain to do two things at once.

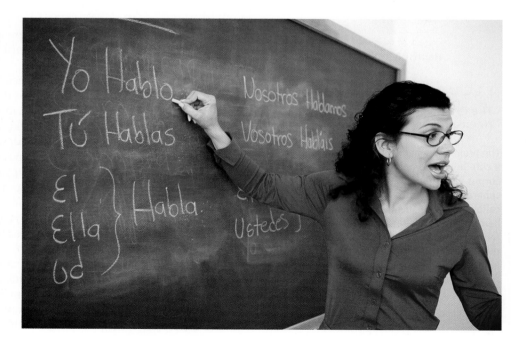

cortex. Neither woman has difficulty speaking or writing nouns, but both have difficulty with verbs (Caramazza & Hillis, 1991). H.W. can write verbs but cannot speak them. S.J.D. can speak verbs but has difficulty writing them. Interestingly, H.W. has difficulty pronouncing *watch* when it is used as a verb in the sentence "I watch TV," but she speaks the same word easily when it appears as a noun in "My watch is slow."

Other association areas in the front of the brain, called the *prefrontal cortex*, are involved in the complex processes necessary for the conscious control of thoughts and actions and for understanding our world (Powell & Voeller, 2004). For example, these areas of association cortex allow us to understand sarcasm or irony—that is, when someone says one thing but means the opposite. In one study, people with prefrontal cortex damage listened to sarcastic stories such as this: "Joe came to work, and instead of beginning to work, he sat down to rest. His boss noticed his behavior and said, 'Joe, don't work too hard'." Normal people immediately realized that the boss was being sarcastic, but people with prefrontal brain damage did not (Shamay-Tsoory & Tomer, 2005).

The Divided Brain: Lateralization

A striking suggestion emerged from observations of people with damage to the language centers of the brain. Researchers noticed that damage to specific areas of the left hemisphere interfered with the ability to use or understand language. Damage to those same areas in the right hemisphere usually did not cause such problems. Could it be that the right and left hemispheres of the brain serve different functions?

This idea was not entirely new. It had long been understood that most sensory and motor pathways cross over from one hemisphere to the other as they enter or leave the brain. As a result, the left hemisphere receives information from, and controls movements of, the right side of the body. The right hemisphere receives input from and controls the left side of the body. Figure 2.12 shows the two hemispheres. The fact that language centers such as Broca's area and Wernicke's area almost always occur on the left side of the brain suggests that each hemisphere might be specialized to perform some functions almost independently of the other hemisphere (Stephan et al., 2003).

In the late 1800s there was great interest in the idea that the hemispheres might be specialized, but no techniques were available for testing it. Renewed interest grew out of studies during the 1960s by Roger Sperry, Michael Gazzaniga, and their colleagues.

Split-Brain Studies   Sperry studied *split-brain* patients—people who had undergone surgery in an attempt to control the severe seizures of epilepsy. Before the surgery, their seizures began in one hemisphere and then spread throughout the brain. As a last resort, surgeons isolated the two hemispheres from each other by cutting the corpus callosum, which had connected them.

After the surgery, researchers used a special device like the one shown in Figure 2.13 to present visual images to only one side of these patients' split brains. They found that cutting the tie between the hemispheres had dramatically changed the way these people thought about and dealt with the world. For example, when the image of a spoon was presented to the left, language-oriented, side of patient N.G.'s split brain, she could say what the spoon was. But when the spoon was presented to the right side of her brain, she could not describe the spoon in words. She still knew what the object was, because she could pick it out from a group of objects by feeling its shape with her left hand (controlled by the right hemisphere). When asked what she had just grasped, she replied, "A pencil." The right hemisphere recognized the object, but the patient could not say what it was because the left (language) half of her brain did not see or feel it (Sperry, 1968).

Although the right hemisphere has no control over spoken language in split-brain patients, it does have important abilities related to nonspoken language. For example, a split-brain patient's right hemisphere can guide the left hand in spelling out words with Scrabble tiles (Gazzaniga & LeDoux, 1978). Thanks to this finding, researchers concluded that split-brain patients have self-awareness and normal learning abilities in

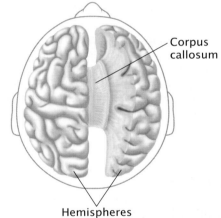

Corpus
callosum

Hemispheres

FIGURE **2.12**

The Brain's Left and Right Hemispheres

The brain's two hemispheres are joined by a core bundle of nerve fibers known as the corpus callosum. In this figure the hemispheres are separated so that the corpus callosum can be seen. The two cerebral hemispheres look nearly the same but perform somewhat different tasks. For one thing, the left hemisphere receives sensory input from, and controls movement on, the right side of the body. The right hemisphere senses and controls the left side of the body.

FIGURE 2.13

Apparatus for Studying Split-Brain Patients

When the person stares at the dot on the screen, images briefly presented on one side of the dot go to only one side of the brain. For example, a picture of a spoon presented on the left side of the screen goes to the right side of the brain. The right side of the brain can find the spoon and direct the left hand to touch it. However, the language areas on the left side of the brain did not see the spoon, so the person is unable to say what it is.

their right hemispheres. In addition, these patients' right hemispheres did better than their left hemispheres at tasks involving spatial relationships (especially drawing three-dimensional shapes) and recognizing human faces.

Having these two somewhat specialized hemispheres allows the normal brain to perform some tasks more efficiently, particularly difficult ones. But the differences between the hemispheres should not be exaggerated. Remember, the corpus callosum usually integrates the functions of the "two brains" (Rueckert et al., 1999). As a result, the hemispheres work closely together, each making up well for whatever lack of ability the other may have (Banich & Heller, 1998; Staudt et al., 2001).

Plasticity in the Central Nervous System

The central nervous system has a remarkable property called **plasticity,** which is the ability to strengthen neural connections at synapses, as well as to establish new connections (Cohen-Cory, 2002; Kolb, Gibb, & Robinson, 2003; Tailby et al., 2005). As a result, even the simplest reflex in the spinal cord can be modified by experience (Chen, Chen, & Wolpaw, 2003). In the brain, plasticity is the basis for our ability to form new memories and learn new things. For example, more cells in the brain's motor cortex become involved in controlling hand movements in people who have learned to play a musical instrument. The process can be seen in brain imaging studies; as nonmusicians get better at making rhythmic finger movements, the amount of motor cortex devoted to this task increases (Munte, Altenmuller, & Jancke, 2002). Even more amazing is that merely *imagining* practicing these movements causes changes in the motor cortex (Pascual-Leone, 2001). Athletes have long engaged in exercises in which they visualize skilled sports movements; brain imaging research reveals that this "mental practice" can change the brain.

Repairing Brain Damage   There are limits to plasticity, though, especially when it comes to repairing damage in the brain and spinal cord. Unlike the skin or the liver, the adult central nervous system does not automatically replace damaged cells. As a result, most victims of severe stroke, Parkinson's disease, Alzheimer's disease, or spinal cord injury are permanently disabled in some way. Nevertheless, scientists are searching for ways to help a damaged central nervous system heal some of its own wounds.

plasticity   A property of the central nervous system that has the ability to strengthen neural connections at synapses, as well as to establish new connections.

HE WAS A SUPER MAN　After a 1995 riding accident left actor/director Christopher Reeve paralyzed below his shoulders, he embarked on a long, intense rehabilitation regimen. He received electrical stimulation to maintain muscle tone and was strapped to a tilting table to maintain bone density. He was suspended in a harness over a treadmill while his legs were put through walking movements. In 1999, he began using a functional electrical stimulation bicycle, which sent computer-controlled electrical impulses to his legs, causing the muscles to contract and move the bike's pedals. By the end of 2002, he could move his fingers, right wrist, and upper legs. In a swimming pool, he could move his knees and upper arms. By the time of his death in 2004, he had also regained feeling in about 70 percent of his body. Research is continuing on other exercise programs to promote recovery from spinal cord injury (Molteni et al., 2004; Taub, 2004).

One approach has been to transplant, or graft, tissue from the still-developing brain of a fetus into the brain of an adult animal. If the receiving animal does not reject it, the graft sends axons out into the brain and makes some functional connections. This treatment has reversed animals' learning difficulties, movement disorders, and other results of brain damage (Noble, 2000). The technique has also been used to treat a small number of people with Parkinson's disease—a disorder characterized by tremors, rigidity of the arms and legs, and poor balance (Lindvall & Hagell, 2001). The initial results have been encouraging (Mendez et al., 2005). Some patients showed improvement for several years, though improvement faded for others, and some patients suffered serious side effects (Freed et al., 2001). Brain tissue transplants in humans are controversial because they require the use of tissue from aborted fetuses. As an alternative, some scientists have tried transplanting neural tissue from another species, such as pigs, into humans (Drucker-Colin & Verdugo-Diaz, 2004). Russian physicians have even tried transplanting neural tissue from fruit flies into the brains of Parkinson's patients. The results were beneficial, and there were no immediate side effects (Saveliev et al., 1997), but the fruit fly neurons were eventually rejected by the patients' bodies (Korochkin, 2000).

The most promising source for new neurons now appears to be an individual's own tissues, because these cells would not be rejected. This is a revolutionary idea, because it was long believed that once humans reached adulthood, the cells of the central nervous system stopped dividing, leaving each of us with a fixed set of neurons (Rakic, 2002). Then came research showing that cell division *does* take place in the adult central nervous systems of humans, nonhuman primates, and other animals (Blakeslee, 2000; Eriksson et al., 1998; Gould et al., 1999; Steindler & Pincus, 2002). It turns out that the adult brain contains *neural stem cells,* a special kind of glial cells that are capable of dividing to form new tissue, including new neurons (Cheng, Tavazoie, & Doetsch, 2005; Sanai et al., 2004).

This discovery has created both excitement and controversy. There is excitement because stem cells raise hope that damaged tissue may someday be replaced by cells created from a person's own body, but there is controversy because stem cells are linked in many people's minds with the cloning of whole individuals. If brain cells can indeed be grown from cells found in bone marrow, the lining of the nose, or other sites, the benefits in treating brain disorders would be substantial (Murrell et al., 2005). Patients suffering from spinal cord injuries, as well as Parkinson's disease and Alzheimer's disease, might someday be cured by treatments that replace damaged or dying neurons with new ones grown from the patients' own stem cells (Chen, Magavi, & Macklis, 2004; Cowan et al., 2005; Horner & Gage, 2002; Mezey et al., 2003; Teng et al., 2002; Zhao et al., 2003).

Generating new neurons is only half the battle, however. The new cells' axons and dendrites would have to reestablish all the synaptic connections that had been lost to damage or disease. Unfortunately, this process is hampered in the central nervous system by glial cells that actively suppress new connections between newly sprouted axons and other neurons (Olson, 1997). Several central nervous system proteins, including one aptly named *Nogo,* have the same suppressant effect.

Despite these challenges, scientists are reporting exciting results in their efforts to promote healing in damaged brains and spinal cords. They have found, for example, that blocking the action of Nogo in mice and rats with spinal cord injuries allows surviving neurons to make new axonal connections and repair the damage (Cummings et al., 2005; Kastin & Pan, 2005). Other research with animals has shown that both spontaneous recovery and the effectiveness of brain-tissue transplants can be greatly enhanced by naturally occurring proteins called *growth factors,* which promote the survival of neurons (Hoglinger et al., 2001). One of these proteins is called *nerve growth factor.* Another, called *glial cell line–derived neurotrophic factor,* or *GDNF,* actually causes neurons to produce the neurotransmitter needed to reverse the effects of Parkinson's disease (Kordower et al., 2000; Theofilopoulos et al., 2001). The best way to increase the amount of these growth factors in humans is still being studied. In one case, nerve growth factor was put directly into the brain of a patient with Alzheimer's disease (Seiger et al., 1993). The early results seemed encouraging, but the continuous infusion of the protein into the brain caused unacceptable side effects (Nabeshima & Yamada, 2000). Another way to deliver growth factors is through gene therapy, in which a gene for the desired growth factor is inserted into a patient's neurons (Bomze et al., 2001; Condic, 2001; Tuszynski, et al., 2002). Early results from the use of this high-tech treatment are encouraging (Tuszynski et al., 2005).

In the meantime, there are things that patients themselves can do to promote the neural plasticity needed to restore lost central nervous system functions. Special mental and physical exercise programs appear useful in restructuring communication in the brains of stroke victims and spinal cord injury patients, thus reversing some forms of paralysis and improving some sensory and cognitive abilities (Blakeslee, 2001; Liepert et al., 2000; Robertson & Murre, 1999; Taub, 2004). Christopher Reeve was an inspiring case in point. After his spinal cord injury, Reeve was told he would never again be able to move or feel his body. He refused to accept this gloomy prediction, and after years of devoted adherence to an exercise-oriented rehabilitation program, he regained some movement and in the years before his death was able to feel sensations from much of his body (Blakeslee, 2001).

 LINKAGES

How do our brains change over a lifetime? (a link to Human Development)

 LINKAGES

Human Development and the Changing Brain

Fortunately, most of the changes that take place in the brain are not the kind associated with damage and disease. How does the human brain change as we develop throughout our lives? Researchers are using PET and fMRI scans to begin to answer that question. For example, they have found that association areas of the cerebral cortex develop later than sensory and motor cortex (Casey, Galvan, & Hare, 2005). There are also some interesting correlations between changes in neural activity and the behavior of newborns and infants. Among newborns, scans show that activity is relatively high in the thalamus but low in a portion of the forebrain related to smooth movement. This finding may be related to the way newborns move. They make random, sweeping movements of the arms and legs—much like patients with Huntington's disease, who have a hyperactive thalamus and a withering of the part of the forebrain that controls smooth movement (Chugani & Phelps, 1986). During the second and third months after birth, activity increases in many regions of the cortex. This change is correlated with the loss of reflexes, such as the grasping reflex. At eight or nine months of age, infants show increased frontal cortex activity, which correlates with the apparent beginnings of cognitive activity (Chugani & Phelps, 1986). The brain continues to mature even through adolescence, showing evidence of ever more efficient neural communication in its major fiber tracts (Gogtay et al., 2004; Paus et al., 1999; Thompson et al., 2000).

Most of these changes reflect plasticity—changes in axons and synapses—not the appearance of new cells. After birth, the number of dendrites and synapses increases. Although different areas of the cortex sprout at different rates, the number of synapses can increase tenfold in the first year after birth (Huttenlocher, 1990). In fact, by the time children are six or seven years old, their brains have more dendrites than those of adults, and they use twice as much energy. In early adolescence, the number of dendrites and neural connections actually drops, so the adult level is reached by about the age of fourteen. During childhood, the brain overproduces neural connections and then "prunes" the extra connections (Sowell et al., 2001). Figure 2.14 shows that as we grow, we develop more brainpower with less brain (Sowell et al., 2003).

At birth

Six years old

Fourteen years old

Source: Conel (1939/1967).

FIGURE **2.14**

Changes in Neurons of the Cerebral Cortex During Development

During childhood, the brain overproduces neural connections, establishes the usefulness of certain connections, and then "prunes" the extra connections. Overproduction of synapses, especially in the frontal cortex, may be essential for infants to develop certain intellectual abilities. Some scientists believe that connections that are used survive, whereas others die.

As already mentioned, the brain's plasticity allows it to restructure itself to form new connections throughout life (Hua & Smith, 2004; Kozorovitskiy et al., 2005). Genes apparently determine the basic pattern of growth and the major lines of connections. However, the details of the connections depend on experience, including how stimulating and interesting the environment is. For example, researchers have compared the brains of rats raised individually with only a boring view of their cages to the brains of rats raised with toys and playmates. The cerebral cortex of the rats from the enriched environment had more and longer dendrites, as well as more synapses, than did the cortex of animals raised alone in bare cages (Klintsova & Greenough, 1999; Torasdotter et al., 1998). Furthermore, the number of synapses increased when old animals who had been living in boring cages were moved to an enriched environment. Such changes in the brain following increased environmental stimulation may help explain why the maze-learning ability of genetically "maze-dull" rats raised in stimulating cages can equal that of genetically "maze-bright" animals.

Researchers have not yet determined whether an enriched environment stimulates the development of new connections or slows down normal pruning. Also not known is whether animals that are moved from a stimulating environment to a boring one will lose synaptic connections. If existing findings apply to humans, however, they have implications for how we raise children and treat the elderly. It is surely the case that within the limits set by genetics, interactions with the world mold the brain itself (Chang & Merzenich, 2003; Holtmaat et al., 2006).

The Chemistry of Behavior: Neurotransmitters

▶ **How do biochemicals affect my mood?**

We have already seen that neurons in the nervous system communicate with each other through chemical messengers called neurotransmitters. The neurotransmitters they use can differ from one set of nerve cells to another. A group of neurons that communicate using the same neurotransmitter is called a *neurotransmitter system.* Let's explore where neurotransmitters operate in the brain, and how they affect behavior.

Three Classes of Neurotransmitters

The process of chemical neurotransmission was first demonstrated in frogs by Otto Loewi in 1921. Since then, about 100 neurotransmitters have been identified, but they fall into three main classes: *small molecules, peptides,* and *gases.* Let's consider some examples of each.

Small Molecules   The most important of the small-molecule chemicals that act as neurotransmitters are acetylcholine, norepinephrine, serotonin, dopamine, GABA, and glutamate. *Acetylcholine* (pronounced "uh-see-tull-KO-leen") was the first to be identified as a neurotransmitter. Among the many neurons that communicate using acetylcholine are those active in controlling movement of the body, in making memories, and in slowing the heartbeat and activating the digestive system. No wonder, then, that disruption of acetylcholine systems can result in a wide variety of problems, including the loss of memory and, eventually, of all mental powers that is seen in Alzheimer's disease.

Systems of neurons that use *norepinephrine* (pronounced "nor-eppa-NEF-rin") affect arousal, wakefulness, learning, and mood. This neurotransmitter is involved when your nervous system prepares you to fight or to run away from a threat. Changes in norepinephrine systems have also been implicated in depression.

PROMOTING RESEARCH ON PARKINSON'S DISEASE Former heavyweight boxing champion Muhammad Ali suffers from Parkinson's disease, a condition related to malfunctioning of dopamine systems in the brain. Even though his shakiness is getting worse, he appeared before these U.S. senators and representatives and encouraged them to sponsor bills to fund more research on curing, and perhaps even preventing, Parkinson's disease.

The neurotransmitter *serotonin* (pronounced "sair-oh-TOE-nin") is similar to norepinephrine in that it affects both sleep and mood. Serotonin may also be involved in the appearance of aggressive and impulsive behaviors. Unlike norepinephrine, though, the amount of serotonin in your brain can be affected by what you eat. For example, eating carbohydrates can increase serotonin, and the increase in serotonin normally reduces the desire for carbohydrates. Some researchers suspect that malfunctions in serotonin systems can result in the mood and appetite problems seen in some types of obesity, premenstrual tension, and depression (Lira et al., 2003; Oquendo & Mann, 2000; Wurtman & Wurtman, 1995). Antidepressant medications such as Prozac, Zoloft, and Paxil appear to relieve some of the symptoms of depression by acting on serotonin systems to maintain proper levels of this neurotransmitter.

Dopamine (pronounced "DOPE-uh-meen") is a neurotransmitter that is important for movement. Malfunctions of dopamine systems contribute to movement disorders such as Parkinson's disease and the shakiness experienced by people who have it. Parkinson's has been treated with some success using drugs that enable neurons to make more dopamine (Chase, 1998). Other dopamine systems are involved in the experiencing of reward, or pleasure, which is vital in shaping and motivating behavior (Spanagel & Weiss, 1999). Animals will work very hard to receive a direct dose of dopamine to certain parts of the brain. These dopamine systems play a role in the rewarding properties of many drugs, including cocaine (Ciccocioppo, Sanna, & Weiss, 2001). Certain dopamine systems are also suspected to be partly responsible for the perceptual, emotional, and thought disturbances associated with schizophrenia, a severe mental disorder (Marenco & Weinberger, 2000).

GABA stands for gamma-amino butyric acid. Unlike most neurotransmitters, which excite neurons to fire action potentials, GABA *reduces* the likelihood that neurons will fire. In fact, it is the main neurotransmitter for slowing, or inhibiting, the brain's activity. When you fall asleep, neurons that use GABA deserve part of the credit. Drugs that cause reduced neural activity often do so by amplifying the "braking" action of GABA. In the case of alcohol, for example, the result is an impairment of thinking, judgment, and motor skills. Malfunctions of GABA systems contribute to severe anxiety and to *Huntington's disease,* an inherited disorder that causes its victims to suffer uncontrollable movement of the arms and legs, along with a progressive loss of thinking abilities. Drugs that interfere with GABA's inhibitory effects produce intense repetitive electrical discharges, known as *seizures.* So researchers suspect that impaired GABA systems contribute to *epilepsy,* another brain disorder associated with seizures and convulsive movements. Repeated or sustained seizures can result in permanent brain damage. Drug treatments can reduce seizure frequency and severity, but completely effective drugs are not yet available.

Glutamate (pronounced "GLOO-tuh-mate") is used by more neurons than any other neurotransmitter. Glutamate is particularly important because it helps the brain to "strengthen" its synaptic connections—that is, to allow messages to more easily cross the synaptic gap between neurons. This strengthening process is necessary for normal development and may be at the root of learning and memory (Bredt & Nicoll, 2003). Yet overactivity of glutamate synapses can cause neurons to die. This overactivity is the main cause of the brain damage that occurs when oxygen is cut off from neurons during a stroke. Glutamate can "excite neurons to death." Blocking glutamate receptors immediately after a brain trauma can prevent permanent brain damage (Colak et al., 2003). Glutamate may also contribute to the loss of brain cells that occurs in Alzheimer's disease (Cha et al., 2001).

Peptides   Hundreds of chemicals called *peptides* have been found to act as neurotransmitters. The first of these, called *endorphins,* were discovered in the 1970s, when scientists were studying *opiates* such as morphine and heroin. Derived from poppy flowers, opiates can relieve pain, produce intense feelings of happiness, and, in high doses, bring on sleep. After marking morphine with a radioactive agent, researchers identified places where it became concentrated in the brain. They found that the opiates bound to receptors that had not been associated with any previously identified neurotransmitter. It is unlikely that the brain had developed opiate receptors just in case a person might want to use morphine or heroin, so researchers reasoned that the body must contain a substance that is similar to opiates. This hypothesis led to the search for a naturally occurring, or *endogenous,* morphine. (*Endogenous* is pronounced "en-DODGE-uh-niss"; *endorphin* is a contraction of the words *endogenous* and *morphine.*) As it turns out, there are many natural opiate-like compounds, and new ones are still being discovered. So the term *endorphin* refers to any neurotransmitter that can bind to the same receptors stimulated by opiates. Endorphins are used by neurons in several parts of the brain, including neuronal pathways that modify pain signals to the brain.

Gases   Ideas about what substances can act as neurotransmitters were radically altered following the recent discovery that these chemicals include *nitric oxide* and *carbon monoxide*—two toxic gases that contribute to air pollution (Boehning & Snyder, 2003). When nitric oxide or carbon monoxide is released by a neuron, it spreads to nearby neurons, sending a signal that affects chemical reactions inside those neurons rather than binding to receptors on their surface. Nitric oxide is not stored in vesicles, as most other neurotransmitters are; it can be released from any part of the neuron. Nitric oxide appears to be one of the neurotransmitters responsible for such diverse functions as penile erection and the formation of memories—not at the same site, obviously.

In summary, neurotransmitters acting throughout the body link our biochemistry with every aspect of our behavior and mental processes. In the chapter on sensation and perception, for example, we describe some of the neurotransmitters that help convey pain messages. In the consciousness chapter, we consider how neurotransmitters are affected by alcohol and illegal drugs. In the chapter on psychological disorders, we discuss the role that neurotransmitters play in schizophrenia and depression, and in the chapter on the treatment of psychological disorders, we explore ways in which prescription drugs act on neurotransmitters to alleviate the symptoms of those disorders. ("In Review: Classes of Neurotransmitters" lists the most important of these neurotransmitters and the consequences of malfunctioning neurotransmitter systems.)

in review

CLASSES OF NEUROTRANSMITTERS

Neurotransmitter Class	Normal Function	Disorder Associated with Malfunction
Small Molecules Acetylcholine	Memory, movement	Alzheimer's disease
Norepinephrine	Mood, sleep, learning	Depression
Serotonin	Mood, appetite, impulsivity	Depression
Dopamine	Movement, reward	Parkinson's disease, schizophrenia
GABA	Sleep, movement	Anxiety, Huntington's disease, epilepsy
Glutamate	Memory	Damage after stroke
Peptides Endorphins	Pain control	No established disorder
Gases Nitric oxide	Memory	No established disorder

1. The main neurotransmitter for slowing, or inhibiting, brain activity is _____.
2. A group of neurons that use the same neurotransmitter is called a _____.
3. Which neurotransmitter's activity causes brain damage during a stroke? _____

The Endocrine System: Coordinating the Internal World

▶ How can my hormones help me in a crisis?

Neurons are not the only cells that use chemicals to communicate with one another in ways that affect behavior and mental processes. Another kind of cell with this ability is found in the **endocrine system** (pronounced "EN-doh-krin"). Operating on orders from the brain, the endocrine system regulates growth, energy consumption, and sexual behavior, and it readies the body for action. The cells of the endocrine organs, or **glands,** communicate by secreting chemicals, much as neurons do. Figure 2.15 shows some major glands of the endocrine system. The chemicals that these glands secrete are called **hormones.**

Hormones from endocrine organs are similar to neurotransmitters. In fact, many such chemicals, including norepinephrine and the endorphins, act both as hormones and as neurotransmitters. However, whereas neurons secrete neurotransmitters into synapses, endocrine organs put their chemicals into the bloodstream, which carries them throughout the body. In this way, endocrine glands can stimulate cells with which they have no direct connection. But not all cells receive the hormonal message. Hormones, like neurotransmitters, can influence only those cells with receptors capable of receiving them. Organs whose cells have receptors for a particular hormone are called *target organs*.

Each hormone acts on many target organs, producing coordinated effects throughout the body. For example, when a woman's ovaries secrete the sex hormone *estrogen*, it activates her reproductive system, causing the uterus to grow in preparation for nurturing

endocrine system Cells that form organs called glands and that communicate with one another by secreting hormones.

glands Organs that secrete hormones into the bloodstream.

hormones Chemicals secreted by glands into the bloodstream, allowing stimulation of cells that are not directly connected.

FIGURE **2.15**

Some Major Glands of the Endocrine System

Each of the glands shown releases its hormones into the bloodstream. Even the hypothalamus, a part of the brain, regulates the nearby pituitary gland by secreting hormones.

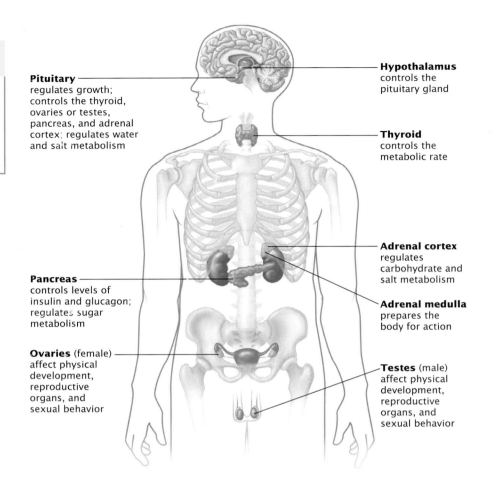

Pituitary regulates growth; controls the thyroid, ovaries or testes, pancreas, and adrenal cortex; regulates water and salt metabolism

Hypothalamus controls the pituitary gland

Thyroid controls the metabolic rate

Adrenal cortex regulates carbohydrate and salt metabolism

Pancreas controls levels of insulin and glucagon; regulates sugar metabolism

Adrenal medulla prepares the body for action

Ovaries (female) affect physical development, reproductive organs, and sexual behavior

Testes (male) affect physical development, reproductive organs, and sexual behavior

Online Study Center

Improve Your Grade
Tutorial: Relationships Among the Nervous, Endocrine, and Immune Systems: Interactions

fight-or-flight response Physical reactions triggered by the sympathetic nervous system that prepare the body to fight or to run from a threatening situation.

an embryo. It enlarges the breasts to prepare them for nursing. It stimulates the brain to increase interest in sexual activity. And it stimulates the pituitary gland to release another hormone that causes a mature egg to be released by the ovary for fertilization. In males, sex organs called *testes* secrete *testosterone*, one of several sex hormones known as *androgens*. Androgens stimulate the maturation of sperm, increase a male's motivation for sexual activity, and increase his aggressiveness (Romeo, Richardson, & Sisk, 2002).

The brain, as a kind of "boss," has ultimate control over the secretion of hormones. The hypothalamus controls the pituitary gland, which in turn controls endocrine organs in the body. The brain is also a target organ for most hormones. In short, the endocrine system typically involves the brain, the pituitary gland, the endocrine organ, and the target organs (which include the brain). Each part in the system uses hormones to signal the next (Dubrovsky, 2005).

The secretion of each hormone is increased or decreased by other hormones. Consider stress-hormone systems, for example. When the brain interprets a situation as threatening, it stimulates the pituitary gland to release *adrenocorticotropic hormone* (*ACTH*), which causes the adrenal glands to release the hormone *cortisol* into the bloodstream. Cortisol, in turn, acts on cells throughout the body, including the brain. One effect of cortisol is to activate the emotion-related limbic system, making it more likely that you will remember stressful or traumatic events (Cahill & McGaugh, 1998). The combined effects of the adrenal hormones and the activation of the sympathetic nervous system result in the **fight-or-flight response.** The many components of this response prepare us for action in response to danger or other stress. The heart beats faster, the liver releases glucose into the bloodstream, fuels are mobilized from fat stores, and the body as a whole is placed in a state of high arousal. Without the endocrine system and the effects of its hormones on the brain, your life would not only be much less emotional, but you also would be less able to escape or avoid threatening situations.

ACTIVE REVIEW | Biology and Behavior

Linkages

As noted in the introductory chapter, all of psychology's subfields are related to one another. Our discussion of developmental changes in the brain illustrates just one way in which the topic of this chapter, biology and behavior, is linked to the subfield of developmental psychology, which is described in the chapter on human development. The Linkages diagram shows ties to two other subfields, and there are many more ties throughout the book. Looking for linkages among subfields will help you see how they all fit together and help you better appreciate the big picture that is psychology.

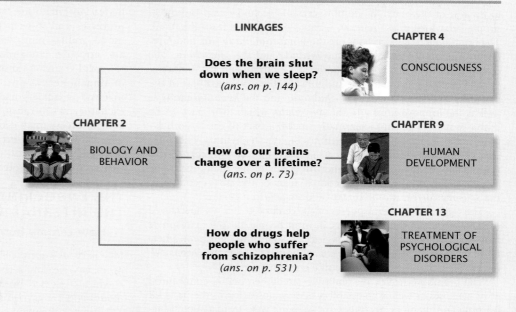

LINKAGES

CHAPTER 2
BIOLOGY AND BEHAVIOR

Does the brain shut down when we sleep?
(ans. on p. 144)

CHAPTER 4
CONSCIOUSNESS

How do our brains change over a lifetime?
(ans. on p. 73)

CHAPTER 9
HUMAN DEVELOPMENT

How do drugs help people who suffer from schizophrenia?
(ans. on p. 531)

CHAPTER 13
TREATMENT OF PSYCHOLOGICAL DISORDERS

Summary

Biological psychology focuses on the biological aspects of our being, which provide the physical basis for behavior and mental processes. Included among these aspects is the *nervous system,* which is composed of billions of cells that allow humans and other organisms to gain information about what is going on inside and outside the body and to respond appropriately.

CELLS OF THE NERVOUS SYSTEM

▶ **What are neurons, and what do they do?**

Much of our understanding of the biological aspects of psychology has stemmed from research on animal and human nervous systems at levels ranging from single cells to complex organizations of cells, including the brain. The fundamental units of the nervous system are cells called *neurons* and *glial cells.* Neurons are especially good at receiving signals from, and transmitting signals to, other neurons. Neurons have cell bodies and two types of fibers, called *axons* and *dendrites.* Axons usually carry signals away from the cell body, whereas dendrites usually carry signals to the cell body.

Neurons can transmit signals because of the structure of the axons and dendrites and the *synapses,* or gaps, between cells. A neuron can transmit, or fire, an *action potential* from one end of its axon to the other. The speed of the action potential is fastest in neurons covered in myelin. The very brief rest between firings is called the *refractory period.*

When an action potential reaches the end of an axon, the axon releases a chemical called a *neurotransmitter.* This chemical crosses the synapse and interacts with the postsynaptic cell at receptors that make the postsynaptic cell either more likely or less likely to fire its own action potential. Because the fibers of neurons have many branches, each neuron can interact with thousands of other neurons. Each neuron constantly integrates signals received at its many synapses; the result of this integration determines how often the neuron fires an action potential.

The cells of the nervous system are organized into two main parts: the *central nervous system (CNS)* and the *peripheral nervous system.*

THE PERIPHERAL NERVOUS SYSTEM: KEEPING IN TOUCH WITH THE WORLD

▶ **How do sights and sounds reach my brain?**

The peripheral nervous system has two components. The first is the *somatic nervous system,* which transmits information from the senses to the CNS and carries signals from the CNS to muscles that move the skeleton. It performs these tasks through sensory systems that receive information from the environment and motor systems that influence the actions of muscles and other organs. The second component of the peripheral nervous system is the *autonomic nervous system,* whose subsystems, the *sympathetic nervous system* and the *parasympathetic nervous system,* carry messages back and forth between the CNS and the heart, lungs, and other organs and glands.

THE CENTRAL NERVOUS SYSTEM: MAKING SENSE OF THE WORLD

▶ **How is my brain "wired"?**

The CNS is laid out in interconnected groups of neuron cell bodies called *nuclei,* whose collections of axons travel together in *fiber tracts,* or pathways. The *spinal cord* receives information from the peripheral senses and sends it to the brain; it also relays messages from the brain to the rest of the body. In addition, cells of the spinal cord can direct simple behaviors, called *reflexes,* without instructions from the brain. The brain's major subdivisions are the *hindbrain, midbrain,* and *forebrain.* The hindbrain includes the *medulla* and the *cerebellum.* The *reticular formation* is found in both the hindbrain and the midbrain.

The forebrain is the largest and most highly developed part of the brain. Its structures include the *thalamus* and the *hypothalamus,* as well as the *hippocampus* and the *amygdala,* which form part of the limbic system. The suprachiasmatic nuclei, a part of the hypothalamus, maintain a clock that determines biological rhythms. The outer surface of the cerebral hemispheres is called the *cerebral cortex;* it is responsible for many of the higher functions of the brain, including speech and reasoning. The functional areas of the cortex consist of the *sensory cortex, motor cortex,* and *association cortex.*

The right and left hemispheres of the cerebral cortex are specialized to some degree in their functions. In most people, the left hemisphere is more active in language and logical tasks and the right hemisphere in spatial tasks. The hemispheres are connected through the *corpus callosum,* allowing them to operate in a coordinated fashion.

The brain's *plasticity,* the ability to strengthen neural connections at its synapses as well as to establish new synapses, forms the basis for learning and memory. Scientists are studying ways to increase plasticity and stimulate formation of new neurons following brain damage.

A child's growing and changing intellectual abilities are based on changing synaptic connections in the brain, not on an increase in the number of brain cells. The brain produces many more synaptic connections than it needs, pruning extra connections as experience strengthens useful connections. The ability to form new synapses continues even into old age.

THE CHEMISTRY OF BEHAVIOR: NEUROTRANSMITTERS

▶ **How do biochemicals affect my mood?**

Neurons that use the same neurotransmitter form a neurotransmitter system. There are three types of neurotransmitters: small molecules, peptides, and gases. Small molecules include acetylcholine, norepinephrine, serotonin, dopamine, GABA, and glutamate. Acetylcholine systems in the brain influence memory processes and movement. Norepinephrine is involved in arousal, mood, and learning. Serotonin is active in systems regulating mood and appetite. Dopamine systems are involved in movement and reward; Parkinson's disease and schizophrenia involve disturbances in dopamine systems. GABA is an inhibitory neurotransmitter involved in anxiety and epilepsy. Glutamate is the most common excitatory neurotransmitter; it is involved in learning and memory and, in excess, may cause neuronal death. Peptide neurotransmitters include the endorphins, which act like morphine by affecting pain pathways. Nitric oxide and carbon monoxide are two gases that can act as neurotransmitters.

THE ENDOCRINE SYSTEM: COORDINATING THE INTERNAL WORLD

▶ **How can my hormones help me in a crisis?**

Like nervous system cells, the cells of the *endocrine system* communicate by releasing a chemical that signals other cells. However, the chemicals released by endocrine organs, or *glands,* are called *hormones* and are carried by the bloodstream to remote target organs. The brain is the main controller: Through the hypothalamus, it controls the pituitary gland, which in turn controls endocrine organs in the body. The brain is also a target organ for most endocrine secretions. The target organs often produce a coordinated response to hormonal stimulation. One example is the *fight-or-flight response,* which is set off by adrenal hormones that prepare for action in times of stress.

Learn by Doing

Put It in Writing

Suppose you are asked to help a young mother choose an infant care center that will be most likely to stimulate her one-year-old son's brain development. Write a page about what biological psychology research tells you about the role of environment on brain development. Does that research provide a useful guide for choosing the best day-care center? Why or why not?

Personal Learning Activity

To get a rough measure of the role played by your brain's left hemisphere in language, try the following test. First, see how long you can balance a yardstick on the tip of your right index finger, and then try the same task with your left hand. The difference in how long you can keep the stick balanced will probably be determined by whether you are right-handed or left-handed. Now try this balancing act eight

more times, alternating hands on each trial so that you use your left index finger four times and your right index finger four times. Now here's where language might come in: On two of the four trials with each hand, count backward from 100 by 3s (100, 97, 94, 91, and so on) out loud while you try to keep the stick balanced. It has been suggested that this language task might interfere with your balancing skill, especially when you are using your right hand (Kemble, Filipi, & Gravlin, 1985; Kinsbourne & Cook, 1971). Why? If the left side of your brain is more involved with language, then counting backward while balancing with your right hand requires the left hemisphere to do two things at once. When counting while balancing with the left hand, the right hemisphere is handling the balancing, and the left hemisphere is dealing with the language task. Is this what happened in your case? Try the same tests on your friends and summarize the results. *For additional projects, see the Personal Learning Activities in the corresponding chapter of the study guide that accompanies this text.*

Step into Action

Courses

Biological Bases of Behavior
Physiological Psychology
Biological Psychology
Brain and Behavior
Introduction to Neuroscience
Anatomy and Physiology

Movies

Awakenings Neurotransmitters and mental functioning.
Iris; Complaints of a Dutiful Daughter Coping with a family member's Alzheimer's disease.

Books

William Calvin, *The Throwing Madonna: Essays on the Brain* (Bantam, 1991) Brain and behavior.
Steven Pinker, *How the Mind Works* (Norton, 1997) Brain and behavior.

V. S. Ramachandran, *Phantoms in the Brain: Probing the Mysteries of the Human Mind* (Quill, 1999) A doctor explores neurological disorders.
Bonnie Sherr Klein, *Slow Dance: A Story of Stroke, Love, and Disability* (PageMill Press, 1998) A personal account of recovery from a series of strokes.

The Web

The World Wide Web is a good source of additional information about the science of psychology, provided you use it carefully and think critically about the information you find. The web site that accompanies this text offers many resources relevant to this chapter. These resources include interactive tutorials and animations; ACE chapter quizzes; recommended web links; and articles on current events, books, and movies. At http://college.hmco.com, select *Psychology* and then this textbook.

Review of Key Terms

Can you define each of the key terms in the chapter? Check your definitions against those on the pages shown in parentheses in the following list or in the Glossary/Index at the end of the text.

action potential *(p. 50)*
amygdala *(p. 63)*
association cortex *(p. 68)*
autonomic nervous system *(p. 54)*
axon *(p. 50)*
biological psychology *(p. 48)*
central nervous system (CNS) *(p. 53)*
cerebellum *(p. 62)*
cerebral cortex *(p. 64)*
corpus callosum *(p. 64)*

dendrites *(p. 50)*
endocrine system *(p. 77)*
fiber tracts *(p. 55)*
fight-or-flight response *(p. 78)*
forebrain *(p. 63)*
glands *(p. 77)*
glial cells *(p. 49)*
hindbrain *(p. 61)*
hippocampus *(p. 64)*
hormones *(p. 77)*
hypothalamus *(p. 63)*

medulla *(p. 62)*
midbrain *(p. 63)*
motor cortex *(p. 66)*
nervous system *(p. 49)*
neurons *(p. 49)*
neurotransmitter *(p. 51)*
nuclei *(p. 54)*
parasympathetic nervous system *(p. 54)*
peripheral nervous system *(p. 53)*

plasticity *(p. 71)*
reflexes *(p. 55)*
refractory period *(p. 51)*
reticular formation *(p. 62)*
sensory cortex *(p. 65)*
somatic nervous system *(p. 54)*
spinal cord *(p. 55)*
sympathetic nervous system *(p. 54)*
synapse *(p. 51)*
thalamus *(p. 63)*

Multiple-Choice Self-Test

Select the best answer for each of the following questions. Then check your responses against the Answer Key at the end of the text.

1. The nucleus of a cell _____, and the mitochondria _____.

   a. produces red blood cells; turn oxygen into glucose.
   b. produces red blood cells; keep a stable chemical environment.
   c. provides genetic information; turn oxygen into glucose.
   d. provides genetic information; keep a stable chemical environment.

2. A nurse has mixed up some test results on neurotransmitter function for several patients at the hospital where you work. To help her out, you tell her that the depressed patient's chart will show malfunctions in _____ systems and the Parkinson's patient's chart will show malfunctions in _____ systems.

   a. dopamine; norepinephrine
   b. dopamine; acetylcholine
   c. serotonin; dopamine
   d. acetylcholine; norepinephrine

3. Hannah had a stroke, and oxygen was cut off from the neurons in her brain. This caused overactivity in _____ synapses, which led to brain damage.

   a. glutamate
   b. dopamine
   c. acetylcholine
   d. serotonin

4. Functional magnetic resonance imaging (fMRI) provides a way to

   a. directly measure brain cell activity.
   b. measure brain areas, showing changes in blood flow and oxygen levels.
   c. locate the causes of particular mental processes.
   d. locate where certain emotions take place in the brain.

5. As you switch on your favorite TV medical show, a doctor charges through the emergency room doors and tells a worried spouse that her husband has a neurological problem. "The nerves that carry signals to his muscles are not functioning," the doctor says, "which means the _____ nervous system has been damaged."

   a. central
   b. autonomic
   c. somatic
   d. sympathetic

6. Kalli finishes a difficult final exam, then hurries home and flops down on her bed to relax. As Kalli relaxes, her _____ nervous system becomes less active, whereas her _____ nervous system becomes more active.

   a. central; somatic
   b. somatic; central
   c. parasympathetic; sympathetic
   d. sympathetic; parasympathetic

7. When Karena accidentally touched a hot stove, she instantly jerked her hand away. This automatic response was directed by neurons entering and leaving the _____, which is part of the _____ nervous system.

   a. spinal cord; central
   b. spinal cord; autonomic
   c. hypothalamus; central
   d. hypothalamus; autonomic

8. A neuron's action potential shoots down its axon with greater speed when the

   a. axon is coated in myelin.
   b. refractory period was longer.
   c. neuron's diameter is smaller.
   d. neuron is in the brain.

9. Jessica has severe damage to her medulla. Most likely, Jessica

   a. is dead.
   b. will have memory problems.
   c. will have difficulty with fine motor movements.
   d. will not feel anything on the left side of her body.

10. Damage in Lily's hindbrain caused her to lapse into a coma. The damage most likely occurred in the

    a. cerebellum.
    b. hippocampus.
    c. hypothalamus.
    d. reticular formation.

11. Riley was an excellent pianist until he suffered brain damage. Now, problems with fine motor skills make it impossible for him to play the piano. Riley most likely had damage to his

    a. cerebellum.
    b. hippocampus.
    c. hypothalamus.
    d. reticular formation.

12. The hippocampus has been found to be significantly smaller in patients who are suffering from which of the following problems?

    a. Parkinson's disease
    b. Alzheimer's disease
    c. depression
    d. an eating disorder

13. A woman was rushed to an emergency room with severely burned hands. She had picked up an iron because she couldn't tell it was hot, and she still doesn't feel pain from her burns. The neurologist who examined her concluded that the woman's _____ system is malfunctioning.

    a. sensory
    b. motor
    c. autonomic
    d. parasympathetic

14. Reginald has suffered damage to his occipital lobe. This means that Reginald will have difficulty

    a. feeling pain.
    b. moving his body.
    c. seeing.
    d. regulating body temperature.

15. Elnora wants to hit a nail with a hammer so she can hang a picture on the wall. This involves voluntary movements that are controlled by neurons in the _____ cortex, which is located in the _____ lobe.

    a. motor; frontal
    b. motor; parietal
    c. association; temporal
    d. sensory; occipital

16. Roberto, an actor, is recovering following a freak accident on the set of his latest movie. When asked about the accident, Roberto, once a confident and fluent speaker, can now only say, "Noise . . . acting . . . hurts." The part of Roberto's brain most likely involved in this type of speech problem is _____ area.

    a. Broca's   c. Wernicke's
    b. Sperry's   d. Sylva's

17. Joe experienced such severe seizures that doctors had to sever his corpus callosum. Following surgery, a psychologist presented the left hemisphere of Joe's brain with a picture of a car and asked Joe what he saw. Most likely, Joe could

    a. correctly say "car."
    b. not identify the car in words.
    c. only draw a car.
    d. not understand the question.

18. Edie is eighty and has suffered a paralyzing stroke. Her doctors are likely to tell her that

    a. if she imagines moving her body, she can increase the number of neurons in her motor cortex.
    b. the Nogo protein will help regenerate nerve cells.
    c. neural stem cells will automatically repair the damage.
    d. mental and physical exercise programs can help reverse some of the effects of the stroke.

19. Ted is creating a study sheet to help him learn the differences between neurotransmitters and hormones. Which of the following statements on his list is *not* correct?

    a. Neurotransmitters travel through the bloodstream, and hormones travel across synapses.
    b. Both hormones and neurotransmitters stimulate only those cells and organs that have receptors for them.
    c. Hormones and neurotransmitters regulate complex behaviors and mental processes.
    d. Hormones operate mainly in the endocrine system; neurotransmitters operate mainly in the nervous system.

20. When Mitch saw a woman in danger of drowning, he jumped into the water to save her. Mitch's endocrine system readied him for this exertion by releasing _____ and other stress hormones into his bloodstream.

    a. cortisol   c. glutamate
    b. GABA   d. BABA

3

Sensation and Perception

As you read and understand this sentence, you are performing a feat of

immense proportions as the lines and squiggles of the letters become meaningful words. This is what sensation and perception are all about. You translate incoming stimulation, such as the light bouncing off this page, into neural activity called *sensations.* Then you interpret these sensations as meaningful experiences—in this case, as letters and words. These processes are so quick and automatic that you probably take them for granted. In this chapter, we draw your attention to these amazing processes. You will learn about how our sensory systems receive stimulation and how that stimulation is coded into patterns of nerve activity that the brain can decode. The sensory systems include vision, hearing, taste, smell, and touch. You will also discover how the brain interprets, or perceives, this information from your senses. Principles for organizing the perceptual world allow you to recognize what you have seen, heard, tasted, smelled, or felt.

Reading this chapter will help you to answer the following questions:

It has been years since Fred Aryee lost his right arm below the elbow in a boating accident, yet he still "feels" sensations from his missing lower arm and hand. Once, his doctor asked Aryee to reach for a cup on the table in front of him with his right arm. When asked what he felt, Aryee said, "I feel my fingers clasping the cup" (Shreeve, 1993). People like Fred may also feel intense pain that seems to be coming from a lost limb (Merzenich, 1998). Where do these "phantom limb" sensations and perceptions come from? Fred no longer has fingers to send messages to the brain, yet he experienced his "feeling" of the cup as real. Cases such as this one remind us that the "objective reality" we assume to be the same for everyone can actually differ from

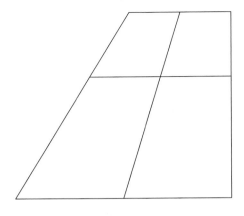

FIGURE 3.1

What Do You See?

person to person (Bartoshuk, Fast, & Snyder, 2005). Just as someone can feel a hand that is not actually "there," every individual's senses actively shape information about the outside world to create a personal reality.

Psychologists distinguish between sensation (the stimulus message coming from the senses) and perception (the process of giving meaning to that message). So you do not actually sense a cat lying on the sofa. You sense shapes and colors, the visual sensations. You then use your knowledge of the world to interpret, or perceive, these sensations as a cat. However, it is impossible to draw a clear line between sensation and perception, because the process of interpreting sensations begins in the sense organs themselves.

Sensing and Perceiving the World

▶ **What is the difference between sensation and perception?**

To understand how sensory systems help us create reality, we need to have some basic information about the senses. A **sense** is a system that translates outside information into activity in the nervous system. For example, your eyes convert light into neural activity that tells the brain something about the source of the light or about the objects reflecting the light. Messages from the senses are called **sensations.** Sensations shape behaviors and mental processes by providing the vital link between the self and the world outside the brain.

Perception is the process of using information and your understanding of the world so that sensations become meaningful experiences. Perception is more than a passive process of absorbing and decoding incoming sensations. For example, look at Figure 3.1. It sends you only raw sensory information about a series of intersecting lines. But your perceptual system automatically interprets this image as a rectangle (or window frame) lying on its side. Perception is so quick and familiar that it is difficult to appreciate the processes that allow you to turn sensory signals into your personal experience of reality. By shaping experience, perceptions influence thoughts, feelings, and actions. But before something can be perceived, it must be sensed.

Sensory Systems

▶ **How does information from my eyes and ears get to my brain?**

Your senses gather information about the world by detecting various forms of energy, such as sound, light, heat, and physical pressure. Your eyes detect light energy, your ears detect the energy of sound, and your skin detects the energy of heat and pressure. Humans depend mainly on vision, hearing, and the skin senses to gain information about the world. We depend less than other animals on smell and taste. To your brain, "the world" also includes the rest of your body, so specific sensory systems provide information about the location and position of your body parts.

All of these senses must detect information about stimuli (the plural of *stimulus*), encode it into neural activity, and then transfer this coded information to the brain. Figure 3.2 illustrates these basic steps in sensation. At each step, sensory information is "processed" in some way. So the information that arrives at one point in the system is not exactly the same information that goes to the next step.

In some sensory systems, the first step in sensation involves **accessory structures,** which modify the incoming stimulus (Step 1 in Figure 3.2). For example, the lens of the eye is an accessory structure that changes incoming light by focusing it. The outer part of the ear is an accessory structure that collects sound.

The second step in sensation is **transduction,** which is the process of converting incoming energy into neural activity (Step 2 in Figure 3.2). Your cell phone receives

sense   A system that translates data from outside the nervous system into neural activity.

sensations   Raw information from the senses.

perception   The process through which people take raw sensations from the environment and give them meaning, using knowledge, experience, and understanding of the world.

accessory structures   Structures, such as the outer part of the ear, that modify a stimulus.

transduction   The process of converting incoming physical energy into neural activity.

FIGURE 3.2

Elements of a Sensory System

Objects in the world generate energy that is focused by accessory structures and detected by sensory receptors, which convert the energy into neural signals. The signals are then relayed through parts of the brain, which processes them into perceptual experiences.

electromagnetic energy and transduces it into sounds. In much the same way, your ears receive sound energy and transduce it into neural activity that you recognize as voices and music. Transduction takes place at structures called **receptors,** which are specialized cells that detect certain forms of energy. These receptors respond to incoming energy by firing an action potential and releasing neurotransmitters that send signals to neighboring cells. Sensory receptors respond best to *changes* in energy (Graziano et al., 2002). A constant level of stimulation usually produces **adaptation,** or a decreasing responsiveness to the stimulus over time. This is the reason that the touch sensations you get from your glasses or wristwatch disappear shortly after you have put them on.

Sensory nerves carry information from receptors to the brain (Step 3 in Figure 3.2). For all the senses except smell (Shepherd, 2005), this information goes first to the thalamus, which does some initial processing before sending it on to the cerebral cortex (Step 4). The most complex processing occurs in the cortex (Step 5). (For a reminder of the location of these brain structures, see Figure 2.9.)

Coding Sensations: Did You Feel That?

When receptors transduce, or convert, energy, they must somehow *code* the physical properties of the stimulus into patterns of neural activity. When organized by the brain, those neural patterns allow you to make sense of the stimulus. This processing lets you determine whether you are looking at a cat, a dog, or your next-door neighbor.

Each psychological dimension of a sensation, such as brightness or color, has a corresponding physical dimension that is encoded by the sensory receptors. In other words, **coding** translates the physical properties of a stimulus, such as the loudness of sound, into a pattern of neural activity that tells us what those physical properties are.

Absolute Thresholds: Is Something Out There?

How much stimulus energy does it take to trigger a conscious perceptual experience? Not much at all. Normal human vision can detect the light equivalent to a candle flame burning in the dark thirty miles away. The minimum detectable amount of light, sound, pressure, or other physical energy is called the *absolute threshold.* Table 3.1 lists absolute thresholds for human vision, hearing, taste, smell, and touch.

Psychologists discovered these thresholds by exploring *psychophysics,* the relationship between *physical* energy in the environment and your *psychological experience* of that energy. In a typical absolute threshold experiment, you would be seated in a darkened laboratory. After your eyes got used to the darkness, the researcher would show you brief flashes of light. These flashes would differ in brightness, or stimulus intensity. Each time, you'd be asked if you saw the light. Averaged over a large number of trials, your responses would probably form a curve like the one shown in Figure 3.3. As you can see, the absolute threshold is not an all-or-nothing affair. A stimulus at an intensity of 3, which is below the absolute threshold in the figure, will still be detected 20 percent of the time it occurs. Because of such variability, psychophysicists redefined the **absolute threshold** as the smallest amount of energy that can be detected 50 percent

receptors Cells specialized to detect certain types of energy and convert it into neural activity.

adaptation Decreasing responsiveness to an unchanging stimulus.

coding Translation of the physical properties of a stimulus into a specific pattern of neural activity.

absolute threshold The minimum amount of stimulus energy that can be detected 50 percent of the time.

TABLE **3.1**

Some Absolute Thresholds

learn by doing Absolute thresholds can be amazingly low. Here are examples of the stimulus equivalents at the absolute threshold for the five primary senses. Set up the conditions for testing the absolute threshold for sound, and see if you can detect this minimal amount of auditory stimulation. If you can't hear it, the signal-detection theory we discuss in this section may help explain why.

Human Sense	Absolute Threshold Is Equivalent to:
Vision	A candle flame seen at 30 miles on a clear night
Hearing	The tick of a watch under quiet conditions at 20 feet
Taste	One teaspoon of sugar in 2 gallons of water
Smell	One drop of perfume diffused into the entire volume of air in a 6-room apartment
Touch	The wing of a fly falling on your cheek from a distance of 1 centimeter

Source: Galanter (1962).

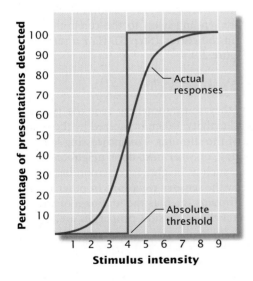

FIGURE **3.3**

The Absolute Threshold

The curved line shows the relationship between the physical intensity of a signal and the chance that it will be detected. If the absolute threshold were truly absolute, or exact, all signals at or above a particular intensity would always be detected, and no signals below that intensity would ever be detected (as shown by the red line). But this response pattern almost never occurs, so the "absolute" threshold is defined as the intensity at which the signal is detected 50 percent of the time.

of the time. Why does a supposedly "absolute" threshold vary? The two most important reasons have to do with internal noise and our response criterion.

Internal noise is the random firing of cells in the nervous system that continues in varying amounts whether or not you are stimulated by physical energy. This ongoing neural activity is a little like "snow" on a television screen or static between radio stations. If the amount of internal noise happens to be high at a particular moment, your sensory systems might mistakenly interpret the noise as an external stimulus.

The second source of variation in absolute threshold, the **response criterion,** reflects a person's willingness to respond to a stimulus. A person's *motivation*—wants and needs—as well as *expectations* affect the response criterion. For example, if you were punished for reporting that a faint light appeared when it did not, then you might be motivated to raise your response criterion. That is, you would report the light only when you were quite sure you saw it. Similarly, expecting a faint stimulus to occur lowers the response criterion. Suppose, for example, that you worked at an airport security checkpoint, examining x-ray images of people's handbags, briefcases, and luggage. The signal to be detected in this situation is a weapon. If there has been a recent terrorist attack, or if the threat level has just been elevated, your airport will be on high alert. So your response criterion for saying that some questionable object on the x-ray image might be a weapon will be much lower than if terrorism were not so likely.

Signal-Detection Theory   Once researchers understood that the detection of a stimulus depends on the combination of its physical energy, the effects of internal noise, and the response criterion, they realized that measurement of absolute thresholds could never be more precise than the 50 percent rule mentioned earlier. So they abandoned the effort to pinpoint absolute thresholds and turned instead to signal-detection theory.

Signal-detection theory presents a mathematical model of how your personal sensitivity and response criterion combine to determine your decision about whether or not a near-threshold stimulus occurred (Green & Swets, 1966). **Sensitivity** refers to your ability to discriminate a stimulus from its background. It is influenced by internal noise, the intensity of the stimulus, and the capacity of your sensory systems. As already mentioned, the response criterion is the internal rule, also known as *bias,* that you use in deciding whether to report a signal. How likely is it that an airport security guard will spot a weapon in a passenger's x-rayed luggage? Signal-detection theory provides a way to understand and predict such responses, because it allows precise measurement of sensitivity to stimuli of any kind (MacMillan & Creelman, 2004; Swets, 1992, 1996).

DETECTING VITAL SIGNALS According to signal-detection theory, the likelihood that security screeners will detect the outline of a bomb or other weapon in a passenger's luggage depends partly on the sensitivity of their visual systems as they look at x-ray images and partly on their response criteria. Those criteria are affected by their expectations that weapons might appear, as well as by how motivated they are to look carefully for them. To help keep inspectors' response criteria sufficiently low, airport security officials occasionally attempt to smuggle a simulated weapon through a checkpoint. This procedure evaluates the inspectors' performance but also helps improve it by keeping inspectors more focused on their vital task (McCarley et al., 2004).

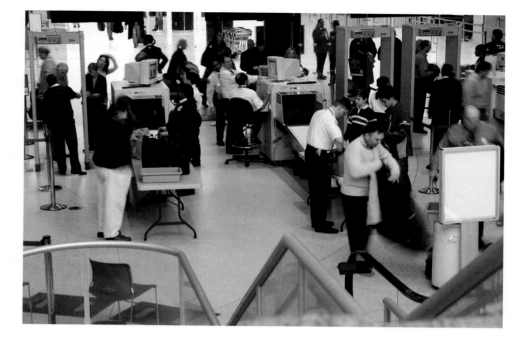

internal noise The spontaneous, random firing of nerve cells that occurs because the nervous system is always active.

response criterion The internal rule a person uses to decide whether or not to report a stimulus.

signal-detection theory A mathematical model of what determines a person's report of a near-threshold stimulus.

sensitivity The ability to detect a stimulus.

Weber's law A law stating that the smallest detectable difference in stimulus energy (just-noticeable difference) is a constant fraction of the intensity of the stimulus.

just-noticeable difference (JND) The smallest detectable difference in stimulus energy. Also called difference threshold.

wavelength The distance between peaks in a wave of light or sound.

frequency The number of complete waves, or cycles, that pass a given point per unit of time.

Judging Differences Between Stimuli Sometimes our task is not to detect a faint stimulus but to notice small changes in a stimulus or to decide whether two stimuli are the same or different. When tuning up for a concert, musicians must discern whether notes played by two instruments are the same. When repainting part of a wall, you have to judge whether the new paint matches the old. And when cooking, you have to decide whether your soup tastes any spicier after you added some pepper.

Your ability to judge differences between stimuli depends on the strength of the stimuli you are dealing with. The weaker the stimuli are, the easier it is to detect small differences between them. For example, if you are comparing the weight of two oranges, you will be able to detect a difference of as little as a fraction of an ounce. But if you are comparing two boxes weighing around fifty pounds each, you may not notice a difference unless it is a pound or more.

One of the oldest laws in psychology, named after German physiologist Ernst Weber (pronounced "VAY-ber"), describes the role of stimulus strength in detecting differences. **Weber's law** states that the smallest detectable difference in stimulus energy is a constant fraction of the intensity of the stimulus. This smallest detectable difference is called the *difference threshold* or **just-noticeable difference (JND)**. According to Weber's law, if an object weighs twenty-five pounds, the JND is only half a pound. So, if you added a container of yogurt to a grocery bag with three gallons of milk in it, you would not be able to tell the difference in weight. But candy snatchers beware: It takes a change of only two-thirds of an ounce to determine that someone has been into a two-pound box of chocolates! The size of the just-noticeable difference differs from one sense to the next. The human visual system, for example, is more sensitive than the human taste system, so we will notice smaller differences in the brightness of a light than in, say, the saltiness of a salad.

Sensory Energy The sensory energies of light and sound vibrate as *waves* passing through space. These waves result from reflected light or from changes in air pressure caused when vocal cords and other objects move. The eye and ear detect the waves as light and sound. Waves of light and sound can be described in terms of wavelength, frequency, and amplitude, and it is these properties that determine what is sensed and perceived. **Wavelength** is the distance from one peak of the wave to the next. Wave **frequency** is the number of complete waves, or cycles, that pass a given point in a

F I G U R E **3 . 4**

The Dimensions of a Wave

Wavelength is the distance from one peak of a wave to the next. *Frequency* is the number of complete waves, or cycles, that pass a given point in a given amount of time, such as one second. *Amplitude* is the height of a wave from baseline to peak.

amplitude The distance between the peak and the baseline of a wave.

visible light Electromagnetic radiation that has a wavelength of about 400 nanometers to about 750 nanometers.

light intensity A physical dimension of light waves that refers to how much energy the light contains and that determines its brightness.

light wavelength A physical dimension of light waves that refers to their length and that produces sensations of different colors.

cornea The curved, transparent, protective layer through which light rays enter the eye.

pupil An opening in the eye, just behind the cornea, through which light passes.

iris The part of the eye that gives it its color and adjusts the amount of light entering it.

lens The part of the eye directly behind the pupil.

retina The surface at the back of the eye onto which the lens focuses light rays.

accommodation The ability of the lens to change its shape and bend light rays so that objects are in focus.

given amount of time. **Amplitude** is the height of the wave from baseline to peak (see Figure 3.4). Different wavelengths, frequencies, and amplitudes create different visual and sound experiences. Let's now consider how these physical properties of light and sound waves become sights and sounds.

Seeing

▶ **Why do some people need eyeglasses?**

Soaring eagles have the incredible ability to see a mouse move in the grass from a mile away. Cats have special "reflectors" at the back of their eyes that help them to see even in very dim light. Nature has provided each species with a visual system uniquely adapted to its way of life. The human visual system is also adapted to do many things well. It combines great sensitivity with great sharpness, enabling us to see objects near and far, during the day and night. Our night vision is not as good as that of some animals, but our color vision is excellent. Not a bad tradeoff; after all, being able to experience a sunset's splendor seems worth an occasional stumble in the dark.

Light

Light is a form of energy known as *electromagnetic radiation*. Most electromagnetic radiation, including x-rays, radio waves, television signals, and radar, is invisible to the human eye. In fact, as shown in Figure 3.5, the range, or spectrum, of **visible light** is just the tiny slice of electromagnetic radiation that vibrates at wavelengths from just under 400 nanometers to about 750 nanometers. (A *nanometer* is one-billionth of a meter.) It is correct to refer to light as either *light waves* or *light rays*.

Sensations of light depend on the intensity and wavelength of light waves. **Light intensity,** which refers to how much energy the light contains, determines the brightness of light. And what color you sense depends mainly on **light wavelength.** At a given intensity, different wavelengths produce sensations of different colors. For instance, 440-nanometer light appears violet blue, and 700-nanometer light appears orangish red.

Focusing Light

The eye transduces light energy into neural activity. First, accessory structures of the eye modify incoming light rays. The light rays enter the eye by passing through the curved, transparent, protective layer called the **cornea.** As shown in Figure 3.6, the light then passes through the **pupil,** the opening just behind the cornea. The **iris,** which gives the eye its color, adjusts the amount of light allowed into the eye by constricting to reduce the size of the pupil or dilating to enlarge it. Directly behind the pupil is the **lens.** Both the cornea and lens of the eye are curved so that they bend light rays. (A camera lens works the same way.) This bending process focuses light rays coming from various angles into a sharp image on the inner surface at the back of the eye. This surface is called the **retina.** Light rays from the top of an object are focused at the bottom of the image on the retinal surface. Light rays from the right side of the object end up on the left side of the retinal image (see Figure 3.7). The brain rearranges this upside-down and reversed image so that we can see the object as it is.

 The muscles that hold the lens adjust its shape so that either near or far objects can be focused on the retina. To illustrate this for yourself, try reading the next sentence while holding the book as close to your face as possible. To maintain a focused image at close range, your muscles have to tighten your lenses, making them more curved. This ability to change the shape of the lens to bend light rays is called **accommodation.** As the lens loses some of its flexibility over the

FIGURE 3.5

The Spectrum of Electromagnetic Energy

The human eye is sensitive to only a narrow range of electromagnetic wavelengths. To detect energy outside this range, we rely on radios, cell phones, TV sets, radar detectors, infrared night-vision scopes, and other electronic instruments that can "see" this energy, just as the eye sees visible light.

Wavelength in meters

10^{-15} 10^{-14} 10^{-13} 10^{-12} 10^{-11} 10^{-10} 10^{-9} 10^{-8} 10^{-7} 10^{-6} 10^{-5} 10^{-4} 10^{-3} 10^{-2} 10^{-1} 10^{1} 10^{2} 10^{3}

Cosmic rays | Gamma rays | X-rays | Ultraviolet | Visible | Infrared | Microwaves | Radar | TV FM AM Radio waves | Short waves

VISIBLE SPECTRUM

400   450   500   550   600   650   700   750

Wavelength in nanometers

FIGURE 3.6

Major Structures of the Eye

As shown in this top view of the eye, light rays bent by the combined actions of the cornea and the lens are focused on the retina, where the light energy is converted into neural activity. Nerve fibers from the retina combine to form the optic nerve, which leaves the back of the eye and continues to the brain.

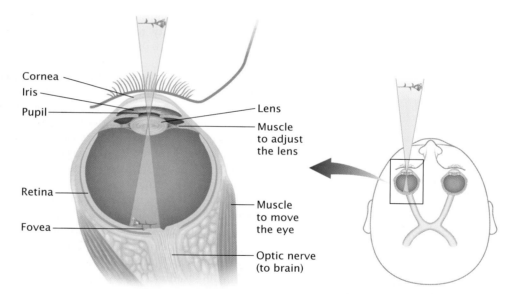

Cornea
Iris
Pupil
Lens
Muscle to adjust the lens
Retina
Fovea
Muscle to move the eye
Optic nerve (to brain)

FIGURE 3.7

The Lens and the Retinal Image

To see objects as they are, your brain must rearrange the upside-down and reversed images that the lens focuses on the retina. If light rays are out of focus when they reach the retina, glasses usually correct the problem. In some older people, vision is impaired by cataracts, a condition in which a "cloudy" lens severely reduces incoming light. Cataracts can be cleared up with laser surgery or by replacing the natural lens with an artificial one (Snellingen et al., 2002).

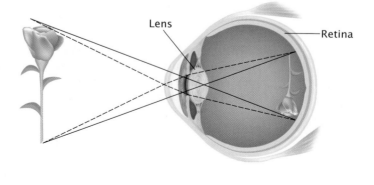

Lens
Retina

years, accommodation becomes more difficult. Converging light rays may come into focus either before or after they reach the retina, causing images to be blurry. This is why most older people become "farsighted," seeing distant objects clearly but needing glasses for reading or close work. A more common problem in younger people is "near-sightedness," in which close objects are in focus but distant ones are blurry. This condition has a genetic component, but it can also be influenced by environmental factors such as reading habits (Quinn et al., 1999; Zadnik, 2001).

Converting Light into Images

The conversion of light energy into neural activity takes place in the retina, which contains neurons that are actually an extension of the brain. The word *retina* is Latin for "net," and the retina is in fact an intricate network of cells (Masland, 2001).

Rods and Cones   Specialized cells in the retina called **photoreceptors** convert light energy into neural activity. There are two main types of photoreceptors: rods and cones. **Rods** and **cones** are retinal cells that are named for their shapes and that contain chemicals that respond to light. When light strikes these chemicals, they break apart, creating a signal that can be transferred to the brain.

The process of rebuilding these light-sensitive chemicals after they break down takes a little time. This explains why you cannot see when you first come from bright sunshine into a dark room (Mahroo & Lamb, 2004). In the dark, as your rods build up their light-sensitive chemicals, your ability to see gradually increases. The increasing ability to see in the dark over time is called **dark adaptation.** You become about 10,000 times more sensitive to light after about half an hour in a darkened room.

There are three kinds of light-sensitive chemicals in cones, and they provide the basis for color vision. Rods have only one kind of chemical, so they cannot discriminate colors. However, rods are more sensitive to light than cones. Rods allow you to see in dim light, as on a moonlit night, but they don't allow you to see colors. It's only at higher light intensities that the cones, with their ability to detect colors, become most active. As a result, you might put on what looked like a matched pair of socks in a darkened bedroom, only to go outside and discover that one is dark blue and the other is dark green.

Cones are concentrated in the center of the retina, in a circular region called the **fovea,** which is where the eye focuses incoming light. Differences in the density of cones in the fovea probably account for differences in various people's visual *acuity,* or ability to see details (Beirne, Zlatkova, & Anderson, 2005). There are no rods in the human fovea. With increasing distance from the fovea, though, the number of cones gradually decreases, and the proportion of rods gradually increases. So, if you are trying to detect a weak light, such as the light from a faint star, it is better to look slightly away from where you expect to see it. This focuses the weak light on the very light-sensitive rods outside the fovea. Because cones do not work well in low light, looking directly at the star will make it seem to disappear.

From the Retina to the Brain   If the eye simply transferred to the brain the images it focused on the retina, we would experience something like a slightly blurry TV picture. Instead, the eye first sharpens visual images. How? The key lies in the interactions among cells of the retina.

Light rays pass through several layers of retinal cells before striking the rods and cones. Signals generated by the rods and cones then go back toward the surface of the retina, making connections with *bipolar cells* and *ganglion cells,* which allow the eye to begin analyzing visual information even before that information leaves the retina. Ganglion cells in the retina have axons that form the **optic nerve,** which then goes to the brain. Because there are no receptors for visual stimuli at the point where the optic nerve exits the eyeball, a **blind spot** is created, as Figure 3.8 demonstrates.

photoreceptors   Specialized cells in the retina that convert light energy into neural activity.

rods   Photoreceptors in the retina that allow sight even in dim light but that cannot discriminate colors.

cones   Photoreceptors in the retina that are less light-sensitive than rods but that can distinguish colors.

dark adaptation   The increasing ability to see in the dark as time passes.

fovea   A region in the center of the retina.

optic nerve   A bundle of fibers that carries visual information to the brain.

blind spot   The point at which the optic nerve exits the eyeball.

RODS AND CONES This electron microscope view of rods (blue) and cones (aqua) shows what your light receptors look like. Rods are more light-sensitive, but they do not detect color. Cones can detect color, but they require more light in order to be activated. To experience the difference in how these cells work, try looking at an unfamiliar color photograph in a room where there is barely enough light to see. This dim light will activate your rods and allow you to make out images in the picture. But because there is not enough light to activate your cones, you will not be able to see colors in the photo.

After leaving the retina, about half the optic nerve fibers cross over to the opposite side of the brain, creating a structure called the *optic chiasm*. (*Chiasm* means "cross" and is pronounced "KYE-az-um.") Fibers from the inside half of each eye, nearest to the nose, cross over. Fibers from the outside half of each eye do not. So no matter where you look, all the visual information about the right half of the visual world goes to the left hemisphere of your brain and all the visual information from the left half of the visual world goes to the right hemisphere (Roth, Lora, & Heilman, 2002).

The optic chiasm is part of the bottom surface of the brain. Beyond this chiasm, optic fibers extend into the brain itself. The axons from most of the retina's ganglion cells form synapses in the thalamus. Neurons there send the visual input to the primary visual cortex in the occipital lobe at the back of the brain. The primary visual cortex sends visual information to many association areas of the brain for processing (see Figure 2.10).

FIGURE 3.8

Find Your Blind Spot

 There is a blind spot where the optic nerve exits the eye. To "see" your blind spot, cover your left eye and stare at the cross inside the circle. Move the page closer and farther away, and at some point the dot to the right should disappear from view. However, the vertical lines around the dot will probably look continuous, because the brain tends to fill in visual information at the blind spot. We are normally unaware of this "hole" in our vision because the blind spot of one eye is in the normal visual field of the other eye.

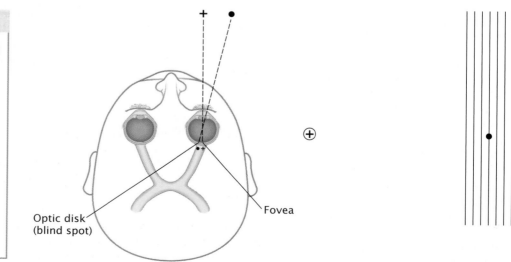

Optic disk (blind spot)

Fovea

Certain cells in the brain's cerebral cortex are called **feature detectors** because they respond to specific characteristics of objects in the visual world (Hubel & Wiesel, 1979). For example, one type of feature detector specializes in responding to straight lines. Others respond to corners, to angles, or to some other feature. The combined responses of several types of feature-detecting cells allow us to sense the shapes of objects, such as rectangles or triangles. Most people can also detect color. Let's explore how color vision works.

Seeing Color

Like beauty, color is in the eye of the beholder. Many animals see only shades of gray, even when they look at a rainbow, but for humans, color is an important feature of vision.

Wavelengths and Color Sensations   At a given intensity, each wavelength of light is sensed as a certain color. However, the eye rarely, if ever, encounters pure light of a single wavelength. Sunlight, for example, is a mixture of all wavelengths of light. When sunlight passes through a droplet of water, each different wavelength of light bends to a different degree, separating into a colorful rainbow. The spectrum of color found in the rainbow illustrates an important concept: The sensation produced by a *mixture* of different wavelengths of light is not the same as the sensations produced by separate wavelengths.

The sensation of a color results from features of the wavelength mixtures striking the eye. The three separate aspects of this sensation are hue, saturation, and brightness. These are *psychological* dimensions that correspond roughly to the physical properties of light. **Hue,** the essential "color," is determined by the dominant wavelength in the mixture of the light. Black, white, and gray are not considered hues, because they do not have a dominant wavelength. **Saturation** is related to the purity of the color. A color is more saturated (purer) if just one wavelength is more intense—contains more energy—than other wavelengths. The yellow of a school bus and the red of a stop sign are saturated colors. Add in many other wavelengths, and the color is said to be *desaturated*. Pastels are colors that have been desaturated by the addition of whiteness. **Brightness** refers to the overall intensity of the wavelengths making up light.

The *color circle* shown in Figure 3.9 arranges hues according to their perceived similarities. Mix two different light wavelengths of equal intensity, and the color you sense is midway between the two original colors on the color circle. This process is called *additive color mixing,* because the effects of the wavelengths are added together. Keep adding different colored lights and you eventually get white, which is the combination of all wavelengths. You are probably more familiar with a different form of color mixing, called *subtractive color mixing,* which occurs when paints are combined. Paint, like other physical objects, reflects certain wavelengths and absorbs others. Grass is green because it absorbs all wavelengths except wavelengths perceived as green. White objects appear white because they reflect all wavelengths. So if you keep combining different colored paints, all of the wavelengths will eventually be subtracted, resulting in black.

Theories of Color Vision

Psychologists have long tried to explain how color vision works, but only two theories have stood the test of time: trichromatic (or "three-color") theory and opponent-process theory.

The Trichromatic Theory of Color Vision   In the early 1800s, Thomas Young and, later, Hermann von Helmholtz proved that by mixing pure versions of blue, green, and red light in different ratios, they could produce any other color. Their theory of color vision is called the **trichromatic theory.**

feature detectors   Cells in the cortex that respond to a specific feature of an object.

hue   The essential color determined by the dominant wavelength of a light.

saturation   The purity of a color.

brightness   The overall intensity of the wavelengths making up light.

trichromatic theory   A theory of color vision stating that information from three types of visual elements combines to produce the sensation of color.

F I G U R E **3 . 9**

The Color Circle

Arranging colors according to their psychological similarities creates a color circle that predicts the result of additive mixing of two colored lights. For example, mixing equal amounts of pure green and pure red light will produce yellow, the color that lies at the midpoint of the line connecting red and green. (Note: *nm* stands for *nanometers,* the unit in which light wavelengths are measured.)

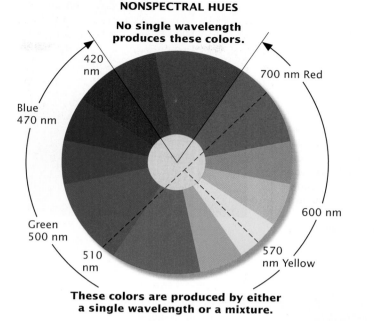

NONSPECTRAL HUES

No single wavelength produces these colors.

420 nm

700 nm Red

Blue 470 nm

600 nm

Green 500 nm

510 nm

570 nm Yellow

These colors are produced by either a single wavelength or a mixture.

SPECTRAL HUES

Support for trichromatic theory comes from research on cones in the retina. There are three types of cones, and each is most sensitive to particular wavelengths. *Short-wavelength* cones respond most to light in the blue range. *Medium-wavelength* cones are most sensitive to light in the green range. *Long-wavelength* cones respond best to light in the reddish-yellow range, but, by tradition, they are known as "red" cones. No single cone by itself can signal the color of a light. It is the *ratio* of the activities of the three types of cones that determines what color will be sensed. As you can see in Figure 3.10, the exact mixture of these three cone types can differ from person to person. The trichromatic theory was applied in the creation of color television screens, which contain microscopic elements of red, green, and blue. A television broadcast excites these elements to varying degrees, mixing their colors to produce many other colors. You see color mixtures, not patterns of red, green, and blue dots, because the dots are too small and close together to be seen individually.

THE SENSATION OF COLOR The vivid array of colored powders offered by this vendor in India allows him to create virtually any combination of hue (color), saturation (purity), and brightness that a customer might request.

(A)   (B)

FIGURE **3.10**

Individual Differences in Cone Types

These photographs show that people can differ widely from one another in the distribution of blue, green, and red cones in their retinas (Roorda & Williams, 1999). J.W., whose retina is shown in Part A, has an especially high population of red cones, whereas green cones predominate in A.N., whose retina is shown in Part B. Both have normal color vision, but J.W. will be somewhat more sensitive to long wavelengths of light, whereas A.N. will be somewhat more sensitive to light of medium wavelengths.

The Opponent-Process Theory of Color Vision   Although essentially correct, the trichromatic theory cannot explain some aspects of color vision, such as afterimages. To see an afterimage, stare at the black dot in the flag in Figure 3.11 for thirty seconds, and then look at the black dot in the white space below it. What was yellow in the original image will be blue in the afterimage. What was green before will appear red, and what was black will now appear white.

This type of observation led Ewald Hering to offer another theory of color vision, called the **opponent-process theory.** Hering suggested that color-sensitive visual elements in the eye are arranged into three kinds of pairs and that the members of each pair oppose, or inhibit, each other. Each element signals one color or the other (red or green, blue or yellow, black or white), but never both. This theory explains color afterimages. When one member of an opponent pair is no longer stimulated, the other is activated. So, in Figure 3.11, if the original image you look at is green, the afterimage will be red.

Summing Up   Together, the trichromatic and opponent-process theories encompass most of what we now know about the complex process of color vision. We see color because our three types of cones have different sensitivities to different wavelengths. We sense different colors when the three cone types are stimulated in different ratios. Because there are three types of cones, any color can be produced by mixing three pure wavelengths of light. But there is more to it than that. The cones connect to ganglion cells containing pairs of opposing elements that respond to different colors and inhibit each other. This arrangement provides the basis for afterimages. Therefore, the trichromatic theory explains color vision as it relates to rods and cones, whereas the opponent-process theory explains color vision as it relates to the ganglion cells. Both theories are needed to account for the complexity of our visual sensations of color. ("In Review: Seeing" summarizes our discussion of vision.)

FIGURE **3.11**

Afterimages Produced by the Opponent-Process Nature of Color Vision

learn by **doing**   Stare at the black dot in the flag for at least thirty seconds, and then focus on the dot in the white space below it. The afterimage you will see can be explained by the opponent process theory of color vision. What colors appeared in the afterimage you saw?

Colorblindness

Cones normally contain three kinds of chemicals, each of which responds best to a particular wavelength of light. People who have cones containing only two of these three color-sensitive chemicals are described as *colorblind* (Carroll et al., 2004). They are not really blind to all color, but they discriminate fewer colors than do other people, as Figure 3.12 shows. Red-green colorblindness, for example, means that reds and greens look the same brownish gray color. Colorblindness is more common in men than in women.

opponent-process theory   A theory of color vision stating that the visual elements sensitive to color are grouped into red-green, blue-yellow, and black-white pairs.

in review

SEEING

Aspect of Sensory System	Elements	Key Characteristics
Energy	Visible light: electromagnetic radiation with a wavelength of about 400 nm to about 750 nm	The intensity, wavelength, and complexity of light waves determine the brightness, hue, and saturation of visual sensations.
Accessory structures of the eye	Cornea, pupil, iris, lens	Light rays are bent to focus on the retina.
Conversion of visual stimuli to neural activity	Photoreceptors (rods and cones) in the retina	Rods are more sensitive to light than cones, but cones discriminate among colors. Sensations of color depend first on the cones, which respond differently to different light wavelengths, and then on processing by ganglion cells.
Pathway to the brain	Optic nerve to optic chiasm to thalamus to primary visual cortex	Neurons in the brain respond to particular aspects of the visual stimulus, such as shape.

?

1. The ability to see in very dim light depends on photoreceptors called _____.
2. Color afterimages are best explained by the _____ theory of color vision.
3. Nearsightedness and farsightedness occur when images are not focused on the eye's _____.

Online Study Center

Improve Your Grade
Tutorial: Opponent Processes

FIGURE **3.12**

Are You Colorblind?

learn by doing   At the upper left is a photo as it appears to people whose cones have all three types of color-sensitive chemicals. The other photos simulate how colors appear to people who are missing chemicals for short wavelengths (lower left), long wavelengths (upper right), or medium wavelengths (lower right). If any of these photos look to you just like the one at the upper left, you may have a form of colorblindness.

Hearing

▶ **How would my voice sound on the moon?**

When Neil Armstrong stepped onto the moon in 1969, millions of people back on earth heard his radio transmission: "That's one small step for a man, one giant leap for mankind." But if Armstrong had taken off his space helmet and shouted, "Whoo-ee! I can moonwalk!" not even an astronaut three feet away could have heard him. Why? Because he would have been speaking into airless, empty space. **Sound** is a repeating fluctuation, a rising and falling, in the pressure of a substance, such as air. Because the moon has almost no atmosphere and almost no air pressure, sound cannot exist there.

Sound

Vibrations of an object produce the fluctuations in pressure that make sound. When you speak, your vocal cords vibrate, causing fluctuations in air pressure that spread as sound waves. Figure 3.13 shows how these changes in air pressure can be represented as sound waveforms. The waveforms are drawn in only two dimensions, but remember that sound waves actually move through the air in all directions. This is the reason that, when people talk to each other during a movie or a lecture, others all around them are distracted by the conversation.

Just as the amplitude and wavelength of light waves affect our experience of light, the characteristics of sound waves affect our experience of sound. The psychological dimension of **loudness** is determined by the amplitude, or height, of the sound wave.

FIGURE 3.13

Sound Waves and Waveforms

Sound is created when objects, such as a tuning fork, vibrate. The vibration creates alternating regions of greater and lesser compression of air molecules, which can be represented as a waveform. The point of greatest compression is the peak of the wave. The lowest point of the wave is where compression is least. In each particular substance, or *medium*, such as air, a sound's wavelength (the distance between peaks) is related to its frequency (the number of waves per second). The longer the wavelength, the lower the sound frequency. The shorter the wavelength, the higher the frequency.

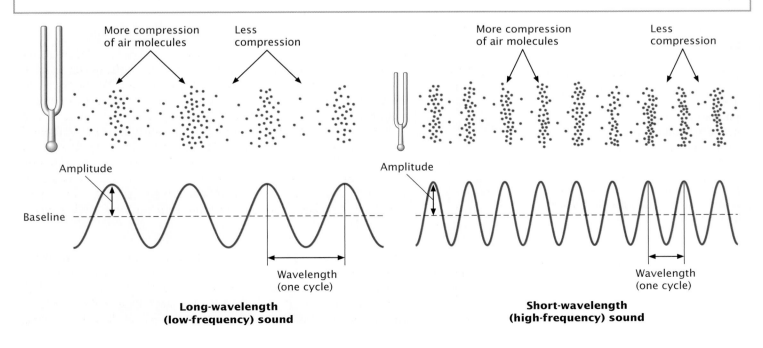

TABLE 3.2

Intensity of Sound Sources

Sound intensity varies across an extremely wide range. A barely audible sound is, by definition, 0 decibels; every increase of 20 decibels reflects a tenfold increase in the amplitude of sound waves. So the 40-decibel sounds of an office are actually 10 times as intense as a 20-decibel whisper; and traffic noise of 100 decibels is 10,000 times as intense as that whisper.

Source	Sound Level (decibels)
Spacecraft launch (from 45 meters)	180
Loudest rock band on record	160
Pain threshold (approximate)	140
Large jet motor (at 22 meters)	120
Loudest human shout on record	111
Heavy auto traffic	100
Conversation (at about 1 meter)	60
Quiet office	40
Soft whisper	20
Threshold of hearing	0

Source: Levine & Schefner (1981).

The greater the amplitude, the louder the sensation of sound. Loudness is described in units called *decibels* (abbreviated *dB*). By definition, 0 decibels is the minimum detectable sound for normal hearing. Table 3.2 gives examples of the intensity, or loudness, of some common sounds.

The psychological dimension of **pitch**—how high or low a tone sounds—depends on the frequency of the sound wave. Frequency is the number of complete waves or cycles that pass a given point in one second. It is described in units called *hertz*, abbreviated *Hz* (for Heinrich Hertz, a nineteenth-century physicist). One cycle per second is 1 hertz. High-frequency waves are sensed as sounds of high pitch. The highest note on a piano has a frequency of about 4,000 hertz, and the lowest note has a frequency of about 50 hertz. Humans can hear sounds ranging from about 20 to 20,000 hertz.

Most sounds are a mixture of many frequencies and amplitudes, and this mixture creates a sound's **timbre** (pronounced "tamber"), the psychological dimension of sound quality. Complex wave patterns added to the *fundamental,* or lowest, frequency of sound determine its timbre. The extra waves allow you to tell the difference between, say, a note played on a flute and the same note played on a clarinet.

The Ear

The human ear converts sound energy into neural activity through a series of accessory structures and transduction mechanisms. The crumpled part of the ear on the side of the head, called the **pinna,** collects sound waves in the outer ear. (People trying to hear a faint sound may cup a hand to their ear, because this action tilts the pinna forward and enlarges the sound-collection area. Try this for a moment, and you will notice a clear difference in how sounds sound.) The pinna funnels sound down through the ear canal. At the end of the ear canal, the sound waves reach the middle ear (see Figure 3.14). There they strike the **eardrum,** a tightly stretched structure also known as the *tympanic membrane.* The sound waves set up vibrations in the eardrum. The *hammer,* the *anvil,* and the *stirrup,* three tiny bones named for their shapes, amplify these vibrations and direct them onto a smaller membrane called the *oval window.*

The Inner Ear   Sound vibrations passing through the oval window enter the inner ear, reaching the **cochlea** (pronounced "COK-lee-ah"), where transduction occurs. The cochlea is rolled into a coiled spiral. (*Cochlea* comes from the Greek word for "snail.") A fluid-filled tube runs down its length. The **basilar membrane** forms the floor of this tube, as you can see in Figure 3.15. When a sound wave passes through the fluid

sound   A repetitive fluctuation in the pressure of a medium such as air.

loudness   A psychological dimension of sound determined by the amplitude of a sound wave.

pitch   How high or low a tone sounds; pitch depends on the frequency of a sound wave.

timbre   The quality of a sound that identifies it.

pinna   The crumpled part of the outer ear that collects sound waves.

eardrum   A tightly stretched membrane in the middle ear that generates vibrations that match the sound waves striking it. Also known as the tympanic membrane.

cochlea   A fluid-filled spiral structure in the inner ear in which auditory transduction occurs.

basilar membrane   The floor of the fluid-filled duct that runs through the cochlea.

FIGURE **3.14**

Structures of the Ear

The outer ear (pinna and ear canal) channels sound waves into the middle ear, where the vibrations of the eardrum are amplified by the delicate bones that stimulate the cochlea. In the cochlea in the inner ear, the vibrations are converted, or transduced, into changes in neural activity, which are sent along the auditory nerve to the brain.

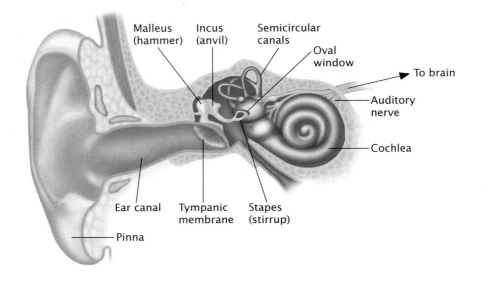

in the tube, it moves the basilar membrane (Ren, 2002). This movement, in turn, bends *hair cells* on the membrane. These hair cells make connections with fibers from the **auditory nerve,** a bundle of axons that goes into the brain. Bending the hair cells stimulates the auditory nerve, which sends coded signals to the brain about the amplitude and frequency of the sound waves (Griesinger, Richards, & Ashmore, 2005). These signals allow you to sense loudness, pitch, and timbre.

Deafness   The middle and inner ear are among the most delicate structures in the body, and damage to them can lead to deafness. One form of deafness is caused by problems with the bones of the middle ear. Over time they can fuse together, preventing accurate conduction of vibrations from one bone to the next. This condition, called *conduction deafness,* can be treated by surgery to break the bones apart or to replace the natural bones with plastic ones (Ayache et al., 2003). Hearing aids that amplify incoming sounds can also help.

Nerve deafness results when the auditory nerve or, more commonly, the hair cells are damaged. Hair cell damage occurs gradually with age, but it can also be caused by very loud sounds, including amplified rock music (Goldstein, 2002). High-intensity sound can actually rip off the hair cells of the inner ear. Generally, any sound loud enough to produce ringing in the ears causes some damage. In humans, small amounts of damage gradually build up and can produce significant hearing loss by middle age—as many older rock musicians, and their fans, are finding out (Levine, 1999).

Hair cells can be regenerated in chickens' ears (Cotanche, 1997), and a related kind of inner-ear hair cell has been regenerated in mammals (Malgrange et al., 1999). Scientists hope that human hair-cell regeneration might someday be accomplished by treating damaged areas with growth factors similar to those being used to repair damaged brain cells (Shepherd et al., 2005; see the chapter on biology and behavior) or by inserting

FIGURE **3.15**

The Cochlea

This drawing shows how the vibrations of the stirrup set up vibrations in the fluid inside the cochlea. The coils of the cochlea are unrolled in this illustration to show the path of the fluid waves along the basilar membrane. Movements of the basilar membrane stimulate hair cells, which transduce the vibrations into changes in neural firing patterns.

SHAPING THE BRAIN The brain region known as the primary auditory cortex is larger in trained musicians than in people whose jobs are less focused on fine gradations of sound. How much larger this area becomes is correlated with how long the musicians have studied their art. This finding reminds us that, as described in the chapter on biology and behavior, the brain can literally be shaped by experience and other environmental factors.

auditory nerve The bundle of axons that carries messages from the hair cells of the cochlea to the brain.

place theory A theory of hearing stating that hair cells at a particular place on the basilar membrane respond most to a particular frequency of sound.

volley theory A theory of hearing stating that the firing rate of an auditory nerve matches a sound wave's frequency. Also called frequency-matching theory.

genes that might direct the regrowth of damaged hair cells (Izumikawa et al., 2005). This achievement could revolutionize the treatment of nerve deafness, which cannot be overcome by conventional hearing aids. In the meantime, scientists have developed an artificial cochlea that can be implanted in the human ear to stimulate the auditory nerve (Seghier et al., 2005; Zeng, 2005).

Auditory Pathways to the Brain Before sounds can be heard, the information coded in the firing of the many axons that make up the auditory nerve must be sent to the brain for further analysis. This transmission process begins when the auditory nerve conveys the information to the thalamus. From there, the information is relayed to the *primary auditory cortex,* an area in the temporal lobe of the brain (see Figure 2.10). Cells in the auditory cortex have *preferred frequencies.* That is, individual cells there respond most vigorously to sounds of a particular frequency. Each neuron in the auditory nerve also has a "favorite," or characteristic, frequency, though each also responds to some extent to a range of frequencies (Schnee et al., 2005). The auditory cortex examines the pattern of activity of many neurons to determine the frequency of a sound. Some parts of the auditory cortex are devoted to processing certain types of sounds. One part, for example, specializes in information from human speech (Belin, Zatorre, & Ahad, 2002); others are particularly responsive to sounds coming from animals, tools, or musical instruments (Lewis et al., 2005; Zatorre, 2003). The auditory cortex receives information from other senses as well. For example, the primary auditory cortex is activated when you watch someone say words (but not when the person makes other facial movements). This is the biological basis for the lip reading that helps you to hear what people say (van Wassenhove, Grant, & Poeppel, 2005).

Coding Sounds

Most people can hear a wide range of sound intensities. The faintest sound that can be heard barely moves the ear's hair cells. Sounds more than a trillion times more intense can also be heard. Between these extremes, the auditory system codes intensity in a rather simple way: The more intense the sound, the more rapid the firing of a given neuron. We are also very good at detecting differences between sound frequencies that allow us to hear differences in pitch (Shera, Guinan, & Oxenham, 2002). Information about frequency differences appears to be coded in two ways: by their location on the basilar membrane and by the rate at which the auditory neurons fire.

As sound waves move down the basilar membrane, they reach a peak and then taper off, much like an ocean wave that crests and then dissolves. High-frequency sounds produce a wave that peaks soon after it starts down the basilar membrane. Lower-frequency sounds produce a wave that peaks farther down the basilar membrane. According to **place theory,** the greatest response by hair cells occurs at the peak of the wave. Because the location of the peak varies with the frequency of sound, it follows that hair cells at a particular place on the basilar membrane are most responsive to a particular frequency of sound. When cells with a particular characteristic frequency fire, we sense a sound of that frequency.

But place theory cannot explain the coding of very low frequencies, such as deep bass notes, because there are no auditory nerve fibers that have very low preferred frequencies. Humans can hear frequencies as low as twenty hertz, though, so they must be coded somehow. The answer appears to be *frequency matching,* a process in which the firing rate of a neuron in the auditory nerve matches the frequency of a sound wave. Frequency-matching theory is sometimes called the **volley theory** of frequency coding, because the outputs of many cells can combine to create a *volley* of firing.

The nervous system apparently uses more than one way to code the range of audible frequencies. The lowest frequencies are coded by frequency matching. Low to moderate frequencies are coded by frequency matching, as well as by the place on the basilar membrane at which the wave peaks. And high frequencies are coded solely by the place at which the wave peaks. ("In Review: Hearing" summarizes the coding process and other aspects of the auditory system.)

in review

HEARING

Aspect of Sensory System	Elements	Key Characteristics
Energy	Sound: pressure fluctuations of air produced by vibrations	Amplitude, frequency, and complexity of sound waves determine the loudness, pitch, and timbre of sounds.
Accessory structures of the ear	Pinna, eardrum, hammer, anvil, stirrup, oval window, basilar membrane	Changes in pressure produced by the original wave are amplified.
Conversion of sound frequencies into neural activity	Hair cells in the inner ear	Frequencies are coded by the location of the hair cells receiving the greatest stimulation (place theory) and by the combined firing rate of neurons (volley theory).
Pathway to the brain	Auditory nerve to thalamus to primary auditory cortex	Auditory cortex examines patterns of information from the auditory nerve, allowing us to sense loudness, pitch, and timbre.

1. *Sound energy is converted to neural activity in an inner ear structure called the _____.*
2. *Hearing loss due to damage to hair cells or the auditory nerve is called _____.*
3. *How high or low a sound sounds is called _____ and is determined by the _____ of a sound wave.*

Online Study Center

Improve Your Grade
Tutorial: The Ear and Sound Waves

The Chemical Senses: Taste and Smell

▶ **Why can't I taste anything when I have a cold?**

There are animals without vision and animals without hearing, but there are no animals without some form of chemical sense. Chemical senses arise from the interaction of chemicals and receptors. Our **sense of smell** (olfaction) detects chemicals that are airborne, or volatile. Our **sense of taste** (gustation) detects chemicals in solution that come into contact with receptors inside the mouth. These systems are connected.

Smell, Taste, and Flavor

If you have a stuffy nose, everything tastes like cardboard. Why? Because smell and taste act as two components of a single system, known as *flavor* (Rozin, 1982). Most of the properties that make food taste good are actually odors detected by the olfactory system, not chemicals detected by the taste system. The scent and taste pathways converge in the cerebral cortex (de Araujo et al., 2003), which is how smell and taste come to seem like one sensation.

Both tastes and odors prompt strong emotional responses. People have an inborn dislike of bitter flavors, but we have to learn to associate emotions with odors (Bartoshuk,

sense of smell The sense that detects chemicals that are airborne. Also called olfaction.

sense of taste The sense that detects chemicals in solution that come into contact with receptors inside the mouth. Also called gustation.

1991). Many animals easily learn taste aversions to particular foods when the taste is associated with nausea, but humans learn aversions to odors more readily than to tastes (Bartoshuk & Wolfe, 1990).

Variations in the state of our nutrition also affect our experience of taste and flavor, as well as our motivation to eat particular foods. Food deprivation or salt deficiency makes sweet or salty things taste better. Influences on protein and fat intake are less direct. Protein and fat molecules have no particular taste or smell. So preferring or avoiding foods that contain these nutrients is based on associations between scent cues from other volatile substances in food and on the nutritional results of eating the foods (Bartoshuk, 1991; Schiffman et al., 1999).

We experience warm foods as sweeter, but temperature does not alter our experience of saltiness (Cruz & Green, 2000). Warming releases aromas that rise from the mouth into the nose and create more flavor sensations. This is why some people find hot pizza delicious and cold pizza disgusting. Spicy "hot" foods actually stimulate pain fibers in the mouth because they contain a substance called *capsaicin* (pronounced "kap-SAY-uh-sin"), which stimulates pain sensing neurons that are also stimulated by heat.

Our Sense of Smell

Pinching your nose prevents you from smelling odors, and a dilator strip on the bridge of your nose opens your nasal passages and intensifies odors (Raudenbush & Meyer, 2002). These effects occur because the nose (and the mouth, to some extent) acts as an accessory structure that collects airborne odor molecules for coding and analysis by the olfactory system (see Figure 3.16). As odor molecules pass into the moist lining of the upper part of the nose—called the *mucous membrane*—they bind to receptors on the dendrites of olfactory neurons, causing a biochemical change. This change, in turn, leads to changes in the firing rates of these neurons, whose axons combine to form the *olfactory nerve* (Dionne & Dubin, 1994). It takes only a single molecule of an odorous substance to cause a change in the activity of an olfactory neuron, but detection of the odor by a human requires about fifty such molecules (Menini, Picco, & Firestein, 1995). The number of molecules needed to trigger an olfactory sensation can vary, however.

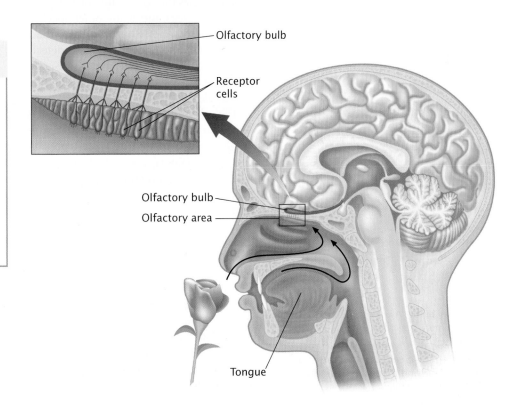

FIGURE 3.16

The Olfactory System: The Nose and the Rose

Airborne odor molecules reach the olfactory area either through the nose or through an opening in the palate at the back of the mouth. This opening allows us to sample odors from our food as we eat. Nerve fibers pass directly from the olfactory area to the olfactory bulb in the brain, and from there signals pass to areas that are involved in emotion. This arrangement helps explain why odors often trigger strong emotional memories.

For example, women are more sensitive to odors during certain phases of their menstrual cycles (Navarrete-Palacios et al., 2003).

There are thousands of different receptors for odors, but there are even more possible odors in the world. Any particular odor is sensed as a particular *pattern* of responses by these odorant receptors (Kajiya et al., 2001; Zou & Buck, 2006). So a rose, a pizza, and your favorite cologne each have a different smell because they stimulate their own unique patterns of activity in your odorant receptors. The question of how smells are coded has been of special interest since the September 11, 2001, terrorist attacks in the United States. Researchers have intensified their efforts to develop an "electronic nose" capable of detecting odorants associated with guns and explosives (Thaler, Kennedy, & Hanson, 2001). Versions of these devices are already in use at some airports.

Unlike other senses, our sense of smell does not send its messages through the thalamus. Instead, axons from olfactory neurons in the nose extend through a bony plate and directly into the brain, where they have a synapse in a structure called the **olfactory bulb.** Connections from the olfactory bulb spread throughout the brain (Zou, Li, & Buck, 2005), but they are especially plentiful in the amygdala, a part of the brain involved in emotional experience and learning. In humans, the amygdala is especially active in response to disgusting odors (Zald & Pardo, 1997).

The unique anatomy of the olfactory system may help account for the unique relationship between smells and emotion (Stevenson & Boakes, 2003). Associations between particular odors and experiences—especially emotional experiences—are not weakened much by time or later experiences (Lawless & Engen, 1977). So catching a whiff of the cologne once worn by a lost loved one can reactivate intense feelings of love or sadness associated with that person. Odors can also bring back accurate memories of experiences linked with them, especially positive experiences (Engen, Gilmore, & Mair, 1991; Mohr et al., 2001).

Species ranging from humans to worms have remarkably similar neural mechanisms for sensing smell. And all mammals, including humans, have brain systems for detecting the source of smells by comparing the strength of sensory inputs reaching the left and right nostrils (Porter et al., 2005). Different species vary considerably, however, in their sensitivity to odor and in the degree to which they depend on it for survival. Humans have about 9 million olfactory neurons, compared with about 225 million in dogs, a species that is far more dependent on smell to identify food, territory, and receptive mates. Dogs and many other species also have an accessory olfactory system that detects pheromones. **Pheromones** (pronounced "FAIR-oh-mohns") are chemicals that, when released by one creature and detected by another, can shape the second animal's behavior or physiology (Silvotti, Montanu, & Tirindelli, 2003). For example, when a male snake detects a chemical on the skin of a female snake, it is stimulated to "court" the female.

The role of pheromones in humans is much less clear, but it appears that we do have some sort of pheromone-like system (Berglund, Lindström, Savic, 2006; Savic, Berglund, & Lindström, 2005). A possible human gene for pheromone receptors has been found (Rodriguez et al., 2000), and pheromones have been shown to cause reproduction-related physiological changes in humans (Grammer, Fink, & Neave, 2005). Specifically, pheromonal signals secreted in women's perspiration can influence nearby women's menstrual cycles. As a result, women living together eventually tend to menstruate at about the same time (Stern & McClintock, 1998). Furthermore, odorants that cannot be consciously detected can nevertheless influence mood and stimulate activity in nonolfactory areas of the brain (Jacob & McClintock, 2000; Jacob et al., 2001; Savic et al., 2001).

Despite steamy ads for cologne and perfume, however, there is not yet any solid evidence that humans give off or can detect pheromones that act as sexual attractants. If a certain scent does enhance a person's readiness for sex, it is probably because the person has learned to associate that scent with previous sexual experiences. There are many other examples of people using olfactory information in social situations. For instance, after just a few hours of contact with their newborn babies, mothers can usually identify them by the infants' smell (Porter, Cernich, & McLaughlin, 1983). And if

olfactory bulb   A brain structure that receives messages regarding smell.

pheromones   Chemicals that are released by one creature and detected by another, shaping the second one's behavior or physiology.

FIGURE 3.17

Are You a Supertaster?

learn by doing This photo shows papillae on the tongue of a "supertaster." If you don't mind a temporary stain on your mouth and teeth, you can look at your own papillae by painting the front of your tongue with a cotton swab soaked in blue food coloring. Distribute the dye by moving your tongue around and swallowing; then look into a magnifying mirror as you shine a flashlight on your tongue. The pink circles you see against the blue background are papillae, each of which has about six taste buds buried in its surface. Get several friends to do this test, and you will see that genes create wide individual differences in taste bud density.

infants are breastfed, they can discriminate their own mother's odor from that of other breastfeeding women and appear to be comforted by it (Porter, 1991). Recognizing this odor may help establish the mother-infant bond discussed in the chapter on human development.

Our Sense of Taste

Our receptors for taste are in the taste buds, which are grouped together in structures called **papillae** (pronounced "puh-PILL-ee"). Normally, there are about ten thousand taste buds in a person's mouth, mostly on the tongue but also on the roof of the mouth and on the back of the throat.

The human taste system detects only a few basic sensations: sweet, sour, bitter, and salty. Each taste bud responds best to one or two of these categories (Zhang et al., 2003) but it also responds weakly to others. Research has also revealed two additional taste sensations (Rolls, 1997). One, called *umami* (which means "delicious" in Japanese), enhances other tastes and is produced by certain proteins, as well as by monosodium glutamate (MSG; DuBois, 2004). The other, called *astringent*, is the taste produced by tannins, which are found in tea, for example. About 25 percent of us are "super-tasters"—individuals whose genes have given them an especially large number of papillae on their tongues (Bartoshuk, 2000; see Figure 3.17). Supertasters are more sensitive than other people to bitterness, as revealed in their reactions to foods such as broccoli, soy products, and grapefruit.

Scientists are learning more and more about how interactions between foods and taste receptors signal various tastes (Small et al., 2003; Stillman, 2002), and they are putting the information to good use. Understanding the chemistry of sweetness, for example, has led to new chemicals that fit into sweetness receptors and taste thousands of times sweeter than sugar. When used in products such as artificial sweeteners, they offer new ways to enjoy good-tasting but low-calorie sweets. ("In Review: Smell and Taste" summarizes our discussion of these senses.)

in review

SMELL AND TASTE

Aspect of Sensory System	Elements	Key Characteristics
Energy	Smell: volatile chemicals Taste: chemicals in solution	The amount, intensity, and location of the chemicals determine taste and smell sensations.
Structures of taste and smell	Smell: chemical receptors in the mucous membrane of the nose Taste: taste buds grouped in papillae in the mouth	Odor and taste molecules stimulate chemical receptors.
Pathway to the brain	Olfactory bulb and taste buds	Axons from the nose and mouth bypass the thalamus and extend directly to the olfactory bulb.

1. The flavor of food arises from a combination of _____ and _____.
2. Emotion and memory are linked especially closely to our sense of _____.
3. Perfume ads suggest that humans are affected by _____ that increase sexual attraction.

papillae Structures in the mouth on which taste buds are grouped.

Sensing Your Body

▶ **Which is the largest organ in my body?**

Some senses are not located in a specific organ, such as the eye or the ear. These are the somatic senses, also called *somatosensory systems,* which are spread throughout the body. The **somatic senses** include the skin senses of touch, temperature, and pain, as well as a body sense, called *kinesthesia,* that tells the brain where the parts of the body are. Kinesthesia is closely related to our sense of balance. Although balance is not strictly a somatosensory system, we describe it here.

Touch and Temperature

People can function and prosper without vision, hearing, or smell. But a person without a sense of touch would have difficulty surviving. Without this sense, you could not even swallow food, because you could tell where it was in your mouth and throat. You receive touch sensations through your skin, which is the body's largest organ. The skin covers nearly two square yards of surface area, weighs more than twenty pounds, and has hair virtually everywhere on it. The hairs on your skin do not sense anything directly. However, when the hairs are bent, they push against the skin beneath them. Receptors in, and just below, the skin send the "touch" message to the brain.

Coding Touch Information   The sense of touch codes information about two aspects of an object contacting the skin: its weight and its location. The *intensity* of the stimulus—how heavy it is—is coded both by the firing rate of individual neurons and by the number of neurons stimulated. A heavy object triggers a higher rate of firing and stimulates more neurons than a light object. The brain "knows" where the touch occurs based on the *location* of the nerves that sense the touch information.

Adapting to Touch Stimuli   Continuous input from all your touch neurons would provide a lot of unnecessary information. Once you get dressed, you do not need to be constantly reminded that you are wearing clothes. Thanks in part to the process of adaptation described earlier, you do not continue to feel your clothes against your skin.

Changes in touch (as when your belt or shoe suddenly feels loose) provide the most important sensory information. The touch sense emphasizes these changes and filters out the excess information. How? Typically, a touch neuron responds with a burst of firing when a stimulus is applied, then quickly returns to its baseline firing rate, even though the stimulus may still be in contact with the skin. If the touch pressure increases, the neuron again responds by increasing its firing rate, then slowing down. A few neurons adapt more slowly, however, continuing to fire as long as pressure is applied. By attending to this input, you can sense a constant stimulus (try doing this by focusing on touch sensations from your glasses or shoes).

Sensing Temperature   Some of the skin's sensory neurons respond to a change in temperature but not to simple contact. "Warm fibers" and "cold fibers" respond to specific temperature changes only. However, many fibers that respond to temperature also respond to touch, so these sensations sometimes interact. For example, if you touch an object made up of alternating warm and cool sections, you will have the sensation of intense heat (Thunberg, 1896, cited in Craig & Bushnell, 1994).

Pain

Touch can feel pleasurable, but if the intensity of touch stimulation increases too much, it can turn into a pain sensation. Pain tells you about the impact of the world on your body. It also has a distinctly negative emotional component that interrupts whatever you are doing (Eccleston & Crombez, 1999).

 TOUCH AND VISION   Just as taste and smell interact, so do touch and vision. To experience an example of this interaction, ask someone sitting across a table from you to stroke the tabletop while stroking your knee under the table in exactly the same way, in exactly the same direction. If you watch the person's hand stroking the table, you will soon experience the touch sensations coming from the table, not your knee! If the person's two hands do not move in synch, however, the illusion will not occur.

somatic senses   Senses including touch, temperature, pain, and kinesthesia that are spread throughout the body rather than located in a specific organ. Also called somatosensory systems.

A LIFE WITH NO PAIN Ashlyn Blocker, shown here at age 5 being checked for injuries, was born with a rare genetic disorder that prevented the development of pain receptors. As a result, she feels no pain if she is cut or bruised, if she bites her tongue while eating, or even if she is burned by hot soup or a hot stove. She only knows she has been injured if she sees herself bleeding, so she will have to find ways to protect herself from danger without the vital information provided by the pain system. Ashlyn doesn't yet understand the seriousness of her condition, but her worried mother says "I would give anything for her to feel pain" (Associated Press, 2004).

Pain as an Information Sense The information-carrying aspect of pain is very similar to that of touch and temperature. The receptors for pain are free nerve endings, which come from the spinal cord, enter the skin, and then simply end. Painful stimuli cause the release of chemicals that fit into these specialized receptors in pain neurons, causing them to fire. The axons of pain-sensing neurons release neurotransmitters not only near the spinal cord (thus sending pain information to the brain) but also near the skin (causing inflammation).

Two types of nerve fibers carry pain signals from the skin to the spinal cord. *A-delta* fibers carry sharp, pricking pain sensations; *C-fibers* carry continuous, dull aches and burning sensations. When you stub your toe, for example, that immediate wave of sharp, intense pain is signaled by A-delta fibers, whereas that slightly delayed wave of gnawing, dull pain is signaled by C-fibers. When pain impulses reach the spinal cord, they form synapses with neurons that relay the pain signals to the thalamus and other parts of the brain. Different pain neurons are activated by different types and degrees of painful stimulation (Ploner et al., 2002).

Emotional Aspects of Pain There are specific pathways that carry the emotional component of a painful stimulus to areas of the hindbrain, reticular formation, and cortex via the thalamus (Johansen, Fields, & Manning, 2001). However, our overall emotional response to pain depends greatly on how we think about it (Spinhoven et al., 2005; Wager, 2005). In one study, some participants were told about the kind of painful stimulus they were to receive and when to expect it. Others were not informed. Those who knew what to expect objected less to the pain, even though the sensation was reported to be equally noticeable in both groups (Mayer & Price, 1982). People can lessen their emotional responses to pain by using pain-reducing strategies (such as distracting thoughts), especially if they expect these strategies to succeed (Bantick et al., 2002). Scientists are also developing special biofeedback systems that may someday allow patients to relieve chronic pain by reducing activity in the brain regions involved in pain perception (deCharms et al., 2005).

Modulating Pain: The Gate Control Theory Pain is useful because it can protect you from harm. There are times, though, when enough is enough. Fortunately, the

NATURAL ANALGESIA   The stress of athletic exertion causes the release of endorphins, natural painkillers that have been associated with pleasant feelings known as "runner's high."

nervous system has several mechanisms for controlling the experience of pain. One theory about how these mechanisms work is called the **gate control theory** (Melzack & Wall, 1965). This theory suggests that there is a "gate" in the spinal cord that either allows pain signals to reach the brain or stops them. Some details of the original theory were incorrect, but more recent work supports the idea that natural mechanisms can indeed block pain sensations (Stanton-Hicks & Salamon, 1997; Sufka & Price, 2002).

For example, input from other skin senses can come into the spinal cord at the same time the pain gets there and "take over" the pathways that the pain impulses would have used. This appears to be the reason we can temporarily relieve pain by rubbing the skin around a wound or using creams that produce temperature sensations. It also helps explain why scratching relieves itching; itchy sensations involve activity in fibers located close to pain fibers (Andrew & Craig, 2001).

The brain itself can close the gate to pain impulses by sending signals down the spinal cord. These messages from the brain block incoming pain signals at spinal cord synapses. The result is **analgesia** (pronounced "ann-nuhl-JEE-zhah"), a reduction in pain sensation in the presence of a normally painful stimulus. Drugs that dull pain sensations, such as aspirin, are called *analgesics.*

Natural Analgesics   As described in the chapter on biology and behavior, natural opiates called *endorphins* play a role in the brain's ability to block pain signals. Endorphins are natural painkillers that act as neurotransmitters at many levels of the pain pathway. In the spinal cord, for example, they block the synapses of the fibers that carry pain signals. Endorphins may also relieve pain when the adrenal and pituitary glands secrete them into the bloodstream as hormones. The more endorphin receptors a person has inherited, the more pain tolerance that person has (Kest, Wilson, & Mogil, 1999; Uhl, Sora, & Wang, 1999).

Several conditions can cause the body to ease its own pain. For example, endorphins are released where inflammation occurs (Cabot, 2001). During the late stages of pregnancy, a spinal cord endorphin system develops to reduce the mother's labor pains (Dawson-Basoa & Gintzler, 1997). An endorphin system is also activated when people believe they are receiving a painkiller, even when they are not (Colloca & Benedetti, 2005; Zubieta et al., 2005); this may be one reason for the placebo effect, discussed in the introductory chapter (Stewart-Williams, 2004). Interestingly, the resulting pain inhibition is experienced in the part of the body where it was expected to occur, but not elsewhere (Benedetti,

gate control theory   A theory suggesting the presence of a "gate" in the spinal cord that either permits or blocks the passage of pain impulses to the brain.

analgesia   Reduction in the sensation of pain in the presence of a normally painful stimulus.

Arduino, & Amanzio, 1999). Physical or psychological stress can also activate natural analgesic systems. Stress-induced release of natural analgesics may account for the fact that injured soldiers and athletes sometimes continue to perform in the heat of battle or competition with no apparent pain (Colloca & Benedetti, 2005).

Does Acupuncture Relieve Pain?

Acupuncture is an ancient and widely used treatment in Asian medicine that is alleged to relieve pain (Ulett, 2003). The method is based on the idea that body energy flows along lines called *channels* (Vincent & Richardson, 1986). According to this theory, there are fourteen main channels, and a person's health depends on the balance of energy flowing in them. Stimulating the channels by inserting fine needles into the skin and twirling them is said to restore a balanced flow of energy. The needles produce an aching and tingling sensation called *Teeh-ch'i* at the site of stimulation, and they relieve pain at distant, seemingly unrelated parts of the body.

■ What am I being asked to believe or accept?

Acupuncturists claim that twirling needles in the skin can relieve pain caused by everything from tooth extraction to cancer.

■ Is there evidence available to support the claim?

There is evidence from positron emission tomography (PET) and magnetic resonance imaging (MRI) studies that stimulating acupuncture sites changes activity in brain regions related to pain regulation and to the targets of treatment (Lewith, White, & Pariente, 2005; Yan et al., 2005). Numerous studies also show positive results in 50 to 80 percent of patients treated by acupuncture for various kinds of pain (Brinkhaus et al., 2006; Manheimer et al., 2005; Witt et al., 2005). In one controlled study of headache pain, 53 percent of the participants reported reduced pain following real acupuncture, whereas only 33 percent of placebo group members improved following fake electrical stimulation (Dowson, Lewith, & Machin, 1985). This latter figure is about the usual proportion of people responding to a placebo.

Another headache study found both acupuncture and drugs to be superior to a placebo. Each reduced the frequency of headaches, but the drugs were more effective than acupuncture at reducing the severity of headache pain (Hesse, Mogelvang, & Simonsen, 1994). Unfortunately, such well-controlled studies are rare, and their results are often contradictory (Ter Riet, Kleijnen, & Knipschild, 1990). Some studies of patients with head, back, or neck pain, for example, found acupuncture to be no better than a placebo or massage therapy (Assefi et al., 2005; Linde et al., 2005; Melchart et al., 2005).

Drugs that slow the breakdown of opiates also prolong the pain relief produced by acupuncture (He, 1987). The pain-reducing effects of acupuncture during electrical stimulation of a tooth can be reversed by naloxone, a substance that blocks the painkilling effects of endorphins and other opiate drugs. These findings suggest that acupuncture somehow activates the body's natural painkilling system. Is this activation brought about only by a placebo effect? Probably not entirely, because acupuncture produces naloxone-reversible pain relief even in monkeys and rats, who obviously have no expectations about acupuncture (Ha et al., 1981; Kishioka et al., 1994).

■ Can that evidence be interpreted another way?

Yes. Evidence about acupuncture might be interpreted as simply confirming that the body's painkilling system can be stimulated by external means. Acupuncture may merely provide one activating method (Pariente et al., 2005). There may be other, even more efficient methods for doing so (Petrovic et al., 2005; Ulett, 2003). We already know, for example, that successful placebo treatments for human pain appear to operate by activating the endorphin system.

■ What evidence would help to evaluate the alternatives?

More placebo-controlled studies of acupuncture are needed, but it is difficult to control for the placebo effect in acupuncture treatment, especially in double-blind fashion (e.g., Kaptchuk, 2001). (How could a therapist not know whether the treatment being given was acupuncture or not? And from the patient's perspective, what placebo treatment could look and feel like having a needle inserted and twirled in the skin?) Nevertheless, researchers have tried to separate the psychological and physical effects of acupuncture—for example, by using blunted or phony needles, mock electrical nerve stimulation (in which electrodes are attached to the skin but no electrical stimulation is given), or stimulation at other sites on the skin (Kaptchuk et al., 2006; Park, White, & Ernst, 2001).

Researchers must also learn more about what factors govern whether acupuncture will activate the endorphin system. Other important unknowns include the types of pain for which acupuncture is most effective, the types of patients who respond best, and the precise procedures that are most effective. Knowing more about the general relationship between internal painkilling systems and external methods for stimulating them would also be valuable.

■ What conclusions are most reasonable?

Although acupuncture is not a cure-all, there seems to be little doubt that, in some circumstances, it does relieve pain and reduce nausea (British Medical Association, 2000; National Institutes of Health Consensus Conference, 1998). One study, for example, found that acupuncture before surgery reduced postoperative pain and nausea, decreased the need for pain-relieving drugs, and reduced patients' stress responses (Kotani et al., 2001). Another found electrical-stimulation acupuncture to be more effective than either drugs or mock stimulation at reducing nausea following major breast surgery; the acupuncture group also reported the least postoperative pain (Gan et al., 2004). So although some critics argue that further expenditures for acupuncture research are not warranted, further studies will probably continue. The quality of their methodology and the nature of their results will determine whether acupuncture finds a more prominent place in Western medicine.

Sensing Body Position

Most sensory systems receive information from the external world, such as the light reflected from a flower or the feeling of cool water. But as far as the brain is concerned, the rest of the body is "out there," too. You know about the position of your body and what each of its parts is doing only because sensory systems provide this information to your brain. These sensory systems are described as **proprioceptive** (meaning "received from one's own," pronounced "pro-pree-oh-SEP-tiv").

Kinesthesia   In the biology and behavior chapter, we describe the case of Christina, a woman who did not recognize her own body. She had lost her sense of **kinesthesia** (pronounced "kin-es-THEE-see-uh"), which tells us where the parts of the body are in relation to one another. To better appreciate kinesthesia, try this: Close your eyes; then hold your arms out in front of you and touch your two index fingers together. You probably did this easily because your kinesthetic sense told you where each finger was with respect to your body. You depend on kinesthetic information to guide all your movements, from walking to complex athletic actions such as running down a basketball court while dribbling a ball and avoiding an opposing player. These movement patterns become simple and fluid because, with practice, the brain uses kinesthetic information automatically. Normally, kinesthetic information comes primarily from the joints and muscles. Receptors in muscle fibers send information to the brain about the stretching of muscles. When the position of the bones

proprioceptive   Referring to sensory systems that tell us about the location of our body parts and what each is doing.

kinesthesia   The proprioceptive sense that tells us where the parts of the body are with respect to one another.

in review

BODY SENSES

Sense	Energy	Conversion of Physical Energy to Nerve Activity	Pathways and Characteristics
Touch	Mechanical deformation of skin	Skin receptors (may be stimulated by hair on the skin)	Nerve endings respond to changes in weight (intensity) and location of touch.
Temperature	Heat	Sensory neurons in the skin	Changes in temperature are detected by warm-sensing and cool-sensing fibers. Temperature interacts with touch.
Pain	Increases with intensity of touch or temperature	Free nerve endings in or near the skin surface	Changes in intensity cause the release of chemicals detected by receptors in pain neurons. Some fibers convey sharp pain; others convey dull aches and burning sensations.
Kinesthesia	Mechanical energy of joint and muscle movement	Receptors in muscle fibers	Information from muscle fibers is sent to the spinal cord, thalamus, cerebellum, and cortex.

1. Gate control theory offers an explanation of why we sometimes do not feel _____.
2. Professional dancers look at the same spot as long as possible during repeated spins. They are trying to avoid the dizziness caused when the _____ sense is overstimulated.
3. Without your sense of _____, you would not be able to swallow food without choking.

changes, receptors in the joints set off neural activity. This coded information goes to the spinal cord and then to the thalamus, along with sensory information from the skin. Finally it goes to the cerebellum and to the somatosensory cortex, both of which help coordinate movements (see Figures 2.8, 2.9, and 2.10).

Balance Have you ever been on a roller coaster? How did you feel when the ride ended? The **vestibular sense** (pronounced "ves-TIB-u-ler") tells the brain about the position of the head (and therefore the body) in space and about its general movements. You have probably heard it referred to as the *sense of balance.* People usually become aware of the vestibular sense only when they overstimulate it and become dizzy or motion sick.

The inner ear contains the organs for the vestibular sense. Each ear has two *vestibular sacs* filled with fluid and containing small crystals called *otoliths* ("ear stones") that rest on hair endings. Three arc-shaped tubes, called the *semicircular canals,* are also fluid filled (see Figure 3.14). Tiny hairs extend into the fluid in the canals. When your head moves, the otoliths shift in the vestibular sacs and the fluid moves in the semicircular canals, stimulating hair endings. This process activates neurons that travel along the auditory nerve, signaling the brain about the amount and direction of head movement.

Neural connections from the vestibular system to the cerebellum help coordinate bodily movements. Connections to the part of the autonomic nervous system that affects the digestive system help create the nausea that may follow overstimulation of the vestibular system—by a roller coaster ride, for instance. Finally, connections to the eye muscles produce *vestibular-ocular reflexes,* which cause your eyes to move opposite to your head movements. These reflexes allow you to focus on one spot even when your head is moving. You can experience these reflexes by having a friend spin you around

learn by doing

on a stool for a while. When you stop, try to fix your gaze on one point in the room. You'll be unable to do so, because the excitation of the vestibular system will cause your eyes to move repeatedly in the direction opposite

vestibular sense The proprioceptive sense that provides information about the position of the head and its movements.

from the way you were spinning. (See "In Review: Body Senses" for a summary of our discussion of touch, temperature, pain, and kinesthesia.)

Perception

▶ **How do sensations become perceptions?**

So far, we have explored how sensory information reaches the brain. Let's now consider the processes of perception that allow the brain to make sense of that information. These perceptual processes can sometimes make the difference between life and death. For example, at a traffic circle in Scotland, fourteen fatal accidents occurred in one year, partly because drivers did not slow down as they approached the circle. After warning signs failed to solve the problem, Gordon Denton, a British psychologist, found a clever solution. He recommended that white lines be painted across the road leading to the circle, in a pattern something like this:

/   /   /   / / / //

Crossing these lines, which were spaced progressively more closely, gave drivers the impression that they were speeding up, so their automatic response was to slow down. During the fourteen months after Denton's idea was implemented, there were only two fatalities at the traffic circle! Similar kinds of striping patterns are now widely used throughout Britain and on approaches to some towns and intersections in the United States, too (Associated Press, 1999). Denton's solution depended partly on his knowledge of sensation but mostly on the principles of human perception.

Some perceptual tasks take attention and effort, as when a child struggles to recognize printed letters. But as experienced readers know, a lot of the perceptual work that transforms sensory information into meaningful experiences happens automatically, without conscious awareness. To illustrate the workings of these complex processes, psychologists draw attention to *perceptual failures*—cases in which we perceive stimuli incorrectly. Just as drivers at the traffic circle incorrectly perceived themselves as speeding up, you will probably perceive the two lines in Figure 3.18 as differing in length, even though they are the same.

FIGURE **3.18**

Misperceiving Reality

 Measure lines A-C and A-B. They are exactly the same length, but you probably perceived A-C as longer. Why? Partly because your visual system tries to interpret all stimuli as three-dimensional, even when they are not. A three-dimensional interpretation of this drawing would lead you to see the two lines as the edges of two parallel paths, one of which ends closer to you than the other. Your eyes tell you that the two paths start at about the same point (the castle entrance), so you assume that the closer line must be the longer of the two.

Source: Gardner (1988).

(A)

(B)

FIGURE **3.19**

Reversible Images

These *reversible images* can be organized by your perceptual system in two ways. If you perceive Part A as the word *figure*, the space around the letters becomes meaningless background. Now emphasize the word *ground*, and what had stood out a moment ago now becomes background. In Part B, when you emphasize the white vase, the black profiles become background; if you organize the faces as the figure, what had been a vase now becomes background. We normally tend to see smaller, lower elements in a scene as figure and larger, higher elements as ground (Vecera, Vogel, & Woodman, 2002), but figures like these don't allow us to use that rule of thumb.

figure   The part of the visual field that has meaning.

ground   The contourless part of the visual field; the background.

Organizing the Perceptual World

▶ **What determines how I perceive my world?**

To further appreciate the wonder of the complicated perceptual work you do every day, imagine yourself driving on a busy road searching for Barney's Diner, an unfamiliar restaurant where you are to meet a friend. The roadside is crammed with signs of all shapes and colors, some flashing, some rotating. If you are ever to recognize the sign that says "Barney's Diner," you will have to impose some sort of organization on this overwhelming mixture of visual information. How do you do this? How do you know where one sign ends and another begins? And how do you know that an apparently tiny sign is not really tiny, but just far away?

Principles of Perceptual Organization

Before you can recognize the "Barney's Diner" sign, your perceptual system must separate that sign from its background of lights, colors, letters, and other competing stimuli. Two basic principles—*figure-ground perception* and *grouping*—guide this initial organization.

Figure and Ground   When you look at a complex scene or listen to a noisy environment, your perceptual apparatus automatically emphasizes certain features, objects, or sounds. These emphasized features become the **figure**. This part of the visual field has meaning, stands in front of the rest, and always seems to include contours or edges. These contours and edges separate the figure from the less relevant background, called the **ground** (Rubin, 1915). So, as you drive toward an intersection, a stop sign will become a figure, standing out clearly against the background of trees or buildings.

To experience how perception creates figure and ground, look at Figure 3.19. Notice that you can decide how to organize the stimuli in the drawings. You can repeatedly reverse figure and ground to see faces, then a vase, then faces again (3.19B), or to see the word *figure* or the word *ground* (3.19A). The fact that you can mentally manipulate these "reversible" images shows that your perceptual systems are not just recording devices that passively absorb incoming sensations; you play an active part in organizing what you perceive. We also usually organize sensory stimulation into only one perceptual category at a time. This is why it is difficult to see both a vase and two faces—or the words *figure* and *ground*—at the same time.

Grouping   Why is it that certain parts of the world become figure and others become ground, even when nothing in particular stands out in the pattern of light that falls on the retina? The answer is that certain properties of stimuli lead you to group them together, more or less automatically.

In the early 1900s, several German psychologists described the principles behind this grouping of stimuli. They argued that people perceive sights and sounds as organized wholes. These wholes, they said, are different from, and more than, the sum of the individual sensations, just as water is something more than just an assortment of hydrogen and oxygen atoms. Because the German word meaning (roughly) "whole figure" is *Gestalt* (pronounced "ge-SHTALT"), these researchers became known as *Gestalt psychologists*. They proposed a number of principles that describe how the perceptual system "glues" raw sensations together in particular ways:

1. *Proximity.*   The closer objects or events are to one another, the more likely they are to be perceived as belonging together, as Figure 3.20(A) illustrates.

2. *Similarity.*   Similar elements are perceived to be part of a group, as in Figure 3.20(B). This is why students wearing the same school colors at a stadium will be perceived as belonging together even if they are not seated close together.

3. *Continuity.*   Sensations that appear to create a continuous form are perceived as belonging together, as in Figure 3.20(C).

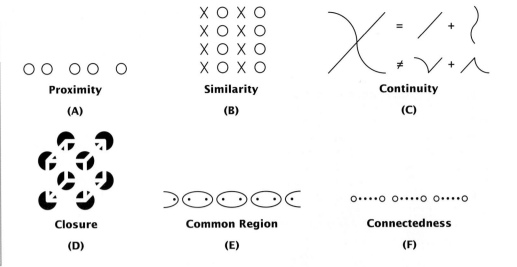

FIGURE **3.20**

Gestalt Principles of Perceptual Grouping

We tend to perceive Part A as two groups of two circles plus one single circle, rather than as, say, five circles. In Part B, we see two columns of Xs and two columns of Os, not four rows of XOXO. We see the X in Part C as being made out of two continuous lines, not a combination of the odd forms shown. In Part D, we fill gaps so as to perceive a hollow cube. In Part E, we tend to pair up dots in the same oval even though they are far apart. Part F shows that connected objects are grouped together.

4. *Closure.*   We tend to mentally "fill in" missing parts of incomplete objects, as in Figure 3.20(D). The gaps are easy to see, but the tendency to link disconnected parts can be so strong that you may perceive faint connections that are not actually there (Meng, Remus, & Tong, 2005).

5. *Texture.*   When basic features of stimuli have the same texture (such as the angle of several elements), we tend to group those stimuli together. So we group standing trees together and perceive them as separate from their fallen neighbors.

6. *Simplicity.*   We tend to group features of a stimulus in a way that provides the simplest interpretation of the world. You can see the simplicity principle in action in Figure 3.20(D), where it is simpler to see a single cube than an assortment of separate, unrelated arrows and Ys.

7. *Common fate.*   Sets of objects that move in the same direction at the same speed are perceived together. So a flock of birds, though separated in space, will be perceived as a group. Choreographers and marching-band directors use the principle of common fate when they arrange for groups or subgroups of dancers or musicians to move in unison, causing the audience to perceive waves of motion or a single large moving object.

Stephen Palmer (1999) has identified three additional grouping principles:

8. *Synchrony.*   Stimuli that occur at the same time are likely to be perceived as coming from the same source. For example, if you see a car up ahead stop violently at the same instant you hear a crash, you will probably perceive these visual and auditory stimuli as part of the same event.

9. *Common region.*   Stimuli located within some boundary tend to be grouped together. The boundary can be created by an enclosing perimeter, as in Figure 3.20(E), a region of color, or other factors.

10. *Connectedness.*   Stimuli that are connected by other elements tend to be grouped together. In Figure 3.20(F), the circles connected by dotted lines seem to go together even though they are farther apart than some pairs of unconnected circles. Here, the principle of connectedness appears more important than the principle of proximity.

Perception of Depth and Distance

We are able to experience the world in three-dimensional depth even though the visual information we receive from it is projected onto two-dimensional retinas. This is possible because of **depth perception,** our ability to perceive distance. Depth perception,

depth perception   Perception of distance, allowing us to experience the world in three dimensions.

FIGURE **3.21**

Stimulus Cues for Depth Perception

learn by doing　　See if you can identify the cues of relative size, interposition, linear perspective, height in the visual field, textural gradient, and shadows that combine to create a sense of three-dimensional depth in this photograph. Notice, too, that sidewalk artist Kurt Wenner has used some of these same cues to create a dramatic illusion of depth in his drawing. (You can see more of Wenner's amazing work at http://www.kurtwenner.com/street/.)

in turn, is made possible by *stimulus cues* provided by the environment and also by the properties of our visual system (Anderson, 2004).

Stimulus Cues　　To some extent, people perceive depth through the same cues that artists use to create the impression of depth and distance on a two-dimensional canvas. Figure 3.21 demonstrates several of these cues:

■ One of the most important depth cues is *interposition*: Closer objects block the view of things farther away. This cue is illustrated in Figure 3.21 by the couple walking away from the camera. Because their bodies block out part of the buildings, we perceive them as being closer to us than the buildings are.

■ You can see the principle of *relative size* operating in Figure 3.21 by measuring the images of that same couple and compare it to the size of the man in the foreground. If two objects are assumed to be about the same size, the object producing a larger image on the retina is perceived as closer than the one producing a smaller image.

■ Another cue comes from *height in the visual field:* On the ground, more-distant objects are usually higher in the visual field than those nearby. Because the building in the center of Figure 3.21 is higher than the people in the restaurant, the building appears to be farther away from you. This is one reason why objects higher in the visual field are more likely to be interpreted as the background for objects that are lower in a scene (Vecera, Vogel, & Woodman, 2002).

■ The tiny figures near the center of Figure 3.21 are seen as very far away because they are near a point where the buildings on each edge of the plaza, like all parallel lines

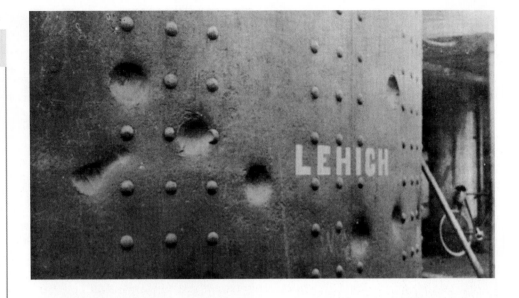

FIGURE **3.22**

Light, Shadow, and Depth Perception

~~learn~~
~~by doing~~ The shadows cast by these protruding rivets and deep dents make it easy to see them in three dimensions. But if you turn the book upside down, the rivets now look like dents, and the dents look like bumps. This reversal in depth perception occurs partly because people normally assume that illumination comes from above and interpret the pattern of light and shadow accordingly (Adams, Graf, & Ernst, 2004). With the picture upside down, light coming from the top would produce the observed pattern of shadows only if the circles were dents, not rivets.

that recede into the distance, appear to converge toward a single point. This apparent convergence provides a cue called *linear perspective.* The closer together two converging lines are, the greater the perceived distance.

■ Notice that the street in Figure 3.21 fades into a hazy background. Increased distance usually produces less clarity, and this *reduced clarity* is interpreted as a cue for greater distance. (Hazy, distant objects also tend to take on a bluish tone, which is why art students are taught to add a little blue when mixing paint for deep background features.)

■ *Light and shadow* also contribute to the perception of three dimensions (Kingdom, 2003; Ramachandran, 1988). The buildings in Figure 3.21 are seen as three-dimensional, not flat, because of the shadows on some of their surfaces. Figure 3.22 shows a more dramatic example.

■ An additional stimulus-based depth cue comes from continuous changes across the visual field, called *gradients.* For example, a *textural gradient* is a graduated change in the texture, or "grain," of the visual field, as you can see in the plaza and the street in Figure 3.21. Texture appears finer and less detailed as distance increases. So, as the texture of a surface changes across the retinal image, you perceive a change in distance.

Cues Based on Properties of the Visual System   Some depth cues result from the way human eyes are built and positioned. Recall that to bring an image into focus on the retina, the lens of the eye changes shape, or *accommodates.* Information about the muscle activity involved is relayed to the brain, and this *accommodation cue* helps create the perception of distance.

Two other depth cues are produced by the relative location of our two eyes. The first is **convergence.** Each eye is located at a different place on the skull, so the eyes must converge, or rotate inward, to project the same image on each retina. The closer the object, the more the eyes must converge. Eye muscles send information about this convergence to the brain, which processes it as a distance cue. You can experience this feedback from your eye muscles by holding up a finger at arm's length and then try to keep it in focus as you move it toward your nose.

Second, because they are in slightly different locations, each eye sees the world from a slightly different angle. The difference between these different retinal images is called **binocular disparity.** The difference, or disparity, between images gets smaller for objects that are far away and larger for objects that are nearby. The brain not only combines the two images of an object but also takes into account how much they differ. This information helps to generate the impression of a single object that has depth,

convergence   A depth cue resulting when the eyes rotate to project the image of an object on each retina.

binocular disparity   A depth cue based on the difference between the retinal images received by each eye.

A CASE OF DEPTH MISPERCEPTION
The runner in this photo is actually farther away than the man on the pitcher's mound. But because he is lower, not higher, in the visual field—and because his leg can be seen as in front of, not behind, the pitcher's leg—the runner appears smaller than normal rather than farther away.

looming A motion cue whereby rapid expansion in the size of an image fills the available space on the retina.

stroboscopic motion An illusion in which lights or images flashed in rapid succession are perceived as moving.

as well as height and width, and that is located at a particular distance. Three-dimensional movies and some virtual reality systems use binocular disparity cues to create the appearance of depth in a two-dimensional stimulus. They show each eye an image of a scene as viewed from a slightly different angle.

In short, many cues—some present in the environment and in retinal images, others arising from the structure of the visual system—combine to give us a powerful and accurate sense of depth and distance.

Perception of Motion

Sometimes the most important property of an object is its motion—how fast it is going and where it is heading. Many of the cues about motion come from *optical flow,* or the changes in retinal images across the entire visual field. As in the case of depth perception, you automatically translate this two-dimensional information into a three-dimensional experience. One particularly meaningful pattern of optical flow is known as **looming,** the rapid expansion in the size of an image so that it fills the retina. When an image looms, there is an automatic tendency to perceive it as an approaching object. If the expansion is as fast to the right as to the left, and as fast above as below, this information signals that the object is directly approaching the eyes. In other words: Duck!

We are lucky that movement of the retinal image is not the only factor contributing to motion perception. If it were, everything in sight would appear to move every time you moved your eyes and head (Ölveczky, Baccus, & Meister, 2003). This does not happen, because as noted earlier, the brain receives and processes information about the motion of the eyes and head (Wexler, 2005). If you look around the room right now, tables, chairs, and other stationary objects will not appear to move, because your brain determines that all the movement of images on your retinas is due to your eye and head movements (Goltz et al., 2003). But now close one eye, and wiggle your open eyeball by gently pushing your lower eyelid. Because your brain receives no signals that your eye is being moved by its own muscles, everything in the room will appear to move.

When your body is moving, as in a car, the flow of visual information across the retina combines with information from the vestibular and touch senses to give you the experience of being in motion. So if the car accelerates, you feel pressure from the back of the seat and feel your head tilting backward. If visual flow is perceived without appropriate sensations from other parts of the body, particularly the vestibular senses, motion sickness may result. This explains why you might feel nauseous while in a motion simulator or playing certain video games, especially those with virtual reality technology. The images suggest that you are moving through space when there is no real motion.

Other illusions of motion are more enjoyable. The most important of these occurs when still images appear, one at a time, in rapid succession, as they do on films, videos, and DVDs. Because each image differs slightly from the preceding one, the brain sees the objects in each image at one location for only a fraction of a second before they disappear and immediately reappear in a slightly different location. The entertaining result is the illusion of **stroboscopic motion;** when objects disappear and then quickly reappear nearby, the brain assumes that they have moved smoothly from one location to another. The same illusion is at work when it appears that flashing lights on a theater or casino sign are moving around the sign.

Perceptual Constancy

Suppose that one sunny day you are watching someone walking toward you along a tree-lined path. The visual sensations produced by this person are actually very strange. For one thing, the size of the image on your retinas keeps getting larger as the person gets closer. To see this for yourself, hold out a hand at arm's length and look at someone far away. The retinal image of that person will be so small that you can cover it with your hand. If you do the same thing when the person is three

BINOCULAR DISPARITY AND DISTANCE There is a smaller difference, or disparity, between each eye's view of an object when the object is far away than when it is close by. The amount of this binocular disparity helps us estimate the object's distance from us. To see for yourself how binocular disparity changes with distance, hold a pencil vertically about six inches in front of your nose; then close one eye and notice where the pencil is in relation to the background. Now open that eye, close the other one, and notice how much the pencil "shifts." These are the two different views your eyes have of the pencil. Repeat this procedure while holding the pencil at arm's length. Notice that there is now less disparity or "shift," because there is less difference in the angles from which your two eyes see the pencil.

feet away, the retinal image will be too large to be covered by your hand, yet you perceive the person as being closer now, not bigger. Similarly, as you watch the person pass from bright sunshine through the shadows of trees, your retinas receive images that shift back and forth from dark to light. Still, you perceive the person's coloring as staying the same.

These examples illustrate **perceptual constancy,** the perception that objects keep their size, shape, color, and other properties despite changes in their retinal image. Without this aspect of perception, you would experience the world as a place in which solid objects continuously changed their properties.

Size Constancy Why does an object's perceived size stay more or less constant, regardless of changes in the size of its retinal image? One reason is that the brain perceives a change in the distance of an object and automatically adjusts the perception of size. Specifically, the *perceived size* of an object is equal to the size of the retinal image multiplied by the perceived distance (Holway & Boring, 1941). As an object moves closer, the size of its retinal image increases, but the perceived distance decreases at the same rate. So the perceived size remains constant. If a balloon is inflated in front of your eyes, perceived distance remains constant, and the perceived size (correctly) increases as the size of the retinal image increases.

Shape Constancy The principles behind shape constancy are closely related to those of size constancy. To see shape constancy at work, remember what page you are on, close this book, and tilt it toward and away from you several times. The book will continue to look rectangular, even though the shape of its retinal image changes dramatically as you move it. Your brain automatically combines information about retinal images and distance as movement occurs. In this case, the distance information has to do with the difference in distance between the near and far edges of the book.

Brightness Constancy Even with dramatic changes in the amount of light striking an object, the object's perceived brightness remains relatively constant. To see this for yourself, place a piece of charcoal in sunlight and a piece of white paper in nearby shade. The charcoal will look very dark and the paper very bright, yet a light meter would tell you that much more light energy is reflected from the sun-bathed coal than from the shaded paper. The reason is partly that the charcoal is

perceptual constancy The perception of objects as retaining the same size, shape, color, and other properties despite changes in their retinal image.

A FAILURE OF SHAPE CONSTANCY
When certain stimuli are viewed from an extreme angle, the brain's ability to maintain shape constancy can break down. Traffic engineers take this phenomenon into account in the design of road markings, as shown in these photos from a London airport. The arrow in the top photo appears to be about the same height as the lettering below it, but it isn't. The arrow had to be greatly elongated, as shown in the side view, so that approaching drivers would see its shape clearly. If the arrow had been painted to match the height of the accompanying letters, it would appear "squashed," and only half as tall as the lettering.

the darkest object relative to its sunlit background and the paper is the brightest object relative to its background of shade. As shown in Figure 3.23, the brightness of an object is perceived in relation to its background.

Size Illusions

Usually, the visual perceptual system works automatically and perfectly to create correct impressions of depth, distance, and size. Sometimes, though, it can fail, resulting in *size illusions* such as the ones shown in Figure 3.24. Why does the monster that is placed higher in Figure 3.24(A) look larger than the lower one, even though they are exactly the same size? The converging lines in the tunnel provide depth cues telling you that the higher monster is farther away. Because the retinal image of the "distant"

FIGURE 3.23

Brightness Contrast

 At first glance, the inner rectangle on the left probably looks lighter than the inner rectangle on the right. But carefully examine the inner rectangles alone (covering their surroundings), and you will see that both are of equal intensity. The brighter surround in the right-hand figure leads you to perceive its inner rectangle as relatively darker.

FIGURE **3.24**

Three Size Illusions

learn by doing These illusions are named for the scientists who described them. In Part A, a version of the *Ponzo illusion,* the upper monster looks bigger but is actually the same size as the lower one. In the *Müller-Lyer illusion* (Part B), both vertical lines are actually of equal length; in the *Ebbinghaus illusion* shown in Part C, both center circles are exactly the same size. To prove that you can't always believe your eyes, measure these drawings for yourself.

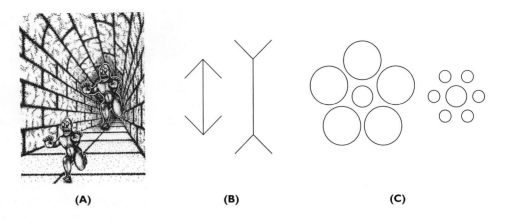

(A)   (B)   (C)

monster is the same size as the "closer" one, your perceptual system calculates that the more distant monster must be bigger. This is the principle of size constancy at work: When two objects have retinal images of the same size, you perceive the one that seems farther away as larger. Now look at Figure 3.24(B). The two vertical lines are the same length, but the one on the right looks longer. Why? One possible reason is that the perceived length of an object is based on what frames it. When the frame is perceived as larger, as on the right side of Figure 3.24(B), so is the line segment within it (Rock, 1978). In Figure 3.24(C), the inner circle at the left looks smaller than the one at the right because, like the brightness of the center rectangles in Figure 3.23, the inner circles are judged in relation to what surrounds them. Because perception is based on many principles, illusions like these probably reflect the violation of more than one of them. (See "In Review: Principles of Perceptual Organization and Constancy.")

in review

PRINCIPLES OF PERCEPTUAL ORGANIZATION AND CONSTANCY

Principle	Description	Example
Figure-ground	Certain objects or sounds automatically become identified as figure, whereas others become meaningless background.	You see a person standing against a building, not a building with a person-shaped hole in it.
Grouping	Properties of stimuli lead us to automatically group them together. These include proximity, similarity, continuity, closure, texture, simplicity, common fate, synchrony, common region, and connectedness.	People who are sitting together, or who are dressed similarly, are perceived as a group.
Depth perception	The world is perceived as three-dimensional, with help from stimulus cues (such as relative size, height in the visual field, interposition, linear perspective, reduced clarity, light and shadow, and gradients) and from visual system cues (such as accommodation, convergence, and binocular disparity).	A person who looks tiny and appears high in the visual field will be perceived as being of normal size, but at a great distance.
Perceptual constancy	Objects are perceived as constant in size, shape, color, and other properties despite changes in their retinal images.	A train coming toward you is perceived as getting closer, not larger; an advertising sign is perceived as rotating, not changing shape.

?
1. The movement we see in movies, videos, and DVDs is due to a perceptual illusion called _____.
2. People who have lost an eye also lose the depth cue called _____.
3. The grouping principle of _____ allows you to identify objects seen through a picket fence.

Recognizing the Perceptual World

► How do I recognize familiar people?

In discussing how people organize the perceptual world, we have set the stage for addressing one of the most vital questions that perception researchers must answer: How do we recognize what objects are? If you are driving in search of Barney's Diner, exactly what happens when your eyes finally locate the pattern of light that spells out its name?

To know that you have finally found what you have been looking for, your brain must analyze incoming patterns of information and compare them with information about the target that you have stored in memory. If the brain finds a match, recognition takes place. Once you recognize a stimulus as belonging to a particular category, your perception of the stimulus may never be the same again. Look at Figure 3.25. Do you see anything familiar? If not, turn to Figure 3.26; then look at Figure 3.25 again. You should now see it in an entirely new light. The difference between your "before" and "after" experiences is the difference between the sensory world before and after a perceptual match occurs and recognition takes place.

How does this matching process occur? Some aspects of recognition begin at the "top." That is, they are guided by knowledge, expectations, and other psychological factors. This phenomenon is called **top-down processing,** because it involves high-level, knowledge-based information. Other aspects of recognition begin at the "bottom," relying on specific, detailed information from the sensory receptors and assembling them into a whole. This phenomenon is called **bottom-up processing,** because it begins with basic information units that serve as a foundation for recognition.

Bottom-Up Processing

All along the path from the eye to the brain, certain cells respond to selected features of a stimulus. The stimulus is first analyzed into these *basic features,* which are then recombined to create the perceptual experience.

What are these features? As mentioned earlier, certain cells specialize in responding to lines, edges, corners, and stimuli having specific orientations in space (Hubel & Wiesel, 1979). For example, some cells in the cerebral cortex fire only in response to a diagonal line, so they act as *feature detectors* for diagonal lines. The analysis by such feature detectors, early in the sensation-perception sequence, may contribute to recognition

FIGURE **3.25**

Categorizing Perceptions

What do you see here? For the identity of this figure, turn to Figure 3.26.

top-down processing Aspects of recognition guided by higher level cognitive processes and psychological factors such as expectations.

bottom-up processing Aspects of recognition that depend first on information about stimuli that come up to the brain from the sensory systems.

of letters or judgments of shape. Color and motion are other sensory features that appear to be analyzed separately, in different parts of the brain, before full perceptual recognition takes place (Beatty, 1995; Cowey, 1994; Treisman, 1999).

The brain also apparently analyzes patterns of light and darkness in the visual scene. Analyzing these patterns may help us to perceive textural gradients, which in turn help us to judge depth and recognize the general shape of blurry images.

Top-Down Processing

Bottom-up feature analysis can explain why you recognize the letters in a sign for Barney's Diner. But why is it that you can recognize the sign more easily if it appears where you were told to expect it rather than a block earlier? And why can you recognize it even if a few letters are missing from the sign? Top-down processing seems to be at work in those cases. In top-down processing, people rely on their knowledge in making inferences, or "educated guesses," that help them recognize objects, words, or melodies, especially when sensory information is vague or ambiguous (DeWitt & Samuel, 1990; Rock, 1983). For example, once you knew that there was a dog in Figure 3.25, it became much easier for you to perceive one. Similarly, police officers find it easy to recognize familiar people on blurry security camera videos, but it is much more difficult for them to recognize strangers (Burton et al., 1999).

Top-down processing illustrates that our experiences create **schemas,** mental representations of what we know and expect about the world. Schemas can bias our perception toward one recognition or another by creating a *perceptual set*—that is, a readiness to perceive a stimulus in a certain way. A tragic example occurred several years ago in London when police shot a man who they were told was carrying a sawed-off shotgun. The object in his hand was actually a table leg, but it was dark, so when he raised his arm, they assumed he was about to fire at them.

Expectancy can be shaped by the *context* in which a stimulus occurs. For example, we know of a woman who saw a masked man in the darkened hallway of a house she was visiting. Her first perception was that the man who lived there was playing a joke; in fact, she had confronted a burglar. Context has biasing effects for sounds as well as sights. When shots are heard on a downtown street, they are often perceived as firecrackers or a car backfiring. The same sounds heard at a shooting range would immediately be interpreted as gunfire.

Motivation is another aspect of top-down processing that can affect perception. A hungry person, for example, might initially mistake a sign for "Burger's Body Shop" as

FIGURE **3.26**

Another Version of Figure 3.25

 Now that you can identify a dog in this figure, it should be much easier to recognize when you look back at the original version.

schemas Mental representations of what we know and expect about the world.

WHAT DOES IT LOOK LIKE TO YOU? Some people see the Devil's face in this photo of smoke from the World Trade Center under attack on September 11, 2001. This perception results partly from top-down processes, such as knowledge about the evil of the attack, that make it easier to see something demonic. People who don't expect to see a face in the smoke—or whose cultural background doesn't include the "devil" concept—may not see one until that interpretation is suggested. To check that possibility, show this photo to people from various religions and cultures (cover the caption). Ask if they see anything in the smoke, but don't immediately tell them what to look for. How many, and which ones, identified a demonic face before you mentioned it?

FIGURE **3.27**

Interaction of Top-Down and Bottom-Up Processing

Which obscured line do you find easier to read: the one on the top or the one on the bottom? Top-down processing should help you read the obscured text on the top line. However, in the bottom line, the words are not related, so top-down processing cannot operate.

indicating a place to eat. Similarly, perhaps you remember a time when an obviously incompetent referee incorrectly called a penalty on your favorite sports team. You knew the call was wrong because you clearly saw the other team's player at fault. But suppose you had been cheering for that other team. The chances are good that you would have seen the referee's call as the right one.

Top-Down and Bottom-Up Processing Together

Bottom-up and top-down processing usually work together to help us recognize the perceptual world. This interaction is beautifully illustrated by the process of reading. When the quality of the raw stimulus on the page is poor, as in Figure 3.27, top-down processes compensate to make continued reading possible. They allow you to fill in where words are not well perceived and processed, thus giving you a general idea of the meaning of the text.

You can fill in the gaps because the world is *redundant;* it provides multiple clues about what is going on. So even if you lose or miss one stimulus in a pattern, other clues can help you recognize the pattern. There is so much redundancy in written language, for instance, that many of the words and letters you see are not needed. Fo- exmp-e, y-u c-n r-ad -hi- se-te-ce -it- ev-ry -hi-d l-tt-r m-ss-ng. Similarly, vision in three dimensions normally provides multiple cues to depth, making recognition of distance easy and clear. It is when many of these cues are eliminated that ambiguous stimuli create the sorts of depth illusions discussed earlier.

In hearing, too, top-down processing can compensate for ambiguous stimuli. In one experiment, participants heard strings of five words in meaningless order, such as "wet brought who socks some." There was so much background noise, however, that only about 75 percent of the words could be recognized (Miller, Heise, & Lichten, 1951). The words were then read to a second group of participants in a meaningful order (e.g., "who brought some wet socks"). The second group was able to recognize almost all of the words, even under the same noisy conditions. In fact, it took twice as much noise to reduce their performance to the level of the first group. Why? When the words were in meaningless order, only bottom-up processing was available. Recognizing one word was no help in identifying the next. Meaningful sentences, however, provided a more familiar context and allowed for some top-down processing. Hearing one word helped the listener make a reasonable guess (based on knowledge and experience) about the others. (See "In Review: Mechanisms of Pattern Recognition" for a summary of bottom-up and top-down processing.)

Culture, Experience, and Perception

We have been talking as if all aspects of perception work or fail in the same way for everyone, everywhere. The truth is, though, that virtually all perceptual abilities are shaped to some extent by the sensory experiences we have or have not had (Kitayama et al., 2003). For example, people are better at judging the size and distance of familiar objects than of unfamiliar ones. Size and shape constancy, too, depend partly on the knowledge and experience that tell us that most solid objects do not suddenly change their size or shape. The experience-based nature of perception can also be seen in brightness constancy: You perceive charcoal to be darker than a sheet of writing paper partly because, no matter how much light the charcoal reflects, you *know* charcoal is black. Experience even teaches us when to ignore certain stimulus cues (Yang & Kubovy, 1999). To fully experience the depth portrayed in a painting, for example, you have to ignore ridges, scratches, dust, or other texture cues from the canvas that would remind you of its flatness. And the next

in review

MECHANISMS OF PATTERN RECOGNITION

Mechanism	Description	Example
Bottom-up processing	Raw sensations from the eye or the ear are analyzed into basic features, such as edges, color, or movement; these features are then recombined at higher brain centers, where they are compared with stored information about objects or sounds.	You recognize a dog as a dog because its features—four legs, barking, panting—match your perceptual category for "dog."
Top-down processing	Knowledge of the world and experience in perceiving allow people to make inferences about the identity of stimuli, even when the quality of raw sensory information is low.	On a dark night, a small, vaguely seen blob pulling on the end of a leash is recognized as a dog because the stimulus occurs at a location where we would expect a dog to be.

1. Your ability to read a battered old sign that has some letters missing is a result of _____ processing.
2. When stimulus features match the stimuli we are looking for, _____ takes place.
3. Schemas can create a _____ that makes us more likely to perceive stimuli in a particular way.

Source: Hudson (1960).

FIGURE **3.28**

Culture and Depth Cues

People in various cultures were shown drawings like these and asked to judge which animal is closer to the hunter. Those in cultures that provide lots of experience with pictured depth cues choose the antelope, which is at the same distance from the viewer as the hunter. Those in cultures less familiar with such cues may choose the elephant, which, though closer on the page, is more distant when depth cues are considered.

time you are watching TV, notice the reflections of objects in the room that appear on the screen. You have learned to ignore these reflections, so it will take a little effort to perceive them and a lot of effort to focus on them for long.

What if you hadn't had a chance to learn or practice these perceptual skills? One way to explore this question is through case studies of people who had been blind for decades and then had surgery that restored their sight. It turns out that these people can immediately recognize simple objects and perceive movement, but they usually have problems with other aspects of perception (Gregory, 2005). For example, M.M. had been blind from early childhood. When his vision was restored in his forties, he adjusted well overall, but he still has difficulty with depth perception and object recognition (Fine et al., 2003). Often, as people move toward or away from him, they appear to shrink or inflate. Identifying common objects can be difficult for him, and faces pose a particular challenge. To recognize individuals, he depends on features such as hair length or eyebrow shape. M.M. has trouble, too, distinguishing male faces from female ones and great difficulty recognizing the meaning of facial expressions. He is also unable to experience many of the perceptual illusions shown in this chapter, such as the closure illusion in Figure 3.20(D) or the size illusions in Figure 3.24.

For the rest of us, too, the ability to experience perceptual illusions depends on our sensory history. So people who grow up in significantly different sensory environments are likely to have noticeably different perceptual experiences. For example, the size illusion shown in Figure 3.24(A) is strongest in the "carpentered world," where seeing straight lines is an everyday experience (Leibowitz et al., 1969). Responses to illusions such as this one are not as strong for people from rural Africa and other places in which the visual environment contains more irregular and curved lines than straight ones (Coren & Girgus, 1978). Similarly, responses to depth cues in pictures and paintings differ in cultures that do and do not use such images to represent reality. People in the Me'n or the Nupa cultures of Africa, who have little experience with pictorial representation, have a more difficult time judging distances shown in pictures than do people in picture-oriented cultures (see Figure 3.28). These individuals also tend to have a harder time sorting pictures of three-dimensional objects into categories, even though they can easily sort the objects themselves (Derogowski, 1989). And residents of dense tropical rain forests, where most objects are seen over relatively short distances, may have some difficulty when asked to judge the distance of remote objects on an open plain (Turnbull, 1961). In other words, although the structure and principles of human perceptual systems tend to create generally similar views of the world for all of us, our perception of reality is also shaped by experience, including the experience of living in a particular culture (Chua, Boland, & Nisbett, 2005).

LINKAGES

How do infants perceive the world? (a link to Human Development)

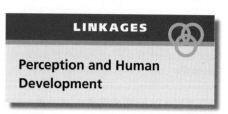

LINKAGES

Perception and Human Development

We have seen that perception is influenced by the knowledge and experience we gain over time, but what perceptual abilities do we start with? To learn about infants' perception, psychologists have studied two inborn patterns called *habituation* and *dishabituation*. Infants stop looking when they repeatedly see stimuli that they perceive to be the same. This is habituation. If they see a stimulus that is perceived to be new and different, they resume looking. This is dishabituation. Using the habituation/dishabituation technique, researchers have found that newborns can perceive differences in stimuli showing various amounts of black-and-white contrast but that they cannot yet distinguish differences between colors (Burr, Morrone, & Fiorentini, 1996). Other studies using the same methods have shown that newborns can perceive differences in the angles of lines (Slater et al., 1991). Taken together, these studies suggest that we are born with the basic components of feature detection.

Are we also born with the ability to combine features into perceptions of whole objects? This is still a matter of debate. We know that at one month of age, infants concentrate their gaze on one part of an object, such as the corner of a triangle (Goldstein, 2002). By two months, though, their eyes systematically scan around the edges of the object. This change suggests that they are now perceiving the pattern, or shape, of the object, not just its component features. However, other researchers have found that newborns show dishabituation (that is, they pay attention) when a familiar set of features are combined in a new way. So even newborns appear to notice and to keep track of the ways some stimulus features are put together (Slater et al., 1991).

Infants may also be innately tuned to perceive at least one important complex pattern of features: the human face. In one study of newborns, patterns such as those in Figure 3.29 were moved slowly past the infants' faces (Johnson et al., 1991). The infants moved their heads and eyes to follow these patterns. But they tracked the face-like pattern shown on the left side of Figure 3.29 significantly farther than any of the nonfaces. The difference in tracking in this study and others indicates that infants can tell faces from nonfaces and are more interested in faces, or at least in face-like patterns (Simion et al., 2003; Valenza et al., 1996). Why should this be? Investigators who take an evolutionary approach suggest that interest in human faces is adaptive because it helps newborns focus on their only source of food and care.

Other research on perceptual development suggests that our ability to accurately perceive depth and distance develops more slowly than our ability to recognize shapes (see Figure 3.30). For example, infants' ability to use binocular disparity and motion cues to judge depth appears to develop sometime after about three months of age. They do not use textural gradients and linear perspective as cues to depth until they are five to seven months old (Arterberry, Craton, & Yonas, 1993; Bhatt & Bertin, 2001).

FIGURE 3.29

Infants' Perceptions of Human Faces

Newborns show significantly greater interest in the face-like pattern at the far left than in any of the other patterns. Evidently, some aspects of face perception are innate.

Source: Johnson et al. (1991).

FIGURE **3.30**

FIGURE **3.30**

The Visual Cliff

The *visual cliff* is a glass-topped table that creates the impression of a sudden dropoff. A ten-month-old placed at what looks like the edge will calmly crawl across the shallow side to reach a parent but will hesitate and cry rather than crawl over the "cliff" (Gibson & Walk, 1960). Changes in heart rate show that infants too young to crawl also perceive the depth but are not frightened by it. Here is another example of the adaptive interaction of nature and nurture: Depth perception appears shortly after birth, but fear and avoidance of dangerous depth do not develop until an infant is old enough to crawl into trouble.

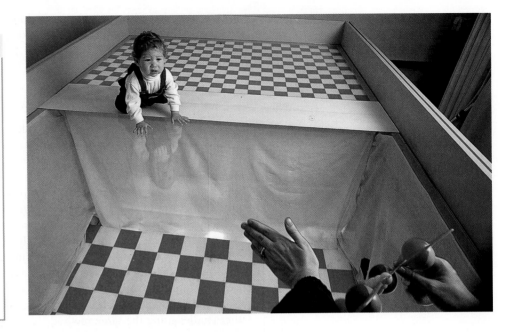

In summary, there is little doubt that many of the basic building blocks of perception are present within the first few days after birth. The basics include such organ-based cues to depth as accommodation and convergence. Maturation of the visual system adds to these basics as time goes by. Over the first few months after birth, the eye's fovea gradually develops the number of cone cells necessary for high visual acuity and perception of fine details (Goldstein, 2002). Visual experience is also necessary. Experience teaches the infant to recognize unified patterns and objects, to interpret depth and distance cues, and to use them in moving safely through the world (Johnson, 2005; Quinn & Bhatt, 2005). Like so many aspects of human psychology, perception is the result of a blending of heredity and environment. From infancy onward, the perceptual system creates a personal reality.

Attention

▶ **Can you run out of attention?**

Believe it or not, you still haven't found Barney's Diner! By now, you understand *how* you will recognize the right sign when you perceive it. But how can you be sure you *will* perceive it? The diner's sign will appear as one small piece of a sensory puzzle that also includes road signs, traffic lights, sirens, talk radio, and dozens of other stimuli. You can't perceive all of them at once. So, to find Barney's, you are going to have to be sure that the information you process includes the stimuli that will help you reach your goal. In short, you are going to have to pay attention.

Attention is the process of directing and focusing certain psychological resources to enhance perception, performance, and mental experience. We use attention to *direct* our sensory and perceptual systems toward certain stimuli, to *select* specific information for further processing, to *allocate* the mental energy required to do that processing, and to *regulate* the flow of resources necessary for performing a task or coordinating several tasks at once (Wickens & Carswell, 2006).

Psychologists have discovered three important characteristics of attention. First, it *improves mental processing.* You often need to concentrate attention on a task to do your best at it. Second, attention takes *effort.* Prolonged concentration of attention can leave

attention   The process of directing and focusing certain psychological resources to enhance perception.

you drained (McNay, McCarty, & Gold, 2001). When you are already tired, focusing attention on anything becomes more difficult. Third, attention is *limited*. When your attention is focused on reading this book, for instance, you will have less attention left over to listen to a conversation in the next room.

Directing Attention

learn by doing To experience the process of attention, try "moving it around" a bit. When you finish reading this sentence, look at something behind you, then face forward and notice the next sound you hear, then visualize your best friend, then focus on how your tongue feels. You just used attention to direct your perceptual systems toward different aspects of your external and internal environments. When you looked behind you, shifting attention involved *overt orienting*—pointing sensory systems at a particular stimulus. But you were able to shift attention to an image of your friend's face without having to move a muscle. This is called *covert orienting*. (We have heard a rumor that students sometimes use covert orienting to shift their attention from their lecturer to thoughts that have nothing to do with the lecture.)

How do you control, or allocate, your attention? Research shows that control over attention can be voluntary or involuntary (Yantis, 1993). *Voluntary*, or goal-directed, control over attention occurs when you purposely focus so that you can perform a task. Voluntary control reflects top-down processing, because attention is guided by knowledge-based factors such as intention, beliefs, expectations, and motivation. As people learn certain skills, they voluntarily direct their attention to information they once ignored. For example, the experienced driver notices events taking place farther down the road than the first-time driver does.

When some aspect of the environment—such as a loud noise—diverts your attention, control is said to be *involuntary*, or stimulus driven. Stimulus characteristics that tend to capture attention include abrupt changes in lighting or color (such as flashing signs), movement, and the appearance of unusual shapes (Folk, Remington, & Wright, 1994). Engineering psychologists' research on which stimuli are most likely to attract—and distract—attention has been used in the design of everything from Internet web sites and billboard ads to operator warning devices for airliners, nuclear power plants, and other complex systems (Clay, 2000; Laughery, 1999). Other psychologists use the results of attention research to help design advertisements, logos, and product packaging that "grab" potential customers' attention.

As already mentioned, attending to some stimuli makes us less able to attend to others. In other words, attention is *selective*. It is like a spotlight that can illuminate only a part of the external or internal environment at any particular moment. So if you focus intently on your reading or on a computer game, you may fail to perceive even dramatic changes in other parts of your environment. This phenomenon has been called *inattentional blindness* (Mack & Rock, 1998; Mack, 2003). In one study, a researcher asked college students for directions to a campus building (Simons & Ambinder, 2005). During each conversation, two "workmen" carrying a large door passed between the researcher and the student. As the door hid the researcher from the student's view, one of the "workmen" took his place. This new person then resumed the conversation with the student as though nothing had happened. Amazingly, only half of the students noticed that they were suddenly talking to a new person! The rest had apparently been paying so much attention to the researcher's question, or to the map he was showing, that they did not notice what he looked like. Magicians take advantage of inattentional blindness when they use sudden movements or other attention-grabbing stimuli to draw our attention away from the actions that lie behind their tricks.

Your search for Barney's Diner will be helped by your ability to overtly allocate attention to a certain part of the environment. It would be made even easier if Barney's had the only flashing sign on the road. As the most intense stimulus around you, it would attract your attention automatically. Psychologists describe this ability to search for targets rapidly and automatically as *parallel processing*. It is as if you can examine all nearby locations at once (in parallel) and rapidly detect the target no matter where it appears.

BLUE   GREEN

GREEN   ORANGE

PURPLE   ORANGE

GREEN   BLUE

RED   RED

GRAY   GRAY

RED   BLUE

BLUE   PURPLE

FIGURE **3.31**

The Stroop Task

learn
by doing

Look at this list of words and, as rapidly as possible, call out the *color of the ink* in which each word is printed. How did you do?

Online Study Center

Improve Your Grade
Tutorial: The Stroop Task

Dividing Attention

Often you can divide your attention efficiently enough to allow you to perform more than one activity at a time (Damos, 1992). You can drive a car, listen to the radio, sing along, and keep a beat by drumming on the steering wheel. However, your attention cannot be divided beyond a certain point without a loss in performance and mental-processing ability. The reason is that attention is a limited resource. If you try to spread it over too many targets, you "run out" of attention.

Still, it can sometimes be hard to keep your attention focused rather than divided. Look at the list of words in Figure 3.31 and, as rapidly as possible, call out the *color of the ink* in which each word is printed. This *Stroop task* (Stroop, 1935) is not easy, because your brain automatically processes the meanings of the familiar words in the list. These meanings then compete for attention with the responses you are supposed to give. To do well, you must focus on the ink color and not allow your attention to be divided between color and meaning. Children just learning to read have far less trouble with this task, because they don't yet process the meanings of words as automatically as experienced readers do.

Although you can walk while talking, or drive while listening to music, you would find it virtually impossible to read and talk at the same time. Why is it sometimes so easy and at other times so difficult to do two things at once? When one task is so automatic as to require little or no attention, it is usually easy to do something else at the same time (Schneider, 1985). Even when two tasks require attention, it may still be possible to perform them simultaneously if each taps into different kinds of attention (Wickens, 2002; Wickens et al., 1992). Some types of attention are devoted to perceiving incoming stimuli. Others handle making responses. This specialization of attention allows a skilled pianist to read musical notes and press keys simultaneously the first time through a piece. Apparently, the human brain can manage more than one type of attention and more than one spotlight of attention (Wickens, 1989). This notion of different types of attention also helps explain why an experienced driver can listen to the radio while steering safely. If two tasks require the same kind of attention, however, performance on both tasks will suffer (Just et al., 2001).

What happens in the brain as people try to attend to more than one source of information at the same time?

■ **What was the researchers' question?**

If directing attention to more than one task causes extra mental work to be done, there should be evidence of that work in brain activity. One possibility is that information-processing activity in the brain should slow down. Does it? This was the question asked by one research team.

■ **How did the researchers answer the question?**

Allan J. Nash and Mercedes Fernandez (1996) examined the brain processing speed of participants engaged in various tasks. Sixteen college students heard high and low tones and saw red and green light flashes. They were asked to respond as quickly as possible to the identified target stimulus. On some trials they were to ignore tones and respond only to one of the lights, and on other trials they were to respond to one light and keep a running count of one of the tones. In short, the participants either attended to one task (responding to a light) or split their attention between two tasks (responding to a light and counting tones). The speed of the participants' reactions to the flashing light was measured throughout the experiment.

■ **What did the researchers find?**

When attention had to be shared between information required for two tasks, reaction times were slower than they were in response to the single-attention task.

■ **What do the results mean?**

The finding that reaction times were slower on split-attention trials suggests that information processing in the brain was slower, too. Further evidence for this conclusion has been provided by positron emission tomography (PET) scans. They reveal increased blood flow to regions of the brain where mental processing is taking place (Corbetta et al., 1991; Just et al., 2001). When attention is focused on only one stimulus feature, increased blood flow appears only in the part of the brain in which that feature is analyzed. But when attention is divided, the added supply of blood is shared between two locations.

■ **What do we still need to know?**

Still to be determined are the limits of attention and processing; the means by which attention is shared; and the specific parts of the brain that are involved in attention, whether divided or undivided. Other research using PET scans, surgery on laboratory animals, and case studies of humans with brain damage has shown that switching the spotlight of visual attention involves at least three different parts of the brain (e.g., Braver, Reynolds, & Donaldson, 2003; Posner & Raichle, 1994). Attention appears to be a linked set of resources that improve mental processing at several levels and locations in the brain. No single brain region has yet been identified as an "attention center" (Posner & Peterson, 1990; Sasaki et al., 2001).

ACTIVE REVIEW | Sensation and Perception

Linkages

As noted in the introductory chapter, all of psychology's subfields are related to one another. Our discussion of the development of perception illustrates just one way in which the topic of this chapter, sensation and perception, is linked to the subfield of developmental psychology, which is described in the chapter on human development. The Linkages diagram shows ties to two other subfields, and there are many more ties throughout the book. Looking for linkages among subfields will help you see how they all fit together and help you better appreciate the big picture that is psychology.

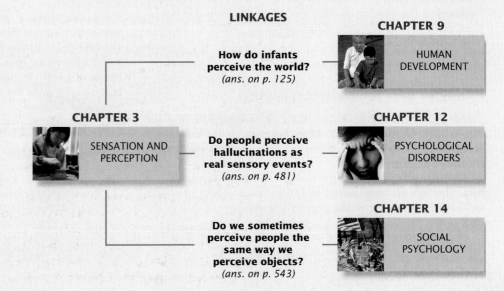

LINKAGES

CHAPTER 3
SENSATION AND PERCEPTION

How do infants perceive the world?
(ans. on p. 125)

CHAPTER 9
HUMAN DEVELOPMENT

Do people perceive hallucinations as real sensory events?
(ans. on p. 481)

CHAPTER 12
PSYCHOLOGICAL DISORDERS

Do we sometimes perceive people the same way we perceive objects?
(ans. on p. 543)

CHAPTER 14
SOCIAL PSYCHOLOGY

Summary

SENSING AND PERCEIVING THE WORLD

▶ **What is the difference between sensation and perception?**

A *sense* is a system that translates information from outside the nervous system into neural activity. Messages from the senses are called *sensations.* *Perception* is the process through which people actively use knowledge and understanding of the world to interpret sensations as meaningful experiences.

SENSORY SYSTEMS

▶ **How does information from my eyes and ears get to my brain?**

The first step in sensation involves *accessory structures,* which collect and modify sensory stimuli. The second step is *transduction,* the process of converting incoming energy into neural activity; it is accomplished by sensory *receptors,* neural cells specialized to detect energy of some type. *Adaptation* takes place when receptors receive unchanging stimulation. Except in the case of smell, neural activity is transferred through the thalamus, which relays it to the cerebral cortex.

Coding is the translation of physical properties of a stimulus into a pattern of neural activity that specifically identifies those physical properties. It is the language that the brain uses to describe sensations.

The minimum amount of light, sound, pressure, or other physical energy that can be detected 50 percent of the time is called the *absolute threshold.* *Internal noise* is the spontaneous, random firing of cells in the nervous system that occurs whether or not you are stimulated by physical energy. The *response criterion* reflects your willingness to respond to a stimulus or ignore it. *Signal-detection theory* addresses whether you will perceive a stimulus. *Sensitivity* refers to your ability to discriminate a stimulus from its background. *Weber's law* states that the smallest detectable difference in stimulus energy is a constant fraction of the intensity of the stimulus. This smallest detectable difference in a stimulus is called the difference threshold or *just-noticeable difference (JND).* *Wavelength* is the distance from one peak of a sound wave or light wave to the next. Wave *frequency* is the number of complete waves, or cycles, that pass a given point per unit of time. *Amplitude* is the height of the wave from baseline to peak.

SEEING

▶ **Why do some people need eyeglasses?**

Visible light is electromagnetic radiation with a wavelength of about 400 to about 750 nanometers. *Light intensity,* or the amount of energy in light, determines its brightness. Differing *light wavelengths* are sensed as different colors.

Accessory structures of the eye include the *cornea, pupil, iris,* and *lens.* Through *accommodation* and other means, these structures focus light rays on the *retina* (the net-like structure of cells at the back of the eye).

Photoreceptors in the retina—*rods* and *cones*—convert light into neural activity. Rods and cones differ in shape, sensitivity to light,

ability to discriminate colors, and distribution across the retina. Photoreceptors, especially rods, contribute to *dark adaptation.* The *fovea,* the area of highest acuity, has only cones, which are color sensitive. Rods are more sensitive to light but do not discriminate colors; they are distributed in areas around the fovea. From the photoreceptors, neural activity is transferred to bipolar cells and then to ganglion cells. A *blind spot* is created at the point where axons of ganglion cells leave the eye as a bundle of fibers called the *optic nerve.* Half of these fibers cross over at the optic chiasm. *Feature detectors* are cells in the cerebral cortex that respond to specific characteristics of objects in the visual field. The color of an object depends on which of the wavelengths striking it are absorbed and which are reflected. The sensation of color has three psychological dimensions: *hue, saturation,* and *brightness.*

According to the *trichromatic* (or Young-Helmholtz) *theory,* color vision results from the fact that the eye includes three types of cones, each of which is most sensitive to short, medium, or long wavelengths. Information from the three types combines to produce the sensation of color. According to the *opponent-process* (or Hering) *theory,* there are red-green, blue-yellow, and black-white visual elements, and the members of each pair inhibit each other so that only one member of a pair may produce a signal at a time. Opponent-process theory explains color afterimages.

HEARING

▶ **How would my voice sound on the moon?**

Sound is a repetitive fluctuation in the pressure of a medium such as air; it travels in waves. The frequency (which is related to wavelength) and amplitude of sound waves produce the psychological dimensions of *pitch* and *loudness,* respectively. *Timbre,* the quality of sound, depends on complex wave patterns added to the basic frequency of sound.

The energy from sound waves is collected and transmitted to the *cochlea* through a series of accessory structures, including the *pinna, eardrum,* hammer, anvil, stirrup, and oval window. Transduction occurs when sound energy stimulates hair cells on the *basilar membrane* of the cochlea, which in turn stimulate the *auditory nerve.* Auditory information is relayed through the thalamus to the primary auditory cortex.

The intensity of a sound stimulus is coded by the firing of auditory neurons. *Place theory* describes the coding of high frequencies. They are coded by the place on the basilar membrane at which the sound wave peaks. Each neuron in the auditory nerve is most sensitive to a specific frequency (its preferred frequency). According to *volley theory,* some frequencies may be matched by the firing rate of a group of neurons.

THE CHEMICAL SENSES: TASTE AND SMELL

▶ **Why can't I taste anything when I have a cold?**

The chemical senses include smell (olfaction) and taste (gustation). Our *sense of smell* detects volatile chemicals that come into contact with olfactory receptors in the nose. Olfactory signals are sent through the olfactory nerve to the *olfactory bulb* in the brain without passing through the thalamus. *Pheromones* are odors from one creature that change the physiology or behavior of another. Our *sense of taste* detects chemicals that come into contact with taste receptors in *papillae* in the mouth, especially on the tongue. The basic taste sensations are sweet, sour, bitter, salty, umami, and astringent. The senses of smell and taste interact to produce flavor.

SENSING YOUR BODY

▶ **Which is the largest organ in my body?**

The *somatic senses,* also called somatosensory systems, include the skin senses and the *proprioceptive* senses. The skin senses detect touch, temperature, and pain. When they are mechanically stimulated, nerve endings in the skin generate touch sensations. Some nerve endings are sensitive to temperature, and some respond to both temperature and touch.

Pain provides information about intense stimuli. Sharp pain is carried by A-delta fibers; dull, chronic pain is carried by C-fibers. The emotional response to pain depends on how the painful stimulus is interpreted. According to the *gate control theory,* pain signals can be blocked on their way to the brain, sometimes by messages sent from the brain down the spinal cord, resulting in *analgesia.* Endorphins act at several levels in pain systems to reduce sensations of pain.

The proprioceptive senses are *kinesthesia,* which provides information about the position of body parts with respect to one another, and the *vestibular sense* (balance), which provides information about the position of the head in space.

PERCEPTION

▶ **How do sensations become perceptions?**

Perception is the knowledge-based interpretation of sensations. Much of this interpretation takes place automatically, but sometimes conscious effort is required to translate sensations into meaningful experience.

ORGANIZING THE PERCEPTUAL WORLD

▶ **What determines how I perceive my world?**

Our perceptual systems automatically discriminate *figure* from *ground.* They also automatically group stimuli into patterns on the basis of the Gestalt principles of proximity, similarity, continuity, closure, texture, simplicity, common fate, and three others known as synchrony, common region, and connectedness.

The perception of distance, or *depth perception,* depends partly on stimulus cues and partly on the physical structure of the visual system. Stimulus cues include relative size, height in the visual field, interposition, linear perspective, reduced clarity, light and shadow, and textural gradients. Cues based on the structure of the visual system include *convergence* of the eyes (the fact that the eyes must move to focus on the same object), *binocular disparity* (the fact that the eyes are set slightly apart), and accommodation (changes in the shape of the lenses as objects are brought into focus).

The perception of motion results, in part, from the movement of stimuli across the retina. Expanding or *looming* stimulation is perceived as an approaching object. Movement of the retinal image is interpreted along with information about movement of the head, eyes, and other body parts, so that one's own movement can be discriminated from the movement of external objects. *Stroboscopic motion* is a movement illusion arising when a series of slightly different still images is seen in rapid succession.

Because of *perceptual constancy,* the brightness, size, and shape of objects are seen as constant despite changes in the sensations received from those objects. Size constancy and shape constancy depend on the relationship between the retinal image of the object and the knowledge-based perception of its distance. Brightness constancy depends on the perceived relationship between the brightness of an object and its background.

Size illusions are distortions of reality that result when principles of perception are applied inappropriately. Many illusions are caused by misreading depth cues and by evaluating stimuli in the context of their surroundings.

RECOGNIZING THE PERCEPTUAL WORLD

▶ **How do I recognize familiar people?**

Both *bottom-up processing* and *top-down processing* contribute to recognition of the world. The ability to recognize objects is based on finding a match between the pattern of sensations organized by the perceptual system and a pattern that is stored in memory. Bottom-up processing seems to be accomplished by the analysis of features, or combinations of features, such as form, color, motion, and depth. Top-down processing is influenced by expectancy and motivation. *Schemas* based on past experience can create a perceptual set, the readiness or predisposition to perceive stimuli in certain ways. Expectancies can also be created by the context in which a stimulus appears. Top-down and bottom-up processing commonly work together to create recognition. Top-down processing can fill in gaps in physical stimuli, in part because the environment provides redundant stimuli.

To the extent that the visual environments of people in different cultures differ, their perceptual experiences—and their responses to perceptual illusions—may differ as well.

The abilities to perceive color, basic shape features, and possibly the human face are present at or near birth. Other abilities, such as recognition of form, develop later. Depth, too, is perceived early, but its meaning is learned later. Perceptual abilities are modified by both experience and maturation.

ATTENTION

▶ **Can you run out of attention?**

Attention is the process of focusing psychological resources to enhance perception, performance, and mental experience. We can shift attention overtly (by moving the eyes, for example) or covertly (without any movement of sensory systems). Attention is selective; it is like a spotlight that illuminates different parts of the external environment or specific mental processes. Control over attention can be voluntary and knowledge based or involuntary and driven by environmental stimuli. People can sometimes attend to two tasks at once, but there are limits to how much they can divide their attention.

Learn by Doing

Put It in Writing

Which of your five sensory systems—vision, hearing, touch, taste, or smell—do you think you could most easily do without? Which could you least easily do without? Write a page describing why you chose each of these sensory systems and listing what you would do to try to make up for the loss of each of these two systems.

Personal Learning Activity

Have you ever noticed how large the moon appears to be when it has just risen above the horizon? Some researchers suggest that the moon appears larger on the horizon than overhead because the horizon moon—seen across a space filled with houses, trees, and terrain—appears to be farther away than when it is overhead (Kauf-

man & Kaufman, 2000). According to principles of size constancy discussed in this chapter, the greater perceived distance causes the horizon moon to be perceived as larger. This explanation has been questioned, though, because the horizon moon sometimes seems larger even when the observer cannot see the intervening terrain. The next time you see what appears to be a bigger-than-normal full moon just above the horizon, turn your back to it, and then bend over and look at the moon, upside down, between your legs. Does the so-called moon illusion remain, or is it destroyed when you look at the moon so that terrain appears above it rather than below it? What do you think causes the moon illusion? *For additional projects, see the Personal Learning Activities in the corresponding chapter of the study guide that accompanies this text.*

Step into Action

Courses

Sensation and Perception
Speech and Hearing
Biological Psychology
Vision
Artificial Intelligence

Movies

The Miracle Worker. The story of Helen Keller, who was both deaf and blind.

Home Before Dark. A thriller about a blind girl menaced by a killer.

Children of a Lesser God. Set in a school for the deaf.

At First Sight. Changes and problems that occur when a man, blind from birth, can suddenly see.

The Matrix. A futuristic film that raises the question, What is reality?

Rashomon. Focuses on a single event perceived in vastly different ways by different people.

The Five Senses. Main characters have heightened sensory powers.

Sound and Fury. Controversy over cochlear implants.

Books

Chandler Burr, *The Emperor of Scent* (Random House, 2003). About the perfume industry and a scientist who is testing a new theory of smell.

Richard Cytowic, *The Man Who Tasted Shapes* (MIT Press, 2003). About synesthesia, a condition in which senses are mixed.

Henry Grunwald, *Twilight: Losing Sight, Gaining Insight* (Knopf, 1999). Former editor-in-chief of *Time* writes about going blind.

Michael Posner and Marcus Raichle, *Images of Mind* (W. H. Freeman, 1997). Brain imaging.

Richard L. Gregory and J. Harris (Eds.), The *Artful Eye* (Oxford University Press, 1995). Visual perception.

Richard L. Gregory and Andrew M. Colman (Eds.), *Sensation and Perception* (Longman, 1995). The senses and psychophysics.

Oliver Sacks, *The Island of the Colorblind* (Knopf, 1997). About a Pacific island where colorblindness is common.

Oliver Sacks, *The Man Who Mistook His Wife for a Hat* (Touchstone Books, 1998). Descriptions of patients with sensory and perceptual disorders.

Oliver Sacks, *Seeing Voices: A Journey into the World of the Deaf* (Vintage, 2000). How deaf people experience the world.

Roger Shepard, *Mind Sights* (W. H. Freeman, 1990). Visual illusions, ambiguous figures.

J. Richard Block and Harold Yuker, *Can You Believe Your Eyes?* (Gardner Press, 1989). More illusions and visual oddities.

The Web

The World Wide Web is a good source of additional information about the science of psychology, provided you use it carefully and think critically about the information you find. The Online Study Center that accompanies this text offers many resources relevant to this chapter. These resources include interactive tutorials; Thinking Critically and Evaluating Research exercises; ACE chapter quizzes; recommended web links; and articles on current events, books, and movies. Please visit the Online Study Center at http://college.hmco.com/pic/bernstein4e.

Review of Key Terms

Can you define each of the key terms in the chapter? Check your definitions against those on the pages shown in parentheses in the following list or in the Glossary/Index at the end of the text.

absolute threshold (p. 87)
accessory structures (p. 86)
accommodation (p. 90)
adaptation (p. 87)
amplitude (p. 90)
analgesia (p. 108)
attention (p. 126)
auditory nerve (p. 100)
basilar membrane (p. 99)
binocular disparity (p. 116)
blind spot (p. 92)
bottom-up processing (p. 121)
brightness (p. 94)
cochlea (p. 99)
coding (p. 87)
cones (p. 92)
convergence (p. 116)
cornea (p. 90)
dark adaptation (p. 92)

depth perception (p. 114)
eardrum (p. 99)
feature detectors (p. 94)
figure (p. 113)
fovea (p. 92)
frequency (p. 89)
gate control theory (p. 108)
ground (p. 113)
hue (p. 94)
internal noise (p. 88)
iris (p. 90)
just-noticeable difference
 (JND) (p. 89)
kinesthesia (p. 110)
lens (p. 90)
light intensity (p. 90)
light wavelength (p. 90)
looming (p. 117)
loudness (p. 98)

olfactory bulb (p. 104)
opponent-process theory
 (p. 96)
optic nerve (p. 92)
papillae (p. 105)
perception (p. 86)
perceptual constancy (p. 118)
pheromones (p. 104)
photoreceptors (p. 92)
pinna (p. 99)
pitch (p. 99)
place theory (p. 101)
proprioceptive (p. 110)
pupil (p. 90)
receptors (p. 87)
response criterion (p. 88)
retina (p. 90)
rods (p. 92)
saturation (p. 94)

schemas (p. 122)
sensations (p. 86)
sense (p. 86)
sense of smell (p. 102)
sense of taste (p. 102)
sensitivity (p. 88)
signal-detection theory (p. 88)
somatic senses (p. 106)
sound (p. 98)
stroboscopic motion (p. 117)
timbre (p. 99)
top-down processing (p. 121)
transduction (p. 86)
trichromatic theory (p. 94)
vestibular sense (p. 111)
visible light (p. 90)
volley theory (p. 101)
wavelength (p. 89)
Weber's law (p. 89)

Multiple-Choice Self-Test

Select the best answer for each of the following questions. Then check your responses against the Answer Key at the end of the text.

1. Sandra reads English, but not Chinese. So when she looks at a Chinese newspaper, the process is _____. When she reads an English newspaper, the process is _____.

   a. sensation; perception
   b. perception; sensation
   c. perception; transduction
   d. sensation; transduction

2. As Jeremy listens to music on his iPod, sound waves are converted by his auditory system into neural signals. This process is called

   a. attention.
   b. transduction.
   c. adaptation.
   d. accommodation.

3. In an experiment, Dante raises his hand each time he hears a tone through a set of headphones. The tone gets quieter and quieter until he fails to hear it half the time. After repeating the same procedure many times, the researcher ends the experiment, because she has found Dante's

   a. absolute threshold.
   b. difference threshold.
   c. internal noise.
   d. response criterion.

4. Jane is told that she will be paid $100 for each needle she can find in a haystack. According to signal detection theory, this information should _____ Jane's _____.

   a. raise; response criterion
   b. lower; response criterion
   c. raise; sensitivity
   d. lower; sensitivity

5. Matt finishes his can of soda as he walks across campus with Brad and Andy, and now he wants to slip the empty can into one of their open backpacks. Brad's pack has several heavy textbooks in it; Andy's contains only a notebook. Weber's law suggests that, to avoid detection, Matt should put the can in _____ pack because the change in weight will be _____ than a just-noticeable difference.

   a. Andy's; less
   b. Brad's; less
   c. Andy's; more
   d. Brad's; more

6. Bianca wants Bruce to see the distant star she wishes on every night. Because it is so faint, to have him see the star she should have him look

   a. directly at the star.
   b. slightly away from where the star is expected to be.
   c. at the star's reflection in a mirror.
   d. at the star when there is a full moon.

7. A projection-screen TV aims green, red, and blue lights at a screen. Because the TV can show a full range of colors by combining the green, red, and blue lights in differing amounts, it best illustrates the _____ theory of color vision.

   a. convergence
   b. frequency-matching
   c. opponent-process
   d. trichromatic

8. When Sarah stubbed her toe, she immediately began to rub it. According to the gate control theory, the rubbing

   a. created sensations that "took over" the pain pathways.
   b. released serotonin.
   c. created an increase in pain tolerance.
   d. shut down the brain's pain-sensing mechanisms.

9. Mick has been a rock musician for forty years. The constant loud noise from his band has caused hair cell damage, literally ripping off hair cells from his inner ear. We would expect that Mick now has

   a. extremely acute hearing.
   b. conduction deafness.
   c. nerve deafness.
   d. normal hearing loss for someone his age.

10. Jeremy developed a disease that destroyed his thalamus. The only sense that was unaffected was

    a. vision.
    b. hearing.
    c. touch.
    d. smell.

11. Your blindspot is located

    a. where the optic nerve leaves the eye.
    b. where visual fibers cross at the optic chiasm.
    c. in the center of the fovea.
    d. where accommodation takes place.

12. In cooking school, Natalie studied flavor. She learned that the flavor of food can be altered by

    a. nutritional state.
    b. changing its temperature.
    c. changing its color.
    d. both a and b.

13. Andrea cannot yet read, but Lorraine can. They are each shown a list of color names (e.g., blue, red, yellow) on which each word is printed in a color that doesn't match the word. They are asked to say the color of the ink each word is printed in, not the word itself. _____ will do better at this Stroop task because _____

    a. Andrea; she can use top-down processing.
    b. Lorraine; she is older.
    c. Andrea; she will not be distracted by word meanings.
    d. Lorraine; word meaning will help focus on the ink color.

14. Ally has lost her kinesthetic sense. She will most likely be unable to

    a. know that her hand is raised without looking at it.
    b. identify the flavor of her ice cream cone.
    c. feel the warmth of the sun on her face.
    d. feel pain.

15. Shanelle likes the lights that appear to race around her Christmas tree as they flash on and off in sequence. This illusion is known as

    a. the motion parallax.
    b. stroboscopic motion.
    c. dishabituation.
    d. texture gradient.

16. Four swimmers practicing their synchronized swimming routine are perceived as a group because they are performing the same movements at the same speed. This is an example of

    a. synchrony.   c. orientation.
    b. common fate.   d. interposition.

17. When you perceive an object as being closer to you because it blocks out part of the background, you are using the depth cue called

    a. linear perspective.   c. interposition.
    b. reduced clarity.   d. movement gradient.

18. As Cliff walks out his front door, he sees a snowball coming straight at him. The retinal image of the snowball is increasing, and he realizes that the snowball is approaching, not getting larger. This example illustrates

    a. induced motion.
    b. looming.
    c. the movement gradient.
    d. stroboscopic motion.

19. Jeff and Larry were making chili. Jeff tasted the chili and thought it was perfectly seasoned. Then, while Jeff's back was turned, Larry added some more salt. When they sat down to eat Jeff immediately said the chili was too salty. Because he didn't know about the added salt, Jeff's perception must have been based on

    a. top-down processing.
    b. bottom-up processing.
    c. pattern recognition.
    d. selective attention.

20. Although José appears to be listening as Rich talks about his new clothes, vacation plans, and exercise routine, José is thinking about the list of errands he has to run. José is

    a. covertly orienting.
    b. overtly orienting.
    c. using parallel distributed processing.
    d. using serial processing.

4

Consciousness

Have you ever "spaced out" while driving on a boring highway? Has your mind wandered

far and wide during a dull lecture? These experiences contrast sharply with how it feels to focus your attention on playing a video game or to concentrate on a complicated recipe, but all of them represent differing versions of consciousness. In this chapter, we delve into both "normal" and altered states of consciousness. Most of the altered states—sleep, dreaming, hypnosis, meditation—differ psychologically and physiologically from normal waking consciousness. We examine how they differ, and we look at the effects of psychoactive drugs, which, in addition to altering consciousness, have complex physiological effects.

Reading this chapter will help you to answer the following questions:

▶ **Can unconscious thoughts affect your behavior? 137**

▶ **Does your brain go to sleep when you do? 144**

▶ **Can you be hypnotized against your will? 152**

▶ **How do drugs affect the brain? 155**

KEEPING AN EYE OUT Humans are not the only creatures capable of processing information while apparently unconscious. While ducks sleep, one hemisphere of their brains can process visual information from an eye that remains open. Birds positioned where they are most vulnerable to predators, such as at the end of a row, may spend twice as much time in this "alert" sleep than do birds in more protected positions (Rattenborg, Lima, & Amlaner, 1999).

There is an old *Sesame Street* episode in which Ernie is trying to find out whether Bert is asleep or awake. In other words, Ernie is trying to determine Bert's state of consciousness. Ernie observes that Bert's eyes are closed, and he comments that Bert usually closes his eyes when he is asleep. Ernie also notes that when Bert is asleep, he does not respond to pokes, so naturally, he delivers a few pokes. At first, Bert does not respond; but after being poked a few times, he awakes, very annoyed, and yells at Ernie for waking him. Ernie then informs Bert that he just wanted to let him know it was time for his nap.

Doctors face a similar situation in dealing with the more than 30 million people each year who receive general anesthesia during surgery. All these patients certainly appear to go to sleep, but there is no reliable way of knowing whether they are actually unconscious. It turns out that about two people in a thousand retain some degree of consciousness during the surgical procedure (Ekman et al., 2004; Sigalovsky, 2003). In rare cases, patients have conscious awareness of pain and remember the trauma. Although their surgical wounds heal, these people may be psychologically scarred by the experience and may even show symptoms of posttraumatic stress disorder (Schwender et al., 1995).

The fact that people can be conscious while "asleep" under the influence of powerful anesthetic drugs makes defining consciousness quite difficult (Edelman, 2003). In fact, after decades of discussion and research by philosophers, psychologists, and even physicists, some believe that consciousness is still not yet understood well enough to be precisely defined (Crick & Koch, 1998; King & Pribram, 1995). Given the ethical and legal concerns raised by the need to ensure that patients are not subjected to pain during surgery, doctors tend to define *consciousness* as awareness that is demonstrated by any ability to recall an experience (Schwender et al., 1995). In psychology, the definition

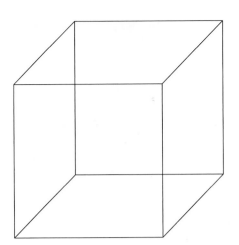

F I G U R E **4 . 1**

The Necker Cube

learn **by doing** Each of the two squares in the Necker cube can be perceived as either the front or rear surface of the cube. Try to make the cube switch back and forth between these two orientations. Now try to hold only one orientation. You probably cannot maintain the whole cube in consciousness for longer than about three seconds before it "flips" from one orientation to the other.

is somewhat broader: **Consciousness** is generally defined as your awareness of the outside world and of your mental processes, thoughts, feelings, and perceptions (Metzinger, 2000; Zeman, 2001). Let's see how this definition applies as we explore the scope of consciousness and various states of consciousness.

The Scope of Consciousness

▶ **Can unconscious thoughts affect your behavior?**

Mental activity changes constantly. The features of consciousness at any instant—what reaches your awareness, the decisions you are making, and so on—make up what is called your **state of consciousness** at that moment (Tassi & Muzet, 2001). Possible states include coma, deep sleep, hypnosis, meditation, daydreaming, and alert wakefulness. Consciousness can also be altered by drugs and other influences.

States of Consciousness

States of consciousness can be viewed as different points along a scale or continuum of consciousness. For example, suppose you were aboard an airliner flying from New York to Los Angeles. The pilot calmly scans instrument displays while talking to an air-traffic controller. In the seat next to you, a lawyer finishes her second cocktail while planning a courtroom strategy. Across the aisle, a young father gazes out the window, daydreaming, while his small daughter sleeps in his lap, dreaming dreams of her own. All these people are experiencing different states of consciousness. Some states are active, and some are passive. The daydreaming father lets his mind wander, passively noticing images, memories, and other mental events that come to mind. Like the pilot, the lawyer actively directs her mental processes. In her case, though, as she evaluates various options and considers their likely outcomes, she is altering her state of consciousness by sipping alcohol.

Generally, people spend most of their time in a *waking* state of consciousness. Mental processing in this state varies with changes in attention or arousal (Taylor, 2002). While reading, for example, you may temporarily ignore sounds around you. Similarly, if you are upset or bored or talking on a cell phone, you may tune out important cues from the environment, making it dangerous to perform complex activities such as driving a car.

Levels of Consciousness

The events and mental processes that you are aware of at any given moment are said to exist at the **conscious level.** For example, look at the Necker cube in Figure 4.1. If you are like most people, you can hold the cube in one orientation for only a few seconds before the other version "pops out" at you. The version that you experience at any moment is at your conscious level of awareness for that moment.

Some events, however, cannot be experienced consciously. For example, you are not directly aware of your brain regulating your blood pressure. Such mental processing occurs at the **nonconscious level,** totally removed from conscious awareness. Some people can learn to alter a nonconscious process through *biofeedback training*. In this training, you receive information about your biological processes and try to change them. Usually, special equipment is required, but you can approximate a biofeedback session by having a friend take your pulse at one-minute intervals while you sit quietly. First, establish a baseline pulse; then imagine a peaceful scene, or think about lowering your pulse rate. Then ask your friend to softly say whether your pulse is higher or lower compared with the baseline. After four or five minutes of having this information "fed back" to you, you will probably be able to keep your pulse below the original baseline. Yet the pulse-regulating processes themselves remain out of consciousness.

consciousness The awareness of external stimuli and our own mental activity

state of consciousness The characteristics of consciousness at any particular moment.

conscious level The level of consciousness at which mental activities accessible to awareness occur.

nonconscious level The level of consciousness at which reside processes that are totally inaccessible to conscious awareness.

Research shows that some surgery patients can hear, and later comply with, instructions or suggestions given while they were under anesthesia, even though they have no memory of what they were told (Bennett, Giannini, & Davis, 1985). Another study found that people have physiological responses to emotionally charged words even when they are not paying attention to them (Von Wright, Anderson, & Stenman, 1975). These and other similar studies provide evidence for the operation of subconscious mental processing (Deeprose & Andrade, 2006).

BLOOM COUNTY   **by Berke Breathed**

Permission granted by International Creative Management Inc. Copyright © 1996 by Burke Breathed. Cartoon first appeared in *The Washington Post.*

Some mental events are not conscious but can become conscious, or can influence conscious experience. These mental events make up the *cognitive unconscious* (Reber, 1992), which includes the preconscious and the subconscious. Mental events that are outside awareness but that can easily be brought into awareness are said to exist at the **preconscious level.** What did you have for dinner last night? The information you needed to answer this question was probably not already in your conscious awareness, but it was at the preconscious level. So when you read the question, you could answer it immediately. Similarly, when you play trivia games, you draw on your large storehouse of preconscious memories to come up with obscure facts.

Other mental activities can alter thoughts, feelings, and actions but are more difficult to bring into awareness (Ratner, 1994). Sigmund Freud suggested that these **unconscious** activities, especially those involving unacceptable sexual and aggressive urges, are actively kept out of consciousness. Most psychologists do not accept Freud's view, but they still use the term *unconscious,* or **subconscious,** to describe mental activity that influences us in various ways but that occurs outside of awareness (Dijksterhuis & Nordgren, 2006.

Mental Processing Without Awareness

A fascinating demonstration of mental processing without awareness was provided by an experiment with patients who had surgery under general anesthesia. After their operations, but while the patients were still unconscious from the anesthesia, an audiotape of fifteen word pairs was played over and over for them in the recovery room. After regaining consciousness, the patients could not say what words were on the tape or even whether a tape had been played at all. However, when given one word from each of the word pairs and asked to say the first word that came to mind, the patients were able to come up with the other member of the word pair from the tape (Cork, Kihlstrom, & Hameroff, 1992).

Even when conscious and alert, you can sometimes process and use information without being aware of it (Gaillard et al., 2006). In one study, participants watched a computer screen as an X flashed in one of four locations. The task was to indicate where the X appeared. The X's location seemed to vary randomly but was actually determined by a set of complex rules. (One such rule was "If the X moves horizontally twice in a row, its next move will be vertical.") Participants' responses became progressively faster and more accurate. Then, unknown to the participants, the rules were abandoned, and the X appeared in *truly* random locations. Participants' accuracy and speed deteriorated instantly. Apparently, the participants had learned the rules without being aware of them and had applied them to improve their performance. However, even when offered $100 to state the rules that had guided the location sequence, they could not do so, nor were they sure that any such rules existed (Lewicki, 1992).

Visual processing without awareness may even occur in certain cases of blindness. When blindness is caused by damage only to the brain's primary visual cortex, pathways from the eyes are still connected to other brain areas that process visual information. Some of these surviving connections may permit visual processing, but without

preconscious level The level of consciousness at which reside mental events that are not currently conscious but can become conscious at will.

unconscious The term used to describe a level of mental activity said by Freud to contain unacceptable sexual, aggressive, and other impulses of which an individual is unaware.

subconscious Another term describing the mental level at which influential, but normally inaccessible, mental processes take place.

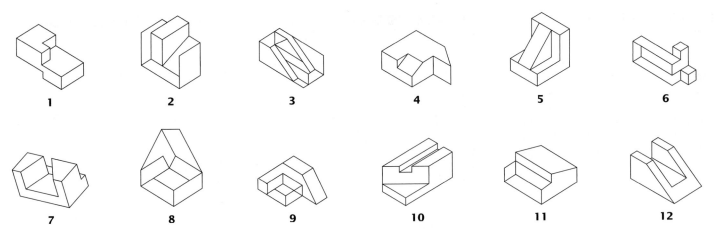

Source: Schacter et al. (1991).

FIGURE **4.2**

Stimuli Used in a Priming Experiment

learn by doing Look at these figures and decide, as quickly as you can, whether each can actually exist. Priming studies show that this task would be easier for figures you have seen in the past, even if you don't recall seeing them. How did you do? The correct answers appear on page 141.

Online Study Center

Improve Your Grade
Tutorial: Priming

visual awareness—a condition known as *blindsight* (Ro et al., 2004; Weiskrantz, 2004). So though patients say they see nothing, if forced to guess, they can still locate visual targets, identify the direction of moving images, reach for objects, name the color of lights, and even discriminate happy from fearful faces (Morris et al., 2001). The same blindsight phenomenon has recently been created in visually normal volunteers using magnetic brain stimulation to temporarily disable the primary visual cortex (Boyer, Harrison, & Ro, 2005; Jolij & Lamme, 2005).

Research on *priming* also demonstrates mental processing without awareness (e.g., Naccache et al., 2005). In a typical priming study, people tend to respond faster or more accurately to stimuli they have seen before. This is true even when they cannot consciously recall having seen those stimuli (Arndt et al., 1997; Bar & Biederman, 1998; Kouider & Dupoux, 2005). In one study, for example, people looked at figures like those in Figure 4.2. They had to decide which figures could actually exist in three-dimensional space and which could not. The participants were better at classifying pictures they had seen before, even when they could not remember having seen them (Schacter et al., 1991).

There is even evidence that some of the decisions and choices we make in everyday life may be guided to some extent by mental processes that occur without our awareness (Dijksterhuis et al., 2006; Myers, 2004). For example, your "lucky" choice of the fastest moving supermarket checkout line might seem to have been based on nothing more than a "hunch," a "gut feeling," or intuition, but previous visits to that store might have given you useful information about the various clerks that you didn't know you had (Adolphs et al., 2005). In a laboratory study that supports this notion, people watched videotaped television commercials while the changing stock prices of fictional companies "crawled" across the bottom of the screen. Later, these people were asked to choose which of these companies they liked best. They couldn't recall anything they had seen about the companies' stock, so they had to make their choice on the basis of their "gut reaction" to the company names. Nevertheless, their choices were not random; they more often chose companies whose stock prices had been rising rather than those whose stock had been falling (Betch et al., 2003).

The research we have described suggests that we don't always have to be aware of information in order for it to affect us (Hassin, Uleman, & Bargh, 2004), but how strong can this influence be? In 1957, an adman named James Vicary claimed that a New Jersey theater flashed messages such as "buy popcorn" and "drink Coke" on a movie screen, too briefly to be noticed, while customers watched the movie *Picnic.*

THINKING CRITICALLY

Can Subliminal Messages Change Your Behavior?

He said that these messages caused a 15 percent rise in sales of Coca-Cola and a 58 percent increase in popcorn sales. Can messages perceived at a *subliminal* level—that is, below conscious awareness—act as a form of "mind control"? Many people seem to think so. Each year, they spend millions of dollars on audiotapes, CDs, and videos whose subliminal messages are supposed to help people lose weight, raise self-esteem, quit smoking, make more money, or achieve other goals.

■ What am I being asked to believe or accept?

Two types of claims have been made about subliminal stimuli. The more general one is that subliminal stimuli can influence our behavior. The second, more specific claim is that subliminal stimuli provide an effective means of changing people's buying habits, political opinions, self-confidence, and other complex attitudes and behaviors, with or without their awareness or consent.

■ Is there evidence available to support the claim?

Evidence that subliminal messages can affect conscious judgments comes in part from laboratory studies that present visual stimuli too briefly to be perceived consciously. In one such study, participants saw slides showing people performing ordinary acts such as washing dishes. Unknown to the participants, each slide was preceded by a subliminal exposure to a photo of "positive" stimuli (such as a child playing) or "negative" stimuli (such as a monster). Later, participants rated the people on the visible slides as more likable, polite, friendly, successful, and reputable when their images had been preceded by a positive subliminal photo (Krosnick et al., 1992). The subliminal photos not only affected participants' liking of the people they saw but also shaped beliefs about their personalities.

In another study, participants were exposed to subliminal presentations of slides showing snakes, spiders, flowers, and mushrooms. Even though the slides were impossible to perceive at a conscious level, participants who were afraid of snakes or spiders showed physiological arousal (and reported feeling fear) in response to slides of snakes and spiders (Öhman & Soares, 1994).

The results of studies such as these support the notion that subliminal information can have an impact on judgments and emotion, but they say little or nothing about the value of subliminal tapes for achieving self-help goals. In fact, no laboratory evidence exists to support the effectiveness of these tapes. Their promoters offer only the reports of satisfied customers.

■ Can that evidence be interpreted another way?

Many claims for subliminal advertising—including the New Jersey movie theater case—have turned out to be publicity stunts using phony data (Haberstroh, 1995; Pratkanis, 1992). And testimonials from satisfied customers could be biased by what these people would like to believe about the subliminal tapes they bought. In one study designed to test this possibility, half the participants were told that they would be listening to tapes containing subliminal messages for improving memory. The rest were told that the subliminal messages would promote self-esteem. However, half the participants in the memory group actually got self-esteem messages, and half of the self-esteem group actually got memory messages. Regardless of which version they received, participants who thought they had heard memory enhancement messages reported improved memory; those who thought they had received self-esteem messages said their self-esteem had improved (Pratkanis, Eskenazi, & Greenwald, 1994). In other words, the effects of the tapes were determined by the listeners' expectations, not by the tapes' subliminal content. These results suggest that customers' reports about the value of subliminal self-help tapes may reflect placebo effects based on optimistic expectations rather than the effects of subliminal messages.

■ **What evidence would help to evaluate the alternatives?**

The effectiveness of self-help tapes and other subliminal products must be evaluated through further experiments, such as the one just mentioned, that carefully control for expectations. Those who support and sell subliminal influence methods are responsible for conducting those experiments, but as long as customers are willing to buy subliminal products on the basis of testimonials alone, scientific evaluation efforts will probably come only from those interested in protecting consumers from fraud.

■ **What conclusions are most reasonable?**

The available evidence suggests that subliminal perception occurs but that it has no potential for "mind control" (Greenwald, Klinger, & Schuh, 1995). Subliminal effects are usually small and short-lived, and they mainly affect simple judgments and general measures of overall arousal. As for subliminal messages aimed at long-term behavior change, most researchers agree that such messages have no special power to create needs, goals, skills, or actions (Pratkanis, 1992). In fact, advertisements, political speeches, and other messages that we *can* perceive consciously have far stronger persuasive effects.

FOCUS ON RESEARCH

Subliminal Messages in Rock Music

Would the persuasive power of subliminal messages be increased if they were presented at normal speed but in reverse, so that we could not consciously understand them? According to numerous Internet web sites, this is exactly how satanic or drug-related messages have been hidden in the recorded music of rock bands such as Marilyn Manson, Nine Inch Nails, Judas Priest, Led Zeppelin, and the Rolling Stones. These alleged "backmasked" subliminal messages are said to have influenced listeners to commit suicide or murder. For this claim to be true, however, the subliminal backward message would have to be perceived at some level of consciousness.

■ **What was the researchers' question?**

There is no good evidence that backward messages are actually present in most of the music cited. However, John R. Vokey and J. Don Read (1985) asked whether any backward messages that might exist could be perceived and understood while the music was playing forward. They also asked whether such a message, if perceived at all, would have any effect on the listener's behavior.

■ **How did the researchers answer the question?**

First, Vokey and Read made tape recordings of a person reading portions of the Twenty-third Psalm and Lewis Carroll's poem "Jabberwocky." This poem includes many nonsense words, but it follows the rules of grammar (e.g., "'Twas brillig, and the slithy toves . . ."). These recordings were then played backward to college students, who were asked to judge whether what they heard would have been meaningful or nonsensical if played forward.

■ **What did the researchers find?**

When the students heard the readings being played backward, they could not discriminate sense from nonsense. Nor could they tell the difference between declarative sentences and questions. They could not even identify the original material on which the recordings were based. In short, the participants could not understand the backward

Answer key to Figure 4.2: Figures 1, 4, 5, 7, 10, and 12 can exist in three dimensional space.

SUBLIMINAL MESSAGES IN ROCK MUSIC? These picketers are protesting at the site of a Marilyn Manson concert. Some people claim that Manson's music, as well as that of rock stars ranging from Michael Jackson to Madonna, contains subliminal messages advocating drug use, violence, and Satanism.

messages at a conscious level. Could they do so subconsciously? To find out, the researchers asked the participants to sort the backward statements they heard into one of five categories: nursery rhymes, Christian, satanic, pornographic, or advertising. They reasoned that if some sort of meaning could be subconsciously understood, the participants would be able to sort the statements nonrandomly. As it turned out, however, the participants did no better at this task than random chance would predict.

Perhaps backward messages might influence people's behavior even if the messages were not perceived consciously. To check on this possibility, Vokey and Read (1985) conducted another study. This time, they presented a backward version of a message whose sentences contained homophones (words that sound alike but have two spellings and two different meanings, such as *feat* and *feet*). When heard in the normal forward direction, such messages affect people's spelling of ambiguous words that are read aloud to them at a later time. (For example, they tend to spell out *f-e-a-t* rather than *f-e-e-t* if they had previously heard the sentence "It was a great feat of strength.") This example of priming occurs even if people do not recall having heard the message. After hearing a *backward* version of the message, however, the participants in this study did not produce the expected spelling bias.

■ What do the results mean?

Obviously, it wasn't possible for the participants to subconsciously understand meaning in the backward messages. Backward messages are evidently not consciously or unconsciously understood, nor do they influence behavior (Vokey, 2002).

■ What do we still need to know?

Researchers would like to understand why the incorrect idea persists that backward messages can influence behavior. Beliefs and suspicions do not simply disappear in the face of contrary scientific evidence (Sagan, 1996; Vyse, 2000; Winer et al., 2002). Perhaps such evidence needs to be publicized more widely in order to lay the misconceptions to rest, but it seems likely that some people so deeply want to believe in the existence and power of backward messages in rock music that such beliefs will forever hold the status of folk myths in Western culture.

altered state of consciousness A condition that exists when changes in mental processes are extensive enough to produce noticeable differences in psychological and behavioral functioning.

Altered States of Consciousness

When changes in mental processes are great enough for you or others to notice significant differences in how you function, you are said to have entered an **altered state of consciousness.** In an altered state, mental processing shows distinct changes unique to that state. Cognitive processes or perceptions of yourself or the world may change, and normal inhibitions or self-control may weaken (Vaitl et al., 2005).

The phrase *altered states of consciousness* recognizes waking consciousness as the most common state, a baseline against which "altered" states are compared. However, this is not to say that waking consciousness is universally considered more normal, proper, or valued than other states. In fact, judgments about the status and meaning of certain states of consciousness vary considerably across cultures (Ward, 1994).

Consider, for instance, *hallucinations,* which are perceptual experiences (such as hearing voices) that occur without sensory stimuli. In the United States, hallucinations are usually viewed as so undesirable that even normal people who develop visual hallucinations

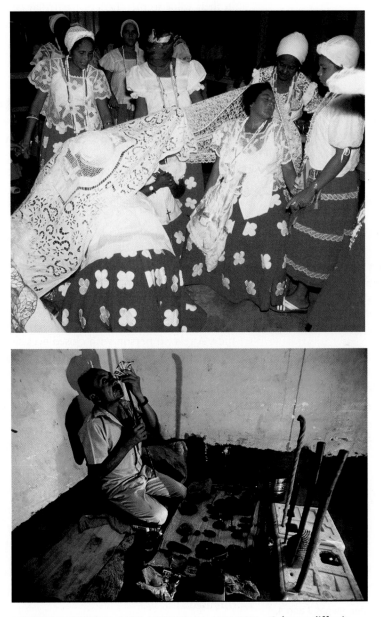

ALTERED STATES AND CULTURAL VALUES   Cultures differ in their definitions of which altered states of consciousness are approved and which are inappropriate. Here we see members of a Brazilian spirit possession cult in various stages of trance and, in Peru, a Moche *curandero*, or "curer," attempting to heal an ailing patient by using fumes from a potion—and a drug from the San Pedro cactus—to put himself in an altered state of consciousness.

due to an eye disorder may be ashamed to seek the medical help they need to solve the problem (Menon et al., 2003). If mental patients hallucinate, they often feel stress and self-blame and may choose not to report their hallucinations. Those who do report them tend to be considered more disturbed and may receive more drastic treatments than patients who keep their hallucinations to themselves (Wilson et al., 1996). Among the Moche of Peru, however, hallucinations have a culturally approved place. When someone experiences illness or misfortune, a healer conducts an elaborate ritual to find causes and treatments. During the ceremony, the healer takes mescaline, a drug that causes hallucinations. These hallucinations are thought to give the healer spiritual insight into the patient's problems (de Rios, 1989). In many other tribal cultures, too, purposeful hallucinations are respected, not rejected (Grob & Dobkin de Rios, 1992).

In other words, states of consciousness differ not only in their characteristics but also in their value to members of particular cultures. In the sections that follow, we describe some of the most interesting altered states of consciousness, beginning with the most common one: sleep.

Sleeping and Dreaming

▶ **Does your brain go to sleep when you do?**

According to ancient myths, sleepers lose control of their minds and flirt with death as their souls wander freely. Early researchers thought sleep was a time of mental inactivity, but sleep is actually an active, complex state (Hobson, 2005).

Stages of Sleep

Sleep researchers study the brain's electrical activity during sleep by taping tiny discs to a person's scalp and connecting them to an *electroencephalograph,* or *EEG.* The resulting EEG recordings, often called *brain waves,* vary in height (amplitude) and speed (frequency) as behavior or mental processes change. The brain waves of an awake, alert person are irregular, small, and closely spaced; that is, high frequency and low amplitude. A relaxed person with closed eyes shows more rhythmic brain waves occurring at slower speeds, about eight to twelve cycles per second (cps). During a normal night's sleep, your brain waves show distinctive and systematic changes in amplitude and frequency as you pass through various stages of sleep (Durka et al., 2005).

Slow-Wave Sleep Imagine that you are participating in a sleep study. You are hooked up to an EEG and various monitors, and a video camera watches as you sleep through the night. If you were to view the results, here's what you'd see: At first, you are relaxed, with eyes closed, but awake. At this point, your muscle tone and eye movements are normal, and your EEG shows the slow brain waves associated with relaxation. Then, as you drift into sleep, your breathing deepens, your heartbeat slows, and your blood pressure falls. Over the next half hour, you descend through four stages of sleep that are characterized by even slower brain waves with even higher amplitude (see Figure 4.3). The last two of these, stages 3 and 4, are called **slow-wave sleep.** When you reach stage 4, the deepest stage of slow-wave sleep, it is quite difficult to be awakened. If you were roused from this stage of deep sleep, you would be groggy and confused.

REM Sleep After thirty to forty-five minutes in stage 4, you quickly return to stage 2 and then enter a special stage in which your eyes move rapidly under your closed eyelids. This is called **rapid eye movement (REM) sleep,** or *paradoxical sleep.* It is called *paradoxical* because its characteristics contain a paradox, or contradiction. In REM sleep, your EEG resembles that of an awake, alert person, and your physiological

---

LINKAGES
Does the brain shut down when we sleep? (a link to Biology and Behavior)

Online Study Center

Improve Your Grade
Tutorial: EEG and Different Stages off Sleep

slow-wave sleep Sleep stages 3 and 4, which are accompanied by slow, deep breathing; a calm, regular heartbeat; and reduced blood pressure.

rapid eye movement (REM) sleep The stage of sleep during which the EEG resembles that of someone who is awake, but muscle tone decreases dramatically.

FIGURE **4.3**

EEG During Sleep

EEG recordings of brain wave activity show four relatively distinct stages of sleep. Notice the regular patterns of brain waves that occur just before a person goes to sleep, followed by the slowing of brain waves as sleep becomes deeper (stages 1 through 4). In REM (rapid eye movement) sleep, the frequency of brain waves increases dramatically. In some ways the brain waves of REM sleep resemble patterns seen in people who are awake.

Awake (resting)

Stage 1 sleep

Stage 2 sleep

Stage 3 sleep

Stage 4 sleep

REM sleep

Seconds

Source: Horne (1988).

arousal—heart rate, breathing, and blood pressure—is also similar to when you are awake. However, your muscles are nearly paralyzed. Sudden, twitchy spasms appear, especially in your face and hands, but your brain actively suppresses other movements (Blumberg & Lucas, 1994). In other words, there are two distinctly different types of sleep, REM sleep and *non-REM,* or *NREM,* sleep. (Lu el al., 2006

A Night's Sleep Most people pass through the cycle of sleep stages four to six times each night. Each cycle lasts about ninety minutes, but with a somewhat changing pattern of stages and stage duration. Early in the night, most of the time is spent in slow-wave sleep, with only a few minutes in REM (see Figure 4.4). As sleep continues, though, it is dominated by stage 2 and REM sleep, from which sleepers finally awaken.

Sleep patterns change with age. The average infant sleeps about sixteen hours a day. The average seventy-year-old sleeps only about six hours (Roffwarg, Muzio, & Dement, 1966), and elderly people tend to wake more often during the night than younger people do (Floyd, 2002). The composition of sleep changes, too. REM accounts for half of total sleep in newborns but less than 25 percent in young adults. Individuals vary widely from these averages, though. Some people feel well rested after four hours of sleep, whereas others of similar age require ten hours to feel satisfied (Clausen, Sersen, & Lidsky, 1974). To some extent, too, sleep patterns are a matter of choice or necessity. For example, North American college students get less sleep than other people their age (Hicks, Fernandez, & Pellegrini, 2001). This trend has grown over the last thirty years as students deal with academic and job responsibilities, along with family obligations and a variety of social and recreational activities—including those late-night sessions playing computer games or surfing the Internet. You have probably noticed the results of sleep deprivation as your classmates (or you?) struggle to stay awake during lectures.

FIGURE **4.4**

A Night's Sleep

During a typical night, a sleeper goes through this sequence of EEG stages. Notice that sleep is deepest during the first part of the night and shallower later on, when REM sleep becomes more prominent.

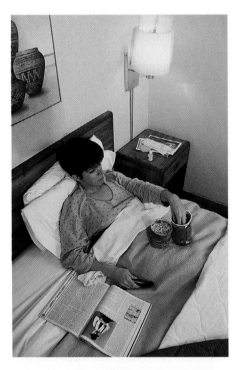

applying psychology

STIMULUS CONTROL THERAPY Insomnia can often be reduced through a combination of relaxation techniques and stimulus control therapy, in which the person goes to bed only when sleepy and gets out of bed if sleep does not come within fifteen to twenty minutes. The goal is to have the bed become a stimulus associated with sleeping, and perhaps sex, but not with reading, eating, watching television, worrying, or anything else that is incompatible with sleep (Edinger et al., 2001).

Sleep Disorders

Sometime in life, most people experience sleep-related problems (Silber, 2001). These can range from occasional nights of tossing and turning to the more serious and long-term sleep disorders that affect as many as 70 million people in the United States alone (Institute of Medicine, 2006). The most common sleep disorder is **insomnia,** in which people feel daytime fatigue due to trouble falling asleep or staying asleep. If you have difficulty getting to sleep or staying asleep that persists for longer than one month at a time, you may be suffering from insomnia. Besides being tiring, insomnia is tied to mental distress and impairment of functioning. Insomnia is especially associated with depressive and anxiety disorders (U.S. Surgeon General, 1999). Overall, insomniacs are three times more likely to show a mental disorder than individuals with no sleep complaints (Ford & Kamerow, 1989; Ohayon & Roth, 2003). It is unclear from such correlations, however, whether insomnia causes mental disorders, mental disorders cause insomnia, or some other factor causes both.

Sleeping pills can relieve insomnia. However, they may interact dangerously with alcohol, may disturb REM sleep, and may eventually lead to increased sleeplessness (Ashton, 1995; Poyares et al., 2004). In the long run, learning-based treatments may be more helpful (Perlis et al., 2001; Stepanski & Perlis, 2000). These include the cognitive behavior therapy methods described in the chapter on treatment of psychological disorders and progressive relaxation training techniques mentioned in the chapter on health, stress, and coping. Both have been shown to promote better sleeping by reducing anxiety, tension, and other stress reactions (Bernstein, Borkovec, & Hazlett-Stevens, 2000; Jacobs et al., 2004). Short daytime naps and moderate evening exercise can also help some people get to sleep more easily, sleep better, and experience better mood and performance the next day (Tanaka et al., 2001).

Narcolepsy is a disturbing daytime sleep disorder that is typically first seen in people who are between fifteen and twenty-five years old (Dyken & Yamada, 2005; Zeman et al., 2004). People with narcolepsy abruptly enter REM sleep directly from the waking state, usually as they are laughing or experiencing some other emotional state. Because of the loss of muscle tone in REM, narcoleptics may experience *cataplexy,* meaning that they collapse and remain briefly immobile even after awakening. The most common cause of narcolepsy appears to be the absence or deficiency of a recently discovered neurotransmitter called *orexin,* which is also known as *hypocretin* (Nishino & Kanbayashi, 2005). A combination of regular naps and stimulant drugs can be a helpful treatment (Rogers, Aldrich, & Lin, 2001; Schwartz, 2005).

SUDDEN INFANT DEATH SYNDROME (SIDS) In SIDS cases, seemingly healthy infants stop breathing while asleep in their cribs. All the causes of SIDS are not known, but health authorities now urge parents to ensure that infants sleep on their backs, as this baby demonstrates.

insomnia A sleep disorder in which a person feels tired during the day because of trouble falling asleep or staying asleep at night.

narcolepsy A daytime sleep disorder in which a person suddenly switches from an active waking state into REM sleep.

sleep apnea A sleep disorder in which people briefly but repeatedly stop breathing during the night.

sudden infant death syndrome (SIDS) A disorder in which a sleeping baby stops breathing but does not awaken and dies.

sleepwalking A phenomenon that starts primarily in non-REM sleep, especially in stage 4, and involves walking while asleep.

nightmares Frightening dreams that take place during REM sleep.

night terrors Horrific dream images during stage 4 sleep, followed by a rapid awakening and a state of intense fear.

REM behavior disorder A sleep disorder in which the decreased muscle tone normally seen in REM sleep does not appear, thus allowing dreams to be acted out.

People who suffer from **sleep apnea** briefly stop breathing hundreds of times each night, waking each time long enough to resume breathing. In the morning, victims do not recall the awakenings. However, they feel tired and tend to suffer headaches, reduced attention, and learning difficulties (Naëgelé et al., 1995). In one tragic case, two members of a train crew—both of whom had apnea—fell asleep on the job, resulting in a collision that killed two people (Pickler, 2002). Apnea has many causes, including genetic predisposition, obesity, problems with brain mechanisms that control breathing, and compression of the windpipe (Kadotani et al., 2001; Macey et al., 2002; Richards et al., 2002). Effective treatments include weight loss and use of a mask that provides a steady stream of air (Ayas et al., 2006; Dixon, Schachter, & O'Brien, 2005; Gupta & Reiter, 2004). In some cases surgery may be required to widen the air passageway in the upper throat (Friedman et al., 2003; Patel et al., 2003).

In cases of **sudden infant death syndrome (SIDS),** sleeping infants stop breathing and die. SIDS is the most common cause of unexpected infant death in Western countries (Daley, 2004). In the United States, it strikes about two of every thousand infants, especially very-low-birth-weight babies, usually when they are two to four months old (Smith & White, 2006; Vernacchio et al., 2003). Some SIDS cases may stem from problems with brain systems that regulate breathing, from exposure to cigarette smoke, or possibly from genetic causes (Anderson, Johnson, & Batal, 2005; Creery & Mikrogianakis, 2004). Correlational evidence suggests that about half of apparent SIDS cases might actually be accidental suffocations caused when infants sleep face down on a soft surface (Gilbert et al., 2005). In the United States, for example, SIDS may be particularly common in families in which babies are placed in the face-down position (Corwin et al., 2003; Hauck et al., 2002; Shields et al., 2005). Observational evidence indicates that the danger of the face-down position is especially great for babies who do not usually sleep in that position or who do not sleep with a pacifier in their mouths (Li et al., 2006; Paluszynska, Harris, & Thach, 2004). Since doctors began a "back to sleep" program, which advises parents to be sure their babies sleep face up, the number of infants dying from SIDS in the United States has dropped by 50 percent (Daley, 2004; Moon, Oden, & Grady, 2004; Rasinski et al., 2003). Babies who sleep face up may also be less likely to inhale potentially toxic bacteria that grow in some foam mattresses (Jenkins & Sherbum, 2005).

Sleepwalking occurs in non-REM sleep, usually in childhood (Guilleminault et al., 2003; Masand, Popli, & Welburg, 1995). By morning, most sleepwalkers have forgotten their travels. Despite myths to the contrary, waking a sleepwalker is not harmful. Drugs help, but most children simply outgrow the problem. One adult sleepwalker was cured when his wife blew a whistle whenever he began a nighttime stroll (Meyer, 1975).

Nightmares are frightening REM dreams that occur in 4 to 8 percent of the general population but in a much higher percentage of people who suffer from posttraumatic stress disorder following military combat or rape (Kryger, Roth, & Dement, 2000; Zadra & Donderi, 2000). **Night terrors** are horrific dream images during stage 4 sleep. Sleepers often awaken from a night terror with a bloodcurdling scream and remain intensely afraid for up to thirty minutes. Yet they may not recall the episode in the morning. Night terrors are especially common in boys, but adults can suffer milder versions. The condition is sometimes treatable with drugs.

In **REM behavior disorder,** the near paralysis that normally accompanies REM sleep does not occur, so sleepers move as if acting out their dreams (Abad & Guilleminault, 2004). If the dreams are violent, the disorder can be dangerous to the dreamer or those nearby. One nine-year-old boy in New York City was seriously injured when he jumped from a third-floor window while dreaming that his parents were being murdered. In another case, a Minnesota man grabbed his wife's throat while dreaming about breaking a deer's neck (Brown, 2003). REM behavior disorder sometimes occurs along with daytime narcolepsy (Schenck & Mahowald, 1992) and in one case was caused by a brain tumor (Zambelis, Paparrigopoulos, & Soldatos, 2002). Fortunately, drug treatments are usually effective (Takeuchi et al., 2001)

Why Do People Sleep?

People need a certain amount of uninterrupted sleep to function normally. In fact, most living creatures sleep. In trying to understand why people sleep, psychologists have studied what sleep does for us and how the brain shapes the characteristics of sleep (Siegel, 2005).

Sleep as a Circadian Rhythm   Humans and almost all animals display cycles of behavior and physiology that repeat about every twenty-four hours. This pattern is called a **circadian rhythm.** (*Circadian* is pronounced "sir-KAY-dee-en." It comes from the Latin *circa dies,* meaning "about a day.") Longer and shorter rhythms also occur, but they are less common.

Circadian rhythms are linked to signals such as the light of day and the dark of night (Ohta, Yamazaki, & McMahon, 2005). However, most of these rhythms continue even when no time signals are available. Volunteers living for months without external light and dark cues maintain daily rhythms in sleeping and waking, eating, urination, hormone release, and other physiological functions. Under such conditions, these cycles repeat about every twenty-four hours (Czeisler et al., 1999).

Disruption of the sleep-wake cycle can create problems. For example, air travel across several time zones often causes **jet lag,** a pattern of fatigue, irritability, inattention, and sleeping problems that can last for several days. The traveler's body feels ready to sleep at the wrong time for the new location. It tends to be easier to stay awake longer than usual than to go to sleep earlier than usual. That is the reason that the symptoms of jet lag are usually more intense after a long eastward trip (when time is lost) than after a long westward journey (when time is gained; Lemmer et al., 2002). Symptoms similar to those of jet lag also appear in workers who repeatedly change between day and night shifts and in people who try to go to sleep early on a Sunday night after a weekend of later-than-usual bedtimes (Czeisler et al., 2005; Di Milla, 2006). For these people, Monday morning "blues" may actually be symptoms of a disrupted sleep-wake cycle (Yang & Spielman, 2001).

The length of circadian sleep rhythms can vary from person to person such that some have a natural tendency to stay up later at night ("owls") or to wake up earlier in the morning ("larks"). But because our sleep-wake rhythms stay about the same even without external cues about light and dark, we must have an internal "biological clock" that keeps track of time. This clock is in the *suprachiasmatic nuclei (SCN)* of the hypothalamus, as shown in Figure 4.5. The SCN receives light information from a special set of photoreceptors in the eyes and then sends signals to hindbrain areas that initiate sleep or wakefulness (Albus et al., 2005; Lee et al., 2003; Saper, Scammell, & Lu, 2005). When animals with SCN damage receive transplanted SCN cells, their circadian rhythms become like those of the donor animal (Menaker & Vogelbaum, 1993). SCN neurons also regulate the release of the hormone *melatonin*. Melatonin, in turn, appears to be important in maintaining circadian rhythms (Beaumont et al., 2004; Cardinali et al., 2002). In fact, many of the symptoms associated with jet lag and other disruptions in sleep-wake cycles can be prevented or treated by taking melatonin (Revell & Eastman, 2005).

The Functions of Sleep   Examining the effects of sleep deprivation may help explain why people sleep at all. People who go without sleep for as long as a week usually don't suffer serious long-term effects. However, extended sleeplessness does lead to fatigue, irritability, and inattention (Drummond et al., 2000; Smith & Maben, 1993). Even short-term sleep deprivation—a common condition among busy adolescents and adults—can also take its toll (Arnedt et al., 2005; Heuer et al., 2004; Stapleton, 2001). For example, serious mistakes in patient care are more likely when medical interns work sleep-disrupting extended hospital shifts than when they work more normal hours (Landrigan et al., 2004). Most fatal car crashes in the United States occur during the "fatigue hazard" hours of midnight to 6 A.M. (Coleman, 1992), and sleepiness resulting

circadian rhythm   A cycle, such as waking and sleeping, that repeats about once a day.

jet lag   Fatigue, irritability, inattention, and sleeping problems caused by air travel across several time zones.

FIGURE **4.5**

Sleep, Dreaming, and the Brain

This diagram shows the location of some of the brain structures thought to be involved in sleep and dreaming, as well as in other altered states discussed later in the chapter. For example, one area near the suprachiasmatic nuclei acts as a "master switch" to promote sleep (Saper, Chou, & Scammell, 2001). If it is damaged, sleep may be nearly impossible. Another nearby area promotes wakefulness; individuals with damage to this area sleep virtually all the time (Salin-Pascual et al., 2001).

from long work shifts or other causes is a major factor in up to 25 percent of all auto accidents (Barger et al., 2005; Garbarino et al., 2001; Philip et al., 2001). The fact that "sleepy driving" can be as dangerous as drunk driving has led at least one U.S. state (New Jersey) to expand the definition of reckless driving to include "driving while fatigued" (i.e., having had no sleep in the previous 24 hours). Fatigue also plays a role in many injuries suffered by sleepy young children at play or in day care (Valent, Brusaferro, & Barbone, 2001). Learning, too, is more difficult after sleep deprivation; but certain parts of the cerebral cortex actually increase their activity when a sleep-deprived person faces a learning task, so we are able to compensate for a while (Drummond et al., 2000).

Scientists are looking for drugs that can combat the effects of sleep deprivation (Porrino et al., 2005), but there appears to be no substitute for sleep itself. Some researchers suggest that sleep helps restore the body and the brain for future activity and helps to consolidate memories of newly learned facts (Gais & Born, 2004; Stickgold, 2005; Orban et al., 2006; Wagner et al., 2004). This restorative function is especially associated with non-REM sleep, which would help explain why most people get their non-REM sleep in the first part of the night (see Figure 4.4).

There is also an apparent need for REM sleep. For example, after total sleep deprivation, people don't need to make up every hour of lost sleep. Instead, they sleep about 50 percent more than usual, then wake up feeling rested. But their "recovery" night includes an unusually high percentage of REM sleep (Feinberg & Campbell, 1993). And if people are deprived *only* of REM sleep, they compensate even more directly. In one study, participants were awakened whenever their EEGs showed REM. When allowed to sleep normally the next night, they "rebounded," nearly doubling the percentage of time spent in REM (Dement, 1960). This research suggests that REM has its own special functions. What those functions might be is still unclear, but there are several interesting possibilities.

First, REM may improve the functioning of neurons that use norepinephrine (Siegel & Rogawski, 1988). Norepinephrine is a neurotransmitter released by cells in the *locus coeruleus* (pronounced "lo-kus seh-ROO-lee-us"; see Figure 4.5). During waking hours, it affects alertness and mood. But the brain's neurons lose their sensitivity to norepinephrine if it is released continuously for too long. Because the locus coeruleus is almost completely inactive during REM sleep, researchers suggest that REM helps restore sensitivity to norepinephrine and thus its ability to keep us alert (Steriade & McCarley, 1990). Animals deprived of REM sleep show unusually high norepinephrine levels and decreased daytime alertness (Brock et al., 1994).

REM sleep may also be a time for creating and strengthening connections between nerve cells in the brain (Graves, Pack, & Abel, 2001; Maquet, 2001; Peigneux et al., 2001). If so, it would explain why infants and children—whose brains are still developing—spend so much time in REM. Evidence favoring this possibility comes from animal research showing that REM sleep helps in the creation of neural connections following new learning experiences (Frank et al., 2001). There is also evidence that REM sleep deprivation slows the creation of these connections (Kim, Mahmoud, & Grover, 2005). So REM sleep may help to solidify and absorb the day's experiences and skills (Fischer et al., 2002; Sejnowski & Destexhe, 2000; Stickgold, James, & Hobson, 2000). In one study, people who were REM deprived showed poorer performance at a skill they had learned the day before when compared with people who were either deprived of non-REM sleep or had slept normally (Karni et al., 1994). Another study found that establishing memories of emotional information was particularly dependent on REM sleep (Wagner, Gais, & Born, 2001). Even 60- to 90-minute naps in which REM sleep appears can be enough to solidify the learning of visual information (Mednick, Nakayama, & Stickgold, 2003).

Dreams and Dreaming

We have seen that the brain is active in all sleep stages (for a summary of our discussion, see "In Review: Sleep and Sleep Disorders"). Some of this brain activity during sleep is experienced as the story-like sensations and perceptions known as **dreams.** Dreams may be as short as a few seconds or last for many minutes. They may be organized or chaotic, realistic or fantastic, peaceful or exciting (Hobson & Stickgold, 1994).

Some dreaming occurs during non-REM sleep, but most dreams—and the most bizarre and vivid dreams—occur during REM (Casagrande et al., 1996; Dement & Kleitman, 1957; Stickgold, Rittenhouse, & Hobson, 1994). Even when they seem to make no sense, dreams may contain a certain amount of logic. For example, when people read dream reports whose segments had been randomly reordered, they could correctly say which had been rearranged and which were intact. And although dreams often involve one person transforming into another or one object turning into another object, it is rare that objects become people or vice versa (Stickgold et al., 1994).

Daytime activities may influence the content of dreams to some extent (Foulkes, 1985; Wegner, Wenzlaff, & Kozak, 2004). In one study, people wore red-tinted goggles for a few minutes just before going to sleep. Although they didn't know the purpose of the study, the next morning they reported more red images in their dreams than people who had not worn the goggles (Roffwarg, Hermann, & Bowe-Anders, 1978). It is also sometimes possible to intentionally direct dream content. This is called **lucid dreaming,** because the sleeper is aware of dreaming while a dream is occurring (Stickgold, Malia, et al., 2000).

Research leaves little doubt that everyone dreams during every night of normal sleep. Even blind people dream, although their perceptual experiences are usually not visual. Whether you remember a dream depends on how you sleep and wake up. Recall is better if you awaken abruptly and lie quietly while writing or tape-recording your recollections.

Why do we dream? Theories abound (Antrobus, 2001; Domhoff, 2001; Eiser, 2005). Some see dreaming as a process through which all species with complex brains analyze and consolidate information that is personally important or has survival value (Payne & Nadel, 2004; Porte & Hobson, 1996; Zadra, Desjardins, & Marcotte, 2006). This view is supported by the fact that dreaming appears to occur in most mammals, as indicated by the appearance of REM sleep. For example, after researchers disabled the neurons that cause REM sleep paralysis, sleeping cats ran around and attacked, or seemed alarmed by, unseen objects, presumably the images from dreams (Winson, 1990).

According to Freud (1900), dreams are a disguised form of *wish fulfillment,* a way to satisfy unconscious urges or resolve unconscious conflicts that are too upsetting to deal with consciously. For example, a person's sexual desires might appear in a dream as the rhythmic motions of a horseback ride. Conflicting feelings about a parent might

dreams   Story-like sequences of images, sensations, and perceptions that last from several seconds to many minutes and occur mainly during REM sleep.

lucid dreaming   Being aware that a dream is a dream while it is occurring.

in review

SLEEP AND SLEEP DISORDERS

Types of Sleep	Characteristics	Possible Functions
Slow wave (stages 3 and 4)	The deepest stages of sleep, characterized by slowed heart rate and breathing, reduced blood pressure, and low-frequency, high-amplitude brain waves	Refreshing of body and brain; memory consolidation
Rapid eye movement (REM) sleep	Characterized by eye movements, waking levels of heart rate, breathing, blood pressure, and brain waves, but near-paralysis in muscles	Restoring sensitivity to norepinephrine, thus improving waking alertness; creating and solidifying nerve cell connections; consolidating memories and new skills

Sleep Disorders	Characteristics	Possible Causes
Insomnia	Difficulty (lasting at least a month) in falling asleep or staying asleep	Worry, anxiety
Narcolepsy	Sudden switching from a waking state to REM sleep	Absence or deficiency in *orexin* (*hypocretin*)
Sleep apnea	Frequent episodes of interrupted breathing while asleep	Genetic predisposition, obesity, faulty breathing-related brain mechanisms, windpipe compression
Sudden infant death syndrome (SIDS)	Interruption of an infant's breathing, resulting in death	Genetic predisposition, faulty breathing-related brain mechanisms
Nightmares	Frightening dreams during REM sleep	Stressful or traumatic events or experiences
Night terrors	Frightening dream images during non-REM sleep	Stressful or traumatic events or experiences
REM behavior disorder	Lack of paralysis during REM sleep allows dreams to be enacted, sometimes with harmful consequences	Malfunction of brain mechanism normally creating REM paralysis

?
1. Jet lag occurs because of a disruption in a traveler's _____ .
2. The importance of non-REM sleep is suggested by its appearance _____ in the night.
3. The safest sleeping position for babies is _____ .

appear as a dream about a fight. Seeing his patients' dreams as a "royal road to a knowledge of the unconscious," Freud interpreted their meaning as part of his psychoanalytic therapy methods (see the chapter on the treatment of psychological disorders).

In contrast, the *activation-synthesis theory* describes dreams as the meaningless byproducts of REM sleep (Hobson, 1997). According to this theory, hindbrain arousal during REM creates random messages that *activate* the brain, especially the cerebral cortex. Dreams result as the cortex connects, or *synthesizes,* these messages as best as it can, using stored memories and current feelings to organize this random brain activity into something more coherent. From this perspective, dreams represent the brain's attempt to make sense of meaningless stimulation during sleep, much as we might try to find meaningful shapes in cloud formations (Bernstein & Roberts, 1995; Rittenhouse, Stickgold, & Hobson, 1994).

Even if dreams arise from random brain activity, their content may still have psychological significance. Some psychologists believe that dreams give people a chance to review and address some of the problems they face during waking hours (Cartwright, 1993).

This view is supported by evidence suggesting that people's current concerns can affect both the content of their dreams and the way in which dreams are organized and recalled (Domhoff, 1996, 1999; Stevens, 1996). However, high-tech imaging research shows that while we are asleep, brain areas involved in emotion tend to be overactivated, whereas those areas controlling logical thought tend to be suppressed (Braun, Balkin, & Wesensten, 1998; Hobson et al., 1998). In fact, as we reach deeper sleep stages, and then enter REM sleep, thinking subsides and hallucinations increase (Fosse, Stickgold, & Hobson, 2001). This is probably why dreams rarely provide realistic, logical solutions to our problems (Blagrove, 1996).

Hypnosis

▶ **Can you be hypnotized against your will?**

The word *hypnosis* comes from the Greek word *hypnos,* meaning "sleep." However, hypnotized people are not sleeping. Even those who say afterward that their bodies felt "asleep" also report that their minds were active and alert. **Hypnosis** has been defined as an altered state of consciousness brought on by special techniques and producing responsiveness to suggestions for changes in experience and behavior (Kirsch, 1994a). Most hypnotized people do not feel forced to follow the hypnotist's instructions. They simply see no reason to refuse (Hilgard, 1965). In fact, the more that people want to cooperate with the hypnotist, the more likely it is they will experience hypnosis (Lynn et al., 2002). People cannot be hypnotized against their will.

Experiencing Hypnosis

Hypnosis often begins with suggestions that the person feels relaxed and sleepy. The hypnotist may then gradually focus the person's attention on a particular, often monotonous, set of stimuli, such as a swinging pendant. The hypnotist suggests that the individual should ignore everything else and imagine certain feelings.

There are special tests to measure **hypnotic susceptibility,** the degree to which people respond to hypnotic suggestions (Gfeller, 1994). These tests show that about 10 percent of adults are difficult or impossible to hypnotize (Hilgard, 1982). At the other extreme are people whose hypnotic experiences are so vivid that they can't tell the difference between images the hypnotist asked them to imagine and images projected on a screen (Bryant & Mallard, 2003). Hypnotically susceptible people typically differ from others in having a better ability to focus attention and ignore distractions (Crawford, Brown, & Moon, 1993). They also tend to have more active imaginations (Spanos, Burnley, & Cross, 1993), a tendency to fantasize (Lynn & Rhue, 1986), a capacity for processing information quickly and easily (Dixon, Brunet, & Laurence, 1990), a tendency to be suggestible (Kirsch & Braffman, 2001), and positive attitudes toward hypnosis (Gfeller, 1994).

The results of hypnosis can be fascinating. People told that their eyes are locked shut may struggle unsuccessfully to open them. They may appear deaf or blind or insensitive to pain. They may seem to forget their own names. Some appear to remember forgotten things. Others show *age regression,* apparently recalling or reenacting their childhoods (see Figure 4.6). These hypnotic effects can be extended for hours or days through *posthypnotic suggestions,* which are instructions about how to behave after hypnosis has ended (such as smiling whenever someone says "England"). Some individuals show *posthypnotic amnesia,* an inability to recall what happened while they were hypnotized, even after being told what happened (Barnier, 2002).

Ernest Hilgard (1965, 1992) described the main changes that people display during hypnosis. First, hypnotized people *tend not to begin actions on their own,* waiting instead for the hypnotist's instructions. One participant said, "I was trying to decide if my legs were crossed, but I couldn't tell, and didn't quite have the initiative to move to find

INDUCING HYPNOSIS In the late 1700s, Austrian physician Franz Anton Mesmer used a forerunner of hypnosis to treat physical disorders. His procedure, known as *mesmerism,* included elaborate trance-induction rituals, but we now know that hypnosis can be induced far more easily, often simply by staring at an object, as this woman did.

hypnosis A phenomenon brought on by special techniques, characterized by varying degrees of responsiveness to suggestions for changes in experience and behavior.

hypnotic susceptibility The degree to which a person responds to hypnotic suggestion

Steve

Steven

Sue

Sue

Source: Hilgard (1965).

FIGURE **4.6**

Hypnotic Age Regression

learn by doing Here are the signatures of two adults before hypnotically induced age regression (top of each pair) and while age regressed (bottom of each pair). The lower signatures in each pair look less mature, but was the change due to hypnosis? To find out, ask a friend to sign a blank sheet of paper, first as usual, and then as if he or she were five years old. If the two signatures look significantly different, what does this say about the cause of certain age-regression effects?

state theory A theory proposing that hypnosis creates an altered state of consciousness.

role theory A theory proposing that hypnotized people act in accordance with a social role that provides a reason to follow a hypnotist's suggestions.

dissociation theory A theory proposing that hypnosis is a socially agreed-upon opportunity to display one's ability to let mental functions become dissociated.

out" (Hilgard, 1965). Second, hypnotized people tend to ignore all but the hypnotist's voice and whatever it points out: Their *attention is redistributed.* Third, hypnosis *enhances the ability to fantasize.* Participants more vividly imagine a scene or relive a memory. Fourth, hypnotized people *readily take on roles.* They more easily act as though they were people of a different age or sex than nonhypnotized people do. Fifth, hypnotized individuals show *reduced reality testing.* They tend not to question whether statements are true, and they are more willing to accept distortions of reality. So a hypnotized person might shiver in a warm room if a hypnotist says it is snowing.

Explaining Hypnosis

Hypnotized people look and act different from nonhypnotized people (Hilgard, 1965). Do these differences indicate an altered state of consciousness?

Advocates of **state theory** say that they do. They point to the notable changes in brain activity that occur during hypnosis (Egner, Jamieson, & Gruzelier, 2005; Mohr et al., 2005; Raij et al., 2005) and to the dramatic effects that hypnosis can produce, including insensitivity to pain and the disappearance of warts (Noll, 1994). They also note that there are slight differences in the way hypnotized and nonhypnotized people carry out suggestions. In one study, hypnotized people and those pretending to be hypnotized were told to run their hands through their hair whenever they heard the word *experiment* (Orne, Sheehan, & Evans, 1968). The pretenders did so only when the hypnotist said the cue word. Hypnotized participants complied no matter who said it. Another study found that hypnotized people complied more often than simulators with a posthypnotic suggestion to mail postcards to the experimenter (Barnier & McConkey, 1998).

Supporters of **role theory** maintain that hypnosis is *not* a special state of consciousness. They point out, for example, that some of the changes in brain activity associated with hypnosis can also be created without hypnosis (Mohr et al., 2005). They suggest that hypnotized people are merely complying with the demands of the situation and acting in accordance with a special social role (Kirsch, 1994b). From this perspective, hypnosis provides a socially acceptable reason to follow someone's suggestions, much as a physical exam provides a socially acceptable reason to remove clothing on request. Support for role theory comes from several sources. First, nonhypnotized people sometimes display behaviors that are usually associated with hypnosis. For example, contestants on television game shows and reality shows do lots of odd, silly, disgusting, or even dangerous things without first being hypnotized. Second, laboratory studies show that motivated but nonhypnotized volunteers can duplicate many aspects of hypnotic behavior, from arm rigidity to age regression (Dasgupta et al., 1995; Orne & Evans, 1965). Other studies have found that people rendered blind or deaf by hypnosis can still see or hear, even though their actions and beliefs suggest that they cannot (Bryant & McConkey, 1989).

Hilgard (1992) proposed a **dissociation theory** to blend role and state theories. He suggested that hypnosis is not a single specific state but a general condition that temporarily reorganizes or breaks down our normal control over thoughts and actions. Hypnosis, he said, activates a process called *dissociation,* meaning a split in consciousness (Hilgard, 1979). Dissociation allows body movements normally under voluntary control to occur on their own and normally involuntary processes (such as overt reactions to pain) to be controlled voluntarily.

Hilgard argued that this relaxation of control is possible because of a social agreement between the hypnotized person and the hypnotist to share control. In other words, people usually decide for themselves how to act or what to attend to, perceive, or remember. During hypnosis, the hypnotist is given permission to control some of these experiences and actions. Compliance with a social role may tell part of the story, Hilgard said, but hypnosis also leads to significant changes in mental processes.

Support for Hilgard's theory comes from brain imaging studies showing that the ability to dissociate certain mental processes is greater in people who are more hypnotically susceptible (Egner et al., 2005). Dissociation was also demonstrated behaviorally by asking hypnotized participants to immerse a hand in ice water (Hilgard,

FIGURE **4.7**

Reports of Pain in Hypnosis

This graph compares the intensity of pain reported by three groups of participants while one of their hands was immersed in ice water. The orange line represents non-hypnotized participants. The blue line represents hypnotized participants who were told they would feel no pain. The purple line shows the reports of hypnotized participants who were told they would feel no pain but were asked to press a key if "any part of them" felt pain. The key pressing by this "hidden observer" suggests that under hypnosis, the experience of pain was dissociated from conscious awareness (Hilgard, 1977).

Morgan, & MacDonald, 1975). They were told that they would feel no pain, but they were asked to press a key with their other hand if "any part of them" felt pain. As shown in Figure 4.7, these participants said they felt almost no pain, but their key pressing told a different story. Hilgard concluded that a "hidden observer" was reporting on pain that was reaching the person but that had been separated, or dissociated, from conscious awareness (Hilgard, 1977).

Much remains to be learned about the nature of hypnosis. However, traditional distinctions between state and role theories have become less important as researchers focus on larger questions, such as why people are susceptible to hypnosis and what roles biological, social, and cognitive factors may play in it (e.g., Lynn & Kirsch, 2006; Raz, Fan, & Posner, 2005).

Applications of Hypnosis

Whatever hypnosis is, it has proven useful, especially in relation to pain (Patterson & Jensen, 2003). Magnetic resonance imaging (MRI) studies of hypnotized pain patients show altered activity in the anterior cingulate cortex, a brain region associated with the emotional component of pain (Faymonville et al., 2000; Mohr et al., 2005). Hypnosis seems to be the only anesthetic some people need to block the pain of dental work, childbirth, burns, and surgery (Patterson, 2004; Van Sickel, 1992). For others, hypnosis relieves chronic pain from arthritis, nerve damage, migraine headaches, and cancer (Stewart, 2005). Hypnotic suggestion can also help eliminate diarrhea (Tan et al., 2005), reduce nausea and vomiting due to chemotherapy (Redd, 1984), limit surgical bleeding (Gerschman, Reade, & Burrows, 1980), and speed postoperative recovery (Astin, 2004).

Other applications of hypnosis are more controversial, especially the use of hypnosis to aid memory. For example, hypnotic age regression is sometimes used in an attempt to help people recover lost memories. However, the memories of past events reported by age-regressed individuals are not as accurate as those of nonhypnotized individuals (Lynn, Myers, & Malinoski, 1997). Similarly, it is doubtful that hypnosis can help witnesses to recall the details of a crime. In fact, their positive expectations about the value of hypnosis may lead them to unintentionally distort or reconstruct memories of what they saw and heard (Garry & Loftus, 1994; Weekes et al., 1992; Wells & Olson, 2003). Being hypnotized may also make witnesses more confident about their reports, even if those reports are inaccurate.

LINKAGES
Does meditation relieve stress? (a link to Health, Stress, and Coping)

M*editation* provides a set of techniques intended to create an altered state of consciousness characterized by inner peace and tranquility (Shapiro & Walsh, 1984; Walsh & Shapiro, 2006). Techniques to achieve a meditative state differ, depending on belief and philosophy (e.g., Eastern meditation, Sufism, yoga, or prayer). However, in the most common meditation methods, attention is focused on just one thing until the meditator stops thinking about anything else and experiences nothing but "pure awareness" (Benson, 1975). In this way, the individual becomes more fully aware of the present moment rather than being caught up in the past or the future.

To organize their attention, meditators may focus on the sound or tempo of their breathing or slowly repeat a soothing word or phrase, called a *mantra*. During a typical meditation session, breathing, heart rate, muscle tension, blood pressure, and oxygen consumption decrease, whereas in the brain blood flow to the thalamus and frontal lobes increases (Cahn & Polich, 2006; Newberg et al., 2001; Wallace & Benson, 1972). During most forms of meditation, EEG activity is similar to that seen in a relaxed, eyes-closed, waking state (see Figure 4.3). Meditation also increases the brain's level of

LINKAGES

Meditation, Health, and Stress

dopamine, the same neurotransmitter that is involved in the experience of reward or pleasure (Kjaer et al., 2002).

Some people claim that meditation increases their awareness and understanding of themselves and their environment. It has also been associated with reduced anxiety; improved immune system functioning; reductions in high blood pressure anxiety and insomnia; longer survival among heart patients; and improved performance in everything from work to tennis (Beauchamp-Turner & Levinson, 1992; Bodian, 1999; Davidson et al., 2003; Paul-Labrador et al., 2006; Schneider et al., 2005). More generally, meditators' scores on personality tests indicate increases in overall mental health, self-esteem, and social openness (Janowiak & Hackman, 1994; Sakairi, 1992). Exactly how meditation produces these benefits is unclear, though its activation of dopamine brain systems may tell an important part of the story. Whatever the mechanism, it is probably not unique to meditation. Many of the same benefits associated with meditation have also been reported in association with other techniques, such as biofeedback, hypnosis, tai chi, or just relaxing (Bernstein et al., 2000; Beyerstein, 1999; Wang, Collet, & Lau, 2004).

SURGERY UNDER HYPNOSIS Bernadine Coady, of Wimblington, England, has a condition that makes general anesthesia dangerous for her. In April 1999, she faced a foot operation that would have been extremely painful without anesthesia. She arranged for a hypnotherapist to help her through the procedure, but when he failed to show up, she was forced to rely on self-hypnosis as her only anesthetic. She said she imagined the pain as "waves lashing against a sea wall . . . [and] going away, like the tide." Coady's report that the operation was painless is believable because, in December 2000, she had the same operation on her other foot, again using only self-hypnosis for pain control (Morris, 2000).

psychoactive drugs Chemical substances that act on the brain to create psychological effects.

psychopharmacology The study of psychoactive drugs and their effects.

blood-brain barrier A feature of blood vessels in the brain that prevents some substances from entering brain tissue.

agonists Drugs that bind to a receptor and mimic the effects of the neurotransmitter that normally fits that receptor.

antagonists Drugs that bind to a receptor and prevent the normal neurotransmitter from binding.

Psychoactive Drugs

▶ **How do drugs affect the brain?**

The altered states we have discussed so far serve a biological need (sleep) or rely on the chemistry of the brain and body (hypnosis and meditation). Other altered states are brought on by outside agents: drugs. Every day, most people in the world use drugs that alter brain activity and consciousness (Levinthal, 2001). For example, 80 to 90 percent of people in North America use caffeine, the stimulant found in coffee and tea. A *drug* is a chemical that is not required for normal physiological functioning yet has an effect on the body. You may say that you "need" a cup of coffee in the morning, but you will still wake up without it; accordingly, the caffeine in coffee is defined as a drug. Drugs that affect the brain, changing consciousness and other psychological processes, are called **psychoactive drugs.** The study of psychoactive drugs is called **psychopharmacology.**

Psychopharmacology

Most psychoactive drugs affect the brain by altering the interactions between neurotransmitters and their receptors, as described in the chapter on biology and behavior. To create their effects, these drugs must cross the **blood-brain barrier,** a feature of blood vessels in the brain that prevents some substances from entering brain tissue (Neuwelt, 2004). Once past this barrier, a psychoactive drug's effects depend on several factors: With which neurotransmitter systems does the drug interact? How does the drug affect those neurotransmitters or their receptors? What psychological functions are normally performed by the brain systems that use those neurotransmitters?

Drugs can affect neurotransmitters or their receptors through several mechanisms. Neurotransmitters fit into their own receptors, as Figure 4.8 shows. Some drugs, such as morphine, are similar enough to a particular neurotransmitter to fool its receptors. These drugs, called **agonists,** bind to receptors and imitate, or mimic, the effects of the normal neurotransmitter. Other drugs, called **antagonists,** are similar enough to a neurotransmitter to occupy its receptors but cannot mimic its effects. When they bind to receptors, they prevent the normal neurotransmitter from binding. Still other drugs work by increasing or decreasing the release of a specific neurotransmitter. Finally, some drugs work by speeding or slowing the *removal* of a neurotransmitter from synapses.

Predicting a psychoactive drug's effects on behavior is complicated. For one thing, most of these drugs interact with many neurotransmitter systems. Also, the nervous system may compensate for a given drug's effects. For instance, repeated exposure to a

Agonists and Antagonists

In Part A, a molecule of neurotransmitter interacts with a receptor on a neuron's dendrites by fitting into and stimulating it. Part B shows a drug molecule acting as an *agonist*, affecting the receptor in the same way a neurotransmitter would. Part C depicts an *antagonist* drug molecule blocking a natural neurotransmitter from reaching and acting on the receptor.

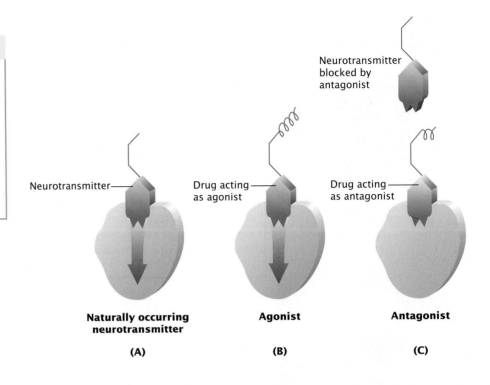

Naturally occurring
neurotransmitter

(A)

Agonist

(B)

Antagonist

(C)

drug that blocks receptors for a certain neurotransmitter often leads to an increase in the number of receptors available to accept that neurotransmitter.

The Varying Effects of Drugs

Unfortunately, chemical properties that give drugs their medically desirable main effects, such as pain relief, often create undesirable side effects as well.

Substance Abuse   One side effect may be the potential for abuse. **Substance abuse** is a pattern of use that causes serious social, legal, or interpersonal problems for the user (American Psychiatric Association, 2000). Of course, as a culture changes, the drugs that cause a person social and legal problems may also change, as Figure 4.9 illustrates.

Substance abuse can lead to psychological or physical dependence. People displaying **psychological dependence** on a drug will continue to use it even though it has harmful effects. They need the drug for a sense of well-being and become preoccupied with getting the drug if it is no longer available. However, they can still function without the drug. Psychological dependence can occur with or without **physical dependence,** also known as *addiction.* **Addiction** is a physiological state in which there is not only a strong craving for the drug but also in which using the drug becomes necessary to prevent an unpleasant **withdrawal syndrome.** Withdrawal symptoms vary depending on the drug, but they often include an intense desire for the drug and physical effects generally opposite to those of the drug itself. Eventually, drug users may develop **tolerance,** a condition in which increasingly larger drug doses are required to produce the same effect (Sokolowska, Siegel, & Kim, 2002). With the development of tolerance, many addicts need the drug just to prevent the negative effects of not taking it. However, most researchers believe that a craving for the positive effects of drugs is what keeps addicts coming back to them (Ciccocioppo, Martin-Fardon, & Weiss, 2004; Everitt & Robbins, 2005; George et al., 2001).

It may be tempting to think of "addicts" as utterly different from the rest of us, but we should never underestimate the ease with which drug dependence can develop in anyone, including ourselves. Physical dependence can develop gradually, without our awareness. In fact, scientists believe that the changes in the brain that underlie addiction may be similar to those that occur during learning (Nestler, 2001; Overton et al., 1999).

substance abuse   The use of psychoactive drugs in ways that deviate from cultural norms and cause serious problems for the user.

psychological dependence   A condition in which a person continues drug use despite adverse effects, needs the drug for a sense of well-being, and becomes preoccupied with obtaining it.

physical dependence (addiction)   Development of a physical need for a psychoactive drug.

withdrawal syndrome   A set of symptoms associated with ending the use of an addictive substance.

tolerance   A condition in which increasingly larger drug doses are needed to produce a given effect.

FIGURE 4.9

Changing Views of Drugs

The legal and social status of a drug can vary across cultures and over time (Weiss & Moore, 1990). For example, in the United States cocaine was once a respectable, commercially available drug; today it is illegal. And alcohol, which is legal in the United States and many other nations, is banned in countries such as Kuwait, Iran, and Saudi Arabia.

FIGURE 4.10

Expectancies and Alcohol Consumption

People may drink more when their expectancies about the positive effects of alcohol have been primed. In this study, some participants watched *Cheers* (a TV show in which people enjoy themselves while drinking alcohol) and were exposed to adjectives associated with positive expectancies about alcohol. They later drank more (nonalcoholic) beer than participants who watched a non-alcohol-related show and were not exposed to the alcohol-positive adjectives (Roehrich & Goldman, 1995).

All addictive drugs stimulate the brain's "pleasure centers," regions that are sensitive to the neurotransmitter dopamine (Nestler, 2005). Neuron activity in these areas of the brain produces intensely pleasurable feelings. It also helps generate the pleasant feelings associated with a good meal, a "runner's high," gambling, or sex (Grunberg, 1994; Harris & Aston-Jones, 1995; Reuter et al., 2005). It is no wonder, then, that addictive drugs have the capacity for creating tremendously rewarding effects in most people (Kelley & Berridge, 2002).

Expectations and Drug Effects   Drug effects are not determined by biochemistry alone. The *expectations* we learn through experience with drugs and/or drug users also play a role (Bartholow & Heinz, 2006; Cumsille, Sayer, & Graham, 2000; Siegel, 2005; Stein, Goldman, & Del Boca, 2000). Several experiments have shown that research participants who consume alcohol-free drinks that they *think* contain alcohol are likely to behave in line with their expectations about alcohol's effects. So they tend to feel drunk and to become more aggressive, more interested in violent and sexual material, and more easily sexually aroused (Darkes & Goldman, 1993; George & Marlatt, 1986; Lang et al., 1975; Lansky & Wilson, 1981). And because they know that alcohol impairs memory, these participants are more vulnerable to developing false memories about a crime they witnessed on videotape (Assefi & Garry, 2003).

Expectations about drug effects develop in part as people watch other people react to drugs (Sher et al., 1996), and these expectations can influence how much of a drug they themselves consume (see Figure 4.10). What they see can differ from one individual and culture to the next, so drug effects vary considerably throughout the world (MacAndrew & Edgerton, 1969). In the United States, for example, drinking alcohol is commonly associated with uninhibited behavior, including impulsiveness, anger, violence, and sexual promiscuity. These effects are not seen in all cultures, however. In Bolivia's Camba culture, people sometimes engage in extended bouts of drinking a brew that is 89 percent alcohol (178 proof). During these binges, the Camba repeatedly pass out, wake up, and start drinking again—all the while maintaining friendly social relations. Other studies have shown that learned expectations also contribute to the effects of heroin, cocaine, and marijuana (Robbins & Everitt, 1999; Schafer & Brown, 1991; Smith et al., 1992).

In short, the effects of psychoactive drugs are complex and variable. Here, we consider several major categories of psychoactive drugs that people use primarily to produce altered states of consciousness. They include depressants, stimulants, opiates, and hallucinogens.

Depressants

Depressants, such as alcohol and barbiturates, reduce or depress central nervous system activity. They do so partly by increasing the effects of the neurotransmitter GABA. As described in the chapter on biology and behavior, GABA reduces the activity of neurons in various brain circuits. So if a drug increases the amount of GABA available, activity in those circuits will be lower than usual, creating feelings of relaxation, drowsiness, and sometimes depression (Hanson & Venturelli, 1995).

Alcohol   The most common depressant drug by far is alcohol. In the United States, more than 100 million people drink alcohol. It is equally popular worldwide (Alvarez, Delrio, & Prada, 1995; Leigh & Stacy, 2004). Alcohol affects several neurotransmitters, including glutamate, serotonin, and GABA, among others (Daglish & Nutt, 2003; Enoch, 2003). The effect on GABA is especially significant. In fact, animal studies show that the intoxicating effects of alcohol can be blocked by drugs that prevent it from interacting with GABA receptors (Suzdak et al., 1986).

Alcohol also enhances the effect of endorphins, the body's natural painkillers. The fact that endorphins produce a sense of well-being may explain why people initially feel "high" when drinking alcohol. It may also explain why drugs that block endorphins are better than placebos at reducing alcohol cravings and relapse rates in recovering alcoholics (Garbutt et al., 2005). The pleasurable effects of alcohol are due in part to its interaction with dopamine systems, which are part of the brain's reward mechanisms (Thanos et al., 2001). Prolonged alcohol use can have lasting effects on the brain's ability to regulate dopamine levels (Tiihonen et al., 1995). Dopamine agonists reduce alcohol cravings and withdrawal effects (Lawford et al., 1995).

Alcohol affects specific brain regions. It depresses activity in the locus coeruleus, an area, as described in our discussion of sleep, that helps activate the cerebral cortex (Koob & Bloom, 1988). This reduced activity, in turn, tends to cause cognitive changes and a loosening of control over normally inhibited behaviors (Casbon et al., 2003). Some drinkers begin talking loudly, acting silly, or telling others what they think of them. Emotional reactions range from giddy happiness to despair. Normally shy people may become impulsive or violent. Alcohol also impairs the hippocampus, making it more difficult to process information and form new memories (Givens, 1995). And it suppresses the cerebellum, causing poor motor coordination, including difficulty in walking (Rogers et al., 1986). Alcohol's ability to depress hindbrain mechanisms required for breathing and heartbeat can make overdoses fatal.

As mentioned earlier, some effects of alcohol—such as anger and aggressiveness—depend on both biochemical factors and learned expectations (Goldman, Darkes, & Del Boca, 1999; Kushner et al., 2000). But other effects—especially disruptions in motor coordination, speech, and thought—result from biochemical factors alone. These biological effects depend on the amount of alcohol the blood carries to the brain. It takes the liver about an hour to break down one ounce of alcohol (the amount in one typical drink), so alcohol has milder effects if consumed slowly. Faster drinking or drinking on an empty stomach speeds absorption of alcohol into the blood and heightens its effects. Even after allowing for differences in average male and female body weight, researchers have found metabolic differences that make male bodies able to tolerate somewhat greater amounts of alcohol. So a given quantity of alcohol may have a stronger effect on a woman than on a man (York & Welte, 1994). Overindulgence by either sex results in unpleasant physical hangover effects that, cannot be prevented or relieved by aspirin, bananas, vitamins, coffee, eggs, exercise, fresh air, honey, pizza, herbal remedies, more alcohol, or any of the dozens of other "surefire" hangover cures you may have heard about (Pittler, Verster, & Ernst, 2005).

Genetics also seems to play a role in determining the biochemical effects of alcohol (Scholz, Franz, & Heberlein, 2005). Evidence suggests that some people have a genetic

depressants   Psychoactive drugs that inhibit the functioning of the central nervous system.

DRINKING AND DRIVING DON'T MIX
Though practice makes it seem easy, driving a car is a complex information-processing task. As described in the chapter on thought, language, and intelligence, such tasks require constant vigilance, quick decisions, and skillful execution of responses. Alcohol can impair all these processes, as well as the ability to judge the degree of impairment—thus making drinking and driving a deadly combination that results in 275,000 injuries and almost 17,000 deaths each year in the United States alone (McDonald, Wang, & Camargo, 2004; National Highway Traffic Safety Administration, 2005).

predisposition toward alcohol dependence (Agarwal, 1997; Enoch, 2003), though the genes involved have not yet been identified (Holden, 1998). Other groups (the Japanese, for example) may have inherited metabolic characteristics that enhance alcohol's adverse effects, possibly inhibiting the development of alcohol abuse (Iwahashi et al., 1995).

Barbiturates   Sometimes called "downers" or sleeping pills, *barbiturates* are highly addictive. In small doses, their psychoactive effects include relaxation, mild pleasure, loss of muscle coordination, and lowered attention. Higher doses cause deep sleep, but continued use actually distorts sleep patterns (Kales & Kales, 1973). So long-term use of barbiturates as sleeping pills may be unwise. Overdoses can be fatal. Withdrawal symptoms are among the most severe for any drug and can include intense agitation, violent outbursts, seizures, hallucinations, and even sudden death.

GHB   *Gamma hydroxybutyrate (GHB)* is a naturally occurring substance similar to the neurotransmitter GABA (Wong, Gibson, & Snead, 2004). In recent years, a laboratory-manufactured version of GHB (also known as "G") has become a popular "club drug" known for creating relaxation, feelings of elation, loss of inhibitions, and increased sex drive. Unfortunately, it can also cause nausea and vomiting, headaches, memory loss, dizziness, loss of muscle control or paralysis, breathing problems, loss of consciousness, and even death—especially when combined with alcohol or other drugs (Miotto et al., 2001; Stillwell, 2002). As with other depressants, long-term use of GHB can lead to dependence. If dependent users abruptly stop taking the drug, they may experience a withdrawal syndrome that can include seizures, hallucinations, agitation, coma, or death (Tarabar & Nelson, 2004).

Stimulants

Whereas depressants slow down central nervous system activity, **stimulants** speed it up. Amphetamines, cocaine, caffeine, and nicotine are all examples of stimulants.

Amphetamines   Often called "uppers" or "speed," *amphetamines* increase the release of norepinephrine and dopamine into synapses, affecting sleep, learning, and mood (Bonci et al., 2003; Kolb et al., 2003). Amphetamines also slow the removal of both

stimulants Psychoactive drugs that increase behavioral and mental activity.

DEADLY DRUG USE John Entwistle, bass player for The Who, died of a cocaine-related heart attack in 2002. He joined a long list of celebrities (including Chris Farley and Righteous Brother Bobby Hatfield) and an even longer list of ordinary people whose lives have been destroyed by the abuse of cocaine or other drugs.

substances at synapses, leaving more of them there, ready to work. The increased activity at these neurotransmitters' receptors results in alertness, arousal, and appetite suppression. These effects are amplified by the fact that amphetamines also reduce activity of the inhibitory neurotransmitter GABA (Centonze et al., 2002). Amphetamines' rewarding properties are probably associated with their effect on dopamine activity, because taking dopamine antagonists reduces amphetamine use (Holman, 1994).

People who abuse amphetamines usually begin taking these drugs in an effort to lose weight, stay awake, or "get high." Continued use leads to anxiety, insomnia, heart problems, brain damage, movement disorders, confusion, paranoia, nonstop talking, and psychological and physical dependence (Thompson et al., 2004; Volkow et al., 2001). In some cases, the symptoms of amphetamine abuse are almost identical to those of paranoid schizophrenia, a serious mental disorder linked to dopamine malfunction.

Cocaine   Like amphetamines, *cocaine* increases norepinephrine and dopamine activity and decreases GABA activity, so it produces many amphetamine-like effects (Kolb et al., 2003). Cocaine's particularly powerful and rapid effect on dopamine activity may underlie its remarkably addictive nature (Bonci et al., 2003; Ciccocioppo et al., 2004; Ungless et al., 2001). In fact, most drugs with rapid onset and short duration are more addictive than others (Kato, Wakasa, & Yamagita, 1987), which helps explain why *crack*—a purified, fast-acting, highly potent, smokable form of cocaine—is especially addictive.

Cocaine stimulates self-confidence, a sense of well-being, and optimism. Continued use, though, brings nausea, overactivity, insomnia, paranoia, a sudden depressive "crash," hallucinations, sexual dysfunction, and seizures (Lacayo, 1995). Overdoses, especially overdoses of crack cocaine, can be deadly. Even small doses can cause a fatal heart attack or stroke (Klausner & Lewandowski, 2002; Marzuk et al., 1995). Using cocaine during pregnancy harms the fetus (e.g., Hurt et al., 1995). However, many of the severe, long-term behavioral problems seen in "cocaine babies" may have as much to do with poverty and neglect after birth as with the mother's cocaine use beforehand. Early intervention can reduce the effects of both cocaine and the hostile environment that confronts most cocaine babies (Mayes et al., 2003; Singer et al., 2004; Wren, 1998).

Caffeine   *Caffeine* may be the world's most popular drug. It is found not only in coffee and tea but also in chocolate and many soft drinks. Caffeine reduces drowsiness and can enhance cognitive performance, including problem solving and vigilance (Beaumont et al., 2001). It also increases the capacity for physical work and raises urine production (Warburton, 1995). At high doses it causes anxiety and tremors. People can develop tolerance to caffeine, and it can be physically addictive (Strain et al., 1994). Withdrawal symptoms—including headache, fatigue, anxiety, shakiness, and craving—appear on the first day of abstinence and last about a week (Silverman et al., 1992). Caffeine may make it harder for women to become pregnant and may increase the risk of miscarriage or stillbirth (Balat et al., 2003; Bech et al., 2005; Rasch, 2003; Wisborg et al., 2003). Moderate daily caffeine use may also cause slight increases in blood pressure (James, 2004), but otherwise it appears to have few, if any, negative effects (Kleemola et al., 2000; Winkelmayer et al., 2005).

Nicotine   A powerful autonomic nervous system stimulant, *nicotine* is the main psychoactive ingredient in tobacco. It enhances the action of acetylcholine and increases the availability of glutamate, the brain's primary excitatory neurotransmitter. It also activates the brain's dopamine-related pleasure systems (Balfour, 2002; McGehee et al., 1995). Nicotine has many psychoactive effects, including elevated mood and improved memory and attention (Domino, 2003; Ernst et al., 2001). Like heroin and cocaine, nicotine can be physically addictive (White, 1998). It doesn't create the "rush" characteristic of many drugs of abuse, but stopping nicotine use often creates a withdrawal syndrome that includes craving, irritability, anxiety, reduced heart rate, and reduced activity in the brain's reward pathways (Epping-Jordan et al., 1998; Hughes, Higgins, & Bickel, 1994). Some smokers appear to develop only a psychological dependence on nicotine (Robinson & Pritchard, 1995), but whether the dependence is physiological or psychological, there is no doubt that tobacco smoking can be a difficult habit to break (Breteler et al., 2004; Shiffman et al., 1997). It is also clearly recognized as a major risk factor for cancer, heart disease, and respiratory disorders (U.S. Department of Health and Human Services, 2001c).

MDMA   The stimulant "Ecstasy," or *MDMA* (short for 3,4-methylenedioxymetham-phetamine), is a popular drug on college campuses in the United States (Strote, Lee, & Wechsler, 2002). MDMA increases the activity of dopamine-releasing neurons, so it leads to some of the same effects as those produced by cocaine and amphetamines (Steele, McCann, & Ricaurte, 1994). These include a sense of well-being, increased sex drive, and a feeling of greater closeness to others. Unfortunately, MDMA may also cause dry mouth, hyperactivity, jaw muscle spasms that may result in "lockjaw," elevated blood pressure, fever, dangerously abnormal heart rhythms, and visual hallucinations (Smith, Larive, & Romananelli, 2002). The hallucinations may appear because MDMA is a serotonin agonist and also increases serotonin release (Green, Cross, & Goodwin, 1995). On the day after using MDMA—also known as "XTC," "clarity," "essence," "E," and "Adam"—people often report muscle aches, fatigue, depression, and poor concentration (Peroutka, Newman, & Harris, 1988).

Even though it does not appear to be physically addictive, MDMA is a dangerous, potentially deadly drug, especially when taken by women (Liechti, Gamma, & Vollenweider, 2001; National Institute on Drug Abuse, 2000). It permanently damages the brain, killing serotonin-sensitive neurons (Green et al., 1995), as well as neurons that use dopamine. As you might expect, the danger of brain damage increases with higher doses and continued use (Battaglia, Yeh, & DeSouza, 1988). MDMA also impairs memory (Reneman et al., 2001; Rodgers, 2000; Zakzanis & Young, 2001), and users may develop the symptoms of *panic disorder,* which include intense anxiety and a sense of impending death (see the chapter on psychological disorders).

Opiates

The **opiates** (opium, morphine, heroin, and codeine) are unique in their capacity for inducing sleep and relieving pain (Julien, 2005). *Opium,* derived from the poppy plant, relieves pain and causes feelings of well-being and dreamy relaxation (Cowan et al., 2001). One of its most active ingredients, *morphine,* was first isolated in the early 1800s. It is used worldwide for pain relief. Percodan and Demerol are some common morphine-like drugs. *Heroin* is derived from morphine but is three times more powerful, causing intensely pleasurable reactions. Opiates have complex effects on consciousness. Drowsy, cloudy feelings occur because opiates depress activity in some areas of the cerebral cortex. They also create excitation in other parts, causing some users to experience euphoria, or elation (Bozarth & Wise, 1984). Opiates exert many of their effects by stimulating the receptors normally stimulated by endorphins, the body's own painkillers. This action "tricks" the brain into an exaggerated activation of its painkilling and mood-altering systems (Julien, 2005).

Opiates are highly addictive, partly because they stimulate a type of glutamate receptor in the brain's neurons that causes physical changes in these neurons. It may be, then, that opiates alter neurons so that they come to require the drug to function properly. Beyond the hazard of addiction itself, heroin addicts risk death through overdoses, contaminated drugs, or AIDS contracted through sharing needles (Hser et al., 2001).

Hallucinogens

Hallucinogens, also called *psychedelics,* create a loss of contact with reality and alter other aspects of emotion, perception, and thought. They can cause distortions in body image (the user may feel gigantic or tiny), loss of identity (confusion about who one actually is), dream-like fantasies, and hallucinations. Because these effects resemble many severe forms of mental disorder, hallucinogens are also called *psychotomimetics* ("mimicking psychosis").

opiates Psychoactive drugs that produce both sleep-inducing and pain-relieving effects.

hallucinogens Psychoactive drugs that alter consciousness by producing a temporary loss of contact with reality and changes in emotion, perception, and thought.

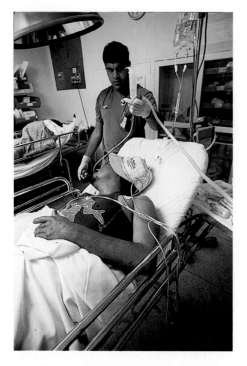

ANOTHER DRUG DANGER Oxycodone, a morphine-like drug prescribed by doctors under the label OxyContin, has become popular among recreational substance abusers. It was designed as a timed-release painkiller, but when people crush OxyContin tablets and then inject or inhale the drug, they get a much stronger and potentially lethal dose, especially when they are also using other drugs such as alcohol or cocaine (Cone et al., 2004). Deaths from OxyContin abuse are already on the rise in the United States (U.S. Drug Enforcement Administration, 2002).

LSD One of the most powerful hallucinogens is *lysergic acid diethylamide,* or *LSD.* It was first synthesized from a rye fungus by a Swiss chemist, Albert Hofmann. In 1938, after Hofmann accidentally ingested a tiny amount of the substance, he discovered the drug's strange effects in the world's first LSD "trip" (Julien, 2005). LSD hallucinations can be quite bizarre. Time may seem distorted, sounds may cause visual sensations, and users may feel as if they have left their bodies. These experiences probably result from LSD's action as a serotonin agonist, because serotonin antagonists greatly reduce LSD's hallucinatory effects (Leonard, 1992).

The effects of LSD on a particular person are unpredictable. Unpleasant hallucinations and delusions can occur during a person's first—or two hundredth—LSD experience. Although LSD is not addictive, tolerance to its effects does develop. Some users suffer lasting side effects, including severe short-term memory loss, paranoia, violent outbursts, nightmares, and panic attacks (Gold, 1994). Sometimes "flashbacks" can occur, in which a person suddenly returns to an LSD-like state of consciousness weeks or even years after using the drug.

Ketamine *Ketamine* is an anesthetic used by veterinarians to ease pain in animals, but because it also has hallucinogenic effects, it is being stolen and sold as a recreational drug known as "Special K." Its effects include dissociative feelings that create what some users describe as an "out-of-body" or "near-death" experience. Ketamine can also lead to lasting memory problems (Curran & Monaghan, 2001; Smith et al., 2002), possibly because it damages memory-related brain structures such as the hippocampus (Jevtovic-Todorovic et al., 2001).

Marijuana A mixture of crushed leaves, flowers, and stems from the hemp plant *(Cannabis sativa)* makes up *marijuana.* The active ingredient is *tetrahydrocannabinol,* or *THC.* When inhaled, THC is absorbed in minutes by many organs, including the brain, and it continues to affect consciousness for a few hours (O'Leary et al., 2002). THC tends to collect in fatty deposits of the brain and reproductive organs, where it can remain for weeks. Low doses of marijuana may initially create restlessness and hilarity, followed by a dreamy, carefree relaxation, an expanded sense of space and time, more vivid sensations, food cravings, and subtle changes in thinking (Kelly et al., 1990).

There is an ongoing debate about the dangers and potential benefits of marijuana (Henquet et al., 2005; Iversen & Snyder, 2000; Strang, Witten, & Hall, 2000). Its dangers are suggested by the fact that a mild withdrawal syndrome has been reported in rats; in humans, withdrawal from marijuana may be accompanied by increases in anxiety, depression, irritability, restlessness, and aggressiveness (Budney et al., 2001, 2003; Haney et al., 1999; Kouri, Pope, & Lukas, 1999; Rodriguez de Fonseca et al., 1997; Smith, 2002). Further, marijuana interacts with the same dopamine and opiate receptors that heroin acts on (Tanda, Pontieri, & Di Chiara, 1997), leading some researchers to speculate that marijuana might be a "gateway" to the use of opiates (Lynskey et al., 2003). Other researchers have cautioned that the interpretation of these results is not clear-cut (Grinspoon, 1999), because sex and chocolate have their rewarding effects by activating those same neurotransmitter receptors—and few people would want to outlaw those pleasures!

Regardless of whether marijuana is addicting or leads to the use of opiates, it can create a number of problems. It disrupts memory formation, making it difficult to carry out mental or physical tasks; and, despite users' impressions, it actually reduces creativity (Bourassa & Vaugeois, 2001; Pope & Yurgelun-Todd, 1996). And because marijuana disrupts muscle coordination, driving while under its influence can be dangerous. In fact, motor impairment continues well after the subjective effects of the drug have worn off. Marijuana easily reaches a developing fetus and therefore should not be used by pregnant women (Fried, Watkinson, & Gray, 1992). Finally, long-term use can lead to psychological dependence (Stephens, Roffman, & Simpson, 1994), as well as to impairments in reasoning and memory that last for months or years after marijuana use stops (Bolla et al., 2002; Solowij et al., 2002). Research has also shown that adults

MAJOR CLASSES OF PSYCHOACTIVE DRUGS

in review

Drug	Trade/Street Name	Main Effects	Potential for Physical/ Psychological Dependence
Depressants			
Alcohol	"booze"	Relaxation, anxiety	High/high
Barbiturates	Seconal, Tuinal, Nembutal ("downers")	reduction, sleep	High/high
GHB	G, Jib, Scoop, GH Buddy	Relaxation, euphoria	High/high
Stimulants			
Amphetamines	Benzedrine, Dexedrine, Methadrine ("speed," "uppers," "ice")	Alertness, euphoria	Moderate/high
Cocaine	"coke," "crack"		Moderate to high/high
Caffeine		Alertness	Moderate/moderate
Nicotine	"smokes," "coffin nails"	Alertness	High (?)/high
MDMA	"Ecstasy," "clarity"	Hallucinations	Low/(?)
Opiates			
Opium		Euphoria	High/high
Morphine	Percodan, Demerol	Euphoria, pain control	High/high
Heroin	"junk," "smack"	Euphoria, pain control	High/high
Hallucinogens			
LSD/ketamine	"acid"/"Special K"	Altered perceptions, hallucinations	Low/low
Marijuana (cannabis)	"pot," "dope," "reefer"	Euphoria, relaxation	Low/moderate

1. Physical dependence on a drug is a condition more commonly known as _____ .
2. Drugs that act as antagonists _____ the interaction of neurotransmitters and receptors.
3. Drug effects are determined partly by what we learn to _____ the effects to be.

who frequently used marijuana scored lower than nonusers with equal IQs on a twelfth-grade academic achievement test (Block & Ghoneim, 1993) and that heavier use in teenagers is associated with the later appearance of anxiety, depression, and other symptoms of mental disorder (Arsenault et al., 2004; Patton et al., 2002; Zammit et al., 2002).

Marijuana may have considerable value in some domains, however. Doctors have successfully used it in the treatment of asthma, glaucoma, epilepsy, chronic pain, and nausea from cancer chemotherapy; it may even help in treating some types of cancer (Gorter et al., 2005; Parolaro et al., 2002; Rog et al., 2005; Tramer et al., 2001). But critics say medical legalization of marijuana is premature until more controlled research is available to establish its medicinal value. They point out, too, that even though patients tend to prefer marijuana-based drugs, other medications may be equally effective and less dangerous (e.g., Campbell et al., 2001; Fox et al., 2004; Hall & Degenhardt, 2003).

Nevertheless, in Canada, it is legal to grow and use marijuana for medicinal purposes, and the same is true in eight U.S. states, despite federal laws to the contrary and the threat of federal intervention to enforce those laws (Okie, 2005). The American Medical Association has rejected the idea of medical uses for marijuana, but scientists are intent on objectively studying its potential value in the treatment of certain diseases, as well as its possible dangers. Their work is being encouraged by the National Institute of Medicine (Joy, Watson, & Benson, 1999), and drug companies are working on new cannabis-based medicines (Altman, 2000; Tuller, 2004). The United Nations, too, has recommended that governments worldwide sponsor additional work on the medical uses of marijuana (Wren, 1999). ("In Review: Major Classes of Psychoactive Drugs" summarizes our discussion of these substances.)

Consciousness

Linkages

As noted in the introductory chapter, all of psychology's subfields are related to one another. Our discussion of meditation, health, and stress illustrates just one way in which the topic of this chapter, consciousness, is linked to the subfield of health psychology, which is described in the chapter on health, stress, and coping. The Linkages diagram shows ties to two other subfields, and there are many more ties throughout the book. Looking for linkages among subfields will help you see how they all fit together and help you better appreciate the big picture that is psychology.

LINKAGES

CHAPTER 4

CONSCIOUSNESS

Do forgotten memories remain in the subconscious?
(ans. on p. 230)

CHAPTER 6

MEMORY

Does meditation relieve stress?
(ans. on p. 154)

CHAPTER 10

HEALTH, STRESS, AND COPING

Can subconscious processes alter our reaction to people?
(ans. on p. 552)

CHAPTER 14

SOCIAL PSYCHOLOGY

Summary

Consciousness can be defined as awareness of the outside world and of one's own thoughts, feelings, perceptions, and other mental processes.

THE SCOPE OF CONSCIOUSNESS

▶ **Can unconscious thoughts affect your behavior?**

A person's *state of consciousness* is constantly changing. When the changes are particularly noticeable, they are called *altered states of consciousness.* Examples of altered states include sleep, hypnosis, meditation, and some drug-induced conditions. Cultures differ in the value placed on particular states of consciousness.

Variations in how much awareness you have for a mental function are described by different levels of consciousness. The *preconscious level* is described as including mental activities that are outside of awareness but that can easily be brought to the *conscious level. Subconscious* and *unconscious* mental activity is said to involve thoughts, memories, and processes that are more difficult to bring to awareness. Mental processes that cannot be brought into awareness are said to occur at the *nonconscious level.*

Awareness is not always required for mental operations. For example, research on priming shows that people's responses to stimuli speed up and improve as stimuli are repeated, even when there is no conscious memory of which stimuli are old and which are new. And some decisions that seem intuitive may be guided by information that is outside of awareness.

SLEEPING AND DREAMING

▶ **Does your brain go to sleep when you do?**

Sleep is an active and complex state. Different stages of sleep are defined on the basis of changes in brain activity (as measured by an electroencephalograph, or EEG) and physiological arousal. Sleep normally begins with stage 1 sleep and progresses gradually to stage 4 sleep. Sleep stages 3 and 4 constitute *slow-wave sleep,* which is part of non-REM sleep. After passing back to stage 2, people enter *rapid eye movement (REM) sleep,* or paradoxical sleep. The sleeper passes through these stages several times each night, gradually spending more time in stage 2 and REM sleep later in the night.

Sleep disorders can disrupt the natural rhythm of sleep. Among the most common is *insomnia,* in which one feels tired because of trouble falling asleep or staying asleep. *Narcolepsy* produces sudden daytime sleeping episodes. In cases of *sleep apnea,* people briefly but repeatedly stop breathing during sleep. *Sudden infant death syndrome (SIDS)* may be due to brain abnormalities or accidental suffocation. *Sleepwalking* happens most frequently during childhood. *Nightmares* and *night terrors* are different kinds of frightening dreams. *REM behavior disorder* is potentially dangerous because it allows people to act out REM dreams. The cycle of waking and sleeping is a natural *circadian rhythm,* controlled by the suprachiasmatic nuclei of the brain. *Jet lag* can be one result of disrupting the normal sleep-wake cycle.

The purpose of sleep is still unclear. Non-REM sleep may aid bodily rest and repair. REM sleep may help maintain activity in brain areas that provide daytime alertness, or it may allow the brain to "check circuits," eliminate useless information, and solidify learning from the previous day.

Most dreaming occurs during REM sleep. *Dreams* are story-like sequences of images, sensations, and perceptions that occur during sleep. Evidence from research on *lucid dreaming* suggests that people may be able to control their own dreams. Some claim that dreams are the meaningless byproducts of brain activity, but our recall of dreams may still have psychological significance.

HYPNOSIS

▶ **Can you be hypnotized against your will?**

Hypnosis is a well-known but still poorly understood phenomenon. Tests of *hypnotic susceptibility* suggest that some people cannot be hypnotized and that others are hypnotized easily. Hypnotized people tend to focus attention on the hypnotist and passively follow instructions. They become better at fantasizing and role taking. They may exhibit apparent age regression, experience posthypnotic amnesia, and obey posthypnotic suggestions.

State theory sees hypnosis as a special state of consciousness. *Role theory* suggests that hypnosis creates a special social role in which people feel free to act in unusual ways. *Dissociation theory* combines aspects of role and state theories, suggesting that hypnotized individuals enter into a social contract with the hypnotist to allow normally integrated mental processes to become dissociated and to share control over these processes.

Hypnosis is useful in the control of pain and the reduction of nausea associated with cancer chemotherapy. Meditation is a set of techniques designed to create an altered state of consciousness characterized by inner peace and increased awareness. The consistent practice of meditation has been associated with reductions in stress-related problems such as anxiety and high blood pressure.

PSYCHOACTIVE DRUGS

▶ **How do drugs affect the brain?**

Psychoactive drugs affect the brain, changing consciousness and other psychological processes. *Psychopharmacology* is the field that studies drug effects and their mechanisms. Psychoactive drugs exert their effects primarily by influencing specific neurotransmitter systems and, hence, certain brain activities. To reach brain tissue, drugs must cross the *blood-brain barrier.* Drugs that mimic the receptor effects of a neurotransmitter are called *agonists;* drugs that block the receptor effects of a neurotransmitter are called *antagonists.* Some drugs alter the release or removal of specific neurotransmitters, thus affecting the amount of neurotransmitter available for receptor effects.

Adverse effects such as *substance abuse* often accompany the use of psychoactive drugs. *Psychological dependence, addiction* (*physical dependence*), *tolerance,* and a *withdrawal syndrome* may result. Drugs that produce dependence share the property of directly stimulating certain dopamine-sensitive areas of the brain known as pleasure centers. The consequences of using a psychoactive drug depend both on how the drug affects neurotransmitters and on the user's expectations.

Alcohol and barbiturates are examples of *depressants.* They reduce activity in the central nervous system, often by enhancing the action of inhibitory neurotransmitters. They have considerable potential for producing both psychological and physical dependence.

Stimulants, such as amphetamines and cocaine, increase behavioral and mental activity mainly by increasing the action of dopamine and norepinephrine. These drugs can produce both psychological and physical dependence. Caffeine, one of the world's most popular stimulants, may also create dependence. Nicotine is a potent stimulant. And MDMA, which has both stimulant and hallucinogenic properties, is one of several psychoactive drugs that can permanently damage brain tissue.

Opiates such as opium, morphine, and heroin are highly addictive drugs that induce sleep and relieve pain.

LSD and marijuana are examples of *hallucinogens,* or psychedelics. They alter consciousness by producing a temporary loss of contact with reality and changes in emotion, perception, and thought.

Learn by Doing

Put It in Writing

Watch a prime-time television program, and make notes on the role played in the story by alcohol, nicotine, cocaine, or other psychoactive drugs. Now think about what you saw, and write a one-page paper describing the messages the show sent to viewers about drugs. Did it directly or indirectly approve or disapprove of drug use? Did it lead viewers to expect particular effects from particular drugs? Conclude by considering what effects these drug-related messages might have on viewers, especially young children.

Personal Learning Activity

For the next two weeks, keep a note pad or tape recorder by your bed, and write down or record your dreams as soon as you awaken. During this same period, use a diary or calendar to jot down significant events, problems, and emotional reactions in your waking life. Then compare the two sets of information. Do you see any correlation? For example, did any of your life events appear in your dreams? Did any dreams contain wished-for solutions to the problems or challenges you were facing at the time? What do you think your own data might say about the meaning of dreams in general? *For additional projects, see the Personal Learning Activities in the corresponding chapter of the study guide that accompanies this text.*

Step into Action

Courses

History of Psychology
Neuropsychology
Cognitive Psychology
Psychopharmacology
Computational Neuroscience
Sleep

Movies

An American Werewolf in London. Nightmares.

Boyz n the Hood. The role of drugs and alcohol in adolescent development.

Days of Wine and Roses; The Lost Weekend; Leaving Las Vegas; When a Man Loves a Woman. Alcoholism.

Deadly Dreams. Portrayal of dreams as glimpses of the future.

Rush; Trainspotting; Basketball Diaries. Drug addiction.

Stir of Echoes; Hypnosis. Myths and misconceptions about hypnosis.

Sacred Sleep: The Power of Dreams. Various cultures view the meaning of dreams.

Books

Susan Cheever, *Note Found in a Bottle: My Life as a Drinker* (Washington Square Press, 2000). Memoir of an alcoholic.

Barnaby Conrad, *Time Is All We Have* (Cameron, 1992). A month at the Betty Ford Treatment Center.

Nicholas Humphrey, *A History of the Mind: Evolution and the Birth of Consciousness* (Copernicus, 1999). Description of how consciousness has arisen from brain activity.

Ernest Keen, *Chemicals for the Mind: Pharmacology and Human Consciousness* (Praeger, 2000). Theories of consciousness and drugs' effects on it.

Caroline Knapp, *Drinking: A Love Story* (Delta, 1997). A woman explores the roots of her alcohol addiction.

Robert M. Julien, *A Primer of Drug Action: A Concise,*

Nontechnical Guide to the Actions, Uses, and Side Effects of Psychoactive Drugs (10th ed.; Worth, 2005). The title says it all.

Daniel Goleman, *The Meditative Mind: Varieties of Meditative Experience* (J. P. Tarcher, 1996). Meditation and its effects.

Steven J. Lynn and Irving Kirsch, *Essentials of Clinical Hypnosis: An Evidence-Based Approach.* (American Psychological Association, 2005). Summary of hypnotic techniques, evidence for clinical use of hypnosis, and theories of hypnosis.

Steven J. Lynn, Irving Kirsh, and Judith Rhue, *Casebook of Clinical Hypnosis* (American Psychological Association, 2006). Case studies in the use of hypnotic techniques in clinical treatment.

Joseph Barber (Ed.), *Hypnosis and Suggestion in the Treatment of Pain* (Norton, 1996). Case studies in pain management using hypnosis.

Stanley Coren, *Sleep Thieves: An Eye-Opening Exploration into the Science and Mysteries of Sleep* (Free Press, 1996). An introduction to sleep research.

Edward F. Pace-Schott, Mark Solms, Mark Blagrove, and Stevan Harnad (Eds.) *Sleep and Dreaming: Scientific Advances and Reconsiderations* (Cambridge University Press, 2003). A comprehensive set of research articles on sleep and dreaming.

The Web

The World Wide Web is a good source of additional information about the science of psychology, provided you use it carefully and think critically about the information you find. The Online Study Center that accompanies this text offers many resources relevant to this chapter. These resources include interactive tutorials; Thinking Critically and Evaluating Research exercises; ACE chapter quizzes; recommended web links; and articles on current events, books, and movies. Please visit the Online Study Center at http://college.hmco.com/pic/bernstein4e.

Review of Key Terms

Can you define each of the key terms in the chapter? Check your definitions against those on the pages shown in parentheses in the following list or in the Glossary/Index at the end of the text.

role theory *(p. 153)*

sleep apnea *(p. 147)*

sleepwalking *(p. 147)*

slow-wave sleep *(p. 144)*

state of consciousness *(p. xxx)*

state theory *(p. 153)*

stimulants *(p. 159)*

subconscious *(p. 138)*

substance abuse *(p. 156)*

sudden infant death syndrome (SIDS) *(p. 147)*

tolerance *(p. 156)*

unconscious *(p. 138)*

withdrawal syndrome *(p. 156)*

Multiple-Choice Self-Test

Select the best answer for each of the following questions. Then check your responses against the Answer Key at the end of the text.

1. Tyrrell is undergoing biofeedback training to help him regulate his blood pressure, a bodily function typically regulated at which level of consciousness?

   a. Nonconscious
   b. Preconscious
   c. Subconscious
   d. Unconscious

2. Dr. Eplort is staying in a cave for several months with no external light cues and no way to keep time. He goes to sleep when he feels sleepy and gets up when he is awake. Dr. Eplort will most likely sleep

   a. fewer hours than he did before.
   b. more hours than he did before.
   c. about the same as he did before.
   d. on a varying and unpredictable schedule.

3. Zandra knew nothing about art, and during her first semester on campus she had not noticed the framed Rembrandt prints in the hallway of her classroom building. But when she took an art appreciation class the next semester, she found that the paintings she liked best were those same Rembrandt images. Her preference was most likely affected by

   a. the prosopagnosia effect.
   b. supraliminal perception.
   c. priming.
   d. visual masking.

4. Edie has purchased a tape that contains subliminal messages designed to help her lose weight. According to the Thinking Critically section in this chapter, Edie's success in losing weight most likely depends on

   a. the content of the subliminal messages.
   b. her expectation that the subliminal messages will help.
   c. how relaxed the subliminal messages make her feel.
   d. the number of times the subliminal messages occur.

5. Mitch noticed that, after his friends smoked marijuana, they soon began giggling, acting silly, and singing "We're Off to See the Wizard." After he smoked marijuana himself for the first time, he found himself doing the very same things. Mitch's specific responses to marijuana were most likely due to

   a. an altered state of consciousness.
   b. reversion to a preconscious state.
   c. priming.
   d. learned expectations.

6. The telephone rang several hours after Leroy fell asleep. It takes Leroy a while to locate the phone, and he is so groggy when he answers that, in the morning, he can't remember who called or what was said. When the phone rang, Leroy was most likely in _____ sleep.

   a. stage 1
   b. stage 2
   c. stage 4
   d. REM

7. Alan's wife is concerned because he often gets out of bed during the night and acts out his dreams. One night he boxed with an invisible opponent, and last night he was fighting a phantom bull. Alan most likely would be diagnosed as having

   a. sleep apnea.
   b. narcolepsy.
   c. REM behavior disorder.
   d. night terrors.

8. The "back to sleep" program, which advises parents to have their babies sleep face up, has greatly reduced the incidence of _____ in the United States.

   a. SIDS
   b. night terrors
   c. REM behavior disorder
   d. insomnia

9. Dr. Franklin was flying from Los Angeles to Paris, where he was to give a speech shortly after arrival. To minimize the effects of jet lag, his physician would most likely recommend that Dr. Franklin should

   a. be sure to sleep eight hours a night for at least a week before his trip.
   b. take melatonin.
   c. stay awake for 24 hours before departure, then sleep throughout the flight.
   d. reverse his sleep-wake cycle for a week before departure.

10. Sleep research suggests that REM sleep may be important for all of the following *except*

   a. improving the functioning of neurons that use norepinephrine.
   b. developing, checking, and expanding the brain's nerve connections.
   c. restoring the body's and brain's energy stores for the next day's activity.
   d. establishing memories of emotional information.

11. According to the activation-synthesis theory, dreams

    a. help our brains analyze and consolidate information.
    b. satisfy unconscious urges and resolve unconscious conflicts.
    c. are hallucinations.
    d. are meaningless, random byproducts of REM sleep.

12. Lavonne, a hypnotist, wanted to present a dramatic demonstration of hypnosis. Which of the following people should she select as her hypnotic subject?

    a. Alex, who is easily distracted.
    b. Bobbi, who doesn't believe in hypnosis.
    c. Carl, who is good at focusing his attention.
    d. Dellena, whose imagination is limited.

13. Hypnosis has been especially effective in

    a. connecting with past lives.
    b. improving memory.
    c. pain control.
    d. lowering cholesterol.

14. Norman has been meditating for over a year. By now, according to your textbook, we would expect Norman to

    a. be less anxious.
    b. need less sleep to feel refreshed.
    c. have a better memory.
    d. daydream more.

15. Candice was given morphine to ease the pain of back surgery. Her doctor explained that morphine occupies the same receptors and has the same effect as endorphins, the body's natural pain killers. In other words, morphine is an endorphin _____

    a. agonist.
    b. antagonist.
    c. reuptake blocker.
    d. placebo.

16. Vincent has been using heroin for some time, and now he finds that he needs larger amounts of the drug to achieve the same effect he used to get from smaller doses. Vincent is experiencing

    a. tolerance.
    b. learned expectations.
    c. withdrawal.
    d. synaptic potential.

17. Which of the following is true about alcohol?

    a. A given amount of alcohol will affect a man more than a woman.
    b. Alcohol's effects are the same whether it is consumed slowly or quickly.
    c. There are no genetic predispositions toward alcohol abuse.
    d. Dopamine agonists reduce alcohol cravings.

18. A young man experiencing hallucinations is brought to a hospital emergency room. Which of the following drugs could his doctor rule out as a likely cause of the hallucinations?

    a. MDMA   c. Caffeine
    b. Cocaine   d. LSD

19. Abel took a drug to reduce the pain in his broken arm. The drug Abel took to reduce his pain would be classified as a(n)

    a. depressant.   c. hallucinogen.
    b. opiate.   d. stimulant.

20. Yeh is doing research for a term paper about legalizing the use of marijuana in the United States. If her research is accurate, she is likely to learn all of the following *except* which one?

    a. Marijuana has been used successfully in treating asthma, glaucoma, chronic pain, and nausea from chemotherapy.
    b. Marijuana increases memory function and creativity.
    c. It is legal to grow and use marijuana for medicinal purposes in Canada.
    d. Doctors have found that marijuana may help treat some types of cancer.

5

Learning

Live and learn. This simple phrase captures the idea that learning is a lifelong

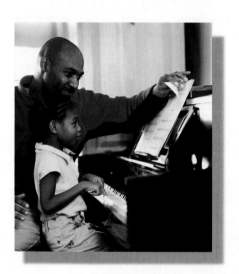

process that affects our behavior every day. Understanding how learning takes place is an important part of understanding ourselves. Sometimes, learning involves one event signaling another, as when we learn to associate wailing sirens with ambulances. Other times, learning depends on what happens after we do something—whether we receive praise or punishment, for example. But learning is more than these kinds of associations. What we think and how we feel about life's signals and consequences also have an impact on what we learn to do and not to do. Blend in practice and feedback about our behavior, mix well, and you have all the ingredients of the learning process.

Reading this chapter will help you to answer the following questions:

▶ **How did Russian dogs teach psychologists about learning?** 171

▶ **How do reward and punishment work?** 178

▶ **Can people learn to be helpless?** 192

▶ **What should teachers learn about learning?** 200

ike most newborn babies, Jeffrey cried until he was fed. He awakened at 3 A.M. nearly every morning, hungry and crying for food. And as she had done every day since he was born, his mother would put on her slippers and walk down the tiled hallway to his bedroom. After a quick change of his diaper came the feeding. By the time he was four months old, Jeffrey would cry for about a minute and then quietly wait a few more minutes for his mother to arrive for his feeding. One particular morning, as his mother was halfway down the hall, she stopped in her tracks as she felt a sneeze coming. She pinched her nostrils together, and the urge to sneeze passed. However, she noticed that Jeffrey had begun to cry again. This was unusual. She began to walk again, and he quieted. Her scientific curiosity aroused, she walked a few steps, then stopped, then started, then stopped. She discovered that Jeffrey stopped crying when he heard her footsteps but resumed crying when the sound of footsteps stopped.

Jeffrey had learned a lot in the four months since his birth. He could anticipate events and predict outcomes based on the meaning of certain sounds. Like the rest of us, he showed an ability to learn about relationships in the environment and to adjust to them. This adjustment to changes in the environment is called *adaptation.* Along with adaptation come expectations and predictions about what is and what is not likely to occur in our world.

The entire process of development, from birth to death, involves adapting to increasingly complex, ever-changing environments, using continuously updated knowledge and skills gained through experience. This ability to adapt is especially impressive in humans, but it appears to varying degrees in every species. Charles Darwin highlighted the importance of adaptation in his theory of evolution, noting that individuals who do not adapt may not survive to reproduce. Many forms of adaptation follow the principles of learning.

Learning is a relatively permanent change in behavior or knowledge due to experience. We are born with some behaviors and knowledge, we acquire others automatically as we grow (through maturation), and we learn still others. Some of our sayings, such as "Once burned, twice shy" and "Fool me once, shame on you; fool me twice, shame on me," reflect this vital learning process. In fact, learning plays a central role in most aspects of human behavior. If you want to know who you are and how you became the person you are today, examining what and how you have learned is a good place to start.

This chapter describes what psychologists now know about the fundamental principles of learning. These include a form of learning called *operant conditioning,* in which rewards and punishments affect the frequency of observable behavior. There is also *classical conditioning,* a form of learning in which specific signals come to trigger behavior. In addition, there are cognitive processes that underlie some of the most complex forms of learning, such as the ability to learn from watching others. Some learning takes place consciously, as when you study for an exam; but as mentioned later, you can also learn things without being aware that you are doing so (Watanabe, Náñez, & Sasaki, 2001). Let's begin by considering classical conditioning.

Online Study Center

Improve Your Grade
Tutorial: Classical
Conditioning—
Pavlov's Study

Classical Conditioning: Learning Signals and Associations

▶ **How did Russian dogs teach psychologists about learning?**

At the first notes of the national anthem, an athlete's heart may start to pound, because those sounds signal that the game is about to begin. A flashing red light on the instrument panel might raise your heart rate, too, because it means that something is wrong with your car. People are not born with these reactions. They have learned them by observing relationships, or *associations,* between events in the world. The experimental study of this kind of learning was begun, almost by accident, by Ivan Petrovich Pavlov.

Pavlov's Discovery

Pavlov is one of the best-known figures in psychology, but he was not a psychologist. He was a Russian physiologist who won the Nobel Prize in 1904 for his research on the digestive system of dogs. In the course of this research, Pavlov noticed a strange phenomenon. His dogs sometimes salivated, or drooled, when no food was present. For instance, they salivated when they saw the assistant who normally brought their food, even if he was empty-handed.

Pavlov devised a simple experiment to determine why salivation occurred without an obvious physical cause, such as food. First he performed an operation to divert a dog's saliva into a container so that the amount of salivation could be measured. Next he placed the dog in an apparatus similar to the one shown in Figure 5.1. The experiment had three phases.

In the first phase, Pavlov and his associates confirmed that when meat powder was placed in the dog's mouth, the dog automatically salivated (Anrep, 1920). They also confirmed that the dog did not automatically salivate in response to a musical tone. The researchers had now established the two basic components of Pavlov's experiment: (1) a quick, automatic response called a *reflex* and (2) a neutral stimulus that does not trigger that reflex.

In the second phase of Pavlov's experiment, the tone was sounded, and then meat powder was placed in the dog's mouth. The dog salivated. This pairing of the tone and the meat powder was repeated several times. So the tone always preceded the arrival of the meat powder, but had the dog learned that relationship? It had. In the third phase of the experiment, the tone was sounded, but no meat powder was presented. Even so, the dog still salivated. The tone alone was now enough to trigger salivation. You may

learning The modification of preexisting behavior and understanding.

FIGURE **5.1**

Apparatus for Measuring Conditioned Responses

In this more elaborate version of Pavlov's original apparatus, the amount of saliva flowing from a dog's mouth is measured precisely and then recorded on a slowly revolving drum of paper.

Pen recording on cylinder

have seen a similar process if you regularly open pet food with an electric can opener. The sound of the opener probably brings your pet running (and salivating) because that sound means that food is on its way.

Pavlov's experiment demonstrated what we now call **classical conditioning.** In this procedure, a neutral stimulus is repeatedly paired with a stimulus that already triggers an automatic, reflexive response. As a result of this pairing, the previously neutral stimulus itself comes to trigger a response that is similar to that reflex. Figure 5.2 shows the basic elements of classical conditioning. The stimulus that naturally elicits a response without conditioning, such as the meat powder in Pavlov's experiment, is called the **unconditioned stimulus (UCS).** The automatic, unlearned, reflexive response to this stimulus is called the **unconditioned response (UCR).** After being paired with the unconditioned stimulus (meat powder), the previously neutral stimulus becomes the **conditioned stimulus (CS),** and the response it comes to trigger is a learned or **conditioned response (CR).**

FIGURE **5.2**

Classical Conditioning

Before classical conditioning has occurred, meat powder on a dog's tongue produces salivation, but the sound of a tone—a neutral stimulus—brings only orienting responses such as turning toward the sound. During the process of conditioning, the tone is repeatedly paired with the meat powder. After classical conditioning has taken place, the sound of the tone alone acts as a conditioned stimulus, producing salivation.

PHASE 1: Before conditioning has occurred

| UCS (meat powder) | → → → → | UCR (salivation) |

| Neutral stimulus (tone) | → → → | Orienting response |

PHASE 2: The process of conditioning

| Neutral stimulus (tone) | followed by | UCS (meat powder) | → | UCR (salivation) |

PHASE 3: After conditioning has occurred

| CS (tone) | → → → | CR (salivation) |

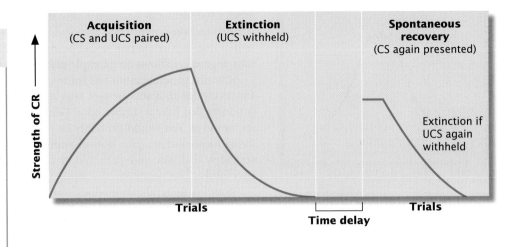

FIGURE **5.3**

Changes over Time in the Strength of a Conditioned Response

As the conditioned stimulus (CS) and the unconditioned stimulus (UCS) are repeatedly paired during initial conditioning, the strength of the conditioned response (CR) increases. If the CS is then repeatedly presented without the UCS, the CR weakens—and eventually disappears—through a process called extinction. If the CS is presented again later on, a weaker version of the CR will reappear (Rescorla, 2004). This phenomenon, called spontaneous recovery, is only temporary, though. Unless the UCS is again paired with the CS, the recovered CR soon disappears.

classical conditioning   A procedure in which a neutral stimulus is paired with a stimulus that triggers a reflexive response until the neutral stimulus alone comes to trigger a similar response.

unconditioned stimulus (UCS)   A stimulus that triggers a response without conditioning.

unconditioned response (UCR)   The automatic, unlearned, reflexive reaction to a stimulus.

conditioned stimulus (CS)   An originally neutral stimulus that now triggers a conditioned response.

conditioned response (CR)   The response triggered by the conditioned stimulus.

extinction   The gradual disappearance of a conditioned response.

reconditioning   The relearning of a conditioned response following extinction.

spontaneous recovery   The temporary reappearance of a conditioned response after extinction.

stimulus generalization   A process in which a conditioned response is triggered by stimuli similar to the original conditioned stimulus.

Conditioned Responses over Time: Extinction and Spontaneous Recovery

If a barking dog once bit you, you might have learned to feel distress whenever you hear a dog's bark. The more bad experiences you might have had with dogs, the stronger will be your learned distress in response to barking sounds. In the language of classical conditioning, continued pairings of a conditioned stimulus (CS/bark) with an unconditioned stimulus (UCS/bite) strengthen the conditioned response (CR/distress). The curve on the left side of Figure 5.3 shows an example: Repeated associations of a tone (CS) with meat powder (UCS) caused Pavlov's dogs to increase their salivation (CR) to the tone alone.

What if the tone (CS) is repeatedly sounded, but the meat powder (UCS) is no longer given? As you might expect, if the unconditioned stimulus is not paired with the conditioned stimulus at least now and then, the conditioned response will gradually disappear. This loss of the conditioned response is known as **extinction** (see the center section of Figure 5.3). The term is not entirely accurate, though. *Extinction* suggests that, like the dinosaurs, the conditioned response has been wiped out, never to return. In fact, though, if the CS (tone) and the UCS (meat powder) are again paired after the conditioned response has been extinguished, that conditioned response will return to its original strength after as few as one or two trials. This quick relearning of a conditioned response after extinction is called **reconditioning.** Because reconditioning takes much less time than the original conditioning, extinction must not have erased the association between the conditioned stimulus and the conditioned response (Bouton, 1993, 2002).

The right side of Figure 5.3 provides more evidence for this conclusion. An extinguished conditioned response will temporarily reappear if, after some time has passed, the conditioned stimulus occurs without the unconditioned stimulus. This is called **spontaneous recovery,** the temporary reappearance of a conditioned response after extinction (and without further CS-UCS pairings). In general, the longer the time between extinction and the reappearance of the CS, the stronger the recovered conditioned response (Devenport, 1998). Even after many years, spontaneous recovery can create a ripple of emotion—a conditioned response—when we hear a song or catch a scent associated with a long-lost lover or a departed relative.

Stimulus Generalization and Discrimination

Once a conditioned stimulus is able to trigger a conditioned response, stimuli similar to the conditioned stimulus will also trigger some version of that response. This phenomenon, called **stimulus generalization,** is illustrated by the fact that a person who was bitten by one particular dog may now show some fear of all dogs. Usually, the

Stimulus Generalization

The strength of a conditioned response (CR) is greatest when the original conditioned stimulus (CS) occurs. However, some version of the CR is also triggered by stimuli that closely resemble the CS. Here, the CS is the sound of a buzzer at a frequency of 1,000 hertz (Hz), and the CR is salivation. Notice that the CR generalizes well to stimuli at 990 or 1,010 Hz but that it gets weaker and weaker as the buzzer sounds less and less similar to the CS.

stimulus discrimination A process through which people learn to differentiate among similar stimuli and respond appropriately to each one.

greater the similarity between a new stimulus and the original conditioned stimulus is, the stronger the conditioned response will be. If the person was bitten by a small, curly-haired dog, fear responses would be strongest to other small dogs with similar types of hair. Figure 5.4 shows an example involving sounds.

Stimulus generalization has some obvious advantages. For example, it is important for survival that, if you get sick after drinking sour-smelling milk, you now avoid dairy products that have a similar odor. Generalization would be a problem if it had no limits, however. You would probably be justifiably frightened if you found a lion in your living room, but imagine how disruptive it would be if your fear response generalized so widely that you were panicked by the sight of lions on TV or even by the word *lion* in a book.

Stimulus generalization does not run wild, because it is usually balanced by a process called **stimulus discrimination.** Through stimulus discrimination, we learn to make distinctions among similar stimuli. Many parents find that the sound of their own baby whimpering soon becomes a conditioned stimulus, triggering a conditioned response that wakes them up. That conditioned response may not occur if a visiting friend's baby whimpers.

The Signaling of Significant Events

Early research suggested that classical conditioning involves nothing more than automatic associations that allow one stimulus (the conditioned stimulus, or CS) to substitute for another (the unconditioned stimulus, or UCS) in triggering a reflex. That view has turned out to be too simplified. For example, a rat's unconditioned, reflexive response to a mild shock (UCS) will be flinching and jumping. But at the sound of a tone (CS) that always precedes shock, the animal's conditioned response will not be to flinch and jump but to freeze—much as it would if threatened by a predator (Domjan, 2005). In other words, classical conditioning involves more than the appearance of robot-like, reflexive responses. Many psychologists now believe that classical conditioning provides a means through which people, and some other animals, develop expectations and other *mental representations* of the relationships between events in their environment (Shanks, 1995). These representations aid in adaptation and survival. When two events repeatedly take place together, we can predict that one will occur based on what we know about the other. Baby Jeffrey predicted his feeding from hearing his mother's footsteps. You have learned that a clear blue sky means dry weather, that too little sleep makes you irritable, that you can reach someone on the telephone by pressing certain buttons, and that yelling orders motivates some people and angers others.

What determines whether conditioned responses are learned? In general, these responses develop when one event *signals* the appearance of another. Other important factors are the timing, predictability, and intensity of the unconditioned stimulus, as well as the amount of attention that is devoted to the conditioned stimulus and how prepared an organism is to associate paired events.

Timing If your instructor always dismisses class at 9:59 and a bell rings at 10:00, the bell cannot prepare you for the dismissal. It comes too late to be a useful signal. For the same reason, classical conditioning works best when the conditioned stimulus comes before the unconditioned stimulus. This arrangement makes sense for adaptation and survival. Usually, the presence of food, predators, or other significant stimuli is most reliably signaled by smells, sounds, or other events that come just before their appearance (Einhorn & Hogarth, 1982). So it is logical that the brain should be "wired" to form associations most easily between things that occur at about the same time. How close together do they have to be? There is no single "best" interval for every situation. Classical conditioning can occur when the interval between the CS and the UCS is less than a second or more than a minute. It all depends on the particular CS, UCS, and UCR that are involved (Longo, Klempay, & Bitterman, 1964; Ross & Ross, 1971). However, classical conditioning will always be weaker if the interval between the CS and the UCS is longer than what is ideal for the stimuli and responses in a given situation.

Predictability   It is not enough for the CS merely to come before the UCS. Suppose your dogs, Moxie and Fang, have very different personalities. When Moxie growls, she sometimes bites, but sometimes she doesn't. Fang growls *only* before biting. Your conditioned fear response to Moxie's growl will probably occur slowly, because her growl does not reliably signal the danger of a bite. However, you are likely to quickly develop a classically conditioned fear response to Fang's growl. It always means that you are in danger of being bitten. Classical conditioning proceeds most rapidly when the CS *always* signals the UCS and *only* the UCS. Even if both dogs provide the same number of pairings of the CS (growl) and the UCS (bite), it is only with Fang that the CS *reliably* predicts the UCS (Rescorla, 1968).

Intensity   A conditioned response will be learned more rapidly if the UCS is strong than if it is weak. For example, a CS that acts as a predictive signal will be more rapidly associated with a strong shock (UCS) than with a weak one. As with the importance of timing, the effect of signal strength on classical conditioning makes adaptive sense. It is more important to be prepared for major events than for those that have little impact.

Attention   In Pavlov's laboratory, just one conditioned stimulus, a tone, was linked to an unconditioned stimulus (meat powder). In the natural environment, a wide variety of stimuli might be present just before a UCS occurs. Suppose you are at the beach. You're eating a hot dog, reading a magazine, listening to your favorite CD, digging your toes in the warm sand, and enjoying the smell of suntan lotion when you are stung by a bee. Which of these stimuli is most likely to become a conditioned stimulus that might later trigger discomfort? It depends partly on where you were focusing your attention at the moment you were stung. The stimulus you most closely attended to— the one you most fully perceived—is most likely to become a CS. In general, loud tones, bright lights, and other intense stimuli tend to get extra attention, so they are the ones most rapidly associated with an unconditioned stimulus.

Biopreparedness   Certain kinds of signals or events are especially likely to become associated with other signals or events (Logue, 1985). So which beach stimulus becomes a conditioned stimulus for fear will depend not only on attention but also on whether the stimulus is a sight, a sound, or a taste and what kind of unconditioned stimulus follows it. The apparently natural tendency for certain events to become linked suggests that organisms are "biologically prepared" or "genetically tuned" to develop certain conditioned associations.

The most dramatic example of this *biopreparedness* phenomenon is seen in conditioned taste aversions. In one study, rats were either shocked or made nauseous in the presence of a light, a buzzer, and flavored water. The rats formed only certain conditioned associations. Animals that had been shocked developed a conditioned fear response to the light and the buzzer, but not to the flavored water. Those that had been made nauseous developed a conditioned avoidance of the flavored water, but they showed no particular response to the light or buzzer (Garcia & Koelling, 1966). These results reflect an adaptive process. Nausea is more likely to be caused by something we eat or drink than by a noise or a light. So nausea is more likely to become a conditioned response to an internal stimulus, such as a flavor, than to an external stimulus. In contrast, the sudden pain of a shock is more likely to have been caused by an external stimulus, so it makes evolutionary sense that the organism should be "tuned" to associate shock or sudden pain with a sight or sound.

Conditioned taste aversion shows that for certain kinds of stimuli, classical conditioning can occur even when there is a long delay between the CS (taste) and the UCS (sickness). Poisons do not usually produce their effects for many minutes or hours, but people who have experienced food poisoning may never again eat the type of food that made them ill. Organisms that are biologically prepared to link taste signals with illness, even a delayed illness, are more likely to survive than organisms not so prepared.

Other evidence for biopreparedness comes from research showing that people are much more likely to develop a conditioned fear of harmless dogs or nonpoisonous

TASTE AVERSIONS   Humans can develop classically conditioned taste aversions, even to preferred foods. For example, Ilene Bernstein (1978) gave one group of cancer patients Mapletoff ice cream an hour before they received nausea-provoking chemotherapy. A second group ate this same kind of ice cream on a day they did not receive chemotherapy. A third group got no ice cream. Five months later, the patients were asked to taste several ice cream flavors. Those who had never tasted Mapletoff and those who had not eaten it in association with chemotherapy chose it as their favorite. Those who had eaten Mapletoff before receiving chemotherapy found it distasteful.

THE POWER OF SECOND-ORDER CONDITIONING Cancer patients may feel queasy when they enter a chemotherapy room because they have associated the room with nausea-producing treatment. Through second-order conditioning, almost anything associated with the room can also become a conditioned stimulus for nausea. One cancer patient, flying out of town on a business trip, became nauseated just by seeing her hospital from the air

© Herb Lingl/aerialarchives.com

snakes than of electrical outlets, knives, or other, more dangerous objects (Öhman & Mineka, 2001, 2003). And experiments with animals suggest that they tend to learn the type of associations that are most relevant to survival in their environment (Staddon & Ettinger, 1989). Birds of prey, which strongly depend on vision to find food, may develop taste aversions on the basis of appearance. Coyotes and rats depend more on their sense of smell, so they tend to develop aversions related to odor.

Second-Order Conditioning Once we learn that a conditioned stimulus (CS) signals the arrival of an unconditioned stimulus (UCS), the CS may operate as if it actually were that UCS. For instance, suppose that a child endures a painful medical procedure (UCS) at the doctor's office, and the pain becomes associated with the doctor's white coat. The white coat might then become a conditioned stimulus (CS) that can trigger a conditioned fear response. Once the white coat is able to set off a conditioned fear response, the coat may take on some properties of an unconditioned stimulus. So if the child later sees a white-coated pharmacist at the drugstore, that once-neutral store can become a conditioned stimulus for fear because it signals the appearance of a white coat, which in turn signals pain. When a conditioned stimulus (the white coat) acts like an unconditioned stimulus, creating conditioned stimuli (the drugstore) out of events associated with it, the process is called **second-order conditioning.**

   This process serves as an adaptive "early warning system." It prepares us for threatening events (UCS) that are signaled not only by a CS but also by associated events that precede, and thus predict, that CS. But second-order conditioning can also cause problems. For example, the high blood pressure seen in medical patients known as *white-coat hypertensives* (Myers et al., 1996; Ugajin et al., 2005) does not reflect a physical disorder. It occurs simply because the sight of a doctor or nurse has become a conditioned stimulus for fear. Medical staff must be alert to such cases in order not to give blood pressure medication to patients who don't need it.

Some Applications of Classical Conditioning

The principles of classical conditioning are summarized in "In Review: Basic Processes of Classical Conditioning." These principles have proven useful in many areas, including in recent efforts to use insects to help detect explosive material. For example, after the taste of sugar water has been associated with the smell of a chemical used in certain explosives, wasps quickly develop a conditioned response to the smell alone. When several of these trained insects are placed in a plastic tube and brought near the target chemical, they display an immediate attraction to it (Rains, Utley, & Lewis, 2006). Researchers hope that it may someday be possible to use these so-called Wasp Hounds

second-order conditioning A process through which a conditioned stimulus comes to signal another conditioned stimulus that is already associated with an unconditioned stimulus.

in review

BASIC PROCESSES OF CLASSICAL CONDITIONING

Process	Description	Example
Acquisition	A neutral stimulus and an unconditioned stimulus (UCS) are paired. The neutral stimulus becomes a conditioned stimulus (CS), eliciting a conditioned response (CR).	A child learns to fear (conditioned response) the doctor's office (conditioned stimulus) by associating it with the reflexive emotional reaction (unconditioned response) to a painful injection (unconditioned stimulus).
Stimulus generalization	A conditioned response is elicited not only by the conditioned stimulus but also by stimuli similar to the conditioned stimulus.	A child fears most doctors' offices and places that smell like them.
Stimulus discrimination	Generalization is limited so that some stimuli similar to the conditioned stimulus do not elicit the conditioned response.	A child learns that his mother's doctor's office is not associated with the unconditioned stimulus.
Extinction	The conditioned stimulus is presented alone, without the unconditioned stimulus. Eventually the conditioned stimulus no longer elicits the conditioned response.	A child visits the doctor's office several times for a checkup, but does not receive a shot. Fear may eventually cease.

?

1. *If your conditioned fear of spiders is triggered by the sight of other creatures that look like spiders, you are demonstrating stimulus _____.*
2. *Because of _____, we are more likely to learn a fear of snakes than a fear of cars.*
3. *Feeling sad upon hearing a song associated with a long-lost relationship illustrates _____.*

and other similar devices to detect explosives or drugs concealed in airline passengers' luggage. Classical conditioning principles have also been applied in overcoming fears and understanding certain aspects of drug addiction.

Phobias Phobias are intense, irrational fears of objects or situations—such as public speaking—that are not dangerous or that are less dangerous than the fear response would suggest. Classical conditioning often plays a role in the development of phobias (Bouton, Mineka, & Barlow, 2001). As mentioned earlier, a person frightened by a dog may learn a fear that is so intense and generalized that it leads the person to avoid all dogs and all situations in which dogs might be encountered. Classically conditioned

applying psychology **PREDATOR CONTROL THROUGH CONDITIONING** In the western United States, some ranchers lace a sheep carcass with enough lithium chloride to make wolves and coyotes nauseous (Pfister et al., 2003). The predators associate nausea with the smell and taste of sheep and afterward stay away from the ranchers' flocks. A similar program in India has greatly reduced the human death toll from tiger attacks. Stuffed dummies are connected to a shock generator and placed in areas where tigers have killed people. When the animals approach the dummies, they receive a shock (UCS). After learning to associate shock with the human form (CS), the tigers tend to avoid people (CR).

fears can be extremely long-lasting, especially when they are based on experiences with strong unconditioned stimuli. Combat veterans and victims of violent crime, terrorism, or other traumatic events may show intense fear responses to trauma-related stimuli for many years afterward.

Classical conditioning has also been used to treat phobias (see the chapter on treatment of psychological disorders). Joseph Wolpe (1958) was a pioneer in this effort. He showed that irrational fears could be relieved through *systematic desensitization,* a procedure that associates a new response, such as relaxation, with a feared stimulus. To treat a thunderstorm phobia, for instance, a therapist might first teach the client to relax deeply and then associate that relaxation with increasingly intense sights and sounds of thunderstorms presented on videotape (Öst, 1978). Because, as Wolpe (1958) noted, a person cannot be relaxed and afraid at the same time, the new conditioned response (relaxation) to thunderstorms replaces the old one (fear).

Drug Addiction   When people repeatedly use heroin or other addictive drugs, their responses to the drugs become weaker. This reduction in responsiveness to a repeated stimulus is called **habituation.** According to Richard Solomon's (1980) *opponent-process theory,* habituation is the result of two processes that balance each other, like a seesaw. The first process is a quick, automatic, involuntary response—essentially an unconditioned response (UCR) to the drug. The second, or opponent, process is a response that follows and counteracts the first. When a person is taking addictive drugs, this opponent response can be learned, or conditioned (McDonald & Siegel, 2004). So if the unconditioned response to a drug injection includes an increase in body temperature, the conditioned response will include an opponent process that reduces body temperature somewhat, creating "chills." As drug injections are repeated day after day, the learned opponent process ("chills") gets stronger and occurs sooner. As this CR strengthens, the rise in temperature caused by the drug gets smaller, resulting in habituation. In the same fashion, the intense pleasure first experienced as an unconditioned response to the drug begins to be weakened over time by an unpleasant opponent process (CR) that becomes faster and stronger. The addict begins to take larger drug doses in an effort to achieve the "high" once created by smaller doses. As described in the chapter on consciousness, people who display this pattern are said to have developed a *tolerance* for the drug.

The place in which a drug is usually taken and the rituals (such as preparing the syringe) that precede an injection can become conditioned stimuli that trigger conditioned opponent-process responses even before the drug enters the bloodstream. These stimuli signal that the drug is coming, and the body begins to brace itself. But what if a person takes the drug in a new location or doesn't follow the usual ritual? According to opponent-process theory, in the absence of these conditioned environmental stimuli, the conditioned responses that normally dampen the user's unconditioned responses to the drug will not be as strong. As a result, the drug dose the addict took in the usual way yesterday might cause a potentially fatal overdose today (Melchior, 1990; Siegel et al., 1982; Siegel, 2005).

Instrumental and Operant Conditioning: Learning the Consequences of Behavior

▶ **How do reward and punishment work?**

Classical conditioning is an important form of learning, but it cannot explain most of what you learn on a daily basis. In classical conditioning, neutral and unconditioned stimuli are predictably paired. The result is an association of the two. This association is reflected in the fact that the conditioned stimulus now triggers the conditioned response. Notice that both stimuli occur before, or along with, the conditioned response. But you also learn many associations between responses and the stimuli that

habituation   Reduced responsiveness to a repeated stimulus.

Thorndike's Puzzle Box

This drawing illustrates the kind of puzzle box used in Thorndike's research. His cats learned to open the door and reach food by stepping on the pedal, but the learning occurred gradually. Some cats actually took longer to get out of the box on one trial than on a previous trial.

follow them, between behavior and its consequences. A child learns to say "please" to get a piece of candy. A headache sufferer learns to take a pill to escape the pain. A dog learns to "shake hands" to get a treat.

From the Puzzle Box to the Skinner Box

Edward L. Thorndike, an American psychologist, did much of the fundamental research on the consequences of behavior. While Pavlov was exploring classical conditioning, Thorndike was studying animals' intelligence, including their ability to solve problems. For example, he placed a hungry cat in a *puzzle box* like the one in Figure 5.5. The cat had to learn some response—such as stepping on a pedal—to unlock the door and get food. During the first few trials in the puzzle box, the cat explored and prodded until it finally hit the pedal. The animal eventually solved the puzzle, but very slowly. It did not appear to understand, or suddenly gain insight into, the problem (Thorndike, 1898). After many trials, though, the cat solved the puzzle quickly each time it was placed in the box. What was it learning? Thorndike argued that any response (such as pacing or meowing) that did not produce a satisfying effect (opening the door) gradually became weaker. And any response (pressing the pedal) that did have a satisfying effect gradually became stronger. The cat's learning, said Thorndike, is governed by the **law of effect.** According to this law, if a response made to a particular stimulus is followed by a satisfying effect (such as food or some other reward), that response is more likely to occur the next time the stimulus is present. In contrast, responses that produce discomfort are less likely to be performed again. Thorndike described this kind of learning as *instrumental conditioning,* because responses are strengthened when they are instrumental in producing rewards (Thorndike, 1905).

About thirty years after Thorndike published his work, B. F. Skinner extended and formalized many of Thorndike's ideas. Skinner noted that, during instrumental conditioning, an organism learns a response by *operating on* the environment. So he used the term **operant conditioning** to refer to the learning process in which behavior is changed by its consequences, specifically by rewards and punishments. To study operant conditioning, Skinner devised some new tools. One of these was a small chamber that, despite Skinner's objections, came to be known as the *Skinner box* (see Figure 5.6).

Basic Components of Operant Conditioning

The chamber Skinner designed allowed researchers to arrange relationships between a particular response and its consequences. If an animal pressed a lever in the chamber, for example, it might receive a food pellet. The researchers could then analyze how consequences affect behavior. It turned out that stimulus generalization, stimulus discrimination, extinction, spontaneous recovery, and other phenomena seen in classical conditioning also appear in operant conditioning. However, research in operant conditioning also focused on concepts known as operants, reinforcers, and discriminative stimuli.

law of effect A law stating that if a response made in the presence of a particular stimulus is rewarded, the same response is more likely to occur when that stimulus is encountered again.

operant conditioning A process in which responses are learned on the basis of their rewarding or punishing consequences.

FIGURE **5.6**

B. F. Skinner (1904–1990)

In the operant conditioning chamber shown here, the rat can press a bar to obtain food pellets from a tube. Operant and instrumental conditioning are similar in most respects, but they do differ in one way. Instrumental conditioning is measured by how long it takes for a response (such as a bar press) to occur. Operant conditioning is measured by the rate at which responses occur. In this chapter, the term operant conditioning refers to both.

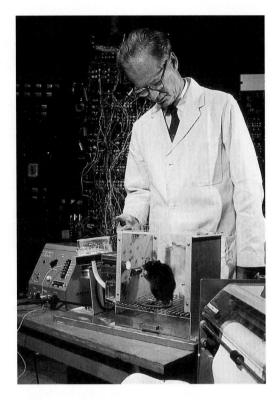

operant   A response that has some effect on the world.

reinforcer   A stimulus event that increases the probability that the response immediately preceding it will occur again.

positive reinforcers   Stimuli that strengthen a response if they follow that response.

negative reinforcers   The removal of unpleasant stimuli.

escape conditioning   The process of learning responses that stop an aversive stimulus.

avoidance conditioning   The process of learning particular responses that avoid an aversive stimulus.

Operants and Reinforcers   Skinner coined the term *operant* or *operant response* to distinguish the responses in operant conditioning from those in classical conditioning. In classical conditioning, the conditioned response does not affect whether or when the stimulus occurs. Pavlov's dogs salivated when a tone sounded. The salivation had no effect on the tone or on whether food was presented. In contrast, an **operant** has some effect on the world. It is a response that operates on the environment. When a child says, "Momma, I'm hungry" and is then fed, the child has made an operant response that influences when food will appear.

A **reinforcer** is a stimulus that increases the probability that the operant behavior will occur again. There are two main types of reinforcers: positive and negative. **Positive reinforcers** strengthen a response if they are presented after that response occurs. The food given to a hungry pigeon after it pecks a key is a positive reinforcer for key pecking. For people, positive reinforcers can include food, smiles, money, and other desirable outcomes. Presentation of a positive reinforcer after a response is called *positive reinforcement*. **Negative reinforcers** are the *removal* of unpleasant stimuli, such as pain or noise. For example, the disappearance of a headache after you take a pain reliever acts as a negative reinforcer that makes you more likely to take that pain reliever in the future. When a response is strengthened by the removal of an unpleasant stimulus such as pain, the process is called *negative reinforcement*.

Notice that reinforcement always increases the likelihood of the behavior that precedes it, whether the reinforcer is adding something pleasant or removing something unpleasant. Figure 5.7 shows this relationship.

Escape and Avoidance Conditioning   The effects of negative reinforcement can be seen in both escape conditioning and avoidance conditioning. **Escape conditioning** occurs when we learn responses that stop an unpleasant stimulus. The left-hand panel of Figure 5.8 shows an example from an animal laboratory, but escape conditioning operates in humans, too. We not only learn to take pills to stop pain, but some parents learn to stop their child's annoying demands for a toy by agreeing to buy it. And television viewers learn to use the mute button to shut off obnoxious commercials.

When an animal or a person responds to a signal in a way that *avoids* an aversive stimulus before it arrives, **avoidance conditioning** has occurred (see the right-hand

FIGURE 5.7

Positive and Negative Reinforcement

learn by doing Remember that behavior is strengthened through positive reinforcement when something pleasant or desirable occurs following the behavior. Behavior is strengthened through negative reinforcement when the behavior results in the removal or termination of something unpleasant. To see how these principles apply in your own life, list two examples of situations in which your behavior was affected by positive reinforcement and two in which you were affected by negative reinforcement.

POSITIVE REINFORCEMENT

| **Behavior** You put coins into a vending machine. | **Presentation of a pleasant or positive stimulus** You receive a cold can of soda. | **Frequency of behavior increases** You put coins in vending machines in the future. |

NEGATIVE REINFORCEMENT

| **Behavior** In the middle of a boring date, you say you have a headache. | **Termination of an unpleasant stimulus** The date ends early. | **Frequency of behavior increases** You use the same tactic on future boring dates. |

sections of Figure 5.8). Avoidance conditioning is an important influence on everyday behavior. We go to work even when we would rather stay in bed, we stop at red lights even when we are in a hurry, and we apologize for our mistakes even before they are discovered. Each of these behaviors helps us avoid a negative consequence, such as lost pay, a traffic ticket, or a scolding.

Avoidance conditioning represents a marriage of classical and operant conditioning. If, as shown in Figure 5.8, a buzzer predicts shock (an unconditioned stimulus), the

FIGURE 5.8

A Shuttle Box

A shuttle box has two sections, usually separated by a barrier, and its floor is an electric grid. Shock can be administered through the grid to either section. The left-hand panel shows escape conditioning, in which an animal learns to get away from a mild shock by jumping over the barrier when the electricity is turned on. The next two panels show avoidance conditioning. Here, the animal has learned to avoid shock altogether by jumping over the barrier when it hears a warning buzzer just before shock occurs.

Escape conditioning   **Avoidance conditioning**

Source: Adapted from Hintzman (1978).

Stimulus Discrimination

This rat could jump from a stand through any of three doors, but it was reinforced only if it jumped through the door that differed from the other two. The rat learned to do this quite well: On this occasion, it discriminated vertical from horizontal stripes.

buzzer becomes a conditioned stimulus (CS). Through classical conditioning, the buzzer (now a CS) triggers a conditioned fear response (CR). Like the shock itself, conditioned fear is an unpleasant internal sensation. The animal then learns the instrumental response of jumping the barrier. The instrumental response (jumping) is reinforced because it reduces fear.

Once learned, avoidance is a difficult habit to break, because avoidance responses continue to be reinforced by fear reduction (Solomon, Kamin, & Wynne, 1953). So even if the shock is turned off in a shuttle box, animals may keep jumping when the buzzer sounds because they never discover that avoidance is no longer necessary. The same is often true of people. Those who avoid escalators out of fear never get a chance to find out that they are safe. Those with limited social skills may avoid potentially embarrassing social situations, but doing so also prevents them from learning how to be successful in those situations.

The study of avoidance conditioning has not only expanded our understanding of negative reinforcement but also has led some psychologists to consider more complex cognitive processes in operant learning. These psychologists suggest, for example, that in order for people to learn to avoid an unpleasant event (such as getting fired or paying a fine), they must have established an expectancy or other mental representation of that event. The role of such mental representations is emphasized in the cognitive theories of learning described later in this chapter.

Discriminative Stimuli and Stimulus Control   The consequences of our behavior often depend on the situation we are in. Most people know that a flirtatious comment about someone's appearance may be welcomed on a date, but not at the office. And even if you have been rewarded for telling jokes, you are not likely to do so at a funeral. In the language of operant conditioning, situations serve as **discriminative stimuli,** which are stimuli that signal whether reinforcement is available if a certain response is made. *Stimulus discrimination* occurs when an organism learns to make a particular response in the presence of one stimulus but not another (see Figure 5.9). The response is then said to be under *stimulus control.* Stimulus discrimination allows people or animals to learn what is appropriate (reinforced) and inappropriate (not reinforced) in particular situations.

Stimulus generalization also occurs in operant conditioning. That is, an animal or person will perform a response in the presence of a stimulus that is similar to, but not exactly like, a stimulus that has signaled reinforcement in the past. The more similar the new stimulus is to the old one, the more likely it is that the response will be performed. Suppose you ate a wonderful meal at a restaurant called "Captain Jack's," which

discriminative stimuli   Stimuli that signal whether reinforcement is available if a certain response is made.

Although the artist may not have intended it, this cartoon nicely illustrates one way in which discriminative stimuli can affect behavior.

"Oh, not bad. The light comes on, I press the bar, they write me a check. How about you?"

was decorated to look like the inside of a sailing ship. You might later be attracted to other restaurants with nautical names or with interiors that look something like the one where you had that great meal.

Stimulus generalization and stimulus discrimination complement each other. In one study, for example, pigeons received food for pecking a key, but only when they saw certain kinds of artwork (Watanabe, Sakamoto, & Wakita, 1995). As a result, these birds learned to *discriminate* the works of the impressionist painter Claude Monet from those of the cubist painter Pablo Picasso. Later, when the birds were shown new paintings by other impressionist and cubist artists, they were able to *generalize* from the original artists to other artists who painted in the same style, as if they had learned the conceptual categories of "impressionism" and "cubism." We humans learn to place people and objects into even more finely detailed categories, such as "honest," "dangerous," or "tax deductible." We discriminate one stimulus from another and then, through generalization, respond similarly to all those we perceive to be in a particular category. This ability to respond in a similar way to all members of a category can save us considerable time and effort, but it can also lead to the development of unwarranted prejudice against certain groups of people (see the chapter on social psychology).

Forming and Strengthening Operant Behavior

Your daily life is full of examples of operant conditioning. You go to movies, parties, classes, and jobs primarily because doing so brings reinforcement. What is the effect of the type or timing of your reinforcers? How do you learn new behaviors? How can you get rid of old ones?

Shaping   Let's say you want to train your dog, Sugar, to sit and "shake hands." You figure that positive reinforcement should work, so you decide to give Sugar a treat every time she sits and shakes hands. But there's a problem with this plan. Smart as Sugar is, she may never make the desired response on her own, so you might never be able to give the reinforcer. The way around this problem is to *shape* Sugar's behavior. **Shaping** is the process of reinforcing *successive approximations*—that is, responses that come successively closer to the desired behavior. For example, you might first give Sugar a treat whenever she sits down. Next, you might reinforce her only when she sits and partially lifts a paw. Finally, you might reinforce only complete paw lifting. Eventually, you would require Sugar to perform the entire sit-lift-shake sequence before giving the treat.

Online Study Center

Improve Your Grade
Tutorial: Shaping

shaping   The reinforcement of responses that come successively closer to some desired response.

GETTING THE HANG OF IT   Learning to eat with a spoon is, as you can see, a hit-and-miss process at first. However, this child will learn to hit the target more and more often as the food reward gradually shapes a more efficient, and far less messy, pattern of behavior.

Shaping is a powerful tool. Animal trainers have used it to teach chimpanzees to roller-skate, dolphins to jump through hoops, and pigeons to play Ping-Pong (Coren, 1999).

Secondary Reinforcement   Operant conditioning often begins with the use of **primary reinforcers,** which are events or stimuli—such as food or water—that satisfy needs basic to survival. The effects of primary reinforcers are powerful and automatic. But constantly giving Sugar food as a reward can disrupt training, because she will stop to eat after every response. Also, once she gets full, food will no longer act as an effective reinforcer. To avoid these problems, animal trainers, parents, and teachers rely on the principle of secondary reinforcement.

Secondary reinforcers are previously neutral stimuli that take on reinforcing properties after being paired with stimuli that are already reinforcing. In other words, they are rewards that people or animals learn to like. If you say "Good girl!" just before feeding Sugar, those words will become reinforcing after a few pairings. "Good girl!" can then be used alone to reinforce Sugar's behavior. It helps if the words are again paired with food every now and then. Does this remind you of classical conditioning? It should, because the primary reinforcer (food) is an unconditioned stimulus. If the words "Good girl!" become a reliable signal for food, they will act as a conditioned stimulus (CS). For this reason, secondary reinforcers are sometimes called *conditioned reinforcers.*

The power of operant conditioning can be greatly increased by using secondary reinforcers. Consider the secondary reinforcer we call money. Some people will do almost anything for it despite the fact that it tastes terrible and won't quench your thirst. Its reinforcing power lies in its association with the many rewards it can buy. Smiles and other forms of social approval (such as the words "Good job!") are also important secondary reinforcers for human beings. However, what becomes a secondary reinforcer can vary widely from person to person and culture to culture. Tickets to a rock concert may be an effective secondary reinforcer for some people, but not for others. A ceremony honoring outstanding job performance might be strongly reinforcing in an individualist culture, but the same experience might be embarrassing for a person in a collectivist culture, where group cooperation is given greater value than personal distinction (Miller, 2001). When carefully chosen, however, secondary reinforcers can build or maintain behavior, even when primary reinforcement is absent for long periods.

Delay and Size of Reinforcement   Much of our behavior is learned and maintained because it is regularly reinforced. But many of us overeat, smoke, drink too much, or procrastinate, even though we know these behaviors are bad for us. We may want to eliminate them, but they are hard to change. We seem to lack "self-control." If behavior is controlled by its consequences, why do we do things that are ultimately self-defeating?

Part of the answer lies in the timing of reinforcers. For example, the good feelings (positive reinforcers) that follow excessive drinking are immediate. But because hangovers and other negative consequences are usually delayed, their effects on future drinking are weakened. In other words, operant conditioning is stronger when reinforcers appear soon after a response occurs (Rachlin, 2000). Under some conditions, delaying a positive reinforcer for even a few seconds can decrease the effectiveness of positive reinforcement. (An advantage of praise and other secondary reinforcers is that they can easily be delivered as soon as the desired response occurs.) The size of the reinforcer is also important. In general, conditioning is faster when the reinforcer is large than when it is small.

Schedules of Reinforcement   When a *continuous reinforcement schedule* is in effect, a reinforcer is delivered every time a particular response occurs. This schedule can be helpful when teaching someone a new skill, but it can be impractical in the long run. Imagine how inefficient it would be, for example, if an employer had to deliver praise or pay following every little task employees performed all day long. In most cases, reinforcement is given only some of the time, on a *partial,* or *intermittent, reinforcement schedule.* Intermittent schedules are described in terms of when and how reinforcers are given. "When" refers to the number of responses that have to occur, or the

primary reinforcers   Events or stimuli that satisfy physiological needs basic to survival.

secondary reinforcers   Rewards that people or animals learn to like.

learn **by doing** **REINFORCEMENT SCHEDULES ON THE JOB** Make a list of all the jobs you have ever held, along with the reinforcement schedule on which you received your pay for each. Which of the four types of schedules (fixed ratio, fixed interval, variable ratio, or variable interval) was most common, and which was most satisfying to you?

amount of time that must pass, before a reinforcer will occur. "How" refers to whether the reinforcer will be delivered in a predictable or unpredictable way.

1. *Fixed-ratio (FR) schedules* provide reinforcement following a fixed number of responses. Rats might receive food after every tenth time they press the lever in a Skinner box (FR 10) or after every twentieth (FR 20). Computer helpline technicians might be allowed to take a break after every fifth call they handle, or every tenth.

2. *Variable-ratio (VR) schedules* also call for reinforcement after a certain number of responses, but that number varies. As a result, it is impossible to predict which particular response will bring reinforcement. On a VR 30 schedule, for example, a rat will be reinforced after an *average* of thirty lever presses. This means that the reward sometimes comes after ten presses, sometimes after fifteen, and other times after fifty or more. Gambling offers humans a similar variable-ratio schedule. Slot machines pay off only after a frustratingly unpredictable number of lever pulls, averaging perhaps one in twenty.

3. *Fixed-interval (FI) schedules* provide reinforcement for the first response that occurs after some fixed time has passed since the last reward. On an FI 60 schedule, for instance, the first response after sixty seconds has passed will be rewarded, regardless of how many responses have been made during that interval. Some radio stations make use of fixed-interval schedules. Listeners who have won a call-in contest might have to wait at least ten days before they are eligible to win again.

4. *Variable-interval (VI) schedules* reinforce the first response after some period of time, but the amount of time varies unpredictably. So on a VI 60 schedule, the first response that occurs after an *average* of 60 seconds is reinforced, but the actual time between reinforcements might vary anywhere from 1 to 120 seconds or more. Police in Illinois once used a VI schedule to encourage seat belt use. They stopped drivers at random times and awarded prizes to those who were buckled up (Mortimer et al., 1988). Kindergarten teachers, too, use VI schedules when they give rewards to children who are in their seats when a chime sounds at random intervals.

As shown in Figure 5.10, different schedules of reinforcement produce different patterns of responding (Skinner, 1961). Both fixed-ratio and variable-ratio schedules produce especially high response rates overall. The reason, in both cases, is that the frequency of reward depends directly on the rate of responding. Under a fixed-interval schedule, it does not matter how many responses are made during the time between rewards. Because the timing of the reinforcement is so predictable, the rate of responding typically drops immediately after reinforcement and then increases as the time for another reward approaches. When teachers schedule quizzes on the same day each week, most students will study just before each quiz and then almost cease studying immediately afterward. By contrast, the possibility of unpredictable "pop" quizzes (on a variable-interval schedule) typically generates more consistent studying patterns (Kouyoumdjian, 2004).

Schedules and Extinction Ending the relationship between an operant response and its consequences weakens that response. In fact, failure to reinforce a response eventually *extinguishes* it. The response occurs less and less often and eventually may disappear. If you keep sending text messages to someone who never replies, you eventually stop trying. But extinction in operant conditioning does not erase learned relationships (Delamater, 2004). If a discriminative stimulus for reinforcement reappears some time after an operant response has been extinguished, that response may recur (spontaneously recover). And if again reinforced, the response will quickly return to its former level, as though extinction had never happened.

In general, behaviors learned under a partial reinforcement schedule are far more difficult to extinguish than those learned on a continuous reinforcement schedule. This phenomenon is called the **partial reinforcement extinction effect**. Imagine,

partial reinforcement extinction effect A phenomenon in which behaviors learned under a partial reinforcement schedule are more difficult to extinguish than those learned on a continuous reinforcement schedule.

Results of Four Partial Reinforcement Schedules

These curves illustrate the patterns of behavior typically seen under different reinforcement schedules. The steeper the curve, the faster the response rate. The thin diagonal lines crossing the curves show when reinforcement was given. In general, the rate of responding is higher under ratio schedules than under interval schedules.

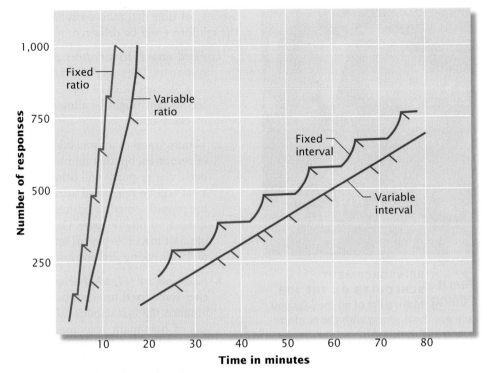

Source: Adapted from Skinner (1961).

for example, that you are in a gambling casino, standing near a broken candy machine and a broken slot machine. You might deposit money in the broken candy machine once, but this behavior will probably stop (extinguish) very quickly. The candy machine should deliver its goodies on a continuous reinforcement schedule, so you can easily tell that it is not going to provide a reinforcer. But you know that slot machines give rewards on an unpredictable, intermittent schedule. So you might put in coin after coin, unsure of whether the machine is broken or is simply not paying off at the moment.

Partial reinforcement helps to explain why superstitious behavior is so resistant to extinction (Vyse, 2000). Suppose you had been out for a run just before hearing that you passed an important exam. The run did nothing to cause this outcome. The reward followed it through sheer coincidence. Still, for some people, this kind of *accidental reinforcement* can strengthen the behavior that appeared to "cause" good news. These people might decide that it is "lucky" to go running after taking an exam. Similarly, someone who wins the lottery or a sports bet while wearing a particular shirt may begin wearing the "lucky shirt" more often (Hendrick, 2003). Of course, if the person wears the shirt often enough, something good is bound to follow every now and then, thus further strengthening the superstitious behavior on a sparse partial schedule.

Why Reinforcers Work

What makes a reinforcer reinforcing? For primary reinforcers, at least, the reason could be that they satisfy basic physiological needs for survival. Yet artificial sweeteners, which have no nutritional value, can be as powerfully reinforcing as sugar, which is nutritious. And what about addictive drugs, which are also powerful reinforcers, even though they threaten the health of those who use them?

Research by biological psychologists suggests that reinforcers may work by exerting particular effects on the brain. In a classic study on this point, James Olds and Peter Milner (1954) discovered that mild electrical stimulation of certain areas of the brain's hypothalamus can be a powerful reinforcer. Hungry rats will ignore food if they can press a lever that stimulates these "pleasure centers" (Olds, 1973). It has since been discovered

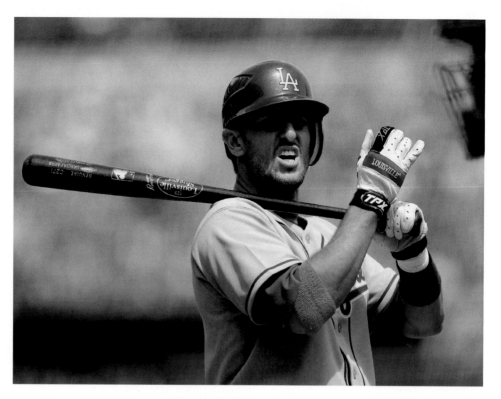

that activation of brain systems that use the chemical dopamine is associated with the pleasure of many stimuli, including food, music, sex, the uncertainty of gambling, and some addictive drugs such as cocaine (Berns et al., 2001; Blood & Zatorre, 2001; Ciccocioppo, Sanna, & Weiss, 2001; Reuter et al., 2005; Tobler, Fiorillo, & Schultz, 2005). Current research suggests that complex and widespread patterns of brain activity are involved in our response to reinforcers, allowing us to enjoy them, to learn to want them, and to learn how to get them (Montague, Hyman, & Cohen, 2004; Robinson et al., 2005).

Punishment

Positive and negative reinforcement *increase* the frequency of a response, either by presenting something pleasurable or by removing something that is unpleasant. In contrast, **punishment** *reduces* the frequency of an operant behavior by presenting an unpleasant stimulus or removing a pleasant one. Shouting "No!" and swatting your cat when it begins chewing on your plants is an example of the kind of punishment that presents an aversive stimulus following a response. Taking away a child's TV privileges because of rude behavior is a second kind of punishment—sometimes called *penalty*—that removes a positive stimulus (see Figure 5.11).

Punishment is often confused with negative reinforcement, but they are quite different. Just remember that reinforcement of any type always *strengthens* behavior, whereas punishment always *weakens* behavior. If shock is *turned off* when a rat presses a lever, this is negative reinforcement. It increases the probability that the rat will press the lever when shock occurs again. But if shock is *turned on* when the rat presses the lever, this is punishment. The rat will be less likely to press the lever again.

Although punishment can change behavior, it has some drawbacks (Gershoff, 2002). First, it does not "erase" an undesirable behavior. It merely suppresses the behavior temporarily. In fact, people often repeat punished acts when they think they can do so without getting caught. Second, punishment can produce unwanted side effects. If you punish a child for swearing, the child may associate the punisher with the punishment and end up fearing you. Third, punishment is often ineffective unless it is given immediately after the undesirable behavior and each time that behavior occurs. If a child gets

punishment The presentation of an aversive stimulus or the removal of a pleasant one following some behavior.

FIGURE 5.11

Two Kinds of Punishment

In one form of punishment, a behavior is followed by an aversive, or unpleasant, stimulus. In a second form of punishment, sometimes called penalty, a pleasant stimulus is removed following a behavior. In either case, punishment decreases the chances that the behavior will occur in the future. Now you decide: When a toddler reaches toward an electric outlet, and her father says "NO!" and gently taps her hand, is that punishment or negative reinforcement? If you said punishment, you are right, because it will reduce the likelihood of her touching outlets in the future.

into the cookie jar and enjoys a few cookies before being discovered and punished, the effect of the punishment will be greatly reduced. Fourth, physical punishment can become aggression, even abuse, if given in anger. And because children tend to imitate what they see, frequent punishment may lead them to behave aggressively themselves (Gilbert, 1997). Finally, punishment lets people know they have done something wrong, but it doesn't specify what they should do instead. An "F" on a term paper means that the assignment was poorly done, but the grade alone tells the student nothing about how to improve.

When used properly, however, punishment can be a valuable tool (Baumrind, Larzelere, & Cowan, 2002). As shown in Figure 5.12, for example, it can help children who suffer from certain developmental disorders or who purposely injure themselves (Flavell et al., 1982). Punishment is especially effective when a few guidelines are

FIGURE 5.12

Life-Saving Punishment

This child suffered from chronic ruminative disorder, a condition in which he vomited everything he ate. At left, the boy was approximately one year old and had been vomiting for four months. At right is the same child thirteen days after punishment with electric shock had eliminated the vomiting response; his weight had increased 26 percent. He was physically and psychologically healthy when tested six months, one year, and two years later (Lang & Melamed, 1969).

Source: Lang & Melamed (1969).

LEARNING CULTURAL VALUES The use of alcohol varies considerably from culture to culture, in part because some cultures reward it more than others. In Japan, for example, drinking alcohol after work is considered appropriate, and even encouraged. In some Islamic cultures, any use of alcohol is actively discouraged and may even be illegal.

followed. First, to prevent the development of a general fear of the punisher, specify why punishment is being given. Second, emphasize that the behavior, not the person, is being punished. Third, without being abusive, make sure the punishment is immediate and noticeable enough to eliminate the undesirable response. A half-hearted "Quit it" may actually reinforce a child's misbehavior, because almost any attention is rewarding to some children. And once a child gets used to mild punishment, the parent may resort to punishment that is far more severe than would have been necessary if stern, but moderate, punishment had been used in the first place. (You may have witnessed this *escalation effect* in grocery stores or restaurants where children ignore their parents' initially weak efforts to stop their misbehavior.) Fourth, identify and positively reinforce more appropriate responses.

When these guidelines are not followed, the beneficial effects of punishment may be wiped out or may be only temporary. As demonstrated in prison systems, punishment alone does not usually lead to rehabilitation. Following their release, about two-thirds of U.S. prison inmates are rearrested for felonies or serious misdemeanors within three years, and about 50 percent will go back to prison (Cassel & Bernstein, 2001; U.S. Department of Justice, 2002).

Some Applications of Operant Conditioning

Although the principles of operant conditioning were originally worked out with animals in the laboratory, they are valuable for understanding human behavior in an endless variety of everyday situations. ("In Review: Reinforcement and Punishment" summarizes some key concepts of operant conditioning.) Effective use of reinforcements and punishments by parents, teachers, and peers is vital to helping children learn what is and is not appropriate behavior at the dinner table, in the classroom, or at a birthday party. People learn how to be "civilized" in their culture partly through experiencing positive and negative responses from others. And differing patterns of rewards and punishments for boys and girls underlie the development of behavior that fits culturally approved *gender roles,* a topic explored in more detail in the chapter on human development.

The scientific study of operant conditioning has led to numerous treatment programs for altering problematic behavior. Behavior modification programs that combine the use of rewards and extinction (or carefully administered punishment) have helped countless mental patients, mentally retarded or brain-damaged individuals, autistic children, and hard-to-manage preschoolers to develop the behaviors they need to live happier and

REINFORCEMENT AND PUNISHMENT

Concept	Description	Example or Comment
Positive reinforcement	Increasing the frequency of a behavior by following it with the presentation of a positive reinforcer—a pleasant, positive stimulus or experience	You say "Good job!" after someone works hard to perform a task.
Negative reinforcement	Increasing the frequency of a behavior by following it with the removal of an unpleasant stimulus or experience	You learn to use the "mute" button on the TV remote control to remove the sound of an obnoxious commercial.
Escape conditioning	Learning to make a response that removes an unpleasant stimulus	A little boy learns that crying will cut short the time that he must stay in his room.
Avoidance conditioning	Learning to make a response that avoids an unpleasant stimulus	You slow your car to the speed limit when you spot a police car, thus avoiding being stopped and reducing the fear of a fine; very resistant to extinction.
Punishment	Decreasing the frequency of a behavior by either presenting an unpleasant stimulus (punishment 1) or removing a pleasant one (punishment 2, or penalty)	You swat the dog after it steals food from the table, or you take a favorite toy away from a child who misbehaves. A number of cautions should be kept in mind before using punishment.

1. *Taking an aspirin can relieve headache pain, so people learn to do so through the process of _____ reinforcement.*
2. *The "walk" sign that tells people it is safe to cross the street is an example of a _____ stimulus.*
3. *Response rates tend to be higher under _____ schedules of reinforcement than under _____ schedules.*

Online Study Center

Improve Your Grade
Tutorial: Reinforcement and Punishment

more productive lives (e.g., Alberto, Troutman, & Feagin, 2002; Pear & Martin, 2002). These programs include establishing goal behaviors, choosing reinforcers and punishers, and developing a systematic plan for applying them to achieve desired changes. Many self-help books also incorporate principles of positive reinforcement, recommending self-reward following each small victory in people's efforts to lose weight, stop smoking, avoid procrastination, or reach other goals (e.g., Grant & Kim, 2002; Rachlin, 2000).

When people cannot do anything to alter the consequences of a behavior, discriminative stimuli may hold the key to changing that behavior. For example, people often find it easier to quit smoking if, at first, they stay away from bars and other places where there are discriminative stimuli for smoking. Old cues can trigger old behavior, so they should avoid the old cues until new behavior can be established. Stimulus control can also help alleviate insomnia. Insomniacs tend to use their beds for activities such as watching television, writing letters, reading magazines, worrying, and so on. Soon the bedroom becomes a discriminative stimulus for so many activities that relaxation and sleep become less and less likely. *Stimulus control therapy* encourages insomniacs to use their beds only for sleeping, and perhaps sex, making it more likely that they will sleep better when in bed (Edinger et al., 2001).

Associations between conditioned stimuli and reflexes or between responses and their consequences play an important role in learning, but how are they actually stored in the brain? No one yet knows for sure, but associative network models provide a good way of thinking about the process. As suggested in the

LINKAGES

Networks of Learning

FIGURE **5.13**

An Associative Network

Here is an example of a network of associations to the word *"dog."* Network theorists suggest that the connections shown here represent patterns of connections among nerve cells in the brain.

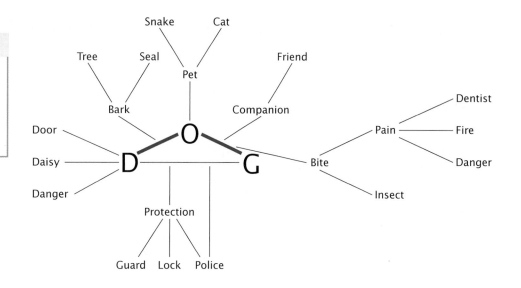

FIGURE **5.13**

An Associative Network

Here is an example of a network of associations to the word *"dog."* Network theorists suggest that the connections shown here represent patterns of connections among nerve cells in the brain.

chapter on memory, the associations we form among stimuli and events are represented in complex networks of connections among brain cells, or neurons. Consider the word *dog*. As shown in Figure 5.13, each person's experience builds many associations to this word, and the strength of each association will reflect the frequency with which *dog* has been mentally linked to the other objects, events, and ideas in that person's life.

Using what they know about the laws of learning and about the way neurons communicate and alter their connections, psychologists have developed computer models of how these associations are established (Messinger et al., 2001). An important feature of these *parallel distributed processing* models is the idea of distributed memory or distributed knowledge. These models suggest, for example, that your knowledge of "dog" does not lie in a single spot, or node, in your brain. Instead, that knowledge is distributed throughout the network of associations that connect the letters *D, O,* and *G*, along with other dog-related experiences. In addition, as shown in Figure 5.13, each of the interconnected nodes that make up your knowledge of "dog" is connected to many other nodes as well. So the letter *D* will be connected to "Daisy," "Danger," and many other concepts.

Neural network models of learning focus on how these connections develop through experience (Hanson & Burr, 1990). For example, suppose you are learning a new word in a foreign language. Each time you read the word and associate it with its English equivalent, you strengthen the neural connections between the sight of the letters forming that word and all of the nodes activated when its English equivalent is brought to mind. Neural network, or *connectionist*, models of learning predict how much the strength of each linkage grows (in terms of the likelihood of neural communication between the two connected nodes) each time the two words are experienced together.

The details of various theories about how these connections grow are very complex, but a theme common to many of them is that the weaker the connection between two items, the greater the increase in connection strength when they are experienced together. So in a classical conditioning experiment, the connections between the nodes that characterize the conditioned stimulus and those that characterize the unconditioned stimulus will show the greatest increase in strength during the first few learning trials. Notice that this prediction nicely matches the typical learning curve shown in Figure 5.3 (Rescorla & Wagner, 1972).

Neural network models have yet to fully explain the learning of complex tasks, nor can they easily account for how people adapt when the "rules of the game" are suddenly changed and old habits must be unlearned and replaced. Nevertheless, a better understanding of what we mean by *associations* may very well lie in future research on neural network models (Anthony & Bartlett, 1999; Goldblum, 2001).

LINKAGES
How are learned associations stored in memory? (a link to memory)

Cognitive Processes in Learning

▶ **Can people learn to be helpless?**

In the first half of the twentieth century, psychologists in North America tended to look at learning through the lens of behaviorism. That is, they saw classical and operant conditioning as the automatic, unthinking formation or modification of associations between observable stimuli and observable responses. They gave little consideration to the role of mental activity that might accompany the learning process.

As mentioned earlier, though, this strictly behavioral view of classical and operant conditioning is now challenged by the cognitive approach, which has become increasingly influential in recent decades. Cognitive psychologists see classical and operant conditioning as helping animals and people to detect and understand what causes what (Young, 1995). They argue that both types of conditioning result not only from automatic associations but also from more complex mental processes—including how information is represented, stored, and used. These processes, they say, underlie our ability to adapt to, and understand, the world around us (Dickinson, 2001).

Cognitive psychologists have found, for example, that a classically conditioned response (such as fear) is more likely to develop if an unconditioned stimulus (such as electric shock) comes as a surprise than if it is expected (Kamin, 1969). Even the brain's reaction to a given stimulus can differ depending on whether that stimulus was expected or unexpected (Waelti, Dickinson, & Schultz, 2001). In other words, according to the cognitive view, learning is affected not only by the nature of the stimuli we experience but also by our expectations about them (Rescorla & Wagner, 1972). Further, just as our perceptions depend on the meaning we attach to sensations (see the chapter on sensation and perception), learning can depend on the meaning we attach to events. So being praised by a boss we respect may be more reinforcing than getting the same good evaluation from a boss we hate.

The importance of cognitive processes has also been demonstrated in research on learned helplessness, latent learning, cognitive maps, insight, and observational learning.

Learned Helplessness

Babies learn that crying attracts attention. Children learn how to make the TV louder. Adults learn what actions lead to success or failure in the workplace. On the basis of this learning people come to expect that certain actions on their part will cause certain consequences. But sometimes events are beyond our control. What happens when our actions have no effect on events, and especially when our escape or avoidance behaviors fail? If these circumstances last long enough, one result may be **learned helplessness,** a tendency to give up on efforts to control the environment (Overmier, 2002; Seligman, 1975).

Learned helplessness was first demonstrated in animals. As described earlier, dogs in a shuttle box will learn to jump over a partition to escape a shock (see Figure 5.8). But if the dogs first receive shocks that they cannot escape, they later do not even try to escape when the shock is turned on in the shuttle box (Overmier & Seligman, 1967). It is as if the animals had learned that "shock happens, and there is nothing I can do about it." Do people learn the same lesson?

learned helplessness A process in which a person or animal stops trying to exert control after experience suggests that no control is possible.

FOCUS ON RESEARCH

The "I Can't Do It" Attitude

What lessons do abused and neglected children learn about their ability to get what they need from the environment? Do they learn that even their best efforts result in failure? Do they give up even trying? Why would a student with above average ability tell a counselor, "I can't do math"? How do people develop an "I can't do it" attitude?

■ What was the researcher's question?

Can lack of control over the environment lead to helplessness in humans? Donald Hiroto (1974) conducted an experiment to test the hypothesis that people develop learned helplessness either after experiencing lack of control or after simply being told that their control is limited.

■ How did the researcher answer the question?

Hiroto (1974) randomly assigned research participants to one of three groups. One group heard a series of thirty bursts of loud, obnoxious noise and, like dogs receiving inescapable shock, had no way to stop it. A second group could control the noise by pressing a button to turn it off. The third group heard no noise at all. After this preliminary phase, all three groups were exposed to eighteen additional bursts of noise, each preceded by a red warning light. During this second phase, all participants could prevent the noise if they pushed a lever quickly enough. However, they didn't know whether to push the lever left or right on any given trial. Before these new trials began, the experimenter told half the participants in each group that avoiding or escaping the noise depended on their skill. The other half were told that their success would be a matter of chance.

■ What did the researcher find?

The people who had previously experienced lack of control now failed to control noise on about four times as many trials as did those who had earlier been in control (50 percent versus 13 percent). This finding was similar to that of the research with dogs and inescapable shock. When the dogs were later placed in a situation in which they could escape or avoid shock, they did not even try. Humans, too, seem to use prior experiences to guide later efforts to try, or not to try, to control their environment.

Expectation of control, whether accurate or not, also had an effect on behavior. In Hiroto's study, those participants who expected that skill could control the noise exerted control on significantly more trials than did those who expected chance to govern the result. This outcome occurred regardless of whether the participants had experienced control before.

Online Study Center

Improve Your Grade
Tutorial: Learned Helplessness

■ What do the results mean?

These results support Hiroto's hypothesis that people, like animals, tend to make less effort to control their environment when prior experience suggests that those efforts will be in vain. But unlike animals, humans need only be *told* that they have no control or are powerless in order for this same effect to occur.

Hiroto's (1974) results appear to reflect a general phenomenon. When prior experience leads people to *believe* that there is nothing they can do to change their lives or control their destiny, they may stop trying to improve their lot (Faulkner, 2001; LoLordo, 2001; Peterson, Maier, & Seligman, 1993). Instead, they may passively endure painful situations. Has this ever happened to you?

■ What do we still need to know?

Further research is needed on when and how learned helplessness affects people's thoughts, feelings, and actions. For example, could learned helplessness explain why some battered women remain with abusive partners? We do know that learned-helplessness experiences are associated with the development of a generally pessimistic way of thinking that can produce depression and other mental disorders (Peterson & Seligman, 1984). People with this *pessimistic explanatory style* see the good things that happen to them as temporary and due to chance and the bad things as permanent and due to internal factors such as lack of ability. This explanatory style has, in fact, been associated with poor grades, inadequate sales performance, health problems, and other negative outcomes (Bennett & Elliott, 2002; Seligman & Schulman, 1986; Taylor, 2002). The exact mechanisms responsible for this connection are still unknown, but understanding how pessimistic (or optimistic) explanatory styles can lead to negative (or positive) consequences remains an important focus of research (e.g., Brennan & Charnetski, 2000). Research is also focusing on how best to min-imize learned helplessness and maximize learned optimism in areas such as education, par-enting, and psychotherapy (e.g., Jackson, Sellers, & Peterson, 2002).

Latent Learning and Cognitive Maps

Decades ago, Edward Tolman studied cognitive processes in learning by watching rats try to find their way to food that was waiting for them at the end of a complex maze. At first, the rats took many wrong turns. Over time, though, they made fewer and fewer mistakes. The behavioral interpretation of this result was that the rats learned a long chain of turning responses that were reinforced by food. Tolman disagreed and offered evidence for a cognitive interpretation.

In one of Tolman's studies, three groups of rats were placed in the same maze once a day for several days (Tolman & Honzik, 1930). For Group A, food was placed in the goal box of the maze on each trial. As shown in Figure 5.14, these rats gradually improved their performance. Group B also ran the maze once a day, but there was never any food in the goal box. The animals in Group B continued to make many errors. Nei-ther of these results is surprising.

The third group of rats, Group C, was the critical one. For the first ten days, they received no reinforcement for running the maze and continued to make many mis-takes. On the eleventh day, food was placed in the goal box for the first time. What do you think happened? On the day after receiving reinforcement, these rats made almost no mistakes (again, see Figure 5.14). In fact, their performance was as good as that of the group that had been reinforced every day. The single reinforcement trial on day 11 produced a dramatic change in their performance the next day.

Tolman argued that these results support two conclusions. First, because the rats in Group C improved their performance the first time they ran the maze after being rein-forced, the reinforcement on day 11 could not have significantly affected their *learning* of the maze. Rather, the reinforcement simply changed their subsequent *performance*. They must have learned the maze earlier as they wandered around making mistakes on their way to the end of the maze. These rats demonstrated **latent learning**—learning that is not evident when it first occurs. (Latent learning occurs in humans, too; for example, after years of experience in your neighborhood, you could probably tell a vis-itor that the corner drugstore is closed on Sundays, even if you had never tried to go there on a Sunday yourself.) Second, the rats' sudden improvement in performance

FIGURE **5.14**

Latent Learning

This graph shows the average number of wrong turns that Tolman's rats made on their way to the goal box of a maze. Notice that when rats in Group C did not receive food reinforcement, they continued to make many errors. The day after first finding food in the goal box, however, they took almost no wrong turns! The reinforcement, argued Tolman, affected only the rats' performance; they must have learned the maze earlier, without reinforcement.

Source: Köhler (1976).

FIGURE 5.15

Insight

Here are three impressive examples of problem solving by chimpanzees. At left, a chimp fixed a fifteen-foot pole in the ground, climbed to the top, and dropped down after grabbing a piece of fruit. In the center photo, the animal stacked two boxes from different areas of the compound, climbed to the top, and used a pole to knock down the fruit. The chimp at right stacked three boxes and climbed them to reach the fruit

latent learning Learning that is not demonstrated at the time it occurs.

cognitive map A mental representation of the environment.

after the first reinforcement trial could have occurred only if the rats had earlier developed a cognitive map of the maze. A **cognitive map** is a mental representation of some physical arrangement—in this case, a maze.

Tolman concluded that cognitive maps develop naturally through experience, even in the absence of any overt response or reinforcement. Research on learning in the natural environment has supported this view. We develop mental maps of shopping malls and city streets, even when we receive no direct reward for doing so (Tversky & Kahneman, 1991). Having such a map allows you to tell that neighborhood visitor exactly how to get to the corner drugstore from where you are standing.

Insight and Learning

Wolfgang Köhler was a psychologist whose work on the cognitive aspects of learning happened almost by accident. He was visiting Tenerife, an island in the Atlantic Ocean, when World War I broke out in 1914. As a German in territory controlled by Germany's enemy, Britain, Köhler was confined there until the war ended in 1918. He used this time to study problem solving in a colony of local chimpanzees (Köhler, 1924).

For example, Köhler would put a chimpanzee in a cage and place a piece of fruit where the chimp could see it but not reach it. He sometimes hung the fruit too high to be reached, or placed it on the ground too far outside the animal's cage to be retrieved. Many of the chimps overcame these obstacles easily. If the fruit was out of reach beyond the cage, some chimps looked around, found a long stick, and used it to rake in the fruit. Surprised that the chimpanzees could solve these problems, Köhler tried more difficult tasks. Again, the chimps quickly got to the fruit, as Figure 5.15 illustrates.

Three aspects of Köhler's observations convinced him that animals' problem solving does not have to depend on trial and error and the gradual association of responses with consequences. First, once a chimpanzee solved one type of problem, it would immediately do the same thing in a similar situation. In other words, it acted as if it understood the problem. Second, Köhler's chimpanzees rarely tried a solution that did not work. Apparently, the solution was not discovered randomly but "thought out" ahead of time and then acted out successfully. Third, the chimps often reached a solution quite suddenly. When confronted with a piece of fruit hanging from a string, for

LEARNING BY IMITATION
Much of our behavior is learned by imitating others, especially those who serve as role models. To appreciate the impact of social learning in your life, list five examples of how your own actions, speech, appearance, or mannerisms have come to match those of a parent, a sibling, a friend, a teacher, or even a celebrity.

instance, a chimp would jump for it several times. Then it would stop jumping, look up, and pace back and forth. Finally it would run over to a wooden crate, place it directly under the fruit, and climb on top of it to reach the fruit. Once, when there were no other objects in the cage, a chimp went over to Köhler, dragged him by the arm until he stood beneath the fruit, and then started climbing up his back!

Köhler believed that the only explanation for these results was that the chimpanzees had experienced **insight,** a sudden understanding of the problem as a whole. Was he right? Possibly, but what Köhler saw as sudden insight might not have been so sudden. Other psychologists found that previous trial-and-error experience with objects, such as boxes and sticks, is necessary for "insight" in chimps (Birch, 1945). In fact, some psychologists argue that all known cases of "insight" include a long history of experience with the objects that are used to solve the problem (Epstein et al., 1984; Wynne, 2004). So although Köhler's work helped establish the importance of cognitive processes in learning, questions remain about whether it demonstrated true insight.

Observational Learning: Learning by Imitation

People and animals learn a lot from personal experience, but they can also learn by observing what others do and what happens to them when they do it (e.g. Akins & Zentall, 1998; Mattar & Gribble, 2005). Learning by watching others—a process called **observational learning,** or *social learning*—is efficient and adaptive. We don't have to find out for ourselves that a door is locked or an iron is hot if we have just seen someone else try the door or suffer a burn.

Children are particularly influenced by the adults and peers who act as *models* for appropriate behavior. In a classic experiment, Albert Bandura showed nursery school children a film starring an adult and a large, inflatable, bottom-heavy "Bobo" doll (Bandura, 1965). The adult in the film punched the Bobo doll in the nose, kicked it, threw things at it, and hit its head with a hammer while saying things like "Sockeroo!" There were different endings to the film. Some children saw an ending in which the aggressive adult was called a "champion" by a second adult and rewarded with candy and soft drinks. Some saw the aggressor scolded and called a "bad person." Some saw a neutral ending in which there was neither reward nor punishment. After the film, each child was allowed to play alone with a Bobo doll. The way they played in this and similar studies led to some important conclusions about learning and the role of cognitive factors in it.

insight   A sudden understanding of what is required to solve a problem.

observational learning   Learning by watching the behavior of others.

FIGURE 5.16

Observational Learning

Bandura found that after observing an aggressive model, many children imitate the model's acts precisely, especially if the model's aggression was rewarded.

Aggressive model rewarded

Aggressive model punished

Nonaggressive model

No model

Source: Bandura, Ross, & Ross (1963).

Bandura found that children who saw the adult rewarded for aggression showed the most aggressive acts in play (see Figure 5.16). They had received **vicarious conditioning,** a kind of observational learning through which a person is influenced by watching or hearing about the consequences of others' behavior. The children who had seen the adult punished for aggressive acts showed less aggression, but they still learned something. When later offered rewards for all the filmed aggressive acts they could perform, these children displayed just as many of these acts as the children who watched the adult being rewarded. Observational learning can occur even when there are no vicarious consequences; many children in the neutral condition also imitated the model's aggression.

Like direct reward and punishment, observational learning is a powerful force in the *socialization* process through which children learn about which behaviors are—and are not—appropriate in their culture (Bandura, 1999). For example, children show long-term increases in their willingness to help and share after seeing a demonstration of helping by a friendly, impressive model (Schroeder et al., 1995). Fears, too, can be learned partly by watching fearfulness in others (Kleinknecht, 1991).

vicarious conditioning A kind of observational learning through which a person is influenced by watching or hearing about the consequences of others' behavior.

If observational learning is important, then surely television—and televised violence—must teach children a great deal. It is estimated that the average child in the United States spends about three hours each day watching television (Annenberg Public Policy Center, 2000). Much of what children see is violent. In addition to the real-life violence portrayed on the news (Van der Molen, 2004), prime-time entertainment programs in the United States present an average of five acts of simulated violence per hour. Some Saturday morning cartoons include

THINKING CRITICALLY

Does Watching Violence on Television Make People More Violent?

more than twenty per hour (American Psychological Association, 1993; Gerbner, Morgan, & Signorielli, 1994). As a result, the average child will have witnessed at least 8,000 murders and more than 100,000 other acts of televised violence before finishing elementary school, and twice that number by age 18 (Annenberg Public Policy Center, 1999; Kunkel et al., 1996; Parents Television Council, 2006).

Psychologists have long speculated that watching so much violence might be emotionally arousing, making viewers more likely to react violently to frustration (Huston & Wright, 1989). In fact, there is evidence that exposure to media violence can trigger or amplify viewers' aggressive thoughts and feelings, thus increasing the likelihood that they will act aggressively (Anderson & Dill, 2000; Bushman, 1998). Televised violence might also provide models that viewers imitate, particularly if the violence is carried out by the "good guys" (Huesmann et al., 2003). Finally, prolonged viewing of violent TV programs might "desensitize" viewers, making them less distressed when they see others suffer and less disturbed about inflicting pain on others (Aronson, 1999; Smith & Donnerstein, 1998). Concern over the influence of violence on television has led to the development of a violence-blocking "V-Chip" for new television sets in the United States.

■ What am I being asked to believe or accept?

Many have argued that watching violence on television causes violent behavior in viewers (Anderson et al., 2003; Anderson & Bushman, 2002b; Bushman & Huesmann, 2000; Eron et al., 1996; Huesmann, 1998). In 1993, a National Academy of Sciences report concluded that "overall, the vast majority of studies, whatever their methodology, showed that exposure to television violence resulted in increased aggressive behavior, both contemporaneously and over time" (Reiss & Roth, 1993, p. 371). An American Psychological Association Commission on Violence and Youth reached the same conclusion (American Psychological Association, 1993).

■ Is there evidence available to support the claim?

Three types of evidence back up the claim that watching violent television programs increases violent behavior. First, there are anecdotes and case studies. Children have poked one another in the eye after watching the Three Stooges appear to do so on television. And adults have claimed that watching TV shows prompted them to commit murders or other violent acts matching those seen on the shows (Werner, 2003).

Second, many correlational studies have found a strong link between watching violent television programs and later acts of aggression and violence (Johnson et al., 2002). One such study tracked people from the time they were six or seven (in 1977) until they reached their early twenties (in 1992). Those who watched more violent television as children were significantly more aggressive as adults (Huesmann et al., 1997, 2003) and more likely to engage in criminal activity (Huesmann, 1995). They were also more likely to use physical punishment on their own children, who themselves tended to be much more aggressive than average. These latter results were found not only in the United States but also in Israel, Australia, Poland, the Netherlands, and even Finland, where the number of violent TV shows is very small (Centerwall, 1990; Huesmann & Eron, 1986).

Finally, the results of numerous experiments support the view that TV violence increases aggression among viewers (American Psychological Association, 1993; Paik & Comstock, 1994; Reiss & Roth, 1993). In one study, groups of boys watched either violent or nonviolent programs in a controlled setting and then played floor hockey (Josephson, 1987). Boys who had watched the violent shows were more likely than those who had watched nonviolent programs to behave aggressively on the hockey floor. This effect was greatest for boys who had the most aggressive tendencies to begin with. More extensive experiments in which children are exposed for long periods to carefully controlled types of television programs also suggest that exposure to large amounts of violent activity on television results in aggressive behavior (Eron et al., 1996).

■ Can that evidence be interpreted another way?

To some, this evidence leaves no doubt that media violence causes increases in aggressive and violent behavior, especially in children (Anderson et al., 2003). Others suggest that the evidence is not conclusive and is open to some qualifications and alternative interpretations (e.g., Browne & Hamilton-Giachritsis, 2005; Freedman, 2002).

Anecdotal reports and case studies are certainly open to different interpretations. If people face imprisonment or execution for their violent acts, how much credibility can we give to their claims that their actions were triggered by television programs? How many other people might say that the same programs made them *less* likely to be violent? Anecdotes alone do not provide a good basis for drawing solid scientific conclusions.

What about the correlational evidence? A correlation between two variables does not necessarily mean that one caused the other. Both might be caused by a third factor. In fact, at least two possible "third factors" might account for the observed relationship between watching TV violence and acting aggressively.

First, certain people may prefer both to watch more violent TV programs and to behave aggressively toward others. In other words, personality may partly account for the observed correlations (e.g., Aluja-Fabregat & Torrubia-Beltri, 1998). Second, perhaps poverty, unemployment, or the effects of drugs and alcohol leave certain people more time to watch television and leave them with frustration or other stressors that trigger aggressive behavior.

Finally, some researchers question whether the results of controlled experiments on the effects of televised violence extend beyond the experimental situation or last more than a short time (Anderson, Lindsay, & Bushman, 1999; Browne & Hamilton-Giachristsis, 2005; Freedman, 2002). Who is to say, for example, whether an increase in aggressive acts during a hockey game has any later bearing on a child's tendency to commit an act of violence?

■ What evidence would help to evaluate the alternatives?

By their nature, correlational studies of the role of TV violence in violent behavior can never be conclusive. As we've pointed out, a third, unidentified causal variable could always be responsible for the results. More important would be further evidence from controlled experiments in which equivalent groups of people were given different, long-term "doses" of TV violence and its effects on their subsequent behavior were observed for many years. Such experiments could also explore the circumstances under which different people (for example, children vs. adults) are affected by various forms of violence. However, studies such as these create an ethical dilemma. If watching violent television programs really does cause violent behavior, are psychologists justified in creating conditions that might lead some people to be more violent? If such violence occurred, would the researchers be partly responsible to the victims and to society? If some participants commit violent acts, should the researchers continue the experiment to establish a pattern, or should they terminate the participation of those individuals? Difficulty in answering questions such as these is partly responsible for the use of short-term experiments and correlational designs in this research area, as well as for some of the remaining uncertainty about the effects of television violence.

■ What conclusions are most reasonable?

The evidence collected so far makes it reasonable to conclude that watching TV violence is one cause of violent behavior, especially in some children, and especially in boys (Anderson & Bushman, 2002a; Browne & Hamilton-Giachritsis, 2005; Bushman & Anderson, 2001; Huesmann et al., 1997; Robinson et al., 2001; Smith & Donnerstein, 1998). Playing violent video games may be another (Anderson, 2004; Anderson & Bushman, 2001). But a cause-effect relationship between watching TV violence and acting violently is not inevitable and may not always be long-lasting (Browne & Hamilton-Giachritsis, 2005). Further, there are many circumstances in which the effect does not occur (Charleton, Gunter, & Coles, 1998; Freedman, 1992, 2002). Parents, peers, and

closetohome@ucomics.com

SMASH!

www.ucomics.com

12-11   ©2003 John McPherson/Dist. by Universal Press Syndicate   McPHERSON

"I have HAD it with you two and your violent video games!"

The violence that may affect children's aggressive behavior may not be limited to what they see on television and in video games.

other environmental influences, along with personality factors, may dampen or amplify the effect of watching televised violence. Indeed, not every viewer interprets violence in the same way, and not every viewer is equally vulnerable (Ferguson, 2002; Wood, Wong, & Chachere, 1991). The most vulnerable may be young boys, and especially those who are most aggressive or violence-prone in the first place, a trait that could well have been acquired by observing the behavior of parents or peers (Huesmann et al., 1997).

Still, the fact that violence on television *can* have a causal impact on violent behavior is reason for serious concern. This issue continues to influence public debate about what should, and should not, be aired on television.

Using Research on Learning to Help People Learn

▶ **What should teachers learn about learning?**

The study of how people learn obviously has important implications for improved teaching in our schools (Bjork & Linn, 2006; Halpern & Hakel, 2003; Lambert, 1999; Li, 2005; Woolfolk-Hoy, 1999) and for helping people develop skills.

Classrooms Across Cultures

Many people have expressed concern that schools in the United States are not doing a very good job (Associated Press, 1997; Carnegie Task Force on Learning in the Primary Grades, 1996; Penner et al., 1994). The average performance of U.S. students on tests of reading, math, and other basic academic skills has tended to fall short of that of youngsters in other countries, especially Asian countries (International Association for the Evaluation of Education Achievement, 1999; National Center for Education Statistics, 2000, 2002; Program for International Student Assessment, 2004, 2005). In one comparison study, Harold Stevenson (1992) followed a sample of pupils in Taiwan, Japan, and the United States from first grade, in 1980, to eleventh grade, in 1991. In the first grade, the Asian students scored no higher than their U.S. peers on tests of mathematical aptitude and skills, nor did they enjoy math more. However, by the fifth grade, the U.S. students had fallen far behind. Corresponding differences were seen in reading skills.

Some possible causes of these differences were found in the classroom itself. In a typical U.S. classroom, teachers talked to students as a group; then students worked at their desks independently. Reinforcement or other feedback about performance on their work was usually delayed until the next day or, often, not provided at all. In contrast, the typical Japanese classroom placed greater emphasis on cooperative work among students (Kristof, 1997). Teachers provided more immediate feedback on a one-to-one basis. And there was an emphasis on creating teams of students with varying abilities, an arrangement in which faster learners help teach slower ones. However, before concluding that the differences in performance are the result of social factors alone, we must consider another important distinction: The Japanese children practiced more. They spent more days in school during the year and, on average, spent more hours doing homework.

Although the significance of these cultural differences in learning and teaching is not yet clear, the educational community in the United States is paying attention to them (e.g., Felder & Brent, 2001). Psychologists and educators are also considering how various principles of learning can be applied to improve education. For example, anecdotal and experimental evidence suggests that some of the most successful educational techniques are those that apply basic principles of operant conditioning, offering frequent testing, positive reinforcement for correct performance, and immediate corrective feedback following mistakes (Kass, 1999; Oppel, 2000; Roediger, McDaniel, & McDermott, 2006; Walberg, 1987).

applying psychology

RECIPROCAL TEACHING Ann Brown and her colleagues (1992) demonstrated the success of reciprocal teaching, in which children take turns teaching each other. This technique, which is similar to the cooperative arrangements seen in Japanese education, has become increasingly popular in North American schools (A. Brown et al., 1992; N. Brown, 2000).

VIRTUAL SURGERY Using a virtual reality system called "Surgery in 3-D," this medical student can actively learn and practice eye surgery skills before working with real patients. Computer-based human body simulators are also giving new doctors active learning experience in emergency room diagnosis and treatment; in heart, lung, and abdominal surgery; and other medical skills (Groopman, 2005).

Further, research in cognitive psychology (e.g., Bjork, 1979, 1999; Pashler, Rohrer, & Cepeda, 2006) suggests that students will retain more of what they learn if they study in several sessions distributed over time rather than in a single "cramming" session on the night before a test. To encourage this kind of "distributed practice," researchers say, teachers should give enough exams and quizzes (some unannounced, perhaps) that students will be reading and studying more or less continuously. And because learning is aided by repeated opportunities to use new information, these exams and quizzes should cover material from throughout the term, not just from recent classes. These recommendations are not necessarily popular with students, but there is good evidence that they promote long-term retention of course material (e.g., Bjork, 1999, 2001).

Active Learning

The importance of cognitive processes in learning is apparent in instructional methods that emphasize *active learning* (Bonwell & Eison, 1991). These methods take many forms, including, for example, small-group problem-solving tasks, discussion of "one-minute essays" written in class, use of "thumbs up" or "thumbs down" to indicate agreement or disagreement with the instructor's lecture, and multiple-choice questions that give students feedback about their understanding of the previous fifteen minutes of a lecture (Goss Lucas & Bernstein, 2005; Heward, 1997). Students typically find classes that include active learning experiences to be interesting and enjoyable (Moran, 2000; Murray, 2000). In addition, active learning methods help students go beyond memorizing isolated facts. These methods encourage students to think more deeply, to consider how new material relates to what they already know, and to apply it in new situations. This kind of thinking also makes the material easier to remember, which is why we have included so many opportunities for you to actively learn, rather than just passively read, the material in this book.

Studies of students in elementary schools, high schools, community colleges, and universities have found that active learning approaches result in better test performance and greater class participation compared with more passive instructional techniques (e.g., Hake, 1998; Kellum, Carr, & Dozier, 2001; Meyers & Jones, 1993). In one study, a fifth-grade teacher spent some days calling only on students whose hands were raised. On other days, all students were required to answer every question by holding up a card with their response written on it. Scores on next-day quizzes and biweekly tests showed that students remembered more of the material covered on the active learning days than on the "passive" days (Gardner, Heward, & Grossi, 1994). In another study of two consecutive medical school classes taught by the same instructor, scores on the final exam were significantly higher when students learned mainly through small-group discussions and case studies than when they were taught mainly through lectures (Chu, 1994). Similarly, among adults being taught to use a new computer program, active learning with "hands-on" practice was more effective than passively watching a demonstration video (Kerr & Payne, 1994). Finally, high school and college students who passively listened to a physics lecture received significantly lower scores on a test of lecture content than did those who participated in a virtual reality lab that allowed them to "interact" with the physical forces covered in the lecture (Brelsford, 1993).

Results like these have fueled the development of other science education programs that place students in virtual laboratory environments in which they actively manipulate materials and test hypotheses (e.g., Horwitz & Christie, 2000). Despite the enthusiasm generated by active learning methods, rigorous experimental research is still needed to compare their short- and long-term effects with those of more traditional methods in teaching various kinds of course content.

Skill Learning

The complex action sequences, or *skills*, that people learn to perform in everyday life develop through learning processes that include feedback and, of course, lots of practice. In fact, *practice*—the repeated performance of a skill—is critical to mastery (Howe, Davidson, & Sloboda, 1998). For perceptual-motor skills such as playing pool or piano, both physical and mental practice are beneficial (Druckman & Bjork, 1994). To be most effective, practice should continue past the point of correct performance until the skill can be performed automatically, with little or no attention. Feedback about the correctness of the response is also necessary. As with any learning process, the feedback should come soon enough to be effective but not so quickly that it interferes with the learner's efforts to learn independently.

Large amounts of guidance may produce very good performance during practice, but too much guidance may hurt later performance (Kluger & DeNisi, 1998; Wickens, 1992). For instance, coaching students about correct responses in math may impair their ability later to retrieve the correct response from memory on their own. Independent practice at retrieving previously learned responses or information requires more effort, but it is critical for skill development (Ericsson & Charness, 1994). There is little or no evidence to support "sleep learning" or similar schemes designed to make learning effortless (Druckman & Bjork, 1994). In short, "no pain, no gain."

ACTIVE REVIEW

Learning

Linkages

As noted in the introductory chapter, all of psychology's subfields are related to one another. Our discussion of associative network models illustrates just one way in which the topic of this chapter, learning, is linked to the subfield of memory, which is described in the chapter by that name. The Linkages diagram shows ties to two other subfields as well, and there are many more ties throughout the book. Looking for linkages among subfields will help you see how they all fit together and help you better appreciate the big picture that is psychology.

LINKAGES

CHAPTER 5

LEARNING

How are learned associations stored in memory?
(ans. on p. 191)

Who teaches boys to be men and girls to be women?
(ans. on p. 369)

Are psychological disorders learned behaviors?
(ans. on p. 459)

CHAPTER 6

MEMORY

CHAPTER 9

HUMAN DEVELOPMENT

CHAPTER 12

PSYCHOLOGICAL DISORDERS

Summary

Individuals adapt to changes in the environment through the process of *learning,* which is the modification, through experience, of preexisting behavior and understanding.

CLASSICAL CONDITIONING: LEARNING SIGNALS AND ASSOCIATIONS

▶ **How did Russian dogs teach psychologists about learning?**

One form of *learning* is *classical conditioning.* It occurs when a previously neutral *conditioned stimulus,* or *CS* (such as a tone), is

repeatedly paired with an *unconditioned stimulus,* or *UCS* (such as meat powder on a dog's tongue), which naturally brings about an *unconditioned response,* or *UCR* (such as salivation). Eventually the conditioned stimulus will elicit a response, known as the *conditioned response,* or *CR,* even when the unconditioned stimulus is not presented.

In general, the strength of a conditioned response grows as CS-UCS pairings continue. If the UCS is no longer paired with the CS, the conditioned response eventually disappears; this is *extinction.* After extinction, the conditioned response often reappears if the CS is presented after some time; this is *spontaneous recovery.* In addition, if the conditioned and unconditioned stimuli are paired once or twice after extinction, *reconditioning* occurs; that is, the conditioned response regains much of its original strength.

Because of *stimulus generalization,* conditioned responses occur to stimuli that are similar, but not identical to, conditioned stimuli. Generalization is limited by *stimulus discrimination,* which prompts conditioned responses to some stimuli but not to others.

Classical conditioning involves learning that the CS is an event that predicts the occurrence of another event, the UCS. Many psychologists see the conditioned response as a means through which animals and people develop mental representations of the relationships between events. Classical conditioning works best when the conditioned stimulus precedes the unconditioned stimulus by intervals ranging from less than a second to a minute or more, depending on the stimuli involved. Conditioning is also more likely when the CS reliably signals the UCS. In general, the speed of conditioning increases as the intensity of the UCS increases. Which particular stimulus is likely to become a CS linked to a subsequent UCS depends in part on which stimulus was being attended to when the UCS occurred; more intense stimuli are more likely to attract attention. *Second-order conditioning* occurs when one conditioned stimulus signals a conditioned stimulus that is already associated with an unconditioned stimulus. Some stimuli become associated more easily than others; taste aversions provide illustrations that organisms seem to be biologically prepared to learn certain associations.

Classical conditioning plays a role in the development and treatment of phobias. *Habituation* is reduced responsiveness to a repeated stimulus. According to Solomon's opponent-process theory, habituation is the result of two processes that balance each other. The first process is a relatively automatic, involuntary response—essentially a UCR. The second, or opponent, process is a learned or conditioned response that follows and counteracts the first. These conditioned responses may help explain the development of drug tolerance and some cases of drug overdoses.

INSTRUMENTAL AND OPERANT CONDITIONING: LEARNING THE CONSEQUENCES OF BEHAVIOR

▶ **How do reward and punishment work?**

Learning occurs not only through associating stimuli but also through associating behavior with its consequences. Thorndike's *law of effect* holds that any response that produces satisfaction becomes more likely to occur again and that any response that produces discomfort becomes less likely to recur. Thorndike referred to this type of learning as *instrumental conditioning.* Skinner called the process *operant conditioning.*

An *operant* is a response that has some effect on the world. A *reinforcer* increases the probability that the operant preceding it will occur again. There are two types of reinforcers: *positive reinforcers,* which are desirable stimuli that strengthen a response if they are presented after that response occurs, and *negative reinforcers,* which are the removal of an unpleasant stimulus following some response. Both kinds of reinforcers strengthen the behaviors that precede them. When behavior is strengthened by a positive reinforcer, the process is called positive reinforcement. When behavior is strengthened by a negative reinforcer, the process is called negative reinforcement. *Escape conditioning* results when a behavior stops an unpleasant stimulus. *Avoidance conditioning* results when behavior prevents an unpleasant stimulus from occurring; it reflects both classical and operant conditioning. Behaviors learned through avoidance conditioning are hard to extinguish. *Discriminative stimuli* signal whether reinforcement is available for a particular behavior.

Complex responses can be learned through *shaping,* which involves reinforcing successive approximations of the desired response. *Primary reinforcers* are innately rewarding; *secondary reinforcers* are rewards that people or animals learn to like because of their association with primary reinforcers. In general, operant conditioning proceeds more quickly when the delay in receiving reinforcement is short rather than long and when the reinforcer is large rather than small. Reinforcement may be delivered on a continuous reinforcement schedule or on one of four types of partial, or intermittent, reinforcement schedules: fixed-ratio (FR), variable-ratio (VR), fixed-interval (FI), and variable-interval (VI) schedules. Ratio schedules lead to a rapid rate of responding. Behavior learned through partial reinforcement is very resistant to extinction; this phenomenon is called the *partial reinforcement extinction effect.* Partial reinforcement is involved in superstitious behavior, which results when some action is followed by, but does not actually cause, a reinforcer.

Research in neuroscience suggests that reinforcers act as rewards largely because of their ability to create activity in "pleasure centers" in the brain's hypothalamus, as well as in other brain areas that use the chemical dopamine.

Punishment decreases the frequency of a behavior by following it either with an unpleasant stimulus or with the removal of a pleasant one. Punishment can be useful when performed properly, but it can have drawbacks. It only suppresses behavior; fear of punishment may generalize to the person doing the punishing; it is ineffective when delayed; it can be physically harmful and may teach aggressiveness; and it teaches only what not to do, not what should be done to obtain reinforcement.

The principles of operant conditioning have been applied in many areas, from teaching social skills to treating sleep disorders.

COGNITIVE PROCESSES IN LEARNING

▶ **Can people learn to be helpless?**

Cognitive processes—how people represent, store, and use information—play an important role in learning. *Learned helplessness* appears to result when people believe that their behavior has no effect on the world. Both animals and humans display *latent learning.* They also form *cognitive maps* of their environments, even in the absence of any reinforcement for doing so. Experiments on *insight* also suggest that cognitive processes play an important role in learning, even by animals. The process of learning by watching others is called *observational learning,* or social learning. Some observational learning occurs through *vicarious conditioning,* in which one is influenced by seeing or hearing about the consequences of others' behavior. Observational learning is more likely to occur when the person observed is rewarded for the observed behavior. It is a powerful source of socialization.

USING RESEARCH ON LEARNING TO HELP PEOPLE LEARN

▶ **What should teachers learn about learning?**

Research on how people learn has implications for improved teaching and for the development of a wide range of skills. The degree to which learning principles, such as immediate reinforcement, are used in teaching varies considerably from culture to culture. The importance of cognitive processes in learning is seen in active learning methods designed to encourage people to think deeply about and apply new information instead of just memorizing isolated

facts. Observational learning, practice, and corrective feedback play important roles in the learning of skills.

Learn by Doing
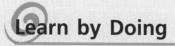

Put It in Writing

Imagine that you have inherited a circus from a long-lost relative, but you discover that all of the animal acts are stale and out of date. At a meeting with your employees, you explain that the principles of classical and operant conditioning could be used to improve these acts. Write a one-page paper describing how classical conditioning could be used to teach elephants a new trick, and how operant conditioning could be used to spice up a trained seal act. Be sure to label all the concepts and principles you use (such as "conditioned stimulus," "conditioned response," "discriminative stimulus," "shaping," and the like).

Personal Learning Activity

Select a pair of friends or relatives of about the same age and intelligence, and try teaching each of them something that is new to

them but that you know well—perhaps the words to a song; a popular dance; or how to operate a digital camera, tie a tie, hit a tennis ball, or use a skateboard. Teach one person simply by telling or showing what you want him or her to learn, but work out a set of active learning methods to use with the second person. (Recall that active learning requires the learner to get involved in the learning process by doing something other than just listening to a lesson.) Keep a record of which student does better at this learning task and how long it takes each student to learn. Which method was more efficient, and which student enjoyed the learning process more? Did your results confirm or conflict with research on active learning in the classroom? *For additional projects, see the Personal Learning Activities in the corresponding chapter of the study guide that accompanies this text.*

Step into Action

Courses

Learning
Animal Behavior
Behavior Modification

Movies

The Deer Hunter; Schindler's List. Learned helplessness.
The Miracle Worker. Shaping and reinforcement.
A Clockwork Orange; The Manchurian Candidate.
   Misconceptions about the power of classical
   conditioning.
Free Willy. Reinforcement and animal behavior.
The War. Observational learning, modeling.
Educating Rita; To Sir, With Love; Dangerous Minds.
   Learning principles in education.

Books

Kieran Egan, *The Educated Mind: How Cognitive Tools Shape Our Understanding* (University of Chicago Press, 1997). How children learn.
James Garbarino, *Lost Boys: Why Our Sons Turn Violent and How We Can Save Them* (Free Press, 1999). Development of violence examined from several perspectives, including learning theories.

Laurence Steinberg, *The Ten Basic Principles of Good Parenting* (Simon & Schuster, 2004). Learning-based parenting skills.
Martin Seligman, *What You Can Change and What You Can't: The Complete Guide to Successful Self-Improvement* (Fawcett Books, 1995). Using learning principles for self-improvement.
Martin Seligman, with Karen Reivich, Lisa Jaycox, and Jane Gillham, *The Optimistic Child* (Harper Perennial Library, 1996). The role of cognitive processes in learning and behavior.

The Web

The World Wide Web is a good source of additional information about the science of psychology, provided you use it carefully and think critically about the information you find. The Online Study Center that accompanies this text offers many resources relevant to this chapter. These resources include interactive tutorials; Thinking Critically and Evaluating Research exercises; ACE chapter quizzes; recommended web links; and articles on current events, books, and movies. Please visit the Online Study Center at http://college.hmco.com/pic/bernstein4e.

Review of Key Terms

Can you define each of the key terms in the chapter? Check your definitions against those on the pages shown in parentheses in the following list or in the Glossary/Index at the end of the text.

avoidance conditioning (p. 180)

classical conditioning (p. 172)

cognitive map (p. 195)

conditioned response (CR) (p. 172)

conditioned stimulus (CS) (p. 172)

discriminative stimuli (p. 182)

escape conditioning (p. 180)

extinction (p. 173)

habituation (p. 178)

insight (p. 196)

latent learning (p. 194)

law of effect (p. 179)

learned helplessness (p. 192)

learning (p. 171)

negative reinforcers (p. 180)

observational learning (p. 196)

operant (p. 180)

operant conditioning (p. 179)

partial reinforcement extinction effect (p. 185)

positive reinforcers (p. 180)

primary reinforcers (p. 184)

punishment (p. 187)

reconditioning (p. 173)

reinforcer (p. 180)

secondary reinforcers (p. 184)

second-order conditioning (p. 176)

shaping (p. 183)

spontaneous recovery (p. 173)

stimulus discrimination (p. 174)

stimulus generalization (p. 173)

unconditioned response (UCR) (p. 172)

unconditioned stimulus (UCS) (p. 172)

vicarious conditioning (p. 197)

Multiple-Choice Self-Test

Select the best answer for each of the following questions. Then check your responses against the Answer Key at the end of the text.

1. Which saying best reflects learning?

   a. "A watched pot never boils."
   b. "A stitch in time saves nine."
   c. "Once burned, twice shy."
   d. "If you will it, it is no dream."

2. In a classical conditioning experiment, a puff of air was blown into Ralph's eye, and he reflexively blinked. The experimenter then began flashing a green light just before presenting the puff of air. After many pairings of the green light and the puff of air, Ralph began to blink as soon as the green light appeared, whether or not the air puff followed. In this experiment, the green light is the

   a. unconditioned stimulus.
   b. conditioned stimulus.
   c. conditioned response.
   d. unconditioned response.

3. Suppose that the experimenter in the previous question continues presenting the green light, but never again follows it with the puff of air. Ralph will soon _____ through the process of _____.

   a. blink faster; reconditioning
   b. stop blinking in response to the green light; extinction
   c. blink slower; stimulus control
   d. stop blinking; spontaneous recovery

4. Kim has gone out with both Alan and Brad this week. Even though she said she hates rock concerts, Alan took her to one, and she came home with a headache. Brad takes her to a movie she had been wanting to see. According to _____, Kim would be more likely to date Brad in the future.

   a. the law of effect
   b. the Premack principle
   c. classical conditioning theory
   d. all of the above

5. After being bitten by a dog at a young age, Najla became fearful of all dogs. Now, when Najla sees a dog, her heart races and she feels like running away. Najla has developed _____ through _____ conditioning.

   a. habituation; operant
   b. habituation; classical
   c. a phobia; operant
   d. a phobia; classical

6. The idea that knowledge is located in many areas throughout the brain rather than in one particular place is a basic assumption of _____.

   a. neural network theories
   b. classical conditioning
   c. observational learning
   d. stimulus generalization

7. Because of birth defects, Justin, a four-year-old, has had to have a number of surgical operations. As a result, just seeing a doctor or nurse in a surgical mask makes Justin fearful and tearful. At Halloween this year, Justin had the same reaction to children wearing masks. This is an example of

   a. stimulus generalization.
   b. stimulus discrimination.
   c. vicarious learning.
   d. observational learning.

8. Laverne lost control and ate an entire coconut cream pie. Later that day she got the flu, complete with nausea and vomiting. After this experience, Laverne associated coconut cream pie with being sick, and now she can't even stand the smell of it. This is an example of _____, which supports the concept of _____.

   a. escape conditioning; spontaneous recovery
   b. discriminative conditioning; biopreparedness
   c. taste aversion; biopreparedness
   d. latent learning; spontaneous recovery

9. When baby Sally cries after being put to bed, her parents check to see that she is all right but otherwise ignore her. After several evenings of this treatment, Sally's bedtime crying stopped. This is an example of

   a. extinction.
   b. habituation.
   c. second-order conditioning.
   d. shaping.

10. Manuel has learned that every time he cleans his room, his mother makes his favorite dessert. This is an example of

    a. classical conditioning.
    b. negative reinforcement.
    c. operant conditioning.
    d. extinction.

11. Loretta gets a backache every day, but if she sits in a hot bath, the pain goes away. So she decides to take a hot bath every day. She has learned to do this through

    a. positive reinforcement.
    b. negative reinforcement.
    c. stimulus discrimination.
    d. shaping.

12. Doug hates to hear children misbehaving in the grocery store, so he always shops late at night when children are not present. Doug's choice of shopping time is an example of

    a. escape conditioning.
    b. avoidance conditioning.
    c. shaping.
    d. secondary reinforcement.

13. Ten minutes before a movie starts, the theater is filled with people who are talking and laughing. As soon as the lights go out, everyone becomes quiet. Sudden darkness serves as a _____ in this example of operant conditioning.

    a. positive reinforcer
    b. negative reinforcer
    c. punishment
    d. discriminative stimulus

14. Craig wanted to teach his dog, JoJo, to sit up and beg using operant conditioning principles. He started by giving JoJo a treat when she was simply standing. Then he gave her a treat only if she was sitting. Next, he gave her a treat only if she was sitting and had raised one paw, and so on. This is an example of

    a. stimulus discrimination.
    b. stimulus generalization.
    c. negative reinforcement.
    d. shaping.

15. When Jamey has washed the dinner dishes on five evenings, his parents take him to the movies. Susan's dad occasionally gives her a dollar after she washes the dishes. What schedules of reinforcement are Jamey and Susan on, respectively?

    a. fixed interval; variable interval
    b. fixed ratio; variable ratio
    c. variable ratio; fixed interval
    d. variable interval; fixed ratio

16. Which of the following is a potential problem with using punishment to change behavior?

    a. It can produce unwanted side effects.
    b. Frequent punishment can teach children to behave aggressively.
    c. It signals that inappropriate behavior occurred but doesn't indicate what should be done instead.
    d. These are all potential problems with using punishment.

17. Whenever Javier asked his next-door neighbor to turn down her loud music, she ignored him. Later, when a new neighbor moved in next door and began playing loud music, Javier did not even bother to complain. His case demonstrates

    a. latent learning.
    b. learned helplessness.
    c. observational learning.
    d. trial and error.

18. When Kenzi got a flat tire not far from campus, he walked down the street to a service station he drove by every day but had never visited. The fact that he immediately knew where it was illustrates

    a. insight learning.
    b. observational learning.
    c. latent learning.
    d. vicarious learning.

19. After watching a number of people petting and playing with a dog, Najla decides that dogs aren't as scary as she'd thought. The next day, at her neighbors' house, she pets their dog. Najla's fear has been reduced through

    a. classical conditioning.
    b. operant conditioning.
    c. spontaneous recovery.
    d. observational learning.

20. Whether the skill you want to learn involves a foreign language, the words of a speech, or a golf swing, the most important thing you can do is

    a. delay feedback until you have almost reached perfection.
    b. read all you can about the task you want to learn.
    c. engage in all the practice you can.
    d. work in a group.

6

Memory

Have you ever forgotten where you parked your car? Have you ever had a name on the tip of your tongue, but couldn't quite recall it? Researchers in the field of memory explore these common experiences. *Memory* is a complex process of storing and retrieving information. You use different kinds of memory for different types of information, such as personal experiences, specific skills, and abstract concepts. Once information is stored in your memory, recalling it can sometimes be difficult. In this chapter, you will learn about some techniques that can help you to retrieve memories. What psychologists have learned about memory has been used to create study techniques that really work!

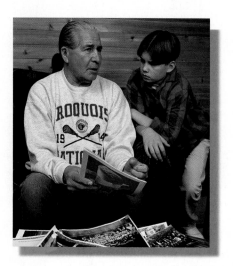

Reading this chapter will help you to answer the following questions:

" 'll make him an offer he can't refuse." "I'll be back." "Trust no one." "Life is like a box of chocolates." "I see dead people." "Show me the money." "Is that your final answer?" Do you remember where you heard these words? They are memorable lines from *The Godfather, The Terminator, The X-Files, Forrest Gump, The Sixth Sense, Jerry Maguire,* and *Who Wants to Be a Millionaire.* Can you say who Private Ryan was and why he needed to be saved? And do you know which classic film character said "Play it again, Sam"? (If you don't, ask a friend who knows about old movies.) The most common answer to the latter question is Rick, the café owner played by Humphrey Bogart in *Casablanca.* Bogart never actually said this often-quoted line, though many people are sure they "remember" it.

Your memory stores vast amounts of useful and not-so-useful information from all of your experiences. This chapter will help you understand the nature of memory—how you form memories, how memory errors happen, and how you forget.

The Nature of Memory

▶ **How does information turn into memories?**

Memory is a funny thing. You might be able to remember the name of your first-grade teacher, but not the name of someone you met five minutes ago. Mathematician John Griffith estimated that in an average lifetime, a person stores roughly five hundred

Basic Memory Processes

Remembering something requires, first, that the information be encoded—put in a form that can be placed in memory. It must then be stored and, finally, retrieved, or recovered. If any of these processes fails, forgetting will occur.

times as much information as can be found in all the volumes of the *Encyclopaedia Britannica* (Hunt, 1982). Keep in mind, however, that although we retain a great deal of information, we also lose a great deal (Wixted, 2004). Consider Tatiana Cooley. She was the U.S. National Memory Champion for three years in a row, but she confesses that she is so absent-minded that she relies on Post-it Notes to remember everyday errands (Schacter, 2001). Obviously, our memory is made up of many different abilities, some of which may be better than others from person to person and from time to time.

Memory plays a critical role in your life. Without it, you wouldn't know how to shut off your alarm, take a shower, get dressed, recognize objects, or communicate. You would be unaware of your own likes and dislikes. You would have no idea of who you are (Craik et al., 1999). The impressive capacity of human memory depends on the operation of a complex mental system (Schacter, 1999).

Basic Memory Processes

In February 2002, prison warden James Smith lost his set of master keys to the Westville Correctional Facility. As a result, 2,559 inmates were kept under partial lockdown for eight days while the Indiana Department of Correction spent $53,000 to change locks in the affected areas. As it turned out, the warden had put the keys in his pocket when he went home, forgot he had done so, and reported the keys "missing" when they were not in their usual place in his office the next day (Associated Press, 2002). What went wrong? There are several possibilities. Memory depends on three basic processes: encoding, storage, and retrieval (see Figure 6.1). Our absent-minded warden might have had problems with any one of these processes.

First, information must be put into memory, a step that requires encoding. **Encoding** is a process that puts information to be remembered into a form that our memory system can accept and use. We use *memory codes* to translate information from the senses into mental representations of that information. **Acoustic codes** represent information as sequences of sounds, such as a tune or a rhyme. **Visual codes** represent information as pictures, such as the image of your best friend's face. **Semantic codes** represent the general meaning of an experience. So if you see a billboard that reads "Huey's Going-Out-of-Business Sale," you might encode the sound of the words as if they had been spoken (acoustic coding), the image of the letters as they were arranged on the sign (visual coding), or the fact that you recently saw an ad for Huey's (semantic coding). The type of coding we use influences what we remember. Semantic coding might allow you to remember the fact that an unfamiliar car was parked in your neighbors' driveway just before their house was robbed. If little or no other coding took place, however, you might not be able to remember the make, model, or color of the car.

The second basic memory process is storage. **Storage** refers to the holding of information in your memory over time. When you recall a vacation you took in childhood

encoding The process of putting information into a form that the memory system can accept and use.

acoustic codes Mental representations of stimuli as sounds.

visual codes Mental representations of stimuli as pictures.

semantic codes Mental representations of experiences by their general meaning.

storage The process of maintaining information in the memory system over time.

HOW DOES SHE DO THAT? As she practices, this young violinist is developing procedural memories of how to play her instrument that may be difficult to put into words. To appreciate the special nature of procedural memory, try writing a step-by-step description of exactly how you tie a shoe.

retrieval   The process of recalling information stored in memory.

episodic memory   Memory for events in one's own past.

semantic memory   Memory for generalized knowledge about the world.

procedural memory   A type of memory containing information about how to do things.

explicit memory   The process through which people deliberately try to remember something.

implicit memory   The unintentional recollection and influence of prior experiences.

or find that you can use a pogo stick many years after you last played with one, you are depending on the storage capacity of your memory.

The third memory process, **retrieval,** occurs when you find information stored in memory and bring it into consciousness. Retrieving stored information such as your address or telephone number is usually so fast and effortless that it seems automatic. The search-and-retrieval process becomes more noticeable, however, when you read a quiz question but cannot quite recall the answer. Retrieval involves both recall and recognition. To *recall* information, you have to retrieve it from memory without much help; this is what is required when you answer an essay test question or play *Jeopardy!* In *recognition,* retrieval is aided by clues, such as the response alternatives given on multiple-choice tests and the questions on *Who Wants to Be a Millionaire.* Accordingly, recognition tends to be easier than recall.

Types of Memory

When was the last time you made a phone call? Who was the first president of the United States? How do you keep your balance on skates? Answering each of these questions involves different aspects of memory. To answer the first question, you must remember a particular event in your life. To answer the second one, you have to recall general knowledge that is unlikely to be tied to a specific event. And the answer to the third question is easier to demonstrate than to describe. So how many types of memory are there? No one is sure, but most research suggests that there are at least three. Each type of memory is named for the kind of information it handles: episodic, semantic, and procedural (Roediger, Marsh, & Lee, 2002).

Any memory of a specific event that happened while you were present is an **episodic memory** (Tulving, 2002). It is a memory of an episode in your life. What you had for dinner yesterday, what you did last summer, or where you were last Friday night are episodic memories. **Semantic memory** contains generalized knowledge of the world—such as that twelve items make a dozen—that does not involve memory of a specific event. So if you were asked "Are wrenches pets or tools?" you could answer using your semantic memory; you don't have to remember a specific episode in which you learned that wrenches are tools. As a general rule, people report episodic memories by saying, "I remember when . . ." whereas they report semantic memories by saying, "I know that . . ." (Tulving, 2000). Memory of how to do things, such as riding a bike, folding a map, or playing golf, is called **procedural memory.** Information in procedural memory often consists of a sequence of movements that are difficult or impossible to put into words. As a result, teachers of music, dance, cooking, woodworking, and other skills usually prefer to first show their students what to do rather than describe how to do it.

Many activities require all three types of memory. Consider the game of tennis. Knowing the official rules or the number of sets needed to win a match involves semantic memory. Remembering who served last requires episodic memory. And knowing how to hit the ball involves procedural memory.

Recalling these three kinds of memories can be either intentional or unintentional. When you deliberately try to remember something, such as where you went on your last vacation, you are relying on **explicit memory.** In contrast, **implicit memory** involves the unintentional recollection and influence of prior experiences (McDermott, 2002; Nelson, 1999). For example, if you were to read this chapter twice, implicit memories from your first reading would help you to read it more quickly the second time. For the same reason, you can solve a puzzle faster if you have solved it in the past. This improvement of performance—often called *priming*—is automatic, and it occurs without conscious effort. In fact, people are often unaware that their actions have been influenced by previous events (see the chapter on consciousness). Have you ever found yourself disliking someone you just met, but you didn't know why? The person might have triggered an implicit memory of a similar-looking person who once treated you badly. In such cases, we are usually unaware of any connection between the two individuals (Lewicki, 1992). Because some influential events cannot be recalled even when people try to do so, implicit memory has been said to involve "retention without remembering" (Roediger, Guynn, & Jones, 1995).

Models of Memory

We remember some information far better than other information. Suppose your friends throw a surprise party for you. When you enter the room, you might barely notice the flash of a camera. Later, you cannot recall it at all. And you might forget in a few seconds the name of a person you met at the party. But if you live to be a hundred, you will never forget where the party took place or how surprised and pleased you were. Why do some things stay in memory forever, whereas others barely make an impression? Each of four ways of thinking about memory, called *models* of memory, provides a somewhat different explanation. Let's see what the levels-of-processing, transfer-appropriate processing, parallel distributed processing, and information-processing models have to say about memory.

Levels of Processing   The **levels-of-processing model** suggests that memory depends on the extent to which you encode and process information when you first encounter it. Consider, for example, the task of remembering a phone number you just heard on the radio. If you were unable to write it down, you would probably repeat the number over and over to yourself until you could get to a phone. This repetition process is called **maintenance rehearsal.** It can be an effective method for encoding information temporarily, but what if you need to remember something for hours, months, or years? In that case, you would be better off using **elaborative rehearsal,** a process in which you relate new material to information you already have stored in memory. For example, instead of trying to remember a new person's name by simply repeating it to yourself, you could try thinking about how the name is related to something you know well. So if you are introduced to a man named Jim Crews, you might think, "He is as tall as my Uncle Jim, who always wears a crew cut."

Study after study has shown that memory is improved when people use elaborative rehearsal rather than maintenance rehearsal (Jahnke & Nowaczyk, 1998). According to the levels-of-processing model, the reason is that material is processed more "deeply" when elaborative rehearsal is used (Lockhart & Craik, 1990; Roediger & Gallo, 2001). The more you think about new information, organize it, and relate it to something you already know, the "deeper" the processing, and the better your memory of the information becomes. Teachers use this idea when they ask students not only to define a new word but also to use it in a sentence. Figuring out how to use the new word takes deeper processing than does merely defining it. (The next time you come across an unfamiliar word in this book, don't just read its definition. Try to use the word in a sentence by coming up with an example of the concept that is related to your knowledge and experience.)

Transfer-Appropriate Processing   Level of processing is not the only factor that affects memory. Another critical factor, suggested by the **transfer-appropriate processing model** of memory, is how the encoding process matches up with what is later retrieved. In one study, for example, half the students in a class were told that their next exam would contain multiple-choice questions. The rest of the students were told to expect essay questions. Only half the students actually got the type of exam they expected, however. These students did much better on the exam than those who took an unexpected type of exam. Apparently, in studying for the exam, the two groups used encoding strategies that were most appropriate to the type of exam they expected. Those who tried to retrieve the information in a way that did not match their encoding method had a harder time (d'Ydewalle & Rosselle, 1978). Results such as these indicate that how well the encoding method transfers to the retrieval task is just as important as the depth of processing.

levels-of-processing model   A model of memory suggesting that differences in how well something is remembered reflect the degree or depth of mental processing.

maintenance rehearsal   A memorization method that involves repeating information over and over to keep it in memory.

elaborative rehearsal   A memorization method that relates new information to information already stored in memory.

transfer-appropriate processing model   A model suggesting that memory depends on how the encoding process matches up with what is later retrieved.

| EXTERNAL STIMULI | → | **Sensory memory** Briefly retains the information picked up by the sensory organs *(information lost after about one second)* | → | **Short-term memory** Temporarily holds information in consciousness *(information stored for about 18 seconds)* | → | **Long-term memory** Can retain information for long periods of time, often for life |

FIGURE 6.2

Three Stages of Memory

This traditional information-processing model describes three stages in the memory system.

Parallel Distributed Processing   A third way of thinking about memory is based on **parallel distributed processing (PDP) models** (Rumelhart & McClelland, 1986). These models of memory suggest that new experiences do more than provide specific facts that are stored and later retrieved one at a time. Those facts are also combined with what you already know, so that each new experience changes your overall understanding of the world and how it operates. For example, when you first arrived at college, you learned lots of specific facts, such as where classes are held, what time the library closes, and where to get the best pizza. Over time, these and many other facts about college life form a network of information that creates a more general understanding of how the whole college system works. The development of this network makes experienced students not only more knowledgeable than new students, but also more sophisticated. It allows them to, say, allocate their study time in order to do well in their most important courses and to plan a schedule that doesn't conflict with work commitments and maybe even avoids early morning classes—and certain professors.

Using this network concept, PDP models of memory see each unit of knowledge as connected with every other unit. The connections between units become stronger as they are experienced together more frequently. In other words, your knowledge about the world is distributed across a network of associations that all operate at the same time, in parallel. This network allows you to quickly and efficiently draw inferences and generalizations about the world. For example, because of your network of associations, just seeing the word *chair* allows you to know immediately what a chair looks like, what it is used for, where it tends to be located, who might buy one, and the like. PDP models of memory explain this process very effectively.

Information Processing   The **information-processing model** is probably the most influential and comprehensive model of memory. It suggests that for information to be firmly implanted in memory, it must pass through three stages of mental processing: sensory memory, short-term memory, and long-term memory (see Figure 6.2).

In *sensory memory*, information from the senses—sights or sounds, for example—is held very briefly before being lost. But if information in sensory memory is attended to, analyzed, and encoded as a meaningful pattern, we say that it has been *perceived* (see the chapter on sensation and perception). Information in sensory memory that has been perceived can now enter *short-term memory*. If nothing further is done with it, that information will disappear in less than twenty seconds. However, if the information in short-term memory is further processed, it may be encoded into *long-term memory*, where it may remain indefinitely.

The act of reading illustrates all three stages of memory processing. As you read any sentence in this book, light energy reflected from the page reaches your eyes, where it is converted to neural activity and registered in your sensory memory. If you pay attention to these visual stimuli, your perception of the patterns of light can be held in short-term memory. This stage of memory holds the early parts of the sentence so that they can be integrated and understood as you read the rest of the sentence. As you read, you are constantly recognizing words by matching your perceptions of them with the patterns and meanings you have stored in long-term memory. In other words, all three stages of memory are necessary for you to understand a sentence.

"In Review: Models of Memory" summarizes the four memory models we have discussed. Each of these models provides an explanation of why we remember some things

learn by doing   **SENSORY MEMORY AT WORK**   In a darkened room, ask a friend to hold a small flashlight and move it very slowly in a circle. You will see a moving point of light. If it appears to have a "tail," like a comet, that is your sensory memory of the light before it fades. Now ask your friend to move the light faster. You should now see a complete circle of light, because as the light moves, its impression on your sensory memory does not have time to fade before the circle is completed. A similar process allows us to see "sparkler circles."

in review

MODELS OF MEMORY

Model	Assumptions
Levels of processing	The more deeply material is processed, the better our memory of it.
Transfer-appropriate processing	Retrieval is improved when we try to recall material in a way that matches how the material was encoded.
Parallel distributed processing (PDP)	New experiences add to and alter our overall knowledge base; they are not separate, unconnected facts. Networks of associations allow us to draw inferences and make generalizations about the world.
Information-processing	Information is processed in three stages: sensory memory, short-term memory, and long-term memory.

1. The value of elaborative rehearsal over maintenance rehearsal has been cited as evidence for the _____ model of memory.
2. Deliberately trying to remember something means using your _____ memory.
3. Playing the piano requires access to _____ memory.

and forget others, but which model offers the best explanation? The answer is that more than one model may be required to understand memory. Just as it is helpful for physicists to characterize light in terms of both waves and particles, psychologists find it useful to think of memory as both a sequential process, as suggested by the information-processing model, and as a parallel process, as suggested by parallel distributed processing models.

Online Study Center

Improve Your Grade
Tutorial: Immediate
Memory Span

Storing New Memories

▶ **What am I most likely to remember?**

The storage of information is critical to memory, because we can retrieve only information that has been stored. According to the information-processing model, sensory memory, short-term memory, and long-term memory each provide a different type of storage. Let's take a closer look at these three memory systems in order to better understand how they work—and sometimes fail.

Sensory Memory

To recognize incoming information, the brain must analyze and compare it with what is already stored in long-term memory. This process is very quick, but it still takes time. The major function of **sensory memory** is to hold information long enough for it to be processed further. This "holding" function is the job of the **sensory registers,** which act as temporary storage bins. There is a separate register for each of the five senses. Each register can store a nearly complete representation of a sensory stimulus, but only briefly, often for less than one second (Eysenck & Keane, 2005).

learn by doing Sensory memory helps us experience a constant flow of information, even if that flow is interrupted. To see this for yourself, move your head and eyes slowly from left to right. It may seem as though your eyes are moving smoothly, like a movie camera scanning a scene, but that's not what is happening. Your

parallel distributed processing (PDP) models Memory models in which new experiences are seen as changing one's overall knowledge base.

information-processing model A model suggesting that information must pass through sensory memory, short-term memory, and long-term memory in order to become firmly embedded in memory.

sensory memory A type of memory that is very brief, but lasts long enough to connect one impression to the next.

sensory registers Memory systems that briefly hold incoming information.

eyes fixate at one point for about one-fourth of a second and then rapidly jump to a new position. You perceive smooth motion because you hold the scene in your visual sensory register until your eyes fixate again. Similarly, when you listen to someone speak, your auditory sensory register allows you to experience a smooth flow of information, even though there are actually short silences between or within words.

The fact that sensory memories fade quickly if they are not processed further is actually an adaptive characteristic of the memory system (Baddeley, 1998). You simply cannot deal with all of the sights, sounds, odors, tastes, and touch sensations that come to your sense organs at any given moment. Using **selective attention,** you focus your mental resources on only part of the stimuli around you, thus controlling what information is processed further in short-term memory.

Short-Term Memory and Working Memory

The sensory registers allow your memory system to develop a representation of a stimulus. However, they can't perform the more thorough analysis needed if the information is going to be used in some way. That function is accomplished by short-term memory and working memory.

Short-term memory (STM) is the part of your memory system that stores limited amounts of information for up to about eighteen seconds. When you check the newspaper or an on-screen guide for the channel number of a TV show you want to watch and then keep that number in mind as you switch channels, you are using short-term memory. **Working memory** is the part of the memory system that allows us to mentally work with, or manipulate, the information being held in short-term memory. When you mentally calculate what time you have to leave home in order to have lunch on campus, return a library book, and still get to class on time, you are using working memory.

Short-term memory is actually a component of working memory, and together these memory systems allow us to do many kinds of mental work (Baddeley, 2003; Engle & Oransky, 1999). Suppose you are buying something for eighty-three cents. You go through your change and pick out two quarters, two dimes, two nickels, and three pennies. To do this you use both short-term memory and working memory to remember the price, retrieve the rules of addition from long-term memory, and keep a running count of how much change you have so far. Now try to recall how many windows there

![learn by doing icon] are on the front of the house or apartment where you grew up. In answering this question, you probably formed a mental image of the building. You used one kind of working-memory process to form that image, and then you maintained the image in short-term memory while you "worked" on it by counting the windows. So working memory has at least two components: *maintenance* (holding information in short-term memory) and *manipulation* (working on that information).

Encoding in Short-Term Memory   The encoding of information in short-term memory is much more elaborate and varied than encoding in the sensory registers (Brandimonte, Hitch, & Bishop, 1992). *Acoustic coding* (by sound) seems to dominate. This conclusion comes from research on the mistakes people make when encoding information in short-term memory. These mistakes tend to involve the substitution of similar sounds. For instance, Robert Conrad (1964) showed people strings of letters and asked them to repeat the letters immediately. Among their most common mistakes was the replacement of the correct letter with another that sounded like it. So if the correct letter was *C*, it was often replaced with a *D, P,* or *T.* The participants made these mistakes even though the letters were presented visually, without any sound. Studies in several cultures have also shown that items are more difficult to remember if they sound similar. For example, native English speakers do less well when they try to remember a string of letters like *ECVTGB* (which all have similar sounds) than when trying to remember one like *KRLDQS* (in which there are different sounds).

Encoding in short-term memory is not always acoustic, however. Information in short-term memory also can be encoded visually, semantically, and even kinesthetically

selective attention   The process of focusing mental resources on only part of the stimulus field.

short-term memory (STM)   A stage of memory in which information normally lasts less than twenty seconds; a component of working memory.

working memory   Memory that allows us to mentally work with, or manipulate, information being held in short-term memory.

```
9 2 5
8 6 4 2
3 7 6 5 4
6 2 7 4 1 8
0 4 0 1 4 7 3
1 9 2 2 3 5 3 0
4 8 6 8 5 4 3 3 2
2 5 3 1 9 7 1 7 6 8
8 5 1 2 9 6 1 9 4 5 0
9 1 8 5 4 6 9 4 2 9 3 7
```

Source: Howard (1983).

FIGURE 6.3

The Capacity of Short-Term Memory

learn by doing Here is a test of your immediate memory span (Howard, 1983). Ask someone to read to you the numbers in the top row at the rate of about one per second; then try to repeat them back in the same order. Then try the next row, and the one after that, until you make a mistake. Your immediate memory span is the maximum number of items you can repeat back perfectly.

immediate memory span The maximum number of items a person can recall perfectly after one presentation of the items.

chunks Stimuli that are perceived as units or meaningful groupings of information.

(in terms of physical movements; Best, 1999). In one study, deaf people were shown a list of words and then asked to immediately write down as many as they could remember (Shand, 1982). When these participants made errors, they wrote words that are expressed through similar *hand movements* in American Sign Language, rather than words that *sounded* similar to the correct words. Apparently, these individuals had encoded the words on the basis of the movements they would use when making the signs for them.

Storage Capacity of Short-Term Memory How much information can you hold in short-term memory? The simple test presented in Figure 6.3 will help you determine your **immediate memory span,** which is the largest number of items you can recall perfectly after one presentation. If your memory span is like most people's, you can repeat six or seven items from the test in this figure. And you should come up with about the same result whether you use digits, letters, words, or virtually anything else (Pollack, 1953). George Miller (1956) noticed that many studies using a variety of tasks showed the same limit on the ability to process information. This "magic number," which is seven plus or minus two, appears to be the immediate memory span or capacity of short-term memory, at least in laboratory settings. In addition, the "magic number" refers not only to discrete elements, such as words or digits, but also to meaningful *groupings* of information, called **chunks.**

learn by doing To see the difference between discrete elements and chunks, read the following letters to a friend, pausing at each dash: *FB-IAO-LM-TVQ-VCB-MW.* The chances are very good that your friend will not be able to repeat this string of letters perfectly. Why? There are fifteen letters, which exceeds most people's immediate memory span. Now, give your friend the test again, but group the letters like this: *FBI-AOL-MTV-QVC-BMW.* Your friend will probably repeat the string easily. Although the same fifteen letters are involved, they will be processed as only five meaningful chunks of information.

The Power of Chunking Chunks of information can be quite complex. If you heard someone say, "The boy in the red shirt kicked his mother in the shin," you could probably repeat the sentence perfectly. Yet, it contains twelve words and forty-three letters. How can you repeat the sentence so effortlessly? The answer is that you are able to build bigger and bigger chunks of information (Ericsson & Staszewski, 1989). In this case, you might represent "the boy in the red shirt" as one chunk of information rather than as six words or nineteen letters. Similarly, "kicked his mother" and "in the shin" represent separate chunks of information.

Learning to use bigger and bigger chunks of information can improve short-term memory. In fact, children's short-term memories improve partly because they gradually become able to hold as many as seven chunks in memory and also because they get better at grouping information into chunks (Servan-Schreiber & Anderson, 1990). Adults also can greatly increase the capacity of their short-term memory by using more efficient chunking. For example, after extensive training, one college student increased his immediate memory span from seven to eighty digits (Neisser, 2000a). So although the capacity of short-term memory is more or less constant (from five to nine chunks of meaningful information), the size of those chunks can vary tremendously.

Duration of Short-Term Memory Why don't you remember every phone number you ever called or every conversation you ever had? The answer is that unless you do something to retain it, information in short-term memory is soon forgotten. This feature of short-term memory is adaptive because it gets rid of a lot of useless information, but it can also be inconvenient. You may have discovered this if you ever looked up a phone number, got distracted before you could call it, and then forgot the number.

Source: Data from Peterson & Peterson (1959).

FIGURE **6.4**

Forgetting in Short-Term Memory

This graph shows the percentage of items recalled after various intervals during which rehearsal was prevented. Notice that forgetting was virtually complete after a delay of eighteen seconds.

How long does information remain in short-term memory if you don't keep rehearsing it? John Brown (1958) and Lloyd and Margaret Peterson (1959) devised the **Brown-Peterson procedure** to measure the duration of short-term memory when no rehearsal is allowed. In this procedure, participants are presented with a group of three letters, such as *GRB*. They then count backward by threes from some number until they get a signal. Counting prevents the participants from rehearsing the letters. At the signal, they stop counting and try to recall the letters. By varying the number of seconds spent counting backward, the experimenter can determine how much forgetting takes place over time. As you can see in Figure 6.4, information in short-term memory is forgotten rapidly: After only eighteen seconds, participants can remember almost nothing. Evidence from other such experiments also suggests that unrehearsed information can be held in short-term memory for no more than about eighteen seconds. However, if the information is rehearsed or processed further in some other way, it may be encoded into long-term memory.

Long-Term Memory

When people talk about memory, they are usually referring to long-term memory. **Long-term memory (LTM)** is the part of the memory system whose encoding and storage capabilities can produce memories that last a lifetime.

Encoding in Long-Term Memory   Some information is encoded into long-term memory even if we make no conscious effort to memorize it (Ellis, 1991). However, putting information into long-term memory is often the result of more elaborate and conscious processing that usually involves *semantic coding*. As we mentioned earlier, semantic encoding often leaves out details in favor of the more general, underlying meaning of the information.

In a classic study, Jacqueline Sachs (1967) demonstrated the dominance of semantic encoding in long-term memory. Her participants first listened to tape recordings of people speaking. She then showed them sets of similar sentences and asked them to say which contained the exact wording heard on the tape. Participants did well at this task when tested immediately, using mainly short-term memory. However, after twenty-seven seconds, they couldn't be sure which of two sentences they had heard. For example, they could not remember whether they had heard "He sent a letter about it to Galileo, the great Italian scientist" or "A letter about it was sent to Galileo, the great Italian scientist." They didn't do as well after the delay because they had to recall information from long-term memory, where they had encoded the general meaning of what they had heard, but not the exact wording.

Perhaps you are thinking, "So what?" After all, the two sentences mean the same thing. Unfortunately, when people encode the general meaning of information they hear or read, they can make mistakes about the details (Brewer, 1977). This can be a problem when recalling exact words is important—such as in the courtroom, during business negotiations, and in discussions between students and teachers about previous agreements. Later in this chapter we show that such mistakes occur partly because people encode into long-term memory not only the general meaning of information but also what they think and assume about that information (McDermott & Chan, 2006).

Counterfeiters depend on the fact that people encode the general meaning of visual stimuli rather than specific details. For example, look at Figure 6.5, and find the correct drawing of a U.S. penny (Nickerson & Adams, 1979). Research shows that most people from the United States are unsuccessful at this task. People from other countries do poorly at recognizing their country's coins, too (Jones, 1990). This research has prompted the U.S. Treasury to begin using more distinctive drawings on the paper currency it distributes.

Storage Capacity of Long-Term Memory   The capacity of long-term memory is extremely large. In fact, many psychologists believe that it is literally unlimited (Matlin, 1998). There is no way to prove this, but we do know that people store vast

Brown-Peterson procedure   A method for determining how long unrehearsed information remains in short-term memory.

long-term memory (LTM)   The stage of memory for which the capacity to store new information is believed to be unlimited.

FIGURE **6.5**

Encoding into Long-Term Memory

 Which is the correct image of a U.S. penny? (See p. 218 for the answer.)

(A)　　　(B)　　　(C)　　　(D)　　　(E)

Source: Nickerson & Adams (1979).

quantities of information in long-term memory that can be remembered remarkably well after long periods of time. For example, people are amazingly accurate at recognizing the faces of their high school classmates after having not seen them for over twenty-five years (Bruck, Cavanagh, & Ceci, 1991). They also do surprisingly well on tests of a foreign language or algebra fifty years after having formally studied these subjects (Bahrick & Hall, 1991; Bahrick et al., 1994).

But long-term memories are also subject to distortion. In one study illustrating this point, students were asked to describe where they were and what they were doing at the moment they heard about the verdict in the O. J. Simpson murder trial (Schmolck, Buffalo, & Squire, 2000). The students first reported their recollections three days after the verdict and then again after either fifteen or thirty-two months. Only half the recollections reported at fifteen months were accurate, and 11 percent contained major errors or distortions. Among those reporting after thirty-two months, 71 percent of their recollections were inaccurate, and just over 40 percent contained major errors or distortions. For example, three days after the verdict, a student said he heard about it while in a campus lounge with many other students around him. Thirty-two months later, this same person recalled hearing the news in the living room of his home with his father and sister. Amazingly, most of the students whose memories had been greatly distorted over time were unaware of the distortion; they were very confident that the reports were accurate. Similar findings have been reported in relation to people's memories of the September 11, 2001, terrorist attacks on New York and Washington, D.C. Even when these memories changed as time went by, people remained confident in their accuracy (Talarico & Rubin, 2003). Later, we see that such overconfidence can also appear in courtroom testimony by eyewitnesses to crime.

A REMARKABLE MEMORY Using only his long-term memory, Franco Magnani created amazingly accurate paintings of his hometown in Italy even though he had not seen it for more than thirty years (Sacks, 1992). People like Magnani display *eidetic imagery,* commonly called *photographic memory.* About 5 percent of school-age children have eidetic imagery, but it is extremely rare in adults (Haber, 1979). You can test yourself for eidetic imagery by drawing a detailed picture or map of a place that you know well but have not seen recently. How did you do?

Magnani's painting

Photo of the same scene

STORING NEW MEMORIES

Storage System	Function	Capacity	Duration
Sensory memory	Briefly holds representations of stimuli from each sense for further processing	Large: absorbs all sensory input from a particular stimulus	Less than 1 second
Short-term and working memory	Holds information in awareness and manipulates it to accomplish mental work	Five to nine distinct items or chunks of information	About 18 seconds
Long-term memory	Stores new information indefinitely	Unlimited	Unlimited

1. If you looked up a phone number but forgot it before you could call it, the information was probably lost from _____ memory.
2. The capacity of short-term memory is about _____ to _____ items.
3. Encoding is usually _____ in short-term memory and _____ in long-term memory.

Online Study Center

Improve Your Grade
Tutorial: Memory:
Primacy and Recency
Effect

Distinguishing Between Short-Term and Long-Term Memory

Some psychologists argue that short-term memory and long-term memory have different features and obey different laws (Cowan, 1988; Talmi et al., 2005). ("In Review: Storing New Memories" summarizes the characteristics of these systems.) Evidence that information is transferred from short-term memory to a distinct storage system comes primarily from experiments on recall.

You can conduct your own recall experiment by reading aloud a list of words at a slow pace (about one word every two seconds). After reading the list just once, look away and write down as many of the words as you can, in any order. Here is a list you can use: *desk, chalk, pencil, chair, paperclip, book, eraser, folder, briefcase, essays, tree, soup, ocean, cabin, monster, bridge.* Did you notice anything about which words you remembered and which ones you forgot? If you are like most people, your recall depended partly on where each word appeared on the list—its serial position. As shown in the *serial-position curve* in Figure 6.6, memory researchers have found that recall tends to be very good for the first two or three words in a list. This result is called the **primacy effect.** The probability of recall decreases for words in the middle of the list and then rises dramatically for the last few words. The ease of recalling words near the end of the list is called the **recency effect.** The primacy effect may reflect the rehearsal that puts early words into long-term memory. The recency effect may occur because the last few words are still in short-term memory when you try to recall the list (Glanzer & Cunitz, 1966; Koppenaal & Glanzer, 1990).

FIGURE 6.6

A Serial-Position Curve

This curve shows the probability of recalling items that appear at various serial positions in a list. Generally, the first several items and the last several items are most likely to be recalled.

Retrieving Memories

▶ **How do I retrieve stored memories?**

Most people have trouble remembering things at one time or another. Have you ever been unable to recall the name of a musical group or movie star, only to think of it the next day? Remembering requires not only the coding and storing of information

Answer key to Figure 6.5: Drawing A shows the correct penny image.

CONTEXT-DEPENDENT MEMORIES
Many people attending a reunion at their old high school find that being in the building again provides context cues that help bring back memories of their school days.

but also the ability to bring it into consciousness. In other words, you have to be able to *retrieve* it.

Retrieval Cues and Encoding Specificity

Retrieval cues are stimuli that help you retrieve information from long-term memory. As mentioned earlier, retrieval cues are what make recognition tasks (such as multiple-choice tests) easier than recall tasks (such as essay exams).

The effectiveness of retrieval cues depends on the extent to which they tap into information that was encoded at the time of learning (Tulving, 1983). This rule is known as the **encoding specificity principle.** Because long-term memories are often encoded in terms of their general meaning, cues that trigger the meaning of the stored information tend to work best. Imagine that you have learned a long list of sentences. One of them was either (1) "The man lifted the piano" or (2) "The man tuned the piano." Now suppose that on a later recall test, you were given the retrieval cue "something heavy." This cue would probably help you to remember the first sentence (because you probably encoded something about the weight of a piano as you read it) but not the second sentence (because it has nothing to do with weight). Similarly, the cue "makes nice sounds" would probably help you recall the second sentence, but not the first (Barclay et al., 1974).

Context and State Dependence

Have you ever taken a test in a classroom other than the one in which you learned the material for that test? If so, was your performance affected? Research has shown that people tend to recall more of what they have learned when they are in the place in which they learned it (Smith, Glenberg, & Bjork, 1978). Why? Because if they have encoded features of the environment in which the learning occurred, these features can later act as retrieval cues (Richardson-Klavehn & Bjork, 1988). In one experiment, people studied a series of photos while in the presence of a particular odor. Later, they reviewed a larger set of photos and tried to recognize the ones they had seen earlier. Half of the people were exposed to the original odor while taking the recognition test. The other half were tested in the presence of another odor. Those who smelled the same odor during learning and testing did significantly better on the recognition task than those tested in the presence of a different odor. The matching odor served as a powerful retrieval cue (Cann & Ross, 1989).

primacy effect A characteristic of memory in which recall is particularly good for the first two or three items in a list.

recency effect A characteristic of memory in which recall is particularly good for the last few items in a list.

retrieval cues Stimuli that allow or help people to recall information.

encoding specificity principle A principle stating that the ability of a cue to aid retrieval depends on how well it taps into information that was originally encoded.

in review

FACTORS AFFECTING RETRIEVAL FROM LONG-TERM MEMORY

Process	Effect on Memory
Encoding specificity	Retrieval cues are effective only to the extent that they tap into information that was originally encoded.
Context dependence	Retrieval is most successful when it occurs in the same environment in which the information was originally learned.
State dependence	Retrieval is most successful when people are in the same psychological state as when they originally learned the information.

?
1. Stimuli called _____ help you recall information stored in long-term memory.
2. If it is easier to remember something in the place where you learned it, you have a _____ memory.
3. The tendency to remember the last few items in a list is called the _____ effect.

Context-dependent memories are those that are helped or hindered by similarities or differences in environmental context. This context-dependency effect is not always strong (Smith, Vela, & Williamson, 1988), but some students do find it helpful to study for a test in the classroom where the test will be given.

Sometimes, we also encode information about how we were feeling during a learning experience, and this information, too, can act as a retrieval cue. When our internal state influences retrieval, we have a **state-dependent memory.** For example, if people learn new material while under the influence of marijuana, they tend to recall it better if they are also tested under the influence of marijuana (Eich et al., 1975). Similar effects have been found with alcohol (Overton, 1984) and other psychoactive drugs (Eich, 1989), although memory is best when people aren't using *any* drugs during encoding or retrieval. Mood states, too, can affect memory (Eich & Macaulay, 2000). College students are more likely to remember pleasant events when they are feeling good at the time of recall (Bower, 1981; Ehrlichman & Halpern, 1988). Negative events are more likely to be recalled when people are feeling sad or angry (Lewinsohn & Rosenbaum, 1987). These *mood congruency* effects are strongest when people try to recall personally meaningful episodes (Eich & Metcalfe, 1989). The more meaningful the experience, the more likely it is that the memory has been colored by their mood. (See "In Review: Factors Affecting Retrieval from Long-Term Memory.")

Retrieval from Semantic Memory

The retrieval situations we have discussed so far are relevant to episodic memory—our memory for events. But how do we retrieve information from semantic memory, in which we store our general knowledge about the world? Researchers studying this question typically ask participants general-knowledge questions, such as (1) Are fish minerals? (2) Is a beagle a dog? (3) Do birds fly? and (4) Does a car have legs? As you might imagine, most people answer such questions correctly. But by measuring how long it takes to answer them, psychologists gain important clues about how semantic memory is organized and how we retrieve information from it.

Semantic Networks   One view of semantic memory suggests that virtually everything we know about, including concepts such as "bird" or "animal," is represented in a dense network of associations (Churchland, 1989). Figure 6.7 presents just a tiny part

context-dependent memories Memories that are helped or hindered by similarities or differences between the contexts in which they are learned and recalled.

state-dependent memory Memory that is helped or hindered by similarities or differences in a person's internal state during learning versus recall.

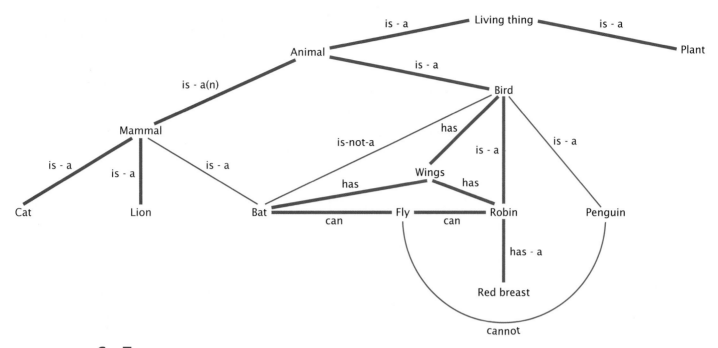

Semantic Memory Networks

This drawing represents just a small part of a network of semantic associations. Semantic network theories of memory suggest that networks like these allow us to retrieve specific pieces of previously learned information, to draw conclusions about how concepts are related, and to make new inferences about the world.

of what our *semantic memory network* might look like. In general, semantic network theories suggest that information is retrieved from memory through the principle of **spreading activation** (Medin, Ross, & Markman, 2001). In other words, when you think about some concept, it becomes activated in the network, and this activation begins to "spread" down all the paths that are related to it. So if you are asked if a robin is a bird, the concepts of both "robin" and "bird" will become activated, and the spreading activation from each will intersect somewhere in these paths. When they do, you know what answer to give.

Some associations in the network are stronger than others, as illustrated by the thicker lines between some concepts in Figure 6.7. For instance, you probably have a stronger association between "bat" and "wings" than between "bat" and "mammal." Spreading activation travels faster along stronger paths than along weaker ones. As a result, you'd probably respond more quickly to "Can a bat fly?" than to "Is a bat a mammal?"

Because of the tight organization of semantic networks and the speed at which activation spreads through them, we can gain access to an enormous body of knowledge about the world quickly and effortlessly. We can retrieve not only facts we have learned from others but also knowledge that allows us to draw our own conclusions and inferences (Matlin, 1998). For example, imagine answering these two questions: (1) Is a robin a bird? and (2) Is a robin a living thing? You can probably answer the first question "directly," because you probably learned this fact at some point in your life. However, you may never have consciously thought about the second question, so answering it requires some inference. Figure 6.7 illustrates the path to that inference. Because you know that a robin is a bird, a bird is an animal, and animals are living things, you infer that a robin must be a living thing. As you might expect, however, it takes slightly longer to answer the second question than the first.

Retrieving Incomplete Knowledge Figure 6.7 shows that concepts such as "bird" or "living thing" are represented in semantic memory as unique sets of features or attributes. As a result, there may be times when you can retrieve some features of a concept from your semantic network, but not enough of them to identify the concept. For example, you might know that there is an animal that has wings, can fly, and is not a bird, and yet be unable to retrieve its name (Connor, Balota, & Neely, 1992). When this happens, you are retrieving *incomplete knowledge*. (The animal in question is a bat.)

spreading activation In semantic network theories of memory, a principle that explains how information is retrieved.

You have probably experienced a particular example of incomplete knowledge called the *tip-of-the-tongue phenomenon*. In a typical experiment on this phenomenon, participants listen to dictionary definitions and are asked to name the word being defined (Brown & McNeill, 1966). If they can't recall the correct word, they are asked if they can recall any feature of it, such as its first letter or how many syllables it has. People are surprisingly good at this task, indicating that they are able to retrieve at least some knowledge of the word (Brennen et al., 1990). Most people experience the tip-of-the-tongue phenomenon about once a week; older people tend to experience it more often than younger people (Brown, 1991; Brown & Nix, 1996).

Constructing Memories

▶ **How accurate are my memories?**

Our memories are affected by what we experience but also by what we already know about the world (Schacter, Norman, & Koutstaal, 1998). We use that existing knowledge to organize the new information we encounter, and we fill in gaps in that information as we encode and retrieve it (Sherman & Bessenoff, 1999). These processes are called *constructive memory*.

In one study of constructive memory, undergraduates were asked to wait for several minutes in the office of a graduate student (Brewer & Treyens, 1981). Later, they were asked to recall everything that was in the office. Most of the students mistakenly "remembered" seeing books, even though there were none. Apparently, the general knowledge that graduate students read many books influenced the participants' memory of what was in the room (Roediger, Meade, & Bergman, 2001). In another study, participants read one of two versions of a story about a man and woman at a ski lodge. One version ended with the man proposing marriage to the woman. The second version was identical until the end, when instead of proposing, the man sexually assaulted the woman. A few days after reading the story, all the participants were asked what they

CONSTRUCTIVE MEMORY Ask a friend to examine this photo for a minute or so (cover the caption). Then close the book and ask whether each of the following items appeared in the office: chair, wastebasket, bottle, typewriter, coffeepot, and book. If your friend reports having seen a wastebasket or a book, you will have demonstrated constructive memory.

remembered from it. Those who had read the "proposal" version recalled nice things about the man, such as that he wanted the woman to meet his parents. Those who read the "assault" version recalled negative things, such as that the man liked to drink a lot. However, neither kind of information had actually been part of the original story. The participants had "recalled" memories of the man that they had constructed in accordance with their overall impression of him (Carli, 1999).

By constructing our own versions of what we have seen and heard, we may remember an event differently from the way it actually happened. These errors, called *false memories*, can occur in relation to anything from the objects present in a room to the identity of an armed robber (Clancy et al., 2000). Later, we consider how false memories might color eyewitness testimony and reports of sexual abuse in childhood. For now, though, let's take a look at how researchers study false memories about less dramatic, everyday experiences.

■ **What was the researchers' question?**

How easy is it for people to form false memories? Henry Roediger and Kathleen McDermott (1995) addressed this question in an experiment to test for false memories as people recalled lists of words that had been read to them.

■ **How did the researchers answer the question?**

On each of sixteen trials, college students heard a different list of words. Each list related to a particular theme. For example, the "cold" list contained fifteen words such as *sleet, slush, frost, white, snow,* and so on. Yet the list's theme word—in this case, *cold*—was not included. On half of these trials, the students were simply asked to recall as many words as possible from the list as they had just heard. But on the other half, the students did math problems instead of trying to recall the words. Once all sixteen lists had been presented, the students were given a new list of words and asked to say which of them they recognized as having been on the lists they had heard earlier. Some of the words on this new list were theme words, such as *cold,* that had not been presented earlier. Would the students "remember" hearing these theme words on the list even though they hadn't? And if so, how confident would they be about their "memory" of these words?

■ **What did the researchers find?**

The students falsely, but confidently, recognized the theme words from twelve of the sixteen lists. In fact, theme words were falsely recognized as often as listed words were correctly recognized. As you might expect, the chance of accurately recognizing the listed words was greater when the students had been allowed to recall them shortly after hearing them. However, false memory of never-presented theme words occurred in both conditions.

■ **What do the results mean?**

The results of this study suggest that the participants could not always distinguish words they had heard from those they had not heard. Why? The never-presented theme words "belonged" with the lists of presented words and apparently were "remembered" because they fit logically into the gaps in the students' memories. In short, the students' knowledge of words that *should* have been included on the lists created a "memory" that they *were* presented.

■ **What do we still need to know?**

Studies such as this one make it clear that memory is constructive and that memory distortion and inaccuracy are commonplace (Schacter et al., 1998; Schmolck et al.,

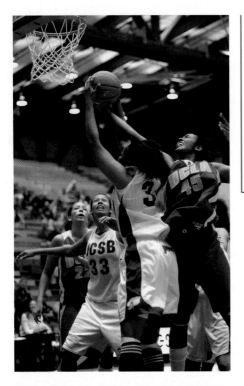

PDP MODELS AND CONSTRUCTIVE MEMORY   If you hear that "our basketball team won last night," your schema about basketball might prompt you to encode, and later retrieve, the fact that the players were men. Such spontaneous, though often incorrect, generalizations associated with PDP models of memory help explain the appearance of constructive memories.

2000). We still need to identify the processes behind such distortion. In addition, we are not yet sure why false memories can seem as real to us as our memories of actual events. Perhaps the more frequently we recall an event (as when students were allowed to rehearse some lists), the stronger is our belief that we have accurately recalled it. There is also evidence that merely thinking about, hearing sounds, or seeing photos associated with certain objects or events appears to make false memories of them more likely (Garry & Gerrie, 2005; Henkel, Franklin, & Johnson, 2000). Questions about how false memories are created lead to even deeper questions about the degree to which our imperfect memory processes might distort our experiences of reality. Is there an objective reality, or do we each experience our own version of reality?

Constructive Memory and PDP Models

Parallel distributed processing models of memory offer one way of explaining how semantic and episodic information become integrated in constructive memories. As mentioned earlier, PDP models suggest that newly learned facts alter our general knowledge of the world. In these network models, learned associations between specific facts come together. Let's say, for example, that your own network "knows" that your friend Joe is a male European American business major. It also "knows" that Claudia is a female African American student, but it has never learned her major. Now suppose that every other student you know is a business major. In this case, the connection between "students you know" and "business majors" would be so strong that you would conclude that Claudia is a business major, too. You would be so confident in this belief that it would take overwhelming evidence for you to change your mind (Rumelhart & McClelland, 1986). In other words, you would have constructed a memory about Claudia.

PDP networks also produce *spontaneous generalizations*. So if your friend tells you that she just bought a new car, you would know without asking that, like all other cars you have experienced, it has four wheels. This is a spontaneous generalization from your knowledge base. Spontaneous generalizations are obviously helpful, but they can also create significant errors if the network is based on limited or biased experience with a class of objects or people.

If it occurs to you that ethnic prejudice can result from spontaneous generalization errors, you are right (Greenwald & Banaji, 1995). Researchers are actually encouraged by this prejudicial aspect of PDP networks, though, because it accurately reflects human thought and memory. Virtually all of us make spontaneous generalizations about males, females, European Americans, African Americans, the young, the old, and many other categories (Rudman et al., 1999). Is prejudice, then, a process that we have no choice in or control over? Not necessarily. Relatively unprejudiced people tend to recognize that they are making generalizations and consciously try to ignore or suppress them (Monteith, Sherman, & Devine, 1998).

Schemas   PDP models also help us understand constructive memory by explaining the operation of the schemas that guide it. As described in the chapters on social psychology and on thought, language, and intelligence, **schemas** are mental representations of categories of objects, places, events, and people. For example, most North Americans have a schema for *baseball game,* so simply hearing these words is likely to activate whole clusters of information in long-term memory, including the rules of the game and images of players, bats, balls, a green field, summer days, and perhaps hot dogs and stadiums. The generalized knowledge contained in schemas provides a basis for making inferences about new information during the encoding stage. So if you hear that a baseball player was injured, your schema about baseball might prompt you to encode the incident as game related, even though the cause was not mentioned. Later, you are likely to recall the injury as having occurred during a game (see Figure 6.8 for another example).

schemas   Mental representations of categories of objects, places, events, and people.

FIGURE **6.8**

The Effect of Schemas on Recall

In a classic experiment, people were shown figures like these, along with labels designed to activate certain schemas (Carmichael, Hogan, & Walter, 1932). For example, when showing the top figure, the experimenter said either "This resembles eyeglasses" or "This resembles a dumbbell." When the participants were later asked to draw these figures from memory, their drawings tended to resemble the items mentioned by the experimenter. In other words, their memory had been altered by the schema-activating labels.

Figure shown to participants	Group 1		Group 2	
	Label given	Figure drawn by participants	Label given	Figure drawn by participants
⊙—⊙	Eyeglasses	◠◠	Dumbbell	⊙—⊙
⋈	Hourglass	⋈	Table	⋈
7	Seven	7	Four	4
⟍▭	Gun	⟍▭	Broom	⟍⋇

LINKAGES
How accurate is eyewitness testimony? (a link to Sensation and Perception)

LINKAGES

Memory and Perception in the Courtroom

There are few situations in which accurate retrieval of memories is more important—and constructive memory is more dangerous—than when an eyewitness testifies in court about a crime. Let's consider the accuracy of eyewitness memory and how it can be distorted. To a jury, the most compelling evidence a lawyer can provide is that of an eyewitness, but eyewitnesses often make mistakes (Loftus & Ketcham, 1991; Wells, Olson, & Charman, 2002). In 1984, for example, North Carolina college student Jennifer Thompson confidently identified Ronald Cotton as the man who had raped her at knifepoint. Mainly on the basis of Thompson's testimony, Cotton was convicted of rape and sentenced to life in prison. He was released eleven years later, when DNA evidence revealed that he was innocent (and identified another man as the rapist). The eyewitness/victim's certainty had convinced a jury, but her memory had been faulty (O'Neill, 2000).

Like the rest of us, eyewitnesses can remember only what they perceive, and they can perceive only what they attend to (Backman & Nilsson, 1991). The witnesses' task is to report as accurately as possible what they saw or heard. But no matter how hard they try to be accurate, there are limits to how valid their reports can be (Kassin, Rigby, & Castillo, 1991). For example, hearing new information about a crime, including in the form of a lawyer's question, can alter a witness's memory (Belli & Loftus, 1996). Experiments show that when witnesses are asked "How fast were the cars going when they *smashed into* each other?" they are likely to recall a higher speed than when asked "How fast were the cars going when they *hit* each other?" (Loftus & Palmer, 1974; see Figure 6.9). There is also evidence that an object mentioned during questioning about an incident is often mistakenly remembered as having been there during the incident (Roediger et al., 2001). So if a lawyer says that a screwdriver was lying on the ground (when it was not), witnesses may recall with great certainty having seen it (Ryan & Geiselman, 1991). This *misinformation effect* can occur in several ways (Loftus & Hoffman, 1989). In some cases, hearing new information can make it harder to retrieve the original memory (Tversky & Tuchin, 1989). In others, the new information may be integrated into the old memory, making it impossible to distinguish from what was originally seen (Loftus, 1992). In still others, an eyewitness report might be influenced by the person's assumption that if a lawyer or police officer says an object was there, or that something happened, it must be true.

FIGURE **6.9**

The Impact of Questions on Eyewitness Memory

After seeing a filmed traffic accident, people were asked, "About how fast were the cars going when they (smashed into, hit, or contacted) each other?" As shown here, the witnesses' responses were influenced by the verb used in the question. "Smashed" was associated with the highest average speed estimates. A week later, people who heard the "smashed" question remembered the accident as being more violent than did people in the other two groups (Loftus & Palmer, 1974).

Jurors' belief in a witness's testimony often depends as much (or even more) on *how* the witness presents evidence as on the content or relevance of that evidence (Leippe, Manion, & Romanczyk, 1992). For example, many jurors are particularly impressed by witnesses who give lots of details about what they saw. Extremely detailed testimony from prosecution witnesses is especially likely to lead to guilty verdicts, even when the details reported are irrelevant (Bell & Loftus, 1989). Apparently, when a witness reports details, such as the exact time of the crime or the color of the criminal's shoes, jurors assume that the witness had paid especially close attention or has a particularly good memory. This assumption seems reasonable, but there are limits on how much people can pay attention to, particularly when they are emotionally aroused and the crime happens quickly. Witnesses whose attention was drawn to details such as shoe color might not have had time to accurately perceive the criminal's facial features (Backman & Nilsson, 1991). So the fact that an eyewitness reports many details doesn't guarantee that all of them were remembered correctly.

Jurors also tend to believe witnesses who are confident about their testimony (Leippe et al., 1992). Unfortunately, research shows that witnesses' confidence is frequently much higher than the accuracy of their reports (Shaw, 1996; Wells et al., 2002). In some cases, repeated exposure to misinformation and the repeated recall of that misinformation can lead witnesses to feel certain about their testimony even when—as in the Jennifer Thompson case—it may not be correct (Lamb, 1998; Mitchell & Zaragoza, 1996; Roediger, Jacoby, & McDermott, 1996).

The weaknesses inherent in eyewitness memory can be amplified by the use of police lineups and certain other criminal identification procedures (Haw & Fisher, 2004; Wells & Olson, 2003). In one study, for example, participants watched a videotaped crime and then tried to identify the criminal from a set of photographs (Wells & Bradfield, 1999). None of the photos showed the person who had committed the crime, but some participants nevertheless identified one of them as the criminal they saw on tape. When these mistaken participants were led to believe that they had correctly identified the criminal, they became even more confident in the accuracy of their false identification (Semmler, Brewer, & Wells, 2004; Wells, Olson, & Charman, 2003). These incorrect, but confident, witnesses became more likely than other participants to claim that it had been easy for them to identify the criminal from the photos because they had had a good view of him and had paid careful attention to him.

Since 1973, at least 123 people, including Ronald Cotton, have been released from U.S. prisons after DNA tests or other evidence revealed that they had been falsely convicted—mostly on the basis of faulty eyewitness testimony (Death Penalty Information Center, 2006; Scheck, Neufeld, & Dwyer, 2000; Wells et al., 2000). DNA evidence

This is exactly the sort of biased police lineup that *Eyewitness Evidence: A Guide for Law Enforcement* (U.S. Department of Justice, 1999) is designed to avoid. Based on research in memory and perception, this guide recommends that no suspect should stand out from all the others in a lineup, that witnesses should not assume that the real criminal is in the lineup, and that they should not be encouraged to "guess" when making an identification.

"Thank you, gentlemen—you may all leave except for No. 3."

freed Charles Fain, who had been convicted of murder and spent almost 18 years on death row in Idaho (Bonner, 2001). Maryland officials approved $900,000 in compensation for Bernard Webster, who served 20 years in prison for rape before DNA revealed that he was innocent (Associated Press, 2003). Frank Lee Smith, too, would have been set free after the sole eyewitness at his murder trial retracted her testimony, but he had already died of cancer while awaiting execution in a Florida prison. Research on memory and perception helps explain how these miscarriages of justice can occur, and it is also guiding efforts to prevent such errors in the future. The U.S. Department of Justice has acknowledged the potential for errors in eyewitness evidence, as well as the dangers of asking witnesses to identify suspects from lineups and photo arrays. The result is *Eyewitness Evidence: A Guide for Law Enforcement* (U.S. Department of Justice, 1999), the first-ever guide for police and prosecutors involved in obtaining eyewitness evidence. The guide warns these officials that asking leading questions about what witnesses saw can distort their memories. It also suggests that witnesses should examine photographs of possible suspects one at a time and points out that false identifications are less likely if witnesses viewing suspects in a lineup are told that the real perpetrator might not be included (Wells & Olson, 2003; Wells et al., 2000).

Forgetting

▶ **What causes me to forget things?**

The frustrations of forgetting—where you left your keys, the answer to a test question, an anniversary—are apparent to most people nearly every day (Neisser, 2000b). Let's look more closely at the nature of forgetting and what causes it.

How Do We Forget?

Hermann Ebbinghaus, a German psychologist, began the systematic study of memory and forgetting in the late 1800s, using only his own memory as his laboratory. He read

FIGURE **6.10**

Ebbinghaus's Curve of Forgetting

learn by **doing** List thirty words, selected at random from a dictionary, and spend a few minutes memorizing them. After an hour has passed, write down as many words as you can remember, but don't look at the original list again. Test yourself again eight hours later, a day later, and two days later. Now look at the original list and see how well you did on each recall test. Ebbinghaus found that most forgetting occurs during the first nine hours after learning, and especially during the first hour. If this was not the case for you, why do you think your results were different?

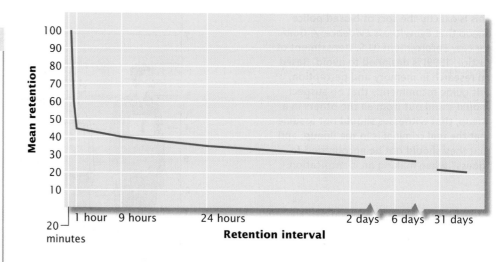

aloud a list of nonsense syllables, such as *POF, XEM,* and *QAL,* at a constant pace, and then tried to recall the syllables.

Ebbinghaus devised the **method of savings** to measure how much he forgot over time. This method compares the number of repetitions (or trials) it takes to learn a list of items and the number of trials needed to relearn that same list later. Any difference in the number of learning trials represents the *savings* from one learning to the next. If it took Ebbinghaus ten trials to learn a list and ten more trials to relearn it, there would be no savings. Forgetting would have been complete. If it took him ten trials to learn the list and only five trials to relearn it, there would be a savings of 50 percent.

Ebbinghaus's research produced two lasting discoveries. One is the shape of the forgetting curve shown in Figure 6.10. Even when psychologists have substituted words, sentences, and stories for nonsense syllables, the forgetting curve shows the same strong initial drop in memory, followed by a more moderate decrease over time (Slamecka & McElree, 1983; Wixted, 2004). Of course, we remember sensible stories better than nonsense syllables, but the shape of the curve is the same no matter what type of material is involved (Davis & Moore, 1935). Even the forgetting of events from daily life tends to follow Ebbinghaus's forgetting curve (Thomson, 1982).

Ebbinghaus also discovered just how long-lasting "savings" in long-term memory can be. Psychologists now know from the method of savings that information about everything from algebra to bike riding is often retained for decades (Matlin, 1998). So, although you may forget something you have learned if you do not use the information, it is very easy to relearn the material if the need arises, indicating that the forgetting was not complete (Hall & Bahrick, 1998).

Why Do We Forget?

We have seen *how* forgetting occurs, but *why* does it happen? In principle, one of two processes can be responsible (Best, 1999). One process is **decay,** the gradual disappearance of the information from memory. Decay occurs in memory in much the same way as the inscription on a ring or bracelet wears away and fades over time. Forgetting might also occur because of interference. Through **interference,** either the storage or the retrieval of information is impaired by the presence of other information. Interference might occur because one piece of information actually displaces other information, pushing it out of memory. It might also occur because one piece of information makes storing or recalling other information more difficult.

In the case of short-term memory, if an item is not rehearsed or thought about, memory of it decreases consistently over the course of about eighteen seconds. So decay appears to play the main role in forgetting information in short-term memory. But interference through displacement can also be operating. Like a desktop, short-term

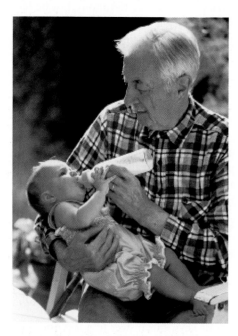

IT'S ALL COMING BACK TO ME This grandfather hasn't fed an infant for decades, but his memory of how to do it is not entirely gone. He showed some "savings"; it took him less time to relearn the skill than it took him to learn it initially.

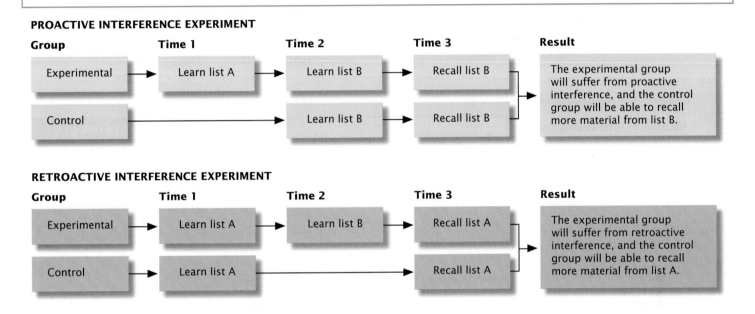

FIGURE **6.11**

Procedures for Studying Interference

To remember the difference between the two types of interference, keep in mind that the prefixes—*pro* and *retro*—indicate directions in time. *Pro* means "forward," and *retro* means "backward." In proactive interference, previously learned material "comes forward" to interfere with new learning; retroactive interference occurs when new information "goes back" to interfere with the recall of past learning.

PROACTIVE INTERFERENCE EXPERIMENT

Group	Time 1	Time 2	Time 3	Result
Experimental	Learn list A	Learn list B	Recall list B	The experimental group will suffer from proactive interference, and the control group will be able to recall more material from list B.
Control		Learn list B	Recall list B	

RETROACTIVE INTERFERENCE EXPERIMENT

Group	Time 1	Time 2	Time 3	Result
Experimental	Learn list A	Learn list B	Recall list A	The experimental group will suffer from retroactive interference, and the control group will be able to recall more material from list A.
Control	Learn list A		Recall list A	

method of savings A method for measuring forgetting.

decay The gradual disappearance of information from memory.

interference The process through which storage or retrieval of information is impaired by the presence of other information.

retroactive interference A cause of forgetting whereby new information placed in memory interferes with the ability to recall information already in memory.

proactive interference A cause of forgetting whereby previously learned information interferes with the ability to remember new information.

memory can hold only so much. Once it is full, adding additional items tends to make others "fall off" and become unavailable (Haberlandt, 1999). Displacement is one reason why the phone number you just looked up is likely to drop out of short-term memory if you read another number immediately afterward. Rehearsal prevents displacement by continually reentering the same information into short-term memory.

The cause of forgetting from long-term memory appears to be more directly tied to interference. Long-term memory can be affected by **retroactive interference,** in which learning new information interferes with our recall of older information (Wixted, 2005). **Proactive interference** can also occur, in which old information interferes with learning or remembering new information. Retroactive interference would help explain why studying French vocabulary this term might make it more difficult to remember the Spanish words you learned last term. And because of proactive interference, the French words you are learning now might make it harder to learn German next term. Figure 6.11 outlines the types of experiments used to study the influence of each form of interference in long-term memory.

Does interference push information out of memory, or does it merely make it harder to retrieve the information? To find out, Endel Tulving and Joseph Psotka (1971) presented people with lists of words that represented a particular category. For example, there was a "buildings" list (e.g., *hut, cottage, cabin, hotel*) and a geographical features list (e.g., *cliff, river, hill, volcano*). Some people learned a list and then recalled as many of its words as possible. Other groups learned one list and then learned up to five additional lists before trying to recall the first one.

The results were dramatic. As the number of additional lists increased, the number of words that people could recall from the original list decreased. This finding reflected strong retroactive interference; the new lists were interfering with recall of the first one. Then the researchers gave a second test, but this time they provided a retrieval cue by telling the category of the words (such as "types of buildings") to be recalled. Now the number of additional lists had almost no effect on the number of words recalled from the original list, as Figure 6.12 shows. These results indicate that the words from the

Number of intervening lists

Source: Tulving & Psotka (1971).

FIGURE **6.12**

Retrieval Failures and Forgetting

Tulving and Psotka (1971) found that people's ability to recall a list of items was strongly affected by the number of other lists they learned before being tested on the first one. When retrieval cues were provided on a second test, however, retroactive interference from the intervening lists almost disappeared.

LINKAGES

Do forgotten memories remain in the subconscious? (a link to Consciousness)

first list were still in long-term memory; they had not been pushed out, but the participants could not remember them without appropriate retrieval cues. In short, faulty retrieval caused the original forgetting. Putting more and more information in long-term memory may be like putting more and more CDs in a storage cabinet. Although none of the CDs disappears, it becomes increasingly difficult to find the one you are looking for.

Some theorists have suggested that all forgetting from long-term memory is due to retrieval failure (Ratcliff & McKoon, 1989). Does this mean that everything in long-term memory remains there for life, even if you cannot always, or ever, recall it? No one yet knows for sure, but as described in the next section, this question lies at the heart of some highly controversial court cases.

I n 1989, Eileen Franklin told California police that when she looked into her young daughter's eyes one day, she suddenly remembered seeing her father kill her childhood friend more than twenty years earlier. On the basis of her testimony about this memory, her father, George Franklin, Sr., was sent to prison for murder (Loftus & Ketcham, 1994).

THINKING CRITICALLY

Can Traumatic Memories Be Repressed, Then Recovered?

■ What am I being asked to believe or accept?

The prosecution in the Franklin case successfully argued that Eileen had recovered her long-buried memory of a murder. Similar arguments in other cases tried in the early 1990s also resulted in imprisonment as now-adult children claimed to have recovered childhood memories of physical or sexual abuse at the hands of their parents. The juries in these trials accepted the assertion that all memory of shocking events can be *repressed,* or pushed into an inaccessible corner of the mind where, for decades, subconscious processes keep it out of awareness, yet potentially subject to accurate recall (Hyman, 2000). Jurors are not the only ones who believe in this phenomenon. A few years ago a large American news organization reported that the United States had illegally used nerve gas during the war in Vietnam. This story was based, in part, on a Vietnam veteran's account of recovered memories of having been subjected to a nerve gas attack.

■ Is there evidence available to support the claim?

Proponents of the recovered-memory argument point to several lines of evidence to support their claims. First, as discussed in the chapter on consciousness, a lot of mental activity occurs outside of awareness (Kihlstrom, 1999). Second, research on implicit memory shows that our behavior can be influenced by information of which we are unaware (Betch et al., 2003; Kouider & Dupoux, 2005; Schacter, Chiu, & Ochsner, 1993). Third, research on *motivated forgetting* suggests that people may sometimes be able to willfully suppress information so that it is no longer accessible on a later memory test (Anderson & Green, 2001). Even suppressing one's emotional reactions to events can interfere with memories of those events (Richards & Gross, 2000). And people appear more likely to forget unpleasant rather than pleasant events (Erdelyi, 1985). In one study, a psychologist kept a detailed record of his daily life over a six-year period. When he later tried to recall these experiences, he remembered more than half of the positive events but only one-third of the negative ones (Waagenaar, 1986). In another study, 38 percent of women who, as children, had been brought to a hospital because of sexual abuse did not report the incident as adults (Williams, 1994). Fourth, retrieval cues can help people recall memories that had previously been inaccessible to conscious awareness (Andrews et al., 2000; Landsdale & Laming, 1995). For example, these cues have helped soldiers remember for the first time the circumstances under which they had been wounded many years before (Karon & Widener, 1997). Finally, there is the confidence with which people report recovered memories; they say they are just too vivid to be anything but real.

■ Can that evidence be interpreted another way?

Those who are skeptical about repressed memories know that subconscious memory and retrieval processes exist (Kihlstrom, 1999). They also recognize that, sadly, child abuse and other traumas are all too common. But to these psychologists, the available evidence is not strong enough to support the conclusion that traumatic memories can be repressed and then accurately recalled. Any given "recovered" memory, they say, may actually be a distorted, or constructed, memory (Clancy et al., 2000; Hyman, 2000; Loftus, 1998). Our recall of past events is affected by what happened at the time, what we knew beforehand, and everything we have experienced since. The people who "remembered" nonexistent books in an office inadvertently used their prior knowledge of what is usually in graduate students' offices to construct a false memory for the books. Similarly, the "recovered memory" of the Vietnam veteran mentioned earlier appears to have no basis in fact; the news story about the alleged nerve gas attack was later retracted.

As we saw in the Focus on Research section, false memories—distortions of actual events and the recall of events that didn't actually happen—can be just as vivid as real, accurate memories, and people can be just as confident in them (Brainerd & Reyna, 2005; Brainerd et al., 2003; Loftus, 2004; Nourkova, Bernstein, & Loftus, 2004; Roediger & McDermott, 2000). Most of us have experienced everyday versions of false memories. It is not unusual to "remember" turning off the coffeepot or mailing the rent check, only to discover later that we didn't. Researchers have demonstrated that false memories can occur in relation to more emotional events, too. In one case study, a teenager named Chris was given descriptions of four incidents from his childhood and asked to write about each of them every day for five days (Loftus, 1997a). One of these incidents—being lost in a shopping mall at age five—never really happened. Yet Chris eventually "remembered" this event, and even added many details about the mall and the stranger whose hand he was supposedly found holding. He also rated this (false) memory as being more vivid than two of the other three (real) incidents he wrote about. Similar results occurred in about half of seventy-seven child participants in more recent case studies (Porter, Yuille, & Lehman, 1999). The same pattern of results has appeared in formal experiments on the planting of emotion-laden false memories (Hyman & Pentland, 1996; Loftus & Pickrell, 1995). Researchers have been able to create vivid and striking, but completely false, memories of events that people thought they experienced when they were one day old (DuBreuil, Garry, & Loftus, 1998). In other experiments, children who were repeatedly asked about a nonexistent trauma (getting a hand caught in a mousetrap) eventually developed a clear and unshakable false memory of experiencing it (Ceci et al., 1994). Some people will even begin to avoid a certain food after researchers create in them a false memory of having been ill after eating that food as a child (Bernstein et al., 2005).

In other words, people sometimes have a difficult time distinguishing between what has happened to them and what they have only imagined, or have come to believe, has happened (Garry & Polaschek, 2000; Henkel, 2004; Johnson & Raye, 1998; Mazzoni & Memon, 2003; Zaragoza et al., 2001). Some studies have found that people who are fantasy-prone, who easily mistake real and imagined stimuli, and who tend to have lapses in attention and memory are more likely than others to develop false memories and possibly more likely to report the recovery of repressed memories (McNally, 2003; McNally et al., 2000a, 2000b, 2005; Porter et al., 2000). Two other studies have found that women who have suffered physical or sexual abuse are more likely to falsely remember words on a laboratory recall test (Bremner, Shobe, & Kihlstrom, 2000; Zoellner et al., 2000). This tendency appears strongest among abused women who show signs of posttraumatic stress disorder (Bremner et al., 2000). Another study found that

EXPLORING MEMORY PROCESSES
Elizabeth Loftus (at the far right) is shown here with her students and Alan Alda, who filmed a documentary about her research. Loftus and other cognitive psychologists have demonstrated mechanisms through which false memories can be created. They have shown, for example, that false memories appear even in research participants who are told about them and asked to avoid them (McDermott & Roediger, 1998). Their work has helped to focus scientific scrutiny on reports of recovered memories, especially those arising from contact with therapists who assume that most people have repressed memories of abuse.

the tendency to have false memories on a word recall task was greater in women who reported recovered memories of sexual abuse than in nonabused women or in those who had always remembered the abuse they suffered (Clancy et al., 2000). False memories on this laboratory recall task are also more common among people who claim to have been abducted by space aliens than among other people (Clancy et al., 2002).

Why would anyone "remember" a trauma that did not actually occur? Elizabeth Loftus (1997b) suggests that, for one thing, popular books such as *The Courage to Heal* (Bass & Davis, 1994) and *Secret Survivors* (Blume, 1998) may lead people to believe that anyone who experiences guilt, depression, low self-esteem, overemotionality, or any of a long list of other problems is harboring repressed memories of abuse. This message, says Loftus, is reinforced and elaborated by some therapists, particularly those who specialize in using guided imagination, hypnosis, and other methods to "help" clients recover repressed memories (Lindsay et al., 2004; Polusny & Follette, 1996; Poole et al., 1995). In so doing, these therapists may influence their clients to construct false memories by encouraging them to imagine experiencing events that might never have actually occurred or that occurred only in a dream (Mazzoni & Loftus, 1996; Olio, 1994). As one client described her therapy, "I was rapidly losing the ability to differentiate between my imagination and my real memory" (Loftus & Ketcham, 1994, p. 25). To such therapists, a client's failure to recover memories of abuse or refusal to accept that they exist is evidence of denial of the truth (Loftus, 1997a; Tavris, 2003).

The possibility that recovered memories might actually be false memories has led to dismissed charges or not-guilty verdicts for defendants in some repressed memory cases. In other cases, previously convicted defendants have been released. (George Franklin's conviction was overturned, but only after he spent five years in prison.) Concern over the potential damage resulting from false memories prompted the establishment in 1992 of the False Memory Syndrome Foundation, an organization of families affected by abuse accusations stemming from allegedly repressed memories. More than a hundred of these families (including George Franklin's) have filed lawsuits against hospitals and therapists. In 1994, California winery executive Gary Ramona received $500,000 in damages from two therapists who had "helped" his daughter recall alleged sexual abuse at his hands. A more recent suit led to a $2 million judgment against a Minnesota therapist whose client discovered that her "recovered" memories of childhood were false; a similar case in Wisconsin brought a $5 million judgment against two therapists. And an Illinois case resulted in a $10.6 million settlement and the suspension of the license of the psychiatrist who had "found" his patient's lost memories (Loftus, 1998).

■ What evidence would help to evaluate the alternatives?

Evaluating reports of recovered memories would be easier if we had more information about whether it is possible for people to repress memories of traumatic events. If it *is* possible, we also need to know how common it is and how accurate recovered memories might be. So far we know that some people apparently forget intense emotional experiences, but that most people's memories of them are vivid and long-lasting (Alexander et al., 2005; Goodman et al., 2003; Pope et al., 1998; Strongman & Kemp, 1991). Some are called *flashbulb memories* because they preserve particular experiences in great detail (Brown & Kulik, 1977). In fact, many people who live through trauma are *unable* to forget it, though they wish they could (Henig, 2004). In the sexual abuse study mentioned earlier, for example (Williams, 1994), 62 percent of the victims recalled as adults the trauma that had been documented in their childhoods. A similar study of a different group of adults found that about 92 percent of them recalled their documented childhood abuse (Alexander et al., 2005; Goodman et al., 2003). The true recall figures might actually be even higher in such studies, because some people who remember abuse may not wish to talk about it. In any case, additional studies like these—studies that track the fate of memories in known abuse cases—would not only help estimate the prevalence of this kind of forgetting but also might offer clues as to the kinds of people and events most likely to be associated with it.

It would also be valuable to know more about the processes through which repression might occur. Is there a mechanism that specifically pushes traumatic memories out of awareness, then keeps them at a subconscious level for long periods? Despite some suggestive results (Anderson & Green, 2001; Anderson et al., 2004; DePrince & Freyd, 2004), cognitive psychologists have so far not found reliable evidence for such a mechanism (Bulevich et al., 2006; Geraerts et al., 2006; Loftus, 1997a; McNally, Clancy, & Schacter, 2001; McNally, 2003; McNally et al., 2000a; Pope et al., 1998).

■ What conclusions are most reasonable?

An objective reading of the research evidence suggests that the recovery of traumatic memories is at least possible but that the implantation of false memories is also possible—and has been demonstrated repeatedly in controlled experiments. With this in mind, it is not easy to decide whether any particular case is an instance of recovered memory or false memory, especially when there is no objective corroborating evidence to guide the decision.

The intense conflict between those who uncritically accept claims of recovered memories and those who are more wary about the accuracy of such claims reflects a fundamental disagreement about evidence (Tavris, 2003). To many therapists who deal daily with victims of sexual abuse and other traumas, clients' reports constitute stronger proof of recovered memories than do the results of laboratory experiments. Client reports are viewed with considerably more skepticism by psychologists who engage in, or rely on, empirical research on the processes of memory and forgetting (Loftus, 2003, 2004; Pope, 1998). They would like to have additional sources of evidence, including brain activity "signatures" that might distinguish true memories from false ones (e.g., Cabeza et al., 2001; Slotnick & Schacter, 2004).

So whether or not you believe a claim of recovered memory may be determined by the relative weight you assign to reports of personal experiences versus evidence from controlled experiments. Still, the apparent ease with which false memories can be created should lead judges, juries, and the general public to exercise great caution before accepting unverified memories of traumatic events as the truth. At the same time, we should not automatically reject the claims of people who appear to have recovered memories. Perhaps the wisest course is to use all the scientific and circumstantial evidence available to carefully and critically examine claims of recovered memories while keeping in mind the possibility that constructive memory processes *might* have influenced those memories. This careful, scientific approach is vital if we are to protect the rights of those who report recovered memories, as well as those who face accusations arising from them.

LINKAGES
Where are memories stored?
(a link to Biology and Behavior)

Biological Bases of Memory

▶ **How does my brain change when I store a memory?**

Many psychologists who study memory focus on explicit and implicit mental processes (e.g. Schott et al., 2005). Others explore the physical, electrical, and chemical changes that take place in the brain when people encode, store, and retrieve information (Abraham, 2006; Jonides, Lacey, & Nee, 2005; Fields, 2005).

The Biochemistry of Memory

As described in the chapter on biology and behavior, communication among brain cells takes place at the synapses between axons and dendrites, using chemicals called *neurotransmitters* that are released at the synapses. The formation and storage of new memories are associated with at least two kinds of changes in synapses.

The first kind of change occurs when stimulation from the environment promotes the formation of *new* synapses. Scientists can now actually see this process occur. As shown in Figure 6.13, repeatedly sending signals across a particular synapse increases the number of special little branches, called *spines,* that appear on the receiving cell's dendrites (Lang et al., 2004; Toni et al., 1999). The second kind of change occurs as new experiences change the operation of *existing* synapses. For example, when two neurons fire at the same time and together stimulate a third neuron, that other neuron will later be more responsive than before to stimulation by either neuron alone. This process of "sensitizing" synapses is called *long-term potentiation* (Li et al., 2003; Rioult-Pedotti, Friedman, & Donoghue, 2000). Other patterns of electrical stimulation can weaken synaptic connections, a process called *long-term depression* (Malenka, 1995). Changes in the sensitivity of synapses could account for the development of conditioned responses and other types of learning (Olson et al., 2006).

In the hippocampus (see Figure 6.14), these changes appear to occur at synapses that use the neurotransmitter *glutamate* (Malenka & Nicoll, 1999). Other neurotransmitters, such as *acetylcholine,* also play important roles in memory formation (e.g., Furey,

FIGURE 6.13

Building Memories

These models are based on electron microscope images of synapses in the brain. The model on the left shows that, before signals were repeatedly sent across the synapse, just one spine (shown in white) appears on this part of the dendrite. Afterward, as shown in the other model, there are two spines, which helps improve communication across the synapse. The creation and changing of many individual synapses in the brain appears to underlie the formation and storage of new memories.

Source: Toni et al. (1999).

Brain Structures Involved in Memory

Combined neural activity in many parts of the brain allows us to encode, store, and retrieve memories. The complexity of the biological bases of these processes is underscored by research showing that different aspects of a memory—such as the sights and sounds of some event—are stored in different parts of the cerebral cortex.

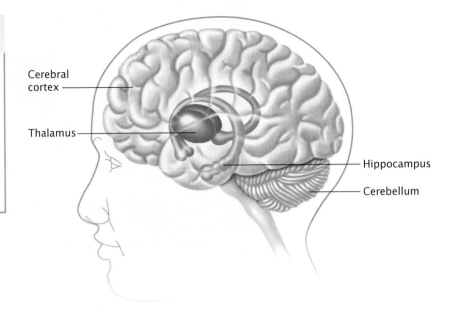

Cerebral cortex

Thalamus

Hippocampus

Cerebellum

Pietrini, & Haxby, 2000; Li et al., 2003). The memory problems seen in Alzheimer's patients are related to a lack of neurons that use acetylcholine and send fibers to the hippocampus and the cortex (Muir, 1997). Drugs that interfere with the action of acetylcholine impair memory, and drugs that increase the amount of acetylcholine in synapses can improve memory somewhat in aging animals and humans (Pettit, Shao, & Yakel, 2001; Sirvio, 1999).

In summary, research has shown that the formation of memories is associated with changes in many individual synapses that, together, strengthen and improve the communication in networks of neurons (Malleret et al., 2001; Rosenzweig & Bennett, 1996).

Brain Structures and Memory

Are the biochemical processes involved in memory concentrated in certain brain regions, or are they distributed throughout the brain? The latest research suggests that memory involves both specialized regions where various types of memories are formed and widespread areas for storage (Takashima et al., 2006).

The Impact of Brain Damage   Studies of how brain injuries affect memory provide evidence about which parts of the brain are involved in various kinds of memory. For example, damage to the hippocampus, nearby parts of the cerebral cortex, and the thalamus often results in **anterograde amnesia,** a loss of memory for any event occurring after the injury. People who suffer this kind of damage are unable to form new memories.

The case of H.M. provides a striking example of anterograde amnesia (Milner, 1966). When H.M. was twenty-seven years old, part of his hippocampus was removed in order to stop his severe epileptic seizures. After the operation, his long-term and short-term memory appeared normal, but something was wrong. Two years later, he still believed that he was twenty-seven. When his family moved into a new house, he couldn't remember the new address or how to get there. When his uncle died, he grieved in a normal way; but soon afterward, he began to ask why his uncle had not visited him. He had to be repeatedly reminded of the death and, each time, H.M. began the mourning process all over again. The surgery had apparently destroyed the mechanism that transfers information from short-term to long-term memory. Now in his seventies,

anterograde amnesia   A loss of memory for events that occur after a brain injury.

A FAMOUS CASE OF RETROGRADE AMNESIA After Ralf Schumacher slammed his race car into a wall during the United States Grand Prix in June of 2004, he sustained a severe concussion that left him with no memory of the crash. Retrograde amnesia is relatively common following concussions, so if you ride a bike or a motorcycle, wear that helmet!

H.M. lives in a nursing home, where his only long-term memories are from fifty years ago, before the operation. He is still unable to recall events and facts he has experienced since then—not even the names of people he sees every day (Corkin, 2002; Hathaway, 2002).

Although patients with damage to the hippocampus cannot form new episodic memories, they may still be able to form implicit memories. For example, H.M.'s performance on a complicated puzzle improved steadily over several days of practice, just as it does with normal people, and eventually it became virtually perfect. But each time he tried the puzzle, he insisted that he had never seen it before (Cohen & Corkin, 1981). A musician with a similar kind of brain damage was able to use his implicit memory to continue leading choral groups (Vattano, 2000). So it appears that the hippocampus is crucial in the formation of new episodic memories, but that implicit memory, procedural memory, and working memory are governed by other regions of the brain (Schott et al., 2005; Squire, 1992).

Retrograde amnesia involves loss of memory for events *prior* to some brain injury. Often, a person with this type of amnesia can't remember anything that took place in the months or years before the injury (Kapur, 1999). In 1994, head injuries from a car crash left thirty-six-year-old Perlene Griffith-Barwell with retrograde amnesia so severe that she forgot virtually everything she had learned about everything and every one she knew over the previous twenty years. She thought she was still sixteen and did not recognize her husband, Malcolm, or her four children. She said, "The children were sweet, but they didn't seem like mine," and she "didn't feel anything" for Malcolm. Her memories of the last twenty years have never fully returned. She is divorced, but, at last report, she still lives with her children and holds a job in a bank (Weinstein, 1999).

Unlike Perlene, most victims of retrograde amnesia gradually recover their memories (Riccio, Millin, & Gisquet-Verrier, 2003). The most distant events are recalled first; then the person gradually regains memory for events leading up to the injury. Recovery is seldom complete, however, and the person may never remember the last few seconds before the injury. One man received a severe blow to the head after being thrown from his motorcycle. Upon regaining consciousness, he claimed that he was eleven years old. Over the next three months, he slowly recalled more and more of his life. He remembered when he was twelve, thirteen, and so on—right up until the time he was riding his motorcycle the day of the accident. But he was never able to remember what happened just before the accident (Baddeley, 1982). Those final events were

retrograde amnesia A loss of memory for events that occurred prior to a brain injury.

probably encoded into short-term memory, but apparently they were never transferred into long-term memory (Dudai, 2004).

Other conditions that suppress neural activity in the brain can also disrupt the transfer of information from short-term to long-term memory. These conditions include anesthetic drugs, poisoning by carbon monoxide or other toxins, and strong electrical impulses such as those in the electroconvulsive therapy that is sometimes used to treat cases of severe depression (see the chapter on treatment of psychological disorders).

Multiple Storage Areas Obviously, the hippocampus does not permanently store long-term memories (Bayley, Hopkins, & Squire, 2003; Rosenbaum et al., 2000). (If it did, H.M. would not have retained memories from the years before part of his hippocampus was removed.) The hippocampus and thalamus send nerve impulses to the cerebral cortex, and it is in and around the cortex that long-term semantic and episodic memories are probably stored—but not just in one place (Levy, Bayley, & Squire, 2004; Maviel et al., 2004; Miceli et al., 2001). As described in the chapter on biology and behavior, different regions of the cortex receive messages from different senses. Specific aspects of an experience are probably stored in or near these regions. For example, damage to the auditory association cortex disrupts memory for sounds (Colombo et al., 1990). A memory, however, involves more than one sensory system. Even in the simple case of a rat remembering a maze, the experience of the maze involves vision, smell, movements, and emotions, each of which may be stored in different regions of the brain (Gallagher & Chiba, 1996). So memories are both localized and distributed. Certain brain areas store specific aspects of each remembered event, but many brain systems are involved in experiencing a whole event (Brewer et al., 1998; Kensinger & Corkin, 2004). For example, the cerebellum (see Figure 6.14) is involved in the storage of procedural memories, such as dance steps and other movements.

What happens in the brain as we retrieve memories? Brain imaging studies show that the hippocampus, as well as various regions of the cerebral cortex, are active during memory retrieval (Buckner & Wheeler, 2001; Cabeza et al., 2001; Davachi, Mitchell, & Wagner, 2003; McDermott & Buckner, 2001; Rugg & Wilding, 2000). There is also evidence to suggest that retrieving memories of certain experiences, such as a conversation or a tennis game, reactivates the sensory and motor regions of the brain that had been involved during the event itself (Nyberg et al., 2001). Research shows, too, that when animals recall an emotional (fear-related) memory, that memory may have to be stored again. During this biological restorage process, it may be open to distortion (Eisenberg et al., 2003; Lee, Everitt, & Thomas, 2004; Nader, Schafe, & Le Doux, 2000). Researchers are exploring the question of whether this process occurs in humans, too (Dudai, 2004; Walker et al., 2003). Cognitive neuroscientists are also trying to determine whether different patterns of brain activity are associated with the storage and retrieval of accurate versus inaccurate memories (Gonsalves & Paller, 2000; Slotnick & Schacter, 2004; Urbach et al., 2005). Future research in these areas will have obvious applications in areas such as lie detection, the understanding of false-memory processes, and the evaluation of claims of recovered memories.

Improving Your Memory

▶ **How can I remember more information?**

Some questions remain about what memory is and how it works, but the results of memory research offer many valuable guidelines to help people improve their memories (Neisser, 2000a).

Mnemonics

One way to improve your memory is to use mnemonics (pronounced "nee-MON-ix"). **Mnemonics** are strategies for putting information into an organized framework in order to remember it more easily. To remember the names of the Great Lakes, for example, you could use the acronym HOMES (for Huron, Ontario, Michigan, Erie, and Superior). Verbal organization is the basis for many mnemonics. You can link items by weaving them into a story, a sentence, or a rhyme. To help customers remember where they left their cars, some large parking lots have replaced traditional section designations such as "A1" or "G8" with the names of colors, months, or animals. Customers can then tie the location of their cars to information already in long-term memory—for example, "I parked in the month of my mother's birthday."

One simple but powerful mnemonic is called the *method of loci* (pronounced "LOW-sigh"), or the "method of places." To use this method, first think about a set of familiar locations. Use your home, for example. You might imagine walking through the front door, around all four corners of the living room, and through each of the other rooms. Next, imagine that each item you want to remember is in one of these locations. Creating vivid or unusual images of how the items appear in each location seems to be particularly effective (Kline & Groninger, 1991). For example, tomatoes smashed against the front door or bananas hanging from the bedroom ceiling might be helpful in recalling these items on a grocery list. Whenever you want to remember a new list, you can create new images using the same locations in the same order.

Guidelines for More Effective Studying

The success of mnemonic strategies demonstrates again the importance of relating new information to knowledge already stored in memory. All mnemonic systems require that you have a well-learned body of knowledge (such as locations) that can be used to provide a framework, or context, for organizing incoming information (Hilton, 1986).

When you want to remember complex material, such as a textbook chapter, the same principle applies (Palmisano & Herrmann, 1991). You can improve your memory for text material by first creating an outline or other overall context for learning, rather than by just reading and rereading (Glover et al., 1990). Repetition may *seem* effective, because it keeps material in short-term memory, but for retaining information over long periods, repetition alone tends to be ineffective, no matter how much time you spend on it (Bjork, 1999; Bjorklund & Green, 1992). In short, "work smarter, not harder."

In addition, spend your time wisely. *Distributed practice* is much more effective than *massed practice* for learning, and retaining, new information. If you are going to spend ten hours studying for a test, you will be much better off studying for ten 1-hour blocks, separated by periods of sleep and other activity. "Cramming" for one 10-hour block will not be as successful. By scheduling more study sessions, you will stay fresh and be able to think about the material from a new perspective during each session. This method will help you elaborate on the material, as in elaborative rehearsal, and thus remember it better.

Reading a Textbook   More specific advice for remembering textbook material comes from a study that examined how successful and unsuccessful college students approached their reading (Whimbey, 1976). Unsuccessful students tended to read the material straight through. They did not slow down when they reached a difficult section. They kept going even when they did not understand what they were reading. In contrast, successful college students monitored their understanding, reread difficult sections, and periodically stopped or reviewed what they had learned. (This book's *In Review* features are designed to help you do that.) In short, effective learners engage in a deep level of processing. They are active learners. They think of each new fact in relation to other material, and they develop a context in which many new facts can be organized effectively.

mnemonics   Strategies for organizing information in order to remember it.

UNDERSTAND AND REMEMBER
Research on memory suggests that students who simply read their textbooks won't remember as much as those who, like this woman, read for understanding using strategies such as the PQ4R method. Further, memory for the material is likely to be better if you read and study it over a number of weeks rather than in one marathon session on the night before a test.

Research on memory suggests two specific guidelines for reading a textbook. First, make sure that you understand what you are reading before moving on (Herrmann & Searleman, 1992). Second, try the *PQ4R method* (Thomas & Robinson, 1972). *PQ4R* stands for six activities to engage in when you read a chapter: *preview, question, read, reflect, recite,* and *review.* These activities are designed to increase the depth to which you process the information you read and should be done as follows:

1. *Preview.* Begin by skimming the chapter. Look at the section headings and any boldfaced or italicized terms. Get a general idea of what material will be discussed, the way it is organized, and how its topics relate to one another and to what you already know. Some people find it useful to survey the entire chapter once and then survey each major section a little more carefully before reading it in detail.

2. *Question.* Before reading each section, ask yourself what content will be covered and what information you should be getting from it.

3. *Read.* Read the text, but think about the material as you read. Are the questions you raised earlier being answered? Do you see the connections between and among the topics?

4. *Reflect.* As you read, think of your own examples—and create visual images—of the concepts and phenomena you encounter. Ask yourself what the material means, and consider how each section relates to other sections in the chapter and other chapters in the book (this book's Linkages features are designed to promote this kind of reflection).

5. *Recite.* At the end of each section, recite the major points. Resist the temptation to be passive and say, "Oh, I remember that." Be active. Put the ideas into your own words by reciting them aloud to yourself or by summarizing the material in a minilecture to a friend or study partner.

6. *Review.* When you reach the end of the chapter, review all of its material. You should now see connections not only within each section but also among sections. The objective is to see how the material is organized. Once you grasp that organization, the individual facts will be far easier to remember.

By following these procedures, you will learn and remember the material better. You will also save yourself considerable time.

Lecture Notes Students and employees often have to learn and remember material from lectures or other presentations. Taking notes will help, but effective note taking is a learned skill that improves with practice (Pauk, 2005). Research on memory suggests some simple strategies for taking and using notes effectively.

Recognize first that in note taking, more is not necessarily better. Taking detailed notes on everything requires that you pay close attention to unimportant as well as important content, leaving little time for thinking about the material. Note takers who concentrate on expressing the major ideas in relatively few words remember more than those who try to catch every detail. In short, the best way to take notes is to think about what is being said. Draw connections with other material in the presentation. Then summarize the major points clearly and concisely (Kiewra, 1989).

Once you have a set of lecture notes, review them as soon as possible after the lecture so that you can fill in missing details. (Remember: Most forgetting from long-term memory occurs during the first hour after learning.) When the time comes for serious study, use your notes as if they were a chapter in a textbook. Write a detailed outline. Think about how various points are related. Once you have organized the material, the details will make more sense and will be much easier to remember. ("In Review: Improving Your Memory" summarizes tips for studying.)

in review

IMPROVING YOUR MEMORY

Goal	Helpful Techniques
Remembering lists of items	Use mnemonics. Look for meaningful acronyms. Try the method of loci.
Remembering textbook material	Follow the PQ4R system. Allocate your time to allow for distributed practice. Read actively, not passively.
Taking lecture notes	Take notes, but record only the main points. Think about the overall organization of the material. Review your notes as soon after the lecture as possible in order to fill in missing points.
Studying for exams	Write a detailed outline of your lecture notes rather than passively reading them.

1. Using mnemonics and the PQ4R system to better remember course material are examples of the value of _____ rehearsal.
2. "Cramming" illustrates _____ practice that usually leads to _____ long-term retention than _____ practice.
3. To minimize forgetting, you should review lecture notes _____ after a lecture ends.

ACTIVE REVIEW

Memory

Linkages

As noted in the introductory chapter, all of psychology's subfields are related to one another. Our discussion of eyewitness testimony illustrates just one way in which the topic of this chapter, memory, is linked to the subfield of sensation and perception, as discussed in the chapter by that name. The Linkages diagram shows ties to two other subfields, and there are many more ties throughout the book. Looking for linkages among subfields will help you see how they all fit together and help you better appreciate the big picture that is psychology.

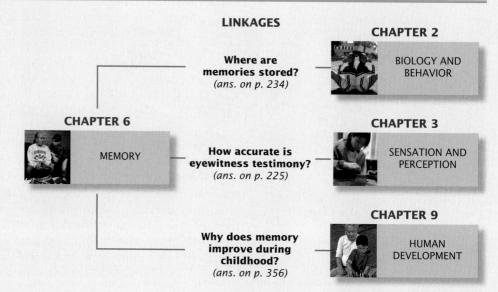

LINKAGES

Where are memories stored?
(ans. on p. 234)

CHAPTER 2
BIOLOGY AND BEHAVIOR

CHAPTER 6
MEMORY

How accurate is eyewitness testimony?
(ans. on p. 225)

CHAPTER 3
SENSATION AND PERCEPTION

Why does memory improve during childhood?
(ans. on p. 356)

CHAPTER 9
HUMAN DEVELOPMENT

Summary

THE NATURE OF MEMORY

▶ **How does information turn into memories?**

Human memory depends on a complex mental system. There are three basic memory processes. *Encoding* transforms stimulus information into some type of mental representation. Material can be encoded by *acoustic* (sound), *visual* (appearance), or *semantic* (meaning) *codes*. *Storage* maintains information in the memory system over time. *Retrieval* is the process of gaining access to previously stored information.

Most psychologists agree that there are at least three types of memory. *Episodic memory* refers to memory for specific events in a person's life. *Semantic memory* refers to generalized knowledge about the world. *Procedural memory* refers to information about how to do things. Research on memory focuses on *explicit memory,* the processes through which people try to remember something, and *implicit memory,* the unintentional recollection and influence of prior experiences.

Four models of memory have guided most research. The *levels-of-processing model* suggests that the most important determinant of memory is how extensively information is encoded or processed when it is first received. In general, *elaborative rehearsal* is more effective than *maintenance rehearsal* in learning new information, because it represents a deeper level of processing. According to the *transfer-appropriate processing model,* the critical determinant of memory is not how deeply information is encoded but whether the processes used during retrieval match those used during encoding. *Parallel distributed processing (PDP) models* of memory suggest that new experiences not only provide specific information but also become part of, and alter, a whole network of associations. The *information-processing model* suggests that for information to become firmly embedded in memory, it must pass through three stages of processing: sensory memory, short-term memory, and long-term memory.

STORING NEW MEMORIES

▶ **What am I most likely to remember?**

Sensory memory maintains incoming stimulus information in the *sensory registers* for a very brief time. *Selective attention,* which focuses mental resources on only part of the stimulus field, controls what information in the sensory registers is actually perceived and transferred to short-term memory.

Working memory is a system that allows us to store, organize, and manipulate information in order to think, solve problems, and make decisions. The storage, or maintenance, component of working memory is referred to as *short-term memory (STM).* Various memory codes can be used in short-term memory, but acoustic codes seem to be used in most verbal tasks. Studies of the *immediate memory span* indicate that the capacity of short-term memory is approximately seven *chunks,* or meaningful groupings of information. Studies using the *Brown-Peterson procedure* show that information in short-term memory is usually forgotten in about eighteen seconds if it is not rehearsed.

Long-term memory (LTM) normally results from semantic coding, which means that people tend to encode the general meaning of information, not the surface details, into long-term memory. The capacity of long-term memory to store new information is extremely large and perhaps unlimited. The appearance of a *primacy effect* and a *recency effect* suggests that short-term and long-term memory may be distinct systems.

RETRIEVING MEMORIES

▶ **How do I retrieve stored memories?**

Retrieval cues help people remember things that they would otherwise not be able to recall. The effectiveness of retrieval cues follows the *encoding specificity principle:* Cues help retrieval only if they match some feature of the information that was originally encoded. All else being equal, memory may be better when we attempt to retrieve information in the same environment in which it was learned; this is called *context-dependent memory.* When our internal state can affect retrieval, we have a *state-dependent memory.* Researchers usually study retrieval from semantic memory by examining how long it takes people to answer general-knowledge questions. It appears that ideas are represented as associations in a dense semantic memory network and that the retrieval of information occurs by a process of *spreading activation.* Each concept in the network is represented as a unique collection of features or attributes. The tip-of-the-tongue phenomenon represents the retrieval of incomplete knowledge.

CONSTRUCTING MEMORIES

▶ **How accurate are my memories?**

In the process of constructive memory, people use generalized knowledge, or *schemas,* to fill in gaps in the information they encode and retrieve. PDP models provide one explanation of how people make spontaneous generalizations about the world.

Eyewitnesses can remember only what they perceive, and they can perceive only what they attend to. As a result, eyewitness testimony is often much less accurate than witnesses—and jurors—think it is.

FORGETTING

▶ **What causes me to forget things?**

In his research on long-term memory and forgetting, Ebbinghaus introduced the *method of savings.* He found that most forgetting from long-term memory occurs during the first hour after learning and that savings can be extremely long-lasting. *Decay* and *interference* are two mechanisms of forgetting. There is evidence of both decay and interference in short-term memory; it appears that most forgetting from long-term memory is due to either *retroactive interference* or *proactive interference.*

BIOLOGICAL BASES OF MEMORY

▶ **How does my brain change when I store a memory?**

Research has shown that memories can result from new synapses forming in the brain and improved communication at existing synapses. Studies of *anterograde amnesia, retrograde amnesia,* and other consequences of brain damage provide information about the brain structures involved in memory. For example, the hippocampus and thalamus are known to play a role in the formation of memories. These structures send nerve impulses to the cerebral cortex, and it is there that memories are probably stored. Memories appear to be both localized and distributed throughout the brain.

IMPROVING YOUR MEMORY

▶ **How can I remember more information?**

Mnemonics are strategies that are used to remember things better. One of the simplest but most powerful mnemonics is the method of loci. It is useful because it provides a context for organizing material effectively. The key to remembering textbook material is to read actively rather than passively. One way to do this is to follow the PQ4R method: preview, question, read, reflect, recite, and review. Similarly, to take lecture notes or to study them effectively, organize the points in a meaningful framework and think about how each main point relates to the others.

Learn by Doing

Put It in Writing

Write a paragraph describing your views on claims of recovered memories of childhood abuse. Be sure to mention what evidence leads you to think as you do about this topic. For example, indicate whether you tend to give more weight to the testimony of clients who say they have recovered traumatic memories or to the results of scientific research on memory and repression. Be sure to say why you prefer one kind of evidence over another and whether you think the debate over recovered memories will ever be resolved to everyone's satisfaction.

Personal Learning Activity

When you study for your next quiz or exam, try using some of the memory tips contained in this chapter. For example, use one or more mnemonic devices to help you to remember lists of information, and try the PQ4R method with the next chapter you read. Did these memory-enhancing methods make it easier for you to study and to do well on your next quiz or exam? Why or why not? *For additional projects, see the Personal Learning Activities in the corresponding chapter of the study guide that accompanies this text.*

Step into Action

Courses

Cognitive Psychology
Social Cognition
Experimental Psychology
Learning and Memory

Movies

The Bourne Identity. Amnesia.
Memento; The Lazarus Man; Anastasia; Blackout; Lapse of Memory; Regarding Henry. Memory loss.
Rashoman; Stagecoach. Constructive memory.
On Golden Pond. Memory and aging.
Total Recall; Eternal Sunshine of the Spotless Mind; Overboard; 50 First Dates. Futuristic, fantasy, and comedy films about constructing and losing memories; try spotting the errors in how memory processes are portrayed.

Books

Douglas J. Herrmann, Cathy McEvoy, and Christopher Hertzog (Eds.), *Basic and Applied Memory Research: Theory in Context* (Lawrence Erlbaum Associates, 1996). Overview of memory research.
Steven Pinker, *How the Mind Works* (Norton, 1997). Biology of memory and thought.
William H. Calvin, *The Cerebral Code: Thinking a Thought in the Mosaics of the Mind* (MIT Press, 1996). Brain function and memory.

Akira Miyake and Priti Shah (Eds.), *Models of Working Memory* (Cambridge University Press, 1999). Theories of short-term memory.
Elizabeth Loftus and Katherine Ketcham, *The Myth of Repressed Memory* (St. Martin's Press, 1996). Research casting doubt on the validity of some recovered memories.
E. Sue Blume, *Secret Survivors: Uncovering Incest and Its Aftereffects in Women* (Ballantine, 1998). Presents the position of some therapists who believe in the validity of all reports of recovered memories.
Elizabeth Loftus, *Eyewitness Testimony* (Harvard University Press, 1996). Summarizes research on limitations of eyewitness testimony.
Lawrence Wright, *Remembering Satan: A Tragic Case of Recovered Memory* (Vintage, 1994). False memories led to convictions of sexual abuse for Paul Ingram.
Kathryn Lyon, *Witch Hunt* (Avon, 1998). Sexual abuse hysteria in Washington State in the 1990s led to dozens of false convictions.
Moira Johnson, *Spectral Evidence* (Westview, 1997). The Gary Ramona case that found a therapist liable for inducing false memories of sexual abuse.
Susan Clancy, *Abducted: How People Come to Believe They Were Kidnapped by Aliens* (Harvard University Press, 2006). A fascinating summary of research on this topic.
Walter Pauk, *How to Study in College* (Houghton Mifflin, 2005). Effective study methods based on the results of memory research.

The Web

The World Wide Web is a good source of additional information about the science of psychology, provided you use it carefully and think critically about the information you find. The Online Study Center that accompanies this text offers many resources relevant to this chapter. These resources include interactive tutorials; Thinking Critically and Evaluating Research exercises; ACE chapter quizzes; recommended web links; and articles on current events, books, and movies. Please visit the Online Study Center at college.hmco.com/pic/bernsteinessentials4e.

Review of Key Terms

Can you define each of the key terms in the chapter? Check your definitions against those on the pages shown in parentheses in the following list or in the Glossary/Index at the end of the text.

acoustic codes (p. 209)

anterograde amnesia (p. 235)

Brown-Peterson procedure (p. 216)

chunks (p. 215)

context-dependent memories (p. 220)

decay (p. 229)

elaborative rehearsal (p. 211)

encoding (p. 209)

encoding specificity principle (p. 219)

episodic memory (p. 210)

explicit memory (p. 210)

immediate memory span (p. 215)

implicit memory (p. 210)

information-processing model (p. 213)

interference (p. 229)

levels-of-processing model (p. 211)

long-term memory (LTM) (p. 216)

maintenance rehearsal (p. 211)

method of savings (p. 229)

mnemonics (p. 238)

parallel distributed processing (PDP) models (p. 213)

primacy effect (p. 219)

proactive interference (p. 229)

procedural memory (p. 210)

recency effect (p. 219)

retrieval (p. 210)

retrieval cues (p. 219)

retroactive interference (p. 229)

retrograde amnesia (p. 236)

schemas (p. 224)

selective attention (p. 214)

semantic codes (p. 209)

semantic memory (p. 210)

sensory memory (p. 213)

sensory registers (p. 213)

short-term memory (STM) (p. 214)

spreading activation (p. 221)

state-dependent memory (p. 220)

storage (p. 209)

transfer-appropriate processing model (p. 211)

visual codes (p. 209)

working memory (p. 214)

Multiple-Choice Self-Test

Select the best answer for each of the following questions. Then check your responses against the Answer Key at the end of the text.

1. Ludwig had an extraordinary memory for sound. Even when he lost his hearing in his later years, he was still able to create beautiful music. This demonstrates his well-developed _____ codes.

   a. acoustic
   b. visual
   c. semantic
   d. auditory

2. Henry is talking about his high school graduation ceremony. He remembers that his parents and grandparents were there and that, afterward, they gave him a laptop computer. Henry's memory of this event is both _____ and _____.

   a. semantic; explicit
   b. episodic; explicit
   c. semantic; implicit
   d. episodic; implicit

3. Riesa was uncomfortable when she was introduced to her roommate's cousin. She was not aware of it, but the cousin reminded her of a hated classmate in elementary school. This incident provides an example of the operation of _____ memory.

   a. procedural
   b. semantic
   c. implicit
   d. explicit

4. Raquel was still studying ten minutes before her test. As she entered the classroom, she kept repeating the last sentence she had read: "Henry VIII had six wives." She was using _____ to keep this information in mind.

   a. elaborative rehearsal
   b. maintenance rehearsal
   c. mnemonics
   d. spreading activation

5. In a memory study, half the students in a class were told to expect multiple-choice questions on their upcoming exam, and the other half were told to expect essay questions. Students did better if they got the type of exam they expected, which is consistent with the _____ model of memory.

   a. levels-of-processing
   b. transfer-appropriate processing
   c. parallel distributed processing
   d. information-processing

6. Reepal listens as her father describes a party the family is planning. She also smells popcorn from the kitchen, hears the radio playing, notices flashes of lightning outside, and feels too warm in her sweater. Yet Reepal is able to transfer the information about the party to her short-term memory, primarily because of

   a. elaborative rehearsal.
   b. implicit memory cues.
   c. selective attention.
   d. transfer-appropriate processing.

7. Larry was thrilled when he met the girl of his dreams at the mall. She told him her phone number before she left, but if Larry doesn't use any rehearsal methods, he will only remember the number for about

   a. one second.
   b. eighteen seconds.
   c. one minute.
   d. five minutes.

8. Remembering your bank account number (2171982) as your birthday (February 17, 1982) is an example of

   a. chunking.
   b. the Brown-Peterson technique.
   c. the PQ4R method.
   d. the method of loci.

9. Lisbeth's mother once told her to remember that "The nail that stands out will get pounded down." But when Lisbeth tried to tell a friend about this saying, she remembered it as "If you stand out too much you'll get in trouble." Her problem in recalling the exact words is probably due to the fact that encoding in long-term memory is usually

   a. acoustic.
   b. visual.
   c. semantic.
   d. state dependent.

10. Raul went to a lecture on the structure of DNA but forgot his notebook and pen. He tried to remember as much of it as possible so that he could make some notes later. Research by Ebbinghaus suggests that Raul will forget most of the lecture within about _____ after it ends

    a. eighteen seconds
    b. a minute
    c. an hour
    d. twenty-four hours

11. Nesta had made a list of twenty CDs that she wanted to check out of the library, but she forgot to bring it with her. Nesta is most likely to remember the CDs that were at the _____ of the list.

    a. beginning
    b. middle
    c. end
    d. beginning and end

12. Janetta has been studying for tomorrow's test while drinking strong, caffeinated coffee. A friend tells Janetta that her test performance can be improved if she takes advantage of state-dependent memory by

    a. drinking strong, caffeinated coffee just before the test.
    b. doing the rest of her studying where the test will be given.
    c. avoiding any kind of coffee just before the test.
    d. using mnemonics to remember key terms.

13. Molly, a high school student, knows that she knows the name of her kindergarten teacher, but she can't quite remember it when asked. This experience is called

    a. constructive memory block.
    b. sensory memory impairment.
    c. the tip-of-the-tongue phenomenon.
    d. the tip-of-the-nose phenomenon.

14. When asked if there was a fever thermometer in her doctor's office, Careen says she remembers seeing one, even though it wasn't actually there. This is an example of _____, which is influenced by _____.

    a. the tip-of-the-tongue phenomenon; schemas
    b. the tip-of-the-tongue phenomenon; selective attention
    c. constructive memory; schemas.
    d. constructive memory; selective attention.

15. Recent use of DNA evidence has had what effect on the U.S. legal system's view of eyewitness testimony?

    a. It has tended to back up eyewitness testimony.
    b. It has demonstrated that eyewitness testimony, though not always accurate, is much better than anyone thought it was.
    c. It has revealed that eyewitness testimony has put many people in prison for crimes they did not commit.
    d. It has had little effect.

16. Robin memorized the names of all of the U.S. presidents when she was ten. Two years later, she had forgotten most of them, so she was pleasantly surprised that she could learn them a second time much more quickly than the first. This is an example of what Ebbinghaus called

    a. mnemonics.
    b. state dependence.
    c. savings.
    d. context dependence.

17. Berean studied French during his first year at college and then started learning Spanish in his second year. Now he is having difficulty remembering his Spanish vocabulary because the French words keep popping into his mind. This is an example of _____ interference.

    a. retrograde
    b. anterograde
    c. proactive
    d. retroactive

18. When her brother said he had gotten a job in a bookstore, Danielle immediately assumed it would be a large room with books along the walls, a magazine section, a children's section, and cash registers near the door. But he had been hired by an online store, so Danielle was wrong. Her mistaken assumptions occurred because of _____, which is/are predicted by the _____ model of memory.

    a. spontaneous generalizations; PDP
    b. spontaneous generalizations; information-processing
    c. constructive memory; depth of processing
    d. semantic memory; transfer-appropriate

19. Jerry, a factory worker, suffered a brain injury when a steel beam fell on his head. Jerry cannot remember anything that happened since the accident. Jerry is experiencing _____ amnesia.

    a. retrograde
    b. anterograde
    c. proactive
    d. retroactive

20. Loretta wanted to remember a list of important memory researchers, so she pictured them all visiting her apartment. She imagined Elizabeth Loftus playing video games in the living room, Hermann Ebbinghaus napping in the bathtub, Henry Roediger and Kathleen McDermott dancing in the kitchen, and so on. Loretta is using the memory strategy called

    a. the method of loci.
    b. procedural memorization.
    c. encoding cues.
    d. context dependence.

7

Thought, Language, and Intelligence

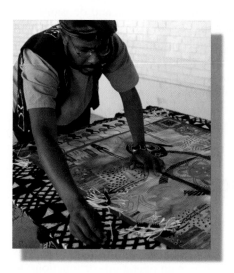
"Say what you mean, and mean what you say." This is good advice,

but following it is not always easy, partly because our thoughts don't always come to us in clear, complete sentences. We have to construct those sentences—using the language we have learned—from the words, images, ideas, and other mental material in our minds. Often, the complexity of that material makes it difficult to accurately express what we are thinking. We all manage to do it, but with varying degrees of success. In this chapter, we explore what thoughts are, what language is, and how people translate one into the other. We also consider how thinking guides decision making and problem solving and how psychologists measure individual differences in these and other cognitive abilities that are commonly described as *intelligence*.

Reading this chapter will help you to answer the following questions:

r. Joyce Wallace, a New York City physician, was having trouble figuring out what was the matter with a forty-three-year-old patient, "Laura McBride." Laura reported pain in her stomach and abdomen, aching muscles, irritability, occasional dizzy spells, and fatigue (Rouéché, 1986). The doctor's first hypothesis was iron-deficiency anemia, a condition in which there is not enough oxygen-carrying hemoglobin in the blood. There was some evidence to support that hypothesis. A physical examination revealed that Laura's spleen was somewhat enlarged, and blood tests showed low hemoglobin and high production of red blood cells, suggesting that her body was attempting to compensate for the loss of hemoglobin. However, other tests revealed normal iron levels. Perhaps she was losing blood through internal bleeding, but other tests ruled that out. Had Laura been vomiting blood? She said no. Blood in the urine? No. Abnormally heavy menstrual flow? No.

As Dr. Wallace puzzled over the problem, Laura's condition worsened. She reported more intense pain, cramps, shortness of breath, and severe loss of energy. Her blood was becoming less and less capable of sustaining her; but if it was not being lost, what was happening to it? Finally, the doctor looked at a smear of Laura's blood on a microscope slide. What she saw indicated that a poison was destroying Laura's red blood cells. What could it be? Laura spent most of her time at home, but her teenage daughters, who lived with her, were perfectly healthy. Dr. Wallace asked herself, "What does Laura do that the girls do not?" She repairs and restores paintings. Paint. Lead! She might be suffering from lead poisoning! When the next blood test showed a lead level seven times higher than normal, Dr. Wallace knew she had found the answer at last.

To solve this medical mystery, Dr. Wallace relied on her intelligence, part of which can be seen in her ability to think, solve problems, and make judgments and decisions. She put these vital cognitive abilities to use in weighing the pros and cons of various hypotheses and in reaching decisions about what tests to order and how to interpret them. In consulting with the patient and other physicians, she relied on another remarkable human cognitive ability known as *language*. Let's take a look at what psychologists have discovered about these complex mental processes, how to measure them, and how to compare people in terms of intelligence. We begin by examining a general framework for understanding human thinking and then go on to look at some specific cognitive processes.

Basic Functions of Thought

▶ **What good is thinking, anyway?**

Understanding the mental processes that Dr. Wallace used to solve her problem begins by realizing that her thinking, like yours, involves five main operations or functions: to *describe*, to *elaborate*, to *decide*, to *plan*, and to *guide action*. Figure 7.1 shows how these functions can be organized into a circle of thought.

The Circle of Thought

Consider how the circle of thought operated in Dr. Wallace's case. It began when she received the information about Laura's symptoms that allowed her to *describe* the problem. Next, Dr. Wallace *elaborated* on this information by using her knowledge, experience, and powers of reasoning to consider what disorders might cause such symptoms. Then she made a *decision* to investigate a possible cause, such as anemia. To pursue this decision, she formulated a *plan*—and then *acted* on that plan. But the circle of thought did not stop there. Information from the blood test provided new descriptive

F I G U R E **7 . 1**

The Circle of Thought

The circle of thought begins as our sensory systems receive information from the world. Our perceptual system describes and elaborates this information, which is represented in the brain in ways that allow us to make decisions, formulate plans, and guide our actions. As those actions change our world, we receive new information, which begins another journey around the circle of thought.

FIGURE **7.2**

An Information-Processing Model

Some stages in the information-processing model depend heavily on both short-term and long-term memory and require some attention—that limited supply of mental resources required for information processing to be carried out efficiently.

information, which Dr. Wallace elaborated further to reach another decision, create a new plan, and guide her next action. Each stage in the circle of thought was also influenced by her overall *intention*—in this case, to find and cure her patient's problem.

The processes making up the circle of thought usually occur so quickly and are so complex that slowing them down for careful analysis might seem impossible. Some psychologists approach this difficult task by studying thought processes as if they were part of a computer-like information-processing system. An **information-processing system** receives information, represents the information with symbols, and then manipulates those symbols (e.g. Anderson et al., 2004). In an information-processing model, **thinking** is defined as the manipulation of mental representations. Figure 7.2 shows how an information-processing model might describe the sequence of mental events that make up one trip around the circle of thought.

In the first stage, information about the world reaches your brain through the senses we discussed in the chapter on sensation and perception. This stage does not require attention. In the second stage, you must perceive and recognize the information—processes that do require attention. In this stage, you also consciously elaborate information using the short-term and working-memory processes described in the memory chapter. These

"AUTOMATIC" THINKING The sensory, perceptual, decision-making, response-planning, and action components of the circle of thought can occur so rapidly that—as when playing a fast-paced video game—we may only be aware of the incoming information and our quick response to it. In such cases, our thinking processes become so well practiced that they are virtually automatic.

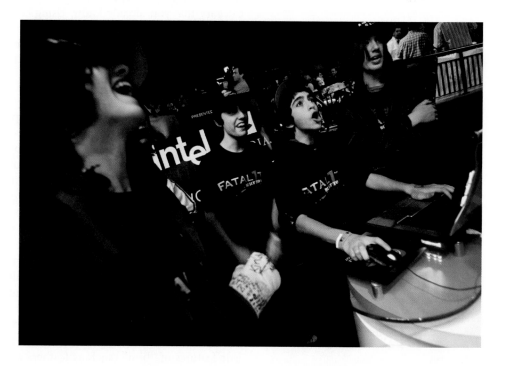

information-processing system
Mechanisms for receiving information, representing it with symbols, and manipulating it.

thinking The manipulation of mental representations.

processes allow you to think about new information in relation to knowledge that is already stored in your long-term memory. Once the information has been elaborated in this way, you must decide what to do with it. This third stage—decision making—demands attention, too. Your decision might be to store the information or to take some action. If the decision is to act, it is at this stage that you plan what to do. In the fourth and fifth stages, the action is carried out. Your action usually affects the environment, providing new information that is "fed back" to the system for processing in the ongoing circle of thought.

Mental Representations: The Ingredients of Thought

▶ **What are thoughts made of?**

Just as measuring, stirring, and baking are only part of the story of cookie making, describing the processes of thinking tells only part of the story behind the circle of thought. Psychologists usually describe the ingredients of thought as *information.* But that is like saying that you make cookies with "stuff." What specific forms can information take in our minds? Cognitive psychologists have found that information can be mentally represented in many ways, including as *concepts, propositions, schemas, scripts, mental models, images,* and *cognitive maps.* Let's explore these ingredients of thought and how people manipulate them as they think.

Concepts

When you think about anything—dogs, happiness, sex, movies, pizza—you are manipulating a basic ingredient of thought called *concepts.* **Concepts** are categories of objects, events, or ideas with common properties. Some concepts, such as "round" and "red," are visual and concrete. Concepts such as "truth" and "justice" are more abstract and harder to define. "To have a concept" is to recognize the properties, or *features,* that tend to be shared by members of a category. For example, the concept of "bird" includes such properties as having feathers, laying eggs, and being able to fly. The concept of "scissors" includes such properties as having two blades, a connecting hinge, and a pair of finger holes. Concepts allow you to relate each object or event you encounter to a category that you already know. Using concepts, you can say, "No, that is not a dog," or "Yes, that is a car." Concepts also make it possible for you to think logically. If you have the concepts "whale" and "bird," you can decide whether a whale is a bird without having either creature in the room with you.

Types of Concepts Some concepts—called **formal concepts**—clearly define objects or events by a set of rules and properties, so that every member of the concept has all of the concept's defining properties and nonmembers do not. For instance, the concept "square" can be defined as "a shape with four equal sides and four right-angle corners." Any object that does not have all of these features is simply not a square. Formal concepts are often used to study concept learning in the laboratory, because the members of these concepts can be neatly defined (Trabasso & Bower, 1968).

learn by doing   In contrast, try to define the concepts "home" or "game." You might say that "home" is the place where you live, and that a "game" is a competition between players. However, some people define "home" as the place they were born, and solitaire is a card game even though it involves only one player. These are just two examples of *natural concepts.* Unlike formal concepts, natural concepts don't have a fixed set of defining features. Instead, **natural concepts** have a set of typical or *characteristic* features, and members don't need to have all of them. For example, the ability to fly is a characteristic feature of the natural concept "bird," but an ostrich is still a bird even though it can't fly. It is a bird because it has enough other characteristic features of "bird" (such as feathers and wings). Having just one bird property is

concepts Categories of objects, events, or ideas that have common properties.

formal concepts Concepts that can be clearly defined by a set of rules or properties.

natural concepts Concepts that have no fixed set of defining features but instead share a set of characteristic features.

Does this person look like a millionaire to you? Our schemas tell us what to expect about objects, places, events, and people, but those expectations can sometimes be wrong. This was dramatically illustrated in October 1999 when Gordon Elwood died. The Medford, Oregon, man, who dressed in rags and collected cans, left over $9 million to charity (McMahon, 2000).

not enough, though. A snake lays eggs and a bat can fly, but neither animal is a bird. It is usually a combination of properties that defines a concept. In most situations outside the laboratory, people are thinking about natural rather than formal concepts. These natural concepts include object categories, such as "bird" or "house." They also include abstract idea categories, such as "honesty" or "justice," and goal-related categories, such as "things to pack for my vacation" (Barsalou, 1993).

The boundaries of a natural concept are fuzzy, so some members are better examples of it than others. A robin, a chicken, an ostrich, and a penguin are all birds. But the robin is a better example of the bird concept than the others, because it is closer to what most people have learned to think of as a typical bird. A member of a natural concept that possesses all or most of its characteristic features is called a **prototype.** The robin is a *prototypical* bird. The more prototypical of a concept something is, the more quickly you can decide whether it is an example of the concept. This is the reason people can answer just a little more quickly when asked "Is a robin a bird?" than when asked "Is a penguin a bird?"

Propositions

We often combine concepts in units known as propositions. A **proposition** is a mental representation that expresses a relationship between concepts. Propositions can be true or false. Suppose you hear someone say that your friend Heather broke up with her boyfriend, Jason. Your mental representation of this event will include a proposition that links your concepts of "Heather" and "Jason" in a particular way. This proposition could be diagrammed (using unscientific terms) as follows: Heather → dumped → Jason.

The diagram looks like a sentence, but it isn't one. Propositions can be expressed as sentences, but they are actually general ideas that can be conveyed in any number of specific ways. In this case, the words "Jason was dumped by Heather" and "Heather is not willing to date Jason anymore" would all express the same proposition. If you later discovered that it was Jason who caused the breakup, the diagram of your proposition about the event would change to reflect this new information, shown here as reversed arrows: Heather ← dumped ← Jason.

Schemas, Scripts, and Mental Models

Sets of propositions are often so closely associated that they form more complex mental representations called *schemas.* As mentioned in the chapters on sensation and perception, memory, and human development, **schemas** are generalizations that we develop about categories of objects, places, events, and people. Our schemas help us to understand the

prototype   A member of a natural concept that possesses all or most of its characteristic features.

propositions   Mental representations that express a relationship between concepts

schemas   Generalizations about categories of objects, places, events, and people.

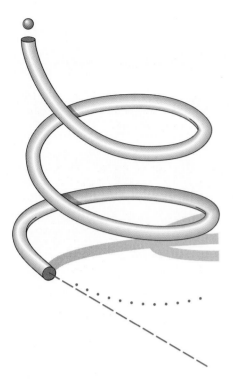

FIGURE 7.3

Applying a Mental Model

learn by doing Try to imagine the path that the ball will follow when it leaves the curved tube. In one study, most people drew the incorrect (curved) path indicated by the dotted line, rather than the correct (straight) path indicated by the dashed line (McCloskey, 1983). Their error was based on the construction of a faulty mental model of the behavior of physical objects.

scripts Mental representations of familiar sequences of activity.

mental models Sets of propositions that represent people's understanding of how things look and work.

images Mental representations of visual information.

cognitive map A mental model that represents familiar parts of the environment.

world. If you borrow a friend's car, your "car" schema will give you a good idea of where to put the ignition key, where the accelerator and brake are, and how to raise and lower the windows. Schemas also generate expectations about objects, places, events, and people—telling us that stereo systems have speakers, that picnics occur in the summer, that rock concerts are loud, and so on.

Scripts Schemas about familiar activities, such as going to a restaurant, are known as **scripts** (Anderson, 2000). Your "restaurant" script represents the sequence of events you can expect when you go out to eat. That script tells you what to do when you are in a restaurant and helps you to understand stories involving restaurants (Whitney, 2001). Scripts also shape your interpretation of events. For example, on your first day of college, you no doubt assumed that the person standing at the front of the class was a teacher, not a security guard or a janitor.

If our scripts are violated, however, it is easy to misinterpret events. In one case, a heart attack victim in London lay for nine hours in the hallway of an apartment building after an ambulance crew smelled alcohol on his breath and assumed he was "sleeping it off." The crew's script for what happens in the poorer sections of big cities told them that someone slumped in a hallway is drunk, not sick. Because script-violating events are unexpected, our reactions to them tend to be slower and less effective than are our reactions to expected events. Your "grocery shopping" script, for example, probably includes pushing a cart, putting items in it, going to the checkout stand, paying, and leaving. But suppose you are at the back of the store when a robber near the entrance fires a gun and shouts at the manager to open the safe. People sometimes ignore these script-violating events, interpreting gunshots as a car backfiring and shouted orders as "someone fooling around." Others simply "freeze," unsure of what to do or not realizing that they could call the police on their cell phones.

Mental Models The relationships among concepts can be organized not only as schemas and scripts but also as **mental models** (Johnson-Laird, 1983). For example, suppose someone tells you, "My living room has blue walls, a white ceiling, and an oval window across from the door." You will mentally represent this information as propositions about how the concepts "wall," "blue," "ceiling," "white," "door," "oval," and "window" are related. However, you will also combine these propositions to create in your mind a three-dimensional model of the room. As more information about the world becomes available, either from existing memories or from new information we receive, our mental models become more complete.

Accurate mental models are excellent guides for thinking about, and interacting with, many of the things we encounter every day (Ashcraft, 2006). If a mental model is incorrect, however, we are likely to make mistakes (see Figure 7.3). For example, people who hold an incorrect mental model of how physical illness is cured might stop taking their antibiotic medication when their symptoms begin to disappear, well before the bacteria causing those symptoms have been eliminated (Medin, Ross, & Markman, 2001). Others overdose on medication because, according to their faulty mental model, "if taking three pills a day is good, taking six would be even better."

Images and Cognitive Maps

Think about how your best friend would look in a clown suit. The "mental picture" you just got illustrates that thinking often involves the manipulation of **images**—which are mental representations of visual information. We can manipulate these images in a way that is similar to manipulating the objects themselves (Reed, 2000; see Figure 7.4). Our ability to think using images extends beyond the manipulation of stimuli such as those in Figure 7.4. We also create mental images that serve as mental models of descriptions we hear or read (Mazoyer et al., 2002). For example, you probably created an image a minute ago when you read about that blue-walled room.

The same thing happens when someone gives you directions to a new pizza place in town. In this case, you scan your **cognitive map**—a mental model of familiar

INGREDIENTS OF THOUGHT

Ingredient	Description	Examples
Concepts	Categories of objects, events, or ideas with common properties; basic building blocks of thought	"Square" (a formal concept); "game" (a natural concept)
Propositions	Mental representations that express relationships between concepts; can be true or false	Assertions such as "The cow jumped over the the moon."
Schemas	Sets of propositions that create generalizations and expectations about categories of objects, places, events, and people	A schema might suggest that all grandmothers are elderly, are gray haired, and bake a lot of cookies.
Scripts	Schemas about familiar activities and situations; guide behavior in those situations	You pay before eating in fast-food restaurants and after eating in fancier restaurants.
Mental models	A representation of how concepts relate to each other in the real world; can be correct or incorrect	Mistakenly assuming that airflow around an open car will send thrown objects upward, a driver tosses a lighted cigarette butt overhead, causing it to land in the back seat.
Images	Mental representations of visual information	Hearing a description of your blind date creates a mental picture of him or her.
Cognitive maps	Mental representations of familiar parts of the world	You can get to class by an alternate route even if your usual route is blocked by construction.

?
1. Thinking is the manipulation of _____.
2. Arguments over what is "fair" occur because "fairness" is a _____ concept.
3. Your _____ of "hotel room" would lead you to expect yours to include a bathroom.

(A)

(B)

Source: Shepard & Metzler (1971).

FIGURE 7.4

Manipulating Images

learn by doing Are these pairs of objects the same or different? To decide, you will have to rotate one member of each pair. Because manipulating mental images, like manipulating actual objects, takes some time, the speed of your decision will depend on how far you have to mentally rotate one object to line it up with the other for comparison. (The top pair matches; the bottom pair does not.) Brain imaging studies have confirmed that manipulating mental images activates some of the same visual and spatial areas of the brain that are active during comparable tasks with real objects (Mazoyer et al., 2002).

parts of your world—to find the location. In doing so, you use a mental process similar to the visual process of scanning a paper map (Anderson, 2000; Taylor & Tversky, 1992). Manipulating images on a different cognitive map would help you if a power failure left your home pitch dark. Even though you couldn't see a thing, you could still find a flashlight or candle, because your cognitive map would show the floor plan, furniture placement, door locations, and other physical features of your home. You would not have this mental map in a hotel room or an unfamiliar house; there, you would have to walk slowly, arms outstretched, to avoid wrong turns and painful collisions. In the chapter on learning we describe how experience shapes cognitive maps that help animals navigate mazes and people navigate shopping malls. ("In Review: Ingredients of Thought" summarizes the ways in which we mentally represent information.)

PITFALLS IN LOGICAL REASONING
"Elderly people cannot be astronauts; this is an elderly man; therefore, he cannot be an astronaut." The logic is correct, but because the first statement is wrong, so is the conclusion. In 1962, John Glenn became the first American astronaut to orbit the earth. Here he is in 1998, at the age of seventy-seven, just before he returned to space as a full-fledged member of the crew of the space shuttle *Discovery*.

Thinking Strategies

▶ **Do people always think logically?**

We have seen that our thinking capacity is based largely on our ability to manipulate mental representations—the ingredients of thought—much as a baker manipulates the ingredients of cookies. The baker's food-processing system combines and transforms these ingredients into a delicious treat. Our information-processing system combines, transforms, and elaborates mental representations in ways that allow us to engage in reasoning, problem solving, and decision making. Let's begin our discussion of these thinking strategies by considering **reasoning**: the process through which we generate and evaluate arguments, as well as reach conclusions about them.

Formal Reasoning

Astronomers tell us that the temperature at the core of the sun is about 27 million degrees Fahrenheit. How do they know this? They can't put a temperature probe inside the sun, so their estimate is based on *inferences* from other things that they know about the sun and about physical objects in general. For example, telescopic observations allowed astronomers to calculate the energy coming from one small part of the sun. They then used what geometry told them about the surface area of spheres to estimate the sun's total energy output. Further calculations told them how hot a body would have to be to generate that much energy.

In other words, astronomers' estimates of the sun's core temperature are based on **formal reasoning** (also called *logical reasoning*)—the process of following a set of rigorous steps for reaching valid, or correct, conclusions. Some of these steps included the application of specific mathematical formulas to existing data in order to generate new data. Such formulas are examples of **algorithms**—systematic methods that always reach a correct solution to a problem, if a correct solution exists.

The astronomers also followed the **rules of logic,** a set of statements that provide a formula for drawing valid conclusions about the world. For example, each step in the astronomers' thinking took the form of "if-then" propositions: If we know how much energy comes from one part of the sun's surface, and if we know how big the whole surface is, then we can calculate the total energy output. You use the same logical reasoning processes when you conclude, for example, that if your friend José is two years older than you are, then his twin brother, Juan, will be two years older, too. This kind of reasoning is called *deductive reasoning*, because it takes a general rule (e.g., twins are the same age) and applies it to deduce conclusions about specific cases (e.g., José and Juan).

Most of us try to use logical or deductive reasoning to reach valid conclusions and avoid invalid ones (Rips, 1994). However, even when our logic is perfect, we can make mistakes if we base our reasoning on false assumptions. Likewise, correct assumptions combined with faulty logic can lead to errors. Do you think the following example leads to a valid conclusion?

> Assumption 1: *All women want to be mothers.*
>
> Assumption 2: *Jill is a woman.*
>
> Conclusion: *Jill wants to be a mother.*

If you said that the first assumption is not necessarily correct, you're right. Now consider this example:

> Assumption 1: *All gun owners are people.*
>
> Assumption 2: *All criminals are people.*
>
> Conclusion: *All gun owners are criminals.*

Here, the assumptions are correct, but the logic is faulty. If "all A's are B" and "all C's are B," it does not follow that "all A's are C."

reasoning The process by which people generate and evaluate arguments and reach conclusions about them.

formal reasoning A set of rigorous procedures for reaching valid conclusions.

algorithms Systematic procedures that cannot fail to produce a correct solution to a problem.

rules of logic A set of statements that provide a formula for drawing valid conclusions.

Formal reasoning follows the rules of logic, but there are no foolproof rules for informal reasoning, as this fool demonstrates.

© Scott Adams/Dist. By United Feature Syndicate, Inc.

Psychologists have discovered that both kinds of pitfalls we just described can lead people to make errors in logical reasoning. This finding is one reason that misleading advertisements or speeches can still attract sales and votes (Cialdini, 2001).

Informal Reasoning

Using the rules of formal logic to deduce answers about specific cases is an important kind of reasoning, but it is not the only kind. A second kind, **informal reasoning,** comes into play when we are trying to assess the *believability* of a conclusion based on the evidence available to support it. Informal reasoning is also known as *inductive reasoning,* because its goal is to induce a general conclusion to appear on the basis of specific facts or examples. Psychologists use informal reasoning when they design experiments and other research methods whose results will provide evidence for (or against) their theories. Jurors use informal reasoning when weighing evidence for the guilt or innocence of a defendant. And air crash investigators use it in their efforts to discover and eliminate the causes of commercial aviation accidents.

Formal reasoning is guided by algorithms, or formulas, but there are no foolproof methods for informal reasoning. For instance, how many white swans would you have to see before concluding that all swans are white? Fifty? A hundred? A million? Formal logic would require that you observe every swan in existence. A more practical approach is to base your conclusion on the number of observations that some mental rule of thumb leads you to believe is "enough." In other words, you would take a mental "shortcut" to reach a conclusion that is probably, but not necessarily, correct (there are, in fact, black swans). Such mental shortcuts are called **heuristics** (pronounced "hyoor-IST-ix").

Heuristics can be helpful, but they can also bias our thinking and cause errors. Suppose your rule of thumb is to vote for all the candidates in a particular political party instead of researching the views of each individual. You might end up voting for someone with whom you strongly disagree on some issues. The extent to which heuristics are responsible for important errors in judgment and decision making is still being studied and debated by cognitive psychologists (e.g., Hilton, 2002; Medin & Bazerman, 1999). Nevertheless, Amos Tversky and Daniel Kahneman (1974; 1993) have described three potentially problematic heuristics that often affect people's judgments. These are the *anchoring heuristic,* the *representativeness heuristic,* and the *availability heuristic.*

The Anchoring Heuristic People use the **anchoring heuristic** when they estimate the probability of some event by adjusting their existing estimate rather than starting from scratch on the basis of new information (Rottenstreich & Tversky, 1997). This strategy sounds reasonable, but their existing estimate biases their final judgment. So even if new information suggests that their first estimate is way off, people may not adjust that estimate enough. It is as if they have dropped a "mental anchor" that keeps them from drifting too far from their original judgment. Suppose you think that the chance of being mugged in Los Angeles is 90 percent, but then you see evidence that the figure is closer to 1 percent. You might reduce your estimate, but only to 80 percent, so your new estimate is still quite inaccurate. The anchoring heuristic

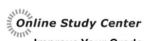
Online Study Center

Improve Your Grade
Tutorial: Common Heuristics

informal reasoning The process of evaluating a conclusion based on the evidence available to support it.

heuristics Mental shortcuts or rules of thumb.

anchoring heuristic A shortcut in the thought process that involves adding new information to existing information to reach a judgment.

presents a challenge for defense attorneys in U.S. criminal courts, because the prosecution presents its evidence first. Once this evidence has created the impression that a defendant is guilty, some jurors mentally anchor to that impression and may not be swayed much by defense evidence to the contrary (Hogarth & Einhorn, 1992). In a similar way, first impressions of people are not easily shifted by later evidence (see the chapter on social psychology).

The Representativeness Heuristic   People use the **representativeness heuristic** when they conclude that something belongs in a certain class based on how similar it is to other items in that class. For example, consider this personality sketch:

Tom W. is of high intelligence, although lacking in true creativity. He has a need for order and clarity and for neat and tidy systems in which every detail finds its appropriate place. His writing is rather dull and mechanical, occasionally enlivened by somewhat corny puns and by flashes of imagination of the sci-fi type. He has a strong drive for competence. He seems to have little feeling and little sympathy for other people and does not enjoy interacting with others. Self-centered, he nonetheless has a deep moral sense.

Do you think it is more likely that Tom is majoring in computer science or psychology? Research by Kahneman and Tversky (1973; Tversky & Kahneman, 1974) showed that most people would choose *computer science*. But this answer would probably be wrong. True, the description given is more similar to the prototypical computer science major than to the prototypical psychology major. However, there are many more psychology majors than computer science majors in the world. So there are probably more psychology majors than computer science majors who match this description. In fact, almost any personality sketch is more likely to describe a psychology major than a computer science major.

The representativeness heuristic affects many real-life judgments and decisions. For example, jury decisions depend partly on the degree to which a defendant's actions are representative of a particular crime category. So someone who abducts a child and asks for ransom is more likely to be convicted of kidnapping than someone who abducts an adult and demands no ransom (Smith, 1991). Both crimes constitute kidnapping, but the first is a more representative example.

The Availability Heuristic   People use the **availability heuristic** when they judge the likelihood of an event or the correctness of a hypothesis by how easy it is to think of that event or hypothesis (Tversky & Kahneman, 1974). In other words, they tend to choose the hypothesis or predict the event that is most mentally "available," much as they might select the box of cereal that happens to be at the front of the supermarket shelf. Although the availability heuristic tends to work well, it, too, can lead to biased judgments—especially when the mental availability of events doesn't match their actual frequency (Morewedge, Gilbert, & Wilson, 2005). For example, news reports about shark attacks and urban shootings lead many people to overestimate how often these memorable, but relatively rare, events actually occur. As a result, people may suffer undue anxiety over swimming in the ocean or being in certain cities (Bellaby, 2003). Similarly, many students stick with their first responses to multiple-choice test questions because it is especially easy to recall those galling occasions on which they changed a right answer to a wrong one. Research shows, though, that changing an answer in light of further reflection is more likely to be correct than incorrect (Kruger, Wirtz, & Miller, 2005).

The three heuristics we have presented represent only a few of the many mental shortcuts that people use more or less automatically in making judgments, and they describe only some of the biases and limitations that operate in human reasoning (Hogarth & Einhorn, 1992). Other biases and limitations are described in the following sections, as we consider two important goals of thinking: problem solving and decision making.

representativeness heuristic   A mental shortcut that involves judging whether something belongs in a given class on the basis of its similarity to other members of that class.

availability heuristic   A mental shortcut through which judgments are based on information that is most easily brought to mind.

Problem Solving

▶ **What's the best way to solve a problem?**

Suppose that you're lost, you don't have a map or a navigation system, and there's nobody around to ask for directions. You have a *problem.* The circle of thought suggests that the most efficient approach to solving it would be to first diagnose the problem in the elaboration stage, then formulate a plan for solving it, then execute the plan, and finally evaluate the results to determine whether the problem remains (Bransford & Stein, 1993). But people's problem-solving efforts are not always so systematic. This is one reason why medical tests are sometimes given unnecessarily, diseases are sometimes misdiagnosed, and auto parts are sometimes replaced when there is nothing wrong with them.

Strategies for Problem Solving

When you are trying to get from one place to another, the best path may not necessarily be a straight line. In fact, obstacles may require going in the opposite direction to get around them. So it is with problem solving. Sometimes, the best strategy does not involve mental steps aimed straight at your goal. For example, when a problem is especially difficult, it can sometimes be helpful to allow it to "incubate" by setting it aside for a while. A solution that once seemed out of reach may suddenly appear after you have been thinking about other things. The benefits of *incubation* probably arise from forgetting incorrect ideas that may have been blocking the path to a correct solution (Anderson, 2000). Other effective problem-solving strategies are more direct.

One of these strategies is called *means-end analysis.* It involves continuously asking where you are in relation to your final goal and then deciding on the means by which you can get one step closer to that goal (Newell & Simon, 1972). In other words, rather than trying to solve the problem all at once, you identify a subgoal that will take you toward a solution (this process is also referred to as *decomposition*). After reaching that subgoal, you identify another one that will get you even closer to the solution, and you continue this step-by-step process until the problem is solved. Some students apply this approach to the problem of writing a major term paper. The task might seem overwhelming at first, but their first subgoal is simply to write an outline of what they think the paper should cover. When the outline is complete, they decide whether a paper based on it will satisfy the assignment. If it will, the next subgoal might be to search the library and the Internet for information about each section. If they decide that this information is adequate, the next subgoal would be to write a rough draft of the introduction, and so on.

A second strategy in problem solving is to *work backward.* Many problems are like a tree. The trunk is the information you are given; the solution is a twig on one of

Simply knowing about problem-solving strategies, such as decomposition, is not enough. As described in the chapter on motivation and emotion, people must believe that the effort required is worth the rewards it can bring.

Calvin and Hobbes   by Bill Watterson

WORKING BACKWARD TO FORGE AHEAD   Whether you are organizing a family vacation or preparing to sail alone in an around-the-world race, as Ellen MacArthur did, working backward from the final goal through all the steps necessary to reach that goal is a helpful approach to solving complex problems.

the branches. If you work forward by taking the "givens" of the problem and trying to find the solution, it's easy to branch off in the wrong direction. Sometimes the more efficient approach is to start at the twig end and work backward (Galotti, 1999). Consider the problem of planning a climb to the summit of Mount Everest. The best strategy is to figure out, first, what equipment and supplies are needed at the highest camp on the night before the attempt to reach the summit, then how many people are needed to stock that camp the day before, then how many people are needed to supply those who must stock the camp, and so on until a plan for the entire expedition is established. People often overlook the working-backward strategy because it runs counter to the way they have learned to think. It is hard to imagine that the first step in solving a problem could be to assume that you have already solved it. Sadly, it was partly because of failure to apply this strategy that six climbers died on Everest in 1996 (Krakauer, 1997).

A third problem-solving strategy is trying to find *analogies,* or similarities, between today's problem and others you have encountered before. A supervisor may discover that a seemingly hopeless problem between co-workers can be resolved by the same compromise that worked during a recent family squabble. Of course, to take advantage of analogies, you must first recognize the similarities between current and previous problems. Then you will be in a position to recall the solution that worked before. Unfortunately, most people are surprisingly poor at seeing the similarities between new and old problems (Anderson, 2000). They tend to concentrate on the surface features that make problems appear different.

FOCUS ON RESEARCH

Problem-Solving Strategies in the Real World

The value of using analogies in problem solving was beautifully illustrated in relation to the Hubble Space Telescope. In 1990, this telescope was placed in an earth orbit to take detailed photographs of distant galaxies, but because its main mirror was not focusing light properly, the pictures were blurry. When NASA engineer James Crocker happened to notice the way a hotel room showerhead pivoted, it gave him the idea for a system of movable mirrors to correct for the flaw in the Hubble's mirror. Shuttle astronauts installed these mirrors in 1993, and the problem was solved (Stein, 1993).

How do people use the other problem-solving strategies we have described to solve other real-world problems? To explore this question, researchers have reconstructed problem-solving strategies associated with major inventions and scientific discoveries (Klahr & Simon, 1999; Weber, 1992).

■ What was the researcher's question?

On December 17, 1903, Wilbur and Orville Wright successfully flew the first heavier-than-air flying machine. Gary Bradshaw (1993a, 1993b) was interested in identifying the problem-solving strategies that led to this momentous event. He found that forty-nine individuals or teams had worked on the problem of heavier-than-air flight, but only the Wright brothers were successful. In fact, it took them only four years to develop the airplane, whereas others worked for decades without success. Bradshaw asked, How did the Wright brothers solve the problem of creating a heavier-than-air flying machine when so many others had failed?

■ How did the researcher answer the question?

Bradshaw compared the written records left by all the individuals and teams who had worked on an airplane design. Using this "comparative case study" method, he was able to see patterns in the ways they approached the flying machine problem.

■ What did the researcher find?

Bradshaw found several factors that might have contributed to the Wright brothers' success. First, as bachelors, they had a lot of spare time to work on their designs. Second, they owned a bicycle shop, so they were familiar with lightweight, but sturdy, structures. Third, they were brothers who had a good working relationship. And finally, as mechanics, they were good with their hands. Were any of these features directly responsible for their successful invention of the airplane?

Perhaps, but Bradshaw's use of the comparative case study method revealed that everyone else working on the problem of flight shared at least one of these features with the Wright brothers. For instance, an engineer named Octave Chanute was good with his hands and familiar with lightweight, sturdy structures. And two other pairs of brothers had worked together to try to invent a flying machine.

However, Bradshaw found one feature that was unique to the Wright brothers' approach. Of all the inventors working on the problem, only the Wrights spent considerable time and energy testing aircraft components before field-testing complete machines. This feature was important because even the best designs of the day flew for only a few seconds—far too briefly to reveal what was working and what was not. As a result, inventors had to guess about what to fix and often ended up with an "improved" model that was worse than the previous one.

■ What do the results mean?

Bradshaw's comparative case study method suggested that the problem-solving strategy of decomposition was the basis for the Wright brothers' success. By testing components, they were able to collect the information they needed to develop an efficient propeller, improve the shape of the wings for maximum lift, and refine other vital components of their aircraft.

■ What do we still need to know?

Decomposition is a strategy often seen in the laboratory, and as demonstrated by the case of the Wright brothers, it is a potentially important aspect of major inventions and discoveries beyond the laboratory. But is decomposition, or means-end analysis, used in other real-world settings as well? To find out, researchers will need to conduct additional studies of people's mental strategies as they attempt to solve problems ranging from how to install a new computer to how to efficiently search the Internet.

Obstacles to Problem Solving

The failure of the Wright brothers' competitors to use decomposition is just one example of the obstacles that face problem solvers every day. Difficulties frequently occur at the start, during the diagnosis stage, when a person forms and then tests hypotheses about a problem.

As a case in point, consider this true story: In September 1998, John Gatiss was in the kitchen of his rented house in Cheltenham, England, when he heard a faint "meowing" sound. Worried that a kitten had become trapped somewhere, he called for the fire brigade to rescue the animal. The sound seemed to be coming from the electric stove, so the rescuers dismantled it, disconnecting the power cord in the process. The sound stopped, but everyone assumed that wherever the kitten was, it was now too frightened to meow. The search was reluctantly abandoned, and the stove was reconnected; four days later, however, the meowing began anew. This time, Gatiss and his landlord called the Royal Society for the Prevention of Cruelty to Animals (RSPCA), whose inspectors heard the kitten in distress and asked the fire brigade

FIGURE **7.5**

The Jar Problem

learn by doing The task here is to come up with the number of quarts of water shown in the first column by using jars with the capacities shown in the next three columns. Each line represents a different problem, and you have an unlimited supply of water for each one. Try to solve all seven problems without looking at the answers in the text.

Quantity	Jar A	Jar B	Jar C
1. 21 quarts	8	35	3
2. 10 quarts	6	18	1
3. 19 quarts	5	32	4
4. 21 quarts	20	57	8
5. 18 quarts	8	40	7
6. 6 quarts	7	17	2
7. 15 quarts	12	33	3

to come back. They spent the next three days searching for the cat. First, they dismantled parts of the kitchen walls and ripped up the floorboards. Next, they called in plumbing and drainage specialists, who used cables tipped with fiber-optic cameras to search remote cavities where a kitten might hide. Rescuers then brought in a disaster search team, which tried to find the kitten with acoustic and ultrasonic equipment normally used to locate victims trapped under earthquake debris. Not a sound was heard. Increasingly concerned about how much longer the kitten could survive, the fire brigade tried to coax it from hiding with the finest-quality fish, but to no avail. Suddenly, there was a burst of "purring" that, to everyone's surprise (and the landlord's dismay), was traced by the ultrasonic equipment to the clock in the electric stove! Later, the landlord commented that everyone assumed Gatiss's original hypothesis was correct—that the "meowing" came from a cat trapped in the kitchen. "I just let them carry on. If there is an animal in there, you have to do what it takes. The funniest thing was that it seemed to reply when we called out to it" (*London Daily Telegraph*, 1998).

How could fifteen fire-rescue workers, three RSPCA inspectors, four drainage workers, and two acoustics experts waste eight days and cause nearly $2,000 in damage to a house in pursuit of a nonexistent kitten? The answer lies in the fact that they, like the rest of us, were prone to four main obstacles to efficient problem solving, described in the following sections.

Multiple Hypotheses   Often, we begin to solve a problem with only a hazy notion of which hypotheses to test. Suppose you heard a strange sound in your kitchen. It could be caused by several different things, but which hypotheses should you test, and in what order?

People have a difficult time working with more than two or three hypotheses at a time (Mehle, 1982). The limited capacity of short-term memory may be part of the reason (Halford et al., 2005). As discussed in the memory chapter, a person can hold only about seven chunks of information in short-term memory. Because a single hypothesis, let alone two or three, might include more than seven chunks, it may be difficult or impossible to keep them all in mind at once. Further, the availability and representativeness heuristics may lead people to choose the hypothesis that comes most easily to mind and seems most likely to fit the circumstances (Tversky & Kahneman, 1974). That hypothesis may be wrong, though, meaning that the correct hypothesis is never considered. Mr. Gatiss diagnosed what he heard as distressed meowing because it sounded more like a kitten than a clock and because it was easier to imagine an animal trapped behind the stove than a suddenly faulty clock inside it.

mental set   The tendency for old patterns of problem solving to persist.

functional fixedness   The tendency to think about familiar objects in familiar ways.

FIGURE **7.6**

The Nine-Dot Problem

learn **by doing**   The problem is to draw no more than four straight lines that run through all nine dots on the page without lifting your pencil from the paper. Figure 7.8 shows two ways of going beyond mental sets to solve this problem.

Mental Sets   Sometimes people are so blinded by one hypothesis or strategy that they stick with it even when better alternatives should be obvious. This is a clear case of the anchoring heuristic at work. Once Gatiss reported hearing a "trapped kitten," his description created an assumption that everyone else accepted and that no one challenged. Figure 7.5 shows a problem-solving situation in which such errors often appear.

learn **by doing**   The first problem in the figure is to come up with 21 quarts of liquid by using 3 jars that have capacities of 8, 35, and 3 quarts, respectively. Before you read any further, try to solve this problem and all the others listed in Figure 7.5.

How did you do? You probably figured out that the solution to the first problem is to fill Jar B to its capacity of 35 quarts, and then use its contents to fill Jar A to its capacity of 8 quarts, leaving 27 quarts in Jar B. Finally, you pour from Jar B to fill Jar C twice, leaving 21 quarts in Jar B [$27 - (2 \times 3) = 21$]. You probably found that a similar solution worked for each problem. In fact, by the time you reached Problem 7, you might have developed a **mental set,** a tendency for old patterns of problem solving to persist (Luchins, 1942; Sweller & Gee, 1978). If so, your mental set probably caused you to use the same old formula (B − A − 2C) even though a simpler one (A + C) would have worked just as well. Figures 7.6 and 7.8 show another way in which mental sets can restrict our perception of the possible solutions to a problem.

Another restriction on problem solving may come from experience with objects. Once people become familiar with using an object for one purpose, they may be blinded to other ways of using it. Long experience may produce **functional fixedness,** a tendency to use familiar objects in familiar, rather than creative, ways (German & Barrett, 2005). Figure 7.7 provides an example. An incubation strategy often helps to break mental sets.

Ignoring Negative Evidence   On September 26, 1983, Lt. Col. Stanislav Petrov was in command of a secret facility that analyzed information from Russian early-warning satellites. Suddenly, alarms went off as computers found evidence of five U.S. missiles being launched toward Russia. Tension between the two countries was high at the time, so, based on the availability heuristic, Petrov hypothesized that a nuclear attack was

FIGURE **7.7**

An Example of Functional Fixedness

learn **by doing**   Before reading further, look at this drawing and ask yourself how you would fasten together two strings that are hanging from the ceiling but are out of reach of each other. Several tools are available, yet most people don't think of attaching, say, a pair of pliers to one string and swinging it like a pendulum until it can be reached while holding the other string. This solution is not obvious because we tend to fixate on the function of pliers as a tool rather than as a weight. People are more likely to solve this problem if the tools are scattered around the room. When the pliers are in a toolbox, their function as a tool is emphasized, and functional fixedness becomes nearly impossible to break.

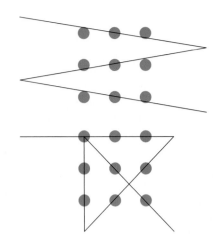

FIGURE **7.8**

Two Creative Solutions to the Nine-Dot Problem

Many people find problems like this diffi-cult because mental sets create artificial limits on the range of solutions. In this case, the mental sets involve the tendency to draw within the frame of the dots and to draw through the middle of each dot. As shown here, however, there are other pos-sibilities.

under way. He was about to alert his superiors to launch a counterattack on the United States when it occurred to him that if this were a real nuclear attack, it would involve many more than five missiles. Fortunately for everyone, he realized that the "attack" was a false alarm (Hoffman, 1999). As this near-disaster shows, the absence of symptoms or events can sometimes provide important evidence for or against a hypothesis. Compared with evidence that is present, however, symptoms or events that do not occur are less likely to be noticed (Hunt & Rouse, 1981). People have a difficult time using the absence of evidence to help eliminate hypotheses from consideration (Hyman, 2002). In the "trapped kitten" case, when the "meowing" stopped for several days after the stove was unplugged and reconnected, rescuers assumed that the animal was frightened into silence. They ignored the possibility that their hypothesis was incorrect in the first place.

Confirmation Bias   Anyone who has had a series of medical tests knows that diag-nosis is not a one-shot affair. Instead, physicians choose their first hypothesis on the basis of observed symptoms and then order tests or evaluate additional symptoms to confirm or eliminate that hypothesis (Trillin, 2001). This process can be distorted by a **confirmation bias:** Humans have a strong bias to confirm rather than reject the hypoth-esis they have chosen, even in the face of strong evidence against the hypothesis. In other words, people are quite willing to perceive and accept data that support their hypothesis, but they tend to ignore information that is inconsistent with it (Groopman, 2000). Con-firmation bias may be seen as a form of the anchoring heuristic. Once you've "anchored" to your first hypothesis, you may be unwilling to abandon it. The would-be rescuers of John Gatiss's "trapped kitten" were so intent on their efforts to pinpoint its location that they never stopped to question its existence. Similarly, as described in the chapter on social psychology, we tend to look for and pay extra attention to information that is consistent with our first impressions of other people. This tendency can create positive or negative bias in, say, a teacher's views of children's cognitive abilities or an interviewer's judgments of a job candidate's skills (Jussim & Eccles, 1992; Reich, 2004). (For a summary of prob-lem solving and its pitfalls, see "In Review: Solving Problems.")

Problem Solving by Computer

Researchers have created artificial limbs, retinas, cochleas, and even hearts to help dis-abled people move, see, hear, and live more normally. They are developing artificial brains, too, in the form of computer systems that not only see, hear, and manipulate objects but also reason and solve problems. These systems are the product of research in **artificial intelligence (AI),** a field that seeks to develop computers that imitate the processes of human perception and thought.

Symbolic Reasoning and Computer Logic   An IBM computer known as Deep Blue has won chess games against the world's best chess masters. This result is not sur-prising, because chess is a clearly defined, logical game at which computers can perform effectively. However, it is precisely their reliance on logic and formulas that accounts for the shortcomings of today's artificial intelligence systems. For example, these systems are successful only in narrowly defined fields, not in general problem solving. This limitation stems from the fact that AI systems are based on logical symbolic manipulations that depend on "if-then" rules. Unfortunately, it is difficult to tell a computer how to recog-nize the "if" condition in the real world. Consider this simple "if-then" rule: "If it is a clock, then set it." Humans recognize all kinds of clocks because they have the natural concept of "clock," but computers are still not very good at forming natural concepts. Doing so requires putting into the same category many examples that have very differ-ent physical features, from your bedside digital alarm clock to London's Big Ben.

Neural Network Models   Recognizing the problems posed by the need to teach computers to form natural concepts, many researchers in AI have moved toward a *connectionist,* or *neural network,* approach. This approach uses computers to simulate

confirmation bias   The tendency to pay more attention to evidence in support of one's hypothesis about a problem than to evidence that refutes that hypothesis.

artificial intelligence (AI)   The field that studies how to program computers to imitate the products of human perception, understanding, and thought.

in review

SOLVING PROBLEMS

Steps	Pitfalls	Remedies
Define the problem.	Inexperience: the tendency to see each problem as unique	Gain experience and practice in seeing the similarity between present problems and previous problems.
Form hypotheses about solutions.	Availability heuristic: the tendency to recall the hypothesis or solution that is most available to memory	Force yourself to write down, and carefully consider, many different hypotheses.
	Anchoring heuristic, or mental set: the tendency to anchor on the first solution or hypothesis, and not adjust your beliefs in light of new evidence or failures of the current approach	Break the mental set, stop, and try a fresh approach.
Test hypotheses.	The tendency to ignore negative evidence	In evaluating a hypothesis, consider the things you should see (but don't) if the hypothesis were true.
	Confirmation bias: the tendency to seek only evidence that confirms your hypothesis	Look for disconfirming evidence that, if found, would show your hypothesis to be false.

?

1. *People stranded without water could use their shoes to collect rain, but they may not do so because of an obstacle to problem solving called* _____ .
2. *Because of the* _____ *heuristic, once sellers set a value on their house, they may refuse to take much less for it.*
3. *If you tackle a massive problem one small step at a time, you are using an approach called* _____ .

the information processing taking place at many different, but interconnected, locations in the brain. Neural network models have helped researchers develop computers that are able to recognize voices, understand speech, read print, guide missiles, and perform many other complex tasks (Ashcraft, 2006). Some of these computer simulations are being used to improve speech recognition software and to test theories of how infants learn to recognize speech (e.g., Roy & Pentland, 2002; Sroka & Braida, 2005). Others have been used to improve on human decision making. One program, called PAPNET, can outperform human technicians at detecting abnormal cells in smears collected during cervical examinations (Kok & Boon, 1996). Indeed, computerized *expert systems* can now perform as well as humans, and sometimes better, at solving complex problems in medical diagnosis and business decision making (Khan et al., 2001; Workman, 2004).

Unfortunately, however, most computer models of neural networks still fall well short of the capacities of the human perceptual system. For example, computers are slow to learn how to classify visual patterns, which has led to disappointment in efforts to develop computerized face recognition systems capable of identifying terrorists and other criminals in public places (Feder, 2004). But even though neural networks are far from perfect "thinking machines," they are sure to play an important role in

ARTIFICIAL INTELLIGENCE Chess master Garry Kasparov had his hands full when he was challenged by "Deep Blue," a chess-playing computer that was programmed so well that it has won games against the world's best competitors, including Kasparov. Still, even the most sophisticated computers cannot perceive and think about the world in general anywhere near as well as humans can. Some observers believe that this situation will eventually change as progress in computer technology—and a deepening understanding of human cognitive processes—leads to dramatic breakthroughs in artificial intelligence.

psychologists' efforts to build ever more intelligent systems and to better understand the principles of human problem solving.

One approach to overcoming the limitations of both computers and humans is to have them work together in ways that create a better outcome than either could achieve alone. In medical diagnosis, for example, the human's role is to establish the presence and nature of a patient's symptoms. The computer then combines this information in a completely unbiased way to identify the most likely diagnosis (Swets, Dawes, & Monahan, 2000). This kind of human-machine teamwork can also help in the assessment of psychological problems (Bernstein, Kramer, & Phares, in press).

Creative Thinking

One of the greatest challenges in the development of artificial intelligence will be to program computers in a way that allows their thinking and problem solving to be as creative as that of humans. Consider the case that opened this chapter. It was Dr. Wallace's knowledge of the chemicals in paint—which has no obvious connection to human body chemistry—that led her to figure out what was causing Laura McBride's illness. Computers are still not nearly as good as humans are at recognizing that information from one area can be used to solve a problem in a seemingly unrelated area.

The ability to blend knowledge from many different domains is only one aspect of the creative thinking that humans display every day. People demonstrate **creativity** by producing original, but useful, solutions to all sorts of challenges (Simonton, 1999; Sternberg & Grigorenko, 2004a). Executives and homemakers, scientists and artists—all may be creative to varying degrees (Klahr & Simon, 1999). How do we know when people are thinking creatively? Psychologists have defined *creativity* as mental activity that can be inferred from performance on certain tests, as well as from the writings, computer programs, artwork, and other products resulting from the creative process (Sternberg & Dess, 2001). To measure creativity, some psychologists have generated tests of **divergent thinking**—the ability to think along many paths to generate multiple solutions to a problem (Diakidoy & Spanoudis, 2002). The Consequences Test is an example. It contains items such as "Imagine all of the things that might possibly happen if all national and local laws were suddenly abolished" (Guilford, 1959). Divergent-thinking tests are scored by counting the number of sensible responses that a person can give to each item and how many of these responses differ from those given by most people.

Only sensible responses to creativity tests are counted, because creativity involves divergent thinking that is appropriate for a given problem or situation. To be productive rather than just weird, a creative person must be firmly anchored in reality, understand society's needs, and learn from the experience and knowledge of others

creativity The capacity to produce original solutions or novel compositions.

divergent thinking The ability to generate many different solutions to a problem.

(Sternberg & Lubart, 1992). Theresa Amabile has identified three kinds of cognitive and personality characteristics necessary for creativity (Amabile, 1996; Amabile, Hennessey, & Grossman, 1986):

1. *Expertise* in the field of endeavor, which is directly tied to what a person has learned. For example, a painter or composer must know the paints, techniques, or instruments available.

2. A set of *creative skills,* including persistence at problem solving, capacity for divergent thinking, ability to break out of old problem-solving habits (mental sets), and willingness to take risks. Amabile believes that training can influence many of these skills, some of which are closely linked to the strategies for problem solving discussed earlier.

3. The *motivation* to pursue creative work for internal reasons, such as satisfaction, rather than for external reasons, such as prize money. In fact, Amabile and her colleagues found that external rewards can deter creativity. They asked groups of children and adults to create artistic products such as paintings or stories. Some were simply asked to work on the project. Others were informed that their project would be judged for its creativity and excellence and that rewards would be given or winners announced. Experts, who had no idea which products were created by which group, judged those from the "reward" group to be significantly less creative. Similar effects have been found in other studies (Deci, Koestner, & Ryan, 1999, 2001).

Is creativity inherited? To some extent, perhaps it is; but evidence suggests that the social, economic, and political environment in which a person grows and lives also influences creative behavior (Amabile, 2001; Nakamura & Csikszentmihalyi, 2001). Do you have to be smart to be creative? Creativity does appear to require a certain degree of intelligence, but you don't have to be a genius (Simonton, 1984, 2002; Sternberg, 2001). In fact, although correlations between scores on creativity tests and intelligence tests are almost always positive, they are relatively modest (Simonton, 1999). This finding is not surprising, because creativity involves divergent thinking about many solutions to a problem. As described later, high scores on most intelligence tests require **convergent thinking,** which uses logic and knowledge to narrow down the number of possible solutions to a problem. Research on creativity and its relationship to intelligence has intensified in recent years (Sternberg & Dess, 2001). One result of that research has been to define the combination of intelligence and creativity in the same person as *wisdom* (Sternberg, 2001; Sternberg & O'Hara, 1999).

Decision Making

▶ **How can I become a better decision maker?**

Paper or plastic? Do I watch TV or study for the test? Should I get out of this relationship? Is it time to start thinking about a nursing home for Mom? Life is full of decisions. Some are easy to make; others are painfully difficult and require considerable time, planning, and mental effort. Even carefully considered decisions can lead to undesirable outcomes, though, because the world is an uncertain place. Decisions made when the outcome is uncertain are called *risky decisions* or *decisions under uncertainty.* Chance aside, psychologists have discovered reasons why human decisions sometimes lead to unsatisfactory outcomes. Let's consider some of these reasons.

Evaluating Options

Suppose that you have to choose between (1) an academic major you love but that is unlikely to lead to steady employment or (2) a boring major that almost guarantees a high-paying job. The fact that each option has positive and negative features greatly

convergent thinking The ability to apply the rules of logic and what one knows about the world to narrow down the possible solutions to a problem.

Analyzing your choices and the possible outcomes of each takes some time and effort, but the results are usually worth it. Like Dilbert's boss, many people prefer to make decisions more impulsively, and although their decisions sometimes turn out well, they often don't. (Gladwell, 2005; Myers, 2004).

© Scott Adams/Dist. By United Feature Syndicate, Inc.

complicates decision making. Deciding which car to buy, which college to attend, or even how to spend the evening are all examples of choices that require you to weigh several options. Such choices are often based on the positive or negative value, or **utility,** that you, personally, place on each feature of each option. Listing the pros and cons of each option is a helpful way of keeping them all in mind as you think about your decisions. You also have to estimate the probabilities and risks associated with the possible outcomes of each choice. For example, you must consider how likely it is that job opportunities in your chosen major will have faded by the time you graduate. In studying risky decision making, psychologists begin with the assumption that the best decision maximizes *expected value*. The **expected value** of a decision is the average benefit you could expect to receive if the decision were repeated on several occasions.

Biases and Flaws in Decision Making

Most people think of themselves as logical and rational, but in making decisions about everything from giving up smoking to investing in the stock market, they don't always act in ways that maximize expected value (Arkes & Ayton, 1999; Farmer, Patelli, & Zovko, 2005; Shiller, 2001). Why not?

Gains, Losses, and Probabilities   For one thing, our pain over losing a certain amount is usually greater than the pleasure we feel after gaining the same amount. This phenomenon is called *loss aversion* (Dawes, 1998; Tversky & Kahneman, 1991). Because of loss aversion, you might go to more trouble to collect a $100 debt than to win a $100 prize. In addition, the value of a gain doesn't depend on the amount of the gain but on what you start with. Suppose you could have a $10 gift certificate from a restaurant, but you have to drive 10 miles to pick it up. This gain has the same monetary value as having an extra $10 added to your paycheck. However, most people tend to behave as if the difference between $0 and $10 is greater than the difference between, say, $300 and $310. So a person who won't drive across town after work to earn a $10 bonus on next week's paycheck might gladly make the same trip to pick up a $10 gift certificate. Understanding these biases and how they affect people's purchasing patterns and other economic decisions has proven so important that Daniel Kahneman received the 2002 Nobel Prize in economics for his research in this area.

People are also biased in how they think about probability. For example, we tend to overestimate the probability of rare events and to underestimate the probability of frequent ones (Kahneman & Tversky, 1984). This bias helps explain why people gamble in casinos and enter lotteries. The odds are against them, and the decision to gamble has a negative expected value, but because people overestimate the probability of winning, they associate a positive expected value with gambling. In one study, not even a course that highlighted gambling's mathematical disadvantages could change university students' gambling behavior (Williams & Connolly, 2006). The tendency to overestimate rare events is amplified by the availability heuristic: Vivid memories of rare gambling successes and the publicity given to lottery winners encourage people to recall gains rather than losses.

utility   In decision making, any subjective measure of value.

expected value   The total benefit to be expected of a decision if it were repeated on several occasions.

A HIGHLY UNLIKELY OUTCOME
Lottery agencies try to attract business by creating memorable images of big winners. They know that, like other decisions, people's ticket buying will be guided by the availability heuristic and the tendency to overestimate the probability of rare events. Did you ever notice that lottery ads and web sites never show or talk about the millions of players who win nothing?

Sometimes, our bias in estimating probability costs more than money. For example, many people underestimate the risk of infection by HIV/AIDS and continue to engage in unprotected sex (Specter, 2005). And after the September 11, 2001, terrorist attacks on the United States, the risks of flying seemed so high that many more people than usual decided to travel by car instead. Yet driving is more dangerous overall than flying, so the decision to drive actually increased these people's risk of death. With more cars on the road, there were 350 more traffic fatalities in the last three months of 2001 than there were during the same period in previous years (Gigerenzer, 2004). Similar bias in risk perception leads many people to buy a big, heavy sport utility vehicle that makes them feel safe, even though the chances of serious injury in an SUV are actually greater than in a minivan or family sedan (Gladwell, 2004).

Another bias in estimating probability is called the *gambler's fallacy:* People believe that the probability of future events in a random process will change depending on past events. This belief is false. For example, if you flip a coin and it comes up heads ten times in a row, what is the likelihood of tails on the next flip? Although some people think otherwise, the chance that it will come up tails on the eleventh flip is still 50 percent, just as it was for the first ten flips. Yet many gamblers continue feeding a slot machine that has not paid off much for hours, because they believe it is "due."

Poor decision making can also stem from the human tendency to be unrealistically confident in the accuracy of our predictions. Baruch Fischoff and Donald MacGregor (1982) devised a clever way to study this bias. People were asked whether they believed a certain event would occur and then were asked to say how confident they were about their prediction. For example, they were asked whether a particular sports team would win an upcoming game. After the events were over, the accuracy of the people's forecasts was compared with their level of confidence. Sure enough, their confidence in their predictions was consistently greater than their accuracy. This overconfidence operates even when people make predictions concerning the accuracy of their own memories (Bjork, 1998).

How Biased Are We? Almost everyone makes decisions that they later regret, but these outcomes may not be due entirely to biased thinking about gains, losses, and probabilities. Some decisions are not intended to maximize expected value but rather to satisfy other goals, such as minimizing expected loss, producing a quick and easy resolution, or preserving a moral principle (Arkes & Ayton, 1999; McCaffery & Baron, 2006; Zsambok & Klein, 1997). Often, decisions depend not just on how likely we are to gain or lose a particular amount of something but also on what that something is. A decision that could cost or save a human life may be made differently than one that could cost or gain a few dollars, even though the probabilities of each outcome are exactly the same in both cases.

Even the "goodness" or "badness" of decisions is often difficult to measure. Many decisions depend on personal values (utilities), which can vary from person to person and from culture to culture. People in individualist cultures, for example, may tend to assign high utilities to attributes that promote personal goals, whereas people in collectivist cultures might place greater value on attributes that bring group harmony and the approval of family and friends (Markus, Kitayama, & Heiman, 1996).

LINKAGES
Do groups solve problems more effectively than individuals? (a link to Social Psychology)

LINKAGES

Group Processes in Problem Solving and Decision Making

Problem solving and decision making often take place in groups. The factors that influence an individual's problem solving and decision making continue to operate when the individual is in a group, but group interactions also shape the outcome.

When groups are trying to make a decision, for example, they usually begin by considering the preferences or opinions stated by various members. Not all of these views have equal influence, though. Views that are shared by the greatest number of group members will have the greatest impact on the group's final decision (Tindale & Kameda, 2000). This means that extreme proposals or opinions will usually have less effect on group decisions than those that are more representative of the majority's views.

Nevertheless, group discussions sometimes result in decisions that are more extreme than the group members would make individually. This tendency toward extreme decisions is called *group polarization* (Rodrigo & Ato, 2002). Two mechanisms appear to underlie group polarization. First, most arguments presented during the discussion favor the majority view, and most criticisms are directed at the minority view. In fact, confirmation bias leads group members to seek additional information that supports the majority position (Schulz-Hardt et al., 2000). In this atmosphere, those who favor the majority view find it reasonable to adopt an even stronger version of it (Stasser, 1991). Second, once some group members begin to agree that a particular decision is desirable, other members may try to associate themselves with it, perhaps by suggesting an even more extreme version (Kaplan & Miller, 1987).

Are people better at problem solving and decision making when they work in groups or on their own? This is one of the questions about human thinking that is studied by social psychologists. In a typical experiment, a group of people is asked to solve a problem like the one in Figure 7.6 or to decide the guilt or innocence of the defendant in a fictional court case. Each person is asked to work alone and then to join with the others to try to agree on a decision. These studies have found that when problems have solutions that can be easily demonstrated to everyone, groups will usually outperform individuals at solving them (Laughlin, 1999). When problems have less obvious solutions, groups may be somewhat better at solving them than their average member, but usually no better than their most talented member (Hackman, 1998). And because of phenomena such as *social loafing* and *groupthink* (discussed in the social psychology chapter), people working in a group are often less productive than people working alone (Williams & Sommer, 1997).

Other research suggests that a critical element in successful group problem solving is the sharing of individual members' unique information and expertise (e.g., Stasser, Stewart, & Wittenbaum, 1995). For example, when asked to diagnose an illness, groups of physicians were much more accurate when they pooled their knowledge (Larson et al., 1998). However, *brainstorming*, a popular strategy that supposedly encourages group members to generate new and innovative solutions to a problem, may actually

One disadvantage of brainstorming sessions is that running comments and bizarre ideas from some group members can interfere with the creative process in others (Nijstad, Stroebe, & Lodewijkx, 2003).

© Scott Adams/Dist. By United Feature Syndicate, Inc.

produce fewer ideas than are generated by individuals working alone (Kerr & Tindale, 2004). This result may occur because comments from other group members may interfere with some members' ability to think clearly and creatively. Further, some participants in a brainstorming session may be reluctant to offer an idea, even a good one, for fear it will be rejected or ridiculed by the group (Kerr & Tindale, 2004). To prevent these problems, some brainstorming groups meet electronically, using a special e-mail system that allows each member to offer suggestions without being identified or interrupted, yet still giving everyone access to the ideas of all the other members. Because this arrangement allows people to think more clearly and express themselves without fear, electronic brainstorming groups may actually outperform groups that meet face to face (Nijstad, Stroebe, & Lodewijkx, 2003).

As they work to solve a problem, group members experience their own thoughts as concepts, propositions, images, or other mental representations. How does each member share these private events to help the group perform its task? The answer lies in the use of language.

Language

▶ **How do babies learn to talk?**

Many pet owners swear that their animals "talk" to them. Maybe Harry barks in a particular way when he wants to go outside, or Cleo meows to be fed. But are Harry's barks and Cleo's meows really language? Probably not. These pets are communicating something to their owners, but the noises they make lack many of the components of human language (Rendall, Cheney, & Seyfarth, 2000; Slocombe & Zuberbühler, 2005). So although Harry may let out three high-pitched yelps when he wants to go outside, he may bark in exactly the same way when his owner asks him whether he agrees with the local leash laws. For this reason, we wouldn't call his barking "language." Humans, however, can use language to express everything from simple requests to abstract principles. They can create stories that pass on cultural information and traditions from one generation to the next. Our language abilities are usually well integrated with our memory, thinking, and other cognitive abilities. As a result, we can speak about our thoughts and memories and think about what people tell us. It is only when strokes or other forms of damage interfere with the brain's language areas that we are reminded that language is a very special kind of cognitive ability (Kohnert, 2004).

A **language** has two basic elements: symbols, such as words, and a set of rules, called **grammar,** for combining those symbols. With their knowledge of approximately 50,000 to 100,000 words (Miller, 1991), humans can create and understand an infinite number of sentences. Yet all of the sentences ever spoken are created from just a few dozen categories of sounds. The power of language comes from the way these rather unimpressive raw materials are organized according to certain rules.

language Symbols, and a set of rules for combining them, used as a means of communicating.

grammar A set of rules for combining the symbols, such as words, used in a given language.

GETTING READY TO TALK Long before they say their first words, babies are getting ready to talk. Experiments in Patricia Kuhl's laboratory show that even six-month-olds tend to look longer at faces whose lip movements match the sounds of spoken words. This tendency reflects babies' abilities to focus on, recognize, and discriminate the sounds of speech, especially in their native language. These abilities are crucial to the development of language (Mayberry, Lock, & Kazmi, 2002).

Learning to Speak: Stages of Language Development

Children the world over develop language with impressive speed; the average six-year-old already has a vocabulary of about 13,000 words (Pinker, 1994). But acquiring language involves more than just learning vocabulary. We also have to learn how words are combined and how to produce and understand sentences. Psychologists who study the development of language have found that the process begins in the earliest days of a child's life and follows some predictable steps (Saffran, Senghas, & Trueswell, 2001).

The First Year In their first year, infants become more and more attuned to the sounds that will be important in acquiring their native language. In fact, this early experience with language appears to be vital. Without it, language development can be impaired (Mayberry & Lock, 2003). The first year is also the time when babies begin to produce **babblings,** which are patterns of meaningless sounds that first resemble speech. These alternating consonant and vowel sounds (such as "bababa," "dadada," and "mamimamima") appear at about four months of age, once the infant has developed the necessary coordination of the tongue and mouth. Though meaningless to the baby, babblings are a delight to parents. Infants everywhere begin with the same set of babbling sounds, but at about nine months of age, they begin to produce only the sounds that occur in the language they hear the most. At about the same time, their babbling becomes more complex and begins to sound like "sentences" in the babies' native language (Goldstein, King, & West, 2003). Infants who hear English begin to shorten some of their vocalizations to "da," "duh," and "ma." They use these sounds to convey joy, anger, interest, and other messages in specific contexts and with obvious purpose (Blake & de Boysson-Bardies, 1992).

By ten to twelve months of age, babies can understand several words—certainly more words than they can say (Fenson et al., 1994). Proper names and object words—such as *mama, daddy, cookie, doggy,* and *car*—are among the earliest words they understand. These are also the first words children are likely to say when, at around twelve months of age, they begin to talk (some talk a little earlier and some a little later). Nouns for simple object categories (*dog, flower*) are acquired before more general nouns (*animal, plant*) or more specific names (*collie, rose*; Rosch et al., 1976).

Of course, these early words do not sound exactly like adult language. English-speaking babies usually reduce them to a shorter, easier form, like "duh" for *duck* or "mih" for *milk*. Children make themselves understood, however, by using gestures, voice

babblings Repetitions of syllables; the first sounds infants make that resemble speech.

tones, facial expressions, and endless repetitions. Once they have a word for an object, they may "overextend" it to cover more ground. So they might use *doggy* to refer to cats, bears, and horses; they might use *fly* for all insects and perhaps for other small things such as raisins and M&Ms (Clark, 1983, 1993). Children make these "errors" because their vocabularies are limited, not because they fail to notice the difference between dogs and cats or because they want to eat a fly (Fremgen & Fay, 1980; Rescorla, 1981). Being around people who don't understand these overextensions encourages children to learn and use more precise words (Markman, 1994). During this period, children build up their vocabularies one word at a time. They also use their limited vocabulary one word at a time; they cannot yet put words together into sentences.

The Second Year   The **one-word stage** of speech lasts for about six months. Then, sometime around eighteen months of age, children's vocabularies expand dramatically (Gleitman & Landau, 1994). They may learn several new words each day, and by the age of two, most youngsters can use fifty to well over one hundred words. They also start using two-word combinations to form efficient little sentences. These two-word sentences are called *telegraphic* because, like telegrams or text messages, they are brief and to the point, leaving out anything that is not absolutely essential. So if she wants her mother to give her a book, a twenty-month-old might first say, "Give book," then "Mommy give," and if that does not work, "Mommy book." The child also uses rising tones to indicate a question ("Go out?") and emphasizes certain words to indicate location ("Play *park*") or new information ("*Big* car").

Three-word sentences come next in the development of language. They are still telegraphic, but more nearly complete: "Mommy give book." The child's sentences now begin to have the subject-verb-object form typical of adult sentences. Other words and word endings begin appearing, too. In English, these include the suffix *-ing*, the prepositions *in* and *on*, the plural *-s*, and irregular past tenses ("It broke," "I ate"; Brown, 1973; Dale, 1976). Children learn to use the suffix *-ed* for the past tense ("I walked"), but they often overapply this rule to irregular verbs that they had previously used correctly, saying, for example, "It breaked," "It broked," or "I eated" (Marcus, 1996). Children also expand their sentences with adjectives, although at first they make some mistakes. For example, they are likely to use both *less* and *more* to mean "more" (Smith & Sera, 1992).

The Third Year and Beyond   By age three or so, children begin to use auxiliary verbs ("Adam is going") and to ask questions using *what, where, who,* and *why.* They begin to put together clauses to form complex sentences ("Here's the ball I was looking for"). By age five, children have acquired most of the grammatical rules of their native language.

How Is Language Acquired?

Despite all that has been learned about the steps children follow in acquiring language, mystery and debate still surround the question of just how they do it. We know that children pick up the specific content of language from the speech they hear around them: English children learn English; French children learn French. But how do children come to follow the rules of grammar?

Conditioning, Imitation, and Rules   Perhaps children learn grammar because their parents reward them for using it. This idea sounds reasonable, but observational research suggests that positive reinforcement (which we describe in the learning chapter) is not the main character in the story of language acquisition. Parents are usually more concerned about what is said than about its grammatical form (Hirsch-Pasek, Treiman, & Schneiderman, 1984). So when the little boy with chocolate crumbs on his face says, "I not eat cookie," his mother is more likely to respond, "Yes, you did" than to ask the child to say, "I did not eat the cookie" and then praise him for his grammatical correctness.

LINKAGES
How do we learn to speak?
(a link to Human Development)

one-word stage   A stage of language development during which children tend to use one word at a time.

Learning through modeling, or imitation, appears to be more influential. Children learn grammar most rapidly when adults demonstrate the correct form in the course of conversation. For example:

Child: Mommy fix.

Mother: Okay, Mommy will fix the truck.

Child: It breaked.

Mother: Yes, it broke.

But if children learn grammar by imitation, why do children who at one time said "I went" later say "I goed"? Adults don't use this form of speech, so neither imitation nor reward can account for its sudden appearance. It appears more likely that children analyze for themselves the underlying patterns in the language they hear around them and then learn the rules governing those patterns (Bloom, 1995).

Biological Bases for Language Acquisition   The ease with which children the world over discover these patterns and develop language has led some to argue that language acquisition is at least partly innate, or automatic. Noam Chomsky (1965) believes that we are born with a built-in *universal grammar,* a mechanism that allows us to identify the basic dimensions of language (Baker, 2002; Chomsky, 1986; Nowak, Komarova, & Niyogi, 2001). According to Chomsky, a child's universal grammar might tell the child that word order is important to the meaning of a sentence. In English, for example, word order tells us who is doing what to whom (the sentences "Heather dumped Jason" and "Jason dumped Heather" contain the same words, but they have different meanings). In Chomsky's view, then, we don't entirely learn language—we develop it as genetic predispositions interact with experience (Senghas & Coppola, 2001). So a child's innate assumption that word order is important to grammar would change if the child heard language in which word order did not have much effect on the meaning of a sentence.

Other theorists disagree with Chomsky, arguing that the development of language reflects the development of more general cognitive skills, not just innate, language-specific mechanisms (e.g., Bates, 1993). Still, there is other evidence to support the existence of biological factors in language acquisition. For example, the unique properties of the human mouth and throat, the language-related brain regions described in the chapter on biology and behavior, and genetic research all suggest that humans are

LEARNING A SECOND LANGUAGE
As these international students are discovering, people who learn a second language as adults do so more slowly, and with less proficiency, than younger people (Johnson & Newport, 1989; Patkowski, 1994) and virtually never learn to speak it without an accent (Lenneberg, 1967). Still, the window of opportunity for learning a second language remains open long after the end of the critical period in childhood during which first-language acquisition must occur (Hakuta, Bialystok, & Wiley, 2003).

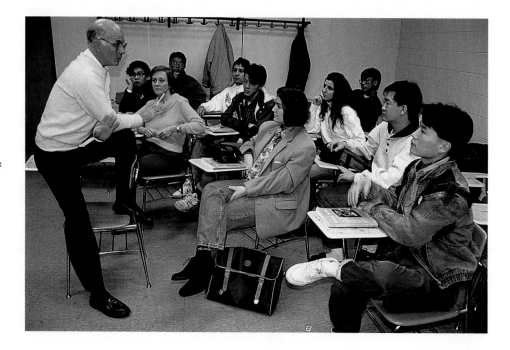

ANIMAL LANGUAGE? Several chimpanzees and gorillas have been taught to use American Sign Language (ASL). Here, Koko the gorilla signs "smoke" as Penny Patterson holds Smoky the cat. Are nonhuman primates' remarkable accomplishments with ASL the same as human language abilities? Probably not (Fitch & Hauser, 2004; Povinelli & Bering, 2002; Rendall, Cheney, & Seyfarth, 2000; Zuberbühler, 2005), but research suggests that with the right tools and training, these animals can master language-like skills.

innately "prewired," or biologically programmed, for language (Buxhoeveden et al., 2001; Lai et al., 2001). In fact, researchers are even beginning to uncover genetic mechanisms behind some speech and language disorders (e.g., Fisher, 2005). In addition, there appears to be a period in childhood during which we can learn language more easily than at any other time (Ridley, 2000). The existence of this *critical period* is supported by evidence from cases in which unfortunate children spent their early years in isolation from human contact and the sound of adult language. Even after years of therapy and language training, these individuals are not able to combine ideas into sentences (Rymer, 1993). Such cases suggest that in order to acquire the complex features of language, we must be exposed to speech before a certain age.

Bilingualism Does trying to learn two languages at once, even before the critical period for language learning is over, impair the learning of either? Research suggests just the opposite. Like some children in any situation, the early language of children from a bilingual environment may be confused or delayed, but they eventually show enhanced performance in each language (de Houwer, 1995). There is also some evidence that *balanced bilinguals*—those who have roughly equal mastery of two languages in childhood—are superior to other children in cognitive flexibility, concept formation, and creativity. It is as if each language offers a slightly different perspective on thinking, and this dual perspective makes the brain more flexible (Hong et al., 2000).

Testing Intelligence

▶ How is intelligence measured?

People who are good at using and understanding language and skilled at thinking, problem solving, and decision making are likely to be seen as *intelligent*. But intelligence is not limited to these abilities alone. Over the years, psychologists studying people in various cultures around the world have proposed that the concept of "intelligence" is a broad umbrella that can also include attributes such as efficiently storing and retrieving memories; effectively focusing—or dividing—attention; rapidly processing information;

quickly learning new things; profiting from experience; adapting well to changing environments; having a good sense of direction; appreciating patterns in nature; being good at music, dance, or athletics; showing eye-hand coordination; understanding oneself and others; and displaying polished social skills (Berry & Bennett, 1992; Eysenck, 1986; Gardner, 1999; Hunt, 1983; Meyer & Salovey, 1997; Sternberg, 1996; Sternberg, Lautrey, & Lubart, 2003).

So what, exactly, is intelligence? Psychologists have never been able to agree on an answer to this question, but many of them accept a working definition proposed by Robert Sternberg (1985, 1997b). According to Sternberg, **intelligence** can be described in terms of three characteristics: (1) being able to learn, remember, reason, and perform other *information-processing skills,* (2) using those skills to *solve problems,* and (3) being able to *alter or adapt to* new or changing environments.

Standard tests of intelligence measure some of these characteristics, but they don't address all of them. Accordingly, some psychologists argue that these tools are not able to capture all that should be tested if we want to get a complete picture of someone's intelligence in its broadest sense. Others say that broadening the definition of intelligence too much will make it meaningless. Still others suggest dropping the term altogether in favor of the more descriptive and less emotionally charged concept of *cognitive ability.* To better understand the controversy, let's take a look at how standard intelligence tests were created, what they are designed to measure, and how well they do their job. Later, we will consider some alternative intelligence tests that have been proposed by those who find fault with traditional ones.

A Brief History of Intelligence Tests

The story of modern intelligence tests begins in 1904, when the French government appointed psychologist Alfred Binet (pronounced "bih-NAY") to a committee whose job was to identify, study, and provide special educational programs for children who were not doing well in school. As part of his work, Binet developed a set of mental tasks that provided the model for today's intelligence tests. Binet assumed that reasoning, thinking, and problem solving all depend on intelligence, so he chose tasks that would highlight individual differences in children's ability to do these things (Binet & Simon, 1905). Children taking Binet's test were asked to unwrap a piece of candy, repeat numbers or sentences from memory, identify familiar objects, and the like (Rogers, 1995).

Binet also assumed that children's cognitive abilities increase with age. So after trying out test items on children of various ages, he categorized each item according to how old a child had to be to get the item right. For example, a "six-year-old item" was one that a large majority of six-year-olds could answer correctly but that five-year-olds could not. In other words, Binet's test contained a set of *age-graded* items (Binet & Simon, 1908). It measured a child's "mental level," later called *mental age,* by determining the age level of the most advanced items that the child could consistently answer correctly. Children whose mental age equaled their actual age, or *chronological age,* were considered to be of "regular" intelligence (Schultz & Schultz, 2000).

At about the time Binet published his test, Lewis Terman at Stanford University began to develop an English-language version that has come to be known as the **Stanford-Binet** test (Terman, 1906, 1916). Table 7.1 gives examples of the kinds of items included on the test. Terman added items to measure the intelligence of adults and revised the scoring scale. Mental age was divided by chronological age, and the result was multiplied by 100. This figure was called the *intelligence quotient,* or *IQ.* So a child whose mental age and chronological age were equal would have an IQ of 100, which is considered "average" intelligence. A ten-year-old who scored at the mental age of twelve would have an IQ of $12/10 \times 100 = 120$. From this method of scoring came the term **IQ test,** a name now widely used for any test designed to measure intelligence on an objective, standardized scale.

The method used to score the Stanford-Binet allowed testers to rank people based on their IQs. This goal was important to Terman and others who promoted the test in

Online Study Center

Improve Your Grade
Tutorial: Determining IQ—Stanford-Binet and IQ Tests

intelligence   The possession of knowledge, the ability to efficiently use that knowledge to reason about the world, and the ability to use that reasoning adaptively in different environments.

Stanford-Binet   A test for determining a person's intelligence quotient, or IQ.

IQ test   A test designed to measure intelligence on an objective, standardized scale.

TABLE **7.1**

The Stanford-Binet

TABLE **7.1**

The Stanford-Binet

Here are samples of the types of items included on Lewis Terman's original Stanford-Binet test. As in Alfred Binet's test, an age level was assigned to each item.

Age	Task
2	Place geometric shapes into corresponding openings; identify body parts; stack blocks; identify common objects.
4	Name objects from memory; complete analogies (e.g., fire is hot; ice is _____); identify objects of similar shape; answer simple questions (e.g., "Why do we have schools?").
6	Define simple words: explain differences (e.g., between a fish and a horse); identify missing parts of a picture; count out objects.
8	Answer questions about a simple story; identify absurdities (e.g., in statements like "John had to walk on crutches because he hurt his arm"); explain similarities and differences among objects; tell how to handle certain situations (e.g., finding a stray puppy).
10	Define more difficult words; give explanations (e.g., about why people should be quiet in a library); list as many words as possible; repeat 6-digit numbers.
12	Identify more difficult verbal and pictured absurdities; repeat 5-digit numbers in reverse order; define abstract words (e.g., *sorrow*); fill in a missing word in a sentence.
14	Solve reasoning problems; identify relationships among points of the compass; find similarities in apparently opposite concepts (e.g., "high" and "low"); predict the number of holes that will appear when folded paper is cut and then opened.
Adult	Supply several missing words for incomplete sentences; repeat 6-digit numbers in reverse order; create a sentence using several unrelated words (e.g., *forest, businesslike,* and *dismayed*); describe similarities between concepts (e.g., "teaching" and "business").

the United States. Terman believed that IQ tests could pinpoint who did and who did not have a suitable "amount" of intelligence. These beliefs were controversial and, in some instances, led to prejudice and discrimination as enthusiasm for testing outpaced understanding of what was being tested. For example, in 1917, as the United States moved closer to entering World War I, a team of psychologists was asked to develop group-administered tests that could identify the cognitive ability of army recruits and then guide their assignment to appropriate jobs. Soldiers who could speak and read English were tested on mental tasks that required verbal skills, such as defining words, whereas the rest were asked to visualize objects and perform other nonverbal tasks. Unfortunately, the verbal tests contained items that were unfamiliar to many recruits. Further, tests were often given under stressful conditions in crowded rooms where instructions were not always audible or, for non-English speakers, understandable. As a result, almost half of the soldiers tested appeared to have a mental age of thirteen or lower (Yerkes, 1921), leading testers to draw seriously incorrect conclusions about their lack of intelligence—especially in the cases of those who did not speak English (Brigham, 1923). Later tests developed by David Wechsler (1939, 1949) were designed to correct some of the weaknesses of earlier ones.

Intelligence Tests Today

Today's editions of the Wechsler tests and the Stanford-Binet are among the most widely used of all individually administered intelligence tests. The Wechsler Adult Intelligence Scale (WAIS-III) includes fourteen subtests. Seven of them require verbal skills

Online Study Center

Improve Your Grade
Tutorial: Wechsler Performance and Verbal Scale Simulation

FIGURE **7.9**

Performance Items Similar to Those on the Wechsler Intelligence Scale for Children (WISC-IV)

The WISC-IV includes ten standard and five supplemental subtests, grouped into four clusters. The *perceptual reasoning* cluster includes tasks, such as those shown here, that involve assembling blocks, solving mazes, and reasoning about pictures. Tests in the *verbal comprehension* cluster require defining words, explaining the meaning of sentences, and identifying similarities between words. Tests in the *working memory* cluster ask children to recall a series of numbers, put a random sequence of numbers into logical order, and the like. The *processing speed* cluster tests children's ability to search for symbols on a page and to decode simple coded messages.

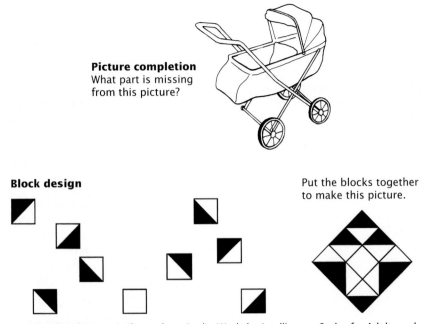

Picture completion
What part is missing from this picture?

Block design

Put the blocks together to make this picture.

Source: Simulated items similar to those in the Wechsler Intelligence Scales for Adults and Children. Copyright © 1949, 1955, 1974, 1981, 1991, and 1997 by Harcourt Assessment, Inc. Reproduced with permission. All rights reserved.

"Wechsler" is a trademark of Harcourt Assessment, Inc. registered in the United States of America and/or other jurisdictions.

verbal scale Subtests in Wechsler tests that measure verbal skills as part of a measure of overall intelligence.

performance scale Subtests in Wechsler tests that measure spatial ability and the ability to manipulate materials as part of a measure of overall intelligence.

IQ score A number that reflects the degree to which a person's score on an intelligence test differs from the average score of others in his or her age group.

test A systematic observation of behavior in a standard situation, described by a numerical scale or category.

norms Descriptions of the frequency of particular scores on a test.

reliability The degree to which test results or other research evidence occurs repeatedly.

and make up the **verbal scale** of the test. These subtests include such items as remembering a series of digits, solving arithmetic problems, defining vocabulary words, and understanding and answering general-knowledge questions. The other seven subtests have little or no verbal content and make up the **performance scale.** They include tasks that require understanding the relationships between objects and manipulation of various materials—tasks such as assembling blocks, solving mazes, arranging pictures to form a story, and completing unfinished pictures. Testers using the WAIS-III can compute a verbal IQ, a performance IQ, and an overall IQ, as well as "index" scores that reflect a person's mental processing speed, memory ability, perceptual skills, and understanding of verbal information. The latest edition of the Wechsler Intelligence Scale for Children (WISC-IV; Wechsler, 2003) yields four similar index scores, along with an overall IQ score (see Figure 7.9).

The latest edition of the Stanford-Binet (SB5) also contains subtests (Roid, 2003). However, the SB5 subtests are designed to measure five different abilities: *fluid reasoning* (e.g., completing verbal analogies, such as "hot is to cold as _____ is to low"), *knowledge* (e.g., defining words, detecting errors in pictures), *quantitative reasoning* (e.g., solving math problems), *visual-spatial processing* (e.g., assembling a puzzle), and working memory (e.g., repeating a sentence). Each of these five abilities is measured by one verbal and one nonverbal subtest, so it is possible to calculate a score for each of the five abilities, a total score on all the verbal tests, a total score on all the nonverbal tests, and an overall score for all ten tests combined.

Calculating IQ

IQ scores are no longer calculated by dividing mental age by chronological age. If you take an intelligence test today, the points you earn for each correct subtest or age-level answer are added up. Your total score is then compared with the scores earned by other people. The average score obtained by people at each age level is given the IQ value of 100. Other scores are given IQ values that reflect how much each score differs from the average. So if you do better on the test than the average person in your age group, you

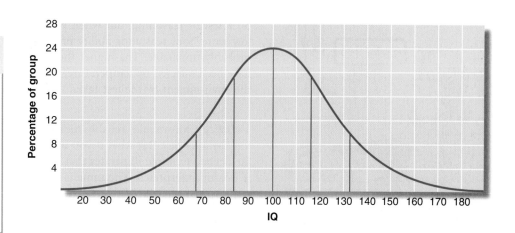

FIGURE 7.10

The Distribution of IQ Scores in the Population

When the IQ scores in the general population are plotted on a graph, a bell-shaped curve appears. The average IQ score of any given age group is 100. Half of the scores are higher than 100, and half are below 100. Approximately 68 percent of the IQ scores of any age group fall between 84 and 116; about 16 percent fall below 84, and about 16 percent fall above 116.

will receive an IQ score above 100. How far above depends on how much better than average you do. Similarly, a person scoring below the age-group average will have an IQ below 100. This procedure is based on a well-supported assumption about many characteristics: Most people's scores fall in the middle of the range of possible scores, creating a bell-shaped curve that approximates the normal distribution (see Figure 7.10). Half of those tested score below 100, the average for any given age group. The other half score above 100. In short, your **IQ score** reflects your relative standing within a population of your age.

Evaluating Intelligence Tests

▶ **How good are IQ tests?**

We have said that no intelligence test can accurately measure all aspects of what various people think of as intelligence. So what does your IQ score say about you? Can it predict your performance in school or on the job? Is it a fair summary of your cognitive abilities? To scientifically answer questions such as these, we have to measure the quality of the tests that yield IQ scores, using the same criteria that apply to tests of personality, language skills, driving, or anything else. Let's review these criteria and then see how they are used to evaluate IQ tests.

A **test** is a systematic procedure for observing behavior in a standard situation and describing it with the help of a numerical scale or system of categories (Cronbach, 1990). Tests are *standardized*, meaning that they present the same tasks, under similar conditions, to each person who takes them. Standardization helps ensure that test results will not be significantly affected by factors such as who gives and scores the test. Because the biases of those giving and scoring a test do not influence the results, a standardized test is said to be *objective*. Test scores can be used to calculate **norms**, which are descriptions of the frequency of particular scores. Norms tell us, for example, what percentage of high school students obtained each possible score on a college entrance exam. They also allow us to say whether a particular IQ score or entrance-exam score is above or below the average score. Any test, including IQ tests, should fairly and accurately measure a person's performance. The two most important things to know about when determining the value of a test are its reliability and validity.

LINKAGES
How do you know if a personality test, or any other kind of test, is any good?
(a link to Personality)

Reliability If you stepped on a scale, checked your weight, stepped off, stepped back on, and found that your weight had increased by twenty pounds, you would know it was time to buy a new scale. A good scale, like a good test, must have **reliability;** in other words, the results must be repeatable or stable. The test must measure the same thing in the same way every time it is used. Let's suppose you receive a very high score

If only measuring intelligence were this easy!

on a test of reasoning, but when you take the same test the next day, you get a very low score. Your reasoning ability probably didn't change much overnight, so the test is probably unreliable. The higher the reliability of a test, the less likely it is that scores have been affected by temperature, hunger, or other random and irrelevant changes in the environment or the test taker.

Validity   Most scales reliably measure your weight, giving you about the same reading day after day. But what if you use these readings as a measure of your height? This far-fetched example illustrates that a reliable scale reading can be incorrect, or *invalid*, if it is misinterpreted. The same is true of tests. Even the most reliable test might not provide a correct, or valid, measure of intelligence, of anxiety, of typing skill, or of anything else if those are not the things the test really measures. In other words, we can't say that a test itself is "valid" or "invalid." Instead, **validity** refers to the degree to which test scores are interpreted appropriately and used properly (American Educational Research Association, American Psychological Association, & National Council on Measurement in Education, 1999; Messick, 1989). As in our scale example, a test can be valid for one purpose but invalid for another.

Researchers evaluate the reliability of a test by obtaining two sets of scores on the same test from the same people. They then calculate a correlation coefficient between the two sets of scores (see the introductory chapter). When the correlation is high and positive (usually above +.80), the test is considered reliable. Evaluating a test's validity usually means calculating a correlation coefficient between test scores and something else. What that "something else" is depends on what the test is designed to measure. Suppose, for example, you wanted to know if a creativity test is valid for identifying creative people. You could do so by computing the correlation between people's scores on the creativity test and experts' judgments about the quality of those same people's artistic creations. If the correlation is high, the test has high validity as a measure of creativity.

The Reliability and Validity of Intelligence Tests

The reliability of intelligence tests is generally evaluated on the basis of their stability, or consistency. The validity of intelligence tests is usually based on their accuracy in guiding statements and predictions about people's cognitive abilities.

Reliability   IQ scores obtained before the age of seven are only moderately correlated with scores on intelligence tests given later. There are two key reasons. First, the test items used with very young children are different from those used with older children. Second, cognitive abilities change rapidly in the early years (see the chapter on human development). Still, during the school years, IQ scores tend to remain stable (Allen & Thorndike, 1995; Mayer & Sutton, 1996). For teenagers and adults, the reliability of intelligence tests is high, generally between +.85 and +.95.

Of course, a person's score may vary from one occasion to another if there are significant changes in motivation, anxiety, health, or other factors. Overall, though, modern IQ tests usually provide exceptionally consistent results, especially compared with most other kinds of mental tests.

Validity   If everyone agreed on exactly what intelligence is (having a good memory, for example), we could evaluate the validity of IQ tests simply by correlating people's IQ scores with their performance on various tasks (in this case, memory tasks). IQ tests whose scores correlated most highly with scores on memory tests would be the most valid measures of intelligence. But because psychologists do not fully agree on a single definition of intelligence, they don't have a single standard against which to compare intelligence tests. Therefore, they cannot say whether these tests are valid measures of intelligence. Because intelligence is always displayed in the course of specific tasks and specific social situations, psychologists can only assess the validity of intelligence tests for specific purposes.

validity   The degree to which test scores are interpreted appropriately and used properly.

The results of their research suggest that intelligence test scores are most valid for assessing aspects of intelligence that are related to schoolwork, such as abstract reasoning and understanding verbal material. Their validity—as measured by correlating IQ scores with high school grades—is reasonably good, about +.50 (Brody & Erlichman, 1998). Scores on tests that focus more specifically on reasoning skills show even higher correlations with school performance (Kuncel, Hezlett, & Ones, 2004; Lohman & Hagen, 2001).

There is also evidence that employees who score high on verbal and mathematical reasoning tests tend to perform better at work than those who earn lower scores (Borman, Hanson, & Hedge, 1997; Johnson & Neal, 1998; Pulakos et al., 2002), especially if their jobs require complex reasoning and judgment skills (Gottfredson, 1997). Later we describe a study that kept track of people for seventy years and found that those who had high IQ scores as children tended to be well above average in terms of academic and financial success in adulthood (Cronbach, 1996; Oden, 1968; Terman & Oden, 1947). IQ scores also appear to be highly correlated with performance on routine tasks such as reading medicine labels and using a telephone book (Gottfredson, 1997, 2004).

So, by the standard measures for judging psychological tests, scores on intelligence tests have good reliability and good validity for predicting success in school and in many life situations and occupations. However, an IQ score is not a perfect measure of how "smart" a person is. Because intelligence tests do not measure the full array of cognitive abilities, a particular test score tells only part of the story, and even that part may be distorted. Many factors other than cognitive ability, including reactions to the testing situation, can influence test performance. For example, children who are suspicious of strangers and adults who fear making mistakes may become anxious and fail even to try answering certain questions, thus artificially lowering their IQ scores (Fagan, 2000). Claude Steele and his colleagues have suggested that some people's test-related anxiety stems from a phenomenon known as *stereotype threat* (Steele & Aronson, 2000). According to Steele, concern over negative stereotypes about the cognitive abilities of the group to which they belong can impair the performance of some women—and some members of ethnic minorities—such that the test scores they earn underestimate those abilities (Blascovich et al., 2001; Cadinu et al., 2005; Inzlicht & Ben-Zeev, 2000). The extent to which stereotype threat actually affects performance on cognitive abilities tests is uncertain, however (Cullen, Hardison, & Sackett, 2004; Sackett, Hardison, & Cullen, 2004).

IQ Scores as a Measure of Inherited Ability

Alfred Binet believed that intelligence could be improved with training and practice at mental tasks. Lewis Terman saw it as an inherited characteristic. Both were partly right. Years of research have led psychologists to conclude that intelligence is *developed ability*. This means that intelligence is influenced partly by genetics but also by educational, cultural, and other environmental factors and experiences that shape the very knowledge, reasoning, and other skills that intelligence tests measure (Atran, Medin, & Ross, 2005; Garlick, 2003; Plomin & Spinath, 2004).

To explore the influence of genetics on individual differences in IQ scores, psychologists have compared the correlations in scores between people who share varying degrees of similarity in genetic makeup and environment. For example, they have examined the IQ scores of identical twins (pairs with exactly the same genes) who were separated when very young and raised in different environments. They have also examined the scores of identical twins raised together. (Research designs used in these *behavioral genetics* studies are described in the introductory chapter.)

These studies find, first, that genetic factors are strongly related to IQ scores. When identical twins who were separated at birth and adopted by different families are tested many years later, the correlation between their scores is usually high and positive, at least +.60 (Bouchard, 1999). If one twin receives a high IQ score, the other probably will, too; if one is low, the other is likely to be low as well. However, studies of IQ correlations also highlight the importance of the environment (Scarr, 1998). Consider any

FIGURE **7.11**

Correlations of IQ Scores

The correlation in IQ between pairs increases with increasing similarity in heredity or environment.

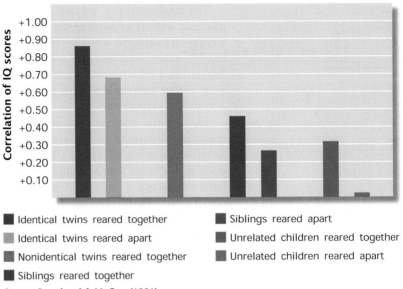

◼ Identical twins reared together   ◼ Siblings reared apart

◼ Identical twins reared apart   ◼ Unrelated children reared together

◼ Nonidentical twins reared together ◼ Unrelated children reared apart

◼ Siblings reared together

Source: Bouchard & McGue (1981).

two people—twins, nontwin siblings, or unrelated children—brought up together in a foster home. No matter what the degree of genetic similarity in these pairs, the correlation between their IQ scores is higher if they share the same home than if they are raised in different homes, as Figure 7.11 shows (Scarr & Carter-Saltzman, 1982).

The role of environmental influences is also seen in studies that compare children's IQ scores before and after environmental changes such as adoption (van IJzendoom & Juffer, 2005). Generally, when children from relatively impoverished backgrounds were adopted into homes offering a more enriching intellectual environment—including interesting materials and experiences, as well as a supportive, responsive adult—they showed modest increases in their IQ scores (Weinberg, Scarr, & Waldman, 1992).

A study of French children who were adopted soon after birth demonstrates the importance of both genetic and environmental influences. These children were tested after years of living in their adopted homes. Those whose biological parents were from higher socioeconomic groups (where higher IQs are more common) had higher IQ scores than those whose biological parents came from lower socioeconomic groups, regardless of the socioeconomic status of the adopted homes (Capron & Duyme, 1989, 1996). These findings are supported by data from the Colorado Adoption Project (Cardon & Fulker, 1993; Cardon et al., 1992), and they suggest that a genetic component of the children's cognitive abilities continued to exert an influence in the adoptive environment. At the same time, when children from low socioeconomic backgrounds were adopted by parents who provided academically enriched environments, their IQ scores rose by twelve to fifteen points (Capron & Duyme, 1989).

Programs designed to enhance young children's school readiness and academic ability have also been associated with improved scores on tests of intelligence (Neisser et al., 1996; Ripple et al., 1999). These early-intervention programs may be partly responsible for the steady increase in average IQ scores seen throughout the world over the past six decades (Flynn, 1999; Neisser, 1998).

Some researchers have concluded that the influences of genetic and environmental factors on intelligence appear to be about equal. Others see a somewhat larger role for genetic factors (Herrnstein & Murray, 1994; Loehlin, 1989; Petrill et al., 1998; Plomin, 1994). One research team has even suggested that specific genes are associated with extremely high IQs (Chorney et al., 1998). Still, it is important to understand that any estimates of the relative contributions of heredity and environment apply only to groups, not to individuals. It would be inaccurate to say that 50 percent of your IQ score is inherited and 50 percent learned. It is more accurate to say that about half of the variability in the IQ scores of a group of people can be

FIGURE **7.12**

A Representation of Ethnic Group Differences in IQ Scores

The average IQ score of Asian Americans is about four to six points higher than the average score of European Americans, who average twelve to fifteen points higher than African Americans and Hispanic Americans. Notice, however, that the variation *within* each of these groups is much greater than the variation *among* them.

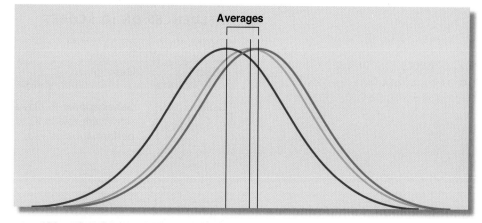

— African Americans and Hispanic Americans
— European Americans
— Asian Americans

attributed to genetic influences and about half can be attributed to environmental influences. (As discussed in the appendix, *variability* is the degree to which scores spread out around an average score.)

Group Differences in IQ Scores

Much of the controversy over the roles played by genes and the environment in intelligence has been sparked by efforts to explain differences in the average IQ scores earned by particular groups of people. For example, the average scores of Asian Americans are typically the highest among various ethnic groups, followed, in order, by European Americans, Hispanic Americans, and African Americans (e.g., Fagan, 2000; Herrnstein & Murray, 1994; Lynn, 1996; Taylor & Richards, 1991). Further, the average IQ scores of people from high-income areas in the United States and elsewhere are consistently higher than those of people from low-income communities with the same ethnic makeup (Jordan, Huttenlocher, & Levine, 1992; McLoyd, 1998; Rowe, Jacobson, & Van den Oord, 1999).

To understand these differences and where they come from, we must remember two things. First, group scores are just that; they do not describe individuals. So even though the average IQ score of Asian Americans is higher than the average IQ score of European Americans, there will still be many European Americans who score well above the Asian American average and large numbers of Asian Americans who score below the European American average (see Figure 7.12). Second, inherited characteristics are not necessarily fixed. As already mentioned, living in a favorable environment can improve a child's intellectual performance somewhat (Humphreys, 1984). There is also evidence that living in an impoverished environment can impair the development of cognitive skills (Turkheimer et al., 2003).

Socioeconomic Differences Why is there a relationship between IQ scores and family income? Four factors seem to account for the correlation. First, parents' jobs and status depend on characteristics related to their own intelligence. And this intelligence is partly determined by a genetic component that, in turn, contributes to their children's cognitive ability level. Second, parents' income affects their children's environment in ways that can increase or decrease the children's IQ scores (Bacharach & Baumeister, 1998). Third, motivational differences may play a role. Parents in upper- and middle-income families tend to provide more financial and psychological support for their children's motivation to succeed and excel in academic endeavors (Atkinson & Raynor, 1974; Erikson et al., 2005; Nelson-LeGall & Resnick, 1998). As a result, children from middle- and upper-income families may exert more effort in testing situations

LINKAGES
How does motivation affect IQ scores? (a link to Motivation and Emotion)

INFLUENCES ON IQ SCORES

Source of Effect	Description	Examples of Evidence for Effect
Genetics	Genes appear to play a significant role in IQ test performance.	The IQ scores of siblings who share no common environment are positively correlated. There is a greater correlation between scores of identical twins than between those of nonidentical twins.
Environment	Environmental conditions interact with genetic inheritance. Nutrition, medical care, sensory and intellectual stimulation, interpersonal relations, and influences on motivation are all significant features of the environment.	IQ scores have risen among children who are adopted into homes that offer a stimulating, enriching environment. Correlations between IQs of twins reared together are higher than for those reared apart.

1. Intelligence is influenced by both _____ and _____.
2. Children living in poverty tend to have _____ IQ scores than those in middle-income families.
3. IQ scores of children whose parents encourage learning tend to be _____ than those of children whose parents do not.

and therefore obtain higher scores (Bradley-Johnson, Graham, & Johnson, 1986; Zigler & Seitz, 1982). Fourth, because colleges, universities, and businesses usually select people with higher scores on various cognitive ability tests, those with higher IQs—who tend to do better on such tests—may have greater opportunities to earn more money (Sackett et al., 2001).

Ethnic Differences　Some have argued that the average differences in IQ among various ethnic groups in the United States and other developed countries are due mostly to heredity (Rowe, 2005; Rushton & Jensen, 2005). However, the existence of hereditary differences among individuals *within* groups does not indicate whether differences *between* groups result from similar genetic causes (Lewontin, 1976). Notice again in Figure 7.12 that variation within ethnic groups is much greater than variation among the mean scores of those groups (Zuckerman, 1990).

We must also take into account the large differences among the environments in which the average African American, Hispanic American, and European American child grows up. To take only the most blatant evidence, the latest U.S. Census Bureau figures show 24.4 percent of African American families and 22.5 percent of Hispanic American families living below the poverty level, compared with 11.8 percent of Asian American families and 8.2 percent of European American families (U.S. Census Bureau, 2004). Compared with European Americans, African American children are more likely to have parents with poor educational backgrounds, as well as inferior nutrition, health care, and schools (Evans, 2004; Wilson, 1997). All of these conditions are likely to pull down scores on intelligence tests (Brooks-Gunn, Klebanov, & Duncan, 1996). Cultural factors may also contribute to differences among the average scores of various ethnic groups. For example, those differing averages may partly reflect differences in the degree to which parents in each group tend to encourage their children's academic achievement (Steinberg, Dornbusch, & Brown, 1992).

In short, it appears that some important nongenetic factors serve to decrease the average scores of African American and Hispanic American children. Whatever heredity might contribute to children's performance, it may be possible for them to improve, given the removal of negative environmental conditions. ("In Review: Influences on IQ Scores" summarizes our discussion of environmental and genetic factors affecting performance on intelligence tests.)

Are Intelligence Tests Unfairly Biased Against Certain Groups?

Summarizing a person's cognitive abilities with an IQ score runs the risk of oversimplifying reality and making errors, but intelligence tests can also prevent errors. If boredom makes a child appear mentally slow, or even retarded, a properly conducted test is likely to reveal the child's potential. And, as Binet had hoped, intelligence tests have been enormously helpful in identifying children who need special educational attention. These tests can minimize the chances of assigning children to special classes that they don't need or to advanced work that they cannot yet handle.

Still, there is great concern over the fact that members of ethnic minorities and other environmentally disadvantaged groups have not had an equal chance to develop the knowledge and skills that are required to achieve high IQ scores.

■ What am I being asked to believe or accept?

Some critics claim that, indeed, standard intelligence tests are not fair. They argue that a disproportionately large number of people in some ethnic minority groups score low on intelligence tests for reasons that are unrelated to cognitive ability, job potential, or other criteria that the tests are supposed to predict (Helms, 1992, 1997; Kwate, 2001; Neisser et al., 1996). They say that using intelligence tests to make decisions about people—such as assigning them to particular jobs or special classes—causes members of certain groups to be unfairly deprived of equal employment or educational opportunities.

■ Is there evidence available to support the claim?

Research reveals several possible sources of bias in intelligence test scores. First, noncognitive factors can influence a person's performance on IQ tests and may put certain groups at a disadvantage. We have seen, for example, that children from some ethnic and socioeconomic groups may be less motivated than other children to perform well on standardized tests. They may also be less comfortable in the testing situation and less likely to trust adult testers (Steele, 1997). So the differences in test scores may partly reflect motivational or emotional differences among various groups, not intellectual ones.

Second, many intelligence test items are still drawn from the vocabulary and experiences of the dominant middle-class culture in the United States. As a result, these tests often measure achievement in acquiring knowledge valued by that culture. Not all cultures value the same things, however (Nisbett, 2003; Serpell, 1994; Sternberg & Grigorenko, 2004b). For example, a study of Cree Indians in northern Canada revealed that words and phrases meaning "competent" included *good sense of direction*. At the "incompetent" end of the scale was the phrase *lives like a white person* (Berry & Bennett, 1992). A European American might not perform well on a Cree intelligence test based on these criteria. In fact, as illustrated in Figure 7.13, poor performance on a culture-specific test is probably due more to unfamiliarity with culture-based concepts than to lack of cognitive ability.

Third, some tests may reward those who interpret questions as expected by the test designer. Conventional intelligence tests have clearly defined "right" and "wrong" answers. Yet a person may interpret test questions in a manner that is "intelligent" or

FIGURE **7.13**

An Intelligence Test?

learn by doing How did you do on this "intelligence test"? If, like most people, you are unfamiliar with the material being tested by these rather obscure questions, your score was probably low. Would it be fair to say, then, that you are not very intelligent?

Take a minute to answer each of these questions, and check your answers against the key below.

1. What fictional detective was created by Leslie Charteris?
2. What planet travels around the sun every 248 years?
3. What vegetable yields the most pounds of produce per acre?
4. What was the infamous pseudonym of broadcaster Iva Toguri d'Aquino?
5. What kind of animal is Dr. Dolittle's Pushmi-Pullyu?

Answers: (1) Simon Templar (2) Pluto (3) Cabbage (4) Tokyo Rose (5) A two-headed llama

"correct," but that produces a "wrong" answer. For example, when one child was asked, "In what way are a pen and a pencil alike?" he replied, "They can both poke holes in paper." The fact that you don't give the answer that the test designer was looking for does not mean that you *can't*. When Liberian rice farmers were asked to sort objects, they tended to put a knife in the same group as vegetables. This was the clever way to do it, they said, because the knife is used to cut vegetables. When asked to sort the objects as a "stupid" person would, the farmers grouped the cutting tools together, the vegetables together, and so on, as most North Americans would (Segall et al., 1990).

■ Can that evidence be interpreted another way?

The same evidence might be interpreted as showing that although traditional intelligence tests do not provide a pure measure of inherited cognitive ability, they do provide a fair test of whether a person is likely to succeed in school or in certain jobs. When some people have had more opportunity than others to develop their abilities, the difference will be reflected in higher IQ scores. From this point of view, intelligence tests are fair measures of the cognitive abilities people have developed while living in a society that, unfortunately, contains some unfair elements. In other words, the tests may be accurately detecting knowledge and skills that are not represented equally in all groups. That doesn't mean that the tests discriminate *unfairly* among those groups.

To some observers, concern over cultural bias in intelligence tests stems from a tendency to think of IQ scores as measures of innate ability. These psychologists suggest instead that intelligence tests are measuring ability that is developed and expressed in a cultural context—much as athletes develop the physical skills needed to play certain sports (Lohman, 2004). Eliminating language and other cultural elements from intelligence tests, they say, would eliminate a vital part of what the term *intelligence* means in any culture (Sternberg, 2004). This may be the reason that "culture-fair" tests do not predict academic achievement as well as conventional intelligence tests do (Aiken, 1994; Lohman, 2005). Perhaps familiarity with the culture reflected in intelligence tests is just as important for success at school or work in that culture as it is for success on the tests themselves. After all, the ranking among groups on measures of academic achievement is similar to the ranking for average IQ scores (Sue & Okazaki, 1990).

■ What evidence would help to evaluate the alternatives?

If the problem of test bias is really a reflection of differences between various groups' opportunities to develop their cognitive skills, it will be important to learn more about how to reduce those differences. Making "unfair" cultures fairer by enhancing the skill development opportunities of traditionally disadvantaged groups should lead to smaller differences between groups on tests of cognitive ability (Martinez, 2000). It will also be important to find better ways to encourage members of disadvantaged groups to take advantage of those opportunities (Sowell, 2005).

At the same time, alternative tests of cognitive ability must also be explored, particularly those that include assessment of problem-solving skills and other abilities not measured by most intelligence tests (e.g., Sternberg & Kaufman, 1998). If new tests show smaller between-group differences than traditional tests but have equal or better predictive validity, many of the issues discussed in this section will have been resolved. So far, efforts in this direction have not been successful.

■ What conclusions are most reasonable?

The effort to reduce unfair cultural biases in tests is well founded, but "culture-fair" tests will be of little benefit if they fail to predict academic or occupational success as well as conventional tests do (Anastasi & Urbina, 1997; Sternberg, 1985). Whether one considers this situation good or bad, fair or unfair, it is important for people to have the information and skills that are valued by the culture in which they live and work. So using tests that are designed to predict success in such areas seems reasonable as long as the tests accurately measure a person's skills and access to culturally valued information.

In other words, there is probably no value-free, or experience-free, or culture-free way to measure the concept known as intelligence. The reason is that the concept is defined in terms of the behaviors that a culture values and that are developed through experience in that culture (Sternberg, 1985, 2004; Laboratory of Comparative Human Cognition, 1982). This conclusion has led some researchers to worry less about how cultural influences might "contaminate" tests of cognitive abilities and to focus instead on how to help people develop the abilities that are required for success in school and society. As mentioned earlier, if more attention were focused on combating poverty, poor schools, inadequate nutrition, lack of health care, and other conditions that result in lower average IQ scores and reduced economic opportunities for certain groups of people, many of the reasons for concern about test bias might be eliminated.

Diversity in Intelligence

▶ Is there more than one type of intelligence?

IQ scores can tell us some things—and predict some things—about people, but we have seen that they don't tell the whole story of intelligence. Let's see how diverse intelligence can be by looking at some nontraditional aspects of intelligence and at some people whose intellectual abilities are unusually high or low.

Practical and Creative Intelligence

According to Robert Sternberg (1988b, 1999), a complete theory of intelligence must deal with three different types of intelligence: analytic, creative, and practical. *Analytic intelligence*, the kind that is measured by traditional intelligence tests, would help you solve a physics problem; *creative intelligence* is what you would use to compose music; and you would draw on *practical intelligence* to figure out what to do if you were stranded on a lonely road during a blizzard. Sternberg's *triarchic theory* of intelligence deals with all three types of intelligence.

Sternberg recognizes the importance of analytic intelligence for success in academics and other areas, but he argues that universities and companies should not select people solely on the basis of tests of this kind of intelligence (Sternberg, 1996; Sternberg & Williams, 1997). Why? Because the tasks posed by tests of analytic intelligence are often of little interest to the people taking them and typically have little relationship to these people's daily experiences. In contrast, the practical problems people face every day are generally of personal interest and are related to more common life experiences (Sternberg et al., 1995). It is no wonder, then, that children who do poorly in school and on intelligence tests may also show high degrees of practical intelligence. Some Brazilian street children, for example, can do the math required for their street businesses despite having failed mathematics in school (Carraher, Carraher, & Schliemann, 1985).

Sternberg and his colleagues have developed new intelligence tests designed to assess analytic, practical, and creative intelligence (see Figure 7.14). They offer evidence that scores on these tests can predict success at some jobs at least as well as standard intelligence tests (Leonhardt, 2000; Sternberg & Kaufman, 1998; Sternberg et al., 1995), but other researchers have questioned this interpretation (Brody, 2003).

Multiple Intelligences

Many people with only average scores on intelligence tests have exceptional ability in specific areas. Even those with very low IQ scores have been known to show incredible ability in narrowly defined skills (Miller, 1999). One such child, whose IQ was only 50, could instantly and correctly state the day of the week for any date between 1880 and 1950 (Scheerer, Rothmann, & Goldstein, 1945). He could also play melodies on the piano by ear and sing Italian operatic pieces he had heard. He could spell—forward or backward—any word spoken to him and could memorize long speeches. However, he had no understanding of what he was doing.

Cases such as this are part of the evidence that led Howard Gardner to suggest that everyone possesses a number of intellectual potentials, or "intelligences," each of which involves a somewhat different set of skills (Gardner, 1993, 2002). Biology, he says, provides raw capacities for each of these *multiple intelligences*; cultures provide symbolic systems—such as language—that enable people to use their raw capacities. According to Gardner, the various intelligences normally interact, but they can function with some independence, and individuals may develop certain intelligences further than others.

The specific intelligences that Gardner (1999) proposes are (1) *linguistic* intelligence (reflected in good vocabulary and reading comprehension), (2) *logical-mathematical* intelligence (as indicated by skill at arithmetic and certain kinds of reasoning), (3) *spatial* intelligence (seen in understanding relationships between objects), (4) *musical* intelligence (as in abilities involving rhythm, tempo, and sound identification), (5) *body-kinesthetic* intelligence (reflected in skill at dancing, athletics, and eye-hand coordination), (6) *intrapersonal* intelligence (displayed by self-understanding), (7) *interpersonal* intelligence (seen in the ability to understand and interact with others), and (8) *naturalistic* intelligence (the ability to see patterns in nature). Other researchers have suggested that people also possess *emotional* intelligence, which involves the capacity to perceive, use, understand, and manage their emotions (Meyer & Salovey, 1997; Salovey & Grewal, 2005).

Gardner says that standard IQ tests sample only the first three of these diverse intelligences, mainly because they are the forms of intelligence most valued in school. To measure specific intelligences that are not tapped by standard IQ tests, Gardner suggests collecting samples of children's writing, assessing their ability to appreciate or produce music, and obtaining teacher reports of their strengths and weaknesses in athletic and social skills.

Gardner's view of intelligence is appealing, partly because it allows virtually everyone to be highly intelligent in at least one way. However, his critics argue that including athletic or musical skill as part of intelligence dilutes the usefulness of the concept, especially as it is applied to school and in many kinds of jobs. Nevertheless, Gardner and his colleagues continue working on new ways of assessing "multiple intelligences." The value of these methods will be determined by further research.

Unusual Intelligence

Psychologists' understanding of intelligence has been advanced by studying people whose cognitive abilities are unusual—especially the gifted and the mentally retarded (Robinson, Zigler, & Gallagher, 2000).

FIGURE 7.14

Testing for Practical and Creative Intelligence

 learn by **doing** Robert Sternberg argues that traditional IQ tests measure mainly analytic intelligence. Here are sample items from tests he developed that test practical and creative intelligence as well. The answers are given at the bottom of the figure. How did you do?

PRACTICAL

1. Think of a problem that you are currently experiencing in real life. Briefly describe the problem, including how long it has been present and who else is involved (if anyone). Then describe three different practical things you could do to try to solve the problem. *(Students are given up to 15 minutes and up to 2 pages.)*

2. Choose the answer that provides the **best** solution, given the specific situation and desired outcome.

   John's family moved to Iowa from Arizona during his junior year in high school. He enrolled as a new student in the local high school two months ago but still has not made friends and feels bored and lonely. One of his favorite activities is writing stories. What is likely to be the most effective solution to this problem?

   A. Volunteer to work on the school newspaper staff.

   B. Spend more time at home writing columns for the school newsletter.

   C. Try to convince his parents to move back to Arizona.

   D. Invite a friend from Arizona to visit during Christmas break.

3. Each question asks you to use information about everyday things. Read each question carefully and choose the best answer.

   Mike wants to buy two seats together and is told there are pairs of seats available only in Rows 8, 12, 49, and 95–100. Which of the following is not one of his choices for the total price of the two tickets?

   A. $10.   **B.** $20.   **C.** $30.   **D.** $40.

CREATIVE

1. Suppose you are the student representative to a committee that has the power and the money to reform your school system. Describe your ideal school system, including buildings, teachers, curriculum, and any other aspects you feel are important. *(Students are given up to 15 minutes and up to 2 pages.)*

2. Each question has a "Pretend" statement. You must suppose that this statement is true. Decide which word goes with the third underlined word in the same way that the first two underlined words go together.

   Colors are audible.

   flavor is to tongue as shade is to

   A. ear.   **B.** light.   **C.** sound.   **D.** hue.

3. First, read how the operation is defined. Then, decide what is the correct answer to the question.

   There is a new mathematical operation called **flix.**
   It is defined as follows:

   $$A \text{ flix } B = A + B, \text{ if } A > B$$
   but $A \text{ flix } B = A \times B, \text{ if } A < B$
   and $A \text{ flix } B = A / B, \text{ if } A = B$
   How much is 4 flix 7?

   A. 28.   **B.** 11.   **C.** 3.   **D.** −11.

ANSWERS. Practical: (2) A, (3) B. Creative: (2) A, (3) A.

Source: Sternberg (1996).

Giftedness   People who show remarkably high levels of accomplishment in particular areas are often referred to as *gifted*. Giftedness is typically measured by school achievement. A child's potential for high achievement is usually measured by intelligence tests, but researchers warn that it is risky to predict academic potential from a single measure, such as an IQ score (Hagen, 1980; Lohman & Hagen, 2001; Thorndike & Hagen, 1996).

For one thing, not all people with unusually high IQs become famous and successful in their chosen fields. One of the best-known studies of the intellectually gifted was conducted by Lewis Terman and his colleagues (Oden, 1968; Sears, 1977; Terman & Oden, 1947, 1959). This study began in 1921 with the identification of more than 1,500 boys and girls whose IQ scores were very high—most higher than 135 by age ten. Periodic interviews and tests over the next seventy years revealed that few, if any, became world-famous scientists, inventors, authors, artists, or composers. But only 11 failed to graduate from high school, and more than two-thirds graduated from college—this at a time when completing a college education was relatively rare, particularly for women. Ninety-seven went on to earn Ph.D.'s; 92, law degrees; and 57, medical degrees. In 1955 their median family income was well above the national average (Terman & Oden, 1959). In general, they were physically and mentally healthier than the general population and appeared to have led happier, or at least more fortunate, lives (Cronbach, 1996). More recent studies also show that people with higher IQ scores tend to live longer (Deary et al., 2004; Gottfredson, 2004; Hart et al., 2003), perhaps because they have the reasoning and problem-solving skills that lead them to take better care of themselves (Deary & Der, 2005; Gottfredson & Deary, 2004; see the Focus on Research section of the chapter on health, stress, and coping).

In other words, higher IQ scores tend to predict greater success in life (Wai, Lubinski, & Benbow, 2005; Lubinski et al., 2006; Whalley & Deary, 2001), but an extremely high IQ does not guarantee special distinction. Some research suggests that gifted children are not fundamentally different kinds of people. They just have "more" of the same basic cognitive abilities seen in all children (Dark & Benbow, 1993; Singh & O'Boyle, 2004). Other work suggests that gifted people may be different in other ways, too, such as having unusually intense motivation to master certain tasks or areas of intellectual endeavor (Lubinski, 2001; Winner, 2000).

Mental Retardation   People whose IQs are lower than about 70 *and* who fail to display the skills at daily living, communication, and other tasks that are expected of those their age have traditionally been described as *mentally retarded* (American Psychiatric Association, 1994). They are now often referred to as *developmentally disabled*, *developmentally delayed*, or *mentally challenged*. People within this very broad category differ greatly in their cognitive abilities and in their ability to function independently in daily life (see Table 7.2).

Some cases of mental retardation have a clearly identifiable cause. The best-known example is *Down syndrome*, which occurs when an abnormality during conception results in an extra copy of chromosome 21 (Hattori et al., 2000). Children with Down syndrome typically have IQ scores in the range of 40 to 55, though some may score higher than that. There are also several inherited causes of mental retardation. The most common of these is *fragile X syndrome*, a defect on chromosome 23 (known as the *X chromosome*). Retardation can also result from environmental causes, such as exposure to German measles (rubella), alcohol, or other toxins before birth; oxygen deprivation during birth; and head injuries, brain tumors, and infectious diseases (such as meningitis or encephalitis) in childhood (U.S. Surgeon General, 1999).

Familial retardation refers to the 30 to 40 percent of (usually mild) cases of mental retardation that have no obvious genetic or environmental cause (American Psychiatric Association, 1994). These cases appear to result from a complex and as yet unknown interaction between heredity and environment that researchers are continuing to explore (Croen, Grether, & Selvin, 2001; Spinath, Harlaar et al., 2004).

familial retardation   Cases of mild retardation for which no environmental or genetic cause can be found.

TABLE **7.2**

Categories of Mental Retardation

These categories are approximate. Especially at the upper end of the scale, many retarded persons can be taught to handle tasks well beyond what their IQ scores might suggest. Furthermore, IQ is not the only diagnostic criterion for retardation. Many people with IQs lower than 70 can function adequately in their everyday environment and so would not be classified as mentally retarded.

Level of Retardation	IQ Scores	Characteristics
Mild	50–70	A majority of all the mentally retarded. Usually show no physical symptoms of abnormality. Individuals with higher IQs can marry, maintain a family, and work in unskilled jobs. Abstract reasoning is difficult for those with the lower IQs of this category. Capable of some academic learning to a sixth-grade level.
Moderate	35–49	Often lack physical coordination. Can be trained to take care of themselves and to acquire some reading and writing skills. Abilities of a 4- to 7-year-old. Capable of living outside an institution with their families.
Severe	20–34	Only a few can benefit from any schooling. Can communicate vocally after extensive training. Most require constant supervision.
Profound	Below 20	Mental age less than 3. Very limited communication. Require constant supervision. Can learn to walk, utter a few simple phrases, and feed themselves.

THE EAGLE HAS LANDED In February 2000, Richard Keebler, twenty-seven, became an Eagle Scout in the Boy Scouts of America. His achievement was notable not only because a mere 4 percent of all Scouts ever reach this rank but also because Keebler has Down syndrome. As we come to better understand the potential, and not just the limitations, of mentally retarded people, their opportunities and their role in society will continue to expand.

People who are mildly retarded differ from other people in three important ways (Campione, Brown, & Ferrara, 1982):

1. They perform certain mental operations more slowly, such as retrieving information from long-term memory. When asked to repeat something they have learned, they are not as quick as a person of normal intelligence.

2. They simply know fewer facts about the world. It is likely that this deficiency is a consequence of the problem listed next.

3. They are not very good at using certain mental strategies that may be important in learning and problem solving. For example, they do not remember to rehearse material that must be held in short-term memory, even though they know how to do so.

Despite such difficulties, the intellectual abilities of mentally retarded people can be improved to some extent. One program that emphasized positive parent-child communications began when the children were as young as two and a half years old. It helped children with Down syndrome to eventually master reading skills at a second-grade level, providing the foundation for further achievement (Rynders & Horrobin, 1980; Turkington, 1987). However, designing effective programs for children who are retarded is complicated by the fact that learning does not depend on cognitive skills alone. It also depends on social and emotional factors, including where children learn. Much debate has focused on *mainstreaming*, the policy of teaching children with disabilities, including those who are retarded, in regular classrooms alongside children without disabilities. Is mainstreaming good for retarded children? A number of studies comparing the cognitive and social skills of children who have been mainstreamed and those who were separated show few significant differences overall. However, it does appear that students at higher ability levels may gain more from being mainstreamed than their less mentally able peers (Cole et al., 1991; Mills et al., 1998).

ACTIVE REVIEW — Thought, Language, and Intelligence

Linkages

As noted in the introductory chapter, all of psychology's subfields are related to one another. Our discussion of group problem solving illustrates just one way in which the topic of this chapter, thought, language, and intelligence, is linked to the subfield of social psychology, which is described in the chapter by that name. The Linkages diagram shows ties to two other subfields, and there are many more ties throughout the book. Looking for linkages among subfields will help you see how they all fit together and help you better appreciate the big picture that is psychology.

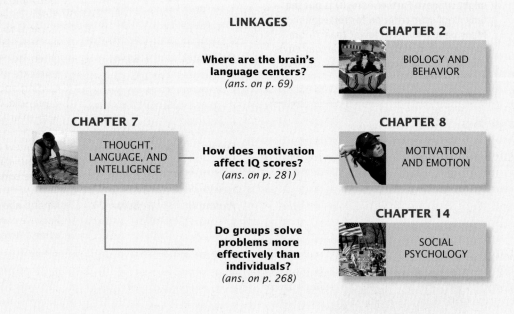

LINKAGES

CHAPTER 7
THOUGHT, LANGUAGE, AND INTELLIGENCE

Where are the brain's language centers?
(ans. on p. 69)

CHAPTER 2
BIOLOGY AND BEHAVIOR

How does motivation affect IQ scores?
(ans. on p. 281)

CHAPTER 8
MOTIVATION AND EMOTION

Do groups solve problems more effectively than individuals?
(ans. on p. 268)

CHAPTER 14
SOCIAL PSYCHOLOGY

Summary

BASIC FUNCTIONS OF THOUGHT

▶ **What good is thinking, anyway?**

The five core functions of thought are to describe, elaborate, decide, plan, and guide action. Many psychologists think of the components of this circle of thought as constituting an *information-processing system* that receives, represents, transforms, and acts on incoming stimuli. *Thinking,* then, is defined as the manipulation of mental representations by this system.

MENTAL REPRESENTATIONS: THE INGREDIENTS OF THOUGHT

▶ **What are thoughts made of?**

Mental representations take the form of concepts, propositions, schemas, scripts, mental models, images, and cognitive maps. *Concepts* are categories of objects, events, or ideas with common properties. They may be formal or natural. *Formal concepts* are precisely defined by the presence or absence of certain features. *Natural concepts* are fuzzy; no fixed set of defining properties determines membership in a natural concept. A member of a natural concept that displays all or most of the concept's characteristic features is called a *prototype.*

  Propositions are assertions that state how concepts are related. Propositions can be true or false. *Schemas* serve as generalized mental representations of concepts and also generate expectations about

them. *Scripts* are schemas about familiar sequences of events or activities. Experience creates accurate or inaccurate *mental models* that help to guide our understanding of, and interaction with, the world. Mental *images* may also be manipulated when people think. *Cognitive maps* are mental representations of familiar parts of one's world.

THINKING STRATEGIES

▶ **Do people always think logically?**

By combining and transforming mental representations, our information-processing system makes it possible for us to engage in *reasoning,* to solve problems, and to make decisions. *Formal reasoning* seeks valid conclusions through the application of rigorous procedures. It is guided by *algorithms,* systematic methods that always reach a correct result, if there is one. To reach a sound conclusion, people should consider both the truth and falsity of their assumptions and whether the argument follows the *rules of logic.* Unfortunately, people are prone to logical errors.

  People use *informal reasoning* to assess the validity of a conclusion based on the evidence supporting it. Errors in informal reasoning often stem from the use of *heuristics,* which are mental shortcuts or rules of thumb. Three important heuristics are the *anchoring heuristic* (estimating the probability of an event by adjusting a starting value), the *representativeness heuristic* (basing conclusions about whether something belongs in a certain class on how similar it is to other items in that class), and the *availability heuristic* (estimating probability by how available an event is in memory).

PROBLEM SOLVING

▶ **What's the best way to solve a problem?**

Steps in problem solving include diagnosing the problem and then planning, executing, and evaluating a solution. Especially when solutions are not obvious, problem solving can be aided by incubation and the use of strategies such as means-end analysis (also called *decomposition*), working backward, and finding analogies.

Many of the difficulties that people experience in solving problems arise when they are dealing with hypotheses. People do not easily consider multiple hypotheses. Because of *mental sets,* they may stick to one hypothesis even when it is incorrect, and, because of *functional fixedness,* they may miss opportunities to use familiar objects in unusual ways. People may be reluctant to revise or change hypotheses on the basis of new data, partly because *confirmation bias* focuses their attention on evidence that supports their hypotheses. They may also fail to use the absence of symptoms or events as evidence in solving problems.

Some specific problems can be solved by computer programs developed by researchers in the field of *artificial intelligence (AI).* There are two approaches to AI. One focuses on programming computers to imitate the logical manipulation of symbols that occurs in human thought; the other (involving connectionist, or neural network, models) attempts to imitate the connections among neurons in the human brain.

Tests of *divergent thinking* are used to measure differences in *creativity.* In contrast, intelligence tests require *convergent thinking.* Although creativity and intelligence are not highly correlated, creative behavior requires a certain amount of intelligence, along with expertise in a creative field, skill at problem solving and divergent thinking, and motivation to pursue a creative endeavor for its own sake.

DECISION MAKING

▶ **How can I become a better decision maker?**

Decisions are sometimes difficult because there are too many alternatives and too many features of each alternative to consider all at once. Furthermore, decisions often involve comparisons of subjective *utility,* not of objective value. Decision making is also complicated by the fact that the world is unpredictable, which makes decisions risky.

People should act in ways that maximize the *expected value* of their decisions. They often fail to do so because losses are perceived differently from gains of equal size and because people tend to overestimate the probability of rare events, underestimate the probability of frequent events, and feel overconfident about the accuracy of their forecasts. The gambler's fallacy leads people to believe that events in a random process are affected by previous events. People also make decisions aimed at goals other than maximizing expected value; these goals may be determined by personal and cultural factors.

Group decisions tend to show group polarization, the selection of more extreme outcomes than would have been chosen by the average group member. Group performance in problem solving and decision making can be effective, but depending on the problem and the people involved, it may be less efficient than when individuals work alone.

LANGUAGE

▶ **How do babies learn to talk?**

Language consists of words or word symbols and rules for their combination—a *grammar.* Children develop grammar according to an orderly pattern. *Babblings* come first, then a *one-word stage* of speech, and then two-word sentences. Next come three-word sentences and certain grammatical forms that appear in a somewhat predictable order. Once children learn certain regular verb forms and plural endings, they may overgeneralize rules. Children acquire most of the grammatical rules of their native language by the time they are five years old.

Both conditioning and imitation play a role in a child's acquisition of language, but neither can provide a complete explanation of how children acquire grammar. Humans may be biologically programmed to learn language. In any event, it appears that language must be learned during a certain critical period if normal language is to occur.

TESTING INTELLIGENCE

▶ **How is intelligence measured?**

Intelligence refers to information-processing skills, problem-solving skills, and the capacity to adapt to changing environments. Binet's pioneering test of intelligence included questions that required reasoning and problem solving at varying levels of difficulty, graded by age. Terman developed a revision of Binet's test that became known as the *Stanford-Binet;* it included items designed to assess the intelligence of adults, as well as that of children, and it became the model for *IQ tests.* Early intelligence tests in the United States required not just cognitive ability but also knowledge of U.S. culture. Wechsler's intelligence tests remedied some of the deficiencies of earlier tests. Made up of subtests, including a *verbal scale* and also a *performance scale* with little verbal content, these tests allowed testers to obtain scores for different aspects of cognitive ability.

In schools, the Stanford-Binet and Wechsler tests are among the most popular individually administered intelligence tests. Both include subtests and provide scores for parts of the test, as well as an overall score. A person's *intelligence quotient,* or *IQ score,* is no longer the result of dividing mental age by actual age. It reflects instead how much the person's performance on the test deviates from the average performance of people in the same age group. An average performance is assigned an IQ of 100.

EVALUATING INTELLIGENCE TESTS

▶ **How good are intelligence tests?**

Tests are standardized, so the performance of different people can be compared; they also produce scores that can be compared with *norms.* A good test must have *reliability,* which means that the results for each person are consistent, or stable. *Validity* refers to the degree to which test scores are interpreted appropriately and used properly.

Intelligence tests are quite reliable and do a reasonable job of predicting academic and occupational success. However, these tests assess only some of the abilities that might be considered aspects of intelligence, and they may favor people who are most familiar with middle-class culture. Nonetheless, this familiarity is important for academic and occupational success in that culture.

Both genes and the environment influence IQ scores, and their effects interact. Genetic influences are reflected in the high correlation between IQ scores of identical twins raised in separate households and in the similarity between the IQ scores of children adopted at birth and those of their biological parents. The influence of the environment is revealed by the higher correlation of IQ between siblings who share the same environment than between those who do not and by the effects of environmental changes such as adoption.

Different socioeconomic and ethnic groups have somewhat different average IQ scores. These differences appear to be due in part to noncognitive factors, such as differences in motivation, family support, educational opportunity, and other environmental conditions. An enriched environment sometimes raises preschool children's IQ scores. Despite their limitations, intelligence tests can help educators to identify a student's strengths and weaknesses and to offer the curriculum that will best serve that student.

DIVERSITY IN INTELLIGENCE

▶ **Is there more than one type of intelligence?**

Sternberg sees three types of intelligence: analytic, practical, and creative. He says that scores on tests of practical intelligence predict job success as well as traditional intelligence test scores do. According to Gardner, biology equips us with the capacities for several intelligences that can function with some independence—specifically, linguistic, logical-mathematical, spatial, musical, body-kinesthetic, intrapersonal, interpersonal, and naturalistic intelligences. Knowledge about cognitive abilities has been expanded by research on giftedness and mental retardation. People with very high IQ scores tend to be successful in life but are not necessarily geniuses. People are considered retarded if their IQ scores are below about 70 and if their communication and daily living skills are less than expected of people their age. In cases of *familial retardation,* no genetic or environmental causes are evident. Compared with people of normal intelligence, people who are retarded process information more slowly, know fewer facts, and are deficient at knowing and using mental strategies. Special teaching programs can, to some extent, improve the intellectual abilities of some people who are mentally retarded.

Learn by Doing

Put It in Writing

Try writing your own definition of *intelligence.* Make a list of at least seven behaviors or characteristics that you feel represent intelligence, and then decide how they could best be tested in children and adults from your own culture and other cultures. Describe the kinds of difficulties you encountered in making your list and designing your assessment devices.

Personal Learning Activity

Consider a problem that you are facing at the moment or one that is being faced by someone you know. In accordance with the problem-solving section of this chapter, write down all the alternative solutions you can think of to solve this problem; then list the pros and cons of each option. Which alternative comes out on top? Does the alternative that seems best on paper also strike you as the best solution to try? Why or why not? *For additional projects, see the Personal Learning Activities in the corresponding chapter of the study guide that accompanies this text.*

Step into Action

Courses

Experimental Psychology
Cognitive Psychology
Psycholinguistics
Engineering Psychology (also called Human Factors)
Tests and Measurement (sometimes called
  Psychometrics)
Behavioral Genetics

Movies

Nell; Dances with Wolves; Clan of the Cave Bear.
  Language development.
Gorillas in the Mist. Animal communication.
Apollo 13; The Negotiator; K-19: The Widowmaker.
  Problem solving.
2001: A Space Odyssey. Artificial intelligence.
My Left Foot. Assessment of ability.
*Forrest Gump; Of Mice and Men; The Other Sister; Charly;
  Rain Man; Little Man Tate.* Diversity of intelligence.
Cast Away. Problem solving, creativity, intelligence.
Searching for Bobby Fischer; Hilary and Jackie; Pi.
  Giftedness.
Born Yesterday; Real Genius. Kinds of intelligence.

Books

Gerd Gigerenzer, Peter M. Todd, and ABC Research
  Group, *Simple Heuristics That Make Us Smart* (Oxford
  University Press, 2000). Research on, and ideas for
  using, mental shortcuts.
Peter Bernstein, *Against the Gods: The Remarkable Story
  of Risk* (Wiley, 1998). History of efforts to understand
  risk and probability in decision making.
James Surowiecki, *The Wisdom of Crowds: Why the
  Many Are Smarter than the Few and How Collective
  Wisdom Shapes Business, Economies, Societies, and
  Nations.* (Doubleday, 2004). Presents theories and
  evidence for the value of group rather than
  individual decisions.
Philip Tetlock, *Expert Political Judgment: How Good is
  it? How Can We Know?* (Princeton University Press,
  2006). Presents evidence that the judgment of even
  revered political experts are subject to the same flaws
  and pitfalls that plague the rest of us.
Howard Gardner, *Intelligence Reframed: Multiple
  Intelligences for the 21st Century* (Basic Books, 1999).
  Theory of multiple intelligences.

Nicholas Lemann, *The Big Test: The Secret History of American Meritocracy* (Farrar, Straus and Giroux, 1999). History of testing in the United States.

Hans Eysenck, with Darrin Evans, *Test Your IQ* (Penguin, 1995). Self-testing.

Steven Fatsis, *Word Freak* (Houghton Mifflin, 2002). Inside the high-stakes world of professional Scrabble.

Richard Herrnstein and Charles Murray, *The Bell Curve* (Free Press, 1994). Controversial book about group differences in intelligence.

Daniel Seligman, *A Question of Intelligence: The IQ Debate in America* (Citadel Press, 1994). Nature, nurture, and IQ.

Steven Fraser (Ed.), *The Bell Curve Wars* (Basic Books, 1995). Essays critical of *The Bell Curve.*

The Web

The World Wide Web is a good source of additional information about the science of psychology, provided you use it carefully and think critically about the information you find. The Online Study Center that accompanies this text offers many resources relevant to this chapter. These resources include interactive tutorials; Thinking Critically and Evaluating Research exercises; ACE chapter quizzes; recommended web links; and articles on current events, books, and movies. Please visit the Online Study Center at college.hmco.com/pic/bernsteinessentials4e.

Review of Key Terms

Can you define each of the key terms in the chapter? Check your definitions against those on the pages shown in parentheses in the following list or in the Glossary/Index at the end of the text.

algorithms *(p. 254)*
anchoring heuristic *(p. 255)*
artificial intelligence (AI) *(p. 262)*
availability heuristic *(p. 256)*
babblings *(p. 270)*
cognitive map *(p. 252)*
concepts *(p. 250)*
confirmation bias *(p. 262)*
convergent thinking *(p. 265)*
creativity *(p. 264)*
divergent thinking *(p. 264)*
expected value *(p. 266)*

familial retardation *(p. 288)*
formal concepts *(p. 250)*
formal reasoning *(p. 254)*
functional fixedness *(p. 260)*
grammar *(p. 269)*
heuristics *(p. 255)*
images *(p. 252)*
informal reasoning *(p. 255)*
information-processing system *(p. 249)*
intelligence *(p. 274)*
IQ score *(p. 276)*

IQ test *(p. 274)*
language *(p. 269)*
mental models *(p. 252)*
mental set *(p. 260)*
natural concepts *(p. 250)*
norms *(p. 276)*
one-word stage *(p. 271)*
performance scale *(p. 276)*
propositions *(p. 251)*
prototype *(p. 251)*
reasoning *(p. 254)*
reliability *(p. 276)*

representativeness heuristic *(p. 256)*
rules of logic *(p. 254)*
schemas *(p. 251)*
scripts *(p. 252)*
Stanford-Binet *(p. 274)*
test *(p. 276)*
thinking *(p. 249)*
utility *(p. 266)*
validity *(p. 278)*
verbal scale *(p. 276)*

Multiple-Choice Self-Test

Select the best answer for each of the following questions. Then check your responses against the Answer Key at the end of the text.

1. *Thinking* is defined as the manipulation of

   a. concepts.
   b. mental models.
   c. heuristics.
   d. mental representations.

2. While trying to describe an unusual bird he saw on his walk, Jarrod asks his friend to "Think of a robin, but with blue tips on the wings, and a tuft of hair on the head. That's what it looked like." Because "bird" is a _____ concept, Jarrod began with the image of a robin, which is the _____ of "bird." He hoped that his description would allow his friend to develop a _____ of the bird he saw.

   a. formal; concept; prototype
   b. natural; image; concept
   c. natural; prototype; mental model
   d. visual; mental model; script

3. Clint is frustrated. His uncle has been winning at checkers all night. During the next game he is going to base his strategy on an algorithm, not a heuristic. What problem will this strategy cause?

   a. Clint still may not win the game.
   b. Clint and his uncle may be playing the same game of checkers for a long time.
   c. Clint will be ignoring overall probabilities.
   d. The representativeness heuristic will bias Clint's choice of strategy.

4. Alicia agreed to go to dinner and a movie with Adam but was surprised and angry when Adam expected her to pay for her half of the evening's expenses. Adam and Alicia apparently had different _____ for what is supposed to happen on a date.

   a. mental models   c. images
   b. propositions   d. scripts

5. Stephanie has worked for hours on a biochemistry problem without success. She decides to put it aside and work on her psychology homework in the hope that a solution might occur to her while she is thinking about something else. Stephanie is trying the _____ strategy to solve her problem.

   a. decomposition   c. working backward
   b. incubation   d. analogies

6. Ebony wanted to leave a note for her husband but couldn't find a pen, so she wrote the note with her lipstick. Ebony was able to overcome the obstacle to problem solving called

   a. absence of information.
   b. multiple hypotheses.
   c. confirmation bias.
   d. functional fixedness.

7. Dr. Sand is sure that Ahmed has appendicitis, and as a result he pays more attention to test results that are consistent with appendicitis than to results that suggest a different problem. Dr. Sand has fallen victim to

   a. functional fixedness.
   b. a mental model.
   c. confirmation bias.
   d. the availability heuristic.

8. While playing a dominos game, Don drew a tile at random and got a "double blank," which costs the most points during the first two rounds. At the start of the third round, he says, "There is no way I will draw the double blank tile next time!" Don is being influenced by

   a. the gambler's fallacy.
   b. loss aversion.
   c. a disregard of negative evidence.
   d. confirmation bias.

9. The fact that children learning language sometimes make errors, such as saying "I goed" instead of "I went," has been used to suggest which of the following?

   a. There is a critical period in language development.
   b. Children are born with a knowledge of grammar.
   c. Children do not learn language entirely through imitation.
   d. Speech is learned mainly through imitation.

10. Children who spend their early years isolated from human contact and the sound of adult language are unable to develop adult language skills despite extensive training efforts later. This phenomenon provides evidence for the notion that

    a. there is a critical period in language development.
    b. children are born with a language acquisition device.
    c. there are no fixed stages in language acquisition.
    d. speech is acquired only through imitation.

11. The earliest IQ test was developed to

    a. identify children who needed special educational programs.
    b. help the armed forces make appropriate assignments of recruits.
    c. identify which immigrants were mentally defective and thus should not be allowed into the United States.
    d. help employers decide which employees were most appropriate for the available jobs.

12. "All monsters are ugly. The Creature from the Black Lagoon is a monster. Therefore, the Creature is ugly." Together, these three statements are an example of

    a. a premise.
    b. a proposition.
    c. a natural concept.
    d. formal reasoning.

13. Jonah's parents are told that their son has an IQ score of 100. According to the intelligence test scoring method used today, this means that Jonah

    a. has a mental age that is higher than his chronological age.
    b. scored higher than half the children in his age group.
    c. can now be considered to be a gifted child.
    d. shows about average skill at divergent thinking.

14. Like all other applicants to medical school, Lavinia took the MCAT admission test. Later, researchers compared all the successful applicants' medical school grades with their MCAT scores. The researchers were obviously trying to measure the MCAT's

    a. reliability.
    b. standardization.
    c. validity.
    d. norms.

15. When Jerrica first took the Handy Dandy Intelligence test, her score was 140. When she took the same test six weeks later, her score was only 102. If other people showed similarly changing score patterns, the Handy Dandy Intelligence test would appear to lack

    a. reliability.
    b. validity.
    c. standardization.
    d. norms.

16. Research shows that today's standardized intelligence tests

    a. have good reliability and reasonably good validity for predicting success in school.
    b. do not do a good job of predicting success on the job.
    c. are not correlated with performance on "real-life" tasks.
    d. measure the full array of cognitive abilities.

17. There are two sets of twins in the Mullis family. Louise and Lanie are identical twins; Andy and Adrian are not. According to research on heredity and intelligence, which pair of twins is likely to show the most similarity in IQ scores?

    a. Andy and Adrian, because they are male siblings.
    b. Andy and Adrian, because they are fraternal twins.
    c. Louise and Lanie, because they are female siblings.
    d. Louise and Lanie, because they are identical twins.

18. Rowena is mildly mentally retarded, but she is attending regular classes at a public school. Rowena most likely _____ and she will _____ from being mainstreamed.

    a. knows fewer facts about the world than others; benefit
    b. knows fewer facts about the world than others; not benefit
    c. learns just as fast as other children, but forgets it faster; not benefit.
    d. has little or no potential for employment; benefit.

19. Betsey took an intelligence test that included items requiring her to say what she would do if she were stranded in a large city with no money and how she would teach music to children who had no musical instruments. This test was most likely based on

    a. Sternberg's triarchic theory of intelligence.
    b. Gardner's concept of multiple intelligences.
    c. Terman's giftedness theory.
    d. the Wechsler Adult Intelligence Scale.

20. Theresa Amabile identified cognitive and personality characteristics necessary for creativity. Which of the following is not one of these characteristics?

    a. A capacity for focusing on the most important element in a problem, which is tied to convergent thinking.
    b. Expertise in the field of endeavor, which is tied to learning.
    c. A set of creative skills, including the capacity for divergent thinking.
    d. The motivation to pursue creative work for internal reasons.

8

Motivation and Emotion

When your alarm clock goes off in the morning, do you jump out of

bed, eager to face the day, or do you bury your head in the blankets, trying to avoid all that's ahead of you? Once you're out of bed, do you eat a big breakfast, or do you just have coffee or tea, no matter how hungry you feel? As you leave home, do you notice your attractive neighbor and find yourself wondering whether the two of you might someday have a romantic relationship? Or, if you're in a long-term relationship, do you find yourself thinking fond thoughts of your partner? Once you're at your job or on campus, do you always try to do your best, or do you work just hard enough to get by? And how do you feel about your life? Are you generally happy? Do you sometimes worry or feel sad? In this chapter, we explore the physical, mental, and social factors that motivate behavior in areas ranging from eating to sexuality to achievement. We also examine what emotions are and how they are expressed.

Reading this chapter will help you to answer the following questions:

When Tiger Woods won the British Open in July 2000, he became the youngest man to win all four tournaments that make up the Grand Slam in men's professional golf. He remains the world's best golfer today. Lance Armstrong, a bicyclist who had overcome cancer to win the Tour de France bicycle race in 1999, won it again every year for six more years, including the 2005 race, after which he finally retired. Serena Williams captured both the 2002 and 2003 women's singles tennis championship at Wimbledon by winning in the finals against her sister, Venus Williams. Venus herself won that same Wimbledon title in 2000, 2001, and 2005.

Success did not come easily to these athletes; it took years of effort and unwavering determination. Why did they work so hard in the face of daunting challenges and tough competition to rise to the top of their fields? For that matter, what prompts any of us to excel, to perform acts of kindness, to look for food, to take dancing lessons, to go

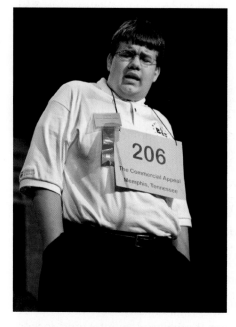

MOTIVATION AND EMOTION The link between motivation and emotion can be seen in many situations. For example, being motivated to win the U.S. National Spelling Bee creates strong emotions as this contestant struggles with a tough word. And the link works both ways. Often, emotions create motivation, as when anger leads a person to become aggressive toward a child or when love leads a person to provide for that child.

bungee jumping, to become violent, or to act in any other particular way? What makes some people go all out to reach a goal, whereas others make only halfhearted efforts and quit at the first obstacle? These are all questions about **motivation,** the factors that influence the initiation, direction, intensity, and persistence of behavior (Reeve, 1996).

Like the study of *how* people and other animals behave and think, the puzzle of *why* they do so has intrigued psychologists for many decades. Part of the motivation for behavior is to feel certain emotions, such as the joy of finishing a race or of becoming a parent. Motivation also affects emotion, as when hunger makes you more likely to become angry if people annoy you. In this chapter we review several aspects of motivation and the features and value of emotions.

Concepts and Theories of Motivation

▶ **Where does motivation come from?**

Suppose that a woman works two jobs, never goes to parties, wears old clothes, drives an old car, eats food left behind by others, ignores charity appeals, and keeps her house at sixty degrees all winter. Why does she do these things? You could suggest a separate explanation for each of these behaviors: Perhaps she likes to work hard, hates parties, doesn't care about new clothes and new cars, enjoys other people's leftovers, has no concern for the poor, and likes cold temperatures. Or you could suggest a **motive,** a reason or purpose that provides a single explanation for all these different behaviors. That unifying motive might be the woman's desire to save as much money as possible. This example illustrates the fact that motivation itself cannot be directly observed. We have to infer, or presume, that motivation is present on the basis of what we can observe.

Motivation helps explain why behavior changes over time. For example, many people are unable to lose weight, quit smoking, or get in shape until they have a heart attack or symptoms of some other serious health problem. At that point, they may suddenly be motivated to eat a healthier diet, give up tobacco, and exercise regularly (West & Sohal, 2006). In other words, a change in motivation can change a person's responses to stimuli such as ice cream, cigarettes, and health clubs.

Sources of Motivation

Human motivation stems from four main sources. First, we can be motivated by *biological factors,* such as the need for food and water (Tinbergen, 1989). Second, *emotional factors* can motivate behavior (Izard, 1993). Panic, fear, anger, love, and hatred can influence behavior ranging from selfless giving to brutal murder. *Cognitive factors* provide a third source of motivation (Weiner, 1993). Your perceptions of the world, your beliefs about what you can do, and your expectations of how others will respond generate certain behaviors. For example, even the least musical contestants who try out for *American Idol* and other talent shows seem utterly confident in their ability to sing. Fourth, motivation can stem from *social factors,* including the influence of parents, teachers, siblings, friends, television, and other sociocultural forces. Have you ever bought a jacket or tried a particular hairstyle not because you liked it but because it was in fashion? This is just one example of how social factors can affect almost all human behavior (Baumeister & Leary, 1995).

Four main theories have been proposed to explain motivation. They include instinct theory, drive reduction theory, optimal arousal theory, and incentive theory. Each of these theories has proven helpful in accounting for some aspects of behavior.

Instinct Theory and Its Descendants

In the early 1900s, many psychologists favored an **instinct theory** of motivation. **Instincts** are automatic, involuntary, and unlearned behavior patterns consistently "released" or triggered by particular stimuli (Tinbergen, 1989). For example, the male

motivation   The influences that account for the initiation, direction, intensity, and persistence of behavior.

motive   A reason or purpose for behavior.

instinct theory   A view that behavior is motivated by automatic, involuntary, and unlearned responses.

instincts   Innate, automatic dispositions to respond in particular ways to specific stimuli.

stickleback fish instantly attacks when it sees the red underbelly of another male. Such behaviors in nonhuman species were originally called *fixed action patterns* because they are unlearned, genetically coded responses to specific "releaser" stimuli.

William McDougall (1908) argued that human behavior, too, is motivated by instincts. He began by listing eighteen human instincts, including self-assertion, reproduction, pugnacity (eagerness to fight), and gregariousness (sociability). Within a few years, McDougall and other theorists had named more than 10,000 instincts, prompting one critic to suggest that his colleagues had "an instinct to produce instincts" (Bernard, 1924). The problem was that instincts had become meaningless labels that described behavior without explaining it. Saying that people gamble because of a gambling instinct or work hard because of a work instinct explains nothing about why these behaviors appear in some people and not others nor about how they develop. Applying instinct theory to human motivation also appeared problematic because people display few, if any, instinctive fixed-action patterns.

Today, psychologists continue to investigate the role played by inborn tendencies in human motivation. They have been stimulated partly by research on a number of human behaviors that are present at birth. Among these are the sucking, grasping, and other reflexes discussed in the human development chapter, as well as certain facial expressions, such as grimacing at bitter tastes (Steiner et al., 2001). Further, as discussed in the chapter on learning, humans appear to be biologically prepared to learn to fear snakes and other potential dangers. But psychologists' thinking about instincts is more sophisticated now than it was a century ago. They recognize that even though certain behaviors reflect inborn motivational tendencies, those behaviors may or may not actually appear, depending on each individual's experience. So although we might be biologically "programmed" to learn to fear snakes, that fear won't develop if we never see a snake. In other words, motivation can be influenced by inherited tendencies, but that doesn't mean that all motivated behavior is genetically determined.

Psychologists who take an evolutionary approach to behavior suggest that a wide range of behavioral tendencies have evolved because, over the centuries, they were adaptive for individual survival in particular circumstances. Those who possessed and expressed these adaptive predispositions were more likely than others to live to father or give birth to offspring. We are descendants of these human survivors. So to the extent that their behavioral predispositions were transmitted genetically, we should have inherited similar predispositions. Evolutionary psychologists also argue that many aspects of human social behavior—including helping, aggression, and the choice of sexual or marriage partners—are motivated by inborn factors, especially by the desire to maximize our genetic contribution to the next generation (Buss, 2004). We may not be consciously aware of this desire (Geary, 2000), so you are more likely to hear someone say "I can't wait to have children" than to say "I want to pass on my genes."

By emphasizing the evolutionary roots of human behavior, modern versions of instinct theory focus on the ultimate, long-term reasons behind much of what we do. The theories of motivation discussed next highlight influences that serve as more immediate causes of behavior (Alcock, 2001).

Drive Reduction Theory

Like instinct theory, the drive reduction theory of motivation emphasizes internal factors, but it focuses mainly on how these factors serve to maintain homeostasis. **Homeostasis** (pronounced "ho-me-oh-STAY-sis") is the tendency to make constant adjustments to maintain body temperature, blood pressure, and other physiological systems at a steady level, or *equilibrium*—much as a thermostat functions to maintain a constant temperature in a house.

According to **drive reduction theory,** any imbalance in homeostasis creates a **need,** which is a biological requirement for well-being. In responding to needs, the brain tries to restore homeostasis by creating a psychological state called **drive**—a feeling that prompts an organism to take action to fulfill the need and thus return to a balanced state. For example, if you have had nothing to drink for some time, the chemical balance of

Online Study Center

Improve Your Grade
Tutorial: Homeostasis and Drive Reduction Theory

homeostasis The tendency for physiological systems to remain stable by constantly adjusting themselves in response to change.

drive reduction theory A theory that motivation arises from imbalances in homeostasis.

need A biological requirement for well-being.

drive A physiological state that arises from an imbalance in homeostasis and prompts action to fulfill a need.

FIGURE **8.1**

Drive Reduction Theory and Homeostasis

The mechanisms of homeostasis, such as the regulation of body temperature or food and water intake, are often compared to thermostats. If the temperature in a house falls below the thermostat setting, the furnace comes on and brings the temperature up to that preset level, achieving homeostasis. When the temperature reaches the preset point, the furnace shuts off.

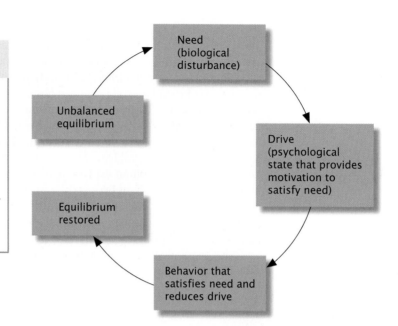

Need
(biological
disturbance)

Unbalanced
equilibrium

Drive
(psychological
state that provides
motivation to
satisfy need)

Equilibrium
restored

Behavior that
satisfies need and
reduces drive

OPTIMAL AROUSAL AND PERSON-ALITY People whose ideal, or optimal, level of arousal is high are more likely to smoke, drink alcohol, engage in frequent sexual activity, listen to loud music, eat "hot" foods, and do other things that are stimulating, novel, and risky (Farley, 1986; Zuckerman, 1993). Those whose optimal level of arousal is lower tend to take fewer risks and behave in ways that are less stimulating. As discussed in the personality chapter, differences in optimal arousal may help shape other characteristics, such as whether we tend to be introverted or extraverted.

your bodily fluids will be disturbed, creating a biological need for water. One consequence of this need is a drive—thirst—that motivates you to find and drink water. After you drink, the need for water is met, so the drive to drink is reduced. In other words, drives push people to satisfy needs, thus reducing the drives that have been created. This cycle is shown in Figure 8.1.

Early drive reduction theorists described two types of drives. **Primary drives** stem from biological needs, such as the need for food or water. People do not have to learn these basic biological needs or the primary drives to satisfy them (Hull, 1951). Other drives, however, are learned through experience. These learned **secondary drives** motivate us to act as if we have unmet basic needs. For example, as people learn to associate money with the ability to buy things to satisfy primary drives for food, shelter, and so on, having money becomes a secondary drive. Having too little money then motivates many behaviors—from hard work to stealing—to obtain more funds.

Optimal Arousal Theory

Drive reduction theory can account for a wide range of motivated behaviors, but not for all of them. Consider curiosity, for example. Monkeys, dogs, cats, and rats will work hard simply to enter a new environment, especially if it is complex and full of novel objects (Loewenstein, 1994). And most people, too, can't resist checking out whatever is new and unusual. We go to the mall opening, watch builders work, surf the Internet, and travel the world just to see what there is to see. People also go out of their way to ride roller coasters, skydive, drive race cars, and do countless other things that do not reduce any known drive (Zuckerman, 1996).

In fact, these behaviors create an increase in **arousal**—the body's general level of activation. Arousal is reflected in heart rate, muscle tension, brain activity, blood pressure, and other bodily systems (Deschaumes et al., 1991; Plutchik & Conte, 1997). It is usually lowest during deep sleep, but arousal can also be lowered by meditation, relaxation techniques, and various depressant drugs. Increases in arousal tend to occur in response to hunger, thirst, stimulant drugs, and, as just mentioned, stimuli that are intense, sudden, new, or unexpected. Because people sometimes try to reduce their arousal and sometimes try to increase it, some psychologists have suggested that motivation is tied to the regulation of arousal.

Specifically, **optimal arousal theory** suggests that we are motivated to behave in ways that keep or restore an ideal, or *optimal level,* of arousal (Hebb, 1955). Too much arousal can hurt performance, as when test anxiety interferes with some students' ability to recall what they have studied. Overarousal can also cause athletes to "choke" so badly that they miss an easy catch or a simple shot (Smith et al., 2000;

in review

THEORIES OF MOTIVATION

Theory	Main Points
Instinct	Innate biological instincts guide behavior.
Drive reduction	Behavior is guided by biological needs and learned ways of reducing drives arising from those needs.
Arousal	People seek to maintain an optimal level of physiological arousal, which differs from person to person. Maximum performance occurs at optimal arousal levels.
Incentive	Behavior is guided by the lure of rewards and the threat of punishment. Cognitive factors influence expectations of the value of various rewards and the likelihood of attaining them.

?

1. The fact that some people like roller coasters and other scary amusement park rides has been cited as evidence for the _____ theory of motivation.
2. Evolutionary theories of motivation are modern outgrowths of _____ theories.
3. The value of incentives can be affected by _____, _____, and _____ factors.

Wright et al., 1995). Underarousal, too, can cause problems, as you probably know if you have ever tried to work, drive, or study when you are sleepy. So we try to increase arousal when it is too low and to decrease it when it is too high. In simpler terms, we seek excitement when we're bored and relaxation when we're stressed or overstimulated.

In general, we perform best, and may feel best, when arousal is moderate (Teigen, 1994), but people differ in the exact level of arousal that is optimal for them (Zuckerman, 1984). These differences in optimal arousal may stem from inherited differences in the nervous system (Bardo, Donohew, & Harrington, 1996; Berns et al., 2001; Eysenck, 1990a) and may motivate boldness, shyness, and many other personality traits and behavioral tendencies.

Incentive Theory

Instinct, drive reduction, and arousal theories of motivation all focus on internal processes that prompt people to behave in certain ways. In contrast, **incentive theory** emphasizes the role of external stimuli that motivate behavior. According to this view, people are pulled toward behaviors that offer positive incentives and pushed away from behaviors associated with negative incentives. In other words, differences in behavior from one person to another or from one situation to another can be traced to the incentives available and the value a person places on those incentives at the time. If you expect that some behavior (such as buying a lottery ticket) will lead to a valued outcome (winning money), you will be motivated to engage in that behavior. The value of incentives can be influenced by inborn physiological factors such as hunger and thirst, as well as by cognitive and social factors that gain their power through learning. As an example of physiological influences, consider that food is a more motivating incentive when you are hungry than when you're full (Balleine & Dickinson, 1994). As for cognitive and social influences, notice that the value of some things we eat—such as communion wafers or diet shakes—isn't determined by hunger or flavor but by what our culture has taught us about spirituality, health, or attractiveness. Perhaps you have also noticed that what early drive reduction theorists called *primary drives* reappear in incentive theory as unlearned influences on an incentive's value. *Secondary drives* reappear as learned influences on the value of incentives.

"In Review: Theories of Motivation" summarizes the theoretical approaches we have outlined. Each theory has helped to guide research on motivated behaviors such as eating, sex, and work, which we consider in the sections that follow.

primary drives Drives that arise from basic biological needs.

secondary drives Stimuli that take on the motivational properties of primary drives through learning.

arousal A general level of activation reflected in several physiological systems.

optimal arousal theory A theory that people are motivated to maintain what is, for them, an optimal level of arousal.

incentive theory A theory that people are pulled toward behaviors that offer positive incentives and pushed away from behaviors associated with negative incentives.

Eating

▶ **What makes me start eating and stop eating?**

At first glance, eating seems to be a simple example of drive reduction theory at work. You get hungry when you haven't eaten for a while. Much as a car needs gasoline, you need fuel from food, so you eat. But what bodily mechanism acts as a "gauge" to signal the need for fuel? What determines which foods you eat, and how do you know when to stop? The answers to these questions involve complex interactions between the brain and the rest of the body (Hill & Peters, 1998).

Signals for Hunger and Satiety

A variety of mechanisms underlie **hunger,** the general state of wanting to eat, and **satiety** (pronounced "seh-TYE-eh-tee"), the general state of no longer wanting to eat.

Signals from the Stomach   The stomach would seem to be a logical source of signals for hunger and satiety. You have probably felt "hunger pangs" from an "empty" stomach and felt "stuffed" after overeating. In fact, the stomach does contract during hunger pangs, and increased pressure within the stomach can reduce appetite (Cannon & Washburn, 1912; Houpt, 1994). But people who have lost their stomachs due to illness still get hungry, and they still eat normal amounts of food (Janowitz, 1967). So stomach cues can affect eating, but they appear to operate mainly when you are very hungry or very full.

Signals from the Blood   The most important signals about the body's fuel level and nutrient needs are sent to the brain from the blood. The brain's ability to "read" blood-borne signals about the body's nutritional needs was discovered when researchers deprived rats of food for a long period and then injected some of the rats with blood from rats that had just eaten. When offered food, the injected rats ate little or nothing (Davis et al., 1969). Something in the injected blood of the well-fed animals apparently signaled the hungry rats' brains that there was no need to eat. What was that satiety signal? Research has shown that the brain constantly monitors both the level of *food nutrients* absorbed into the bloodstream from the stomach and the level of *hormones* released into the blood in response to those nutrients (Korner & Leibel, 2003).

The nutrients that the brain monitors include *glucose* (the main form of sugar used by body cells), *fatty acids* (from fat), and *amino acids* (from protein). When the level of blood glucose drops, eating increases sharply (Mogenson, 1976). The brain also monitors hormone levels to regulate hunger and satiety. For example, when glucose levels rise, the pancreas releases *insulin,* a hormone that most body cells need in order to use the glucose they receive. Insulin itself may also provide a satiety signal by acting directly on brain cells (Brüning et al., 2000; Schwartz et al., 2000).

The hormone *leptin* (from the Greek word for "thin") also appears to provide a satiety signal to the brain (Farooqi et al., 2001; Margetic et al., 2002). Unlike glucose and insulin, whose satiety signals help us know when to end a particular meal, leptin appears to be involved mainly in the long-term regulation of body fat (Huang & Li, 2000). The process works like this: Cells that store fat normally have genes that produce leptin. As the fat supply in these cells increases, leptin is released into the blood, helping to reduce food intake. Animals with defects in these genes make no leptin and are obese (Bouret, Draper, & Simerly, 2004). When these animals are given leptin injections, though, they rapidly lose weight and body fat, but not muscle tissue (Forbes et al., 2001). Leptin injections can produce the same changes in normal animals, too (Fox & Olster, 2000). These results initially raised hope that leptin might be a "magic bullet" for treating human obesity, but this is not the case. Although it can help those rare individuals whose fat cells make no leptin (Farooqi et al., 1999), injections of leptin are

hunger   The general state of wanting to eat.

satiety   The condition of no longer wanting to eat.

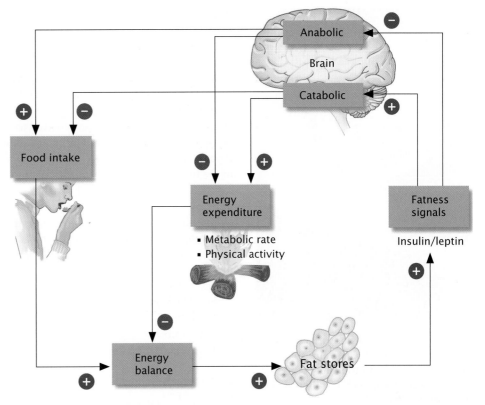

Source: Adapted from Schwartz et al. (2000).

far less effective in people who are obese because they eat a high-fat diet (Gura, 1999; Heymsfield et al., 1999). In these far more common cases of obesity, the brain appears to have become less sensitive to leptin's satiety signals (Ahima & Flier, 2000; Lin et al., 2000; Lustig et al., 2004).

Hunger and the Brain

Many parts of the brain contribute to the control of eating. However, research has focused on regions of the hypothalamus that may play primary roles in detecting and reacting to the blood's signals about the need to eat. As shown in Figure 8.2, the hypothalamus influences both how much food is taken in and how quickly its energy is used, or metabolized.

Some regions of the hypothalamus detect leptin and insulin; these regions generate signals that either increase hunger and reduce energy expenditure or reduce hunger and increase energy expenditure. There are at least twenty neurotransmitters that convey these signals to networks in various parts of the hypothalamus and in the rest of the brain (Cota et al., 2006; Woods et al., 1998, 2000).

Activity in a part of the network that passes through the *ventromedial nucleus* in the hypothalamus tells an animal that there is no need to eat. So if a rat's ventromedial nucleus is stimulated, the animal will stop eating (Kent et al., 1994). However, if the ventromedial nucleus is destroyed, the animal will eat much more than usual and maintain a much higher body weight.

In contrast, the *lateral hypothalamus* contains networks that tell an animal to start eating. So when the lateral hypothalamus is stimulated, rats begin to eat huge quantities, even if they have just had a large meal (Stanley et al., 1993). When the lateral hypothalamus is destroyed, however, rats stop eating almost entirely.

Decades ago, these findings led to the suggestion that these two hypothalamic regions interact to maintain some homeostatic level, or *set point*, based on food intake, body weight, or other eating-related signals (Powley & Keesey, 1970). According to this

FIGURE **8.2**

The Hypothalamus and Hunger

Regions of the hypothalamus generate signals that either increase hunger and reduce energy expenditure, called *anabolic effects*, or reduce hunger and increase energy expenditure, called *catabolic effects*.

LINKAGES
How does the brain know when we are hungry? (a link to Biology and Behavior)

ONE FAT MOUSE   After surgical damage to its ventromedial nucleus, this mouse ate enough to triple its body weight. Results such as this initially led many psychologists to conclude that food intake is regulated by a combination of "start-eating" signals from the lateral hypothalamus and "stop-eating" signals from the ventromedial nucleus. We now know that the regulation process is far more complex and involves more than just these two brain regions.

application of drive reduction theory, normal animals eat until their set point is reached, then stop eating until desirable intake falls below the set point (Cabanac & Morrissette, 1992).

This theory turned out to be too simplistic. More recent research shows that the brain's control of eating involves more than just the interaction of a pair of "stop-eating" and "start-eating" areas (Winn, 1995). For example, the *paraventricular nucleus* in the hypothalamus also plays an important role. As with the ventromedial nucleus, stimulating the paraventricular nucleus reduces food intake. Damaging it causes animals to become obese (Leibowitz, 1992). In addition, hunger—and the eating of particular types of food—is related to the effects of various neurotransmitters on certain neurons in the brain. One of these neurotransmitters, called *neuropeptide Y,* stimulates increased eating of carbohydrates (Kishi & Elmquist, 2005; Schwartz et al., 2000). Another one, *serotonin,* suppresses carbohydrate intake. *Galanin* motivates eating of high-fat food (Krykouli et al., 1990), and *enterostatin* reduces it (Lin et al., 1998). *Endocannabinoids* stimulate eating in general. They affect the same hypothalamic receptors as does the active ingredient in marijuana, which may account for "the munchies," a sudden hunger that marijuana use often creates (Cota et al., 2003; Di Marzo et al., 2001). *Peptide YY3–36* causes a feeling of fullness and reduced food intake (Batterham et al., 2002, 2003).

In other words, several brain regions and many brain chemicals regulate hunger and food selection. These internal regulatory processes are themselves affected by the physical environment (e.g., what foods are available), by learning experiences with particular foods, and, for humans, by social and cultural traditions about eating.

Flavor, Sociocultural Experience, and Food Selection

For example, eating is powerfully affected by the *flavor* of food—the combination of its taste and smell (Carlson, 2001). In general, people eat more when differently flavored foods are served, as in a multicourse meal, than when only one food is served (Raynor & Epstein, 2001). Apparently the flavor of a food becomes less enjoyable as more of it is eaten (Swithers & Hall, 1994). In one study, people rated how much they liked four kinds of food; then they ate one of the foods and rated all four again. The food they had just eaten now got a lower rating, whereas liking increased for all the rest (Johnson & Vickers, 1993).

Eating is also affected by the appearance and smell of certain foods. These signals come to elicit conditioned physiological responses—including the secretion of saliva, digestive juices, and insulin—in anticipation of eating those foods (see the learning chapter for more on conditioned responses). So merely seeing a pizza on television may prompt you to order one. And if you see a delicious-looking cookie, you don't have to be hungry to start eating it. In fact, many people who have just pronounced themselves "full" after a huge holiday meal still manage to find room for an appetizing dessert. In other words, humans eat not just to satisfy nutritional needs but also to experience enjoyment.

Eating is stimulated by other kinds of signals, too. Do you usually eat while reading or watching television? If so, you may find that merely settling down with a book or your favorite show can trigger the desire to have a snack, even if you just finished dinner! This happens partly because situations associated with eating in the past can become signals that stimulate eating in the future (Birch et al., 1989; Weingarten, 1983). People also learn social rules and cultural traditions that influence eating. In North American culture, having lunch at noon, munching popcorn at movies, and eating hot dogs at ball games are common examples of how certain social situations can stimulate eating particular items at particular times. How much you eat may also depend on what others do. Politeness or custom might prompt you to try foods you would otherwise have avoided. Generally, the mere presence of others, even strangers, tends to increase food consumption. Most people consume 60 to 75 percent more food when they are with others than when eating alone (Clendenen, Herman, & Polivy, 1995), and the same effect has been observed in other species, from monkeys to chickens (Galloway et al., 2005; Keeling & Hurink, 1996).

learn by doing **BON APPÉTIT!** The definition of delicacy differs from culture to culture. At this elegant restaurant in Mexico, diners pay to feast on baby alligators, insects, and other dishes that some people from other cultures would not eat even if the restaurant paid *them*. To appreciate your own food culture, make a list of foods that are traditionally valued by your family or cultural group but that people from other groups do not, or might even be unwilling to, eat.

Celebrations, holidays, vacations, and even daily family interactions often revolve around food and what some call a *food culture* (Rozin, 1996). There are wide cultural variations in food use and selection. For example, chewing coca leaves is popular in the Bolivian highlands but illegal in the United States (Burchard, 1992). Insects called palm weevils, a delicacy for people in Papua New Guinea (Paoletti, 1995), are regarded by many Westerners as disgusting (Springer & Belk, 1994), and the beef enjoyed by many Westerners is morally repugnant to devout Hindus in India. Even within the same culture, different groups may have sharply contrasting food traditions. Squirrel brains won't be found on most dinner tables in the United States, but some people in the rural South consider them to be a tasty treat. In short, eating serves functions beyond nutrition—functions that help to remind us of who we are and with whom we identify.

Eating Disorders

Problems in the processes that regulate hunger and eating may cause an *eating disorder*. The most common and dangerous examples are obesity, anorexia nervosa, and bulimia nervosa.

Obesity The World Health Organization (WHO, 1998) defines **obesity** as a condition in which a person's body-mass index, or BMI, is greater than 30. BMI is determined by dividing a person's weight (in kilograms) by the square of the person's height (in meters). So someone who is 5 feet 2 inches and weighs 164 pounds would be classified as obese, as would someone 5 feet 10 inches who weighs 207 pounds. BMI calculators are available at web sites such as www.consumer.gov/weightloss/bmi.htm. People whose BMI is 25 to 29.9 are considered to be overweight, but not obese. (Keep in mind, though, that a given volume of muscle weighs more than the same volume of fat, so very muscular individuals may have an elevated BMI without being overweight.) Using the BMI criterion, about 32 percent of adults in the United States are obese and about 17 percent of children are overweight (Flegal et al., 2002; Hedley et al., 2004; Mokdad et al., 2003; Ogden et al., 2006). The problem has become so common that commercial jets have to burn excess fuel to carry heavier loads, parents of obese young children have trouble finding car safety seats to fit them, and the funeral industry has to offer larger than normal coffins and order wider hearses (Dannenberg, Burton, & Jackson, 2004; St. John, 2003; Trifiletti et al., 2006). And obesity among adults and children is rising, not only in the United States but also in regions as diverse as Asia, Europe, South America, and Africa (e.g., Hedley et al., 2004; Manson et al., 2004; McCarthy, Ellis, & Cole, 2003; Rolland-Cachera et al., 2002; Sturm, 2003; Vasan et al., 2005; Wang & Lobstein, 2006; WHO, 2002a). Obesity is associated with health problems such as diabetes, high blood pressure, an increased risk of heart attack, and possibly Alzheimer's disease (Gustafson et al., 2003; Lakdawalla, Bhattacharya, & Goldman, 2004; Nanchahal et al., 2005). In the United States alone, obesity is blamed for about 30,000 deaths each year and for a predicted shortening of life expectancy in the twenty-first century (Flegel et al., 2005; Olshansky et al., 2005).

Why do some people become obese? Body weight is determined by a combination of food intake and energy output (Keesey & Powley, 1986). Obese people get more energy from food than their body metabolizes, or "burns up." The excess energy, measured in calories, is stored as fat. Obese people tend to eat above-average amounts of high-calorie, tasty foods but below-average amounts of less tasty foods (Kauffman, Herman, & Polivy, 1995). Further, they may be less active than lean people, a pattern that often begins in childhood (Jago et al., 2005; Marshall et al., 2004; Strauss & Pollack, 2001). Spending long hours watching television or playing computer games is a major cause of the inactivity seen in overweight children (Hancox & Poulton, 2006).

In short, inadequate physical activity, combined with overeating—especially of the high-fat foods so prevalent in most Western cultures—has a lot to do with obesity.

obesity A condition in which a person is severely overweight.

But not everyone who is inactive and eats a high-fat diet becomes obese, and some obese people are as active as lean people, so other factors must also be involved (Blundell & Cooling, 2000; Parsons, Power, & Manor, 2005). Some people probably have a genetic predisposition toward obesity (Farooqi & O'Rahilly, 2004; Loos et al., 2006; Meyre et al., 2005). For example, although most obese people have the genes to make leptin, they may not be sensitive to its weight-suppressing effects—perhaps because of differing genetic codes for leptin receptors in the hypothalamus. These genetic factors, along with the presence of certain viruses in the body (Dhurandhar et al., 2000), may help explain obese people's tendency to eat more, to accumulate fat, and to feel hungrier than lean people.

Other explanations for obesity focus on factors such as learning from the examples set by parents who overeat (Hood et al., 2000), too little parental control over what and how much children eat (Johnson & Birch, 1994), and maladaptive reactions to stress. Many people do tend to eat more when under stress, a reaction that may be especially extreme among those who become obese (Dallman et al., 2003; Friedman & Brownell, 1995).

For most people, and especially for people who are obese, it is a lot easier to gain weight than to lose it and keep it off (Jain, 2005; McTigue et al., 2003). The problem arises partly because our evolutionary ancestors—like nonhuman animals in the wild today—could not always be sure that food would be available. Those who survived lean times were the ones whose genes created tendencies to build and maintain fat reserves (e.g., Hara et al., 2000). These "thrifty genes" are adaptive in famine-plagued environments, but they can be harmful and even deadly in affluent societies in which overeating is unnecessary and in which donut shops and fast food restaurants are on every corner (Brown, 1991). Further, if people starve themselves to lose weight, their bodies may burn calories more slowly. This drop in metabolism saves energy and fat reserves and slows weight loss (Leibel, Rosenbaum, & Hirsch, 1995). No wonder health and nutrition experts warn that obese people (and others) should not try to lose a great deal of weight quickly by dramatically cutting food intake (Brownell & Rodin, 1994).

An even more radical approach to the problem of obesity is *bariatric surgery* (Hamad, 2004), which restructures the stomach and intestines so that less food energy is absorbed and stored. Bariatric surgery was performed on about 103,000 people in 2003 alone (Santry, Gillen, & Lauderdale, 2005). Its popularity has been fueled partly by the examples of NBC-TV personality Al Roker and other celebrities whose surgery resulted in dramatic weight loss. Still, due to its costs and risks—postoperative mortality rates range from 0.1 to 2 percent—bariatric surgery is recommended only for extreme and life-threatening cases of obesity.

Drugs offer yet another approach. Several antiobesity drugs have been developed, including one that prevents fat in foods from being digested (e.g., Finer et al., 2000; Hauptman et al., 2000). Another drug has been found to interfere with an enzyme that forms fat. This "fatty acid synthase inhibitor" not only caused rapid weight loss in mice but also reduced their hunger (Loftus et al., 2000). The drug has not yet been tested for safety and effectiveness in humans, but researchers hope that it may someday be possible to give obese people medications that alter the brain mechanisms involved in overeating and fat storage (Arterburn, Crane, & Veenstra, 2004; Chanoine et al., 2005; Wynne et al., 2005).

Millions of people are taking various kinds of antiobesity medication (Stafford & Radley, 2003), but drug treatments alone are unlikely to solve the problem of obesity. In fact, no single antiobesity treatment is likely to be a safe, effective solution that works for everyone. To achieve the kind of gradual weight loss that is most likely to last, obese people are advised to make lifestyle changes in addition to, or instead of, drugs or surgery. The most effective weight-loss programs include components designed to reduce food intake, to change eating habits and attitudes toward food, and to increase energy expenditure through regular exercise (Bray & Tartaglia, 2000; Stice & Shaw, 2004; Wadden et al., 2001). Exercise is especially important because it burns calories while raising metabolism rather than lowering it (Binzen, Swan, & Manore, 2001; Curioni & Lourenço, 2005; Wadden et al., 2005).

THIN IS IN In Western cultures today, thinness is a much-sought-after ideal, especially among young women. This ideal is seen in fashion models, as well as in Miss America pageant winners, whose body mass index has decreased from the "normal" range of 20 to 25 in the 1920s to an "undernourished" 18.5 in recent years (Rubinstein & Caballero, 2000; Voracek & Fisher, 2002). In the United States, 35 percent of normal-weight girls—and 12 percent of underweight girls!—begin dieting when they are as young as nine or ten. Correlational studies suggest that many of these children's efforts to lose weight may have come in response to criticism from family members (Barr Taylor et al., 2006a; Schreiber et al., 1996); for some, the result is anorexia.

anorexia nervosa An eating disorder characterized by self-starvation and dramatic weight loss.

bulimia nervosa An eating disorder that involves eating massive quantities of food, then eliminating it by self-induced vomiting or laxatives.

Anorexia Nervosa At the opposite extreme of eating disorders is **anorexia nervosa** (pronounced "ann-or-EX-ee-ah nuhr-VO-suh"). It is characterized by some combination of self-starvation, self-induced vomiting, excessive exercise, and laxative use that results in weight loss to below 85 percent of normal (Kaye et al., 2000). About 95 percent of people who suffer from anorexia are young females. Anorexics often feel hungry, and many are obsessed with food and its preparation, yet they refuse to eat. Anorexic self-starvation causes serious, often irreversible, physical damage, including reduction in bone density that increases the risk of fractures (Grinspoon et al., 2000). The health dangers may be especially high in anorexic dancers, gymnasts, and other female athletes, who are at risk for stress fractures and heart problems (Sherman & Thompson, 2004). It is estimated that from 4 to 30 percent of those suffering severe anorexia eventually die of starvation, biochemical imbalances, or suicide; their death rate is twelve times higher than for other young women (Herzog et al., 2000; Millar et al., 2005; National Association of Anorexia Nervosa and Associated Disorders, 2002). Anorexia tends to first appear in adolescence and affects about 1 percent of young women in the United States. It is also a growing problem in many other industrialized nations (American Psychiatric Association Work Group on Eating Disorders, 2000; Bulik et al., 2006; Rome et al., 2003).

The appearance of anorexia has been attributed to a combination of factors, including genetic predispositions, biochemical imbalances, social influences, and psychological characteristics (Bulik et al., 2000, 2006; Jacobi et al., 2004; Kaye et al., 2000; Keel & Klump, 2003; Ribases et al., 2005; Vink et al., 2001). Psychological factors that may contribute to the problem include a self-punishing, perfectionistic personality and a culturally reinforced obsession with thinness and attractiveness (Bulik et al., 2003; Dittmar, Halliwell, & Ive, 2006; Francis & Birch, 2005; Moradi, Dirks, & Matteson, 2005; Ricciardelli & McCabe, 2004). Anorexics appear to develop a fear of being fat, which they take to dangerous extremes (de Castro & Goldstein, 1995). Many anorexics continue to view themselves as fat or misshapen even as they are wasting away (Feingold & Mazzella, 1998).

Drugs, hospitalization, and psychotherapy are all used to treat anorexia. In many cases, treatment brings recovery and the maintenance of normal weight (National Institutes of Health, 2001; Pike et al., 2003), but more effective treatment and early intervention methods are still needed (Agras et al., 2004; Lo et al., 2003). Prevention programs now being tested with college women at high risk for developing anorexia are showing promising results (e.g., Barr Taylor et al., 2006b; Franko et al., 2005).

Bulimia Nervosa Like anorexia, bulimia nervosa (pronounced "bu-LEE-mee-uh nuhr-VO-suh") involves intense fear of being fat, but the person may be thin, normal in weight, or even overweight. **Bulimia nervosa** involves eating huge amounts of food (say, several boxes of cookies, a half-gallon of ice cream, and a bucket of fried chicken) and then getting rid of the food through self-induced vomiting or strong laxatives. These "binge-purge" episodes may occur as often as twice a day (Weltzin et al., 1995).

Like people with anorexia, bulimic individuals are usually female; and, like anorexia, bulimia usually begins with a desire to be slender. However, bulimia and anorexia are separate disorders (Pryor, 1995). For one thing, most bulimics see their eating habits as problematic, whereas most anorexics do not. In addition, bulimia nervosa is usually not life threatening (Thompson, 1996). There are consequences, however, including dehydration, nutritional problems, and intestinal damage. Many bulimics develop dental problems from the acids associated with vomiting. Frequent vomiting and the insertion of objects to cause it can also damage the throat.

Estimates of the frequency of bulimia in the United States range from 1 to 3 percent of adolescent and college-age women (National Institutes of Health, 2001; U.S. Surgeon General, 1999). The combination of factors that contribute to bulimia includes perfectionism, low self-esteem, stress, culturally encouraged preoccupation with being thin, and depression and other emotional problems. Problems in the brain's satiety mechanisms may also be involved (Crowther et al., 2001; Steiger et al., 2001; Stice, 2001; Stice & Fairburn, 2003; Zalta & Keel, 2006). Treatment for bulimia, which typically includes

MAJOR FACTORS CONTROLLING HUNGER AND EATING

Theory	Stimulate Eating	Inhibit Eating
Biological factors	Levels of glucose and insulin in the blood provide signals that stimulate eating; neurotransmitters that affect neurons in different regions of the hypothalamus also stimulate food intake and influence hungers for specific kinds of foods, such as fats and carbohydrates. Stomach contractions are associated with subjective feelings of hunger, but they do not play a substantial role in the stimulation of eating.	Hormones released into the bloodstream produce signals that inhibit eating; hormones such as leptin and insulin affect neurons in the hypothalamus and inhibit eating.
Nonbiological factors	Sights and smells of particular foods elicit eating because of prior associations; family customs and social occasions often include norms for eating in particular ways.	Values in contemporary U.S. society encourage thinness and thus can inhibit eating.

1. People may eat when they are "full," suggesting that eating is not controlled by _____ alone.
2. People with _____ nervosa know that they have a problem; those with _____ nervosa tend not to.
3. The best strategy for lasting weight loss includes regular _____, as well as improved eating habits.

individual or group psychotherapy and sometimes antidepressant drugs, can help most bulimic people to eat more normally (Herzog et al., 1999; Wilson et al., 1999).

For a summary of the processes involved in hunger and eating, see "In Review: Major Factors Controlling Hunger and Eating."

Sexual Behavior

▶ **How often does the average person have sex?**

Unlike food, sex is not necessary for an individual's survival, but it is obviously vital for reproduction. The various factors that shape sexual motivation and behavior differ in strength across species. These factors often include physiology, learned behavior, and the physical and social environments. For example, one species of desert bird requires adequate sex hormones, a suitable mate, and a particular environment before it engages in sexual behavior. As long as the dry season lasts, it shows no interest in sex, but within ten minutes of the first rainfall, the birds vigorously copulate.

Rainfall is obviously much less influential as a sexual trigger for humans. In fact, people show an amazing diversity of *sexual scripts,* or patterns of behavior that lead to sex. One survey of college-age men and women identified 122 specific acts and 34 different tactics used for promoting sexual encounters (Greer & Buss, 1994). What actually happens during sex? The matter is exceedingly difficult to address scientifically, partly because most people are reluctant to allow researchers to observe their sexual behavior. Many won't even answer questions about their sexual practices (Bancroft, 1997). Yet having valid information about the nature of human sexual behavior is a vital first step for psychologists and other scientists who study such topics as individual differences in sexuality, gender differences in sexual motivation and behavior, sources of sexual orientation, types of sexual dysfunctions, and pathways through which AIDS and other sexually transmitted diseases (STDs) reach new victims. This information can also help people think about their own sexual behavior in relation to trends in the general population.

The first extensive studies of sexual behavior in the United States were completed in the 1950s and 1960s by Alfred Kinsey (Kinsey, Pomeroy, & Martin, 1948; Kinsey et al., 1953) and by William Masters and Virginia Johnson (1966). In the Kinsey studies, volunteers were asked about their sexual practices, whereas Masters and Johnson actually recorded volunteers' physiological responses during natural or artificial sexual stimulation in a laboratory. Together, these pioneering studies broke new ground in the exploration of human sexuality. However, the people who volunteered for them were probably not a representative sample of the adult population. So the results, and the conclusions drawn from them, might not apply to people in general. Further, the data are now so old that they may not reflect sexual practices today. Unfortunately, the results of more recent surveys, such as reader polls in *Cosmopolitan* and other magazines, are also flawed by the use of unrepresentative samples (Davis & Smith, 1990).

■ What was the researchers' question?

Is it possible to gather data about sexual behavior that are more representative and therefore more applicable to people in general? A team of researchers at the University of Chicago believe it is, so they undertook the National Health and Social Life Survey, the first extensive survey of sexual behavior in the United States since the Kinsey studies (Laumann et al., 1994).

■ How did the researchers answer the question?

This survey included important design features that had been neglected in most other surveys of sexual behavior. First, the study did not depend on self-selected volunteers. The researchers sought out a particular sample of 3,432 people, ranging in age from eighteen to fifty-nine. Second, the sample was carefully constructed so as to reflect the sociocultural diversity of the U.S. population in terms of gender, ethnicity, socioeconomic status, geographical location, and the like. Third, unlike previous mail-in surveys, the Chicago study was based on face-to-face interviews. This approach made it easier to ensure that the participants understood each question and allowed them to explain their responses. To encourage honesty, the researchers allowed participants to answer some of the survey's questions anonymously by placing written responses in a sealed envelope.

■ What did the researchers find?

For one thing, the researchers found that people in the United States have sex less often and with fewer partners than many had assumed. For most, sex occurs about once a week, and only with the partner with whom they share a stable relationship. About a third of the participants reported having had sex only a few times, or not at all, in the preceding year. And, in contrast to various celebrities' splashy tales of dozens, even hundreds, of sexual partners per year, the average male survey participant had had only six sexual partners in his entire life. The average female respondent reported a lifetime total of two. Further, the survey data suggested that people in committed, one-partner relationships had the most frequent and the most satisfying sex. And, although a wide variety of specific sexual practices were reported, the overwhelming majority of heterosexual couples said they tend to engage mainly in penis-vagina intercourse.

■ What do the results mean?

The Chicago survey challenges some of the cultural and media images of sexuality in the United States. In particular, it suggests that people in the United States may be more sexually conservative than one might think on the basis of magazine reader polls and the testimony of guests on daytime talk shows.

■ What do we still need to know?

Many questions remain. The Chicago survey did not ask about some of the more controversial aspects of sexuality, such as the effects of pornography or the role in sexual activity of sexual fetishes such as shoes or other clothing. Had the researchers asked about such topics, their results might have painted a different picture. Further, because the Chicago survey focused on people in the United States, it told us little or nothing about the sexual practices, traditions, and values of people in the rest of the world.

The Chicago team has continued to conduct interviews, and the results are beginning to fill in the picture about sexual behavior in the United States and around the world (Youm & Laumann, 2002). They have found, for example, that nearly one-quarter of U.S. women prefer to achieve sexual satisfaction without partners of either sex. And, although people in the United States tend to engage in a wider variety of sexual behaviors than do those in Britain, people in the United States appear to be less tolerant of disapproved sexual practices (Laumann & Michael, 2000; Michael et al., 1998). Other researchers have found a number of consistent gender differences in sexuality. For example, men tend to have a stronger interest in and desire for sex than women, whereas women are more likely than men to associate sexual activity with a committed relationship (Baumeister, Catanese, & Vohs, 2001; Peplau, 2003; Regan & Berscheid, 1999).

The results of even the best survey methods—like those of the best of all other research methods—usually raise as many questions as they answer. When do people become interested in sex, and why? How do they choose to express these desires, and why? What determines their sexual likes and dislikes? How do learning and sociocultural factors modify the biological forces that seem to provide the raw material of human sexual motivation? These are some of the questions about human sexual behavior that a survey cannot easily or accurately explore (Benson, 2003).

The Biology of Sex

Observations in Masters and Johnson's laboratory led to important findings about the **sexual response cycle,** the pattern of physiological arousal before, during, and after sexual activity (see Figure 8.3). Masters and Johnson (1966) found that men show one primary pattern of sexual response and that women display at least three different patterns from time to time. In both men and women, the first, or *excitement,* phase begins with sexually stimulating input from the environment or from one's own thoughts. Further stimulation leads to intensified excitement in the second, or *plateau,* phase. If stimulation continues, the person reaches the third, or *orgasmic,* stage. Although orgasm lasts only a few seconds, it provides an intensely pleasurable release of physical and psychological tension. The *resolution* phase follows, during which the person returns to a state of relaxation. At this point, men enter a *refractory period,* during which they are temporarily unable to be aroused. Women are capable of immediately repeating the cycle if stimulation continues.

People's motivation to engage in sexual activity has biological roots in **sex hormones.** The female sex hormones are **estrogens** and **progestins;** the main ones are *estradiol* and *progesterone.* The male hormones are **androgens;** the principal example is *testosterone.* Each sex hormone flows in the blood of both sexes, but males have relatively more androgens, and women have relatively more estrogens and progestins.

Sex hormones have both organizing and activating effects on the brain. The *organizing effects* are permanent changes in the brain that influence the brain's response to hormones. The *activating effects* are temporary behavioral changes that last only as long as a sex hormone's level is elevated—such as in the ovulation phase of the monthly menstrual cycle. In mammals, including humans, the organizing effects of hormones occur around the time of birth. It is then that certain brain areas are sculpted into a "female-like" or "male-like" pattern. For example, a brain area called *BnST* is generally

sexual response cycle   The pattern of arousal before, during, and after sexual activity.

sex hormones   Chemicals in the blood that organize and motivate sexual behavior.

estrogens   Feminine hormones that circulate in the bloodstream.

progestins   Feminine hormones that circulate in the bloodstream.

androgens   Masculine hormones that circulate in the bloodstream.

FIGURE **8.3**

The Sexual Response Cycle

Masters and Johnson (1966) found that men show one primary pattern of sexual response, depicted in Part A, and that women display at least three different patterns from time to time—labeled A, B, and C in Part B. For both men and women, sexual stimulation begins with the excitement phase, which is followed by intensified excitement in the plateau phase and the pleasurable release of tension in the orgasmic stage. During the resolution phase, both men and women return to a state of relaxation. Following resolution, men (but not women) enter a refractory phase, during which they are unresponsive to sexual stimulation.

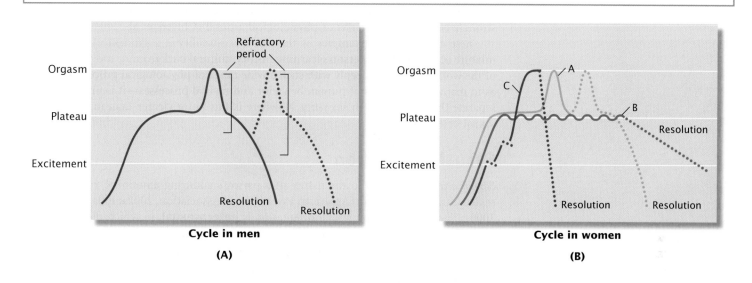

Cycle in men
(A)

Cycle in women
(B)

larger in men than in women. Its possible role in some aspects of human sexuality was suggested by a study that compared the brains of men with a male gender identity to those of male-to-female transsexuals (genetic males who feel like women and may request surgery and hormone treatments to create more female-looking bodies). The BnST in the male-identified men was larger than in the transsexuals. In fact, the transsexuals' BnST was about the size usually seen in women (Zhou et al., 1995).

Rising levels of sex hormones during puberty activate increased sexual desire and interest in sexual behavior. Generally, estrogens stimulate females' sexual interest (Burleson, Gregory, & Trevarthen, 1995). Androgens raise males' sexual interest (Davidson, Camargo, & Smith, 1979), but they may also do so in females (Sherwin & Gelfand, 1987). The activating effects of hormones are also seen in reduced sexual motivation and behavior among people whose hormone-secreting ovaries or testes have been removed for medical reasons. Injections of hormones help restore these people's sexual interest and activity (Sherwin, Gelfand, & Brender, 1985).

Generally, hormones affect sexual desire, not the physical ability to have sex (Wallen & Lovejoy, 1993). This fact may explain why castration (removal of the testes) does not prevent sex crimes by male offenders. Men with low testosterone levels due to medical problems or castration show less sexual desire, but they still have erections in response to erotic stimuli (Kwan et al., 1983). So a sex offender treated by chemical or physical castration would be less likely to seek out sex, but he would still respond as before to his favorite sexual stimuli (Wickham, 2001).

Social and Cultural Factors in Sexuality

Human sexuality is shaped not only by hormones but also by a lifetime of learning and thinking. For example, children learn some of their sexual attitudes and behaviors as part of the development of *gender roles*, as described in the human development chapter. The specific attitudes and behaviors they learn depend partly on the nature of gender roles in their culture (Baumeister, 2000; Hyde & Durik, 2000; Peplau, 2003).

There are differences, too, in what women and men find sexually arousing. For example, in many cultures, men are far more interested in, and responsive to, erotic visual images than women are (Herz & Cahill, 1997; Symons, 1979). A biological basis for this difference was investigated in a study that scanned the brain activity of males and females while they looked at erotic photographs (Hamann et al., 2004). As expected, the men showed greater activity in the amygdala and hypothalamus than the women did. But even though there were gender differences in brain activity, the male and female participants rated the photos as equally attractive and sexually arousing. In another study, when men reported sexual arousal in response to erotic films, they showed signs of physiological arousal, too. For women, self-reports of arousal were not strongly correlated with signs of physiological arousal (Chivers et al., 2004).

These are just a few examples of the fact that sexuality is a product of a complex mixture of factors. Each person's learning history, cultural background, and perceptions of the world interact so deeply with such a wide range of physiological processes that—as in many other aspects of human behavior and mental processes—it is impossible to separate their influence on sexuality. Nowhere is this point clearer than in the case of sexual orientation.

Sexual Orientation

Sexual orientation refers to the nature of a person's enduring emotional, romantic, or sexual attraction to others (American Psychological Association, 2002a; Ellis & Mitchell, 2000). The most common sexual orientation is **heterosexual,** in which the attraction is to members of the opposite sex. When attraction focuses on members of one's own sex, the orientation is called **homosexual,** and more specifically, *gay* (for men) and *lesbian* (for women). People who are attracted to members of both sexes are said to have a **bisexual** orientation. Sexual orientation involves feelings that may or may not be translated into corresponding patterns of sexual behavior. For example, some people whose orientation is gay, lesbian, or bisexual may have sex only with opposite-sex partners. Similarly, people whose orientation is heterosexual may have had one or more same-sex encounters.

In many cultures, heterosexuality has long been regarded as a moral norm, and homosexuality seen as a disease, a disorder, or even a crime (Hooker, 1993). Yet attempts to alter the sexual orientation of gay men and lesbians—using psychotherapy, brain surgery, or electric shock—have usually been ineffective (American Psychiatric Association, 1999; Haldeman, 1994). In 1973 the American Psychiatric Association dropped *homosexuality* from the *Diagnostic and Statistical Manual of Mental Disorders,* thus ending its official status as a mental disorder. The same change was made by the World Health Organization in its *International Classification of Diseases* in 1993, by Japan's psychiatric organization in 1995, and by the Chinese Psychiatric Association in 2001.

Nevertheless, some people still disapprove of homosexuality. Because gays, lesbians, and bisexuals are often the victims of discrimination and even hate crimes, many of them are reluctant to let their sexual orientation be known (Bernat et al., 2001; Meyer, 2003). It is difficult, therefore, to obtain an accurate picture of the mix of heterosexual, gay, lesbian, and bisexual orientations in a population. In the Chicago sex survey mentioned earlier, 1.4 percent of women and 2.8 percent of men identified themselves as exclusively gay or lesbian (Laumann et al., 1994). These figures are much lower than the 10 percent found earlier in Kinsey's studies. However, the Chicago survey's face-to-face interviews did not allow respondents to give anonymous answers to questions about sexual orientation. Some researchers suggest that if anonymous responses to those questions had been permitted, the prevalence figures for gay, lesbian, and bisexual orientations would have been higher (Bullough, 1995). In fact, studies that have allowed anonymous responding estimate that gay, lesbian, and bisexual people make up between 2 and 21 percent of the population in the United States, Canada, and Western Europe (Aaron et al., 2003; Bagley & Tremblay, 1998; Binson et al., 1995; Savin-Williams, 2006; Sell, Wells, & Wypij, 1995).

heterosexual Referring to sexual desire or behavior that is focused on members of the opposite sex.

homosexual Referring to gay men and lesbians, whose sexual desire or behavior is focused on members of their own sex.

bisexual Referring to sexual desire or behavior that is focused on members of both sexes.

The question of where sexual orientation comes from is a topic of intense debate in scientific circles, on talk shows, in Internet chat rooms, and in everyday conversations.

■ What am I being asked to believe or accept?

One point of view suggests that genes dictate our sexual orientation. According to this view, we do not learn a sexual orientation but, rather, are born with it.

■ Is there evidence available to support the claim?

In 1995, a report by a respected research group suggested that one kind of sexual orientation—namely, that of gay men—is associated with a particular gene on the X chromosome (Hu et al., 1995). This finding was not supported by later studies (Rice et al., 1999), but a growing body of evidence from research in behavioral genetics suggests that genes might indeed influence sexual orientation in humans (Kendler et al., 2000; Pillard & Bailey, 1998). One study examined pairs of monozygotic male twins (whose genes are identical), pairs of dizygotic, or nonidentical, twins (whose genes are no more alike than those of any pair of brothers), and pairs of adopted brothers (who are genetically unrelated). To participate in this study, at least one brother in each pair had to be gay. As it turned out, the other brother was also gay or bisexual in 52 percent of the identical-twin pairs but in only 22 percent of the nonidentical pairs and in just 11 percent of the adoptive pairs (Bailey & Pillard, 1991). Similar findings have been reported for male identical twins raised apart. In such cases, a shared sexual orientation cannot be due to the effects of a shared environment (Whitam, Diamond, & Martin, 1993). The few available studies of female sexual orientation have yielded similar results (Bailey & Benishay, 1993; Bailey, Dunne, & Nicholas, 2000).

Other evidence for the role of biological factors in sexual orientation comes from research on the impact of sex hormones. In adults, differences in the levels of these hormones are not generally associated with differences in sexual orientation. However, hormonal differences during prenatal development might be involved in the shaping of sexual orientation (Lalumière, Blanchard, & Zucker, 2000; Lippa, 2003; Williams et al., 2000). For example, one study found that women who had been exposed to high levels of androgens during their fetal development were much more likely to become lesbians than their sisters who were not similarly exposed (Meyer et al., 1995). Studies of nonhuman animals have found that such hormonal influences alter the structure of the hypothalamus, a brain region known to underlie some aspects of sexual functioning (Swaab & Hofman, 1995). In humans, too, prenatal exposure to hormones and other chemicals may be responsible for anatomical differences in the hypothalamus. These hormone-related differences are seen not only between males and females but between heterosexual and gay men as well (Bogaert, 2003, 2006; LeVay, 1991; Savic, Berglund, & Lindström, 2005; Swaab et al., 2001).

Finally, a biological basis for sexual orientation is suggested by the relatively weak effects of the environment on sexual orientation. For example, the sexual orientation of children's caregivers has little or no effect on those children's own orientation. Several studies have shown that children adopted by homosexual parents are no more or less likely to display a homosexual orientation than are children raised by heterosexual parents (Anderssen, Amlie, & Ytteroy, 2002; Bailey et al., 1995; Tasker & Golombok, 1995).

■ Can that evidence be interpreted another way?

Like all correlational data, correlations between genetics and sexual orientation are open to alternative interpretations. As discussed in the introductory chapter, a correlation describes the strength and direction of the relationship between two variables, but it does not guarantee that one variable actually influences the other. Consider again the

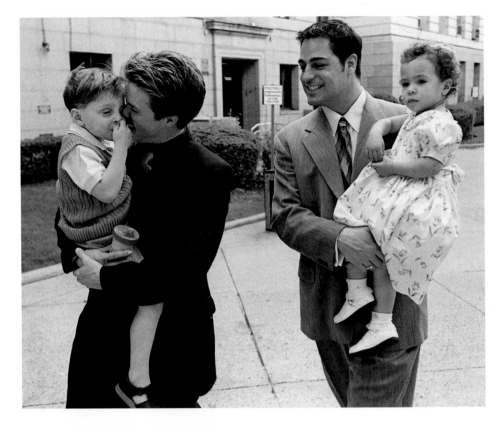

A COMMITTED RELATIONSHIP, WITH CHILDREN Like heterosexual relationships, gay and lesbian relationships can be brief and stormy or stable and long lasting (Kurdek, 2005). These gay men are committed to each other for the long haul, as evidenced by their decision to adopt two children together. The strong role of biological factors in sexual orientation is seen in research showing that these children's orientation will not be influenced much, if at all, by that of their adoptive parents (Anderssen, Amlie, & Ytteroy, 2002; Patterson, 2004; Stacey & Biblarz, 2001; Tasker & Golombok, 1995).

data showing that the brothers who shared the most genes were also most likely to share a gay orientation. What they shared was probably not a "gay gene" but, rather, a set of genes that influenced the boys' activity levels, emotionality, aggressiveness, and the like. One example is "gender nonconformity" in childhood, the tendency for some boys to display "feminine" behaviors and for some girls to behave in "masculine" ways (Bailey, Dunne, & Martin, 2000; Knafo, Iervolino, & Plomin, 2005). Such general aspects of their temperaments or personalities—and other people's reactions to them—could influence the likelihood of a particular sexual orientation (Bem, 1996). In other words, sexual orientation could arise as a reaction to the way people respond to a genetically determined but nonsexual aspect of personality. The influence of prenatal hormone levels could also influence sexual orientation by shaping aggressiveness or other nonsexual aspects of behavior.

It is also important to look at behavioral genetics evidence for what it can tell us about the role of *environmental* factors in sexual orientation. When we read a study showing that 52 percent of the time, both members of identical-twin pairs have a gay, lesbian, or bisexual orientation, it is easy to ignore the fact that the sexual orientation of the twin pair members *differed* in 48 percent of the cases. Viewed in this way, the results suggest that genes do not tell the entire story of sexual orientation. In other words, it is not determined by unlearned, genetic forces alone. As described in the chapter on biology and behavior, the brains and bodies we inherit are quite responsive to environmental influences. In fact, the behaviors we engage in and the experiences we have often result in physical changes in the brain and elsewhere (Wang et al., 1995). For example, physical changes occur in the brain's synapses as we form new memories. So differences seen in the brains of adults with differing sexual orientations could be the effect, not the cause, of their behavior or experiences.

■ **What evidence would help to evaluate the alternatives?**

Much more evidence is needed regarding the role of genes in shaping sexual orientation. We also have a lot to learn about the extent to which genes and hormones shape physical and psychological characteristics that lead to various sexual orientations. In studying these topics, researchers will want to learn more about the genetic makeup, mental style, and behavioral characteristics of people with different sexual orientations. Are there personality characteristics associated with particular sexual orientations? If so, do those characteristics have a strong genetic component? To what extent are heterosexuals, gays, lesbians, and bisexuals similar—and different—in terms of biases, coping skills, developmental histories, and the like (Bailey, Dunne, & Martin, 2000)? The more we learn about sexual orientation in general, the easier it will be to interpret data relating to its origins.

Yet even classifying sexual orientation is not simple, because people do not always fall into sharply defined categories (American Psychological Association, 2002a; Savin-Williams, 2006). Should a man who identifies himself as gay be considered bisexual because he occasionally has heterosexual daydreams? What sexual orientation label would be appropriate for a forty-year-old woman who experienced a few lesbian encounters in her teens but has engaged in exclusively heterosexual sex since then? Progress in understanding the origins of sexual orientation would be enhanced by a generally accepted system for describing and defining exactly what is meant by the term *sexual orientation* (Stein, 1999).

■ What conclusions are most reasonable?

The evidence available so far suggests that genetic factors, probably operating via prenatal hormones, create differences in the brains of people with different sexual orientations. However, the manner in which a person expresses a genetically influenced sexual orientation will be profoundly shaped by what that person learns through social and cultural experiences (Bancroft, 1994). In short, as is true of other psychological phenomena, sexual orientation reflects the complex interplay of both genetic and nongenetic mechanisms—of both nature and nurture.

Sexual Dysfunctions

The biological, social, and psychological factors that shape human sexual behavior can also contribute to **sexual dysfunctions,** which are problems in a person's desire for, or ability to have, satisfying sexual activity (Goldstein & Rosen, 2002). For men, a common problem is *erectile disorder*, a persistent inability to have or maintain an erection adequate for sex. Physical causes—such as fatigue, diabetes, high blood pressure, the use of alcohol or other drugs, and perhaps even genetics—account for some cases (Fischer et al., 2004; Heiman, 2002). Psychological causes such as anxiety are also common (Everaerd & Laan, 1994). As its name implies, *premature ejaculation* is a recurring tendency to ejaculate during sex sooner than the man or his partner desires.

For women, the most common sexual dysfunction is *sexual arousal disorder* (once called *frigidity*), which involves a recurring inability to become aroused during sexual activity (Phillips, 2000; Wilson et al., 1996). Sexual arousal disorder can stem from inadequate genital stimulation, hormonal imbalances, insufficient vaginal lubrication, or inadequate blood flow to the clitoris (Anastasiadis et al., 2002; Mansfield, Voda, & Koch, 1995; Wilson et al., 1996). However, it is also often tied to psychological factors such as guilt or self-consciousness, which can affect men as well as women (Davidson & Moore, 1994; Laan et al., 1993).

Many people experience episodes of at least one of these problems at some point in their lives (Heiman, 2002; Laumann, Paik, & Rosen, 1999; Mercer et al., 2003), but these episodes are considered dysfunctions only if they become a persistent and distressing obstacle to sexual functioning (American Psychiatric Association, 1994; Mercer et al., 2003). Fortunately, most sexual dysfunctions can be overcome through psychotherapy, medication, or both (Braunstein et al., 2005; de Silva, 1994). For example, Viagra and other drugs that affect blood flow in the penis are effective in treating many cases of erectile disorder.

sexual dysfunctions Problems with sexual motivation, arousal, or orgasmic response.

Source: Murray (1971).

FIGURE **8.4**

Assessing Achievement Motivation

This picture is similar to those included in the Thematic Apperception Test, or TAT (Morgan & Murray, 1935). The strength of people's achievement motivation is inferred from the stories they tell about TAT pictures. A response like "The young woman is hoping that she will be able to make her grandmother proud of her" would be seen as reflecting high achievement motivation.

Achievement Motivation

▶ **Why do some people try harder than others to succeed?**

This sentence was written at 6 A.M. on a beautiful Sunday in June. Why would someone get up that early to work on a weekend? Why do people take their work seriously and try to do the best that they can? People work hard partly due to *extrinsic motivation,* a desire for external rewards such as money. But work and other human activities also reflect *intrinsic motivation,* a desire for internal satisfaction.

The next time you visit someone's home or office, notice the mementos displayed there. Perhaps there are framed diplomas and awards, trophies and ribbons, and photos of children and grandchildren. These badges of achievement affirm that a person has accomplished tasks that merit approval or establish worth. Much of human behavior is motivated by a desire for approval, admiration, and a sense of achievement—in short, for esteem—from others and from within. In this section, we examine two of the most common avenues to esteem: achievement in general and achievement in one's work.

Need for Achievement

Many athletes who already hold world records still train intensely; many people who have built multimillion-dollar businesses still work fourteen-hour days. What motivates these people? One answer is a motive called **need achievement** (Murray, 1938). People with a high need for achievement seek to master tasks—such as sports, business ventures, occupational skills, intellectual puzzles, or artistic creation—and feel intense satisfaction from doing so. They work hard at striving for excellence, enjoy themselves in the process, and take great pride in achieving at a high level.

Individual Differences   How do people with strong achievement motivation differ from others? To find out, researchers gave children a test to measure their need for achievement (Figure 8.4 shows a test for adults) and then asked them to play a ring-toss game. Most of the children who scored low on the need-for-achievement test stood either so close to the ring-toss target that they couldn't fail or so far away that they could not succeed. In contrast, children scoring high on the need-for-achievement test stood at a moderate distance from the target, making the game challenging but not impossible (McClelland, 1958).

Experiments with adults and children suggest that people with high achievement needs tend to set challenging but realistic goals. They actively seek success, take risks when necessary, can wait for rewards, and are intensely satisfied when they do well (Mayer & Sutton, 1996). Yet if they feel they have tried their best, people with high achievement motivation are not too upset by failure. Those with low achievement motivation also like to succeed, but instead of joy, success tends to bring them relief at having avoided failure (Winter, 1996).

Differences in achievement motivation also appear in the kinds of goals people seek in achievement-related situations (Molden & Dweck, 2000). Some tend to adopt *learning goals.* When they play golf, take piano lessons, work at problems, go to school, and engage in other achievement-oriented activities, they do so mainly to get better at those activities. They realize that they may not yet have the skills necessary to achieve at a high level, so they tend to learn by watching others and to struggle with problems on their own rather than asking for help (Mayer & Sutton, 1996). When they do seek help, people with learning goals are likely to ask for explanations, hints, and other forms of task-related information, not for quick, easy answers that remove the challenge from the situation. In contrast, people who adopt *performance goals* are usually more concerned with demonstrating the competence they believe they already possess. They tend to seek information about how well they have performed compared with others rather than about how to improve their performance (Butler, 1998). When they seek help, it is usually to ask for "the "right answer" rather than for tips on how to find the answer

need achievement   A motive reflected in the degree to which a person establishes specific goals, cares about meeting them, and experiences satisfaction by doing so.

HELPING THEM DO THEIR BEST

Learning-oriented goals are especially appropriate in classrooms, where students typically have little knowledge of the subject matter. This is why most teachers tolerate errors and reward gradual improvement. They do not usually encourage performance goals, which emphasize doing better than others and demonstrating immediate competence (Reeve, 1996). Still, to help students do their best in the long run, teachers may promote performance goals, too. The proper combination of both kinds of goals may be more motivating than either kind alone (Barron & Harackiewicz, 2001).

themselves. Because their primary goal is to display competence, people with performance goals tend to avoid new challenges if they are not confident that they will be successful, and they tend to quit in response to failure (Grant & Dweck, 2003; Weiner, 1980). Those with learning goals tend to be more persistent and less upset when they don't immediately perform well (Niiya, Crocker, & Bartmess, 2004).

Development of Achievement Motivation   Achievement motivation develops in early childhood under the influence of both genetic and environmental factors. As described in the personality chapter, children inherit general behavioral tendencies, such as impulsiveness and emotionality, and these tendencies may support or undermine the development of achievement motivation. The motivation to achieve is also shaped by what children learn from watching and listening to others, especially their parents. Evidence for the influence of parental teachings about achievement comes from a study in which young boys were given a task so difficult that they were sure to fail. Fathers whose sons scored low on achievement motivation tests often became annoyed as they watched their boys work on the task, discouraged them from continuing, and interfered or even completed the task themselves (Rosen & D'Andrade, 1959). A much different response pattern emerged among parents of children who scored high on tests of achievement motivation. Those parents tended to (1) encourage the child to try difficult tasks, especially new ones; (2) give praise and other rewards for success; (3) encourage the child to find ways to succeed rather than merely complaining about failure; and (4) prompt the child to go on to the next, more difficult challenge (McClelland, 1985). Other research with adults shows that even the slightest cues that bring a parent to mind can boost some people's efforts to achieve a goal (Shah, 2003).

More general cultural influences also affect the development of achievement motivation. Subtle messages about a culture's view of the importance and value of achievement often appear in the books children read, the stories they hear, and the programs they see on television. Does the story's main character work hard and overcome obstacles, thus creating expectations of a payoff for persistence? Or does a lazy main character drift aimlessly and then win the lottery, suggesting that rewards come randomly, regardless of effort? And if the main character succeeds, is it the result of personal effort, as is typical of stories in individualist cultures? Or is success based on ties to a cooperative and supportive group, as is typical of stories in collectivist cultures? These themes appear to act as blueprints for reaching one's goals. It is not surprising, then,

"Maybe they didn't try hard enough."

that ideas about achievement motivation differ from culture to culture. In one study, individuals from Saudi Arabia and from the United States were asked to comment on short stories describing people succeeding at various tasks. Saudis tended to see the people in the stories as having succeeded because of the help they got from others, whereas Americans tended to attribute success to the internal characteristics of each story's main character (Zahrani & Kaplowitz, 1993).

In short, achievement motivation is strongly influenced by social and cultural learning experiences and by the beliefs about oneself that these experiences help to create. People who come to believe in their ability to achieve are more likely to do so than those who expect to fail (Butler, 1998; Dweck, 1998; Wigfield & Eccles, 2000).

Achievement and Success in the Workplace

In the workplace, there is usually more concern with employees' motivation to work hard during business hours than with their general level of need achievement. In fact, employers tend to set up jobs in accordance with their ideas about how intrinsic and extrinsic motivation combine to shape employees' performance (Riggio, 1989). Employers who see workers as lazy, dishonest, and lacking in ambition tend to offer highly structured, heavily supervised jobs. They give the employees little say in deciding what to do or how to do it. These employers assume that workers are motivated mainly by extrinsic rewards—especially money. So they are often surprised when, in spite of good pay and benefits, some employees are dissatisfied with their jobs and show little motivation to work hard (Diener & Seligman, 2004; Igalens & Roussel, 1999).

If good pay and benefits alone don't bring job satisfaction and the desire to excel on the job, what does? In Western cultures low worker motivation appears to come largely from negative thoughts and feelings about having little or no control over the work environment (Rosen, 1991). Compared with those in highly structured jobs, workers tend to be happier, more satisfied, and more productive if they are (1) encouraged to participate in decisions about how work should be done; (2) given problems to solve, without being told how to solve them; (3) taught more than one skill; (4) given individual responsibility; and (5) given public recognition, not just money, for good performance (Fisher, 2000).

Allowing people to set and achieve clear goals is one way to increase both job performance and job satisfaction (Abramis, 1994). Goals that most effectively maintain work motivation have three features (Katzell & Thompson, 1990). First, they are personally meaningful. When a memo from a high-level administrator tells employees that

GOAL SETTING AND ACHIEVEMENT MOTIVATION Clear and specific goals motivate the most persistent of achievement efforts on the job and in other areas, too (Locke & Latham, 2002). These women are more likely to stick with their exercise program if they are pursuing the goal of "losing twenty pounds" or "doing aerobics three times a week," rather than the vague goal of "getting in shape." Similarly, you are more likely to keep reading this chapter if your goal is to "read the motivation section of the motivation and emotion chapter today" than if it is to "do some studying." Clarifying your goal makes it easier to know when you have reached it and when it is time to take a break. Without clear goals, a person can be more easily distracted by fatigue, boredom, or frustration and more likely to give up before completing a task.

subjective well-being A cognitive judgment of satisfaction with life, the frequent experiencing of positive moods and emotions, and the relatively infrequent experiencing of unpleasant moods and emotions.

their goal should be to increase production, they tend to feel unfairly burdened and not particularly motivated to meet the goal. Second, effective goals are specific and concrete (Locke & Latham, 2002). The goal of "doing better" is usually not a strong motivator. A specific target, such as increasing sales by 10 percent, is a far more motivating goal. It is there for all to see, and it is easy to determine whether, and when, the goal has been reached. Finally, goals are most effective if management supports the workers' own goal setting, offers special rewards for reaching goals, and gives encouragement for renewed efforts after failure (Kluger & DeNisi, 1998).

To summarize, motivating jobs offer personal challenges, independence, and both intrinsic and extrinsic rewards. They provide enough satisfaction for people to feel excitement and pleasure in working hard. For employers, the rewards are more productivity, less absenteeism, and fewer resignations (Ilgen & Pulakos, 1999).

Achievement and Subjective Well-Being

Some people believe that the more they achieve and the more money and other material goods they have as a result, the happier they will be. Do you agree? Researchers studying *positive psychology* (Seligman et al., 2005; Sheldon & King, 2001) have become increasingly interested in the systematic study of what it actually takes to achieve happiness, or, more formally, *subjective well-being* (Lyubomirsky, 2001). **Subjective well-being** is a combination of a cognitive judgment of satisfaction with life, the frequent experiencing of positive moods and emotions, and the relatively infrequent experiencing of unpleasant moods and emotions (Diener, 2000; Diener & Biswas-Diener, 2002; Frederickson & Losada, 2005; Urry et al., 2004).

Research on subjective well-being indicates that, as you might expect, people living in extreme poverty or in war-torn or politically chaotic countries are less happy than people in better circumstances. And people everywhere react to good or bad events with corresponding changes in mood. As described in the chapter on health, stress, and coping, for example, severe or long-lasting stressors—such as the death of a loved one—can lead to psychological and physical problems. But although events do have an impact, the depressing or elevating effects of major changes, such as being promoted or fired—or even being imprisoned, seriously injured, or disabled—tend not to last as long as we might think they would. In other words, how happy you are may have less to do with what happens to you than you might expect (Bonanno, 2004; Gilbert & Wilson, 1998; Kahneman et al., 2006; Lyubomirsky, 2001; Riis et al., 2005).

Most event-related changes in mood subside within days or weeks, and most people then return to their previous level of happiness (Suh, Diener, & Fujita, 1996). Even when events create permanent changes in circumstances, most people adapt by changing their expectancies and goals, not by radically and permanently changing their baseline level of happiness. For example, people may be thrilled after getting a big salary increase, but as they get used to having more money, the thrill fades, and they may eventually feel just as underpaid as before. In fact, although there are exceptions (Fujita & Diener, 2005; Lucas et al., 2004), most people's level of subjective well-being tends to be remarkably stable throughout their lives. This stable baseline may be related to temperament, or personality, and it has been likened to the homeostatic processes that maintain body temperature or weight (Lykken, 1999). And like many other aspects of temperament, our baseline level of happiness may be influenced by genetics. Twin studies have shown, for example, that individual differences in happiness are more strongly associated with inherited personality characteristics than with environmental factors such as money, popularity, or physical attractiveness (Lykken, 1999; Tellegen et al., 1988).

Beyond inherited tendencies, the things that appear to matter most in generating happiness are close social ties (including friends and a satisfying marriage or partnership), religious faith, and having the resources necessary to make progress toward one's goals (Diener, 2000; Myers, 2000). So you don't have to be a smart, rich, physically attractive high achiever to be happy, and it turns out that most people in Western cultures are relatively happy (Diener & Diener, 1995; Gow et al., 2005).

These results are consistent with the views expressed over many centuries by philosophers, psychologists, and wise people in all cultures (e.g., Ekman et al., 2005). As discussed in the personality chapter, for example, Abraham Maslow (1970) noted that when people in Western cultures experience unhappiness and psychological problems, those problems can often be traced to a *deficiency orientation*. He said that these people tend to seek happiness by trying to acquire the goods and status they don't have—but think they need—rather than by appreciating life itself, as well as the material and nonmaterial riches they already have. Others have amplified this point, suggesting that our efforts to get more of the things we think will bring happiness may actually contribute to unhappiness if what we get is never "enough" (Diener & Seligman, 2004; Luthar & Latendresse, 2005; Nickerson et al., 2003; Srivastava, Locke, & Bartol, 2001).

Relations and Conflicts Among Motives

▶ **Which motives move me most?**

It is far too early to tell whether research on subjective well-being will help to channel people's achievement motivation toward a more balanced set of goals, but there is no doubt that people will continue striving to meet whatever needs they perceive to be important. What are those needs?

Maslow's Hierarchy

Maslow (1970) suggested that human behavior is influenced by a hierarchy, or ranking, of five classes of needs, or motives (see Figure 8.5). He said that needs at the lowest level of the hierarchy must be at least partially satisfied before people can be motivated by the ones at higher levels. From the bottom to the top of Maslow's hierarchy, these five motives are as follows:

1. *Physiological,* such as the need for food, water, oxygen, and sleep.

2. *Safety,* such as the need to be cared for as a child and to have a secure income as an adult.

3. *Belongingness and love,* such as the need to be part of groups and to participate in affectionate sexual and nonsexual relationships.

4. *Esteem,* such as the need to be respected as a useful, honorable individual.

FIGURE **8.5**

Maslow's Hierarchy of Motives

learn by doing Abraham Maslow saw human motives as organized in a hierarchy in which motives at lower levels come before those at higher levels. According to this view, self-actualization is the essence of mental health; but Maslow recognized that only rare individuals, such as Mother Teresa or Martin Luther King, Jr., approach full self-actualization. Take a moment to consider which level of Maslow's hierarchy you are focused on at this point in your life. Which level do you ultimately hope to reach?

Self-actualization (i.e., maximizing one's potential)

Esteem (e.g., respect)

Belongingness and love (e.g., acceptance, affection)

Safety (e.g., nurturance, money)

Physiological (e.g., food, water, oxygen)

Source: Adapted from Maslow (1943).

5. *Self-actualization,* which means reaching one's full potential. People motivated by this need explore and enhance relationships with others; follow interests for intrinsic pleasure rather than for money, status, or esteem; and are concerned with issues affecting all people, not just themselves.

Maslow's hierarchy has been very influential over the years, partly because the needs associated with basic survival and security do generally take precedence over those related to self-enhancement or personal growth (Baumeister & Leary, 1995; Oishi et al., 1999). But critics see the hierarchy as too simplistic (Hall, Lindzey, & Campbell, 1998; Neher, 1991). It doesn't predict or explain, for example, the motivation of people who starve themselves to draw attention to political or moral causes. Further, people may not have to satisfy one kind of need before addressing others; we can seek to satisfy several needs at once. Finally, the ordering of needs within the survival/security and enhancement/growth categories differs from culture to culture, suggesting that there may not be a single, universal hierarchy of needs.

To address some of the problems in Maslow's theory, Clayton Alderfer (1969) proposed *existence, relatedness, growth (ERG) theory,* which places human needs into just three categories: *existence needs* (such as for food and water), *relatedness needs* (e.g., for social interactions and attachments), and *growth needs* (such as for developing one's capabilities). Unlike Maslow, Alderfer doesn't assume that these needs must be satisfied in a particular order. Instead, he sees needs in each category as rising and falling from time to time and from situation to situation. When a need in one area is fulfilled, or even if it is frustrated, a person will be motivated to pursue some other needs. For example, if a breakup frustrates relatedness needs, a person might focus on existence or growth needs by eating more or volunteering to work late.

LINKAGES
Can motivational conflicts cause stress? (a link to Health, Stress, and Coping)

LINKAGES

Conflicting Motives and Stress

As in the case of hunger strikes, in which the desire to promote a cause is pitted against the desire to eat, human motives can sometimes conflict. The usual result is some degree of discomfort. For example, imagine that you are alone and bored on a Saturday night and you think about going out for a snack. What are your motives? Hunger might play a part, and so might the prospect of the increased arousal that a change of scene will provide. Even sexual motivation might be involved, as you consider the chances of meeting someone exciting in the convenience store. But safety-related motives may also kick in: Is your neighborhood safe enough for you to go out alone? Even an esteem motive might come into play, making you hesitate to be seen on your own on a weekend night.

These are just a few of the motives that may shape a trivial decision. When the decision is more important, the number and strength of motivational pushes and pulls are often greater, creating far more internal conflict and indecision. There are four basic types of motivational conflicts (Miller, 1959):

1. *Approach-approach conflicts.* When we must choose only one of two desirable activities—say, going to a movie or to a concert—an *approach-approach conflict* exists.

2. *Avoidance-avoidance conflicts.* An *avoidance-avoidance conflict* arises when we must select one of two undesirable alternatives. Someone forced either to sell the family home or to declare bankruptcy faces an avoidance-avoidance conflict.

3. *Approach-avoidance conflicts.* If someone you couldn't stand had tickets to your favorite group's sold-out concert and invited you to come along, what would you do? When a particular event or activity has both attractive and unattractive features, an *approach-avoidance* conflict is created.

4. *Multiple approach-avoidance conflicts.* Suppose you must choose between two jobs. One offers a high salary with a well-known company but requires long

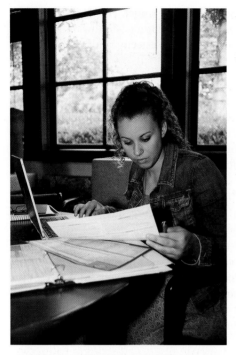

working hours and relocation to a miserable climate. The other boasts advancement opportunities, fringe benefits, and a better climate, but it doesn't pay as much and involves an unpredictable work schedule. This is an example of a *multiple approach-avoidance conflict,* in which two or more alternatives each have both positive and negative features. Such conflicts are especially difficult to resolve, partly because the features of each option may not be easy to compare. For example, how many dollars a year does it take to compensate you for living in a bad climate?

The difficulties associated with resolving each of these conflicts can create stress, a topic explored in the chapter on health, stress, and coping. Most people who have motivational conflicts are tense, irritable, and more vulnerable than usual to physical and psychological problems. These reactions are especially likely when no choice is obviously "right," when varying motives have approximately equal strength, and when a choice can have serious consequences (as in decisions to marry, to split up, or to place an elderly parent in a nursing home). Some people may spend a long time agonizing over these conflicts, whereas others may make a choice quickly, impulsively, and thoughtlessly, simply to end the discomfort of uncertainty. Even after resolving the conflict on the basis of careful thought, people may continue to experience stress responses, such as worrying about whether they made the right decision or blaming themselves for bad choices. These and other consequences of conflicting motives can even lead to depression or other serious disorders.

learn by doing   A STRESSFUL CONFLICT
Think back to when you were deciding which college to attend. Was the decision easy and obvious, or did it create a motivational conflict? If there was a conflict, was it an approach-approach, approach-avoidance, or multiple approach-avoidance conflict? What factors were most important in deciding how to resolve the conflict, and what emotions and signs of stress did you experience during and after the decision-making process?

The emotions associated with motivational conflicts provide just one example of the close links between motivation and emotion. Motivation can intensify emotion, as when hunger leads a normally calm person to angrily complain about slow service at a restaurant. But emotions can also create motivation. Happiness, for example, is an emotion that people want to feel, so they engage in whatever behaviors—studying, artwork, investing, beachcombing—they think will achieve it. Similarly, as an emotion that most people want to avoid, anxiety motivates many behaviors, from leaving the scene of an accident to avoiding poisonous snakes. Let's take a closer look at emotions.

The Nature of Emotion

▶ **How do feelings differ from thoughts?**

Everyone seems to agree that joy, sorrow, anger, fear, love, and hate are emotions. However, it is often hard to identify the shared features that make these experiences emotions rather than, say, thoughts or impulses.

Defining Characteristics

Most psychologists in Western cultures tend to see emotions as organized psychological and physiological reactions to changes in our relationship to the world. These reactions are partly private, or *subjective,* experiences and partly measurable patterns of behavior and physiological arousal. The subjective experience of emotion has several characteristics:

1. Emotion is usually *temporary.* In other words, it tends to have a relatively clear beginning and end and a relatively short duration. Moods, by contrast, tend to last longer.

2. Emotional experience can be *positive,* as in joy, or *negative,* as in sadness. It can also be a mixture of both, as in the bittersweet feelings of watching one's child leave for the first day of kindergarten (Larsen et al., 2004).

WINNERS AND LOSERS Emotional experiences depend in part on our interpretation of situations and how those situations relate to our goals. A single event—the announcement of the results of a cheerleading contest—triggered drastically different emotional reactions in these women, depending on whether they perceived it as making them winners or losers.

3. Emotion can vary in intensity. You can feel pleased, happy, or ecstatic. You can also feel mildly disappointed, sad, or deeply depressed.

4. Emotional experience is triggered partly by thoughts, especially by a *mental assessment* of how a situation relates to your goals. The same event can bring on different emotions depending on what it means to you. An exam score of 75 percent may thrill you if your best previous score had been 50 percent, but it may upset you if you had never before scored below 90 percent.

5. Emotional experience *alters thought processes,* often by directing attention toward some things and away from others. Negative emotions tend to narrow attention, and positive emotions tend to broaden it. Anxiety about terrorism, for example, narrows our attention to focus on potential threats in airports and other public places (Craske, 1999; Yovel & Mineka, 2005).

6. Emotional experience brings on an *action tendency,* a motivation to behave in certain ways. Grieving parents' anger, for example, might motivate them to harm their child's killer. But for John Walsh, whose son was kidnapped and murdered, grief led to helping to prevent such crimes by creating *America's Most Wanted,* a TV show dedicated to bringing criminals to justice.

7. Emotional experiences are *passions* that you feel, whether you want to or not. You do have some control over emotions, though, because they depend partly on how you interpret situations (Gross, 2001). For example, you can reduce your emotional reaction to a car accident by reminding yourself that no one was hurt and that you are insured. Still, you can't just *decide* what emotions you experience; instead, you "fall in love" or "explode in anger" or are "overcome by grief."

In other words, the subjective aspects of emotions are experiences that are both triggered by the thinking self and felt as happening to the self. The extent to which we are "victims" of our passions versus rational controllers of our emotions is a central dilemma of human existence.

The objectively measurable aspects of emotion include learned and innate *expressive displays* and *physiological responses.* Expressive displays—such as a smile or a frown—communicate feelings to others. Physiological responses—changes in heart rate, for example—provide the biological adjustments needed to perform actions generated by the emotional experience. If you throw a temper tantrum, for instance, your heart must deliver additional oxygen and fuel to your muscles.

In summary, an **emotion** is a temporary experience with positive, negative, or mixed qualities. People experience emotion with varying intensity as happening to the self, generated in part by a mental assessment of situations, and accompanied by both learned and innate physical responses. Through emotion, whether they mean to or not, people communicate their internal states and intentions to others. Emotion often disrupts thinking and behavior, but it also triggers and guides thinking and organizes, motivates, and sustains behavior and social relations.

The Biology of Emotion

The biological systems described in the chapter on biology and behavior play a major role in emotion. In the *central nervous system,* numerous brain areas are involved in the generation of emotions, as well as in our experience of those emotions (Barrett & Wager, 2006). The *autonomic nervous system* gives rise to many of the physiological changes associated with emotional arousal.

emotion A temporary positive or negative experience that is felt as happening to the self, that is generated partly by interpretation of situations, and that is accompanied by learned and innate physical responses.

Brain Mechanisms Although many questions remain, researchers have described three main aspects of how emotion is processed in the brain. First, it appears that activity in the *limbic system,* especially in the *amygdala,* is central to emotion (Kensinger & Corkin, 2004; Phelps & LeDoux, 2005; see Figure 2.9 in the chapter on biology and behavior). Normal functioning in the amygdala appears critical to the ability to learn emotional associations, recognize emotional expressions, and perceive emotionally charged words (Anderson & Phelps, 2001; Suslow et al., 2006; Whalen et al., 2004). For example, victims of a disease that destroys only the amygdala are unable to judge other people's emotional states by looking at their faces (Adolphs, Tranel, & Damasio, 1998).

A second aspect of the brain's involvement in emotion is seen in its control over our emotional and nonemotional facial expressions (Rinn, 1984). Take a moment **learn by doing** to look in a mirror, and put on your best fake smile. The voluntary facial movements you just made, like all voluntary movements, are controlled by the brain's *pyramidal motor system,* a system that includes the motor cortex. However, a smile that expresses genuine happiness is involuntary. That kind of smile, like the other facial movements associated with emotions, is governed by the *extrapyramidal motor system,* which depends on areas beneath the cortex. Brain damage can disrupt either system (see Figure 8.6). People with pyramidal motor system damage show normal facial expressions during genuine emotion, but they cannot fake a smile. In contrast, people with damage to the extrapyramidal system can pose facial expressions at will, but they remain straight-faced even when feeling genuine joy or profound sadness (Hopf, Muller, & Hopf, 1992).

A third aspect of the brain's role in emotion is revealed by research on the two sides, or hemispheres, of the cerebral cortex (Davidson, 2000; Davidson, Shackman, & Maxwell, 2004). For example, after suffering damage to the right, but not the left, hemisphere, people no longer laugh at jokes—even though they can still understand their words, the logic (or illogic) underlying them, and their punch lines (Critchley, 1991). And when people are asked to name the emotions shown in slides of facial expressions, blood flow increases in the right hemisphere more than in the left hemisphere (Gur, Skolnic, & Gur, 1994). But smiling while experiencing a positive emotion is correlated with greater activity in the *left* side of the brain (Davidson et al., 1990). Similarly, when an area of one patient's left hemisphere was stimulated, she began to smile, then laugh (Fried et al., 1998). She attributed her emotional expression to the situation ("You guys are just so funny . . . standing around").

The fact that different brain areas appear to be involved in displaying and experiencing positive and negative emotions (Harmon-Jones, 2004; Harmon-Jones & Sigelman, 2001; Heller, 1993) makes it difficult to map the exact roles the two hemispheres play in emotion (Vingerhoets, Berckmoes, & Stroobant, 2003). Generally, however, most aspects of emotion—the experiencing of negative emotion, the perception of any emotion exhibited in faces or other stimuli, and the facial expression of any emotion—depend more on the right hemisphere than on the left (Heller, Nitschke, & Miller, 1998; Kawasaki et al., 2001).

If the right hemisphere is relatively dominant in emotion, which side of the face would you expect to be somewhat more involved in expressing emotion? If you said the left side, you are correct, because, as described in the chapter on biology and behavior, movements of each side of the body are controlled by the opposite side of the brain.

Mechanisms of the Autonomic Nervous System The autonomic nervous system (ANS) triggers many of the physiological changes that accompany emotions (Vernet, Robin, & Dittmar, 1995; see Figure 8.7). If your hands get cold and clammy when you are nervous, it is because the ANS has increased perspiration and decreased the blood flow in your hands.

As described in the chapter on biology and behavior, the ANS carries information between the brain and most organs of the body—the heart and blood vessels, the digestive system, and so on. Each of these organs is active on its own, but input from the ANS can increase or decrease that activity. By doing so, the ANS coordinates the functioning of these organs to meet the body's general needs and to prepare the body for change (Porges, Doussard, & Maita, 1995). If you are aroused to take action, such as running to catch a bus, you need more glucose to fuel your muscles. The ANS frees

FIGURE **8.6**

Control of Voluntary and Emotional Facial Movements

This man has a tumor in his motor cortex that prevents him from voluntarily moving the muscles on the left side of his face. In the top photograph he is trying to smile in response to instructions from the examiner. He cannot smile on command, but he can smile with happiness, as the bottom photograph shows, because the movements associated with genuine emotion are controlled by the extrapyramidal motor system, which is beneath the motor cortex.

Parasympathetic functions　　　**Sympathetic functions**

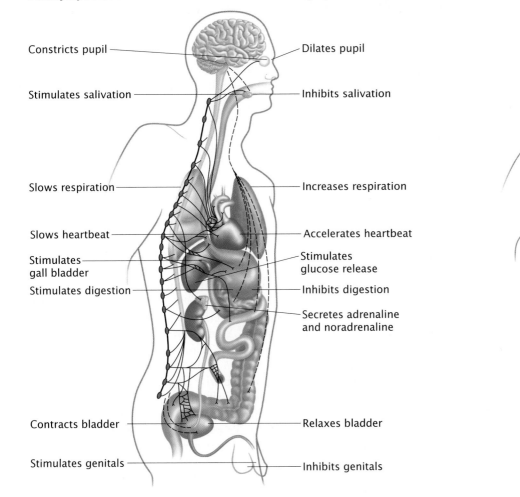

Constricts pupil — Dilates pupil

Stimulates salivation — Inhibits salivation

Slows respiration — Increases respiration

Slows heartbeat — Accelerates heartbeat

Stimulates gall bladder — Stimulates glucose release

Stimulates digestion — Inhibits digestion

— Secretes adrenaline and noradrenaline

Contracts bladder — Relaxes bladder

Stimulates genitals — Inhibits genitals

CNS

Sympathetic ganglion

Norepinephrine released

Target organ

Acetylcholine released

Parasympathetic ganglion

FIGURE 8.7

The Autonomic Nervous System

learn by doing Emotional responses involve activation of the autonomic nervous system, which is organized into sympathetic and parasympathetic subsystems. Which of the bodily responses shown here do you associate with emotional experiences?

parasympathetic nervous system The subsystem of the autonomic nervous system that typically influences activity related to the protection, nourishment, and growth of the body.

sympathetic nervous system The subsystem of the autonomic nervous system that readies the body for vigorous activity.

fight-or-flight syndrome Physical reactions triggered by the sympathetic nervous system that prepare the body to fight or flee a threatening situation.

needed energy by stimulating secretion of glucose-generating hormones and promoting blood flow to the muscles.

Figure 8.7 shows that the autonomic nervous system is organized into two parts: the sympathetic nervous system and the parasympathetic nervous system. Emotions can activate either part, both of which send axon fibers to each organ in the body. Generally, the sympathetic and parasympathetic fibers have opposite effects on these *target organs*. Axons from the **parasympathetic nervous system** release the neurotransmitter *acetylcholine* onto target organs, leading to activity related to the protection, nourishment, and growth of the body. Axons from the **sympathetic nervous system** release a different neurotransmitter, *norepinephrine*, onto target organs, helping to prepare the body for vigorous activity. When one part of the sympathetic system is stimulated, other parts are activated "in sympathy" with it (Gellhorn & Loofbourrow, 1963). The result is the **fight-or-flight syndrome,** a pattern of increased heart rate and blood pressure, rapid or irregular breathing, dilated pupils, perspiration, dry mouth, increased blood sugar, "goose bumps," and other changes that help prepare the body to confront or run from a threat.

You cannot consciously experience the brain mechanisms that alter the activity of your autonomic nervous system. This is why most people cannot exert direct, conscious control over blood pressure or other aspects of ANS activity. However, you can do things that have indirect effects on the ANS. For example, to create autonomic arousal of your sex organs, you might imagine an erotic situation. To raise your blood pressure, you might hold your breath or strain your muscles. And to lower your blood pressure, you can lie down, relax, and think calming thoughts.

Theories of Emotion

▶ **Is emotion in the heart, in the head, or both?**

Are the physiological responses associated with emotion enough to create an emotional experience? Or are those responses the *result* of emotional experiences that begin in the brain? And how does our mental interpretation of events affect our emotional reactions to them? For over a century now, psychologists have worked at finding the answers to these questions. In the process, they have developed a number of theories that explain emotion mainly in terms of biological or cognitive factors. The main biological theories are those of William James and Walter Cannon. The most prominent cognitive theories are those of Stanley Schachter and Richard Lazarus. Let's review these theories, along with some research designed to evaluate them.

James's Peripheral Theory

Suppose you are camping in the woods when a huge bear approaches your tent in the middle of the night. You would no doubt be afraid and run for your life, but would you run because you're afraid, or are you afraid because you run? This was the example and the question posed by William James, one of the first psychologists to offer a formal account of how physiological responses relate to emotional experience. He argued that you are afraid because you run. Your running and the physiological responses associated with it, he said, follow directly from your perception of the bear.

At first, James's claim sounds ridiculous; it would be silly to run from something unless you already feared it. James concluded otherwise after examining his own mental processes. He decided that once you strip away all physiological responses—such as changes in heart rate, breathing, and other peripheral nervous system activity—nothing remains of the experience of an emotion (James, 1890). Without these responses, he said, you would feel no fear, because it is the experiencing of physiological responses that creates fear and other emotions. The same argument was made by Carle Lange, a Danish physician, so James's view is sometimes called the *James-Lange theory* of emotion. It is also known as a *peripheral theory* of emotion, because it emphasizes activity in the peripheral nervous system, not in the central nervous system, as the main cause of emotional experience.

Observing Peripheral Responses   Figure 8.8 outlines the components of emotional experience, including those emphasized by James. First, perception affects the cerebral cortex. The brain interprets a situation and automatically directs a particular set of physiological changes, such as increased heart rate, sinking stomach, perspiration, and certain patterns of blood flow. It is when we become *aware* of this pattern of bodily changes, said James, that we experience an emotion. According to this view, each particular emotion is created by a particular pattern of physiological responses.

Notice that according to James's theory, emotional experience is not generated by the brain alone. There is no special "emotion center" in the brain where the firing of neurons creates a direct experience of emotion. If this theory is accurate, it might account for the difficulty we sometimes have in knowing our true feelings: We must figure out what emotions we feel by perceiving small differences in specific physiological response patterns (Katkin, Wiens, & Öhman, 2001).

Evaluating James's Theory   Research shows that certain emotional states are indeed associated with particular patterns of autonomic changes (Damasio et al., 2000; Keltner & Buswell, 1996; Sinha & Parsons, 1996). For example, blood flow to the hands and feet increases in association with anger and decreases in association with fear (Levenson, Ekman, & Friesen, 1990). So fear involves "cold feet"; anger does not. A pattern of activity associated with disgust includes increased muscle activity but no change in heart rate. And when people mentally relive different kinds of emotional experiences,

1. Sensation/perception
(It's a bear!)

2. Cognitive interpretation
(That bear can kill me!)

3. Activation of CNS and peripheral nervous system
(Cannon)

5. Perception of peripheral responses
(James)

4. Peripheral responses
(e.g., increase in heart rate, change in facial expression)

6. Cognitive interpretation of peripheral responses
(Schachter)

F I G U R E 8.8

Components of Emotion

Emotion is associated with activity in the brain, as well as with responses elsewhere in the body (called peripheral responses) and with cognitive interpretations of events. Emotion theorists have argued about which of these components are essential for emotion. William James emphasized the perception of peripheral responses, such as changes in heart rate. Walter Cannon asserted that emotion could occur entirely within the brain. Stanley Schachter emphasized cognitive factors, including how we interpret events and label peripheral responses.

they show different patterns of autonomic activity (Ekman, Levenson, & Friesen, 1983). These emotion-specific patterns of physiological activity have been found in widely different cultures (Levenson et al., 1992). Further, people who are more keenly aware of physiological changes in their bodies are likely to experience emotions more intensely than those who are less aware of such changes (Schneider, Ring, & Katkin, 1998; Wiens, Mezzacappa, & Katkin, 2000). It has even been suggested that the "gut feelings" that cause us to approach or avoid certain situations might be the result of physiological changes that are perceived without conscious awareness (Bechara et al., 1997; Damasio, 1994; Katkin et al., 2001; Winkielman & Berridge, 2004).

Different patterns of autonomic activity are also related to specific emotional facial expressions. In one study, research participants were asked to make a series of facial movements that, when combined, would create the appearance of sadness, fear, happiness, anger, or some other emotion (Levenson, Ekman, & Friesen, 1990). Making these movements led to autonomic changes that resembled those normally accompanying emotion (see Figure 8.9). In addition, almost all of the participants reported feeling the emotion associated with the expression they had created, even though they couldn't see their own expressions and didn't realize that they had made an "emotional" face.

Other studies have confirmed these results (Schnall & Laird, 2003) and have also shown that emotional feelings can be eased by relaxing facial muscles (Duclos & Laird, 2001). To get an idea of how facial expressions can alter, as well as communicate, emotion, look at a photograph of someone whose face is showing a strong emotion, and try your best to imitate it. Did this create in you the same feelings and autonomic responses that the other person appears to be experiencing?

FIGURE **8.9**

Patterns of Physiological Change Associated with Different Emotions

In this experiment, facial movements characteristic of different emotions produced different patterns of change in (A) heart rate; (B) peripheral blood flow, as measured by finger temperature; (C) skin conductance; and (D) muscle activity (Levenson, Ekman, & Friesen, 1990). For example, making an angry face caused heart rate and finger temperature to rise, whereas making a fearful face raised heart rate but lowered finger temperature.

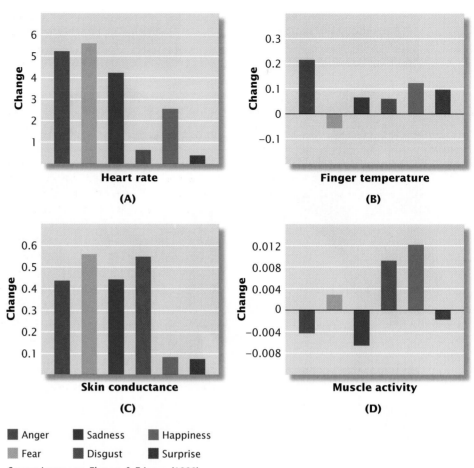

Source: Levenson, Ekman, & Friesen (1990).

A variation on James's theory, called the *facial feedback hypothesis,* suggests that involuntary facial movements provide enough information about activity in the rest of the body to create an emotional experience (Ekman & Davidson, 1993). If so, it would help to explain how posed facial expressions create the emotions normally associated with them. Try taking advantage of this notion in your own life. The next time you want to cheer yourself up, it might help to smile—even though you don't feel like it (Fleeson, Malanos, & Achille, 2002)!

Lie Detection   James's view that different patterns of physiological activity are associated with different emotions forms the basis for the lie detection industry. If people experience anxiety or guilt when they lie, specific patterns of physiological activity accompanying these emotions should be detectable on instruments, called *polygraphs,* that record heart rate, breathing rate, perspiration, and other autonomic responses.

To identify the perpetrator of a crime using the *control question test,* a polygraph tester might ask questions specific to the crime, such as "Did you stab someone on May 31, 2006?" Responses to such *relevant questions* are then compared with responses to *control questions,* such as "Have you ever lied to get out of trouble?" Innocent people might have lied at some time in the past and might feel guilty when asked about it, but they should have no reason to feel guilty about what they did on May 31, 2006. Accordingly, an innocent person should have a stronger emotional response to control questions than to relevant questions (Rosenfeld, 1995). Another approach, called the *directed lie test,* compares a person's physiological reactions when asked to lie about something and when telling what is known to be the truth. Finally, the *guilty knowledge test* seeks to determine whether a person reacts in a notable way to information about a crime that only the guilty party would know (Ben-Shakhar, Bar-Hillel, & Kremnitzer, 2002).

SEARCHING FOR THE TRUTH Polygraph tests are not foolproof, though they may intimidate people who believe that they are. In one small town where the police could not afford a polygraph, a guilty suspect confessed his crime when a "lie detector" consisting of a kitchen colander was placed on his head and attached by wires to a copy machine (Shepherd, Kohut, & Sweet, 1989).

Most people do have emotional responses when they lie, but statistics about the accuracy of polygraphs are difficult to obtain. Estimates vary widely, from those suggesting that polygraphs detect 90 percent of guilty, lying individuals (Honts & Quick, 1995; Kircher, Horowitz, & Raskin, 1988; Raskin, 1986) to those suggesting that polygraphs mislabel as many as 40 percent of truthful, innocent persons as guilty liars (Ben-Shakhar & Furedy, 1990; Saxe & Ben-Shakhar, 1999). Obviously, the results of a polygraph test are not determined entirely by whether a person is telling the truth. What people think about the act of lying and about the value of the test can also influence the accuracy of its results. For example, people who believe that lying is acceptable and who don't believe in the power of polygraphs are not likely to display emotion-linked physiological responses while lying during the test. However, an innocent person who believes in such tests and who thinks that "everything always goes wrong" might show a large fear response when asked about a crime, thus wrongly indicating "guilt" (Lykken, 1998).

Polygraphs can catch some liars, but most researchers agree that a guilty person can "fool" a polygraph lie detector and that some innocent people can be mislabeled as guilty (Ruscio, 2005). After reviewing the relevant research literature, a panel of distinguished psychologists and other scientists in the United States expressed serious reservations about the value of polygraph tests in detecting deception and argued against their use as evidence in court or in employee screening and selection (Committee to Review the Scientific Evidence on the Polygraph, 2003). Scientists are working on other lie-detecting techniques that focus on brain activity and other measures that do not depend on a link between deception and autonomic nervous system responses (Gronau, Ben-Shakhar, & Cohen, 2005; Kozel, Padgett, & George, 2004; Langleben et al., 2005).

Cannon's Central Theory

James said that the experience of emotion depends on feedback from physiological responses occurring outside the brain, but Walter Cannon disagreed (Cannon, 1927/1987). According to Cannon, you feel fear at the sight of a wild bear even before you start to run because emotional experience starts in the brain—specifically, in the thalamus, the brain structure that relays information from most sense organs to the cortex.

According to Cannon's *central theory* of emotion (called the *Cannon-Bard theory*, in recognition of Philip Bard's contribution), information about emotional situations goes first to the thalamus. The thalamus then sends signals to the autonomic nervous system and—at the same time—to the cerebral cortex, where the emotion becomes conscious. So when you see a bear, the brain receives sensory information about it, interprets that information as a bear, and instantly creates the experience of fear while at the same time sending messages to your heart, lungs, and legs to get you out of the situation. According to Cannon's theory, then, there is a *direct*, central-nervous-system experience of emotion, whether or not the brain receives feedback about responses in other parts of the body (see Figure 8.8).

Updating Cannon's Theory Later research indicates that the thalamus is not the "seat" of emotion, as Cannon had suggested. Still, the thalamus is indeed involved in some aspects of emotional processing (Lang, 1995). For example, studies of humans and laboratory animals show that the emotion of fear is generated by connections from the thalamus to the amygdala (Anderson & Phelps, 2000; LeDoux, 1995). The implication is that strong emotions can sometimes bypass the cortex without requiring conscious thought to activate them. This process helps to explain why people find it so difficult to overcome an intense fear, or phobia, even though they may consciously know the fear is irrational.

An updated version of Cannon's theory suggests that activity in specific brain areas produces the feelings of pleasure or discomfort associated with emotion. This idea arose when researchers found that rats kept returning to the place in their cage at which electrical stimulation had been delivered to a certain area of their brains. The stimulation was obviously pleasurable, because when the animals were allowed to control delivery of the stimulation by pressing a lever, they pressed it until they were exhausted, ignoring even food and water (Olds & Milner, 1954). The brain areas in which stimulation is experienced as especially pleasurable include the dopamine systems, which, as described in the chapter on consciousness, are activated by cocaine and other psychoactive drugs (Bardo, 1998). In contrast, stimulation of other brain regions is so unpleasant that animals will work hard to avoid it.

Presumably, part of the direct central experience of emotion involves areas of the brain whose activity is experienced as either pleasant or aversive. In humans, these areas have extensive connections throughout the brain (Fossati et al., 2003). As a result, the representation of emotion in the brain probably involves activity in widely distributed neural circuits, not just in a narrowly localized emotion "center" (Derryberry & Tucker, 1992).

Cognitive Theories

Suppose you are about to be interviewed for your first job, or to go out on a blind date, or to take your first ride in a hot-air balloon. In such situations, it is not always easy to be sure of what you are feeling. Is it fear, excitement, anticipation, worry, happiness, dread, or what? Stanley Schachter suggested that the emotions we experience every day are shaped partly by how we interpret the arousal we feel. His cognitive theory of emotion is known as the *Schachter-Singer theory* in recognition of the contributions of Jerome Singer. The theory took shape in the early 1960s, when many psychologists were raising questions about the validity of James's theory of emotion. Schachter argued that the theory was essentially correct—but required a few modifications (Cornelius, 1996).

According to the Schachter-Singer theory, emotions result from a combination of feedback from the body's responses and our interpretation of what caused those responses. So cognitive interpretation comes into play twice: first when you perceive the situation that leads to bodily responses and again when you interpret those responses as a particular emotion (see Figure 8.8). Schachter said that a given pattern of physiological responses can be interpreted in many different ways and so might give rise to many different emotions. According to Schachter, then, the emotion you experience when that bear approaches your campsite might be fear, excitement, astonishment, or surprise, depending on how you label your bodily reactions to seeing it (Schachter & Singer, 1962).

Schachter also said that how we label arousal depends on **attribution,** the process of identifying the cause of some event. We attribute our physiological arousal to different emotions depending on the information we have about the situation. For example, if you are watching the final seconds of a close ball game, you might attribute your racing heart, rapid breathing, and perspiration to excitement; but you might attribute the same physiological reactions to anxiety if you are waiting for a big exam to begin. Schachter predicted that our emotional experiences will be less intense if we attribute arousal to a nonemotional cause. So if you notice your heart pounding before an exam but say to yourself, "Sure my heart's pounding—I just drank five cups of coffee!" then you should feel "wired" from caffeine rather than afraid or worried. This prediction has received some support (Mezzacappa, Katkin, & Palmer, 1999; Sinclair et al., 1994), but other aspects of Schachter's theory have not.

Few researchers today fully accept the Schachter-Singer theory, but it did stimulate an enormous amount of valuable research. That research includes studies of **excitation transfer,** a phenomenon in which physiological arousal from one experience carries over to affect emotion in an independent situation (Reisenzein, 1983; Zillmann, 1984). For example, people who have been aroused by physical exercise become angrier when provoked and experience more intense sexual feelings around an attractive person than do people who have been less physically active (Allen et al., 1989). Arousal from fear, like arousal from exercise, can also enhance emotions, including sexual feelings. One study of this transfer took place in Canada, near a deep river gorge. The gorge

attribution   The process of explaining the cause of some event.

excitation transfer   The process by which arousal is carried over from one experience to an independent situation.

LABELING AROUSAL Schachter's cognitive theory of emotion predicts that these people will attribute their physiological arousal to the game they are watching and will label their emotion "excitement." Further, as described in the chapter on health, stress, and coping, the emotions they experience will also depend partly on their cognitive interpretation of the outcome (Lazarus & Folkman, 1984). Those who see their team's defeat as a disaster will experience more negative emotions than those who think of it as a challenge to improve.

could be crossed either by a shaky swinging bridge or by a more stable structure. A female researcher asked men who had just crossed each bridge to fill out a questionnaire that included a measure of sexual imagery. The men who met the woman after crossing the more dangerous bridge had much higher sexual imagery scores than the men who had crossed the stable bridge. Furthermore, they were more likely to rate the researcher as attractive (Dutton & Aron, 1974). When the person giving out the questionnaire was a male, however, the type of bridge crossed had no impact on sexual imagery. You might be wondering whether the men who crossed the dangerous bridge were simply more adventurous than other men in both bridge crossing and heterosexual encounters. To check this possibility, the researcher repeated the study, but with one change. This time, the woman approached the men farther down the trail, long after arousal from the bridge crossing had subsided. Now the apparently adventurous men were no more likely than others to rate the woman as attractive. So it was probably excitation transfer, not differing amounts of adventurousness, that produced the original result.

Schachter focused on the way we interpret our bodily responses to events. Other cognitive theorists have argued that it is our interpretation of events themselves that are most important in shaping emotional experiences. For example, as we mentioned earlier, a person's emotional reaction to receiving exam results can depend partly on whether the score is seen as a sign of improvement or as a disaster. According to Richard Lazarus's (1966, 1991) *cognitive appraisal theory* of emotion, these differing reactions can be best explained by how we think exam scores, job interviews, blind dates, bear sightings, and other events will affect our personal well-being. According to Lazarus, the process of cognitive appraisal, or evaluation, begins when we decide whether or not an event is relevant to our well-being; that is, do we even care about it? If we don't, as might be the case when an exam doesn't count toward our grade, we are unlikely to have an emotional experience when we get the results. If the event is relevant to our well-being, we will probably have a significant emotional reaction to it. That reaction will be positive or negative, said Lazarus, depending on whether we interpret the event as advancing our personal goals or blocking our progress. The *specific* emotion we experience depends on our individual goals, needs, standards, expectations, and past experiences. As a result, a second-place finisher in a marathon race might experience bitter disappointment at having "lost," whereas someone at the back of the pack may be thrilled just to have completed the race alive (Larsen et al., 2004).

"In Review: Theories of Emotion" summarizes key elements of the theories we have discussed. Research on these theories suggests that both bodily responses (including

in review

THEORIES OF EMOTION

Theory	Source of Emotions	Example
James-Lange	Emotions are created by awareness of specific patterns of peripheral (autonomic) responses.	Anger is associated with increased blood flow in the hands and feet; fear is associated with decreased blood flow in these areas.
Cannon-Bard	The brain generates direct experiences of emotion.	Stimulation of certain brain areas can create pleasant or unpleasant emotions.
Cognitive (Schachter-Singer and Lazarus)	Cognitive interpretation of events, and of physiological reactions to them, shapes emotional experiences.	Autonomic arousal can be experienced as anxiety or excitement, depending on how it is labeled. A single event can lead to different emotions, depending on whether it is perceived as threatening or challenging.

?

1. *Research showing that there are pleasure centers in the brain has been cited in support of the _____ theory of emotion.*
2. *The use of polygraphs in lie detection is based on the _____ theory of emotion.*
3. *The process of attribution is most important to _____ theories of emotion.*

Online Study Center

Improve Your Grade
Tutorial: Three Theories
of Emotion

facial responses) and the cognitive interpretation of those responses add to emotional experience. So does cognitive appraisal of events themselves. In addition, the brain can apparently generate emotional experience, independent of physiological arousal. So emotion is probably both in the heart and in the head (including the face). The most basic emotions probably occur directly within the brain, whereas the many shades of emotion probably arise from attributions, including evaluations of physiological responses. No theory has completely resolved the issue of which, if any, component of emotion is primary. However, the theories we have discussed have helped psychologists better understand how these components interact to produce emotional experience.

Communicating Emotion

▶ **Which emotional expressions are innate, and which are learned?**

So far, we have described emotions and how people experience them. Let's now consider how people communicate emotions to one another.

One way they do this is, of course, through words. Some people describe their feelings relatively simply, and mainly in terms of pleasantness or unpleasantness; others include information about the intensity of their emotions (Barrett, 1995; Barrett et al., 2001). In general, women are more likely than men to talk about their emotions and the complexity of their feelings (Barrett et al., 2000; Kring & Gordon, 1998). But humans also communicate emotion through the movement and posture of their bodies (de Gelder et al., 2004; Hadjikhani & de Gelder, 2003), through their tone of voice, and especially through their facial movements and expressions.

WHAT ARE THEY FEELING?
People's emotions are usually "written on their faces." Jot down what emotions you think these people are feeling, and then look at the footnote on page 334 to see how well you "read" their emotions.

Imagine a woman watching television. You can see her face, but not what she sees on the screen. She might be deep in complex thought, perhaps comparing her investment decisions with those of the experts being interviewed on CNBC. Or she might be thinking of nothing at all as she loses herself in a rerun of *Seinfeld*. In other words, you can't tell much about what she is thinking just by looking at her. But if the TV program creates an emotional experience, you will be able to make a reasonably accurate guess about which emotion she is feeling based on her facial expressions. The human face can create thousands of different expressions, and people—especially females—are good at detecting them (McClure, 2000; Zajonc, 1998). Observers can see even very small facial movements: A twitch of the mouth can carry a lot of information (Ambadar, Schooler, & Cohn, 2005). Are emotional facial expressions innate, or are they learned? And how are they used in communicating emotion?

Innate Expressions of Emotion

Charles Darwin observed that some facial expressions seem to be universal (Darwin, 1872/1965). He proposed that these expressions are genetically determined, passed on biologically from one generation to the next. The facial expressions seen today, said Darwin, are those that have been most effective over the centuries for telling others something about how a person is feeling. If someone is scowling with teeth clenched, for example, you will probably assume that the person is angry. And you will be unlikely to choose that particular moment to ask for a loan (Marsh, Ambady, & Kleck, 2005).

Infants provide one source of evidence that some facial expressions are innate. Newborns do not have to be taught to grimace in pain, to smile in pleasure, or to blink when startled (Balaban, 1995). Even blind infants, who cannot imitate adults' expressions, show the same emotional expressions as do sighted infants (Goodenough, 1932).

A second line of evidence for innate facial expressions comes from studies showing that for the most basic emotions, people in all cultures show similar facial responses to similar emotional stimuli (Hejmadi, Davidson, & Rozin, 2000; Zajonc, 1998). Participants in these studies looked at photographs of people's faces and then tried to name the emotion each person was feeling. The pattern of facial movements we call a smile, for example, is universally related to positive emotions. Sadness is almost always accompanied by slackened muscle tone and a "long" face. Likewise, in almost all cultures, people contort their faces in a similar way when shown something they find disgusting. And a furrowed brow is frequently associated with frustration or unpleasantness (Ekman, 1994).

Anger is also linked with a facial expression recognized by almost all cultures. One study examined ceremonial masks of various Western and non-Western cultures (Aronoff, Barclay, & Stevenson, 1988). The angry, threatening masks of all eighteen cultures contained similar elements, such as triangular eyes and diagonal lines on the cheeks. In particular, angular and diagonal elements carry the impression of threat (see Figure 8.10).

THE UNIVERSAL SMILE The idea that some emotional expressions are inborn is supported by the fact that the facial movement pattern we call a smile is related to happiness, pleasure, and other positive emotions in cultures throughout the world.

Social and Cultural Influences on Emotional Expression

Not all basic emotional expressions are innate or universal (Ekman, 1993). Some are learned through contact with a particular culture, and all of them, even innate expressions, are flexible enough to change as necessary in the social situations in which they occur (Fernández-Dols & Ruiz-Belda, 1995). For example, facial expressions become more intense and change more frequently when people are imagining social scenes as opposed to solitary scenes (Fridlund et al., 1990). Similarly, facial expressions in response to odors tend to be more intense when others are watching than when people are alone (Jancke & Kaufmann, 1994).

Further, although a core group of emotional responses is recognized by all cultures (Hejmadi et al., 2000), a certain degree of cultural variation exists in recognizing some emotions (Russell, 1995). In one study, for example, Japanese and North American people agreed about which facial expressions signaled happiness, surprise, and sadness, but they frequently disagreed about which faces showed anger, disgust, and fear (Matsumoto & Ekman, 1989). Members of cultures such as the Fore of New Guinea agree even less with people in Western cultures on the labeling of facial expressions (Russell, 1994). In addition, there are variations in the ways that cultures interpret emotions expressed by tone of voice (Mesquita & Frijda, 1992). An example is provided by a study showing that Taiwanese participants were best at recognizing a sad tone of voice, whereas Dutch participants were best at recognizing happy tones (Van Bezooijen, Otto, & Heenan, 1983).

People learn how to express certain emotions in ways specified by cultural rules. Suppose you say, "I just bought a new car," and all your friends stick their tongues out at you. In North America, this display probably means they are envious or resentful. But in some regions of China, it expresses surprise.

Even smiles can vary as people learn to use them to communicate certain feelings. Paul Ekman and his colleagues categorized seventeen types of smiles, including "false smiles," which fake enjoyment, and "masking smiles," which hide unhappiness. They called the smile that occurs with real happiness the *Duchenne smile* (pronounced "do-SHEN"), after the French researcher who first noticed a difference between spontaneous, happy smiles and posed smiles. A genuine, Duchenne smile includes contractions of the muscles around the eyes (creating a distinctive wrinkling of the skin in these areas), as well as contractions of the muscles that raise the lips and cheeks. Few people can successfully contract the muscles around the eyes during a posed smile, so this feature can be used to distinguish "lying smiles" from genuine ones (Frank, Ekman, & Friesen, 1993).

Learning About Emotions   The effects of learning are seen in a child's growing range of emotional expressions. Although infants begin with a set of innate emotional responses, they soon learn to imitate facial expressions and use them to express a wide range of emotions. In time, these expressions become more precise and personalized, so that a particular expression conveys a clear message to anyone who knows that person well.

If facial expressions become too personalized, however, no one will know what the expressions mean, and they will fail to bring responses from others. Operant shaping, described in the chapter on learning, probably helps keep emotional expressions within certain limits. If you could not see other people's facial expressions or observe their responses to yours, you might show fewer, or less intense, facial signs of emotion. In

FIGURE **8.10**

Elements of Ceremonial Facial Masks That Convey Threat

learn by doing Certain geometric patterns are common to threatening masks in many cultures. "Scary" Halloween pumpkins tend to include these patterns, too. When people in various cultures were asked which member of each of these pairs was more threatening, they consistently chose those, shown here on the left, containing triangular and diagonal elements. Cover this caption, then ask a few friends to try the same task. How many of them chose the left-hand elements as being more threatening?

The photo on page 333 shows the wife and daughter of a U.S. Marine helicopter pilot waving goodbye as he departs for duty in a war zone. Their emotions probably included sadness, anxiety, worry, dread, uncertainty, hope, and perhaps anger.

fact, as congenitally blind people grow older, their facial expressions tend to become less animated (Izard, 1977).

As children grow, they learn an *emotion culture*—rules that govern what emotions are appropriate in what circumstances and what emotional expressions are allowed. These rules can vary between genders and from culture to culture (LaFrance, Hecht, & Paluck, 2003; Matsumoto et al., 2005). For example, TV news cameras showed that men in the U.S. military being deployed to Iraq tended to keep their emotions in check as they said goodbye to wives, girlfriends, and parents. However, many male soldiers in Italy—where mother-son ties are particularly strong—wailed with dismay and wept openly as they left for duty in Kosovo. In a laboratory study, when viewing a distressing movie with a group of peers, Japanese students exerted much more control over their facial expressions than did North American students. When they watched the film while alone, however, the Japanese students' faces showed the same emotional expressions as those of the North American students (Ekman, Friesen, & Ellsworth, 1972).

Emotion cultures also shape how people describe and categorize feelings, resulting in both similarities and differences across cultures (Russell, 1991). At least five of the seven basic emotions listed in an ancient Chinese book called the *Li Chi*—joy, anger, sadness, fear, love, disliking, and liking—are considered primary emotions by most Western theorists. Yet although English has more than 500 emotion-related words, some emotion words in other languages have no English meaning. The Czech word *litost* apparently has no English word equivalent: "It designates a feeling that is the synthesis of many others; grief, sympathy, remorse, and an indefinable longing. . . . Litost is a state of torment caused by a sudden insight into one's own miserable self" (Russell, 1991). The Japanese word *ijirashii* also has no English equivalent; it describes the feeling of seeing a praiseworthy person overcoming an obstacle (Russell, 1991).

Similarly, other cultures have no equivalent for some English emotion words. Many cultures do not see anger and sadness as different, for example. The Ilongot, a head-hunting group in the Philippines, have only one word, *liget*, for both anger and grief (Russell, 1991). Tahitians have different words for forty-six types of anger, but no word for sadness and, apparently, no concept of it. One Westerner described a Tahitian man as being sad over separation from his wife and child. The man himself said that he felt *pe'a pe'a*—a general word for feeling ill, troubled, or fatigued—and did not attribute it to the separation.

Social Referencing Facial expressions, tone of voice, body postures, and gestures can do more than communicate emotion. They can also influence other people's behavior, especially people who are not sure what to do. An inexperienced chess player, for instance, might reach out to move the queen, catch sight of a spectator's pained expression, and infer that another move would be better. The process of letting another person's emotional state guide our own behavior is called **social referencing** (Campos, 1980). This process begins early; even three-month-old infants will look in the direction in which an adult's eyes have moved (Hood, Willen, & Driver, 1998).

The visual-cliff studies described in the sensation and perception chapter have been used to create an uncertain situation for infants. To reach its mother, an infant in these experiments must cross the visual cliff. If the apparent drop-off is very small or very large, there is no doubt about what to do. One-year-olds crawl across in the first case and stay put in the second case. However, if the apparent drop-off is just large enough (say, two feet) to create uncertainty, the infant relies on its mother's facial expressions to decide what to do. In one study, mothers were asked to make either a fearful or a joyful face. When the mothers made a fearful face, no infant crossed the glass floor. But when they made a joyful face, most infants crossed (Sorce et al., 1981). Here is yet another example of the adaptive value of sending, and receiving, emotional communications.

social referencing A phenomenon in which people's communication of emotion serves to guide another person's behavior in uncertain situations.

ACTIVE REVIEW

Motivation and Emotion

Linkages

As noted in the introductory chapter, all of psychology's sub-fields are related to one another. Our discussion of motivational conflicts and stress illustrates just one way in which the topic of this chapter, motivation and emotion, is linked to the subfield of health psychology, discussed in the chapter on health, stress, and coping. The Linkages diagram shows ties to two other subfields, and there are many more ties throughout the book. Looking for link-ages among subfields will help you see how they all fit together and help you better appreciate the big picture that is psychology.

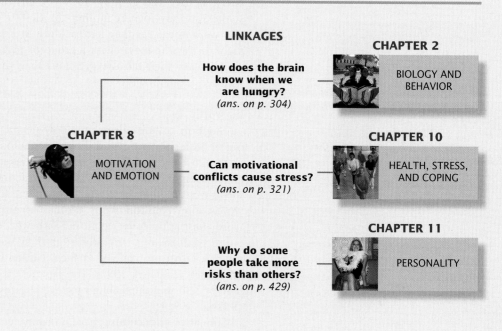

Summary

Motivation refers to factors that influence the initiation, direction, intensity, and persistence of behavior. Emotion and motivation are often linked: Motivation can influence emotion, and people are often motivated to seek certain emotions.

attaining desired stimuli (positive incentives) and avoiding unde-sirable ones (negative incentives). Each of these theories has con-tributed to our understanding of the basis for various kinds of motivated behavior.

CONCEPTS AND THEORIES OF MOTIVATION

▶ **Where does motivation come from?**

Focusing on a *motive* often reveals a single theme within apparently diverse behaviors. The many sources of motivation fall into four cat-egories: biological factors, emotional factors, cognitive factors, and social factors.

An early argument held that motivation follows from *instincts*—automatic, involuntary, and unlearned behavior patterns consis-tently "released" by particular stimuli. Modern versions of *instinct theory* are seen in evolutionary accounts of helping, aggression, mate selection, and other aspects of social behavior. *Drive reduc-tion theory* is based on *homeostasis,* a tendency to maintain equi-librium in a physical or behavioral process. When disruption of equilibrium creates a *need* of some kind, people are motivated to reduce the resulting *drive* by behaving in some way that satisfies the need and restores balance. *Primary drives* are unlearned; *sec-ondary drives* are learned. According to the *optimal arousal the-ory* of motivation, people are motivated to behave in ways that maintain a level of *arousal* that is optimal for their functioning. Finally, *incentive theory* highlights behaviors that are motivated by

EATING

▶ **What makes me start eating and stop eating?**

Eating is controlled by a complex mixture of learning, culture, and biochemistry. The desire to eat (*hunger*) or to stop eating (*satiety*) depends on signals from the stomach and from blood-borne sub-stances such as glucose, fatty acids, amino acids, insulin, and lep-tin. Activity in the ventromedial nucleus of the hypothalamus results in satiety, whereas activity in the lateral hypothalamus results in hunger. Other areas of the hypothalamus, such as the par-aventricular nucleus, are also involved. Further, several neurotrans-mitters act in various regions of the hypothalamus to motivate the eating of certain types of foods. Eating may also be influenced by the flavor of food and by the pleasure it can bring. Food selection is influenced by many factors, including social contexts and cultural traditions.

Obesity has been linked to overconsumption of certain kinds of foods, low energy metabolism, genetic factors, and even viruses. Peo-ple suffering from *anorexia nervosa* starve themselves. Those who suffer from *bulimia nervosa* engage in binge eating, followed by purging through self-induced vomiting or laxatives.

SEXUAL BEHAVIOR

▶ **How often does the average person have sex?**

Sexual motivation and behavior result from a rich interplay of biology and culture. Sexual stimulation produces a *sexual response cycle,* a predictable pattern of physiological arousal before, during, and after sexual activity. *Sex hormones,* which include male hormones *(androgens)* and female hormones *(estrogens* and *progestins),* occur in different relative amounts in both sexes. They can have organizing effects, which create physical differences in the brain, and activating effects, which temporarily increase the desire for sex.

Gender-role learning, educational experiences, media influences, and family dynamics are examples of cultural factors that can bring about variations in sexual attitudes and behaviors. Sexual orientation—*heterosexual, homosexual* (gay or lesbian), or *bisexual*—is increasingly viewed as a sociocultural variable that affects many other aspects of behavior and mental processes. Although undoubtedly shaped by a lifetime of learning, sexual orientation appears to have strong biological roots.

Common male *sexual dysfunctions* include erectile disorder and premature ejaculation. Females may experience such problems as sexual arousal disorder.

ACHIEVEMENT MOTIVATION

▶ **Why do some people try harder than others to succeed?**

People gain esteem from achievement in many areas, including the workplace. The motive to succeed is called *need achievement.* Individuals with high achievement motivation strive for excellence, persist despite failures, and set challenging but realistic goals.

Workers are most satisfied when they are working toward their own goals and getting concrete feedback. Jobs that offer clear and specific goals, a variety of tasks, individual responsibility, and other intrinsic rewards are the most motivating. People tend to have a characteristic level of happiness, or *subjective well-being,* that is not necessarily related to the attainment of money, status, or other material goals.

RELATIONS AND CONFLICTS AMONG MOTIVES

▶ **Which motives move me most?**

People's behavior reflects many motives, some of which may be in conflict. Maslow proposed a hierarchy of five types of human motives, from meeting basic physiological needs to attaining self-actualization. Motives at the lowest levels, according to Maslow, must be at least partially satisfied before people can be motivated by higher level goals. Alderfer's three-level version does not assume that needs are met in a particular order.

Four types of motivational conflict have been identified: approach-approach, avoidance-avoidance, approach-avoidance, and multiple approach-avoidance conflicts. These conflicts act as stressors, and people caught in them often experience physical and psychological problems.

THE NATURE OF EMOTION

▶ **How do feelings differ from thoughts?**

An *emotion* is a temporary experience with negative or positive qualities that is felt with some intensity as happening to the self, is generated in part by interpretation of a situation, and is accompanied by both learned and innate physical responses.

Several brain mechanisms are involved in emotion, including the amygdala in the limbic system. The expression of emotion through involuntary facial movement is controlled by the extrapyramidal motor system. Voluntary facial movements are controlled by the pyramidal motor system. The brain's right and left hemispheres play somewhat different roles in emotion. In addition to specific brain mechanisms, both the *sympathetic nervous system* and the *parasympathetic nervous system,* which are divisions of the autonomic nervous system, are involved in physiological changes that accompany emotional activation. The *fight-or-flight syndrome,* for example, follows from activation of the sympathetic nervous system.

THEORIES OF EMOTION

▶ **Is emotion in the heart, in the head, or both?**

James said that peripheral physiological responses are the primary source of emotion and that awareness of these responses creates emotional experience. James's peripheral theory is supported by evidence that, at least for several basic emotions, physiological responses are distinguishable enough for emotions to be generated in this way. Distinct facial expressions are linked to particular patterns of physiological change.

Cannon's central theory of emotion proposes that emotional experience is independent of bodily responses and that there is a direct experience of emotion based on activity of the central nervous system. Updated versions of this theory suggest that various parts of the central nervous system may be involved in different emotions and different aspects of emotional experience. Some pathways in the brain, such as the pathway from the thalamus to the amygdala, allow strong emotions to occur before conscious thought can take place. Specific parts of the brain appear to be responsible for the feelings of pleasure or pain in emotion.

Cognitive theories of emotion include the Schachter-Singer theory. It suggests that physiological responses are primary sources of emotion but that interpretation of these responses in light of the situation is required to label the emotion. This interpretation process depends on *attribution.* Attributing arousal from one situation to stimuli in another situation can produce *excitation transfer,* which intensifies the emotion experienced in the second situation. Cognitive theorists such as Lazarus have argued that emotional experience is significantly affected by how we interpret events themselves, not just by how we interpret physiological responses to those events.

COMMUNICATING EMOTION

▶ **Which emotional expressions are innate, and which are learned?**

In humans, emotion can be communicated by words, voice tones, postures, bodily movements, and facial movements and expressions. Darwin suggested that certain facial expressions of emotion are innate and universal and that these expressions evolved because they effectively communicate one creature's emotional condition to other creatures. Some facial expressions of basic emotions do appear to be innate, and certain facial movements are universally associated with certain emotions.

Other emotional expressions are learned, and even innate expressions are modified by learning and social contexts. As children grow, they learn an emotion culture, the rules of emotional expression appropriate to their culture. Accordingly, the same emotion may be communicated by different facial expressions in different cultures.

Especially in ambiguous situations, one person's emotional expressions may serve to guide another person's behavior, a phenomenon called *social referencing.*

Learn by Doing

Put It in Writing

Write a page or two about what goals you hope to achieve in life, what motivates you to strive for them, and how important it is for you to reach them. In light of our discussion about achievement and subjective well-being, consider the question of whether reaching your goals will make you happy and contented or leave you always wanting more.

Personal Learning Activity

Videotape a session in which you ask a friend four questions, such as "Who was the best teacher you ever had?" "What's the strangest thing that ever happened to you?" "What is your most surprising talent?" or "Where would you most like to live?" Ask your friend to give truthful answers to two of these questions but to lie as convincingly as possible while answering the other two. Now play the tape for a group of people and ask them to say which answers are true and which are lies. How well did your participants do? If they are like most people, they probably were right about half the time on this lie detection task (DePaulo, 1994). Did the participants' accuracy differ depending on whether or not they knew the person on the tape? If so, why do you think this was so? *For additional projects, see the Personal Learning Activities in the corresponding chapter of the study guide that accompanies this text.*

Step into Action

Courses

Health Psychology
Motivation and Emotion
Human Sexuality
Personality
Industrial-Organizational Psychology

Movies

Entrapment; The Edge. Motivational conflict.
The Heidi Chronicles. Secondary drives.
Super Size Me. Diet and obesity.
La Cage aux Folles; Wild Reeds; Wilde; Southern Comfort; Boys Don't Cry; Venus Boyz. Sexual orientation.
Wall Street; The Family Man; Rudy; Cool Runnings; Fame; Endurance. Achievement motivation.

Books

Gelsey Kirkland, *Dancing on My Grave* (Doubleday, 1987). Eating disorders.
Joyce Murdoch and Deb Price, *Courting Justice: Gay Men and Lesbians v. the Supreme Court* (Basic Books, 2001). Homosexuality and the law.
Lillian Rubin, *Intimate Strangers: Men and Women Together* (Harper, 1983). Gender differences in intimacy and sexuality.
David C. Edwards, *Motivation and Emotion: Evolutionary, Physiological, Cognitive, and Social Influences* (AltaMira Press, 1998). A basic introduction to the field of motivation and emotion.
Steven Pinker, *The Blank Slate: The Modern Denial of Human Nature* (Viking Press, 2002). Wide-ranging

description of evolutionary and genetic explanations of motivation.
David Goldstein (Ed.), *The Management of Eating Disorders and Obesity* (Humana Press, 2005). A summary of research on and treatment of eating disorders.
William H. Masters, Virginia E. Johnson, and Robert C. Kolodny, *Heterosexuality* (Grammercy Press, 1998). An overview of sexuality between males and females.
Aldert Vrij, *Detecting Lies and Deceit: The Psychology of Lying and Implications for Professional Practice* (Wiley, 2000). A summary of various approaches.
David Lykken, *Happiness: The Nature and Nurture of Joy and Contentment* (Griffin, 2000). A summary of research on the "happiness set point" and other aspects of subjective well-being.
Antonia Damasio, *Looking for Spinoza* (Harcourt, 2003). A discussion of emotions as bodily sensations.

The Web

The World Wide Web is a good source of additional information about the science of psychology, provided you use it carefully and think critically about the information you find. The Online Study Center that accompanies this text offers many resources relevant to this chapter. These resources include interactive tutorials; Thinking Critically and Evaluating Research exercises; ACE chapter quizzes; recommended web links; and articles on current events, books, and movies. Please visit the Online Study Center at college.hmco.com/pic/bernsteinessentials4e.

Review of Key Terms

Can you define each of the key terms in the chapter? Check your definitions against those on the pages shown in parentheses in the following list or in the Glossary/Index at the end of the text.

androgens *(p. 310)*

anorexia nervosa *(p. 307)*

arousal *(p. 301)*

attribution *(p. 330)*

bisexual *(p. 312)*

bulimia nervosa *(p. 307)*

drive *(p. 299)*

drive reduction theory *(p. 299)*

emotion *(p. 323)*

estrogens *(p. 310)*

excitation transfer *(p. 330)*

fight-or-flight syndrome *(p. 325)*

heterosexual *(p. 312)*

homeostasis *(p. 299)*

homosexual *(p. 312)*

hunger *(p. 302)*

incentive theory *(p. 301)*

instinct theory *(p. 298)*

instincts *(p. 298)*

motivation *(p. 298)*

motive *(p. 298)*

need *(p. 299)*

need achievement *(p. 316)*

obesity *(p. 305)*

optimal arousal theory *(p. 301)*

parasympathetic nervous system *(p. 325)*

primary drives *(p. 301)*

progestins *(p. 310)*

satiety *(p. 302)*

secondary drives *(p. 301)*

sex hormones *(p. 310)*

sexual dysfunctions *(p. 315)*

sexual response cycle *(p. 310)*

social referencing *(p. 335)*

subjective well-being *(p. 319)*

sympathetic nervous system *(p. 325)*

Multiple-Choice Self-Test

Select the best answer for each of the following questions. Then check your responses against the Answer Key at the end of the text.

1. Although most researchers do not believe in instinct theories of motivation, psychologists who advocate _____ theory argue that many aspects of human behavior are motivated by efforts to pass on our genes to the next generation.

   a. drive reduction
   b. evolutionary
   c. arousal
   d. incentive

2. Steve is cold, so he turns up the thermostat in his house. As soon as it starts to get too warm, the thermostat shuts off the furnace. This process is similar to the biological concept of

   a. homeostasis.
   b. secondary drive.
   c. incentive.
   d. arousal.

3. Lisbeth and Harriet work as instructors in an exercise class. After class, Lisbeth prefers to go home and read quietly, whereas Harriet is ready to party. Which theory of motivation *best* explains the difference between these two women?

   a. Drive reduction
   b. Incentive
   c. Evolutionary
   d. Arousal

4. Monica wants her daughter to get high grades, so she offers her $10 for each A that she earns and $5 for each B. Monica appears to believe in the _____ theory of motivation.

   a. drive reduction
   b. incentive
   c. evolutionary
   d. arousal

5. Ahmed is desperate to lose weight. To keep from eating, he buys an electrical device that allows him to stimulate various areas of his brain. Which areas should he stimulate if he wants his brain to help him reduce food intake?

   a. Ventromedial nucleus and paraventricular nucleus
   b. Lateral hypothalamus and ventromedial nucleus
   c. Lateral hypothalamus and paraventricular nucleus
   d. Thalamus and pineal gland

6. Ronia is on a diet, again! She is *most* likely to eat less food if she

   a. eats only with friends, never alone.
   b. eats only one or two kinds of food at each meal.
   c. changes her food culture.
   d. focuses on the flavor of what she eats.

7. Dr. Stefan is working in the emergency room when a very dehydrated young woman comes in. She is of normal weight, but a medical exam reveals nutritional imbalances and intestinal damage. The woman is *most* likely suffering from

   a. anorexia nervosa.
   b. bulimia nervosa.
   c. lateral hypothalamic disorder.
   d. ventromedial disorder.

8. The University of Chicago's National Health and Social Life Survey found that people in the United States

   a. are more sexually active than previously thought.
   b. have sex more often if they are not in an exclusive relationship.
   c. have sex less often and with fewer people than previously thought.
   d. do not enjoy sex very much.

9. According to the Thinking Critically section of this chapter, sexual orientation is *most* likely influenced by

   a. prenatal hormones.
   b. genetic factors.
   c. sociocultural learning.
   d. all of the above.

10. Edwina wants her son, Egbert, to develop high need achievement and to be successful in life. According to research on need achievement, Edwina should do all of the following *except*

    a. encourage Egbert to try difficult tasks.
    b. encourage Egbert to avoid failure at all costs.
    c. give praise and rewards for success.
    d. read achievement-oriented stories to him.

11. Liang wants his employees to work hard. As a psychologist specializing in motivation, you tell Liang that the *best* way to increase employee performance is to

    a. increase their pay and benefits.
    b. allow them to set their own goals.
    c. remind them regularly of the need to do better.
    d. keep all tasks as simple as possible.

12. According to Maslow, which of the following would you *most* likely do first if you were shipwrecked on a desert island?

    a. Look for food and fresh water
    b. Look for firewood
    c. Start keeping a diary
    d. Build a place to live

13. Jill would like to send her son to an expensive private school, but this would create a financial hardship for her. Jill is faced with a(n) _____ motivational conflict.

    a. approach-approach
    b. avoidance-avoidance
    c. approach-avoidance
    d. multiple approach-avoidance

14. Which of the following is *not* a characteristic associated with emotion? They

    a. tend to last a relatively short time.
    b. can be triggered by thoughts.
    c. are always intense.
    d. can motivate behavior.

15. When people are afraid to do something, they are said to have "cold feet." The fact that fear is associated with decreased blood flow to the feet and hands supports _____ theory of emotion.

    a. James's peripheral
    b. Cannon's central
    c. Schachter's cognitive
    d. Lazarus's cognitive

16. After she finished a vigorous workout, Lydia saw Thaddeus walk into the gym, and she instantly fell in love. This is an example of _____, which is consistent with _____ theory of emotion.

    a. social referencing; James's
    b. social referencing; Schachter's
    c. excitation transfer; James's
    d. excitation transfer; Schachter's

17. When Yatsira saw someone trying to open her car door while she was stopped at a light, her heart raced, and at the exact same time she felt fear. This is *most* consistent with _____ theory of emotion.

    a. James's
    b. Cannon's
    c. Schachter's
    d. Lazarus's

18. As Jarrod got older, he learned that he could not express his anger by throwing his toys. Jarrod is learning

    a. to use facial feedback.
    b. Darwin's universal rules.
    c. to use social referencing.
    d. his emotion culture.

19. Suppose that Dick, Sally, Harry, and Tommy, the space aliens on the TV show *Third Rock from the Sun,* first came to earth in your backyard. They tell you they want to learn how to communicate their emotions so that humans will understand them. What should you focus on teaching them?

    a. Body postures
    b. Facial movements
    c. Hand gestures
    d. Voice inflections

20. Sam is unsure how to react to a comment from one of his friends, so he glances at his girlfriend, Diane, to see what her reaction is. In doing so, he is using

    a. facial feedback.
    b. social referencing.
    c. attribution.
    d. excitation transfer.

9

Human Development

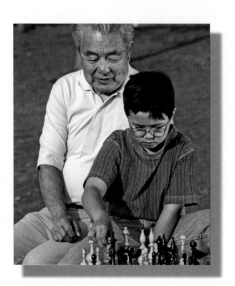
A colt begins walking within an hour of being born, but it typically takes a human baby about a year to reach this milestone—a year in which the baby also first smiles, eats solid food, learns to recognize familiar people and objects, and gets ready to talk, to name just a few accomplishments. Four years later, the child is entering school, where learning, development, and change continue. Ten years after that, the adolescent is still changing and developing, becoming more independent and mature with each passing day. In young adulthood, change and development take the form of decisions about jobs, families, and relationships—decisions whose effects echo throughout adulthood. Development occurs in late adulthood, too, as the person adjusts to the joys and challenges of growing older. Developmental psychologists explore how people change and grow over the course of the life span.

Reading this chapter will help you to answer the following questions:

Over the past several years, the tragedy of school shooting sprees has plagued all too many towns and cities in the United States and Canada, and thwarted mass murder plots by disgruntled students continue to make news (Associated Press, 2006). Though the number of school homicides has been dropping, this trend is of little solace to the friends and families of the more than 100 students or teachers who have died or been injured in these horrific events. Why do these things happen? In each case, the killers were boys ranging in age from six to eighteen. Had they watched too many violent movies and television shows? Were their actions the fault of a "gun culture" that allows children access to firearms? Had they been victims of abuse and neglect? Were their parents too strict—or not strict enough? Did they come from "broken homes" or witness physical violence between family members? Did they behave violently because they were going through a difficult "stage," because they had not been taught right from wrong, because they wanted to impress their peers, because males are more aggressive in general, or because their brains were "defective"? Or were they just "bad kids"?

Developmental psychologists try to find answers to questions like these. They explore the times at which certain kinds of behavior first appear, how those behaviors change with age, and whether the changes are sudden or gradual. They look into how development in one area, such as moral reasoning, relates to development in other areas,

A DEADLY CHILD Andrew Golden was barely out of diapers when he was given camouflage clothing and taught to fire a hunting rifle. In March 1998, at the age of eleven, he and a thirteen-year-old friend, Mitchell Johnson, used their rifles to kill four classmates and a teacher at their elementary school in Jonesboro, Arkansas. Many youngsters learn to hunt; what led these two to commit murder? Researchers in developmental psychology study the genetic and environmental factors that underlie violent aggression and many other patterns of behavior and mental processes.

developmental psychology The psychological specialty that documents the course of people's social, emotional, moral, and intellectual development over the life span.

maturation Natural growth or change triggered by biological factors independent of the environment.

such as aggressive behavior. Developmental psychologists attempt to discover whether everyone develops at the same rate and, if not, whether slow starters ever catch up to early bloomers. They ask how and why some children develop into well-adjusted, socially competent, caring individuals, whereas others become murderers; or why some adolescents go on to win honors in college and others drop out of high school. They seek to explain how development through infancy, childhood, and adolescence is affected by both genetics and the environment. They analyze the extent to which development is a product of what we arrive with at birth (our inherited, biological *nature*) and the extent to which it is a product of what the world provides (the *nurture* of the environment). And, of course, they also study the development that occurs over the years of adulthood and try to determine how these changes are related to earlier abilities and the events of life. In short, **developmental psychology** is concerned with the course and causes of developmental changes over a person's entire lifetime.

This chapter focuses on many of these changes, beginning with the physical and biological changes that take place from the moment of conception to the moment of birth.

Exploring Human Development

▶ **What does "genetic influence" mean?**

Arguments about how nature and nurture affect development can be traced back through centuries of philosophy. In essays published in the 1690s, the British empiricist philosopher John Locke argued for the importance of nurture. He believed that what happens in childhood has a profound and permanent effect on the individual. Empiricists saw the newborn as a blank slate, or *tabula rasa*. Adults write on that slate, said Locke, as they teach children about the world and how to behave in it. About seventy years later, Jean-Jacques Rousseau (pronounced "roo-SOH"), a French philosopher, argued just the opposite, claiming that children are capable of discovering how the world operates and how they should behave without instruction from adults. According to Rousseau, children should be allowed to grow as nature commands, with little guidance or pressure from parents.

The first American psychologist to investigate systematically the role of nature in behavior was Arnold Gesell (pronounced "geh-ZELL"). In the early 1900s, Gesell made many observations of children of all ages. He found that motor skills, such as standing and walking, picking up a cube, and throwing a ball, develop in a fixed sequence of stages in all children, as illustrated in Figure 9.1. Gesell argued that the order of the stages and the age at which they appear are determined by nature and are relatively unaffected by nurture. Only under extreme conditions, such as famine, war, or poverty, he claimed, are children thrown off their biologically programmed timetable. This type of natural growth or change, which unfolds in a fixed sequence relatively independent of the environment, is called **maturation.** The broader term *development* encompasses not only maturation but also the behavioral and mental processes that are influenced by learning.

John B. Watson disagreed with Gesell's views. He argued that the environment, not nature, molds and shapes development. As described in the introductory chapter, Watson founded the behaviorist approach to psychology. In the early 1900s he began conducting experiments with children. From these experiments Watson inferred that children learn *everything,* from skills to fears. In his words, "There is no such thing as an inheritance of capacity, talent, temperament, mental constitution and characteristics. These things . . . depend on training that goes on mainly in the cradle" (Watson, 1925, pp. 74–75).

It was the Swiss psychologist Jean Piaget (pronounced "p-ah-ZHAY") who first suggested that nature and nurture work together and that their influences are inseparable and interactive. Through a series of books published from the 1920s until his death in 1980, Piaget's ideas influenced the field of developmental psychology more than those of any other person before or since (Flavell, 1996).

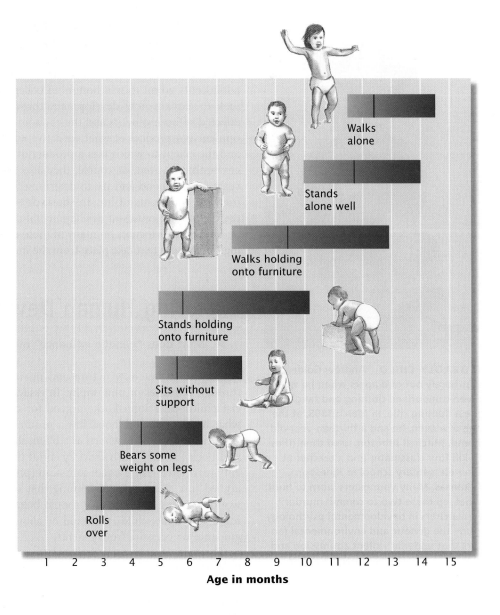

FIGURE **9.1**

Motor Development

When did you start walking? The left end of each bar indicates the age at which 25 percent of infants were able to perform a particular behavior; 50 percent of the babies were performing the behavior at the age indicated by the vertical line in the bars; the right end indicates the age at which 90 percent could do so (Frankenberg & Dodds, 1967). Although different infants, especially in different cultures, achieve milestones of motor development at slightly different ages, all infants—regardless of their ethnicity, social class, or temperament—achieve them in the same order.

Walks alone

Stands alone well

Walks holding onto furniture

Stands holding onto furniture

Sits without support

Bears some weight on legs

Rolls over

1 2 3 4 5 6 7 8 9 10 11 12 13 14 15

Age in months

Understanding Genetic Influence

Most developmental psychologists now accept Piaget's idea that both nature and nurture contribute to development. Guided by research in **behavioral genetics,** the study of how genes affect behavior, they explore how genes and the environment influence specific aspects of development. Their studies have demonstrated that nature and nurture jointly contribute to development in two ways. First, nature and nurture operate together to make all people *similar* in some respects. For example, nature influences all of us to achieve milestones of motor development in the same order and at roughly the same rate. But supportive nurture, in the form of proper nutrition and exercise, is also necessary to allow normal maturation to unfold. Second, nature and nurture operate together to make each person *unique*. The nature of inherited genes and the nurture of widely different family and cultural environments produce differences among individuals in athletic abilities, intelligence, speech patterns, personality, and many other dimensions (Plomin et al., 2002; Spinath et al., 2004).

Behavioral geneticists are concerned with the *differences* between individuals or groups of individuals, not with the characteristics of a single individual. Consider height. Whether raised together or apart, identical twins (who have identical genes) are much more similar in height than fraternal twins (who share no more genes than other siblings) or unrelated individuals. This finding suggests that height is more strongly

behavioral genetics The study of the effect of genes on behavior.

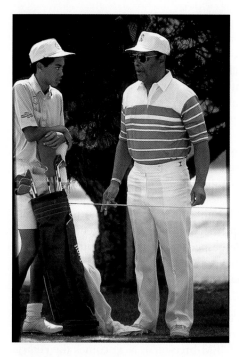

A TIGER IN TRAINING The development of human behavior is shaped by both heredity and environment—by nature and nurture. The joint and inseparable influence of these two factors in development is perfectly illustrated in the case of professional golfer Tiger Woods, shown here as a youngster with his father, who not only provided some of Tiger's genes but also served as his golf teacher.

influenced by genes than by the environment. Does this mean that a person who is six feet tall grew, say, four of those feet because of genes and the other two feet because of environment? No. It means that more of the variability in height that we see among people can be explained by the genetic differences among them than by the environmental differences. In fact, genes do account for about 80 to 95 percent of the variability in height. So if a person is taller or shorter than average, genetic factors are probably the primary cause. We say "probably" because determination of a genetic influence on height refers only to the origins of average individual differences in the population. So even though the differences in people's heights are due mainly to genetic factors, a particular person's height could be due mainly to an early illness or other growth-stunting environmental factors.

To see how the logic of behavioral genetics applies to conclusions about psychological characteristics, suppose a researcher discovered that a certain personality trait is 50 percent heritable. This finding would mean that approximately half of the *differences between people* on that trait can be explained by genetic factors. It would not mean that each person inherits half of the trait and gets the other half from environmental influences. In other words, the results of behavioral genetics research allow us to draw general conclusions about the influence of nature and nurture on certain characteristics, but those conclusions do not necessarily apply to the origins of a *particular person's* characteristics. Keep in mind, too, that the effects of genes on our traits and behaviors are not always simple or fixed. Complex traits such as intelligence and personality are influenced by many genes, as well as by many environmental factors. So genetic influence means just that: *influence* (Plomin et al., 2002). Genes can affect a trait without completely determining whether that trait will actually appear in a particular individual.

Genes and the Environment

The relative contributions of nature and nurture differ for specific aspects of development, but their influences on all human characteristics are forever intertwined. They are also mutually influential. Just as the environment encourages or discourages the expression of an individual's inherited characteristics, those inherited characteristics determine the individual's environment to some extent. In short, heredity creates predispositions that interact with the immediate environment, including family and teachers, books, and computers (Caspi et al., 2002). This interaction is what produces developmental outcomes. Let's now consider how it all begins.

Beginnings

▶ **Why should pregnant women stay away from tobacco and alcohol?**

Nowhere are the intertwined contributions of heredity and environment clearer than during the eventful nine months before birth, when a single fertilized egg develops into a functioning newborn infant.

Prenatal Development

chromosomes Long, thin structures in every biological cell that contain genetic information in the form of genes.

genes Hereditary units, located on chromosomes, that contain biological instructions inherited from both parents, providing the blueprint for physical development.

deoxyribonucleic acid (DNA) The molecular structure of a gene that provides the genetic code.

The process of development begins when sperm from a father-to-be fertilizes the egg of a mother-to-be and forms a brand-new cell. Most human cells contain forty-six **chromosomes** (pronounced "KROH-muh-sohmz"), arranged in twenty-three matching pairs. Each chromosome is made up of thousands of **genes,** the biochemical units of heredity that govern the development of an individual. Genes, in turn, are composed of **deoxyribonucleic acid (DNA).** (*Deoxyribonucleic* is pronounced "dee-OKS-ee-rye-boh-noo-KLAY-ic.") The DNA in genes provides coded messages that serve as blueprints for constructing every aspect of a physical human being, including eye color, height, blood type, inherited disorders, and the like. All of this information fits in less space than the period that ends this sentence.

A FETUS AT TWELVE WEEKS   In this photo of a fetus at three months after conception, the umbilical cord and placenta are clearly visible. At this point in prenatal development, the fetus can kick its legs, curl its toes, make a fist, turn its head, squint, open its mouth, swallow, and take a few "breaths" of amniotic fluid.

New cells in the body are constantly being produced by the division of existing cells. Most of the body's cells divide through a process called *mitosis* (pronounced "mye-TOH-sis"), in which the cell's chromosomes duplicate themselves so that each new cell contains copies of the twenty-three pairs of chromosomes in the original cell.

A different kind of cell division occurs when a male's sperm cells and a female's egg cells, called *ova,* are formed. This process is called *meiosis* (pronounced "mye-OH-sis"). In meiosis, the chromosome pairs are not copied. Instead, they are randomly split and rearranged, leaving each new sperm and egg cell with just one member of each chromosome pair, or twenty-three *single* chromosomes. No two of these special new cells are quite the same, and none contains an exact copy of the person who produced it. So, at conception, when a male's sperm penetrates, or *fertilizes,* the female's ovum, a truly new cell is formed. The fertilized cell, called a *zygote,* carries the usual twenty-three pairs of chromosomes, but half of each pair comes from the mother and half from the father. The zygote represents a unique heritage—a complete genetic code for a new person that combines randomly selected aspects from both parents. The zygote divides first into copies of itself; then it divides and redivides into the billions of specialized cells that form a complete new human being.

Stages of Prenatal Development   The first two weeks after conception are called the *germinal stage* of development. By the end of this stage, the cells of the dividing zygote have formed an **embryo** (pronounced "EM-bree-oh"). Next comes the *embryonic stage* of development, during which the embryo quickly forms a heart, nervous system, stomach, esophagus, and ovaries or testes. By two months after conception, when the embryonic stage ends, the embryo looks decidedly human, with eyes, ears, nose, jaw, mouth, and lips. The tiny arms have elbows, hands, and stubby fingers; the legs have knees, ankles, and toes.

The seven-month period remaining until birth is called the *fetal stage* of prenatal development. During this stage, the various organs grow and start to function. By the end of the third month, the **fetus** can kick, make a fist, turn its head, open its mouth, swallow, and frown. In the sixth month, the eyelids, which have been sealed, open. The fetus is now capable of making sucking movements and has a well-developed grasp, taste buds, eyebrows, and eyelashes.

By the end of the seventh month, the organ systems, though immature, are all functional. In the eighth and ninth months, the fetus can respond to light and touch, and it can hear what is going on outside. It can also learn. When it hears its mother's familiar voice, its heart beats a little faster, but the heart slows if the fetus hears a stranger (Kisilevsky et al., 2003).

Prenatal Risks   During prenatal development, a spongy organ called the *placenta* appears and attaches itself to the mother's uterus through an *umbilical cord.* (The cord is detached at birth, but you can see where yours was by looking at your navel.) The placenta sends nutrients from the mother to the developing baby and carries away wastes. It also screens out many potentially harmful substances, including most bacteria. This screening is imperfect, however: Gases, viruses, nicotine, alcohol, and other drugs can pass through. Severe damage can occur if the baby's mother takes certain drugs, is exposed to certain toxic substances such as mercury, or has certain illnesses while organs are forming in the embryonic stage (Koger, Schettler, & Weiss, 2005).

Harmful external substances that invade the womb and result in birth defects are called **teratogens** (pronounced "tuh-RAT-uh-jens"). Teratogens are especially damaging in the embryonic stage, because it is a **critical period** in prenatal development, a time during which certain kinds of growth must occur if development is to proceed normally. If the heart, eyes, ears, hands, and feet do not appear during the embryonic stage, they cannot form later on. If they form incorrectly, the defects will be permanent. So even before a mother knows she is pregnant, she may accidentally damage her infant by exposing it to teratogens. For example, a baby whose mother has rubella (German measles) during the third or fourth week after conception has a 50 percent

embryo   The developing individual from two weeks to two months after fertilization.

fetus   The developing individual from the third month after conception until birth.

teratogens   Harmful substances, such as alcohol and other drugs, that can cause birth defects.

critical period   An interval during which certain kinds of growth must occur if development is to proceed normally.

chance of being blind, deaf, or mentally retarded or of having a malformed heart. If the mother has rubella later in the pregnancy, after the infant's eyes, ears, brain, and heart have formed, the likelihood that the baby will have one of these defects is much lower. Later, during the fetal stage, teratogens affect the baby's size, behavior, intelligence, and health, rather than the formation of organs and limbs.

Of special concern today are the effects of drugs on infants' development (e.g., Gendle et al., 2004; Jones, 2006). Pregnant women who use substances such as cocaine create a substantial risk for their fetuses, which do not yet have the enzymes necessary to break down the drugs. "Cocaine babies" or "crack babies" may be born premature, underweight, tense, and fussy (Inciardi, Surratt, & Saum, 1997). They may also suffer delayed physical growth and motor development (Tarr & Pyfer, 1996). Current research suggests, however, that although cocaine babies are more likely to have behavioral and learning problems (Singer et al., 2001; Singer et al., 2002; Tan-Laxa et al., 2004), their mental abilities are not necessarily different from those of any baby born into an impoverished environment (Frank et al., 2001; Jones, 2006). How well these children ultimately do in school depends on how supportive that environment turns out to be (Begley, 1997; Messinger et al., 2004; Singer et al., 2004).

Alcohol is another dangerous teratogen, because it interferes with infants' brain development (Avaria et al., 2004). Almost half the children born to expectant mothers who abuse alcohol will develop **fetal alcohol syndrome,** a pattern of defects that includes mental retardation and malformations of the face (Jenkins & Culbertson, 1996). Pregnant women who drink as little as a glass or two of wine a day can harm their infants' intellectual functioning (Streissguth et al., 1999). Those who engage in bouts of heavy drinking triple the odds that their child will develop alcohol-related problems by the age of twenty-one (Baer et al., 2003).

Smoking, too, can affect the developing fetus. Smokers' babies often suffer from respiratory problems, irritability, and attention problems, and they are at greater risk for nicotine addiction in adolescence and adulthood (Buka, Shenassa, & Niaura, 2003; Gilliland, Li, & Peters, 2001; Law et al., 2003; Linnet et al., 2005; Niaura et al., 2001). Worse, they may be born prematurely, and they are usually underweight. Babies who are premature and/or underweight—for whatever reason—are likely to have cognitive and behavioral problems that continue throughout their lives (Bhutta et al., 2002; Jefferis, Power, & Hertzman, 2002).

Defects due to teratogens are most likely to appear when the negative effects of nature and nurture combine. The worst-case scenario is one in which a genetically vulnerable infant receives a strong dose of a damaging substance during a critical period of prenatal development. The risk of behavioral and psychological difficulties in later life is also increased for children whose mothers were under significant stress during the first six months of pregnancy (Huizink, Mulder, & Buitelaar, 2004; Van den Bergh & Marcoen, 2004) or who got the flu during that period (Brown et al., 2005).

Fortunately, mental or physical problems resulting from all harmful prenatal factors affect fewer than 10 percent of the babies born in Western nations. The vast majority of fetuses arrive at the end of their nine-month gestation averaging a healthy seven pounds and ready to continue a normal course of development in the world.

The Newborn

Determining what newborns can see, hear, or do is one of the most fascinating and frustrating challenges for researchers in developmental psychology. Babies are extremely difficult to study because they sleep about 70 percent of the time. When they are not sleeping, they are drowsy, crying, awake and active, or awake and inactive. It is only when they are in this latter state, which is infrequent and lasts only a few minutes, that researchers can assess the infants' abilities.

To do so, psychologists show infants objects or pictures and record where they look and for how long. They film the infants' eye movements and note changes in heart rates, sucking rates, brain waves, bodily movements, and skin conductance (a measure of perspiration that accompanies emotion) when objects are shown or sounds are

fetal alcohol syndrome A pattern of defects found in babies born to women who drink heavily during pregnancy.

A BABY'S-EYE VIEW OF THE WORLD
The top photograph simulates what a mother looks like to her infant at three months of age. Although their vision is blurry, infants particularly seem to enjoy looking at faces.

made. From studies using these techniques, researchers have pieced together a fair picture of what infants can see and hear (Kellman & Arterberry, 2006).

Vision and Other Senses   Infants can see at birth, but their vision is blurry. Researchers estimate that newborns have 20/300 eyesight. In other words, an object 20 feet away looks as clear as it would if viewed from 300 feet by an adult with normal vision. The reason infants' vision is so limited is that their eyes and brains still need time to grow and develop. Newborns' eyes are smaller than those of adults, and the cells in their foveas—the area in each eye on which images are focused—are fewer and far less sensitive. Their eye movements are slow and jerky. And pathways connecting the eyes to the brain are still inefficient, as is the processing of visual information within the brain.

Although infants cannot see small objects across the room, they can see large objects up close—the distance at which most interactions with caregivers take place. Infants look longest at objects that have large elements, movement, clear contours, and a lot of contrast—all of which can be found in the human face (Farroni et al., 2005; Turati, 2004).

Newborns actively use their senses to explore the world around them. At first they attend to sights and sounds for only short periods, but gradually their attention span lengthens, and their exploration becomes more systematic. In the first two months, they focus only on the edges of objects, but after two months of age, they scan whole objects (Banks & Salapatek, 1983). Then, when they see an object, they get all the information they can from it before going on to something new (Hunter & Ames, 1988). Newborns stare at human faces longer than at other figures (Valenza et al., 1996). They are particularly interested in eyes, as shown in their preference for faces that are looking directly at them (Farroni et al., 2002).

At two or three days of age, newborns can hear soft voices and notice differences between tones about one note apart on the musical scale (Aslin, Jusczyk, & Pisoni, 1998). In addition, they turn their heads toward sounds (Clifton, 1992). But their hearing is not as sharp as that of adults' until well into childhood. This condition is not merely a hearing problem; it also reflects an inability to listen selectively to some sounds over others (Bargones & Werner, 1994). As infants grow, they develop sensory capacities and the skill to use them.

Infants pay special attention to speech. When they hear someone talking, they open their eyes wider and search for the speaker. Infants also prefer certain kinds of speech. They like rising tones spoken by women or children (Sullivan & Horowitz, 1983). They also like high-pitched, exaggerated, and expressive speech. In other words, they like to hear the "baby talk" used by most adults in all cultures when talking to babies (Fernald, 1990). They even seem to learn language faster when they hear baby talk (Thiessen, Hill, & Saffran, 2005).

Newborns also like certain smells and tastes better than others. When given something sweet to drink, they suck longer and slower, pause for shorter periods, and smile and lick their lips (Ganchrow, Steiner, & Daher, 1983). Within a few days after birth, breastfed babies prefer the odor of their own mother to that of another mother (Porter et al, 1992).

Reflexes and Motor Skills   In the first weeks and months after birth, babies show involuntary, unlearned reactions called **reflexes**. These swift, automatic movements occur in response to external stimuli. Figure 9.2 illustrates the *grasping reflex*, one of more than twenty reflexes that have been observed in newborn infants. Another is the *rooting reflex,* whereby the infant turns its mouth toward a finger or nipple that touches its cheek. And the newborn exhibits the *sucking reflex* in response to anything that touches its lips. Many of these reflexive behaviors evolved because they help infants to survive. The absence of reflexes in a newborn signals problems in brain development. So does a failure of reflexes to disappear as brain development during the first three or four months allows the infant to control muscles voluntarily.

reflexes   Simple, involuntary, unlearned behaviors directed by the spinal cord without instructions from the brain.

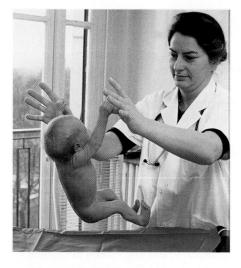

F I G U R E **9 . 2**

Reflexes in the Newborn

When a finger is pressed into a newborn's palm, the *grasping reflex* causes the infant to hold on tightly enough to suspend its entire weight. And when a newborn is held upright over a flat surface, the *stepping reflex* leads to walking movements.

Voluntary control permits the development of motor skills, allowing the infant to roll over, sit up, crawl, stand, and walk. Until a few years ago, most developmental psychologists accepted Gesell's view that, except under extreme environmental conditions, these motor abilities occur spontaneously as the central nervous system and muscles mature. Research demonstrates, however, that maturation does not tell the whole story, even in normal environments (Thelen, 1995).

Consider the fact that many babies today aren't learning to crawl on time—or at all. Why? One reason has to do with the "Back to Sleep" campaign begun a decade ago in an effort to prevent sudden infant death syndrome (see the chapter on consciousness). This public health campaign urges parents to put babies to sleep on their backs rather than face down. The campaign has been successful, but researchers have discovered that many babies who were never placed on their tummies went directly from sitting to toddling, skipping the crawling stage but reaching all other motor milestones on schedule (Kolata & Markel, 2001).

Observation of infants who do learn to crawl has shown that it does not happen suddenly. It takes the development of enough muscle strength to support the abdomen—and some active experimentation—to get the job done. Six infants in one study tried various crawling techniques—moving backward, moving one limb at a time, using the arms only, and so on (Freedland & Bertenthal, 1994). After a week or two of trial and error, all six infants arrived at the same method: moving the right arm and left leg together, then the left arm and right leg. This pattern turned out to be the most efficient way of getting around quickly without tipping over. Such observations suggest that as maturation increases infants' strength, they try out various motor patterns and select the ones that work best (Nelson, 1999).

In other words, motor development results from a combination of maturation and experience. It is not the result of an entirely automatic sequence that is genetically etched in the brain. Yet again, we see that nature and nurture influence each other. The brain controls developing behavior, but its own development is affected by experience, including efforts at building motor skills.

Infancy and Childhood: Cognitive Development

▶ **How do babies think?**

In less than ten years, a tiny infant becomes a person who can read a book, write a poem, and argue logically for access to the family's new computer. What leads to the dramatic shifts in thinking, knowing, and remembering that occur between early infancy and later childhood? Researchers studying *cognitive development* try to answer this question.

The Development of Knowledge: Piaget's Theory

Foremost among these researchers was Jean Piaget, who dedicated his life to a search for the origins of intelligence and the factors that lead to changes in knowledge over the life span. Piaget was the first to chart the journey from the simple reflexes of the newborn to the complex understandings of the adolescent. Although his theory turned out to be incomplete, and in some respects incorrect, his ideas about cognitive development are still guiding research (Fischer & Hencke, 1996).

Intensive observations of infants (including his own) and extensive interviews with children led Piaget to propose that cognitive development proceeds in a series of distinct stages, or periods. He believed that all children's thinking goes through the same stages, in the same order, without skipping. (Table 9.1 outlines these stages.) According to Piaget, the thinking of infants is different from the thinking of children, which in turn is different from that of adolescents. He said that children are not just miniature

TABLE 9.1

Piaget's Periods of Cognitive Development

According to Piaget, a predictable set of features characterizes each period of children's cognitive development. The ages associated with the stages are approximate; Piaget realized that some children move through the stages slightly faster or slower than others.

Period	Activities and Achievements
Sensorimotor Birth–2 years	Infants discover aspects of the world through their sensory impressions, motor activities, and coordination of the two. They learn to differentiate themselves from the external world. They learn that objects exist even when they are not visible and that they are independent of the infants' own actions. Infants gain some appreciation of cause and effect.
Preoperational 2–4 years 4–7 years	Children cannot yet manipulate and transform information in logical ways, but they now can think in images and symbols. They become able to represent something with something else, acquire language, and play games of pretend. Intelligence at this stage is said to be intuitive, because children cannot make general, logical statements.
Concrete operational 7–11 years	Children can understand logical principles that apply to concrete external objects. They can appreciate that certain properties of an object remain the same, despite changes in appearance, and they can sort objects into categories. They can appreciate the perspective of another viewer. They can think about two concepts, such as longer and wider, at the same time.
Formal operational Over 11 years	Only adolescents and adults can think logically about abstractions, can speculate, and can consider what might or what ought to be. They can work in probabilities and possibilities. They can imagine other worlds, especially ideal ones. They can reason about purely verbal or logical statements. They can relate any element or statement to any other, manipulate variables in a scientific experiment, and deal with proportions and analogies. They can reflect on their own activity of thinking.

---

schemas   Mental representations of what we know and expect about the world.

assimilation   The process of taking in new information about objects by using existing schemas on objects that fit those schemas.

accommodation   The process of modifying schemas as an infant tries out familiar schemas on objects that do not fit them.

sensorimotor period   According to Piaget, the first stage of cognitive development, when the infant's mental activity is confined to sensory perception and motor skills.

object permanence   The knowledge that an object exists even when it is not in view.

---

adults and that they are not dumber than adults; they just think in completely different ways at different stages of development. In other words, entering each stage involves a *qualitative* change from whatever preceded it, much as a caterpillar is transformed into a butterfly.

Building Blocks of Development   To explain how infants and children move to ever higher stages of understanding and knowledge, Piaget introduced the concept of *schemas* as the basic units of knowledge, the building blocks of intellectual development. As noted in other chapters, **schemas** are the mental images or generalizations that form as people experience the world. Schemas, in other words, organize past experiences and provide a framework for understanding future experiences.

At first, infants form simple schemas. For example, a sucking schema combines their experiences of sucking into images of what objects can be sucked on (bottles, fingers, pacifiers) and what kinds of sucking can be done (soft and slow, speedy and vigorous). Later, children form more complex schemas, such as a schema for tying a knot or making a bed. Still later, adolescents form schemas about what it is to be in love.

Two related processes guide this development: assimilation and accommodation. In **assimilation,** infants and children take in information about new objects by trying out

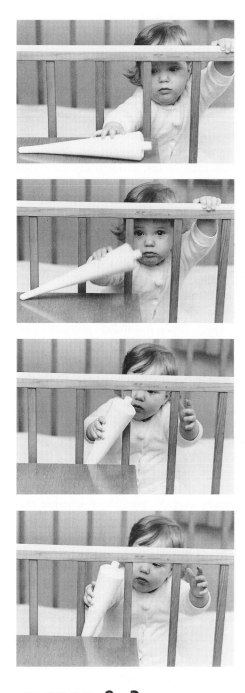

Accommodation

Because the bars of the playpen are in the way, this child discovers that her schema for grasping and pulling objects toward her will not work. So she adjusts, or accommodates, her schema to achieve her goal.

existing schemas and finding schemas that the new objects will fit. They *assimilate* the new objects into their existing schemas. So when an infant is given a squeaker toy, he will suck on it, thus assimilating it into the sucking schema he has developed with his bottle and pacifier. In the same way, a toddler who sees a butterfly for the first time may assimilate it into her "birdie" schema, because, like a bird, it's colorful and it flies. Now suppose an older toddler encounters a large dog. How she assimilates this new experience depends on her existing schema of dogs. If she has had positive experiences with the family dog, she will have a positive schema, and, expecting the dog to behave like her pet, she will greet it happily. In other words, past experiences affect what and how children think about new ones.

Sometimes, like Cinderella's stepsisters squeezing their oversized feet into the glass slipper, people distort information about a new object to make it fit an existing schema. When squeezing won't work, though, people are forced to change, or *accommodate*, their schemas to the new objects. In **accommodation,** the person tries out familiar schemas on a new object, finds that the schemas cannot be made to fit the object, and changes the schemas so that they will fit (see Figure 9.3). So when the infant discovers that the squeaker toy is more fun when it makes a noise, he accommodates his sucking schema and starts munching on the squeaker instead. When the toddler realizes that butterflies are not birds because they don't have beaks and feathers, she accommodates her "birdie" schema to include two kinds of "flying animals"—birds and butterflies. And if the child with the positive "doggie" schema meets a snarling stray, she discovers that her original schema does not extend to all dogs and refines it to distinguish between friendly dogs and aggressive ones.

Sensorimotor Development   Piaget (1952) called the first stage of cognitive development the **sensorimotor period,** a time when mental activity is confined to schemas about sensory functions, such as seeing and hearing, and to schemas about motor skills, such as grasping and sucking. Piaget believed that during the sensorimotor stage, infants can form schemas only of objects and actions that are present—things they can see, hear, or touch. They cannot think about absent objects, he said, because they cannot act on them. For infants, then, thinking is doing. They do not lie in the crib thinking about their mother or their teddy bear, because they are not yet able to form schemas that are *mental representations* of objects and actions that are not present.

The sensorimotor period ends when infants do become able to form such mental representations. At that point, they can think about objects or actions when the objects are not visible or the actions are not occurring. This milestone, according to Piaget, frees the child from the here-and-now of the sensory environment. It allows for the development of thought. One sign of this milestone is the child's ability to find a hidden object. This behavior reflects the infant's knowledge that an object exists even if it cannot be seen, touched, or sucked. Piaget called this knowledge **object permanence.**

Piaget believed that before infants acquire knowledge of object permanence, they do not search for objects that are placed out of sight. For infants, out of sight is literally out of mind. He said that evidence of object permanence begins to appear when infants are four to eight months old. At this age, for the first time, they can recognize a familiar object even if part of it is hidden: They know it's their bottle even if they can see only the nipple peeking out from under the blanket. Infants now have some primitive mental representations of objects. If an object is completely hidden, however, they will not search for it.

Several months later, infants will search briefly for a hidden object, but their search is random and ineffective. Not until they are about eighteen to twenty-four months old, said Piaget, do infants appear able to picture and follow events in their minds. They look for the object in places other than where they saw it last, sometimes in entirely new places. According to Piaget, their concept of object permanence is now fully developed. They have a mental representation of the object that is completely separate from their immediate perception of it.

FIGURE **9.4**

Infant Memory

This infant has learned to move a mobile by kicking her left foot, which is connected to the mobile by a ribbon. Even a month later, the baby will show recognition of this particular mobile by kicking more vigorously when she sees it than when she sees another one.

New Views of Infants' Cognitive Development   In the years since Piaget's death, psychologists have found new ways to measure what is going on in infants' minds. They use infrared photography to record infants' eye movements, time-lapse photography to detect slight hand movements, special equipment to measure infants' sucking rates, and computer technology to track and analyze it all. Their research shows that infants know a lot more, and know it sooner, than Piaget ever thought they did (Onishi & Baillargeon, 2005).

For example, it turns out that infants in the sensorimotor period are doing more than just sensing and moving; they are thinking as well. They are not just experiencing isolated sights and sounds but combining these experiences. In one study, for example, infants were shown two different videotapes at the same time, while the soundtrack for only one of them came from a speaker placed between the two TV screens. The infants tended to look at the video that went with the soundtrack—at a toy bouncing in synch with a tapping sound, at Dad's face when his voice was on the audio, or at an angry face when an angry voice was heard (Soken & Pick, 1992). Infants remember, too. Babies as young as two to three months of age can recall a mobile that was hung over their crib a few days before (Rovee-Collier, 1999; see Figure 9.4).

Young babies even seem to have a sense of object permanence. Piaget had required infants to demonstrate object permanence by making effortful responses, such as removing a cover that had been placed over an object. Today, researchers recognize that finding a hidden object under a cover requires several abilities: mentally representing the hidden object, figuring out where it might be, and pulling off the cover. Piaget's tests did not allow for the possibility that infants know a hidden object still exists but don't yet have the skill to find it. When researchers have created situations in which infants merely have to stare to indicate that they know where an object is hidden, even infants under the age of one have demonstrated this cognitive ability, especially when the object is a familiar one (Hespos & Baillargeon, 2001; Shinskey & Munakata, 2005). And when experimenters simply turn off the lights in a room, infants as young as five months of age may reach for now-unseen objects in the dark (Clifton et al., 1991).

Developmental psychologists generally agree that infants develop some mental representations earlier than Piaget suggested. However, they disagree about whether this knowledge is "programmed" in infants (Spelke et al., 1992), whether it develops quickly through interactions with the world (Baillargeon, 1995), or whether it is constructed by combining old schemas into new ones (Fischer & Bidell, 1991).

To explore how infants develop mental representations, Renee Baillargeon (pronounced "by-ar-ZHAN") investigated infants' early understanding of the principles of physics. Whether you realize it or not, you have quite a storehouse of knowledge about physics. You know about gravity and balance, for example. But when did you understand that "what goes up must come down" and that an unbalanced tray will tip over? Are these things you have always known, or did you figure them out through trial and error?

FOCUS ON RESEARCH

What Do Infants Know About Physics?

■ **What was the researcher's question?**

Baillargeon wanted to know when and how babies first develop knowledge about balance and gravity—specifically, about the tendency of unsupported objects to fall.

■ **How did the researcher answer the question?**

In one series of creative experiments, Baillargeon (1994a, 1994b, 2002) showed infants a red-gloved hand pushing a box from left to right along the top of a platform. On some trials, they saw physically possible events, as when the hand pushed the box to

(A)

(B)

Source: Baillargeon (1992). **(C)**

(D)

Events Demonstrating Infants' Knowledge of Physics

Infants look longer at things that interest them—that is, at new things rather than things they have seen before and find boring. In her research on the development of knowledge, Renee Baillargeon (1995) has found that physically impossible events B and C—made possible by an experimenter's reaching through a hidden door to support a moving box—attract the most attention from infants. These results suggest that humans understand some basic laws of physics quite early in life.

the edge of the platform or held onto the object as it went beyond the edge of the platform (see events A and D in Figure 9.5). On other trials, they saw physically impossible events, as when the hand pushed the box until only the end of its bottom surface rested on the platform or went beyond the platform (see events B and C in the figure). Trials continued until the infants had seen at least four pairs of possible and impossible events in alternating order. Baillargeon measured the length of time the infants looked at the objects in each event. Their tendency to look longer at unexpected events provided an indication of which events violated what the babies knew about the world.

■ **What did the researcher find?**

Baillargeon found that three-month-old infants looked longest at impossible event C, in which the box was entirely off the platform. They were not particularly interested in either event D (box held by the gloved hand) or event A (box still on the platform). But at six and a half months, infants stared intently at both event C (box off the platform) and event B (in which only the end of the box was resting on the platform).

■ **What do the results mean?**

According to Baillargeon (2002), these results suggest that three-month-old babies know something about physical support. They expected the box to fall if it was entirely off the platform and acted surprised when it did not. But they did not yet know that a box should fall if its center of gravity is unsupported, as in event B. By six and a half months of age, they had apparently developed this understanding.

■ **What do we still need to know?**

Baillargeon may have demonstrated that very young infants possess fundamental knowledge about the world that implies an understanding of complex physical principles. But a question remains: Does an infant's tendency to stare longer at a particular sight necessarily indicate "surprise," or could it mean that babies simply recognize that certain images are different from, or more interesting than, things they have seen before (Bogartz, Shinskey, & Speaker, 1997)? The answer to this question will require further research using varied visual stimuli that allow researchers to determine whether infants stare longer at physically possible events that are just as novel and vivid as physically impossible events.

Researchers also want to discover *how* babies know about physics (Johnson, Amso, & Slemmer, 2003). Does their knowledge develop from their experience with objects, or is it innate? In an attempt to answer this question, Baillargeon conducted another experiment with infants ranging from three to six and a half months old. Half the children were randomly selected to receive extra experience watching objects falling when unsupported. After only a few demonstrations of such events, infants in the extra-experience group stared longer than the other babies when an unsupported object did *not* fall. Other studies found similar results (Needham & Baillargeon, 1999). It is still too early to say for sure whether Baillargeon's hypothesis about the importance of experience in developing knowledge is correct, but her results seem to support it (Baillargeon, 2004; Wang & Baillargeon, 2005). So the next time you see an infant stacking blocks and watching them fall, consider the possibility that you are watching a little scientist testing hypotheses about the workings of the universe.

THE FAMILY CIRCUS.   **By Bil Keane**

"I think the moon likes us. It keeps on followin' us."

During the second half of the preopera- tional period, according to Piaget, chil- dren believe that inanimate objects are alive and have intentions, feelings, and consciousness.

preoperational period According to Piaget, the second stage of cognitive development, during which children be- gin to understand, create, and use sym- bols that represent things that are not present.

conservation The ability to recognize that the important properties of a sub- stance, such as number, volume, or weight, remain constant despite changes in shape, length, or position.

Preoperational Development   According to Piaget, the **preoperational period** follows the sensorimotor stage of development. During the first half of this period, he observed, children begin to understand, create, and use *symbols* that represent things that are not present. They draw, pretend, and talk.

Using and understanding symbols opens up a new world for two- to four-year-olds. At two, for the first time, children are able to play "pretend." They make their fingers "walk" or "shoot" and use a spoon to make a bridge. By the age of three or four, children can symbolize complex roles and events as they play "house," "doctor," or "super-hero." They also can use drawing symbolically: Pointing to their scribble, they might say, "This is Mommy and Daddy and me going for a walk."

During the second half of the preoperational stage, according to Piaget, four- to seven-year-olds begin to make intuitive guesses about the world as they try to figure out how things work. However, Piaget observed that they cannot tell the difference between imagination and reality. For example, children in this age range might claim that dreams are real and take place outside of themselves as "pictures on the window," "a circus in the room," or "something from the sky." And they believe that inanimate objects are alive and have intentions, feelings, and consciousness: "Clouds go slowly because they have no legs"; "Flowers grow because they want to"; and "Empty cars feel lonely." Children in the preoperational period are also *egocentric,* meaning that they assume that their own view of the world is shared by everyone else. (This helps to explain why they stand between you and the TV screen and assume you can still see it, or ask "What's this?" as they look at a picture book in the back seat of the car you're driving.)

Children's thinking at this stage is so dominated by what they can see and touch for themselves that they do not realize something is the same if its appearance is changed. In one study, preoperational children thought that a cat wearing a dog mask was actually a dog, because that's what it looked like (DeVries, 1969). These children do not yet have what Piaget called **conservation,** the ability to recognize that important properties of a substance or a person remain the same despite changes in shape or appearance.

In a test of conservation, Piaget showed children water from each of two equal-sized glasses being poured into either a tall, thin glass or a short, wide one. They were then asked if one glass contained more water than the other. Children at the preoperational stage of development said that one glass (usually the taller one) contained more. They were dominated by the evidence of their eyes. If the glass looked bigger, then they thought it contained more.

Children at this stage do not understand the logic of *reversibility*—that if you just poured the water from one container to another, you can pour it back, and it will be the same amount. Nor do they understand the concept of *complementarity*—that one glass is taller but narrower, and the other is shorter but wider. They focus on only one dimension at a time—the most obvious or important one—and make their best guess. In fact, Piaget named this stage *preoperational* because children at this stage do not yet understand logical mental *operations* such as reversibility and complementarity.

**TESTING FOR CONSERVA-
TION** If you know a child who is between the ages of four and seven, get parental permission to test the child for what Piaget called *conservation.* Show the child two identical lumps of clay and ask which lump is bigger. The child will probably say they are the same. Now roll one lump into a long "rope" and again ask which lump is bigger. If the child says that they are still the same, this is evidence of conservation. If the longer one is seen as bigger, conservation has not yet developed—at least not for this task. The older the child, the more likely it is that conservation will appear, but some children display conservation much earlier than Piaget thought was possible.

Concrete and Formal Operational Thought   At around the age of six or seven, Piaget observed, children do develop conservation. When this happens, they enter what he called the stage of **concrete operations.** Now, he said, they can count, measure, add, and subtract. Their thinking is no longer dominated by the appearance of things. They can use simple logic and perform simple mental manipulations and mental operations on things. They can sort objects into classes (such as tools, fruit, and vehicles) or series (such as largest to smallest) by systematic searching and ordering.

Still, concrete operational children can perform their logical operations only on real, concrete objects, such as sticks, glasses, tools, and fruit—not on abstract concepts, such as justice or freedom. They can reason only about what *is,* not about what is *possible.* The ability to think logically about abstract ideas comes in the next stage of cognitive development, as children enter adolescence. This new stage is called the **formal operational period,** and it is marked by the ability to engage in hypothetical thinking, including the imagining of logical consequences. For example, adolescents who have reached this level can consider various strategies for finding a part-time job and recognize that some methods are more likely to succeed than others. They can form general concepts and understand the impact of the past on the present and the present on the future. They can question social institutions; think about the world as it might be and ought to be; and consider the consequences and complexities of love, work, politics, and religion. They can think logically and systematically about symbols and propositions.

Piaget explored adolescents' formal operational abilities by asking them to perform science experiments that involved forming and investigating hypotheses. Research indicates that only about half the people in Western cultures ever reach the formal operational level necessary to succeed in Piaget's experiments (Kuhn & Franklin, 2006). People who have not studied science and math at a high school level are less likely to do well in those experiments (Keating, 1990). In adulthood, people are more likely to use formal operations for problems based on their own occupations; this is one reason that people who think logically at work may still become victims of a home-repair or investment scam (Cialdini, 2001).

Modifying Piaget's Theory

Piaget's observations and demonstrations of children's cognitive development are vivid and fascinating. He was right in pointing out that significant shifts in children's thinking occur with age and that thinking becomes more systematic, consistent, and integrated as

concrete operations   According to Piaget, the third stage of cognitive development, during which children can learn to count, measure, add, and subtract.

formal operational period   According to Piaget, the fourth stage of cognitive development, characterized by the ability to engage in hypothetical thinking.

children get older. His idea that children are active explorers and constructors of knowledge, not passive recipients of input from the environment, influenced our contemporary views of child development. Piaget also inspired other psychologists to test his findings and theory with experiments of their own. The results of these experiments suggest that Piaget's theory needs some modification.

What needs to be modified most is Piaget's notion of developmental stages. Several studies have shown that changes from one stage to the next are less consistent and global than Piaget had described them. For example, three-year-olds can sometimes make the distinction between physical and mental events; they know the characteristics of real dogs versus pretend dogs (Woolley, 1997). And they are not always egocentric. In one study, children of this age knew that a white card, which looked pink to them because they were wearing rose-colored glasses, looked white to someone who was not wearing the glasses (Liben, 1978). Preoperational children can even succeed at conservation tasks if they are allowed to count the number of objects or have been trained to focus on relevant dimensions such as number, height, and width (Gelman & Baillargeon, 1983).

Taken together, these studies suggest that children's knowledge and mental strategies develop at different ages in different areas and in "pockets" rather than at global levels of understanding. Knowledge in particular areas is demonstrated sooner in children who are given specific experience in those areas or who are faced with very simple questions and tasks. In other words, children's reasoning depends not only on their general level of development but also on (1) how easy the task is, (2) how familiar they are with the objects involved, (3) how well they understand the language being used, and (4) what experiences they have had in similar situations (Siegal, 1997). Research has also shown that the level of a child's thinking varies from day to day and may even shift when the child solves the same problem twice in the same day (Siegler, 1994).

In summary, psychologists now tend to think of cognitive development as occurring in rising and falling "waves" rather than in fixed stages characterized by permanent shifts from one way of thinking to another (Siegler, 2006). Children appear to systematically try out many different solutions to problems and gradually come to select the best of them.

Information Processing During Childhood

An alternative to Piaget's theory of cognitive development is based on the concept of information processing described in the chapters on memory and on thought, language, and intelligence. The **information-processing** approach to development describes cognitive activities in terms of how people take in information, use it, and remember it. Developmental psychologists taking this approach focus on gradual quantitative changes in children's mental capacities, rather than on qualitative advances or stages in development.

Research by these psychologists demonstrates that as children get older, their information-processing skills gradually get better (Munakata, 2006). Older children have longer attention spans. They take in information and shift their attention from one task to another more rapidly. (This is how they manage to do their homework while watching TV.) They are also more efficient in processing information once it is received (Miller & Vernon, 1997). Children's memory storage capacity also improves (Schneider & Bjorklund, 1998). Preschoolers can keep only two or three pieces of information in mind at the same time; older children can hold four or five. And compared with younger children, older children are better at choosing problem-solving strategies that fit the task they are facing (Siegler, 2006).

We don't yet know exactly what causes these increases in children's attention, information-processing, and memory capacities. A full explanation will undoubtedly include both nature (specifically, maturation of the brain; Luciana et al., 2005) and nurture (including increased familiarity with the information to be processed and memorized). Researchers have noticed that the cognitive abilities of children improve dramatically when they are dealing with familiar rather than unfamiliar material. In one experiment, Mayan children in Mexico lagged behind their age-mates in the United States on standard memory tests of pictures and nouns. But they did a lot better when

LINKAGES
Why does memory improve during childhood? (a link to Memory)

information processing   The process of taking in, remembering or forgetting, and using information.

in review

MILESTONES OF COGNITIVE DEVELOPMENT IN INFANCY AND CHILDHOOD

Age*	Achievement	Description
3–4 months	Maturation of senses	Immaturities that limit the newborn's vision and hearing are overcome.
	Voluntary movement	Reflexes disappear, and infants begin to gain voluntary control over their movements.
12–18 months	Mental representation	Infants can form images of objects and actions in their minds.
	Object permanence	Infants understand that objects exist even when out of sight.
18–24 months	Symbolic thought	Young children use symbols to represent things that are not present in their pretend play, drawing, and talk.
4 years	Intuitive thought	Children reason about events, real and imagined, by guessing rather than by engaging in logical analysis.
6–7 years	Concrete operations Conservation	Children can apply simple logical operations to real objects. For example, they recognize that important properties of a substance, such as number or amount, remain constant despite changes in shape or position.
7–8 years	Information processing	Children can remember more information; they begin to learn strategies for memorization.

? 1. *Research in cognitive development suggests that children form mental representations _____ than Piaget thought they did.*
2. *Recognizing that changing the shape of clay doesn't change the amount of clay is evidence of a cognitive ability called _____.*
3. *The appearance of object permanence signals the end of the _____ period.*

*These ages are approximate; they indicate the order in which children first reach these milestones of cognitive development rather than the exact ages.

Online Study Center

Improve Your Grade
Tutorial: Preoperational Inability to Conserve Matter

researchers gave them a more familiar task, such as recalling miniature objects in a model of a Mayan village (Rogoff & Waddell, 1982).

Better memorization strategies may also help account for the improvement in children's memories. To a great extent, children learn these strategies in school. They learn how to memorize and how to study. They learn to repeat information over and over to help fix it in memory, to place information into categories, and to use other memory aids to help them remember.

After about age seven, schoolchildren are also better at remembering more complex and abstract information. Their memories are more accurate, extensive, and well organized. The knowledge they have accumulated allows them to draw more inferences and to integrate new information into a more complete network of facts. (See "In Review: Milestones of Cognitive Development in Infancy and Childhood.")

LINKAGES
What happens to our memories of infancy?
(a link to Memory)

LINKAGES

Development and Memory

learn by doing

The ability to remember facts, figures, pictures, and objects improves as we get older and more expert at processing information. But take a minute right now and try to recall anything that happened to you when you were, say, one year old. Most people can accurately recall a few memories from age five or six but remember virtually nothing from before the age of three (Bauer, 2006; Bruce, Dolan, & Phillips-Grant, 2000).

Psychologists have not yet found a fully satisfactory explanation for this "infantile amnesia." Some have suggested that young children lack the memory encoding and storage processes described in the chapter on memory. Yet children of two or three can clearly recall experiences that happened weeks or even months earlier (Bauer, 2006). Others suggest that infantile amnesia occurs because very young children lack a sense of self. Because they don't even recognize themselves in the mirror, they may not have a framework for organizing memories about what happens to them (Howe, 2003). However, this explanation would hold for only the first two years or so, because after that children do recognize their own faces and even their taped voices (Legerstee, Anderson, & Schaffer, 1998).

Another possibility is that early memories, though "present," are implicit rather than explicit. As mentioned in the memory chapter, *implicit memories* form automatically and can affect our emotions and behavior even when we do not consciously recall them. However, children's implicit memories of their early years, like their explicit memories, are quite limited. One study found that when ten-year-old children were shown photographs of preschool classmates they hadn't seen in five years, the children had little implicit or explicit memory of them (Newcombe & Fox, 1994). In contrast, adults can correctly identify 90 percent of photographs of high-school classmates they have not seen for thirty years (Bahrick, Bahrick, & Wittlinger, 1975).

Other explanations of infantile amnesia suggest that our early memories are lost because in early childhood we don't yet have the language skills to talk about, and thus solidify, those memories. This possibility was explored in a study in which two- to three-year-old children played with a machine that supposedly shrunk toys (Simcock & Hayne, 2002). Six months later, they were asked what they remembered about this event. If they had not yet developed language at the time they played with the machine, the children were now able to say little or nothing about the experience. However, most of these same children could correctly identify pictures of the machine and act out what they had done with it. It appears that they had memories of the event that could be recalled nonverbally but not in words. Another possibility is that early experiences tend to be fused into *generalized event representations,* such as "going to Grandma's" or "playing at the beach," so it becomes difficult to remember any specific event.

Research on hypotheses such as these may someday unravel the mystery of infantile amnesia (Nelson & Fivush, 2004; Newcombe et al., 2000).

Culture and Cognitive Development

To explain cognitive development, Piaget focused on the physical world of objects. Russian psychologist Lev Vygotsky (pronounced "vah-GOT-skee") focused on the social world of people. He viewed cognitive abilities as the product of cultural history. The child's mind, said Vygotsky, grows through contact with other minds. It is through interaction with parents, teachers, and other representatives of their culture that children acquire the ideas of that culture (Vygotsky, 1991).

Vygotsky's followers have studied the effects of the social world on children's cognitive development—especially how participation in social routines affects children's developing knowledge of the world (Gauvain, 2001). In Western societies, those routines include shopping, eating at McDonald's, going to birthday parties, and attending religious services. In other cultures they might include helping to make pottery, going hunting, and weaving baskets (Larson & Verma, 1999). Quite early, children develop mental representations, called *scripts,* for these activities (see the chapter on thought, language, and intelligence). By the time they are three, children can describe routine activities quite accurately. Scripts, in turn, affect children's knowledge and understanding of cognitive tasks. For example, in cultures in which pottery making is important, children display conservation about the mass of objects sooner than children do in other cultures (Gardiner & Kosmitzki, 2005).

Children's cognitive abilities are also influenced by the language of their culture. Korean and Chinese children, for instance, show exceptional ability at adding and subtracting large numbers (Miller et al., 1995). As third-graders, they do in their heads three-digit problems (such as 702 minus 125) that their peers in the United States labor over or fail to solve. The difference seems traceable in part to the clear and explicit words that Asian languages use for the numbers from eleven to nineteen. In English, the meaning of the words *eleven* and *twelve,* for instance, is not as clear as the Asian *ten-one* and *ten-two.* Moreover, Asians use the abacus and the metric system of measurement, both of which are structured around the number ten. Korean math textbooks emphasize this tens structure by presenting the ones digits in red, the tens in blue, and the hundreds in green. Above all, for children in Asian cultures, educational achievement, especially in mathematics, is encouraged at home and strongly encouraged in school (Naito & Miura, 2001). In short, children's cognitive development is affected in ways large and small by the culture in which they live (Tomasello, 2000).

Individual Variations in Cognitive Development

Even within a single culture, some children are mentally advanced, whereas others lag behind their peers. Why? As already suggested, heredity is an important factor, but experience also plays a role. To explore how significant that role is, psychologists have studied the cognitive development of children raised in many different environments.

Cognitive development is seriously delayed if children are raised in environments in which they are deprived of the everyday sights, sounds, and feelings provided by conversation and loving interaction with family members, by pictures and books, and even by television, radio, and the Internet. Children subjected to this kind of severe deprivation show significant impairment in intellectual development by the time they are two or three years old. "Genie" was one such child. When rescued at age fourteen, she weighed only fifty-nine pounds. The only things she could say were "stop it" and "no

BABIES AT RISK The cognitive development of infants raised in this understaffed Russian orphanage will be permanently impaired if they are not given far more stimulation in the orphanage or, better yet, adopted into a loving family at a young age.

WHEN DOES STIMULATION BECOME OVERSTIMULATION?   A child's cognitive development is enhanced by a stimulating environment, but can there be too much stimulation? In the face of an avalanche of electronic media aimed specifically at babies and toddlers, some people are beginning to wonder. These stimulating media include computer "lapware," such as this baby is enjoying, videos and DVDs for even the tiniest infants, and, of course, the *Teletubbies.* Many babies in Western countries are immersed in electronic media for hours each day. In the United States, more than 25 percent of children under two have a TV set in their rooms, and one-third of them have videos in the "Baby Einstein" series (Lewin, 2003). We don't yet know how all this well-intentioned electronic stimulation is affecting young children because we don't yet have enough evidence on which to base conclusions.

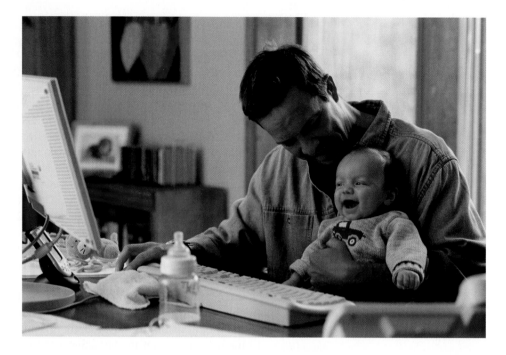

more." Investigators discovered that she had spent her life confined to a small bedroom, harnessed to a potty chair during the day and caged in a crib at night. She had not been permitted to hear or make many sounds. Although scientists and therapists worked intensively with Genie in the years after her discovery, she never learned to speak in complete sentences, and she remains in an adult care facility.

Cognitive development may also be impaired by less extreme conditions of deprivation, including the neglect, malnourishment, noise, and chaos that occur in some homes. A study of the effects of poverty found that by the time they were five years old, children raised in poverty scored nine points lower on IQ tests than did children in families whose incomes were at twice the poverty level—even after the researchers had controlled for all other family variables, such as family structure and parents' education (Duncan, Brooks-Gunn, & Klebanov, 1994). A more recent study of more than 10,000 children found that the economic status of the family into which a child is born is a much better predictor of the child's later cognitive development than are physical risk factors such as low birth weight (Jefferis, Power, & Hertzman, 2002).

In families with incomes above the poverty line, too, children's cognitive development is related to their surroundings and experiences. Parents can often make the difference between a child's getting A's or getting C's. To help children achieve those A's, adults can expose them, from the early years, to a variety of interesting materials and experiences— though not so many that the child is overwhelmed. Children's cognitive development is also enhanced when parents read and talk to them, encourage and help them to explore, and actively teach them (Gottfried, 1997)—in short, when they provide both support and challenge for their children's talents (Yeung, Linver, & Brooks-Gunn, 2002).

To improve the cognitive skills of children who do not get these kinds of stimulation, developmental psychologists have provided some children with extra lessons, materials, and educational contact with sensitive adults. In the United States, the most comprehensive effort to provide this kind of help has been through Project Head Start, a preschool program for poor children. Many smaller, more intensive programs have also been carried out. In a variety of such programs, children's cognitive abilities have been enhanced (Love et al., 2005; Ramey, Ramey, & Lanzi, 2006), and some effects can last into adulthood (Campbell et al., 2001). Music lessons can also promote children's cognitive development, especially verbal memory (Ho, Cheung, & Chan, 2003; Rauscher et al., 1997; Schellenberg, 2004). Even electronic games, although they are no substitute for adult attention, can provide opportunities for school-age children to hone spatial skills that can help improve their performance in math and science (Green & Bavelier, 2003; Greenfield et al., 1994).

FORMING A BOND Mutual eye contact, exaggerated facial expressions, and shared "baby talk" are an important part of the early social interactions that promote an enduring bond of attachment between parent and child.

temperament An individual's basic, natural disposition, evident from infancy.

Infancy and Childhood: Social and Emotional Development

▶ **How do infants become attached to their caregivers?**

Life for the child is more than learning about objects, doing math problems, and getting good grades. It is also about social relationships and emotional reactions. From the first months onward, infants are sensitive to those around them (Mumme & Fernald, 2003), and they are both attracted by and attractive to other people—especially parents and other caregivers.

During the first hour or so after birth, mothers gaze into their infants' eyes and give them gentle touches (Klaus & Kennell, 1976). This is the first opportunity for the mother to display her *bond* to her infant—an emotional tie that begins even before the baby is born. Psychologists once believed that this immediate contact was critical—that the mother-infant bond would never be strong if the opportunity for early interaction was missed. Research has revealed, however, that such interaction is a luxury, not a requirement for a close relationship (Myers, 1987). Mothers and fathers, whether biological or adoptive, gradually form close attachments to their infants by interacting with them day after day.

As the mother gazes at her baby, the baby is gazing back. By the time infants are two days old, they recognize—and like—their mother's face. They will suck more vigorously to see a videotaped image of her face than to see that of a stranger (Walton, Bower, & Bower, 1992). Soon, they begin to respond to the mother's facial expressions as well. By the time they are a year old, children use their mothers' emotional expressions to guide their own behavior in uncertain situations (Hertenstein & Campos, 2004; Saarni, 2006). If the mother looks frightened when a stranger approaches, for example, the child is more likely to avoid the stranger.

Individual Temperament

From the moment infants are born, they differ from one another in the emotions they express. Some infants are happy, active, and vigorous; they splash, thrash, and wriggle. Others lie still most of the time. Some infants approach new objects with enthusiasm; others turn away or fuss. Some infants whimper; others kick, scream, and wail. Characteristics such as these make up the infant's temperament. **Temperament** refers to the infant's individual style and frequency of expressing needs and emotions; it is constitutional, biological, and genetically based. Although temperament mainly reflects nature's contribution to the beginning of an individual's personality, it can also be affected by the prenatal environment, including—as noted earlier—the mother's smoking and drug use.

In some of the earliest research on infant temperament, Alexander Thomas and Stella Chess (1977) found three main temperament patterns. *Easy babies,* the most common kind, get hungry and sleepy at predictable times, react to new situations cheerfully, and seldom fuss. *Difficult babies* are irregular and irritable. Those in the third group, *slow-to-warm-up babies,* react warily to new situations but eventually come to enjoy them.

Traces of early temperamental characteristics weave their way throughout childhood (Rothbart & Bates, 2006). Easy infants usually stay easy (Zhou et al., 2004); difficult infants often remain difficult, sometimes developing attention and aggression problems in childhood (Else-Quest et al., 2006; Guerin, Gottfried, & Thomas, 1997). Timid toddlers tend to become shy preschoolers, restrained and inhibited eight-year-olds, and somewhat anxious teenagers (Roberts, Caspi, & Moffitt, 2001). However, in temperament, as in cognitive development, nature interacts with nurture. Many events take place between infancy and adulthood that can shift the individual's development in one direction or the other.

One influential factor suggested by Thomas and Chess is the match between the infant's temperament and the parents' expectations, desires, and personal styles. When parents believe they are responsible for the infant's behavior, an easy child might reassure

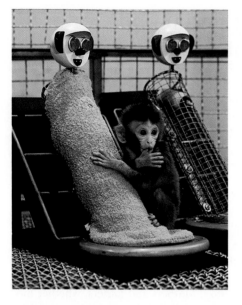

FIGURE **9.6**

Wire and Terry Cloth "Mothers"

Here are the two types of artificial mothers used in Harlow's research. Although baby monkeys received milk from the wire mother, they spent most of their time with the terry cloth version, and they clung to it when frightened.

attachment A deep, affectionate, close, and enduring relationship with a person with whom a baby has shared many experiences.

them. If parents are looking for signs of assertiveness, a difficult child might be just what they want.

If parent and infant are in tune, chances increase that temperamental qualities will be stable. Consider the temperament patterns of Chinese American and European American children. At birth, Chinese American infants are calmer, less changeable, less excitable, and more easily comforted when upset than European American infants (Kagan et al., 1994). This tendency toward self-control is powerfully reinforced by the Chinese culture. Compared with European American parents, Chinese parents are less likely to reward and stimulate babbling and smiling and more likely to maintain close control of their young children. The children, in turn, are more dependent on their mothers and less likely to play by themselves. They are less vocal, noisy, and active than European American children (Smith & Freedman, 1983).

These temperamental differences between children in different ethnic groups illustrate the combined contributions of nature and nurture. Mayan infants, for example, are relatively inactive from birth. The Zinacantecos, a Mayan group in southern Mexico, reinforce this innate predisposition toward restrained motor activity by tightly wrapping their infants and by nursing at the slightest sign of movement (Greenfield & Childs, 1991). This combination of genetic predisposition and cultural reinforcement is adaptive. Quiet infants do not kick off their covers at night, which is important in the cold highlands where they live. Inactive infants are able to spend long periods on their mothers' backs as the mothers work. And infants who do not begin to walk until they can understand some language do not wander into the open fire at the center of the house. This adaptive interplay of innate and cultural factors in the development of temperament operates in all cultures.

The Infant Grows Attached

As infants and caregivers respond to one another in the first year, the infant begins to form an **attachment**—a deep, affectionate, close, and enduring relationship—to these important figures. John Bowlby, a British psychoanalyst, drew attention to the importance of attachment after he observed children who had been orphaned in World War II. These children's depression and other emotional scars led Bowlby to propose a theory about the importance of developing a strong attachment to one's primary caregivers—a tie that normally keeps infants close to those caregivers and, therefore, safe (Bowlby, 1973). Soon after Bowlby first described his theory, researchers in the United States began to investigate how such attachments are formed and what happens when they fail to form or are broken by loss or separation. The most dramatic of these studies was conducted with monkeys by Harry Harlow.

Motherless Monkeys—and Children   Harlow (1959) separated newborn monkeys from their mothers and raised them in cages containing two artificial mothers. One "mother" was made of wire with a rubber nipple from which the infant could get milk (see Figure 9.6). It provided food but no physical comfort. The other artificial mother had no nipple but was made of soft, comfortable terry cloth. If attachments form entirely because caregivers provide food, the infants would be expected to prefer the wire mother. In fact, they spent most of their time with the terry cloth mother. And when they were frightened, the infants immediately ran to their terry cloth mother and clung to it. Harlow concluded that the monkeys were motivated by the need for comfort. The terry cloth mother provided feelings of softness and cuddling, which were things the infants needed when they sensed danger.

Harlow also investigated what happens when attachments do not form. He isolated some monkeys from all social contact from birth. After a year of this isolation, the monkeys showed dramatic disturbances. When visited by normally active, playful monkeys, they withdrew to a corner, huddling or rocking for hours. These monkeys' problems continued into adulthood. As adults, they were unable to have normal sexual relations. When some of the females became pregnant through artificial means, their maternal behaviors were woefully inadequate. In most cases, these mothers ignored their infants. When the infants became distressed, the mothers physically abused and sometimes even killed them.

Humans who spend their first few years without a consistent caregiver react in a tragically similar manner. At Romanian and Russian orphanages in which many children were neglected by institutional caregivers, visitors discovered that the children, like Harlow's deprived monkeys, were withdrawn and engaged in constant rocking (Holden, 1996). These effects tend to remain even after the children are adopted. In one study, researchers observed the behavior of four-year-old children who had been in a Romanian orphanage for at least eight months before being adopted (Chisholm, 1997). Compared with children who had been adopted before they were four months old, the late-adopted children were found to have many more serious problems. Depressed or withdrawn, they stared blankly, demanded attention, and could not control their tempers. Although they interacted poorly with their adoptive mothers, they were friendly with strangers, usually trying to cuddle and kiss them. At age six, a third of late-adopted children still showed no preference for their parents or any tendency to look to them when stressed (Rutter, O'Connor, & ERA Study Team, 2004). Neuroscientists suggest that the dramatic problems seen in isolated monkeys, as well as in humans, are the result of developmental brain dysfunction and damage brought on by a lack of touch and body movement in infancy (Wismer Fries et al., 2005; Prescott, 1996).

Forming an Attachment Fortunately, most infants do have a consistent caregiver, usually the mother, to whom they can form an attachment. They learn to recognize her and are able to distinguish her from a stranger at an early age. Some infants vocalize more to their mothers than to a stranger when they are only three months old. By the age of six or seven months, infants show signs of preferring the mother to anyone else. They crawl after her, call out to her, hug her, climb into her lap, and protest when she leaves (Ainsworth & Marvin, 1995). Babies who recognize and prefer their mothers even earlier—at three months—may be especially bright. One study found that such babies eventually achieve higher-than-average grades in high school, score higher on college entrance exams, and complete more years of education (Roe, 2001).

Infants also develop attachments to their fathers, but usually a little later (Lamb, 1997). Father-infant interaction is also less frequent than mother-infant interaction, and most studies show that it has a somewhat different nature (Parke, 2002). Mothers tend to feed, bathe, dress, cuddle, and talk to their infants, whereas fathers are more likely to play with, jiggle, and toss them, especially sons.

Online Study Center

Improve Your Grade
Tutorial: Strange Situation Test and Attachment

Variations in Attachment The amount of closeness and contact the infant seeks with either mother or father depends to some extent on the infant. Babies who are ill, tired, or slow to warm up may require more closeness. Closeness also depends to some extent on the parent. An infant whose parent has been absent or unresponsive is likely to need more closeness than one whose parent is accessible and responsive.

Researchers have studied the differences in infants' attachments in a special situation that simulates the natural comings and goings of parents and infants—the so-called *Strange Situation* (Ainsworth et al., 1978). Testing occurs in an unfamiliar playroom where the infant interacts with the mother and an unfamiliar woman in brief episodes: The infant plays with the mother and the stranger, the mother leaves the baby with the stranger for a few minutes, the mother and the stranger leave the baby alone in the room briefly, and the mother returns to the room.

Videotapes of these sessions show that most infants display a *secure attachment* to the mother in the Strange Situation (Thompson, 2006). In the unfamiliar room, the infant uses the mother as a home base, leaving her side to explore and play but returning to her periodically for comfort or contact. Securely attached children can tolerate the brief separation from their mothers, but they are always happy to see them return, and they are always receptive to the mothers' offers of contact. These mother-child pairs, researchers have found, tend to have harmonious interactions from the earliest months. The mothers themselves tend to be sensitive and responsive (DeWolff & van IJzendoorn, 1997).

Some infants, however, form *insecure attachments*. If the relationship is *avoidant*, the infant avoids or ignores the mother when she approaches or when she returns after the brief separation. If the relationship is *ambivalent*, the infant is upset when the mother leaves, but when she returns the child acts angry and rejects the mother's efforts at contact; when picked up, the child squirms to get down. If the relationship is *disorganized,* the infant's behavior is inconsistent, disturbed, and disturbing; the child may begin to cry again after the mother has returned and provided comfort, or may reach out for the mother while looking away from her (Moss et al., 2004).

The nature of a child's attachment to caregivers can have long-term and far-reaching effects (NICHD Early Child Care Research Network, 2006b). For example, unless disrupted by the loss of a parent, abuse by a family member, chronic depression in the mother, or some other severe negative event (Weinfield, Sroufe, & Egeland, 2000), an infant's secure attachment continues into young adulthood—and probably throughout life (Hamilton, 2000; Mattanah, Hancock, & Brand, 2004; Waters et al., 2000). A secure attachment to the mother is also reflected in relationships with other people. Children who are securely attached receive more positive reactions from other children when they are toddlers (Fagot, 1997) and have better relations with peers in middle childhood and adolescence (Carlson, Sroufe, & Egeland, 2004; Schneider, Atkinson, & Tardif, 2001).

Patterns of child care and attachment vary widely in different parts of the world. In northern Germany, for example, where parents are quite strict, the proportion of infants who display avoidant attachments is much higher than in the United States (Spangler, Fremmer-Bombik, & Grossman, 1996). Kibbutz babies in Israel, who sleep in infant houses away from their parents, are relatively likely to show insecure attachments and other related problems (Aviezer et al., 1999). In Japan, where mothers are expected to be completely devoted to their children and are seldom apart from them, even at night, children develop an attachment relationship that emphasizes harmony and union (Rothbaum et al., 2000). These attachment patterns differ from the secure type that is most common in the United States: With their parents' encouragement, U.S. children balance closeness and proximity with exploration and autonomy.

THINKING CRITICALLY

Does Day Care Harm the Emotional Development of Infants?

With about 60 percent of mothers of infants in the United States working outside the home, concern has been expressed about how daily separations from their mothers might affect children, especially infants (Clarke-Stewart & Allhusen, 2005). Some have argued that putting infants in day care, with a baby sitter or in a day-care center, damages the quality of the mother-infant relationship and increases the babies' risk for psychological problems later on (Gallagher, 1998).

■ **What am I being asked to believe or accept?**

The claim is that daily separations created by day care damage the formation of an attachment between the mother and infant and harm the infant's emotional development.

■ **Is there evidence available to support the claim?**

There is clear evidence that separation from the mother is painful for young children. If separation lasts a week or more, children who have formed an attachment to their mother tend to protest, then become apathetic and mournful, and finally seem to lose interest in the missing mother (Robertson & Robertson, 1971). But day care does not involve such lasting separations. Research has shown that infants who are in day care do form attachments to their mothers. In fact, they prefer their mothers to their daytime caregivers (Lamb & Ahnert, 2006).

Are these attachments as secure as the attachments formed by infants whose mothers do not work outside the home? Researchers have examined this question by comparing how infants react to brief separations from their mothers in the Strange Situation. A

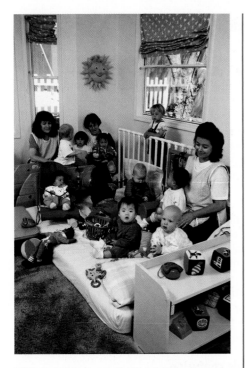

THE EFFECTS OF DAY CARE Parents are understandably concerned that leaving their infants in a day-care center all day long might interfere with the mother-infant attachment or with other aspects of the child's development. Research shows that most infants in day care do form healthy bonds with their parents but that if children spend many hours in day care between infancy and kindergarten, they are more likely to have behavior problems in school, such as talking back to the teacher or getting into fights with other children (NICHD Early Child Care Research Network, 2001, 2006b). Time will tell whether other problems develop in the future.

review of about twenty studies done in the 1980s revealed that infants in full-time day care were somewhat more likely to be classified as insecurely attached. About 36 percent of them were classified as insecure; only 29 percent of the infants who were not in full-time day care were counted as insecure (Clarke-Stewart, 1989). These results appear to support the suggestion that day care harms infants' attachments to their mothers.

■ Can that evidence be interpreted another way?

Perhaps factors other than day care could explain the difference between infants in day care and those at home with their mothers. One such factor could be the method that was used to assess attachment. Infants in these studies were judged insecure if they did not run to their mothers after a brief separation in the Strange Situation. But maybe infants who experience daily separations from their mothers during day care feel more comfortable in the Strange Situation and therefore seek out less closeness with their mothers. A second factor concerns the possible differences between the infants' mothers. Perhaps mothers who value independence in themselves and in their children are more likely to be working and to place their children in day care, whereas mothers who emphasize closeness with their children are more likely to stay home.

■ What evidence would help to evaluate the alternatives?

Finding insecure attachment to be more common among the infants of working mothers does not, by itself, demonstrate that day care is harmful. To judge the effects of day care, we must consider other measures of emotional adjustment as well. If day-care infants showed consistent signs of impaired emotional relations in other situations (at home, say) and with other caregivers (such as the father), this evidence would support the argument that day care harms children's emotional development. Another useful method would be to statistically control for differences in the behavior and attitudes of parents who do and do not put their infants in day care, and then look for differences in their children.

In fact, this research design has already been employed. In 1990, the U.S. government funded a study of infant day care in ten sites around the country. The psychological and physical development of more than 1,300 randomly selected infants was tracked from birth through age three. The results available so far show that when factors such as parents' education, income, and attitudes were statistically controlled, infants in day care were no more likely to have emotional problems or to be insecurely attached to their mothers than infants not in day care. However, in cases in which infants were placed in poor-quality day care with caregivers who were insensitive and unresponsive and in which mothers were insensitive to their babies' needs at home, the infants were less likely to develop a secure attachment to their mothers (NICHD Early Child Care Research Network, 2005, 2006a).

■ What conclusions are most reasonable?

Based on available evidence, the most reasonable conclusion appears to be that day care by itself does not lead to insecure attachment. But if that day care is of poor quality, it can worsen a risky situation at home and increase the likelihood that infants will have problems forming a secure attachment to their mothers. The U.S. government study is still under way, and the children's progress is being followed into adolescence.

Relationships with Parents and Peers

Erik Erikson (1968) saw the first year of life as a time when infants develop a feeling of trust (or mistrust) about the world. According to his theory, an infant's first year represents the first of eight stages of lifelong psychosocial development (see Table 9.2). Each stage focuses on an issue, or "crisis," that is especially important at that time of

TABLE 9.2

Erikson's Stages of Psychosocial Development

In each of Erikson's stages of development, a different psychological issue presents a new crisis for the person to resolve. The person focuses attention on that issue and, by the end of the period, has worked through the crisis and resolved it either positively, in the direction of healthy development, or negatively, hindering further psychological development.

Age	Central Psychological Issue or Crisis
First Year	**Trust versus mistrust** Infants learn to trust that their needs will be met by the world, especially by the mother—or they learn to mistrust the world.
Second year	**Autonomy versus shame and doubt** Children learn to exercise will, to make choices, and to control themselves—or they become uncertain and doubt that they can do things by themselves.
Third to fifth year	**Initiative versus guilt** Children learn to initiate activities and enjoy their accomplishments, acquiring direction and purpose—or, if they are not allowed initiative, they feel guilty for their attempts at independence.
Sixth year through puberty	**Industry versus inferiority** Children develop a sense of industry and curiosity and are eager to learn—or they feel inferior and lose interest in the tasks before them.
Adolescence	**Identity versus role confusion** Adolescents come to see themselves as unique and integrated persons with an ideology—or they become confused about what they want out of life.
Early adulthood	**Intimacy versus isolation** Young people become able to commit themselves to another person—or they develop a sense of isolation and feel they have no one in the world but themselves.
Middle age	**Generativity versus stagnation** Adults are willing to have and care for children and to devote themselves to their work and the common good—or they become self-centered and inactive.
Old age	**Integrity versus despair** Older people enter a period of reflection, becoming assured that their lives have been meaningful and becoming ready to face death with acceptance and dignity—or they are in despair for their unaccomplished goals, failures, and ill-spent lives.

life. Erikson believed that the ways in which people resolve these crises shape their personalities and social relationships. Resolving a crisis in a positive way provides the foundation for characteristics such as trust, independence, initiative, or industry. But if the crisis is not resolved positively, according to Erikson, the person will be psychologically troubled and cope less effectively with later crises. In Erikson's theory, trusting caregivers during infancy forms the bedrock for all future social and emotional development.

After children have formed strong emotional attachments to their parents, their next psychological task is to develop a more independent relationship with them. In Erikson's theory, this task is reflected in the second stage (again, see Table 9.2). Children begin to exercise their wills, to develop some independence from their parents, and to begin activities on their own. According to Erikson, children who are not allowed to exercise their wills or start their own activities will feel uncertain about doing things for themselves and guilty about seeking independence. The extent to which parents allow or encourage their children's independence is related to their parenting style.

Parenting Styles Most parents try to channel children's impulses into socially accepted outlets and teach them the skills and rules needed to function in their society. Cultural values strongly shape this **socialization** process. Parents in Hispanic cultures of Mexico, Puerto Rico, and Central America, for example, tend to be influenced by the collectivist tradition discussed in the introductory chapter, in which family and community interests are emphasized over individual goals. Children in these cultures are expected to respect and obey their elders, and they are taught to do less of the questioning, negotiating, and arguing that is encouraged—or at least tolerated—in many middle-class European American families (Greenfield, Suzuki, & Rothstein-Fisch, 2006; Parke & Buriel, 2006).

European American parents tend to employ one of three distinct parenting styles, as described by Diana Baumrind (1991). **Authoritarian parents** tend to be strict, punishing, and unsympathetic. They value obedience from children and try to shape their children's behavior to meet a set standard and to curb the children's wills. They do not encourage independence. They are detached and seldom praise their youngsters. In contrast, **permissive parents** give their children complete freedom and provide little discipline. **Authoritative parents** fall between these two extremes. They reason with their children, encouraging give and take. They allow children increasing responsibility as they get older and better at making decisions. They are firm but understanding. They set limits but also encourage independence. Their demands are reasonable, rational, and consistent.

In her research with middle-class parents, Baumrind found these three parenting styles to be consistently related to young children's social and emotional development. Authoritarian parents had children who were unfriendly, distrustful, and withdrawn. The children of permissive parents were immature, dependent, and unhappy; they were likely to have tantrums or to ask for help when they encountered even slight difficulties. Children raised by authoritative parents were friendly, cooperative, self-reliant, and socially responsible.

Other researchers who followed Baumrind's lead found that authoritative parenting styles were associated with additional positive outcomes, including better school achievement, greater popularity, and better psychological adjustment to parental divorce (Hetherington & Clingempeel, 1992; Hinshaw et al., 1997; Steinberg et al., 1994). In contrast, children of authoritarian parents are more likely to cheat and to be aggressive and less likely to experience guilt or accept blame after doing something wrong (Eisenberg, Fabes, & Spinrad, 2006).

The results of these parenting studies are interesting, but they are limited in several ways. First, they are based on correlations, which, as discussed in the introductory chapter, do not prove causation. Finding consistent correlations between parents' and children's behavior does not establish that the parents are *creating* the differences seen in their children. Even evidence that differences between the children of authoritative and nonauthoritative parents tend to increase over time can only show that parents' socialization styles *might* have a direct influence on children's behavior (Steinberg et al., 1994). It is also possible, for example, that parents' behavior might be shaped to some extent by their children. Children's temperament, size, and appearance may influence the way parents treat them (Bugental & Grusec, 2006) and may alter the effects of parenting styles (Zhou et al., 2004).

Second, some developmental psychologists suggest that it is not the parents' socialization practices that influence children but, rather, how the children perceive the discipline they receive—as stricter or more lenient than what an older sibling received, for example (Reiss et al., 2000). A third limitation of parenting studies is that the correlations between parenting styles and children's behavior, though statistically significant, are usually not terribly strong. Expected outcomes do not always appear. For example, Baumrind (1971) found a small group of "harmonious" families in which discipline was never observed, yet the children were thriving.

In all likelihood, it is the "fit" between parenting style and children's characteristics that affects children the most. There is no universally "best" style of parenting (Parke & Buriel, 2006). So authoritative parenting, which is so consistently linked with positive outcomes in European American families, is not related to better school performance among African American or Asian American youngsters (Kim & Rohner,

socialization The process by which parents, teachers, and others teach children the skills and social norms necessary to be well-functioning members of society.

authoritarian parents Parents who are firm, punitive, and unsympathetic.

permissive parents Parents who give their children complete freedom and lax discipline.

authoritative parents Parents who reason with their children and are firm but understanding.

CHILDREN'S FRIENDSHIPS
Although relationships with peers may not always be this friendly, they are often among the closest and most positive in a child's life. Friends are more interactive than nonfriends; they smile and laugh together more, pay closer attention to equality in their conversations, and talk about mutual goals. Having at least one close friend in childhood predicts good psychological functioning later on.

2002; Steinberg, Dornbusch, & Brown, 1992). And frequent spankings in the first two years increases the risk of behavior problems by school age for European American children, but not for African American and Hispanic American children (Slade & Wissow, 2004). One possible reason for these differing patterns is that disciplinary styles can have different meanings in different cultures. When Chinese American parents use authoritarian discipline—which they do to a greater extent than European American parents—their goal is usually to "train" *(chiao shun)* and "govern" *(guan)* children so that they will know what is expected of them (Chao, 1994). By contrast, European American parents who use authoritarian discipline are more likely to do so to "break the child's will." In other words, each parenting style must be evaluated in its cultural context.

Some people have suggested that parenting styles are a less significant influence on children's social development than are the influences they encounter outside the home—especially peer influences (Harris, 1995, 1998). Research evidence does not justify dismissing the impact of parenting styles, but there is no denying the impact of peer influences, either (Collins et al., 2000; Leventhal & Brooks-Gunn, 2000).

Relationships with Peers   Social development over the years of childhood spans an ever-enlarging social world that broadens to include brothers and sisters, playmates, and classmates. Psychologists have observed that from a remarkably early age—as young as one year—children are interested in the behavior of other children (usually their siblings) and that by the time they are a year and a half old, they know how to hurt or comfort other children (Rubin, Bukowski, & Parker, 2006).

It takes time for children to learn how to interact with other children. Two-year-olds in Western cultures are only able to exchange or fight over toys. By the time they are three, they can use toys to get a response from peers. At age four, children converse about the toys they are playing with, and at the end of the preschool period, they are able to share toys and tasks cooperatively. This kind of play is important because it shows children how to communicate what they are feeling and gives them the chance to form their first friendships (Dunn & Hughes, 2001; Rubin et al., 2006).

In the school years, peer interaction becomes more complex and structured as children play games with rules, play on teams, tutor each other, and cooperate—or compete—in achieving goals. The school years are also the time when friends become important and friendships become long lasting (Hartup & Stevens, 1997). At this age, the most important aspects of friendship are companionship and fun; psychological intimacy does not enter the picture until children become teenagers (Parker et al., 2001).

Social Skills

The changes in peer interactions and relationships over the years of childhood reflect children's increasing social competence and understanding. *Social skills,* like cognitive skills, must be learned (Rubin et al., 2006).

One important social skill is the ability to engage in sustained, responsive interactions with peers. These interactions require cooperation, sharing, and taking turns—behaviors that first appear in the preschool years. A second social skill that children learn is the ability to detect and correctly interpret other people's emotional signals. Much as children's school performance depends on processing academic information, their social performance depends on processing information about other people (Slomkowski & Dunn, 1996). A related set of social skills involves the ability to feel what another person is feeling, or something close to it (*empathy*), and to respond with comfort or help if the person is in distress.

Children whose social skills allow them to understand another person's perspective, appreciate how that person might be feeling, and offer sympathy, cooperation, and help tend to be the most popular members of a peer group (Izard et al., 2001; Rubin et al., 2006). Children without these skills tend to be rejected or neglected; they may become bullies or the victims of bullies. Parents, other adults, and even older siblings can help

LEARNING GENDER ROLES In every culture, socialization by parents and others typically encourages the interests, activities, and other characteristics traditionally associated with a child's own gender.

their children to develop these skills by engaging them in lots of "pretend" play and other prosocial activities and by encouraging them to express their emotions constructively (Eisenberg et al., 2006; Ladd, 2005; Lopes et al., 2005).

Gender Roles

LINKAGES
Who teaches boys to be men and girls to be women?
(a link to Learning)

An important aspect of understanding other people is knowing about social roles, including those linked to being male or female. All cultures establish expectations about **gender roles,** the general patterns of work, appearance, and behavior associated with being a man or a woman. Gender roles appear in every culture, but they are more pronounced in some cultures than in others. One analysis revealed, for example, that where smaller differences in social status exist between males and females, gender-role differences are smaller as well (Wood & Eagly, 2002). In North America, some roles—such as homemaker and firefighter—have traditionally been tied to gender, although these traditions are weakening. Research by Deborah Best suggests that children show gender-role expectations earliest in Muslim countries (where the differences in roles are perhaps most extreme), but children in all twenty-five countries she studied eventually developed them (Best, 1992; Williams & Best, 1990).

Gender roles appear and persist because they are deeply rooted in both nature and nurture. Small physical and behavioral differences between the sexes appear early on and tend to increase over the years. For example, girls tend to speak and write earlier and to be better at grammar and spelling than boys (Halpern, 1997). Girls are also able to read emotional signals at younger ages than boys (Dunn et al., 1991), and their play tends to be more orderly. Boys tend to be more skilled than girls at manipulating objects, constructing three-dimensional forms, and mentally manipulating complex figures and pictures (Choi & Silverman, 2003). They are more physically active and aggressive and more inclined to hit obstacles or people. They play in larger groups and spaces and enjoy noisier, more strenuous physical games (Fabes, Martin, & Hanish, 2003).

Biological Factors A biological contribution to these and other male-female differences is supported by studies of differences in anatomy, hormones, and brain organization and functioning (Geary, 1999; Ruble, Martin, & Berenbaum, 2006). A biological basis for male-female differences is also supported by cross-cultural research that shows consistency in gender patterns despite differing socialization (Simpson & Kenrick, 1997). In virtually every culture, for example, males are more violent than females.

gender roles Patterns of work, appearance, and behavior that society associates with being male or female.

SOCIAL AND EMOTIONAL DEVELOPMENT DURING INFANCY AND CHILDHOOD

Age	Relationships with Parents	Relationships with Other Children	Social Understanding
Birth–2 years	Infants form an attachment to the primary caregiver.	Play focuses on toys, not on other children.	Infants respond to emotional expressions of others.
2–4 years	Children become more independent and no longer need their parents' constant attention.	Toys are a way of eliciting responses from other children.	Young children can recognize emotions of others.
4–10 years	Parents actively socialize their children.	Children begin to cooperate, compete, play games, and form friendships with peers.	Children learn social rules, such as politeness, and roles, such as being a male or female.

1. As part of their social development, children learn _____ , which tell them what patterns of appearance and behavior are associated with being male or female.
2. Teaching children to talk quietly in a restaurant is part of the process called _____ .
3. Strict rules and the threat of punishment are typical of _____ parenting.

Finally, research with nonhuman primates has found sex differences that parallel those seen in human children. In one study, young female animals preferred playing with dolls and young males preferred playing with a toy car (Alexander & Hines, 2002).

Social Factors   There is no doubt, though, that socialization also influences gender roles, partly by exaggerating whatever gender differences may already exist (Hyde, 2005). From the moment they are born, boys and girls are treated differently. Adults usually play more gently with, and talk more to, infants they believe to be girls than infants they believe to be boys (Culp, Cook, & Housley, 1983). They often shower their daughters with dolls and tea sets, their sons with trucks and tools. They tend to encourage boys to achieve, compete, and explore; to control their feelings; to be independent; and to assume personal responsibility. They more often encourage girls to be expressive, nurturant, reflective, dependent, domestic, obedient, and unselfish (Ruble et al., 2006). In short, parents, teachers, and television role models consciously or accidentally pass on their ideas about "appropriate" behaviors for boys and girls (Parke & Buriel, 2006; Ruble et al., 2006).

Children also pick up ideas about gender-appropriate behavior from their peers (Martin & Fabes, 2001). For example, boys tend to be better than girls at computer or video games (Greenfield, 1994). However, this difference stems partly from the fact that boys encourage and reward each other for skilled performance at these games more than girls do (Law, Pellegrino, & Hunt, 1993). Children are also more likely to play with children of the same sex, and in gender-typical ways, on the playground than they are in private, at home, or in the classroom (Luria, 1992). An analysis of 143 studies of sex differences in aggression showed that boys acted significantly and consistently more aggressively than girls, but especially so when they knew they were being watched (Hyde, 1986). Among girls, aggression is less obvious; it is usually "relational aggression" that shows up in nasty words, not punching (Crick et al., 2004).

In short, social and cultural training tends to support and amplify any biological predispositions that distinguish boys and girls. Gender roles reflect a mix of nature and nurture. (Gender roles and other elements of early development are summarized in "In Review: Social and Emotional Development During Infancy and Childhood.")

The efforts of some parents to deemphasize gender roles in their children's upbringing may be helping to reduce the size of gender differences in areas such as verbal and quantitative skills. However, the evolutionary approach to psychology suggests that other gender differences are unlikely to change much. These differences include males' greater ability to visualize the rotation of objects in space and females' greater ability to read facial expressions. Evolutionary psychologists see these differences as deeply rooted reflections of gender-related hunting versus child-rearing duties that were adaptive eons ago for the survival of both sexes (Buss, 2004). Others have suggested that such differences result from prenatal exposure to male or female hormones that shape brain development in different ways (Halpern, 1997). Still others see gender differences as reflecting social inequality, not just biological destiny (Wood & Eagly, 2002).

Adolescence

▶ **What threatens adolescents' self-esteem?**

The years of middle childhood usually pass smoothly, as children busy themselves with schoolwork, hobbies, friends, and clubs. But in adolescence, things change dramatically. All adolescents undergo significant changes in size, shape, and physical capacities. In Western cultures, many adolescents also experience huge changes in their social lives, reasoning abilities, and views of themselves.

The Challenges of Change

A sudden spurt in physical growth is a visible signal that adolescence has begun. This growth spurt peaks at about age twelve for girls and at about age fourteen for boys (Tanner, 1978; see Figure 9.7). Suddenly, adolescents find themselves in new bodies. At the end of the growth spurt, menstruation begins in females, and live sperm are produced in males. This condition of being able for the first time to reproduce is called **puberty.**

In Western cultures, *early adolescence* (the period from age eleven to fourteen or so) is filled with challenges. Sexual interest stirs, and there are opportunities to smoke, drink alcohol, and take other drugs (Patton et al., 2004). All of this can be disorienting. Adolescents—especially early-maturing girls—may experience bouts of depression and other psychological problems (Ge, Conger, & Elder, 2001; Ohring, Graber, & Brooks-Gunn, 2002).

Some of these problems appear as adolescents begin to face challenges to their *self-esteem,* their sense of being worthy, capable, and deserving of respect (Harter, 2006). Adolescents are especially vulnerable if other stressors occur at the same time (DuBois et al., 1992; Kling et al., 1999). The switch from elementary school to middle school is particularly challenging. Declining grades are especially likely among students who were already having trouble in school or who don't have confidence in their own abilities (Rudolph et al., 2001). But grades do not affect self-esteem in all teens; many base their self-esteem primarily on what others think of them or on other social factors that might affect their feelings of self-worth (Crocker & Wolfe, 2001).

The changes and pressures of adolescence are often played out at home. Many teenagers become discontented with their parents' rules and values, leading to arguments over everything from taking out the garbage to who left the gallon of milk on top of the refrigerator. Serious conflicts may lead to serious problems, including running away, pregnancy, stealing, drug taking, or even suicide—especially among teens who do not feel close to their parents (Blum, Beuhring, & Rinehart, 2000; Goldstein, Davis-Kean, & Eccles, 2005). Fortunately, although the bond with parents weakens during the transition from early to mid-adolescence, most adolescents and young adults maintain reasonably good relationships with their parents (van Wel, ter Bogt, & Raaijmakers, 2002). In fact, research suggests that in Western cultures, more than half

puberty The condition of being able, for the first time, to reproduce.

FIGURE **9.7**

Physical Changes in Adolescence

At about ten and a half years of age, girls begin their growth spurt, and by age twelve, they are taller than their male peers. When boys, at about twelve and a half years of age, begin their growth spurt, they usually grow faster and for a longer period of time than girls. Adolescents may grow as much as five inches a year. The development of sexual characteristics accompanies these changes in height. The ages at which these changes occur vary considerably across individuals, but the sequence of changes is the same.

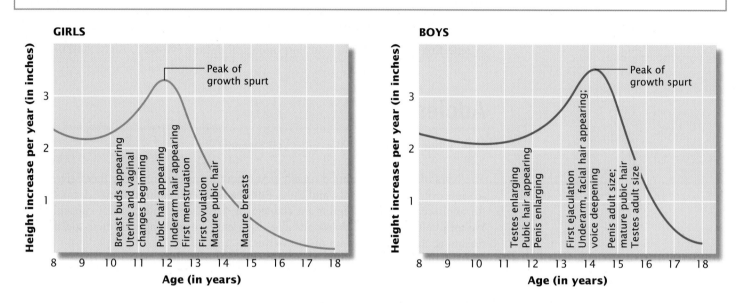

of today's teens find early adolescence relatively trouble free (Arnett, 1999); only about 15 percent of the adolescents studied experience serious turmoil.

Love and Sex in Adolescence   Surveys suggest that nearly half of fifteen-year-olds and 70 percent of eighteen-year-olds have romantic relationships (Carver, Joyner, & Udry, 2003) and that by age sixteen almost half of North America's young people have had sexual intercourse (National Center for Chronic Disease Prevention and Health Promotion, 2002). Teens who have sex differ from those who do not in a number of ways. They hold less conventional attitudes and values, and they are more likely to smoke, drink alcohol, and use other drugs (National Center on Addiction and Substance Abuse, 2004). They also have more unsupervised time after school (Cohen et al., 2002), and they are more likely to have sexually active best friends (Jaccard, Blanton, & Dodge, 2005). Their parents tend to be less educated, less likely to exert control over them, and less likely to talk openly with them. The typical pairing of sexually active teens is a "macho" male and a "girly" female (Udry & Chantala, 2003). Adolescents who displayed poorer self-control skills as children are the ones most likely to take greater sexual risks, such as having multiple partners and not using condoms (Raffaelli & Crockett, 2003).

Too often, sexual activity leads to declining school achievement and interest, sexually transmitted diseases, and unplanned and unwanted pregnancies. Teenagers have the highest rates of sexually transmitted diseases (such as gonorrhea, chlamydia, and pelvic inflammatory disease) of any age group (National Center for Health Statistics, 2000; Ross, 2002). One-fifth of all AIDS cases start in adolescence, and although teenage pregnancy rates have been declining of late, nearly 9 percent of all teenage girls in the United States get pregnant before they reach age nineteen (National Center for Health Statistics, 2003; Starkman & Rajani, 2002). The teens most likely to become pregnant are those with little confidence in themselves or in their educational futures (Young et al., 2004). More than half of the U.S. adolescents who become pregnant elect to keep their babies and become single mothers.

A teenage pregnancy can create problems for the mother, the baby, and others in the family. Teenage parents tend to be less positive and stimulating with their children than older parents and more likely to abuse them (Brooks-Gunn & Chase-Lansdale, 2002). The children of teenage parents, in turn, are more likely to develop behavior problems and to do poorly in school than those whose parents are older (Moffitt, 2002; National Center for Health Statistics, 2000).

Identity and Development of the Self

In many less economically developed nations today, and in the United States during earlier times, the end of early adolescence (around the age of fourteen) marks the onset of adulthood—a time when work, parenting, and grown-up responsibilities begin. In modern North America, the transition from childhood to adulthood often lasts well into the twenties. Adolescents spend a lot of time being students or trainees. This lengthened adolescence has created special problems—among them, the matter of finding or forming an identity.

Forming a Personal and Ethnic Identity   Preschool children asked to describe themselves often mention a favorite or habitual activity: "I watch TV" or "I play in the yard." At eight or nine, children identify themselves by giving facts such as their sex, age, name, physical appearance, and likes and dislikes. They may still describe themselves in terms of what they do, but they now include how well they do it compared with other children. Then, at about age eleven, children begin to describe themselves in terms of social relationships, personality traits, and other general, stable psychological characteristics such as "smart" or "friendly" (Shaffer, 1999). These changes in the way children and adolescents describe themselves suggest changes in the way they think about themselves. As they become more self-conscious, they gradually develop a personal identity as unique individuals.

Their personal identity may be affected by their **ethnic identity**—the part of a person's identity that reflects the racial, religious, or cultural group to which the person belongs (French et al., 2006). In melting-pot nations such as the United States, some members of ethnic minorities may identify with their ethnic group—Chinese, Mexican, or Italian, for example—even more than with their national citizenship. Children are aware of ethnic cues such as skin color before they reach the age of three. Minority-group children notice these cues earlier than other children and prefer to play with children from their own group (Milner, 1983). In high school, most students hang out with members of their own ethnic group. They tend not to know classmates in other ethnic groups well, seeing them more as members of those groups than as individuals (Steinberg, Dornbusch, & Brown, 1992). A positive ethnic identity contributes to self-esteem, partly because seeing their own group as superior makes people feel good about themselves (Fiske, 1998). However, as described in the chapter on social psychology, the same processes that create ethnic identity can also sow the seeds of ethnic prejudice. Adolescents who regularly interact with members of other ethnic groups usually become less prejudiced adults (Phinney, Ferguson, & Tate, 1997).

Facing the Identity Crisis   Identity formation is the central task of adolescence in Erikson's theory of psychosocial development. According to Erikson (1968), events of late adolescence—graduating from high school, going to college, and forming new relationships—challenge the adolescent's self-concept and trigger an **identity crisis** (see Table 9.2). In this crisis, the adolescent must develop the self-image of a unique person by pulling together self-knowledge acquired during childhood. If infancy and childhood brought trust, autonomy, and initiative, according to Erikson, adolescents will resolve the identity crisis positively, feeling self-confident and competent. If infancy and childhood resulted in feelings of mistrust, shame, guilt, and inferiority, adolescents will be confused about their identity and goals.

In Western cultures there is some limited empirical support for Erikson's ideas about the identity crisis. In late adolescence, young people do consider alternative identities (Waterman, 1982). They may "try out" being rebellious, studious, or detached as they attempt to resolve questions about sexuality, self-worth, industriousness, and

ethnic identity The part of a person's identity that reflects the racial, religious, or cultural group to which he or she belongs.

identity crisis The phase during which an adolescent attempts to develop an integrated self-image as a unique person by pulling together self-knowledge acquired during childhood.

HANGING OUT, SEPA-RATELY Ethnic identity is that part of our personal identity that reflects the racial, religious, or cultural group to which we belong. Ethnic identity often leads people to interact mainly with others who share that same identity. To what extent is this true of you? You can get a rough idea by jotting down the ethnicity of all the people you chose to spend time with over the past week or so.

independence, but late adolescence is also a time when many people become more aware of their obligations to their families (Fuligni & Pedersen, 2002). By the time they are twenty-one, about half of the adolescents studied have resolved the identity crisis in a way that is consistent with their self-image and the historical era in which they are living. They enter young adulthood with self-confidence. Basically the same people who entered adolescence, they now have more mature attitudes and behavior, more consistent goals and values, and a clearer idea of who they are (Savin-Williams & Demo, 1984). Many have become more aware of their obligations to their families (Fuligni & Pedersen, 2002). For those who fail to resolve identity issues—either because they avoided the identity crisis by accepting the identity their parents set for them or because they postponed dealing with the crisis and remain uncommitted and lacking in direction—there are often problems ahead (Lange & Byrd, 2002).

Moral Reasoning

Adolescents are able to develop an identity partly because, according to Piaget's theory, they have entered the *formal operational period*, which allows them to think logically and reason about abstract concepts. Adolescents often find themselves applying these advanced cognitive skills to questions of morality.

Kohlberg's Stages of Moral Reasoning   To examine how people think about morality, psychologists have asked them how they would resolve moral dilemmas, and why. Perhaps the most famous of these is the "Heinz dilemma," in which people must decide whether a man named Heinz should steal a rare and unaffordably expensive drug in order to save his wife from cancer.

By posing moral dilemmas such as this one, Lawrence Kohlberg found that the reasons given for moral choices change systematically and consistently with age (Kohlberg & Gilligan, 1971). Young children make moral judgments that differ from those of older children, adolescents, or adults. Kohlberg proposed that moral reasoning develops in six stages, which are summarized in Table 9.3. These stages, he said, are not tightly linked to a person's chronological age. Instead, there is a range of ages for reaching each stage, and not everyone reaches the highest level.

Stage 1 and Stage 2 moral judgments, which are most typical of children under the age of nine, tend to be selfish in nature. Kohlberg called this level of moral reasoning **preconventional,** because it is not based on the conventions or rules that usually guide social interactions in society. People at this level of moral development are mainly concerned with avoiding punishment or following rules when it is to their own advantage. At the **conventional** level of moral reasoning, Stages 3 and 4, people care about other

preconventional   Referring to moral reasoning that is not based on the conventions or rules that guide social interactions in a society.

conventional   Referring to moral reasoning that reflects a concern about other people, as well as the belief that morality consists of following rules and conventions.

TABLE 9.3

Kohlberg's Stages of Moral Development

Kohlberg's stages of moral reasoning describe differences in how people think about moral issues. Here are some examples of answers that people at different stages of development might give to the "Heinz dilemma" described in the text. This dilemma is more realistic than you might think. In 1994, a man was arrested for robbing a bank after being turned down for a loan to pay for his wife's cancer treatments.

Stage	What Is Right?	Should Heinz Steal the Drug?
Preconventional		
1	Obeying and avoiding punishment from a superior authority	"Heinz should not steal the drug, because he will be jailed."
2	Making a fair exchange, a good deal	"Heinz should steal the drug, because his wife will repay him later."
Conventional		
3	Pleasing others and getting their approval	"Heinz should steal the drug, because he loves his wife and because she and the rest of the family will approve."
4	Doing your duty, following rules and social order	"Heinz should steal the drug for his wife, because he has a duty to care for her," or "Heinz should not steal the drug, because stealing is illegal."
Postconventional		
5	Respecting rules and laws, but recognizing that they may have limits	"Heinz should steal the drug, because life is more important than property."
6	Following universal ethical principles, such as justice, reciprocity, equality, and respect for human life and rights	"Heinz should steal the drug because of the principle of preserving and respecting life."

people. They think that morality consists of following rules and conventions such as duty to the family, to marriage vows, and to the country. The moral reasoning of children and adolescents from nine to nineteen is most often at this level. Stages 5 and 6 represent the highest level of moral reasoning, which Kohlberg called **postconventional** because it occurs after conventional reasoning. Moral judgments at this level are based on personal standards or universal principles of justice, equality, and respect for human life, not just on the demands of authority figures or society. People who have reached this level view rules and laws as arbitrary but respect them because they protect human welfare. They believe that individual rights can sometimes justify violating these laws if the laws become destructive. People do not usually reach this level until sometime after the end of adolescence. Stage 6 is seen only rarely, in extraordinary individuals. Studies of Kohlberg's stages have generally supported the sequence he proposed (Turiel, 2006).

Limitations of Kohlberg's Stages Do Kohlberg's stages appear across cultures? In general, yes. Forty-five studies in twenty-seven cultures from Alaska to Zambia showed that people do tend to make upward progress through Kohlberg's stages, without reversals (Snarey, 1987). Stages 5 and 6, however, did not always appear. Further, the moral judgments made in some cultures do not always fit neatly into Kohlberg's stages. For example, some people in collectivist cultures, such as Papua New Guinea, Taiwan, and Israeli kibbutzim, explained their answers to moral dilemmas by pointing to the importance of the community. And people in India included in their moral reasoning the importance of acting in accordance with one's caste (social class) and with

postconventional Referring to moral reasoning that reflects moral judgments based on personal standards or universal principles of justice, equality, and respect for human life.

maintaining personal purity (Shweder et al., 1994). As in other areas of cognitive development, culture plays a significant role in shaping moral judgments.

Gender may also play a role. Carol Gilligan (1982, 1993) has suggested that Kohlberg's research documented mainly the abstract, impersonal concept of justice typically seen in males. When Gilligan asked people about moral conflicts, the majority of men focused on justice, but only half of the women did. The other half focused on caring. This finding supports Gilligan's belief that, for North American females, the moral ideal is to protect enduring relationships and fulfill human needs. This difference between men and women has not been found consistently, however (Jaffee & Hyde, 2000). In fact, it appears that males and females are capable of using either approach to moral reasoning (Johnston, 1988). The tendency for females to focus on caring more than males do and for males to focus on justice more than females do appears most clearly when they are resolving hypothetical moral dilemmas (Turiel, 2006). When resolving real-life moral issues, both men and women focus more on caring than on justice (Walker, 1995).

Taken together, the results of research in different countries and with both genders suggest that moral ideals are not absolute and universal. Moral development is apparently an adaptation to the moral world—and the specific situations in which people find themselves (Bersoff, 1999). Formal operational reasoning may be necessary for people to reach the highest level of moral reasoning, but formal operational reasoning alone is not sufficient. To some extent, at the highest levels, moral reasoning is a product of culture and history, of situations, and of people's emotions and goals in those situations (Krebs & Denton, 2005; Turiel, 2006).

Adulthood

▶ **What developmental changes occur in adulthood?**

Development does not end with adolescence. Adults, too, go through transitions and experience physical, cognitive, and social changes. It has been suggested that adulthood emerges as early as eighteen (Arnett, 2000), but for our purposes, adulthood can be divided into three periods: *early adulthood* (ages twenty to thirty-nine), *middle adulthood* (ages forty to sixty-five), and *late adulthood* (beyond age sixty-five).

Physical Changes

In early adulthood, physical growth continues. Shoulder width, height, and chest size increase, and people continue to develop their athletic abilities. By their mid-thirties nearly everyone shows some hearing impairment, but for most people, the years of early adulthood are the prime of life.

In middle adulthood, other physical changes slowly emerge. The most common of these involve the further loss of sensory sharpness (Fozard et al., 1977). People become less sensitive to light, less accurate at perceiving differences in distance, and slower and less able at seeing details. At about age forty, increased farsightedness is common, and glasses may be necessary to correct for it. In their late forties or early fifties, women generally experience *menopause*, the shutdown of reproductive capability. Estrogen and progesterone levels drop, and the menstrual cycle eventually ceases.

Most people are well into late adulthood before their bodily functions show noticeable impairment. However, inside the body, bone mass is dwindling, and the risk of heart disease is increasing. Men shrink about an inch in height, and women about two inches, as their posture changes and cartilage disks between the spinal vertebrae become thinner. Older adults tend to go to sleep earlier but may find it harder to sleep through the night without awakening to use the bathroom (Park et al., 2002). Hardening of the arteries and a buildup of fat deposits on the artery walls may lead to heart disease. The digestive system slows down and becomes less efficient. Both digestive disorders and heart disease sometimes result from problems of diet—too little fluid, too little fiber, too much fat—and inactivity. In addition, the brain shrinks during late adulthood. The few reflexes that remained after infancy, such as the knee-jerk reflex, weaken or disappear. The flow of blood to the brain slows. As in earlier years, many of these changes can be delayed or diminished by a healthy diet and exercise (Brach et al., 2003; Larson et al., 2006; Seeman & Chen, 2002).

Cognitive Changes

Adulthood is marked by increases, as well as decreases, in cognitive abilities. Abilities that involve intensive information processing begin to decline in early adulthood, but those that depend on accumulated knowledge and experience increase until beginning to tail off in old age, if at all. In fact, older adults may function as well as, or better than, younger adults in situations that tap their long-term memories and well-learned skills (Park et al., 2002; Park & Gutchess, 2006). The experienced teacher may deal with an unruly child more skillfully than the new teacher, and the senior lawyer may understand the implications of a new law better than the recent graduate. Their years of accumulating and organizing information can make older adults practiced, skillful, and wise.

Early and Middle Adulthood   Until age sixty at least, important cognitive abilities improve. During this period, adults do better on tests of vocabulary, comprehension, and general knowledge—especially if they use these abilities in their daily lives or engage in enriching activities such as travel or reading (Park, 2001). Young and middle-aged adults learn new information and new skills; they remember old information and hone old skills. In fact, it is in their forties through their early sixties that people tend to put in the best performance of their lives on complex mental tasks such as reasoning, verbal memory, and vocabulary (Willis & Schaie, 1999).

The nature of thought may also change during adulthood. Adult thought is often more complex and adaptive than adolescent thought (Labouvie-Vief, 1992). Unlike adolescents, adults see both the possibilities and the problems in every course of action—in deciding whether to start a new business, back a political candidate, move to a new place, or change jobs. Middle-aged adults are more expert than adolescents or young adults at making rational decisions and at relating logic and abstractions to actions, emotions, social issues, and personal relationships (Tversky & Kahneman, 1981). As they appreciate these relationships, their thought becomes more global, more concerned with broad moral and practical issues (Labouvie-Vief, 1982). It has been suggested that the achievement of these new kinds of thinking reflects a stage of cognitive development that goes beyond Piaget's formal operational period (Lutz & Sternberg, 1999). In this stage, people's thinking becomes *dialectical,* which means they understand that knowledge is relative, not absolute—such that what is seen as wise today may have been thought foolish in times past. They see life's contradictions as an inevitable part of reality, and they tend to weigh various solutions to problems rather than just accepting the first one that springs to mind.

Late Adulthood   It is not until late in adulthood, after the age of sixty-five or so, that some intellectual abilities decline noticeably. Generally, these are abilities that require rapid and flexible manipulation of ideas and symbols, active thinking and reasoning, and sheer mental effort (Baltes, 1993, 1994; Finkel et al., 2003; see Figure 9.8). Older adults do just as well as younger ones at tasks they know well, such as naming familiar objects (Radvansky, 1999). However, when asked to perform an unfamiliar task or to solve a complex problem they have not seen before, older adults are generally slower and less effective than younger ones (Craik & Rabinowitz, 1984). When faced with complex problems, older people apparently suffer from having too much information to sift through. They have trouble considering, choosing, and executing solutions (Arenberg, 1982). As people age, they grow less efficient at organizing the elements of a problem and at holding and mentally manipulating more than one idea at a time. They have difficulty doing tasks that require them to divide their attention

Online Study Center

Improve Your Grade
Tutorial: Crystallized
Intelligence

FIGURE **9.8**

Mental Abilities over the Life Span

Mental abilities collectively known as "fluid" intelligence—speed and accuracy of information processing, for example—begin to decline quite early in adult life. Changes in these biologically based aspects of thinking are usually not noticeable until late adulthood, however. "Crystallized" abilities learned over a lifetime—such as reading, writing, comprehension of language, and professional skills—decline too, but later and at a slower pace (Li et al., 2004).

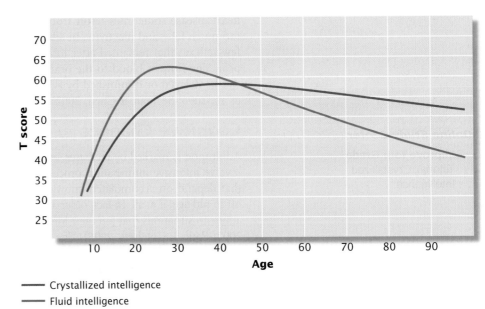

———— Crystallized intelligence
———— Fluid intelligence

Source: Adapted from Baltes (1994).

between two activities and are slower at shifting their attention back and forth between those activities (Smith et al., 2001; Wecker et al., 2005). If older adults have enough time, though, and can separate the two activities, they can perform just as well as younger adults (Hawkins, Kramer, & Capaldi, 1993).

Usually, the loss of intellectual abilities is slow and need not cause severe problems (Bashore & Ridderinkhof, 2002). A study of older adults in Sweden (Nilsson, 1996) showed, for example, that their memory problems were largely confined to *episodic memory* (e.g., remembering what they had for lunch yesterday) rather than *semantic memory* (remembering general information, such as the capital of Italy). In other words, everyday abilities that involve verbal processes are likely to remain intact into advanced old age (Freedman, Aykan, & Martin, 2001).

The risk of cognitive decline is significantly lower for people who are healthy and psychologically flexible and who have a high level of education, income, and occupation. Environmental factors are important, too (Reynolds et al., 2005). Cognitive decline is slower among those who live in an intellectually stimulating atmosphere with mentally able spouses or companions (Albert et al., 1995; Chodosh et al., 2002; Shimamura et al., 1995). Continued mental exercise—such as doing puzzles, painting, and having intellectually stimulating conversations with friends—can also help older adults think and remember effectively and creatively (Verghese et al., 2003, 2006; Wilson, Beckett, et al., 2002). Practice at memory and other information-processing tasks may even lead to some improvement in skills already impaired by old age and disuse (Kramer & Willis, 2002; Rapp, Brenes, & Marsh, 2002). Maintaining physical fitness through dancing or other forms of aerobic exercise has been associated with better maintenance of skills on a variety of mental tasks, including those involving reaction time, reasoning, and divided attention (Abbott et al., 2004; McAuley, Kramer, & Colcombe, 2004; Weuve et al., 2004). And a life full of organized activities and opportunities to interact with a lots of different people—not just family members—seems best for preventing decline in communication abilities (Keller-Cohen et al., 2004).

The greatest threat to cognitive abilities in late adulthood is Alzheimer's disease. As the disease progresses, it leaves even the brightest minds incapable. Victims become emotionally flat, then disoriented, then mentally vacant. They usually die prematurely. The average duration of the disease, from onset to death, is seven years. But the age of onset and rate of decline depends on a number of factors, such as intelligence (Rentz et al., 2004), gender (Molsa, Marttila, & Rinne, 1995), and education (Mortimer, Snowdon, & Markesbery, 2003). Highly intelligent people show clinical signs of Alzheimer's later than the general population. Women and well-educated people of either gender deteriorate more slowly.

Social Changes

Adulthood is a time when changes occur in social relationships and positions. These changes do not come in neat, predictable stages but instead follow various paths, depending on individual experiences. Transitions—such as divorcing, being fired, going back to school, remarrying, losing a spouse to death, being hospitalized, getting arrested, moving back home, or retiring—are just a few of the turning points that can redirect a person's life path and lead to changes in personality (Caspi & Shiner, 2006; Roberts, Helson, & Klohnen, 2002).

Early Adulthood Men and women in Western cultures usually enter the adult world in their twenties. The process may begin with an "emerging adulthood" period during which they explore life's possibilities through education, dating, and travel before they settle into stable adult roles and responsibilities (Arnett, 2000; Roisman et al., 2004). They decide on an occupation, or at least take a job, and become preoccupied with their careers (Srivastava et al., 2003). Nevertheless, by age 25 about 20 percent of young adults are still living with their parents, and just under half are still financially dependent (Cohen et al., 2003). It is in their twenties, too, that young adults become more concerned with matters of romantic love. Having reached the sixth of Erikson's stages of psychosocial development noted in Table 9.2 (intimacy versus isolation), they begin to focus on forming mature relationships based on sexual intimacy, friendship, or mutual intellectual stimulation. The result may be marriage or some other form of committed relationship.

Just how willing and able people are to make intimate commitments may depend on their earlier attachment relationships (Scharf, Mayseless, & Kivenson-Baron, 2004; Treboux, Crowell, & Waters, 2004). Researchers have discovered that young adults' views of intimate relationships parallel the patterns of infant attachment that we described earlier (Campbell et al., 2005; Horowitz, Rosenberg, & Bartholomew, 1993). If their view reflects a secure attachment, they tend to feel valued and worthy of support and affection; they develop closeness easily. They have relationships characterized by joy, trust, and commitment. If their view reflects an insecure attachment, however, they tend to be preoccupied with relationships and may feel misunderstood, underappreciated, and worried about being abandoned. Their relationships are often negative, obsessive, and jealous. Alternatively, they may be aloof and unable to trust or to commit themselves to a partner. Overall, young adults whose parents have been accepting and

BUILDING MONUMENTS Middle adulthood tends to be a time during which people become deeply committed to building personal monuments, through either child raising or achievements outside the home. This graduating parent seems to have accomplished both goals.

supportive tend to develop warm and supportive romantic relationships (Conger et al., 2000; Dresner & Grolnick, 1996).

For many young adults, the experience of becoming parents represents entry into a major new developmental phase often accompanied by personal, social, and occupational changes (Palkovitz, Copes, & Woolfolk, 2001). This milestone usually comes earlier for young adults from lower income backgrounds, who are more likely to be in full-time employment and less likely to be living at home (Cohen et al., 2003). Often, satisfaction with the marriage or partnership declines once a baby is born (Belsky & Kelly, 1994), and about half of all marriages break under the strain (National Center for Health Statistics, 2001). Young mothers may experience particular dissatisfaction—especially if they resent the constraints infants bring, if they see their careers as important, if the infants are temperamentally difficult, if the partnerships are not strong, and if the partners are not supportive (Shapiro, Gottman, & Carrere, 2000). When the father does not do his share of caring for the baby, both mothers and fathers are dissatisfied (Levy-Shiff, 1994). The ability of young parents to provide adequate care for their babies is related to their own attachment histories. New mothers whose attachments to their own mothers were secure tend to be more responsive to their infants, and the infants, in turn, are more likely to develop secure attachments to them (Adam, Gunnar, & Tanaka, 2004; van IJzendoorn, 1995).

The challenges of young adulthood are complicated by the nature of family life today (Halpern, 2005). Forty years ago, about half of North American households consisted of married couples in their twenties and thirties—a breadwinner husband and a homemaker wife—raising at least two children together. This description now applies to only about 10 percent of households (Demo, Allen, & Fine, 2000; Hernandez, 1997). Parents are older now because young adults are delaying marriage longer and waiting longer to have children. Many are having children without marrying or choosing to raise children on their own (Weinraub, Horvath, & Gringlas, 2002). Those who divorce face many unanticipated stressors, including money problems, changes in living circumstances and working hours, loneliness, anxiety, and, for custodial parents, a dramatic increase in housework and child-care tasks (Clarke-Stewart & Brentano, 2006). In short, the changes seen in families and family life over the past several decades have made it more challenging than ever to successfully navigate the years of early adulthood.

Middle Adulthood   At around age forty, people go through a **midlife transition,** during which they may rethink and modify their lives and relationships. Many feel invigorated and liberated; some may feel upset and have a "midlife crisis" (Beck, 1992; Levinson et al., 1978). The contrast between youth and middle age may be especially

midlife transition A point at around age forty when adults take stock of their lives.

generativity The concern of adults in their forties with generating something enduring.

THE "SANDWICH" GENERATION
During their midlife transition, many people feel "sandwiched" between generations—pressured by the social, emotional, and financial needs of their children on one side and of their aging parents on the other.

upsetting for men who matured early in adolescence and were sociable and athletic rather than intellectual (Block, 1971). Women who chose a career over a family now hear the biological clock ticking out their last childbearing years. Women who have had children, however, become more independent and confident and more oriented toward achievement and events outside the family (Helson & Moane, 1987). For both men and women, the emerging sexuality of their teenage children, the emptiness of the nest as children leave home, or the declining health of a parent may precipitate a crisis.

Following the midlife transition, the middle years of adulthood are often a time of satisfaction and happiness (MacArthur Foundation, 1999; Mroczek & Spiro, 2005). Many people become concerned with producing something that will outlast them— usually through parenthood and/or job achievements (Sheldon & Kasser, 2001; Zucker, Ostrove, & Stewart, 2002). Erikson called this concern the crisis of **generativity,** because people are focused on producing or generating something. If people do not resolve this crisis, he suggested, they stagnate.

In their fifties, most people become grandparents (Smith & Drew, 2002), though they may find it hard to believe they are no longer young (Karp, 1991). At this age, spending lots of time caring for young grandchildren can be stressful and may even increase the risk of heart disease (Lee et al., 2003). Caring for grown children can be stressful, too. Most people in their sixties want their children to be independent; they may have mixed feelings toward adult children who still need financial support (Pillemer & Suitor, 2002). One study of more than 7,000 adults suggested that the degree of happiness and health-iness people experience during middle adulthood depends on how much control they feel they have over their work, finances, marriages, children, and sex lives, as well as how many years of education they completed and what kind of jobs they have (Azar, 1996).

STILL ON A ROLL   At the age of 80, actor and race car driver Paul Newman remains a famous example of the many people whose late adulthood is healthy and vigorous. In January 2000, at the age of seventy-five, Newman received bruised ribs in a minor accident while preparing to drive his race car in the 24 Hours of Daytona. He was racing again the following month, and he is still racing today.

Late Adulthood   Most people between sixty-five and seventy-five years of age think of themselves as middle-aged, not old (Neugarten, 1977). They are active and influential politically and socially, and they often are physically vigorous. Ratings of life satisfaction and self-esteem are, on average, as high in old age as during any other period of adult-hood (Ben-Zur, 2002; Charles, Mather, & Carstensen, 2003; Hamarat et al., 2002). Men and women who have been employed usually retire from their jobs during this period. They adjust most easily to retirement if they view it as a choice (Swan, 1996).

Today, more people than ever are reaching old age. In fact, those over 75 make up the fastest-growing segment of the population, a group that is 25 times larger than it was a century ago. Today, 77,000 people in the United States are over 100, and the Census Bureau predicts that number will rise to 834,000 by 2050 (Volz, 2000). Old age is not necessarily

MILESTONES OF ADOLESCENCE AND ADULTHOOD

Age	Physical Changes	Cognitive Changes	Social Events and Psychological Changes
Early adolescence (11–15 years)	Puberty brings reproductive capacity and marked bodily changes.	Formal operations and principled moral reasoning become possible for the first time. (This occurs only for some people.)	Social and emotional changes result from growing sexual awareness; adolescents experience mood swings, physical changes, and conflicts with parents.
Late adolescence (16–19 years)	Physical growth continues.	Formal operations and principled moral reasoning become more likely.	An identity crisis accompanies graduation from high school.
Early adulthood (20–39 years)	Physical growth continues.	Increases continue in knowledge, problem-solving ability, and moral reasoning.	People choose a job and often a mate; they may become parents.
Middle adulthood (40–65 years)	Size and muscle mass decrease; fat increases; eyesight declines; reproductive capacity in women ends.	Thought becomes more complex, adaptive, and global.	Midlife transition may lead to change; for most, the middle years are satisfying.
Late adulthood (over 65 years)	Size decreases; organs become less efficient.	Reasoning, mathematical ability, comprehension, novel problem solving, and memory may decline.	Retirement requires adjustments; people look inward; awareness of death precipitates life review.

1. The greatest threat to cognitive abilities in late adulthood is _____ disease.
2. Adolescents' _____ identity may be more defining than their national citizenship.
3. Not stealing because "I might get caught" reflects the _____ stage of moral reasoning.

a time of loneliness and desolation, but it is a time when people generally become more inward looking, cautious, and conforming (Reedy, 1983). It is a time when people develop coping strategies that increasingly take into account the limits of their control—accepting what they cannot change, such as chronic health problems (Brandtstadter & Renner, 1990). Although they interact with others less frequently, older adults enjoy these interactions more (Carstensen, 1997). They find relationships more satisfying, supportive, and fulfilling than they did earlier in life. As they sense that time is running out, they value positive interactions and become selective about their social partners. As long as they have a network of at least three close relatives or friends, they are usually content.

The many changes associated with adolescence and adulthood are summarized in "In Review: Milestones of Adolescence and Adulthood."

Death and Dying

With the onset of old age, people become aware that death is approaching. They watch as their friends disappear. They may feel their health failing, their strength waning, and their intellectual capabilities declining. A few years or a few months before death, some people experience a sharp decline in mental functioning known as **terminal drop** (Small & Bäckman, 1999).

The awareness of impending death brings about the last psychological crisis, according to Erikson's theory. During this stage, people evaluate their lives and accomplishments and see them as meaningful (leading to a feeling of integrity) or meaningless (leading to a feeling of despair). They tend to become more philosophical and reflective. They

terminal drop A sharp decline in mental functioning that tends to occur in late adulthood, a few months or years before death.

attempt to put their lives into perspective. They revisit old memories, resolve past conflicts, and integrate past events. They may also become more interested in the religious and spiritual side of life. This "life review" may trigger anxiety, regret, guilt, and despair; the risk of suicide does increase with age (Anderson & Conwell, 2002). But it may also help people to face their own deaths and the deaths of friends and relatives with a feeling of peace and acceptance (Lieberman & Tobin, 1983).

Even the actual confrontation with death does not have to bring despair and depression. When death finally is imminent, old people strive for a death with dignity, love, affection, physical contact, and no pain (Schulz, 1978). As they think about death, they are comforted by their religious faith, their achievements, and the love of their friends and family (Kastenbaum, Kastenbaum, & Morris, 1989).

Longevity Facing death with dignity and openness helps people to complete the life cycle with a sense of life's meaningfulness, but most of us want to live as long as possible. How can we do so? Research suggests that longevity is greater in women and in people who do not have a history of heavy drinking or smoking. Longevity is also related to personality characteristics such as conscientiousness as a child (Friedman et al., 1995a) and curiosity as an adult (Swan & Carmelli, 1996). People with higher IQ scores and faster reaction times tend to live longer, too (Deary & Der, 2005), as do those who typically experienced happiness, enthusiasm, contentment, and other forms of *positive affect* during adulthood (Cohen & Pressman, 2006). Adults who had more positive self-perceptions when they were in their fifties and sixties lived seven and a half years longer than those with less positive self-perceptions. This factor was more predictive of longevity than were health problems such as high blood pressure, high cholesterol, smoking, lack of exercise, or being overweight (Levy et al., 2002). Still, people who restrict their caloric intake, engage in regular physical and mental exercise, and have a sense of control over important aspects of their lives are likely to live longer (Krause & Shaw, 2000; Yaffe et al., 2001). So eat your veggies, stay physically fit, and continue to think actively—not just to live longer later, but to live better now.

ACTIVE REVIEW

Human Development

Linkages

As noted in the introductory chapter, all of psychology's subfields are related to one another. Our discussion of infantile amnesia illustrates just one way in which the topic of this chapter, human development, is linked to the subfield of memory, which is discussed in the chapter on memory. The Linkages diagram shows ties to two other subfields, and there are many more ties throughout the book. Looking for linkages among subfields will help you see how they all fit together and help you better appreciate the big picture that is psychology.

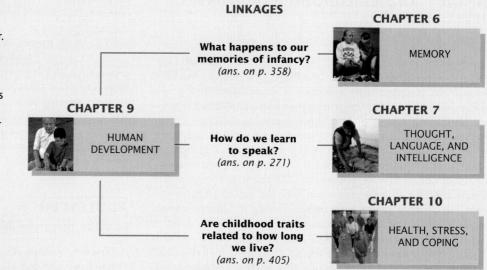

LINKAGES

CHAPTER 6
MEMORY

What happens to our memories of infancy?
(ans. on p. 358)

CHAPTER 9
HUMAN DEVELOPMENT

CHAPTER 7
THOUGHT, LANGUAGE, AND INTELLIGENCE

How do we learn to speak?
(ans. on p. 271)

CHAPTER 10
HEALTH, STRESS, AND COPING

Are childhood traits related to how long we live?
(ans. on p. 405)

Summary

Developmental psychology is the study of the course and causes of systematic, sequential, age-related changes in mental abilities, social relationships, emotions, and moral understanding over the life span.

EXPLORING HUMAN DEVELOPMENT

▶ **What does "genetic influence" mean?**

A central question in developmental psychology concerns the relative influences of nature and nurture. Gesell stressed nature in his theory of development, proposing that development is **maturation**—the natural unfolding of abilities with age. Watson took the opposite view, claiming that development is learning, as shaped by the external environment. In his theory of cognitive development, Piaget described how nature and nurture work together. Today we accept the notion that both nature and nurture affect development and ask not whether, but how and to what extent, each contributes. Research in **behavioral genetics** shows that complex traits, such as intelligence and personality, are influenced by many genes, as well as by many environmental factors.

BEGINNINGS

▶ **Why should pregnant women stay away from tobacco and alcohol?**

Development begins with the union of an ovum and a sperm to form a zygote, which develops into an **embryo. Genes,** which consist of **deoxyribonucleic acid (DNA),** make up the **chromosomes** that are in each body cell. The embryonic stage is a **critical period** for development, a time when certain organs must develop properly or they never will. The development of organs at this stage is permanently affected by harmful **teratogens** such as tobacco, alcohol, or other drugs. After the embryo develops into a **fetus,** adverse conditions may harm the infant's size, behavior, intelligence, or health. Babies born to women who drink heavily are at risk for **fetal alcohol syndrome.**

Newborns have limited, but effective, senses of vision, hearing, taste, and smell. They exhibit many **reflexes**—swift, automatic responses to external stimuli. Motor development proceeds as the nervous system matures and muscles grow and as the infant experiments with and selects the most efficient movement patterns.

INFANCY AND CHILDHOOD: COGNITIVE DEVELOPMENT

▶ **How do babies think?**

Cognitive development refers to the development of thinking, knowing, and remembering. According to Piaget, **schemas** are modified through the complementary processes of **assimilation** (fitting new objects or events into existing schemas) and **accommodation** (changing schemas when new objects will not fit existing schemas). During the **sensorimotor period,** infants progress from using only their senses and simple reflexes to forming mental representations of objects and actions. As a result, the child becomes capable of thinking about objects that are not present. The ability to recognize that objects continue to exist even when they are hidden from view is what Piaget called **object permanence.** During the **preoperational period,** children can use symbols, but they do not have the ability to think logically and rationally. Their understanding of the world is intuitive. When children develop the ability to think logically about concrete objects, they enter the period of **concrete operations.** At this time they can solve simple problems and have a knowledge of **conservation,** recognizing that, for example, the amount of a substance is not altered when its shape changes. The **formal operational period** begins in adolescence and allows thinking and logical reasoning about abstract ideas.

Today, developmental psychologists believe that new levels of cognition do not appear in sharply separated stages of global understanding, but more gradually, and that children's reasoning can be affected by factors such as task difficulty and degree of familiarity with the objects and language involved.

Psychologists who explain cognitive development in terms of **information processing** have documented age-related improvements in children's attention, their abilities to explore and focus on features of the environment, and their memories. "Infantile amnesia" leaves us with virtually no memory of events from before the age of three. Several explanations have been suggested, but this phenomenon is not yet fully understood.

The specific content of cognitive development, including the development of scripts, depends on the cultural context in which children live. How fast children develop cognitive abilities depends to some extent on how stimulating and supportive their environments are. Children growing up in poverty are likely to have delayed or impaired cognitive abilities.

INFANCY AND CHILDHOOD: SOCIAL AND EMOTIONAL DEVELOPMENT

▶ **How do infants become attached to their caregivers?**

Infants and their caregivers, from the early months, respond to each other's emotional expressions. Most infants can be classified as having easy, difficult, or slow-to-warm-up **temperaments.** Whether they retain these temperamental styles depends to some extent on their parents' expectations and demands. Over the first year after birth, infants form a deep, long-lasting emotional **attachment** to their mothers or other primary caregivers. This attachment may be secure or insecure, depending largely on whether the caregiver is responsive and loving or rejecting. The process of **socialization** begins as parents teach their children the skills and rules needed in their culture, using parenting styles described as **authoritarian, permissive,** or **authoritative.** Among European American parents, those with authoritative styles tend to have more competent and cooperative children. Patterns of socialization depend on the culture and conditions in which parents find themselves.

Over the childhood years, interactions with peers evolve into cooperative and competitive encounters, and friendships become more important. Changes in children's relationships are based in part on their growing social competence. Children become increasingly able to interpret and understand social situations and emotional signals. They also learn social rules and roles, including those related to gender. **Gender roles** are based both on biological differences between the sexes and on implicit and explicit socialization by parents, teachers, and peers.

ADOLESCENCE

▶ **What threatens adolescents' self-esteem?**

Adolescents undergo significant changes not only in size, shape, and physical capacity but also, typically, in their social lives, reasoning abilities, and views of themselves. **Puberty** brings about physical changes that lead to psychological changes. Early adolescence is a period of shaky self-esteem. It is also a time when conflict with parents, as well as closeness and conformity to friends, is likely to arise. Later adolescence focuses on finding an answer to the question, Who am I? Events such as graduating from high school and going to college challenge the adolescent's self-concept, precipitating an **identity crisis.** To resolve this crisis, the adolescent must develop an integrated self-image as a unique person, an image that often includes **ethnic identity.** Moral reasoning progresses from **preconventional** to **conventional** and, possibly, **postconventional** stages. Principled moral judgment—shaped by gender and culture—becomes possible for the first time.

ADULTHOOD

▶ **What developmental changes occur in adulthood?**

Physical, cognitive, and social changes occur throughout adulthood. Middle adulthood sees changes that include decreased sharpness of the senses, increased risk of heart disease, and declining fertility. Nevertheless, most people do not experience major health problems until late adulthood.

The cognitive changes that occur in early and middle adulthood are generally positive, including improvements in reasoning and problem-solving ability. In late adulthood, some intellectual abilities decline—especially those involved in tasks that are unfamiliar, complex, or difficult. Other abilities, such as recalling facts or making wise decisions, tend not to decline.

In their twenties, young adults make occupational choices and form intimate commitments. By the end of their thirties, they settle down and decide what is important. They become concerned with **generativity**—with producing something that will outlast them. Sometime around age forty, adults experience a **midlife transition,** which may or may not be a crisis. The forties and fifties are often a time of satisfaction. In their sixties, people contend with the issue of retirement. They generally become more inward looking, cautious, and conforming. In their seventies, eighties, and beyond, people confront their own mortality. They may become more philosophical and reflective as they review their lives. A few years or months before death, many experience a sharp decline in mental functioning known as **terminal drop.** Still, they strive for a death with dignity, love, and no pain.

Death is inevitable, but healthy diets, exercise, conscientiousness and curiosity, and a sense of control over one's life are associated with living longer and happier lives. Older adults feel better and live longer if they receive attention from other people, maintain an open attitude toward new experiences, and keep their minds active.

Learn by Doing

Put It in Writing

Write a short paper describing some of the ways in which you have developed over the past five years. Include comments on physical changes, as well as changes in your thoughts, feelings, and behavior. Imagine yourself in another five years and describe what further changes you expect in your physical condition, lifestyle, relationships, ideas, emotional state, and behavior. Compare the changes that have taken place in your life with those we have described in this chapter for the average person of your age.

Personal Learning Activity

Ask several of your friends about the way their parents raised them, and especially about how strict or permissive they were in providing discipline. Take notes on these interviews, and then try to categorize your friends' parents as authoritarian, permissive, or authoritative. (You might try categorizing your own parents, as well.) Was it easy to decide which category to use in each case? Do you think that additional categories are necessary to describe parenting styles? Do you think that your friends' personalities reflect the effects of the parenting styles described in this chapter? *For additional projects, see the Personal Learning Activities in the corresponding chapter of the study guide that accompanies this text.*

Step into Action

Courses

Infancy
Child Development
Adolescence
Life-Span Development
Social Development
Cognitive Development
Death and Dying

Movies

Antwone Fisher. Overcoming abuse and abandonment.
Wrestling Ernest Hemingway. Aging.
About Schmidt. Aging, Erikson's stage of generativity versus stagnation.
The War; Pop and Me. Parenting styles.
Schindler's List. Moral development.
Lord of the Flies. Nature-nurture.

Stand by Me; A Christmas Story. Childhood.
Parenthood. Child rearing.
Little Man Tate; Searching for Bobby Fischer; What's Eating Gilbert Grape. Raising special children.
Revenge of the Nerds; Ferris Bueller's Day Off; The Breakfast Club; My Life in Pink; Rushmore. Adolescence.
St. Elmo's Fire; Good Will Hunting; Reality Bites; Clerks; Chasing Amy. Young adulthood.
The Big Chill; American Beauty; Same Time, Next Year. Adulthood.
City Slickers. Midlife transition.
On Golden Pond; Cocoon; Space Cowboys. Aging.
Do the Right Thing. Moral reasoning and moral action.
The Color Purple. Development of self-esteem.

Books

Deborah Blum, *Love at Goon Park: Harry Harlow and the Science of Affection* (Perseus, 2002). Study of Harlow's famous research.

Sampson Davis, George Jenkins, and Rameck Hunt, *The Pact: Three Young Men Make a Promise and Fulfill a Dream* (Penguin/Putnam, 2002). How three young men overcame their criminogenic backgrounds and became doctors.

Lawrence J. Friedman, *Identity's Architect: A Biography of Erik H. Erikson* (Scribner's, 1999). Focusing on Erikson's own identity crisis.

Thomas Hine, *The Rise and Fall of the American Teenager* (Avon, 1999). Social and cultural history of adolescence.

Jeffrey W. Trawick-Smith, *Early Childhood Development: A Multicultural Perspective* (Prentice Hall, 1999).

Introduction to cultural influences on development.

Alison Gopnik, Andrew N. Meltzoff, and Patricia K. Kuhl, *The Scientist in the Crib: Minds, Brains, and How Children Learn* (William Morrow, 1999). Readable summary of research in cognitive development.

Richard Shulz and Timothy A. Salthouse, *Adult Development and Aging: Myths and Emerging Realities* (Prentice Hall, 1998). The title says it all.

Rachel Simmons, *Odd Girl Out: The Hidden Culture of Aggression in Girls* (Harcourt Books, 2002). Study of girls' relational aggression.

Robin Karr-Morse and Meredith S. Wiley, *Ghosts from the Nursery: Tracing the Roots of Violence* (Grove/Atlantic, 1999). How biological predispositions may lead to violence.

Robert Karen, *Becoming Attached: First Relationships and How They Shape Our Capacity to Love* (Oxford University Press, 1995). Emotional development.

The Web

The World Wide Web is a good source of additional information about the science of psychology, provided you use it carefully and think critically about the information you find. The Online Study Center that accompanies this text offers many resources relevant to this chapter. These resources include interactive tutorials; Thinking Critically and Evaluating Research exercises; ACE chapter quizzes; recommended web links; and articles on current events, books, and movies. Please visit the Online Study Center at college.hmco.com/pic/bernsteinessentials4e.

Review of Key Terms

Can you define each of the key terms in the chapter? Check your definitions against those on the pages shown in parentheses in the following list or in the Glossary/Index at the end of the text.

accommodation *(p. 350)*
assimilation *(p. 350)*
attachment *(p. 362)*
authoritarian parents *(p. 367)*
authoritative parents *(p. 367)*
behavioral genetics *(p. 344)*
chromosomes *(p. 345)*
concrete operations *(p. 355)*
conservation *(p. 354)*
conventional *(p. 374)*

critical period *(p. 346)*
deoxyribonucleic acid (DNA) *(p. 345)*
developmental psychology *(p. 343)*
embryo *(p. 346)*
ethnic identity *(p. 373)*
fetal alcohol syndrome *(p. 347)*
fetus *(p. 346)*
formal operational period *(p. 355)*

gender roles *(p. 369)*
generativity *(p. 380)*
genes *(p. 345)*
identity crisis *(p. 373)*
information processing *(p. 356)*
maturation *(p. 343)*
midlife transition *(p. 380)*
object permanence *(p. 350)*
permissive parents *(p. 367)*
postconventional *(p. 375)*

preconventional *(p. 374)*
preoperational period *(p. 354)*
puberty *(p. 371)*
reflexes *(p. 348)*
schemas *(p. 350)*
sensorimotor period *(p. 350)*
socialization *(p. 367)*
temperament *(p. 361)*
teratogens *(p. 346)*
terminal drop *(p. 382)*

Multiple-Choice Self-Test

Select the best answer for each of the following questions. Then check your response against the Answer Key at the end of the text.

1. Ralph read an article that described intelligence as 50 percent heritable. Ralph can reasonably conclude that

   a. half of his intelligence came from his genes and half from his environment.
   b. about half of the variation in intelligence among groups of people can be accounted for by genetic influences.
   c. about half of a person's intelligence can be changed by environmental influences.
   d. about half the population got their intelligence from their genes alone.

2. When she became pregnant, Alyse was advised to quit smoking, but she didn't. Her baby is likely to be born

   a. mentally retarded.
   b. with facial deformities.
   c. underweight.
   d. with an irritable temperament.

3. When they brought their newborn, Tyrone, home from the hospital, they always laid him on his back, especially at night. As the baby grew, he began to roll over, sit up, pull himself up on furniture, and walk. He skipped the crawling stage. Tyrone's physical development is the result of

   a. behavioral genetics alone.
   b. maturation alone.
   c. environmental influences alone.
   d. maturation and environmental influences.

4. Keshawn is one month old. He is most likely to look longest at

   a. small figures on the wallpaper.
   b. a ribbon hanging above his crib.
   c. colorful figures.
   d. a nearby human face.

5. At six months of age, Jacob still demonstrates the grasping and rooting reflexes. This could signal that Jacob

   a. has advanced motor skills.
   b. has muscles that cannot support his body.
   c. has a problem with brain development.
   d. needs less environmental stimulation than the average baby.

6. When two-year-old Jesse sees a scuba diver emerge on the beach, he says "Big fish!" According to Piaget, Jesse used _____ to try to understand the new stimulus of a scuba diver.

   a. assimilation
   b. accommodation
   c. object permanence
   d. conservation

7. Adriana is crying because her teddy bear, Boyd, has fallen off the table and landed face down. She insists that her mother put a bandage on Boyd's nose. According to Piaget's theory, Adriana is most likely in the _____ stage of cognitive development.

   a. sensorimotor
   b. preoperational
   c. concrete operational
   d. formal operational

8. Renee Baillargeon's research focused on infants' understanding about objects and gravity. Baillargeon found that infants

   a. looked longer at "possible" events that they had experienced many times.
   b. looked longer at "impossible" events that defied physical principles.
   c. have no knowledge of physical principles until they have actual experience with such principles.
   d. show no difference in their understanding of physical principles between the ages of three months and one year.

9. According to research on information processing and memory, when you try to recall your first birthday, you are likely to

   a. recall a general schema of "birthday," as well as details about your first one.
   b. be unable to recall anything about your first birthday due to infantile amnesia.
   c. recall information about your first birthday if you are shown pictures of yourself taken that day.
   d. recall information about the birthday if you hear a tape recording of your party.

10. Tara is a difficult baby. She is irritable, sleeps at irregular intervals, and cries at unpredictable times. According to research on temperament, Tara will most likely

    a. outgrow her difficult temperament and become an easier child.
    b. remain difficult in childhood, and may display aggressiveness.
    c. develop a dependent relationship with her parents.
    d. become independent and especially successful in school.

11. Harlow's research with infant monkeys and artificial mothers demonstrated that

    a. infant monkeys become attached to the "mothers" that feed them.
    b. infant monkeys become attached to the "mothers" that provide contact comfort.
    c. attachment is entirely innate, with no learned component.
    d. "mothering" is instinctive, with no learned component.

12. When young Habib's mother drops him off at the day care center, he always cries when she leaves. When his mother returns and lifts him up, Habib tries to squirm away. Habib is demonstrating a(n) _____ attachment to his mother.

    a. secure
    b. anxious insecure
    c. avoidant insecure
    d. ambivalent insecure

13. Sam and Alex are sixteen and want to drive to a rock concert in a big city that is five hours away. Sam's parents explain that it is too dangerous for him to drive that distance and to be in a major city without an adult. They offer to drive him and Alex to the concert. Alex's parents tell him that it is no problem if he wants to drive their car and stay in the city overnight. According to Baumrind's research, Sam's parents are displaying a(n) _____ style of parenting, whereas Alex's parents are displaying a(n) _____ style.

    a. authoritative; authoritarian
    b. authoritarian; authoritative
    c. authoritative; permissive
    d. authoritarian; permissive

14. Pat is seven years old and lives in the Midwestern United States. Pat learned to speak early and writes well. Pat is able to "read" people's emotional reactions by watching their faces. From this information we can conclude that Pat is most likely

    a. female.
    b. male.
    c. African American.
    d. Asian American.

15. Ludmilla recently graduated from high school but can't decide whether to attend a local community college or work full time. She doesn't know what career she would like to pursue, and she is also uncertain whether she should stay with her current boyfriend. According to Erikson, Ludmilla is most likely experiencing the psychosocial crisis characterized by

    a. trust versus mistrust.
    b. initiative versus guilt.
    c. identity versus role confusion.
    d. integrity versus despair.

16. Louise is sixteen and having a difficult time with adolescence. She became sexually active two years ago and doesn't worry about using condoms or other safe sex practices. Louise is most likely to

    a. hold conventional attitudes and values and feel ashamed of herself.
    b. avoid smoking and drinking alcohol.
    c. have average or better grades at school.
    d. have parents who are not highly educated.

17. Jeanine and Helen are in a drugstore when Jeanine suggests that they steal some candy. Helen says that they should not steal the candy because they might get caught and put into jail. According to Kohlberg's theory, Helen is at the _____ stage of moral reasoning.

    a. preconventional
    b. conventional
    c. postconventional
    d. universal

18. In the past ten years, Vernon has gained weight, especially around the middle. He also now needs glasses. If he is typical of most people his age, Vernon has most likely reached

    a. adolescence.
    b. early adulthood.
    c. middle adulthood.
    d. late adulthood.

19. Verna is fifty years old. Based on developmental research, we would assume that Verna

    a. has less general knowledge than younger people.
    b. has a more limited vocabulary than younger people.
    c. understands that knowledge is relative, not absolute.
    d. is experiencing a slow but steady decay of all of her cognitive skills.

20. Patrice is eighty years old and has recently been unable to understand what she reads. She can't make sense of her checkbook, even though she was once an expert accountant. Her health is deteriorating, and her strength is waning. Patrice is most likely experiencing

    a. cognitive dissonance.
    b. terminal drop.
    c. the crisis of initiative versus guilt.
    d. androgyny.

10

Health, Stress, and Coping

In North America, people are living longer than ever.

In fact, those over 100 constitute the fastest growing age group in the United States. Will you eventually join them? To some extent, the answer lies in your genes, but how long you live is also determined in large measure by how you behave, how you think, and what stressors you face. Health psychologists explore how illness and death are related to these behavioral, psychological, and social factors, and they apply their research to preventing illness and promoting health. They develop programs to help people make lifestyle changes that can lower their risk of illness and premature death. And they study how stress affects people's mental and physical health. Of particular importance is the immune system's response to stress. In this chapter, you will learn about several kinds of stressors, how people respond to them, and the relationship between stress reactions and illness. You will also discover what you can do to protect your own health and change risky behaviors that may affect it.

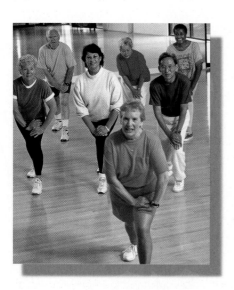

Reading this chapter will help you to answer the following questions:

health psychology A field focused on understanding how psychological factors affect health and illness and which interventions help maintain health and combat illness.

I n Bangor, Maine, where snow and ice have paralyzed the community, Angie's headache gets worse as her four-year-old daughter and six-year-old son start bickering again. The day-care center and elementary school are closed, so Angie must stay home from her job at the grocery store. She probably couldn't have gotten there anyway, because the buses have stopped running. During the latest storm the power went out, and the house is now almost unbearably cold; the can of spaghetti Angie opens is nearly frozen. Worry begins to creep into her head: "If I can't work, how will I pay for rent and day care?" Her parents have money problems, too, so they can't offer financial help, and her ex-husband rarely makes his child-support payments. On top of everything else, Angie is coming down with the flu.

How do people manage such adversity, and what are its consequences for the individual? Psychologists who study questions such as these have established a specialty known as **health psychology,** "a field within psychology devoted to understanding psychological influence on how people stay healthy, why they become ill, and how they respond when they do get ill" (Taylor, 1999, p. 4).

Health Psychology

▶ What do health psychologists do?

The themes underlying health psychology date back to ancient times. For thousands of years, in many cultures around the world, people have believed that their mental state, their behavior, and their health are linked. Today, there is scientific evidence to support this belief (Schneiderman, 2004; Taylor, 2002). We now know that the stresses of life influence health through their impact on psychological and physical processes. Researchers have also associated anger, hostility, pessimism, depression, and hopelessness with the appearance of physical illnesses. Traits such as optimism are associated with good health. Similarly, poor health has been linked to behavioral factors such as lack of exercise, inadequate diet, smoking, and abuse of alcohol and other drugs (Freedman et al., 2006; Vollset, Tverdal, & Gjessing, 2006). Good health has been associated with behaviors such as adequate exercise and following medical advice.

Health psychology has become increasingly prominent in North America, in part because of changing patterns of illness. Until the middle of the twentieth century, acute infectious diseases such as influenza, tuberculosis, and pneumonia were the major causes of illness and death in the United States and Canada. With these deadly diseases now tamed, chronic illnesses—such as coronary heart disease, cancer, and diabetes—have joined accidents and injury as the leading causes of disability and death (Guyer et al., 2000). Compared with acute diseases, these chronic diseases develop more slowly and are more strongly associated with people's psychological makeup, lifestyle, and environment (Centers for Disease Control and Prevention, 2001; D'Agostino et al., 2001; see Table 10.1). The psychological and behavioral factors that contribute to these illnesses can be changed by intervention programs such as those that promote nonsmoking, exercise, and healthy eating (e.g., Bazzano et al., 2003; Kraus et al., 2002). In fact, about half the deaths in the United States are due to potentially preventable health-risky behaviors (Greenland et al., 2003; Khot et al., 2003; Taylor, 2002).

Yet as few as 3 percent of people in the United States follow a lifestyle that includes maintaining a healthy weight, getting regular exercise, eating a proper diet, and not smoking (Reeves & Rafferty, 2005). One goal of health psychology is to help people understand the role they can play in controlling their own health and life expectancy (Nash et al., 2003; Nicassio, Meyerowitz, & Kerns, 2004). For example, health psychologists have been active in educating people about the warning signs of cancer, heart disease, and other serious illnesses, encouraging them to engage in self-examinations, and emphasizing the importance of seeking medical attention while lifesaving treatment is still possible. Health psychologists also study, and help people to understand, the role played by stress in physical health and illness. And clinical health psychologists help individuals cope as effectively as possible with cancer and many other kinds of serious illness.

TABLE 10.1

Lifestyle Behaviors That Affect the Leading Causes of Death in the United States

This table shows five of the leading causes of death in the United States today, along with behavioral factors that contribute to their development (Centers for Disease Control and Prevention, 2001; Jemal et al., 2005).

Cause of Death	Alcohol	Smoking	Diet	Exercise	Stress
Cancer	x	x	x		?
Heart disease	x	x	x	x	x
Stroke	x	x	x	?	?
Lung disease		x			
Accidents and injury	x	x			x

Source: Data from Centers for Disease Control and Prevention (2001).

Understanding Stress and Stressors

▶ **How do psychological stressors affect physical health?**

You have probably heard that death and taxes are the only two things guaranteed in life. If there is a third, it surely must be stress. Stress is woven into the fabric of life. No matter how wealthy, powerful, attractive, or happy you might be, stress happens. It comes in many forms: a difficult exam, an automobile accident, standing in a long line, reading about frightening world events, or just having a day when everything goes wrong. Some stress experiences, such as waiting to be with that special person, can be stimulating, motivating, and even desirable, but when circumstances begin to exceed our ability to cope with them, the result can be stress that creates physical, psychological, and behavioral problems. Stress in the workplace, for example, costs U.S. businesses more than $150 billion each year as a result of employee absenteeism, reduced productivity, and health care costs (Chandola, Brunner, & Marmot, 2006; Sauter et al., 1999; Schwartz, 2004; Spector, 2002).

Stress is the negative emotional and physiological process that occurs as individuals try to adjust to or deal with stressors. **Stressors,** in turn, are environmental circumstances (such as exams or accidents) that disrupt, or threaten to disrupt, people's daily functioning and cause people to make adjustments. **Stress reactions** are the physical, psychological, and behavioral responses (such as nervousness, nausea, or fatigue) that occur in the face of stressors (Taylor, 2002).

Some of us are more strongly affected by stressors than others, and we may be more strongly affected on some occasions than on others. Why? As described in more detail later, several *mediating factors* influence the relationship between people and their environments. These mediating factors include (1) the extent to which we can *predict* and *control* our stressors, (2) how we *interpret* the threat involved, (3) the *social support* we get, and (4) our stress-coping *skills.* Mediating factors can either minimize or magnify a stressor's impact. In other words, as shown in Figure 10.1, stress is not a specific event but a transaction between people and their environments. It is a *process* in which the nature and intensity of our responses depend on what stressors occur and how they are affected by factors such as the way we think about them and how much confidence we have in our coping skills and resources.

FIGURE 10.1

The Process of Stress

Stressful events, stress reactions, and stress mediators are all important components of the stress process. Notice that the process involves many two-way relationships. For example, if a person has effective coping skills, stress responses will be less severe. Having milder stress responses can act as a "reward" that strengthens those skills. Further, as coping skills (such as refusing unreasonable demands) improve, certain stressors (such as a boss's unreasonable demands) may become less frequent.

stress The process of adjusting to circumstances that disrupt, or threaten to disrupt, a person's daily functioning.

stressors Events or situations to which people must adjust.

stress reactions Physical and psychological responses to stressors.

COPING WITH CATASTROPHE
Catastrophic events such as terrorism, explosions, hurricanes, plane crashes, school shootings, and other traumas are stressors that can be psychologically devastating for victims, their families, and rescue workers. As was the case in the wake of the 2005 terrorist attacks on the London transit system, health psychologists and other professionals provide on-the-spot counseling and follow-up sessions to help people deal with the consequences of trauma.

Psychological Stressors

Most of our stressors have both physical and psychological components. Because these components overlap, it is often difficult to separate them for analysis. For example, students are challenged by psychological demands to do well in their courses, as well as by physical fatigue resulting from a heavy load of classes, and maybe a job and family responsibilities, too. So although we focus here on psychological stressors, remember that physical stressors almost always accompany them.

Any event that forces a person to change or adapt can be a psychological stressor. Even pleasant events can be stressful. For example, a vacation is supposed to be relaxing and a wedding is supposed to be wonderful, but both can also be exhausting. And a promotion that brings higher pay can also bring new pressures (Schaubroeck, Jones, & Xie, 2001). Still, it is usually unpleasant circumstances that produce the most adverse psychological and physical effects (e.g., Kiecolt-Glaser et al., 2005). These circumstances include catastrophic events, life changes and strains, chronic stressors, and daily hassles.

Catastrophic events are sudden, unexpected, potentially life-threatening experiences or traumas. Physical or sexual assault, military combat, natural disasters, terrorist attacks, and accidents fall into this category. *Life changes* and *strains* include divorce, illness in the family, difficulties at work, moving to a new house, and other circumstances that create demands to which people must adjust (see Table 10.2). *Chronic stressors*—those that continue over a long period of time—include such circumstances as living under the threat of terrorism, having a serious illness, being unable to earn a decent living, residing in a high-crime neighborhood, being the victim of discrimination, and even enduring years of academic pressure. Finally, *daily hassles* involve irritations, pressures, and annoyances that may not be major stressors by themselves but whose effects add up to become significant (Almeida, 2005; Evans & Wener, 2006). The frustrations of daily commuting in heavy traffic, for example, can become so intense for some drivers that they display a pattern of aggression called "road rage" (Levy et al., 1997; Rathbone & Huckabee, 1999).

TABLE 10.2

The Undergraduate Stress Questionnaire

Here are some items from the Undergraduate Stress Questionnaire, which asks students to indicate whether various stressors have occurred in their lives during the previous week.

Has this stressful event happened to you at any time during the last week? If it has, please check the space next to it. If it has not, please leave it blank.

_____ 1. Assignments in all classes due the same day

_____ 2. Having roommate conflicts

_____ 3. Lack of money

_____ 4. Trying to decide on major

_____ 5. Can't understand your professor

_____ 6. Stayed up late writing a paper

_____ 7. Sat through a boring class

_____ 8. Went into a test unprepared

_____ 9. Parents getting divorced

_____ 10. Incompetence at the registrar's office

Source: Crandall, Priesler, & Aussprung (1992).

Measuring Stressors

Which stressors are the most harmful? To study stress more precisely, psychologists have tried to measure the impact of particular stressors. In 1967, Thomas Holmes and Richard Rahe (pronounced "ray") pioneered the effort to find a standard way of measuring the stress in a person's life. Working on the assumption that both positive and negative changes produce stress, they asked a large number of people to rate—in terms of *life-change units,* or *LCUs*—the amount of change and demand for adjustment caused by events such as divorcing, being fired, retiring, losing a loved one, or becoming pregnant. On the basis of these ratings, Holmes and Rahe (1967) created the *Social Readjustment Rating Scale,* or *SRRS.* People taking the SRRS receive a stress score equal to the sum of the LCUs for all the stressful events they have recently experienced. Numerous studies have shown that people scoring high on the SRRS and other life-change scales are more likely to suffer physical illness, mental disorder, or other problems than those with lower scores (e.g., Monroe, Thase, & Simons, 1992).

Some researchers wondered, though, whether life changes alone tell the whole story about the impact of stressors. Accordingly, some investigators have used face-to-face interviews to more precisely measure stressors and their impact (e.g., Dohrenwend et al., 1993). Others developed scales such as the *Life Experiences Survey,* or *LES* (Sarason, Johnson, & Siegel, 1978), which measure not just which life events occurred but also people's perceptions of how positive or negative the events were and how well they were able to cope with the events. The LES also allows respondents to write in and rate any stressors they have experienced that are not on the printed list. This individualized approach can capture the differing impact and meaning that certain experiences might have for men compared with women and for members of various cultural groups. Divorce, for example, may have different meanings to people of different religious backgrounds. And members of some ethnic groups may experience prejudice and discrimination that is not felt by other groups (Lewis et al., 2006; Matthews et al., 2005; Steffen et al., 2003).

Stress Responses

▶ **How do people react to stressors?**

Physical and psychological stress reactions often occur together, especially as stressors become more intense. Furthermore, one type of stress response can set off a stress response in another dimension. For example, a physical stress reaction such as mild

FIGURE **10.2**

The General Adaptation Syndrome

Hans Selye found that physical reactions to stressors include an initial alarm reaction, followed by resistance and then exhaustion. During the alarm reaction, the body's resistance to stress temporarily drops below normal as it absorbs a stressor's initial impact. Resistance increases and then levels off in the resistance stage, but it ultimately declines if the exhaustion stage is reached.

Source: Adapted from Selye (1974).

Online Study Center

Improve Your Grade
Tutorial: Physical Reactions to Stressors—General Adaptation Syndrome

general adaptation syndrome (GAS)
A three-stage pattern of responses triggered by the effort to adapt to stressors.

chest pains might trigger the psychological stress response of worrying about a heart attack. Still, it is useful to consider each category of stress responses one at a time.

Physical Responses

If you have experienced a near accident or some other sudden, frightening event, you know that the physical responses to stressors include rapid breathing, increased heartbeat, sweating, and, a little later, shakiness. These reactions make up a general pattern known as the *fight-or-flight syndrome.* As described in the chapters on biology and behavior and on motivation and emotion, this syndrome prepares the body to face or to flee an immediate threat. Once the danger passes, fight-or-flight responses subside.

When stressors are longer lasting, however, the fight-or-flight syndrome is only the beginning of a longer sequence of reactions. Observation of animals and humans led Hans Selye (pronounced "SELL-yay") to suggest that this extended sequence of physical stress responses occurs in a consistent pattern. He called this sequence the **general adaptation syndrome,** or **GAS** (Selye, 1956, 1976). The GAS occurs in three stages (see Figure 10.2), and it is activated by efforts to adapt to any stressor, whether it is physical or psychological.

The first stage, called the *alarm reaction,* involves some version of the fight-or-flight syndrome. The alarm reaction to a mild stressor, such as a hot room, might be no more than changes in heart rate, respiration, and perspiration that help the body regulate its temperature. More severe stressors prompt more dramatic alarm reactions, rapidly mobilizing the body's adaptive energy, much as a burglar alarm alerts the police to take action (Kiecolt-Glaser et al., 1998).

Alarm reactions are controlled by the sympathetic nervous system through organs and glands that make up the *sympatho-adreno-medullary (SAM) system.* As shown on the right side of Figure 10.3, stressors trigger a process that begins when the brain's hypothalamus activates the sympathetic branch of the autonomic nervous system (ANS), which stimulates the medulla (inner part) of the adrenal glands. The adrenals, in turn, secrete *catecholamines* (pronounced "kat-uh-KOH-luh-meens")—especially adrenaline and noradrenaline—which circulate in the bloodstream, activating the liver, kidneys, heart, lungs, and other organs. The result is increased blood pressure, muscle tension, and blood sugar, along with other physical changes needed to cope with stressors. Even brief exposure to a stressor can produce major changes in these coordinated regulatory body systems (Cacioppo et al., 1995).

As shown on the left side of Figure 10.3, stressors also activate the *hypothalamic-pituitary-adrenocortical (HPA) system,* in which the hypothalamus stimulates the pituitary gland in the brain. The pituitary, in turn, secretes hormones such as adrenocorticotropic hormone (ACTH). Among other things, ACTH stimulates the cortex (outer surface) of the adrenal glands to secrete *corticosteroids;* these hormones release the body's energy supplies and fight inflammation. The pituitary gland also triggers the release of *endorphins,* which are some of the body's natural painkillers.

FIGURE **10.3**

Organ Systems Involved in the GAS

Stressors produce a variety of physiological responses that begin in the brain and spread to organs throughout the body. For example, the pituitary gland triggers the release of painkilling endorphins. It also stimulates the release of corticosteroids, which help resist stress but, as described later, also tend to suppress the immune system. Some of these substances may interact with sex hormones to create different physical stress responses and coping methods in men and women (Taylor et al., 2000, 2006).

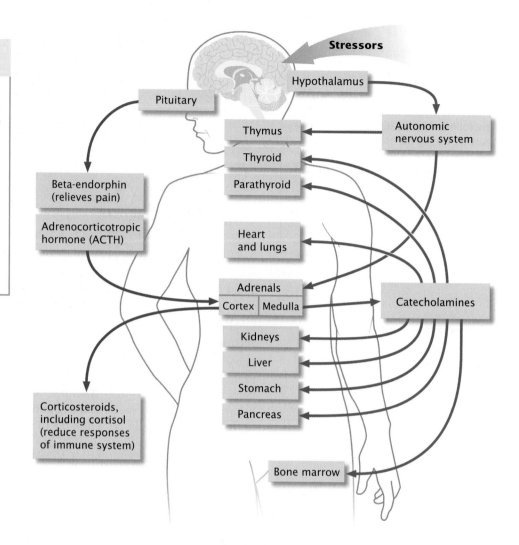

Together, these stress systems generate emergency energy. The more stressors there are and the longer they last, the more resources the body must spend in responding to them. If the stressors persist, the *resistance stage* of the GAS begins. Here, obvious signs of the initial alarm reaction fade as the body settles in to resist the stressor on a long-term basis. The drain on adaptive energy is less during the resistance stage compared with the alarm stage, but the body is still working hard to cope with stress.

This continued campaign of biochemical resistance is costly. It slowly but surely uses up the body's reserves of adaptive energy. The body then enters the third GAS stage, known as *exhaustion*. In extreme cases, such as prolonged exposure to freezing temperatures, the result is death. More commonly, the exhaustion stage brings signs of physical wear and tear. Especially hard-hit are the organ systems that were weak to begin with or that were heavily involved in the resistance process. For example, if adrenaline and cortisol (which help fight stressors during the resistance stage) remain elevated for an extended time, the result can be damage to the heart and blood vessels; suppression of the body's disease-fighting immune system; and vulnerability to illnesses such as heart disease, high blood pressure, arthritis, colds, and flu (e.g., Robles, Glaser, & Kiecolt-Glaser, 2005). Selye referred to illnesses caused or worsened by stressors as **diseases of adaptation**.

Psychological Responses

Selye's research focused mainly on the physiological aspects of stress responses, but stressors also create a variety of psychological responses, including changes in emotion and cognition (thinking), and accompanying changes in behavior.

diseases of adaptation Illnesses caused or worsened by stressors.

Emotional Changes   The physical stress responses we have described are usually accompanied by emotional stress responses. If someone pulls a gun and demands your money, you will most likely experience physiological changes, such as a spike in heart rate, but you will also feel some strong emotion—probably fear, maybe anger. In describing stress, people tend to say, "I was angry and frustrated!" rather than "My heart rate increased, and my blood pressure went up." In other words, they tend to mention changes in the emotions they are experiencing.

In most cases, emotional stress reactions fade soon after the stressors are gone. Even severe emotional stress responses ease eventually. However, if stressors continue for a long time or if lots of them occur in a short time, emotional stress reactions may persist. When people don't have a chance to recover their emotional equilibrium, they feel tense, irritable, short-tempered, or anxious, and they may experience increasingly intense feelings of fatigue, depression, and hopelessness. These reactions can become severe enough to be diagnosed as major depressive disorder, generalized anxiety disorder, or other stress-related problems discussed in the chapter on psychological disorders.

Cognitive Changes   In 1995, in the busy, noisy intensive care unit of a London hospital, a doctor misplaced a decimal point while calculating the amount of morphine a one-day-old premature baby should receive. The child died of a massive overdose (Davies, 1999). Reductions in the ability to concentrate, to think clearly, or to remember accurately are typical cognitive stress reactions (Beilock & Carr, 2005; Hygge, Evans, & Bullinger, 2002). These problems appear partly because of *ruminative thinking,* the repeated intrusion of thoughts about stressful events (Lyubomirsky & Nolen-Hoeksema, 1995). Ruminative thoughts about relationship problems, for example, can seriously interfere with studying for a test. A related phenomenon is *catastrophizing,* which means dwelling on and overemphasizing the possible negative consequences of events. During exams, test-anxious college students are likely to say to themselves, "I'm falling behind" or "Everyone is doing better than I am." As catastrophizing or ruminative thinking impairs cognitive functioning, resulting feelings of anxiety and other emotional arousal add to the total stress response, further hampering performance (Beilock et al., 2004; Mendl, 1999).

Overarousal created by stressors also tends to narrow the scope of attention, making it harder to scan the full range of possible solutions to complex problems (Craske, 1999; Keinan, Friedland, & Ben-Porath, 1987). In addition, stress-narrowed attention may increase the problem-solving errors described in the chapter on thought, language, and intelligence. People under stress are more likely to cling to *mental sets,* which are well-learned, but not always efficient, approaches to problems. Stress may also intensify *functional fixedness,* the tendency to use objects for only one purpose. Victims of hotel fires, for example, sometimes die trapped in their rooms because, in the stress of the moment, it did not occur to them to use the telephone or a piece of furniture to break a window.

Stressors may also impair decision making. Under stress, people who normally consider all aspects of a situation before making a decision may act impulsively and sometimes foolishly. High-pressure salespeople often take advantage of this stress response by creating time-limited offers or by telling indecisive customers that others are waiting to buy the item they are considering (Cialdini, 2001).

Behavioral Responses   Clues about people's physical and emotional stress reactions come from changes in how they look, act, or talk. Strained facial expressions, a shaky voice, tremors, and jumpiness are common behavioral stress responses. Posture can also convey information about stress, a fact well known to skilled interviewers.

Even more obvious behavioral stress responses appear as people try to escape or avoid stressors. Some people quit their jobs, drop out of school, turn to alcohol, or even attempt suicide. In the month after Hurricane Katrina struck the U.S. gulf coast in 2005, for example, more than double the normal number of calls were placed from the affected area to the National Suicide Prevention Hotline (Breed, 2006). Unfortunately,

STRESS FOR $500, ALEX   The negative effects of stress on memory, thinking, decision making, and other cognitive functions are often displayed by players on TV game shows such as *Jeopardy!* and *Who Wants to be a Millionaire.* Under the intense pressure of time, competition, and the scrutiny of millions of viewers, contestants may miss questions that seem ridiculously easy to those calmly recalling the correct answers at home.

as discussed in the chapter on learning, escape and avoidance tactics deprive people of the opportunity to learn more adaptive ways of coping with stressful environments, including college (Cooper et al., 1992). Aggression is another common behavioral response to stressors. All too often, this response is directed at members of one's own family (Polusny & Follette, 1995). So areas devastated by hurricanes and other natural disasters are likely to see not only suicides, but dramatic increases in reports of domestic violence (Curtis, Miller, & Berry, 2000; Rotton, 1990).

LINKAGES
When do stress responses become mental disorders?
(a link to Psychological Disorders)

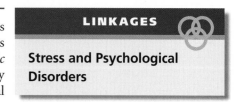

LINKAGES

Stress and Psychological Disorders

Physical and psychological stress responses sometimes appear together in patterns known as *burnout* and *posttraumatic stress disorder*. **Burnout** is an increasingly intense pattern of physical and psychological dysfunction in response to a continuous flow of stressors or to chronic stress (Maslach, 2003). As burnout nears, previously reliable workers or once-attentive spouses become indifferent, disengaged, impulsive, or accident prone. They miss work frequently; oversleep; perform their jobs poorly; abuse alcohol or other drugs; and become irritable, suspicious, withdrawn, and depressed (Taylor, 2002). Burnout is particularly common among those who do "people work," such as teachers and nurses, and those who perceive themselves as being treated unjustly by employers (Elovainio, Kivimäki, & Vahtera, 2002; Schultz & Schultz, 2002).

A different pattern of severe stress reactions is illustrated by the case of Mary, a thirty-three-year-old nurse who was raped at knifepoint by an intruder in her apartment. In the weeks following this trauma, she was fearful about being alone and was preoccupied with thoughts about the attack and about the risk of it happening again. She installed additional locks on her doors and windows but experienced difficulty concentrating and could not immediately return to work. The thought of sex repelled her.

Mary suffered from **posttraumatic stress disorder (PTSD),** a pattern of severe negative reactions following a traumatic event. Among the characteristic reactions are anxiety, irritability, jumpiness, inability to concentrate or work productively, sexual dysfunction, and difficulty in getting along with others. PTSD sufferers also experience sleep disturbances, intense startle responses to noise or other sudden stimuli, and long-term suppression of their immune systems (e.g., Goenjian et al., 2001; Guthrie & Bryant, 2005; Johnson et al., 2002; Kawamura, Kim, & Asukai, 2001). High-tech scanning techniques reveal that PTSD symptoms are accompanied by noticeable changes in brain functioning, and even in brain structure (Kitayama et al., 2005). The most common feature of posttraumatic stress disorder is reexperiencing the trauma through nightmares or vivid memories. In rare cases, *flashbacks* occur in which the person behaves for minutes, hours, or days as if the trauma were occurring again.

Posttraumatic stress disorder is usually associated with events such as war, rape, terrorism, assault, or abuse in childhood (e.g., Galea, Ahern, et al., 2002; Galea, Resnick, et al, 2002; Goldberg & Garno, 2005; Shalev & Freedman, 2005; Shalev et al., 2006), but researchers now believe that some PTSD symptoms can be triggered by any major stressor, from car accidents to being stalked (Ironson et al., 1997; Kamphuis & Emmelkamp, 2001). PTSD may appear immediately following a trauma, or it may not occur until weeks, months, or even years later (Gilboa-Schechtman & Foa, 2001; Heim et al., 2000; Port, Engdahl, & Frazier, 2001). Many people affected by PTSD require professional help, although some seem to recover without it (Bradley et al., 2005; Perkonigg et al., 2005). For most, improvement takes time; for nearly all, the support of family and friends is vital to recovery (Foa et al., 1999; Foa et al., 2005; LaGreca et al., 1996). For some people, though, PTSD never appears, even after severe trauma (Breslau et al., 2005). Researchers are working to discover what protective factors are operating in these individuals and whether those factors can be strengthened through PTSD treatment programs (Yehuda et al., 2005).

---

burnout   A pattern of physical and psychological dysfunctions in response to continuous stressors.

posttraumatic stress disorder (PTSD) A pattern of adverse reactions following a traumatic event, commonly involving reexperiencing the event through nightmares or vivid memories.

LIFE HANGING IN THE BALANCE
Symptoms of burnout and posttraumatic stress disorder often plague firefighters, police officers, emergency medical personnel, and others who are repeatedly exposed to time pressure, trauma, danger, and other stressors (Fullerton, Ursano, & Wang, 2004). Posttraumatic stress disorder can also occur following a single catastrophic event. Surveys taken in the weeks and months following the terrorist attacks on the World Trade Center revealed that 7.5 percent of adults and 10.6 percent of children who lived near the devastated area experienced symptoms of PTSD. Even higher rates of PTSD symptoms were reported by adult survivors of the massive tidal waves that devastated south and southeast Asia in 2004. (DeLisi et al., 2003; Galea, Ahern, et al., 2002; Galea, Resnick, et al., 2002; Hoven et al., 2005; Simeon et al., 2003; van Griensven et al., 2006).

Stress is also thought to play a role in the development of many other psychological disorders, including depression and schizophrenia (e.g., Cutrona et al., 2005). This point is emphasized in the chapter on psychological disorders, especially in relation to the *diathesis-stress approach* to psychopathology. This approach suggests that certain individuals may be predisposed to develop certain disorders but that whether or not these disorders actually appear depends on the frequency, nature, and intensity of the stressors the people encounter.

Stress Mediators

▶ **Why doesn't everyone react to stressors in the same way?**

The ways in which particular people interact with particular stressors can be seen in many areas of life. The stress of combat, for example, is partly responsible for the errors in judgment and decision-making that lead to "friendly fire" deaths and injuries in almost every military operation (Adler, 1993). But not everyone in combat makes these mistakes. Why does stress disrupt the performance of some individuals and not others? And why does one individual survive, and even thrive, under the same circumstances that lead another to break down, give up, and burn out? The answer may lie in *psychobiological models,* which recognize the importance of psychological, as well as biological, factors in the stress process (Folkman et al., 2000; Suls & Rothman, 2004; Taylor, 2002). These models emphasize that, as shown in Figure 10.1, the impact of stressors depends not only on the stressors themselves but on several important mediating factors as well (Bonanno, 2004, 2005; Kemeny, 2003; McEwen & Seeman, 1999).

How Stressors Are Perceived

As described in the chapter on sensation and perception, our view of the world depends partly on how we interpret sensory information. Similarly, our physical and psychological reactions to stressors depend somewhat on how we think about them, a process known as *cognitive appraisal*. A potential stressor usually has a stronger negative impact on people who perceive it as a threat than on people who see it as a challenge (Lazarus, 1999; Maddi & Khoshaba, 2005).

Evidence for the effects of cognitive factors on stress responses comes from both surveys and experiments (e.g., Abelson et al., 2005). In one of the first laboratory demonstrations of these effects, Richard Lazarus gave differing instructions to three groups of students who were about to watch a film showing bloody industrial accidents (Lazarus et al., 1965). One group (the "intellectualizers") was instructed to remain mentally detached from the gruesome scenes; a second group (the "denial" group) was instructed to think of the scenes as unreal; and a third group (the "unprepared" group) was not told anything about the film. As Figure 10.4 shows, the intensity of physiological arousal during the film, as measured by sweat-gland activity, depended on how the viewers were instructed to think about the film. The unprepared students were more upset than either of the other two groups. In a more recent study, students who were first trained to see the threatening aspects of information showed more emotional arousal to a stressful video than those who had been trained to see information as nonthreatening (Wilson et al., 2006). Similarly, physical and psychological symptoms associated with the stress of airport noise, of being diagnosed with a serious illness, of learning about toxins in local soil, or of living with terrorism threats are more common in people who engage in more catastrophic thinking about these problems (Bryant & Guthrie, 2005; Lerner et al., 2003; Matthies, Hoeger, & Guski, 2000; Speckhard, 2002). Those who hold a more optimistic outlook tend to show milder stress responses and better health outcomes (de Moor et al., 2006; Taylor et al., 2000; Taylor et al., 2003).

The influence of cognitive factors weakens somewhat as stressors become extreme. Still, even the impact of major stressors, such as natural disasters or divorce, may be less severe for those who think of them as challenges to be overcome. In other words, many stressful events are not inherently stressful; their impact depends partly on how people perceive them. An important part of this appraisal is the degree to which the stressors are perceived to be predictable and controllable, or at least manageable.

Predictability and Control

Why is the threat of terrorism so terrorizing? For one thing, knowing that a stressor might occur but being uncertain whether, or when, it will occur tends to increase the stressor's impact (Lerner et al., 2003; Sorrentino & Roney, 2000). In other words,

FIGURE 10.4

Cognitive Influences on Stress Responses

Richard Lazarus and his colleagues found that students' physiological stress reactions to a film showing bloody industrial accidents were affected by the way they thought about what they saw. Those who had been instructed to remain detached from the film (the "intellectualizers") or to think of it as unreal (the "denial" group) were less upset—as measured by sweat-gland activity—than those in an "unprepared" group. These results were among the first to show that people's cognitive appraisal of stressors can affect their responses to those stressors.

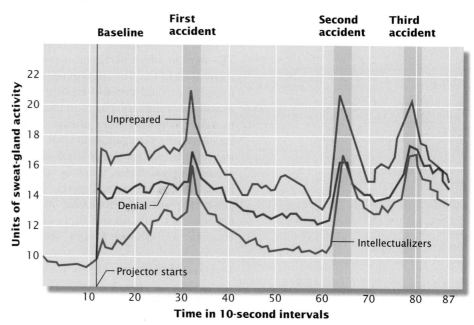

Source: Adapted from Lazarus et al. (1965).

unpredictable stressors tend to have more impact than those that are predictable (Lazarus & Folkman, 1984; Pham, Taylor, & Seeman, 2001)—especially when the stressors are intense and relatively brief. For example, people whose spouses died suddenly tend to display more immediate disbelief, anxiety, and depression than those who had weeks or months to prepare for the loss (Schulz et al., 2001; Swarte et al., 2003). However, predictability does not provide total protection against stressors. Research with animals shows that predictable stressors can be even more damaging than unpredictable ones if they occur over long periods of time (Abbott, Schoen, & Badia, 1984).

The *perception of control* also mediates the effects of stressors. If people feel they have some control over stressors, those stressors usually have less impact (e.g. Johnson & Krueger, 2005). For example, studies of several thousand employees in the United States, Sweden, and the United Kingdom have found that those who felt they had little or no control over their work environment were more likely to suffer heart disease and other health problems than workers with a high degree of perceived control over their work environment (Bosma et al., 1997; Cheng et al., 2000; Spector, 2002). And at many hospitals, it is now standard procedure to help patients to manage or control the stress of emergency treatment or the side effects of surgery, because doing so helps people to heal faster and go home sooner (Broadbent et al., 2003; Chamberlin, 2000; Gordon et al., 2005; Kiecolt-Glaser et al., 1998).

Simply *believing* that a stressor is controllable, even if it isn't, can also reduce its impact. This effect was demonstrated in a study in which participants with panic disorder inhaled a mixture of oxygen and carbon dioxide that typically causes a panic attack (Sanderson, Rapee, & Barlow, 1989). Half the participants were led to believe (falsely) that they could control the concentration of the mixture. Compared with those who believed that they had no control, significantly fewer of the "in-control" participants experienced full-blown panic attacks during the session, and their panic symptoms were fewer and less severe.

People who feel they have no control over negative events appear especially prone to physical and psychological problems. They often experience feelings of helplessness and hopelessness that, in turn, may promote depression or other mental disorders (Sarin, Abela, & Auerbach, 2005; Taylor & Aspinwall, 1996).

Coping Resources and Coping Methods

People usually suffer fewer ill effects from a stressor if they have adequate coping resources and effective coping methods. *Coping resources* include, among other things, the money and time to deal with stressful events. For example, the physical and psychological responses you experience if your car breaks down tend to be more negative if you are broke and pressed for time than if you have the money for repairs and the freedom to take a day off from work.

The impact of stressors can also be reduced by effective coping methods (Benight et al., 1999; Cote & Pepler, 2002; Poczwardowski & Conroy, 2002). Most of these methods can be classified as either problem focused or emotion focused. *Problem-focused* coping methods involve efforts to change or eliminate a source of stress, whereas *emotion-focused* techniques attempt to control the negative emotional consequences of stressors (Folkman et al., 1986). Some people use both kinds of coping. For example, you might deal with the problem of noise from a nearby factory by forming a community action group to push for tougher noise-reduction laws and, at the same time, calm your anger when noise occurs by mentally focusing on the group's efforts to improve the situation (Folkman & Moskowitz, 2000; Hatfield et al., 2002). Susan Folkman and Richard Lazarus (1988) devised a widely used questionnaire to assess the specific ways in which people cope with stressors; Table 10.3 shows some examples from their questionnaire.

Particularly when a stressor is difficult to control, it is sometimes helpful to fully express and think about the emotions you are experiencing in relation to the stressful event (Low, Stanton, & Danoff-Burg, 2006; Niederhoffer & Pennebaker, 2002). The benefits of this coping strategy have been observed in many individuals whose religious

TABLE 10.3

Ways of Coping

Coping is defined as cognitive and behavioral efforts to manage specific demands that people perceive as taxing their resources (Folkman et al., 1986). This table illustrates two major approaches to coping measured by the Ways of Coping Questionnaire: problem focused and emotion focused. Ask yourself which approach you usually take when faced with stressors. Now rank the coping skills under each major approach in terms of how often you tend to use each. Do you rely on just one or two, or do you adjust your coping strategies to fit different kinds of stressors?

Coping Skills	Example
Problem-focused coping	
Confronting	"I stood my ground and fought for what I wanted."
Seeking social support	"I talked to someone to find out more about the situation."
Planful problem solving	"I made a plan of action, and I followed it."
Emotion-focused coping	
Self-controlling	"I tried to keep my feelings to myself."
Distancing	"I didn't let it get to me; I tried not to think about it too much."
Positive reappraisal	"I changed my mind about myself."
Accepting responsibility	"I realized I brought the problem on myself."
Escape/avoidance (wishful thinking)	"I wished that the situation would go away or somehow be over with."

Source: Adapted from Folkman et al. (1986); Taylor (1995).

beliefs allow them to bring meaning to the death of a loved one or the devastation of natural disasters that might otherwise seem senseless tragedies (Heppner et al., 2006; Powell, Shahabi, & Thoreson, 2003; VandeCreek et al., 2002). Some individuals who use humor to help them cope also show better adjustment and milder physiological reactivity to stressful events (Martin, 2001; Moran, 2002).

Social Support

Has a good friend ever given you comfort and reassurance during troubled times? If so, you have experienced the value of *social support* in easing the impact of stressful events. Social support consists of emotional, tangible, or informational resources provided by other people. These people might help to eliminate a stressor (by, say, fixing your car), suggest how to deal with the stressor (by recommending a good mechanic), or reduce a stressor's impact by providing companionship and reassurance (Sarason, Sarason, & Gurung, 1997). The people you can depend on for support make up your **social support network** (Burleson, Albrecht, & Sarason, 1994).

The stress-reducing effects of social support have been documented in people dealing with a wide range of stressors, including cancer, stroke, military combat, loss of loved ones, natural disasters, arthritis, AIDS, and even ethnic discrimination (e.g., Boden-Albala et al., 2005; Foster, 2000; Jason, Witter, & Torres-Harding, 2003; Penner, Dovidio, & Albrecht, 2001; Savelkoul et al., 2000). Social support can have health benefits, too. For example, students who get emotional support from friends show better immune system functioning and than those with less adequate social support (Cohen & Herbert, 1996). This may be why people in strong social support networks are less vulnerable to colds and flu during exams and other periods of high academic stress (Kop et al., 2005; Pressman et al., 2005; Taylor, Dickerson, & Klein, 2002). Having strong social support is also associated with faster recovery from surgery or illness, possibly because helpful friends and family members encourage patients to follow medical advice (Brummett et al., 2005; Grassi et al., 2000; Krohne & Slangen, 2005; Taylor, 2002). Stronger social networks are even associated with better mental functioning in old age (Barnes et al., 2004). According to some researchers, having inadequate social support can be as dangerous as smoking, obesity, or lack of exercise in that it nearly doubles a person's risk of dying from disease, suicide, or other causes (House, Landis, & Umberson, 1988a, 1988b; Kiecolt-Glaser & Newton, 2001; Rutledge et al., 2004).

social support network   The friends and social contacts on whom one can depend for help and support.

applying
psychology **YOU'VE GOT A FRIEND** Even when social support cannot eliminate stressors, it can help people, such as these breast cancer survivors, to feel less anxious, more optimistic, more capable of control, and more willing to try new ways of dealing with stressors (Trunzo & Pinto, 2003). Those who provide support may feel better, too (Brown et al., 2003).

Exactly how social support brings about its positive effects is not entirely clear. James Pennebaker (1995, 2000) has suggested that social support may help prevent illness by providing the person under stress with an opportunity to express pent-up thoughts and emotions. Keeping important things to yourself, says Pennebaker, is itself a stressor. In a laboratory experiment, for example, participants who were asked to deceive an experimenter showed elevated physiological arousal (Pennebaker & Chew, 1985). Further, the spouses of suicide or accidental-death victims who do not or cannot confide their feelings to others are especially likely to develop physical illness during the year following the death (Pennebaker & O'Heeron, 1984). Disclosing, even anonymously, the stresses and traumas one has experienced is associated with enhanced immune functioning, reduced physical symptoms, and decreased use of health services (Broderick, Junghaenel, & Schwartz, 2005; Campbell & Pennebaker, 2003; Epstein, Sloan, & Marx, 2005; Sloan, Marx, & Epstein, 2005). This may explain why support groups for problems ranging from bereavement to overeating to alcohol and drug abuse tend to promote participants' physical health (Taylor et al., 2002).

Research in this area is made more challenging by the fact that the relationship between social support and the impact of stressors is not a simple one. For one thing, the quality of social support can influence the ability to cope with stress, but the reverse may also be true: Your ability to cope may determine the quality of the social support you receive (McLeod, Kessler, & Landis, 1992). People who complain endlessly about stressors but never do anything about them may discourage social support, whereas those with an optimistic, action-oriented approach may attract support.

Second, *social support* refers not only to your relationships with others but also to the recognition that others care and will help (Demaray & Malecki, 2002). Some relationships in a seemingly strong social network can be stormy, fragile, or shallow, resulting in interpersonal conflicts that can have an adverse effect on health (Ben-Ari & Gil, 2002; Malarkey et al., 1994).

Third, having too much support or the wrong kind of support can be as bad as not having enough (Reynolds & Perrin, 2004). Dangerous behaviors such as smoking, for example, can be harder to give up if one's social support network consists entirely of smokers. People whose friends and family overprotect them from stressors may actually put less energy into coping efforts or have less opportunity to learn effective coping strategies. And if the efforts of people in a social support network become annoying, disruptive, or interfering, they can increase stress and intensify psychological problems (Newsome, 1999; Newsome & Schulz, 1998). It has even been suggested that among people under intense stress, the benefits of having a large social support network may be offset by the dangers of catching a cold or the flu from people in that network (Hamrick, Cohen, & Rodriguez, 2002).

Finally, the value of social support may depend on the kind of stressor being encountered. So although having a friend nearby might reduce the impact of some stressors, it might amplify the impact of others. In one study, participants who were about to make a speech experienced the task as more threatening—and showed stronger physical and psychological stress responses—when a friend was watching than when they were alone (Stoney & Finney, 2000).

Stress, Personality, and Gender

The impact of stress on health appears to depend not only on how people think about particular stressors but also to some extent on how they think about, and react to, the world in general. For instance, stress-related health problems tend to be especially common among people whose "disease-prone" personalities lead them to (1) try to ignore stressors when possible; (2) perceive stressors as long-term, catastrophic threats that they brought on themselves; and (3) be pessimistic about their ability to overcome stressors (e.g., Penninx et al., 2001; Peterson et al., 1998; Segerstrom et al., 1998; Suinn, 2001).

Other cognitive styles, such as those characteristic of "disease-resistant" personalities, help insulate people from the ill effects of stress. These people tend to think of stressors as temporary challenges to be overcome, not catastrophic threats. And they don't constantly blame themselves for causing these stressors. One particularly important component of the "disease-resistant" personality seems to be *dispositional optimism,* the belief or expectation that things will work out positively (Folkman & Moskowitz, 2000; Pressman & Cohen, 2005; Rosenkranz et al., 2003; Taylor et al., 2000). Optimistic people tend to live longer (Giltay et al., 2004, 2006) and to have more resistance than pessimists to colds and other infectious diseases (Cohen et al., 2003a, 2003b; Pressman & Cohen, 2005), which helps explain why optimistic students experience fewer physical symptoms at the end of the academic term (Aspinwall & Taylor, 1992; Ebert, Tucker, & Roth, 2002). Optimistic coronary bypass surgery patients tend to heal faster and stay healthier than pessimists (Scheier et al., 1989, 1999) and perceive their quality of life following coronary surgery to be higher than do patients with less optimistic outlooks (Fitzgerald et al., 1993). And among HIV-positive men, dispositional optimism has been associated with lower psychological distress, fewer worries, and lower perceived risk of acquiring full-blown AIDS (Johnson & Endler, 2002; Taylor et al., 1992). These effects appear due in part to optimists' tendency to use challenge-oriented, problem-focused coping strategies that attack stressors directly, in contrast to pessimists' tendency to use emotion-focused coping strategies, such as denial and avoidance (Bosompra et al., 2001; Brenes et al., 2002). They also tend to be happier than pessimists, a tendency associated not only with less intense and less dangerous physiological responses to stressors but also with greater success in life (e.g. Lyubomirsky, King, & Diener, 2005; Steptoe, Wardle, & Marmot, 2005).

Gender may also play a role in responses to stressors. In a review of 200 studies of stress responses and coping methods, Shelley Taylor and her colleagues found that males under stress tended to get angry, avoid stressors, or both, whereas females were more likely to help others and to make use of their social support network (Taylor et al., 2000; Taylor, Lewis et al., 2002). Further, in the face of equally intense stressors, men's physical responses tend to be more intense than women's (Stoney & Matthews, 1988). This is not true in every case, of course, but why should such gender differences show up at all? The gender-role learning discussed in the human development chapter surely plays a part (Eagly & Wood, 1999). But Taylor also proposes that women's "tend and befriend" style differs from the "fight or flight" pattern so often seen in men because of gender differences in how hormones combine under stress. Consider, for example, oxytocin (pronounced "ox-see-TOH-sin"), a hormone released in both sexes in response to social stressors (Taylor et al., 2006; Uvnas-Moberg, Arn, & Magnusson, 2005). Taylor suggests that oxytocin interacts differently with male and female sex hormones—amplifying men's physical stress responses and reducing women's (Light et al., 2005). This gender difference could lead to the more intense emotional and behavioral stress responses typical of men, and it might be partly responsible for men's greater vulnerability to heart disease and other stress-related illnesses (Kajantie & Phillips, 2006). If that is the case, gender differences in stress responses may help to explain why women live an average of 5.3 years longer than men (Hoyert, Kung, & Smith, 2005). The role of gender-related hormones in stress responding is supported by the fact that there are few, if any, gender differences in children's stress responses. Those differences begin to appear only around adolescence, when sex hormone differences become pronounced (Allen & Matthews, 1997).

LINKAGES
Are childhood traits related to how long we live? (a link to Human Development)

The way people think and act in the face of stressors, the ease with which they attract social support, and their tendency to be optimists or pessimists are but a few aspects of *personality*.

■ What was the researchers' question?

Are there other personality characteristics that protect or threaten people's health? This was the question asked by Howard Friedman and his associates (Friedman, 2000; Friedman et al., 1995a, 1995b). In particular, they attempted to identify aspects of personality that increase the likelihood that people will die prematurely from heart disease, high blood pressure, or other chronic diseases.

■ How did the researchers answer the question?

Friedman suspected that an answer might lie in the results of the Terman Life Cycle Study of Intelligence, which was named after Louis Terman, author of the Stanford-Binet intelligence test. As described in the chapter on thought, language, and intelligence, the study was originally designed to measure the long-term development of 1,528 gifted California children (856 boys and 672 girls), nicknamed the "Termites" (Terman & Oden, 1947).

Starting in 1921, and every five to ten years thereafter, Terman's research team had gathered information about the Termites' personality traits, social relationships, stressors, health habits, and many other variables. The data were collected through questionnaires and interviews with the Termites themselves, as well as with their teachers, parents, and other family members. By the early 1990s, about half of the Termites had died. It was then that Friedman realized that the Terman Life Cycle Study could shed light on the relationship between personality and health, because the personality traits identified in the Termites could be related to how long they lived. So he examined the Termites' death certificates, noting the dates and causes of death, and then looked for associations between their personalities and the length of their lives.

■ What did the researchers find?

Friedman and his colleagues found that one of the most important predictors of long life was a dimension of personality known as *conscientiousness,* or social dependability (described in the personality chapter). Termites who, in childhood, had been seen as truthful, prudent, reliable, hard working, and humble tended to live longer than those whose parents and teachers had identified them as impulsive and lacking in self-control.

Friedman also examined the Terman Life Cycle Study for what it suggested about the relationship between health and social support. In particular, he compared Termites whose parents had divorced or who had been in unstable marriages themselves with those who grew up in stable homes and who had stable marriages. He discovered that people who had experienced parental divorce during childhood, or who themselves had

in review

STRESS RESPONSES AND STRESS MEDIATORS

Category	Examples
Responses	
Physical	Fight-or-flight syndrome (increased heart rate, respiration, and muscle tension; sweating; pupillary dilation); SAM and HPA activation (involving release of catecholamines and corticosteroids); eventual breakdown of organ systems involved in prolonged resistance to stressors
Psychological	*Emotional:* anger, anxiety, depression, and other emotional states. *Cognitive:* inability to concentrate or think logically, ruminative thinking, catastrophizing. *Behavioral:* aggression and escape/avoidance tactics (including suicide attempts)
Mediators	
Appraisal	Thinking of a difficult new job as a challenge will create less discomfort than focusing on the threat of failure.
Predictability	A tornado that strikes without warning may have a more devastating emotional impact than a long-predicted hurricane.
Control	Repairing a disabled spacecraft may be less stressful for the astronauts doing the work than for their loved ones on earth, who can do nothing to help.
Coping resources and methods	Having no effective way to relax after a hard day may prolong tension and other stress responses.
Social support	Having no one to talk to about a rape or other trauma may amplify the negative impact of the experience.

?
1. The friends and family we can depend on to help us deal with stressors are called our _____ network.
2. Fantasizing about winning money is a(n) _____ -focused way of coping with financial stress.
3. Sudden, extreme stressors may cause psychological and behavioral problems known as _____.

unstable marriages, died an average of four years earlier than those whose close social relationships had been less stressful.

■ What do the results mean?

Did these differences in personality traits and social support actually cause some Termites to live longer than others? Friedman's research is based mainly on correlational analyses, so it was difficult for the investigators to draw conclusions about what caused the relationships they observed. Still, Friedman and his colleagues searched the Terman data for clues to mechanisms through which personality and other factors might have exerted a causal influence on how long the Termites lived (Peterson et al., 1998). For example, they evaluated the hypothesis that conscientious, dependable Termites who lived socially stable lives might have followed healthier lifestyles than those who were more impulsive and socially stressed. They found that people in the latter group did, in fact, tend to eat less healthy diets and were more likely to smoke, drink to excess, or use drugs. But health behaviors alone did not fully account for their shorter average life spans. Another possible explanation is that conscientiousness and stability in social relationships reflect a general attitude of caution that goes beyond eating right and avoiding substance abuse. Friedman found some support for this idea in the Terman data. Termites who were impulsive or low on conscientiousness were somewhat more likely to die from accidents or violence than those who were less impulsive.

■ **What do we still need to know?**

The Terman Life Cycle Study does not provide final answers about the relationship between personality and health. However, it has generated some important clues and a number of intriguing hypotheses to be evaluated in research with more representative samples of participants. Some of that research has already taken place and tends to confirm Friedman's findings about conscientiousness (Hampson et al., 2006). Further, Friedman's decision to reanalyze a set of data on psychosocial development as a way of exploring issues in health psychology stands as a fine example of how a creative researcher can pursue answers to complex questions that are difficult or impossible to study via controlled experiments.

Our discussion of personality and other factors that can alter the impact of stressors should make it obvious that what is stressful for a given individual is not determined fully and simply by predispositions, coping styles, or situations. (See "In Review: Stress Responses and Stress Mediators.") Even more important are interactions between the person and the situation, the mixture of each individual's coping resources with the specific characteristics of the situation encountered.

The Physiology and Psychology of Health and Illness

▶ **How does stress affect your immune system?**

Several studies mentioned so far show that people under stress are more likely than less-stressed people to develop infectious diseases. Other research shows that they are also more likely to experience flare-ups of the latent viruses responsible for oral herpes (cold sores) or genital herpes (Cohen & Herbert, 1996). In the following sections we focus on some of the ways in which these and other illnesses are related to the impact of stress on the immune system and the cardiovascular system.

Stress, Illness, and the Immune System

LINKAGES
Can stress give you the flu?
(a link to Biology and Behavior)

On March 19, 1878, at a seminar before the Académie de Médecine de Paris, Louis Pasteur showed his distinguished audience three chickens. One bird had been raised normally and was healthy. A second bird had been intentionally infected with bacteria but given no other treatment; it was also healthy. The third chicken that Pasteur presented was dead. It had been infected with the same bacteria as the second bird, but it had also been physically stressed by being exposed to cold temperatures; as a result, the bacteria killed it (Kelley, 1985).

Research conducted since Pasteur's time has greatly expanded our knowledge about how stressors affect the body's reaction to disease. **Psychoneuroimmunology** is the field that examines the interaction of psychological and physiological processes that strengthen or weaken the body's ability to defend itself against disease (Ader, 2001).

psychoneuroimmunology The field that examines the interaction of psychological and physiological processes affecting the body's ability to defend itself against disease.

immune system The body's first line of defense against invading substances and microorganisms.

The Immune System and Illness The body's first line of defense against invading substances and microorganisms is the **immune system.** The immune system is perhaps as complex as the nervous system, and it contains as many cells as the brain (Guyton, 1991). Some of these cells are in organs such as the thymus and spleen,

THE FIRST LINE OF DEFENSE   A patrolling immune system cell sends out an extension known as a pseudopod (pronounced "SUE-doh-pod") to engulf and destroy a bacterial cell before alerting more defenders. These immune cells are able to squeeze out of the bloodstream and enter organs, where they destroy foreign cells.

whereas others circulate in the bloodstream, entering tissues throughout the body. Components of the immune system kill or inactivate foreign or harmful substances in the body, such as viruses and bacteria (Simpson, Hurtley, & Marx, 2000). If our immune systems are impaired, we are left more vulnerable to colds, mononucleosis, and many other infectious diseases (Potter & Zautra, 1997). It is by disabling the immune system that the human immunodeficiency virus (HIV) leads to AIDS and leaves the HIV-infected person defenseless against other infections or cancers. The immune system can also become overactive, with devastating results. Many chronic, progressive diseases—including arthritis, diabetes, and lupus erythematosus—are now recognized as *autoimmune disorders*. In these cases, cells of the immune system begin to attack and destroy normal body cells (Oldenberg et al., 2000).

An important aspect of the human immune system is the action of the white blood cells, called *leukocytes* (pronounced "LU-koh-sites"). These cells are formed in the bone marrow and serve as the body's mobile defense units. Leukocytes are called to action when foreign substances are detected. Among the varied types of leukocytes are *B-cells*, which produce *antibodies* to fight foreign toxins; *T-cells*, which kill other cells; and *natural killer cells*, which destroy a variety of foreign organisms and are particularly important in fighting viruses and tumors. The brain can influence the immune system indirectly by altering the secretion of adrenal hormones, such as cortisol, that modify the circulation of T-cells and B-cells. The brain can also influence the immune system directly by making connections with the immune organs, such as the thymus, where T-cells and B-cells are stored (Felten et al., 1991; Maier & Watkins, 2000).

The Immune System and Stress   A wide variety of stressors can lead to suppression of the immune system. The effects are especially strong in the elderly (Penedo & Dahn, 2004), but they occur in everyone (Kiecolt-Glaser & Glaser, 2001; Kiecolt-Glaser et al., 2002). One study showed that as first-year law students participated in class, took exams, and experienced other stressful aspects of law school, they showed a decline in several measures of immune functioning (Segerstrom et al., 1998). Similarly, decreases in natural killer cell activity have been observed in both men and women following the deaths of their spouses (Irwin et al., 1987), and a variety of immune system impairments have been found in people suffering the effects of prolonged marital conflict, divorce, or extended periods of caring for elderly relatives (Cacioppo et al., 1998; Kiecolt-Glaser et al., 2003, 2005; Vitaliano, Zhang, & Scanlan, 2003).

The relationship between stress and the immune system can be critical to people who are HIV-positive but do not yet have AIDS. Because their immune systems are already fragile, further stress-related impairments could be life threatening. Research indicates that psychological stressors are associated with the progression of HIV-related illnesses (e.g., Antoni et al., 2000; Nott & Vedhara, 2000). Unfortunately, people with HIV (and AIDS) face a particularly heavy load of immune-suppressing psychological stressors, including uncertainty about the future. A lack of perceived control and resulting depression and anxiety can further magnify their stress responses (e.g., Sewell et al., 2000).

Stress, Illness, and the Cardiovascular System

Earlier we mentioned the role of the sympatho-adreno-medullary (SAM) system in mobilizing the body's defenses during times of threat. Because the SAM system is linked to the cardiovascular system, its repeated activation in response to stressors has been linked to the development of coronary heart disease (CHD), high blood pressure (hypertension), and stroke (Krantz & McCeney, 2002). The link appears especially strong in people who display strong physical reactions to stressors (Andre-Petersson et al., 2001; Ming et al., 2004; Treiber et al., 2001). For example, among healthy young adult research participants, those whose blood pressure rose most dramatically in response to a mild stressor or a series of stressors were the ones most likely to develop

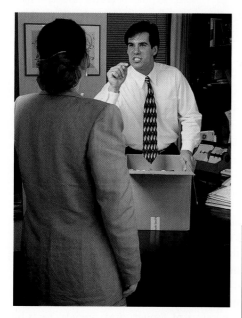

YOU CAN'T FIRE ME—I QUIT! For a time, researchers believed that anyone who displayed the pattern of aggressiveness, competitiveness, and nonstop work known as Type A behavior was at increased risk for heart disease (Friedman & Rosenman, 1974). More recent research shows, however, that the danger lies not in these characteristics alone but in hostility, which is seen in some, but not all, Type A people.

hypertension later in life (Kasagi, Akahoshi, & Shimaoki, 1995; Light et al., 1999; Matthews et al., 2004).

As also mentioned earlier, these physical reactions to stressors—and the chances of suffering stress-related health problems—depend partly on personality, especially on how people tend to think about stressors and about life in general. For example, the trait of *hostility*—especially when accompanied by irritability and impatience—has been associated with the appearance of coronary heart disease (Bunde & Suls, 2006; Day & Jreige, 2002; Krantz & McCeney, 2002; Smith, 2003).

Health psychologists see hostility as characterized by suspiciousness, resentment, frequent anger, antagonism, and distrust of others (Helmers & Krantz, 1996; Krantz & McCeney, 2002; Williams, 2001). The identification of hostility as a risk factor for coronary heart disease and heart attack may be an important breakthrough in understanding these illnesses, which remain chief causes of death in the United States and most other Western nations. But is hostility as dangerous as health psychologists suspect?

■ What am I being asked to believe or accept?

Many researchers claim that individuals who display hostility increase their risk for coronary heart disease and heart attack (e.g., Bleil et al., 2004; Boyle et al., 2004). This risk, they say, is independent of other risk factors such as heredity, diet, smoking, and drinking.

■ Is there evidence available to support the claim?

There is evidence that hostility and heart disease are related, but scientists are still not sure about what causes the relationship. Some suggest that the risk of coronary heart disease and heart attack is elevated in hostile people because these people tend to be unusually reactive to stressors, especially when challenged. During interpersonal conflicts, for example, people predisposed to hostile behavior display not only overt hostility but also unusually large increases in blood pressure, heart rate, and other aspects of autonomic reactivity (Brondolo et al., 2003; Suls & Wan, 1993). In addition, it takes hostile individuals longer than normal to get back to their resting levels of autonomic functioning (Gerin et al., 2006). Like a driver who damages a car's engine by pressing the accelerator and applying the brakes at the same time, these "hot reactors" may create excessive wear and tear on the arteries of the heart as their increased heart rate forces blood through tightened vessels. Increased sympathetic nervous system activation not only puts stress on the coronary arteries but also leads to surges of stress-related hormones from the adrenal glands. High levels of these hormones are associated with increases in cholesterol and other fatty substances that are deposited in arteries and contribute to coronary heart disease (Bierhaus et al., 2003; Stoney & Hughes, 1999; Stoney, Bausserman, et al., 1999; Stoney, Niaura, et al., 1999). Cholesterol levels do appear to be elevated in the blood of hostile people (Dujovne & Houston, 1991; Engebretson & Stoney, 1995).

Hostility may affect heart disease risk less directly, as well, through its impact on social support. Some evidence suggests that hostile people get fewer benefits from their social support networks (Lepore, 1995). Failing to use this support—and possibly offending potential supporters in the process—may intensify the impact of stressful events on hostile people. The result may be increased anger, antagonism, and, ultimately, additional stress on the cardiovascular system.

■ Can that evidence be interpreted another way?

Studies suggesting that hostility causes coronary heart disease are not true experiments. Researchers cannot manipulate the independent variable by creating hostility in randomly selected people in order to assess its effects on heart health. Accordingly, we have to consider other possible explanations of the observed relationship between hostility and heart disease.

For example, some researchers suggest that higher rates of heart problems among hostile people are not due entirely to the impact of hostility on blood pressure, heart rate, and hormone surges. It may also be that a genetically determined tendency toward autonomic reactivity increases the likelihood of both hostility and heart disease (Cacioppo et al., 1998; Krantz et al., 1988). If this is the case, then the fact that hostility and coronary heart disease often appear in the same people might reflect not just the effects of hostility but also a third factor—autonomic reactivity—that contributes to both of them.

It has also been suggested that hostility may be only one of many traits linked to heart disease. Depressiveness, hopelessness, pessimism, anger, and anxiety may be involved, too (Frasure-Smith & Lespérance, 2005; Kubzansky, Davidson, & Rozanski, 2005; Nicholson, Fuhrer, & Marmot, 2005; Suls & Bunde, 2005).

■ What evidence would help to evaluate the alternatives?

Research on the role these other traits may play in heart disease will be vital, and that work is now under way. One way to test whether hostile people's higher rates of heart disease are related specifically to their hostility or to a more general tendency toward intense physiological arousal is to examine how these individuals react to stress when they are not angry. Some researchers have done this by observing the physiological reactions of hostile people during the stress of surgery. One study found that even under general anesthesia, such people show unusually strong autonomic reactivity (Krantz & Durel, 1983). Because these patients were not conscious, it appears that oversensitivity to stressors, not hostile thinking, caused their exaggerated stress responses. This possibility is supported by research showing that, compared with other people, individuals who have strong blood pressure responses to stressors also show different patterns of brain activity during stress (Gianaros et al., 2005).

■ What conclusions are most reasonable?

Most studies continue to find that hostile individuals are at greater risk for heart disease and heart attacks than other people (Krantz & McCeney, 2002; Stansfeld & Marmot, 2002). But the relationship between hostility and heart disease is probably more complex than any current theory suggests; it appears that many factors underlie this relationship.

A more elaborate psychobiological model may be required—one that takes into account that (1) some individuals may be biologically predisposed to react to stress with hostility and increased cardiovascular activity, each of which can contribute to heart disease; (2) hostile people help to create and maintain stressors through aggressive thoughts and actions, which can provoke others to be aggressive; and (3) hostile people are more likely than others to smoke, drink to excess, overeat, fail to exercise, and engage in other heart-damaging behaviors.

We must also keep in mind that the relationship between heart problems and hostility may not be universal. Although this relationship appears to hold for women, as well as men, and for individuals in various ethnic groups (e.g., Davidson, Hall, & MacGregor, 1996; Nakano & Kitamura, 2001; Olson et al., 2005; Powch & Houston, 1996; Yoshimasu et al., 2002), final conclusions must await further research that examines the relationship between hostility and heart disease in other cultures.

Promoting Healthy Behavior

▶ **Who is most likely to adopt a healthy lifestyle?**

Health psychologists are deeply involved in the development of smoking cessation programs, in campaigns to prevent young people from taking up smoking, in alcohol-education efforts, in the prevention of skin cancer through sun-safety education, and in the fight against the spread of HIV and AIDS (e.g., Buller, Buller, & Kane, 2005; Carey et al., 2004; Durantini et al, 2006; Latkin, Sherman, & Knowlton, 2003; Taylor, 2002). They have also helped promote early detection of disease. Encouraging women to perform breast self-examinations and men to do testicular self-examinations are just two examples of health psychology programs that can save thousands of lives each year (Taylor, 2002). Health psychologists have also explored the reasons behind some people's failure to follow doctors' orders that are vital to the control of diseases such as diabetes, heart disease, AIDS, and high blood pressure (Bartlett, 2002; Gonzalez et al., 2004). Understanding these reasons and finding ways to encourage better adherence to medical advice could speed recovery, prevent unnecessary suffering, and save many lives (Simpson et al., 2006).

Efforts to reduce, eliminate, or prevent behaviors that pose health risks and to encourage healthy behaviors are called **health promotion** (Smith, Orleans, & Jenkins, 2004). For example, health psychologists have developed programs that teach children as young as nine to engage in healthy behaviors and avoid health-risky behaviors. School systems now offer a variety of these programs, including those that give children and adolescents the skills necessary to turn down cigarettes, drugs, and unprotected sex. Health psychologists also go into workplaces and communities with the goal of helping people to adopt healthier lifestyles by altering diet, smoking, and exercise patterns. They teach stress-management techniques, too (Langenberg et al., 2000; Tuomilehto et al., 2001). These programs can create savings in future medical treatment costs (Blumenthal et al., 2002; Schneiderman et al., 2001) and better health for those who participate (Lisspers et al., 2005).

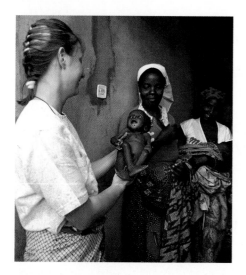

DOCTOR'S ORDERS Despite physicians' instructions, many patients fail to take their blood pressure medication and continue to eat an unhealthy diet. Non-compliance with medical advice is especially common when cultural values and beliefs conflict with that advice. Aware of this problem, health psychologists are developing culture-sensitive approaches to health promotion and disease prevention (Kazarian & Evans, 2001).

Health Beliefs and Health Behaviors

Health psychologists are also trying to understand the thought processes that lead people to engage in health-endangering behaviors and that can interfere with efforts to adopt healthier lifestyles (Klepp, Kelder, & Perry, 1995). Their research has led to intervention programs that seek to change these patterns of thinking, or at least take them into account. In one study, for example, women who avoid thinking about the risks of breast cancer were more likely to get a mammogram screening after receiving health information that was tailored to their cognitive styles (Williams-Piehota et al., 2005).

This cognitive approach to health psychology can be seen in various *health-belief models*. Irwin Rosenstock (1974) developed one of the most influential and extensively tested of these models (e.g., Aspinwall & Duran, 1999). He based his model on the assumption that people's decisions about health-related behaviors (such as smoking) are guided by four main factors:

1. Perceiving a *personal threat* of risk for getting a specific illness. (Do you believe that *you* will get lung cancer from smoking?)

2. Perceiving the seriousness of the illness and the consequences of having it. (How serious do you think lung cancer is? What will happen to you if you get it?)

3. Believing that changing a particular behavior will reduce the threat. (Will stopping smoking prevent you from getting lung cancer?)

4. A comparison of the *perceived costs* of changing a health-risky behavior and the *benefits expected* from making that change. (Will the reduced risk of getting cancer in the future be worth the discomfort and loss of pleasure from not smoking?)

health promotion The process of altering or eliminating behaviors that pose risks to health and, at the same time, fostering healthier behavior patterns.

© Reprinted by permission, Steve Kelley, *The Times-Picayune,* New Orleans.

As described in the chapter on thought, language, and intelligence, humans tend to underestimate the likelihood of common outcomes and to overestimate the likelihood of rare events. When this tendency causes people to ignore the dangers of smoking and other health-risky behaviors, the results can be disastrous.

According to this health-belief model, the people most likely to quit smoking would be those who believe that they are at risk for getting cancer from smoking, that cancer is serious and life threatening, and that the benefits of reducing cancer risks are greater than the costs of quitting (McCaul et al., 2006).

Other cognitive factors are emphasized in other health-belief models. For example, people generally do not try to quit smoking unless they believe they can succeed. So *self-efficacy,* the belief that you are able to perform some behavior, is an additional consideration in making decisions about health behaviors (Armitage, 2005; Bandura, 1992; Dijkstra, DeVries, & Bakker, 1996). A related factor is the *intention* to engage in a healthy behavior (Albarracin et al., 2001; Schwarzer, 2001; Webb & Sheeran, 2006).

Health-belief models have been useful in predicting a variety of health behaviors, including exercise (McAuley, 1992), safe-sex practices (Fisher, Fisher, & Rye, 1995), adherence to doctors' orders (Bond, Aiken, & Somerville, 1992), and having routine mammogram tests for breast cancer (Champion & Huster, 1995).

Changing Health Behaviors: Stages of Readiness

Changing health-related behaviors depends not only on a person's health beliefs but also on that person's readiness to change. According to James Prochaska and his colleagues, successful change occurs in five stages (Prochaska, DiClemente, & Norcross, 1992; Schumann et al., 2005):

1. *Precontemplation.*   The person does not perceive a health-related problem and has no intention of changing anytime soon.

┌ **T A B L E** **10.4**

Steps for Coping with Stress

Many successful programs for systematically coping with stress guide people through several steps and are aimed at removing stressors that can be changed and at reducing responses to stressors that cannot be changed (Taylor, 2002).

Step	Task
1. Assessment	Identify the sources and effects of stress.
2. Goal setting	List the stressors and stress responses to be addressed. Designate which stressors are and are not changeable.
3. Planning	List the specific steps to be taken to cope with stress.
4. Action	Implement coping plans.
5. Evaluation	Determine the changes in stressors and stress responses that have occurred as a result of coping methods.
6. Adjustment	Alter coping methods to improve results, if necessary.

TAKING TIME OUT The workplace is the number one source of stress for many people. On January 1, 2000, Raymond Fowler, who was then chief executive officer of the American Psychological Association, joined the ranks of those whose elevated blood pressure, heart problems, and other physical stress responses required a leave of absence from stressful jobs (Fowler, 2000). The National Institute for Occupational Safety and Health (1999) suggests a wide range of other behavioral coping options for stressed employees who cannot afford to take time off. You can view this advice online at http://www.cdc.gov/niosh/stresswk.html.

LINKAGES
How can people manage stress? (a link to Treatment of Psychology Disorders)

2. *Contemplation.* A problem behavior has been identified and the person is seriously thinking about changing it.

3. *Preparation.* The person has a strong intention to change and has made specific plans to do so.

4. *Action.* The person is engaging successfully in behavior change.

5. *Maintenance.* The healthy behavior has continued for at least six months, and the person is using newly learned skills to prevent relapse, or "backsliding."

The road from precontemplation through maintenance can be a bumpy one (Prochaska, 1994). Usually, people relapse and go through the stages repeatedly until they finally achieve stability in the healthy behavior they desire (Polivy & Herman, 2002). Smokers, for example, typically require three to four cycles through the stages over several years before they finally reach the maintenance stage (Piasecki, 2006).

Programs for Coping with Stress and Promoting Health

An important part of health psychologists' health promotion work has been to improve people's stress-coping skills (e.g., Keogh, Bond, & Flaxman, 2006). Let's consider a few specific procedures and programs associated with this effort.

Planning to Cope Just as people with extra money in the bank have a better chance of weathering a financial crisis, those with effective coping skills have a better chance of escaping some of the more harmful effects of intense stress. Like family money, the ability to handle stress appears to come naturally to some people, but coping strategies can also be learned. Programs for teaching these strategies include several stages, which are summarized in Table 10.4.

Bear in mind, though, that no single method of coping with stressors is right for everyone or every stressor. For example, denying the existence of an uncontrollable stressor may be fine in the short run but may lead to problems if no other coping method is used. Similarly, people who rely entirely on active, problem-focused coping might handle controllable stressors well but find themselves nearly helpless in the face of uncontrollable ones (Murray & Terry, 1999). The most successful stress managers may be those who can adjust their coping methods to the demands of changing situations and differing stressors (Taylor, 2002).

Developing Coping Strategies Strategies for coping with stress can be cognitive, emotional, behavioral, or physical. *Cognitive coping strategies* involve changing the way we think. These changes include thinking more calmly, rationally, and constructively in the face of stressors and may lead to a more hopeful emotional outlook. For example, students with heavy course loads may experience anxiety, confusion, discouragement, lack of motivation, and the desire to run away from it all. Frightening, catastrophizing thoughts (such as "What if I fail?") magnify these stress responses. Cognitive coping strategies replace catastrophic thinking with thoughts in which stressors are seen as challenges, not threats. This substitution process is called *cognitive restructuring* (Lazarus, 1971; Meichenbaum, 1977). It involves first identifying upsetting thoughts (such as "I'll never figure this out!") and then developing and practicing more constructive thoughts to use when under stress (such as "All I can do is the best I can"). Cognitive coping doesn't eliminate stressors, of course, but it can help us to perceive them as less threatening and therefore less disruptive (Antoni et al., 2000; Chesney et al., 2003).

Seeking and finding social support are effective *emotional coping strategies.* As mentioned earlier, feeling that you are cared about and valued by others can be an

DEALING WITH CHEMOTHERAPY
Progressive relaxation training involves briefly tensing groups of muscles throughout the body, one at a time, then releasing the tension and focusing on the resulting feelings of relaxation. It can be used to ease a variety of health-related problems, including the anxiety, physiological arousal, and nausea associated with cancer chemotherapy (Bernstein, Borkovec, & Hazlette-Stevens, 2000).

effective buffer against the ill effects of stressors, leading to enhanced immune functioning (Kiecolt-Glaser & Newton, 2001) and quicker recovery from illness (Taylor, 2002).

Behavioral coping strategies involve changing behavior in order to minimize the negative impact of stressors. Time management is one example. If it seems that you are always pressed for time, consider developing a time management plan. The first step is to use a calendar or day planner to record how you spend each hour of each day in a typical week. Next, analyze the information to locate when and how you might be wasting time and how you might use your time more efficiently. Then set out a schedule for the coming week and stick to it. Make adjustments in subsequent weeks as you learn more realistic ways to manage your time. Time management can't create more time, but it can help control catastrophizing thoughts by providing reassurance that there is enough time for everything and a plan for handling everything you have to do.

Physical coping strategies can be used to alter the undesirable physical responses that occur before, during, or after the appearance of stressors. The most common physical coping strategy is some form of drug use. Prescription medications are sometimes an appropriate coping aid, especially when stressors are severe and acute, such as the sudden death of one's child. However, people who rely on prescribed or nonprescription drugs, including alcohol, to help them face stressors may come to believe that their coping success is due to the drug, not to their own skill. This belief can make people more and more psychologically dependent on the drug. Furthermore, the drug effects that blunt stress responses may also interfere with the ability to apply coping strategies. The resulting loss of perceived control over stressors may make those stressors even more threatening and disruptive.

Nonchemical methods of reducing physical stress reactions and improving stress coping include progressive relaxation training (Bernstein, Borkovec, & Hazlette-Stevens, 2000; Scheufele, 2000), physical exercise (Anshel, 1996), biofeedback (Sarafino & Goehring, 2000), and meditation and tai chi (Carlson et al., 2003; Davidson et al., 2003; Li et al., 2001), among others (Taylor, 2002).

"In Review: Methods for Coping with Stress" summarizes our discussion of stress-coping methods.

in review

METHODS FOR COPING WITH STRESS

Type of Coping Method	Examples
Cognitive	Thinking of stressors as challenges rather than as threats; avoiding perfectionism
Emotional	Seeking social support; getting advice
Behavioral	Implementing a time-management plan; where possible, making life changes to eliminate stressors
Physical	Progressive relaxation training; exercise; meditation

1. Catastrophizing thoughts are best overcome through _____ coping strategies.
2. The first step in coping with stress is to _____ the sources and effects of your stressors.
3. True or false: It is best to rely on only one good coping strategy. _____

| Health, Stress, and Coping

Linkages

As noted in the introductory chapter, all of psychology's subfields are related to one another. Our discussion of how stressors can lead to the development of mental disorders illustrates just one way in which the topic of this chapter, health, stress, and coping, is linked to the subfield of abnormal psychology, which is described in the chapter on psychological disorders. The Linkages diagram shows ties to two other subfields, and there are many more ties throughout the book. Looking for linkages among subfields will help you see how they all fit together and help you better appreciate the big picture that is psychology.

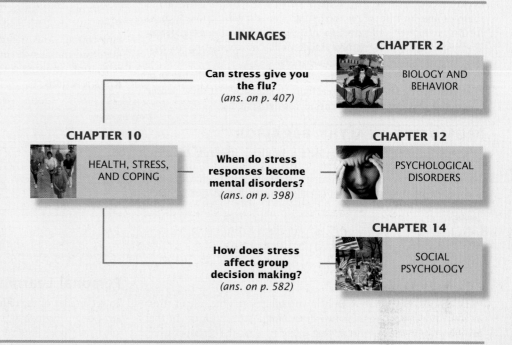

LINKAGES

CHAPTER 10

HEALTH, STRESS, AND COPING

Can stress give you the flu?
(ans. on p. 407)

CHAPTER 2

BIOLOGY AND BEHAVIOR

When do stress responses become mental disorders?
(ans. on p. 398)

CHAPTER 12

PSYCHOLOGICAL DISORDERS

How does stress affect group decision making?
(ans. on p. 582)

CHAPTER 14

SOCIAL PSYCHOLOGY

Summary

HEALTH PSYCHOLOGY

▶ **What do health psychologists do?**

The development of **health psychology** was prompted by recognition of the link between stress and illness and of the role of behaviors such as smoking in increasing the risk of illness. Health psychologists work to understand how psychological factors are related to physical disease and to help people behave in ways that prevent or minimize disease and promote health.

UNDERSTANDING STRESS AND STRESSORS

▶ **How do psychological stressors affect physical health?**

The term **stress** refers in part to **stressors,** which are physical or psychological events and situations to which people must adjust. The term is also used to refer to **stress reactions.** Most generally, however, stress is viewed as an ongoing, interactive process that takes place as people adjust to, and cope with, their environment. Psychological stressors include catastrophic events, life changes and strains, chronic stressors, and daily hassles. Stressors can be measured by tests such as the Social Readjustment Rating Scale (SRRS) and the Life Experiences Survey (LES), but scores on such tests provide only a partial picture of the stress in a person's life.

STRESS RESPONSES

▶ **How do people react to stressors?**

Responses to stressors can be physical and psychological. These stress responses can occur alone or in combination, and the appearance of one can often stimulate others.

Physical stress responses include changes in heart rate, respiration, and many other processes that are part of a pattern known as the **general adaptation syndrome,** or **GAS.** The GAS has three stages: alarm reaction, resistance, and exhaustion. The GAS helps people resist stress but, if activated for too long, it can lead to impairment of immune system functions, as well as to physical illnesses, which Selye called **diseases of adaptation.**

Psychological stress responses can be emotional, cognitive, and behavioral. Anxiety, anger, and depression are among the most common emotional stress reactions. Cognitive stress reactions include ruminative thinking; catastrophizing; and disruptions in the ability to think clearly, remember accurately, and solve problems efficiently. Behavioral stress responses include irritability, aggression, absenteeism, health-risky behaviors, and even suicide attempts. Severe or long-lasting stressors can lead to **burnout** or to psychological disorders such as **posttraumatic stress disorder (PTSD).**

STRESS MEDIATORS

▶ **Why doesn't everyone react to stressors in the same way?**

The key to understanding stress appears to lie in observing the interaction of specific stressors with particular people. Stressors are likely to have greater impact if they are perceived as threats or if they are unpredictable, uncontrollable, or unmanageable. The people most likely to react strongly to a stressor are those whose coping resources, coping methods, and **social support networks** are inadequate or perceived as inadequate.

THE PHYSIOLOGY AND PSYCHOLOGY OF HEALTH AND ILLNESS

▶ **How does stress affect your immune system?**

Psychoneuroimmunology is the field that examines the interaction of psychological and physiological processes that affect the body's ability to defend itself against disease. When a person is under stress, some of the hormones released from the adrenal glands, such as cortisol, reduce the effectiveness of the cells of the *immune system* (T-cells, B-cells, and natural killer cells) in combating foreign invaders, such as viruses and cancer cells.

People who are hostile appear at greater risk for heart disease than other people. The heightened reactivity to stressors that these people experience may damage their cardiovascular systems.

PROMOTING HEALTHY BEHAVIOR

▶ **Who is most likely to adopt a healthy lifestyle?**

The process of altering or eliminating health-risky behaviors and encouraging healthy behaviors is called *health promotion.* People's health-related behaviors are partly guided by their beliefs about health risks and what they can do about them.

The process of changing health-related behaviors appears to involve several stages, including precontemplation, contemplation, preparation, action, and maintenance. Understanding which stage people are in and helping them move through these stages is an important task in health psychology.

To cope with stress, people must identify the stressors affecting them and develop a plan for coping with these stressors. Important coping skills include cognitive restructuring, acting to minimize the number or intensity of stressors, and using progressive relaxation training and other techniques for reducing physical stress reactions.

Learn by Doing

Put It in Writing

What is stress like for you? To help you understand the role of stress in your life, write a page or two describing a stressful incident that you had to face in the recent past. Identify what the stressors were, and classify each of them as physical or psychological. List your physical, emotional, cognitive, and behavioral responses to these stressors, and how long the responses lasted. Include a brief summary of how you coped with these stressors and how successful your coping efforts were. Some research suggests that writing about stressful experiences can help people to deal with those experiences. Did this writing project have any such benefits for you? For more about writing and health, visit http://homepage.psy.utexas.edu/homepage/faculty/pennebaker/Home2000/WritingandHealth.html

Personal Learning Activity

To get an idea of the differences in people's stress-coping methods, create a one-paragraph story about a stressful situation (such as losing a job, having one's home destroyed by fire, working for an obnoxious boss, or being overburdened by schoolwork). Now show this description to ten people and ask each of them to tell you how they would cope with the situation if it happened to them. Classify each of their coping methods as problem focused or emotion focused. Did you notice any relationships between the kind of coping responses these people chose and their personal characteristics, such as age, gender, ethnicity, or experience with stress? If so, why do you think those relationships appeared? *For additional projects, see the Personal Learning Activities in the corresponding chapter of the study guide that accompanies this text.*

Step into Action

Courses

Biological Psychology
Health Psychology
Stress Management
Stress and Coping

Movies

Black Hawk Down. General adaptation syndrome.
Falling Down; *All That Jazz*; *Girlhood.* Behavioral stress responses.
The Deer Hunter. Posttraumatic stress disorder.
Do the Right Thing. Social support networks.
Women on the Verge of a Nervous Breakdown. Impact of a sudden stressor.
Glengarry Glen Ross; *The Paper.* Effects of stress in the workplace.
Angela's Ashes. Impact of stress on development.

Saving Private Ryan. Individual differences in responses to traumatic stress.

Books

David J. Mahoney, *The Longevity Strategy: How to Live to 100 Using the Brain-Body Connection* (Wiley, 1998). The origins of longevity.
Lance Armstrong and Sally Jenkins, *It's Not About the Bike: My Journey Back to Life* (Berkley Books, 2001). Armstrong focuses on the origins of his survival of a deadly form of cancer.
Lewis B. Puller, *Fortunate Son* (Bantam, 1996). Son of a famous Marine deals with posttraumatic stress and multiple amputations after the Vietnam War.
Richard Sorrentino and Christopher Roney, *The Uncertain Mind: Individual Differences in Facing the Unknown* (Psychology Press, 2000). Discusses the impact of uncertainty on physical and mental health.

Tony Cassidy, *Stress, Cognition, and Health* (Routledge, 1999). Summarizes research on the effects of stress on thinking and physical well-being.

Jerrold Greenberg, *Comprehensive Stress Management* (McGraw-Hill, 1999). Ideas for stress management.

Robert M. Sapolsky, *Why Zebras Don't Get Ulcers* (Owl Books, 2004). Describes the stress process, stress-related diseases, and coping skills.

James W. Pennebaker, *Opening Up: The Healing Power of Expressing Emotions* (Guilford, 1997). Describes research on the benefits of self-disclosure.

The Web

The World Wide Web is a good source of additional information about the science of psychology, provided you use it carefully and think critically about the information you find. The Online Study Center that accompanies this text offers many resources relevant to this chapter. These resources include interactive tutorials; Thinking Critically and Evaluating Research exercises; ACE chapter quizzes; recommended web links; and articles on current events, books, and movies. Please visit the Online Study Center at college.hmco.com/pic/bernsteinessentials4e.

Review of Key Terms

Can you define each of the key terms in the chapter? Check your definitions against those on the pages shown in parentheses in the following list or in the Glossary/Index at the end of the text.

burnout *(p. 398)*

diseases of adaptation *(p. 396)*

general adaptation syndrome (GAS) *(p. 395)*

health promotion *(p. 411)*

health psychology *(p. 390)*

immune system *(p. 407)*

posttraumatic stress disorder (PTSD) *(p. 398)*

psychoneuroimmunology *(p. 407)*

social support network *(p. 402)*

stress *(p. 391)*

stress reactions *(p. 391)*

stressors *(p. 391)*

Multiple-Choice Self-Test

Select the best answer for each of the following questions. Then check your response against the Answer Key at the end of the text.

1. Health research statistics show that your great-grandparents' generation was most likely to die from _____ diseases, whereas your own generation is most likely to die from _____ diseases.

   a. infectious; infectious
   b. chronic; chronic
   c. infectious; chronic
   d. chronic; infectious

2. Stephanie married a wonderful guy, moved to a new city, and took a great new job, all in the same month. We would expect her to

   a. display physical and/or psychological stress responses.
   b. experience little stress, because these are all desirable changes.
   c. experience little stress, because these are not chronic stressors.
   d. experience physical stress responses only.

3. Doug lives next to a family that includes several teenagers. He is forever reminding them not to run across his front lawn; their loud music often keeps him awake at night; and their cars are parked so that it is hard for him to back out of his driveway. These stressors can best be classified as

   a. life changes and strains.   c. catastrophic.
   b. traumatic.   d. daily hassles.

4. Aaron's sympathetic nervous system is engaged in the fight-or-flight syndrome. Which stage of the general adaptation syndrome (GAS) is he experiencing?

   a. Alarm
   b. Resistance
   c. Exhaustion
   d. Precontemplative

5. Bill and Ellen's car breaks down and it takes two hours for help to arrive. According to Shelley Taylor's research on stress and gender, Bill is likely to _____, and Ellen is likely to _____.

   a. get angry; get angry, too
   b. be supportive of Ellen; be supportive of Bill
   c. get angry; seek and offer support
   d. seek and offer support; get angry

6. Enrico finds that, no matter what else he is doing, he can't stop thinking about all the stressful events in his life. Enrico is experiencing

   a. catastrophizing.
   b. ruminative thinking.
   c. functional fixedness.
   d. cognitive restructuring.

7. Caitlin just failed her high school math test. She says to herself, "Mom is going to be furious with me! She will probably ground me, which means I won't be able to go to the prom. If I don't go to the prom, I will be a social outcast, and no one will talk to me. I'll never have any friends or find a partner, and no one will ever love me!" This is an example of

   a. cognitive restructuring.
   b. catastrophizing.
   c. posttraumatic stress disorder.
   d. the fight-or-flight syndrome.

8. Dr. Zarro finds that one of her patients, Juan, has a disease-resistant personality. This means that Juan is likely to

   a. ignore his stressors.
   b. be optimistic.
   c. blame himself for his stressors.
   d. ruminate about his stressors.

9. Shane, a veteran, occasionally experiences flashbacks involving vivid recollections of his wartime experiences. Flashbacks are associated with

   a. generalized anxiety disorder.
   b. posttraumatic stress disorder.
   c. the general adaptation syndrome.
   d. the fight-or-flight syndrome.

10. When Robin finds out he didn't get the promotion he had been hoping for, he tries to laugh it off. He goes out with friends and jokingly tells them that it is all for the best, because the promotion would have forced him to buy a lot of new clothes. Robin is using _____ coping strategies.

    a. problem-focused   c. social-focused
    b. emotion-focused   d. posttraumatic

11. Postsurgery patients who are allowed to adjust their own levels of pain medication tend to use less medication than patients who must ask for it. This phenomenon is consistent with research showing that

    a. social support can mediate stress.
    b. predictable stressors are easier to manage.
    c. the perception of control reduces the impact of stressors.
    d. thinking of stressors as threats amplifies their effects.

12. Laton, the head of human resources at his company, knows that the employees have stressful jobs. He schedules group picnics and lunches to help employees get better acquainted. Laton is trying to ease the employees' stressors by

    a. promoting cognitive restructuring.
    b. improving social support networks.
    c. increasing employees' sense of control.
    d. helping employees think of their stressors as challenges rather than threats.

13. In the Focus on Research section of this chapter, on the relationship between personality and life expectancy, the researchers found

    a. no relationship between the two.
    b. that conscientiousness was associated with longer life.
    c. that social relationships had no impact on longevity.
    d. that impulsiveness was associated with longer life.

14. Porter has a flu virus. Research on the immune system shows that Porter's _____ will be working to fight off this virus.

    a. B-cells
    b. T-cells
    c. natural killer cells
    d. macrophages

15. Fred is at high risk for coronary heart disease. As his friend, you tell him that current research suggests that he could lower his risk if he

    a. takes up fishing as a hobby.
    b. works at being less hostile.
    c. reduces his workload.
    d. restructures his thinking about stress.

16. When Larry finds out that he has arthritis, an autoimmune disease, he is very upset. His stress reactions are likely to be reduced *most* if Larry

    a. goes to a spa to try to ignore the situation.
    b. keeps his worries to himself.
    c. focuses all his attention on worrying about his medical condition.
    d. joins an arthritis support group.

17. According to Rosenstock's health-belief model, which of the following would *most* help Bridgit decide to quit smoking?

    a. Perceiving a personal threat of getting cancer from her smoking
    b. Knowing that smoking causes cancer
    c. Knowing that quitting can lower people's risk of cancer
    d. Carefully reading the statistics on smoking and health in general

18. Amanda is severely overweight. She knows that, for her health's sake, she needs to limit her caloric intake, but she loves to eat and has made no specific plans to go on a diet. Amanda is at the _____ stage of readiness to change a health-risky behavior.

    a. precontemplation
    b. contemplation
    c. preparation
    d. maintenance

19. Sayumi is trying to control her stress. In response to a hurtful comment from a friend, Sayumi thinks to herself, "Don't jump to conclusions; he probably didn't mean it the way it sounded," instead of "That jerk! Who does he think he is?" Sayumi is using the coping strategy of

    a. cognitive restructuring.
    b. emotional restructuring.
    c. catastrophizing.
    d. contemplation.

20. Loretta, a marriage counselor, finds her job very stressful. She has found that physical coping strategies help her the most. This means that Loretta most likely

    a. constantly reminds herself about the good she is doing.
    b. organizes a support group for therapists.
    c. practices progressive relaxation every evening.
    d. works on her time-management plan.

11

Personality

If you have ever been stuck in heavy traffic, you have probably noticed

differences in how drivers deal with the situation. Some are tolerant and calm; others become so cautious that they worsen the congestion; still others react with such impatience and anger that they may trigger a shouting match or cause an accident. Variations in how people handle traffic jams and other frustrating situations reflect just one aspect of their *personality*—the consistent patterns of thinking, feeling, and behaving that make each person different from, and in some ways similar to, others. In this chapter, we examine four views of personality and review some of the personality tests that psychologists have developed to measure and compare people's personalities. We also describe some of the ways in which personality theory and research are being applied in areas such as diagnosing mental disorders and screening potential employees.

Reading this chapter will help you to answer the following questions:

▶ **How did paralyzed patients lead Freud to psychoanalysis? 421**

▶ **What personality traits are most basic? 426**

▶ **Do we learn our personalities? 433**

▶ **Is everyone basically good? 436**

▶ **How do psychologists measure personality? 443**

personality   The pattern of psychological and behavioral characteristics by which each person can be compared and contrasted with other people.

psychodynamic approach   A view developed by Freud that emphasizes unconscious mental processes in explaining human thought, feelings, and behavior.

id   According to Freud, a personality component containing basic instincts, desires, and impulses with which all people are born.

pleasure principle   The operating principle of the id, which guides people toward whatever feels good.

ego   According to Freud, the part of the personality that makes compromises and mediates conflicts between and among the demands of the id, the superego, and the real world.

reality principle   The operating principle of the ego, which takes into account the constraints of the social world.

learn by doing

Take out your wallet, look through it, and select the four most important things you carry with you. One person we know picked a driver's license, a credit card, a friend's phone number, and a witty prediction from a fortune cookie. The driver's license describes his physical traits. The credit card represents information about his buying history and responsibility in paying debts. His friends provide support, affection, and intimacy. And the fortune cookie prediction says something about his wishes, beliefs, or hopes. In other words, the selected items form a crude personality sketch.

There is no universally accepted definition, but psychologists generally view **personality** as the unique pattern of enduring thoughts, feelings, and actions that characterize a person. Personality research, in turn, seeks to understand how and why our consistent patterns of thinking, emotion, and behavior make each of us different in some ways and alike in others.

To gain a full understanding of just one individual's personality, a researcher would have to learn about many things, including the person's developmental experiences and cultural influences, genetic and other biological characteristics, perceptual and other information-processing habits and biases, typical patterns of emotional expression, and social skills. Psychologists also want to know about personality in general, such as how it develops and changes across the life span. They ask why some people are usually

FOUNDER OF THE PSYCHOANALYTIC APPROACH Here is Sigmund Freud with his daughter, Anna, who became a psychoanalyst herself and eventually developed a revised version of her father's theories.

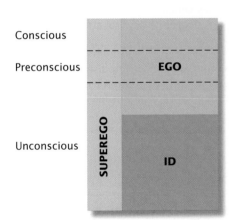

Source: Adapted from Liebert & Spiegler (1994).

FIGURE **11.1**

A Freudian View of Personality Structure

According to Freud, some parts of the personality are conscious, whereas others are unconscious. Between these levels is the *preconscious*, which Freud saw as the home of memories and other material that we are not usually aware of but that we can easily bring into consciousness.

optimistic, whereas others are usually pessimistic, and whether people respond consistently or inconsistently from one situation to the next.

The specific questions psychologists ask and the methods they use to investigate personality often depend on which of the four main approaches to personality they take. These four are known as the *psychodynamic, trait, social-cognitive,* and *humanistic* approaches.

The Psychodynamic Approach

► **How did paralyzed patients lead Freud to psychoanalysis?**

Some people think that personality reveals itself in behavior alone. A person with an "obnoxious personality," for example, shows it by acting obnoxiously. But is that all there is to personality? Not according to Sigmund Freud. As a physician in Vienna, Austria, during the 1890s, Freud specialized in treating "neurotic" disorders, such as blindness or paralysis, for which there was no physical cause and that hypnosis could often remove. One patient sleepwalked on legs that were paralyzed during the day. These cases led Freud to believe in *psychic determinism,* the idea that personality and behavior are determined more by psychological factors than by biological conditions or current events (Allen, 2006). He proposed that people may not know why they feel, think, or act the way they do because they are partly controlled by the unconscious portion of the personality—the part of which people are normally unaware (Funder, 2004). From these ideas Freud created *psychoanalysis,* a theory of personality and a way of treating mental disorders. Freud's theory became the basis of the **psychodynamic approach** to personality, which assumes that various unconscious psychological processes interact to determine our thoughts, feelings, and behavior (Schultz & Schultz, 2005).

The Structure of Personality

Freud believed that people are born with basic needs or instincts—not only for food and water but also for sex and aggression. He believed that needs for love, knowledge, security, and the like arise from these more fundamental desires. He said that each of us has to find ways of meeting our needs in a world that often frustrates our efforts. Our personalities develop, said Freud, as we struggle with this task and are reflected in the way we satisfy a wide range of urges.

Id, Ego, and Superego Freud described the personality as having three major components: the id, the ego, and the superego (Allen, 2006; see Figure 11.1). The **id** represents the inborn, unconscious portion of the personality where life and death instincts reside. The *life instincts* promote positive, constructive behavior; the *death instincts* are responsible for human aggression and destructiveness (Carver & Scheier, 2004). The id operates on the **pleasure principle,** seeking immediate satisfaction of both kinds of instincts, regardless of society's rules or the rights and feelings of others. The hungry person who pushes to the front of the line at Burger King would be satisfying an id-driven impulse.

As parents, teachers, and others place ever greater restrictions on the expression of id impulses, a second part of the personality, called the *ego* (or "self"), emerges from the id. The **ego** is responsible for organizing ways to get what a person wants in the real world, as opposed to the fantasy world of the id. Operating on the **reality principle,** the ego makes compromises as the id's demands for immediate satisfaction run into the practical realities of the social world. The ego would influence that hungry person at Burger King to wait in line and think about what to order rather than risk punishment by pushing ahead.

As children gain experience with the rules and values of society, they tend to adopt them. This process of *internalizing* parental and cultural values creates the third

TABLE 11.1

Ego Defense Mechanisms

learn by doing According to Freud, defense mechanisms prevent anxiety or guilt in the short run, but they sap energy. Further, using them to avoid dealing with the source of problems can make those problems worse in the long run. Try listing some incidents in which you or someone you know might have used each of the defenses described here. What questions would a critical thinker ask to determine whether these behaviors were unconscious defense mechanisms or actions motivated by conscious intentions?

Defense Mechanism	Description
Repression	Unconsciously pushing threatening memories, urges, or ideas from conscious awareness: A person may experience loss of memory for unpleasant events.
Rationalization	Attempting to make actions or mistakes seem reasonable: The reasons or excuses given (e.g., "I spank my children because it is good for them") sound rational, but they are not the real reasons for the behavior.
Projection	Unconsciously attributing one's own unacceptable thoughts or impulses to another person: Instead of recognizing that "I hate him," a person may feel that "He hates me."
Reaction formation	Defending against unacceptable impulses by acting opposite to them: Sexual interest in a married co-worker might appear as strong dislike instead.
Sublimation	Converting unacceptable impulses into socially acceptable actions, and perhaps symbolically expressing them: Sexual or aggressive desires may appear as artistic creativity or devotion to athletic excellence.
Displacement	Deflecting an impulse from its original target to a less threatening one: Anger at one's boss may be expressed through hostility toward a clerk, a family member, or even the dog.
Denial	Simply discounting the existence of threatening impulses: A person may vehemently deny ever having had even the slightest degree of physical attraction to a person of the same sex.
Compensation	Striving to make up for unconscious impulses or fears: A business executive's extreme competitiveness might be aimed at compensating for unconscious feelings of inferiority.

superego According to Freud, the component of personality that tells people what they should and should not do.

defense mechanisms Unconscious tactics that either prevent threatening material from surfacing or disguise it when it does.

psychosexual stages In Freud's psychodynamic theory, periods of personality development in which internal and external conflicts focus on particular issues.

oral stage The first of Freud's psychosexual stages, occurring during the first year of life, in which the mouth is the center of pleasure.

anal stage The second of Freud's psychosexual stages, occurring during the second year of life, in which the focus of pleasure shifts from the mouth to the anus.

phallic stage The third of Freud's psychosexual stages, lasting from approximately ages three to five, in which the focus of pleasure shifts to the genital area.

Oedipus complex The notion that young boys' impulses involve sexual feelings for the mother and the desire to eliminate the father.

Electra complex The notion that young girls develop an attachment to the father and compete with the mother for the father's attention.

component of personality. It is called the **superego,** and it tells us what we should and should not do. The superego becomes our moral guide, and it is just as relentless and unreasonable as the id in its demands to be obeyed. The superego would make the person at Burger King feel guilty for even thinking about violating culturally approved rules about waiting in line.

Conflicts and Defenses Freud described the inner clashes among id, ego, and superego as *intrapsychic,* or *psychodynamic, conflicts.* He believed that each individual's personality is shaped by the number, nature, and outcome of these conflicts. Freud said that the ego's main job is to prevent the anxiety or guilt that would arise if we became conscious of socially unacceptable id impulses, especially those that would violate the superego's rules (Engler, 2003). Sometimes, the ego guides sensible actions, as when a parent asks for help because of impulses to abuse a child. However, the ego also uses **defense mechanisms,** which are unconscious tactics that protect against anxiety and guilt by either preventing threatening material from surfacing or disguising it when it does (Porcerelli et al., 2004; see Table 11.1).

Which of Freud's ego defense mechanisms is operating here? (Check the answer at the bottom of page 424.)

© Scott Adams/Dist. By United Feature Syndicate, Inc.

Stages of Personality Development

Freud proposed that personality develops during childhood through a series of **psychosexual stages.** Failure to resolve the conflicts that appear at any of these stages can leave a person *fixated*—that is, unconsciously preoccupied with the area of pleasure associated with that stage. Freud believed that the stage at which a person became fixated in childhood can be seen in the person's adult personality characteristics.

The Oral Stage   In Freud's theory, a child's first year or so is called the **oral stage** because the mouth—which infants use to eat and to explore everything from toys to their own hands and feet—is the center of pleasure during this period. Personality problems arise, said Freud, when oral needs are either neglected or overindulged. For example, early or late weaning from breastfeeding or bottle feeding may leave a child fixated at the oral stage. The resulting adult characteristics may range from overeating or childlike dependence (late weaning) to the use of "biting" sarcasm (early weaning).

The Anal Stage   The **anal stage** occurs during the second year, when the child's ego develops to cope with parental demands for socially appropriate behavior. For example, in most Western cultures, toilet training clashes with the child's freedom to have bowel movements at will. Freud said that if toilet training is too harsh or begins too early, it can produce an anal fixation that leads, in adulthood, to stinginess or excessive neatness (symbolically withholding feces). If toilet training is too late or too lax, however, the result could be a kind of anal fixation that is reflected in adults who are disorganized or impulsive (symbolically expelling feces).

The Phallic Stage   According to Freud, between the ages of three and five, the focus of pleasure shifts to the genital area. Because he emphasized the psychosexual development of boys, Freud called this period the **phallic stage** (*phallus* is another word for penis). It is during this stage, he claimed, that the boy experiences sexual feelings for his mother and a desire to eliminate, or even kill, his father, with whom the boy competes for the mother's affection. Freud called this set of impulses the **Oedipus complex,** because it reminded him of the plot of the classical Greek play *Oedipus Rex.* (In the play, Oedipus unknowingly kills his father and marries his mother.) The boy's fantasies create so much fear, however, that the ego represses his incestuous desires and leads him to "identify" with his father and try to be like him. In the process, the child's superego begins to develop.

According to Freud, a girl begins the phallic stage with a strong attachment to her mother. However, when she realizes that boys have penises and girls don't, she supposedly develops *penis envy* and transfers her love to the father. (This sequence has been called the **Electra complex** because it echoes the plot of *Electra,* another classical Greek play, but Freud never used this term.) To avoid her mother's disapproval, the girl identifies with and imitates her, thus forming the basis for her own superego.

Freud believed that unresolved conflicts during the phallic stage create a fixation that is reflected in many kinds of adult problems. These problems can include difficulties with authority figures and an inability to maintain a stable love relationship.

THE ORAL STAGE   According to Freud, personality develops in a series of psychosexual stages. At each stage, a different part of the body becomes the primary focus of pleasure. This baby would appear to be in the oral stage.

The Latency Period   As the phallic stage draws to a close and its conflicts are coped with by the ego, there is an interval of psychological peace. During this **latency period,** which lasts through childhood, sexual impulses stay in the background as the youngster focuses on education, same-sex peer play, and the development of social skills.

The Genital Stage   During adolescence, when sexual impulses reappear at the conscious level, the genitals again become the focus of pleasure. Thus begins what Freud called the **genital stage,** which lasts for the rest of the person's life. The quality of relationships and the degree of fulfillment experienced during this final stage, he claimed, are influenced by how intrapsychic conflicts were resolved during the earlier stages.

Variations on Freud's Personality Theory

Freud's ideas—especially those concerning infantile sexuality and the Oedipus complex—were, and still are, controversial. Even many of Freud's followers did not entirely agree with him. Some of these followers are known as *neo-Freudian* theorists, because they maintained many of the basic ideas in Freud's theory but developed their own approaches. Others are known as *ego-psychologists,* because their theories focus more on the ego than on the id (Larsen & Buss, 2005).

Jung's Analytic Psychology   Carl Jung (pronounced "yoong") was the most prominent of Freud's early followers to chart his own theoretical course. Jung (1916) argued that people are born with a general life force that, in addition to a sex drive, includes a drive for creativity, for growth-oriented resolution of conflicts, and for the productive blending of basic impulses with real-world demands. Jung did not identify specific stages in personality development. He suggested instead that people gradually develop differing degrees of *introversion* (a tendency to reflect on one's own experiences) or *extraversion* (a tendency to focus on the social world), along with differing tendencies to rely on specific psychological functions, such as thinking or feeling. The combination of these tendencies and functions, said Jung (1933), creates personalities that show distinctive and predictable patterns of behavior.

Other Neo-Freudian Theorists   Alfred Adler, once a loyal follower of psychoanalysis, came to believe that the power behind the development of personality comes not from id impulses but from an innate desire to overcome infantile feelings of helplessness and gain some control over the environment. Other prominent neo-Freudians emphasized social relationships in the development of personality. Some, including Erik Erikson, Erich Fromm, and Harry Stack Sullivan, argued that once biological needs are met, the attempt to meet social needs (to feel protected, secure, and accepted, for example) is the main force that shapes personality. According to these theorists, the strategies that people use to meet social needs, such as dominating other people or being dependent on them, become core features of their personalities.

The first feminist personality theorist, Karen Horney (pronounced "horn-eye"), challenged Freud's view that women's lack of a penis causes them to envy men and feel inferior to them. Horney (1937) argued that it is men who envy women. Realizing that they cannot bear children, males see their lives as having less meaning and substance than women's. Horney called this condition *womb envy.* She believed that when women feel inferior, it is because of cultural factors—such as the personal and political restrictions that men have placed on them—not because of penis envy (Larsen & Buss, 2005).

Contemporary Psychodynamic Theories

Today, some of the most influential psychodynamic approaches to personality focus on *object relations*—that is, on how early relationships, particularly with their parents, affect how people perceive and relate to other people later in life (Pervin, Cervone, &

latency period   The fourth of Freud's psychosexual stages, usually beginning during the fifth year of life, in which sexual impulses become dormant and the child focuses on education and other matters.

genital stage   The fifth and last of Freud's psychosexual stages, which begins during adolescence, when sexual impulses begin to appear at the conscious level.

The defense mechanism illustrated in the cartoon on page 423 is displacement.

John, 2005) According to object relations theorists, early relationships between infants and their love objects (usually the mother and other primary caregivers) are vital influences on the development of personality (Greenberg & Mitchell, 1983; Klein, 1975; Kohut, 1984; Sohlberg & Jansson, 2002). These relationships, they say, shape our thoughts and feelings about social relationships in later life.

A close cousin of object relations theory is called *attachment theory* because it focuses specifically on the early attachment process that we describe in the chapter on human development. Ideally, infants form a secure bond, or attachment, to their mothers, gradually tolerate separation from this "attachment object," and eventually develop the ability to relate to others as independent, secure individuals (Ainsworth & Bowlby, 1991). Attachment theorists have studied how variations in the nature of this early bond are related to differences in self-image, identity, security, and social relationships in adolescence, adulthood, and even old age (Consedine & Magai, 2003; Shaver & Mikulincer, 2005). In one study, women who had been securely attached in childhood were more likely to have happy marriages than women whose childhood attachments had been insecure (Klohnen & Bera, 1998). Another study found that people with insecure attachments were less likely to be helpful when they encountered a person in distress (Mikulincer & Shaver, 2005). Still other research suggests that children who, because of abuse, neglect, or rejection, miss the opportunity to become securely attached may suffer severe disturbances in their later relationships (Aizawa, 2002).

Evaluating the Psychodynamic Approach

Freud's personality theory is probably the most comprehensive and influential psychological theory ever proposed. His ideas have shaped a wide range of psychotherapy techniques (see the chapter on treatment of psychological disorders) and stimulated the development of several personality assessments, including the projective tests described later in this chapter. Some of Freud's ideas have received support from research on cognitive processes (Andersen & Chen, 2002). It appears, for example, that people employ several of the defense mechanisms Freud described (Cramer, 2003), although these may not always operate at an unconscious level. There is also evidence that our thoughts and actions can be influenced by events and experiences that we don't recall (Andersen & Chen, 2002; Andersen & Miranda, 2000; Ferguson & Bargh, 2004) and possibly by emotions we don't consciously experience (Winkielman & Berridge, 2004).

However, Freud's theories have several weaknesses. For one thing, his conclusions about personality are based almost entirely on case studies of a few individuals. As discussed in the introductory chapter, conclusions drawn from case studies may not apply to people in general. Freud's sample of cases was certainly not representative of people in general. Most of his patients were upper-class Viennese women who not only had psychological problems but also were raised in a society that considered the discussion of sex to be uncivilized. Second, Freud's theory reflected Western European and North American cultural values, which may or may not be helpful in understanding people in other cultures (Feist & Feist, 2002). For example, the concepts of ego and self that are so central to Freud's personality theory are based on the self-oriented values of individualist cultures and thus may be less descriptive of personality development in collectivist cultures, such as those of Asia and South America (Matsumoto, 2000).

Freud's conclusions may have been distorted by other biases as well. Some Freud scholars believe he might have (perhaps unconsciously) modified reports of what happened during therapy to better fit his theory (Esterson, 2001; Powell & Boer, 1995; Schultz & Schultz, 2005). He may also have asked leading questions that influenced patients to "recall" events from their childhoods that never happened (Esterson, 2001). Today, as described in the memory chapter, there are similar concerns that some patients who recover allegedly repressed memories about childhood sexual abuse may actually be reporting false memories implanted by their therapists (Loftus, 2004).

Freud's focus on male psychosexual development and his notion that females envy male anatomy have also been attacked. In the tradition of Horney, some contemporary neo-Freudians have proposed theories that focus specifically on the psychosexual development of women (Sayers, 1991).

Finally, as judged by modern standards, Freud's theory is not very scientific. His definitions of *id, ego, unconscious conflict,* and other concepts lack the precision required for scientific measurement and testing (Pervin et al., 2005). Further, his belief that unconscious desires drive most human behavior ignores evidence showing that much of that behavior goes beyond impulse gratification. For example, the conscious drive to attain personal, social, and spiritual goals is an important determinant of behavior, as is learning from others. Taken together, these shortcomings have made the psychodynamic approach to personality less popular today than it was in past decades (Allen, 2006; Carver & Scheier, 2004).

The Trait Approach

▶ **What personality traits are most basic?**

You could probably describe the personality of someone you know well with just a few statements. For example, you might say,

She's a really caring person, and very outgoing. She's generous with her time, and she works very hard at everything she does. Yet sometimes I think she also lacks self-confidence. She always gives in to other people's demands because she wants to be accepted by them.

In other words, most people describe others by referring to the kind of people they are ("outgoing"); to the thoughts, feelings, and actions that are most typical of them ("caring," "lacks self-confidence"); or to their needs ("wants to be accepted"). Together, these statements describe personality *traits*—the tendencies that help direct how a person usually thinks and behaves (Pervin et al., 2005).

The trait approach to personality makes three main assumptions:

1. Personality traits are relatively stable, and therefore predictable, over time. So a gentle person tends to stay that way day after day, year after year (Costa & McCrae, 2002).

2. Personality traits are relatively stable across situations, and they can explain why people act in predictable ways in many different situations. A person who is competitive at work will probably also be competitive on the tennis court or at a party.

3. People differ in how much of a particular personality trait they possess; no two people are exactly alike on all traits. The result is an endless variety of unique personalities.

In short, psychologists who take the **trait approach** see personality as a combination of stable internal characteristics that people display consistently over time and across situations (Pervin et al., 2005). Trait theorists seek to measure the relative strength of the many personality characteristics that they believe are present in everyone (see Figure 11.2).

Early Trait Theories

Today's trait theories of personality are largely based on the work of Gordon Allport and Raymond Cattell. (The contributions of another early trait theorist, Hans Eysenck, are discussed later.) Allport spent thirty years searching for the traits that combine to form personality. When he looked at the nearly 18,000 dictionary terms that can be used to describe human behavior (Allport & Odbert, 1936), he noticed that there are clusters of terms referring refer to the same thing. For example, *hostile, nasty,* and *mean* all convey a similar meaning. To better understand this clustering, think of a close relative, and jot down all the personality traits that describe this person. If you are like most people, you were able to capture your relative's personality using only a few trait labels. Allport believed that the set of labels that describe a particular person reflects that person's *central traits*—those that are usually obvious to others and

trait approach A perspective on personality that views it as the combination of stable characteristics that people display over time and across situations.

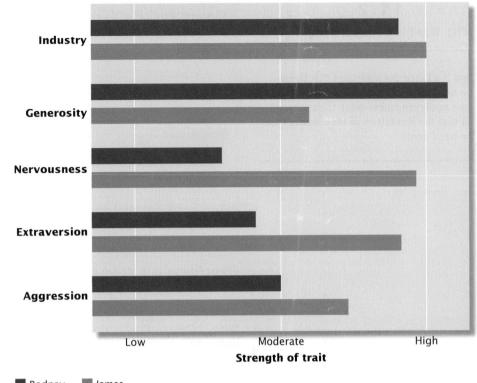

FIGURE **11.2**

Two Personality Profiles

learn **by doing** Trait theory describes personality in terms of the strength of particular dimensions, or traits. Here are trait profiles for Rodney, an inner-city social worker, and James, a sales clerk. Compared with James, Rodney is about equally industrious; more generous; and less nervous, extraverted, and aggressive. Just for fun, mark this figure to indicate how strong you think you are on each of the listed traits. Trait theorists suggest that this should be easy for you to do because, they say, virtually everyone displays a certain amount of almost any personality characteristic.

■ Rodney   ■ James

Source: Costa & McCrae (1992).

that organize and control behavior in many different situations. Central traits are roughly equivalent to the descriptive terms used in letters of recommendation (*reliable* or *distractible,* for example) that are meant to tell what can be expected from a person most of the time (Schultz & Schultz, 2005). Allport also believed that people possess *secondary traits*—those that are more specific to certain situations and control far less behavior. "Dislikes crowds" is an example of a secondary trait.

applying psychology **SELECTING A JURY** Some psychologists employ trait theories of personality in advising prosecution or defense attorneys about which potential jurors are most likely to be sympathetic to their side of a court case.

TABLE 11.2

The Big-Five Personality Dimensions

Here is a list of the adjectives that define the big-five personality factors. You can more easily remember these factors by noting that the first letters of their names spell the word *ocean*.

Dimension	Defining Descriptors
Openness	Artistic, curious, imaginative, insightful, original, wide interests, unusual thought processes, intellectual interests
Conscientiousness	Efficient, organized, planful, reliable, thorough, dependable, ethical, productive
Extraversion	Active, assertive, energetic, outgoing, talkative, gesturally expressive, gregarious
Agreeableness	Appreciative, forgiving, generous, kind, trusting, noncritical, warm, compassionate, considerate, straightforward
Neuroticism	Anxious, self-pitying, tense, emotionally unstable, impulsive, vulnerable, touchy, worrying

Source: Adapted from McCrae & John (1992).

Allport's research helped to lay the foundation for modern research on personality traits. However, his focus on the uniqueness of each personality made it difficult to draw conclusions about the structure of personality in general. In contrast, British psychologist Raymond Cattell was interested in the personality traits that people share. He used a mathematical technique called *factor analysis* to study which traits are correlated with one another. Factor analysis can reveal, for example, whether people who are moody are also likely to be anxious, rigid, and unsociable. Cattell found sixteen clusters of traits that he believed make up the basic dimensions, or factors, of personality (Cattell, Eber, & Tatsuoka, 1970).

The Big-Five Model of Personality

Building on the work of Allport and Cattell, today's trait theorists use factor-analytic techniques to bring the structure of personality into even sharper focus. The results of their research have led many of these theorists to conclude that personality is organized around just five basic factors (McCrae & Costa, 2004). The components of this **big-five model,** or **five-factor model,** of personality have been given slightly different labels by different researchers, but the most widely used names are *openness, conscientiousness, extraversion, agreeableness,* and *neuroticism* (see Table 11.2). The fact that some version of the big-five factors reliably appear in many countries and cultures—including Canada, China, the Czech Republic, Germany, Greece, Finland, India, Japan, Korea, the Philippines, Poland, and Turkey (Allik & McCrae, 2004; Ashton et al., 2004; McCrae et al, 2004; Saucier et al., 2005)—provides evidence that these factors may indeed represent the most important components of human personality (McCrae & Terracciano, 2005).

The emergence of the big-five model is considered by many trait theorists to be a major breakthrough in examining the personalities of all people, regardless of where they live or the nature of their economic, social, and cultural backgrounds (Carver & Scheier, 2004) The big-five model also allows researchers to precisely describe the similarities and differences in people's personalities and to explore how these factors are related to everything from personality disorders and political beliefs to substance abuse, happiness, and a sense of well-being (DeNeve, 1999; Lynam & Widiger, 2001; Roberts & Bogg, 2004; Van Hiel & Merviedle, 2004).

Biological Trait Theories

Some personality theorists are interested not only in what traits form the core of human personality but also in why people differ on these traits. Their research suggests that differences in traits might be due to biological factors.

big-five model   A view based on factor-analytic studies suggesting the existence of five basic components of human personality: openness, conscientiousness, extraversion, agreeableness, and neuroticism. Also called the five-factor model.

ANIMAL PERSONALITIES The idea that personality can be described in terms of five main dimensions seems to hold for some animals, as well as humans. The five animal dimensions differ from, but are still related to, human traits. For example, hyenas differ among themselves in terms of dominance, excitability, agreeableness (toward people), sociability (toward each other), and curiosity. Some of these same traits have been observed in a wide variety of other species, including dogs, horses, orangutans, and chimpanzees (Gosling, 2001; Gosling, Kwan, & John, 2003; King, Weiss, & Farmer, 2005; Weiss, King, & Perkins, 2006). Cat lovers often report such traits in their pets, too.

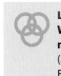

LINKAGES
Why do some people take more risks than others?
(a link to Motivation and Emotion)

Eysenck's Biological Trait Theory The biological basis for personality was emphasized in the work of British psychologist Hans Eysenck (pronounced "eye-sink"). Like other trait theorists who helped lay the groundwork for the big-five model, Eysenck used factor analysis to study personality. His research led him to focus on two main personality dimensions known as *introversion-extraversion* and *emotionality-stability* (Eysenck, 1990a, 1990b):

1. *Introversion-extraversion.* Extraverts are sociable and outgoing, enjoy parties and other social activities, take risks, and love excitement and change. Introverts tend to be quiet, thoughtful, and reserved, enjoying solitary pursuits and avoiding excitement and social involvement.

2. *Emotionality-stability.* At one extreme of this dimension are people who exhibit such characteristics as moodiness, restlessness, worry, anxiety, and other negative emotions. People at the opposite end are calm, even-tempered, relaxed, and emotionally stable. (This dimension is also often called *neuroticism.*)

According to Eysenck, personality can be described in terms of where a person falls along these two dimensions. For example, an introverted but stable person is likely to be controlled and reliable. An introverted but emotional person is likely to be rigid and anxious (see Figure 11.3).

Eysenck argued that the variations in personality characteristics that we see among individuals can be traced to inherited differences in their nervous systems, especially in their brains. These biological differences, he said, create differences in people's typical levels of physiological arousal and in their sensitivity to stress and other environmental stimulation. For example, people who inherit a nervous system that normally operates below some ideal level of arousal will always be on the lookout for excitement, change, and social contact in order to increase their arousal. As a result, they will be *extraverted*. In contrast, people whose nervous system is normally "overaroused" will tend to avoid excitement, change, and social contact in order to reduce arousal to their ideal level. In short, they will be *introverted*. What about the emotionality-stability dimension? Eysenck said that people who fall toward the stability side have nervous systems that are relatively insensitive to stress; those who are more emotional have nervous systems that react more strongly to stress.

Gray's Approach-Inhibition Theory Jeffrey Gray, another British psychologist, agrees with Eysenck about the two basic dimensions of personality but offers a different explanation of the biological factors underlying them (Gray, 1991). According to Gray, differences among people in introversion-extraversion and emotionality-stability

FIGURE **11.3**

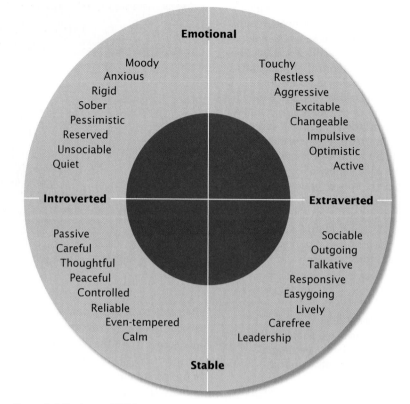

Source: Eysenck & Rachman (1965).

stem from two related systems in the brain. These are called the behavioral approach system and the behavioral inhibition system (Pickering & Gray, 1999). The *behavioral approach system*, or *BAS*, is made up of brain regions that affect people's sensitivity to rewards and their motivation to seek these rewards. The BAS has been called a "go" system because it is responsible for how impulsive or uninhibited a person is. The *behavioral inhibition system*, or *BIS*, includes brain areas that affect sensitivity to possible punishment and the motivation to avoid being punished. The BIS is a "stop" system that is responsible for how fearful or inhibited a person is. Gray says that people with an active behavioral approach system tend to experience positive emotions; people with an active behavioral inhibition system are more likely to experience negative ones (Larsen & Buss, 2005). Gray's theory is now more widely accepted than Eysenck's theory—primarily because it is supported by what neuroscientists have learned about brain structures and neurotransmitters and how they operate (Avila, 2001; Franken, Muris, & Georgieva, 2006; Larsen & Buss, 2005; Wacker, Chavanon, & Stemmler, 2006).

Gray's approach-inhibition theory is one of several biologically oriented explanations of the origins of personality traits (e.g., Zuckerman, 2004). A related approach involves exploring the role of genetics in these traits. For example, consider a pair of identical twins who had been separated at five weeks of age and did not meet again for thirty-nine years. Both men drove Chevrolets, chain-smoked the same brand of cigarettes, had divorced a woman named Linda, were remarried to a woman named Betty, had sons named James Allan, had dogs named Toy, enjoyed similar hobbies, and had served as sheriff's deputies (Tellegen et al., 1988).

THINKING CRITICALLY

Are Personality Traits Inherited?

FAMILY RESEMBLANCE Do children inherit personality traits in the same direct way as they inherit facial features, coloration, and other physical characteristics? Research in behavioral genetics suggests that personality is the joint product of genetically influenced behavioral tendencies and the environmental conditions each child encounters.

■ What am I being asked to believe or accept?

Cases like this have helped focus the attention of behavioral geneticists on the possibility that some core aspects of personality might be partly, or even largely, inherited (Bouchard, 2004; Ebstein, 2006; Johnson et al., 2004; Krueger, Markon, & Bouchard, 2003; Noblett & Coccaro, 2005).

■ Is there evidence available to support the claim?

Some of the evidence for this assertion comes from the many familiar cases in which children seem to "have" their parents' or grandparents' bad temper, generosity, or shyness. More systematic studies have also found moderate but significant correlations between children's personality test scores and those of their parents and siblings (Davis, Luce, & Kraus, 1994; Loehlin, 1992).

Even stronger evidence comes from studies conducted around the world that compared identical twins raised together, identical twins raised apart, nonidentical twins raised together, and nonidentical twins raised apart (Grigorenko, 2002). Whether they are raised apart or together, identical twins (who have exactly the same genes) tend to be more alike in personality than nonidentical twins (whose genes are no more similar than those of other siblings). This research also shows that identical twins are more alike than nonidentical twins in general temperament, such as how active, sociable, anxious, and emotional they are (Pickering & Gray, 1999; Borkenau et al., 2002; Wolf et al., 2004). On the basis of such twin studies, behavioral geneticists have concluded that at least 30 percent, and perhaps as much as 60 percent, of the differences among people in terms of personality traits is due to genetic factors (Caspi, Roberts, & Shiner, 2005).

■ Can that evidence be interpreted another way?

Family resemblances in personality could reflect inheritance or social influence. So an obvious alternative interpretation of this evidence might be that family similarities come not from common genes but from a common environment. Children learn many rules, skills, and behaviors by watching parents, siblings, and others; perhaps they learn their personalities as well (Funder, 2004). And the fact that nontwin siblings are less alike than twins may well result from what is called *nonshared environments* (Plomin, 2004). Nonshared factors include, for example, a child's place in the family birth order, differences in the way parents treat each of their children, and accidents, illnesses, or events that alter a particular child's life or health (Paulhus, Trapnell, & Chen, 1999). Nontwins are more likely than twins, especially identical twins, to be affected by these nonshared environmental factors.

■ What evidence would help to evaluate the alternatives?

One way to evaluate the idea that personality is inherited would be to locate genes that are associated with certain personality characteristics (Ebstein, 2006). Genetic differences have already been tentatively associated with certain behavior disorders, but most behavioral genetics researchers doubt that there are direct links between particular genes and particular personality traits (Caspi et al., 2005; Reif & Lesch, 2003).

Another way evaluate the role of genes in personality is to study people in infancy, before the environment has had a chance to exert its influence. If the environment were entirely responsible for personality, newborns should be essentially alike. However, as discussed in the chapter on human development, infants show immediate differences in activity level, sensitivity to the environment, the tendency to cry, and interest in new stimuli (Rothbart & Derryberry, 2002). These differences in *temperament* suggest biological, and perhaps genetic, influences.

To evaluate the relative contributions of nature and nurture beyond infancy, psychologists have examined the personality characteristics of adopted children. If adopted children are more like their biological than their adoptive parents, this suggests the influence of heredity in personality. If they are more like their adoptive families, a strong role for environmental factors in personality is suggested. In actuality, adopted children's personalities tend to resemble the personalities of their biological parents and siblings more closely than they do those of the families in which they are raised (Plomin et al., 1998).

Further research will determine more clearly what aspects of the environment are most important in shaping personality (Turkheimer & Waldron, 2000). So far, the evidence suggests that personality is not influenced very strongly by elements of the shared environment—such as socioeconomic status—that equally affect all children in the same family. However, nonshared environmental influences, at home and elsewhere, appear to be very important in personality development (Harris, 2000; Loehlin, Neiderhiser, & Reiss, 2003). We need to know more about the exact impact on personality development of nonshared environmental factors that may be different for twins and nontwin siblings.

■ What conclusions are most reasonable?

Even those researchers, such as Robert Plomin, who support genetic theories of personality caution that we should not replace "simple-minded environmentalism" with the equally incorrect view that personality is almost completely biologically determined (Plomin & Crabbe, 2000). It is pointless to talk about heredity *versus* environment as causes of personality, because nature and nurture always intertwine to exert joint and simultaneous influences (Dodge, 2004; Johnson, McGue, & Krueger, 2005).

With this caution in mind, we would be well advised to draw only tentative conclusions about the origins of personality differences. The evidence available so far suggests that genetic influences do appear to contribute significantly to the differences among people in many personality traits (Plomin & Crabbe, 2000). As noted earlier, however, there is no evidence of a specific gene for any specific personality trait. The genetic contribution to personality most likely comes as genes influence people's nervous systems and general predispositions toward certain temperaments (Arbelle et al., 2003; Ebstein, 2006; Grigorenko, 2002). Temperamental factors (e.g., emotionality and sociability) then interact with environmental factors, such as family experiences, to produce specific features of personality (Caspi et al., 2005). For example, children who inherit a tendency toward emotionality might play less with other children and withdraw from social interactions and thus tend to fail to learn important social skills (Eisenberg, Fabes, & Murphy, 1995). These experiences and tendencies, in turn, might foster the self-consciousness and shyness seen in introverted personalities.

Notice, though, that genetic predispositions toward particular personality characteristics may or may not appear in behavior, depending on whether the environment supports or stifles them. Changes in genetically predisposed traits are not only possible but may actually be quite common as children grow (Cacioppo et al., 2000). So even though there is a strong genetic basis for shyness, many children learn to overcome this tendency and become quite outgoing (Rowe, 1997). In summary, rather than inheriting specific traits, people appear to inherit the behavioral and emotional raw materials out of which their personalities are shaped by the world.

Evaluating the Trait Approach

The trait approach, and especially the big-five model, tends to dominate contemporary research in personality. Yet there are several problems and weaknesses associated with this approach.

For one thing, trait theories seem better at describing people than at understanding them. It is easy to say, for example, that Marilyn is nasty because she has a strong hostility trait; but other factors, such as the way people treat her, could also be responsible. In other words, trait theories say a lot about how people behave, but they don't always explain why (Mischel, 2004a, 2004b). Nor do trait theories say much about how traits are related to the thoughts and feelings that precede, accompany, and follow behavior. Do introverts and extraverts decide to act as they do? Can they behave otherwise? And how do they feel about their actions and experiences (Cervone & Shoda, 1999)? Some personality psychologists are linking their research with that of cognitive psychologists in an effort to better understand how thoughts and emotions influence, and are influenced by, personality traits (Shoda & LeeTiernan, 2002).

The trait approach has also been criticized for offering a short list of traits that provides, at best, a fixed and rather shallow description of personality that fails to capture how traits combine to form a complex and dynamic individual (Block, 2001; Funder, 2001). Even if the big-five model of personality proves to be correct and universal, its factors are not all-powerful. Situations, too, affect behavior. For example, people high in extraversion are not always sociable. Whether they behave sociably depends, in part, on where they are and who else is present.

In fairness, early trait theorists such as Allport acknowledged the importance of situations in influencing behavior, but it is only recently that consideration of person-situation interactions has become an important part of trait-based approaches to personality. This change is largely the result of research conducted by psychologists who have taken a social-cognitive approach to personality, which we describe next.

The Social-Cognitive Approach

▶ **Do we learn our personalities?**

To social-cognitive researchers, psychodynamic theories place too much emphasis on unconscious forces in personality and trait theories presume more consistency in people's behavior than there really is. In contrast, researchers who take a **social-cognitive approach** see personality as the full set of behaviors that people have acquired through *learning* and that they then display in particular situations. Some aspects of this approach reflect the view of traditional behaviorists, namely that all behavior is learned through classical and operant conditioning (see the chapter on learning). However, the social-cognitive approach expands that view by emphasizing (1) the role played by *learned patterns of thinking* in guiding behavior and (2) the fact that personality is learned in social situations as people observe and interact with other people (Bandura & Walters, 1963; Funder, 2004). The social-cognitive approach is sometimes called the *social-learning approach* because it defines personality as the sum of the behaviors and cognitive habits that develop as people learn through experience in the social world. Social-cognitive theorists are interested in how our thinking affects our behavior, as well as how our behavior and its consequences affect our thinking and our future actions.

Prominent Social-Cognitive Theories

Julian Rotter, Albert Bandura, and Walter Mischel have presented the most influential social-cognitive personality theories.

Rotter's Expectancy Theory   Julian Rotter (1982) argued that learning creates cognitions known as *expectancies* and that these expectancies guide behavior. He suggested that a person's decision to engage in a behavior is determined by (1) what the person expects to happen following the behavior and (2) the value the person places on the outcome. For example, people spend a lot of money on new clothes to wear at job interviews because past learning leads them to expect that doing so will help get them the job, and they place a high value on having the job. To Rotter, then, behavior is shaped by the positive or negative consequences it brings and also by the expectancy that a particular behavior will be rewarded or punished (Mischel, Shoda, & Smith, 2004).

Personality researchers influenced by Rotter have suggested that in addition to learning expectancies about particular behaviors in particular situations, we also learn more

social-cognitive approach   An approach that views personality as a label summarizing the unique patterns of thinking and behavior that a person learns.

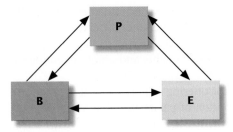

B = Behavior

E = The external environment

P = Personal factors, such as thoughts, feelings, and biological events

F I G U R E **11.4**

Reciprocal Determinism

Bandura's notion of reciprocal determinism suggests that thoughts, behavior, and the environment are constantly affecting each other. For example, a person's hostile thoughts might lead to hostile behavior, which generates even more hostile thoughts. At the same time, the hostile behavior offends others, thus creating a threatening environment that causes the person to think and act in even more negative ways. As increasingly negative thoughts alter the person's perceptions of the environment, that environment seems to be more threatening than ever (e.g., Bushman et al., 2005).

general expectancies, especially about how life's rewards and punishments are controlled (e.g., Phares, 1976). Some people (called *internals*) come to expect that events are controlled mainly by their own efforts. These people assume, for example, that what they achieve and the rewards they get are determined by what they themselves do. Others (*externals*) tend to expect events to be controlled by external forces over which they have no control. So when externals succeed, they tend to believe that their success was based on chance or luck.

Research on differences in generalized expectancies does show that they are correlated with differences in behavior. For example, when threatened by a hurricane or other natural disaster, internals—in accordance with their belief that they can control what happens to them—are more likely than externals to buy bottled water and make other preparations (Sattler, Kaiser, & Hittner, 2000). Internals also tend to work harder than externals at staying physically healthy, and as a result may lower their risk of cancer and heart disease (Stürmer, Hasselbach, & Amelang, 2006). They are less likely to drink alcohol, or—if they do drink—to drive while intoxicated (Cavaiola & Desordi, 2000). Internals tend to be more careful with money (Lim, Teo, & Loo, 2003), and internal college students tend to be better informed about the courses they take, including what they need to do to get a high grade. Perhaps as a result, internals tend to get better grades than externals (Dollinger, 2000).

Bandura and Reciprocal Determinism   In his social-cognitive theory, Albert Bandura (1999, 2006) sees personality as shaped by the ways in which thoughts, behavior, and the environment interact and influence one another. He points out that whether people learn through direct experience with rewards and punishments or through watching what happens to others, their behavior creates changes in their environment. Observing these changes, in turn, affects how they think, which then affects their behavior, and so on in a constant web of mutual influence that Bandura calls *reciprocal determinism* (see Figure 11.4).

An especially important cognitive element in this mutual-influence system is perceived **self-efficacy,** the learned expectation of success. Bandura says that what we do and what we try to do are largely controlled by our perceptions or beliefs about the chances of success at a particular task or problem. People with a high degree of perceived self-efficacy believe that they can successfully perform a behavior regardless of past failures or current obstacles. So the higher your perceived self-efficacy is in a particular situation or task, the greater your actual accomplishments in that situation or task are likely to be (Zimmerman & Schunk, 2003). For example, going into a job interview believing that you have the skills for the job may help you to get the job. (Perhaps you recall the classic children's story *The Little Engine That Could:* Trying to get up a steep hill, the scared little engine starts by saying "I think I can, I think I can" and ends up saying "I know I can, I know I can." And it did.)

According to Bandura, self-efficacy interacts with expectancies about the outcome of behavior in general, and the result of this interplay helps to shape a person's psychological well-being (Bandura, 1997; Maddux & Gosselin, 2003). So if a person has low self-efficacy and also expects that nothing anyone does has much effect on the world, apathy may result. But if a person with low self-efficacy believes that other people enjoy the benefits of their efforts, the result may be self-criticism and depression.

Mischel's Cognitive/Affective Theory   Social-cognitive theorists argue that learned beliefs, feelings, and expectancies characterize each individual and make that individual different from other people. Walter Mischel calls these characteristics *cognitive person variables*. He believes that they outline the dimensions along which individuals differ (Mischel & Shoda, 1999).

According to Mischel, the most important cognitive person variables are (1) *encodings* (the person's beliefs about the environment and other people), (2) *expectancies* (including self-efficacy and what results the person expects will follow from various behaviors), (3) *affects* (feelings and emotions), (4) *goals and values* (the things a person

self-efficacy According to Bandura, the learned expectation of success in given situations.

THE IMPACT OF SITUATIONS Like the rest of us, Arnold Schwarzenegger behaves differently in different situations, including when acting in his *Terminator* movies and when serving as the governor of California. Mischel's theory of personality emphasizes that person-situation interactions are important in determining behavior.

believes in and wants to achieve), and (5) *competencies and self-regulatory plans* (the things the person can do and the ability to thoughtfully plan behaviors; Mischel & Shoda, 1999).

To predict how a person might behave in a particular situation, says Mischel, we need to know about these cognitive person variables and about the features of that situation. In short, the person and the situation interact to produce behavior. Mischel's ideas have been called an "if-then" theory, because he proposes that *if* people encounter a particular situation, *then* they will engage in the characteristic behaviors (called *behavioral signatures*) that they typically show in this situation (Kammrath, Mendoza-Denton, & Mischel, 2005).

Mischel was once highly critical of the trait approach to personality, but now he sees his own theory as generally consistent with that approach. In fact, the concept of behavioral signatures is quite similar to the concept of traits. However, Mischel still argues that trait theorists underestimate the power of situations to alter behavior and do not pay enough attention to the cognitive and emotional processes that underlie people's overt actions. Despite their remaining differences, most advocates of the trait and social-cognitive approaches are now focusing on the similarities between their views (Cervone, 2005; Fleeson, 2004). This search for similarities between the trait approach and the social-cognitive approach has helped to clarify the relationship between personal and situational variables and how they affect behavior under various conditions. Many of the conclusions that have emerged are consistent with Bandura's concept of reciprocal determinism:

1. Personal dispositions (which include traits and cognitive person variables) influence behavior only in relevant situations. The trait of anxiousness, for example, may predict anxiety, but mainly in situations in which an anxious person feels threatened.

2. Personal dispositions can lead to behaviors that alter situations that, in turn, promote other behaviors. For example, a hostile child can trigger aggression in others and thus start a fight.

3. People choose to be in situations that are in accord with their personal dispositions. Introverts, for instance, are likely to choose quiet environments, whereas extraverts tend to seek out livelier, more social circumstances.

4. Personal dispositions are more important in some situations than in others. Where many different behaviors would be appropriate—at a picnic, for example—what people do can usually be predicted from their dispositions (extraverts will probably play games and socialize while introverts watch). However, in situations such as a funeral, where fewer options are socially acceptable, personal dispositions will not differentiate one person from another; everyone is likely to be quiet and somber.

Today, social-cognitive theorists are attempting to discover how person variables develop, how they relate to stress and health, and how they interact with situational variables to affect behavior.

Evaluating the Social-Cognitive Approach

The social-cognitive approach to personality is valuable because it blends behavioral learning theories with concepts from cognitive psychology and applies them to such socially important topics as aggression, the effects of mass media on children, and the development of techniques that enhance personal control over behavior. Social-cognitive principles have also been translated into cognitive-behavioral treatment procedures (O'Donohue, Fisher, & Hayes, 2003; see the chapter on treatment of psychological disorders).

The social-cognitive approach has not escaped criticism, however. Psychodynamic theorists point out that social-cognitive theories leave no role for unconscious thoughts and feelings in determining behaviors (e.g., Westen, 1998). Some advocates of trait theory complain that social-cognitive theorists have focused more on explaining why traits are unimportant than on why situations are important and that they have failed to identify what it is about specific situations that brings out certain behaviors (Friedman & Schustack, 2003; Funder, 2001). Finally, some critics feel that the social-cognitive approach cannot capture the complexities, richness, and uniqueness that are inherent in human personality (Carver & Scheier, 2004). For these critics, a far more attractive alternative is offered by the humanistic approach to personality.

The Humanistic Approach

▶ **Is everyone basically good?**

Unlike theories that emphasize the instincts and learning processes that humans seem to share with other animals, the humanistic approach to personality focuses on mental capabilities that set humans apart: self-awareness, creativity, planning, decision making, and responsibility. Those who adopt the **humanistic approach** view human behavior as motivated mainly by an innate drive toward growth that prompts people to fulfill their unique potential. And, like the planted seed whose natural potential is to become a flower, people are seen as naturally inclined toward goodness, creativity, love, and joy. Humanistic psychologists also believe that to explain people's actions, it is more important to understand their view of the world than their instincts, traits, or learning experiences. To humanists, that world view is a bit different for each of us, and it is this unique *phenomenology* (pronounced "feh-naw-men-ALL-oh-gee"), or way of perceiving and interpreting the world, that shapes personality and guides behavior (Kelly, 1980). Because of its emphasis on the importance of looking at people's perceptions, this approach to personality is also sometimes called the *phenomenological approach.*

Prominent Humanistic Theories

The most prominent humanistic theories of personality are those of Carl Rogers and Abraham Maslow.

Rogers's Self Theory   In his extensive writings, Carl Rogers (1961, 1970, 1980) emphasized the **actualizing tendency,** which he described as an innate inclination

humanistic approach   A view of behavior as controlled by the decisions that people make about their lives based on their perceptions of the world.

actualizing tendency   An innate inclination toward growth and fulfillment that motivates all human behavior.

"Just remember, son, it doesn't matter whether you win or lose—unless you want Daddy's love."

Parents are not usually this obvious about creating conditions of worth, but according to Rogers, the message gets through in many more subtle ways.

toward growth and fulfillment that motivates all human behavior (Raskin & Rogers, 2001). To Rogers, personality is the expression of that actualizing tendency as it unfolds in each person's uniquely perceived reality (Allen, 2006).

The centerpiece of Rogers's theory is the *self,* the part of experience that a person identifies as "I" or "me." According to Rogers, those who accurately experience the self—with all its preferences, abilities, fantasies, shortcomings, and desires—are on the road to *self-actualization.* The progress of those whose experiences of the self become distorted, however, is likely to be slowed or stopped.

Rogers saw personality development beginning early, as children learn to need the approval, or *positive regard,* of others. Evaluations by parents, teachers, and others soon begin to affect children's self-evaluations. When these evaluations by others are in agreement with a child's own self-evaluations, the child reacts in a way that matches, or is *congruent* with, self-experience. The child not only feels the other person's positive regard but also evaluates the self as "good" for having earned approval. This positive self-experience becomes part of the **self-concept,** which is the way one thinks of oneself. Unfortunately, things may not always go so smoothly. If a pleasurable self-experience is evaluated negatively by others, the child must either do without their positive regard or reevaluate the experience. So a little boy who is teased by his father for having fun playing with dolls might adopt a distorted self-experience—deciding, perhaps, that "I don't like dolls" or that "Feeling good is bad."

In other words, said Rogers, personality is shaped partly by the actualizing tendency and partly by other people's evaluations. In this way, people come to like what they are "supposed" to like and to behave as they are "supposed" to behave. This socialization process helps people to get along in society, but it often requires that they suppress their self-actualizing tendencies and distort their experiences. Rogers argued that psychological discomfort, anxiety, or mental disorder can result when the feelings people experience or express are *incongruent,* or at odds, with their true feelings.

Incongruence is likely, Rogers said, when parents and teachers lead children to believe that their personal worth depends on displaying the "right" attitudes, behaviors, and values. These **conditions of worth** are created whenever *people* are evaluated instead of their behavior. For example, parents who find their child drawing on the wall are not likely to say, "I love you, but I don't approve of this behavior." They are more likely to shout, "Bad boy!" or "Bad girl!" This reaction suggests that the child is lovable and worthwhile only when well behaved. As a result, the child's self-experience is not "I like drawing on the wall, but Mom and Dad don't approve," but instead, "Drawing on the wall is bad, and I am bad if I like it, so I don't like it." The child may eventually show overly neat and tidy behaviors that do not reflect the real self but, rather, are part of an ideal self that is dictated by the parents.

As with Freud's concept of superego, conditions of worth are first set up by external pressure but eventually become part of the person's belief system. To Rogers, then, rewards and punishments are important in personality development not just because they shape behavior but also because they so easily create distorted self-perceptions and incongruence.

Maslow's Growth Theory Like Rogers, Abraham Maslow (1954, 1971a, 1971b) viewed personality as the expression of a basic human tendency toward growth and self-actualization. In fact, Maslow believed that self-actualization is not just a human capacity but a human need; as described in the chapter on motivation and emotion, he placed self-actualization as the highest in a hierarchy of needs. Yet, said Maslow, people are often distracted from seeking self-actualization because they are focusing on needs that are lower in the hierarchy.

Maslow saw most people as controlled by a *deficiency orientation,* a preoccupation with perceived needs for material things. Ultimately, he said, deficiency-oriented people come to see life as a meaningless exercise in disappointment and boredom, and they may begin to behave in problematic ways. For example, in an attempt to satisfy the need for love, many people focus on what love can give them (security), not on what

self-concept The way one thinks of oneself.

conditions of worth According to Rogers, circumstances in which an individual experiences positive regard from others only when displaying certain behaviors or attitudes.

SEEKING SELF-ACTUALIZATION
According to Rogers, conditions of worth can make it harder for children to become aware of and accept the aspects of themselves that conflict with their parents' values. Progress toward self-actualization can be enhanced by associating with those whose positive regard does not depend on displaying any particular set of behaviors.

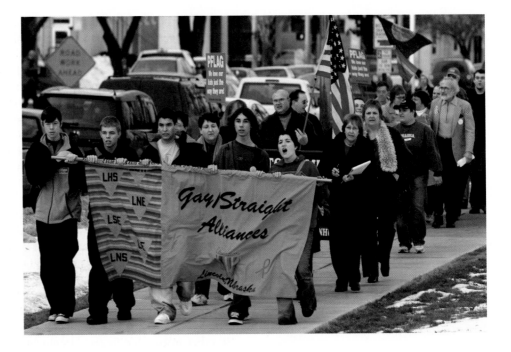

they can give to someone else. This deficiency orientation may lead a person to be jealous and to focus on what is missing in relationships; as a result, the person will never truly experience love or security.

In contrast, people with a *growth orientation* do not focus on what is missing but draw satisfaction from what they have, what they are, and what they can do. This orientation opens the door to what Maslow called *peak experiences*, in which people feel joy, and even ecstasy, in the mere fact of being alive, being human, and knowing that they are utilizing their fullest potential.

Evaluating the Humanistic Approach

The humanistic approach to personality is consistent with the way many people view themselves. It gives a central role to immediate experience and emphasizes each person's uniqueness. The best-known application of the humanistic approach is the client-centered

THE JOYS OF A GROWTH ORIENTATION　According to Maslow's theory of personality, the key to personal growth and fulfillment lies in focusing on what we have, not on what we don't have or on what we have lost. Rachel Barton could have let the accident that took her leg destroy her career as a concert violinist, and with it, her joy in life—but she didn't.

therapy of Carl Rogers, which is discussed in the chapter on treatment of psychological disorders. The humanistic approach has also inspired other therapies, as well as short-term personal-growth experiences such as sensitivity training and encounter groups that are designed to help people become more aware of themselves and the way they relate to others (e.g., Cain & Seeman, 2002). It has also led to programs designed to teach parents how to avoid creating conditions of worth while maximizing their children's potential. Further, the humanistic approach is consistent with the rapidly growing field of *positive psychology*, which, as described in the motivation and emotion chapter, focuses on subjective well-being and other positive aspects of human thought and feelings (Diener, 2003; Snyder & Lopez, 2006).

Yet to some, the humanistic approach is naive, romantic, and unrealistic. Are people all as inherently good and "growth oriented" as this approach suggests? Critics wonder about that, and they also fault humanists for paying too little attention to the role of inherited characteristics, learning, situational influences, and unconscious motivation in shaping personality. Further, the idea that personality development is directed only by an innate growth potential is seen by many as an oversimplification. So, too, is the humanistic assumption that all human problems stem from blocked self-actualization. Personality researchers also see many humanistic concepts as too vague to be tested empirically. Accordingly, the humanistic approach is not popular among those who conduct empirical research to learn about personality (Friedman & Schustack, 2003).

Finally, humanists' tendency to define ideal personality development in terms of personal growth, independence, and self-actualization has been criticized for emphasizing culture-specific concepts about mental health that may not apply outside North America and other Western cultures (Heine, 2003). As discussed in the next section, the foundations of humanistic self theories may be in direct conflict with the values of non-Western, collectivist cultures.

"In Review: Major Approaches to Personality" summarizes key features of the humanistic approach, along with those of the other approaches we have described. Which approach is most accurate? There is no simple answer to that question, partly

in review

MAJOR APPROACHES TO PERSONALITY

Approach	Basic Assumptions About Behavior	Typical Research Method
Psychodynamic	Determined by largely unconscious intrapsychic conflicts	Case studies
Trait	Determined by traits or needs	Analysis of tests for basic personality dimensions
Social-cognitive	Determined by learning, cognitive factors, and specific situations	Analysis of interactions between people and situations
Humanistic	Determined by innate growth tendency and individual perception of reality	Studies of relationships between perceptions and behavior

1. Tests that measure the big-five dimensions of personality are based on the _____ approach to personality.
2. The role of learning is most prominent in the _____ approach to personality.
3. Object relations and attachment theories are modern variants on _____ personality theories.

because each approach emphasizes different aspects of personality. Accordingly, it has been suggested that a full understanding of the origins and development of personality will come only by recognizing the roles of all the factors that various approaches have shown to be important. Some psychologists are now working on theoretical models that take this promising integrative approach (Mayer, 2005; McAdams & Pals, 2006).

LINKAGES
Does culture determine personality? (a link to Human Development)

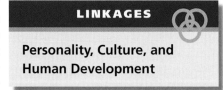

LINKAGES

Personality, Culture, and Human Development

In many Western cultures, people encourage others to "stand up for yourself" or to "blow your own horn" in order to "get what you have coming to you." In middle-class North America, the values of achievement and personal distinction are taught to children, particularly male children, very early in life (Kitayama, Duffy, & Uchida, in press). North American children are encouraged to feel special, to have self-esteem, and to feel good about themselves, partly because these characteristics are associated with happiness, popularity, and superior performance in school. Whether self-esteem is the cause or the result of these good outcomes (Baumeister et al., 2003), children who learn and display these values nevertheless tend to receive praise for doing so. (The goal of esteem building is clear in day-care centers, summer camps, and children's clothing stores with names such as Starkids, Little Wonders, Incredible Me!, Superkids, and Precious Jewels.)

As a result of this cultural training, many people in North America and Europe develop personalities that are largely based on a sense of high self-worth. In a study by Hazel Markus and Shinobu Kitayama (1991), for example, 70 percent of a sample of U.S. students believed that they were superior to their peers. In addition, 60 percent believed that they were in the top 10 percent on a wide variety of personal attributes! This tendency toward self-enhancement is evident as early as age four.

It is no wonder that many Western personality theorists see a sense of independence, uniqueness, and self-esteem as fundamental to mental health. As noted in the chapter on human development, for example, Erik Erikson included the appearance of personal identity and self-esteem as part of normal psychosocial development. Middle-class North Americans who fail to value and strive for independence, self-promotion, and unique personal achievement may be seen as having a personality disorder, some form of depression, or other psychological problems.

Do these ideas reflect universal truths about personality development or, rather, the influence of the cultures that generated them? It is certainly clear that people in many non-Western cultures develop personal orientations that are quite different from those of North Americans and Europeans (Lehman, Chiu, & Schaller, 2004). In China and Japan, for example, an independent, unique self is not emphasized (Ho & Chiu, 1998). In fact, children there are encouraged to develop and maintain pleasant, respectful relations with others and not to stand out from the crowd, because doing so might make others seem inferior by comparison. In fact, the Japanese word for "different" *(tigau)* also means "wrong" (Kitayama & Markus, 1992). So whereas children in the United States hear that "the squeaky wheel gets the grease" (meaning that you don't get what you want unless you ask for it), Japanese children are warned that "the nail that stands up gets pounded down" (meaning that it is not a good idea to draw attention to yourself). From a very young age, they are taught to be modest, to play down the value of personal contributions, and to appreciate the joy and value of group work (Kitayama & Uchida, 2003).

In contrast to the *independent* self-system common in individualist cultures such as Great Britain, Switzerland, and the United States, cultures with a more collectivist orientation (such as Brazil, China, Japan, and Nigeria) promote an *interdependent* self-system through which people see themselves as a fraction of the social whole. Each person has little or no meaningful definition without reference to the group. These

learn by doing **CULTURE AND PERSONALITY** In individualist cultures, most children learn early that personal distinction is valued by parents, teachers, and peers. In collectivist cultures, having a strong sense of self-worth may be seen as less important. In other words, the features of "normal" personality development vary from culture to culture. Make a list of the core values you have learned. Which of them are typical of individualist cultures, which are typical of collectivist cultures, and which reflect a combination of both?

differences in self-systems may produce differences in what gives people a sense of well-being and satisfaction (Tsai, Knutson, & Fung, 2006). For example, in the United States, a sense of well-being is usually associated with *having positive attributes,* such as intelligence, creativity, competitiveness, persistence, and so on. In Japan and other Asian countries, feelings of well-being are more likely to be associated with *having no negative attributes* (Eliot et al., 2001). Studies of thousands of people all over the world indicate that in collectivist cultures, life satisfaction is associated with having social approval and harmonious relations with others. In individualist cultures, life satisfaction is associated with having high self-esteem and good feelings about one's own life (Uchida et al., 2001).

Because cultural factors shape ideas about how the ideal personality develops, it is important to evaluate various approaches to personality in terms of how well they apply to cultures other than the one in which they were developed (Cross & Markus, 1999). Their applicability to males and females must be considered as well. Even within North American cultures, for example, there are gender differences in the development of self-esteem. Females tend to show an interdependent self-system, achieving their sense of self and self-esteem from attachments to others. By contrast, males' self-esteem tends to develop in relation to personal achievement, in a manner more in keeping with an independent self-system (Cross & Madson, 1997). Cross-gender and cross-cultural differences in the nature and determinants of a sense of self highlight the widespread effects of gender and culture on the development of many aspects of human personality (Zakriski, Wright, & Underwood, 2005).

FOCUS ON RESEARCH

Personality Development over Time

Psychologists have long been interested in how people's personalities differ, but they also want to know why those differences appear. Some search for the source of personality differences by looking at infants' differing temperaments. As noted in the chapter on human development, temperament is reflected in the unlearned, generalized patterns of emotional expression and other behavior that humans display from birth (Buss, 1997).

■ **What was the researchers' question?**

Can young children's temperaments predict their personality characteristics and behaviors as adults?

■ **How did the researchers answer the question?**

To try to answer this question, Avshalom Caspi and his colleagues conducted a longitudinal study in which the same people were assessed at several different times in their lives (Caspi, 2000; Caspi & Silva, 1995; Caspi et al., 1997; Caspi et al., 1995, 2003). The research sample included all the children born in Dunedin, New Zealand, between April 1972 and March 1973—a total of about 1,000 people. When these children were three years old, research assistants observed them in a standard situation and rated them on a number of dimensions, including the degree to which they showed explosive or uncontrolled behavior, interacted easily with others, or acted withdrawn and unresponsive. These observations were used to place each child into one of five temperament categories: *undercontrolled* (irritable, impatient, emotional), *inhibited* (shy, fearful, easily distracted), *confident* (eager to perform, responsive to questions), *reserved* (withdrawn, uncomfortable), and *well adjusted* (friendly, well controlled). The children were observed and categorized again when they were five, seven, and nine years old. If it occurs to you that seeing a child at one point in life might bias an observer's ratings of that child later on, you are right. To ensure that ratings would not be influenced by this kind of observer bias, the researchers arranged for different people to make the ratings at each point in time. These ratings indicated that the children's temperaments stayed about the same over the years from age three to age nine.

When the research participants were twenty-one, they were interviewed about their involvement in risky and unhealthy behaviors, such as excessive drinking, violent criminal activities, unprotected sex, and unsafe driving habits. To avoid bias, the interviewers were given no information about the participants' childhood temperaments. At age twenty-six, the participants took a standard personality test and were rated by friends on the big-five personality dimensions.

■ **What did the researchers find?**

Several significant differences were found in the personality test results of the five original temperament groups. For example, the average test scores of twenty-six-year-olds who had been classified as "undercontrolled" in childhood showed that they were more alienated, uninhibited, and stressed than the other temperament groups. Further, people who had been classified as "confident" or "well adjusted" as children tended to be better adjusted and more extraverted at twenty-six than people who had been classified as "inhibited" or "reserved." These findings held true for males and females alike.

There were also small but significant correlations between childhood temperament and risky behavior in young adulthood. For example, "undercontrolled" children were about twice as likely as others to develop personalities that are associated with violence, excessive drinking, and other health-risky behaviors (Caspi et al., 2003).

■ **What do the results mean?**

The results of this research provide support for a hypothesis long endorsed by personality psychologists, namely that we can make relatively accurate predictions about people's personalities and behaviors as adults if we know about their temperaments as children (e.g. Schwartz et al., 2003). But as critical thinkers, we must be careful not to overstate the strength of these results. Although the correlations between temperament and personality and between temperament and various problematic behaviors were statistically significant, they were also relatively small. In other words, not all children classified as "undercontrolled" at age three turned out to be aggressive or violent at eighteen. So it is more accurate to say that personality may be influenced and shaped by temperament, but not completely determined by it (Roberts, Walton, & Viechtbauer, 2006).

■ What do we still need to know?

Valuable as it is, this study leaves a number of unanswered questions about the relationship between temperament and personality (Roberts & DelVecchio, 2000). For example, why is there a connection between temperament as a child and personality as an adult? The link is probably a complex one, involving both nature and nurture. Caspi and his colleagues (1989) offered one explanation that draws heavily on social-cognitive theories, especially Bandura's notion of reciprocal determinism. They proposed that long-term consistencies in behavior result from the mutual influence that temperament and environmental events have on one another. For example, people may put themselves in situations that reinforce their temperament. So undercontrolled people might choose to spend time with people who accept, and even encourage, rude or impolite behavior. When such behavior brings negative reactions, the world seems that much more hostile, and the undercontrolled people become even more aggressive and negative. Caspi and his colleagues see the results of their studies as evidence that this process of mutual influence between personality and situations can continue over a lifetime (Caspi et al., 2003).

Assessing Personality

▶ **How do psychologists measure personality?**

Suppose you are an industrial/organizational psychologist whose job is to ensure that your company hires only honest, cooperative, and hard-working employees. How would you know which candidates had these characteristics? There are four basic methods of assessing and describing personality (Funder, 2004): *life outcomes* (such as records of education, income, or marital status), *situational tests* (observations of behavior in situations designed to measure personality), *observer ratings* (judgments about a person made by friends or family), and *self-reports* (responses to interviews and personality test items). Data gathered through these methods assist in employee selection, in the diagnosis of psychological disorders, in making predictions about a convict's or mental patient's dangerousness, and in other risky decision situations (Meyer et al., 2001; Bernstein, Kramer, & Phares, in press).

Life outcomes, observer ratings, and situational tests allow direct assessment of many aspects of personality and behavior, including how often, how effectively, and how consistently various actions occur. *Interviews* provide information about personality from the person's own point of view. Some interviews are *open-ended*, meaning that questions are tailored to the intellectual level, emotional state, and special needs of the person being assessed. Others are *structured*, meaning that the interviewer asks a fixed set of questions about specific topics in a particular order. Structured interviews are routinely used in personality research because they are sure to cover matters of special interest to the researcher.

Personality tests offer a way to gather self-report information that is more standardized and economical than interviews. To be useful, however, a personality test must be reliable and valid. As described in the chapter on thought, language, and intelligence, *reliability* refers to how stable or consistent the results of a test are; *validity* reflects the degree to which test scores are interpreted appropriately and used properly in making inferences about people. The many personality tests available today are traditionally classified as either *objective* or *projective*.

Objective Personality Tests

Objective personality tests ask clear questions about a person's thoughts, feelings, or behavior (such as "Do you like parties?"). The answers are used to draw conclusions about the individual's personality. These self-report tests are usually set up in a multiple-choice

objective personality test A form listing clear, specific questions, statements, or concepts to which people are asked to respond.

TABLE **11.3**

Sample Summary of Results from the NEO-PI-R

The NEO-PI-R assesses the big-five personality dimensions. In this example of the results a person might receive, the five factors scored are, from the top row to the bottom row, neuroticism, extraversion, openness, agreeableness, and conscientiousness. Because people with different NEO profiles tend to have different psychological problems, this test has been used to aid in the diagnosis of personality disorders (Trull & Sher, 1994).

Compared with the responses of other people, your responses suggest that you can be described as:

☐ Sensitive, emotional, and prone to experience feelings that are upsetting.	☒ Generally calm and able to deal with stress, but you sometimes experience feelings of guilt, anger, or sadness.	☐ Secure, hardy, and generally relaxed even under stressful conditions.
☐ Extraverted, outgoing, active, and high-spirited. You prefer to be around people most of the time.	☐ Moderate in activity and enthusiasm. You enjoy the company of others, but you also value privacy.	☒ Introverted, reserved, and serious. You prefer to be alone or with a few close friends.
☐ Open to new experiences. You have broad interests and are very imaginative.	☐ Practical but willing to consider new ways of doing things. You seek a balance between the old and the new.	☒ Down-to-earth, practical, traditional, and pretty much set in your ways.
☐ Compassionate, good-natured, and eager to cooperate and avoid conflict.	☒ Generally warm, trusting, and agreeable, but you can sometimes be stubborn and competitive.	☐ Hardheaded, skeptical, proud, and competitive. You tend to express your anger directly.
☒ Conscientious and well organized. You have high standards and always strive to achieve your goals.	☐ Dependable and moderately well organized. You generally have clear goals but are able to set your work aside.	☐ Easygoing, not very well organized, and sometimes careless. You prefer not to make plans.

or true-false format that allows them to be given to many people at once, much like the academic tests used in many classrooms. And as in the classroom, objective personality tests can be scored by machine and then compared with the responses of other people. So before interpreting your score on an objective test of extraversion, for example, a psychologist would compare it to a *norm*, or the average score of thousands of others of your age and gender. You would be considered unusually extraverted only if you scored well above that norm.

Some objective personality tests focus on one particular trait, such as optimism (Carver & Scheier, 2002). Others measure a small group of related traits, such as empathy and social responsibility (Penner, 2002). Still other objective tests measure the strength of a wider variety of traits to reveal general psychological functioning. For example, the *Neuroticism Extraversion Openness Personality Inventory, Revised,* or *NEO-PI-R* (Costa & McCrae, 1992), is designed to measure the big-five personality traits described earlier. Table 11.3 shows how the test's results are presented. The NEO-PI-R is quite reliable (Viswesvaran & Ones, 2000), and people's scores on its various scales have been successfully used to predict a number of criteria, including performance on specific jobs and overall career success (Barrick & Mount, 1991; Siebert & Kraimer, 2001), social status (Anderson et al., 2001), and the likelihood that people will engage in criminal activities and risky sexual behaviors (Clower & Bothwell, 2001; Miller et al., 2004).

When the goal of personality assessment is to diagnose psychological disorders, the most commonly used objective test is the *Minnesota Multiphasic Personality Inventory,* better known as the *MMPI* (Butcher & Rouse, 1996). This 556-item true-false test was developed during the 1930s at the University of Minnesota by Starke Hathaway and

LINKAGES
Can personality tests be used to diagnose mental disorders?
(a link to Psychological Disorders)

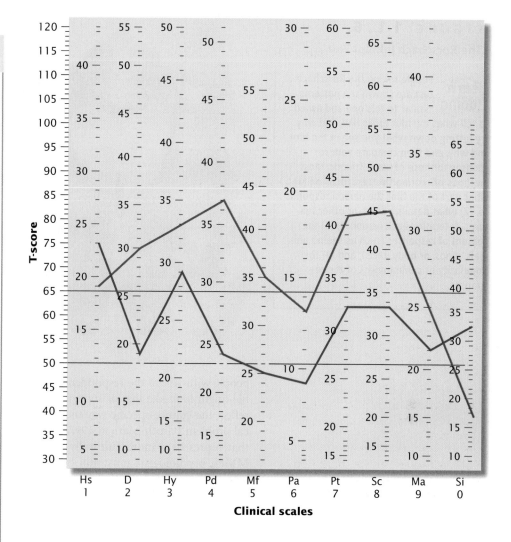

F I G U R E **1 1 . 5**

The MMPI: Clinical Scales and Sample Profiles

A score of 50 on the MMPI's clinical scales is average. Scores at or above 65 mean that responses on that scale are more extreme than at least 95 percent of the normal population. The red line represents the profile of Kenneth Bianchi, the "Hillside Strangler" who murdered thirteen women in the late 1970s. His profile is characteristic of a shallow person with poor self-control and little personal insight who is sexually preoccupied and unable to reveal himself to others. The profile in green comes from a more normal man, but it is characteristic of someone who is self-centered, passive, and unwilling to accept personal responsibility for his behavior and who, when under stress, complains of numerous vague physical symptoms.

The clinical scales abbreviated in the figure are as follows:

1. Hypochondriasis (Hs; concern with bodily functions and symptoms).
2. Depression (D; pessimism, hopelessness, slowed thinking).
3. Hysteria (Hy; use of physical or mental symptoms to avoid problems).
4. Psychopathic deviate (Pd; disregard for social customs, emotional shallowness).
5. Masculinity/femininity (Mf; interests associated with a particular gender).
6. Paranoia (Pa; delusions, suspiciousness).
7. Psychasthenia (Pt; worry, guilt, anxiety).
8. Schizophrenia (Sc; bizarre thoughts and perceptions).
9. Hypomania (Ma; overactivity, excitement, impulsiveness).
10. Social introversion (Si; shy, insecure).

J. C. McKinley. It has since been revised and updated in the MMPI-2 (National Computer Systems, 1992).

The MMPI is organized into ten groups of items called *clinical scales*. Certain patterns of responses to the items on these scales have been associated with people who display particular psychological disorders or personality characteristics. The MMPI and MMPI-2 also contain four *validity scales*. Responses to these scales detect whether respondents are distorting their answers, misunderstanding the items, or being uncooperative. For example, someone who responds "true" to items such as "I never get angry" may not be giving honest answers to the test as a whole.

To interpret the meaning of MMPI test results, a person's scores on the ten clinical scales are plotted as a *profile* (see Figure 11.5). This profile is then compared with the profiles of people who are known to have certain personality characteristics or problems. It is presumed that people taking the MMPI share characteristics with people whose profiles are most similar to their own. So although a high score on a particular clinical scale, such as depression, might suggest a problem in that area, interpreting the MMPI usually focuses on the overall pattern in the clinical scale scores—particularly on the combination of two or three scales on which a person's scores are unusually high.

There is considerable evidence for the reliability and validity of MMPI clinical scales, but even the latest editions of the test are far from perfect measurement tools (Carr, Moretti, & Cue, 2005; Munley, 2002). The validity of MMPI interpretations may be particularly suspect when—because of cultural factors—the perceptions, values, and experiences of the test taker differ significantly from those of the test developers and the

FIGURE **11.6**

The Rorschach Inkblot Test

learn by doing People taking the Rorschach test are shown ten patterns similar to this one and asked to tell what the blot looks like, and why. Try jotting down what you see in the blot, and why, and then compare your responses to those of some friends. Most methods of scoring this test focus on (1) what part of the blot the person responds to; (2) what details, colors, or other features determine each response; (3) the content of responses (such as seeing animals, maps, or body parts); and (4) the popularity or commonness of the responses.

people with whom the respondent's results are compared. So although an MMPI profile might look like that of someone with a mental disorder, the profile might actually reflect the culture-specific way the person interpreted the test items, not a psychological problem (Groth-Marnat, 1997). Even though the MMPI-2 uses comparison norms that represent a more culturally diverse population than did those of the original MMPI, psychologists must still be cautious when interpreting the profiles of people who identify with minority subcultures (Butcher, 2004.)

Projective Personality Tests

Unlike objective tests, **projective personality tests** contain items or tasks that are ambiguous, meaning that they can be perceived in many different ways. People taking projective tests might be asked to draw a house, a person, a family, or a tree; to fill in the missing parts of incomplete pictures or sentences; to say what they associate with particular words; or to report what they see in a drawing or picture. Projective techniques are sometimes employed in personality research, but they are far more popular among clinical psychologists, who use them in the assessment of psychological disorders (Wood et al., 2003) These psychologists tend to take a psychodynamic approach to their work. They believe that people's responses to these tests are guided by unconscious needs, motives, fantasies, conflicts, thoughts, and other hidden aspects of personality.

One prominent projective test, called the *Thematic Apperception Test,* or *TAT,* is described in the motivation and emotion chapter as a measure of need for achievement. Henry Murray and Christina Morgan developed this test to assess the needs they saw as the basis of personality. Another well-known projective test, the *Rorschach Inkblot Test,* features a series of ten inkblots similar to the one in Figure 11.6. The respondent is asked to tell what the blot might be and then to explain why.

Those who support projective testing claim that using ambiguous test items makes it difficult for respondents to detect what is being measured and what the "best" answers would be. They argue, therefore, that these tests can measure aggressive and sexual impulses and other personality features that people might be able to hide on an objective test. The tests' supporters also point to specific instances, such as in studies assessing achievement motivation with the TAT, in which projective tests show acceptable reliability and validity (Grønnerød, 2003; Schultheiss & Rohde, 2002).

projective personality tests Personality tests made up of relatively unstructured stimuli in which responses are seen as reflecting the individuals' unconscious needs, fantasies, conflicts, thought patterns, and other aspects of personality.

in review

PERSONALITY TESTS

Type of Test	Characteristics	Advantages	Disadvantages
Objective	Paper-and-pencil format; quantitatively scored	Efficiency, standardization	Subject to deliberate distortion
Projective	Ambiguous stimuli create maximum freedom of response; scoring is relatively subjective	"Correct" answers not obvious; designed to tap unconscious impulses; flexible use	Reliability and validity lower than those of objective tests

1. Projective personality tests are based on the _____ approach to personality.
2. The NEO-PI-R and the MMPI-2 are examples of _____ tests.
3. Most personality researchers use _____ tests in their work.

Nonetheless, most researchers agree that projective personality tests, especially the Rorschach, are substantially less reliable and valid than objective tests (Garb et al., 2005). In fact, because of their generally poor ability to predict behavior, they often add little information about people beyond what might be inferred from interviews or other sources (Hunsley, Lee, & Wood, 2003). "In Review: Personality Tests" summarizes the characteristics of objective and projective personality tests, along with some of their advantages and disadvantages.

Personality Tests and Employee Selection

How good are objective personality tests at selecting people for jobs? Most industrial/organizational psychologists believe that they are valuable tools for the selection of good employees. Tests such as the MMPI (and even some projective tests) are sometimes used to help guide hiring decisions, but large organizations usually choose objective tests that are designed to measure the big-five personality dimensions or related characteristics (Borman et al., 1997; Costa, 2001). Several researchers have found significant relationships between scores on the big-five dimensions and measures of job performance and effective leadership (Kieffer, Schinka, & Curtiss, 2004; Lim & Ployhart, 2004; Silverthorne, 2001). A more general review of studies involving thousands of people has shown that objective personality tests are of value in helping businesses reduce theft, absenteeism, and other disruptive employee behaviors (Ones & Viswesvaran, 2001; Ones, Viswesvaran, & Schmidt, 2003).

Still, personality tests are far from perfect predictors of workplace behavior. Many tests measure traits that may be too general to predict specific aspects of job performance (Furnham, 2001). In fact, features of the work situation are often better predictors of employee behavior than are personality tests (Mumford et al., 2001). Further, some employees see personality tests as an invasion of their privacy. They worry that test results in their personnel files might later be misinterpreted and hurt their chances for promotion or for employment by other companies. Lawsuits have resulted in a ban on the use of personality tests in the selection of U.S. federal employees. Concerns about privacy and other issues surrounding personality testing have also led the American Psychological Association and related organizations to publish joint ethical standards relating to procedures for the development, distribution, and use of all psychological tests (American Educational Research Association, American Psychological Association, & National Council on Measurement in Education, 1999; American Psychological Association, 2002b). The goal is not only to improve the reliability and validity of tests but also to ensure that their results are properly used and do not infringe on individuals' rights (Turner et al., 2001).

ACTIVE REVIEW   Personality

Linkages

As noted in the introductory chapter, all of psychology's subfields are related to one another. Our discussion of personality, culture, and human development illustrates just one way in which the topic of this chapter, personality, is linked to the subfield of developmental psychology, which is described in the chapter on human development. The Linkages diagram shows ties to two other subfields, and there are many more ties throughout the book. Looking for linkages among subfields will help you see how they all fit together and help you better appreciate the big picture that is psychology.

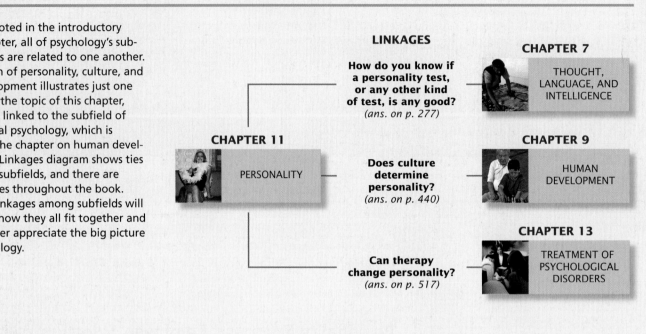

LINKAGES

CHAPTER 11

PERSONALITY

How do you know if a personality test, or any other kind of test, is any good?
(ans. on p. 277)

Does culture determine personality?
(ans. on p. 440)

Can therapy change personality?
(ans. on p. 517)

CHAPTER 7

THOUGHT, LANGUAGE, AND INTELLIGENCE

CHAPTER 9

HUMAN DEVELOPMENT

CHAPTER 13

TREATMENT OF PSYCHOLOGICAL DISORDERS

Summary

Personality refers to the unique pattern of psychological and behavioral characteristics by which each person can be compared and contrasted with other people. The four main theoretical approaches to personality are the psychodynamic, trait, social-cognitive, and humanistic approaches.

THE PSYCHODYNAMIC APPROACH

▶ **How did paralyzed patients lead Freud to psychoanalysis?**

The *psychodynamic approach,* pioneered by Freud, assumes that personality arises out of unconscious psychological processes that interact to determine our thoughts, feelings, and behavior. Freud believed that personality has three components—the *id,* which operates according to the *pleasure principle;* the *ego,* which operates according to the *reality principle;* and the *superego,* which internalizes society's rules and values. The ego uses *defense mechanisms* to prevent unconscious conflicts among these components from becoming conscious and causing anxiety or guilt.

Freud proposed that the focus of conflict changes as the child passes through *psychosexual stages* of development. These include the *oral stage,* the *anal stage,* the *phallic stage* (during which the *Oedipus complex* or *Electra complex* occurs), the *latency period,* and the *genital stage.*

Many of Freud's followers developed new theories that differed from his. Among these theorists were Jung, Adler, and Horney. They tended to downplay the role of instincts and the unconscious, emphasizing instead the importance of conscious processes, ego functions, and social and cultural factors. Horney also challenged the male-oriented nature of Freud's original theory.

Current psychodynamic theories reflect the neo-Freudians' emphasis on family and social relationships. According to object relations and attachment theorists, personality development depends mainly on the nature of early interactions between individuals and their caregivers.

The psychodynamic approach is reflected in many forms of psychotherapy, but critics fault the approach for its lack of a scientific base and for its view of human behavior as driven by forces that are difficult or impossible to measure.

THE TRAIT APPROACH

▶ **What personality traits are most basic?**

The *trait approach* assumes that personality is made up of stable internal characteristics that appear at varying strengths in different people and guide their thoughts, feelings, and behavior. Allport believed that personality is created by a small set of central traits and a larger number of secondary traits in each individual. Allport studied unique patterns of traits, whereas later researchers such as Cattell used factor analysis to explore common traits or core dimensions of personality. Most recently, these factor analyses have identified five basic dimensions of personality, collectively referred to as the *big-five model* or *five-factor model.* These dimensions—openness, conscientiousness, extraversion, agreeableness, and neuroticism—have been found in many different cultures, may arise partly from inherited differences in temperament and other biological factors that provide the raw materials out of which experience molds each personality. These biological factors are the focus of trait theories proposed by Eysenck and by Gray.

The trait approach has been criticized for being better at describing personality than at explaining it, for failing to consider mechanisms that motivate behavior, and for underemphasizing the role of situational factors. Nevertheless, the trait approach—particularly the big-five model—currently dominates the field.

THE SOCIAL-COGNITIVE APPROACH

▶ **Do we learn our personalities?**

The *social-cognitive approach* assumes that personality is a set of unique patterns of thinking and behavior that a person acquires through learning and then displays in particular situations. The social-cognitive approach has expanded on traditional behavioral approaches by emphasizing the role of cognitive factors, such as observational learning, in personality development.

Rotter's theory focuses on expectancies that guide behavior, and it generated interest in assessing general beliefs about whether rewards occur because of personal efforts (internal control) or chance (external control). Bandura believes that personality develops largely through cognitively mediated learning, including observational learning. He sees personality as reciprocally determined by interactions among cognition, environmental stimuli, and behavior. *Self-efficacy*—the belief in one's ability to accomplish a given task—is an important determinant of behavior. Mischel emphasizes the importance of situations and their interactions with cognitive person variables in determining behavior. According to Mischel, we must look at both cognitive person variables and situational variables in order to understand human consistencies and inconsistencies.

The social-cognitive approach has led to new forms of psychological treatment and many other applications. However, critics of this approach consider even its latest versions to be incapable of capturing all the unlearned factors that some psychologists see as important in personality.

THE HUMANISTIC APPROACH

▶ **Is everyone basically good?**

The *humanistic approach,* also called the *phenomenological approach,* is based on the assumption that personality is determined by the unique ways in which each individual views the world. These perceptions form a personal version of reality and guide people's behavior as they strive to reach their fullest potential.

Rogers believed that personality development is driven by an innate *actualizing tendency* but also that one's *self-concept* is shaped

by social evaluations. He proposed that *conditions of worth* imposed on children by parents and others interfere with personal growth and can lead to psychological problems. Maslow saw self-actualization as the highest in a hierarchy of needs. Personality development is healthiest, he said, when people have a growth orientation rather than a deficiency orientation.

Applications of the humanistic approach include certain forms of psychotherapy, parent training, and group experiences designed to enhance personal growth. This approach has considerable popularity, but it has been faulted for being too idealistic, for failing to explain personality development, for being vague and unscientific, and for underplaying cultural differences in "ideal" personalities.

Many people in the individualist cultures of North America and Europe are taught to believe in the importance of self-worth and personal distinction. This independent self-system contrasts with the interdependent self-system often fostered in collectivist cultures, in which the self is defined mainly in relation to family or other groups. Contrasting definitions of the self in different cultures and among males versus females tend to exert differing influences on the development of personality.

Research suggests that temperament in childhood may influence personality development into adulthood.

ASSESSING PERSONALITY

▶ **How do psychologists measure personality?**

Personality is usually assessed through some combination of life outcomes, observer ratings, situational tests, and self-reports. To be useful, personality assessments must be both reliable and valid.

Objective personality tests usually present clear, direct items; their scores can be compared with group norms. The NEO-PI-R and the MMPI are examples of objective personality tests.

Based on psychodynamic theories, *projective personality tests* present ambiguous stimuli in an attempt to tap unconscious personality characteristics. Two popular projective tests are the TAT and the Rorschach. In general, projective personality tests are less reliable and valid than objective personality tests.

Objective personality tests are often used to identify the people best suited for certain occupations. Although such tests can be helpful in this regard, those who use them must be aware of the tests' limitations and take care not to violate the rights of test respondents.

Learn by Doing

Put It in Writing

Choose a well-known person who interests you. It could be a rock star; an actor; a television personality; a political, religious, or business figure; or even a famous criminal. Write a one-paragraph description of this individual's personality traits as they seem to you. Now continue by writing a page or two about how you think the development of these traits would be explained by psychodynamic, biological trait, social-cognitive, and humanistic personality theories.

Personal Learning Activity

To get an idea of the problems involved in scoring projective personality tests, try creating your own projective test that contains

pictures, drawings, or other stimuli that can be interpreted in many different ways. Administer your test to some friends and record their responses to each stimulus (in writing or on tape). How will you decide what your friends' responses tell you about their personalities? Do you think your conclusions about their personalities were affected mainly by their test responses or by what you already knew about them? Now give your test to someone you don't know. Was it easier or harder to draw conclusions about this person's personality? How will you know if your conclusions about this new person are correct, or valid? *For additional projects, see the Personal Learning Activities in the corresponding chapter of the study guide that accompanies this text.*

Step into Action

Courses

Personality Psychology
Personality Research Methods
Personality Theories
History and Systems of Psychology

Movies

Good Will Hunting; Unforgiven; The Cider House Rules.
   Personality development.
Hoop Dreams. Self-efficacy.
Freud. Development of psychoanalytic theory.
Girl, Interrupted; Bridget Jones's Diary. Conditions of
   worth and self-concept.
Gandhi. Self-actualization.
Adrenaline Rush: The Science of Risk. Personality factors
   associated with risk-taking.

Books

David C. Funder et al. (Eds.), *Studying Lives Through
   Time* (American Psychological Association, 1996).
   Famous studies in personality and development.
Harry Stack Sullivan, *The Interpersonal Theory of
   Psychiatry* (Norton, 1968). Sullivan's neo-Freudian
   theory.

Frank J. Sulloway, *Born to Rebel: Birth Order, Family
   Dynamics and Creative Lives* (Vintage, 1997).
   Psychodynamics in personality development.
Duane P. Schultz and Sydney E. Schultz, *Theories of
   Personality* (Brooks-Cole, 2005). Summary of
   personality theories.
Stella Chess and M. D. Alexander, *Temperament: Theory
   and Practice* (Brunner/Mazel, 1996). Differences in
   temperament.
Edward Chang and Lawrence Sanna, *Virtue, vice, and
   personality: The complexity of behavior* (American
   Psychological Association, 2003). Readable chapters on
   how cultural factors alter evaluation of personality traits.

The Web

The World Wide Web is a good source of additional information about the science of psychology, provided you use
it carefully and think critically about the information you
find. The Online Study Center that accompanies this text
offers many resources relevant to this chapter. These
resources include interactive tutorials; Thinking Critically
and Evaluating Research exercises; ACE chapter quizzes;
recommended web links; and articles on current events,
books, and movies. Please visit the Online Study Center
at college.hmco.com/pic/bernsteinessentials4e.

Review of Key Terms

Can you define each of the key terms in the chapter? Check your definitions against those on the pages shown in parentheses in the
following list or in the Glossary/Index at the end of the text.

actualizing tendency *(p. 436)*
anal stage *(p. 422)*
big-five model *(p. 428)*
conditions of worth *(p. 437)*
defense mechanisms *(p. 422)*
ego *(p. 420)*
Electra complex *(p. 422)*
genital stage *(p. 424)*

humanistic approach *(p. 436)*
id *(p. 420)*
latency period *(p. 424)*
objective personality test
   (p. 443)
Oedipus complex *(p. 422)*
oral stage *(p. 422)*
personality *(p. 420)*

phallic stage *(p. 422)*
pleasure principle *(p. 420)*
**projective personality
   tests** *(p. 446)*
**psychodynamic
   approach** *(p. 420)*
psychosexual stages *(p. 422)*
reality principle *(p. 420)*

self-concept *(p. 437)*
self-efficacy *(p. 434)*
social-cognitive approach
   (p. 433)
superego *(p. 422)*
trait approach *(p. 426)*

Multiple-Choice Self-Test

Select the best answer for each of the following questions. Then check your responses against the Answer Key at the end of the text.

1. When psychologists talk about the unique pattern of enduring
    psychological and behavioral characteristics by which each
    person can be compared and contrasted with other people,
    they are referring to

    a. motivation.
    b. personality.
    c. reciprocal determinism.
    d. conditions of worth.

2. As Jared is jostled by a passerby he thinks, "I'd like to hit that
    guy!" Freud would say that this impulse comes from Jared's
    _____, which operates on the _____ principle.

    a. id; pleasure
    b. id; reality
    c. ego; pleasure
    d. ego; reality

3. Nine-year-old Jeffrey has just bounded into the room with his latest artistic creation. He chatters about his friends at school and how much he likes reading and working math problems. According to Freud, Jeffrey is most likely in the _____ stage of psychosexual development.

   a. oral
   b. anal
   c. phallic
   d. latency

4. Elizabeth's therapist suggests that Elizabeth's inability to trust her boyfriend could stem from her parents' neglecting her when she was a child. This therapist most likely follows the _____ theory of personality.

   a. reciprocal deterministic
   b. social-cognitive
   c. humanistic
   d. object relations

5. Oscar strives to be the best at everything he does. He believes that he is successful because he is intelligent, works hard, and never gives up. Oscar most likely has a(n) _____ self-system.

   a. independent
   b. interdependent
   c. reciprocal
   d. growth-oriented

6. Which of the following is not a common criticism of Freud's psychodynamic approach to personality?

   a. His sample of patients was small and unrepresentative of the general population.
   b. His theory reflects Western European and North American cultural values.
   c. The theory was not developed scientifically and thus is subject to bias.
   d. The theory was not comprehensive and has had little influence on psychology.

7. Rajeem believes that he is unique because no one else has exactly the same combination of internal characteristics (such as high intelligence, low sociability, average creativity) that he does. In other words, Rajeem believes in the _____ approach to personality.

   a. psychodynamic   c. social-cognitive
   b. trait   d. humanistic

8. A politician is described by her critics as dishonest, intelligent, industrious, extraverted, aggressive, generous, and charming. This method of describing personality most closely matches _____ model of personality.

   a. Eysenck's biological   c. Allport's trait
   b. Rotter's expectancy   d. the big-five

9. Tamerika has been described as high on openness (very curious and imaginative), low in conscientiousness (disorganized and unproductive), high in extraversion (very active, talkative, and energetic), high in agreeableness (generous, kind, and trusting), and high in neuroticism (impulsive, touchy, and vulnerable). This description reflects _____ model of personality

   a. Eysenck's biological trait
   b. Rotter's expectancy
   c. Allport's trait
   d. the big-five

10. David is very sociable and tends to seek out situations in which other people are appreciative of his work and his jokes. He is usually happy and loves to try new activities, such as bungee jumping. According to Gray, David has an active _____ system.

    a. external control
    b. internal control
    c. behavioral approach
    d. behavioral inhibition

11. According to the Thinking Critically section of this chapter, research on the question of whether or not personality is inherited concludes that

    a. there are specific genes for specific personality traits.
    b. there are genetic predispositions toward particular personality characteristics.
    c. the environment is the strongest influence on personality development.
    d. personality is essentially determined by the age of six months.

12. Sandy believes that if she works hard, she will be rewarded. So when she gets a D on her psychology test, she decides that she didn't study hard enough. When she wins the "Outstanding Senior of the Month" award, she believes that she earned it. According to one type of social-cognitive personality theory, Sandy would be described as

    a. internal.
    b. external.
    c. deficiency oriented.
    d. growth oriented.

13. Darma was standing in line at a movie theater, thinking about how her boyfriend had dumped her, when she was accidentally shoved from behind. She shouted "Hey! Back off, you jerks!" This prompted angry comments from the people behind her, which made Darma even angrier, so she refused to move forward in line. This case is an example of

    a. conditions of worth.
    b. growth orientation.
    c. reciprocal determinism.
    d. internal locus of control.

14. At college basketball games, Melinda jumps up and down and yells and screams continuously. Otherwise, however, she is a quiet person who chooses peaceful environments without much social stimulation. She finds that when she is around other people, they often become quiet, too. Melinda's personality can best be explained by _____ theory.

     a. psychodynamic
     b. Allport's trait
     c. Rotter's expectancy
     d. Mischel's person-situation

15. Rolf believes that his children's personalities are shaped by the way he rewards and punishes them. His wife, Jena, believes that the children were born with an innate drive toward growth and that their personalities are shaped by their unique perceptions of the world. Rolf's beliefs most closely match the _____ approach to personality, and Jena's most closely match the _____ approach.

     a. psychodynamic; trait
     b. social-cognitive; trait
     c. social-cognitive; humanistic
     d. psychodynamic; humanistic

16. When Lizzie finger-paints on the wall, her mother gets angry and shouts, "You are a very bad girl!" Rogers would say that Lizzie's mother is creating

     a. growth-oriented development.
     b. deficiency-orientated development.
     c. conditions of worth.
     d. psychodynamic conflicts.

17. Ruben is preoccupied with what is missing from his life. He has a good job and just got a raise, but he still feels underpaid. He has a great wife, but he wishes she were more attractive. He bought a new car, but he just saw a better one that has become his latest obsession. Maslow would say that Ruben is controlled by

     a. growth orientation.
     b. deficiency orientation.
     c. conditions of worth.
     d. self-actualization.

18. Which of the following techniques would a psychodynamic psychologist be most likely to use to assess personality?

     a. Behavioral observations
     b. Objective tests
     c. Measurements of physiological activity
     d. Projective tests

19. Paul is an undercontrolled eight-year-old who regularly has tantrums. The longitudinal study described in this chapter's Focus on Research section would suggest that, when Paul is an adult, he will most likely

     a. join the military or live in some other highly structured environment.
     b. have outgrown his lack of control.
     c. be more aggressive than most other men.
     d. keep jobs longer than most other men.

20. Peggy is responsible for hiring new employees for her company. To guide her selections, she decides to use _____, which have been shown to have value in screening out employees who are likely to be unreliable or dishonest.

     a. structured interviews
     b. objective personality tests
     c. projective personality tests
     d. life outcome measures

12

Psychological Disorders

A man sits alone in a restaurant booth, giving his order to a waitress. But

when she leaves, he continues talking and laughing as though someone were sitting with him. When his lunch arrives he thanks the waitress, then continues his "conversation." Later, he pays his bill, leaves a tip, and walks outside, chatting to his invisible companion all the while. Is this person crazy or just eccentric? When does oddness become abnormality? When does sadness become depression? What are psychological disorders? In this chapter, we describe the major categories of psychological disorders, discuss some of their possible causes, consider how they have been explained over the centuries, and examine their role in the insanity defense.

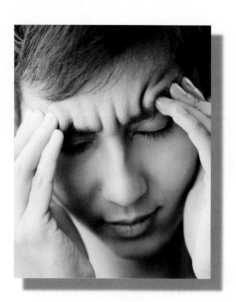

Reading this chapter will help you to answer the following questions:

J osé is a fifty-five-year-old electronics technician. A healthy and vigorous father of two adult children, he was recently forced to take medical leave because of a series of sudden, uncontrollable panic attacks in which dizziness, a racing heart, sweating, and other terrifying symptoms made him fear that he was about to die. José is suffering from a psychological disorder, also called a *mental disorder* or *psychopathology*. **Psychopathology** involves patterns of thought, emotion, and behavior that are maladaptive, disruptive, or uncomfortable either for the person affected or for others.

The number of people worldwide who exhibit some form of psychological disorder is staggering (World Health Organization Mental Health Survey Consortium, 2004). Surveys reveal that in any given year in the United States alone, about 86 million people, or about 30 percent of the adult population, have displayed some form of mental disorder and that as many as 48 percent have experienced a disorder at some point in their lives (Bjil et al., 2003; Kessler, Berglund, Demier, et al., 2005, Kessler, Chiu, et al.,

psychopathology Patterns of thinking and behaving that are maladaptive, disruptive, or uncomfortable for the affected person or for others.

FIGURE 12.1

Incidence of Specific Psychological Disorders

Several large-scale surveys of adults in the United States revealed that about 30 percent of them experience some form of mental disorder in any given year and that almost half of them have displayed a disorder at some time in life. The data shown here summarize these findings by category of disorder. The same general patterns appear among the more than 400 million people worldwide who suffer from some form of psychological disorder (Andrade et al., 2002; Bjil et al., 2003; Liu et al., 2002; World Health Organization, 2002b; World Health Organization Mental Health Survey Consortium, 2004).

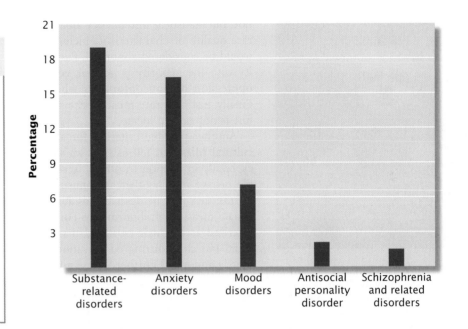

2005; Narrow et al., 2002; see Figure 12.1). In addition, about 20 percent of U.S. children display significant mental disorder in any given year (Costello et al., 2003; U.S. Surgeon General, 1999). These rates of mental disorder have remained steady in recent years and are seen in all segments of U.S. society. As described later, though, some disorders are more prevalent in males or females or in certain ethnic groups (Beals et al., 2005; Peterson et al., 1993). The overall prevalence rates may actually be higher than the survey percentages suggest, because major studies have examined fewer than half of all known psychological disorders. In short, psychological disorders are enormously costly in terms of human suffering, wasted potential, economic burden, and lost resources (Druss, Rosenheck, & Sledge, 2000; Lyons & McLoughlin, 2001; Marcotte & Wilcox-Goek, 2001; Stewart et al., 2003).

Defining Psychological Disorders

▶ **How do psychologists define abnormal behavior?**

A woman's husband dies. In her grief, she stays in bed all day, weeping, refusing to eat, at times holding "conversations" with him. In India, a Hindu holy man on a pilgrimage rolls along the ground for more than 1,000 miles of deserts and mountains, in all kinds of weather, until he reaches the sacred place he seeks. A British artist randomly scratches parked cars as part of his "creative process" (Telegraph Correspondent, 2005). Eight percent of U.S. adults surveyed say they have seen a UFO (CNN/Time, 1997), and hundreds claim to have been abducted by space aliens (Appelle, Lynn, & Newman, 2000). These examples and countless others raise the question of where to draw the line between normality and abnormality, between eccentricity and mental disorder (Kanner, 1995).

What Is Abnormal?

There are several criteria for judging whether a person's thinking, emotions, or behaviors are abnormal. Each criterion has value but also some flaws.

If we define *normality* as what most people do, then the criterion for abnormality becomes *statistical infrequency,* or that which is unusual or rare. By this criterion, the few people who believe that space aliens steal their thoughts would be judged as abnormal; the many people who worry about becoming victims of crime or terrorism would

IS THIS PERSON ABNORMAL?
Whether unusual individuals are labeled "abnormal" and perhaps given treatment for psychological disorders depends on a number of factors, including how *abnormality* is defined by the culture in which they live, who is most directly affected by their behavior, and how much distress they suffer or cause.

not. But statistical infrequency alone is a poor criterion for abnormality, because any rare quality or characteristic, including creative genius or world-class athletic ability, would be considered abnormal. Further, because this definition implies that conformity with the majority is normal, equating rarity with abnormality may result in the oppression of nonconformists who express unusual or unpopular views or ideas. Finally, just how rare must a behavior be in order to call it "abnormal"? The dividing line is not easy to locate.

Another possible criterion for abnormality is the violation of social norms—the cultural rules that tell us how we should and shouldn't behave in various situations, especially in relation to others. According to this *norm violation* criterion, when people behave in ways that are unusual enough or disturbing enough to violate social norms, they may be described as abnormal. However, norm violation alone is an inadequate measure of abnormality. For one thing, some norm violations are better characterized as eccentric or illegal than as abnormal. People who seldom bathe or who stand too close during conversation violate social norms, but are they abnormal or merely annoying? Further, whose norms are we talking about? Social norms vary across cultures, subcultures, and historical eras, so certain behaviors that qualify as abnormal in one part of the world might be perfectly acceptable elsewhere (Giosan, Glovsky, & Haslam, 2001; Phelan et al., 2000).

Abnormality can also be described in terms of *personal suffering*. In fact, experiencing distress is the criterion that people often use in deciding that their psychological problems are severe enough to require treatment. But personal suffering alone is not an adequate criterion for abnormality. For one thing, it does not take into account the fact that people are sometimes distressed about characteristics (such as being gay or lesbian) that are not mental disorders. Second, some people display serious psychological disorders but experience little or no distress. Those who sexually abuse children, for example, create far more distress in victims and their families than they suffer themselves.

Behavior in Context: A Practical Approach

Obviously, no single criterion fully defines abnormality. So mental health practitioners and researchers tend to adopt a *practical approach* that combines aspects of all the criteria we've discussed. They consider the *content* of behavior (that is, what the person does), the sociocultural *context* in which the person's behavior occurs, and the *consequences* of the behavior for that person and for others. This practical approach pays special attention to whether a person's thoughts, behavior, or emotions cause **impaired functioning**—that is, difficulty in fulfilling appropriate and expected roles in family, social, and work-related situations (U.S. Surgeon General, 1999; Wakefield, 1999).

What is "appropriate" and "expected" depends on age, gender, culture, and the particular situation and historical era in which people live. For example, a short attention span is considered normal in a two-year-old but inappropriate and problematic in an adult. In some countries, expressing certain emotions is considered more appropriate for women than for men. So kisses, tears, and long embraces are common when women in the U.S. greet each other after a long absence; men tend to simply shake hands or hug briefly. And because of cultural differences, hearing a dead relative's voice calling from the afterlife would be more acceptable in certain American Indian tribes than among, say, the families of suburban Toronto. Situational factors are important as well. Falling to the floor and "speaking in tongues" is considered appropriate, and even desirable, during the worship services of some religious groups; but the same behavior would be seen as inappropriate, and possibly a sign of disorder, in a college classroom. Finally, judgments about behavior are shaped by changes in social trends and cultural values. For example, the American Psychiatric Association once listed homosexuality as a mental disorder but dropped this category from its official list of disorders in 1973. In taking this step, it was responding to changing views of sexual orientation prompted in part by the political and educational efforts of gay and lesbian rights groups.

impaired functioning   Difficulty in fulfilling appropriate and expected social roles.

biopsychosocial model   Explaining mental disorders as the combined result of biological, psychological, and sociocultural factors.

In summary, it is difficult, and probably impossible, to define a specific set of behaviors that everyone, everywhere, will agree constitutes abnormality. Instead, the practical approach sees abnormality as including those patterns of thought, behavior, and emotion that impair functioning, cause discomfort, and/or disrupt the lives of others.

Explaining Psychological Disorders

▶ **What causes abnormality?**

Since the dawn of civilization, people have tried to understand the causes of psychological disorder. Centuries ago, explanations of abnormal behavior focused on gods or demons. Disordered people were seen either as innocent victims of evil spirits or as social or moral deviants suffering supernatural punishment. In Europe during the late Middle Ages, for example, people who engaged in threatening or unusual behavior were seen as controlled by the devil or other evil beings. Supernatural explanations of psychological disorders are still invoked today in many cultures around the world—including certain ethnic and religious subcultures in North America (Nickell, 2001; Tagliabue, 1999).

The Biopsychosocial Model

More generally, however, mental health researchers in Western cultures attribute the appearance of psychopathology to three other causes: biological factors, psychological processes, and sociocultural contexts. For many decades, there was controversy over which of these three causes was most important, but it is now widely agreed that they can all be important. Most researchers have adopted a **biopsychosocial model** in which mental disorders are seen as caused by the combination and interaction of biological, psychological, and sociocultural factors, each of which contributes in varying degrees to particular problems in particular people (Krueger & Markon, 2006; U.S. Surgeon General, 1999).

Biological Factors The biological factors thought to be involved in causing mental disorders include physical illnesses and disruptions or imbalances of bodily

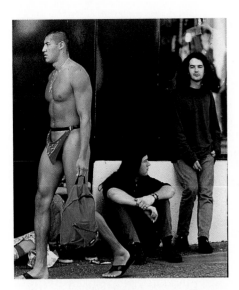

learn by doing **SITUATIONAL FACTORS IN DEFINING *ABNORMALITY*** When this college student attended classes virtually nude to protest "social repression," complaints from other students led to his dismissal. Yet if he lived in a nudist colony, he might be seen as overdressed. Make a list of the reasons you would give for or against labeling him "abnormal." Which criteria for abnormality did you use in making your list?

AN EXORCISM The exorcism being performed by this Buddhist monk in Thailand is designed to cast out the evil forces seen as causing this child's disorder. Supernatural explanations of mental disorder remain influential among religious groups in many cultures and subcultures around the world (Fountain, 2000). Awareness of this influence in the United States and Europe has increased recently following cases in which people have died during exorcism rituals (e.g., Christopher, 2003; Radford, 2005).

VISITING BEDLAM   As shown in William Hogarth's portrayal of "Bedlam" (slang for London's Saint Mary's of Bethlehem hospital), most asylums of the 1700s were little more than prisons. Notice the well-dressed visitors. In those days, the public could buy tickets to look at mental patients, much as people go to the zoo today.

processes. This *medical model* of psychological disorder has a long history. For example, Hippocrates, a physician in ancient Greece, said that psychological disorders result from imbalances among four *humors,* or bodily fluids (blood, phlegm, black bile, and yellow bile). In ancient Chinese cultures, psychological disorders were seen as arising from an imbalance of *yin* and *yang,* the dual forces of the universe flowing in the physical body.

As the medical model gained prominence in Western cultures after the Middle Ages, special hospitals for the insane were established throughout Europe. Treatment in these early *asylums* consisted mainly of physical restraints, laxative purges, bleeding of "excess" blood, and induced vomiting. Cold baths, fasts, and other physical discomforts were also used in efforts to "shock" patients back to normality.

The medical model gave rise to the concept of abnormality as *mental illness*—and in fact, most people in Western cultures today still tend to seek medical doctors and hospitals for the diagnosis and treatment of psychological disorders. The medical model is now more properly called the **neurobiological model,** because it explains psychological disorders in terms of particular disturbances in the anatomy and chemistry of the brain and in other biological processes, including genetic influences (e.g., Kendler, 2005; Plomin & McGuffin, 2003). Neuroscientists and others who adopt a neurobiological approach investigate these disorders as they would investigate any physical illness, seeing problematic symptoms stemming primarily from an underlying illness that can be diagnosed, treated, and cured.

Psychological Processes   The biological factors we have described are constantly influencing, and being influenced by, a variety of psychological processes, such as our wants, needs, and emotions; our learning experiences; and our way of looking at the world. The roots of the **psychological model** of disorder can be found in ancient Greek literature and drama dealing with *psyche,* or mind—and especially with the problems people experience as they struggle to resolve inner conflicts or to overcome the effects of stressful events.

These ideas took center stage in the late 1800s, when Sigmund Freud challenged the assumption that psychological disorders had only physical causes. As described in the chapter on personality, Freud viewed psychological disorders as resulting mainly from the effects of unresolved, mostly unconscious clashes between people's inborn impulses and the limits placed on those impulses by the environment. These conflicts, he said, begin early in childhood. Today's versions of this psychodynamic model focus less on

neurobiological model   A view of mental disorder as caused by physical illness or an imbalance in bodily processes, including disturbances in the anatomy and chemistry of the brain.

psychological model   An approach that views mental disorder as arising from inner conflicts or other psychological processes.

instinctual urges and more on the role of attachment and other early interpersonal relationships (Schultz & Schultz, 2005).

Other theories discussed in the personality chapter suggest still other psychological processes that contribute to the appearance of mental disorders. For example, *social-cognitive* theorists, also known as *social-learning* theorists, see most psychological disorders as the result of past learning and current situations. These theorists say that just as people learn to avoid touching hot stoves after being burned, bad experiences in school or a dental office can "teach" people to fear such places. Social-cognitive theorists also emphasize the effects of expectancies and other mental processes. They see depression, for example, as stemming from negative events, such as losing a job, and from learned patterns of thoughts about these events, such as "I never do anything right."

According to the *humanistic,* or phenomenological, approach to personality, behavior disorders appear when a person's natural tendency toward healthy growth is blocked, usually by a failure to be aware of and to express true feelings. When this happens, the person's perceptions of reality become distorted. The greater the distortion, the more serious the psychological disorder.

LINKAGES
Are psychological disorders learned behaviors? (a link to Learning)

LINKAGES
How do societies define what is abnormal? (a link to Social Psychology)

Sociocultural Context   Together, neurobiological and psychological factors can go a long way toward explaining many forms of mental disorder. Still, they focus mainly on causes residing within the individual. The **sociocultural model** of disorder suggests that we cannot fully explain all forms of psychopathology without also looking outside the individual—especially at the social and cultural factors that form the context, or background, of abnormal behavior. Looking for causes of disorders in this *sociocultural context* means paying attention to factors such as gender, age, and marital status; the physical, social, and economic situations in which people live; and the cultural values, traditions, and expectations in which they are immersed (Evans et al., 2000; Johnson et al., 1999; Whisman, 1999). Sociocultural context influences not only what is and is not labeled "abnormal" but also who displays what kind of disorder.

Consider gender, for instance. The greater tolerance in many cultures for open expression of emotional distress among women, but not men, may contribute to the higher rates of depression reported by women compared with men (Nolen-Hoeksema, Larson, & Grayson, 1999). Similarly, the view held in many cultures that excessive alcohol consumption is less appropriate for women than for men is a sociocultural factor that may set the stage for higher rates of alcohol abuse in men (Helzer et al., 1990).

Sociocultural factors also influence the form that abnormality takes (Kyrios et al., 2001). For example, depression is considered a *culture-general* disorder because it appears virtually everywhere in the world. However, specific symptoms tend to differ depending on a person's cultural background (Hopper & Wanderling, 2000). In Western cultures, in which the emotional and physical components of disorders are generally viewed separately, symptoms of depression tend to revolve around despair and other signs of emotional distress (Kleinman, 1991). But in China and certain other Asian cultures, in which emotional and physical experiences tend to be viewed as one, depressed people are as likely to report stomach or back pain as to complain of sadness (Kleinman, 2004; Parker, Gladstone, & Chee, 2001).

There are also *culture-specific* forms of disorder. For instance, Puerto Rican and Dominican Hispanic women sometimes experience *ataques de nervios* ("attacks of nerves"), a unique way of reacting to stress that includes heart palpitations, shaking, shouting, nervousness, depression, and possibly fainting or seizure-like episodes (Spiegel, 1994). In Asia, Khmer refugees sometimes suffer from panic-related fainting spells known as *kyol goeu* (Hinton, Um, & Ba, 2001). And in Southeast Asia, southern China, and Malaysia, a condition called *koro* is occasionally observed. Victims of this disorder, usually men, fear that their penis will shrivel, retract into the body, and cause death. In females, the fear relates to shriveling of the breasts. *Koro* appears only in cultures that hold the specific supernatural beliefs that explain it (Tseng et al., 1992).

In short, sociocultural factors create differing social roles, stressors, opportunities, and experiences for people who differ in age, gender, and cultural traditions. They also

sociocultural model   An approach to explaining mental disorder that emphasizes the role of factors such as gender and age, physical situations, cultural values and expectations, and historical era.

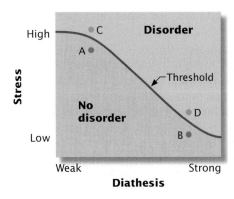

F I G U R E **12.2**

Diathesis, Stress, and Disorder

Diathesis-stress explanations suggest that psychological disorders can result from many combinations of predisposition and stress. Point D shows disorder stemming from a strong predisposition and relatively little stress. At Point C, disorder resulted from a weak predisposition but a lot of stress. Points A and B represent blends of diathesis and stress that are not potent enough to trigger disorder.

Online Study Center

Improve Your Grade
Tutorial: Disorder
Categories

diathesis-stress   An approach that recognizes the roles of both predispositions and situational factors in the appearance of psychological disorders.

help shape the disorders and symptoms to which certain categories of people are prone. Any attempt to fully explain psychological disorders must take these sociocultural factors into account.

Diathesis-Stress as an Integrative Explanation

The biopsychosocial model is currently the most comprehensive and influential approach to explaining psychological disorders. It is prominent partly because it encompasses so many important causal factors, including biological imbalances, genetically inherited characteristics, brain damage, psychological traits, socioculturally influenced learning experiences, stressful life events, and many more.

But how do all these factors actually interact to create disorder? Most researchers who study psychopathology believe that inherited characteristics, biological processes, learning experiences, and sociocultural forces combine to create a predisposition, or *diathesis* (pronounced "dye-A-thuh-sis"), for psychological disorders. Whether or not a person eventually develops symptoms of disorder, they say, depends on the nature and amount of stress the person encounters (Turner & Lloyd, 2004; U.S. Surgeon General, 1999). For example, a person may have inherited a biological tendency toward depression or may have learned depressing patterns of thinking. But these predispositions might not result in a depressive disorder unless the person is faced with a severe financial crisis or suffers the loss of a loved one. If major stressors don't occur, or if the person has good stress-coping skills, depressive symptoms may never appear or may be relatively mild.

So according to the **diathesis-stress** explanation of psychological disorder, biological, psychological, and sociocultural factors can predispose us toward disorder, but it takes a certain amount of stress to actually trigger it. For those with a strong diathesis, relatively mild stress might be enough to create a problem. Those whose predisposition is weaker might not show signs of disorder until stress becomes extreme or prolonged (see Figure 12.2). Another way to think about the notion of diathesis-stress is in terms of *risk:* The more risk factors for a disorder a person has—whether they take the form of genetic tendencies, personality traits, cultural traditions, or stressful life events—the more likely it is that the person will display a form of psychological disorder associated with those risk factors.

Table 12.1 shows how a particular case of psychopathology might be explained by various biopsychosocial factors and how it might be summarized in terms of diathesis and stress. Later, you'll see these same biopsychosocial factors combined within a diathesis-stress framework to explain a number of other psychological disorders.

Classifying Psychological Disorders

▶ **How many psychological disorders have been identified?**

Although definitions of abnormality differ within and across cultures, there does seem to be a set of behavior patterns that roughly defines the range of most abnormality in most cultures. The majority of these behavior patterns qualify as disorders because they result in impaired functioning, a main criterion of the practical approach to defining abnormality. It has long been the goal of those who study abnormal behavior to classify these patterns into a set of diagnostic categories.

The purpose of diagnosis is to determine the nature of people's psychological problems. Once the characteristics of these problems are understood, the most appropriate method of treatment can be chosen. Diagnoses are also important for research on the causes of psychopathology. If researchers can accurately classify people into particular disorder categories, they will have a better chance of spotting genetic features, biological abnormalities, cognitive processes, and environmental experiences that people in the same category might share. Finding that people in one category share a set of

TABLE 12.1

Explaining Psychopathology

Here are the factors that would be highlighted by the biopsychosocial model in the case of José, the man described at the beginning of this chapter. At the bottom is a summary of how these factors might be combined within a diathesis-stress framework.

Explanatory Domain	Possible Contributing Factors
Neurobiological/medical	José may have organic disorders (e.g., genetic tendency toward anxiety; brain tumor, endocrine dysfunction; neurotransmitter imbalance).
Psychological: psychodynamic	José has unconscious conflicts and desires. Instinctual impulses are breaking through ego defenses into consciousness, causing panic.
Psychological: social-cognitive	Physical stress symptoms are interpreted as signs of serious illness or impending death. Panic is rewarded by avoidance of work stress and the opportunity to stay home.
Psychological: humanistic	José fails to recognize his genuine feelings about work and his place in life, and he fears expressing himself.
Sociocultural	A culturally based belief that "a man should not show weakness" amplifies the intensity of stress reactions and delays José's decision to seek help.
Diathesis-stress summary	José has a biological (possibly genetic) predisposition to be overly responsive to stressors. The stress of work and extra activity exceeds his capacity to cope and triggers panic as a stress response.

features that differs from those shared by people in other categories could provide clues about which features are related to the development of each disorder.

In 1952 the American Psychiatric Association published the first edition of what has become the "official" North American diagnostic classification system, the *Diagnostic and Statistical Manual of Mental Disorders (DSM)*. Each edition of the *DSM* has included more categories. The latest editions, *DSM-IV* and *DSM-IV-TR* (text revision), include more than 300 specific diagnostic labels (American Psychiatric Association, 1994, 2000). Mental health professionals outside North America diagnose mental disorders using classification systems that appear in the tenth edition of the World Health Organization's *International Classification of Diseases (ICD-10)* and its companion volume, the second edition of the *International Classification of Impairments, Disabilities and Handicaps (ICIDH-2)*. To facilitate international communication about—and cross-cultural research on—psychopathology, *DSM-IV* was designed to be compatible with these manuals, and efforts are under way to remove inconsistencies existing between the systems (DeAngelis, 2001; Ottosson et al., 2002).

A Classification System: *DSM-IV*

DSM-IV describes the patterns of thinking, emotion, and behavior that define various mental disorders. For each disorder, *DSM-IV* provides specific criteria outlining the conditions that must be present before a person is given that diagnostic label. In keeping with the biopsychosocial model, diagnosticians using *DSM-IV* can evaluate troubled people on five dimensions, or *axes* (the plural of *axis*). Together, these axes provide a broad picture of each person's biological and psychological problems, as well as of any sociocultural context factors that might contribute to them. As shown in Table 12.2, mental disorders such as schizophrenia or major depressive disorder are recorded on Axis I, whereas evidence of personality disorders or mental retardation is noted on Axis II. Any medical conditions that might be important in understanding the person's cognitive, emotional, or behavioral problems are listed on Axis III. On Axis IV, the diagnostician notes any

┌─ TABLE **12.2**

The *Diagnostic and Statistical Manual of Mental Disorders (DSM)* of the American Psychiatric Association

Axis I of the fourth edition (*DSM-IV*) lists the major categories of mental disorders. Personality disorders and mental retardation are listed in Axis II.

Axis I (Clinical Syndromes)

1. ***Disorders usually first diagnosed in infancy, childhood, or adolescence.*** Problems such as hyperactivity, childhood fears, conduct disorders, frequent bed-wetting or soiling, and other problems in normal social and behavioral development. Autistic spectrum disorders (severe impairment in social, behavioral, and language development), as well as learning disorders.

2. ***Delirium, dementia, and amnesic and other cognitive disorders.*** Problems caused by physical deterioration of the brain due to aging, disease, drugs or other chemicals, or other possible unknown causes. These problems can appear as an inability to "think straight" (delirium) or as loss of memory and other intellectual functions (dementia).

3. ***Substance-related disorders.*** Psychological, behavioral, physical, social, or legal problems caused by dependence on, or abuse of, a variety of chemical substances, including alcohol, heroin, cocaine, amphetamines, hallucinogens, marijuana, and tobacco.

4. ***Schizophrenia and other psychotic disorders.*** Severe conditions characterized by abnormalities in thinking, perception, emotion, movement, and motivation that greatly interfere with daily functioning. Problems involving false beliefs (delusions).

5. ***Mood disorders*** (also called ***affective disorders***). Severe disturbances of mood, especially depression, overexcitement (mania), or alternating episodes of each extreme (as in bipolar disorder).

6. ***Anxiety disorders.*** Specific fears (phobias); panic attacks; generalized feelings of dread; rituals of thought and action (obsessive-compulsive disorder) aimed at controlling anxiety; and problems caused by traumatic events, such as rape or military combat (see the chapter on health, stress, and coping for more on posttraumatic stress disorder).

7. ***Somatoform disorders.*** Physical symptoms, such as paralysis and blindness, that have no physical cause. Unusual preoccupation with physical health or with nonexistent physical problems (hypochondriasis, somatization disorder, pain disorder).

8. ***Factitious disorders.*** False mental disorders that are intentionally produced to satisfy some psychological need.

9. ***Dissociative disorders.*** Psychologically caused problems of consciousness and self-identification—e.g., loss of memory (amnesia) or the development of more than one identity (multiple personality).

10. ***Sexual and gender identity disorders.*** Problems of (a) finding sexual arousal through unusual objects or situations (like shoes or exposing oneself), (b) unsatisfactory sexual activity (sexual dysfunction; see the chapter on motivation and emotion), or (c) identifying with the opposite gender.

11. ***Eating disorders.*** Problems associated with eating too little (anorexia nervosa) or binge eating followed by self-induced vomiting (bulimia nervosa). (See the chapter on motivation and emotion.)

12. ***Sleep disorders.*** Severe problems involving the sleep-wake cycle, especially an inability to sleep well at night or to stay awake during the day. (See the chapter on consciousness.)

13. ***Impulse control disorders.*** Compulsive gambling, stealing, or fire setting.

14. ***Adjustment disorders.*** Failure to adjust to, or deal well with, such stressors as divorce, financial problems, family discord, or other unhappy life events.

Axis II (Personality Disorders and Mental Retardation)

1. ***Personality disorders.*** Diagnostic labels given to individuals who may or may not receive an Axis I diagnosis but who show lifelong behavior patterns that are unsatisfactory to them or that disturb other people. These patterns may involve unusual suspiciousness, unusual ways of thinking, self-centeredness, shyness, overdependency, excessive concern with neatness and detail, or overemotionality, among others.

2. ***Mental retardation.*** As described in the chapter on thought, language, and intelligence, the label of "mental retardation" is applied to individuals whose measured IQ is less than about 70 *and* who fail to display the skills at daily living, communication, and other tasks expected of people their age.

psychosocial or environmental problems (such as the loss of a loved one, physical or sexual abuse, discrimination, unemployment, poverty, homelessness, inadequate health care, or conflict with religious or cultural traditions) that are important for understanding the person's psychological problems. Finally, on Axis V, the person is rated (from 100 down to 1) on current psychological, social, and occupational functioning. Here is a sample *DSM-IV* diagnosis for someone who received labels on all five axes:

Axis I: Major depressive disorder, single episode; alcohol abuse.

Axis II: Dependent personality disorder.

Axis III: Alcoholic cirrhosis of the liver.

Axis IV: Problems with primary support group (death of spouse).

Axis V: Global assessment of functioning = 50.

Notice that *neurosis* and *psychosis* are no longer listed in *DSM*, because they are not specific enough. However, some mental health professionals still sometimes use these terms as shorthand descriptions. *Neurosis* refers to conditions in which some form of anxiety is the major characteristic. *Psychosis* refers to conditions involving more extreme problems that leave people "out of touch with reality" or unable to function on a daily basis. The disorders once listed under these headings now appear in various Axis I categories in *DSM-IV.*

Further changes in the diagnostic system will surely appear in *DSM-V,* a new edition of the *DSM* currently under development for publication in 2010 (Beutler & Malik, 2002; Helzer & Hudziak, 2002; Maj et al., 2002; McHugh, 2005). For example, some experts are proposing that diagnoses should consist not just of specific labels, such as "major depression," but also of symptom clusters or dimensions that would be rated in terms of severity (Vollebergh et al., 2001; Widiger & Clark, 2000). The idea behind this *dimensional approach* would be to create a set of symptom "building blocks" that could be combined in many different ways so as to better recognize and describe the precise nature of each person's problems (Hankin et al., 2005; Krueger & Markon, 2006; Krueger, Watson, & Barlow, 2005; Markon, Krueger, & Watson, 2005; Widiger & Samuel, 2005).

Evaluating the Diagnostic System

How good is the diagnostic system now in use? One way to evaluate *DSM-IV* is to consider *interrater reliability,* the degree to which different mental health professionals agree on what diagnostic label a particular person should have. Some studies indicate that interrater agreement is as high as 83 percent for schizophrenia and mood disorders; agreement on many other Axis I categories—such as anxiety disorders—is also high (e.g., Brown et al., 2001; Nathan & Langenbucher, 1999; Simpson et al., 2002). Still other categories, such as Axis II personality disorders, remain more difficult to diagnose reliably (Shedler & Westen, 2004; Westen, Shedler, & Bradley, 2006; Zanarini et al., 2000). Overall, interrater agreement appears highest when diagnosis is based on structured interviews that systematically address each area of functioning and provide guidelines for interpreting people's responses (Brown et al., 2001; Rogers, 2001; Widiger & Sanderson, 1995).

Do diagnostic labels give accurate information that guides correct inferences about people? This *validity* question is difficult to answer because accuracy can be judged in different ways. A diagnosis could be evaluated, for example, on how well it predicts a person's future behavior, or perhaps on whether the person is helped by treatment that has helped others in the same diagnostic category. Still, evidence does support the validity of most *DSM* criteria (Clark, Watson, & Reynolds, 1995; Keenan & Wakschlag, 2004; Kim-Cohen et al., 2005). And validity is likely to improve even more as diagnostic labels—and the diagnostic system—are refined in *DSM-V* to reflect what researchers are learning about the characteristics, causes, courses, and cultural factors involved in various disorders.

The diagnostic system is far from perfect, however (Beutler & Malik, 2002; Kendell & Jablensky, 2003; Krueger & Markon, 2006; Nestadt et al., 2005). First, people's problems often do not fit neatly into a single category. For example, a person may suffer both

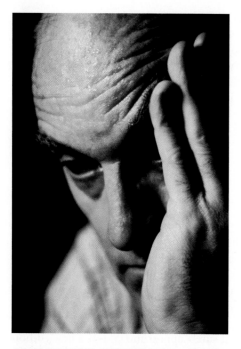

ANXIETY AND DEPRESSION People
who experience anxiety disorders—particularly panic disorder, generalized anxiety disorder, or posttraumatic stress disorder—are likely to display some other mental disorder as well, most often depression (Kaufman & Charney, 2000; Roy-Byrne et al., 2000). Accordingly, the next edition of the *DSM* may include *mixed anxiety-depression disorder*, a new category describing people whose symptoms of anxiety and depression combine to impair their daily functioning (Barlow & Campbell, 2000; Widiger & Clark, 2000).

anxiety and depression. Second, the same symptom (such as difficulty sleeping) can appear as part of more than one disorder. Third, although *DSM-IV* provides many useful diagnostic criteria, some of them—such as "clinically significant impairment"—are open to a certain amount of interpretation. When mental health professionals must decide for themselves whether a particular person's symptoms are severe enough to warrant a particular diagnosis, personal bias can creep into the system (Kim & Ahn, 2002; Widiger & Clark, 2000). All of these factors may lead to misdiagnosis in some cases. Concern over this possibility has grown as the nations of North America and Western Europe become increasingly multicultural and as diagnosticians encounter more and more people whose cultural backgrounds they may not fully understand or appreciate.

Some people whose behavior differs enough from cultural norms to cause annoyance feel that society should tolerate their "neurodiversity" instead of giving them a diagnostic label (Harmon, 2004). In the same vein, Thomas Szasz (pronounced "zaws") and other critics argue that the entire process of labeling people instead of describing problems is dehumanizing, because it ignores people's strengths and the features that make each case unique (Caplan, 1995; Kutchins & Kirk, 1997; Snyder & Lopez, 2006, 2007; Szasz, 2003; Wampold, Ahn, & Coleman, 2001). Calling people "schizophrenics" or "alcoholics," he says, actually encourages the behaviors associated with these labels and undermines the confidence of clients and therapists about the chances of improvement.

In summary, it is unlikely that any diagnostic system will ever satisfy everyone. No shorthand label can fully describe a person's problems or predict exactly how that person will behave. All that can be reasonably expected of a diagnostic system is that it provide informative, general descriptions of the types of problems displayed by people who have been placed in various categories (First et al., 2004).

THINKING CRITICALLY

Is Psychological Diagnosis Biased?

Some researchers and clinicians worry that problems with the reliability and validity of the diagnostic system are due partly to bias in its construction and use. They point out, for example, that if the criteria for diagnosing a certain disorder were based on research that focused on only one gender, one ethnic group, or one age group, those criteria might not apply to other groups. Moreover, diagnosticians, like other people, hold expectations and make assumptions about males versus females and about individuals from differing cultures or ethnic groups. These cognitive biases could color their judgments and might lead them to apply diagnostic criteria in ways that are slightly but significantly different from one case to the next (Garb, 1997; Hartung & Widiger, 1998).

■ What am I being asked to believe or accept?

Here, we focus on ethnicity as a possible source of bias in diagnosing psychopathology. It is of special interest because there is evidence that, like social class and gender, ethnicity is an important sociocultural factor in the development of mental disorder. The assertion to be considered is that clinicians in the United States base their diagnoses partly on a client's ethnic background and, more specifically, that there is bias in diagnosing African Americans.

■ What evidence is available to support the claim?

Several facts suggest the possibility of ethnic bias in psychological diagnosis. For example, African Americans receive the diagnosis of schizophrenia more frequently than European Americans do (Manderscheid & Barrett, 1987; Minsky et al., 2003; Pavkov, Lewis, & Lyons, 1989). Further, relative to their presence in the general population, African Americans are overrepresented in public mental hospitals, where the most serious forms of disorder are seen, and they are underrepresented in private hospitals and outpatient clinics, where less severe problems are treated (Lindsey & Paul, 1989; Snowden & Cheung, 1990; U.S. Surgeon General, 1999). Other research suggests that emergency room physicians are less likely to recognize psychiatric disorders in African American patients than in patients from other groups (Kunen et al., 2005).

There is also evidence that members of ethnic minorities, including African Americans, are underrepresented in research on psychopathology (Iwamasa, Sorocco, & Koonce, 2002). This lack of minority representation may leave clinicians less aware of sociocultural factors that could influence diagnosis. For example, they might more easily misinterpret an African American's unwillingness to trust a European American diagnostician as evidence of paranoid symptoms (Whaley, 2001).

■ Can that evidence be interpreted another way?

Differences among ethnic groups in diagnosis or treatment do not automatically indicate bias based on ethnicity. Perhaps there are real differences in psychological functioning among different ethnic groups. If, relative to other groups, African Americans are exposed to more risk factors for disorder, including poverty, violence, and other major stressors, they could be especially vulnerable to more serious forms of mental disorder (Plant & Sachs-Ericsson, 2004; Turner & Lloyd, 2004). And poverty, not diagnostic bias, could be responsible for the fact that African Americans are more often seen at less expensive public hospitals than at more expensive private ones. Finally, there is no guarantee that diagnostic criteria would be significantly different if more African Americans had been included in psychopathology research samples.

■ What evidence would help to evaluate the alternatives?

So do African Americans actually display more signs of mental disorder, or do diagnosticians just perceive them as more disordered? One way of approaching this question is to conduct experiments in which diagnosticians assign labels to clients on the basis of case histories, test scores, and the like. In some studies, the cases are selected so that pairs of clients show about the same amount of disorder, but one member of the pair is identified as European American and the other as African American. In other studies, the same case materials, identified as representing either African American or European American clients, are presented to different diagnosticians. Bias in diagnosis would be suggested if, for example, patients identified as African American were seen as more seriously disordered than others.

Most studies of this type have actually found little or no ethnic bias (e.g., Angold et al., 2002; Garb, 1997; Littlewood, 1992). These results are difficult to interpret, however, because the diagnosticians may be aware of the purpose of the study and so may go out of their way to be unbiased (Abreu, 1999; Gushue, 2004). In fact, researchers *have* found evidence of some diagnostic bias against African Americans when clinicians were unaware of the purpose of the research (e.g., Baskin, Bluestone, & Nelson, 1981; Jones, 1982).

Bias has also appeared in studies aimed at identifying the factors that influence clinicians' diagnostic judgments following extensive interviews with patients. For example, one hospital study found that, in arriving at their diagnoses, psychiatrists were more likely to attribute hallucinations and paranoid thinking to African American patients than to non–African American patients. Symptoms of mood disorders were more likely to be attributed to non–African Americans (Trierweiler et al., 2000). As noted earlier, these differences could reflect ethnic differences in the rate of disorder in the population, but when people were interviewed in their own homes as part of large-scale mental health surveys, the diagnosis of schizophrenia was given only slightly more often to African Americans than to European Americans (Robins & Regier, 1991; Snowden & Cheung, 1990). So the presence of ethnic bias is suggested, at least for some diagnoses, for patients who are evaluated in mental hospitals (Trierweiler et al., 2000).

■ What conclusions are most reasonable?

Just as *DSM-IV* is imperfect, so are the people who use it. As described in the chapters on social psychology and on thought, language, and intelligence, cognitive biases and stereotypes affect human thinking to some extent in virtually every social situation. It is not surprising, then, that they operate in diagnosis as well. Diagnostic bias does not necessarily reflect deliberate discrimination, however. At least one study has shown that, like the processes of prejudice discussed in the social psychology chapter, diagnostic bias based on ethnicity can operate unconsciously, without the diagnostician's being aware of it (Abreu, 1999). So no matter how precisely researchers specify the criteria for assigning diagnostic labels, biases and stereotypes are likely to threaten the objectivity of the diagnostic process (Funtowicz & Widiger, 1999; Trierweiler et al., 2000).

Minimizing diagnostic bias requires a better understanding of it. Hope Landrine (1991) suggests that diagnosticians should focus more intently than ever on the fact that their concepts of "normality" and "abnormality" are affected by sociocultural values that a given client might not share. Steven Lopez (1989) argues that mental health professionals must become more aware that the same cognitive shortcuts and biases that affect everyone else's thinking and decision making can impair their own clinical judgments. In fact, future research on memory, problem solving, decision making, social attributions, and other aspects of culture and cognition may turn out to hold the key to reducing bias in the diagnosis of psychological disorders. Meanwhile, perhaps the best way to counteract clinicians' cognitive shortcomings is to teach them to base their diagnoses solely on standard diagnostic criteria and decision rules rather than relying on their (potentially biased) clinical impressions (Garb, 1997; Bernstein, Kramer, & Phares, in press).

We do not have space to cover all the *DSM-IV* categories, so we focus on several of the most prevalent and socially significant examples. As you read, try not to catch "medical student's disease." Just as medical students often think that they have the symptoms of every illness they read about, some psychology students worry that certain aspects of their behavior (or that of a relative or friend) might reflect a mental disorder. Remember that everyone has problems sometimes. Before deciding that you or someone you know needs psychological help, consider whether the content, context, and functional impairment associated with the behavior would qualify it as abnormal according to the criteria of the practical approach.

Anxiety Disorders

▶ **What is a phobia?**

If you have ever been tense before an exam, a date, or a job interview, you have some idea of what anxiety feels like. Increased heart rate, sweating, rapid breathing, dry mouth, and a sense of dread are all common features of anxiety. Brief episodes of moderate anxiety are a normal part of life for most people. But when anxiety is so intense and long-standing that it disrupts a person's daily functioning, it is called an **anxiety disorder.**

Types of Anxiety Disorders

Here, we discuss four types of anxiety disorders: *phobia, generalized anxiety disorder, panic disorder,* and *obsessive-compulsive disorder.* Another type, called *posttraumatic stress disorder,* is described in the chapter on health, stress, and coping. Together, these are the most common psychological disorders in North America.

anxiety disorder   A condition in which intense feelings of fear and dread are long-standing or disruptive.

phobia   An anxiety disorder that involves strong, irrational fear of an object or situation that does not objectively justify such a reaction.

Phobia   An intense, irrational fear of an object or situation that is not likely to be dangerous is called a **phobia.** Even though people who experience phobias may realize that their fears are groundless, their efforts to avoid some object or event greatly interfere with daily life. Thousands of phobias have been described; some of them are listed in Table 12.3.

TABLE 12.3

Some Phobias

Phobia, the Greek word for "morbid fear," refers to *Phobos*, the Greek god of terror. The names of most phobias begin with the Greek word for the feared object or situation.

Name	Feared Stimulus
Acrophobia	Heights
Aerophobia	Flying
Claustrophobia	Enclosed places
Cynophobia	Dogs
Entomophobia	Insects
Gamophobia	Marriage
Gephyrophobia	Crossing a bridge
Hematophobia	Blood
Kenophobia	Empty rooms
Melissophobia	Bees
Ophidiphobia	Snakes
Xenophobia	Strangers

specific phobias Phobias that involve fear and avoidance of heights, blood, animals, and other specific stimuli and situations.

social phobias Strong, irrational fears relating to social situations.

agoraphobia A strong fear of being alone or away from the safety of home.

generalized anxiety disorder A condition that involves long-lasting anxiety that is not focused on any particular object or situation.

panic disorder Anxiety in the form of severe panic attacks that come without warning or obvious cause.

DSM-IV classifies phobias into three subtypes: specific phobia, social phobia, and agoraphobia. **Specific phobias** are fear and avoidance of heights, blood, animals, automobile or air travel, and other specific stimuli and situations. In the United States and other developed nations, they are the most prevalent of the anxiety disorders, affecting 7 to 11 percent of adults and children (American Psychiatric Association, 2000; Kessler et al., 1994; Lichtenstein & Annas, 2000; U.S. Surgeon General, 1999). Here is an example:

> *Mr. L., a fifty-year-old office worker, became terrified whenever he had to drive over a bridge. For years, he avoided bridges by taking roundabout ways to and from work, and he refused to be a passenger in anyone else's car, in case they used a bridge. Even these inconvenient strategies failed when Mr. L. was transferred to a job requiring frequent automobile trips, many of which were over bridges. He refused the transfer and lost his job.*

Social phobias involve anxiety about being criticized by others or acting in a way that is embarrassing or humiliating. The anxiety is so intense and persistent that it impairs the person's normal functioning. Common social phobias include fear of public speaking or performance ("stage fright"), fear of eating in front of others, and fear of using public restrooms (Kleinknecht, 2000). *Generalized social phobia* is a more severe form of social phobia in which fear occurs in virtually all social situations (Mannuzza et al., 1995). Sociocultural factors can alter the form of social phobias. For example, in Japan, where cultural training emphasizes group-oriented values and goals, a common social phobia is *tai-jin kyofu sho,* fear of embarrassing those around you (Kleinknecht, 1994).

Agoraphobia is a strong fear of being away from a safe place, such as home; of being away from a familiar person, such as a spouse or close friend; or of being in crowds or in other situations that are difficult to leave. People who suffer from agoraphobia prefer to stay at home, thus avoiding the intense anxiety associated with shopping, driving, or using public transportation. In Western cultures, agoraphobia is more often reported by women, many of whom are totally homebound by the time they seek help. In other cultures, such as India, where homebound women are considered less unusual than in the United States, those diagnosed as agoraphobic tend to be male (Raguram & Bhide, 1985). Although agoraphobia occurs less frequently than specific phobias (affecting about 5 percent of the U.S. population), it is the phobia that most often leads people to seek treatment—mainly because it so severely disrupts everyday life (U.S. Surgeon General, 1999).

Generalized Anxiety Disorder Strong and long-lasting anxiety that is not focused on any particular object or situation marks **generalized anxiety disorder.** Because the problem occurs in virtually all situations and because the person cannot pinpoint its source, this disorder is sometimes called *free-floating anxiety.* For weeks at a time, the person feels anxious and worried, sure that some disaster is about to occur. The person becomes jumpy and irritable and cannot sleep soundly. Fatigue, inability to concentrate, and physiological signs of anxiety are also common. Generalized anxiety disorder affects about 3.4 percent of the U.S. population in any given year and about 5 percent of the population at some point in their lives (Kessler, Keller, & Wittchen, 2001; U.S. Surgeon General, 1999). It is more common in women, often accompanying other problems such as depression or substance abuse (Wittchen & Hoyer, 2001).

Panic Disorder For some people, anxiety takes the form of **panic disorder.** Like José, whom we met at the beginning of this chapter, people suffering from panic disorder experience recurrent, terrifying *panic attacks* that seem to come without warning or obvious cause. These attacks are marked by intense heart palpitations, pressure or pain in the chest, sweating, dizziness, and feeling faint. Often, victims believe they are having a heart attack. They may worry so much about having panic episodes that they limit their activities to avoid possible embarrassment. In fact, it is the fear of experiencing

A CLEANING COMPULSION Obsessive-compulsive disorder is diagnosed when a culturally expected degree of cleanliness turns into an obsessive preoccupation with germs and a life-disrupting compulsion to clean things. Learning and stress appear to play the major role in shaping and triggering this and other anxiety disorders, but biological factors, including genetically inherited characteristics and problems in certain neurotransmitter systems, may result in an oversensitive nervous system and a predisposition toward anxiety.

obsessive-compulsive disorder (OCD) An anxiety disorder in which a person becomes obsessed with certain thoughts or feels a compulsion to do certain things.

panic attacks that may lead to agoraphobia as the person begins to fear and avoid places in which help won't be available should panic recur (Carter & Barlow, 1995; Kessler et al., 2006). Panic disorder may last for many years, with periods of improvement followed by recurrence (Ehlers, 1995). As many as 30 percent of the U.S. population have experienced at least one panic attack within the past year, but full-blown panic disorder is seen in only about 1 to 2 percent of the population in any given year (American Psychiatric Association, 2000; Kessler, Chiu, et al., 2006; U.S. Surgeon General, 1999). Here is one example:

> *Geri, a thirty-two-year-old nurse, had her first panic attack while driving on a freeway. Afterward, she would not drive on freeways. Her next attack occurred while with a patient and a doctor in a small examining room. A sense of impending doom flooded over her, and she burst out of the office and into the parking lot, where she felt immediate relief. From then on, fear of another attack made it impossible for her to tolerate any close quarters, including crowded shopping malls. She eventually quit her job because of terror of the examining rooms.*

Obsessive-Compulsive Disorder Anxiety is also at the root of **obsessive-compulsive disorder (OCD),** which affects about 2.4 percent of the U.S. population in any given year (American Psychiatric Association, 2000; Howarth & Weissman, 2000; U.S. Surgeon General, 1999). People displaying this disorder are plagued by persistent, upsetting, and unwanted thoughts—called *obsessions*—that often focus on the possibility of infection, contamination, or doing harm to themselves or others. They don't actually carry out harmful acts, but the obsessive thoughts motivate repetitive behaviors—called *compulsions*—that the person believes will prevent infection, aggressive acts, or other events associated with the obsessions (Foa & Kozak, 1995). Common compulsions include rituals such as checking locks; repeating words, images, or numbers; counting things; or arranging objects "just so." Obsessions and compulsions are much more intense than the familiar experience of having a thought or tune running "in the back of your mind" or rechecking a door to see that it is locked. In OCD, the obsessions and compulsions are intense, disturbing, and often strange intrusions that can severely impair daily activities. (*DSM-IV* defines compulsions as taking up more than one hour a day.) Many of those who display OCD recognize that their thoughts and actions are irrational, but they still experience severe anxiety if they try to interrupt their obsessions or give up their compulsive rituals.

Causes of Anxiety Disorders

As with all the forms of psychopathology we consider, the exact causes of anxiety disorders are a matter of some debate. However, there is good evidence that biological, psychological, and social factors all contribute. Biological predispositions, distortions in thinking, and certain learning experiences appear to be particularly important causal factors (U.S. Surgeon General, 1999).

Biological Factors Most anxiety disorders appear to run in families (Kendler et al., 1995, 2001; Pauls et al., 1995; Skre et al., 2000; Wittchen et al., 1994), suggesting that these disorders are influenced by a genetic predisposition (Hettema et al., 2003, 2005; Maron et al., 2005). For example, if one identical twin suffers an anxiety disorder, the other is more likely to share that disorder than is the case in nonidentical twin pairs (e.g., Hettema, Neale, & Kendler, 2001; Kendler et al., 1992, 2002; Neumeister et al., 2004). What is actually inherited? Anxiety disorders might stem from a tendency to react with anxiety to a wide range of situations, and this tendency, in turn, might result partly from inheriting an autonomic nervous system that is oversensitive to stress (Ahmad et al., 2002; Hamilton et al., 2003; Zinbarg & Barlow, 1996). There may be more specific predispositions as well. One study found that identical twins were more likely than other siblings to share phobias of small animals and social situations but not of heights or enclosed spaces (Skre et al., 2000).

A predisposition to develop anxiety disorders may also stem from abnormalities in brain structure (Szeszko et al., 2005) or in the brain's neurotransmitter systems, which are discussed in the chapter on biology and behavior. Excessive activity of norepinephrine in certain parts of the brain has been linked with panic disorder, and problems involving serotonin have been associated with obsessive-compulsive disorder. There is also evidence that anxiety-generating nerve impulses may run unchecked when the neurotransmitter GABA is prevented from exerting its normal inhibitory influence in certain brain pathways (Friedman, Clark, & Gershon, 1992; Zorumski & Isenberg, 1991).

Psychological Factors Biological predispositions combine with environmental stressors and psychological factors—especially cognitive processes and learning—to bring about most anxiety disorders (Mineka & Zinbarg, 2006; Schmidt et al., 2000; Stein, Chavira, & Jang, 2001). To see the effects of environmental stressors, one need only look at the dramatic rise in cases of posttraumatic stress disorder following natural disasters or terrorist attacks (Galea, Ahern, et al., 2002; Galea, Resnick, et al., 2002; Hoven et al., 2005). The impact of learning can be seen, for example, in families in which parents don't socialize much, tend to be suspicious of others, and exaggerate life's everyday dangers. These parents might unwittingly promote social anxiety in their children—especially in those born with a tendency toward shyness—by influencing them to interpret social situations as threatening. Abuse or other traumatic childhood experiences also increase the risk of developing an anxiety disorder, particularly panic disorder (Safren et al., 2002).

Learned ways of thinking play their part, too. Many people suffering from anxiety disorders exaggerate dangers in their environment, thereby creating an unrealistic expectation that bad things are going to happen (Wenzel et al., 2006; Wilson et al., 2006). In addition, they tend to underestimate their own capacity for dealing with threatening events, thus triggering anxiety and desperation when feared events do occur (Beck & Emery, 1985). Consider the development of a panic attack. Unexplained symptoms of physical arousal may set the stage for a panic attack, but it is the person's sensitivity to and cognitive interpretation of those symptoms that can determine whether or not the attack actually develops (Lim & Kim, 2005; Schmidt, Lerew, & Jackson, 1999). In the chapter on health, stress, and coping we describe a study in which patients with panic disorder breathed air rich in carbon dioxide. Some were told that they could control the amount of carbon dioxide they were inhaling by turning a dial on a control panel. Others were told they could not control it. In fact, the dial had no effect for either group, but the patients who believed they had control were far less likely to have a full-blown panic attack (Rapee et al., 1992; Sanderson, Rapee, & Barlow, 1989). In another study, patients with panic disorder who inhaled carbon dioxide in the presence of a person they associated with safety were significantly less fearful than patients whose "safe person" was not present (Carter et al., 1995). Results like these suggest that cognitive factors play an important role in panic disorder.

LINKAGES
Can we learn to become "abnormal"? (a link to Learning)

LINKAGES

Anxiety Disorders and Learning

Money troubles, illness, final exams, unhappy relationships, and other problems often create upsetting thoughts. And upsetting thoughts create worry and anxiety, especially for people who are under stress or feel incapable of dealing with their problems. As these thoughts become more persistent, anxiety increases. If doing something such as cleaning the kitchen temporarily relieves the anxiety, that action may be strengthened through the process of negative reinforcement (see the learning chapter). But cleaning can't eliminate the obsessive thoughts, so when they return, the cleaning may begin again. Eventually, cleaning or other actions may become compulsive, endlessly repeated rituals that keep the person trapped in a vicious circle

BIOLOGICAL PREPARED-NESS Being predisposed to learn to fear snakes and other potentially dangerous stimuli makes evolutionary sense. Like other animals, humans who rapidly learn a fear response to objects or situations that they see frightening their parents or peers are more likely to survive to pass on their genes to the next generation. Are there things you are especially afraid of? If so, list them and make a note of how you think these fears developed. How many of them appear to have "survival value"?

of anxiety (Barlow, 1988). Based on this kind of analysis, social-cognitive theorists see obsessive-compulsive disorder as a learned pattern sparked by distressing thoughts and maintained by operant conditioning (Abramowitz et al., 2006).

They also see phobias as based in part on the principles of learning, especially classical conditioning and observational learning. The object of the phobia becomes a conditioned aversive stimulus through association with a traumatic event that acts as an unconditioned stimulus (Öst, 1992). Fear of dogs, for example, may result from a dog attack. Observing or hearing about other people's bad experiences can produce the same result: Most people who fear flying have never been in a plane crash. Once the fear is learned, avoidance of the feared object or situation prevents the person from finding out that there is no need to be afraid. This cycle of avoidance helps explain why many fears do not disappear on their own.

Why are phobias involving snakes and spiders so common, even though people are seldom harmed by them? And why are there so few cases of electrical-shock phobia, even though lots of people receive accidental shocks? The answer may be that people are *biologically prepared* to learn to fear and avoid things that had the potential to harm their evolutionary ancestors (Öhman & Mineka, 2001, 2003; Skre et al., 2000). Laboratory research supports the idea that people are biologically prepared to learn certain phobias (Hamm, Vaitl, & Lang, 1989). In one study, a group of Swedish psychologists created conditioned fear reactions to certain stimuli by associating photographs of those stimuli with electrical shocks (Öhman, Dimberg, & Öst, 1985). Their volunteer participants developed approximately equal conditioned anxiety reactions to photos of houses, human faces, and snakes. Later, however, when the participants were shown the photos alone, their conditioned reaction to snakes remained long after their response to houses and faces had faded. These results suggest that anxiety disorders probably arise through the combined effects of genetic predispositions and learning.

Somatoform Disorders

▶ **Can mental disorder cause blindness?**

A young athlete was suffering fainting spells that prevented her from competing in track and field events. Doctors found no physical problems, and it was only after a program of stress management that her symptoms disappeared and she was able to rejoin her

FIGURE 12.3

Glove Anesthesia

In a form of conversion disorder called *glove anesthesia*, lack of feeling stops abruptly at the wrist (Part B). But as shown in Part A, the nerves of the hand and arm blend, so if they were actually impaired, part of the arm would also lose sensitivity. Other neurologically impossible symptoms of conversion disorder include sleepwalking at night on legs that are "paralyzed" during the day.

(A)　　　　　(B)

somatoform disorders Psychological problems in which a person shows the symptoms of some physical (somatic) disorder for which there is no physical cause.

conversion disorder A somatoform disorder in which a person appears to be, but actually is not, blind, deaf, paralyzed, or insensitive to pain.

hypochondriasis A strong, unjustified fear of physical illness.

somatization disorder A psychological problem in which a person has numerous physical complaints without verifiable physical illness.

pain disorder A somatoform disorder marked by complaints of severe, often constant pain with no physical cause.

team (Lively, 2001). Sometimes people show symptoms of a *somatic,* or bodily, disorder even though there is nothing physically wrong. When psychological problems take somatic form, they are called **somatoform disorders.** The classic example is **conversion disorder,** a condition in which a person appears to be, but is not, blind, deaf, paralyzed, or insensitive to pain in various parts of the body. (An earlier term for this disorder was *hysteria.*) Conversion disorders are rare, accounting for only about 2 percent of diagnoses (American Psychiatric Association, 2000). Although they can occur at any point in life, they usually appear in adolescence or early adulthood.

Conversion disorders differ from true physical disabilities in several ways. First, they tend to appear when a person is under severe stress. Second, they often help reduce that stress by enabling the person to avoid unpleasant situations. Third, the symptoms may be physiologically impossible or improbable, as Figure 12.3 illustrates. Finally, the person may show remarkably little concern about what most people would think was a rather serious problem. One college student, for example, experienced visual impairment that began each Sunday evening and became total blindness by Monday morning. Her vision would begin to return on Friday evenings and was fully restored in time for weekend social activities. She expressed no particular concern over her condition (Holmes, 1991). In such cases, the visual system remains intact, but the person appears to be unaware of the sensory information that the brain is still processing (Blake, 1998; Halligan & David, 1999).

Another type of somatoform disorder is **hypochondriasis** (pronounced "hye-poh-kon-DRY-a-sis"), a strong, unjustified fear that one has, or might get, cancer, heart disease, AIDS, or some other serious medical problem. The fear prompts frequent visits to doctors and reports of numerous symptoms. Their preoccupation with illness often leads people with hypochondriasis to become "experts" on their most feared diseases. In a related condition called **somatization disorder,** individuals make dramatic but vague reports about a multitude of physical problems rather than any specific illness. **Pain disorder** is marked by complaints of severe, often constant pain (typically in the neck, chest, or back) with no physical cause.

Some cases of somatoform disorder may be related to childhood experiences in which a person learns that symptoms of physical illness bring special attention and care (Barsky et al., 1994). Others, including conversion disorder, may be triggered by severe stressors (Spiegel, 1994). Cognitive factors also come into play. When given information about their health, people who display hypochondriasis are strongly biased to focus on threat-confirming information but to ignore reassuring information (Smeets, de Jong, & Mayer, 2000).

Based on such findings, many researchers have adopted a diathesis-stress approach to explaining somatoform disorders. The results of their work suggest that certain people may have biological and psychological traits that make them especially vulnerable to somatoform disorders, particularly when combined with a history of physical illness. Among these traits are self-consciousness and oversensitivity to physical sensations. If such people experience a number of long-lasting stressors, intense emotional conflicts, or severe traumas, they are more likely than others to display physical symptoms in association with emotional arousal.

Sociocultural factors may also shape some somatoform disorders. In many Asian, Latin American, and African cultures, it is not unusual for people to experience severe headaches and other physical symptoms in association with psychological or interpersonal conflicts. In North America such conflicts are more likely to be accompanied by anxiety or depression (Brislin, 1993). Genetic factors appear to play only a minor role in somatoform disorders.

Dissociative Disorders

▶ **What disorders create sudden memory loss?**

Have you ever been driving all day on a boring highway and suddenly realized that you had almost no memory of what happened during the past half-hour? This common experience does not signal a mental disorder, but when disruptions in a person's memory, consciousness, or identity are more intense and long-lasting, they are known as **dissociative disorders.** These disruptions can come on gradually, but they usually occur suddenly and last from a few hours to many years. Consider the case of John, a thirty-year-old computer executive. When his wife announced that she was leaving him to live with his younger brother, John did not go to work the next day. In fact, his whereabouts were unknown until, two weeks later, he was arrested for public drunkenness and assault in a city more than 300 miles away. The police discovered that during those two weeks, John lived under a different name at a cheap hotel and worked selling tickets at a pornographic movie theater. He did not know his real name or his home address, couldn't explain how he got to his new location, and could not remember much about the previous two weeks.

John displayed a disorder known as **dissociative fugue** (pronounced "fewg"), a sudden loss of personal memory and the adoption of a new identity in a new place. A related disorder called **dissociative amnesia** also involves sudden memory loss for personal information, but the person does not leave home or create a new identity. These conditions are rare, but they tend to attract intense publicity because they are so dramatic.

The most famous dissociative disorder is **dissociative identity disorder (DID)**, formerly known as—and still commonly called—*multiple personality disorder (MPD)*. A person with DID appears to have more than one identity, each of which speaks and acts in a different way. Each personality seems to have its own memories, wishes, and (often conflicting) impulses. Here is a case example:

Mary, a pleasant and introverted thirty-five-year-old social worker, was referred to a psychiatrist for hypnotic treatment of chronic pain. At an early interview she mentioned the odd fact that though she had no memory of using her car after coming home from work, she often found that it had been driven 50 to 100 miles overnight. It turned out that she also had no memory of large parts of her childhood. Mary rapidly learned self-hypnosis for pain control, but during one hypnotic session, she suddenly began speaking in a hostile manner. She told the doctor her name was Marian, and that it was "she" who had been taking long evening drives. She also called Mary "pathetic"

dissociative disorders Conditions involving sudden and usually temporary disruptions in a person's memory, consciousness, or identity.

dissociative fugue A psychological disorder involving sudden loss of memory and the assumption of a new identity in a new locale.

dissociative amnesia A psychological disorder marked by a sudden loss of memory for one's own name, occupation, or other identifying information.

dissociative identity disorder (DID) A dissociative disorder in which a person appears to have more than one identity, each of which behaves in a different way.

"Would it be possible to speak with the personality that pays the bills?"

Debate and skepticism about the nature and origins of dissociative identity disorder are not confined to professional journals. This drawing appeared in *The New Yorker* magazine.

for *"wasting time" trying to please other people. Eventually, six other identities emerged, some of whom told of having experienced parental abuse in childhood. (Spitzer et al., 1994)*

How do dissociative disorders develop? Psychodynamic theorists see massive repression of unwanted impulses or memories as the basis for creating a "new person" who acts out otherwise unacceptable impulses or recalls otherwise unbearable memories (e.g., Ross, 1997). Social-cognitive theorists focus on the fact that everyone is capable of behaving in different ways depending on circumstances (e.g., rowdy in a bar, quiet in a museum). In rare cases, they say, this variation can become so extreme that a person feels, and is perceived by others as, a "different person." Further, sudden memory loss or unusual behavior may be rewarded by providing escape from unpleasant situations, responsibilities, or punishment for misbehavior (Lilienfeld et al., 1999).

Evaluating these hypotheses has been difficult, partly because dissociative disorders have been so rare. Recently, however, DID has been diagnosed more frequently, either because clinicians are looking for it more carefully or because the conditions leading to it are more widespread. Research available so far suggests three conclusions. First, many people displaying DID have experienced events they would like to forget or avoid. The majority (some clinicians believe all) have suffered severe, unavoidable, persistent abuse in childhood (Ross et al., 1991). Second, like Mary, most of these people appear to be skilled at self-hypnosis, through which they can induce a trance-like state. Third, most found that they could escape the trauma of abuse, at least temporarily, by creating "new personalities" to deal with stress (Spiegel, 1994). However, not all abused children display DID, and there is evidence that some cases of DID may be triggered by media stories or by suggestions made to clients by their therapists (Spanos, 1996).

This evidence has led some skeptics to question the existence of multiple personalities (Acocella, 1998; Merckelbach, Devilly, & Rassin, 2002). Others suggest that the increased incidence of dissociative identity disorder may simply reflect its status as a culturally approved method of expressing distress (Hacking, 1995; Spanos, 1994). In fact, concerns such as these were partly responsible for the change in designation from *multiple personality disorder* to *dissociative identity disorder*. The authors of *DSM-IV* wanted to downplay the idea that people harbor multiple personalities that can easily be "contacted" through hypnosis or related techniques. The new name was chosen to suggest, instead, that dissociation, or separation, between one's memories and other aspects of identity can be so dramatic that people experiencing it may come to believe that they have more than one personality (Gleaves, May, & Cardena, 2001; Spiegel, 1994). They point to research showing, for example, that people who display DID may be more aware than they think they are of the memories and actions of each apparent identity (Allen, 2002; Allen & Iacono, 2001). Research on the existence and effects of repressed memories (discussed in the memory chapter) is sure to have an impact on our understanding of, and the controversy over, the causes of dissociative identity disorder. ("In Review: Anxiety, Somatoform, and Dissociative Disorders" presents a summary of our discussion of these topics.)

Mood Disorders

▶ **How common is depression?**

mood disorder A condition in which a person experiences extremes of mood for long periods, shifts from one extreme mood to another, and experiences moods that are inconsistent with events.

Everyone's mood, or *affect,* tends to rise and fall from time to time. However, when people experience long periods of extreme moods such as wild elation or deep depression, when they shift from one extreme to another, and especially when their moods are not consistent with the events around them, they are said to show a **mood disorder,** also known as *affective disorder.* We describe two main types: depressive disorders and bipolar disorders.

in review

ANXIETY, SOMATOFORM, AND DISSOCIATIVE DISORDERS

Disorder	Subtypes	Major Symptoms
Anxiety disorders	Phobias	Intense, irrational fear of objectively nondangerous situations or things, leading to disruptions of behavior.
	Generalized anxiety disorder	Excessive anxiety not focused on a specific situation or object; free-floating anxiety.
	Panic disorder	Repeated attacks of intense fear involving physical symptoms such as faintness, dizziness, and nausea.
	Obsessive-compulsive disorder	Persistent ideas or worries accompanied by ritualistic behaviors performed to neutralize the anxiety-driven thoughts.
Somatoform disorders	Conversion disorder	A loss of physical ability (e.g., sight, hearing) that is related to psychological factors.
	Hypochondriasis	Preoccupation with, or belief that one has, serious illness in the absence of any physical evidence.
	Somatization disorder	Wide variety of somatic complaints that occur over several years and are not the result of a known physical disorder.
	Pain disorder	Preoccupation with pain in the absence of physical reasons for the pain.
Dissociative disorders	Dissociative amnesia/fugue	Sudden, unexpected loss of memory, which may result in relocation and the assumption of a new identity.
	Dissociative identity disorder (multiple personality disorder)	Appearance within the same person for two or more distinct identities, each with a unique way of thinking and behaving.

1. Concern that it may be triggered by media stories or therapists' suggestions has made _____ the most controversial of the dissociative disorders.
2. A person who sleepwalks but is not able to walk when awake is showing signs of _____.
3. Panic disorder sometimes leads to another anxiety disorder called _____.

Depressive Disorders

Depression can range from occasional, normal "down" periods to episodes severe enough to require hospitalization. A person suffering **major depressive disorder** feels sad and overwhelmed for weeks or months, typically losing interest in activities and relationships and taking pleasure in nothing (Coryell et al., 1993; Rapaport et al., 2005; Sloan, Strauss, & Wisner, 2001). Exaggerated feelings of inadequacy, worthlessness, hopelessness, or guilt are common. Despite the person's best efforts, anything from conversation to bathing can become an unbearable, exhausting task (Solomon, 1998). Changes in eating habits resulting in weight loss or weight gain often accompany major depressive disorder. So does disturbed sleeping or, sometimes, excessive sleeping. Problems in working, concentrating, making decisions, and thinking clearly are also common, as are symptoms of an accompanying anxiety disorder (Zimmerman, McDermut, & Mattia, 2000). In extreme cases, depressed people may express false beliefs, or **delusions**—worrying, for example, that government agents are planning to punish them. Major depressive disorder may come on suddenly or gradually. It may consist of a single episode or, more commonly, repeated depressive periods. Here is a case example:

Mr. J. was a fifty-one-year-old industrial engineer …. Since the death of his wife five years earlier, he had been suffering from continuing episodes of depression marked by extreme social withdrawal and occasional thoughts of suicide …. He drank, and when

major depressive disorder A condition in which a person feels sad and hopeless for weeks or months, often losing interest in all activities and taking pleasure in nothing.

delusions False beliefs, such as those experienced by people suffering from schizophrenia or severe depression.

thoroughly intoxicated would plead to his deceased wife for forgiveness. He lost all capacity for joy. ... Once a gourmet, he now had no interest in food and good wine ... and could barely manage to engage in small talk. As might be expected, his work record deteriorated markedly. Appointments were missed and projects haphazardly started and left unfinished. (Davison & Neale, 1990, p. 221)

Depression is not always so extreme. In a less severe pattern of depression, called **dysthymic disorder,** the person shows the sad mood, lack of interest, and loss of pleasure associated with major depression but less intensely and for a longer period. (The duration must be at least two years to qualify as dysthymic disorder.) Mental and behavioral disruptions are also less severe. People exhibiting dysthymic disorder rarely require hospitalization.

Major depressive disorder occurs sometime in the lives of about 13 to 17 percent of people in North America and Europe (Hasin et al., 2005; Kessler et al., 1994, 2003; U.S. Surgeon General, 1999). The incidence of the disorder varies considerably across cultures and subcultures, however. For example, it occurs at much higher rates in urban Ireland than in urban Spain (Judd et al., 2002). There are gender differences in some cultures, too. North American and European women are two to three times more likely than men to experience major depressive disorder (American Psychiatric Association, 2000; Weissman et al., 1993), but this difference does not appear in the less economically developed countries of the Middle East, Africa, and Asia (Ayuso-Mateos et al., 2001; Culbertson, 1997). Depression can occur at any age, but it frequently first appears in late adolescence or young adulthood. Increased rates of depression are also found among the elderly (Cross-National Collaborative Group, 2002; Fassler & Dumas, 1997; Sowdon, 2001).

Suicide and Depression   Suicide is associated with a variety of psychological disorders, but it is most closely tied to depression. Some form of depression has been implicated in 40 to 60 percent of all suicides (Angst, Angst, & Stassen, 1999; Oquendo & Mann, 2001; Rihmer, 2001). In fact, thinking about suicide is a symptom of depressive disorders. Hopelessness about the future—another depressive symptom—and a desire to seek instant escape from problems are also related to suicide attempts (Beck et al., 1990; Brown et al., 2000).

About 31,000 people in the United States commit suicide each year, and 10 to 20 times that many people attempt it (Centers for Disease Control and Prevention, 2004). This puts the U.S. suicide rate at about 11 per 100,000 individuals, making suicide the eleventh leading cause of death. Worldwide, the suicide rate is as high as 25 per 100,000 in some northern European countries, China, and Japan and as low as 6 per 100,000 in countries with stronger religious prohibitions against suicide, such as Greece, Italy, Ireland, and the nations of the Middle East (Lamar, 2000; Phillips, Li, & Zhang, 2002).

Suicide rates differ considerably depending on sociocultural factors such as age, gender, and ethnicity (Centers for Disease Control and Prevention, 2002b; Oquendo et al., 2001). In the United States, suicide is most common among people sixty-five and older, especially males (Centers for Disease Control and Prevention, 2004). However, since 1950, suicide among adolescents has tripled, making it the third leading cause of death, after accidents and homicides, among fifteen- to twenty-four-year-olds (Centers for Disease Control and Prevention, 2002a). Suicide is the second leading cause of death among college students; about 10,000 try to kill themselves each year, and about 1,000 succeed. These figures are much higher than for young people in general, but much lower than for the elderly. Women attempt suicide three times as often as men, but men are four times as likely to actually kill themselves (Centers for Disease Control and Prevention, 2002b). Suicide rates also differ across ethnic groups (see Figure 12.4). Among males in the United States, for example, the overall rate for American Indians is 19.1 per 100,000, compared with 19.4 for European Americans, 9.7 for Asian Americans, 10.7 for Hispanic Americans, and 10.4 for African Americans. The same pattern of ethnic differences appears among women, though the actual rates are much lower (Centers for Disease Control and Prevention, 2002a).

dysthymic disorder   A pattern of depression in which the person shows the sad mood, lack of interest, and loss of pleasure associated with major depressive disorder but to a lesser degree and for a longer period.

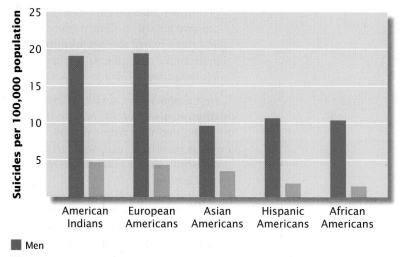

FIGURE **12.4**

Suicide Rates by Gender and Ethnicity

The suicide rates among ethnic groups in the United States vary widely. In 2002, more teenagers and young adults died from suicide than from cancer, heart disease, AIDS, birth defects, stroke, pneumonia and influenza, and chronic lung disease *combined* (National Center for Health Statistics, 2004).

■ Men
■ Women

Source: Centers for Disease Control and Prevention (2002d).

Surveys indicate that, sometime during the previous year, about 3 percent of all adults and as many as 10 percent of college students have thought about committing suicide (Brener, Hassan, & Barrios, 1999; Kessler, Berglund, Borges, et al., 2005). Predicting who will actually do so is difficult, but the results of hundreds of research studies provide some guidance. In the United States, at least, suicide is most likely among European American males, especially those older than forty-five, single or divorced, and living alone. The risk of suicide is also heightened among people diagnosed with a mood disorder, anxiety disorder, or schizophrenia (Boardman & Healy, 2001; Khan et al., 2002; Rihmer, 2001). Among the elderly, suicide is most common in males who suffer depression over health problems (e.g., Brown, Bongar, & Cleary, 2004). The risk is higher, too, in people who have made a specific plan, given away possessions, and are impulsive (Centers for Disease Control and Prevention, 2004; Corruble, Damy, & Guelfi, 1999). A previous suicide attempt may not always be a good predictor of eventual suicide, because such attempts may have been help-seeking gestures, not failed efforts to die (Nock & Kessler, 2006). In fact, although about 10 percent of unsuccessful attempters try again and succeed, most people who commit suicide had made no prior attempts (Clark & Fawcett, 1992).

It is often said that people who talk about suicide will never try it. This is a myth (Shneidman, 1987). Those who say they are thinking of suicide are much more likely than other people to try suicide. In fact, most suicides are preceded by some kind of warning, whether direct ("I think I'm going to kill myself") or vague ("Sometimes I wonder if life is worth living"). Although not everyone who threatens suicide follows through, if you suspect that someone you know is thinking about suicide, encourage the person to contact a mental health professional or a crisis hotline. If the danger is immediate, make the contact yourself, and ask for advice about how to respond. Many suicide attempts—including those triggered by other suicides in the same town or school—can be prevented by social support and other forms of help for people at high risk (Centers for Disease Control and Prevention, 2004; Mann et al., 2005). For more information, visit suicide-related web sites, such as that of the American Association of Suicidology (www.suicidology.org).

Bipolar Disorders

The alternating appearance of two emotional extremes, or poles, characterizes **bipolar disorder.** We have already described one emotional pole: depression. The other is **mania,** which is an agitated, usually elated, emotional state. During periods of mania, people tend to be overly optimistic, boundlessly energetic, certain of having extraordinary powers and abilities, and bursting with all sorts of ideas. They are irritated by

bipolar disorder   A condition in which a person alternates between the two emotional extremes of depression and mania.

mania   An elated, active emotional state.

in review

MOOD DISORDERS

Type	Typical Symptoms	Related Features
Major depressive disorder	Deep sadness, feelings of worthlessness, changes in eating and sleeping habits, loss of interest and pleasure	Lasts weeks or months; may occur in repeating episodes; severe cases may include delusions
Dysthymic disorder	Similar to major depressive disorder, but less severe and longer lasting	Hospitalization usually not necessary
Bipolar disorder	Alternating extremes of mood, from deep depression to mania, and back	Manic episodes include impulsivity, unrealistic optimism, high energy, severe agitation
Cyclothymic disorder	Similar to bipolar disorder, but less severe	Hospitalization usually not necessary

1. The risk of suicide is associated with _____ more than with any other symptom of disorder.
2. Cyclothymic disorder is the bipolar version of _____.
3. Women are _____ likely than men to try suicide, but men are _____ likely to succeed.

anyone who tries to reason with them or "slow them down," and they may make impulsive and unwise decisions, including spending their life savings on foolish schemes.

In bipolar disorder, episodes of mania may alternate with periods of deep depression. Sometimes, periods of relatively normal mood separate these extremes (Tohen et al., 2003). This pattern has also been called *manic depression*. Compared with major depressive disorder, bipolar disorder is rare. It occurs in only about 1 percent of adults, and it affects men and women about equally. Even less common is *bipolar II disorder*, in which major depressive episodes alternate with episodes known as *hypomania*, which are less severe than the manic phases seen in bipolar I disorder.

Slightly more common is a pattern of milder mood swings known as **cyclothymic disorder,** the bipolar equivalent of dysthymic disorder. Like major depressive disorder, bipolar disorders are extremely disruptive to a person's ability to work or maintain social relationships (Goldberg, Harrow, & Grossman, 1995), and they are often accompanied by anxiety disorders (Freeman, Freeman, & McElroy, 2002). "In Review: Mood Disorders" summarizes the main types of mood disorders.

Causes of Mood Disorders

Research on the causes of mood disorders has focused on biological, psychological, and sociocultural risk factors. The more of these risk factors people have, the more likely they are to experience a mood disorder.

LINKAGES
Are some psychological disorders inherited? (a link to Biology and Behavior)

Biological Factors The role of genetics is suggested by twin studies and family studies showing that mood disorders tend to run in families (Cho et al., 2005; Kendler et al., 2006; Kieseppä et al., 2004; Weissman et al., 2005). For example, bipolar disorder is much more likely to be seen in both members of genetically identical twin pairs than in genetically nonidentical twins (Bowman & Nurnberger, 1993; Egeland et al., 1987; McGuffin et al., 2003). Family studies also show that those who are closely related to people with bipolar disorder are more likely than others to develop the disorder themselves

cyclothymic disorder A mood disorder characterized by an alternating pattern of mood swings that are less extreme than those of bipolar disorder.

TREATING SAD Seasonal affective disorder (SAD) can often be relieved by exposure to full-spectrum light for as little as a couple of hours a day (Terman & Terman, 2005).

(Blackwood, Visscher, & Muir, 2001). Major depressive disorder, too, is more likely to occur in both members of identical, compared with nonidentical, twins (Klein et al., 2001; Levinson, 2006). This genetic influence is especially strong in female twins (Bierut et al., 1999). Researchers continue to look for the specific genes that might be involved in the transmission of elevated risk for mood disorders (Cheng et al., 2006; Greenwood et al., 2006; Hariri et al., 2005; Konradi et al., 2004; MacQueen, Hajek, & Alda, 2005).

Other biological factors that may contribute to mood disorders include malfunctions in regions of the brain involved in mood, imbalances in the brain's neurotransmitter systems, malfunctioning of the endocrine system, disruption of biological rhythms, and underdevelopment in the frontal lobes, hippocampus, or other brain areas (Blumberg et al., 2003; Geuze, Vermetten, & Bremner, 2005; Jacobs, 2004; MacQueen et al., 2005; Milak et al., 2005; Staley et al., 2006; Strakowski, DelBello, & Adler, 2005). All of these conditions may themselves be influenced by genetics.

As for the role of neurotransmitters, norepinephrine, serotonin, and dopamine were implicated decades ago when scientists discovered that drugs capable of altering these substances also relieved mood disorders. However, the precise nature of the relationship between neurotransmitters and mood disorders is still not fully understood (Martinot et al., 2001; Schloss & Williams, 1998; U.S. Surgeon General, 1999).

Mood disorders have also been related to malfunctions of the endocrine system, especially the subsystem involved in the body's responses to stress (see the chapter on health, stress, and coping). For example, research shows that as many as 70 percent of depressed people secrete abnormally high levels of the stress hormone cortisol (Dinan, 2001; Posener et al., 2000).

The cycles of mood swings seen in bipolar disorders and in recurring episodes of major depressive disorder suggest that mood disorders may be related to stressful triggering events (Miklowitz & Alloy, 1999). They may also be related to disturbances in the body's biological clock, which is described in the chapter on biology and behavior (Goodwin & Jamison, 1990). This second possibility seems especially likely to apply to the 15 percent of depressed people who consistently experience a calendar-linked pattern of depressive episodes known as *seasonal affective disorder (SAD)*. During months of shorter daylight, these people slip into severe depression, accompanied by irritability and excessive sleeping. Their depression tends to lift as daylight hours increase (Faedda et al., 1993). Disruption of biological rhythms is also suggested by the fact that many depressed people tend to have trouble sleeping—partly because during the day, their biological clocks may be telling them it is the middle of the night. Resetting the biological clock through methods such as sleep deprivation or light stimulation has relieved depression in many cases (Golden et al., 2005; Lewy et al., 2006; Terman et al., 2001).

Psychological and Social Factors Researchers have come to recognize that the biological factors involved in mood disorders always operate in combination with psychological and social factors (Jacobs, 2004). As mentioned earlier, the very nature of depressive symptoms can depend on the culture in which a person lives. Biopsychosocial explanations of mood disorders also emphasize the impact of anxiety, negative thinking, and the other psychological and emotional responses triggered by trauma, losses, and other stressful events (Kendler, Hettema, et al., 2003; Kendler, Kuhn, & Prescott, 2004; Monroe et al., 1999). For example, the higher rate of depression among females—and especially among poor, ethnic-minority single mothers—has been attributed to their greater exposure to stressors of all kinds (Brown & Moran, 1997; Miranda & Green, 1999). Environmental stressors affect men, too (Bierut et al., 1999), which may be one reason that gender differences are smaller in countries in which men and women face equally stressful lives. Still, differing stressors may not be the only source of these gender differences (Kendler, Thornton, & Prescott, 2001).

A number of social-cognitive theories suggest that the way people think about their stressors can increase or decrease the likelihood of mood disorders. One of these theories is based on the *learned helplessness* research described in the chapter on learning. Just as animals become inactive and appear depressed when they have no control over negative events (El Yacoubi et al., 2003), humans may experience depression as a result of feeling incapable of controlling their lives, especially the stressors confronting them (Klein & Seligman, 1976; Seligman, 1991). But most of us have limited control, so why aren't we all depressed? The ways in which people learn to think about events in their lives may hold the key. For example, Aaron Beck's (1967, 1976) cognitive theory of depression suggests that depressed people develop mental habits of (1) blaming themselves when things go wrong, (2) focusing on and exaggerating the negative side of events, and (3) jumping to overly generalized, pessimistic conclusions. Such cognitive habits, says Beck, are errors that lead to depressing thoughts and other symptoms of depression (Beck & Beck, 1995). Depressed people, in fact, do tend to think about significant negative events in ways that are likely to increase or prolong their depression (Gotlib & Hammen, 1992; Gotlib et al., 2004; Strunk, Lopez, & DeRubeis, 2006).

Severe, long-lasting depression is especially likely among people who blame their lack of control or other problems on a permanent, generalized lack of personal competence rather than on a temporary mistake or some external cause (Seligman et al., 1988). This *negative attributional style* may be another important cognitive factor in depression (Alloy, Abramson, & Francis, 1999; Hankin, Fraley, & Abela, 2005; Hunt & Forand, 2005). Are depressed people's unusually negative beliefs about themselves actually helping to cause their depression, or are they merely symptoms of it? A number of studies have assessed the attributional styles of large samples of nondepressed people and then kept in touch with them to see whether individuals with negative self-beliefs are more likely to become depressed when stressors occur. These longitudinal studies suggest that a negative attributional style is, in fact, a risk factor for depression, not just a result of being depressed (Garber, Keiley, & Martin, 2002; Gibb et al., 2004; Runyon & Kenny, 2002; Satterfield, Folkman, & Acree, 2002). In one study, for example, adolescents who held strong negative self-beliefs were more likely than other youngsters to develop depression when faced with stress later in life (Lewinsohn, Joiner, & Rohde, 2001).

Social-cognitive theorists also suggest that whether depression continues or worsens depends in part on how people respond once they start to feel depressed. Those who continuously think about negative events, about why they occur, and even about being depressed are likely to feel more and more depressed (Just & Alloy, 1997; Sarin, Abela, & Auerbach, 2005). According to Susan Nolen-Hoeksema (1990, 2001), this *ruminative style* is especially characteristic of women and may help explain gender differences in the frequency of depression. When men start to feel sad, she says, they tend to use a *distracting style.* In other words, they engage in activity that distracts them from their concerns and helps bring them out of their depressed mood (Hankin & Abramson, 2001; Just & Alloy, 1997; Nolen-Hoeksema, Morrow, & Fredrickson, 1993).

Notice that social-cognitive explanations of depression are consistent with the diathesis-stress explanation of disorder (Hankin & Abramson, 2001). These explanations suggest that certain cognitive styles serve as a predisposition (or diathesis) that makes a person vulnerable to depression, which is made even more likely by stressors. As suggested in the chapter on health, stress, and coping, the depressing effects of these stressors are likely to be magnified by lack of social support, inadequate coping skills, and the presence of other stressful conditions, such as poverty (e.g., Stice, Ragan, & Randall, 2004).

Given the number and complexity of biological, psychological, social, and situational factors potentially involved in causing mood disorders, the diathesis-stress approach appears to be an especially appropriate guide to future research (Kendler, Gardner, & Prescott, 2006). One study based on this approach looked at the role of genetics and stressful events in shaping mood disorders in a large group of female twin pairs. Both factors were associated with major depression; the women at highest genetic risk were the most likely to become depressed following a significant stressor (Kendler, Thornton, & Gardner, 2000, 2001; Kendler et al., 2005). Another study found that people with a particular version of a single gene were more likely than others to experience depressive symptoms in relation to stressful events (Caspi et al., 2003). Further, different biological and psychological risk factors may be of particular importance at different stages in life (Kendler, Gardner, & Prescott, 2002). In the final analysis, it may turn out that each subtype of mood disorder is caused by a unique combination of factors. The challenge for researchers is to identify these subtypes and map out their causal ingredients.

Schizophrenia

▶ **Is schizophrenia the same as "split personality"?**

Here is part of a letter that arrived in the mail several years ago:

Dear Sirs:
Pertaining to our continuing failure to prosecute violations of minor's rights to sovereign equality which are occurring in gestations being compromised by the ingestation of controlled substances, ... the skewing of androgyny which continues in female juveniles even after separation from their mother's has occurred, and as a means of promulflagitating my paying Governor Hickel of Alaska for my employees to have personal services endorsements and controlled substance endorsements, ... the Iraqi oil being released by the United Nations being identified as Kurdistanian oil, and the July, 1991 issue of the Siberian Review spells President Eltsin's name without a letter y.

The disorganization and strange content of this letter suggest that its writer might be displaying **schizophrenia** (pronounced "skit-so-FREE-nee-uh"), a pattern of severely disturbed thinking, emotion, perception, and behavior that seriously impairs the ability to communicate and relate to others and disrupts most other aspects of daily functioning (Freedman, 2003). Schizophrenia is one of the most severe and disabling of all mental disorders. Its core symptoms are seen virtually everywhere in the world, occurring in about 1 to 2 percent of the population (American Psychiatric Association, 2000). In the United States, it appears about equally in various ethnic groups, but, like most disorders, it tends to be diagnosed more frequently in economically disadvantaged populations. Schizophrenia is seen about equally in men and women, although in women it may appear later in life, be less severe, and respond better to treatment (Aleman, Kahn, & Selten, 2003; American Psychiatric Association, 2000; U.S. Surgeon General, 1999).

Schizophrenia tends to develop in adolescence or early adulthood. In about three out of four cases, symptoms appear gradually over a period of years; in other cases, the onset is more rapid. About 40 percent of people diagnosed with schizophrenia improve with treatment and are able to function reasonably well; the rest continue to display symptoms that permanently impair their functioning (Van der Heiden & Haefner, 2000;

schizophrenia A pattern of severely disturbed thinking, emotion, perception, and behavior that constitutes one of the most serious and disabling of all mental disorders.

Hegarty et al., 1994). It has been estimated that 10 to 13 percent of homeless individuals suffer from schizophrenia (Fischer & Breakey, 1991; Olfson et al., 1999).

One of the best predictors of the outcome of schizophrenia is *premorbid adjustment,* the level of functioning a person had achieved before schizophrenia symptoms first appeared. Improvement is more likely in those who had reached higher levels of education and occupation and who had established supportive relationships with family and friends (Rabinowitz et al., 2002; Watt & Saiz, 1991).

Symptoms of Schizophrenia

The main problems seen in people displaying schizophrenia relate to thinking—both how they think and what they think (Heinrichs, 2005). Indeed, the very word *schizophrenia,* or "split mind," refers to the oddities of schizophrenic thinking, including a splitting of normally integrated mental processes, such as thoughts and feelings. So the person may giggle while talking about sad events and claiming to feel unhappy. Contrary to common usage, schizophrenia does not refer to the "split personality" seen in dissociative identity disorder (multiple personality disorder), discussed earlier in this chapter.

Schizophrenic thought and language are often disorganized. *Neologisms,* or words that have meaning only to the person speaking them, are common. The word "promulflagitating" in the preceding letter is one example. That letter also illustrates *loose associations,* the tendency for one thought to be logically unconnected or only loosely connected to the next. In the most severe cases, thought becomes just a jumble known as *word salad.* For example, one patient was heard to say, "Upon the advisability of held keeping, environment of the seabeach gathering, to the forest stream, reinstatement to be placed, poling the paddleboat, of the swamp morass, to the forest compensation of the dunce" (Lehman, 1967, p. 627).

The content of schizophrenic thinking is also disturbed. Often it includes a bewildering assortment of delusions (false beliefs), especially *delusions of persecution.* Some patients believe that space aliens or government agents are trying to steal their internal organs, and they may interpret everything from TV commercials to casual hand gestures as part of the plot. Delusions that such common events are somehow related to oneself are called *ideas of reference. Delusions of grandeur* may also appear; one young man was convinced that the president of the United States was trying to contact him for advice. Other types of delusions include (1) *thought broadcasting,* in which patients believe that their thoughts can be heard by others; (2) *thought blocking* or *thought withdrawal,* the belief that someone is either preventing thoughts or "stealing" them as they appear; and (3) *thought insertion,* the belief that other people's thoughts are appearing in one's own mind. Some patients believe that their behavior is being controlled by others; in one case, a man claimed that the CIA had placed a control device in his brain.

People with schizophrenia often report that they cannot focus their attention, and they may feel overwhelmed as they try to attend to everything at once. Various perceptual disorders may also appear. The person may feel detached from the world and see other people as flat cutouts. The body may feel as though it is a machine or as though parts of it are dead or rotting. **Hallucinations,** or false perceptions, are common, often emerging as voices. These voices may sound like an overheard conversation, or they may urge the person to do or not to do things; sometimes they comment on, narrate, or (most often) criticize the person's actions. Hallucinations can also involve the experience of nonexistent sights, smells, tastes, and touch sensations. Emotional expression is often muted—a pattern called *flat affect.* But when schizophrenics do display emotion, it is often exaggerated or inappropriate. For example, they may cry for no apparent reason or fly into a rage in response to a simple question.

Some people with schizophrenia are quite agitated, constantly fidgeting, grimacing, or pacing the floor in ritualized patterns. Others become so withdrawn that they move very little. Lack of motivation and poor social skills, deteriorating personal hygiene, and an inability to function in everyday situations are other common characteristics of schizophrenia.

LINKAGES
Do people perceive hallucinations as real sensory events? (a link to Sensation and Perception)

hallucinations   False or distorted perceptions of objects or events.

These traditional categories of schizophrenia convey some useful information, but subtype labels are not always accurate. Some symptoms of schizophrenia appear in more than one subtype, and people first placed in one subtype might later display characteristics of another. These concerns, plus the fact that *DSM-IV* subtypes may not be linked to different causal factors, have led researchers to develop additional ways of categorizing schizophrenia, such as whether positive or negative symptoms are most prominent in a given case (Villalta-Gil et al., 2006).

Type	Frequency	Prominent Features
Paranoid schizophrenia	40 percent of people with schizophrenia; appears late in life (after age 25–30)	Delusions of grandeur or persecution; anger; anxiety; argumentativeness; extreme jealousy; onset often sudden; signs of impairment may be subtle.
Disorganized schizophrenia	5 percent of all people with schizophrenia; high prevalence in homeless population	Delusions; hallucinations; incoherent speech; facial grimaces; inappropriate laughter/giggling; neglected personal hygiene; loss of bladder/bowel control.
Catatonic schizophrenia	8 percent of all people with schizophrenia	Disordered movement, alternating between total immobility (stupor) and wild excitement. In stupor, the person does not speak or attend to communication.
Undifferentiated schizophrenia	40 percent of all people with schizophrenia	Patterns of disordered behavior, thought, and emotion that do not fall easily into any other subtype.
Residual schizophrenia	Varies	Applies to people who have had prior episodes of schizophrenia but are not currently displaying symptoms.

Categorizing Schizophrenia

DSM-IV lists five major subtypes of schizophrenia: paranoid, disorganized, catatonic, undifferentiated, and residual. These subtypes are summarized in Table 12.4.

Researchers have also made other useful distinctions among various forms of schizophrenia. One of these distinctions involves the positive-negative symptom dimension. Disorganized thoughts, delusions, and hallucinations are sometimes called *positive symptoms* of schizophrenia, because they appear as undesirable *additions* to a person's mental life (Andreasen et al., 1995; Racenstein et al., 2002). In contrast, the absence of pleasure and motivation, lack of emotion, social withdrawal, reduced speech, and other deficits seen in schizophrenia are sometimes called *negative symptoms,* because they appear to *subtract* elements from normal mental life (Nicholson & Neufeld, 1993). Many patients exhibit both positive and negative symptoms, but when the negative symptoms are stronger, schizophrenia generally has a more severe course, including long-term disability and relative lack of response to treatment (e.g., Milev et al., 2005; Racenstein et al., 2002). Yet another way of categorizing schizophrenic symptoms focuses on whether they are *psychotic* (e.g., hallucinations, delusions), *disorganized* (e.g., incoherent speech, chaotic behavior, inappropriate affect), or *negative* (e.g., lack of speech or motivation). Some researchers believe that each symptom cluster or dimension may ultimately be traceable to different causes. For this reason, schizophrenia is often referred to as the *schizophrenia spectrum* (Tsuang, Stone, & Faraone, 2000).

CATATONIC STUPOR The symptoms of schizophrenia often occur in characteristic patterns. This woman's lack of motivation and other negative symptoms of schizophrenia are severe enough that she appears to be in a catatonic stupor. Such patients may become rigid or, as in this case, show a waxy flexibility that allows them to be "posed" in virtually any position. Diagnosticians using the traditional subtype system would probably label her as displaying catatonic schizophrenia.

Causes of Schizophrenia

The search for causes of schizophrenia has been more intense than for any other psychological disorder. The findings so far confirm one thing for certain: As with other disorders, biological, psychological, and sociocultural factors combine to cause or worsen all forms of schizophrenia (Sullivan, Kendler, & Neale, 2003).

Biological Factors Research in behavioral genetics shows that schizophrenia runs in families (Asarnow et al., 2001; Gottesman, 1991). One family study found that 16 percent of the children of mothers with schizophrenia—compared with 2 percent of those of mothers without schizophrenia—developed schizophrenia themselves over a twenty-five-year period (Parnas et al., 1993). Even if they are adopted by families without schizophrenia, the children of parents with schizophrenia are ten times more likely to develop schizophrenia than adopted children whose biological parents do not have schizophrenia (Kety et al., 1994). Still, it is unlikely that a single gene transmits schizophrenia (Chumakov et al., 2002; Plomin & McGuffin, 2003). Among identical-twin pairs in which one of the members displays schizophrenia, 40 percent of the other members display it, too; but 60 percent of them do not (McGue, 1992). It is more likely that some people inherit a predisposition, or diathesis, for schizophrenia that involves many genes (e.g., Harrison & Law, 2006; Ma et al., 2006; Mah et al., 2006; Peirce et al., 2006). This diathesis then combines with other genetic and nongenetic factors to cause the disorder (Moldin & Gottesman, 1997).

The search for biological factors in schizophrenia also focuses on a number of abnormalities in the structure, functioning, and chemistry of the brain that tend to appear in people with schizophrenia (e.g., Andrews et al., 2006; Neves-Pereira et al., 2005; Tamminga & Holcomb, 2005). For example, brain imaging studies have compared patients with schizophrenia with other mental patients. Many patients with schizophrenia (especially those who display mostly negative symptoms) have less tissue in areas of the brain that are involved in emotional expression, thinking, and information processing—functions that are disordered in schizophrenia (Conklin & Iacono, 2002; Csernansky et al., 2004; Gilbert et al., 2001; Highley et al., 2003; Pol et al., 2002; Selemon et al., 2003; Sigmundsson et al., 2001; Velakoulis et al., 2006). There is also evidence that worsening symptoms are associated with continued tissue loss in these areas (Ho et al., 2003). Patients with mainly positive symptoms tend to have essentially normal-looking brains (Andreasen, 1997).

Researchers are also investigating the possibility that abnormalities in brain chemistry—especially in neurotransmitter systems that use dopamine—play a role in causing or intensifying the symptoms of schizophrenia (Seeman et al., 2005). Because drugs that block the brain's dopamine receptors often reduce the hallucinations, disordered thinking, and other positive symptoms of schizophrenia, some investigators speculate that schizophrenia results from excess dopamine. However, the relationship between dopamine and schizophrenia is a complex one (Albert et al., 2002; Koh et al., 2002). Some research suggests, for example, that excessive activity in dopamine systems may be related to the appearance of hallucinations, delusions, and other positive symptoms of schizophrenia. Abnormally low dopamine system activity, especially in prefrontal brain areas, has been associated with negative symptoms such as withdrawal (e.g., Cohen & Servan-Schreiber, 1992).

Some researchers are integrating genetic and environmental explanations of schizophrenia by looking for *neurodevelopmental* abnormalities (e.g., Rapoport, Addington, & Frangou, 2005). Perhaps, they say, some forms of schizophrenia arise from disruptions in brain development during the period from before birth through childhood, when the brain is growing and its various functions are maturing. For instance, prenatal exposure to physical trauma, flu, or other infections is associated with increased risk for developing schizophrenia (AbdelMalik et al., 2003; Brown et al., 2004, 2005; Malaspina et al., 2001). It may be that the expression of a genetically transmitted predisposition for brain abnormality is enhanced by environmental stressors such as maternal drug use during pregnancy, complications during birth, and childhood malnutrition

in review

SCHIZOPHRENIA

Aspect	Key Features
Common Symptoms	
Disorders of thought	Disturbed *content*, including delusions; disorganization, including loose associations, neologisms, and word salad
Disorders of perception	Hallucinations or false perceptions; poorly focused attention
Disorders of emotion	Flat affect; inappropriate tears, laughter, or anger
Possible Causes	
Biological	Genetics; abnormalities in brain structure; abnormalities in dopamine systems; neurodevelopmental problems
Psychological and sociocultural	Learned maladaptive behavior; disturbed patterns of family communication

?

1. The _____ approach forms the basis of the vulnerability theory of schizophrenia.
2. Hallucinations are _____ symptoms of schizophrenia; lack of emotion is a _____ symptom.
3. Patients with schizophrenia who were able to finish school are _____ likely to show improvement.

(Sørenson et al., 2003). Neurodevelopmental factors may help explain why children of parents with schizophrenia tend to show cognitive and intellectual problems associated with brain abnormalities (Ashe, Berry, & Boulton; 2001; Cannon et al., 1994; McGlashan & Hoffman, 2000; Neumann et al., 1995).

Psychological and Sociocultural Factors Psychological factors alone are not considered to be primary causes of schizophrenia (Bassett et al., 2001), but psychological processes and sociocultural influences can contribute to the appearance of schizophrenia and influence its course. These influences include poverty and other adverse living situations, maladaptive learning experiences, dysfunctional cognitive habits, and stressful family communication patterns (Cantor-Graae & Selten, 2005; Wicks et al., 2005). For example, individuals with schizophrenia who live with relatives who are critical, unsupportive, or emotionally overinvolved are especially likely to relapse following improvement (Hooley, 2004; Rosenfarb et al., 2000; Wearden et al., 2000). Family members' negative attitudes may be a source of stress that actually increases the chances that disruptive or odd behaviors will persist or worsen (Rosenfarb et al., 1995). Patients who are helped to cope with these potentially damaging influences tend to have better long-term outcomes (Bustillo et al., 2001; Velligan et al., 2000).

Vulnerability Theory All the causal theories of schizophrenia we have outlined are consistent with the diathesis-stress approach, which assumes that stress activates a person's predisposition for disorder. ("In Review: Schizophrenia" summarizes these theories, as well as the symptoms of schizophrenia.) In fact, a diathesis-stress framework forms the basis for the *vulnerability theory* of schizophrenia (Cornblatt & Erlenmeyer-Kimling, 1985; Zubin & Spring, 1977). This theory suggests that (1) vulnerability to schizophrenia is mainly biological; (2) different people have differing degrees of vulnerability; (3) vulnerability is influenced partly by genetic influences on development and partly by abnormalities that arise from environmental risk factors; and (4) psychological components, such as exposure to poor parenting, a high-stress environment, or inadequate coping skills, may help determine whether schizophrenia actually appears and may also influence the course of the disorder (Walker & Diforio, 1998; Wearden et al., 2000).

Many different blends of vulnerability and stress can lead to schizophrenia. People whose genetic characteristics or prenatal experiences leave them vulnerable to developing schizophrenia may be especially likely to do so if they are later exposed to learning experiences, family conflicts, or other stressors that trigger and maintain schizophrenic patterns of thought and action. Those same experiences and stressors would not be expected to lead to schizophrenia in people who are less vulnerable to developing the disorder. In other words, schizophrenia is a highly complex disorder—probably more than one disorder (Kirkpatrick et al., 2001; Tsuang, Stone, & Faraone, 2000)—whose origins appear to lie in numerous biological, psychological, and sociocultural domains, some of which are yet to be discovered.

Personality Disorders

▶ **Which personality disorder often leads to crime?**

Personality disorders are long-standing, inflexible ways of behaving that are not so much severe mental disorders as dysfunctional styles of living (Shea et al., 2002). These disorders affect all areas of functioning and, from childhood or adolescence on, create problems for those who display them and for others (Millon & Davis, 1996). Some psychologists view personality disorders as interpersonal strategies (Kiesler, 1996) or as extreme, rigid, and maladaptive expressions of personality traits (Widiger, 1997).

The ten personality disorders found on Axis II of *DSM-IV* are grouped into three clusters that share certain features (see Table 12.5). The *odd-eccentric* cluster includes

TABLE 12.5

Personality Disorders

Here are brief descriptions of the ten personality disorders listed on Axis II of *DSM-IV*.

Type	Typical Features
Paranoid	Suspiciousness and distrust of others, all of whom are assumed to be hostile
Schizoid	Detachment from social relationships; restricted range of emotion
Schizotypal	Detachment from, and great discomfort in, social relationships; odd perceptions, thoughts, beliefs, and behaviors
Dependent	Helplessness; excessive need to be taken care of; submissive and clinging behavior; difficulty in making decisions
Obsessive-compulsive	Preoccupation with orderliness, perfection, and control
Avoidant	Inhibition in social situations; feelings of inadequacy; oversensitivity to criticism
Histrionic	Excessive emotionality and preoccupation with being the center of attention; emotional shallowness; overly dramatic behavior
Narcissistic	Exaggerated ideas of self-importance and achievements; preoccupation with fantasies of success; arrogance
Borderline	Lack of stability in interpersonal relationships, self-image, and emotion; impulsivity; angry outbursts; intense fear of abandonment; recurring suicidal gestures
Antisocial	Shameless disregard for, and violation of, other people's rights

personality disorders Long-standing, inflexible ways of behaving that become styles of life that create problems, usually for others.

A CLASSIC CASE OF ANTISOCIAL PERSONALITY DISORDER Alfred Jack Oakley meets women through personal ads, claiming to be a millionaire movie producer, pilot, and novelist. In reality, he is a penniless con artist who uses his smooth-talking charm to gain the women's trust so he can steal from them. In January 2000, after being convicted of stealing a Florida woman's Mercedes, Oakley complimented the prosecutor's skills and the jury's wisdom and claimed remorse. The judge appeared to see through this ploy ("I don't believe there is a sincere word that ever comes out of your mouth"), but it was still effective enough to get Oakley probation instead of jail time!

paranoid, schizoid, and schizotypal personality disorders. People diagnosed as having *schizotypal personality disorder,* for example, display some of the peculiarities seen in schizophrenia but are not disturbed enough to be labeled as having schizophrenia. The *anxious-fearful* cluster includes dependent, obsessive-compulsive, and avoidant personality disorders. The *avoidant personality disorder,* for example, is similar to social phobia in the sense that persons labeled with this disorder tend to be "loners" with a long-standing pattern of avoiding social situations and of being particularly sensitive to criticism or rejection. Finally, the *dramatic-erratic* cluster includes the histrionic, narcissistic, borderline, and antisocial personality disorders. The main characteristics of *narcissistic personality disorder,* for example, are an exaggerated sense of self-importance, extreme sensitivity to criticism, a constant need for attention, and a tendency to arrogantly overestimate personal abilities and achievements.

The most serious, costly, and intensively studied personality disorder is **antisocial personality disorder** (e.g., Scott, 2001). It is marked by a long-term pattern of irresponsible, impulsive, unscrupulous, and sometimes criminal behavior, beginning in childhood or early adolescence. In the nineteenth century, the pattern was called *moral insanity* because the people displaying it appear to have no morals or common decency. Later, people in this category were called *psychopaths* or *sociopaths.* The current "antisocial personality" label more accurately portrays them as troublesome but not "insane" by the legal standards we discuss later. About 3 percent of men and about 1 percent of women in the United States fall into this diagnostic category (American Psychiatric Association, 2000).

At their least troublesome, these people are a nuisance. They are often charming, intelligent "fast talkers" who borrow money and fail to return it; they are arrogant, selfish manipulators who "con" people into doing things for them, usually by lying and taking advantage of the decency and trust of others. A hallmark of those displaying antisocial personality is a lack of anxiety, remorse, or guilt, whether they have wrecked a borrowed car or killed an innocent person (Gray et al., 2003; Hare, 1993). No method has yet been found for permanently altering the behavior of these people (Rice, 1997). Research suggests that the best hope for dealing with them is to identify their antisocial personalities early, before the most treatment-resistant traits are fully developed (Compton et al., 2005; Crawford, Cohen, & Brooks, 2001; Lynam, 1996; Stoff, Breiling, & Maser, 1997).

There are numerous theories about the causes of antisocial personality. Some research suggests a genetic predisposition (Slutske et al., 2001), possibly in the form of abnormal brain development, impaired neurological functioning, or chronic underarousal of both the autonomic and central nervous systems (Dolan & Park, 2002; Fung et al., 2005; Kiehl et al., 2006; Raine et al., 2000, 2005). This underarousal may render people less sensitive to punishment, and more likely to seek excitement, than is normally the case (Birbaumer et al., 2005; Verona et al., 2004). Broken homes, rejection by parents, poor discipline, lack of good parental models, lack of attachment to early caregivers, impulsivity, conflict-filled childhoods, and poverty have all been suggested as psychological and sociocultural factors contributing to the development of antisocial personality disorder (Caspi et al., 2004; Lahey et al., 1995; Raine, Brennan, & Mednick, 1994; Tremblay et al., 1994). The biopsychosocial model suggests that antisocial personality disorder results when these psychosocial and environmental conditions combine with genetic predispositions to low arousal and the sensation seeking and impulsivity associated with it (Gray et al., 2003).

antisocial personality disorder A long-term, persistent pattern of impulsive, selfish, unscrupulous, even criminal behavior.

One of the most prominent environmental factors associated with the more violent forms of antisocial personality disorder is the experience of abuse in childhood (MacMillan et al., 2001). However, most of the studies that have found a relationship between childhood abuse and antisocial personality disorder were based on potentially biased reports (Monane, Leichter, & Lewis,

FOCUS ON RESEARCH

Exploring Links Between Child Abuse and Antisocial Personality Disorder

1984; Rosenbaum & Bennett, 1986). People with antisocial personalities—especially those with criminal records—are likely to make up stories of abuse in order to shift the blame for their behavior onto others. Even if their reports were accurate, however, most of these studies didn't compare the abuse histories of antisocial people with those of a control group from similar backgrounds who did not become antisocial. This research design flaw makes it almost impossible to separate the effects of reported child abuse from the effects of poverty or other factors that might also have contributed to the development of antisocial personality disorder.

■ What was the researcher's question?

Can childhood abuse cause antisocial personality disorder? To help answer this question and to correct some of the flaws in earlier studies, Cathy Widom (1989) used a *prospective* research design, first finding cases of childhood abuse and then looking for the effects of that abuse on adult behavior.

■ How did the researcher answer the question?

Widom began by identifying 416 adults whose backgrounds included official records of their having been physically or sexually abused before the age of eleven. She then explored the stories of these people's lives, as told in police and school records, as well as in a two-hour diagnostic interview. To reduce experimenter bias and distorted reporting, Widom ensured that the interviewers remained "blind" to the purpose of the study and that the respondents were told only that the study's purpose was to talk to people who had grown up in an urban area of the midwestern United States in the late 1960s and early 1970s. Widom also selected a comparison group of 283 people who had no histories of abuse but who were similar to the abused sample in terms of age, gender, ethnicity, hospital of birth, schools attended, and area of residence. Her goal was to obtain a nonabused control group that had been exposed to approximately the same environmental risk factors and socioeconomic conditions as the abused children.

■ What did the researcher find?

First, Widom (1989) tested the hypothesis that exposure to abuse in childhood is associated with criminality and/or violence in later life. She found that 26 percent of the abused youngsters went on to commit juvenile crimes, 29 percent were arrested as adults, and 11 percent committed violent crimes. These percentages were significantly higher than the figures for the nonabused group. The correlations between criminality and abuse were higher for males than for females and higher for African Americans than for European Americans. And overall, victims of physical abuse were more likely to commit violent crimes as adults than were victims of sexual abuse.

Next, Widom tested the hypothesis that childhood abuse is associated with the development of antisocial personality disorder (Luntz & Widom, 1994). She found that the abused group did show a significantly higher rate of antisocial personality disorder (13.5 percent) than did the comparison group (7.1 percent). The apparent role of abuse in antisocial personality disorder was particularly pronounced in men, and it remained strong even when other factors—such as age, ethnicity, and socioeconomic status—were accounted for in the statistical analyses. One other factor—failure to graduate from high school—was also strongly associated with the appearance of antisocial personality, whether or not childhood abuse had occurred.

■ What do the results mean?

Widom's research supported earlier studies in finding an association between childhood abuse and criminality, violence, and antisocial personality disorder. Further, although her study did not permit a firm conclusion that abuse alone causes antisocial personality disorder, the data from its prospective design added strength to the argument that abuse may be an important causal factor (Widom, 2000). This interpretation is supported by the results of research by other investigators (Jaffee et al., 2004). Finally,

Widom's work offers yet another reason—as if more reasons were needed—why it is so important to prevent the physical and sexual abuse of children. The long-term consequences of such abuse can be tragic not only for its immediate victims but also for those victimized by the criminal actions and antisocial behavior of some abused children as they grow up (Weiler & Widom, 1996).

■ **What do we still need to know?**

Widom's results suggest that one or more of the factors that lead teenagers to drop out (or be thrown out) of high school might help create antisocial personality disorder even in children who were not abused. Some of her more recent work suggests, too, that exposure to poverty and other stressors can be as important as abuse in promoting antisocial personality disorder (Horwitz et al., 2001). More research is obviously needed to discover whether antisocial personality disorder stems from abuse itself, from one of the factors accompanying it, or from some specific combination of known and still-unknown risk factors. The importance of combined and interacting risk factors is suggested by the fact that abuse is often part of a larger pool of experiences, such as exposure to deviant models, social rejection, poor supervision, and various stressful events. Until we understand how all these potentially causal pieces fit together, we will not fully understand the role played by childhood abuse in the chain of events leading to antisocial personality disorder.

We need to know more, too, about why such a small percentage of the abused children in Widom's sample displayed violence, criminal behavior, and antisocial personality disorder. These results raise the question of what genetic characteristics or environmental experiences serve to protect children from at least some of the devastating effects of abuse (Flores, Cicchetti, & Rogosch, 2005; Rind & Tromovitch, 1997; Rind, Tromovitch, & Bauserman, 1998). An understanding of what these protective elements are might go a long way toward the development of programs for the prevention of antisocial personality disorder.

A Sampling of Other Psychological Disorders

▶ **How do children's disorders differ from adults' disorders?**

The disorders described so far represent some of the most prevalent and socially disruptive psychological problems encountered in cultures around the world. Several others are mentioned in other chapters. In the chapter on consciousness, for example, we discuss insomnia, night terrors, and other sleep disorders; mental retardation is covered in the chapter on thought, language, and intelligence; sexual dysfunctions are mentioned in the chapter on motivation and emotion; and posttraumatic stress disorder is described in the chapter on health, stress, and coping. Here we consider two other significant psychological problems: disorders of childhood and substance-related disorders.

Psychological Disorders of Childhood

The physical, cognitive, emotional, and social changes seen in childhood—and the stress associated with them—can create or worsen psychological disorders in children. Stress can do the same in adults, but childhood disorders are not just miniature versions of adult psychopathology. Because children's development is still incomplete, and because their capacity to cope with stress is limited, children are often vulnerable to special types of disorders. The majority of childhood behavior problems can be placed in two broad categories: externalizing disorders and internalizing disorders (Achenbach, 1997; Lahey et al., 2004; Nigg, 2000).

ACTIVE OR HYPERACTIVE? Normal behavior for children in one culture might be considered hyperactive in other cultures. Do people in the same culture disagree on what is hyperactive? To find out, ask two or three friends to join you in observing a group of children at a playground, a schoolyard, a park, or some other public place. Ask your friends to privately identify which children they would label as "hyperactive" and then count how many of their choices agree with yours and with one another's.

The *externalizing,* or *undercontrolled,* category includes behaviors that disturb people in the child's environment. Lack of control shows up as *conduct disorders* in from 1 to 10 percent of children and adolescents, mostly boys (American Psychiatric Association, 2000; Martin & Hoffman, 1990). Conduct disorders are characterized by a relatively stable pattern of aggression, disobedience, destructiveness, and other obnoxious behaviors (Kalb & Loeber, 2003; Lahey et al., 1995). Often these behaviors involve criminal activity, and they may signal the development of antisocial personality disorder (Lahey et al., 2005). A genetic predisposition toward conduct disorders is suggested by the fact that many such children have parents who display antisocial personality disorder (Hicks et al., 2004). Children who are temperamentally inclined toward high activity levels are at greater risk for externalizing disorders (Mesman & Koot, 2000). There is no doubt, though, that parental and peer influences, as well as academic problems at school, also help to shape these children's antisocial behavior (Laird et al., 2001; Scourfield et al., 2004; Shaw et al., 2001).

Another kind of externalizing problem, *attention deficit hyperactivity disorder (ADHD),* is seen in 3 to 7 percent of children, mainly boys (and in about 4 percent of adults, mainly men; Kessler, Adler, et al., 2006). An ADHD diagnosis is given to children who, compared with other children their age, are impulsive, inattentive, or both (Nigg, 2001; Wolraich et al., 2005). Many of these children also have great difficulty sitting still or otherwise controlling their physical activity. Their impulsiveness and lack of self-control contribute to significant impairments in learning and to an astonishing ability to annoy and exhaust those around them. Children diagnosed with ADHD also tend to perform poorly on tests of attention, memory, decision making, and other information-processing tasks. As a result, ADHD is being increasingly viewed as a neurological condition rather than just "bad" behavior (Halperin & Schulz, 2006; Konrad et al., 2006; Krain & Castellanos, 2006; Ollendick & Prinz, 2002; Sergeant, Geurts, & Oosterlaan, 2002).

ADHD may result from a genetic predisposition (Waldman & Gizer, 2006), but other factors, such as brain damage, poisoning from lead or other household substances, and low birth weight may also play causal roles (Hudziak et al., 2005; Linnet et al., 2003; Mick et al., 2002; Sergeant, Geurts, & Oosterlaan, 2002; Spencer, 2002). In some cases, problems in parenting may increase the risk for this disorder (Clarke et al., 2002). Exactly how all these factors might combine is still not clear. Also uncertain is exactly what constitutes hyperactivity. Cultural standards about acceptable activity levels in children vary, so a "hyperactive" child in one culture might be considered merely "active" in another. In fact, when mental health professionals from four cultures used the same rating scale to judge hyperactivity in a videotaped sample of children's behavior, the Chinese and Indonesians rated the children as significantly more hyperactive than did their U.S. and Japanese colleagues (Jacobson, 2002; Mann et al., 1992). Such findings remind us that sociocultural factors can be important determinants of what is acceptable, and thus what is abnormal, in various parts of the world.

The second broad category of child behavior problems involves *internalizing,* or *overcontrol.* Children in this category experience significant distress, especially depression and anxiety, and may be socially withdrawn. Those displaying *separation anxiety disorder,* for example, constantly worry that they will be lost, kidnapped, or injured or that some harm may come to a parent (usually the mother). The child clings desperately to the parent and becomes upset or sick at the prospect of separation. Refusal to go to school (sometimes called "school phobia") is often the result. Children who are temperamentally shy or withdrawn are at higher risk for internalizing disorders, but these disorders are also associated with environmental factors, including rejection by peers and (especially for girls) being raised by a single parent (Mesman & Koot, 2000; Prinstein & La Greca, 2002).

A few childhood disorders, such as *pervasive developmental disorders,* do not fall into either the externalizing or internalizing category. Children diagnosed with these disorders show severe deficits in communication and impaired social relationships. They also often show repetitive, stereotyped behaviors and unusual preoccupations and interests (American Psychiatric Association, 2000; Filipek et al., 1999). The disorders in this group, also known as *autistic spectrum disorders* (Filipek et al., 1999; Rutter & Schopler, 1992; U.S. Surgeon General, 1999), share many of these core symptoms, although the severity of the symptoms may vary (Çeponien et al., 2003; Constantino & Todd, 2003). Estimates of the prevalence of autistic spectrum disorders vary from 10 to 20 children per 10,000 births (Bryson & Smith, 1998; Filipek et al., 1999) to as high as 62 per 10,000 (Chakrabarti & Fombonne, 2001), depending largely on the diagnostic criteria employed (Gernsbacher, Dawson, & Goldsmith, 2005). About half of these children suffer *autistic disorder,* which can be the most severe disorder of the group. The earliest signs of autistic disorder usually occur within the first thirty months after birth, as these babies show little or no evidence of forming an attachment to their caregivers. Language development is seriously disrupted in most of these children; half of them never learn to speak at all. However, those who display "high functioning autism" or a less severe autistic spectrum disorder called *Asperger's disorder* are able to function adaptively and, in some cases, independently as adults (e.g., Grandin, 1996).

Possible biological roots of autistic disorder include genetic factors (Segurado et al., 2005; Skaar et al., 2005; Vorstman et al., 2006) or neurodevelopmental abnormalities that affect language and communication (Baron-Cohen, Knickmeyer, & Belmonte, 2005; Belmonte et al., 2004; Courchesne et al., 2001; Grossberg & Seidman, 2006). The more specific causes of autistic disorder remain unknown, but it is likely that genetic influences, along with prenatal damage leading to structural brain abnormalities, are involved (Carper & Courchesne, 2000; Juul-Dam, Townsend, & Courchesne, 2001; Rodier, 2000; Szatmari et al., 1998; Vidal et al., 2006). Researchers today have rejected the once-popular hypothesis that autistic disorder is caused by cold and unresponsive parents.

Disorders of childhood differ from adult disorders not only because the patterns of behavior are distinct but also because their early onset disrupts development. To take one example, children whose separation anxiety causes spotty school attendance may not only fall behind academically but also may fail to form the relationships with other children that promote normal social development (Wood, 2006). Some children never make up for this deficit. They may drop out of school and risk a life of poverty, crime, and violence. Moreover, children depend on others to get help for their psychological problems, but all too often those problems may go unrecognized or untreated. For some, the long-term result may be adult forms of mental disorder.

Substance-Related Disorders

Childhood disorders, especially externalizing disorders, often lead to substance-related disorders in adolescence and adulthood. *DSM-IV* defines **substance-related disorders** as the use of psychoactive drugs for months or years in ways that harm the user or others. These disorders create major political, economic, social, and health problems worldwide. The substances involved most often are alcohol and other depressants (such as barbiturates), opiates (such as heroin), stimulants (such as cocaine or amphetamines), and hallucinogens (such as LSD).

One effect of using some substances (including alcohol, heroin, and amphetamines) is **addiction,** a physical need for the substance. *DSM-IV* calls addiction *physiological dependence.* Even when the use of a drug does not create physical addiction, some people may overuse, or *abuse,* it because the drug gives them temporary self-confidence, enjoyment, or relief from tension. *DSM-IV* defines *substance abuse* as a pattern of use that causes serious social, legal, or interpersonal problems. In other words, people can become psychologically dependent on psychoactive drugs without becoming physiologically addicted to them. People who are psychologically dependent on a drug often have problems that are at least as serious as those of people who are addicted and that may be even more difficult to treat. In the consciousness chapter, we describe how consciousness is affected by a wide range of psychoactive drugs. Here, we focus more specifically on the problems associated with the use and abuse of alcohol, heroin, and cocaine.

substance-related disorders   Problems involving the use of psychoactive drugs for months or years in ways that harm the user or others.

addiction   Development of a physical need for a psychoactive drug.

Alcohol Use Disorders   In the United States, about 8.4 percent of people over the age of twelve display *alcohol dependence* or *alcohol abuse* (Grant et al., 2004). This means that about 19 million individuals engage in a pattern of continuous or off-and-on drinking that may lead to addiction and that almost always causes severe social, physical, and other problems (e.g., Murphy et al., 2005). Males outnumber females in this category by a ratio of about three to one, although the problem is on the rise among women and among teenagers of both genders (Chassin, Pitts, & Prost, 2002; Grant et al., 2004). Prolonged overuse of alcohol can result in life-threatening liver damage, reduced cognitive abilities, vitamin deficiencies that can lead to severe and permanent memory loss, and a host of other physical ailments (Hommer et al., 2001; Pfefferbaum et al., 2001). Alcohol dependence or abuse, commonly referred to as **alcoholism,** has been implicated in half of all the traffic fatalities, homicides, and suicides that occur each year (National Institute on Alcohol Abuse and Alcoholism [NIAAA], 2001; Yi, Williams, & Smothers, 2004). Alcoholism also figures prominently in rape and child abuse, as well as in elevated rates of hospitalization and absenteeism from work, resulting in total costs to society of over $184 billion each year (Harwood, Fountain, & Livermore, 1998; NIAAA, 2001). It is estimated that about half of U.S. adults have a close relative who has or had displayed alcoholism and that about 25 percent of children are exposed to adults who display alcohol abuse or dependence (NIAAA, 2001). Children growing up in families in which one or both parents abuse alcohol are at increased risk for developing a host of mental disorders, including substance-related disorders (Hoffmann & Cerbone, 2002). And as described in the chapter on human development, children of mothers who abused alcohol during pregnancy may be born with fetal alcohol syndrome.

The biopsychosocial model suggests that alcohol abuse stems from a combination of genetic characteristics (including inherited aspects of temperament such as impulsivity and emotionality) and what people learn in their social and cultural environments (Elkins et al., 2006; Kendler, Jacobson, et al., 2003; Petry, 2001; Sher et al., 1991; Wall et al., 2001). For example, the children of people with alcoholism are more likely than others to develop alcoholism themselves; and if the children are identical twins, both are at increased risk for alcoholism, even when raised apart (Kendler et al., 1992; McGue, 1999; Slutske et al., 1998). It is still unclear just what might be inherited or which genes are involved. One possibility involves inherited abnormalities in the brain's neurotransmitter systems or in the body's metabolism of alcohol (Martinez et al., 2005; Nurnberger et al., 2001; Petrakis et al., 2004). Males with alcoholism do tend to be less sensitive than other people to the effects of alcohol—a factor that may contribute to greater consumption (Pollack, 1992; Schuckit, 1998). Now that the human genome has been decoded, researchers are focusing on specific chromosomes as the possible location of genes that predispose people to—or protect them from—the development of alcoholism (Cheng et al., 2004; NIAAA, 2000, 2001; Wall et al., 2005). However, the genetics of addiction is highly complex; there is probably not a single gene for alcoholism (Crabbe, 2002). As with other disorders, many genes interact with each other and with environmental events, including parental influences (Rhee et al., 2003). One study found that, as expected, the sons of identical twins were at elevated risk for alcoholism if their father had alcoholism, but not if it was the father's identical twin who had alcoholism (Jacob et al., 2003). In these cases, something in the boys' nonalcoholic family environment had apparently moderated whatever genetic tendency toward alcoholism they might have inherited.

Youngsters typically learn to drink by watching their parents and their peers. The observations help shape their expectations, such as that alcohol will make them feel good and help them cope with stressors (Chassin, Pitts, & Prost, 2002; Schell et al., 2005). But alcohol use can become abuse, and perhaps addiction, if drinking is a person's main coping strategy (NIAAA, 2001). The importance of learning is supported by evidence that alcoholism is more common among ethnic and cultural groups (such as the Irish and English) in which frequent drinking tends to be socially approved than among groups (such as Jews, Italians, and Chinese) in which all but moderate drinking tends to be discouraged (Gray & Nye, 2001; Wilson et al., 1996). Moreover, different forms of social support for drinking can result in different consumption patterns within a cultural group. For example, one study found significantly more drinking among Japanese men living in Japan (where social norms for males' drinking are most permissive) compared with Japanese men living in Hawaii or California, where excessive drinking is less strongly supported (Kitano et al., 1992).

alcoholism A pattern of continuous or intermittent drinking that may lead to addiction and that almost always causes severe social, physical, and other problems.

Heroin and Cocaine Dependence   Like people with alcoholism, those with heroin and cocaine addiction suffer many serious health problems as a result of both the drugs themselves and the poor eating and health habits related to use of those drugs. The risk of death from overdose, contaminated drugs, or AIDS (contracted through blood in shared needles), as well as from suicide, is also always present. Drug dependence tends to be more prevalent among males, especially young males (Warner et al., 1995).

Addiction to such substances as heroin and cocaine appears in about 4 percent of the adult population in the United States (Compton et al., 2005) and is mainly a biological process brought about by the physical effects of the drugs (Kalivas & Volkow, 2005; Phillips et al., 2003). Explaining why people first use these drugs is more complicated. One line of theorizing suggests that there might be a genetic tendency toward behavioral compulsions that predisposes some people to abuse many kinds of drugs (Crabbe, 2002; NIAAA, 2000). One study supporting this idea found a link between alcoholism in biological parents and drug abuse in the sons they had given up for adoption (Cadoret et al., 1995). The same study also found a link between antisocial personality traits in biological parents and antisocial acts—including drug abuse—in the sons they had put up for adoption.

A number of psychological and environmental factors have been proposed as promoting initial drug use (Alessi et al., 2002; Brems & Namyniuk, 2002; Hoffmann & Cerbone, 2002). These include seeing parental drug use, being abused in childhood, efforts to cope with stressors or to ease anxiety or depression, associating drug use with pleasant experiences, peer pressure, thrill seeking, and poor social adjustment (Dube et al., 2003; Putnam, 2003). Research has not yet established why continued drug use occurs in some people and not in others, but, again, it is likely that a biological predisposition interacts with psychological processes and stressors that play out their roles in specific social and cultural contexts (Kendler et al., 2003; Kreek et al., 2005).

Mental Illness and the Law

► **Can insanity protect criminals from punishment?**

Have you wondered why the word *insanity* doesn't appear in our definition of *mental disorder* or in the *DSM-IV* categories we have described? The reason is that *insanity* is a legal term, not a psychiatric diagnosis (Cassel & Bernstein, 2007). For example, in 1984 John Hinckley, Jr., was found "not guilty by reason of insanity" for his attempted assassination of President Ronald Reagan. This verdict reflected U.S. laws and rules that protect people with severe psychological disorders when they are accused of crimes.

This protection takes two forms. First, under certain conditions, people designated as mentally ill may be protected from prosecution. If, at the time of trial, individuals accused of crimes are unable to understand the proceedings and charges against them or to help in their own defense, they are declared *mentally incompetent* to stand trial. When that happens, defendants are sent to a mental institution until they are judged to have become mentally competent. If they are still not competent after some specified period—two years, in most cases—a defendant may be ruled permanently ineligible for trial and either committed to a mental institution or released. Release is rare, however, because competency to stand trial requires only minimal mental abilities. If drugs can produce even temporary mental competence, the defendant will usually go to trial.

Second, the mentally ill may be protected from punishment. In most U.S. states, defendants may be judged *not guilty by reason of insanity* if, at the time of the crime, mental illness prevented them from (1) understanding what they were doing, (2) knowing that what they were doing was wrong, and (3) resisting the impulse to do wrong. The first two of these criteria relate to a person's ability to think clearly and are called

applying psychology

ASSESSMENT OF MENTAL COMPETENCE Andrea Yates admitted to drowning her five children in the bathtub of her Houston, Texas, home in 2001. She had twice tried to kill herself in previous years, and she was reportedly depressed at the time of the murders. Accordingly, she pleaded not guilty by reason of insanity. The first legal step in deciding her fate was to confine her in a mental institution for assessment of her mental competency to stand trial. Following testimony of psychologists who examined her, she was found competent and sentenced to life in prison. Her conviction was overturned on appeal, though, and at a second trial in 2006, she was found not guilty by reason of insanity and committed to a mental hospital.

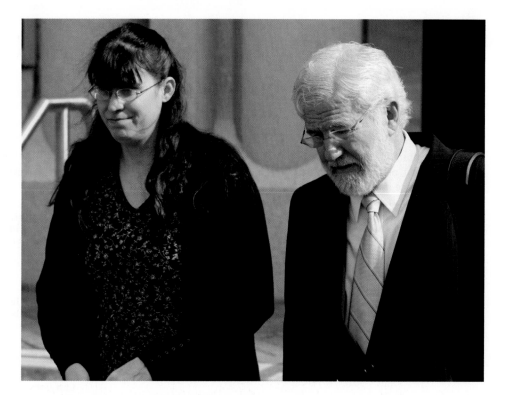

the *M'Naughton rule,* for the defendant in the 1843 case that established it. The third criterion, which relates to the defendant's emotional state during a crime, is known as the *irresistible impulse test.* All three criteria were combined in a rule proposed by the American Law Institute in 1962—a rule that is now followed in about one-third of the U.S. states.

After the Hinckley verdict, the U.S. Congress passed the Insanity Defense Reform Act, which eliminated the irresistible impulse criterion from the definition of insanity in federal cases. About 75 percent of the U.S. states have passed similar or related reform laws (Giorgi-Guarnieri et al., 2002); in about half the states, these laws require the use of some version of the narrower M'Naughton rule (American Psychiatric Association, 2003). Whatever criteria are used, when defendants plead insanity, judges and juries must decide whether or not a defendant should be held responsible for criminal acts. Defendants who are judged not guilty by reason of insanity and who still display a psychological disorder are usually required to receive treatment, typically through commitment to a hospital, until judged to be cured or no longer dangerous. Thirteen U.S. states have laws allowing jurors to find defendants *guilty but mentally ill.* These defendants are to receive treatment while in prison, though they seldom do (Cassel & Bernstein, 2007).

Critics of insanity rules complain that these rules allow criminals to "get away with murder." Actually, such outcomes are rare. Insanity pleas occur in only 1 out of every 200 felony cases in the United States, and they are successful in only 2 of every 1,000 attempts (American Psychiatric Association, 2003; Silver, Cirincione, & Steadman, 1994). Even the few defendants found not guilty by reason of insanity are usually hospitalized for two to nine times as long as they would have spent in prison had they been convicted (Silver, 1995; Steadman, 1993). John Hinckley, Jr., has been in Saint Elizabeth's Hospital in Washington, D.C., since 1982, and in spite of his annual efforts to be released and court approval for some visits with his parents outside the hospital, he is unlikely to be freed anytime soon.

In summary, society is constantly seeking the proper balance between protecting the rights of defendants and protecting society from dangerous criminals. In the process, the sociocultural values that shape our views about what is abnormal also influence judgments about the extent to which abnormality should relieve people of responsibility for criminal behavior.

ACTIVE REVIEW
Psychological Disorders

Linkages

As noted in the introductory chapter, all of psychology's subfields are related to one another. Our discussion of how mental disorders might be learned illustrates just one way in which the topic of this chapter, psychological disorders, is linked to the subfield of learning, which is discussed in the chapter by that name. The Linkages diagram shows ties to two other subfields, and there are many more ties throughout the book. Looking for linkages among subfields will help you see how they all fit together and help you better appreciate the big picture that is psychology.

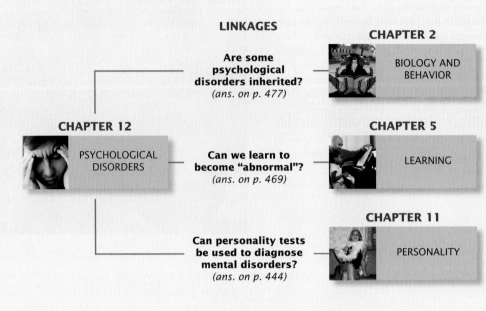

LINKAGES

CHAPTER 12
PSYCHOLOGICAL DISORDERS

Are some psychological disorders inherited?
(ans. on p. 477)

CHAPTER 2
BIOLOGY AND BEHAVIOR

Can we learn to become "abnormal"?
(ans. on p. 469)

CHAPTER 5
LEARNING

Can personality tests be used to diagnose mental disorders?
(ans. on p. 444)

CHAPTER 11
PERSONALITY

Summary

Psychopathology involves patterns of thinking, feeling, and behaving that are maladaptive, disruptive, or distressing—either for the person affected or for others.

DEFINING PSYCHOLOGICAL DISORDERS

▶ **How do psychologists define abnormal behavior?**

Some psychological disorders show considerable similarity across cultures, but the definition of *abnormality* is largely determined by social and cultural factors. The criteria for judging abnormality include statistical infrequency (a comparison with what most people do), norm violations, and personal suffering. Each of these criteria is flawed to some extent. The practical approach, which considers the content, context, and consequences of behavior, emphasizes the question of whether people show **impaired functioning** in fulfilling the roles appropriate for particular people in particular settings, cultures, and historical eras.

EXPLAINING PSYCHOLOGICAL DISORDERS

▶ **What causes abnormality?**

At various times and places, abnormal behavior has been attributed to the action of gods or the devil. Mental health professionals in Western cultures rely on a **biopsychosocial model,** which attributes mental disorders to the interaction of biological, psychological, and sociocultural factors. Biological factors, such as brain chemistry, are emphasized in the medical or **neurobiological model** of disorder. The

psychological model focuses on processes such as inner conflicts, maladaptive learning experiences, or blocked personal growth. The *sociocultural model* helps to explain disorder by highlighting gender, ethnicity, and other social and cultural factors that form the context of abnormality. *Diathesis-stress* explanations suggest that biological, psychological, and sociocultural characteristics create predispositions for disorder that are translated into symptoms in the face of sufficient amounts of stress.

CLASSIFYING PSYCHOLOGICAL DISORDERS

▶ **How many psychological disorders have been identified?**

The dominant system for classifying abnormal behavior in North America is the fourth edition of the *Diagnostic and Statistical Manual of Mental Disorders (DSM-IV and DSM-IV-TR)* of the American Psychiatric Association. It includes more than 300 specific categories of mental disorder that can be described using five dimensions, or axes. Diagnosis helps to identify the features, causes, and most effective methods of treating various psychological disorders. Research on the reliability and validity of *DSM-IV* shows that it is a useful, but not perfect, classification system.

ANXIETY DISORDERS

▶ **What is a phobia?**

Long-standing and disruptive patterns of anxiety characterize *anxiety disorders.* The most prevalent type of anxiety disorder is *phobia,* a category that includes **specific phobias, social phobias,** and **agoraphobia.** Other anxiety disorders are **generalized anxiety disorder,** which involves nonspecific anxiety; **panic disorder,** which brings unpredictable attacks of intense anxiety; and **obsessive-compulsive disorder (OCD),** which is characterized by uncontrollable repetitive thoughts and ritualistic actions.

The most influential explanations of anxiety disorders suggest that they may develop when a biological predisposition for strong anxiety reactions combines with fear-enhancing thought patterns and learned anxiety responses. Many anxiety disorders appear to develop in accordance with the principles of classical and operant conditioning, as well as with those of observational learning. People may be biologically prepared to learn fear of certain objects and situations.

SOMATOFORM DISORDERS

▶ **Can mental disorder cause blindness?**

Somatoform disorders include **conversion disorder,** which involves physical problems, such as blindness, deafness, and paralysis, that have no apparent physical cause; **hypochondriasis,** an unjustified concern over being or becoming ill; **somatization disorder,** in which the person complains of numerous unconfirmed physical complaints; and **pain disorder,** in which pain is felt in the absence of a physical cause.

DISSOCIATIVE DISORDERS

▶ **What disorders create sudden memory loss?**

Dissociative disorders involve rare conditions such as **dissociative fugue** and **dissociative amnesia,** both of which involve sudden and severe memory loss, and **dissociative identity disorder (DID),** or multiple personality disorder, in which a person appears to have two or more identities. There is considerable controversy about the origins of dissociative identity disorder.

MOOD DISORDERS

▶ **How common is depression?**

Mood disorders, also known as *affective disorders*, are quite common and involve extreme moods that may be inconsistent with events. **Major depressive disorder** is marked by feelings of inadequacy, worthlessness, and guilt; in extreme cases, **delusions** may also occur. **Dysthymic disorder** includes similar but less severe symptoms that persist for a long period. Suicide is often related to these disorders. Alternating periods of depression and **mania** characterize **bipolar disorders,** which are also known as manic depression. **Cyclothymic disorder,** an alternating pattern of less extreme mood swings, is a slightly more common variant.

Mood disorders have been attributed to biological causes such as genetic inheritance, disruptions in neurotransmitter and endocrine systems, and irregularities in biological rhythms. These interact with stressors and psychological factors such as maladaptive patterns of thinking. A predisposition toward some of these disorders may be inherited, although their appearance is probably determined by a diathesis-stress process.

SCHIZOPHRENIA

▶ **Is schizophrenia the same as "split personality"?**

Schizophrenia is perhaps the most severe and puzzling disorder of all. Among its symptoms are problems in thinking, perception (often including **hallucinations**), attention, emotion, movement, motivation, and daily functioning. Positive symptoms of schizophrenia include hallucinations or disordered speech; negative symptoms can include withdrawal, immobility, and the absence of affect.

Genetic influences, neurotransmitter problems, abnormalities in brain structure and functioning, and neurodevelopmental abnormalities are biological factors implicated in schizophrenia. Psychological factors such as maladaptive learning experiences and disturbed family interactions can affect the severity and course of this disorder. Diathesis-stress explanations, including vulnerability theory, provide a promising framework for research into the multiple causes of schizophrenia.

PERSONALITY DISORDERS

▶ **Which personality disorder often leads to crime?**

Personality disorders are long-term patterns of maladaptive behavior that, although not always associated with personal discomfort, may be disturbing to others. These include odd-eccentric types (paranoid, schizoid, and schizotypal personality disorders), anxious-fearful types (dependent, obsessive-compulsive, and avoidant personality disorders), and dramatic-erratic types (histrionic, narcissistic, borderline, and antisocial personality disorders). **Antisocial personality disorder** is marked by impulsive, irresponsible, and unscrupulous behavior patterns that often begin in childhood. Childhood abuse may be related to the appearance of this potentially dangerous personality disorder.

A SAMPLING OF OTHER PSYCHOLOGICAL DISORDERS

▶ **How do children's disorders differ from adults' disorders?**

Childhood psychological disorders can be categorized as externalizing conditions (such as conduct disorders or attention deficit hyperactivity disorder) and internalizing disorders, in which children show overcontrol and experience distress (as in separation anxiety disorder). Pervasive developmental disorders do not fall into either category and include the autistic spectrum disorders. In autistic disorder, which can be the most severe of these, children show no interest in, or attachment to, others.

Substance-related disorders involving alcohol and other drugs affect millions of people. **Addiction** to and psychological dependence on these substances contribute to disastrous personal and social problems, including physical illnesses, accidents, and crime. Genetic factors probably create a predisposition for **alcoholism,** but learning, cultural traditions, and other nonbiological processes are also important. Stress reduction, imitation, thrill seeking, and social maladjustment have been proposed as important factors in drug addiction, along with genetic predisposition; but the exact causes of initial use of these drugs are unknown.

MENTAL ILLNESS AND THE LAW

▶ **Can insanity protect criminals from punishment?**

"Insanity" is a legal term, not a psychiatric diagnosis. Current rules protect people accused of crimes from prosecution or punishment if they are declared mentally incompetent at the time of their trials or if they were legally insane at the time of their crimes. Defendants judged not guilty by reason of insanity and who still display a psychological disorder are usually required to receive treatment until judged to be cured or no longer dangerous. Those found guilty but mentally ill are to receive treatment in prison.

Learn by Doing

Put It in Writing

Think about something you have seen someone do recently that you considered truly abnormal. Now write a page describing what happened and the specific rules or criteria—such as statistical infrequency, norm violation, personal suffering, or impaired functioning—that you used in deciding that this person's behavior qualifies as abnormal. Include a statement about whether you think this person should be treated for his or her behavior problem and why. Predict the degree to which this behavior would be considered abnormal by other people in your culture. Finally, tell whether and why people in other cultures might have a different view of the case.

Personal Learning Activity

To what extent do people agree on what is abnormal? To find out, ask at least twenty friends, family members, teachers, classmates in other courses, casual acquaintances, and maybe even some strangers to read your description of the behavior you diagnosed as abnormal in the Put It in Writing exercise. (Show them only the description, not your comments.) Ask these people to tell you whether they think the behavior is normal, merely odd, or seriously abnormal and whether they think the person is in need of treatment. Analyze the results in terms of how many of these people agreed with your diagnosis and with one another. Did you notice any trends in their responses based on age, gender, educational status, or cultural background? What do your results say about how easy or difficult it is to precisely define abnormality? *For additional projects, see the Personal Learning Activities in the corresponding chapter of the study guide that accompanies this text.*

Step into Action

Courses

Abnormal Psychology
Child Psychopathology
Psychology and the Law

Movies

A Beautiful Mind. Schizophrenia.
Boys Don't Cry. Gender identity disorder.
The Fisher King. Psychosis, depression, substance abuse, avoidant personality disorder.
Mercury Rising. Autism.
The Hours; Ordinary People. Depression and suicidality.
The Silence of the Lambs; The Talented Mr. Ripley; In Cold Blood; Natural Born Killers; Dahmer. Antisocial personality disorder.
Copycat. Agoraphobia.
Blue Sky. Borderline personality disorder, substance abuse.
One Flew over the Cuckoo's Nest. Life in a state mental hospital of the 1960s.
The Three Faces of Eve; Sybil; Identity. Dissociative identity disorder.
Vertigo. Anxiety disorders.
As Good as It Gets. Obsessive-compulsive disorder.
Days of Wine and Roses; Leaving Las Vegas. Alcoholism.
Trainspotting; Permanent Midnight. Drug addiction.
Man on the Moon; Fast, Cheap, and Out of Control. Defining abnormality.
The Exorcism of Emily Rose. Supernatural explanations of abnormality.
Anatomy of a Murder. Use of the insanity defense in a murder case.

Books

Robert Spitzer et al., *DSM-IV Casebook: A Learning Companion to the Diagnostic and Statistical Manual of Mental Disorders* (American Psychiatric Press, 1994). A casebook illustrating the disorders listed in *DSM-IV.*
Karen Eriksen and Victoria Kress, *Beyond the DSM Story: Ethical Quandaries, Challenges, and Best Practices* (Sage, 2005). A summary of DSM, its problems, and alternative approaches.
Larry Beutler and Mary Malik, *Rethinking the DSM: A Psychological Perspective* (American Psychological Association, 2002). A critical analysis of the standard diagnostic system.
William Styron, *Darkness Visible* (Vintage, 1992). Depression and suicidality.
Sylvia Plath, *The Bell Jar* (Harper & Row, 1971). Major depression, suicidality.
Kay Redfield Jamison, *An Unquiet Mind: A Memoir of Moods and Madness* (Vintage, 1997). A psychiatrist writes about her own bipolar disorder.
Patty Duke, *A Brilliant Madness* (Bantam, 1993). Bipolar disorder.
Sally Bedell Smith, *Diana: In Search of Herself—Portrait of a Troubled Princess* (Signet, 2000). Eating disorders, depression, borderline personality disorder.
Vaslav Nijinsky, *The Diary of Vaslav Nijinsky* (Farrar, Straus and Giroux, 1999). Insight into schizophrenia from one of Eugen Bleuler's most famous patients, the Russian ballet dancer.
Jerald J. Kriesman and Hal Straus, *I Hate You—Don't Leave Me: Understanding the Borderline Personality* (Avon, 1991). Descriptions and explanations of borderline behaviors, focusing on conflicted relationships.

Lewis B. Pullen, *Fortunate Son* (Bantam, 1996). Posttraumatic stress disorder.

Judith Rapoport, *The Boy Who Couldn't Stop Washing* (New American Library, 1997). Obsessive-compulsive disorder.

Karlene K. Hale, *Being There: Profiles of Mental Illness* (Dilligaf, 1997). Case studies of mental disorder.

Clark R. Clipson and Jocelyn M. Steer, *Case Studies in Abnormal Psychology* (Houghton Mifflin, 1998). More case studies.

Joan Acocella, *Creating Hysteria: Women and Multiple Personality Disorder* (Jossey-Bass, 1999). A description of the influence of culture and other social forces in shaping dissociative identity disorder.

Meyer Glantz and Christine Hartel (Eds.), *Drug Abuse: Origins and Interventions* (American Psychological Association, 2000). Information that challenges various myths about drug abuse.

The Web

The World Wide Web is a good source of additional information about the science of psychology, provided you use it carefully and think critically about the information you find. The Online Study Center that accompanies this text offers many resources relevant to this chapter. These resources include interactive tutorials; Thinking Critically and Evaluating Research exercises; ACE chapter quizzes; recommended web links; and articles on current events, books, and movies. Please visit the Online Study Center at college.hmco.com/pic/ bernsteinessentials4e.

Review of Key Terms

Can you define each of the key terms in the chapter? Check your definitions against those on the pages shown in parentheses in the following list or in the Glossary/Index at the end of the text.

addiction *(p. 490)*

agoraphobia *(p. 467)*

alcoholism *(p. 491)*

antisocial personality disorder *(p. 486)*

anxiety disorder *(p. 466)*

biopsychosocial model *(p. 456)*

bipolar disorder *(p. 476)*

conversion disorder *(p. 471)*

cyclothymic disorder *(p. 477)*

delusions *(p. 474)*

diathesis-stress *(p. 460)*

dissociative disorders *(p. 472)*

dissociative fugue *(p. 472)*

dissociative amnesia *(p. 472)*

dissociative identity disorder (DID) *(p. 472)*

dysthymic disorder *(p. 475)*

generalized anxiety disorder *(p. 467)*

hallucinations *(p. 481)*

hypochondriasis *(p. 471)*

impaired functioning *(p. 456)*

major depressive disorder *(p. 474)*

mania *(p. 476)*

mood disorder *(p. 473)*

neurobiological model *(p. 458)*

obsessive-compulsive disorder (OCD) *(p. 468)*

pain disorder *(p. 471)*

panic disorder *(p. 467)*

personality disorders *(p. 485)*

phobia *(p. 466)*

psychological model *(p. 458)*

psychopathology *(p. 454)*

schizophrenia *(p. 480)*

social phobias *(p. 467)*

sociocultural model *(p. 459)*

somatization disorder *(p. 471)*

somatoform disorders *(p. 471)*

specific phobias *(p. 467)*

substance-related disorders *(p. 490)*

Multiple-Choice Self-Test

Select the best answer for each of the following questions. Then check your responses against the Answer Key at the end of the text.

1. According to the statistics on psychopathology, _____ percent of people in the United States experience a mental disorder in their lifetimes.

   a. Less than 5 percent
   b. Approximately 25 percent
   c. Almost 50 percent
   d. Over 75 percent

2. Babette, a successful opera singer, believes that aliens could snatch her at any time if she isn't wearing her lucky charm. She is constantly worried and insists that the stage be rimmed with foil to ward off evil spirits. According to which criterion of abnormality would Babette *not* be considered abnormal?

   a. Statistical
   b. Norm violation
   c. Practical
   d. Personal suffering

3. Herman murdered a man who bumped into him in a bar. In order to be found not guilty by reason of insanity, the jury would have to find that he

   a. was under the influence of alcohol when he committed the crime.
   b. is currently insane.
   c. was insane when he committed the crime.
   d. knew the crime was wrong but did it anyway.

4. Roberta and Rhonda are identical twins who inherited identical predispositions for depression. Roberta has lived an easy life and has not developed any depressive symptoms. Rhonda, who has been divorced and lost several jobs over the years, has been diagnosed with major depressive disorder. The difference between these twins is most consistent with the _____ approach to abnormality.

   a. neurobiological
   b. psychological
   c. sociocultural
   d. diathesis-stress

5. Dr. Kramer is evaluating a patient brought in for psychiatric treatment. In his report he indicates that his global assessment of the patient's functioning is about 30 on a 100-point scale. Dr. Kramer is using _____ to evaluate the patient.

   a. the M'Naughton rule
   b. norm violation criteria
   c. insanity criteria
   d. *DSM-IV*

6. Kat stopped going to classes because of worry that she will embarrass herself by saying something silly. She takes her meals to her dorm room so that no one will see her eat. According to *DSM-IV*, Kat is probably displaying

   a. agoraphobia.
   b. simple phobia.
   c. generalized anxiety disorder.
   d. social phobia.

7. Terraba had a difficult time driving to work. Every time she went over a bump she had to drive back around to make sure that she had not run over anything. This occurred ten or twelve times each day, so Terraba was always late for everything. Terraba appears to be suffering from

   a. specific phobia.
   b. panic attacks.
   c. obsessive-compulsive disorder.
   d. generalized anxiety disorder.

8. Conversion disorder is characterized by

   a. impairment of movement or sensory ability with no apparent physical cause.
   b. severe pain with no apparent physical cause.
   c. fear of becoming seriously ill.
   d. frequent, vague complaints of physical symptoms.

9. Tomas has been suffering severe back pain for several weeks, but extensive medical tests reveal no physical problem. Tomas appears to be displaying

   a. pain disorder.
   b. hypochondriasis.
   c. paranoid schizophrenia.
   d. somatization disorder.

10. When Jennifer, a newspaper reporter, disappeared while covering a crime story that put her under constant threat, everyone assumed she had been kidnapped. But she was found several months later, now married and calling herself Emily, working as a waitress in a city a thousand miles from her home. She had no memory of her previous life, even after being reunited with her parents. Jennifer would most likely be diagnosed as displaying

    a. dissociative fugue.
    b. dissociative identity disorder.
    c. dissociative amnesia.
    d. schizophrenia.

11. Over the past three months, Barb has been feeling very sad; she has been sleeping as much as fifteen hours a day and has gained thirty pounds. Debbie, too, feels very low, but she can barely sleep and has lost both her appetite and fifteen pounds. Both Barb and Debbie have symptoms of

    a. obsessive-compulsive disorder.
    b. major depressive disorder.
    c. bipolar disorder.
    d. hypochondriasis.

12. Suicide is closely tied to depression. Studies of suicide in the United States have found that

    a. people who talk about suicide typically don't attempt suicide.
    b. older males who are living alone are the most likely to commit suicide.
    c. suicide rates are about the same across ethnic groups and gender.
    d. depressed women almost never actually attempt suicide.

13. Carlisle has been very depressed. He can't face his responsibilities and often spends days at a time in bed. A psychologist who adopts the social-cognitive approach would be most likely to see this depression as caused by Carlisle's

    a. attributional style.
    b. brain chemicals.
    c. unconscious conflicts.
    d. blocked growth tendencies.

14. As you sit down next to a messy-looking man on a bus, he says, "Ohms vibrate orange and dishwrings obvious dictionary." As he continues talking in this manner, you begin to suspect that he is displaying _____, a _____ symptom of _____.

    a. anxiety; negative; obsessive-compulsive disorder.
    b. thought disorder; positive; schizophrenia.
    c. thought disorder; negative; schizophrenia.
    d. flat affect; negative; depression.

15. Juan can't explain why, but he worries constantly that something terrible is going to happen to him. This vague feeling of impending doom is associated with a diagnosis of

    a. conversion disorder.
    b. specific phobia.
    c. social phobia.
    d. generalized anxiety disorder.

16. Forty-year-old Richard believes that he was ordered by God to save the world. He is suspicious of other people because he thinks they want to prevent him from fulfilling his mission. He is unable to keep a job because he is angry and argumentative most of the time. Richard would most likely be diagnosed as displaying

    a. mood disorder.
    b. dissociative identity disorder.
    c. paranoid schizophrenia.
    d. catatonic schizophrenia.

17. Al is charming and intelligent, but he has always been irresponsible, impulsive, and unscrupulous. None of his girlfriends knows he is dating other women. He borrows money from friends and doesn't pay them back. He doesn't care about anyone else, including his family. Al would probably be diagnosed as displaying _____ personality disorder.

    a. antisocial
    b. narcissistic
    c. passive-aggressive
    d. inadequate

18. Cathy Widom's research study, discussed in the Focus on Research section of this chapter, found that there was a relationship between antisocial personality disorder and

    a. narcissistic personality disorder.
    b. schizophrenia.
    c. high intelligence.
    d. being abused in childhood.

19. Angelo drinks alcohol until he passes out. Unable to hold a job or take care of himself, Angelo is diagnosed as having a substance-related disorder. Research on alcoholism suggests that Angelo's problems are caused by

    a. a single inherited gene.
    b. a culture that did not tolerate drinking.
    c. alcoholic parents.
    d. a combination of genetic and environmental factors.

20. Aaron is an infant who shows no signs of attachment to his parents. He dislikes being held and doesn't smile or laugh. Aaron's symptoms are most consistent with

    a. infantile schizophrenia.
    b. autistic disorder.
    c. antisocial personality disorder.
    d. an externalizing disorder of childhood.

13

Treatment of Psychological Disorders

In old Hollywood movies, such as *The Dark Past* or *The Three Faces of Eve,* troubled

people find instant cures when a psychotherapist helps them discover an unconscious memory that holds the key to their psychological disorder. Somewhat more realistic versions of psychotherapy have been presented in recent movies and television shows, such as *Good Will Hunting* and *The Sopranos.* Unfortunately, even these portrayals do not convey what psychotherapy is really like, and even the best of them tell only part of the story of how psychological disorders can be treated. In this chapter we describe a wide range of treatment options, including methods based on psychodynamic, humanistic, behavioral, and biological theories of psychological disorders. We also consider research on the effectiveness of treatment and methods for preventing disorders.

Reading this chapter will help you to answer the following questions:

I n the chapter on psychological disorders, we described José, an electronics technician who had to take medical leave from his job because of his panic attacks. After four months of diagnostic testing turned up no physical problems, José's physician suggested that he see a psychologist. José resisted at first, insisting that his condition was not "just in his head," but he eventually began psychological treatment. Within a few months, his panic attacks had ceased, and José had returned to all his old activities. After the psychologist helped him to reconsider his workload, José decided to take early retirement from his job in order to pursue more satisfying work at his home-based computer business.

José's case is by no means unique. During any given year in the United States alone, about 15 percent of adults and about 21 percent of children and adolescents are receiving some form of treatment for psychological disorders, including substance abuse problems (Kancelbaum, Singer, & Wong, 2004; Kessler et al., 2005; Wang, Lane, et al., 2005; U.S. Surgeon General, 1999). This treatment can be expensive, but its cost is made up for by the savings it creates. Compared with untreated patients, those who receive treatment typically need fewer mental and physical health services later on (American

Psychological Association, 2002c; Schoenbaum, Sherbourne, & Wells, 2005; U.S. Surgeon General, 1999).

The most common targets of treatment are problems involving anxiety, mood, impulse control, substance abuse, or some combination of these (Kessler et al., 2005). Many people also seek treatment for problems that are not officially diagnosed as disorders, such as relationship conflicts or difficulties associated with grief, divorce, retirement, or other life transitions.

In this chapter, we describe a variety of treatment methods, most of which are based on the theories of stress and coping, personality, and psychological disorders reviewed in the chapters on those topics. First, we examine the basic features common to all forms of treatment. Then we discuss approaches that rely on **psychotherapy,** the treatment of psychological disorders through psychological methods, such as talking about problems and exploring new ways of thinking and acting. Next, we consider biological approaches to treatment, which depend mainly on drugs and other physical therapies. (Many clients receive psychoactive drugs in addition to psychotherapy during the course of psychological treatment.)

Basic Features of Treatment

▶ **What features do all treatment techniques have in common?**

All treatments for psychological disorders share certain basic features—not only with one another but also with efforts to help the physically ill (Frank, 1978). These common features include a *client* or *patient,* a *therapist* or helper who is accepted as capable of helping the client, and a *special relationship* between the client and the therapist. In addition, all forms of treatment are based on some *theory* about the causes of the client's problems (Dumont & Corsini, 2000). The presumed causes can range from magic spells to infections and everything in between (Frank & Frank, 1991). These theories form the basis of *treatment procedures* for dealing with the client's problems. Traditional healers combat supernatural forces with ceremonies and prayers, medical doctors treat chemical imbalances with drugs, and psychologists focus on altering psychological processes through psychotherapy.

People can receive treatment as inpatients or outpatients. *Inpatients* are treated in a hospital or other residential institution. They are hospitalized because their impairments are severe enough to create a threat to their own well-being or that of others. Depending on their level of functioning, inpatients may stay in the hospital for a few days or weeks or—in rare cases—several years. Their treatment almost always includes psychoactive drugs. *Outpatients* receive psychotherapy and/or psychoactive drugs while living in the community.

Those who provide psychological treatment are a diverse group. **Psychiatrists** are medical doctors who complete specialty training in the treatment of mental disorders. Like other physicians, they are authorized to prescribe drugs for the relief of psychological problems. **Psychologists** who offer psychotherapy have usually completed a doctoral degree in clinical or counseling psychology, often followed by additional specialized training. Except in Louisiana and New Mexico, psychologists in the United States are not authorized to prescribe drugs, though this privilege may eventually be granted to specially trained psychologists elsewhere (Dittmann, 2003; Heiby, DeLeon, & Anderson, 2004; Mantell, Ortiz, & Planthara, 2004; Sammons, Paige, & Levant, 2003). Other therapy providers include *clinical social workers, marriage and family therapists,* and *licensed professional counselors,* all of whom typically hold a master's degree in their respective fields. They provide treatment in many settings, including hospitals, clinics, and private practice. *Psychiatric nurses, substance abuse counselors,* members of the clergy working as *pastoral counselors,* and a host of *paraprofessionals* also provide therapy services, often as part of a hospital or outpatient treatment team (Bernstein, Kramer, & Phares, in press).

psychotherapy The treatment of psychological disorders through psychological methods, such as analyzing problems, talking about possible solutions, and encouraging more adaptive ways of thinking and acting.

psychiatrists Medical doctors who have completed special training in the treatment of mental disorders.

psychologists In the area of treatment, therapists with advanced training in clinical or counseling psychology.

MEDIEVAL TREATMENT METHODS
Methods used to treat psychological disorders have always been related to the presumed causes of those disorders. In medieval times, when abnormal behavior was associated with demonic possession, physician-priests tried to make the victim's body an uncomfortable place for evil spirits. In this depiction, demons are shown fleeing as an afflicted person's head is placed in an oven.

The overall goal of treatment is to help troubled people change their thinking, feelings, and behavior in ways that relieve discomfort; promote happiness; and improve functioning as parents, students, employees, and the like. More specific goals and the methods chosen to reach them are included in a treatment plan that the therapist and client develop together. The details of this plan depend on the nature of the client's problems, preferences, and financial circumstances and on the time available for treatment (Johnson, 2003). They depend, too, on the therapist's training and qualifications, theoretical leanings and methodological preferences, and the degree to which the therapist is guided by the results of experimental research on treatment. Later, we discuss drugs and other biological treatments; for now, however, let's consider several forms of psychotherapy, each of which is based on psychodynamic, humanistic, behavioral, or cognitive-behavioral explanations of mental disorder.

Although we describe different approaches in separate sections, keep in mind that the majority of mental health professionals describe themselves as *eclectic* therapists. In other words, they might lean toward one set of treatment methods, but when working with particular clients or particular problems, they may employ other methods as well (Hayes & Harris, 2000; Norcross, Hedges, & Castle, 2002; Slife & Reber, 2001).

Psychodynamic Psychotherapy

▶ **How did Freud get started as a therapist?**

The field of formal psychotherapy began in the late 1800s when, as described in the personality chapter, Sigmund Freud established the psychodynamic approach to personality and mental disorders. Freud's method of treatment, **psychoanalysis,** was aimed at understanding unconscious conflicts and how they affect clients. Almost all forms of psychotherapy reflect some of Freud's ideas, including (1) his one-to-one treatment method; (2) his search for relationships between an individual's life history and current problems; (3) his emphasis on thoughts, emotions, and motivations in treatment; and (4) his focus on the client-therapist relationship. We describe Freud's original methods first and then consider some more recent treatments that are rooted in his psychodynamic approach.

psychoanalysis A method of psychotherapy that seeks to help clients gain insight into, and work through, unconscious thoughts and emotions presumed to cause psychological problems.

FREUD'S CONSULTING ROOM During psychoanalytic sessions, Freud's patients lay on this couch, free associating or describing dreams and events in their lives, while he sat in the chair behind them. According to Freud, even apparently trivial actions may carry messages from the unconscious. Forgetting a dream or missing a therapy appointment might reflect a client's unconscious resistance to treatment. Even accidents may be meaningful. The waiter who spills hot soup on an older male customer might be seen as acting out unconscious aggressive impulses against a father figure.

Classical Psychoanalysis

Classical psychoanalysis developed mainly out of Freud's medical practice. He was puzzled by patients who suffered from blindness, paralysis, or other disabilities that had no physical cause (see our discussion of *conversion disorders* in the chapter on psychological disorders). Freud tried to cure these patients with hypnotic suggestions, but he found this method to be only partially and temporarily successful. Later, he asked hypnotized patients to recall events that might have caused their symptoms. Eventually, however, he stopped using hypnosis and merely had patients lie on a couch and report whatever thoughts, memories, or images came to mind. Freud called this process *free association.*

Freud's "talking cure" produced surprising results. He was struck by how many patients reported childhood memories of sexual abuse, usually by a parent or other close relative (Esterson, 2001). Was child abuse rampant in Vienna, or were his patients' reports distorted by psychological factors? Freud concluded that these reports of childhood seduction probably reflected unconscious impulses and fantasies, not reality. He also concluded that his patients' physical symptoms were based on unconscious conflicts about those fantasies. So psychoanalysis came to focus on exploring the unconscious and resolving the conflicts raging within it.

Classical psychoanalytic treatment involves the use of free association, dream analysis, and analysis of the client's reactions to the therapist (called *transference*) to help the client gain insight into problems. Clients are encouraged, first, to recognize unconscious thoughts and emotions. Then they are encouraged to discover, or *work through,* the many ways in which those unconscious elements continue to motivate maladaptive thinking and behavior in everyday life. The treatment may require as many as three to five sessions per week, usually over several years. Generally, the psychoanalyst remains compassionate but neutral as the client slowly develops insight into how past conflicts have shaped current problems (Gabbard, 2004).

Contemporary Variations on Psychoanalysis

Classical psychoanalysis is still practiced, but not as much as it was several decades ago (Gabbard, 2004; Horgan, 1996). The decline is due in part to the growth of several alternative forms of treatment, including variations on classical psychoanalysis. Many of these variations were developed by neo-Freudian theorists. As noted in the personality chapter, these theorists placed less emphasis than Freud did on the past and on unconscious impulses driven by the id. They focused instead on the role played by social relationships in clients' problems and on how the power of the ego can be harnessed to solve them. Psychotherapists who adopt various neo-Freudian treatment methods tend to take a much more active role than classical analysts do—in particular, by directing the client's attention to evidence of certain conflicts in social relationships.

Many of these methods have come to be known as *short-term psychodynamic psychotherapy* because they aim to provide benefits in far less time than is required in classical psychoanalysis (Davanloo, 1999; Levenson, 2003; Rawson, 2003, 2006). In a particularly popular short-term psychodynamic approach known as *object relations therapy* (Scharff & Scharff, 2004; St. Clair, 1999), the powerful need for human contact and support takes center stage. Object relations therapists believe that most of the problems that bring clients to treatment ultimately stem from their relationships with others, especially their mothers or other early caregivers. (The term *object* usually refers to a person who has emotional significance for the client.) Accordingly, these therapists work to create a nurturing relationship in which the client's problems can be understood and corrected (Kahn & Rachman, 2000; Lieberman & Pawl, 1988; Wallerstein, 2002). This relationship provides a "second chance" for the client to receive the support that might have been missing in infancy and to counteract some of the consequences of maladaptive early attachment patterns. For example, object relations therapists take pains to show that they will not abandon their clients, as might have happened to these people in the past. *Interpersonal therapy,* too, is rooted partly in neo-Freudian theory (Sullivan, 1954). Often used in cases of depression, it focuses on

Ψapplying psychology **A PLAY THERAPY SESSION** Modern versions of psychoanalytic treatment include fantasy play and other techniques that make the approach more useful with children. A child's behavior and comments while playing with puppets representing family members, for example, are seen as a form of free association that the therapist hopes will reveal important unconscious material, such as fear of abandonment (Booth & Lindaman, 2000).

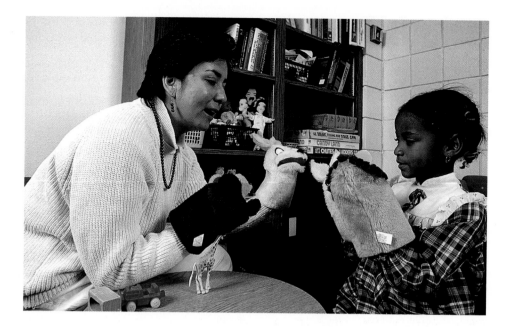

helping clients explore and overcome the problematic effects of interpersonal events that occur *after* early childhood—events such as the loss of a loved one, conflicts with a parent or a spouse, job loss, or social isolation (Mufson et al., 2004; Weissman, Markowitz, & Klerman, 2000).

With their focus on interpersonal relationships rather than instincts, their emphasis on clients' potential for self-directed problem solving, and their reassurance and emotional supportiveness, contemporary variants on classical psychoanalysis have helped the psychodynamic approach to retain its influence among mental health professionals (Norcross, Hedges, & Castle, 2002; Westen & Gabbard, 1999).

Humanistic Psychotherapy

▶ **Why won't some therapists give advice?**

Whereas some therapists revised Freud's ideas, others developed radical new therapies based on the humanistic approach to personality, which we describe in the personality chapter. *Humanistic psychologists,* sometimes called *phenomenologists,* emphasize the ways in which people interpret the events in their lives. They view people as capable of consciously controlling their own actions and taking responsibility for their decisions. Most humanistic therapists believe that human behavior isn't motivated by inner conflicts but by an innate drive toward growth that is guided by the way people perceive their world. Disordered behavior, they say, reflects a blockage in natural growth brought on by distorted perceptions or lack of awareness about feelings. Accordingly, humanistic (or phenomenological) therapy operates on the following assumptions:

1. Treatment is an encounter between equals, not a "cure" given by an expert. It is a way to help clients restart their natural growth and to feel and behave in a more genuine way.

2. Clients will improve on their own, given the right conditions. These ideal conditions promote clients' awareness, acceptance, and expression of their feelings and perceptions.

3. Ideal conditions in therapy can best be established through a therapeutic relationship in which clients are made to feel accepted and supported as human beings, no matter how problematic or undesirable their behavior may be. It is the

client's experience of this relationship that brings beneficial changes. (Notice that this assumption is shared with object relations and some other forms of brief psychodynamic therapy.)

4. Clients must remain responsible for choosing how they will think and behave.

Of the many humanistically oriented treatments in use today, the most influential are client-centered therapy, developed by Carl Rogers, and Gestalt therapy, developed by Frederick and Laura Perls (Cain & Seeman, 2002; Patterson, 2000; Woldt & Toman, 2005).

Client-Centered Therapy

Carl Rogers was trained in psychodynamic therapy methods during the 1930s, but he soon began to question their value. He especially disliked being a detached expert whose task is to "figure out" the client. Eventually convinced that a less formal approach would be more effective, Rogers allowed his clients to decide what to talk about and when, without direction, judgment, or interpretation by the therapist. This approach, now called **client-centered therapy** or **person-centered therapy,** relies on the creation of a relationship that reflects three intertwined therapist attitudes: unconditional positive regard, empathy, and congruence.

Unconditional Positive Regard　The attitude Rogers called **unconditional positive regard** consists of treating the client as a valued person, no matter what. This attitude is communicated through the therapist's willingness to listen without interrupting and to accept what is said without evaluating it. The therapist doesn't have to approve of everything the client says, but must accept it as reflecting that client's view of the world. Because Rogerian therapists trust clients to solve their own problems, they rarely give advice (Merry & Brodley, 2002). Doing so, said Rogers, would send clients an unspoken message that they are incompetent, making them less confident and more dependent on help.

Empathy　In addition, the client-centered therapist tries to see the world as the client sees it. In other words, the therapist tries to develop **empathy,** an emotional understanding of what the client might be thinking and feeling. Client-centered therapists convey empathy by showing that they are actively listening to the client. Like other skillful interviewers, they make eye contact with the client, nod in recognition as the client speaks, and give other signs of careful attention. They also use **reflection,** a paraphrased summary of the client's words that emphasizes the feelings and meanings that appear to go along with them. Reflection confirms what the client has said while also expressing the therapist's interest and helping the client to be aware of the thoughts and feelings expressed. Here is an example:

Client:　This has been such a bad day. I've felt ready to cry any minute, and I'm not even sure what's wrong!

Therapist:　You really do feel so bad. The tears just seem to well up inside, and I wonder if it is a little scary to not even know why you feel this way.

Notice that in rephrasing the client's statements, the therapist reflected back not only the obvious feelings of sadness but also the fear in the client's voice. Most clients respond to empathic reflection by elaborating on their feelings. This client went on to say, "It *is* scary, because I don't like to feel in the dark about myself. I have always prided myself on being in control."

Empathic listening tends to be so effective in promoting self-understanding and awareness that it is used across a wide range of therapies (Corsini & Wedding, 2001). Even beyond the realm of therapy, people who are thought of as easy to talk to are usually "good listeners" who reflect back the important messages they hear from others.

Congruence　Rogerian therapists also try to convey **congruence** (sometimes called *genuineness*) by acting in ways that are consistent with their feelings during therapy.

client-centered therapy (person-centered therapy)　A type of therapy in which the client decides what to talk about and when, without direction, judgment, or interpretation from the therapist.

unconditional positive regard　In client-centered therapy, the therapist's attitude that expresses caring for and acceptance of the client as a valued person.

empathy　In client-centered therapy, the therapist's attempt to appreciate how the world looks from the client's point of view.

reflection　Restating or paraphrasing what the client has said.

congruence　In client-centered therapy, a consistency between the way therapists feel and the way they act toward clients.

Ψapplying psychology   **A CLIENT-CENTERED THERAPY GROUP** Carl Rogers (shown here in shirtsleeves) believed that people in successful client-centered therapy become more self-confident, more aware of their feelings, more accepting of themselves, more comfortable and genuine with other people, more reliant on self-evaluation than on the judgments of others, and more effective and relaxed.

For example, if they are confused by what a client has said, they would say so rather than trying to pretend that they always understand everything. When the therapist's unconditional positive regard and empathy are genuine, the client is able to see that relationships can be built on openness and honesty. Ideally, this experience will help the client become more congruent in other relationships.

Gestalt Therapy

Another form of humanistic treatment was developed by Frederick S. (Fritz) Perls, along with his wife, Laura Perls. A European psychoanalyst, Frederick Perls was greatly influenced by Gestalt psychology. (As noted in the chapter on sensation and perception, Gestalt psychologists emphasized the idea that people actively organize their perceptions of the world.) As a result, he believed that (1) people create their own versions of reality and (2) people's natural psychological growth continues only as long as they perceive, remain aware of, and act on their true feelings. Growth stops and symptoms of mental disorder appear, said Perls, when people are not aware of all aspects of themselves (Perls, 1969; Perls, Hefferline, & Goodman, 1951).

Like client-centered therapy, **Gestalt therapy** seeks to create conditions in which clients can become more unified, self-aware, and self-accepting and thus ready to grow again. However, Gestalt therapists use more direct and dramatic methods than do Rogerians. Often working with groups, Gestalt therapists prod clients to become aware of feelings and impulses that they have disowned and to discard feelings, ideas, and values that are not really their own. For example, the therapist or other group members might point out inconsistencies between what clients say and how they behave. Gestalt therapists pay particular attention to clients' gestures and other forms of "body language" that appear to conflict with what the clients are saying (Kepner, 2001). The therapist may also ask clients to engage in imaginary dialogues with other people, with parts of their own personalities, and even with objects (Elliott, Watson, & Goldman, 2004a, 2004b). Like a shy person who can be socially outgoing only while at a costume party, clients often find that these dialogues help to get them in touch with and express their feelings (Paivio & Greenberg, 1995; Woldt & Toman, 2005).

In recent years, client-centered and other forms of humanistic therapy have declined in popularity (Norcross, Hedges, & Castle, 2002), but Carl Rogers's contributions to psychotherapy remain significant. In particular, his emphasis on the importance of the therapeutic relationship in bringing about change has been adopted by many other treatment approaches (Kirschenbaum & Jourdan, 2005).

Gestalt therapy   A form of treatment that seeks to create conditions in which clients can become more unified, more self-aware, and more self-accepting.

Behavior Therapy and Cognitive-Behavior Therapy

▶ **Can we learn to conquer fears?**

Psychodynamic and humanistic approaches to therapy assume that if clients gain insight or self-awareness about underlying problems, the symptoms created by those problems will disappear. Behavior therapists emphasize a different kind of self-awareness: They help clients to think about psychological problems as *learned behaviors* that can be changed without first searching for hidden meanings or unconscious causes (Miltenberger, 2003). For example, suppose you have a panic attack every time you leave home and find relief only when you return. Making excuses when friends invite you out temporarily eases your anxiety but does nothing to solve the problem. Could you reduce your fear without first seeking its "underlying meaning"? Behavior therapists say yes. They would begin by helping you to understand the learning principles that maintain your fear and then guide you in learning new responses in feared situations.

These goals are based on the behavioral approach to psychology in general and, in particular, on the social-cognitive approach to personality and disorder. As described in the personality chapter, social-cognitive theorists see learning as the basis both of normal personality and of most behavior disorders. According to this perspective, disordered behavior and thinking are examples of the maladaptive thoughts and actions that the client has developed through the processes described in the chapter on learning. For example, fear of leaving home (called *agoraphobia*) would be seen by behavior therapists as stemming from classically conditioned associations between being away from home and having panic attacks. The problem is partly maintained, they say, through operant conditioning: Staying home, and making excuses for doing so, is rewarded by reduced anxiety.

Some behavior therapists also emphasize that fears and other problems are maintained by what we think about situations and about ourselves. As discussed later, these *cognitive-behavior* therapists focus their treatment efforts on changing maladaptive thoughts, as well as problematic behaviors. In short, behavior therapists believe that if problems can be created through learning, they can also be eliminated through learning. So whether phobias and other problems were based on childhood experiences or were learned more recently, behavior therapists address them by arranging for clients to have beneficial new experiences.

The application of learning principles to change troublesome overt behavior has its roots in the work of John B. Watson, Ivan Pavlov, and others who studied the learned nature of fear in the 1920s. It stems, too, from B. F. Skinner's research on the impact of reward and punishment on behavior. In the late 1950s and early 1960s, researchers began to use classical and operant conditioning in treatment programs designed to eliminate fears, improve the behavior of disruptive schoolchildren and mental patients, and deal with many other problems (Plaud, 2003; Ullmann & Krasner, 1965). By 1970, behavioral treatment had become a popular alternative to psychodynamic and humanistic methods. The most notable features of behavioral treatment include the following:

1. Development of a productive therapist-client relationship. As in other therapies, this relationship enhances clients' confidence that change is possible and makes it easier for them to speak openly and to cooperate in and benefit from treatment (Creed & Kendall, 2005; Lejuez et al., 2005; Wilson, 1995).

2. A careful listing of the behaviors and thoughts to be changed. This assessment and the establishment of specific treatment goals sometimes replace the formal diagnosis used in some other therapy approaches. So instead of treating "depression" or "obsessive-compulsive disorder," behavior therapists work to change the specific thoughts, behaviors, and emotional reactions that cause people to receive these diagnostic labels.

behavior therapy Treatments that use classical conditioning principles to change behavior.

behavior modification Treatments that use operant conditioning methods to change behavior.

cognitive-behavior therapy Behavioral treatment methods that help clients change the way they think, as well as the way they behave.

systematic desensitization A behavioral method for treating anxiety in which clients visualize a graduated series of anxiety-provoking stimuli while remaining relaxed.

TABLE 13.1

A Desensitization Hierarchy

Desensitization hierarchies are lists of increasingly fear-provoking stimuli or situations that clients visualize while using relaxation methods to remain calm. Here are a few items from the beginning and the end of a hierarchy that was used to help a client overcome fear of flying.

1. You are reading a newspaper and notice an ad for an airline.
2. You are watching a television program that shows a group of people boarding a plane.
3. Your boss tells you that you need to take a business trip by air.
4. You are in your bedroom packing your suitcase for your trip.
.
.
.
12. Your plane begins to move as you hear the flight attendant say, "Be sure your seat belt is securely fastened."
13. You look at the runway as the plane is readied for takeoff.
14. You look out the window as the plane rolls down the runway.
15. You look out the window as the plane leaves the ground.

3. A therapist who acts as a kind of teacher/assistant by providing learning-based treatments, giving "homework" assignments, and helping the client make specific plans for dealing with problems rather than just talking about them.

4. Continuous monitoring and evaluation of treatment, along with constant adjustments to any procedures that do not seem to be effective. (Because ineffective procedures are soon altered or abandoned, behavioral treatment tends to be one of the briefer forms of therapy.)

Behavioral treatment can take many forms. By tradition, those that rely mainly on classical conditioning principles are usually referred to as **behavior therapy.** Those that focus on operant conditioning methods are usually called **behavior modification.** And behavioral treatment that focuses on changing thoughts, as well as overt behaviors, is called **cognitive-behavior therapy.** These methods, especially cognitive-behavior therapy, have become increasingly influential in recent years.

Techniques for Modifying Behavior

LINKAGES
Can people learn their way out of a disorder? (a link to Learning)

Some of the most important and commonly used behavioral treatment methods are those that laid the foundations of behavior therapy and behavior modification. These include systematic desensitization, modeling, positive reinforcement, extinction, aversion conditioning, and punishment.

Systematic Desensitization Joseph Wolpe (1958) developed one of the first behavioral methods for helping clients overcome phobias and other forms of anxiety. Called **systematic desensitization,** it is a treatment in which the client visualizes a series of anxiety-provoking stimuli while remaining relaxed. Wolpe believed that this process gradually weakens the learned association between anxiety and the feared object until the fear disappears.

Wolpe first helped his clients learn to relax, often using the *progressive relaxation training* procedures described in the chapter on health, stress, and coping. While relaxed, clients would be asked to imagine the easiest item on a *desensitization hierarchy,* which is a list of increasingly fear-provoking situations (see Table 13.1). As treatment progressed, clients imagined each item in the hierarchy, one at a time, moving to a more difficult

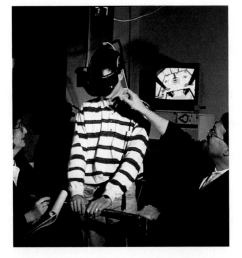

applying psychology   **VIRTUAL DESENSITIZATION**   This client fears heights. He is wearing a virtual reality display that creates the visual experience of being in a glass elevator, which, under the therapists' careful control, seems to gradually rise higher and higher. After learning to tolerate these realistic images without anxiety, clients are better able to fearlessly face the situations they once avoided.

item only after learning to imagine the previous one without distress. Wolpe found that once clients could calmly imagine being in feared situations, they were better able to deal with them in reality later on.

Desensitization appears especially effective when it slowly and carefully presents clients with real, rather than imagined, hierarchy items (Bouton, 2000; Marks, 2002; McGlynn et al., 1999; Tryon, 2005). This *in vivo*, or "real life," desensitization was once difficult to arrange or control, especially in treating fear of flying, heights, or highway driving, for example. Recently, however, *virtual reality graded exposure* has made it possible for clients to "experience" vivid and precisely graduated versions of feared situations without actually being exposed to them. In one study, clients who feared heights wore a virtual reality helmet that gave the impression of standing on bridges of gradually increasing heights, on outdoor balconies at higher and higher floors, and in a glass elevator as it slowly rose forty-nine stories (Rothbaum et al., 1995). The same technology has been used successfully in the treatment of fears caused by spiders, dentists, air travel, social interactions, and posttraumatic stress disorder (Anderson, Rothbaum, & Hodges, 2003; Choi et al., 2001; Dittman, 2005; Gershon et al., 2002; Glantz, Rizzo, & Graap, 2003; Maltby, Kirsch, & Mayers, 2002; Rothbaum et al., 1999, 2000, 2002; Winerman, 2005).

Modeling   Therapists often teach clients desirable behaviors by first demonstrating those behaviors. In **modeling** treatments, the client learns important skills by watching other people perform desired behaviors (Bidwell & Rehfeldt, 2004). For example, modeling can teach fearful clients how to respond fearlessly and confidently. In one case, a therapist showed a spider-phobic client how to calmly kill spiders with a fly swatter and then assigned her to practice this skill at home with rubber spiders (Mac-Donald & Bernstein, 1974). This combination of fearless demonstrations and firsthand practice, called *participant modeling,* is one of the most powerful treatments for fear (e.g., Bandura, Blanchard, & Ritter, 1969; Faust, Olson, & Rodriguez, 1991).

Modeling is also a major part of assertiveness training and social skills training, which help clients learn how to deal with people more comfortably and effectively. Social skills training has been used to help children interact more effectively with peers, to help social-phobic college students make conversation on dates, and to help rebuild mental patients' ability to have normal conversations with people outside the hospital (McQuaid, Granholm, et al., 2000; Spence, 2003; Spence, Donovan, & Brechman-Toussaint, 2000; Trower, 1995; Wong et al., 1993). In **assertiveness training,** the therapist helps clients learn to express their feelings and stand up for their rights in social situations (Alberti & Emmons, 1986; Ballou, 1995). Assertiveness training is often done in groups and involves both modeling and role playing of specific situations. For example, group assertiveness training has helped wheelchair-bound adults and learning-disabled students more comfortably handle the socially awkward situations in which they sometimes find themselves (Gleuckauf & Quittner, 1992; Weston & Went, 1999).

Positive Reinforcement   Behavior therapists also use **positive reinforcement** to alter problematic behaviors and to teach new skills in cases ranging from childhood tantrums and juvenile delinquency to schizophrenia and self-starvation. Employing operant conditioning principles, they set up *contingencies,* or rules, that specify the behaviors to be strengthened through reinforcement. In one study, children with autistic disorder, who typically speak very little, were given grapes, popcorn, or other items they liked in return for saying "please," "thank you," and "you're welcome" while exchanging crayons and blocks with a therapist. After the therapist modeled the desired behavior by saying the appropriate words at the appropriate times, the children began to say these words on their own. Their use of language also began to appear in other situations, and, as shown in Figure 13.1, the new skills were still evident six months later (Matson et al., 1990).

When working with severely retarded or disturbed clients in institutions or with unruly juveniles in residential facilities, behavior therapists sometimes establish a

modeling   A behavioral therapy method in which desirable behaviors are demonstrated for clients.

assertiveness training   A set of methods for helping clients learn to express their feelings and stand up for their rights in social situations.

positive reinforcement   Presenting a positive reinforcer (reward) after a desired response.

FIGURE **13.1**

Positive Reinforcement for an Autistic Child

applying psychology During each pretreatment baseline period, an autistic child rarely said "please," "thank you," or "you're welcome," but these statements began to occur once they were demonstrated, then reinforced. Did modeling and reinforcement actually cause the change? Probably, because each type of response did not start to increase until the therapist began demonstrating it.

Source: Matson et al. (1990).

token economy, which is a system for reinforcing desirable behaviors with points or coin-like tokens that can be exchanged later for snacks, access to television, or other desired rewards (Ayllon, 1999; Ayllon & Azrin, 1968; Field et al., 2004; LePage et al., 2003; Paul & Lentz, 1977; Seegert, 2003). The goal is to shape more adaptive behavior patterns that will persist outside the institution (Moore et al., 2001; Paul, 2000; Paul, Stuve, & Cross, 1997).

Extinction Just as reinforcing desirable behaviors can make them more likely to occur, failing to reinforce undesirable behaviors can make them less likely to occur, a process known as **extinction.** Treatment methods that use extinction change behavior slowly but offer a valuable way of reducing inappropriate behavior in children and adolescents and in retarded or seriously disturbed adults. For example, a client who gets attention by disrupting a classroom, damaging property, or violating hospital rules might be placed in a quiet, boring "time out" room for a few minutes to eliminate reinforcement for misbehavior (e.g., Kee, Hill, & Weist, 1999; Reitman & Drabman, 1999).

Extinction is also the basis of a fear-reduction treatment called **flooding,** in which clients are kept in a feared but harmless situation and not permitted to use their normally rewarding escape strategies (O'Donohue, Hayes, & Fisher, 2003). The client is flooded with fear at first, but after an extended period of exposure to the feared stimulus (a frog, say) without experiencing pain, injury, or any other dreaded result, the association between the feared stimulus and the fear response gradually weakens, and the conditioned fear response is extinguished (Basoglu, Livanou, & Salcioglu, 2003; Harris & Goetsch, 1990; Öst et al., 2001). In one study, twenty clients who feared needles were exposed for two hours to the sight and feel of needles, including mild finger pricks, harmless injections, and blood samplings (Öst, Hellström, & Kåver, 1992). Afterward, all except one client were able to have a blood sample drawn without experiencing significant anxiety. (Because they continuously expose clients

token economy A system for improving the behavior of clients in institutions by rewarding desirable behaviors with tokens that can be exchanged for various rewards.

extinction The gradual disappearance of a conditioned response.

flooding A procedure for reducing anxiety that involves keeping a client in a feared but harmless situation.

applying psychology

TREATING FEAR THROUGH FLOODING Flooding is designed to extinguish anxiety by allowing it to occur without the harmful consequences the person dreads. This man's fear of flying is obvious here on takeoff, but it is likely to diminish during and after an uneventful flight. Like other behavioral treatments, flooding is based on the idea that phobias and other psychological disorders are learned and can thus be "unlearned." Some therapists prefer more gradual exposure methods similar to those of *in vivo* desensitization, which start with situations that are lower on the client's fear hierarchy (Back et al., 2001; Fava et al., 2001; Fritzler, Hecker, & Losee, 1997).

aversion conditioning A method for reducing unwanted behaviors by using classical conditioning principles to create a negative response to some stimulus.

punishment The presentation of an aversive stimulus or the removal of a pleasant one following some behavior.

rational-emotive behavior therapy (REBT) A treatment that involves identifying illogical, self-defeating thoughts that clients have learned, then helping clients replace these thoughts with more realistic and beneficial ones.

to feared stimuli, flooding and other similar methods are also called *exposure techniques*.)

Aversion Therapy   Some unwanted behaviors, such as excessive gambling or using addictive drugs, can become so habitual and temporarily rewarding that they must be made less attractive if a client is to have any chance of giving them up. Methods for reducing the appeal of certain stimuli are known as *aversion therapy*. The name reflects the fact that these methods rely on a classical conditioning process called **aversion conditioning** to associate shock, nausea, or other physical or psychological discomfort with stimuli, thoughts, or actions the client wants to avoid (e.g., Bordnick et al., 2004).

Because aversion conditioning is unpleasant and uncomfortable, because it may not work with all clients (Flor et al., 2002), and because its effects are often temporary, most behavior therapists use this method relatively rarely, only when it is the best treatment choice, and only long enough to allow the client to learn more appropriate alternative behaviors.

Punishment   Sometimes the only way to eliminate a dangerous or disruptive behavior is to punish it with an unpleasant but harmless stimulus, such as a shouted "No!" or a mild electric shock. Unlike aversion conditioning, in which the unpleasant stimulus occurs along with the behavior that is to be eliminated (a classical conditioning approach), **punishment** is an operant conditioning technique; it presents the unpleasant stimulus *after* the undesirable response occurs.

Before using electric shock or other forms of punishment, behavior therapists are required by ethical and legal guidelines to ask themselves several important questions: Have all other methods failed? Would the client's life be in danger without treatment? Has an ethics committee reviewed and approved the procedures? Has the adult client or a close relative of a child client agreed to the treatment (Kazdin, 1994a)? When the answer to these questions is yes, punishment can be an effective, sometimes life-saving, treatment—as in the case illustrated in Figure 5.12 in the chapter on learning. As with extinction and aversion conditioning, punishment works best when it is used just long enough to eliminate undesirable behavior and is combined with other behavioral methods designed to reward more appropriate behavior.

Cognitive-Behavior Therapy

Like psychodynamic and humanistic therapists, most behavior therapists recognize that depression, anxiety, and many other behavior disorders can stem from how clients think about themselves and the world. And like other therapists, most behavior therapists try to change clients' troublesome ways of thinking, not just their overt behavior. Unlike other therapists, however, behavior therapists rely on learning principles to help clients change the way they think. Their methods are known collectively as *cognitive-behavior therapy* (Dobson, 2001; O'Donohue, Hayes, & Fisher, 2003). Suppose, for example, that a client has good social skills but suffers intense anxiety around other people. In a case like this, social skills training would obviously be unnecessary. Instead, the behavior therapist would use cognitive-behavioral methods designed to help the client identify habitual thoughts (such as "I shouldn't draw attention to myself") that create awkwardness and discomfort in social situations. Once these cognitive obstacles are brought to light, the therapist describes new and more adaptive ways of thinking—and encourages the client to learn and practice them. As these cognitive skills develop (e.g., "I have as much right to give my opinion as anyone else"), it becomes easier and more rewarding for clients to let these new thoughts guide their behavior (Meichenbaum, 1995).

Rational-Emotive Behavior Therapy   One prominent form of cognitive-behavior therapy is **rational-emotive behavior therapy (REBT),** which was developed by Albert Ellis (1962, 1993, 1995; 2004a, 2004b). REBT aims first at identifying unrealistic and self-defeating thoughts, such as "I must be loved or approved of by everyone" or "I

ALBERT ELLIS Rational-emotive behavior therapy (REBT) focuses on altering the self-defeating thoughts that Ellis believes underlie people's behavior disorders. Ellis argues, for example, that students do not get upset because they fail a test but because they have learned to believe that failure is a disaster that indicates they are worthless. Many of Ellis's ideas have been incorporated into various forms of cognitive-behavior therapy.

must always be competent to be worthwhile." After the client learns to recognize such thoughts as these and to see how they can cause problems, the therapist uses suggestions, encouragement, and logic to help the client replace such thoughts with more realistic and beneficial ones. The client is then given "homework" assignments to try these new ways of thinking in everyday situations. Here is part of an REBT session with a woman who suffered from panic attacks. She has just said that it would be "terrible" if she had an attack in a restaurant and that people "should be able to handle themselves!"

Therapist: ... *The reality is that* ... *"shoulds" and "musts" are the rules that other people hand down to us, and we grow up accepting them as if they are the absolute truth, which they most assuredly aren't.*

Client: *You mean it is perfectly okay to, you know, pass out in a restaurant?*

Therapist: *Sure!*

Client: *But ... I know I wouldn't like it to happen.*

Therapist: *I can certainly understand that. It would be unpleasant, awkward, inconvenient. But it is illogical to think that it would be terrible, or ... that it somehow bears on your worth as a person.*

Client: *What do you mean?*

Therapist: *Well, suppose one of your friends calls you up and invites you back to that restaurant. If you start telling yourself, "I might panic and pass out and people might make fun of me and that would be terrible," ... you might find you are dreading going to the restaurant, and you probably won't enjoy the meal very much.*

Client: *Well, that is what usually happens.*

Therapist: *But it doesn't have to be that way .... The way you feel, your reaction ... depends on what you choose to believe or think, or say to yourself.* (Masters et al., 1987)

Cognitive-behavior therapists use many techniques related to REBT to help clients learn to think in more adaptive ways. Techniques aimed at replacing upsetting thoughts with alternative thinking patterns were originally described by behaviorists as *cognitive restructuring* (Lazarus, 1971). They help clients plan calming thoughts to use during exams, tense conversations, and other anxiety-provoking situations. These thoughts might include "OK, stay calm, you can handle this. Just focus on the task, and don't worry about being perfect." Sometimes, these techniques are expanded to include *stress inoculation training,* in which clients imagine being in a stressful situation and then practice newly learned cognitive skills to remain calm (Meichenbaum, 1995; Sheehy & Horan, 2004).

Beck's Cognitive Therapy Behavior therapists seek a different kind of cognitive restructuring when they use Aaron Beck's **cognitive therapy** (Beck, 1976, 1995, 2005). Beck's treatment approach is based on the idea that certain psychological disorders can be traced to errors in logic (e.g., "If I fail my driver's test the first time, I will never pass it") and false beliefs (e.g., "Everyone ignores me"). Beck says that over time, these learned *cognitive distortions* occur so quickly and automatically that the client never stops to consider that they might not be true (see Table 13.2).

Cognitive therapy takes an active, organized, problem-solving approach in which the therapist first helps clients learn to identify the errors in logic, false beliefs, and other cognitive distortions that precede anxiety, depression, conduct problems, eating disorders, and other psychological problems (Beck & Rector, 2005; Drinkwater & Stewart, 2002; Hendricks & Thompson, 2005; Pardini & Lochman, 2003; Turkington, Kingdon, & Weiden, 2006). Then, much as in the five-step critical thinking system illustrated throughout this book, these thoughts and beliefs are considered as hypotheses to be tested, not as "facts" to be uncritically accepted (Hatcher, Brown, & Gariglietti, 2001). In other words, the therapist and client become a team of "investigators" as they plan ways to test beliefs such as "I'm no good around the house." For example, they might agree on tasks that the client will attempt as "homework"—such as cleaning out the basement,

cognitive therapy An organized problem-solving approach in which the therapist actively collaborates with clients to help them notice how certain negative thoughts precede anxiety and depression.

TABLE 13.2

Some Examples of Negative Thinking

learn by doing   Here are just a few examples of the kinds of thoughts that cognitive-behavior therapists see as underlying anxiety, depression, and other behavior problems. After reading this list, try writing an alternative thought that clients could use to replace each of these in-grained cognitive habits. Then jot down a "homework assignment" that you would recommend to help clients challenge each maladaptive statement and thus develop new ways of thinking about themselves.

"I shouldn't draw attention to myself."

"I will never be any good at this."

"It would be so awful if I don't know the answer."

"Everyone is smarter than I am."

"Nobody likes me."

"I should be able to do this job perfectly."

"What if I panic?"

"I'll never be happy."

"I should have accomplished more by this point in my life."

getting advice on hanging a picture, or cutting the grass. Success at accomplishing even one of these tasks provides concrete evidence to challenge a false belief that has supported depression or anxiety, thus helping to reduce it (Beck et al., 1992; Mullin, 2000).

As described in the chapter on psychological disorders, however, depression, anxiety, and some other disorders may not be due entirely to specific thoughts or beliefs about specific situations (Beck, 2002). Sometimes they stem from a more general cognitive style that leads people to expect that the worst will always happen to them and to assume that negative events occur because they are completely and permanently incompetent and worthless (Peterson, 1995; Peterson & Seligman, 1984). So cognitive-behavior therapists also help clients to develop more optimistic ways of thinking and to reduce their tendency to blame themselves for negative outcomes (Persons, Davidson, & Tompkins, 2001). In some cases, cognitive restructuring is combined with practice at using logical thinking, anxiety management techniques, and skill training—all designed to help clients experience success and develop confidence in situations in which they had previously expected to fail (Beck & Beck, 1995).

Group, Family, and Couples Therapy

▶ **How does group therapy differ from individual therapy?**

The one-to-one methods of psychodynamic, humanistic, and behavioral treatment we have described are often adapted for use with groups of clients or family units (Petrocelli, 2002; Rosen, Stukenberg, & Saeks, 2001; Scheidinger, 2004; Thorngren & Kleist, 2002).

Group Therapy

Group therapy refers to the treatment of several clients under the guidance of a therapist who encourages helpful interactions among group members. Many groups are organized around one type of problem (such as alcoholism) or one type of client (such as adolescents). In most cases, six to twelve clients meet with their therapist at least once a week for about two hours. All group members agree to hold confidential everything that occurs within group sessions.

Group therapy offers features not found in individual treatment (Marmarosh, Holtz, & Schottenbauer, 2005; Ogrondniczuk & Piper, 2003; Yalom, 1995). First, group therapy allows the therapist to observe clients interacting with one another. Second, groups encourage their members to talk about themselves and explore their feelings. As they listen to each other, clients often feel less alone because they realize that many people are struggling with difficulties at least as severe as their own. This realization tends to raise each client's expectations for improvement, a factor important in all forms of treatment. Third, group members can boost one another's self-confidence and self-acceptance as they come to trust and value one another. Fourth, clients learn from one another. They share ideas for solving problems and give one another honest feedback

group therapy Psychotherapy involving six to twelve unrelated individuals.

TABLE **13.3**

Some "Rules for Talking" in Couples Therapy

learn by doing Many forms of couples therapy help partners improve communication through establishing rules such as these. Think about your own experience in relationships or your observations of couples as they interact, and then write down some rules you would add to this list. Why do you think it would be important for couples to follow the rules on your list?

1. Always begin with something positive when stating a problem.

2. Use specific behaviors rather than derogatory labels or overgeneralizations to describe what is bothersome about the other person.

3. Make connections between those specific behaviors and feelings that arise in response to them (e.g., "It makes me sad when you . . .").

4. Admit your own role in the development of the problem.

5. Be brief; don't lecture or harangue.

6. Maintain a focus on the present or the future; don't review all previous examples of the problem or ask "why" questions such as "Why do you always . . .?"

7. Talk about observable events; don't make inferences about them (e.g., say "I get angry when you interrupt me" rather than "Stop trying to make me feel stupid").

8. Paraphrase what your partner has said, and check out your own perceptions of what was said before responding. (Note that this suggestion is based on the same principle as Rogers's empathic listening.)

about their attitudes and behavior. Fifth, perhaps through mutual modeling, the group experience makes clients more sensitive to other people's needs, motives, and messages. Finally, group therapy allows clients to try out new skills in a supportive environment.

Family and Couples Therapy

As its name implies, **family therapy** involves treatment of two or more individuals from the same family. One of these, often a troubled adolescent or child, is the initially identified client. Whether family therapy is based on psychodynamic, humanistic, or cognitive-behavioral approaches, the family is usually considered as a functioning unit known as a *family system*. As with group therapy, the family therapy format gives the therapist an excellent view of how the initially identified client interacts with others, thus providing a basis for discussion of topics important to each family member. And as with group therapists, family therapists usually have special training that helps them understand how the problems of individual family members affect and are affected by problems in the complex interactions taking place within the family system as a whole (Beels, 2002; Pilling et al., 2002; Williams, 2005). Ultimately, the client in family therapy is the family itself, and treatment involves as many members as possible. In fact, the goal of family therapy is not just to ease the identified client's problems but also to create greater harmony and balance within the family by helping each member understand family interaction patterns and the problems they create (Blow & Timm, 2002; Goldenberg & Goldenberg, 1995).

In **couples therapy**, improving communication between partners is one of the most important targets of treatment (Christensen et al., 2004; Gurman & Jacobson, 2002). Discussion in couples therapy sessions typically focuses on identifying and improving the miscommunication or lack of communication that is interfering with the couples' happiness and intimacy. Often, the sessions revolve around learning to abide by certain "rules for talking," such as those listed in Table 13.3. For some therapists, helping couples become closer also means helping them to express emotions more honestly and to be more accepting of one another (Shadish & Baldwin, 2005; Wood et al., 2005). Some therapists even offer preventive treatment to couples who are at risk for relationship problems (Jacobson et al., 2000; Laurenceau et al., 2004). ("In Review: Approaches to Psychological Treatment" summarizes key features of the main approaches to treatment that we have discussed so far.)

family therapy A type of treatment involving two or more clients from the same family.

couples therapy A form of therapy that focuses on improving communication between partners.

APPROACHES TO PSYCHOLOGICAL TREATMENT

Dimension	Classical Psychoanalytic	Contemporary Psychodynamic	Humanistic	Behavioral/ Cognitive-Behavioral
Nature of the human being	Driven by sexual and aggressive urges	Driven by the need for human relationships	Has free will, choice, and capacity for self-actualization	Is a product of social learning and conditioning; behaves on the basis of past experience
Therapist's role	Neutral; helps client explore meaning of free associations and other material from the unconscious	Active; develops relationship with client as a model for other relationships	Facilitates client's growth; some therapists are active, some are nondirective	Teacher/trainer who helps client replace undesirable thoughts and behaviors; active, action oriented
Focus	Unresolved unconscious conflicts from the distant past	Understanding the past, but focusing on current relationships	Here and now; focus on immediate experience	Current behavior and thoughts; may not need to know original causes to create change
Goals	Psychosexual maturity through insight; strengthening of ego functions	Correction of effects of failures of early attachment; development of satisfying intimate relationships	Expanded awareness; fulfillment of potential; self-acceptance	Changes in thinking and behaving in particular classes of situations; better self-management
Typical methods	Free association; dream analysis, analysis of transference	Analysis of interpersonal relationships, including the client-therapist relationship	Reflection-oriented interviews designed to convey unconditional positive regard, empathy, and congruence; exercises to promote self-awareness	Systematic desensitization, modeling, assertiveness and social skills training, positive reinforcement, extinction, aversion conditioning, punishment, cognitive restructuring

? 1. *Object relations therapy and interpersonal therapy are both contemporary examples of the _____ approach to psychological treatment.*
2. *Imagining increasingly fear-provoking stimuli is a _____ treatment method called _____.*
3. *Reflection is an interviewing technique associated mainly with the _____ approach to treatment.*

Online Study Center

Improve Your Grade
Tutorial: Phobia
Treatments

Evaluating Psychotherapy

▶ **How effective is psychotherapy?**

Most psychotherapists and their clients find psychotherapy effective (*Consumer Reports*, 1995), but confirming that effectiveness through experimental research has proven to be challenging and controversial (Dawes, 1994; DeRubeis & Crits-Christoph, 1998; Norcross, Beutler, & Levant, 2005; Seligman, 1995; Weisz, Weersing, & Henggeler, 2005; Westen, Novotny, & Thompson-Brenner, 2004).

LINKAGES
Can therapy change personality? (a link to Personality)

The value of psychotherapy was first widely questioned in 1952, when British psychologist Hans Eysenck reviewed studies in which thousands of clients had received either traditional psychodynamic therapy, various other therapies, or no treatment. To the surprise and dismay of many therapists, Eysenck (1952) found that the percentage of clients who improved following any kind of psychotherapy was actually lower than among people who received no treatment.

Critics argued that Eysenck was wrong (e.g., Bergin, 1971; de Charms, Levy, & Wertheimer, 1954; Luborsky, 1972). They claimed that he had ignored studies supporting the value of psychotherapy and misinterpreted his data. In fact, when some of these critics reviewed treatment successes and failures themselves, they concluded that psychotherapy tends to be *more* helpful than no treatment (e.g., Bergin, 1971).

Debate over Eysenck's findings—and the contradictory reports that followed them—highlight several factors that make it so hard to answer the apparently simple question, Does psychotherapy work? For one thing, there is the problem of how to measure improvement in psychotherapy. Should the yardstick be psychological test results, behavioral observations, interviews, or a combination of all three? Different measurements may tell somewhat different stories about improvement, making it difficult for researchers to compare or combine the results of different studies and draw conclusions about the overall effectiveness of treatment (De Los Reyes & Kazdin, 2006; Krause, 2005; Sass, Twohig, & Davies, 2004).

The question of effectiveness is further complicated by the broad range of clients, therapists, and treatments involved in psychotherapy. Clients differ in the problems they present, in their motivation to solve those problems, and in the amount of stress and social support present in their environments. Therapists differ, too, not only in skill, experience, and personality but also in which of the hundreds of available treatment procedures they decide to use (Feltham, 2000). In addition, differences in the nature and quality of the client-therapist relationship from one case to another can significantly alter the course of treatment, the clients' faith in the procedures, and their willingness to cooperate (Lambert & Barley, 2001; Norcross, 2002). Because clients' responses to psychotherapy can be influenced by all these factors, results from any particular treatment evaluation study might not tell us much about how well different therapists using different methods would do with other kinds of clients and problems (Kazdin, 1994b).

In short, the question of whether psychotherapy "works" is difficult or impossible to answer scientifically in a way that applies to all therapies for all disorders. However, several research reviews (Galatzer-Levy et al., 2000; Shadish et al., 2000; Smith, Glass, & Miller, 1980; Weisz & Jensen, 1999) have demonstrated that, in general, psychotherapy does work (see Figure 13.2).

FIGURE **13.2**

An Analysis of Psychotherapy's Effects

These curves show the results of one large-scale analysis of the effects of psychotherapy. Notice that on average, people who received therapy were better off than 80 percent of troubled people who did not. The overall effectiveness of psychotherapy has also been confirmed in a more recent analysis of ninety treatment outcome studies (Shadish et al., 2000).

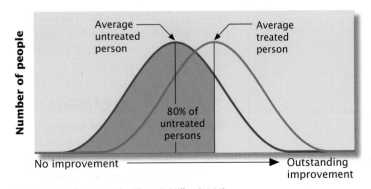

Source: Data from Smith, Glass, & Miller (1980).

LINKAGES
Does psychotherapy work? (a link to Introduction to the Science of Psychology)

As you might imagine, most therapists agree with this assessment, and most believe that the theoretical approach and treatment methods *they* use work better than those of other therapists (e.g., Giles, 1990; Mandelid, 2003).

THINKING CRITICALLY

Are All Forms of Therapy Equally Effective?

■ What am I being asked to believe or accept?

They can't all be right, of course, and some researchers claim that they are all wrong. These researchers argue that, in fact, various theories of behavior disorder and the specific treatment methods based on them don't have much to do with the success of psychotherapy. All approaches, they say, are equally effective. This has been called the "Dodo Bird Verdict," after the *Alice in Wonderland* creature who, when called on to judge who had won a race, answered, "Everybody has won and all must have prizes" (Duncan, 2002; Luborsky, Singer, & Luborsky, 1975).

■ Is there evidence available to support the claim?

Some evidence does suggest that there are no significant differences in the overall effectiveness of psychodynamic, humanistic, and behavioral therapies. Statistical analyses that combine the results of a large number of therapy studies show that the three approaches are associated with about the same degree of success (Lambert & Bergin, 1994; Luborsky et al., 2002; Luborsky, Rosenthal, & Diguer, 2003; Shadish et al., 2000; Smith et al., 1980; Weisz, McCarty, & Valeri, 2006).

■ Can that evidence be interpreted another way?

It is possible, however, that evidence in favor of the Dodo Bird Verdict is based on statistical methods that cannot detect genuine differences among treatments. A statistical analysis that averages the results of many different studies might not reveal important differences in the impact of particular treatments for particular problems (Beutler, 2002; Eysenck, 1978; Wilson, 1985; Rounsaville & Carroll, 2002). Suppose, for example, that Therapy A works better than Therapy B in treating anxiety but that Therapy B works better than Therapy A in cases of depression. If you combined the results of treatment studies with both kinds of clients, the average effects of each therapy would be about the same, making it appear that the two treatments are about equally effective. Differences among the effects of specific treatment procedures might also be overshadowed by the beneficial *common factors* shared by almost all forms of therapy—such as the support of the therapist, the hope and expectancy for improvement that therapy creates, and the trust that develops between client and therapist (Barber et al., 2000; Martin, Garske, & Davis, 2000; Vocisano et al., 2004). Therapists whose personal characteristics can motivate clients to change might promote that change no matter what specific therapeutic methods they use (Elkin, 1999; Hubble, Duncan, & Miller, 1999).

■ What evidence would help to evaluate the alternatives?

Debate over the question of whether all forms of psychotherapy are about equally effective on the average is likely to continue, but to many researchers, it is the wrong question. They argue that is pointless to compare the effects of psychodynamic, humanistic, and behavioral methods in general. It is more important, they say, to address what Gordon Paul called the "ultimate question" about psychotherapy: "What treatment, by whom, is most effective for this individual with that specific problem, under what set of circumstances?" (Paul, 1969, p. 44).

■ What conclusions are most reasonable?

Statistical analyses show that various treatment approaches appear about equally effective overall. But this does not mean that every psychotherapy experience will be equally helpful. Potential clients must realize that the success of their treatment can still be affected by how severe their problems are, by the quality of the relationship they form with a therapist, by their motivation to change, and by the appropriateness of the therapy methods chosen for their problems (Goldfried & Davila, 2005).

Like those seeking treatment, many clinical psychologists, too, are eager for more specific scientific evidence about the effectiveness of particular therapies for particular kinds of clients and disorders. These empirically oriented clinicians are concerned that, all too often, therapists' choice of therapy methods depends more heavily on personal preferences or current trends than on scientific evidence of effectiveness (Lynn, Lilienfeld, & Lohr, 2003; Nathan, Stuart, & Dolan, 2000; Norcross, Beutler, & Levant, 2005; Tavris, 2003). They believe that advocates of any treatment—whether it is object relations therapy or systematic desensitization—must demonstrate that its benefits are the result of the treatment itself and not just of the passage of time, the effects of repeated assessment, the client's motivation and personal characteristics, or other confounding factors (Chambless & Hollon, 1998). A movement toward the same kind of *evidence-based practice* has also appeared in the medical and dental professions (Borry, Schotsmans, & Dierickx, 2006; Niederman & Richards, 2005).

Empirically oriented clinicians also want to see evidence that the benefits of treatment are clinically significant. To be *clinically significant,* therapeutic changes must be great enough to make treated clients' feelings and actions similar to those of people who have not experienced these clients' disorders (Kendall, 1999; Kendall & Sheldrick, 2000). The need to demonstrate clinical significance has become more important than ever as increasingly cost-conscious clients—and their health insurance companies—decide whether, and how much, to pay for various psychotherapy services (Levant, 2005; Makeover, 2004; Nelson & Steele, 2006). The most scientific way to evaluate treatment effects is through experiments in which clients are randomly assigned to various treatments or control conditions and their progress is objectively measured.

To help clinicians select treatment methods on the basis of this kind of empirical evidence, the American Psychological Association's Division of Clinical Psychology created a task force on effective psychotherapies (Task Force on Promotion and Dissemination of Psychological Procedures, 1995).

FOCUS ON RESEARCH

Which Therapies Work Best for Which Problems?

■ What was the researchers' question?

The question addressed by this task force was, "What therapies have proven themselves most effective in treating various kinds of psychological disorders?"

■ How did the researchers answer the question?

Working with other empirically oriented clinical psychologists, members of this task force examined the outcomes of thousands of well-controlled experiments that evaluated psychotherapy methods used to treat mental disorder, marital distress, and health-related behavior problems in children, adolescents, and adults (Baucom et al., 1998; Chambless & Ollendick, 2001; Compas et al., 1998; DeRubeis & Crits-Christoph, 1998; Foley, 2004; Kazdin & Weisz, 1998; Kendall & Chambless, 1998).

TABLE **13.4**   **Examples of Empirically Supported Therapies for Selected Disorders**

Treatments listed as "efficacious and specific" (pronounced "effeh-KAY-shus") were shown to be superior to no treatment or to some alternative treatment in at least two experiments in which clients were randomly assigned to various treatment conditions. These experiments are called *randomized clinical trials,* or *RCTs.* Also included in this category are treatments supported by scientific outcome measures from a large number of carefully conducted case studies. Treatments listed as "probably efficacious" are supported by at least one RCT or by a smaller number of rigorously evaluated case studies. Those listed as "possibly efficacious" are supported by a mixture of data, generally from single-case studies or other nonexperimental studies (Chambless & Ollendick, 2001).

Problem	Efficacious and Specific	Probably Efficacious	Possibly Efficacious
Major depressive disorder	Behavior therapy Cognitive-behavior therapy Interpersonal therapy	Brief dynamic therapy Social problem solving Self-control therapy	
Specific phobia	Exposure therapy	Systematic desensitization	
Agoraphobia/panic disorder	Cognitive-behavior therapy	Couples training + exposure therapy	
Generalized anxiety disorder	Cognitive-behavior therapy	Applied relaxation therapy	
Obsessive-compulsive disorder	Exposure therapy + response prevention	Cognitive therapy Family-assisted exposure therapy + response prevention + relaxation	Rational emotive behavior therapy + exposure therapy
Posttraumatic stress disorder		Exposure Stress inoculation Cognitive therapy + stress inoculation + exposure	Structured psychodynamic treatment
Schizophrenia	Behavioral family therapy	Family systems therapy Social skills training Supportive group therapy	Cognitive therapy (for delusions)
Alcohol abuse and dependence	Community reinforcement	Cue exposure therapy Behavioral marital therapy + anti-alcohol drug, disulfiram Social skills training (with inpatients)	
Opiate abuse and dependence		Behavior therapy Brief dynamic therapy Cognitive therapy	
Marital discord	Behavioral marital therapy	Insight-oriented marital therapy	

Source: Chambless & Ollendick (2001).

empirically supported therapies (ESTs)
Treatments for psychological disorders whose effectiveness has been validated by controlled experimental research.

■ **What did the researchers find?**

The task force found that a number of treatments—known as **empirically supported therapies or ESTs**—have been validated by controlled experimental research (Chambless & Ollendick, 2001; DeRubeis & Crits-Christoph, 1998; Kendall & Chambless, 1998). Table 13.4 contains some examples of these therapies. Notice that the treatments identified as effective for particular problems in adult clients are mainly behavioral, cognitive, and cognitive-behavioral methods, but that certain psychodynamic therapies (e.g., interpersonal therapy and brief dynamic therapy) also made the list (Chambless & Ollendick, 2001; Svartberg, Stiles, & Seltzer, 2004).

■ What do the results mean?

The authors of the report on empirically supported therapies and those who support their efforts claim that by relying on analysis of experimental research they have scientifically evaluated various treatments and generated a list of methods from which clinicians and consumers can choose with confidence when facing specific disorders (e.g., Hunsley & Rumstein-McKean, 1999; Kendall & Chambless, 1998). Therapists are even being urged to follow *treatment manuals* stemming from this research to help them deliver empirically supported therapies exactly as they were intended (Addis, 1997; Wade, Treat, & Stuart, 1998). The state of Kansas has been the first in the United States to formally encourage the use of empirically supported treatments for children (Roberts, 2002).

Not everyone agrees with the conclusions and recommendations of the APA Task Force. Critics note, first, that treatments missing from the latest list of ESTs haven't necessarily been discredited. Some of those treatments might not yet have been studied or validated according to the efficacy criteria selected by the task force. These critics also have doubts about the value of some of those criteria. They point to research showing that had the task force used different outcome criteria, it might have reached different—and perhaps less optimistic—conclusions about the value of some empirically supported treatments (Bradley et al., 2005; Thompson-Brenner, Glass, & Westen, 2003). There is concern, too, about the wisdom of categorizing treatments as either "supported" or "unsupported." These simple either-or judgments seem reassuring, but may fail to give a complete picture of the impact of various treatments on various clients with various problems (Westen & Bradley, 2005). Critics argue further that the list of empirically supported therapies is based on research that may not be relevant to clinicians working in the real world of clinical practice. They note that experimental studies of psychotherapy have focused mainly on relatively brief treatments for highly specific disorders, even though most clients' problems tend to be far more complex (Westen & Bradley, 2005). These studies focus, too, on the therapeutic procedures used rather than on the characteristics and interactions of therapists and clients (Cornelius-White, 2002; Garfield, 1998; Hilliard, Henry, & Strupp, 2000; Westen et al., 2004). This emphasis on procedure is a problem, critics say, because the outcome of therapy in these experiments might have been strongly affected by client-therapist factors, such as whether the random pairing of clients and therapists resulted in a match or a mismatch on certain personal characteristics. In real clinical situations, clients and therapists are not paired up at random (Goldfried & Davila, 2005; Hill, 2005; Hohman & Shear, 2002). Finally, because therapists participating in experimental research were required to follow standard treatment manuals, they were not free to adapt treatment methods, as they normally would, to the needs of particular clients (Garfield, 1998). Perhaps, say critics, when there is less experimental control over the treatment situation, all therapies really are about equally effective, as suggested by the statistical analyses of outcome research we mentioned earlier (Shadish et al., 2000; Smith et al., 1980).

In short, critics reject the empirically supported therapies list as a useful guide. In fact, some see it as an incomplete and ultimately misleading document (Westen & Bradley, 2005). They also worry that widespread use of treatment manuals would make psychotherapy mechanical and less effective and would discourage therapists' from developing new treatment methods (Addis & Krasnow, 2000; Beutler, 2000; Garfield, 1998).

■ What do we still need to know?

The effort to identify empirically supported treatments and to develop evidence-based practice in clinical psychology (Levant, 2005) represent important steps in responding to Paul's (1969) "ultimate question" about psychotherapy: "What treatment, by whom, is most effective for this individual with that specific problem, under what set of circumstances?" We still have a long way to go to answer the rest of Paul's complex question, but empirically oriented clinical psychologists are determined to do so.

The combinations of treatment methods and therapist and client characteristics that are best suited to solving particular psychological problems have not yet been mapped out, but there are a few trends. For example, when differences do show up in comparative studies of adult psychotherapy, they tend to reveal a small to moderate advantage for behavioral and cognitive-behavioral methods, especially in the treatment of phobias and certain other anxiety disorders (Barrowclough et al., 2001; Borkovec & Costello, 1993; DeRubeis & Crits-Christoph, 1998; Eddy et al., 2004; Hunsley & Di Giulio, 2002; Lambert & Bergin, 1994; Weisz et al., 1995), as well as bulimia nervosa, an eating disorder (Hendricks & Thompson, 2005; Wilson, 1997). The same tends to be true for child and adolescent clients (Epstein et al., 1994; Weiss & Weisz, 1995; Weisz et al., 1995).

Further, the client-therapist relationship seems to play a significant role in the success of many forms of treatment (Brown & O'Leary, 2000; Constantino et al., 2005; Horvath, 2005; Martin, Garske, & Davis, 2000; Messer & Wampold, 2002; Uwe, 2005). Certain people seem to be particularly effective in forming productive human relationships. Even without formal training, these people can sometimes be as helpful as professional therapists because of personal qualities that are inspiring, healing, and soothing to others (Stein & Lambert, 1995). These qualities may help account for the success of many kinds of therapy.

In summary, the Dodo Bird Verdict is probably incorrect, and it is certainly incomplete. Although different treatments can be equally effective in addressing some disorders, empirical research shows that for other disorders certain therapies are more effective than others. That research provides valuable guidelines for matching treatments to disorders, but it doesn't guarantee success. The outcome of any given case will also be affected by client characteristics, therapist characteristics, and the therapeutic relationship that develops between them (e.g., Hill, 2005; Sherer & Schreibman, 2005). The challenge now is to combine research on empirically supported therapy methods with research on the common factors they share and to create a picture of psychotherapy effectiveness that is based on both sets of data (Messer, 2004; Westen & Bradley, 2005). Such a comprehensive view would be a useful guide for clinicians practicing today and an ideal training model for the clinicians of tomorrow.

Given what is known so far, potential clients are well advised to choose a treatment approach and a therapist based on (1) what treatment approach, methods, and goals the person finds comfortable and appealing; (2) information about the potential therapist's "track record" with a particular method for treating problems similar to those the person faces; and (3) the likelihood of forming a productive relationship with the therapist. This last consideration assumes special importance when client and therapist do not share similar social or cultural backgrounds.

Sociocultural Factors in Therapy

Sociocultural differences between clients and therapists—in religious faith, gender, age, ethnicity, sexual orientation, socioeconomic background, and the like—can sometimes create miscommunication or mistrust. If it does, their working relationship and the clients' motivation to change may both be impaired (Jones, Botsko, & Gorman, 2003; Pachankis & Goldfried, 2004). Suppose, for example, that a therapist suggests that a client's insomnia is a reaction to stress, but the client is sure that it comes as punishment for having offended a long-dead ancestor. That client may not easily accept a treatment based on the principles of stress management (Wohl, 1995). Similarly, a therapist who believes that people should confront and overcome life's problems might run into trouble when treating clients whose cultural or religious training encourages calmly

PREPARING FOR THERAPY Special pretreatment orientation programs may be offered to clients who, because of sociocultural factors, are unfamiliar with the rules and procedures of psychotherapy. These programs provide a preview of what psychotherapy is, how it can help, and what the client is expected to do to make it more effective (Reis & Brown, 2006; Sue, Zane, & Young, 1994).

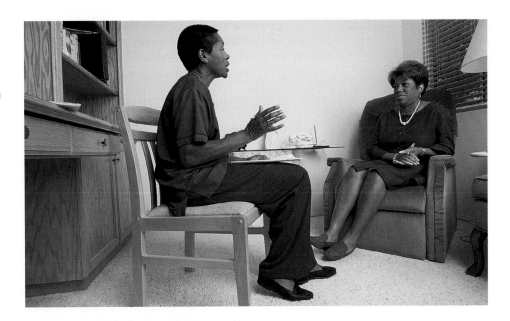

accepting such problems (Sundberg & Sue, 1989). In such cases, the result may be much like two people singing a duet using the same music but different lyrics (Johnson & Thorpe, 1994; Martinez-Taboas, 2005).

In the United States, cultural clashes may be partly to blame for the underuse of, or withdrawal from, mental health services by recent immigrants, as well as by African Americans, Asian Americans, Hispanic Americans, American Indians, and members of other minority populations (Dingfelder, 2005; Gone, 2004; Sanders Thompson, Bazile, & Akbar, 2004; Wang, Lane, et al., 2005). Accordingly, major efforts are under way to ensure that such differences do not impede the delivery of treatment to anyone who wants or needs it (Richards & Bergin, 2000). Virtually every mental health training program in North America is seeking to recruit more students from traditionally underserved minority groups to eventually make it easier to match clients with therapists from similar cultural backgrounds (e.g., Kersting, 2004; Norcross, Hedges, & Prochaska, 2002; Rogers & Molina, 2006). In the meantime, many minority clients are likely to encounter a therapist from a differing background, so researchers have also examined the value of matching therapeutic techniques with clients' culturally based expectations and preferences (Li & Kim, 2004; Preciado, 1994; Sue, 1998; Tanaka-Matsumi & Higginbotham, 1994).

Today, psychotherapists are more sensitive than ever to the cultural values of particular groups and the difficulties that can impair intercultural communication (Ali, Liu, & Humedian, 2004; Carrillo & Lopez, 2001; LaRoche & Martin, 2005; Weisman, 2005). Some U.S. states now require psychologists to complete courses on the role of cultural factors in therapy before being licensed. This cultural sensitivity training helps clinicians appreciate, for example, that it is considered impolite in some cultures to make eye contact with a stranger. Armed with this information, a therapist is more likely to realize that clients from those cultures are not necessarily depressed, lacking in self-esteem, or overly submissive just because they look at the floor during an interview. More and more graduate students in clinical and counseling psychology are receiving this training, too (Kersting, 2004; Smith et al. 2006).

There is no guarantee that ethnic matching or cultural sensitivity training for therapists will improve treatment results (McCabe, 2002; Pope-Davis et al., 1995; Quintana & Bernal, 1995; Ramirez et al., 1996; Shin et al., 2005), but there is some evidence that sensitivity training can help (e.g., Constantine, 2002; Razali, Aminah, & Umeed, 2002). And although it is unrealistic to expect all therapists to be equally effective with clients of all sociocultural backgrounds, cultural sensitivity training offers a way to improve their *cultural competence,* an extension of Carl Rogers's concept of "empathy." When therapists appreciate the client's view of the world, it is easier for them to set goals that are in harmony with that view (Dyche & Zayas, 2001; Pedersen & Draguns, 2002; Stuart, 2004; Ulrich, Richards, & Bergin, 2000). Minimizing misunderstanding and miscommunication is one of the many ethical obligations that therapists assume when working with clients (Tomes, 1999). Let's consider some others.

Rules and Rights in the Therapeutic Relationship

Treatment can be an intensely emotional experience, and the relationship established with a therapist can profoundly affect a client's life. Professional ethics and common sense require the therapist to ensure that this relationship does not harm the client. For example, the American Psychological Association's *Ethical Principles of Psychologists and Code of Conduct* forbids a sexual relationship between therapist and client—during treatment and for at least two years afterward—because of the severe harm it can cause the client (American Psychological Association, 2002b; Behnke, 2004).

These ethical standards also require therapists, with a few exceptions, to keep strictly confidential everything a client says in therapy. Confidentiality is one of the most important features of a successful therapeutic relationship. It allows the client to reveal unpleasant or embarrassing impulses, behaviors, or events without fear that this information will be repeated to anyone else. Professionals do sometimes consult with one another about a client, but each is required not to reveal information to outsiders (including members of the client's family) without the client's consent. The APA's code of ethics even includes standards for protecting confidentiality for the growing number of clients who seek psychological services via *telehealth* or *e-health* channels, which include telephone, video conferencing, e-mail, or other Internet links (APA, 2002b; Barnett & Scheetz, 2003; Christensen, Griffiths, & Jorm, 2004; Fisher & Fried, 2003; Mohr et al., 2005; Ruskin et al., 2004). One of these standards requires therapists to inform clients that others might be able to gain access to their e-mail messages and that no formal client-therapist relationship exists in e-mail exchanges.

Professional standards about confidentiality are backed up in most U.S. states and in federal courts by laws recognizing that information revealed in therapy (like information given to a priest, a lawyer, or a physician) is privileged communication. This means that a therapist can refuse, even in court, to answer questions about a client or to provide personal notes or recordings from therapy sessions. Only under special circumstances can therapists be legally required to violate confidentiality. These circumstances include those in which (1) a client is so severely disturbed or suicidal that hospitalization is needed, (2) a client uses his or her mental condition and history of therapy as part of his or her defense in a civil or criminal trial, (3) the therapist must defend against a client's charge of malpractice, (4) a client reveals information about sexual or physical abuse of a child, and (5) the therapist believes a client may commit a violent act against a specific person.

Source: The Museum of the History of Medicine of the University of Zurich, accessed on-line at http://www.nobel.se/medicine/articles/moniz/.

HOSPITAL RESTRAINTS Here are examples of the chains, straitjackets, belts, and covered bathtubs that were used to restrain disruptive patients in North American and European mental hospitals in the 1800s and well into the 1900s. These devices were gentle compared with some of the methods endorsed in the late 1700s by Benjamin Rush. Known as the "father of American psychiatry," Rush advocated curing patients by frightening or disorienting them—for example, by placing them in a coffin-like box that was then briefly immersed in water.

Biological Treatments

▶ **Is electric shock still used to treat disorders?**

So far, we have described psychological approaches to the treatment of mental disorders. But biological treatments are also available—primarily through psychiatrists and other medical doctors, who often work in cooperation with psychologists. Today, biological treatments for psychological problems mainly involve the prescribing of psychoactive drugs. In the mid-1900s, however, the most common biological treatment for severe psychological problems was to create seizures using electric shock.

Electroconvulsive Therapy

In the 1930s, a Hungarian physician named Ladislaus Von Meduna used a drug to induce convulsions in people with schizophrenia. He believed—incorrectly—that

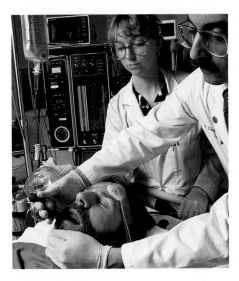

ELECTROCONVULSIVE THERAPY
Estimates of the number of people receiving ECT each year in the United States range from 30,000 to over 100,000 (Hermann et al., 1995; Mathew, Amiel, & Sackeim, 2005). A survey in the United Kingdom suggests that about 12,000 patients a year are receiving ECT (U.K. Statistical Bulletin, 1999). Because of its dramatic and potentially dangerous nature, the use of ECT remains controversial (Breggin, 1997). Critics want it outlawed, but proponents say the benefits of ECT for certain patients outweigh its potential costs.

Online Study Center

Improve Your Grade
Tutorial: Different Drug Effects.

---

electroconvulsive therapy (ECT) A brief electric shock administered to the brain, usually to reduce severe depression that does not respond to drug treatments.

neuroleptics Drugs that relieve the symptoms of schizophrenia or other severe forms of psychological disorder. Also called antipsychotics.

---

because schizophrenia and epilepsy rarely occur in the same person, epileptic-like seizures might combat schizophrenia. In 1938, Italian physicians Ugo Cerletti and Lucio Bini created seizures by passing an electric current through the brains of people with schizophrenia. During the next twenty years or so, this procedure, called **electroconvulsive therapy (ECT),** became a routine treatment for schizophrenia, depression, and sometimes mania. Although many patients improved, they often relapsed. The benefits of ECT also had to be weighed against side effects such as memory loss, confusion, speech disorders, and, in some cases, death due to cardiac arrest (Lickey & Gordon, 1991; Shiwach, Reid, & Carmody, 2001).

To make ECT safer, patients are now given an anesthetic so that they are unconscious before the shock is delivered, along with a muscle relaxant to prevent bone fractures during convulsions. Also, the shock now lasts only about half a second and is usually delivered to only one side of the brain (Sackeim et al., 2000). Finally, in contrast to the dozens of treatments administered decades ago, patients now receive only about six to twelve shocks, one approximately every two days (Fink, 1999).

Although we still don't know for sure how and why ECT works (Greenberg & Kellner, 2005; Rudorfer, Henry, & Sackheim, 1997; Sackeim, 1994), it is being performed more frequently in the United States than coronary bypass operations, appendectomies, and tonsillectomies (Mathew, Amiel, & Sackeim, 2005). It is administered mainly to patients suffering severe depression (and occasionally to manic patients) who do not respond to less drastic treatments (Daly et al., 2001; de Macedo-Soares et al., 2005; Rasmussen, 2003). ECT can be effective in such cases—especially when followed up with medication—and it does not appear to cause brain damage, even when administered repeatedly (e.g., Anghelescu et al., 2001; Dwork et al., 2004; Kellner et al., 2005; Sackeim et al., 2001). Nevertheless, researchers are looking for even safer methods of inducing seizures. Among the techniques being investigated are *magnetic seizure therapy (MST),* which creates seizures with timed pulses of magnetic energy (Lisanby, 2004), and a related but less intense procedure called *repetitive transcranial magnetic stimulation (rTMS*; Avery et al., 2006; Couturier, 2005; Schutter, 2005).

Psychoactive Drugs

The use of ECT declined after the 1950s, in part because psychoactive drugs had begun to emerge as more convenient and effective treatment alternatives. In the chapters on biology and behavior and on consciousness, we discuss the effects of psychoactive drugs on neurotransmitter systems, autonomic activity, emotions, thinking, and behavior. Here, we describe their role in combating schizophrenia, depression, mania, and anxiety.

Neuroleptics One group of drugs, called **neuroleptics** or *antipsychotics,* dramatically reduces the intensity of psychotic symptoms such as hallucinations, delusions, paranoid suspiciousness, disordered thinking, and confused speech in many mental patients, especially those with schizophrenia. The most widely used antipsychotic drugs are the *phenothiazines* (pronounced "fee-noh-THIGH-uh-zeens"), of which the first, chlorpromazine (marketed as Thorazine in the United States and as Largactil in Canada and the United Kingdom), has been especially popular. Another neuroleptic, haloperidol (Haldol), is about as effective as the phenothiazines, but it creates less sedation (Julien, 2005). Patients who do not respond to one type of neuroleptic may respond to the other (Davis, Chen, & Glick, 2003). Between 60 and 70 percent of patients receiving these drugs show improvement, though fewer than 30 percent respond well enough to live successfully on their own.

Neuroleptics have side effects ranging from dry mouth and dizziness to symptoms similar to those of Parkinson's disease, including muscle rigidity, restlessness, tremors, and slowed movement. Some of these side effects can be treated with medication, but at least 25 percent of patients who take chlorpromazine or haloperidol for several years develop an irreversible movement disorder. This disorder, called *tardive dyskinesia (TD),* causes uncontrollable, repetitive actions, often including twitching of the face, flailing of the arms and legs, and thrusting of the tongue.

A NATURAL CURE?   An herbal remedy from a plant called *Saint John's wort* has become a popular nonprescription treatment for depression. One of its active ingredients, *hypericin*, is thought to affect neurotransmitters in the brain much as Prozac does. Double-blind, placebo-controlled studies have shown Saint John's wort to be as effective as Prozac for depression (e.g., Hammerness, Basch, & Ulbricht, 2003; Hypericum Depression Trial Study Group, 2002; Szegedi et al., 2005). The design of some of these studies has been questioned, however (e.g., Spira, 2001), so final conclusions about the safety and effectiveness of Saint John's wort must await the results of further research.

Among a newer generation of antipsychotic drugs (also called *atypical neuroleptics*) is clozapine (Clozaril), which has effects like those of the phenothiazines but is less likely to cause movement disorders except at high doses (Louzá & Bassitt, 2005; Rochon et al., 2005). Although no more effective overall than the phenothiazines, clozapine has helped many patients who did not respond to the phenothiazines or haloperidol (Green & Patel, 1996; Rabinowitz et al., 2001). Unfortunately, taking clozapine carries a slight risk of developing a fatal blood disease called *agranulocytosis* (Alvir et al., 1993). Weekly blood tests to detect early signs of this disease greatly increase the cost of using this drug (Meltzer, 1997).

Several other atypical neuroleptics have been introduced recently, including risperidone (Risperdal), olanzapine (Zyprexa), quetiapine (Seroquel), ziprasidone (Geodon), and, most recently, aripiprazole (Abilify). These medications are expensive, but they have fewer side effects than clozapine, and they do not cause agranulocytosis (Correll, Leucht, & Kane, 2004). Like clozapine, they also appear to reduce the "negative" symptoms of schizophrenia, such as lack of emotion, social withdrawal, and reduced speech (e.g., Kane et al., 2003; Kapur, Sridhar & Remington, 2004; Lieberman et al., 2003; Potkin et al., 2003). There is some doubt, though, whether these newest atypical neuroleptics are significantly more effective than older drugs, partly because 60 to 80 percent of patients may stop taking them because of weight gain, nervous tics, and other bothersome side effects (Lieberman et al., 2005; Miyamoto et al., 2005).

Antidepressants   Soon after antipsychotic drugs appeared, they were joined by **antidepressants,** a class of drugs that is now widely prescribed for relieving the symptoms of depression (National Institute for Clinical Excellence, 2004; Olfson et al., 2002). There are several classes of antidepressant drugs. The *monoamine oxidase inhibitors (MAOIs)* are used to treat many cases of depression, especially with clients who also experience anxiety and panic (Julien, 2005). The *tricyclic antidepressants (TCAs)* are another popular class of antidepressants. The TCAs have been prescribed more frequently than MAOI drugs because they seem to work somewhat better and have fewer side effects. However, overdoses of TCAs can be fatal, as can taking TCAs and drinking alcohol at the same time (Nutt, 2005a).

The most prominent of several newer antidepressants is fluoxetine (Prozac). Introduced in 1986, fluoxetine quickly became the most widely used antidepressant in North America. Its popularity is due to the fact that it is about as effective as older drugs and, in most cases, has fewer and milder side effects—mainly weight gain, sexual dysfunction, and gastrointestinal problems (Cookson & Duffett, 1998; Nutt, 2005a; Patten et al., 2005). An improved version of Prozac, *R-fluoxetine,* is currently being developed, and other, even newer antidepressants also show promise. These include bupropion (Wellbutrin), venlafaxine (Effexor), nefazodone (Serzone), escitalopram (Lexapro), and duloxetine (Cymbalta; Appleton, 2000; Brambilla et al., 2005; Hirschfeld & Vornik, 2004, Zimmerman et al., 2005).

About 50 to 60 percent of patients who take antidepressant drugs show improved mood, greater physical activity, increased appetite, and better sleep (Hollon, Thase, & Markowitz, 2002). However, only about 10 to 20 percent of people suffering the most severe psychotic depression show this same amount of improvement (U.S. Surgeon General, 1999). It has long been assumed that the effects of antidepressant drugs were due to the chemical action of their active ingredients, but there is some doubt about this assumption. An analysis of clinical trial data submitted to the U.S. Food and Drug Administration by the makers of six widely prescribed antidepressant drugs showed that in 57 percent of the trials, antidepressant drugs did only a little better than placebo medications ("sugar pills") at relieving depression (Kirsch et al., 2002; Kirsch, Scoboria, & Moore, 2002). Defenders of antidepressant medications argue that even relatively small effects are better than none (e.g., Thase, 2002), whereas critics contend that those effects are too small to matter (Moncrieff & Kirsch, 2005).

Lithium and Anticonvulsants   The mineral salt lithium carbonate, when taken regularly, prevents both the depression and the mania associated with bipolar disorder

antidepressants   Drugs that reduce depression.

in some patients (Baldessarini & Tondo, 2000; Geddes et al., 2004). Without lithium, the typical patient with bipolar disorder has a manic episode about every fourteen months and a depressive episode about every seventeen months; with lithium, attacks of mania occur as rarely as every nine years (Geddes et al., 2004). The lithium dosage must be exact and carefully controlled, however, because taking too much can cause vomiting, nausea, tremor, fatigue, slurred speech, and, with severe overdoses, coma or death. Combining lithium with other mood stabilizing drugs, such as carbamazepine, has shown enhanced benefits but also more adverse side effects (Baethge et al., 2005).

In recent years, anticonvulsant drugs such as divalproex and lamotrigine (Epival/Depakote; Lamictal) have been used as an alternative to lithium in treating mania (e.g., Goodwin, Bowden, & Calabrese, 2004; McElroy, Zarate, & Cookson, 2004). Compared with lithium, these drugs cause fewer side effects, are less dangerous at higher doses, and are easier to regulate (Bowden et al., 2000; Bowden et al., 2003; Hirschfeld et al., 1999). However, their long-term benefits in reducing mania and the risk of suicide are not as well established, so lithium is still considered the treatment of choice against which others are measured (Baldessarini et al., 2002; Carney & Goodwin, 2005).

Anxiolytics During the 1950s, a new class of drugs called *tranquilizers* was shown to reduce mental and physical tension and the symptoms of anxiety. The first of these drugs, meprobamate (Miltown or Equanil), acts somewhat like barbiturate sleeping pills, meaning that overdoses can cause sleep and even death. Because they do not pose this danger, the *benzodiazepines*—particularly chlordiazepoxide (Librium) and diazepam (Valium)—became the worldwide drug treatment of choice for anxiety (Blackwell, 1973). Today, these and other anti-anxiety drugs, now called **anxiolytics** (pronounced "ang-zee-oh-LIT-ix"), continue to be the most widely prescribed and used of all legal drugs (Stevens & Pollack, 2005). Anxiolytics have an immediate calming effect and are quite useful in treating the symptoms of generalized anxiety and posttraumatic stress disorder.

One of the benzodiazepines, alprazolam (Xanax), has become especially popular for the treatment of panic disorder and agoraphobia (Verster & Volkerts, 2004). But benzodiazepines can have bothersome side effects, such as sleepiness, lightheadedness, and impaired memory and thinking. Combining these drugs with alcohol can be fatal, and continued use can lead to tolerance and physical dependence (Chouinard, 2004). Further, suddenly discontinuing benzodiazepines after heavy or long-term use can cause severe withdrawal symptoms, including seizures and anxiety attacks (Rickels et al., 1993).

The anxiolytic called *buspirone (BuSpar)* provides an alternative anxiety treatment that eliminates some of these problems (Lickey & Gordon, 1991; Stahl, 2002; Wagner et al., 2003). Its effects do not occur for days or weeks after treatment begins, but buspirone can ultimately equal diazepam in reducing generalized anxiety (Gorman, 2003; Rickels & Rynn, 2002; U.S. Surgeon General, 1999). Further, it does not seem to promote dependence, it causes less interference with thinking, and it does not interact dangerously with alcohol.

Because depression often accompanies anxiety, antidepressant drugs such as fluoxetine (Prozac), paroxetine (Paxil), clomipramine (Anafranil), fluvoxamine (Luvox), and sertraline (Zoloft) are also used in treating anxiety-related problems such as panic disorder, social phobia, obsessive-compulsive disorder, and posttraumatic stress disorder (e.g., Gorman, 2003; Julien, 2005; Nutt, 2005b; Rickels et al., 2003). Table 13.5 lists the effects and side effects of some of the psychoactive drugs we have described.

Human Diversity and Drug Treatment

Drug treatments are designed to benefit everyone in the same way, but it turns out that the same psychoactive drug dose can have significantly different effects in each sex, and in people from various ethnic groups (e.g., Esel et al., 2005; Seeman, 2004). For example, compared with Asians, Caucasians must take significantly higher doses of the

anxiolytics Drugs that reduce tension and symptoms of anxiety.

TABLE **13.5** **A Sampling of Psychoactive Drugs Used for Treating Psychological Disorders**

Psychoactive drugs have been successful in dramatically reducing the symptoms of many psychological disorders. Critics point out that drugs can have troublesome side effects, however, and they may create dependence, especially after years of use (e.g., Breggin, 1997). They note, too, that drugs do not "cure" mental disorders (National Institute of Mental Health, 1995), that their effects are not always strong (Kirsch et al., 2002), and that temporary symptom relief may make some patients less likely to seek a permanent solution to their psychological problems.

For Schizophrenia: Neuroleptics (Antipsychotics)

Chemical Name	Trade Name	Effects and Side Effects
Chlorpromazine	Thorazine	Reduce hallucinations, delusions, incoherence, jumbled thought processes;
Haloperidol	Haldol	cause movement-disorder side effects, including tardive dyskinesia
Clozapine	Clozaril	Reduces psychotic symptoms; causes no movement disorders, but raises risk of serious blood disease
Risperidone	Risperdal	Reduces positive and negative psychotic symptoms without risk of blood disease
Ziprasidone	Geodon	Reduces positive and negative psychotic symptoms without causing weight gain
Aripiprazole	Abilify	Reduces positive and negative psychotic symptoms without weight gain and with few side effects

For Mood Disorders: Antidepressants and Mood Elevators

Tricyclics

Imipramine	Tofranil	Act as antidepressants, but also have antipanic action; cause sleepiness and other moderate side effects; potentially dangerous if taken with alcohol
Amitriptyline	Elavil, Amitid	

Other Antidepressants

Fluoxetine	Prozac	Have antidepressant, antipanic, and anti-obsessive action
Clomipramine	Anafranil	
Fluvoxamine	Luvox	
Sertraline	Zoloft	
Escitalopram	Lexapro	

Other Drugs

Lithium carbonate	Carbolith, Lithizine	Calms mania; reduces mood swings of bipolar disorder; overdose harmful, potentially deadly
Divalproex	Depakote	Is effective against mania, with fewer side effects
Lamotrigine	Lamictal	Is effective in delaying relapse in bipolar disorder; most benefits associated with depression

For Anxiety Disorders: Anxiolytics

Benzodiazepines

Chlordiazepoxide	Librium	Act as potent anxiolytics for generalized anxiety, panic, stress; extended use may
Diazepam	Valium	cause physical dependence and withdrawal syndrome if abruptly discontinued
Alprazolam	Xanax	Also has antidepressant effects; often used in agoraphobia (has high dependence potential)
Clonazepam	Klonopin	Often used in combination with other anxiolytics for panic disorder

Other Anti-anxiety Agents

Buspirone	BuSpar	Has slow-acting anti-anxiety action; no known dependence problems

There is widespread concern that psychiatrists, and especially general practitioners, rely too heavily on drugs to deal with psychological problems, partly because of drug ads that fuel consumer demand (Kravitz et al., 2005; Zuvekas, 2005). In one case, dramatically increased medication failed to stop a patient with paranoid schizophrenia from repeatedly running away from a mental hospital. But allowing him to use a telephone at a nearby shopping mall eliminated the problem. A psychologist discovered that the man had been afraid to use "bugged" hospital phones and kept escaping to call his mother (Rabasca, 1999).

"I medicate first and ask questions later."

benzodiazepines, haloperidol, clozapine, lithium, and possibly the tricyclic antidepressants in order to obtain equally beneficial effects (Lin & Poland, 1995; Matsuda et al., 1996). In addition, African Americans may show a faster response to tricyclic antidepressants than European Americans and may respond to lower doses of lithium (Strickland et al., 1991). There is also some evidence that, compared with European Americans or African Americans, Hispanic Americans require lower doses of antipsychotic drugs to get the same benefits (Ruiz et al., 1999). Some of these ethnic differences are thought to be related to genetically regulated differences in drug metabolism, whereas others may be due to dietary practices.

Males and females may respond in about the same way to tricyclic antidepressants (Wohlfarth et al., 2004), but women may maintain higher blood levels of these and other therapeutic psychoactive drugs and may show better response to neuroleptics (Hildebrandt et al., 2003; Salokangas, 2004). They also may be more vulnerable to adverse effects such as tardive dyskinesia (Yonkers et al., 1992). These gender differences in drug response appear less related to estrogen than to other hormonal or body-composition differences between men and women, such as the ratio of body fat to muscle (Dawkins & Potter, 1991; Salokangas, 2004). Continued research on these and other dimensions of human diversity will undoubtedly lead to more effective and safer drug treatments for all clients (Thompson & Pollack, 2001).

Drugs and Psychotherapy

Despite their widespread success in the treatment of psychological disorders, psychoactive drugs do have some drawbacks. As we have seen, some of them can result in physical or psychological dependence, and their side effects can range from minor problems, such as the thirst and dry mouth caused by some antidepressants, to movement disorders such as tardive dyskinesia caused by some neuroleptics. Although the most serious of these side effects are relatively rare, some are irreversible, and it is impossible to predict in advance who will develop them. For example, although a clear causal link has not yet been confirmed (Gibbons et al., 2005), the U.S. National Institute of Mental Health (NIMH) and regulatory agencies in Canada and Britain have recently issued warnings about the danger of suicidal behavior in children and adolescents who are given Prozac and similar antidepressant drugs (Breggin, 2005; Hammad, Laughren, &

Racoosin, 2006; Martinez et al., 2005; NIMH, 2004; Jureidini et al., 2004; Vitiello & Swedo, 2004; Whittington, Kendall, & Pilling, 2005). There is concern, too, about whether psychoactive drugs are as effective as they appear to be, especially in research sponsored by the drug companies that make them (Chan et al, 2004; Heres et al., 2006; Melander et al, 2003; Moncrieff & Kirsch, 2005).

With these issues in mind, many clinicians and clients wonder which is better: drugs or psychotherapy. Can they be effectively combined? A considerable amount of research is being conducted to address these questions.

Although occasionally a study shows that one form of treatment or the other is more effective, neither drugs nor psychotherapy has been shown to be clearly superior overall for treating problems such as anxiety disorders and major depressive disorder (Antonuccio, Danton, & DeNelsky, 1995; DeJonghe et al., 2004). For example, several studies of treatment for severe depression have found that behavior therapy, cognitive-behavior therapy, and interpersonal psychotherapy can be as effective as an antidepressant drug (DeRubeis et al., 2005; Dimidjian et al., 2006; Hollon et al., 2002; March et al., 2004; Spanier et al., 1996). Cognitive-behavior therapy has also equaled drug effects in the treatment of phobias (Clark et al., 2003; Davidson et al., 2004; Otto et al., 2000; Thom, Sartory, & Jöhren, 2000), panic disorder (Klosko et al., 1990), generalized anxiety disorder (Gould et al., 1997), and obsessive-compulsive disorder (Abramowitz, 1997; Kozak, Liebowitz, & Foa, 2000). Further, the dropout rate from psychotherapy may be lower than from drug therapies, and the benefits of many kinds of psychotherapy may last longer than those of drug therapies (e.g., Casacalenda, Perry, & Looper, 2002; Hollon, Stewart, & Strunk, 2006; Segal, Gemar, & Williams, 2000; Thom et al., 2000).

What about combining drugs and psychotherapy? Recent research suggests that doing so can sometimes be helpful (Hofmann et al., 2006; Winston, Been, & Serby, 2005). Combined treatment is recommended in cases of bipolar disorder (Otto, Bruce, & Deckersbach, 2005) and produces slightly better results than either psychotherapy or drugs alone in people suffering from severe, long-term depression (Hegerl, Plattner, & Moller, 2004). The combination of drugs and psychotherapy has been also shown to be more effective than either method alone in treating attention deficit hyperactivity disorder, obsessive-compulsive disorder, alcoholism, stammering, compulsive sexual behavior, and panic disorder (Barlow et al., 2000; deBeurs et al., 1995; Engeland, 1993; Keller et al., 2000; March et al., 2004; Roy-Byrne et al., 2005). The combined approach may be especially useful for clients who are initially too distressed to cooperate in psychotherapy. A related approach, already shown successful with clients who had been taking drugs for panic disorder and depression, is to use psychotherapy to prevent relapse and to make further progress as drug treatment is discontinued (e.g., Bruce, Spiegel, & Hegel, 1999; Klein et al., 2004; Lam et al., 2003). Preliminary evidence also suggests that a drug called D-cycloserine might be helpful in preventing the reappearance of fears being extinguished through exposure techniques or other forms of behavior therapy (Davis et al., 2005; Hofmann et al., 2006; Ressler et al., 2004).

However, many studies have found little advantage in combining drugs and psychotherapy (e.g., Davidson et al., 2004; Elkin, 1994; Nemeroff et al., 2003; Spiegel & Bruce, 1997). One research team compared the effects of a form of *in vivo* desensitization called *gradual exposure* and an anti-anxiety drug (Xanax) in the treatment of agoraphobia. Clients receiving gradual exposure alone showed better short- and long-term benefits than those getting either the drug alone or a combination of the drug and gradual exposure (Echeburua et al., 1993). Other studies, too, have found that combining drugs and psychotherapy may produce surprisingly little added benefit (e.g., Elkin, 1994; Spiegel & Bruce, 1997).

Perhaps the most conservative strategy for treating most cases of anxiety and depression is to begin with cognitive or interpersonal psychotherapy (which have no major negative side effects) and then to add or switch to drug treatment if psychotherapy alone is ineffective (Jacobs et al., 2004; Schatzberg et al., 2005). Someday, research may offer better guidelines as to which clients should be treated with psychotherapy alone, medication alone, or a combination of the two (Hollon et al., 2005).

LINKAGES
How do psychoactive drugs work? (a link to Biology and Behavior)

As described in the chapter on biology and behavior, human feelings, thoughts, and actions—whether normal or abnormal—are ultimately the result of biological processes, especially those involving neurotransmitters and their receptors in the brain. Because different neurotransmitters are especially prominent in particular brain regions or circuits, altering the functioning of particular neurotransmitter systems will have relatively specific psychological and behavioral effects.

LINKAGES

Biology, Behavior, and the Treatment of Psychological Disorders

Let's consider some of the ways in which therapeutic psychoactive drugs affect neurotransmitters and their receptors. Some therapeutic drugs cause neurons to fire, whereas others reduce, or inhibit, firing. For example, benzodiazepines (e.g., Valium and Xanax) exert their anti-anxiety effects by helping the inhibitory neurotransmitter GABA bind to receptors and thus suppress neuron firing. This increased inhibitory effect acts as a sort of braking system that slows the activity of GABA-sensitive neurons involved in the experience of anxiety. However, benzodiazepines also slow the action of all neural systems that use GABA, including those associated with motor activity and mental processing, which are spread throughout the brain. The result is the decreased motor coordination and clouded thinking that appear as benzodiazepines' side effects. Research suggests that it might soon be possible to develop drugs that will bind only to certain kinds of GABA receptors and thus greatly reduce these side effects (Gorman, 2005; Löw et al., 2000; Stahl, 2002).

Other therapeutic drugs are receptor antagonists (see Figure 4.8 in the consciousness chapter), acting to block the receptor site normally used by a particular neurotransmitter. The phenothiazines and haloperidol, for example, exert their antipsychotic effects by blocking receptors for dopamine, a neurotransmitter that is important for movement, as described in the chapter on biology and behavior. Blocking dopamine seems to normalize the jumbled thinking of many schizophrenia patients, but it can create severe disorders—including tardive dyskinesia—in the movement systems that are also controlled by dopamine.

LINKAGES
How do drugs help people who suffer from schizophrenia? (a link to Biology and Behavior)

Some psychoactive drugs exert their therapeutic influence by increasing the amount of a neurotransmitter available to act on receptors. This effect usually occurs because the drug slows a process called *reuptake,* by which the neurotransmitter would normally return to the brain cell from which it was released. The tricyclic antidepressants, for example, operate by slowing the reuptake of norepinephrine. Prozac, Anafranil, and some other antidepressants are called *selective serotonin reuptake inhibitors (SSRIs)* because they slow the reuptake of serotonin. Others, such as Effexor, slow the reuptake of both serotonin and norepinephrine.

Community Psychology

▶ **How can we prevent psychological disorders?**

It has long been argued that even if psychologists and psychiatrists knew exactly how to treat every psychological problem, there would never be enough mental health professionals to help everyone who needs it (Albee, 1968). This view helped fuel the rise of **community psychology,** an approach whose goals are to treat people in their local communities and to work for social changes that can prevent psychological disorders.

community psychology A mental health approach whose goal is to minimize or prevent psychological disorders by promoting social change and making treatment methods more accessible to those who normally have little or no access to psychological services.

One aspect of community psychology, the *community mental health movement,* appeared during the 1960s as an attempt to make treatment available to people in their own communities. As antipsychotic drugs became available, and as concern grew that patients were not improving—and might be getting worse—after years of confinement in mental hospitals, thousands of these patients were released. The plan was for them

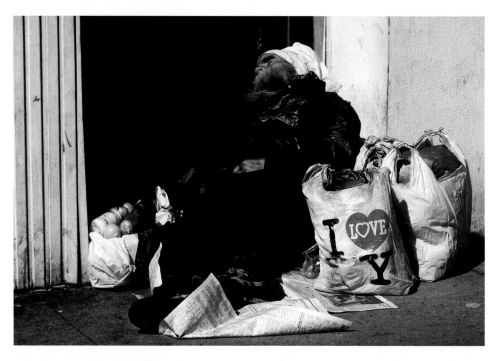

COMMUNITY MENTAL HEALTH EFFORTS Professional and nonprofessional staff members at community mental health centers provide traditional therapy and mental health education, as well as walk-in facilities and hotlines for people who are suicidal or in crisis because of rape or domestic violence. They also offer day treatment to former mental patients, many of whom are homeless.

to receive drugs and other mental health services in newly funded community mental health centers. This *deinstitutionalization* process spared patients the boredom and isolation of the hospital environment, but the mental health services available in the community never matched the need for them. Some former hospital patients and many people whose disorders might once have sent them to mental hospitals are now living in halfway houses and other community-based facilities where they receive *psychosocial rehabilitation.* These community support services are not designed to "cure" them but to help them cope with their problems and develop the social and occupational skills necessary for semi-independent living (Cook et al., 2005; Liberman et al., 1998; Talbott, 2004). All too many others with severe psychological disorders did not receive or respond to rehabilitation and are to be found enduring the dangers of homelessness on city streets or of confinement in jails and prisons (Teplin et al., 2005; U.S. Department of Health and Human Services, 2001b).

Community psychology also attempts to prevent psychopathology by addressing unemployment, poverty, overcrowded substandard housing, and other stressful social situations that may put vulnerable people at greater risk for some disorders (Albee, 1985; Tucker & Herman, 2002; Weissberg, Kumpfer, & Seligman, 2003; Xue et al., 2005). Less ambitious but perhaps even more significant are efforts to detect psychological problems in their earliest stages and keep them from becoming worse (e.g., Bond & Hauf, 2004; President's New Freedom Commission on Mental Health, 2003; Sanders et al., 2000). Some examples include prevention of depression and suicide (Beardslee et al., 2003; Freres et al., 2002; Horowitz & Garber, 2006; Oyama et al., 2004; Spence, Sheffield, & Donovan, 2005); programs, including Project Head Start, that help preschoolers whose backgrounds hurt their chances of doing well in school and put them at risk for delinquency (Shaw et al., 2006; Tremblay et al., 1995); and identification of children who are at risk for disorder because of parental divorce or being rejected or victimized at school (e.g., Frey et al., 2005; Greenberg et al., 1999; Martinez & Forgatch, 2001). There are also interventions designed to head off anxiety disorders or schizophrenia in children and adults (Dadds et al., 1999; McGorry et al., 2002; Rapee et al., 2005); to prevent domestic violence and child abuse (Duggan et al., 2004; Whitaker et al., 2006), and to promote health consciousness in ethnic minority communities (Borg, 2002).

Further, community psychology supports the notion that nonprofessionals—including the relatives and friends of troubled clients—can be enlisted in efforts to combat psychological disorders (e.g., Bright, Baker, & Neimeyer, 1999). This idea is compatible with and has encouraged the development of *self-help* or *mutual-help* organizations. Self-help groups, such as Alcoholics Anonymous (AA), are made up of people who share some problematic experience and want to help one another. Millions of people in the United States and Canada take part each year in face-to-face or Internet-based self-help groups for alcohol and drug addiction, childhood sexual abuse, pain, depression, anxiety, cancer, HIV/AIDS, overeating, overspending, bereavement, compulsive gambling, schizophrenia, and many other problems (Barlow et al., 2000; Dittman, 2004; Norcross et al., 2000; Swindle et al., 2000; Zuckerman, 2003).

Lack of reliable data makes it difficult to assess the value of many self-help programs, but available information suggests that active members may obtain some moderate improvement in their lives (Kelly, 2003; Mains & Scogin, 2003; Moos et al., 2001). Some professional therapists view these groups with suspicion; others encourage clients to participate in them as part of their treatment or as a first step toward more formal treatment (Haaga, 2000; Salzer, Rappaport, & Segre, 1999). This recommendation is especially likely for clients with problems such as eating disorders, alcoholism, and other substance-related disorders (Dunne & Fitzpatrick, 1999; Guimon, 2004; Scheidinger, 2004).

ACTIVE REVIEW | Treatment of Psychological Disorders

Linkages

As noted in the introductory chapter, all of psychology's subfields are related to one another. Our discussion of the psychopharmacology of drug treatment illustrates just one way in which the topic of this chapter, treatment of psychological disorders, is linked to the subfield of biological psychology, which is described in the chapter on biology and behavior. The Linkages diagram shows ties to two other subfields, and there are many more ties throughout the book. Looking for linkages among subfields will help you see how they all fit together and help you better appreciate the big picture that is psychology.

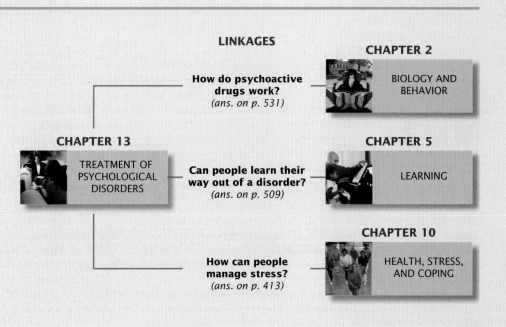

Summary

BASIC FEATURES OF TREATMENT

▶ **What features do all treatment techniques have in common?**

Psychotherapy for psychological disorders is usually based on psychodynamic, humanistic, or behavioral theories of personality and behavior disorder. Many therapists employ elements of more than one approach. The biological approach is reflected in the use of drugs and other physical treatment methods.

All forms of treatment include a client, a therapist, a theory of behavior disorder, a set of treatment procedures suggested by the theory, and a special relationship between the client and therapist.

Therapy may be offered to inpatients and outpatients in many different settings by *psychologists, psychiatrists,* and other helpers. The goal of treatment is to help people change their thinking, feelings, and behavior so that they will be happier and function better.

PSYCHODYNAMIC PSYCHOTHERAPY

▶ **How did Freud get started as a therapist?**

Psychodynamic psychotherapy began with Freud's *psychoanalysis,* which seeks to help clients gain insight into unconscious conflicts and impulses and then to explore how those factors have created disorders. Exploration of the unconscious is aided by the use of free association, dream interpretation, and related methods. Some variations on psychoanalysis retain most of Freud's principles but are typically shorter in duration and tend to stress social and interpersonal factors, such as early relationships with caregivers.

HUMANISTIC PSYCHOTHERAPY

▶ **Why won't some therapists give advice?**

Humanistic psychotherapy helps clients to become more aware of discrepancies between their feelings and their behavior. According to the humanistic approach, these discrepancies are at the root of behavior disorders and can be resolved by the client once they are brought to light in the context of a genuine, trusting relationship with the therapist.

Therapists using Rogers's *client-centered therapy,* also known as *person-centered therapy,* help mainly by adopting attitudes toward the client that express *unconditional positive regard, empathy,* and *congruence.* These attitudes create a nonjudgmental atmosphere that makes it easier for clients to be open and honest with the therapist, with themselves, and with others. One way of creating this atmosphere is through *reflection.* Therapists employing the *Gestalt therapy* of Fritz and Laura Perls use more active techniques than Rogerian therapists, often pointing out inconsistencies between what clients say and how they behave.

BEHAVIOR THERAPY

▶ **Can we learn to conquer fears?**

Behavior therapy and *behavior modification* apply learning principles to eliminate undesirable behavior patterns and to strengthen more desirable alternatives. The methods they employ include *systematic desensitization, modeling, assertiveness training* and social skills training, *positive reinforcement* (sometimes within a *token economy*), *extinction* techniques (such as *flooding*), *aversion conditioning,* and *punishment.*

Many behavior therapists also employ *cognitive-behavior therapy* to help clients alter the way they think, as well as the way they behave. Among the specific cognitive-behavioral methods are *rational-emotive behavior therapy (REBT),* cognitive restructuring, stress inoculation training, and *cognitive therapy.*

GROUP, FAMILY, AND COUPLES THERAPY

▶ **How does group therapy differ from individual therapy?**

Therapists of all theoretical persuasions offer *group therapy, family therapy,* and *couples therapy.* These forms of treatment take advantage of relationships in the group, family, or couple to enhance the effects of treatment.

EVALUATING PSYCHOTHERAPY

▶ **How effective is psychotherapy?**

Research has found that clients who receive psychotherapy are better off than most clients who receive no treatment, but that no single approach is uniformly better than all others for all clients and problems. Still, some methods appear effective enough in the treatment of particular disorders to have been listed as *empirically supported therapies (ESTs).* The outcome of treatment is also affected by the characteristics of the client and the therapist and the relationship that develops between them. More research is needed to discover all the combinations of therapists, clients, and treatments ideally suited to treating particular psychological problems. Several factors, including personal preferences, must be considered when choosing a form of treatment and a therapist. The effects of cultural differences in the values and goals of therapist and client have also attracted increasing attention. In all forms of treatment, the client's rights include the right to confidentiality.

BIOLOGICAL TREATMENTS

▶ **Is electric shock still used to treat disorders?**

Biological treatment methods seek to relieve psychological disorders by physical, rather than psychological, means. *Electroconvulsive therapy (ECT)* involves passing an electric current through the patient's brain, usually in an effort to relieve severe depression. Today, the most prominent form of biological treatment involves psychoactive drugs, including those with antipsychotic (*neuroleptic*), *antidepressant,* or tranquilizing (*anxiolytic*) effects. Psychoactive drugs appear effective in many cases, but critics point out a number of undesirable side effects associated with these drugs. Drugs may be no more effective than some forms of psychotherapy for many people. Combining drugs and psychotherapy may help in some cases and in the treatment of certain disorders, but their joint effect may be no greater than the effect of either one alone.

COMMUNITY PSYCHOLOGY

▶ **How can we prevent psychological disorders?**

The realization that there will never be enough therapists to treat all who need help prompted the development of *community psychology.* Community mental health programs and efforts to prevent mental disorders are the two main elements of community psychology. The growth of self-help or mutual-help organizations is compatible with the goals of community psychology.

Learn by Doing

Put It in Writing

Imagine that you have decided to get help for depression, anxiety, or some other psychological problem. Using what you have learned in this chapter, write a page describing what approach to treatment you would prefer and why. Tell whether you would choose that approach for all kinds of problems or whether your choice would depend on the nature of the problem. Finally, list the characteristics of your ideal therapist, and say why you think those characteristics might lead to successful treatment.

Personal Learning Activity

To get a better idea of how practicing therapists choose their treatment methods, ask a local psychologist, psychiatrist, or coun-

selor (at the student counseling center on campus, perhaps) to meet with you for a short research interview. Ask this person what treatment approach and methods he or she prefers, how this preference developed, and what convinces him or her to continue using these methods. Write a summary of what you learned in this interview, and don't forget to include your impressions of whether this therapist's choice of treatment methods depends mainly on personal experience, empirical research evidence, or a combination of both. *For additional projects, see the Personal Learning Activities in the corresponding chapter of the study guide that accompanies this text.*

Step into Action

Courses

Clinical Psychology
Methods of Psychotherapy
Psychopharmacology
Behavior Modification
Community Psychology

Movies

Good Will Hunting; Analyze This; Analyze That; Vertigo. Hollywood portrayals of psychotherapy.

One Flew over the Cuckoo's Nest; Girl, Interrupted. Institutional treatment.

A Beautiful Mind. Biological treatment of schizophrenia.

I Never Promised You a Rose Garden. Psychodynamic treatment for schizophrenia.

Antwone Fisher. Psychotherapy.

Books

Peter Wyden, *Conquering Schizophrenia: A Father, His Son, and a Medical Breakthrough* (Knopf, 1998). A father searches for a cure for his son with schizophrenia.

Ken Kesey, *One Flew over the Cuckoo's Nest* (New American Library, 1989). The book from which the award-winning movie was adapted.

Michael Winerip, *9 Highland Road* (Vintage, 1995). The aftermath of deinstitutionalization.

Peter Kramer, *Listening to Prozac* (Penguin, 1997). Psychotropic antidepressant medications.

Susan Sheehan, *Is There No Place on Earth for Me?* (Vintage, 1983). Inadequate treatment for a woman with schizophrenia.

Raymond J. Corsini and Danny Wedding, *Current Psychotherapies* (6th ed.; Peacock, 2001) A

comparison of numerous approaches to psychotherapy.

Frank Dumont and Raymond J. Corsini (Eds.), *Six Therapists and One Client* (Springer, 2000). Therapists representing six different treatment methods describe how they would help the same client.

W. S. Appleton, *Prozac and the New Antidepressants: What You Need to Know About Prozac, Zoloft, Paxil, Luvox, Wellbutrin, Effexor, Serzone, Vestra, Celexa, St. John's Wort, and Others* (rev. ed.; Plume Books, 2000). A summary of modern drug treatment alternatives for depression.

T. M. Luhrmann, *Of Two Minds: The Growing Disorder in American Psychiatry* (Knopf, 2000). Summary of the conflict between biological and psychological approaches to treatment.

Christina Hoff Summers and Sally Satel, *One Nation Under Therapy: How the Helping Culture is Eroding Self-Reliance* (St. Martin's Press, 2005). Argues that people have become overly dependent on psychotherapy and drugs to solve their problems.

The Web

The World Wide Web is a good source of additional information about the science of psychology, provided you use it carefully and think critically about the information you find. The Online Study Center that accompanies this text offers many resources relevant to this chapter. These resources include interactive tutorials; Thinking Critically and Evaluating Research exercises; ACE chapter quizzes; recommended web links; and articles on current events, books, and movies. Please visit the Online Study Center at college.hmco.com/pic/bernsteinessentials4e.

Review of Key Terms

Can you define each of the key terms in the chapter? Check your definitions against those on the pages shown in parentheses in the following list or in the Glossary/Index at the end of the text.

antidepressants *(p. 526)*

anxiolytics *(p. 527)*

assertiveness training *(p. 510)*

aversion conditioning *(p. 512)*

behavior therapy *(p. 508)*

behavior modification *(p. 508)*

client-centered therapy (person-centered therapy) *(p. 506)*

cognitive therapy *(p. 513)*

cognitive-behavior therapy *(p. 508)*

community psychology *(p. 531)*

congruence *(p. 506)*

couples therapy *(p. 515)*

electroconvulsive therapy (ECT) *(p. 525)*

empathy *(p. 506)*

empirically supported therapies (ESTs) *(p. 520)*

extinction *(p. 511)*

family therapy *(p. 515)*

flooding *(p. 511)*

Gestalt therapy *(p. 507)*

group therapy *(p. 514)*

modeling *(p. 510)*

neuroleptics *(p. 525)*

positive reinforcement *(p. 510)*

psychiatrists *(p. 502)*

psychoanalysis *(p. 503)*

psychologists *(p. 502)*

psychotherapy *(p. 502)*

punishment *(p. 512)*

rational-emotive behavior therapy (REBT) *(p. 512)*

reflection *(p. 506)*

systematic desensitization *(p. 508)*

token economy *(p. 511)*

unconditional positive regard *(p. 506)*

Multiple-Choice Self-Test

Select the best answer for each of the following questions. Then check your responses against the Answer Key at the end of the text.

1. Claudia's therapist asks her to talk about whatever thoughts, memories, or ideas come into her mind. He asks her not to "edit" any of her thoughts. This technique is called _____ and is part of _____ therapy.

   a. reflection; psychodynamic
   b. reflection; humanistic
   c. free association; psychodynamic
   d. free association; humanistic

2. Vicki tells Dr. Denter, her therapist, that she is very happy in her marriage. Dr. Denter points out that, as she says this, she is clenching her fist. He asks her to have a dialogue with herself by "becoming" her fist and saying what it would say to her. Dr. Denter is most likely a _____ therapist.

   a. Gestalt
   b. psychodynamic
   c. behavior
   d. cognitive

3. Melinda is a licensed clinical psychologist, which means she probably has

   a. a doctoral degree in psychology.
   b. a psychodynamic approach to therapy.
   c. the right to prescribe drugs in all but two U.S. states.
   d. a medical degree.

4. A primary aim of classical psychoanalysis is to

   a. help clients get in touch with their current feelings.
   b. help clients gain insight into their unconscious conflicts.
   c. replace clients' problematic behaviors with more desirable behaviors.
   d. teach clients new ways of thinking.

5. Dr. Margent listens as her client, Eric, talks at length about his problems at work, including the fact that he hates the job, often sneaks out early, sometimes ignores his manager's instructions, and generally avoids working hard. Dr. Margent doesn't interrupt or criticize him but often rephrases what he says to be sure she understands it. Dr. Margent is using methods most closely associated with _____ therapy.

   a. psychodynamic   c. behavioral
   b. client-centered   d. cognitive behavioral

6. Carl's therapist is helping him to overcome his fear of heights by imagining increasingly frightening images while relaxed. The therapist is using methods known as

   a. assertion training.   c. flooding.
   b. systematic desensitization. d. modeling.

7. Shanobi is tearfully telling a friend that she is depressed and does not know why. Her friend says, "You seem so unhappy, and maybe a bit scared, too." The friend's response is most like which method used in client-centered therapy?

   a. Sympathy   c. Reflection
   b. Empathy   d. Actualization

8. Rebecca is convinced that she will never get the promotion she wants because she "is just not good at job interviews." Her therapist asks her to close her eyes and say the first thing that comes into her mind as she thinks about her job. He also asks Rebecca for details of the dreams she has been having lately. Rebecca's therapist appears to prefer the _____ approach to treatment.

   a. behavioral   c. Gestalt
   b. cognitive-behavioral   d. psychodynamic

9. Brandon complains that he has an intense need to touch all four walls of any room he enters for the first time. His therapist suggests that Brandon might have learned this compulsive behavior because it helped him avoid anxiety. The therapist appears to favor the _____ approach to treatment.

    a. psychodynamic
    b. humanistic
    c. behavioral
    d. neurobiological

10. Your friend Rallo is considering entering psychotherapy, but he wonders if it will help. Based on the research you read about in this chapter, you tell Rallo that

    a. therapy does not help the average client.
    b. therapy helps the average client.
    c. humanistic therapies are most effective overall.
    d. there is no experimental research on the effectiveness of therapy.

11. According to the American Psychological Association's *Ethical Principles of Psychologists and Code of Conduct,* a therapist may reveal information learned about a client during therapy if

    a. the client's employer requests this information in confidence.
    b. the client drops out of therapy.
    c. the client is suicidal and needs immediate hospitalization.
    d. the therapist feels it will do no harm.

12. Juanita is trying to influence her state legislature to pass laws that will help prevent psychological problems caused by malnutrition, overcrowding, and homelessness. She is most likely a _____ psychologist.

    a. behavioral
    b. community
    c. humanistic
    d. psychodynamic

13. Rafer's intense fear of spiders greatly interferes with his job as a forest ranger. His therapist suggests that he stay in a room full of harmless spiders until he feels no further anxiety. This therapy technique is known as

    a. flooding.
    b. punishment.
    c. systematic desensitization.
    d. aversion conditioning.

14. Sally constantly tells herself that she is "worthless" and "will never succeed at anything." Her therapist helps her practice new thoughts such as "I'm as good as the next person" and "I am going to try my best." Her therapist is using the technique of _____, which is part of _____ therapy.

    a. free association; psychodynamic
    b. reflection; humanistic
    c. stress inoculation; behavioral
    d. cognitive restructuring; cognitive-behavior

15. Lucinda is experiencing severe depression that leaves her unable to enjoy life. She has not responded to psychotherapies or medication. Lucinda would be a candidate for

    a. neuroleptics.
    b. ECT.
    c. aversion conditioning.
    d. cognitive restructuring.

16. Therapeutic drugs can work in many ways, but NOT by

    a. increasing the amount of neurotransmitters released in the brain.
    b. decreasing the amount of neurotransmitters released in the brain.
    c. blocking the action of neurotransmitters in the brain.
    d. changing the kind of neurotransmitters released by neurons in the brain.

17. An important common element in the success of many forms of psychotherapy is

    a. the client-therapist relationship.
    b. randomly assigning therapists to clients.
    c. having a therapist trained in a variety of therapeutic methods.
    d. having appropriate assessment methods to measure outcomes.

18. When prescribing neuroleptics for schizophrenia, psychiatrists must consider that patients may

    a. become addicted to them.
    b. become insensitive to them after an extended period of time.
    c. develop side effects such as tardive dyskinesia.
    d. experience hallucinations after extensive use.

19. Jon's therapist has prescribed anxiolytics for him. Jon is probably being treated for

    a. depression.
    b. an anxiety disorder.
    c. schizophrenia.
    d. somatoform disorder.

20. Which of the following is *not* an advantage of group therapy?

    a. It allows the therapist to observe clients interacting with one another.
    b. Clients learn from one another.
    c. Clients improve more quickly.
    d. Clients feel less alone.

14

Social Psychology

If you are like most people, there is probably at least one thing you do in private that you would never do when someone else is around. The tendency to behave differently when others are present is just one aspect of social psychology. This chapter describes many other ways in which the presence and behavior of other people affect our own thoughts and actions and how we, in turn, affect the thoughts and actions of others. It explores how perception, learning, memory, thinking, and emotion occur in relation to other people; how people think about themselves and others; why we may like one person but dislike another; how people form and change attitudes; and why and how we judge other people, sometimes in biased ways. Social pressure, ranging from unspoken social rules to commands for obedience, is another concern of social psychologists. The chapter also reviews some of the helpful, cooperative, competitive, and aggressive ways in which people behave toward one another in the workplace and in other social situations. Finally, it considers group decision making and other group processes.

Reading this chapter will help you to answer the following questions:

The death toll in the September 11, 2001, attacks on the World Trade Center and the Pentagon exceeded 3,000, the largest number of people to die violently on American soil in a single day since 1862, during the U.S. Civil War. Almost all of the questions that can be asked about this horrendous tragedy and about terrorism in general relate to human behavior. For example, what could lead people to kill themselves, along with thousands of innocent people, in the name of political or religious beliefs? Why did hundreds of firefighters, police officers, emergency medical workers, and others enter the World Trade Center's burning towers to save the lives of others while risking, and ultimately losing, their own? Why did some of the people who were fleeing the damaged buildings return to their offices after hearing an announcement telling them to do so? Is there any reason to hope that the hatred and distrust that brought about this disaster can someday be reduced or eliminated?

We may never have final answers to such questions as these, but some partial answers may lie in the study of **social psychology,** the scientific study of how people's thoughts and feelings influence their behavior toward others and how the behavior of others influences people's own thoughts, feelings, and behavior. In this chapter, we focus on several topics in social psychology, including **social cognition** (the mental processes associated with how people perceive and react to other individuals and groups) and group and interpersonal behaviors such as conformity, aggression, and helping. One important aspect of social cognition is how it affects the way we see ourselves.

Social Influences on the Self

▶ **How do we compare ourselves with others?**

Each of us lives in both a personal and a social world. This means that although you experience your thoughts and feelings as your own, they have been strongly influenced by other people.

The thoughts, feelings, and beliefs about what characteristics you have and who you are make up your **self-concept.** Although your self-concept is unique to you, it is a product of your social and cultural environment. In the chapters on human development and personality, we describe how each individual develops within a cultural context and how collectivist and individualist cultures emphasize different core values and encourage contrasting definitions of the self. As you will see in this chapter, culture also provides the context for **self-esteem,** the evaluations you make of your worth as a human being. Let's look at how self-esteem develops.

Social Comparison

People spend a lot of time thinking about themselves, trying to evaluate their own perceptions, opinions, values, abilities, and so on (Mussweiler, 2003). Decades ago, Leon Festinger (1954) noted that self-evaluation involves two distinct types of questions: those that can be answered by taking objective measurements and those that cannot. You can determine your height or weight by measuring it, but for other types of questions—about your creativity or attractiveness, for example—there are no objective criteria, no obvious yardsticks. In these cases, according to Festinger's theory of **social comparison,** people evaluate themselves in relation to others. When you use others as a basis for evaluating how intelligent, athletic, interesting, or attractive you are, you are engaging in social comparison (Buunk et al., 2005).

Who serves as your basis of comparison? Festinger said that people usually look to others who are similar to themselves. For example, if you are curious about how good you are at swimming or science, you will probably compare yourself with people who are at about your own level of experience and ability, not with Olympic champions or Nobel Prize winners (Major, Sciacchtinano, & Crocker, 1993). The categories of people you feel you belong to and usually compare yourself with are called your **reference groups.**

The performance of individuals in your reference groups can affect your self-esteem (Baumeister, 1998). For example, if being good at science is important to you, knowing that someone in your reference group always scores much higher than you on science tests can lower your self-esteem. To protect their self-esteem and make themselves feel better, people sometimes compare themselves with those who are not as good, a strategy called *downward social comparison.* They may also sometimes engage in *upward social comparison,* in which they compare themselves with people who are doing much better than they are (Buunk et al., 2005; Frieswijk et al., 2004). At first glance, this might

social psychology   The subfield of psychology that explores the effects of the social world on the behavior and mental processes of individuals and groups.

social cognition   Mental processes associated with people's perceptions of and reactions to other people.

self-concept   The way one thinks of oneself.

self-esteem   The evaluations people make about their worth as human beings.

social comparison   Using other people as a basis of comparison for evaluating oneself.

reference groups   Categories of people with whom individuals compare themselves.

not seem sensible, but upward social comparison can create optimism about improving our own situations (Buunk & Oldersma, 2001). We may tell ourselves "If they can do it, so can I!" Or we might tell ourselves that the superior performer is not really similar enough to be in our reference group, or even that the ability in question is not that important to us (Alicke et al., 1997).

An unfavorable comparison of your own status with that of others can produce **relative deprivation**—the belief that whatever you are getting, it is less than what you deserve (Brehm, Kassin, & Fein, 2005). The concept of relative deprivation explains why a movie star who receives $5 million per film feels abused if a costar is receiving $10 million. It also explains the far more common situation in which employees become dissatisfied when they see themselves as underpaid or underappreciated in comparison to their coworkers (Feldman & Turnley, 2004). Relative deprivation can create depression and anxiety (Taylor & Lobel, 1989), and when large groups of people experience relative deprivation, political unrest may follow. The turmoil usually starts after the members of an oppressed group experience some improvement in their lives and begin to compare their circumstances with those of people in other groups (Worchel et al., 2000). This improvement brings higher expectations about what they deserve. It is likely, for example, that resentment over U.S. prosperity and global influence plays a role in creating the hatred that leads some people to engage in terrorist attacks against the United States.

Self-Esteem and the Ultimate Terror

Why is self-esteem so important to so many people? An intriguing answer to this question comes from the *terror management theory* proposed by Jeff Greenberg, Tom Pyszczynski, and Sheldon Solomon. This theory is based on the notion that humans are the only creatures capable of thinking about the future and realizing that we will all eventually die. Terror management theory suggests that humans cope with anxiety, including the terror that thoughts about death might bring, by developing a variety of self-protective psychological strategies. One of these is the effort to establish and maintain high self-esteem (Greenberg, Pyszczynski, & Solomon, 2003; Pyszczynski et al., 2004).

■ What was the researchers' question?

In one series of experiments, Greenberg and his colleagues (1992) asked whether high self-esteem would, in fact, serve as a buffer against anxiety—specifically, the anxiety brought on by thoughts about death and pain.

■ How did the researchers answer the question?

About 150 students at several North American universities participated in one of three studies, each of which followed a similar format. The first step was to temporarily alter the participants' self-esteem. To do so, the researchers gave the students feedback about a personality or intelligence test they had taken earlier in the semester. Half the participants received positive feedback designed to increase their self-esteem. The other half received feedback that was neutral—it was neither flattering nor depressing. (Measurement of the students' self-esteem showed that the positive feedback actually did create higher self-esteem than the neutral feedback.) In the next phase of each experiment, the researchers used either a film about death or the (false) threat of a mild electric shock to provoke some anxiety in half the participants in the positive-feedback group and half the participants in the neutral-feedback group. The amount of anxiety created was measured by the participants' self-reports or by monitoring galvanic skin resistance (GSR), a measure of perspiration in their skin that reflects anxiety-related physiological arousal (Dawson, Schell, & Filion, 2000).

relative deprivation The sense that one is not getting all that one deserves.

■ **What did the researchers find?**

Self-reports and GSR measures revealed that participants in all three experiments were significantly less upset by an anxiety-provoking experience (the death film or the threat of shock) if they had first received esteem-building feedback about their previous test performance.

■ **What do the results mean?**

The researchers concluded that their results support the notion that self-esteem can act as a buffer against anxiety and other negative feelings. This conclusion would help explain why people are so eager to maintain or enhance their self-esteem (Tesser, 2001): We don't like to feel anxious, and increased self-esteem reduces most people's anxiety.

■ **What do we still need to know?**

These results certainly support terror management theory, but by themselves, they are not broad enough to confirm all of its assumptions. For example, the theory also predicts that when people are sensitized to the threat of death, they will seek to protect themselves by suppressing thoughts of death and also by doing things that increase the approval and support of others in the society in which they live. Consistent with this prediction, people have been found to make larger contributions to charity after they have been made more aware of their own mortality (Jonas et al., 2002). Similarly, dramatic increases in volunteering for charity work occurred after the events of September 11, 2001 (Penner, Dovidio, et al., 2005).

But which strategies are people most likely to use, and why? Are some strategies more or less likely to be adopted at different times in a person's life or among people in certain cultures? And what forms of self-esteem are most important in different cultures? So far, most of the research on terror management theory has been done in individualistic cultures such as North America, where self-esteem is largely based on personal accomplishments. However, terror management theory has also been supported by preliminary studies in Japan, aboriginal Australia, and other collectivist cultures in which feelings of self-worth tend to be more closely tied to the performance and status of the groups to which people belong (Halloran & Kashima, 2004; Heine, Harihara, & Niiya, 2002). It will take many more experiments to test all the predictions derived from the theory.

Social Identity Theory

learn by doing

Stop reading for a moment, and complete the following sentence: I am a(n) _____ . Some people fill in the blank using characteristics such as "hard worker," "good sport," or some other aspect of their *personal* identity. However, many others identify themselves using a word or phrase that refers to their nationality, gender, or religion (Lee & Yoo, 2004). These latter responses reflect **social identity,** our beliefs about the groups to which we belong. Our social identity is therefore a part of our self-concept (Tropp & Wright, 2001; Vignoles et al., 2006).

Our social or group identity permits us to feel part of a larger whole (Ashmore et al., 2004). Its importance is seen in the pride that people feel when a member of their family graduates from college or when a local team wins a big game (Burris, Branscombe, & Klar, 1997). In wars between national, ethnic, or religious groups, individuals sacrifice and sometimes die for the sake of their group identity. A group identity is also one reason people donate money to those in need, support friends in a crisis, and display other helping behaviors. As we shall see later, however, defining ourselves in terms of a group identity can foster an "us versus them" mentality that sets the stage for prejudice, discrimination, intergroup conflict, and even terrorism (Brewer & Pierce, 2005).

social identity The beliefs we hold about the groups to which we belong.

Social Perception

▶ **Do we perceive people and objects in similar ways?**

There is a story about a company president who was having lunch with a man being considered for an executive position. When the man salted his food without first tasting it, the president decided not to hire him. The reason, she explained, was that the company had no room for a person who acted before collecting all relevant information. The candidate lost his chance because of the president's **social perception,** the processes through which people interpret information about others, form impressions of them, and draw conclusions about the reasons for their behavior. In this section we examine how and why social perception influences our thoughts, feelings, and actions.

The Role of Schemas

The perception of people follows many of the same laws that govern the perception of objects, including the Gestalt principles discussed in the chapter on sensation and perception (Cloutier, Mason, & Macrae, 2005). Consider Figure 14.1. Consistent with Gestalt principles, most people would describe it as "a square with a notch in one side," not as eight straight lines (Woodworth & Schlosberg, 1954). The reason is that they interpret new information using the mental representations, or **schemas,** that they already have about squares. In other words, they interpret this diagram as a square with a slight modification.

Schemas about people, too, can affect our perception of them. For one thing, schemas influence what we pay attention to and what we ignore. We tend to process information about the other person more quickly if it confirms our beliefs about that person's gender or ethnic group, for example, than if it violates those beliefs. Second, schemas influence what we remember about others. In one study, if people thought a woman they saw in a videotape was a waitress, they recalled that she had a beer with dinner and owned a TV set. Those who thought she was a librarian remembered that she was wearing glasses and liked classical music (Cohen, 1981). Finally, schemas affect our judgment about the behavior of others (Moskowitz, 2005). Thomas Hill and his colleagues (1989) found that participants' ratings of male and female friends' sadness were influenced not only by the friends' actual behavior but also by the participants' general schemas about how much sadness men versus women experience.

In other words, through top-down processing (discussed in the sensation and perception chapter), our schemas about people influence our perceptions of them. And just as schemas help us read sentences whose words have missing letters, they also allow us to efficiently "fill in the blanks" about people. Our schemas tell us, for example, that someone wearing a store uniform or name tag is likely to know where merchandise is located, so we usually approach that person for help. Accurate schemas help us to categorize people quickly and respond appropriately in social situations, but if schemas are incorrect they can create false expectations and errors in judgment about people that can lead to narrow-mindedness and even prejudice.

First Impressions

Our schemas about people act as lenses that alter our first impressions of them. Those impressions, in turn, affects both our later perceptions of their behavior and our reactions to it. First impressions are formed quickly, sometimes in less than one second (Willis & Todorov, 2006), usually change slowly, and typically have a long-lasting influence. No wonder they are so important in the development of social relations (Brehm et al., 2005). How do people form impressions of other people? And why are these impressions so resistant to change?

 Forming Impressions Think about your first impression of a close friend. It was probably formed quickly, because existing schemas create a

LINKAGES
Do we sometimes perceive people the same way we perceive objects? (a link to Sensation and Perception)

social perception   The processes through which people interpret information about others, draw inferences about them, and develop mental representations of them.

schemas   Mental representations about people and social situations.

MAY I HELP YOU? Schemas help us to quickly categorize people and respond appropriately to them, but schemas can also create narrow-mindedness and, as we shall see later, prejudice. If this woman does not fulfill your schema—your mental representation—of how carpenters are supposed to look, you might be less likely to ask her advice on your home improvement project. One expert carpenter who manages the hardware department of a large home improvement store told us that most customers walk right past her in order to ask the advice of one of her less experienced male clerks.

tendency to automatically assume a great deal about a person on the basis of limited information (Smith & Quellar, 2001). An ethnic name, for example, might have caused you to draw inferences about your friend's religion, food preferences, or temperament. Clothing or hairstyle might have led you to make assumptions about political views or taste in music. These inferences and assumptions may or may not be accurate. How many turned out to be true in your friend's case?

One schema has a particularly strong influence on first impressions: We tend to assume that the people we meet have attitudes and values similar to our own (Hoyle, 1993). So, all else being equal, we are inclined to like other people. However, even a small amount of negative information can change our minds. Why? The main reason is that most of us don't expect other people to act negatively toward us. When unexpectedly negative behaviors do occur, they capture our attention and lead us to believe that these behaviors reflect something negative about the other person (Taylor, Peplau, & Sears, 2003). The result is that negative information attracts more attention and carries more weight than positive information in shaping first impressions (Smith & Mackie, 2000).

Lasting Impressions Does your friend seem the same today as when you first met? First impressions can change, but the process is usually slow. One reason is that negative first impressions may cause us to avoid certain people, thus reducing our exposure to new information that might change our view of them (Denrell, 2005). Further, most people want to keep their social environment simple and easy to understand (Kenrick, Neuberg, & Cialdini, 2005). We cling to our beliefs about the world, often using our schemas to preserve a reality that fits our expectations. Holding on to existing impressions

Noticeable features or actions help shape our impressions of others. Those impressions may or may not be correct.

© Scott Adams/Dist. By United Feature Syndicate, Inc.

SELF-FULFILLING PROPHECIES IN THE CLASSROOM If teachers inadvertently spend less time helping children who at first seem "dull," those children may not learn as much, thus fulfilling the teachers' expectations. If the girl in the back row has not impressed this teacher as being bright, how likely do you think it is that she will be called on?

appears to be part of this effort. If your friend recently violated your expectations by being impatient, your view of her probably did not change much, if at all. In fact, you may have acted to preserve your impression of her by thinking something like, "She is not herself today." In other words, impressions change slowly because the meaning we give to new information about people is shaped by what we already know or believe about them (Kenrick et al., 2005).

Self-Fulfilling Prophecies Another reason first impressions tend to be stable is that we often do things that cause others to confirm our impressions (Franzoi, 2003). If teachers expect particular students to do poorly in mathematics, those students may sense this expectation, exert less effort, and perform below their ability level. And if mothers expect their young children to eventually abuse alcohol, they are more likely to do so than the children of mothers who didn't convey that expectation (Madon et al., 2003; Madon et al., 2004). When, without our awareness, schemas cause us to subtly lead people to behave in line with our expectations, a **self-fulfilling prophecy** is at work.

Self-fulfilling prophecies also help maintain judgments about groups. If you assume that members of a certain ethnic group are a threat, you might be defensive or even hostile when you meet a member of that group. That person might react to your behavior with hostility and anger. These reactions fulfill your prophecy and strengthen the impressions that created it (Kenrick et al., 2005).

Explaining Behavior: Attribution

So far, we have examined how people form impressions about other people's characteristics. But our perceptions of others also include our explanations of their behavior. People tend to form ideas about why people (including themselves) behave as they do and about what behavior to expect in the future (Brehm et al., 2005). Psychologists use the term **attribution** to describe the process we go through to explain the causes of behavior (including our own).

Suppose a classmate borrows your notes but fails to return them. You could attribute this behavior to many causes, from an emergency situation to selfishness. Which of these explanations you choose is important, because it will help you *understand* your

self-fulfilling prophecy A process in which an initial impression causes us to bring out behavior in another that confirms the impression.

attribution The process of explaining the causes of people's behavior, including our own.

classmate's behavior, *predict* what will happen if this person asks to borrow something in the future, and decide how to *control* the situation should it arise again. Similarly, whether a person attributes a partner's nagging to temporary stress or to loss of affection can influence whether that person will work on the relationship or end it.

People usually attribute behavior in a particular situation to either internal causes (characteristics of the person) or external causes (characteristics of the situation). For example, if you thought your classmate's failure to return your notes was due mainly to lack of consideration or laziness, you would be making an *internal attribution*. If you thought that the oversight was due mainly to preoccupation with a family crisis, you would be making an *external attribution*. Similarly, if you failed an exam, you could explain it by concluding that you're not very smart (internal attribution) or that your work schedule left you too little time to study (external attribution). The attribution that you make, in turn, might determine how much you study for the next exam or even whether you decide to stay in school.

Biases in Attribution

Most people are usually logical in their attempts to explain behavior (Trope, Cohen, & Alfieri, 1991). However, they are also prone to *attributional biases,* or errors, that can distort their view of behavior (Gilbert, 1998).

The Fundamental Attribution Error   North American psychologists have paid special attention to the **fundamental attribution error,** a tendency to overattribute the behavior of others to internal factors (Moskowitz, 2005). Imagine that you hear a student give an incorrect answer in class. You will probably attribute this behavior to an internal cause and infer that the person is not very smart. In doing so, however, you might be ignoring possible external factors (such as lack of study time).

A related attributional bias is called the *ultimate attribution error.* Through this error, the positive actions of people from a different ethnic or social group are attributed to external causes, such as easy opportunities, whereas their negative actions are attributed to internal causes, such as dishonesty (Pettigrew, 1979). The ultimate attribution error also causes people to see good deeds done by those in their own group as due to kindness or other internal factors and bad deeds as stemming from external causes, such as unemployment. In this way, the ultimate attribution error helps to create and maintain people's negative views of other groups and positive views of their own group (Fiske, 1998).

These attributional biases may not be universal (Miyamoto & Kitayama, 2002). For example, research suggests that the fundamental attribution error and the ultimate attribution error are less likely to appear among people in collectivist cultures such as India, China, Japan, and Korea compared with people in the individualist cultures of North America and Europe (Lehman, Chiu, & Schaller, 2004). And even within individualist cultures, some people hold a stronger individualist orientation than others. So some people in these cultures are more likely than others to make attribution errors (Miller, 2001; Vandello & Cohen, 1999).

Other Attributional Biases   The tendency to make internal attributions is much less pronounced when people explain their own behavior. In fact, people tend to show an **actor-observer bias:** that is, we often attribute other people's behavior to internal causes but attribute our own behavior to external factors, especially when our behavior is inappropriate or inadequate (Baumeister, 1998). For example, when Australian students were asked why they sometimes drive too fast, they focused on circumstances, such as being late, but saw other people's dangerous driving as a sign of aggressiveness or immaturity (Harré, Brandt, & Houkamau, 2004). Similarly, when you are driving too slowly, the reason is that you are looking for an address, not that you are a big loser like that jerk who crawled along in front of you yesterday.

The actor-observer bias occurs mainly because people have different kinds of information about their own behavior and the behavior of others. When *you* are in some

Online Study Center

Improve Your Grade
Tutorial: Fundamental
Attribution Error

fundamental attribution error   A bias toward attributing the behavior of others to internal factors.

actor-observer bias   The tendency to attribute other people's behavior to internal causes while attributing one's own behavior to external causes.

WHY ARE THEY HELPING? Attributional biases are more common in some cultures than others. In one study, students in an individualist culture were more likely than those in a collectivist culture to explain acts of helping as being due to internal causes such as kindness or enjoyment of helping (Miller & Bersoff, 1994).

situation—giving a speech, perhaps—the information most available to you is likely to be external and situational, such as the temperature of the room and the size of the audience. You also have a lot of information about other external factors, such as the amount of time you had to prepare your talk or the upsetting conversation that occurred this morning. If your speech is disorganized and boring, you can easily attribute it to one or all of these external causes. But when you observe someone else, the most obvious information in the situation is *that person*. You do not know what happened to the person last night or this morning, so you are likely to attribute the quality of the performance to stable, internal characteristics (Moskowitz, 2005).

Of course, people do not always attribute their own behavior to external forces. In fact, whether they do so often depends on whether the outcome is positive or negative. In one study, when people were asked what they saw as the cause of their good and bad experiences when shopping online, they tended to take personal credit for positive outcomes but to blame the computer for the negative ones (Moon, 2003). In other words, these people showed a **self-serving bias,** the tendency to take personal credit for success but to blame external causes for failure. This bias has been found in almost all cultures, but as with the fundamental attribution error, it is usually more pronounced among people from individualistic Western cultures than among those from collectivist Eastern cultures (Mezulis et al., 2004).

The self-serving bias occurs, in part, because people are motivated to maintain their self-esteem—and ignoring negative information about themselves is one way to do so. If you just failed an exam, it is painful to admit that the exam was fair. Like the other attributional biases we have discussed, self-serving bias helps people think about their failures and shortcomings in ways that protect their self-esteem (Dunning et al., 2003; Gilbert et al., 2004; Tesser, 2001). These self-protective cognitive biases can help us temporarily escape from unpleasant thoughts and feelings, but they may also create a distorted view of reality that can lead to other problems. One such problem is *unrealistic optimism,* the tendency to believe that good things (such as financial success or having a gifted child) are likely to happen to you but that bad things (e.g., accidents or illness) are not (Lin & Raghubir, 2005). Unrealistic optimism tends to persist even when there is strong evidence against it, and it can lead to potentially harmful behaviors. For example, people who are unrealistically optimistic about their health may not bother to exercise and may ignore information about how to prevent heart disease (Radcliffe & Klein, 2002). ("In Review: Some Biases in Social Perception" summarizes the common cognitive biases discussed here.)

self-serving bias The tendency to attribute one's successes to internal characteristics while blaming one's failures on external causes.

SOME BIASES IN SOCIAL PERCEPTION

Bias	Description
Importance of first impression	Ambiguous information is interpreted in line with a first impression, and the initial schema is recalled better and more vividly than any later correction to it. Actions based on this impression may elicit behavior that confirms it.
Fundamental attribution error	The tendency to overattribute the behavior of others to internal factors.
Actor-observer bias	The tendency for actors to attribute their own behavior to external causes and for observers to attribute the behavior of others to internal factors.
Self-serving bias	The tendency to attribute one's successes to internal factors and one's failures to external factors.
Unrealistic optimism	The tendency of people to believe that good things will happen to them but that bad things will not.

?
1. The fundamental attribution error appears to be somewhat less likely to occur among people in _____ cultures.
2. First impressions form _____, but change _____.
3. If you believed that immigrants' successes are due to government help but that their failures are due to laziness, you would be committing the _____ error.

Attitudes

▶ **Do attitudes always determine behavior?**

Our views about health, safety, or any other topic reflect our *attitudes*. Social psychologists have studied this aspect of social cognition longer and more intensely than any other. An **attitude** is the tendency to think, feel, or act positively or negatively toward objects in our environment (Albarracín, Johnson, & Zanna, 2005). Attitudes play an important role in guiding how we react to other people, what causes and politicians we support, which products we buy, and countless other daily decisions.

The Structure of Attitudes

Social psychologists have long viewed attitudes as having three components (Fabrigar, MacDonald, & Wegener, 2005). The *cognitive* component is a set of beliefs about the attitude object. The emotional, or *affective*, component includes feelings about the object. And the *behavioral* component is the way people act toward the object. If these three components were always in harmony, we would be able to predict people's behavior toward the homeless, for example, on the basis of the thoughts or feelings they express, and vice versa. This is often not the case, however (Schwarz & Bohner, 2001). Many people's charitable thoughts and sympathetic emotions regarding the homeless are never translated into actions aimed at helping them.

What determines whether people's behavior will be consistent with the cognitive and affective components of their attitudes? Several factors are important. For one thing, behavior is more likely to be consistent with attitude when people see the attitude as important and relevant to their lives (Kenrick et al., 2005; Skitka, Bauman, & Sargis, 2005). Attitude-behavior consistency is also more likely when the behavioral component

attitude   A tendency toward a particular cognitive, emotional, or behavioral reaction to objects in one's environment.

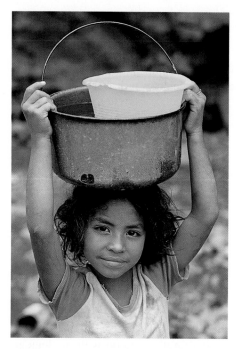

A REMINDER ABOUT POVERTY Photographs such as this one are used by fund-raising organizations to remind us of the kind thoughts and charitable feelings we have toward needy people and other worthy causes. As a result, we may be more likely to behave in accordance with the cognitive and affective components of our attitudes and make a donation to these causes. Browse through several newspapers and popular magazines and calculate the percentage of such photos you find in ads for charitable organizations.

of the attitude is in line with a *subjective norm,* our view of how the important people in our lives want us to act. If there is a conflict between what we want to do and what a subjective norm tells us we should do, we may end up behaving in ways that are inconsistent with our attitudes (Ajzen & Fishbein, 2005). For example, someone who believes that the rights of gay men and lesbians should be protected might not go out and campaign for this cause, because doing so would upset valued family members or co-workers who are strongly against it. Third, attitude-consistent behavior is more likely when people have *perceived control,* a belief that they can actually perform the behavior (Ajzen & Fishbein, 2005). The cognitive and emotional components of your attitude toward the homeless might be positive, but if you don't believe you can do anything to help them, you are not likely to even try. Finally, *direct experience* with the object of an attitude increases the likelihood of attitude-consistent behavior (Kenrick et al., 2005). So you might be more likely to actively support, and perhaps even participate in, efforts to help the homeless if you have come to know a homeless person on your campus than if you have only read about their plight.

Forming Attitudes

People's attitudes about objects begin to appear in early childhood and continue to emerge throughout life. How do these attitudes form? Genetics may have a certain amount of influence on some attitudes (Abrahamson, Baker, & Caspi, 2002), but social learning—what children learn from their parents and others—appears to play the major role in attitude formation. Children learn not only the names of objects but also what they should believe and feel about them and how they should act toward them. For example, a parent may teach a child not only that snakes are reptiles but also that they should be feared and avoided. So as children learn concepts such as "reptile" or "work," they learn attitudes about those concepts, too (Bohner & Schwarz, 2001).

Classical and operant conditioning can also shape positive or negative attitudes (Baron, Byrne, & Branscombe 2006). Advertisers pair up enjoyable music, soothing colors, or sexy images with the products they try to sell (Pratkanis & Aronson, 2001), and parents, teachers, and peers reward children for stating particular views. The *mere-exposure effect* is influential as well. All else being equal, attitudes toward an object become more positive the more frequently people are exposed to the object (Zajonc, 2001). One study even found that newborns preferred to listen to stories that had been read aloud while they were still in the womb (Cacioppo, Berntson, & Petty, 1997). This exposure effect helps explain why commercials and political ads are aired over and over and why some rock bands won't include new songs in a live concert until their fans have repeatedly heard and come to like the recorded versions.

Changing Attitudes

The nearly $100 billion a year spent on advertising in the United States alone provides just one example of how people constantly try to change our attitudes. Stop for a moment and make a list of other examples, starting, perhaps, with the persuasive messages of groups concerned with abortion or gun control or recycling—and don't forget about friends who want you to think the way they do.

Two Routes to Attitude Change Whether a persuasive message succeeds in changing attitudes depends mainly on three factors: (1) the person communicating the message, (2) the content of the message, and (3) the audience who receives it (Johnson, Maio, & Smith-McLallen, 2005). The **elaboration likelihood model** of attitude change—illustrated in Figure 14.2—provides a framework for understanding when and how these factors affect attitude change. The model is based on the idea that persuasive messages can change people's attitudes through one of two main routes.

The first is called the *peripheral route* because, when it is activated, we devote little attention to the central content of the persuasive message. We tend to be affected instead by peripheral, or surrounding, persuasion cues, such as the confidence, attractiveness, or

elaboration likelihood model A model of attitude change suggesting that people can change their attitudes through a central route (by considering an argument's content) or through a peripheral route (by relying on irrelevant persuasion cues).

FIGURE **14.2**

The Elaboration Likelihood Model of Attitude Change

The central route to attitude change involves carefully processing and evaluating a message's content (high elaboration). The peripheral route involves little processing and evaluation of message content (low elaboration) and relying instead on persuasion cues such as the attractiveness of the person making the argument (Cacioppo, Petty, & Crites, 1993).

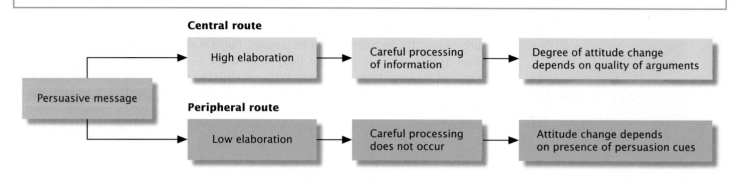

other characteristics of the person who delivers the message. These persuasion cues influence attitude change even though they may have nothing to do with the logic or accuracy of the message itself. Commercials in which movie stars or other attractive nonexperts endorse pain relievers or denture cleaners are designed to encourage the peripheral route to attitude change.

By contrast, when the *central route* to attitude change is activated, the core content of the message becomes more important than the communicator's characteristics in determining attitude change. A person following the central route uses logical steps—such as those outlined in the Thinking Critically sections of this book—to analyze the content of the persuasive message, including the validity of its claims, whether it leaves out pertinent information, alternative interpretations of evidence, and so on.

What determines which route people will follow? Personal involvement with the content of a message is an important factor. The elaboration likelihood model predicts that the more personally involving a topic is, the more likely it is that the central route will be activated (Fabrigar et al., 2005; Holbrook et al., 2006). Suppose, for example, that you hear someone arguing for the cancellation of all student loans in Chile. This message might persuade you through the peripheral route if it comes from someone who looks attractive and sounds intelligent. However, you are more likely to follow the central route if the message proposes eliminating student loans at your own school. You might still be persuaded, but only if the logic of the message is clear and convincing. This is why celebrity endorsements tend to be more effective when the products being advertised are relatively unimportant to the audience.

Persuasive messages are not the only means of changing attitudes. Another approach is to get people to act in ways that are inconsistent with their attitudes in the hope that they will adjust those attitudes to match their behavior. Often, such adjustments do occur. Cognitive dissonance theory attempts to explain why.

cognitive dissonance theory A theory that attitude change is driven by efforts to reduce tension caused by inconsistencies between attitudes and behaviors.

Cognitive Dissonance Theory Leon Festinger's (1957) classic **cognitive dissonance theory** holds that people want their thoughts, beliefs, and attitudes to be in harmony with one another and with their behavior. When people experience inconsistency, or *dissonance*, among these elements, they become anxious and are motivated to make them more consistent (Elliot & Devine, 1994; Olson & Stone, 2005). For example, someone who believes that "smoking is dangerous" but who must also admit that "I smoke" would be motivated to reduce the resulting dissonance. Because it is often difficult to change behavior, people usually reduce cognitive dissonance by changing attitudes that are inconsistent with the behavior. So rather than quit smoking, the smoker might decide that smoking is not so dangerous after all.

Favorable

Unfavorable

$20.00 $1.00
Experimental condition

■ High justification (low dissonance)

■ Low justification (high dissonance)

Source: Festinger & Carlsmith (1959)

FIGURE **14.3**

Cognitive Dissonance and Attitude Change

According to cognitive dissonance theory, people given $20 to say that a boring task was enjoyable had clear justification for lying. So they should experience little dissonance between what they said and what they felt about the task. In fact, their attitude toward the task did not change much. However, people who received only $1 had little justification to lie and reduced their dissonance mainly by displaying a more positive attitude toward the task.

In one of the first studies of cognitive dissonance, Festinger and his colleague Merrill Carlsmith (1959) asked people to turn pegs in a pegboard, a very dull task. Later, some of these people were asked to persuade a person who was waiting to participate in the study that the task was "exciting and fun." Some were told that they would be paid $1 to tell this lie. Others were promised $20. After they had talked to the waiting person, their attitudes toward the dull task were measured. Figure 14.3 shows and explains the surprising results. The people who were paid just $1 to lie liked the dull task more than those who were paid $20 (Festinger & Carlsmith, 1959).

Hundreds of other experiments have also found that when people publicly engage in behaviors that are inconsistent with their privately held attitudes, they are likely to change their attitudes to be consistent with their behavior (Stone & Cooper, 2001). These experiments have found that attitude-behavior inconsistency is likely to change attitudes when (1) the inconsistency causes some distress or discomfort in a person and (2) changing attitudes will reduce that discomfort. But why should attitude-behavior inconsistency cause discomfort in the first place? There is considerable debate among attitude researchers about this question (Wood, 2000).

Currently, the most popular of several possible answers is that discomfort results when people's positive self-concept (e.g., "I am honest") is threatened by recognizing that they have done something inconsistent with that self-concept. For example, if they have encouraged another person to do something that they themselves didn't believe in or that they themselves wouldn't do, this inconsistency makes most people feel uncomfortable. So they change their attitudes to reduce or eliminate the discomfort (Stone & Cooper, 2001; Stone, 2003). In other words, if people can persuade themselves that they really believe in what they have said or done, the inconsistency disappears, their positive self-concept is restored, and they can feel good about themselves again.

The circumstances that lead to cognitive dissonance may be different in the individualist cultures of Europe and North America than in collectivist cultures such as Japan and China. In individualist cultures, dissonance typically arises from behaving in a manner inconsistent with one's own beliefs, because this behavior causes self-doubt. But in collectivist cultures, dissonance typically arises when such behavior causes the person to worry about one's reputation with others (Kitayama et al., 2004). Cultural values also operate in shaping dissonance-reducing strategies. For example, people from individualistic cultures can reduce the unpleasant feelings that accompany

in review

FORMING AND CHANGING ATTITUDES

Type of Influence	Description
Social learning and conditioning	Attitudes are usually formed through observation of how others behave and speak about an attitude object, as well as through classical and operant conditioning.
Elaboration likelihood model	People change attitudes through either a central or peripheral route, depending on factors such as personal involvement.
Cognitive dissonance	Holding inconsistent cognitions can motivate attitude change.

?

1. According to the elaboration likelihood model, people are more likely to pay close attention to the content and logic of a persuasive message if the _____ route to attitude change has been activated.

2. Holding attitudes that are similar to those of your friends illustrates the importance of _____ in attitude formation

3. According to cognitive dissonance theory, we tend to reduce conflict between attitudes and behaviors by changing our _____.

dissonance by affirming their value as unique individuals, whereas people from collectivist cultures can reduce the same kind of feelings by affirming the value of the groups to which they belong (Hoshino-Browne et al., 2005). ("In Review: Forming and Changing Attitudes" summarizes some of the main processes through which attitudes are formed and changed.)

Prejudice and Stereotypes

▶ **How does prejudice develop?**

All of the principles behind impression formation, attribution, and attitudes come together in prejudice and stereotypes. **Stereotypes** are the perceptions, beliefs, and expectations a person has about members of some group. They are schemas about entire groups of people (Dion, 2003). Usually, they involve the false assumption that all members of a group share the same characteristics. The characteristics that make up the stereotype can be positive, but more often they are negative. The most prevalent and powerful stereotypes focus on observable personal attributes, particularly ethnicity, gender, and age (Operario & Fiske, 2001).

The stereotypes people hold can be so ingrained that their effects on behavior can be automatic and unconscious (Banaji, Lemm, & Carpenter, 2001; Blair, Judd, & Fallman, 2004). In one study, for example, European American and African American participants played a video game in which white or black men suddenly appeared on a screen, holding an object that might be a weapon (Correll et al., 2002; see Figure 14.4). The participants had to immediately "shoot" armed men but not unarmed ones. Under this time pressure, participants' errors were not random. If they "shot" an unarmed man, he was more likely to be black than white; when they failed to "shoot" an armed man, he was more likely to be white than black. These differences appeared in both European American and African American participants, but was most pronounced among those who held the strongest cultural stereotypes about blacks.

Stereotyping often leads to **prejudice,** which is a positive or negative attitude toward an individual based simply on that individual's membership in some group (Dion, 2003). The word *prejudice* means "to prejudge." Many theorists believe that prejudice, like other attitudes, has cognitive, affective, and behavioral components. Stereotyped thinking is the cognitive component of prejudicial attitudes. The hatred, admiration, anger, and other feelings people have about stereotyped groups constitute the affective component. The behavioral component of prejudice involves **discrimination,** which is differing treatment of individuals who belong to different groups.

Theories of Prejudice and Stereotyping

Prejudice and stereotyping may occur for several reasons. Let's consider three explanatory theories, each of which has been supported by research and accounts for many instances of stereotyping and prejudice.

Motivational Theories For some people, prejudice serves to meet certain needs and increases their sense of security. This idea was first proposed by Theodor W. Adorno and his associates more than fifty years ago (Adorno et al., 1950) and was elaborated more recently by Bob Altemeyer (1996, 2004). These researchers suggest that prejudice is especially likely among people who display a personality trait called *authoritarianism.* According to Altemeyer, authoritarianism is composed of three main elements: (1) acceptance of conventional or traditional values, (2) willingness to unquestioningly follow the orders of authority figures, and (3) an inclination to act aggressively toward individuals or groups identified by authority figures as threats to the person's values or well-being. In fact, people with an authoritarian orientation tend to view the world as a threatening place (Winter, 1996). One way to protect themselves from the

LINKAGES
Can subconscious processes alter our reaction to people?
(a link to Consciousness)

FIGURE 14.4

The Impact of Stereotypes on Behavior

learn by doing When these men suddenly appeared on a video screen, participants were supposed to "shoot" them, but only if they appeared to be armed (Correll et al., 2002). Stereotypes about whether white men or black men are more likely to be armed significantly affected the errors made by participants in firing their video game "weapons." Cover these photos with a pair of index cards; then ask a few friends to watch as you show each photo, one at a time, for just an instant, before covering it again. Then ask your friends to say whether either man appeared to be armed. Was one individual more often seen as armed? If so, which one?

SCHEMAS AND STEREOTYPES The use of schemas to assign certain people to certain categories can be helpful when deciding who is a customer and who is a store employee, but it can also lead to inaccurate stereotypes. After the September 11, 2001, terrorist attacks on New York and Washington, D.C., many people began to think of all Muslims as potential terrorists and to discriminate against them. This false assumption and the problems it has created for Muslims in the United States was one of the many awful side effects of the terrorist attacks.

threats they perceive all around them is to strongly identify with people like themselves—their *in-group*—and to reject, dislike, and maybe even punish people from groups that are different from their own (Cottrell & Neuberg, 2005). Looking down on, and discriminating against, members of these *out-groups*—such as gay men and lesbians, African Americans, or Muslims, for example—may help authoritarian people feel safer and better about themselves (Haddock & Zanna, 1998).

Another motivational explanation of prejudice involves the concept of social identity discussed earlier. Recall that whether or not they display authoritarianism, most people are motivated to identify with their in-group and tend to see it as better than other groups (Brewer & Pierce, 2005). As a result, members of an in-group often see all members of out-groups as less attractive and less socially acceptable than members of the in-group and may thus treat them badly (Jackson, 2002). In other words, prejudice may result when people's motivation to enhance their own self-esteem causes them to disrespect other people.

Cognitive Theories Stereotyping and prejudice may also result from the thought processes that people use in dealing with the world. There are so many other people, so many situations in which we meet them, and so many behaviors that others might display that we cannot possibly attend to and remember them all. Therefore, people must use schemas and other cognitive shortcuts to organize and make sense of their social world (Moskowitz, 2005). Often these cognitive processes provide accurate and useful summaries of other people, but sometimes they lead to inaccurate stereotypes.

For example, one effective way to deal with social complexity is to group people into *social categories*. Rather than remembering every detail about everyone we have ever encountered, we tend to put other people into categories such as doctor, senior citizen, Republican, student, Italian, and the like (Dovidio, Kawakami, & Gaertner, 2000). To further simplify perception of these categories, we tend to see group members as being quite similar to one another. This tendency can be seen in the fact that members of one ethnic group may find it harder to distinguish among specific faces in other ethnic groups than in their own (Anthony, Cooper, & Mullen, 1992; Michel et al., 2006). People also tend to assume that all members of a different group hold the same beliefs and values and that those beliefs and values differ from those of their own group (Dion, 2003). Finally, because particularly noticeable stimuli tend to draw a lot of attention, rude behavior by even a few members of an easily identified ethnic group may lead people to see an *illusory correlation* between rudeness and ethnicity (Hamilton & Sherman, 1994). As a result, they may incorrectly believe that all members of that group are rude.

stereotypes False assumptions that all members of some group share the same characteristics.

prejudice A positive or negative attitude toward people in certain groups.

discrimination Differential treatment of people in certain groups; the behavioral component of prejudice.

FIGHTING ETHNIC PREJUDICE Negative attitudes about members of ethnic groups are often based on negative personal experiences or on the negative experiences and attitudes people hear about from others. Cooperative contact between equals can help promote mutual respect and reduce ethnic prejudice.

Learning Theories Like other attitudes, prejudice can be learned. Some prejudice is learned as a result of personal conflicts with members of different groups, but people also develop negative attitudes toward groups with whom they have had little or no contact. Learning theories suggest that children can pick up prejudices just by watching and listening to parents, peers, and others (Rohan & Zanna, 1996). There may even be a form of biopreparedness (described in the learning chapter) that makes us especially likely to learn to fear people who are strangers or who look different from us (Olson et al., 2001). Movies and television also portray ethnic or other groups in ways that teach stereotypes and prejudice (Brehm et al., 2005). One study revealed that local news coverage often gives the impression that African Americans are responsible for a higher percentage of crimes than is actually the case (Romer, Jamieson, & deCoteau, 1998). No wonder so many young children know about the supposed negative characteristics of other ethnic groups, sometimes long before they ever meet people in those groups (Baron & Banaji, 2006; Quintana, 1998).

Reducing Prejudice

One clear implication of the cognitive and learning theories of prejudice and stereotyping is that members of one group are often ignorant or misinformed about the characteristics of people in other groups. Before 1954, for example, most black and white schoolchildren in the United States knew very little about one another because they went to separate schools. Then the Supreme Court declared that segregated public schools should be prohibited. In doing so, the court created a real-life test of the **contact hypothesis,** which states that stereotypes and prejudice toward a group will decrease as contact with that group increases (Pettigrew & Tropp, 2006).

Did the desegregation of U.S. schools confirm the contact hypothesis? In a few schools, integration was followed by a decrease in prejudice, but in most places, either no change occurred or prejudice actually increased (Oskamp & Schultz, 1998). However, these results did not necessarily disprove the contact hypothesis. In-depth studies of schools with successful desegregation suggested that contact alone was not enough. Integration reduced prejudice only when certain social conditions were created (Pettigrew & Tropp, 2006). First, members of the two groups had to be of roughly equal social and economic status. Second, school authorities had to promote cooperation and interdependence between ethnic groups by having members of the two groups work together on projects that required reliance on one another to achieve success. Third, the contact between group members had to occur on a one-to-one basis. It was only when *individuals* got to know each other that the errors contained in stereotypes became apparent. Finally, the members of each group had to be seen as typical and not unusual in any significant way. When these four conditions were met, the children's attitudes toward one another became more positive.

Elliot Aronson (Aronson & Patnoe, 2000) describes a teaching strategy, called the *jigsaw technique,* that helps create these conditions. Children from several ethnic groups must work together on a team to complete a task, such as writing a report about a famous person in history. Each child learns a separate piece of information about this person, such as place of birth or greatest achievement, then provides this information to the team (Aronson, 1990). Studies show that children from various ethnic groups who take part in the jigsaw technique and other cooperative learning experiences display substantial reductions in prejudice toward other groups (e.g., Aronson, 1997). The success reported in these studies has greatly increased the popularity of cooperative learning exercises in U.S. classrooms. Such exercises may not eliminate all aspects of ethnic prejudice in children, but they seem to be a step in the right direction.

Can friendly, cooperative, interdependent contact reduce the more entrenched forms of prejudice seen in adults? It may. When equal-status adults from different ethnic groups work jointly toward a common goal, bias and distrust can be reduced, particularly among those in ethnic majority groups (Tropp & Pettigrew, 2005). This is especially true if they come to see themselves as members of the same group rather than as belonging to opposing groups (Dovidio, Kawakami, & Gaertner, 2000; Fiske, 2000).

contact hypothesis The idea that stereotypes and prejudice toward a group will diminish as contact with the group increases.

learn by doing

PROXIMITY AND LIKING
Research on environmental factors in attraction suggests that, barring bad first impressions, the more often we make contact with someone—as neighbors, classmates, or co-workers, for example—the more we tend to like that person. Does this principle apply in your life? To find out, think about how and where you met each of your closest friends. If you can think of cases in which proximity did not lead to liking, what do you think interfered with the formation of friendship?

The challenge to be met in creating such cooperative experiences in the real world is that the participants must be of equal status—a challenge made more difficult in many countries by the status differences that still exist between ethnic groups (Dixon, Durrheim, & Tredoux, 2005; Kenworthy et al., 2006).

In the final analysis, contact can provide only part of the solution to the problems of stereotyping, prejudice, and discrimination. To reduce ethnic prejudice, we must develop additional techniques to address the social cognitions and perceptions that lie at the core of bigotry and hatred toward people who are different from ourselves (Monteith, Zuwerink, & Devine, 1994). Altering these mental processes will be difficult because, as we saw earlier, they can operate both consciously and unconsciously, causing even those who do not see themselves as prejudiced to discriminate against individuals who are different (Banaji et al., 2001; Uleman, Blader, & Todorov, 2005). However, recent research suggests that it may be possible to change even unconscious forms of stereotyping and prejudice (Kawakami, Dovidio, & van Kamp, 2005; Plant & Peruche, 2005; Wheeler & Fiske, 2005).

Interpersonal Attraction

▶ **What factors affect who likes whom?**

Research on prejudice suggests some of the reasons why people may come to dislike or even hate other people. An equally fascinating aspect of social cognition is why people like or love other people. Folklore tells us that "opposites attract" but also that "birds of a feather flock together." Each statement is partly true, but neither is entirely accurate in all cases. We begin our coverage of interpersonal attraction by discussing the factors that draw people toward one another. We then examine how liking sometimes develops into more intimate relationships.

Keys to Attraction

Whether you like someone or not depends partly on situational factors and partly on personal characteristics.

The Environment   One of the most important determinants of attraction is simple physical proximity (Berscheid & Reis, 1998). As long as you do not initially dislike a person, your liking for that person will increase with additional contact (Brehm et al., 2005). This proximity phenomenon—another example of the *mere-exposure effect* mentioned earlier—helps account for why next-door neighbors are usually more likely to become friends than people who live farther from one another. Chances are, most of your friends are people you met as neighbors, co-workers, or classmates (Liben-Nowell et al., 2005).

The circumstances under which people first meet also influence attraction. You are much more likely to be attracted to a stranger if you meet in comfortable, as opposed to uncomfortable, physical conditions. Similarly, if you receive a reward in the presence of a stranger, the chances are greater that you will like that stranger, even if the stranger is not the one giving the reward (Clark & Pataki, 1995). In one study, for example, an experimenter judged one person's creativity while another person watched. Compared with those who received a negative evaluation, participants who were evaluated positively tended to like the observer more (Griffitt & Guay, 1969). At least among strangers, then, liking can occur through associating someone with something pleasant.

Similarity   People also tend to like those they perceive as similar to themselves on variables such as age, religion, smoking or drinking habits or being a "morning" or "evening" person (Buston & Emlen, 2003; Rushton & Bons, 2005). Similarity in attitudes is another important influence on attraction (Brehm et al., 2005).

FIGURE **14.5**

Balanced and Imbalanced Relationships

Here are some common examples of balanced and imbalanced relationships among three people. The plus and minus signs refer to liking and disliking, respectively. Balanced relationships are comfortable and harmonious; imbalanced ones often bring conflict.

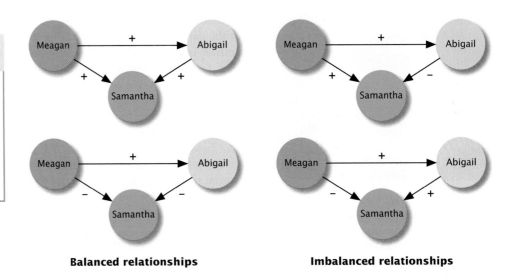

Balanced relationships   **Imbalanced relationships**

An especially good predictor of liking is similarity in attitudes about mutual acquaintances, because in general, people prefer relationships that are *balanced*. As illustrated in Figure 14.5, if Meagan likes Abigail, the relationship is balanced as long as they agree on their evaluation of a third person, regardless of whether they like or dislike that third person. However, the relationship will be imbalanced if Meagan and Abigail disagree on their evaluation of a third person.

One reason why we like people whose attitudes are similar to our own is that we expect such people to think highly of us (Condon & Crano, 1988). It's hard to say, though, whether attraction is a cause or an effect of similarity. For example, you might like someone because his attitudes are similar to yours, but it is also possible that as a result of liking him, your attitudes will become more similar to his (Davis & Rusbult, 2001). Even if your own attitudes do not change, you may change your perceptions of the liked person's attitudes such that those attitudes now seem more similar to yours (Brehm, 1992).

Physical Attractiveness   Physical characteristics are another important factor in attraction, particularly in the early stages of a relationship. From preschool through adulthood, physical attractiveness is a key to popularity with members of both sexes (Langlois et al., 2000; Lemly, 2000). Consistent with the **matching hypothesis** of interpersonal attraction, however, people tend to date, marry, or form other committed relationships with those who are similar to themselves in physical attractiveness (Yela & Sangrador, 2001). One possible reason for this outcome is that although people tend to be most attracted to those with the greatest physical appeal, they also want to avoid being rejected by such individuals. So it may be compromise, not preference, that leads people to pair off with those who are roughly equivalent to themselves in physical attractiveness (Carli, Ganley, & Pierce-Otay, 1991).

Intimate Relationships and Love

There is much about intimate relationships that psychologists do not and may never understand, but they are learning all the time. For example, evolutionary psychologists suggest that men and women employ different strategies to ensure the survival of their genes and that each gender looks for different attributes in a potential mate (Kenrick et al., 2005; Li & Kenrick, 2006; Schmitt, 2003). The physical appearance of a partner tends to be more important to men than to women, whereas the partner's intelligence tends to be more important to women than to men (Buss, 2004; see Figure 14.6).

matching hypothesis   The notion that people are most likely to form committed relationships with others who are similar to themselves in physical attractiveness.

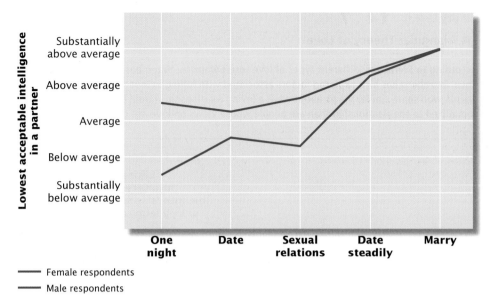

Sex Differences in Date and Mate Preferences

According to evolutionary psychologists, men and women have developed different strategies for selecting sexual partners. These psychologists say that women became more selective than men because they can have relatively few children and want a partner who is best able to help support those children. Here are some data that support this idea. When asked about the intelligence of people they would choose for one-night stands, dating, and sexual relationships, women preferred much smarter partners than men did. Only when the choices concerned steady dating and marriage did the men's preference for bright partners equal that of the women. Critics of the evolutionary approach explain such sex differences as reflecting learned social norms and expectations of the way men and women should behave (Eagly & Wood, 1999; Miller, Putcha-Bhagavatula, & Pedersen, 2002).

Source: Kenrick et al. (1993).

Intimate Relationships Eventually, people who are attracted to each other usually become *interdependent,* which means that the thoughts, emotions, and behaviors of one person affect the thoughts, emotions, and behaviors of the other (Rusbult, Arriaga, & Agnew, 2001). Interdependence is one of the defining characteristics of intimate relationships (Agnew et al., 1998).

Another key component of successful intimate relationships is *commitment,* which is the extent to which each person is psychologically attached to the relationship and wants to remain in it (Rusbult & Van Lange, 1996). People feel committed to a relationship when they are satisfied with the rewards they receive from it, when they have invested significant tangible and intangible resources in it, and when they have few attractive alternative relationships available to them (Bui, Peplau, & Hill, 1996).

Analyzing Love Although some people think love is simply a strong form of liking, recent research suggests that romantic love and liking are quite separate emotions, at least in the sense that they are associated with differing patterns of brain chemistry and brain activity (Aron et al., 2005; Emanuele et al., 2006). And although romantic love and sexual desire are often experienced together, they, too, seem to be separate emotions associated with different patterns of physiological arousal (Diamond, 2004). Further, most theorists agree that there are several different types of love (Brehm et al., 2005). One widely accepted view distinguishes between passionate (romantic) love and companionate love (Hendrick & Hendrick, 2003). *Passionate love* is intense, arousing, and marked by both strong physical attraction and deep emotional attachment. Sexual feelings are intense, and thoughts of the other intrude on each person's awareness frequently. *Companionate love* is less arousing but psychologically more intimate. It is marked by mutual concern for the welfare of the other and a willingness to disclose personal information and feelings. People who experience companionate love seem especially satisfied with their lives (Brehm et al. 2005; Hendrick & Hendrick, 2003; Kim & Hatfield, 2004).

Robert Sternberg (1988a, 1997a) has offered an even broader analysis of love. According to his *triangular theory,* the three basic components of love are passion, intimacy, and commitment (see Figure 14.7). Various combinations of these components result in various types of love. For example, Sternberg suggests that *romantic love* involves a high degree of passion and intimacy, yet lacks substantial commitment to the other person. *Companionate love* is marked by a great deal of intimacy and commitment but little passion. *Consummate love* is the most complete and satisfying. It is the most complete because it includes a high level of all three components. It is

FIGURE **14.7**

A Triangular Theory of Love

According to Sternberg, different types of love result when the three basic components in his triangular theory occur in different combinations. Sternberg has also explored factors associated with falling in love (Sternberg, Hojjat & Barnes, 2001). Preliminary results suggest that people who share similar views about what a loving relationship should be like are much more likely to fall in love with each other and remain committed to the relationship than are people whose views on love are dissimilar.

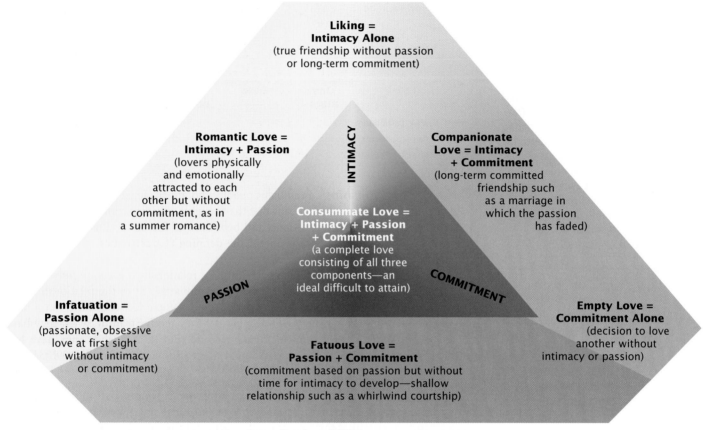

Source: Sternberg (1988a).

the most satisfying because the relationship is likely to fulfill many of the needs of each partner.

Cultural factors have a strong influence on the way people think about love and marriage. In North America and the United Kingdom, for example, the vast majority of people believe that they should love the person they marry. By contrast, in India and Pakistan, about half the people interviewed in a survey said they would marry someone they did not love if that person had other qualities that they desired (Levine et al., 1995). In Russia, only 40 percent of respondents said that they married for love. Most reported marrying because of loneliness, shared interests, or an unplanned pregnancy (Baron & Byrne, 1994).

Strong and Weak Marriages   Long-term research on successful and unsuccessful marriages suggests that premarital attitudes, feelings, and perceptions can predict marital success. For example, couples who have a close, intimate relationship, similar attitudes, and realistic views of each other's strengths and weaknesses when they are dating are more likely than other couples to remain married (Hill & Peplau, 1998; Neff & Karney, 2005).

Among married couples, women—but not men—generally tend to be more satisfied with their marriages when the partners talk a lot about the relationship (Acitelli,

1992). Partners in successful marriages also tend to share each other's view of themselves and the other, even if that view is a negative one (Swann, De La Ronde, & Hixon, 1994). The perception that the relationship is fair and equitable also increases marital satisfaction (Grote & Clark, 2001). After the birth of a first child, for example, many wives find that they have much more work than they had anticipated. If their husbands do not share this work to the degree they had expected, wives' marital satisfaction tends to decrease (Hackel & Ruble, 1992; McNulty & Karney, 2004).

One particularly interesting line of research suggests that even brief observations of couples' interactions can predict whether couples will divorce and when (Driver & Gottman, 2004). Among couples who divorced relatively soon after marriage, the partners tended to express both positive and negative feelings toward one another, but they were unable to control the way they expressed these feelings, especially the negative ones. Communication became increasingly hurtful and eventually broke down (Driver et al., 2003). A different picture emerged, however, in couples who divorced after many years of marriage. These people did not necessarily express negative emotions toward one another. They simply became less and less likely to communicate *any* feelings. The increasing emotional distance between the spouses created a sense of isolation that eventually led to divorce (Gottman & Levenson, 2002). These findings can help us understand why people in a long, and apparently strong, marriage might suddenly announce that they are divorcing—and why they may remain friends afterward. These people may still like each other, but no longer love each other.

Social Influence

▶ **What social rules shape our behavior?**

So far, we have considered social cognition, the mental processes associated with people's perceptions of, and reactions to, other people. Let's now explore *social influence,* the process through which individuals and groups directly and indirectly influence a person's thoughts, feelings, and behavior. Research has shown, for example, that suicide rates increase following well-publicized suicides and that murder rates increase after well-publicized homicides (Jamieson, Jamieson, & Romer, 2003). Do these correlations mean that media coverage of violence triggers similar violence? As described in the chapter on learning, televised violence can play a causal role in aggressive behavior, but there are other reasons to believe that when murders or suicides become media events, they stimulate imitators. For one thing, many of the people who kill themselves after a widely reported suicide are similar to the original victim in some respect (Cialdini, 2001). For example, after German television reported a story about a young man who committed suicide by jumping in front of a train, there was a dramatic increase in the number of young German men who committed suicide in the same way (Schmidtke & Hafner, 1988). This phenomenon—known as "copycat" violence—illustrates the effects of social influence.

Social Norms

The most common, yet subtle, form of social influence is communicated through social norms. **Norms** are learned, socially based rules that tell people what they should or should not do in various situations (Cialdini & Goldstein, 2004). Parents, teachers, members of the clergy, peers, and other agents of culture transmit these norms. Because of the power of norms, people often follow them automatically. In North America and Britain, for example, norms tell us that we should get in line to buy a movie ticket rather than crowd around the box office window. They also lead us to expect that others will do the same. By informing people of what is expected of them and others, norms make social situations clearer, more predictable, and more comfortable.

One particularly powerful norm is *reciprocity,* the tendency to respond to others as they have acted toward you (Cialdini & Goldstein, 2004). Restaurant servers often take

norms Learned, socially based rules that prescribe what people should or should not do in various situations.

DEINDIVIDUATION   Robes, hoods, and group rituals help create deindividuation in these Ku Klux Klansmen by focusing their attention on membership in their organization and on its values. The hoods also hide their identities, which reduces their sense of personal responsibility and accountability and makes it easier for them to engage in hate crimes and other cowardly acts of bigotry. Deindividuation operates in other groups, too, ranging from lynch mobs and terrorist cells to political protesters and urban rioters. Through deindividuation, people appear to become "part of the herd," and they may do things that they might not do on their own (Spears et al., 2001).

advantage of this norm by leaving some candy with the bill. Customers who receive this gift tend to reciprocate by leaving a larger tip than customers who don't get candy (Strohmetz et al., 2002). The reciprocity norm probably exists in every culture, but other norms are not universal (Miller, 2001). For instance, people around the world differ greatly in terms of the physical distance they keep between themselves and others while talking. People from South America usually stand much closer to each other than do people from North America. And as suggested in the chapter on psychological disorders, behavior considered normal and friendly in one culture may be seen as offensive, or even abnormal, in another.

The social influence exerted by norms creates orderly social behavior. But social influence can also lead to a breakdown in order. For example, **deindividuation** is a psychological state in which a person becomes "submerged in the group" and loses the sense of individuality (Cialdini & Goldstein, 2004). When people experience deindividuation, they become emotionally aroused and feel intense closeness with their group. This increased awareness of group membership may lead people to follow the group's norms, even if those norms promote antisocial behavior (Spears et al., 2001). Normally mild-mannered adults may throw rocks at police during political protests, and youngsters who would not ordinarily commit hate crimes have done so as part of gangs. Such behavior becomes more extreme as people feel less identifiable. An analysis of newspaper accounts of lynchings in the United States over a fifty-year period showed that larger lynch mobs were more savage and vicious than smaller ones (Mullen, 1986). Deindividuation provides an example of how, given the right circumstances, quite normal people can engage in destructive, even violent, behavior.

Conformity and Compliance

When people change their behavior or beliefs to match those of other members of a group, they are said to conform. **Conformity** occurs as a result of unspoken group pressure, real or imagined (Cialdini & Goldstein, 2004). You probably have experienced group pressure when everyone around you stands to applaud a performance that you thought was not particularly great. You may conform by standing as well, though no one told you to do so; the group's behavior creates a silent, but influential, pressure to follow suit. **Compliance,** in contrast, occurs when people adjust their behavior because of a request. The request can be clear and direct, such as "Please do me favor," or it can

deindividuation   A psychological state occurring in group members that results in loss of individuality and a tendency to do things not normally done when alone.

conformity   Changing one's behavior or beliefs to match those of others, generally as a result of real or imagined, though unspoken, group pressure.

compliance   Adjusting one's behavior because of a direct request.

Standard line

(A)

Test lines

(B)

FIGURE **14.8**

Types of Stimulus Lines Used in Experiments by Asch

learn by doing Participants in Asch's experiments saw a new set of lines like these on each trial. The middle line in Part B matches the one in Part A, but when several of Asch's assistants claimed that a different line matched, so did many of the participants. Try re-creating this experiment with four friends. Secretly ask three of them to say that the test line on the left matches the standard line; then show this drawing to all four. Did the fourth person conform to the group norm? If not, do you think it was something about the person, the length of the incorrect line chosen, or both that led to nonconformity? Would conformity be more likely if the first three people had chosen the line on the right? (Read on for more about this possibility.)

be more subtle—as when someone simply looks at you in a way that lets you know the person needs a favor.

Conformity and compliance are usually generated by spoken or unspoken norms. In a classic experiment, Muzafer Sherif (1937) charted the formation of a group norm by taking advantage of a visual illusion: If you look at a fixed point of light in a pitch-dark room, the light will appear to move. Estimates of how far the light seems to move tend to stay the same over time if an observer is alone. But when Sherif tested several people at once, asking each person to say aloud how far the light moved on repeated trials, their estimates tended to converge; they had established a group norm. Even more important, when individuals who had been in the group were later tested alone, they continued to be influenced by this norm.

In another classic experiment, Solomon Asch (1956) explored what people do when faced with a norm that is obviously wrong. The participants in this experiment saw a standard line like the one in Figure 14.8(A); then they saw a display like that in Figure 14.8(B). Their task was to pick out the line in the display that was the same length as the one they had first been shown.

Each participant performed this task in a small group of people who posed as fellow participants but who were actually the experimenter's assistants. There were two conditions. In the control condition, the real participant responded first. In the experimental condition, the participant did not respond until after the other people did. The experimenter's assistants chose the correct response on 6 trials, but on the other 12 trials they all gave the same, obviously incorrect, response. So, on 12 trials, each participant was confronted with a "social reality" created by a group norm that conflicted with the physical reality created by what the person could clearly see. Only 5 percent of the participants in the control condition ever made a mistake on this easy perceptual task. However, among participants who heard the assistants' incorrect responses before giving their own, about 70 percent made at least one error by conforming to the group norm. An analysis of 133 studies conducted in seventeen countries reveals that conformity in Asch-type situations has declined somewhat in the United States since the 1950s but that it still occurs. It is especially likely in collectivist cultures, where conformity to group norms is emphasized (Cialdini et al., 2001).

Why Do People Conform? Why did so many people in Asch's experiment give incorrect responses when they were capable of near-perfect performance? One possibility, called *public conformity,* is that they didn't really believe in their responses but gave them simply because it was the socially desirable thing to do. Another possibility is that the participants experienced *private acceptance.* Perhaps they used the other people's responses as a guide, became convinced that their own perceptions were wrong, and actually changed their minds. Which possibility is more likely? Morton Deutsch and Harold Gerard (1955) reasoned that if people still conformed even when the other group members couldn't hear their response, then Asch's findings must reflect private acceptance, not just public conformity. Actually, although conformity does decrease when people respond privately, it doesn't disappear (Deutsch & Gerard, 1955). So people sometimes say things in public that they don't believe in, but hearing other people's responses also appears to influence their private beliefs (Moscovici, 1985).

Why are group norms so powerful? Research suggests several influential factors (Cialdini & Goldstein, 2004). First, people are motivated to be correct, and norms provide information about what is right and wrong. This factor may help explain why some extremely disturbed or distressed people consider stories about suicide to be "social proof" that self-destruction is a reasonable way out of their problems (Cialdini, 2001). Second, people want others to like them, so they may seek favor by conforming to the norms that those others have established. Third, conforming to group norms may increase a person's sense of self-worth, especially if the group is valued or has high prestige (Cialdini & Goldstein, 2004). The process may occur without our awareness (Lakin & Chartrand, 2003). For example, observations of interviews by Larry King, the television talk show host, revealed that he tended to imitate the speech patterns of

MASS CONFORMITY   The faithful who gather at Mecca, at the Vatican, and at other holy places around the world exemplify the power of religion and other social forces to produce conformity to group norms.

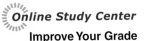
Online Study Center

Improve Your Grade

Tutorial: Conformity and the Asch experiment

high-status guests but not low-status ones (Gregory & Webster, 1996). Finally, norms affect the distribution of social reward and punishment (Cialdini, 1995). From childhood on, people in many cultures learn that going along with group norms is good and earns rewards. (These positive outcomes presumably help compensate for not always saying or doing exactly what we please.) People also learn that breaking a norm may bring punishments ranging from scoldings for small transgressions to imprisonment for violation of norms that have been translated into laws.

When Do People Conform?   People do not always conform to group influence. In the Asch studies, for example, nearly 30 percent of the participants did not go along with the assistants' obviously wrong judgments. Countless experiments have probed the question of what combinations of people and circumstances do and do not lead to conformity.

For example, *ambiguity,* or uncertainty, is important in determining how much conformity will occur. As the features of a situation become less clear, people rely more and more on others' opinions, and conformity to a group norm becomes increasingly likely (Cialdini & Goldstein, 2004). You can demonstrate this aspect of conformity on any street corner. First, create an ambiguous situation by having several people look at the sky or the top of a building. When passersby ask what is going on, be sure everyone excitedly reports seeing something interesting, but fleeting—perhaps a faint flashing light or a tiny, shiny high-flying object. If you are especially successful, conforming newcomers will begin persuading other passersby that there is something fascinating to be seen.

If ambiguity contributes so much to conformity, though, why did so many of Asch's participants conform to a judgment that was clearly wrong? The answer has to do with the *unanimous* nature of the group's judgment and the number of people expressing that judgment. Specifically, people experience intense pressure to conform as long as the rest of the group all agree with each other. If even one other person in the group disagrees with the majority view, conformity drops greatly. When Asch (1951) arranged for just one assistant to disagree with the others, fewer than 10 percent of the real participants conformed. Once unanimity is broken, it becomes much easier to disagree with the majority, even if the other nonconformist does not agree with the person's own view (Turner, 1991).

Conformity also depends on the *size of the majority.* Asch (1955) demonstrated this phenomenon by varying the number of assistants in the group from one to fifteen.

Conformity to incorrect norms grew as the number of people in the group increased. However, most of the growth in conformity occurred as the size of the majority rose from one to about three or four members. This effect probably occurs because pressure to conform has already reached a peak after someone has heard three or four people agree. Hearing more people confirm the majority view has little additional social impact (Latané, 1981).

Conformity can also occur through *minority influence,* by which a minority of group members influence the behavior or beliefs of the majority (Kenrick et al., 2005). This phenomenon is less common than majority influence, but when members of a numerical minority are established group members, agree with one another, and persist in their views, they can be influential (Martin, Gardikiotis, & Hewstone, 2002). Perhaps because the views of a numerical minority are examined especially carefully (Martin & Hewstone 2003), minority-influenced change often takes a while to occur. And these changes may involve only a moderate adjustment of the majority view (Alvaro & Crano, 1997; Crano & Chen, 1998).

Does gender affect conformity? Early research suggested that women conform more than men, but the gender difference stemmed mainly from the fact that the tasks used in those studies were often more familiar to men than to women. This fact is important because people are especially likely to conform when they are faced with an unfamiliar situation (Cialdini & Goldstein, 2004). No male-female differences in conformity have been found in research using materials that are equally familiar to both genders (Maupin & Fisher, 1989). So why do some people still perceive women as more conforming than men, despite evidence to the contrary? Part of the answer may lie in their perception of the relative social status of men and women. People who think of women as having lower social status than men in most social situations are likely to see women as easier to influence, even though men and women conform equally often (Eagly, 1987).

Creating Compliance   In the experiments just described, the participants experienced psychological pressure to conform to the views or actions of others, even though no one specifically asked them to do so. In contrast, *compliance* involves changing what you say or do because of a direct request.

How is compliance brought about? Many people believe that the direct approach is always best: If you want something, ask for it. But salespeople, political strategists, social psychologists, and other experts have learned that often the best way to get something is to ask for something else. Three examples of this strategy are the foot-in-the-door technique, the door-in-the-face procedure, and the low-ball approach.

The *foot-in-the-door technique* works by getting a person to agree to small requests and then working up to larger ones. In the original experiment on this strategy, homeowners were asked to do one of two things. Some were asked to allow a large, unattractive "Drive Carefully" sign to be placed on their front lawns. About 17 percent of the people approached in this way complied with the request. In the foot-in-the-door condition, however, homeowners were first asked only to sign a petition supporting laws aimed at reducing traffic accidents. Several weeks later, when a different person asked these same homeowners to put the "Drive Carefully" sign on their lawns, 55 percent of them complied (Freedman & Fraser, 1966).

Why should the granting of small favors lead to granting larger ones? First, people are usually far more likely to comply with a request that doesn't cost much in time, money, effort, or inconvenience. Second, complying with a small request makes people think of themselves as being committed to the cause or issue involved (Burger & Guadagno, 2003). In the study just described, participants who signed the petition might have thought, "I must care enough about traffic safety to do something about it." Compliance with the higher-cost request (displaying the sign) increased because it was consistent with these people's self-perceptions and past actions (Burger & Guadagno, 2003).

The foot-in-the-door technique can be amazingly effective. Steven Sherman (1980) created a 700 percent increase in the rate at which people volunteered to work for a

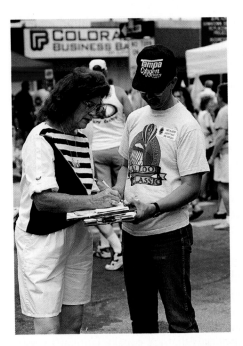

applying psychology

PROMOTING COMPLIANCE Have you ever been asked to sign a petition favoring some political, social, or economic cause? Supporters of these causes know that people who comply with this small request are the best people to contact later with requests to do more. Complying with larger requests is made more likely because it is consistent with the signer's initial commitment to the cause. If you were contacted after signing a petition, did you agree to donate money or become a volunteer?

charity simply by first getting them to say that, in a hypothetical situation, they would volunteer if asked. For some companies, the foot in the door is a request that potential customers merely answer a few questions; the request to buy something comes later. Others offer a small gift, or "door opener," as salespeople call it. Acceptance of the gift not only gives the salesperson a foot in the door but also may activate the reciprocity norm: Many people who get something for free feel obligated to reciprocate by buying something—especially if the request to do so is delayed for a while (Cialdini, 2001; Guadagno et al., 2001).

The *door-in-the-face procedure* offers a second effective way of obtaining compliance (Cialdini, 2001; Pascual & Guéguen, 2005). This strategy begins with a request for a favor that is likely to be refused. The person making the request then concedes that this favor was too much to ask and substitutes a lesser alternative—which is what the person really wanted in the first place! Because the person appears willing to compromise, and because the second request seems small in comparison with the first one, it is more likely to be granted than if it had been made at the outset. The door-in-the-face strategy is at the heart of bargaining among political groups and between labor and management.

The third technique, called the *low-ball approach,* is commonly used by car dealers and other businesses (Cialdini, 2001). The first step in this strategy is to get people to say that they will do something, such as to purchase a car. Once this commitment is made, the cost of fulfilling it is increased, often because of an "error" in computing the car's price. Why do buyers end up paying much more than originally planned for "low-balled" items? Apparently, once people commit themselves to do something, they feel obligated to follow through, especially when the initial commitment was made in public and when the person who obtained that commitment also makes the higher-cost request (Burger & Cornelius, 2003).

Obedience

▶ **How far will people go in obeying authority?**

Compliance involves a change in behavior in response to a request. In the case of **obedience,** the behavior change comes in response to a *demand* from an authority figure (Blass, 2004). In the 1960s, Stanley Milgram developed a laboratory procedure at Yale University to study obedience. For his first experiment, he used newspaper ads to find forty male volunteer participants. They ranged in age from twenty to fifty, lived in the local community, and included professionals, white-collar businessmen, and unskilled workers (Milgram, 1963).

Imagine you are one of the people who answered the ad. When you arrive for the experiment, you join a fifty-year-old gentleman who has also volunteered and has been scheduled for the same session. The experimenter explains that the purpose of the experiment is to examine the effects of punishment on learning. One of you—the "teacher"—will help the "learner" remember a list of words by administering an electric shock whenever the learner makes a mistake. Then the experimenter turns to you and asks you to draw one of two cards out of a hat. Your card says, "TEACHER." You think to yourself that this must be your lucky day.

Now the learner is taken into another room and strapped into a chair, and, as illustrated in Figure 14.9, electrodes are attached to his arm. You are shown a shock generator with thirty switches. The experimenter explains that the switch on the far left administers a mild, 15-volt shock and that each succeeding switch increases the shock by 15 volts. The one on the far right delivers 450 volts. The far left section of the shock generator is labeled "Slight shock." Looking across the panel, you see "Moderate shock," "Very strong shock," and at the far right, "Danger—severe shock." The last two switches are ominously labeled "XXX." The experimenter explains that you, the teacher, will begin by reading a list of word pairs to the learner. Then you will go through the list again, presenting just

obedience Changing behavior in response to a demand from an authority figure.

FIGURE **14.9**

Studying Obedience in the Laboratory

In this photograph from Milgram's original experiment, a man is being strapped into a chair with electrodes on his arm. Although participants in the experiment didn't know it, the man was actually the experimenter's research assistant and received no shock.

one word of each pair. The learner will have to say which word went with it. After the first mistake, you are to throw the switch to deliver 15 volts of shock. Each time the learner makes another mistake, you are to increase the shock by 15 volts.

You begin, following the experimenter's instructions. But after the learner makes his fifth mistake and you throw the switch to give him 75 volts, you hear a loud moan. At 90 volts, the learner cries out in pain. At 150 volts, he screams and asks to be let out of the experiment. You look to the experimenter, who says, "Proceed with the next word."

No shock was actually delivered in Milgram's experiments. The learner was always an employee of the experimenter, and the moans and other sounds of pain came from a prerecorded tape. But you do not know that. What would you do in this situation? Suppose you continue and eventually deliver 180 volts. The learner screams that he cannot stand the pain any longer and starts banging on the wall. The experimenter says, "You have no other choice; you must go on." Would you continue? Would you keep going even when the learner begged to be let out of the experiment and then fell silent? Would you administer 450 volts of potentially deadly shock to an innocent stranger just because an experimenter demanded that you do so?

Figure 14.10 shows that only 5 participants in Milgram's experiment stopped before 300 volts and that 26 out of 40 (65 percent) went all the way to the 450-volt level. The decision to continue was difficult and stressful for the participants. Many protested repeatedly. But each time the experimenter told them to continue, they did so. Here is a partial transcript of what a typical participant said:

[After throwing the 180-volt switch]: *He can't stand it. I'm not going to kill that man in there. Do you hear him hollering? He's hollering. He can't stand it. What if something happens to him? I'm not going to get that man sick in there. He's hollering in there. Do you know what I mean? I mean, I refuse to take responsibility. He's getting hurt in there. . . . Too many left here. Geez, if he gets them wrong. There are too many of them left. I mean, who is going to take responsibility if anything happens to that gentleman?*

[After the experimenter accepts responsibility]: *All right. . . .*

[After administering 240 volts]: *Oh, no, you mean I've got to keep going up the scale? No sir, I'm not going to kill that man. I'm not going to give him 450 volts.*

[After the experimenter says, "The experiment requires that you go on"]: *I know it does, but that man is hollering in there, sir.*

This participant administered shock up to 450 volts (Milgram, 1974).

FIGURE **14.10**

Results of Milgram's Obedience Experiment

When Milgram asked a group of college students and a group of psychiatrists to predict how participants in his experiment would respond, they estimated that fewer than 2 percent would go all the way to 450 volts. In fact, 65 percent of the participants did so. What do you think you would have done in this situation?

Source: Milgram (1963).

PROXIMITY AND OBEDIENCE Milgram's research showed that close physical proximity to an authority figure is one of several factors that can enhance obedience to authority (Rada & Rogers, 1973). This proximity principle is used in the military, where no one is ever far away from the authority of a higher-ranking person.

Factors Affecting Obedience

Milgram had not expected so many people to deliver such apparently intense shocks. Was there something about his procedure that produced this high level of obedience? To find out, Milgram and other researchers varied the original procedure in a number of ways. The overall level of obedience to an authority figure was usually quite high, but the degree of obedience was affected by several aspects of the situation and procedure.

Experimenter Status and Prestige

One possibility is that the experimenter's status as a Yale University professor helped produce high levels of obedience in Milgram's original experiment (Blass & Schmitt, 2001). To test the effects of status and prestige, Milgram rented an office in a rundown building in Bridgeport, Connecticut. He then placed a newspaper ad for research sponsored by a private firm. There was no mention of Yale. In all other ways, the experimental procedure was identical to the original.

Under these less impressive circumstances, the level of obedience dropped, but not as much as Milgram expected: 48 percent of the participants continued to the maximum level of shock, compared with 65 percent in the original study. Milgram concluded that people are willing to obey orders to do great harm to another person even when the authority making the demand is not especially reputable or prestigious.

The Behavior of Other People

To study how the behavior of fellow participants might affect obedience, Milgram (1965) created a situation in which there appeared to be three teachers. Teacher 1 (in reality, a research assistant) read the words to the learner. Teacher 2 (another research assistant) stated whether or not the learner's response was correct. Teacher 3 (the actual participant) was to deliver shock when the learner made mistakes. At 150 volts, when the learner began to complain that the shock was too painful, Teacher 1 refused to participate any longer and left the room. The experimenter asked him to come back, but he refused. The experimenter then instructed Teachers 2 and 3 to continue by themselves. The experiment continued for several more trials. However, at 210 volts, Teacher 2 said that the learner was suffering too much and also refused to participate further. The experimenter then told Teacher 3 (the actual participant) to continue the procedure. In this case, only 10 percent of the participants (compared with 65 percent in the original study) continued to deliver shock all the way up to 450 volts. In other words, as research on conformity would suggest, the presence of others who disobey appears to be the most powerful factor in reducing obedience.

Personality Characteristics

Were the participants in Milgram's original experiment heartless creatures who would have given strong shocks even if there had been no pressure on them to do so? Quite the opposite; most of them were nice people who were influenced by experimental situations to behave in apparently antisocial ways. In a later demonstration of the same phenomenon, college students playing the role of prison guards behaved with aggressive heartlessness toward other students who were playing the role of prisoners (Zimbardo, 1973). A more recent illustration of this phenomenon occurred among some U.S. soldiers who were assigned to guard or interrogate prisoners in Afghanistan and Iraq.

Still, not everyone is equally obedient to authority. For example, people who display what we described earlier as *authoritarianism* are more likely than others to obey an experimenter's instructions to shock the learner (Blass, 2000). Support for this idea comes from recent findings that German soldiers who may have obeyed orders to kill Jews during World War II were higher on authoritarianism than other German men of the same age and background (Steiner & Fahrenberg, 2000).

Evaluating Obedience Research

Milgram's obedience studies were conducted forty years ago. How relevant are they today? Consider this fact: The U.S. Federal Aviation Authority attributes some commercial airplane accidents to what it calls "captainitis." In this phenomenon, the pilot of an airliner makes an obvious error, but none of the other crew members are willing to challenge the captain's authority by pointing out the error. As a result, planes have crashed and people have died (Kanki & Foushee, 1990). Captainitis might have been operating aboard the nuclear submarine USS *Greeneville* on February 9, 2001, when, as it surfaced off the coast of Hawaii, it struck and sank a Japanese fishing boat, killing nine people. A navy board of inquiry found that crew members had been reluctant to challenge their captain's order to surface, even though they felt he had not checked carefully enough for other vessels in the area (Myers, 2001). Obedience to authority may also have operated during the World Trade Center attack on September 11, 2001, when some people returned to their offices after hearing an ill-advised public address announcement telling them to do so. Most of these people died as a result.

These tragic events suggest that Milgram's findings are still relevant and important (Blass, 2004). Similar kinds of obedience have been observed in experiments conducted in many countries, from Europe to the Middle East, with female, as well as male, participants. In short, people appear to be as obedient today as they were when Milgram conducted his research (Blass, 2004; Smith & Bond, 1999). Nevertheless, there is still debate over the ethics and meaning of Milgram's work. (For a summary of Milgram's results, plus those of studies on conformity and compliance, see "In Review: Types of Social Influence.")

Questions About Ethics Although the "learners" in Milgram's experiment suffered no discomfort, the participants did. Milgram (1963) observed participants "sweat, stutter, tremble, groan, bite their lips, and dig their fingernails into their flesh" (p. 375). Against the potential harm inflicted by Milgram's experiments stand the potential gains. For example, people who learn about Milgram's work often take his findings into account when deciding how to act in social situations (Sherman, 1980). But even if social value has come from Milgram's studies, a question remains: Was it ethical for Milgram to treat his participants as he did?

In the years before his death in 1984, Milgram defended his experiments (e.g., Milgram, 1977). He argued that the way he dealt with his participants after the experiment prevented any lasting harm. For example, he explained to them that the learner did not experience any shock; in fact, the learner came in and chatted with each participant. On a later questionnaire, 84 percent of the participants said that they had learned something important about themselves and that the experience had been worthwhile. Milgram argued, therefore, that the experience was actually a positive one. Still, the committees charged with protecting human participants in research today would be unlikely to approve Milgram's experiments, and less controversial ways to study obedience have now been developed (Blass, 2004).

Questions About Meaning Do Milgram's dramatic results mean that most people are putty in the hands of authority figures and that most of us would blindly follow inhumane orders from our leaders? Some critics have argued that Milgram's results cannot be interpreted in this way because his participants knew they were in an experiment and may simply have been playing a cooperative role. If so, the social influence processes identified in his studies may not explain obedience in the real world today (Berkowitz, 1999).

Most psychologists believe, however, that Milgram demonstrated a basic truth about human behavior—namely, that under certain circumstances people are capable of unspeakable acts of brutality toward other people. Sadly, examples abound. And one of the most horrifying aspects of human inhumanity—whether it is the Nazis' campaign of genocide against Jews sixty years ago or the campaigns of terror under way today—is that the perpetrators are not necessarily demented, sadistic fiends. Most of them are normal people who have been prompted by economic, political, or religious influences and the persuasive power of their leaders to behave in a demented and fiendish manner (Moghaddam, 2005).

LINKAGES
Is it ethical to deceive people to learn about their social behavior? (a link to Introduction to the Science of Psychology)

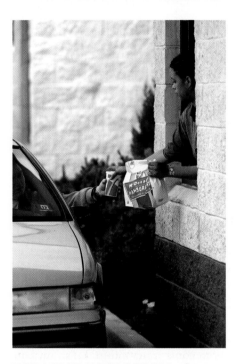

MAY I TAKE YOUR ORDER? In February of 2004, the managers of four fast food restaurants in Boston, Massachusetts, received calls from someone claiming to be a police detective on the trail of a robbery suspect. The caller said the suspect might be one of the restaurant's employees and told the managers to strip search all of them for evidence of guilt. The calls turned out to be hoaxes, but every manager obeyed this bizarre order, apparently because it appeared to come from a legitimate authority. In a similar case, hospital nurses obeyed medical treatment orders given by a teenager who claimed he was a doctor (Kenrick, Neuberg, & Cialdini, 2005).

in review

TYPES OF SOCIAL INFLUENCE

Type	Definition	Key Findings
Conformity	A change in behavior or beliefs to match those of others	In cases of ambiguity, people develop a group norm and then adhere to it. Conformity occurs because people want to be right, because they want to be liked by others, and because conformity to group norms is usually reinforced. Conformity usually increases with the ambiguity of the situation, as well as with the unanimity and size of the majority.
Compliance	A change in behavior because of a request	Compliance increases with the foot-in-the-door technique, which begins with a small request and works up to a larger one. The door-in-the-face procedure can also be used. After making a large request that is denied, the person substitutes a less extreme alternative that was desired all along. The low-ball approach also elicits compliance. An oral commitment for something is first obtained; then the person claims that only a higher cost version of the original request will suffice.
Obedience	A change in behavior in response to an explicit demand, typically from an acknowledged authority figure	People may inflict great harm on others when an authority demands that they do so. Even when people obey orders to harm another person, they often agonize over the decision. People are most likely to disobey orders to harm someone else when they see another person disobey.

?

1. Joining the end of a ticket line is an example of _____, whereas forming two lines when a theater employee requests it is an example of _____.
2. Seeing someone disobey a questionable order makes people _____ likely to obey the order themselves.
3. Pricing your used car for more than you expect to get, then agreeing to reduce it to make a sale, is an example of the _____ approach to gaining compliance.

In short, inhumanity can occur even without pressure to obey. A good deal of people's aggressiveness toward other people appears to come from within. Let's now consider human aggressiveness and some of the circumstances that influence its expression.

Aggression

▶ **Are people born aggressive?**

Aggression is an action intended to harm another person. It is all too common. More than 1.3 million violent crimes are committed each year in the United States alone, including more than 93,000 rapes and 16,000 murders (Federal Bureau of Investigation, 2004). In fact, homicide is the second leading cause of death for people in the United States between the ages of 15 and 24 (National Center for Injury Prevention and Control, 2002). One of the most disturbing aspects of these figures is that about 43 percent of all murder victims knew their assailants and that over 70 percent of rapists were romantic partners, friends, relatives, or acquaintances of their victims (U.S.

aggression   An act that is intended to harm another person.

Department of Justice, 2005). Further, as many as one-third of married and unmarried couples in the United States have engaged in aggressive acts toward each other that range from pushing, shoving, and slapping to beatings and the threatened or actual use of weapons (Archer, 2000; Durose et al., 2005).

Why Are People Aggressive?

Sigmund Freud proposed that aggression is an instinctive biological urge that builds up in everyone and must be released. Evolutionary psychologists offer a different view, suggesting that in prehistoric times, aggression helped people compete for mates, thus ensuring the survival of their genes in the next generation (Malamuth & Addison, 2001). Through natural selection, they say, aggressive tendencies have been passed on through countless generations.

Evolutionary theories of aggression are popular, but even evolutionary theorists recognize that "nature" alone cannot fully account for aggression. "Nurture," in the form of environmental factors, also plays a large role in when and why people are aggressive. We know this partly because there are large differences in aggression from culture to culture. The murder rate in the Philippines, for example, is forty-six times higher than in China or Finland; and the U.S. murder rate is almost nine times higher than in those latter two countries (Barclay & Tavares, 2002). These data suggest that even if aggressive *impulses* are universal, the appearance of aggressive *behavior* reflects the influence of both nature and nurture (Malamuth & Addison, 2001). No equation can predict exactly when people will be aggressive, but years of research have revealed a number of important biological, learning, and environmental factors that combine in various ways to produce aggression in various situations.

Genetic and Biological Mechanisms   There is strong evidence for hereditary influences on aggression, especially in animals (Cairns, Gariepy, & Hood, 1990). In one study, the most aggressive members of a large group of mice were interbred; then the most aggressive of their offspring were also interbred. After this procedure was followed for twenty-five generations, the resulting animals would immediately attack any mouse put in their cage. Continuous inbreeding of the least aggressive members of the original group produced animals that were so nonaggressive that they would refuse to fight even when attacked (Lagerspetz & Lagerspetz, 1983). Research in which human twins—reared together or apart—were rated on aggressiveness suggests that there is a genetic component to aggression in people as well (Hudziak et al., 2003). However, other research suggests that people do not necessarily inherit the tendency to be aggressive. Instead, they may inherit certain temperaments, such as impulsiveness, or certain aspects of brain chemistry that in turn make aggression more likely (Hennig et al., 2005).

Several parts of the brain influence aggression (Anderson & Bushman, 2002a). One of these is the limbic system, which includes the amygdala, the hypothalamus, and related areas. Damage to these structures may produce *defensive aggression,* which includes aggressiveness to stimuli that are not usually threatening or a decrease in the responses that normally inhibit aggression (Coccaro, 1989; Eichelman, 1983). The cerebral cortex may also be involved in aggression (Pietro et al., 2000).

Hormones such as *testosterone*—the masculine hormone that is present in both sexes—may also play an important role in aggression (Dabbs & Dabbs, 2001). Experiments have shown that aggressive behavior increases or decreases dramatically with the amount of testosterone in an animal's body (Pope, Kouri, & Hudson, 2000; Yates, 2000). Among criminals, those who commit violent crimes have higher levels of testosterone than those whose crimes are nonviolent. And among murderers, those with higher levels of testosterone are more likely than others to have known their victims and to have planned their crimes before committing them (Dabbs, Riad, & Chance, 2001).

Testosterone may have its most significant and durable influence through its impact on early brain development. One natural test of this hypothesis occurred when pregnant women were given testosterone in an attempt to prevent miscarriage. As a result, their children were exposed to high doses of testosterone during prenatal development.

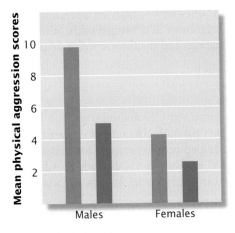

FIGURE 14.11

Testosterone and Aggression

In the study illustrated here, the children of women who had taken testosterone during pregnancy to prevent miscarriage became more aggressive than the mothers' other children of the same sex who had not been exposed to testosterone during prenatal development. This outcome appeared in both males and females.

Figure 14.11 shows that these children grew up to be more aggressive than their same-sex siblings who were not exposed to testosterone during prenatal development (Reinisch, Ziemba-Davis, & Sanders, 1991).

Drugs that affect the central nervous system also affect the likelihood that a person will act aggressively. Even relatively small amounts of alcohol, for example, can greatly increase some people's aggressiveness. Canadian researchers have found that in almost 70 percent of the acts of aggression they studied, the aggressors had been drinking alcohol. And the more alcohol the aggressors consumed, the more aggressive they were (Wells, Graham, & West, 2000). No one knows exactly why alcohol increases aggression, but research suggests that the drug may affect areas of the brain that normally inhibit aggressive responses (Lau, Pihl, & Peterson, 1995).

Learning and Cultural Mechanisms   Biological factors may increase or decrease the likelihood of aggression, but cross-cultural research makes it clear that learning also plays a role. Aggressive behavior is much more common in individualist than in collectivist cultures, for example (Oatley, 1993). Cultural differences in the expression of aggression appear to stem in part from differing cultural values (Cohen, 1998). For example, the Utku (an Inuit culture) view aggression in any form as a sign of social incompetence. In fact, the Utku word for "aggressive" also means "childish" (Oatley, 1993). The effects of culture on aggression can also be seen in the fact that the amount of aggression in a given culture changes over time as cultural values change (Matsumoto, 2000).

In addition, people learn many aggressive responses by watching others (Bingheimer, Brennan, & Earls, 2005; Bushman & Anderson, 2001). Children, in particular, learn and perform many of the aggressive responses that they see modeled by others. Bandura's "Bobo" doll experiments, which are described in the chapter on learning, provide impressive demonstrations of the power of observational learning. The significance of observational learning is highlighted, too, by studies described in that chapter on the effects of televised violence. For example, the amount of violent content eight-year-olds watch on television predicts aggressiveness in these children even fifteen years later (Huesmann et al., 2003). Fortunately, not everyone who sees aggression becomes aggressive. Individual differences in temperament, the modeling of nonaggressive behavior by parents, and other factors can reduce the effects of violent television. Nevertheless, observational learning, including the learning that comes through exposure to violent television and violent video and computer games, does play a significant role in the development and display of aggressive behavior (Anderson & Murphy, 2003; Bushman & Anderson, 2001).

Reward or punishment can also alter the frequency of aggressive acts. People become more aggressive when rewarded for aggressiveness and less aggressive when punished for aggression (Geen, 1998). In short, a person's life experiences, including culturally transmitted teachings, combine with daily rewards and punishments to influence whether, when, and how aggressive acts occur (Baron & Richardson, 1994).

When Are People Aggressive?

In general, people are more likely to be aggressive when they are both physically aroused and experiencing a strong emotion such as anger (Anderson & Bushman, 2002). People tend either to lash out at those who make them angry or to displace, or redirect, their anger toward children, pets, or other defenseless targets. However, aggression can also be made more likely by other forms of emotional arousal. One emotion that has long been considered to be a major cause of aggression is *frustration*, which occurs when we are prevented from reaching some goal.

Frustration and Aggression   Suppose that a friend interrupts your studying for an exam by asking to borrow a book. If things have been going well that day and you are feeling confident about the exam, you will probably be friendly and helpful. But what if you are feeling frustrated because your friend's visit was the fifth interruption

FOLLOWING ADULT EXAMPLES
Learning to express aggression is especially easy for children who, like these youngsters in Iraq, see aggressive acts modeled for them all too often.

in the last hour? Under these emotional circumstances, you may react aggressively, perhaps snapping at your startled visitor for bothering you.

Your aggressiveness in this situation would be predicted by the **frustration-aggression hypothesis,** which suggests that frustration leads to aggression (Dollard et al., 1939). Research on this hypothesis has shown that it is too simple and too general, however. For one thing, frustration sometimes produces depression and withdrawal, not aggression (Berkowitz, 1998). In addition, not all aggression is preceded by frustration (Berkowitz, 1994).

After many years of research, Leonard Berkowitz suggested that the frustration-aggression hypothesis be modified in two ways. First, he proposed that it may be stress in general, not just frustration, that is involved in aggression. Stress, he said, produces a readiness for aggression that may or may not be translated into aggressive behavior (Berkowitz, 1998). Once this readiness exists, however, aggression can be more easily triggered by stimuli in the environment. The triggering stimuli might be guns or knives, televised scenes of people arguing, violent song lyrics, or other cues associated with aggression. In other words, neither stress alone nor environmental cues alone are enough to set off aggression. When combined, however, they often do. Support for this aspect of Berkowitz's theory has been quite strong (Anderson & Bushman, 2002).

Second, Berkowitz argues that the direct cause of most kinds of aggression is negative feelings, or *negative affect* (Berkowitz, 1998). Research suggests that the more negative affect people experience, regardless of what caused it, the stronger is their readiness to be aggressive. Participants in one study experienced negative affect caused by the pain of immersing their hands in ice water. They became more aggressive than participants in a control group whose hands were in water of room temperature (Berkowitz, 1998).

Generalized Arousal Imagine that you've just jogged three miles. You are hot, sweaty, and out of breath, but you aren't angry. Still, the physiological arousal caused by jogging may increase the probability that you will become aggressive if, say, a passerby shouts an insult (Zillmann, 1988). Why? The answer lies in a phenomenon described in the chapter on motivation and emotion: Arousal from one experience may carry over to a new situation, producing what is called *excitation transfer.* So the physiological arousal caused by jogging may intensify your reaction to an insult (Harrison, 2003).

By itself, however, arousal does not lead to aggression. It is most likely to produce aggression when a situation presents some reason, opportunity, or target for aggression

frustration-aggression hypothesis A proposition stating that frustration always leads to some form of aggressive behavior.

(Zillmann, 2003). In one study, for example, people engaged in two minutes of vigorous exercise. Then they had the opportunity to deliver electric shock to another person. The participants chose to give high levels of shock only if they had first been insulted (Zillmann, Katcher, & Milavsky, 1972). Apparently, the arousal resulting from the exercise made aggression more likely; the insult "released" it. These findings are in keeping with the notion that aggression is caused not by internal impulses alone or by particular situations alone but by the interaction of the two (Klinesmith, Kasser, & McAndrew, 2006).

THINKING CRITICALLY

Does Pornography Cause Aggression?

In both men and women, sexual stimulation produces strong, generalized physiological arousal, especially in the sympathetic nervous system. If arousal in general can make a person more likely to be aggressive (given a reason, opportunity, and target), could stimuli that create sexual arousal be dangerous? In particular, does viewing or reading pornographic material make people more likely to be aggressive? Prior to the mid-1980s, several scholars had concluded that there was no evidence for an overall relationship between any type of antisocial behavior and mere exposure to pornographic material (Donnerstein, 1984). However, in 1986 the U.S. Attorney General's Commission on Pornography reexamined the question and concluded that pornography is dangerous.

■ What am I being asked to believe or accept?

Specifically, the commission proposed that there is a cause-effect link between exposure to erotic material and several forms of antisocial behavior, including sexually related violent crimes.

■ Is there evidence available to support the claim?

The commission cited several types of evidence in support of its conclusion. First, there was the testimony of men convicted of sex crimes. Rapists, for example, are unusually heavy users of pornography, and they often say that they were aroused by erotic material immediately before committing a rape (Silbert & Pines, 1984). Similarly, child molesters often view child pornography immediately before committing their crimes (Marshall, 1989).

In addition, the commission cited experimental evidence that men who are most aroused by aggressive themes in pornography are also the most potentially sexually aggressive. One study, for example, showed that men who said they could commit a rape became sexually aroused by scenes of rape and less aroused by scenes of mutually consenting sex; this was not true for men who said they could never commit a rape (Malamuth & Check, 1983).

Perhaps the strongest evidence cited by the commission, however, came from excitation transfer studies. In one experiment, male participants were told that a person in another room (actually an employee of the experimenter) would be performing a learning task and that they were to administer an electric shock every time the person made a mistake. The intensity of shock could be varied (as in the Milgram studies, no shock actually reached the employee), but participants were told that changing the intensity would not affect the speed of learning. So the shock intensity (and presumed pain) that they chose to administer was considered to be a measure of aggression. Before the learning trials began, some participants watched a film in which several men had sex with the same woman. These participants' aggressiveness during the learning experiment was greater than that of men who did not watch the film (Donnerstein, 1984).

■ Can that evidence be interpreted another way?

The commission's interpretation of all this evidence was questioned for several reasons. First, critics argued that some of the evidence should be given little weight. In particular, how much should we rely on what convicted sex offenders say? Their testimony may reflect self-serving attempts to lay the blame for their crimes on pornography. These reports cannot establish that exposure to pornography causes aggression. In fact, it may be that pornography partially *satisfies* sex offenders' aggressive impulses rather than creating them (Aronson, Wilson, & Akert, 2005). Similarly, the fact that potential rapists are most aroused by rape-oriented material may show only that they prefer violence-oriented pornography, not that such materials created their impulse to rape.

What about the evidence from excitation transfer studies? To interpret these studies, you need to know that the pornography that led to increased aggression contained violence, as well as sex. The sexual activity depicted was painful for, or unwanted by, the woman. So the higher levels of aggression that followed viewing these films could have been due to the transfer of sexual arousal, the effects of observing violent behavior, or the effects of seeing sex combined with violence (Donnerstein, Slaby, & Eron, 1995).

Several careful experiments have found that highly arousing sexual themes, in and of themselves, do not produce aggression. When men in excitation transfer studies experience pleasant arousal by viewing a film depicting nudity or mutually consenting sexual activity, they are actually less aggressive than when they viewed no film or a neutral film (Lord, 1997). In short, excitation transfer studies might be interpreted as showing that aggressiveness is influenced by portrayals of sexual violence, but not by watching other kinds of sexually arousing material.

■ What evidence would help to evaluate the alternatives?

Two types of evidence are needed to better understand the effects of pornography on aggression. First, because pornography can include sexual acts, aggressive acts, or both, the effects of each of these components must be more carefully examined. Second, factors affecting men's reactions to pornography, particularly pornography that involves violence, must be more clearly understood. Work is in progress on each of these fronts.

Whether specifically paired with sexual activity or not, aggressive themes do appear to increase subsequent aggression (Bushman & Anderson, 2001). Research has focused on *aggressive pornography*, which contains sexual themes but also scenes of violence against women (Malamuth, Addison, & Koss, 2000). In laboratory experiments, males often administer stronger electric shocks to females after viewing aggressive pornographic films as compared with neutral films. Yet there is no parallel increase in aggression against other men, suggesting that aggressive pornography creates an increase in aggressiveness that is specifically directed toward women (Aronson, Wilson, & Akert, 2005). Similarly, viewing aggressive pornography in which a rape victim appears aroused by the aggression usually leads males to become less sympathetic toward the victim and more tolerant of aggressive acts toward women (Donnerstein & Linz, 1995). Sexually explicit films that do not contain violence have no effects on attitudes toward rape (Linz, Donnerstein, & Penrod, 1987).

Are all men who are exposed to aggressive pornography equally likely to become rapists? The evidence available so far suggests that the answer is no (Seto, Maric, & Barbaree, 2001). Whether aggressive pornography alters men's behavior and attitudes toward women depends to some extent on the men. For example, one study of about 2,700 men in the United States collected data on their sexual aggressiveness, their use of pornography, their history of sexual promiscuity, and their feelings of hostility toward women (Malamuth, 1998). Among men low in promiscuity and hostility, viewing pornography had little, if any, impact on sexual aggression; but among men who were high in promiscuity and hostility, pornography dramatically increased the chances that these men would engage in sexual aggression. In fact, 72 percent of the men who were high in all three factors—use of pornography, promiscuity, and hostility—had actually engaged in sexually aggressive acts (see Figure 14.12).

■ What conclusions are most reasonable?

The attorney general's commission appeared to ignore numerous studies showing that the relationship between sexual arousal and aggression is neither consistent nor simple

FIGURE 14.12

Pornography and Sexual Aggression

Extensive exposure to pornography does not, by itself, increase most men's sexual aggressiveness. Such aggressiveness is much more likely, however, among men who not only view or read a lot of pornography but also are hostile toward women and are sexually promiscuous.

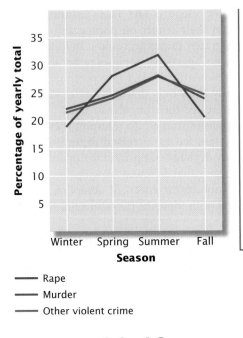

- Rape
- Murder
- Other violent crime

FIGURE **14.13**

Temperature and Aggression

Studies from around the world indicate that aggressive behaviors are most likely to occur during the hottest months of the year. These studies support the hypothesis that environmental factors can affect aggression.

environmental psychology   The study of the effects of the physical environment on people's behavior and mental processes.

helping behavior   Any act that is intended to benefit another person.

altruism   An unselfish concern with another's welfare.

(Seto et al., 2001). Analysis of this relationship reveals that it is important to distinguish between pornography in general and aggressive pornography in particular. Aggressive pornography can lead to violence against women, especially in men who are already inclined to abuse and exploit them. So there is reason for concern over the impact of sexual violence commonly seen on television and in movies—especially in "slasher" films. Remarkably, such films are sometimes given less restrictive ratings ("R" or even "PG-13") than films that are nonviolent but erotic.

The effects of nonaggressive pornography are more complicated. For most men, it has little or no impact on their behavior toward women. But among men who are inclined to abuse and exploit women, exposure to a lot of pornography might increase the chances that they would act on their abusive impulses (Malamuth et al., 2000; Seto et al., 2001). In summary, pornography is probably not, by itself, a major cause of violence against women. In combination with other factors, however, pornography—and especially aggressive pornography—can play a role in sexual aggression.

Environmental Influences on Aggression   The link between stress, arousal, and the likelihood of aggressive behavior suggests that stressful environmental conditions can create enough arousal to make aggressive behavior more likely (Anderson, 2001). This possibility is one of the research topics in **environmental psychology,** the study of the relationship between people's physical environment and their behavior (Bell et al., 2000). One aspect of the environment that clearly affects social behavior is the weather, especially temperature. High temperatures are a source of stress; as Figure 14.13 indicates, murder and other violent crimes are most likely to occur during the hottest months of the year (Anderson et al., 2000).

Living arrangements also influence aggressiveness. Compared with the tenants of crowded apartment buildings, those in buildings with relatively few residents are less likely to behave aggressively (Bell et al., 2000). This difference appears to be due in part to how people feel when they are crowded. Crowding tends to create physiological arousal and to make people tense, uncomfortable, and more likely to experience negative feelings (Oskamp & Schultz, 1998). This arousal and tension can influence people to like one another less and to be more aggressive (Ray et al., 1982).

Altruism and Helping Behavior

▶ **What motivates people to help one another?**

Like all acts of terrorism, the attacks on the World Trade Center and the Pentagon in September 2001 were horrifying examples of human behavior at its worst. But like all tragedies, they drew responses that provide inspiring examples of human behavior at its best. For example, Michael Benfante and John Cerqueira were working in the World Trade Center when one of the hijacked planes struck their building. They headed for a stairwell, but they did not just save themselves. Although it slowed their own escape, they chose to carry Tina Hansen, a wheelchair-bound co-worker, down sixty-eight flights of stairs to safety. Acts of selflessness and sacrifice were common that day and in the days and weeks and months that followed. Police officers, medical personnel, search-and-rescue specialists, and just ordinary people came to New York from all over the United States to help clear wreckage, look for survivors, and recover bodies. More than $1 billion in donations to the Red Cross and other charity organizations poured in to help victims, and volunteering in general more than tripled in the weeks following the attacks (Penner, Dovidio, et al., 2005).

All of these actions are examples of **helping behavior,** which is defined as any act that is intended to benefit another person. Helping can range from picking up dropped packages to donating a kidney. Closely related to helping is **altruism,** an unselfish

A YOUNG HELPER Even before their second birthday, some children offer help to those who are hurt or crying by snuggling, patting, or offering food or even their own teddy bears. Their helpful actions are shaped by the norms established by their families and the broader culture (Grusec & Goodnow, 1994).

concern for another's welfare (Penner et al., 2005b). Let's consider some of the reasons behind helping and altruism, along with some of the conditions under which people are most likely to help others.

Why Do People Help?

The tendency to help others begins early in life, although at first it is not automatic. Children have to learn to be helpful (Eisenberg & Fabes, 1998). In most cultures, very young children usually help others only when they are asked to do so or are offered a reward (Grusec, Davidov, & Lundell, 2002). Still, observational studies have shown that many children as young as eighteen months will spontaneously act to help a friend, a family member, or even a stranger (Warneken & Tomasello, 2006; Zahn-Waxler et al., 1992). As they grow older, children use helping behavior to gain social approval, and their efforts at helping become more elaborate. The role of social influence in the development of helping is seen as children follow the examples set by people around them. In addition, children are usually praised and given other rewards for helpfulness but scolded for selfishness. Eventually most children come to believe that being helpful is good and that they are good when they are helpful. By the late teens, people often help others even when no one is watching and no one will know that they did so (Grusec et al., 2002). There are three major theories about why people help even when they cannot expect any external rewards for doing so.

Arousal: Cost-Reward Theory One approach to explaining why people help is called the **arousal: cost-reward theory** (Piliavin et al., 1981). This theory proposes that people find the sight of a victim distressing and anxiety-provoking and that this experience motivates them to do something to reduce the unpleasant arousal. Before rushing to a victim's aid, however, the bystander will first evaluate two aspects of the situation: the costs associated with helping and the costs (to the bystander and the other person) of not helping. Whether or not the bystander actually helps depends on the outcome of this evaluation (Dovidio et al., 1991). If the costs of helping are low (as when helping someone pick up a dropped grocery bag) and the costs of not helping are high (as when the other person is physically unable to do this alone), the bystander will almost certainly help. However, if the costs of helping are high (as when helping someone lift a heavy box into a car) and the costs of not helping are low (as when the other person is obviously strong enough to do the job alone), the bystander is unlikely to offer help. One of the strengths of the arousal: cost-reward theory is that it is broad enough to explain several factors that affect helping.

The first of these factors is the *clarity of the need for help* (Dovidio et al., 1991). In a laboratory study of this factor, undergraduate students waiting alone in a campus building saw what appeared to be an accident involving a window washer. The man screamed as he and his ladder fell to the ground; then he clutched his ankle and groaned in pain. All the students looked out of the window to see what had happened, but only 29 percent of them did anything to help. Other students witnessed the same "accident," but with one important added element: The man said he was hurt and needed help. In this case, more than 80 percent of the participants came to his aid (Yakimovich & Saltz, 1971). Why so many? Apparently, this one additional cue eliminated any uncertainty about whether help was needed. The man's more obvious need for help served to raise the perceived costs of not helping him, thus making helping more likely.

If this laboratory study seems unrealistic, consider the March 2000 case of a sixty-two-year-old woman in Darby, Pennsylvania. She was walking to the grocery store when she was pushed from behind by an attacker. She fended him off and then did her shopping as usual. It was only when she got home and her daughter saw the handle of a knife protruding from her back that she realized that the assailant had stabbed her! No one in the grocery store said anything to her about the knife, let alone offered to help. Why? The most likely explanation is that the woman did nothing to suggest that help was necessary.

The *presence of others* also has a strong influence on the tendency to help. Somewhat surprisingly, however, their presence actually tends to suppress helping behavior

arousal: cost-reward theory A theory that attributes helping behavior to people's efforts to reduce the unpleasant arousal they feel when confronted with a suffering victim, while also considering the costs involved.

DIFFUSION OF RESPONSIBILITY
Does the man on the sidewalk need help?
The people walking by him are probably
not sure, and they might assume that if
he does need help, someone else will assist him. Research on factors affecting
helping suggests that if you are ever in
need of help, especially in a crowd, it is
important not only to clearly ask for help
but also to tell a specific onlooker to take
specific action (e.g., "You, in the yellow
shirt, please call an ambulance!").

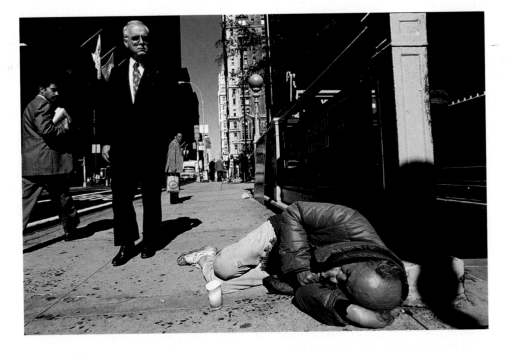

(Garcia et al., 2002). One of the most highly publicized examples of this phenomenon
occurred on a New York City street in 1964. During a thirty-minute struggle, a man
repeatedly stabbed a woman named Kitty Genovese, but none of the dozens of neighbors who witnessed the attack intervened or even called the police until it was too late
to save her life. A similar case occurred on November 27, 2000, in London, when a ten-
year-old boy who had been stabbed by members of a street gang lay ignored by
passersby as he bled to death. After every such case, journalists and social commenta-
tors express dismay about the cold, uncaring attitudes that seem to exist among people
who live in big cities.

That description may apply to some people, but research stimulated by the Genovese
case has revealed a social phenomenon that offers a different explanation of why her
neighbors, like those passersby in London, took no action to help. This phenomenon,
called the **bystander effect,** can be described as follows: The chance that someone will
help in an emergency usually decreases as the number of people present increases (Garcia
et al., 2002). Why does the bystander effect occur? One explanation is that each witness assumes someone else will take responsibility for helping the victim. This *diffusion
of responsibility* among all the witnesses leaves each witness feeling less obligated to help
and thus lowers the perceived cost of not helping (Dovidio & Penner, 2001).

The degree to which the presence of other people will suppress helping may depend
on who those other people are. When they are strangers, perhaps poor communication
interferes with helping. Many people have difficulty speaking to strangers, particularly in
an emergency; and without speaking, they have difficulty knowing what the others intend
to do. According to this logic, if people are with friends rather than strangers, they should
be less embarrassed, more willing to discuss the problem, and more likely to help.

In a study designed to test this idea, an experimenter left a research participant in a
waiting room, either alone, with a friend, with a stranger, or with a stranger who was
actually the experimenter's assistant (Latané & Rodin, 1969). The experimenter then
stepped behind a curtain into an office. For a few minutes, she could be heard opening
and closing the drawers of her desk, shuffling papers, and so on. Then there was a loud
crash, and she screamed, "Oh, my god—my foot, I—I can't move it. Oh, my ankle—I
can't get this—thing off me." Then the participant heard her groan and cry.

Would the participant go behind the curtain to help? Once again, people were most
likely to help if they were alone. When one other person was present, participants were
more likely to communicate with one another and to offer help if they were friends
than if they were strangers. When the stranger was the experimenter's assistant—who

bystander effect A phenomenon in
which the chances that someone will
help in an emergency decrease as the
number of people present increases.

had been instructed not to help—very few participants offered to help. Other studies have confirmed that bystanders' tendency to help increases when they know one another (Rutkowski, Gruder, & Romer, 1983).

Research suggests that the *personality of the helper* also plays a role in helping. Some people are simply more likely to help than others. Consider, for example, the Christians who risked their lives to save Jews from the Nazi Holocaust. Researchers interviewed these rescuers many years later and compared their personalities with those of people who had a chance to save Jews but did not do so (Midlarsky, Jones, & Corley, 2005; Oliner & Oliner, 1988). The rescuers were found to have more *empathy* (the ability to understand or experience another's emotional state; Davis, 1994), more concern about others, a greater sense of responsibility for their own actions, and greater confidence that their efforts would succeed. Louis Penner and his associates (Penner, 2002; Penner & Finkelstein, 1998) have found that these kinds of personality traits predict a broad range of helping behaviors, from how quickly bystanders intervene in an emergency to how much time volunteers spend assisting AIDS patients. Consistent with the arousal: cost-reward theory, these personality characteristics are correlated with people's estimates of the costs of helping and not helping. For example, empathic individuals usually estimate the costs of not helping as high, and people who are confident about their ability to help usually rate the costs of helping as low (Penner et al., 1995).

Valuable as it is, the arousal: cost-reward theory cannot account for all aspects of helping. For instance, it cannot easily explain why environmental factors affect helping. Research conducted in several countries has shown that people in urban areas are generally less helpful than those in rural areas (Aronson et al., 2005). Why? The explanation probably has more to do with the stressors found in cities than with city living itself. Studies of cities in the United States, the United Kingdom, the Middle East, and Africa found that people's tendency to help was more strongly related to the population density (the number of people per square mile) where they lived than to the overall size of their city (Hedge & Yousif, 1992; Levine et al., 1994; Yousif & Korte, 1995). The higher the density, the less likely people were to help others. Why should stress make people less helpful? Two explanations have been suggested. The first is that stressful environments create bad moods—and, generally speaking, people in bad moods are less likely to help (Salovey, Mayer, & Rosenhan, 1991). A second possibility is that noise, crowding, and other urban stressors create too much stimulation. To reduce this stimulation, people may pay less attention to their surroundings, including less attention to individuals who need help.

Empathy-Altruism Theory There are also situations in which matters of cost are not the major cause of a decision to help or not help. A second approach to explaining helping considers some of these situations. This second approach is embodied in the **empathy-altruism theory,** which maintains that people are more likely to engage in altruistic, or unselfish, helping—even at a high cost—if they feel empathy toward the person in need (Batson, 1998). In one experiment illustrating this phenomenon, students listened to a tape-recorded interview in which a young woman told how her parents had died in an automobile accident, leaving no life insurance (Batson et al., 1997). She said that she was trying to take care of her younger brother and sister while going to college but that time and money were so tight that she might have to quit school or give up her siblings for adoption. None of this was true, but the participants were told that it was. Before hearing the tape, half the participants were given information about the woman that would increase their empathy for her; the other half were not. After listening to the tape, all participants were asked to help the woman raise money for herself and her siblings. Consistent with the empathy-altruism theory, more participants in the empathy group offered to help than did those in the control group.

Were the students who offered help in this experiment being utterly unselfish, or could there have been other reasons for their apparent altruism? This is a hotly debated

empathy-altruism theory A theory suggesting that people help others because they feel empathy toward them.

question. Some researchers dispute the claim that this study illustrated truly altruistic helping. They suggest instead that people help in such situations for more selfish reasons, such as relieving the distress they experienced after hearing of the woman's problems (Maner et al., 2002). The final verdict on this question is not yet in.

Evolutionary Theory   The evolutionary approach to psychology offers a third way to explain helping. According to this approach, many human social behaviors are a reflection of actions that contributed to the survival of our prehistoric ancestors (Buss, 2003). At first glance, it might not seem reasonable to apply evolutionary theory to helping and altruism, because helping others at the risk of our own well-being does not appear adaptive. If we die while trying to save others, it will be their genes, not ours, that will survive. In fact, according to Darwin's concept of the "survival of the fittest," helpers—and their genes—should have disappeared long ago. Today's evolutionary theorists suggest, however, that Darwin's thinking about natural selection focused too much on the survival of the fittest *individuals* and not enough on the survival of their genes in *others*. Accordingly, the concept of survival of the fittest has been replaced by the concept of *inclusive fitness*, the survival of one's genes in future generations (Hamilton, 1964; Kruger, 2003). Because we share genes with our relatives, helping—or even dying for—a cousin, a sibling, or, above all, our own child increases the likelihood that at least some of our genetic characteristics will be passed on to the next generation through the beneficiary's future reproduction. So *kin selection,* or helping a relative to survive, may produce genetic benefits for the helper even if it provides no personal benefits (Kruger, 2003).

There is considerable evidence that kin selection occurs among birds, squirrels, and other animals. The more closely the animals are related, the more likely they are to risk their lives for one another. Studies in a wide variety of cultures show the same pattern of helping among humans (Buss, 2003). For example, people in the United States are three times as likely to donate a kidney to a relative as to a nonrelative (Borgida, Conner, & Monteufel, 1992). (See "In Review: Helping Behavior" for a summary of the major reasons why people help and the conditions under which they are most likely to do so.)

Cooperation, Competition, and Conflict

Helping is one of several ways in which people *cooperate* with one another. **Cooperation** is any type of behavior in which people work together to attain a goal (Penner et al., 2005b). For example, several law students might form a study group to help one another pass the bar exam. But people also compete with others for limited resources. Those same students might later try to outdo one another to be chosen for a single job opening at a top law firm. **Competition** exists whenever individuals try to reach a goal themselves while denying that goal to others. Finally, there is **conflict,** which occurs when a person or group believes that another person or group interferes with the attainment of a goal. When the law students become attorneys and represent opposing parties in a trial, they will be in conflict with one another. One way in which psychologists have learned about all three of these phenomena is by studying social dilemmas (Weber, Kopelman, & Messick, 2004).

Social dilemmas are situations in which an action that is most rewarding for each individual will, if adopted by all others in the situation, create problems for everyone (Dawes & Messick, 2000). For instance, during a drought, each homeowner is better off in the short run by watering the lawn as often as necessary to keep it from dying; but if everyone ignores local water restrictions, there will be no drinking water for anyone in the long run. Social dilemmas reflect conflicts between the interests of the individual and those of the group and between short-term and long-term interests (Schroeder, 1995). Are people from collectivist cultures (which emphasize cooperation) less likely to act competitively or selfishly in social dilemma situations? In general, they may be, but interpersonal conflict in such situations still appears to some extent in all cultures (Smith & Bond, 1999).

cooperation   Any type of behavior in which people work together to attain a goal.

competition   Any type of behavior in which individuals try to attain a goal for themselves while denying that goal to others.

conflict   What occurs when a person or group believes that another person or group interferes with the attainment of a goal.

social dilemmas   Situations in which actions that produce rewards for one individual will produce negative consequences if they are adopted by everyone.

in review

HELPING BEHAVIOR

Theory	Basic Premise	Important Variables
Arousal: cost-reward	People help in order to reduce the unpleasant arousal caused by another person's distress. They attempt to minimize the costs of doing this.	Factors that affect the costs of helping and of not helping
Empathy-altruism	People sometimes help for unselfish reasons if they feel empathy for a person in need. They are motivated by a desire to increase another person's well-being.	The amount of empathy that one person feels for another
Evolutionary	People help relatives because it increases the chances that the helper's genes will survive in future generations.	The biological relation-ship between the helper and the recipient of help

?

1. If you could save only one person from a burning house, the _____ theory of helping would predict that it would be your own child rather than, say, a grandparent.
2. Are you more likely to receive help in a nearly empty bus or a crowded bus terminal? _____.
3. People who have empathy for others are _____ likely to be helpful.

Group Processes

▶ **What makes a good leader?**

Although Western industrialized cultures tend to emphasize individuals over groups, the fact remains that most important decisions and efforts by governments and businesses in those cultures and elsewhere are made by groups, not individuals (Kerr & Tindale, 2004). Sometimes groups function very well. Perhaps you recall the extraordinary teamwork by engineers, emergency workers, and volunteers that led to the dramatic rescue of nine men trapped in a flooded Pennsylvania coal mine in July 2002. At other times, though, groups have been known to make bad, or even disastrous, decisions. To begin to understand why, let's consider some of the social psychological processes that often occur in groups to alter the behavior of individuals and the quality of their collective efforts.

The Presence of Others

In 1897, in what was probably the first social psychological experiment ever conducted, Norman Triplett demonstrated that an individual's behavior is affected by the mere presence of other people. Triplett found that bicycle racers went much faster when another racer was nearby than when they were simply racing against time. This effect occurred even when the cyclists were not competing against each other. There was something about the presence of another person, not just competition, that made riders go faster.

The term **social facilitation** describes circumstances in which the presence of other people can improve performance (Aiello & Douthitt, 2001). This improvement does not always occur, however. In fact, having other people present sometimes hurts performance,

social facilitation A phenomenon in which the presence of others improves a person's performance.

SOCIAL FACILITATION Premier athletes like Lindsay Davenport, shown here winning the women's singles championship at Wimbledon in 2005, are able to perform at their best even though large crowds are present. In fact, the crowds probably help them do well, because the presence of others tends to increase arousal, which enhances the performance of familiar and well-learned skills, such as tennis strokes. However, arousal created by an audience tends to interfere with the performance of unfamiliar and poorly developed skills. This is one reason that professional athletes who show flawless grace in front of thousands of fans are likely to freeze up or blow their lines in front of a small production crew when trying for the first time to tape a TV ad or a public service announcement.

a process known as **social impairment.** For decades, these results seemed contradictory; then Robert Zajonc (pronounced "ZYE-onze") suggested that both effects could be explained by one process: arousal.

The presence of other people, said Zajonc, increases a person's general level of arousal or motivation (Zajonc, 1965). Why? One reason is that being watched by others increases our sense of being evaluated, producing worry that in turn increases emotional arousal (Penner & Craiger, 1992). Arousal increases the tendency to perform those behaviors that are most *dominant*—the ones you know best. This tendency can either help or hinder performance. When you are performing an easy, familiar task, such as riding a bike, increased arousal due to the presence of others should allow you to ride even faster than normal. But when a task is hard or unfamiliar—such as trying new dance steps or playing a newly learned piano piece in front of an audience—the most dominant responses may be incorrect and cause performance to suffer. In other words, the impact of other people on performance depends on whether the task is easy or difficult.

What if a person is not merely in the presence of others, but is working with them on some task? In these situations, people often exert less effort than when performing alone, a phenomenon called **social loafing** (Liden et al., 2004). Whether the task is pulling on a rope, clapping as loudly as possible, or trying to solve mental puzzles, people tend to work harder when alone than with others. Research in industrial/organizational psychology suggests that social loafing is most likely when large groups work on the same task (making each member's contribution harder to evaluate), when the group is not closely knit, and when members feel they are not being rewarded according to their performance (Liden et al., 2004; Szymanski, Garczynski, & Harkins, 2000).

In Western cultures, social loafing appears in groups of all sorts, from volunteer committees to search parties. It is much less likely among people in Eastern cultures such as those in China and Japan. In fact, in these collectivist cultures, working in a group usually produces *social striving*—defined as greater individual effort when working in a group (Matsumoto, 2000). This difference in the effects of group membership on individual efforts probably reflects the high value that collectivist cultures place on coordinated and cooperative group activities.

Group Leadership

The role of group leaders is especially important when social loafing and other obstacles threaten to impair the effectiveness of group efforts. A good leader can help a group

social impairment A reduction in performance due to the presence of other people.

social loafing Exerting less effort when performing a group task than when performing the same task alone.

pursue its goals, but a bad one can get in the way of a group's functioning. What makes a good leader? Psychologists once thought that the personalities of good and bad leaders were about the same, but we now know that certain personality traits often distinguish effective from ineffective leaders. For example, using tests similar to those that measure the big-five traits described in the personality chapter, Colin Silverthorne (2001) examined the characteristics of leaders in the United States, Thailand, and China. He found that effective leaders in all three countries tended to score high on agreeableness, emotional stability, extraversion, and conscientiousness. Other researchers have found that, in general, effective leaders are intelligent, success oriented, flexible, and confident (Chemers, Watson, & May, 2000).

Having particular personality traits does not guarantee good leadership ability, however. People who are effective leaders in one situation may be ineffective in another (Chemers, 2000). The reason is that effective leadership also depends on the characteristics of the group members; the task at hand; and, most important, the interaction between these factors and the leader's style (Yun, Faraj, & Sims, 2005).

For many years, leadership research focused on two main types of leaders. The first, called **task-oriented leaders,** provide close supervision, lead by giving orders, and generally discourage group discussion (Yukl & Van Fleet, 1992). Their style may make them unpopular. The second, called **person-oriented leaders,** provide loose supervision, ask for group members' ideas, and are generally concerned with subordinates' feelings. They are usually well liked by the group, even when they must discipline a group member (Brehm, Kassin, & Fein, 2005). More recently, additional leadership styles have been identified. One of these styles is seen in *transactional leaders*; whose actions depend on the actions of those they lead. They reward those who behave as the leader wishes, and they correct or punish those who don't. There are also *transformational* or *charismatic leaders* (Bass & Riggio, 2006). These people concentrate on creating a vision of the group's goals, inspiring others to pursue that vision, and giving their followers reason to respect and admire them.

Do men or women make better leaders? Research by Alice Eagly and her colleagues at first found that, overall, men and women are equally capable leaders. It also looked as though men tend to be more effective when success requires a task-oriented leader and that women tend to be more effective when success requires a more person-oriented leader. In other words, it appeared that people of each gender tend to be most effective when they are acting in a manner consistent with gender-role traditions (Eagly & Karau, 1991; Eagly, Karau, & Makhijani, 1995). Perhaps the reason was that some people did not like female leaders who act in a "masculine" manner or occupy leadership positions traditionally held by men (Eagly, Makhijani, & Klonsky, 1992).

A somewhat different picture of gender and leadership has emerged from Eagly's more recent research. For one thing, she found that females are generally more likely than males to display a transformational leadership style. Further, when women display a transactional style, they tend to be more encouraging than transactional male leaders, focusing more on using rewards rather than punishments to modify group members' behaviors. Finally, and in contrast to earlier findings, Eagly's results now suggest that women may be slightly more effective leaders overall than men (Eagly, Johannesen-Schmidt, & van Engen, 2003).

Groupthink

The emphasis on group decisions in most large organizations is based on the belief that several people working together will make better decisions than will individuals working alone. As noted in the chapter on thought, language, and intelligence, this belief is generally correct; yet under certain circumstances groups have been known to make amazingly bad decisions (Kerr & Tindale, 2004). Consider, for example, the fact that, in 1986, administrators at the National Aeronautics and Space Administration (NASA) ignored engineers' warnings about the effects of cold weather and decided to launch the space shuttle *Challenger*. The spacecraft exploded seventy-three seconds after liftoff, killing all aboard. After analyzing these and other disastrous decisions, Irving Janis

task-oriented leaders Leaders who provide close supervision, lead by giving directions, and generally discourage group discussion.

person-oriented leaders Leaders who provide loose supervision, ask for group members' ideas, and are generally concerned with subordinates' feelings.

(1989) proposed that they can be attributed to a phenomenon called *groupthink*. **Groupthink** occurs, he said, when group members are unable to realistically evaluate the options available to them or to fully consider the potential negative consequences of the option they are about to choose.

Groupthink is particularly likely when four conditions exist: (1) the decision is not based on all the facts at hand, (2) group members all share certain biases, (3) members who express disagreement with the majority view are punished or even ejected from the group, and (4) the group leader puts pressure on the members to reach agreement. This last condition appeared to play a crucial role in the U.S. government's decision to support a disastrously unsuccessful invasion of Cuba by anti-Castro Cubans in 1961. Before the final decision was made, several advisers were told that President John F. Kennedy had made up his mind to support the invasion and that it was time to "close ranks with the president." This situation created enormous pressure for conformity (May & Zelikow, 1997).

Some researchers have questioned the prevalence and dangers of groupthink (e.g., Aldag & Fuller, 1993; Park, 2000), but because it does occur, other researchers have worked on developing techniques to help groups avoid it (Galinsky & Kray, 2004; Kray & Galinsky, 2003).

One way to avoid groupthink is to teach group members to imagine all the negative outcomes of each course of action. Another is to designate someone to play the "devil's advocate," a person who constantly challenges the group's emerging decision and forces everyone to consider all the facts and other decisions that are possible (Risen, 1998). Yet another technique is to encourage diverse opinions by allowing people to express them anonymously. For example, group members might communicate by e-mail on networked computers that hide the sender's identity. Research suggests that allowing groups to discuss decision options without knowing who is saying what stimulates logical debate and makes it easier for people to disagree with the group (O'Brien, 1991).

LINKAGES
How does stress affect group decision making? (a link to Health, Stress, and Coping)

LINKAGES
Can we "see" prejudice in the brain? (a link to Biology and Behavior)

LINKAGES

Biological and Social Psychology

Research in social psychology was once thought to be entirely separate from research on the biological processes that underlie social behavior (Winkielman, Berntson, & Cacioppo, 2001). Social psychologists believed it was impossible to reduce complex social psychological processes to the firing of neurons or the secretion of hormones. For their part, biological psychologists, more commonly known as *neuroscientists*, viewed the study of social psychology as having little, if any, relevance to the understanding of, say, behavioral genetics or the functioning of the nervous system. Recently, however, scientists in both subfields have begun to take a closer look at each other's research and at how their subfields are linked. The result has been the emergence of a new specialty called **social neuroscience** or *social cognitive neuroscience* (Adolphs, 2003; Heatherton, Macrae, & Kelley, 2004; Ochsner, 2004). This new specialty focuses on the influence of social processes on biological processes and on the influence of biological processes, including genetics, on social psychological phenomena (e.g. Bielsky et al., 2005; Thompson et al., 2006).

There are many reasons to believe that this approach will be valuable. For example, the chapter on health, stress, and coping contains numerous examples of how social stressors can have health-related biological consequences. Health psychologists have also found that the availability and quality of a person's social support network can affect biological processes ranging from blood pressure to the healing of wounds (Kiecolt-Glaser et al., 1998; Uchino, Cacioppo, & Kiecolt-Glaser, 1996; Robles & Kiecolt-Glaser, 2003). In addition, as discussed in the chapter on psychological disorders, some problems in social behavior can result from the interaction of environmental stressors with genetic influences. One study compared the amount of antisocial behavior displayed

groupthink   A pattern of thinking that renders group members unable to evaluate realistically the wisdom of various options and decisions.

social neuroscience   A specialty that focuses on the influence of social processes on biological processes and on the influence of biological processes on social psychological phenomena.

by men who either had or had not suffered the stress of parental abuse in childhood. Antisocial behavior was much more common among men who had been abused, but this behavior was most common among abused men who also had inherited characteristics associated with antisocial behaviors (Caspi et al., 2002).

Researchers are beginning to identify the biological aspects of many social processes. One example can be seen in studies of how the amygdala—a brain structure involved in emotion—is related to the stereotyping and prejudice discussed earlier in this chapter (Eberhardt, 2005). Researchers found that European Americans who were prejudiced against African Americans showed significantly more amygdala activity when looking at pictures of black people than when looking at pictures of white people (Cunningham et al., 2004; Hart et al., 2000; Phelps et al., 2000).

In short, social cognitive neuroscience shows great promise for creating a better understanding of the linkages among social, cognitive, and biological phenomena, as well as a better understanding of complex social and physiological processes.

ACTIVE REVIEW   Social Psychology

Linkages

As noted in the introductory chapter, all of psychology's subfields are related to one another. Our discussion of social neuroscience illustrates just one way in which the topic of this chapter, social psychology, is linked to the subfield of biological psychology, which is discussed in the chapter on biology and behavior. The Linkages diagram also shows ties to two other subfields, and there are many more ties throughout the book. Looking for linkages among subfields will help you see how they all fit together and help you better appreciate the big picture that is psychology.

LINKAGES

Can we "see" prejudice in the brain? (ans. on p. 582)

CHAPTER 2
BIOLOGY AND BEHAVIOR

CHAPTER 14
SOCIAL PSYCHOLOGY

Do groups solve problems more effectively than individuals? (ans. on p. 268)

CHAPTER 7
THOUGHT, LANGUAGE, AND INTELLIGENCE

How do societies define what is abnormal? (ans. on p. 459)

CHAPTER 12
PSYCHOLOGICAL DISORDERS

Summary

Social cognition, the mental processes through which people perceive and react to others, is one aspect of *social psychology,* the study of how people influence and are influenced by other people. Through social cognition, each person creates a unique perception of reality.

SOCIAL INFLUENCES ON THE SELF

▶ **How do we compare ourselves with others?**

People's social and cultural environments affect their thoughts and feelings about themselves, including their *self-concept* and their *self-*

esteem. When people have no objective criteria by which to judge themselves, they look to others as the basis for *social comparison.* Such comparison can affect self-evaluation or self-esteem. Categories of people that are regularly used for social comparison are known as *reference groups.* Comparison with reference groups sometimes produces *relative deprivation,* which in turn can cause personal and social turmoil.

A person's *social identity* is formed from beliefs about the groups to which the person belongs. Social identity affects the beliefs we hold about ourselves, our self-concept. Social identity permits people to feel part of a larger group, generating loyalty and sacrifice from group members but also potentially creating bias and discrimination toward people who are not members of the group.

SOCIAL PERCEPTION

▶ **Do we perceive people and objects in similar ways?**

Social perception concerns the processes by which people interpret information about others, form impressions of them, and draw conclusions about the reasons for their behavior. *Schemas,* the mental representations about people and social situations that we carry into social interactions, affect what we pay attention to, what we remember, and how we judge people and events.

First impressions are formed easily and quickly, in part because people apply existing schemas to their perceptions of others. First impressions change slowly, because once we form an impression about another person, we try to maintain it. Schemas, however, can create *self-fulfilling prophecies,* leading us to act in ways that bring out behavior in others that is consistent with our expectations of them.

Attribution is the process of explaining the causes of people's behavior, including our own. Observers tend to attribute behavior to causes that are either internal or external to the actor. Attributions are also affected by biases that systematically distort our view of behavior. The most common attributional biases are the *fundamental attribution error* (and its cousin, the ultimate attribution error), the *actor-observer bias,* and the *self-serving bias.* Personal and cultural factors can affect the extent to which people exhibit these biases.

ATTITUDES

▶ **Do attitudes always determine behavior?**

An *attitude* is the tendency to respond positively or negatively to a particular object. Attitudes affect a wide range of behaviors. Most social psychologists see attitudes as composed of three components: cognitive (beliefs), affective (feelings), and behavioral (actions). However, it is often difficult to predict a specific behavior from a person's beliefs or feelings about an object. Cognitive theories suggest that the likelihood of attitude-behavior consistency depends on the importance of the attitude, subjective norms, perceived control over the behavior, and prior direct experience with the attitude object.

Attitudes can be learned through modeling, as well as through classical or operant conditioning. They are also subject to the mere-exposure effect: All else being equal, people develop greater liking for a new object the more often they are exposed to it.

The effectiveness of a persuasive message in changing attitudes is influenced by the characteristics of the person who communicates the message, by its content, and by the audience receiving it. The *elaboration likelihood model* suggests that attitude change can occur through either the peripheral or the central route, depending on a person's ability and motivation to carefully consider an argument. Accordingly, different messages will produce attitude change under different circumstances. Another approach is to change a person's behavior in the hope that attitudes will be adjusted to match the behavior. *Cognitive dissonance theory* holds that if inconsistency between attitude and behavior creates discomfort related to a person's self-concept, the attitude may change in order to reduce the conflict.

PREJUDICE AND STEREOTYPES

▶ **How does prejudice develop?**

Stereotypes often lead to *prejudice* and *discrimination.* Motivational theories of prejudice suggest that some people have a need to dislike people who differ from themselves. This need may stem from the trait of authoritarianism, as well as from a strong social identity with one's in-group. In either case, feeling superior to members of out-groups helps these people to feel better about themselves. As a result, in-group members tend to discriminate against out-groups. Cognitive theories suggest that people categorize others into groups in order to reduce social complexity. Learning theories maintain that stereotypes, prejudice, and discriminatory behaviors can be learned from parents, peers, and the media. The *contact hypothesis* proposes that intergroup contact can reduce prejudice and lead to more favorable attitudes toward the stereotyped group—but only if the contact occurs under specific conditions, such as equal status between groups.

INTERPERSONAL ATTRACTION

▶ **What factors affect who likes whom?**

Interpersonal attraction is affected by many variables. Physical proximity is important because it allows people to meet. The situation in which they meet is important because positive or negative aspects of the situation tend to be associated with the other person. Characteristics of the other person are also important. Attraction tends to be greater when two people share similar attitudes and personal characteristics. Physical appearance plays a role in attraction; initially, attraction is strongest to those who are most physically attractive. But for long-term relationships, the *matching hypothesis* applies: People tend to choose others whose physical attractiveness is about the same as theirs.

Two key components of successful intimate relationships are interdependence and mutual commitment. Sternberg's triangular theory suggests that love is a function of three components: passion, intimacy, and commitment. Varying combinations of these three components create qualitatively different types of love. Marital satisfaction depends on communication, the perception that the relationship is equitable, the couple's ability to deal effectively with conflict and anger, and agreement on important issues in the marriage.

SOCIAL INFLUENCE

▶ **What social rules shape our behavior?**

Norms establish the rules for what should and should not be done in a particular situation. One particularly powerful norm is reciprocity, the tendency to respond to others as they have acted toward us. *Deindividuation* is a psychological state in which people temporarily lose their individuality, their normal inhibitions are relaxed, and they may perform aggressive or illegal acts that they would not do otherwise.

When behavior or beliefs change as the result of unspoken or implicit group pressure, *conformity* has occurred. When the change is the result of a request, *compliance* has occurred. People tend to follow the normative responses of others, and groups create norms when none already exist. People sometimes display public conformity without private acceptance; at other times, the responses of others have an impact on private beliefs. People conform because they want to be right, because they want to be liked, and because they tend to be rewarded for conformity. People are most likely to conform when the situation is unclear, as well as when others in the group are in unanimous agreement. Up to a point, conformity usually increases as the number of people holding the majority view grows larger. Effective strategies for creating compliance include the foot-in-the-door technique, the door-in-the-face procedure, and the low-ball approach.

OBEDIENCE

▶ How far will people go in obeying authority?

Obedience involves complying with an explicit demand from an authority figure. Research by Milgram indicates that obedience is likely even when obeying an authority appears to result in pain and suffering for another person. Obedience declines when the status of the authority figure declines, as well as when others are observed to disobey. Some people are more likely to obey orders than others. Because participants in Milgram's studies experienced considerable stress, the experiments have been questioned on ethical grounds. Nevertheless, his research showed that people do not have to be psychologically disordered to inflict pain on others.

AGGRESSION

▶ Are people born aggressive?

Aggression is an act intended to harm another person. Freud saw aggression as due partly to instincts. More recent theories attribute aggressive tendencies to genetic and evolutionary factors, brain dysfunctions, and hormonal influences. Learning is also important; people learn to display aggression by watching others and by being rewarded for aggressive behavior. There are wide cultural differences in the occurrence of aggression.

A variety of emotional factors play a role in aggression. The *frustration-aggression hypothesis* suggests that frustration can lead to aggression, particularly in the presence of cues that invite or promote aggression. Arousal from sources unrelated to aggression, such as exercise, can also make aggressive responses more likely, especially if aggression is already a dominant response in that situation. Research in *environmental psychology* suggests that factors such as high temperature and crowding increase the likelihood of aggressive behavior, particularly among people who are already angry.

ALTRUISM AND HELPING BEHAVIOR

▶ What motivates people to help one another?

Humans often display *helping behavior* and *altruism.* There are three major theories of why people help others. According to the *arousal:*

cost-reward theory, people help in order to reduce the unpleasant arousal they experience when others are in distress. Their specific reaction to a suffering person depends on the costs associated with helping or not helping. Helping behavior is most likely when the need for help is clear and when diffusion of responsibility is not created by the presence of other people—a phenomenon called the *bystander effect.* Environmental and personality factors also affect willingness to help. The *empathy-altruism theory* suggests that helping can be truly unselfish if the helper feels empathy for the person in need. Finally, evolutionary theory suggests that humans have an innate tendency to help others, especially relatives, because doing so increases the likelihood that family genes will survive.

Cooperation is any type of behavior in which people work together to attain a goal; *competition* exists whenever individuals try to attain a goal for themselves while denying that goal to others. Interpersonal or intergroup *conflict* occurs when one person or group believes that another stands in the way of reaching some goal. Psychologists study conflict by observing behavior in *social dilemmas,* situations in which behavior that benefits individuals in the short run may spell disaster for an entire group in the long run.

GROUP PROCESSES

▶ What makes a good leader?

People's behavior is affected by the mere presence of other people. By enhancing one's most likely behavior in a situation, the presence of others sometimes creates *social facilitation* (which improves performance) and sometimes creates *social impairment* (which interferes with performance). When people work in groups, they often exert less effort than when alone, a phenomenon called *social loafing.* Effective group leaders tend to score high on emotional stability, agreeableness, and conscientiousness. In general, they are also intelligent, success oriented, flexible, and confident. *Task-oriented leaders* provide close supervision, lead by giving orders, and generally discourage group discussion. *Person-oriented leaders* provide loose supervision, ask for group members' ideas, and are generally concerned with subordinates' feelings. Transactional leaders focus on rewarding or correcting group members' performance; transformational leaders tend to lead by example, thus inspiring good performance.

When *groupthink* occurs, decisions are not based on all the facts, group members share certain biases, dissenting members' views are rejected, and the group leader pressures members to reach agreement.

A new specialty called *social neuroscience* focuses on the influence of social processes on biological processes and on the influence of biological processes on social psychological phenomena.

Learn by Doing

Put It in Writing

A survey reveals that first-graders from various ethnic groups in a local school hold prejudiced attitudes toward one another. Imagine that you have been hired to develop a program to help these children become less prejudiced and more accepting of members of other ethnic groups. Write a one-page description of two or three classroom activities that would help you to accomplish this goal, and tell why you think they

would do so. Do you think these activities could be successful in eliminating all prejudiced thinking in the children? Why or why not?

Personal Learning Activity

Research mentioned in this chapter suggests that the physical appearance of a partner tends to be more important to men, whereas a partner's intelligence tends to be more important to women. If that is true, what qualities would you hypothesize that men versus women will say they are looking for when they place ads for a partner in a personals column or web site? Develop a research plan to test your hypothesis, and then collect some data by reading and analyzing personals ads in your local newspaper or on a web site for singles. Was your hypothesis supported? Did gender differences in the content of the ads hold true for homosexuals and bisexuals, as well as heterosexuals? Write a brief report of your findings, and summarize what you think they can and cannot say about the factors that attract people to each other. *For additional projects, see the Personal Learning Activities in the corresponding chapter of the study guide that accompanies this text.*

Step into Action

Courses

Social Psychology
Social Conflict
Marriage and Family
Social Cognition
Interpersonal Processes
Prejudice and Discrimination

Movies

The Last of the Mohicans. Reference groups.
Snow Falling on Cedars; Ray; Rosewood; A Patch of Blue. Stereotypes, prejudice, and discrimination.
The Breakfast Club; The Defiant Ones. Prejudice and the contact hypothesis.
Higher Learning; Revenge of the Nerds; Legally Blonde. Cultural diversity and stereotypes.
Gangs of New York; Mississippi Burning. Deindividuation; aggression.
Schindler's List. Obedience, compliance.

Books

Henry Louis Gates, Jr., *Colored People: A Memoir* (Vintage, 1994). Growing up black in segregated West Virginia.
James Goodman, *Stories of Scottsboro* (Vintage, 1994). Prejudice and discrimination lead to wrongful rape convictions of young black men in Alabama in 1931.
Elliot Aronson, *Nobody Left to Hate* (W. H. Freeman, 2000). A social psychologist explores the social roots of the Columbine school massacre.
Alex Kotlowitz, *The Other Side of the River: A Story of Two Towns, a Death, and America's Dilemma* (Doubleday, 1998). A story of discrimination in law enforcement and prejudice in a town that is racially and geographically divided.
John Gray, *Men Are from Mars, Women Are from Venus* (HarperCollins, 1993). Interpersonal relationships.
Hans-Werner Bierhoff, *Prosocial Behaviour* (Psychology Press, 2002). An introductory overview of research on helping and altruism.
Charles Stangor (Ed.), *Stereotypes and Prejudice: Essential Readings* (Psychology Press, 2000). A collection of research articles on prejudice.
Robert Cialdini, *Influence: Science and Practice* (Addison-Wesley, 2001). Summary of research on influence and how it is applied in everyday life.
Russell Geen and Edward Donnerstein (Eds.), *Human Aggression: Theory, Research, and Implications for Social Policy* (Academic Press, 1998). Readings on the origins of and factors in aggression.
Malcolm Gladwell, *The Tipping Point: How Little Things Can Make a Big Difference* (Back Bay Books, 2002). Describes how concepts from social psychology can help explain the development of popular fads and trends.

The Web

The World Wide Web is a good source of additional information about the science of psychology, provided you use it carefully and think critically about the information you find. The Online Study Center that accompanies this text offers many resources relevant to this chapter. These resources include interactive tutorials; Thinking Critically and Evaluating Research exercises; ACE chapter quizzes; recommended web links; and articles on current events, books, and movies. Please visit the Online Study Center at college.hmco.com/pic/bernsteinessentials4e.

Review of Key Terms

Can you define each of the key terms in the chapter? Check your definitions against those on the pages shown in parentheses in the following list or in the Glossary/Index at the end of the text.

actor-observer bias (p. 546)	**attitude** (p. 548)	**competition** (p. 578)	**cooperation** (p. 578)
aggression (p. 568)	**attribution** (p. 545)	**compliance** (p. 560)	**deindividuation** (p. 560)
altruism (p. 574)	**bystander effect** (p. 576)	**conflict** (p. 578)	**discrimination** (p. 553)
arousal: cost-reward theory (p. 575)	**cognitive dissonance theory** (p. 550)	**conformity** (p. 560)	**elaboration likelihood model** (p. 549)
		contact hypothesis (p. 554)	

empathy-altruism
 theory (p. 577)
environmental
 psychology (p. 574)
frustration-aggression
 hypothesis (p. 571)
fundamental attribution
 error (p. 546)
groupthink (p. 582)
helping behavior (p. 574)

matching hypothesis (p. 556)
norms (p. 559)
obedience (p. 564)
person-oriented leaders (p. 581)
prejudice (p. 553)
reference groups (p. 540)
relative deprivation (p. 541)
schemas (p. 543)

self-concept (p. 540)
self-esteem (p. 540)
self-fulfilling prophecy (p. 545)
self-serving bias (p. 547)
social cognition (p. 540)
social comparison (p. 540)
social dilemmas (p. 578)
social facilitation (p. 579)

social identity (p. 542)
social impairment (p. 580)
social loafing (p. 580)
social neuroscience (p. 582)
social perception (p. 543)
social psychology (p. 540)
stereotypes (p. 553)
task-oriented leaders (p. 581)

Multiple-Choice Self-Test

Select the best answer for each of the following questions. Then check your responses against the Answer Key at the end of the text.

1. Jack took an entry-level job after completing college with honors and having his senior research paper published. Now Jack is depressed because the older people around him make more money than he does and are more advanced in their careers. Jack is experiencing

   a. cognitive dissonance.
   b. relative deprivation.
   c. social facilitation.
   d. a self-fulfilling prophecy.

2. One of the assumptions of terror management theory is that

   a. having high self-esteem helps to reduce the impact of thoughts about death.
   b. people who engage in terrorism have antisocial personalities.
   c. it is better to dwell on negative thoughts than avoid them.
   d. people cope better with terrifying thoughts when they do not seek social support.

3. When Rowland first met Jacob, Jacob wasn't feeling well and threw up on Rowland's shoes. According to research on first impressions, we would expect Rowland to

   a. feel sorry for Jacob and thus have a positive first impression of him.
   b. develop a negative impression of Jacob because of the negative first experience with him.
   c. have an initial negative impression that will become positive later, no matter what Jacob does.
   d. have a positive first impression of Jacob because he is a male.

4. Gena is in a bad mood because she is convinced that she won't like her blind date, Pat. When Pat arrives, he is outgoing and considerate, but Gena is short-tempered and rude to him. Soon Pat becomes irritable and ends the date early. Gina's prediction that she wouldn't have a good time came true mainly because of

   a. cognitive dissonance.
   b. prejudice.
   c. a self-fulfilling prophecy.
   d. the fundamental attribution error.

5. "I earned an A on my history test because I studied hard and I'm smart, but I failed my philosophy test because its questions were poorly worded and the teacher doesn't like me." This statement is an example of

   a. actor-observer bias.
   b. the fundamental attribution error.
   c. a self-fulfilling prophecy.
   d. a self-serving bias.

6. Richard is listening to a student government leader suggest that professors on campus should stop giving grades. Richard is most likely to be convinced if the speaker

   a. introduces a famous celebrity who supports this idea.
   b. circulates a petition in support of the idea.
   c. presents evidence that eliminating grades does not hurt students' job prospects.
   d. is personable and funny.

7. Rachel and Matteus listen to a boring lecture. Afterward, Rachel is offered $100 and Matteus is offered $1 to tell the lecturer's next class that the lecture was interesting and fun. Both agree to do so. According to cognitive dissonance theory, we would expect real attitude change about the lecture to occur in

   a. Rachel, but not Matteus.
   b. Matteus, but not Rachel.
   c. both Rachel and Matteus.
   d. neither Rachel nor Matteus.

8. In an attempt to reduce prejudice between ethnic groups at Lincoln School, the principal asks members of all groups to help build a new playground. Prejudice would be most likely to decrease as a result if

   a. teams from each ethnic group competed to see which could work the fastest.
   b. one member of each group was appointed to a committee to lead the project.
   c. members of all the groups worked together in teams to complete various parts of the playground.
   d. members of each ethnic group wore the same kind of t-shirt.

9. Rhona, a pretty woman with conservative political views, has just moved into an apartment building on campus. All else being equal, which neighbor will Rhona probably like the most?

    a. Jill, whose hair color, height, and weight, are similar to Rhona's.
    b. Shauna, president of the Young Conservatives club.
    c. Patrice, president of the Young Liberals club.
    d. Yolanda, who comes from Rhona's home town.

10. Giorgio and Louisa share their thoughts, hopes, and daily worries. They plan to stay married throughout their lifetime, and they enjoy an active and satisfying sex life. According to Sternberg's theory, Giorgio and Louisa are experiencing _____ love.

    a. consummate
    b. companionate
    c. temporary
    d. romantic

11. When her best friend stopped by with a Christmas gift, Jen was upset because she had nothing to give in return. Jen was uncomfortable because she had

    a. experienced deindividuation.
    b. engaged in social loafing.
    c. made the ultimate attribution error.
    d. violated the reciprocity norm.

12. In Harper Lee's novel *To Kill a Mockingbird*, an angry mob tries to lynch a prisoner. The prisoner's attorney, Atticus Finch, and his young daughter, "Scout," talk to the crowd, calling people by name, and reminding them that they know their families. Soon the mob disperses, no longer a faceless crowd but a group of identifiable individuals. Atticus and Scout disrupted the phenomenon of

    a. diffusion of responsibility.
    b. deindividuation.
    c. situational ambiguity.
    d. social facilitation.

13. Shawn's teacher doesn't keep track of her students' performance in groups, so Shawn does not put as much effort into his group project as he does into his individual project. Shawn is exhibiting

    a. a self-serving bias.
    b. social facilitation.
    c. social loafing.
    d. diffusion of responsibility.

14. Keyonna thought that the play she had just seen was boring, but everyone else seemed to like it. At the closing curtain, the audience gave the actors a standing ovation. Keyonna stood up and applauded, too, even though she didn't believe the actors deserved it. Keyonna's behavior in this situation is an example of

    a. conformity.
    b. compliance.
    c. obedience.
    d. a self-fulfilling prophecy.

15. Colleen knows she should take a day off from work to study for a big exam, but she also knows her boss won't like it. So she first asks for the entire week off. When the boss refuses, she asks for the one day off instead, and he agrees. Colleen used the _____ approach to gain her boss's compliance.

    a. foot-in-the-door
    b. door-in-the-face
    c. low-ball
    d. peripheral

16. Which of the following is not a major factor in determining whether or not a person will obey an order?

    a. The status of the authority figure giving the order.
    b. The personality characteristics of the person receiving the order.
    c. The presence of another person who disobeys the order.
    d. The gender of the person given the order.

17. Leonard is upset because he just can't get his new iPod to work. When his roommate comes home and accidentally knocks over Leonard's glass of lemonade, Leonard becomes abusive, screaming at his roommate and throwing books and pillows at him. This is an example of the _____ theory of aggression.

    a. frustration-aggression
    b. generalized arousal
    c. authoritarian
    d. biological

18. While shopping, Lenora falls and breaks her ankle. She is most likely to receive help from a stranger if she

    a. is in a quiet area where only a few people saw her fall.
    b. is in the midst of a large crowd.
    c. is in a large city.
    d. doesn't ask for help.

19. Which of the following summarizes the evolutionary view of helping behavior?

    a. People feel good when they help others.
    b. People help others in order to improve the chance that some of their genes will survive in future generations.
    c. People are motivated to protect others if the costs of helping are outweighed by the benefits.
    d. People are helpful because it improves everyone's chances of survival.

20. When groups fail to consider all the facts and all their options, when they share similar biases, and when they are pressured to reach an agreement, they often make poor decisions because of a phenomenon called

    a. deindividuation.
    b. groupthink.
    c. social facilitation.
    d. social impairment.

Appendix
Statistics in Psychological Research

Understanding and interpreting the results of psychological research depend on *statistical analyses,* the methods for describing and drawing conclusions from data. The introductory chapter introduced some terms and concepts associated with these analyses. *Descriptive statistics* are the numbers that psychologists use to describe and present their data. *Inferential statistics* are the mathematical procedures they use to draw conclusions from data and to make inferences about what the data mean. Here, we present more details about these statistical analyses that will help you to evaluate research results.

Describing Data

To illustrate our discussion, let's imagine a hypothetical experiment on the effects of rewards on performance. The experimenter presents a set of mathematics problems to two groups of people. Each group must solve the problems within a fixed time. For each correct answer, the low-reward group is paid ten cents. The high-reward group gets one dollar. The hypothesis to be tested is the **null hypothesis,** the assertion that the independent variable manipulated by the experimenter will have no effect on the dependent variable measured by the experimenter. In this case, the null hypothesis is that the size of the reward (the independent variable) will not affect performance on the mathematics task (the dependent variable).

Assume that the experimenter has obtained a sample of participants, assigned them randomly to the two groups, and done everything possible to avoid the influence of confounding variables and other research problems discussed in the introductory chapter. The experiment has been run, and the researcher now has the data, a list of the number of correct answers given by each participant in each group. Now comes the first task of statistical analysis. We must describe the data in a way that makes them easy to understand.

The Frequency Histogram

The simplest way to describe the data is to draw up something like Table 1, in which all the numbers are simply listed. After examining the table, you might notice that the high-reward group seems to have done better than the low-reward group. But the difference is not immediately obvious. It might be even harder to see if more participants had been involved or if the scores included three-digit numbers. A more satisfactory way of presenting the same data is in a picture-like graphic known as a **frequency histogram** (see Figure 1).

Construction of a histogram is simple. First, divide the scale for measuring the dependent variable (in this case, the number of correct solutions) into a number of categories, or "bins." The bins in our example are 1–2, 3–4, 5–6, 7–8, and 9–10. Next, sort the raw data into the appropriate bin. (For example, the score of a participant who had 5 correct answers would go into the 5–6 bin, a score of 8 would go into the 7–8 bin, and so on.) Finally, for each bin, count the number of scores in that bin, and draw a bar up to the height of that number on the vertical axis of the graph. The set of bars makes up the frequency histogram. Figure 1 shows a histogram comparing the scores of the high-reward group and the low-reward group. Now the difference between groups that was difficult to see in Table 1 becomes clearly visible. More people in the high-reward group obtained high scores than in the low-reward group.

null hypothesis A testable statement that the independent variable manipulated by an experimenter will have no effect on the dependent variable being measured by the experimenter.

frequency histogram A pictorial presentation of how often each possible score on a dependent variable occurs in a set of research data.

TABLE 1

A Simple Data Set

Here are the test scores obtained by thirteen participants performing under low-reward conditions and thirteen participants performing under high-reward conditions.

Low Reward	High Reward
4	6
6	4
2	10
7	10
6	7
8	10
3	6
5	7
2	5
3	9
5	9
9	3
5	8

FIGURE 1

A Frequency Histogram

The height of each bar of a histogram represents the number of scores falling within each range of score values. The pattern formed by these bars gives a visual image of how research results are distributed.

Histograms and other "pictures" of data are useful for visualizing and better understanding the "shape" of research data. But in order to analyze data statistically, we need to use other ways of handling the numbers that make up these graphic presentations. For example, before we can tell whether two histograms are different statistically or just visually, the data they represent must be summarized using descriptive statistics.

Descriptive Statistics

The four basic categories of descriptive statistics do the following: (1) count the number of observations made; (2) summarize the typical value of a set of data; (3) summarize the spread, or variability, in a set of data; and (4) express the correlation between two sets of data, using the correlation coefficient described in the introductory chapter.

N   The easiest statistic to compute, abbreviated as N, simply describes the number of observations that make up the data set. In Table 1, for example, $N = 13$ for each group, or 26 for the entire data set. Simple as it is, N plays a very important role in more sophisticated statistical analyses.

Measures of Central Tendency   It is apparent in Figure 1 that there is a difference in the pattern of scores between the two groups. But how much of a difference? What is the typical value, the *central tendency*, that represents each group's performance? There are three measures that capture this typical value: the mode, the median, and the mean. The *mode* is the value or score that occurs most frequently in the data set. The *median* is the halfway point in a set of data; half the scores fall above the median, and half fall below it. The *mean* is the arithmetic average. To find the mean, add the values of all the scores and divide by the number of scores (N).

Measures of Variability   The variability (or spread or dispersion) of a set of data is often just as important as its central tendency. This variability can be quantified by measures known as the *range* and the *standard deviation*. The range is simply the difference between the highest and the lowest values in a data set. For the data in Table 1, the range for the low-reward group is $9 - 2 = 7$; for the high-reward group, the range is $10 - 3 = 7$. The standard deviation, or SD, describes the average difference between each score and the mean of the data set.

The Normal Distribution   In most subfields in psychology, when researchers collect many measurements and plot their data in histograms, the pattern that results often resembles that shown for the low-reward group in Figure 1. That is, the majority of

Statistics can be valuable for describing research results, but critical thinking demands that we evaluate them carefully before drawing conclusions about what they mean. Knowing this pointy-haired executive's tendency toward uncritical thinking, you can bet that Dogbert's impressive-sounding restatement of the definition of *median* will win him an extension of his pricey consulting contract.

DILBERT: ©Scott Adams/Dist. By United Feature Syndicate, Inc.

scores tend to fall in the middle of the distribution, whereas fewer and fewer scores occur as one moves toward the extremes. As more and more data are collected, and as smaller and smaller bins are used (perhaps containing only one value each), the histogram tends to smooth out until it resembles the bell-shaped curve known as the **normal distribution,** or normal curve, which is shown in Figure 2. When a distribution of scores follows a truly normal curve, its mean, median, and mode all have the same value. Furthermore, if the curve is normal, we can use its standard deviation to describe how any particular score stands in relation to the rest of the distribution.

The distribution of IQ scores shown in Figure 2 provides an example. They are distributed in a normal curve, with a mean, median, and mode of 100 and a standard deviation (SD) of 16. In such a distribution, half of the population will have an IQ above 100, and half will have one below 100. The shape of the true normal curve is such that 68 percent of the area under it lies within 1 standard deviation above and below the mean. In terms of IQ, this means that 68 percent of the population has an IQ somewhere between 84 (100 minus 16) and 116 (100 plus 16). Of the remaining 32 percent of the population, half falls more than 1 SD above the mean, and half falls more than 1 SD below the mean. Thus, 16 percent of the population has an IQ above 116, and 16 percent scores below 84.

The normal curve is also the basis for percentiles. A **percentile score** indicates the percentage of people or observations that fall at or below a given score in a normal distribution. In Figure 2, for example, the mean score (which is also the median) lies at a point below which 50 percent of the scores fall. Thus, the mean of a normal distribution

FIGURE **2**

The Normal Distribution

Many kinds of research data approximate the shape of the normal curve, in which most scores fall toward the center of the range.

normal distribution A smooth, bell-shaped curve representing a set of data in which most scores occur in the middle of the possible range, with fewer and fewer scores occurring toward the extremes of the range.

percentile score A way of stating what percentage of scores in a data set fall at or below a certain score.

The normal distribution of IQ

is at the 50th percentile. What does this mean for IQ? If you score 1 SD above the mean, your score is at a point above which only 16 percent of the population falls. This means that 84 percent of the population (100 percent minus 16 percent) must be below that score. So this IQ score is at the 84th percentile. A score at 2 SDs above the mean is at the 97.5 percentile, because 97.5 percent of the scores are below it in a normal distribution.

Scores may also be expressed in terms of their distance in standard deviations from the mean, producing what are called **standard scores.** A standard score of 1.5, for example, is 1.5 standard deviations from the mean.

Inferential Statistics

It can be hard to understand the meaning of research results summarized in descriptive statistics alone. Is a correlation between college grade-point averages and the eating of certain foods large enough to support the hypothesis that diet is important for mental functioning? Is the difference in the effects of two different kinds of psychotherapy large enough to recommend one over the other? The answers to questions such as these are based largely on the results of analyses that use inferential statistics.

Consider again the descriptive statistics from our rewards experiment. They tell us that the performances of the high- and low-reward groups differ, but there is some uncertainty. Is the difference large enough to be important? Does it represent a real effect or a fluke? The researcher would like to have some measure of confidence that the difference between groups did not occur by chance alone. **Inferential statistics** use certain rules to estimate the likelihood that a particular correlation or a particular difference between groups was due to chance. If that likelihood is small enough, the researcher can usually conclude that the correlation or difference is *statistically significant.*

Differences Between Means: The *t* Test

One of the most important tools of inferential statistics is the *t* test. It allows the researcher to ask how likely it is that the difference between two means occurred by chance rather than because of the independent variable. When the *t* test or another inferential statistic says that the probability of chance effects is small enough (usually less than 5 percent), the results are said to be *statistically significant.* Conducting a *t* test of statistical significance requires the use of three descriptive statistics.

The first component of the *t* test is the size of the observed effect, the difference between the means. Recall that the mean is calculated by summing a group's scores and dividing by the number of scores. In the example shown in Table 1, the mean of the high-reward group is 94/13, or 7.23, and the mean of the low-reward group is 65/13, or 5. Thus the difference between the means for the high- and low-reward groups is $7.23 - 5 = 2.23$.

Second, the standard deviation of scores in each group must be known. If the scores in the groups are quite variable, their standard deviations will be large, indicating that chance may have played a large role in producing the results. If the scores within each group are all very similar, however, their standard deviations will be small, which suggests that the participants in each group reacted in about the same way to the rewards they were given. Thus, the difference between groups is more likely to be significant when each group's standard deviation is small. In Table 1, some people in the low-reward group actually did better on the math test than some in the high-reward group. If variability is high enough that the scores of two groups overlap, the difference between group means, though large, may not be statistically significant.

Third, we need to take the sample size, N, into account. The larger the number of participants or observations, the more likely it is that a given difference between means is significant. This is so because with larger samples, random factors within a group will have less impact on the group's mean. The unusual performance of a few people who were sleepy or anxious or hostile, for example, will likely be canceled out by the

standard score A way of stating how many standard deviations separate a particular score from the mean of all the scores in a data set.

inferential statistics A form of statistical analysis designed to provide a measure of confidence about how likely it is that a certain result appeared by chance.

scores of the more representative majority of people. The same effect of sample size can be seen in coin tossing. If you toss a quarter 5 times, you might not be too surprised if heads come up 80 percent of the time. But if you get 80 percent heads after 100 tosses, you might begin to suspect that this is probably not due to chance alone. Some other effect, perhaps some bias in the coin, is probably producing the results. For the same reason, a relatively small correlation coefficient—between diet and grades, say—might be statistically significant if it was based on 50,000 students. As the number of participants increases, it becomes less likely that the correlation reflects the influence of a few oddball cases.

To summarize, as the difference between the means gets larger, as N increases, and as standard deviations get smaller, t increases. This increase in t raises the researcher's confidence in the significance of the difference between means.

Beyond the t Test

Many experiments in psychology are considerably more complex than simple comparisons between two groups. They often involve three or more experimental and control groups. Some experiments also include more than one independent variable. For example, suppose we were interested not only in the effect of reward size on performance but also in the effect of problem difficulty. We might then create six groups whose members would perform easy, moderate, or difficult problems under low- or high-reward conditions.

In an experiment like this, the results might be due to the size of the reward, the difficulty of the problem, or the combined effects (known as the *interaction*) of the two. Analyzing the size and source of these effects is typically accomplished through procedures known as *analysis of variance*. The details of analysis of variance are beyond the scope of this book, but note that, as in the t test, the statistical significance of each effect is influenced by differences between means, standard deviation, and sample size.

For more detailed information about how analysis of variance and other inferential statistics are used to understand and interpret the results of psychological research, consider taking courses in research methods and statistical or quantitative methods.

Answer Key to Multiple-Choice Self-Test Questions

Chapter 1   Introduction to the Science of Psychology

1A The first research laboratory in psychology was established to study consciousness *(p. 10)*.   **2B** A community psychologist would believe that low-income families who live in crowded conditions are more likely to need mental health services *(p. 5)*.   **3B** Someone who believes that human behavior is influenced by genetic inheritance, unconscious motivations, and environmental influences exemplifies the multiple perspectives of the eclectic approach *(p. 14)*.   **4C** An educational psychologist studies what teachers actually do when they are teaching students to read *(p. 5)*.   **5A** Behaviorists say that people think and behave in ways that have previously been rewarded *(pp. 12–13)*.   **6C** In collectivist cultures, people tend to think of themselves as part of a family or work group *(p. 20)*.   **7D** Recognition of a smile is a behavior that cross-cultural psychologists find to be similar around the world *(p. 19)*.   **8D** "What am I being asked to believe or accept?" is the first of five critical thinking questions discussed in this chapter *(pp. 22–23)*.   **9D** An operational definition defines a variable so that it can be measured. In this case the score on the mood survey is the operational definition of mood *(p. 25)*.   **10C** Case Studies are used to collect descriptive data *(pp. 25–26)*.   **11D** Before using survey results to support a hypothesis, we must be sure that the questions are properly worded, the sample used is representative of the population of interest, and the responses are not biased by efforts to appear "socially acceptable" *(pp. 27–28)*.   **12A** When research results are statistically significant it means that the probability that the results occurred by chance are extremely small *(p. 40)*.   **13D** To avoid the possibility that experimenter bias may confound the results of an experiment aimed at testing a hypothesis, a researcher should use a double-blind study *(p. 35)*.   **14A** In an experiment, the outcome behavior being measured (such as memory) is the dependent variable *(p. 30)*.   **15B** In an experiment, the group that receives the "treatment" or intervention is the experimental group *(p. 32)*.   **16B** Using a true experiment to try to scientifically study this problem would pose the greatest ethical problems for Jose because it is not ethical to purposely create abusive conditions for children *(pp. 40–41)*.   **17B** The number closest to ±1.00 is the strongest correlation coefficient *(p. 29)*.   **18D** A correlation coefficient can tell us the strength, direction, and existence of a relationship between two variables, but not its cause *(pp. 29–30)*.   **19C** To select participants for study such as smoking habits of a group of students, you would use a representative sample *(p. 35)*.   **20D** All are good reasons for ethical behavior *(pp. 40–41)*.

Chapter 2   Biology and Behavior

1D The nucleus of a cell provides genetic information, and the mitochondria keep a stable chemical environment *(p. 50)*.   **2C** Malfunctions of serotonin systems contribute to depression, and malfunctions in dopamine systems contribute to Parkinson's disease *(p. 75)*.   **3A** Overactivity of glutamate, which occurs when oxygen is cut off from neurons in the brain, can result in a stroke *(p. 76)*.   **4B** Functional magnetic resonance imaging (fMRI) combines the advantages of PET and MRI and is capable of detecting changes in blood flow and blood oxygen that reflect ongoing changes in the activity of neurons *(p. 56)*.   **5C** The somatic system carries information to and from the central nervous system *(p. 54)*.   **6D** The sympathetic nervous system is less active, and the parasympathetic system is more active, now that Kalli is relaxing *(p. 54)*.   **7A** Some simple behaviors like reflexes occur automatically via the spinal cord and without instructions from the other portion of the central nervous system, the brain *(p. 55)*.   **8A** A neuron's action potential shoots down its axon with greater speed when the axon is coated in myelin *(pp. 50–51)*.   **9A** The medulla, located in the hindbrain, helps to regulate heart rate, blood pressure, and breathing *(p. 62)*.   **10D** If the reticular formation fibers in Lily's hindbrain were damaged, she would go into a coma *(p. 62)*.   **11A** The cerebellum is that part of the hindbrain that controls finely coordinated movements *(p. 62)*.   **12B** Defects in the hippocampus have been found in people with Alzheimer's disease *(p. 64)*.   **13A** The sensory system provides information about the environment *(pp. 54–56)*.   **14C** The sensory cortex in the occipital lobe receives information concerning vision *(p. 65)*.   **15A** Voluntary movements are controlled by neurons in the motor cortex, located in the frontal lobe *(p. 66)*.   **16A** Damage to Broca's area creates difficulties in speaking *(p. 69)*.   **17A** The left hemisphere of the brain is specialized for language *(p. 70)*.   **18A** Brain imaging research reveals that imagining practicing movements causes changes in the motor cortex *(p. 71)*.   **19A** Neurons secrete neurotransmitters across synapses and endocrine organs release hormones into the blood stream *(pp. 51; 77)*.   **20A** Glands release hormones such as cortisol into the bloodstream *(p. 77)*.

Chapter 3   Sensation and Perception

1A Perception is the process of using information and your understanding of the world so that messages from the senses become meaningful experiences *(p. 86)*.   **2B** Transduction is the process of converting incoming energy into neural activities *(p. 86)*.   **3A** The described procedure defines absolute threshold *(p. 87)*.   **4B** Expecting a stimulus to occur lowers the response criterion *(p. 88)*.   **5C** According to Weber's law, the lighter the objects being compared, the smaller the weight difference needed to detect a change in weight *(p. 89)*.   **6B** When a star is faint, it is more easily seen by looking slightly away from where the star is expected to be *(pp. 94–95)*.   **7D** The trichromatic theory proposes that combining three primary colors can produce any other color *(p. 88)*.   **8A** According to the gate control theory, input from other skin senses can come into the spinal cord at the same time the pain gets there and "take over" the pathways that the pain impulses would have used *(pp. 107–108)*.   **9C** Constant loud noise causes hair cell damage, literally ripping off hair cells form his inner ear, resulting in nerve deafness *(p. 100)*.   **10D** Unlike other senses, our sense of smell does not send its messages through the thalamus *(p. 104)*.   **11A** Your blind spot is located where the optic nerve leaves the eyeball *(pp. 92–93)*.   **12D** Nutritional state and temperature can both contribute to food's flavor *(p. 103)*.   **13C** The Stroop task is difficult because one must divide attention between the meaning of the word and the color of the word. Without knowing the meaning of the word, there is no divided attention *(p. 128)*.   **14A** Kinesthesia gives us knowledge of the position of our body parts *(p. 106)*.   **15B** Stroboscopic motion is an illusion in which lights or images flashed in rapid succession are perceived as moving *(p. 117)*.   **16B** People moving at the same speed, in a sense having a "common fate," are perceived as a group *(p. 114)*.   **17C** Interposition is the depth perception cue that operates on this basis *(p. 115)*.   **18B** Looming is a motion cue such that objects increasingly fill the retinal space as they get closer *(p. 117)*.   **19B** Bottom-up processing involves basic sensory feature analysis, including the sensation of changes in salt level *(p. 121)*.   **20A** Covert orienting involves a shift of attention that isn't easily observed *(p. 127)*.

Chapter 4   Consciousness

1A Mental processing of bodily processes, such as the brain regulating blood pressure, occur at the nonconscious level, and some people are able to learn to control these processes through biofeedback *(p. 137)*.   **2C** Dr. Eplort will most likely sleep about the same as he did before *(p. 148)*.   **3C** Zandra's preference for the Rembrandt paintings was most likely affected by priming *(p. 139)*.   **4B** Edie's success depends on her expectation that the messages will help her *(pp. 140–141)*.   **5D** Mitch's responses to marijuana were most likely due to learned expectations *(pp. 157–158)*.   **6C** Leroy was most likely in stage 4 sleep, the deepest stage of slow-wave sleep *(p. 144)*.   **7C** Alan is most likely suffering from REM behavior disorder, a condition that allows dreams to be acted out *(p. 147)*.   **8A** SIDS (sudden infant death syndrome) has been greatly reduced in the United States by the "back to sleep" program, which advises parents to have their babies sleep face up *(p. 147)*.   **9B** Disruptions of your circadian rhythm can make you grouchy and less productive. Melatonin has been used to maintain these circadian rhythms *(p. 148)*.   **10C** It is non-REM sleep that researchers believe is important for restoring the body and brain's energy stores for the next day's activity, the other three responses are functions of REM sleep *(p. 149)*.   **11D** According to the activation-synthesis theory, dreams are meaningless, random byproducts of REM sleep *(p. 151).* **12C** People susceptible to hypnosis are able to focus and redistribute their attention on the hypnotist *(p. 152).* **13C** Hypnosis has been used to help people reduce nausea from chemotherapy, surgical bleeding, and pain *(p. 154).* **14A** Research on meditation has shown that meditators report a decrease in stress-related problems and anxiety *(p. 155).* **15A** Agonists are drugs that bind to a receptor and mimic the effects of the neurotransmitter that normally fits that receptor *(pp. 146–155).* **16A** Tolerance is a condition in which increasingly larger drug doses are required to produce the same effect *(p. 156).* **17D** Since alcohol's physiological effects involve dopamine, dopamine agonists can reduce cravings and withdrawal effects *(p. 158).* **18C** Caffeine is a stimulant, which does not cause hallucinations *(p. 160).* **19B** Opiates relieve pain and cause sleep *(p. 161).* **20B** Marijuana disrupts memory function and reduces creativity *(p. 162).*

Chapter 5   Learning

1C The expression "Once burned, twice shy" reflects a change in knowledge (or behavior) due to experience *(p. 171).* **2B** After repeated pairings with a stimulus that already triggers a reflexive response, the conditioned stimulus alone elicits the reflexive-like response *(pp. 172–173).* **3B** Extinction is the gradual disappearance of a conditioned response when the UCS is eliminated *(p. 173).* **4A** The law of effect predicts that Kim will be more likely to date Brad because he is associated with a positive outcome, her enjoyment of the movie *(p. 179).* **5D** Najla has developed a phobia through classical conditioning *(pp. 171–172).* **6A** The idea that knowledge is located in many areas throughout the brain rather than in one particular place is a basic assumption of neural network theories *(p. 191).* **7A** Stimulus generalization is a process in which a conditioned response is triggered by stimuli similar to the original conditioned stimulus *(pp. 173–174).* **8C** For survival reasons, people are biologically prepared to link taste signals with illness *(p. 175).* **9A** Extinction occurs because the behavior is no longer being rewarded *(pp. 185–186).* **10B** Operant conditioning involves learning that behaviors have consequences *(p. 171).* **11B** Negative reinforcement strengthens behavior that is followed by the removal of an unpleasant event or stimulus *(p. 180).* **12B** Once avoidance conditioning is learned, avoidance can be a difficult habit to break *(pp. 180–181).* **13D** A discriminative stimulus signals that a reward will occur if a certain response is given *(p. 185).* **14D** Shaping is the process of reinforcing successive approximations to the target behavior *(p. 183).* **15B** Jamey must exhibit a fixed number of behaviors while Susan must work a variable amount of time *(p. 185).* **16D** They are all problems with using punishment *(p. 187).* **17B** Learned helplessness occurs when people learn they are unable to control circumstances or outcomes *(p. 192).* **18C** Latent learning is learning that is not demonstrated when it is first learned *(p. 194).* **19D** Najla has learned from the experience of watching others pet a dog *(pp. 196–197).* **20D** Working in groups is an active learning method that improves students' recall of information *(p. 201).*

Chapter 6   Memory

1A Acoustic codes represent information as sequences of sounds, such as a tune or a rhyme *(p. 209).* **2B** Episodic memory is a person's recall of a specific event that happened while that person was present; explicit memory involves the processes through which people try to remember something, *(p. 210).* **3C** Implicit memories are not purposefully recalled but do influence behavior *(p. 210).* **4B** Maintenance rehearsal is a method of keeping information in short-term memory by repeating it *(p. 211).* **5B** The transfer-appropriate processing model of memory suggests that a critical factor in memory is how the encoding process matches up with what is later retrieved *(p. 211).* **6C** Selective attention allows Reepal to focus on the most important information *(p. 214).* **7B** Unrehearsed information stays in short-term memory for about eighteen seconds *(p. 216).* **8A** Chunking involves grouping information into meaningful units that can be stored *(p. 215).* **9C** Semantic memory contains general knowledge not linked to a specific event *(p. 210).* **10C** Ebbinghaus found that most forgetting occurs during the first nine hours after learning, and especially during the first hour *(pp. 227–228).* **11D** The serial position curve predicts that first items (primacy effect) and last items (recency effect) will be best remembered. *(p. 218).* **12A** State-dependent memory memory that is helped or hindered by similarities or differences in a person's internal state during learning versus recall *(p. 220).* **13C** The tip-of-the-tongue phenomenon represents the retrieval of incomplete knowledge *(p. 222).* **14C** In the process of constructive memory, people use generalized knowledge, or schemas, to fill in gaps in the information they encode and retrieve *(p. 224).* **15C** Recent use of DNA evidence has revealed that many people in prison for serious crimes did not commit those crimes *(p. 225).* **16C** As Ebbinghaus discovered, relearning takes much less time than original learning. This difference represents the savings

from one learning to the next learning *(p. 228).* **17C** Proactive interference occurs when old information disrupts the learning of new information *(p. 229).* **18A** Spontaneous generalizations are produced by PDP networks *(p. 224).* **19B** Anterograde amnesia is the inability to form new long-term memories following a brain injury *(p. 235).* **20A** The method of loci involves mentally placing objects in various spots in a familiar location (loci) *(p. 238).*

Chapter 7   Thought, Language, and Intelligence

1D Thinking is part of an information processing system that manipulates mental representations *(p. 249).* **2C** A natural concept has no fixed set of defining characteristics but a prototype possesses most of its characteristic features *(p. 250).* **3B** Basing his strategy on an algorithm would require Clint to evaluate every possible move and countermove *(p. 254).* **4D** Scripts are mental representations of familiar sequences of activity *(p. 252).* **5B** Setting aside a difficult problem, hoping for a solution to occur while working on something else, is called incubation *(p. 257).* **6D** Functional fixedness occurs when a person fails to use a familiar object in a novel way to solve a problem *(p. 261).* **7C** Confirmation bias is a strong tendency to confirm rather than refute the preferred hypothesis, even in the face of strong evidence against the hypothesis *(p. 262).* **8A** The gambler's fallacy has led Richard to believe that the probability of a random event will change over time *(p. 267).* **9C** Incorrect words or word endings are not likely to have been reinforced. They are overgeneralizations of a language rule the child has learned *(p. 271).* **10A** A critical period is a limited window of opportunity for language learning. If the critical period is missed, normal language development will not occur *(p. 273).* **11A** Alfred Binet designed the first IQ test to identify children with special educational needs *(p. 274).* **12D** Formal reasoning is based on the rules of logic *(p. 254).* **13B** The average score obtained by people at each age level is assigned the IQ value of 100 with half of the scores lower than 100 and half higher than 100 *(p. 274).* **14C** If the scores from this preemployment test predict future performance on the job, the test is valid for the purpose of employee selection *(p. 279).* **15A** A reliable test yields consistent and stable scores over time *(p. 278).* **16A** IQ tests appear to be most valid for assessing aspects of intelligence that are related to school work *(p. 279).* **17D** The highest correlation is likely to be found between the identical twins' scores *(pp. 279–280).* **18A** Individuals with mild mental retardation will have most difficulty with academic material and abstract reasoning but are able to learn new material *(p. 288).* **19A** This test was most likely based on Sternberg's triarchic theory of intelligence which proposes three types of intelligences: creative, analytic, and practical *(pp. 285–286).* **20A** Creative people are internally motivated, have a set of creative skills, use divergent thinking, and have expertise in the field of pursuit *(pp. 264–265).*

Chapter 8   Motivation and Emotion

1B The evolutionary approach suggests that adaptive behaviors that promote the survival of the species reflect inborn motivations to pass on genes *(p. 299).* **2A** Homeostasis is the tendency to maintain physiological systems at a steady, stable level by adjusting to changes *(p. 299).* **3D** Arousal theory states that people are motivated to behave in ways that maintain an individual, optimal level of arousal *(p. 300).* **4B** Incentive theory states that behavior is goal directed to obtain positive stimuli and avoid negative stimuli *(p. 301).* **5A** When stimulated, the ventromedial nucleus tells Ahmed that there is no need to eat *(p. 303).* **6B** Research shows that we tend to eat less when given only one food than when given several choices of food *(p. 303).* **7B** Although bulimics can maintain normal weight, they may experience dehydration and other symptoms *(p. 307).* **8C** The Chicago survey found that people in the United States have sex less frequently and with fewer partners than was earlier believed *(p. 309).* **9D** According to the Thinking Critically section of this chapter, sexual orientation is *most* likely influenced by prenatal hormones, genetic factors and sociocultural learning. *(pp. 313–314).* **10B** Edwina will encourage her son to try difficult tasks, praise his efforts, and help him learn from his mistakes *(p. 316).* **11B** Studies have shown that allowing people to set and achieve clear goals is one way to increase both job performance *(p. 318).* **12A** Physiological needs, including those for food and water, come first in Maslow's hierarchy *(p. 320).* **13B** An avoidance-avoidance conflict arises when we must select one of two undesirable alternatives *(p. 321).* **14C** Emotion can vary in intensity from ecstatic to mildly disappointed *(p. 323).* **15A** James's theory states that we experience emotions only by perceiving our physiological response to an event *(p. 326).* **16D** Excitation transfer occurs when arousal from an experience carries over to a different situation. This is consistent with Schachter's theory of emotion *(p. 330).* **17B** Cannon's theory maintains that emotional experience originates in the thalamus and simultaneously triggers physiological arousal and cognitive awareness *(p. 329)*. **18D** As children grow up, they learn an emotional culture, which are rules that govern what emotions are appropriate, in what situations, and what expressions are allowed *(p. 335)*. **19B** Human emotions are communicated mainly through facial movements and expressions *(p. 324)*. **20B** In allowing Diane's emotional state to guide his behavior, Sam is using social referencing *(p. 335)*.

Chapter 9   Human Development

1B Behavioral genetics is concerned with the differences between groups of individuals, not with the characteristics of a single individual *(pp. 344–345)*. **2C** Smokers' babies are usually underweight *(p. 347)*. **3D** Tyrone's physical development is the result of maturation and environmental influences *(p. 343)*. **4D** Newborns visually prefer novelty and shapes that resemble human faces *(p. 348)*. **5C** With normal brain development, grasping and rooting reflexes should have disappeared by 6 months of age *(p. 348)*. **6A** Assimilation is the process of taking in information that adds to an existing schema *(pp. 350–351)*. **7B** Adriana is probably four to six years old; she is in the preoperational stage *(p. 354)*. **8B** Babies stare longer when natural physical laws are defied *(pp. 353–354)*. **9B** We are unlikely to recall anything about our first year due to infantile amnesia *(p. 358)*. **10B** Difficult babies tend to remain difficult into childhood *(p. 361)*. **11B** Harlow's attachment studies demonstrate that infant monkeys form attachments based on contact comfort needs *(p. 362)*. **12D** With ambivalent insecure attachment, the child sometimes prefers and sometimes rejects the primary caregiver *(pp. 363–364)*. **13C** Authoritative parents are sympathetic but firm; permissive parents give lots of freedom *(p. 367)*. **14A** Girls tend to speak and write earlier and are able to read emotional signals at younger ages than boys *(p. 369)*. **15C** Ludmilla is still confused about her identity *(pp. 373–374)*. **16D** Teens who have sex tend to have parents who are less educated and less likely to exert control over them than teens who do not have sex *(p. 372)*. **17A** People at the Stage 1 (preconventional) level of moral reasoning are concerned with avoiding punishment *(p. 374)*. **18C** These changes occur mainly in middle adulthood *(p. 376)*. **19C** Up until at least age sixty, people's thinking becomes dialectical, which means they understand that knowledge is relative, not absolute *(p. 377)*. **20B** Terminal drop is the decline in mental functioning that occurs in the months or years preceding death *(p. 382)*.

Chapter 10   Health, Stress, and Coping

1C Your great-grandparents' generation was most likely to die from infectious diseases, whereas your own generation is most likely to die from chronic diseases *(p. 391)*. **2A** The more stressors Lila has, the more physical, psychological, and behavioral responses she will probably experience *(p. 396)*. **3D** Daily hassles involve irritations, pressures, and annoyances that may not be major stressors by themselves but whose effects add up to become significant *(p. 393)*. **4A** The first stage of the GAS, the alarm reaction, involves some version of the fight-or-flight syndrome *(p. 395)*. **5C** Males under stress tended to get angry, avoid stressors, or both, whereas females are more likely to help others and to make use of their social support network *(p. 404)*. **6B** Rumination is continuously thinking about negative events and it tends to intensify negative emotional states *(p. 397)*. **7B** Catastrophizing involves the exaggeration of negative consequences *(p. 397)*. **8B** People with disease-resistant personalities tend to think of stressors as temporary challenges to be overcome, not catastrophic threats *(p. 404)*. **9B** Flashbacks are associated with posttraumatic stress disorder *(pp. 379–380)*. **10B** Emotion-focused coping strategies include denial and avoidance *(p. 404)*. **11C** Perceived control over stressful events helps reduce their negative effects *(p. 401)*. **12B** Laton is trying to improve the employees' social support networks *(p. 402)*. **13B** People who are impulsive or low on conscientiousness are more likely to die from accidents or violence *(p. 405)*. **14C** Natural killer cells of the immune system have antiviral properties and help prevent tumors *(p. 408)*. **15B** Hostility is a risk factor in heart disease *(pp. 409–410)*. **16D** Social support is a mediating factor on stress *(pp. 413–414)*. **17A** Personalizing the risk of danger to the individual should increase the likelihood of behavioral change *(pp. 411–412)*. **18B** Being aware of a problem behavior and thinking about changing it occur during the contemplation stage of readiness to alter a health-related behavior *(p. 413)*. **19A** Sayumi is using the coping strategy of cognitive restructuring, or changing her thinking about an event or person *(p. 413)*. **20C** Progressive relaxation trains a person to physically relax muscles, thus reducing heart rate and blood pressure *(p. 414)*.

Chapter 11   Personality

1B Personality is defined as a person's unique pattern of enduring psychological and behavioral characteristics *(p. 420)*. **2A** The id contains the life and death instincts, is impulsive and pleasure seeking *(p. 421)*. **3D** During the latency period, which lasts from about age five until puberty, an individual's focus is on education and social development *(p. 424)*. **4B** Displacement is deflecting an impulse from its original target to a less threatening one *(p. 422)*. **5A** Overly strict toilet training can lead to an anal fixation that appears as sloppy, disorganized, and impulsive behavior in adulthood *(p. 423)*. **6D** Although based on a small, culturally biased sample and not scientifically derived, Freud's theory is comprehensive and has profoundly affected psychology *(p. 425)*. **7B** Trait theory assumes that personality traits are relatively stable, consistent, and predictable *(p. 426)*. **8C** Allport believed that personality can be described using about seven central traits *(pp. 426–427)*. **9D** Trait theorists have identified five (called "the big-five") main factors that make up personality *(p. 428)*. **10C** According to Gray, people with an active behavioral approach system tend to experience positive emotions *(p. 430)*. **11B** Twin studies suggest that there are genetic predispositions toward particular personality traits and temperament *(p. 431)*. **12A** Internals expect outcomes and events to be controlled mainly by their own efforts *(p. 434)*. **13C** Reciprocal determinism is a mutually influential interaction among cognitive patterns, the environment, and behavior *(p. 434)*. **14D** According to Mischel, person variables and situation variables are important in explaining particular behaviors *(pp. 434–435)*. **15C** Social-cognitive theories describe personality as patterns of thought and behavior that are learned though experience in social situations *(p. 433)*. **16C** Conditions of worth are created when "people" are evaluated instead of their behavior *(p. 437)*. **17B** A preoccupation with perceived need for material things and a devaluation of what one does have, reflects a deficiency orientation *(p. 437)*. **18D** Unconscious needs, motives, and conflicts supposedly guide responses to the relatively unstructured stimuli of projective tests *(p. 446)*. **19C** Research has found that those rated as ill-tempered as children are more likely to be aggressive in adulthood *(pp. 441–442)*. **20B** Objective personality tests are often used by potential employers to screen out employees who are likely to be unreliable or dishonest *(pp. 443–444)*.

Chapter 12   Psychological Disorders

1C Approximately 48 percent of the population in the United States have experienced a mental disorder at some point in their lives *(p. 454)*. **2C** The practical approach defines abnormality based on the content, context, and consequence of behavior *(p. 456)*. **3C** To be found not guilty by reason of insanity, they jury would have to find that Herman was insane at the time he committed the crime *(p. 492)*. **4D** Diathesis-stress approach attributes abnormal behavior to the interaction of stress with biological, environmental, and psychological predispositions *(p. 460)*. **5D** The global assessment of functioning is one evaluation axis of the *DSM IV (p. 463)*. **6D** Social phobias involve anxiety about being criticized by others or acting in a way that is embarrassing or humiliating *(p. 467)*. **7C** OCD involves an obsession with particular thoughts or images, which motivates repetitive, uncontrollable behaviors called compulsions *(p. 468)*. **8A** Conversion disorder involves functional impairment with no physical cause *(p. 471)*. **9A** Severe pain in the absence of any physical problem is symptomatic of pain disorder *(p. 471)*. **10A** Dissociative fugue is disorder that includes a sudden loss of personal memory and the adoption of a new identity in a new place *(p. 472)*. **11B** Sleep changes and weight gain or loss are typical of major depressive disorder *(p. 474)*. **12B** Depressed women, certain ethnic groups, males over forty-five and living alone, and those who talk about suicide do tend to be at elevated risk for committing suicide *(p. 475)*. **13A** Attribution is the process of explaining the causes of one's own and other's behavior; social-cognitive theorists see a depressive attributional style as partly responsible for depression *(p. 479)*. **14B** Schizophrenia is characterized by abnormality in thinking, writing, speaking, affect, perception and attention, and personal identity. Positive symptoms are undesirable *additions* to a person's mental life *(p. 481)*. **15D** Strong and long-lasting anxiety that is not focused on any particular object or situation marks generalized anxiety disorder *(p. 467)*. **16C** The most common symptoms of paranoid schizophrenia include delusions of grandeur or persecution, which are often accompanied by anger, anxiety, or jealousy *(p. 481)*. **17A** People diagnosed with antisocial personality disorder display impulsive, selfish, unscrupulous behavior and have few morals or deep feelings for others *(p. 486)*. **18D** The more violent forms of antisocial personality disorder are associated with the experience of abuse in childhood *(p. 486)*. **19D** Studies have shown that genetics and what people learn in their social and cultural environment play a role in alcoholism *(p. 491)*. **20B** Children with autistic disorder usually show little attachment, poor eye contact, and asocial behavior *(p. 490)*.

Chapter 13   Treatment of Psychological Disorders

1C As a part of psychodynamic therapy, the client reports all feelings, thoughts, memories, and images that come to mind in free association *(p. 504)*. **2A** Gestalt therapy uses role playing, among other techniques, to help clients become more self-aware and self-accepting *(p. 507)*. **3A** Licensed clinical psychologists generally hold a doctoral degree in clinical or counseling psychology *(p. 502)*. **4B** Psychoanalysis focuses on revealing and working through unconscious conflicts *(p. 503)*. **5B** Client-centered therapists use reflection, a paraphrased summary of the client's words that emphasizes the feelings and meanings that appear to go along with them *(p. 506)*. **6B** systematic desensitization is a behavioral method for treating anxiety in which clients visualize a graduated series of anxiety-provoking stimuli while remaining relaxed *(p. 509)*. **7C** By paraphrasing what Shanobi has said, her friend is responding in a manner consistent with reflection *(p. 506)*. **8D** Psychodynamic therapists seek to help clients gain insight by recognizing and understanding unconscious thoughts and emotions *(p. 503)*. **9C** Behavioral therapists see compulsive behaviors as learned habits *(p. 508)*. **10B** Although there is much controversy about the effectiveness of therapy, there are therapies that have been empirically found to help clients. And over-all, those seeking therapy get better more often than those who do not *(pp. 519–520)*. **11C** Confidentiality is a critical aspect of therapy than can be violated only under special circumstances, as when the therapist believes the client's life is in danger *(p. 524)*. **12B** Community psychologists are concerned with promoting social changes that prevent psychological problems *(pp. 531–532)*. **13A** Flooding is a behavior therapy technique that places a client in a feared but harmless situation to extinguish the fear *(p. 511)*. **14D** Cognitive restructuring replaces stress-provoking thoughts with more constructive thoughts thereby using thoughts to change behavior *(p. 513)*. **15B** ECT involves passing electric current through the brain to treat depression when other treatments have failed *(p. 525)*. **16D** Therapeutic psychoactive drugs may alter the functioning of particular neurotransmitter systems but they cannot change the type of neurotransmitters released into the brain *(p. 531)*. **17A** One of the most important elements of success with any therapy is the client-therapist relationship, which involves trust, disclosure, and empathy *(p. 522)*. **18C** Neuroleptics are drugs that can reduce psychotic symptoms but some of these drugs can cause severe side effects *(p. 525)*. **19B** Anxiolytics are drugs that reduce anxiety and tension *(p. 527)*. **20C** Simultaneous treatment of several clients has many positive features, but client improvement is not more rapid with this technique than with others *(p. 514)*.

Chapter 14   Social Psychology

1B Jack is experiencing relative deprivation, comparing himself to others around him *(p. 541)*. **2A** An experiment conducted by Green et al. revealed that participants were significantly less upset by an anxiety-provoking experience if they had first received esteem-building feedback about their previous test performance *(pp. 541–542)*. **3B** The first impression is formed quickly and is difficult to change *(pp. 543–544)*. **4C** The change in her date's behavior was probably due to a self-fulfilling prophecy *(p. 545)*. **5D** A self-serving bias is the tendency to take credit for success and blame external causes for failures *(p. 547)*. **6C** Richard will more likely be persuaded by evidence from the presenter (central route) since he is personally involved in the content of the presenter's message *(p. 550)*. **7B** The amount of money Matteus received was too small to justify lying about what he thought about the lecture, so he changed his attitude toward the lecture, thus making his attitude consistent with his behavior *(p. 550)*. **8C** The contact hypothesis suggests that stereotypes and prejudices can be reduced through cooperation and interdependence *(p. 554)*. **9B** People tend to like others who have attitudes similar to their own, especially attitudes about other people *(p. 555)*. **10A** Intimacy, commitment, and passion are characteristic of consummate love *(pp. 557–558)*. **11D** A particularly powerful norm is reciprocity, the tendency to respond to others as they have acted toward you *(p. 559)*. **12B** Deindividuation occurs when people in a group temporarily lose their individuality and behave in ways they otherwise would not *(p. 560)*. **13C** Shawn is exhibiting social loafing by not putting in as much effort as other group members *(p. 580)*. **14A** Conformity results from unspoken group pressure *(p. 560)*. **15B** Colleen used the door-in-the-face procedure, first asking for an unrealistic favor, then a smaller one *(p. 564)*. **16D** The gender of the person giving the order is not a major factor determining whether someone will obey the order *(p. 567)*. **17A** According to frustration-aggression

hypothesis, frustration produces a readiness to respond aggressively, which can later be environmentally triggered *(p. 571)*. **18A** The presence of others actually tends to suppress helping behavior so the fewer people who witness Lenora's fall, the better chance she will have that one of them will help her *(pp. 575–576)*. **19B** According to the evolutionary view, people display helping behaviors to improve the chances that some of their genes will survive in future generations *(p. 569)*. **20B** Groupthink impairs a group's ability to realistically evaluate options and their own decisions *(p. 582)*.

Chapter 15   Industrial/Organizational Psychology

1A I/O psychologists conduct research on behavior and mental processes in the workplace *(p. 591)*. **2C** The information from a job analysis of the position is used to guide decisions about whom to hire *(p. 592)*. **3A** A job-oriented approach describes the tasks involved in doing a job *(p. 592)*. **4B** A job analysis identifies the KSAOs required for a specific position *(pp. 592–593)*. **5C** KSAOs are attributes or characteristics necessary to successfully perform a job *(p. 592)*. **6C** Research has consistently shown that structured interviews are far more effective than unstructured interviews in leading to good hiring decisions *(p. 594)*. **7A** Assessment centers are used primarily to determine an individual's suitability for a position and are often used to hire or promote managers *(p. 594)*. **8D** Performance appraisals are used for all of these purposes *(pp. 595–596)*. **9C** A theoretical criterion is a general statement of what we mean by good or poor performance *(p. 595)*. **10A** Subjective measures of job performance take the form of judgments about various aspects of an employee's work *(p. 596)*. **11C** A critical incident provides an example of what is considered to be effective or ineffective behavior by an employee *(p. 597)*. **12B** The most valuable training programs are those that teach knowledge or skills that can be applied or transferred to the workplace *(p. 602)*. **13C** Massed training is less expensive and disruptive to employees' work schedules but people do not retain as much after mass training as they do after distributed or spaced training *(p. 603)*. **14B** I/O psychologists usually conduct a training needs assessment; design the training; and evaluate the training but do not usually deliver the training *(p. 601)*. **15D** In Maslow's theory the need for water is a physiological need; in Alderfer's theory it is an existence need *(p. 605)*. **16B** The facet approach to job satisfaction presumes that employees can be satisfied with some aspects of their jobs, but dissatisfied with others *(p. 606)*. **17B** Knowing that salary and pay raise decisions are made in a fair way can be more important to job satisfaction than to the amount of money employees receive *(p. 608)*. **18A** Employees steal more from their employers than do shoplifters *(p. 611)*. **19B** A work team is a special kind of workgroup in which the members' activities depend on one another; each person has a specialized task, and everyone is working toward a common goal *(p. 615)*. **20A** Leader-member exchange theory suggests that most leaders tend to adopt different styles with different kinds of subordinates *(p. 617)*.

Chapter 16   Neuropsychology

1A The experimental neuropsychologist's aim is to add to our knowledge of brain functioning among people in general, whereas the clinical neuropsychologists aim is to use this knowledge to try to understand the problems that appear in particular individuals *(p. 626)*. **2C** Phrenology originated from the idea that particular brain areas, indicated by corresponding bumps in the skull just above them, controlled particular aspects of mental life *(p. 627)*. **3B** Broca's area was identified when people experiencing language difficulties were found to have left frontal brain lesions *(p. 628)*. **4B** Lesion analysis is research conducted by experimental neuropsychologists in an attempt to understand localization of function by looking at the results of brain damage *(p. 629)*. **5A** The neuropsychologist evaluating Damian will most likely give him a battery of psychometric tests and compare his scores to established norms *(p. 627)*. **6C** A stroke is the loss of blood supply to some part of the brain, resulting in disruption of some aspect of behavior or mental processes *(pp. 632–633)*. **7D** Neurodegenerative disease affects a particular kind of brain cell, or cells in a particular part of the brain, causing them to be the first to stop working properly *(pp. 633–634)*. **8D** Patients with Korsakoff's syndrome are prone to creating false memories *(p. 636)*. **9B** People with delirium enter alternating periods of abnormally impaired consciousness and abnormally elevated levels of consciousness *(p. 637)*. **10C** Anosognosia is a disorder of consciousness in which a person has difficulty becoming aware of the loss of neurological function *(p. 638)*. **11C** The pathway leading toward the ventrolateral temporal lobe has been called the "what" system because the cortical regions along this pathway help us to decide what it is that we are seeing *(p. 640)*.   **12D** Prosopagnosia is a condition in which a person can no longer recognize faces, even their own *(p. 641)*.   **13A** Hemineglect is a condition, usually occurring after a stroke, that involves difficulty in seeing, responding to, or acting on information coming from either the right, or more often, the left side of the world *(p. 642)*.   **14A** In the study cited, patients exhibiting hemineglect were not found to have visual deficits that explained their symptoms *(pp. 642–643)*.   **15B** People who suffer damage to Broca's area display Broca's aphasia, which is seen mainly in the loss of language fluency *(pp. 644–645)*.   **16A** People with Wernicke's aphasia can still speak fluently and effortlessly, but what they say sounds like gibberish *(p. 645)*.   **17C** Alexia without agraphia is a neurological deficit in which people have difficulty reading the letters that they themselves wrote *(p. 629)*.   **18D** Alfreda is most likely experiencing *aprosodia*, a condition whereby she has lost the ability to use tone of voice to express meaning *(p. 646)*.   **19A** Dementia is a neuropsychological disorder in which there are significant and disruptive impairments in memory, as well as in perceptual ability, language, or learned motor skills *(p. 647)*.   **20C** Research on Alzheimer's disease has found that patient's with Alzheimer's have a different brain pathology than those experiencing normal aging *(p. 588)*.

Answer Key to In Review Chart Questions

The questions at the bottom of each chapter's In Review charts are listed here, followed in parentheses by the correct answers. The questions are grouped under each chapter's title and by the name and page number of the In Review chart in which they appear. The answer keys for the optional Industrial/Organizational Psychology and Neuropsychology chapters appear in blue.

Chapter 1   Introduction to the Science of Psychology

The Development of Psychology *(p. 13)*
1. Darwin's theory of evolution had an especially strong influence on _____ ism and _____ ism. *(functionalism; behaviorism)*
2. Which school of psychological thought was founded by a medical doctor? _____ *(Psychoanalysis)*
3. In the history of psychology, _____ was the first school of thought to appear. *(structuralism)*

Approaches to Psychology *(p. 18)*
1. Teaching people to be less afraid of heights reflects the _____ approach. *(behavioral)*
2. Charles Darwin was not a psychologist, but his work influenced the _____ approach to psychology. *(evolutionary)*
3. Assuming that people inherit mental disorders suggests a _____ approach. *(biological)*

Methods of Psychology *(p. 36)*
1. The _____ method is most likely to use a double-blind design. *(experimental)*
2. Research on a new treatment method is most likely to begin with _____. *(case studies)*
3. Studying language by listening to people in public places is an example of _____ research. *(naturalistic observation)*

Chapter 2   Biology and Behavior

Neurons, Neurotransmitters, and Receptors *(p. 52)*
1. For one neuron to communicate with another, a _____ has to cross the _____ between them. *(neurotransmitter; synapse)*
2. The nervous system's main functions are to _____, _____, and _____ information. *(receive; process; act on)*
3. The two main types of cells in the nervous system are _____ and _____. *(neurons; glial cells)*

Organization of the Brain *(p. 66)*
1. The oldest part of the brain is the _____. *(hindbrain)*
2. Cells that operate as the body's twenty-four-hour "time clock" are found in the _____. *(hypothalamus)*
3. Memory problems seen in Alzheimer's disease are related to shrinkage of the _____. *(hippocampus)*

Classes of Neurotransmitters *(p. 77)*
1. The main neurotransmitter for slowing, or inhibiting, brain activity is _____. *(GABA)*
2. A group of neurons that use the same neurotransmitter is called a _____. *(neurotransmitter system)*
3. Which neurotransmitter's activity causes brain damage during a stroke? _____ *(glutamate)*

Chapter 3   Sensation and Perception

Seeing *(p. 97)*
1. The ability to see in very dim light depends on photoreceptors called _____. *(rods)*
2. Color afterimages are best explained by the _____ theory of color vision. *(opponent-process)*
3. Nearsightedness and farsightedness occur when images are not focused on the eye's _____. *(retina)*

Hearing *(p. 102)*
1. Sound energy is converted to neural activity in an inner ear structure called the _____. *(cochlea [or basilar membrane])*
2. Hearing loss due to damage to hair cells or the auditory nerve is called _____. *(nerve deafness)*
3. How high or low a sound sounds is called _____ and is determined by the _____ of a sound wave. *(pitch; frequency)*

Smell and Taste *(p. 105)*
1. The flavor of food arises from a combination of _____ and _____. *(taste; smell)*
2. Emotion and memory are linked especially closely to our sense of _____. *(smell)*
3. Perfume ads suggest that humans are affected by _____ that increase sexual attraction. *(pheromones)*

Body Senses *(p. 111)*
1. Gate control theory offers an explanation of why we sometimes do not feel _____. *(pain)*
2. Professional dancers look at the same spot as long as possible during repeated spins. They are trying to avoid the dizziness caused when the _____ sense is overstimulated. *(vestibular)*
3. Without your sense of _____, you would not be able to swallow food without choking. *(touch)*

Principles of Perceptual Organization and Constancy *(p. 120)*
1. The movement we see in movies, videos, and DVDs is due to a perceptual illusion called _____. *(stroboscopic motion)*
2. People who have lost an eye also lose the depth cue called _____. *(binocular disparity)*
3. The grouping principle of _____ allows you to identify objects seen through a picket fence. *(closure)*

Mechanisms of Pattern Recognition *(p. 124)*
1. Your ability to read a battered old sign that has some letters missing is a result of _____ processing. *(top-down)*
2. When stimulus features match the stimuli we are looking for, _____ takes place. *(recognition)*
3. Schemas can create a _____ that makes us more likely to perceive stimuli in a particular way. *(perceptual set)*

Chapter 4   Consciousness

Sleep and Sleep Disorders *(p. 151)*
1. Jet lag occurs because of a disruption in a traveler's _____. *(circadian rhythms [or sleep-wake cycle])*
2. The importance of non-REM sleep is suggested by its appearance _____ in the night. *(early)*
3. The safest sleeping position for babies is _____. *(face up)*

Major Classes of Psychoactive Drugs (p. 163)
1. Physical dependence on a drug is a condition more commonly known as _____. (addiction)
2. Drugs that act as antagonists _____ the interaction of neurotransmitters and receptors. (block)
3. Drug effects are determined partly by what we learn to _____ the effects to be. (expect)

Chapter 5   Learning

Basic Processes of Classical Conditioning (p. 177)
1. If your conditioned fear of spiders is triggered by the sight of other creatures that look like spiders, you are demonstrating stimulus _____. (generalization)
2. Because of _____, we are more likely to learn a fear of snakes than a fear of cars. (biopreparedness)
3. Feeling sad upon hearing a song associated with a long-lost relationship illustrates _____. (spontaneous recovery)

Reinforcement and Punishment (p. 190)
1. Taking an aspirin can relieve headache pain, so people learn to do so through the process of _____ reinforcement. (negative)
2. The "walk" sign that tells people it is safe to cross the street is an example of a _____ stimulus. (discriminative)
3. Response rates tend to be higher under _____ schedules of reinforcement than under _____ schedules. (ratio; interval)

Chapter 6   Memory

Models of Memory (p. 213)
1. The value of elaborative rehearsal over maintenance rehearsal has been cited as evidence for the _____ model of memory. (levels-of-processing)
2. Deliberately trying to remember something means using your _____ memory. (explicit)
3. Playing the piano requires access to _____ memory. (procedural)

Storing New Memories (p. 218)
1. If you looked up a phone number but forgot it before you could call it, the information was probably lost from _____ memory. (short-term)
2. The capacity of short-term memory is about _____ to _____ items. (five; seven)
3. Encoding is usually _____ in short-term memory and _____ in long-term memory. (acoustic; semantic)

Factors Affecting Retrieval from Long-Term Memory (p. 220)
1. Stimuli called _____ help you recall information stored in long-term memory. (retrieval cues)
2. If it is easier to remember something in the place where you learned it, you have a _____ memory. (context-dependent)
3. The tendency to remember the last few items in a list is called the _____ effect. (recency)

Improving Your Memory (p. 240)
1. Using mnemonics and the PQ4R system to better remember course material are examples of the value of _____ rehearsal. (elaborative)
2. "Cramming" illustrates _____ practice that usually leads to _____ long-term retention than _____ practice. (massed; poorer [or less]; distributed)
3. To minimize forgetting, you should review lecture notes _____ after a lecture ends. (immediately [as soon as possible])

Chapter 7   Thought, Language, and Intelligence

Ingredients of Thought (p. 253)
1. Thinking is the manipulation of _____. (mental representations)
2. Arguments over what is "fair" occur because "fairness" is a _____ concept. (natural)
3. Your _____ of "hotel room" would lead you to expect yours to include a bathroom. (schema)

Solving Problems (p. 263)
1. People stranded without water could use their shoes to collect rain, but they may not do so because of an obstacle to problem solving called _____. (functional fixedness)
2. Because of the _____ heuristic, once sellers set a value on their house, they may refuse to take much less for it. (anchoring)
3. If you tackle a massive problem one small step at a time, you are using an approach called _____. (decomposition or means-end analysis)

Influences on IQ Scores (p. 282)
1. Intelligence is influenced by both _____ and _____. (heredity; environment)
2. Children living in poverty tend to have _____ IQ scores than those in middle-class families. (lower)
3. IQ scores of children whose parents encourage learning tend to be _____ than those of children whose parents do not. (higher)

Chapter 8   Motivation and Emotion

Theories of Motivation (p. 301)
1. The fact that some people like roller coasters and other scary amusement park rides has been cited as evidence for the _____ theory of motivation. (optimal arousal)
2. Evolutionary theories of motivation are modern outgrowths of _____ theories. (instinct)
3. The value of incentives can be affected by _____, _____, and _____ factors. (physiological [or biological]; cognitive; social)

Major Factors Controlling Hunger and Eating (p. 308)
1. People may eat when they are "full," suggesting that eating is not controlled by _____ alone. (hunger)
2. People with _____ nervosa know that they have a problem; those with _____ nervosa tend not to. (bulimia; anorexia)
3. The best strategy for lasting weight loss includes regular _____, as well as improved eating habits. (exercise)

Theories of Emotion (p. 332)
1. Research showing that there are pleasure centers in the brain has been cited in support of the _____ theory of emotion. (Cannon-Bard)
2. The use of polygraphs in lie detection is based on the _____ theory of emotion. (James-Lange)
3. The process of attribution is most important to _____ theories of emotion. (cognitive)

Chapter 9   Human Development

Milestones of Cognitive Development in Infancy and Childhood (p. 357)
1. Research in cognitive development suggests that children form mental representations _____ than Piaget thought they did. (earlier)
2. Recognizing that changing the shape of clay doesn't change the amount of clay is evidence of a cognitive ability called _____. (conservation)
3. The appearance of object permanence signals the end of the _____ period. (sensorimotor)

Social and Emotional Development During Infancy and Childhood (p. 370)
1. As part of their social development, children learn _____, which tell them what patterns of appearance and behavior are associated with being male or female. (gender roles)
2. Teaching children to talk quietly in a restaurant is part of the process called _____. (socialization)
3. Strict rules and the threat of punishment are typical of _____ parenting. (authoritarian)

Milestones of Adolescence and Adulthood (p. 382)
1. The greatest threat to cognitive abilities in late adulthood is _____ disease. (Alzheimer's)
2. Adolescents' _____ identity may be more defining than their national citizenship. (ethnic)
3. Not stealing because "I might get caught" reflects the _____ stage of moral reasoning. (preconventional)

Chapter 10   Health, Stress, and Coping

Stress Responses and Stress Mediators (p. 406)
1. The friends and family we can depend on to help us deal with stressors are called our _____ network. (*social support*)
2. Fantasizing about winning money is a(n) _____-focused way of coping with financial stress. (*emotion*)
3. Sudden, extreme stressors may cause psychological and behavioral problems known as _____. (*posttraumatic stress disorder*)

Methods for Coping with Stress (p. 414)
1. Catastrophizing thoughts are best overcome through _____ coping strategies. (*cognitive*)
2. The first step in coping with stress is to _____ the sources and effects of your stressors. (*identify*)
3. True or false: It is best to rely on only one good coping strategy. _____ (*false*)

Chapter 11   Personality

Major Approaches to Personality (p. 439)
1. Tests that measure the big-five dimensions of personality are based on the _____ approach to personality. (*trait*)
2. The role of learning is most prominent in the _____ approach to personality. (*social-cognitive*)
3. Object relations and attachment theories are modern variants on _____ personality theories. (*psychodynamic*)

Personality Tests (p. 447)
1. Projective personality tests are based on the _____ approach to personality. (*psychodynamic*)
2. The NEO-PI-R and the MMPI-2 are examples of _____ tests. (*objective*)
3. Most personality researchers use _____ tests in their work. (*objective*)

Chapter 12   Psychological Disorders

Anxiety, Somatoform, and Dissociative Disorders (p. 474)
1. Concern that it may be triggered by media stories or therapists' suggestions has made _____ the most controversial of the dissociative disorders. (*dissociative identity disorder*)
2. A person who sleepwalks but is not able to walk when awake is showing signs of _____. (*conversion disorder*)
3. Panic disorder sometimes leads to another anxiety disorder called _____. (*agoraphobia*)

Mood Disorders (p. 477)
1. The risk of suicide is associated with _____ more than with any other symptom of disorder. (*depression*)
2. Cyclothymic disorder is the bipolar version of _____. (*dysthymic disorder*)
3. Women are _____ likely than men to try suicide, but men are _____ likely to succeed. (*more; more*)

Schizophrenia (p. 484)
1. The _____ approach forms the basis of the vulnerability theory of schizophrenia. (*diathesis-stress*)
2. Hallucinations are _____ symptoms of schizophrenia; lack of emotion is a _____ symptom. (*positive; negative*)
3. Patients with schizophrenia who were able to finish school are _____ likely to show improvement. (*more*)

Chapter 13   Treatment of Psychological Disorders

Approaches to Psychological Treatment (p. 516)
1. Object relations therapy and interpersonal therapy are both contemporary examples of the _____ approach to psychological treatment. (*psychodynamic*)
2. Imagining increasingly fear-provoking stimuli is a _____ treatment method called _____. (*behavioral; systematic desensitization*)
3. Reflection is an interviewing technique associated mainly with the _____ approach to treatment. (*humanistic [or nondirective]*)

Chapter 14   Social Psychology

Some Biases in Social Perception (p. 548)
1. The fundamental attribution error appears to be somewhat less likely to occur among people in _____ cultures. (*collectivist*)
2. First impressions form _____, but change _____. (*quickly; slowly*)
3. If you believed that immigrants' successes are due to government help but that their failures are due to laziness, you would be committing the _____ error. (*ultimate attribution error*)

Forming and Changing Attitudes (p. 551)
1. According to the elaboration likelihood model, people are more likely to pay close attention to the content and logic of a persuasive message if the _____ route to attitude change has been activated. (*central*)
2. Holding attitudes that are similar to those of your friends illustrates the importance of _____ in attitude formation (*learning*)
3. According to cognitive dissonance theory, we tend to reduce conflict between attitudes and behaviors by changing our _____. (*attitudes*)

Types of Social Influence (p. 568)
1. Joining the end of a ticket line is an example of _____, whereas forming two lines when a theater employee requests it is an example of _____. (*conformity; compliance*)
2. Seeing someone disobey a questionable order makes people _____ likely to obey the order themselves. (*less*)
3. Pricing your used car for more than you expect to get, then agreeing to reduce it to make a sale, is an example of the _____ approach to gaining compliance. (*door-in-the-face*)

Helping Behavior (p. 579)
1. If you could save only one person from a burning house, the _____ theory of helping would predict that it would be your own child rather than, say, a grandparent. (*evolutionary*)
2. Are you more likely to receive help in a nearly empty bus or a crowded bus terminal? _____. (*a nearly empty bus*)
3. People who have empathy for others are _____ likely to be helpful. (*more*)

Chapter 15   Industrial/Organizational Psychology

Assessing People, Jobs, and Job Performance (p. 598)
1. Lists of critical incidents are contained in _____-focused employee rating forms. (*behavior*)
2. A potential employer might use a two-day _____ to measure your skill at the job you want. (*assessment center*)
3. In general, _____ interviews are more useful in employee selection than _____ interviews. (*structured; unstructured*)

Recruiting, Selecting, and Training Employees (p. 604)
1. Employees tend to remember more from a training program when it is set up on a _____ rather than a _____ schedule. (*distributed; massed*)
2. Depending on "walk-in" applications is usually acceptable when hiring _____-level employees. (*low*)
3. Assuring that your hiring criteria actually predict employees' job performance requires a _____. (*validation study*)

Chapter 16   Neuropsychology

Foundations of Neuropsychology (p. 631)
1. A person who studies individual patients to determine what kind of brain damage each one happens to have is called a _____. (*clinical neuropsychologist*)
2. The case of "Tan" helped to establish the principle of _____. (*localization of function*)
3. In alexia without agraphia, the brain areas that control reading and writing are intact but cannot interact. This condition is called a _____. (*disconnection syndrome*)

Mechanisms of Brain Dysfunction (p. 634)
1. The brain floats in a bath of _____ inside the skull. (*cerebrospinal fluid*)
2. The brain needs a constant flow of fresh _____ all the time. (*blood*)
3. Strokes rank as the number _____ cause of death in the United States. (*three*)

Major Neuropsychological Problems *(p. 650)*

1. A patient who has become forgetful but has no problems in other areas of cognitive function may be said to have _____. *(mild cognitive impairment)*

2. A dementia patient whose hippocampus is relatively intact and can still form new memories probably has _____ dementia. *(vascular)*

3. A patient with thiamine deficiency who is forgetful but makes up memories and believes they are real probably has _____. *(Korsakoff's amnesia)*

References

A

Aaron, D. J., Chang, Y.-F., Markovic, N., & LaPorte, R. E. (2003). Estimating the lesbian population: A capture-recapture approach. *Journal of Epidemiology and Community Health, 57,* 207–209.

Abad, V. C., & Guilleminault, C. (2004). Review of rapid eye movement behavior sleep disorders. *Current Neurology and Neuroscience Reports, 4,* 157–163.

Abbott, B. B., Schoen, L. S., & Badia, P. (1984). Predictable and unpredictable shock: Behavioral measures of aversion and physiological measures of stress. *Psychological Bulletin, 96,* 45–71.

Abbott, R. D., White, L. R., Ross, G. W., Masaki, K. H., Curb, J. D., & Petrovitch, H. (2004). Walking and dementia in physically capable elderly men. *Journal of the American Medical Association, 292,* 1447–1453.

AbdelMalik, P., Husted, J., Chow, E. W., & Bassett, A. S. (2003). Childhood head injury and expression of schizophrenia in multiply affected families. *Archives of General Psychiatry, 60,* 231–236.

Abelson, J. L., Liberzon, I., Young, E. A., & Khan, S. (2005). Cognitive modulation of the endocrine stress response to a pharmacological challenge in normal and panic disorder subjects. *Archives of General Psychiatry, 62,* 668–675.

Abi-Hashem, N. (2000). Psychology, time, and culture. *American Psychologist, 55,* 342–343.

Abraham, W. C. (2006). Memory maintenance: The changing nature of neural mechanisms. *Current Directions in Psychological Science, 15,* 5–8.

Abrahamson, A. C., Baker, L. A., & Caspi, A. (2002). Rebellious teens? Genetic and environmental influences on the social attitudes of adolescents. *Journal of Personality and Social Psychology, 83,* 1392–1408.

Abramis, D. J. (1994). Work role ambiguity, job satisfaction, and job performance: Meta-analyses and review. *Psychological Reports, 75,* 1411–1433.

Abramowitz, J. S. (1997). Effectiveness of psychological and pharmacological treatments for obsessive-compulsive disorder: A quantitative review. *Journal of Consulting and Clinical Psychology, 65,* 44–52.

Abramowitz, J. S., Khandker, M., Nelson, C. A., Deacon, B. J., & Rygwall, R. (2006). The role of cognitive factors in the pathogenesis of obsessive-compulsive symptoms: A prospective study. *Behaviour Research and Therapy, 44,* 1361–1374.

Abreu, J. M. (1999). Conscious and unconscious African American stereotypes: Impact on first impression and diagnostic ratings by therapists. *Journal of Consulting and Clinical Psychology, 67,* 387–393.

Achenbach, T. M. (1997). *Empirically based assessment of child and adolescent psychopathology.* Thousand Oaks, CA: Sage.

Acitelli, L. K. (1992). Gender differences in relationship awareness and marital satisfaction among young married couples. *Personality and Social Psychology Bulletin, 18,* 102–110.

Acker, T., & Acker, H. (2004). Cellular oxygen sensing need in CNS function: Physiological and pathological implications. *Journal of Experimental Biology, 207*(Pt. 18), 3171–3188.

Acocella, J. (1998, April 6). The politics of hysteria. *New Yorker,* pp. 64–79.

Adair, J. C., Gilmore, R. L., Fennell, E. B., Gold, M., & Heilman, K. M. (1995). Anosognosia during intracarotid barbiturate anesthesia: Unawareness or amnesia for weakness. *Neurology, 45*(2), 241–243.

Adam, E. K., Gunnar, M. R., & Tanaka, A. (2004). Adult attachment, parent emotion, and observed parenting behavior: Mediator and moderator models. *Child Development, 75,* 110–122.

Adams, W. J., Graf, E. W., & Ernst, M. O. (2004). Experience can change the "light from above" prior. *Nature Neuroscience, 7,* 1057–1058.

Addis, M. E. (1997). Evaluating the treatment manual as a means of disseminating empirically validated psychotherapies. *Clinical Psychology: Science and Practice, 4,* 1–11.

Addis, M. E., & Krasnow, A. D. (2000) A national survey of practicing psychologists' attitudes toward psychotherapy treatment manuals. *Journal of Consulting and Clinical Psychology, 68,* 331–339.

Ader, R. (2001). Psychoneuroimmunology. *Current Directions in Psychological Science, 10,* 94–98.

Adler, T. (1993, March). Bad mix: Combat stress, decisions. *APA Monitor,* p. 1.

Adolphs, R. (2003). Investigating the cognitive neuroscience of social behavior. *Neuropsychologia, 41,* 119–126.

Adolphs, R., Tranel, D., & Damasio, A. R. (1998). The human amygdala in social judgment. *Nature, 393*(6684), 470–474.

Adolphs, R., Tranel, D., Koenigs, M., & Damasio, A. R. (2005). Preferring one taste over another without recognizing either. *Nature Neuroscience, 8,* 860–861.

Adorno, T. W., Frenkel-Brunswik, E., Levinson, D. J., & Sanford, R. N. (1950). *The authoritarian personality.* New York: Harper & Row.

Agarwal, D. P. (1997). Molecular genetic aspects of alcohol metabolism and alcoholism. *Pharmacopsychiatry, 30*(3), 79–84.

Agnew, C. R., Van Lange, P. A. M., Rusbult, C. E., & Langston, C. A. (1998). Cognitive interdependence: Commitment and the mental representation of close relationships. *Journal of Personality and Social Psychology, 74,* 939–954.

Agras, W. S., Brandt, H. A., Bulik, C. M., Dolan-Sewell, R., Fairburn, C. G., Halmi, K. A., et al. (2004). Report of the National Institutes of Health workshop on overcoming barriers to treatment research in anorexia nervosa. *International Journal of Eating Disorders, 35,* 509–521.

Aharonov, R., Segev, L., Meilijson, I., & Ruppin, E. (2003). Localization of function via lesion analysis. *Neural Computation, 15*(4), 885–913.

Ahima, R. S., & Flier, J. S. (2000). Leptin. *Annual Review of Physiology, 62,* 413–437.

Ahmad, R. H., Venkata, S. M., Alessandro, T., Bhaskar, K., Francesco, F., Goldman, D., et al. (2002). Serotonin transporter genetic variation and the response of the human amygdala. *Science, 297,* 400–403.

Aiello, J. R., & Douthitt, E. A. (2001). Social facilitation from Triplett to electronic performance monitoring. *Group Dynamics, 5,* 163–180.

Aiken, L. R. (1994). *Psychological testing and assessment* (8th ed.). Boston: Allyn & Bacon.

Ainsworth, M. D. S., Blehar, M. D., Waters, E., & Wall, S. (1978). *Patterns of attachment: A psychological study of the Strange Situation.* Hillsdale, NJ: Erlbaum.

Ainsworth, M. D. S., & Bowlby, J. (1991). An ethological approach to personality development. *American Psychologist, 46,* 333–341.

Ainsworth, M. D. S., & Marvin, R. S. (1995). On the shaping of attachment theory and research: An interview with Mary D. S. Ainsworth (Fall 1994). *Monographs of the Society for Research in Child Development, 60,* 3–21.

Aizawa, N. (2002). Grandiose traits and hypersensitive traits of the narcissistic personality. *Japanese Journal of Educational Psychology, 50,* 215–224.

Ajzen, I., & Fishbein, M. (2005). The influence of attitudes on behavior. In D. Albarracín, B. T. Johnson, & M. P. Zanna (Eds.), *Handbook of attitudes* (pp. 173-221). Mahwah, NJ: Erlbaum.

Akins, C. K., & Zentall, T. R. (1998). Imitation in Japanese quail: The role of reinforcement of demonstrator responding. *Psychonomic Bulletin and Review, 5,* 694–697.

Albarracín, D., Johnson, B. T., Fishbein, M., & Muellerleile, P. A. (2001). Theories of reasoned action and planned behavior as models of condom use: A meta-analysis. *Psychological Bulletin, 127,* 142–161.

Albarracín, D., Johnson, B. T., & Zanna, M. P. (Eds.). (2005). *Handbook of attitudes.* Mahwah, NJ: Erlbaum.

Albee, G. W. (1968). Conceptual models and manpower requirements in psychology. *American Psychologist, 23,* 317–320.

Albee, G. W. (1985, February). The answer is prevention. *Psychology Today, 19,* 60–62.

Albert, K. A., Hemmings, H. C., Adamo, A. I. B., Potkin, S. G., Akbarian, S., Sandman, C. A. (2002). Evidence for decreased DARPP-32 in the prefrontal cortex of patients with schizophrenia. *Archives of General Psychiatry, 59,* 705–712.

Albert, M. S., Savage, C. R., Blazer, D., Jones, K., Berkman, L., & Seeman, T. (1995). Predictors of cognitive change in older persons: MacArthur studies of successful aging. *Psychology and Aging, 10,* 578–589.

Alberti, R. E., & Emmons, M. L. (1986). *Your perfect right: A guide to assertive living* (5th ed.). San Luis Obispo, CA: Impact.

Alberto, P. A., Troutman, A. C., & Feagin, J. R. (2002). *Applied behavior analysis for teachers* (6th ed.). Englewood Cliffs, NJ: Prentice Hall.

Albus, H., Vansteensel, M. J., Michel, S., Block, G. D., & Meijer, J. H. (2005). A GABAergic mechanism is necessary for coupling dissociable ventral and dorsal regional oscillators within the circadian clock. *Current Biology, 15,* 886–893.

Alcock, J. (2001). *Animal behavior: An evolutionary approach* (7th ed.). Sunderland, MA: Sinauer.

Aldag, R. J., & Fuller, S. R. (1993). Beyond fiasco: A reappraisal of the groupthink phenomenon and a new model of group decision processes. *Psychological Bulletin, 113,* 533–552.

Alderfer, C. P. (1969). An empirical test of a new theory of human needs. *Organizational Behavior and Human Performance, 4,* 142–175.

Aldridge, J. W. (2005). Interpreting correlation as causation? *Science, 308*(5724), 954.

Aleman, A., Kahn, R. S., & Selten, J.-P. (2003). Sex differences in the risk of schizophrenia: Evidence from meta-analysis. *Archives of General Psychiatry, 60,* 565–571.

Alessi, S. M., Roll, J. M., Reilly, M. P., & Johanson, C.-E. (2002). Establishment of a diazepam preference in human volunteers following a differential-conditioning history of placebo versus diazepam choice. *Experimental and Clinical Psychopharmacology, 10,* 77–83.

Alexander, G. M., & Hines, M. (2002). Sex differences in response to children's toys in nonhuman primates (*Cercopithecus aethiops sabaeus*). *Evolution and Human Behavior, 23,* 467–479.

Alexander, K. W., Quas, J. A., Goodman, G. S., Ghetti, S., Edelstein, R. S., Redlich, A. D., et al. (2005). Traumatic impact predicts long-term memory for documented child sexual abuse. *Psychological Science, 16,* 33–40.

Ali, R., Liu, W. M., & Humedian, M. (2004). Islam 101: Understanding the religion and therapy implications. *Professional Psychology: Research and Practice, 35,* 635–642.

Alicke, M., LoSchiavo, F. M., Zerbst, J., & Zhang, S. (1997). The person who outperforms me is a genius: Maintaining perceived competence in upward social comparisons. *Journal of Personality and Social Psychology, 73,* 781–789.

Allen, B. P. (2006). *Personality theories: Development, growth, and diversity* (5th ed.). Boston, MA: Pearson.

Allen, J. B., Kenrick, D. T., Linder, D. E., & McCall, M. A. (1989). Arousal and attraction: A response-facilitation alternative to misattribution and negative-reinforcement models. *Journal of Personality and Social Psychology, 57,* 261–270.

Allen, J. J. B. (2002). The role of psychophysiology in clinical assessment: ERPs in the evaluation of memory. *Psychophysiology, 39,* 261–280.

Allen, J. J. B., & Iacono, W. G. (2001). Assessing the validity of amnesia in dissociative identity disorder: A dilemma for the DSM and the courts. *Psychology, Public Policy and Law, 7,* 311–344.

Allen, M. T., & Matthews, K. A. (1997). Hemodynamic responses to laboratory stressors in children and adolescents: The influences of age, race and gender. *Psychophysiology, 34,* 329–339.

Allen, S. R., & Thorndike, R. M. (1995). Stability of the WPPSI-R and WISC-III factor structure using cross-validation of covariance structure models. *Journal of Psychoeducational Assessment, 13,* 3–20.

Allen, T. D., Herst, D. E. L., Bruck, C. S., & Sutton, M. (2000). Consequences associated with work-to-family conflict: A review and agenda for future research. *Journal of Occupational Health Psychology, 5,* 278–308.

Alliger, G. M., & Dwight, S. A. (2000). A meta-analytic investigation of the susceptibility of integrity tests to faking and coaching. *Educational and Psychological Measurement, 60,* 59–72.

Allik, J., & McCrae, R. R. (2004). Toward a geography of personality traits: Patterns of profiles across 36 cultures. *Journal of Cross-Cultural Psychology, 35,* 13–28.

Alloy, L. B., Abramson, L. Y., & Francis, E. L. (1999). Do negative cognitive styles confer vulnerability to depression? *Current Directions in Psychological Science, 8,* 128–132.

Allport, G. W., & Odbert, H. S. (1936). Trait names: A psycholexical study. *Psychological Monographs, 47*(1, Whole No. 211).

Almeida, D. M. (2005). Resilience and vulnerability to daily stressors assessed via diary methods. *Current Directions in Psychological Science, 14,* 64–68.

Alston, J. H. (1920). Spatial condition of the fusion of warmth and cold in heat. *American Journal of Psychology, 31,* 303–312.

Altemeyer, B. (1996). *The authoritarian specter.* Cambridge: Harvard University Press.

Altemeyer, B. (2004). Highly dominating, highly authoritarian personalities. *Journal of Social Psychology, 144,* 421–447.

Altman, L. K. (2000, April 10). Company developing marijuana for medical uses. *New York Times.* Retrieved December 13, 2004, from http://www.mapinc.org/drugnews/v00/n474/a01.html

Aluja-Fabregat, A., & Torrubia-Beltri, R. (1998). Viewing of mass media violence, perception of violence, personality and academic achievement. *Personality and Individual Differences, 25,* 973–989.

Alvarez, F. J., Delrio, M. C., & Prada, R. (1995). Drinking and driving in Spain. *Journal of Studies on Alcohol, 56*(4), 403–407.

Alvarez, K., Salas, E., & Garofano, C. M. (2004). An integrated model of training evaluation and effectiveness. *Human Resource Development and Review, 3,* 385–416.

Alvaro, E. M., & Crano, W. D. (1997). Indirect minority influence: Evidence for leniency in source evaluation and counterargumentation. *Journal of Personality and Social Psychology, 72,* 949–964.

Alvir, J. M., Lieberman, J. A., Safferman, A. Z., Schwimmer, J. L., & Schaaf, J. A. (1993). Clozapine-induced agranulocytosis: Incidence and risk factors in the United States. *New England Journal of Medicine, 329,* 162–167.

Amabile, T. M. (1996). *Creativity in context: Update to "The Social Psychology of Creativity."* Boulder, CO: Westview.

Amabile, T. M. (2001). Beyond talent: John Irving and the passionate craft of creativity. *American Psychologist, 56,* 333–336.

Amabile, T. M., Hennessey, B. A., & Grossman, B. S. (1986). Social influences on creativity: The effects of contracted-for reward. *Journal of Personality and Social Psychology, 50,* 14–23.

Amaro, E., Jr., & Barker, G. J. (2006). Study design in fMRI: Basic principles. *Brain and Cognition, 60,* 220–232.

Ambadar, Z., Schooler, J. W., & Cohn, J. F. (2005) Deciphering the enigmatic face. *Psychological Science, 16,* 403–410.

Amedi, A., Merabet, L. B., Bermpohl, F., & Pascual-Leone, A. (2005). The occipital cortex in the blind. *Current Directions in Psychological Science, 14,* 306–311.

American Educational Research Association, American Psychological Association, & National Council on Measurement in Education. (1999). *Standards for educational and psychological testing.* Washington, DC: American Educational Research Association.

American Psychiatric Association. (1994). *Diagnostic and statistical manual of mental disorders* (4th ed.). Washington, DC: Author.

American Psychiatric Association. (1999). Position statement on psychiatric treatment and sexual orientation. *American Journal of Psychiatry, 156,* 1131.

American Psychiatric Association. (2000). *Diagnostic and statistical manual of mental disorders* (4th ed., text rev.). Washington DC: Author.

American Psychiatric Association. (2003). *The insanity defense.* Retrieved May 26, 2004, from http://www.psych.org/public_info/insanity.cfm.

American Psychiatric Association Work Group on Eating Disorders. (2000). Practice guidelines for the treatment of patients with eating disorders (Revision). *American Journal of Psychiatry, 157,* 1–39.

American Psychological Association. (1993). *Violence and youth: Psychology's response.* Washington: DC: Author.

American Psychological Association. (2000). *1998–1999 Survey of undergraduate departments of psychology.* Washington, DC: Author.

American Psychological Association. (2002a). *Answers to your questions about sexual orientation and homosexuality.* Retrieved December 13, 2004, from http://www.apa.org/pubinfo/answers.html#whatis

American Psychological Association. (2002b). Ethical principles of psychologists and code of conduct. *American Psychologist, 57,* 1060–1073.

American Psychological Association. (2002c). *Medical cost offset.* Retrieved December 13, 2004, from http://www.apa.org/practice/offset3.html

American Society for Microbiology. (2000, September 18). *America's dirty little secret—our hands.* Washington, DC: Author.

an der Heiden, W., & Haefner, H. (2000). The epidemiology of onset and course of schizophrenia. *European Archives of Psychiatry and Clinical Neuroscience, 250,* 292–303.

Anastasi, A. (1997). *Psychological testing* (7th ed.). Upper Saddle River, NJ: Prentice-Hall.

Anastasi, A., & Urbina, S. (1997). *Psychological testing* (7th ed.). Upper Saddle River, NJ: Prentice-Hall.

Anastasiadis, A.G., Davis, A. R., Salomon, L., Burchardt, M., & Shabsigh, R. (2002). Hormonal factors in female sexual dysfunction. *Current Opinion in Urology, 12,* 503–507.

Andersen, S. M., & Chen, S. (2002). The relational self: An interpersonal social-cognitive theory. *Psychological Review, 109,* 619–645.

Andersen, S. M., & Miranda, R. (2000). Transference: How past relationships emerge in the present. *Psychologist, 13,* 608–609.

Anderson, A., & Conwell, Y. (2002). Doctors study why elderly so prone to suicide. *American Journal of Geriatric Psychiatry.* Retrieved September 26, 2006, from http://www.stopgettingsick.com/templates/news_template.cfm/6086.

Anderson, A. K., & Phelps, E. A. (2000). Expression without recognition: Contributions of the human amygdala to emotional communication. *Psychological Science, 11,* 106–111.

Anderson, A. K., & Phelps, E. A. (2001). Lesions of the human amygdala impair enhanced perception of emotionally salient events. *Nature, 411,* 305–309.

Anderson, B. L. (2004). The role of occlusion in the perception of depth, lightness, and opacity. *Psychological Review, 110,* 785–801.

Anderson, C. A. (2001). Heat and violence. *Current Directions in Psychological Science, 10,* 33–38.

Anderson, C. A. (2004). An update on the effects of playing violent video games. *Journal of Adolescence, 27,* 113–122.

Anderson, C. A., Anderson, K. B., Dorr, N., DeNeve, K. M., & Flanagan, M. (2000). Temperature and aggression. In M. Zanna (Ed.), *Advances in experimental social psychology* (Vol. 32, pp. 63–133). New York: Academic Press.

Anderson, C. A., Berkowitz, L., Donnerstein, E., Huesmann, L. R., Johnson, J. D., Linz, D., et al. (2003). The influence of media violence on youth. *Psychological Science in the Public Interest, 4,* 81–110.

Anderson, C. A., & Bushman, B. J. (2001). Effects of violent video games on aggressive behavior, aggressive cognition, aggressive affect, physiological arousal, and prosocial behavior: A meta-analytic review of the scientific literature. *Psychological Science, 12,* 353–359.

Anderson, C. A., & Bushman, B. J. (2002a). Human aggression. *Annual Review of Psychology, 53,* 27–51.

Anderson, C. A., & Bushman, B. J. (2002b). Media violence and the American public revisited. *American Psychologist, 57,* 448–450.

Anderson, C. A., & Dill, K. E. (2000). Video games and aggressive thoughts, feelings, and behavior in the laboratory and in life. *Journal of Personality and Social Psychology, 78,* 772–790.

Anderson, C., John, O. P., Keltner, D., & Kring, A. M. (2001). Who attains social status? Effects of personality and physical attractiveness in social groups. *Journal of Personality and Social Psychology, 81,* 116–132.

Anderson, C. A., Lindsay, J. J., & Bushman, B. J. (1999). Research in the psychological laboratory: Truth or triviality? *Current Directions in Psychological Science, 8,* 3–9.

Anderson, C. A., & Murphy, C. R. (2003). Violent video games and aggressive behavior in young women. *Aggressive Behavior, 29,* 423–429.

Anderson, J. R. (2000). *Cognitive psychology and its implications* (5th ed). New York: Worth.

Anderson, J. R., Bothell, D., Byrne, M.D., Douglass, S., Lebiere, C., & Qin, Y. (2004). An integrated theory of the mind. *Psychological Review, 111,* 1036–1060.

Anderson, M. C., & Green, C. (2001). Suppressing unwanted memories by executive control. *Nature, 410,* 366–369.

Anderson, M. C., Ochsner, K. N., Kuhl, B., Cooper, J., Robertson, E., Gabrieli, S. W., et al. (2004). Neural systems underlying the suppression of unwanted memories. *Science, 303,* 232–235.

Anderson, M. E., Johnson, D. C., & Batal, H. A. (2005). Sudden infant death syndrome and prenatal maternal smoking: Rising attributed risk in the *Back to Sleep* era. *BMC Medicine, 3,* 4.

Anderson, P., Rothbaum, B. O., & Hodges, L. F. (2003). Virtual reality exposure in the treatment of social anxiety. *Cognitive and Behavioral Practice, 10*(3), 240–247.

Anderssen, N., Amlie, C., & Ytteroy, E. A. (2002). Outcomes for children with lesbian or gay parents: A review of studies from 1978 to 2000. *Scandinavian Journal of Psychology, 43,* 335–351.

Andrade, L., Walters, E. E., Gentil, V., & Laurenti, R. (2002). Prevalence of ICD-10 mental disorders in a catchment area in the city of San Paolo, Brazil. *Social Psychiatry and Psychiatric Epidemiology, 37,* 316–325.

Andreasen, N. C. (1997). Linking mind and brain in the study of mental illnesses: A project for a scientific psychopathology. *Science, 275,* 1586–1593.

Andreasen, N. C., Arndt, S., Alliger, R., Miller, D., & Flaum, M. (1995). Symptoms of schizophrenia. *Archives of General Psychiatry, 52,* 341–351.

Andre-Petersson, L., Engstroom, G., Hagberg, B., Janzon, L., Steen, G., Lane, D. A., et al. (2001). Adaptive behavior in stressful situations and stroke incidence in hypertensive men: Results from prospective cohort study "Men Born in 1914" in Malmo, Sweden. *Stroke, 32,* 1712–1720.

Andrew, D., & Craig, A. D. (2001). Spinothalamic lamina I neurons selectively sensitive to histamine: A central neural pathway for itch. *Nature Neuroscience, 4,* 72–77.

Andrews, B., Brewin, C., Ochera, J., Morton, J., Bekerian, D. A., Davies, G. M., & Mollon, P. (2000). The timing, triggers, and quality of recovered memories in therapy. *British Journal of Clinical Psychology, 39,* 11–26.

Andrews, J., Wang, L., Csernansky, J. G., Gado, M. H., & Barch, D. M. (2006). Abnormalities of thalamic activation and cognition in schizophrenia. *American Journal of Psychiatry, 163,* 463–469.

Anghelescu, I., Klawe, C. J., Bartenstein, P., & Szegedi, A. (2001). Normal PET after long-term ETC. *American Journal of Psychiatry, 158,* 1527.

Angold, A., Erkanli, A., Farmer, E. M. Z., Fairbank, J. A., Burns, B. J., Keeler, G., & Costello, E. J. (2002). Psychiatric disorder, impairment, and service use in rural African American and white youth. *Archives of General Psychiatry, 59,* 893–901.

Angst, J., Angst, F., & Stassen, H. H. (1999). Suicide risks inpatients with major depressive disorder. *Journal of Clinical Psychiatry, 60*(Suppl. 2), 57–62.

Annenberg Public Policy Center. (1999). *The 1999 state of children's television report: Programming for children over broadcast and cable television.* Washington, DC: Author.

Annenberg Public Policy Center. (2000). *Media in the home: The fifth annual survey of parents and children 2000.* Washington, DC: Author.

Anrep, G. V. (1920). Pitch discrimination in the dog. *Journal of Physiology, 53,* 367–385.

Anshel, M. (1996). Coping styles among adolescent competitive athletes. *Journal of Social Psychology, 136,* 311–323.

Anthony, M., & Bartlett, P. L. (1999). *Neural network learning: Theoretical foundations.* Cambridge, UK: Cambridge University Press.

Anthony, T., Cooper, C., & Mullen, B. (1992). Cross-racial facial identification: Five studies of sex differences in facial prominence. *Personality and Social Psychology Bulletin, 18,* 296–301.

Antoni, M. H., Cruess, D. G., Cruess, S., Lutgendorf, S., Kumar, M., Ironson, G., et al. (2000). Cognitive-behavioral stress management intervention effects on anxiety, 24-hr urinary norepinephrine output, and t-cytotoxic/suppressor cells over time among symptomatic HIV-infected gay men. *Journal of Consulting and Clinical Psychology, 68,* 31–45.

Antonuccio, D. O., Danton, W. G., & DeNelsky, G. Y. (1995). Psychotherapy versus medication for depression: Challenging the conventional wisdom with data. *Professional Psychology: Research and Practice, 26,* 574–585.

Antrobus, J. (2001). Rethinking the fundamental process of dream and sleep mentation production: Defining new questions that avoid the distraction of REM versus NREM comparisons. *Sleep and Hypnosis, 3,* 1–8.

APA Office of Ethnic Minority Affairs. (2000). *Guidelines for research in ethnic minority communities.* Washington, DC: American Psychological Association.

Appelle, S., Lynn, S. J., & Newman, L. (2000). Alien abduction experiences. In E. Cardena, S. J. Lynn, & S. Krippner (Eds.), *Varieties of anomalous experience: Examining the scientific evidence* (pp. 253–282). Washington, DC: American Psychological Association.

Appleton, W. S. (2000). *Prozac and the new antidepressants: What you need to know about Prozac, Zoloft, Paxil, Luvox, Wellbutrin, Effexor, Serzone, Vestra, Celexa, St. John's Wort, and others* (Rev. ed.). New York: Plume Books.

Aquino, K., Tripp, T. M., & Bies, R. J. (2006). Getting even or moving on? Power, procedural justice, and types of offense as predictors of revenge, forgiveness, reconciliation, and avoidance in organizations. *Journal of Applied Psychology, 91,* 653–668.

Arbelle, S., Benjamin, J., Golin, M., Kremer, I., Belmaker, R. H., & Ebstein, R. P. (2003). Relation of shyness in grade school children to the genotype for the long form of the serotonin transporter promoter region polymorphism. *American Journal of Psychiatry, 160,* 671–676.

Archer, J. (2000). Sex differences between heterosexual partners: A meta-analytic review. *Psychological Bulletin, 126,* 651–680.

Arenberg, D. (1982). Changes with age in problem solving. In F. I. M. Craik & S. Trehub (Eds.), *Aging and cognitive processes* (pp. 221–236). New York: Plenum.

Arkes, H. R., & Ayton, P. (1999). The sunk cost and Concorde effects: Are humans less rational than lower animals? *Psychological Bulletin, 125,* 591–600.

Armitage, C. J. (2005). Can the theory of planned behavior predict the maintenance of physical activity? *Health Psychology, 24,* 235–245.

Arndt, J., Greenberg, J., Pyszczynski, T., & Solomon, S. (1997). Subliminal exposure to death-related stimuli increases defense of the cultural worldview. *Psychological Science, 8,* 379–385.

Arnedt, J. T., Owens, J., Crouch, M., Stahl, J., & Carskadon, M. A. (2005). Neurobehavioral performance of residents after heavy night call vs after alcohol ingestion. *Journal of the American Medical Association, 294,* 1025–1033.

Arnett, J. J. (1999). Adolescent storm and stress, reconsidered. *American Psychologist, 54,* 317–326.

Arnett, J. J. (2000). Emerging adulthood: A theory of development from the late teens through the twenties. *American Psychologist, 55,* 469–480.

Aron, A., Fisher, H. E., Mashek, D. J. Strong, G., Li, H-F. & Brown, L. L. (2005) Reward, motivation and emotion systems associated with early-stage intense romantic love. *Journal of Neurophysiology, 94,* 327–337.

Aronoff, J., Barclay, A. M., & Stevenson, L. A. (1988). The recognition of threatening stimuli. *Journal of Personality and Social Psychology, 54,* 647–655.

Aronson, E. (1990). Applying social psychology to desegregation and energy conservation. *Personality and Social Psychology Bulletin, 16,* 118–132.

Aronson, E. (1997). *The jigsaw classroom.* New York: Longman.

Aronson, E. (1999). *The social animal* (8th ed.). New York: Worth/Freeman.

Aronson, E. (2004). Reducing hostility and building compassion: Lessons from the jigsaw classroom. In A. G. Miller (Ed.), *The social psychology of good and evil* (pp. 469–488). New York: Guilford Press.

Aronson, E., & Patnoe, S. (1997). *The jigsaw classroom: Building cooperation in the classroom* (2nd ed.). New York: Addison Wesley Longman.

Aronson, E., Wilson, T. D., & Akert, R. M. (2005). *Social psychology* (5th ed.). Upper Saddle River, NJ: Prentice Hall.

Arseneault, L., Cannon, M., Witton, J., & Murray, R. M. (2004). Causal association between cannabis and psychosis: Examination of the evidence. *British Journal of Psychiatry, 184,* 110–117.

Arterberry, M. E., Craton, L. G., & Yonas, A. (1993). Infants' sensitivity to motion-carried information for depth and object properties. In C. Granrud (Ed.), *Visual perception and cognition in infancy. Carnegie Mellon symposia on cognition* (pp. 215–234). Hillsdale, NJ: Erlbaum.

Arterburn, D. E., Crane, P. K., & Veenstra, D. L. (2004). The efficacy and safety of sibutramine for weight loss: A systematic review. *Archives of Internal Medicine, 164,* 994–1003.

Arvey, R. D., Bouchard, T. J., Segal, N. L., & Abraham, L. M. (1989). Job satisfaction: Environmental and genetic components. *Journal of Applied Psychology, 74,* 187–192.

Asarnow, R. F., Nuechterlein, K. H., Fogelson, D., Subotnik, K. L., Payne, D. A., Russell, A. T., et al. (2001). Schizophrenia and schizophrenia-spectrum personality disorders in the first-degree relatives of children with schizophrenia: The UCLA family study. *Archives of General Psychiatry, 58,* 581–588.

Asch, S. E. (1951). Effects of group pressure upon the modification and distortion of judgments. In H. Guetzkow (Ed.), *Groups, leadership, and men* (pp. 177–190). Pittsburgh, PA: Carnegie Press.

Asch, S. E. (1955). Opinions and social pressure. *Scientific American, 193,* 31–35.

Asch, S. E. (1956). Studies of independence and conformity: A minority of one against a unanimous majority. *Psychological Monographs, 70,* 1–70.

Ashcraft, M. H. (2006). *Cognition* (4th ed.). Upper Saddle River, NJ: Prentice Hall.

Ashe, P. C., Berry, M. D., & Boulton, A. A (2001). Schizophrenia, a neurodegenerative disorder with neurodevelopmental antecedents. *Progress in Neuro-Psychopharmacology and Biological Psychiatry, 25,* 691–707.

Ashmore, R. D., Deaux, K., McLaughlin-Volpe, T. (2004). An organizing framework for collective identity: Articulation and significance of multidimensionality. *Psychological Bulletin, 130,* 80–114.

Ashton, H. (1995). Protracted withdrawal from benzodiazepines: The post-withdrawal syndrome. *Psychiatric Annals, 25*(3), 174–179.

Ashton, M. C., Lee, K., Perugini, M., Szarota, P., de Vries, R. E., Di Blas, L., et al. (2004). A six-factor structure of personality-descriptive adjectives: Solutions from psycholexical studies in seven languages. *Journal of Personality and Social Psychology, 86,* 356–366.

Aslin, R. N., Jusczyk, P. W., & Pisoni, D. B. (1998). Speech and auditory processing during infancy: Constraints on and precursors to language. In W. Damon (Ed.), *Handbook of child psychology* (5th ed., pp. 147–198). New York: Wiley.

Aspinwall, L. G., & Duran, R. E. F. (1999). Psychology applied to health. In A. M. Stec & D. A. Bernstein (Eds.), *Psychology: Fields of application* (pp. 17–38). Boston: Houghton Mifflin.

Aspinwall, L. G., & Taylor, S. E. (1992). Modeling cognition adaptation: A longitudinal investigation of the impact of individual differences and coping on college adjustment and performance. *Journal of Personality and Social Psychology, 63,* 989–1003.

Assefi, N. P., Sherman, K. J., Jacobsen, C., Goldberg, J., Smith, W. R., & Buchwald, D. (2005). A randomized clinical trial of acupuncture compared with sham acupuncture in fibromyalgia. *Annals of Internal Medicine, 143,* 10–19.

Assefi, S. L., & Garry, M. (2003). Absolut® memory distortions: Alcohol placebos influence misinformation effect. *Psychological Science, 14,* 77–80.

Associated Press. (1997, October 22). Forty percent in senior classes fail at science. *Chicago Tribune.*

Associated Press. (1999, November 17). Stripes near Waldo mean slow down. *St. Petersburg Times.*

Associated Press. (2002, March 9). Odds and ends. *Naples Daily News.* Retrieved August 27, 2003, from http://www.nctimes.net/news/2002/20020313/wwww.html

Associated Press. (2003, January 10). Man to get $900,000 for 20 years spent in prison for rape he did not commit. *Naples Daily News.*

Associated Press. (2004, November 1). *Genetic disorder deprives kindergartner of natural alarms.* Retrieved September 26, 2006, from http://www.msnbc.msn.com/id/6379795/.

Associated Press. (2006, April 23). *Six middle schoolers arrested after planning massacre.* Retrieved September 26, 2006, from http://www.foxnews.com/story/0,2933,192726,00.html.

Astin, J. A. (2004). Mind-body therapies for the management of pain. *Clinical Journal of Pain, 20,* 27–32.

Atkinson, J. W., & Raynor, J. O. (1974). *Personality, motivation, and achievement.* Washington, DC: Hemisphere.

Atran, S., Medin, D. L., & Ross, N. O. (2005). The cultural mind: Environmental decision making and cultural modeling within and across populations. *Psychological Review, 112,* 744–776.

Avaria, M., Mills, J. L., Kleinsteuber, K., Aros, S., Conley, M. R., Cox, C., et al. (2004). Peripheral nerve conduction abnormalities in children exposed to alcohol in utero. *Journal of Pediatrics, 144,* 338–343.

Avery, D. H., Holtzheimer, P. E., III, Fawaz, W., Russo, J., Neumaier, J., Dunner, D. L., et al. (2006).A controlled study of repetitive transcranial magnetic stimulation in medication-resistant major depression. *Biological Psychiatry, 59,* 187–194.

Aviezer, O., Sagi, A., Joels, T., & Ziv, Y. (1999). Emotional availability and attachment representations in kibbutz infants and their mothers. *Developmental Psychology, 35,* 811–821.

Avila, C. (2001). Distinguishing BIS-mediated and BAS-mediated disinhibition mechanisms: A comparison of the disinhibition models of Gray (1981, 1987) and of Patterson and Newman (1993). *Journal of Personality and Social Psychology, 80,* 311–324.

Axtell, R. (Ed.). (1998). *Gestures: The do's and taboos of body language around the world.* Hoboken, NJ: Wiley.

Ayache, D., Corre, A., Can Prooyen, S., & Elbaz, P. (2003). Surgical treatment of otosclerosis in elderly patients. *Otolaryngological Head and Neck Surgery, 129,* 674–677.

Ayas, N. T., FitzGerald, J. M., Fleetham, J. A., White, D. P., Schulzer, M., Ryan, C. F., et al. (2006). Cost-effectiveness of continuous positive airway pressure therapy for moderate to severe obstructive sleep apnea/hypopnea. *Archives of Internal Medicine, 166,* 977–984.

Ayllon, T. (1999). *How to use token economy and point systems* (2nd ed.). Austin, TX: Pro-Ed.

Ayllon, T., & Azrin, N. H. (1968). *The token economy: A motivational system for therapy and rehabilitation.* New York: Appleton-Century-Crofts.

Ayuso-Mateos, J. L., Vazquez-Barquero, J. L., Dowrick, C., Lehtinen, V., Dalgard, O. S., Casey, P., et al. (2001). Depressive disorders in Europe: Prevalence figures fromt he ODIN study. *British Journal of Psychiatry, 179,* 308–316.

Azar, B. (1996, November). Project explores landscape of midlife. *APA Monitor,* p. 26.

B

Babinski, J. (1914). Contribution a l'etude dies troubles mentaux dans l'hemiplegie organique cerebrale (anosognosia). *Reveu Neurologie (Paris), 27,* 845–847.

Bacharach, V. R., & Baumeister, A. A. (1998). Direct and indirect effects of maternal intelligence, maternal age, income, and home environment on intelligence of preterm, low-birth-weight children. *Journal of Applied Developmental Psychology, 19,* 361–375.

Back, S. E., Dansky, B. S., Carroll, K. M., Foa, E. B., & Brady, K. T. (2001). Exposure therapy in the treatment of PTSD among cocaine-dependent individuals: Description of procedures. *Journal of Substance Abuse Treatment, 21,* 35–45.

Backman, L., & Nilsson, L. (1991). Effects of divided attention on free and cued recall of verbal events and action events. *Bulletin of the Psychonomic Society, 29,* 51–54.

Baddeley, A. (1982). *Your memory: A user's guide.* New York: Macmillan.

Baddeley, A. (1998). *Human memory: Theory and practice.* Boston: Allyn & Bacon.

Baddeley, A. D. (2003). Working memory: Looking back and looking forward. *Nature Reviews Neuroscience, 4,* 829–839.

Baer, J. S., Sampson, P. D., Barr, H. M., Connor, P. D., & Streissguth, A. P. (2003) A 21–year longitudinal analysis of the effects of prenatal alcohol exposure on young adult drinking. *Archives of General Psychiatry, 60,* 377–385.

Baethge, C., Baldessarini, R. J., Mathiske-Schmidt, K., Hennen, J., Berghofer, A., et al., (2005). Long-term combination therapy versus monotherapy with lithium and carbamazepine in 46 bipolar I patients. *Journal of Clinical Psychiatry, 66,* 174–182.

Bagley, C., & Tremblay, P. (1998). On the prevalence of homosexuality and bisexuality, in a random survey of 750 men aged 18–27. *Journal of Homosexuality, 36,* 1–18.

Bahrick, H. P., & Hall, L. K. (1991). Lifetime maintenance of high school mathematics content. *Journal of Experimental Psychology: General, 120,* 20–33.

Bahrick, H. P., Bahrick, P. O., & Wittlinger, R. P. (1975). Fifty years of memory for names and faces: A cross-cultural approach. *Journal of Experimental Psychology: General, 104,* 54–75.

Bahrick, H. P., Hall, L. K., Noggin, J. P., & Bahrick, L. E. (1994). Fifty years of language maintenance and language dominance in bilingual Hispanic immigrants. *Journal of Experimental Psychology: General, 123,* 264–283.

Bailey, J. M., & Benishay, D. S. (1993). Familial aggregation of female sexual orientation. *American Journal of Psychiatry, 150,* 272–277.

Bailey, J. M., Bobrow, D., Wolfe, M., & Mikach, S. (1995). Sexual orientation of adult sons of gay fathers. *Developmental Psychology, 31*(1), 124–129.

Bailey, J. M., Dunne, M. P., & Martin, N. G. (2000). Genetic and environmental influences on sexual orientation and its correlates in an Australian twin sample. *Journal of Personality and Social Psychology, 78,* 524–536.

Bailey, J. M., Dunne, M. P., & Nicholas, G. (2000). Genetic and environmental influences on sexual orientation and its correlates in an Australian twin sample. *Journal of Personality and Social Psychology, 78,* 524–536.

Bailey, J. M., & Pillard, R. C. (1991). A genetic study of male sexual orientation. *Archives of General Psychiatry, 48,* 1086–1096.

Baillargeon, R. (1994a). How do infants learn about the physical world? *Current Directions in Psychological Science, 3,* 133–139.

Baillargeon, R. (1994b). Physical reasoning in young infants: Seeking explanations for impossible events. *Journal of Development Psychology, 12,* 9–33.

Baillargeon, R. (1995). Physical reasoning in infancy. In M. S. Gazzaniga (Ed.), *The cognitive neurosciences* (pp. 181–204). Cambridge, MA: MIT Press.

Baillargeon, R. (2002). The acquisition of physical knowledge in infancy: A summary in eight lessons. In U. Goswami (Ed.), *Blackwell handbook of childhood cognitive development* (pp. 47–83). Malden, MA: Blackwell.

Baillargeon, R. (2004). Infants' physical world. *Current Directions in Psychological Science 13,* 89–94.

Baker, M. C. (2002). *The atoms of language: The mind's hidden rules of grammar.* New York: Basic Books.

Balaban, M. T. (1995). Affective influences on startle in five-month-old infants: Reactions to facial expressions of emotion. *Child Development, 66*(1), 28–36.

Balat, O., Balat, A., Ugur, M. G., & Pence, S. (2003). The effect of smoking and caffeine on the fetus and placenta in pregnancy. *Clinical and Experimental Obstetrics and Gynecology, 30,* 57–59.

Baldessarini, R. J., & Tondo, L. (2000). Does lithium treatment still work? Evidence of stable responses over three decades. *Archives of General Psychiatry, 57,* 187–190.

Baldessarini, R. J., Tondo, L., Hennen, J., Viguera, A. C. (2002). Is lithium still worth using? An update of selected research. *Harvard Review of Psychiatry, 10,* 59–75.

Baldwin, T. T., & Ford, J. K. (1988). Transfer of training: A review and directions for future research. *Personnel Psychology, 41,* 63–105.

Balfour, D. J. (2002). The neurobiology of tobacco dependence: A commentary. *Respiration, 69,* 7–11.

Balleine, B., & Dickinson, A. (1994). Role of cholecystokinin in the motivational control of instrumental action in rats. *Behavioral Neuroscience, 108*(3), 590–605.

Ballou, M. (1995). Assertiveness training. In M. Ballou (Ed.), *Psychological interventions: A guide to strategies* (pp. 125–136). Westport, CT: Praeger.

Baltes, P. B. (1993). The aging mind: Potential and limits. *The Gerontologist, 33,* 580–594.

Baltes, P. B. (1994, August). *Life-span developmental psychology: On the overall landscape of human development.* Invited address presented at the annual meeting of the American Psychological Association, Los Angeles.

Baltes, B. B., Briggs, T. E., Huff, J. W., Wright, J. A., & Neumann, G. A. (1999). Flexible and compressed workweek schedules: A meta-analysis of their effects on work-related criteria. *Journal of Applied Psychology, 84,* 496–513.

Baltes, B. B., & Heydens-Gahir, H. A. (2003). Reduction of work–family conflict through the use of selection, optimization, and compensation behaviors. *Journal of Applied Psychology, 88,* 1005–1018.

Balzer, W. K., & Sulsky, L. M. (1992). Halo and performance appraisal research: A critical examination. *Journal of Applied Psychology, 77,* 975–985.

Banaji, M., Lemm, K. M., & Carpenter, S. J. (2001). The social unconscious. In A. Tesser & N. Schwarz (Eds.), *Blackwell handbook of social psychology: Intraindividual processes* (pp. 134–158). Oxford, UK: Blackwell.

Bancroft, J. (1994). Homosexual orientation: The search for a biological basis. *British Journal of Psychiatry, 164,* 437–440.

Bancroft, J. (1997). *Researching sexual behavior: Methodological issues.* Bloomington, IN: Indiana University Press.

Bandura, A. (1965). Influence of a model's reinforcement contingencies on the acquisition of imitative responses. *Journal of Personality and Social Psychology, 1,* 589–595.

Bandura, A. (1992). Self-efficacy mechanism in psychobiologic functioning. In R. Schwarzer (Ed.), *Self-efficacy: Thought control of action* (pp. 355–394). Washington, DC: Hemisphere.

Bandura, A. (1997). *Self-efficacy: The exercise of control.* New York: Freeman.

Bandura, A. (1999). Social cognitive theory of personality. In L. Pervin & O. John (Eds.), *Handbook of personality: Theory and research* (2nd ed., pp. 154–196). New York: Guilford.

Bandura, A. (2006). Toward a psychology of human agency. *Perspectives on Psychological Science, 1,* 164–180.

Bandura, A., Blanchard, E. B., & Ritter, B. (1969). The relative efficacy of desensitization and modeling approaches for inducing behavioral, affective, and attitudinal changes. *Journal of Personality and Social Psychology, 13,* 173–199.

Bandura, A., Ross, D., & Ross, S. A. (1963). Imitation of film-mediated aggressive models. *Journal of Abnormal and Social Psychology, 66,* 3–11.

Bandura, A., & Walters, R. H. (1963). *Social learning and personality development.* New York: Holt, Rinehart & Winston.

Banich, M. T. (2004). *Cognitive neuroscience and neuropsychology.* Boston: Houghton Mifflin.

Banich, M. T., & Heller, W. (1998). Evolving perspectives on lateralization of function. *Current Directions in Psychological Science, 7,* 1–2.

Banker, R. D., Field, J. M., Schroeder, R. G., & Sinha, K. K. (1996). Impact of work teams on manufacturing performance: A longitudinal field study. *Academy of Management Journal, 39,* 867–890.

Banks, M. S., & Salapatek, P. (1983). Infant visual perception. In P. H. Mussen (Ed.), *Handbook of child psychology: Vol. 2. Infancy and developmental psychobiology* (pp. 435–571). New York: Wiley.

Bantick, S. J., Wise, R. G., Ploghaus, A., Clare, S., Smith, S. M., & Tracey, I. (2002). Imaging how attention modulates pain in humans using functional MRI. *Brain, 125,* 310–319.

Bar, M., & Biederman, I. (1998). Subliminal visual priming. *Psychological Science, 9,* 464–469.

Barber, J. P., Connolly, M. B., Crits-Christoph, P., Gladis, L., & Siqueland, L. (2000). Alliance predicts patients' outcome beyond in-treatment change in symptoms. *Journal of Consulting & Clinical Psychology, 68,* 1027–1032.

Barclay, G., & Tavares, C. (2002). *International comparisons of crime statistics.* London: Home Office.

Barclay, J. R., Bransford, J. D., Franks, J. J., McCarrell, N. S., & Nitsch, K. (1974). Comprehension and semantic flexibility. *Journal of Verbal Learning and Verbal Behavior, 13,* 471–481.

Bardo, M. T. (1998). Neuropharmacological mechanisms of drug reward: Beyond dopamine in the nucleus accumbens. *Critical Reviews of Neurobiology, 12*(1–2), 37–67.

Bardo, M. T., Donohew, R. L., & Harrington, N. G. (1996). Psychobiology of novelty-seeking and drug-seeking behavior. *Behavioral Brain Research, 77*(1–2), 23–43.

Barger, L. K., Cade, B. E., Ayas, N. T., Cronin, J. W., Rosner, B., Speizer, F. E., et al. (2005). *New England Journal of Medicine, 352,* 125–134.

Bargones, J. Y., & Werner, L. A. (1994). Adults listen selectively; infants do not. *Psychological Science, 5,* 170–174.

Barling, J., & Frone, M. R. (Eds.). (2004). The psychology of workplace safety. Washington, DC: APA Books.

Barling, J., Weber, T., & Kelloway, E. K. (1996). Effects of transformational leadership training on attitudinal and financial outcomes: A field experiment. *Journal of Applied Psychology, 81*, 827–832.

Barlow, D. H. (1988). *Anxiety and its disorders: The nature and treatment of panic and anxiety.* New York: Guilford.

Barlow, D. H., & Campbell, L. A. (2000). Mixed anxiety-depression and its implications for models of mood and anxiety disorders. *Comprehensive Psychiatry, 41*, 55–60.

Barlow, D. H., Gorman, J. M., Shear, M. K., & Woods, S. W. (2000). Cognitive-behavioral therapy, imipramine, or their combination for panic disorder: A randomized controlled trial. *Journal of the American Medical Association, 283*, 2529–2536.

Barnes, L. L., Mendes de Leon, C. F., Wilson, R. S., Bienias, J. L., & Evans, D. A. (2004). Social resources and cognitive decline in a population of older African Americans and whites. *Neurology, 63*, 2322–2326.

Barnett, J. E., & Scheetz, K. (2003). Technological advances and telehealth: Ethics, law, and the practice of psychotherapy. *Psychotherapy: Theory, Research, Practice, and Training, 40*, 86–93.

Barnier, A. J. (2002). Posthypnotic amnesia for autobiographical episodes: A laboratory model of functional amnesia? *Psychological Science, 13*, 232–237.

Barnier, A. J., & McConkey, K. M. (1998). Posthypnotic responding away from the hypnotic setting. *Psychological Science, 9*, 256–262.

Baron, A. S., & Banaji, M. R. (2006). The development of implicit attitudes. *Psychological Science 17*, 53–58.

Baron, J. C. (2005). How healthy is the acutely reperfused ischemic penumbra? *Cerebrovascular Disease, 20*(Suppl. 2), 25–31.

Baron, R. A., & Byrne, D. (1994). *Social psychology: Understanding human interaction* (7th ed.). Boston: Allyn & Bacon.

Baron, R. A., Byrne, D., & Branscombe, N. R. (2006). *Social psychology* (11th ed.). Boston: Allyn & Bacon.

Baron, R. A., & Richardson, D. C. (1994). *Human aggression* (2nd ed.). New York: Plenum.

Baron-Cohen, S., Knickmeyer, R. C., & Belmonte, M. K. (2005). Sex differences in the brain: Implications for explaining autism. *Science, 310*, 819–823.

Barrett, L. F. (1995). Valence focus and arousal focus: Individual differences in the structure of affective experience. *Journal of Personality and Social Psychology, 69*, 153–166.

Barrett, L. F., Gross, J., Christensen, T. C., & Benvenuto, M. (2001). Knowing what you're feeling and knowing what to do about it: Mapping the relation between emotion differentiation and emotion regulation. *Cognition and Emotion, 15*, 713–724.

Barrett, L. F., Lane, R. D., Sechrest, L., & Schwartz, G. E. (2000). Sex differences in emotional awareness. *Personality and Social Psychology Bulletin, 26*, 1027–1035.

Barrett, L. F., & Wager, T. D. (2006). The structure of emotion. *Current Directions in Psychological Science, 15*, 79–83.

Barrick, M. R., & Mount, M. K. (1991). The Big Five personality dimensions and job performance: A meta-analysis. *Personnel Psychology, 44*, 1–26.

Barron, K. E., & Harackiewicz, J. M. (2001). Achievement goals and optimal motivation: Testing multiple goal models. *Journal of Personality and Social Psychology, 80*, 706–722.

Barrowclough, C., King, P., Colville, J., Russell, E., Burns, A., & Tarrier, N. (2001). A randomized trial of the effectiveness of cognitive-behavioral therapy and supportive counseling for anxiety symptoms in older adults. *Journal of Consulting and Clinical Psychology, 69*, 756–762.

Barsalou, L. W. (1993). Flexibility, structure, and linguistic vagary in concepts: Manifestations of a compositional system of perceptual symbols. In A. F. Collins, S. E. Gathercole, M. A. Conway, & P. E. Morris (Eds.), *Theories of memory* (pp. 29–102). Hillsdale, NJ: Erlbaum.

Barsky, A. J., Wool, C., Barnett, M. C., & Cleary, P. D. (1994). Histories of childhood trauma in adult hypochondriacal patients. *American Journal of Psychiatry, 151*, 397–401.

Barr Taylor, C., Bryson, S., Celio Doyle, A. A., Luce, K. H., Cunning, D., Abascal, L. B., et al. (2006a). The adverse effect of negative comments about weight and shape from family and siblings on women at high risk for eating disorders. *Pediatrics, 118*, 731–738.

Barr Taylor, C., Bryson, S., Luce, K. H., Cunning, D., Celio Doyle, A. A., Abascal, L. B., et al. (2006b). Prevention of eating disorders in at-risk college-age women. *Archives of General Psychiatry, 63*, 881–888.

Bartels, A., & Zeki, S. (2000). The neural basis of romantic love. *Neuroreport, 11*, 3829–3834.

Bartholow, B. D. & Heinz, A. (2006). Alcohol and aggression without consumption. *Psychological Science, 17*, 30–37.

Bartlett, J. A. (2002). Addressing the challenges of adherence. *Journal of Acquired Immune Deficiency Syndrome, 29*(Suppl. 1), S2–S10.

Barton, J. J., Cherkasova, M. V., Press, D. Z., Intriligator, J. M., & O'Connor, M. (2004). Perceptual functions in prosopagnosia. *Perception, 33*(8), 939–956.

Barton, J., & Folkard, S. (1991). The response of day and night nurses to their work schedules. *Journal of Occupational Psychology, 64*, 207–218.

Barton, J. J., Press, D. Z., Keenan, J. P., & O'Connor, M. (2002). Lesions of the fusiform face area impair perception of facial configuration in prosopagnosia. *Neurology, 58*(1), 71–78.

Bartoshuk, L. M. (1991). Taste, smell, and pleasure. In R. C. Bollef (Ed.), *The hedonics of taste* (pp. 15–28). Hillsdale, NJ: Erlbaum.

Bartoshuk, L. M. (2000). Comparing sensory experiences across individuals: Recent psychophysical advances illuminate genetic variation in taste perception. *Chemical Senses, 25*, 447–460.

Bartoshuk, L. M., Fast, K., & Snyder, D. J. (2005). Differences in our sensory worlds: Invalid comparisons with labeled scales. *Current Directions in Psychological Science, 14*, 122–125.

Bartoshuk, L. M., & Wolfe, J. M. (1990). Conditioned taste aversion in humans: Are there olfactory versions? *Chemical Senses, 15*, 551.

Bashore, T. R., & Ridderinkhof, K. R. (2002). Older age, traumatic brain injury, and cognitive slowing: Some convergent and divergent findings. *Psychological Bulletin, 128*, 151–198.

Baskin, D., Bluestone, H., & Nelson, M. (1981). Ethnicity and psychiatric diagnosis. *Journal of Clinical Psychology, 37*, 529–537.

Basoglu, M., Livanou, M., & Salcioglu, E. (2003). A single session with an earthquake simulator for traumatic stress in earthquake survivors. *American Journal of Psychiatry, 160*, 788–790.

Bass, B. M., Avolio, B. J., Jung, D. I., & Berson, Y. (2003). Predicting unit performance by assessing transformational and transactional leadership. *Journal of Applied Psychology, 88*, 207–218.

Bass, B. M., & Riggio, R. E. (2006). *Transformational leadership* (2nd ed.). Mahwah, NJ: Erlbaum.

Bass, E., & Davis, L. (1994). *The courage to heal* (3rd ed.). New York: Harper Perennial Library.

Bassett, A. S., Chow, E. W. C., O'Neill, S., & Brzustowicz, L. M. (2001). Genetic insights into the neurodevelopmental hypothesis of schizophrenia. *Schizophrenia Bulletin, 27*, 417–430.

Bates, E. (1993, March). *Nature, nurture, and language development.* Paper presented at the biennial meeting of the Society for Research in Child Development, New Orleans.

Bates, E., Appelbaum, M., Salcedo, J., Saygin, A. P., & Pizzamiglio, L. (2003). Quantifying dissociations in neuropsychological research. *Journal of Clinical and Experimental Neuropsychology, 25*(8), 1128–1153.

Batson, C. D. (1998). Altruism and prosocial behavior. In D. Gilbert, S. T. Fiske, & G. Lindzey (Eds.), *Handbook of social psychology* (Vol. 2, 4th ed., pp. 282–316). Boston: McGraw-Hill.

Batson, C. D., Sager, K., Garst, E., & Kang, M. (1997). Is empathy-induced helping due to self-other merging? *Journal of Personality and Social Psychology, 73*, 495–509.

Battaglia, G., Yeh, S. Y., & De Souza, E. B. (1988). MDMA-induced neurotoxicity: Parameters of degeneration and recovery of brain serotonin neurons. *Pharmacology, Biochemistry and Behavior, 29*, 269–274.

Batterham, R. L., Cohen, M. A., Ellis, S. M., Le Roux, C. W., Withers, D. J., Frost, G. S., et al. (2003). Inhibition of food intake in obese subjects by peptide YY3-36. The *New England Journal of Medicine, 349*, 941–948.

Batterham, R. L., Cowley, M. A., Small, C. J., Herzog, H., Cohen, M. A., Dakin, C. L., et al. (2002). Gut hormone PYY3-36 physiologically inhibits food intake. *Nature, 418*, 650–654.

Baucom, D. H., Shoham, V., Mueser, K. T., Daiuto, A. D., & Stickle, T. R. (1998). Empirically supported couple and family interventions for marital distress and adult mental health problems. *Journal of Consulting and Clinical Psychology, 66*, 53–88.

Bauer, P. J. (2006). Event memory. In W. Damon & R. M. Lerner (Series Eds.) & D. Kuhn & R. Siegler (Vol. Eds.), *Handbook of child psychology: Vol. 2. Cognition, perception, and language* (6th ed.). New York: Wiley.

Bauer, R. M., & Demery, J. A. (2003). Agnosia. In K. M. Heilman & E. Valenstein (Eds.), *Clinical neuropsychology* (4th ed.). New York: Oxford.

Bauer, T. N., & Green, S. G. (1996). Development of leader-member exchange: A longitudinal test. *Academy of Management Journal, 39*, 1538–1567.

Baumeister, R. F. (1998). The self. In D. Gilbert, S. T. Fiske, & G. Lindzey (Eds.), *Handbook of social psychology* (Vol. 1, 4th ed., pp. 680–740). Boston: McGraw-Hill.

Baumeister, R. F. (2000). Gender differences in erotic plasticity: The female sex drive as socially flexible and responsive. *Psychological Bulletin, 126,* 347–374.

Baumeister, R. F., Campbell, J. D., Krueger, J. I., & Vohs, K. D. (2003). Does high self-esteem cause better performance, interpersonal success, happiness, or healthier lifestyles? *Psychological Science in the Public Interest, 4,* 1–44.

Baumeister, R. F., Catanese, K. R., & Vohs, K. D. (2001). Is there a gender difference in strength of sex drive? *Personality and Social Psychology Review, 5,* 242–273.

Baumeister, R. F., & Leary, M. R. (1995). The need to belong: Desire for interpersonal attachments as a fundamental human motivation. *Psychological Bulletin, 117*(3), 497–529.

Baumrind, D. (1971). Current patterns of parental authority. *Developmental Psychology Monographs, 4*(1, part 2).

Baumrind, D. (1991). Effective parenting during the early adolescent transition. In P. A. Cowan & E. M. Hetherington (Eds.), *Family transition* (pp. 111–163). Hillsdale, NJ: Erlbaum.

Baumrind, D., Larzelere, R. E., & Cowan, P. A. (2002). Ordinary physical punishment: Is it harmful? Comment on Gershoff. *Psychological Bulletin, 128,* 580–589.

Bayley, P. J., Hopkins, R. O., & Squire, L. R. (2003). Successful recollection of remote autobiographical memories by amnesic patients with medial temporal lobe lesions. *Neuron, 38,* 135–144.

Bazzano, L. A., He, J., Ogden, L. G., Loria, C. M., & Whelton, P. K. (2003). Dietary fiber intake and reduced risk of coronary heart disease in US men and women. *Archives of Internal Medicine, 163,* 1897–1904.

Beals, J., Novins, D. K., Whitesell, N. R., Spicer, P., Mitchell, C. M., & Manson, S. M. (2005). Prevalence of mental disorders and utilization of mental health services in two American Indian reservation populations: Mental health disparities in a national context. *American Journal of Psychiatry, 162,* 1723–1732.

Beardslee, W. R., Gladstone, T. R. G., Wright, E. J., & Cooper, A. B. (2003). A family-based approach to the prevention of depressive symptoms in children at risk: Evidence of parental and child change. *Pediatrics, 112,* 119–131.

Beatty, J. (1995). *Principles of behavioral neuroscience.* Dubuque: Brown and Benchmark.

Beauchamp-Turner, D. L., & Levinson, D. M. (1992). Effects of meditation on stress, health, and affect. *Medical Psychotherapy: An International Journal, 5,* 123–131.

Beaulieu, D. (2003). *Eye movement integration therapy: The comprehensive clinical guide.* Williston, VT: Crown House.

Beaumont, M., Batejat, D., Pierard, C., Coste, O., Doireau, P., Van Beers, P., et al. (2001). Slow release caffeine and prolonged (64-h) continuous wakefulness: effects on vigilance and cognitive performance. *Journal of Sleep Research, 10*(4), 265.

Beaumont, M., Batejat, D., Pierard, C., Van Beers, P., Denis, J. B., Coste, O., et al. (2004). Caffeine or melatonin effects on sleep and sleepiness after rapid eastward transmeridian travel. *Journal of Applied Physiology, 96,* 50–58.

Bech, B. H., Nohr, E. A., Vaeth, M., Henriksen, T. B., & Olsen, J. (2005). Coffee and fetal death: A cohort study with prospective data. *American Journal of Epidemiology, 162,* 983–990.

Bechara, A., Damasio, H., Tranel, D., & Damasio, A. R. (1997). Deciding advantageously before knowing the advantageous strategy. *Science, 275,* 1293–1295.

Beck, A. T. (1967). *Depression: Clinical, experimental and theoretical aspects.* New York: Harper & Row.

Beck, A. T. (1976). *Cognitive therapy and the emotional disorders.* New York: International Universities Press.

Beck, A. T. (1995). Cognitive therapy: A 30-year retrospective. In S. O. Lilienfeld (Ed.), *Seeing both sides: Classic controversies in abnormal psychology* (pp. 303–311). Pacific Grove, CA: Brooks/Cole. (Original work published 1991)

Beck, A. T. (2002). Cognitive models of depression. In R. L. Leahy & E. T. Dowd (Eds.), *Clinical advances in cognitive psychotherapy: Theory and Application* (pp. 29–61). New York: Springer.

Beck, A. T. (2005). The current state of cognitive therapy: A 40-year retrospective. *Archives of General Psychiatry, 62,* 953–959.

Beck, A. T., Brown, G., Berchick, R. J., Stewart, B. L., & Steer, R. A. (1990). Relationship between hopelessness and ultimate suicide: A replication with psychiatric outpatients. *American Journal of Psychiatry, 147,* 190–195.

Beck, A. T., & Emery, G. (1985). *Anxiety disorders and phobias: A cognitive perspective.* New York: Basic Books.

Beck, A. T., & Rector, N. A. (2005). Cognitive approaches to schizophrenia: Theory and therapy. *Annual Review of Clinical Psychology, 1,* 577–606. Behnke, S. (2004,

December). Sexual involvements with former clients: A delicate balance of core values. *Monitor on Psychology,* 76–77.

Beck, A. T., Sokol, L., Clark, D., Berchick, R., & Wright, F. (1992). A crossover study of focused cognitive therapy for panic disorder. *American Journal of Psychiatry, 149,* 778–783.

Beck, J. S., & Beck, A. T. (1995). *Cognitive therapy: Basics and beyond.* New York: Guilford.

Beck, M. (1992, December 7). The new middle age. *Newsweek,* pp. 50–56.

Beels, C. C. (2002). Notes for a cultural history of family therapy. *Family Process, 41,* 67–82.

Begley, S. (1997, September 29). Hope for "snow babies. " *Newsweek,* pp. 62–63.

Beilock, S. L., & Carr, T. H. (2005). When high-powered people fail: Working memory and "choking under pressure" in math. *Psychological Science, 16,* 101–105.

Beilock, S. L., Kulp, C. A., Holt, L. E., & Carr, T. H. (2004). More on the fragility of performance: Choking under pressure in mathematical problem solving. *Journal of Experimental Psychology: General, 133,* 584–600.

Beirne, R. O., Zlatkova, M. B., & Anderson, R. S. (2005). Changes in human short-wavelength-sensitive and achromatic resolution acuity with retinal eccentricity and meridian. *Visual Neuroscience, 22,* 79–86.

Bekinschtein, T., Tiberti, C., Niklison, J., Tamashiro, M., Ron, M., Carpintiero, S., et al. (2005). Assessing level of consciousness and cognitive changes from vegetative state to full recovery. *Neuropsychological Rehabilitation, 15*(3–4), 307–322.

Belin, P., Zatorre, R. J., & Ahad, P. (2002). Human temporal-lobe response to vocal sounds. *Brain Research and Cognitive Brain Research, 13,* 17–26.

Bell, B. E., & Loftus, E. F. (1989). Trivial persuasion in the courtroom: The power of (a few) minor details. *Journal of Personality and Social Psychology, 56,* 669–679.

Bell, P. A., Greene, T. C., Fisher, J. D., & Baum, A. (2000). *Environmental psychology* (5th ed.). Belmont, CA: Wadsworth.

Bellaby, P. (2003). Communication and miscommunication of risk: Understanding UK parents' attitudes to combined MMR vaccination. *British Medical Journal, 327,* 725–728.

Belli, R. F., & Loftus, E. F. (1996). The pliability of autobiographical memory: Misinformation and the false memory problem. In D. C. Rubin (Ed.), *Remembering our past: Studies in autobiographical memory* (pp. 157–179). New York: Cambridge University Press.

Belmonte, M. K., Cook, E. H., Jr, Anderson, G. M., Rubenstein, J. L., Greenough, W. T., Beckel-Mitchener, A., et al. (2004). Autism as a disorder of neural information processing: Directions for research and targets for therapy [Electronic version]. *Molecular Psychiatry, 9,* 646–663.

Belsky, J., & Kelly, J. (1994). *The transition to parenthood.* New York: Dell.

Bem, D. J. (1996). Exotic becomes erotic: A developmental theory of sexual orientation. *Psychological Review, 103,* 320–335.

Ben-Ari, A., & Gil, S. (2002). Traditional support systems: Are they sufficient in a culturally diverse academic environment? *British Journal of Social Work, 32,* 629–638.

Benecke, M. (1999). Spontaneous human combustion: Thoughts of a forensic biologist. *Skeptical Inquirer, 22,* 47–51.

Benedetti, F., Arduino, C., & Amanzio, M. (1999). Somatotopic activation of opioid systems by target-directed expectations of analgesia. *Journal of Neuroscience, 19,* 3639–3648.

Benight, C. C., Swift, E., Sanger, J., Smith, A., & Zeppelin, D. (1999). Coping self-efficacy as a mediator of distress following a natural disaster. *Journal of Applied Social Psychology, 29,* 2443–2464.

Benjamin, L. T., Jr. (2000). The psychology laboratory at the turn of the 20th century. *American Psychologist, 55,* 318–321.

Benjamin, L. T., Jr., & Baker, D. (2004). *From séance to science: A history of the profession of psychology in America.* Belmont, CA: Wadsworth.

Bennett, H. L., Giannini, J. A., & Davis, H. S. (1985). Nonverbal response to intraoperational conversation. *British Journal of Anaesthesia, 57,* 174–179.

Bennett, K. K., & Elliott, M. (2002). Explanatory style and health: Mechanisms linking pessimism to illness. *Journal of Applied Social Psychology, 32,* 1508–1526.

Bennett, R. J., & Robinson, S. L. (2000). Development of a measure of workplace deviance. *Journal of Applied Psychology, 85,* 349–360.

Ben-Shakhar, G., Bar-Hillel, M., & Kremnitzer, M. (2002). Trial by polygraph: Reconsidering the use of the guilty knowledge technique in court. *Law & Human Behavior, 26,* 527–541.

Ben-Shakhar, G., & Furedy, J. J. (1990). *Theories and applications in the detection of deception: A psychophysiological and international perspective.* New York: Springer-Verlag.

Benson, D. F., & Geschwind, N. (1971). Aphasia and related cortical disturbances. In A. B. Baker & L. H. Baker (Eds). *Clinical neurology*. New York: Harper & Row.

Benson, E. (2003). Sex: The science of sexual arousal. *Monitor on Psychology, 34,* 50.

Benson, H. (1975). *The relaxation response.* New York: Morrow.

Ben-Zur, H. (2002). Coping, affect and aging: The roles of mastery and self-esteem. *Personality & Individual Differences, 32*(2), 357–372.

Bergin, A. E. (1971). The evaluation of therapeutic outcomes. In A. E. Bergin & S. L. Garfield (Eds.), *Handbook of psychotherapy and behavior change: An empirical analysis* (pp. 217–270). New York: Wiley.

Berglund, H., Lindström, P., & Savic, I. (2006). Brain response to putative pheromones in lesbian women. *Proceedings of the National Academy of Sciences of the USA, 103,* 8269—8274.

Berkowitz, L. (1994). Is something missing? Some observations prompted by the Cognitive-neoassociationist view of anger and emotional aggression. In L. R. Huesmann (Ed.), *Human aggression: Current perspectives* (pp. 35–60). New York: Plenum.

Berkowitz, L. (1998). Affective aggression: The role of stress, pain, and negative affect. In R. G. Geen & E. Donnerstein (Eds.), *Human aggression* (pp. 49–72). San Diego: Academic Press.

Berkowitz, L. (1999). Evil is more than banal: Situationism and the concept of evil. *Personality and Social Psychology Review, 3,* 246–253.

Bernard, L. L. (1924). *Instinct.* New York: Holt, Rinehart & Winston.

Bernardin, H. J., & Beatty, R. W. (1984). *Performance appraisal: Assessing human behavior at work.* Boston: Kent.

Bernat, J. A., Calhoun, K. S., Adams, H. E., & Zeichner, A. (2001). Homophobia and physical aggression toward homosexual and heterosexual individuals. *Journal of Abnormal Psychology, 110,* 179–187.

Berns, G. S., McClure, S. M., Pagnoni, G., & Montague, P. R. (2001). Predictability modulates human brain response to reward. *Journal of Neuroscience, 21,* 2793–2798.

Bernstein, D. A. (1970). The modification of smoking behavior: A search for effective variables. *Behaviour Research and Therapy, 8,* 133–146.

Bernstein, D. A., Borkovec, T. D., & Hazlett-Stevens, H. (2000). *Progressive relaxation training: A manual for the helping professions* (2nd ed.) New York: Praeger.

Bernstein, D. A., Kramer, G. P., & Phares, V. (in press). *Introduction to clinical psychology* (7th ed.). Upper Saddle River, NJ: Prentice Hall.

Bernstein, D. M., Laney, C., Morris, E. K., & Loftus, E. F. (2005). False beliefs about fattening foods can have healthy consequences. *Proceedings of the National Academy of Sciences of the USA, 102,* 13724–13731.

Bernstein, D. M., & Roberts, B. (1995). Assessing dreams through self-report questionnaires: Relation with past research and personality. *Dreaming: Journal of the Association for the Study of Dreams, 5,* 13–27.

Bernstein, I. L. (1978). Learned taste aversions in children receiving chemotherapy. *Science, 200,* 1302–1303.

Berry, J. W., & Bennett, J. A. (1992). Cree conceptions of cognitive competence. *International Journal of Psychology, 27,* 73–88.

Berscheid, E., & Reis, H. T. (1998). Attraction and close relationships. In D. Gilbert, S. T. Fiske, & G. Lindzey (Eds.), *Handbook of social psychology* (Vol. 2, 4th ed., pp. 193–281). Boston: McGraw-Hill.

Bersoff, D. M. (1999). Why good people sometimes do bad things: Motivated reasoning and unethical behavior. *Personality and Social Psychology Bulletin, 25,* 28–39.

Bertau, C., Anderson, N., & Salgado, J. F. (2005). The predictive validity of cognitive ability tests: A UK meta-analysis. *Journal of Occupational and Organizational Psychology, 78,* 387–409.

Berti, A., Ladavas, E., & Corti, M. D. (1996). Anosognosia for hemiplegia, neglect dyslexia, and drawing neglect: Clinical findings and theoretical implications. *Journal of the International Neuropsychological Association, 2,* 426–440.

Best, D. (1992, June). *Cross-cultural themes in developmental psychology.* Paper presented at workshop on cross-cultural aspects of psychology. Western Washington University, Bellingham.

Best, J. B. (1999). *Cognitive psychology* (5th ed.) Belmont, CA: Brooks/Cole.

Betch, T., Hoffman, K., Hoffrage, U., & Plessner, H. (2003). Intuition beyond recognition: When less familiar events are liked more. *Experimental Psychology, 50,* 49–54.

Beutler, L. E. (2000). David and Goliath: When empirical and clinical standards of practice meet. *American Psychologist, 55,* 997–1007.

Beutler, L. E. (2002). The dodo bird is extinct. *Clinical Psychology: Science and Practice, 9,* 30–34.

Beutler, L. E., & Malik, M. L. (Eds.). (2002). *Rethinking DSM: A psychological perspective.* Washington DC: American Psychological Association.

Beyerstein, B. L. (1999). Pseudoscience and the brain: Tuners and tonics for aspiring superhumans. In S. Della Sala (Ed.), *Mind myths: Exploring popular assumptions about the mind and brain* (pp. 59–82). Chichester, UK: Wiley.

Bhagat, R. S., Kedia, B. L., Harveston, P. D., & Triandis, H. C. (2002). Cultural variations in the cross-border transfer of organizational knowledge: An integrative framework. *Academy of Management Review, 27,* 204–221.

Bhatt, R. S., & Bertin, E. (2001). Pictorial cues and three-dimensional information processing in early infancy. *Journal of Experimental Child Psychology, 80,* 315–332.

Bhopal, R., Vettini, A., Hunt, S., Wiebe, S., Hanna, L., & Amos, A. (2004). Review of prevalence data in, and evaluation of methods for cross cultural adaptation of, UK surveys on tobacco and alcohol in ethnic minority groups. *British Medical Journal, 328,* 76.

Bhutta, A. T., Cleves, M. A., Casey, P. H., Cradock, M. M., & Anand, K. J. S. (2002). Cognitive and behavioral outcomes of school-aged children who were born preterm. *JAMA, 288,* 728–737.

Bickis, M., Kelly, I. W., & Byrnes, G. (1995). Crisis calls and temporal and lunar variables: A comprehensive study. *Journal of Psychology, 129,* 701–711.

Bidwell, M. A., & Rehfeldt, R. A. (2004). Using video modeling to teach a domestic skill with an embedded social skill to adults with severe mental retardation. *Behavioral Interventions, 19,* 263–274.

Bielsky, I. F., Hu, S.-B., Ren, X., Terwilliger, E. F., & Young, L. J. (2005). The V1a Vasopressin receptor is necessary and sufficient for normal social recognition: A gene replacement study. *Neuron, 47,* 503–513.

Bierhaus, A., Wolf, J., Andrassy, M., Rohleder, N., Humpert, P. M., Petrov, D., et al. (2003). A mechanism converting psychosocial stress into mononuclear cell activation. *Proceedings of the National Academy of Sciences, 100,* 1920–1925.

Bierut, L. J., Heath, A. C., Bucholz, K. K., Dinwiddie, S. H., Madden, P. A., Statham, D. J., et al. (1999). Major depressive disorder in a community-based twin sample: Are there different genetic and environmental contributions for men and women? *Archives of General Psychiatry, 56,* 557–563.

Bies, R. J., Tripp, T. M., & Kramer, R. M. (1997). At the breaking point: Cognitive and social dynamics of revenge in organizations. In R. A. Giacalone & J. Greenberg (Eds.), *Antisocial behavior in organizations* (pp. 18–36). Thousand Oaks, CA: Sage.

Binet, A., & Simon, T. (1905). Methodes nouvelles pour le diagnostic du niveau intellectuel des anormaux. *L'Annee Psychologique, 11,* 191–244.

Binet, A., & Simon, T. (1908). The development of intelligence in the child. *L'Annee Psychologique, 14,* 1–94.

Bingheimer, J. B., Brennan, R. T., & Earls, F. J. (2005). Firearm violence exposure and serious violent behavior. *Science, 308,* 1323–1326.

Binson, D., Michaels, S., Stall, R., Coates, T. J., Gagnon, J. H., & Catania, J. A. (1995). Prevalence and social distribution of men who have sex with men: United States and its urban centers. *Journal of Sex Research, 32*(3), 245–254.

Binzen, C. A., Swan, P. D., & Manore, M. M. (2001). Postexercise oxygen consumption and substrate use after resistance exercise in women. *Medicine and Science in Sports and Exercise, 33,* 932–938.

Birbaumer, N., Veit, R., Lotze, M., Erb, M., Hermann, C., Grodd, W., & Flor, H. (2005). Deficient fear conditioning in psychopathy: A functional magnetic resonance imaging study. *Archives of General Psychiatry, 62,* 799–805.

Birch, H. G. (1945). The relation of previous experience to insightful problem solving. *Journal of Comparative Psychology, 38,* 367–383.

Birch, L. L., McPhee, L., Sullivan, S., & Johnson, S. (1989). Conditioned meal initiation in young children. *Appetite, 13,* 105–113.

Bisiach, E., Capitani, E., & Tansini, E. (1979). Detection from left and right hemifields on single and double simultaneous stimulation. *Perceptual and Motor Skills, 48*(3, Pt. 1), 960.

Bisiach, E., Luzzatti, C., & Perani, D. (1979). Unilateral neglect, representational schema and consciousness. *Brain, 102*(3), 609–618.

Bisiach, E., Vallar, G., Perani, D., Papagano, C., & Berti, A. (1986). Unawareness of disease following lesions of the right hemisphere: Anosognosia for hemiplegia and anosognosia for hemianopia. *Neuropsychologia, 24,* 471–482.

Bjil, R. V., de Graaf, R., Hiripi, E., Kessler, R. C., Kohn, R., Offord, D. R., et al. (2003). The prevalence of treated and untreated mental disorders in five countries. *Health Affairs, 22,* 122–133.

Bjork, R. A. (1979). An information-processing analysis of college teaching. *Educational Psychologist, 14,* 15–23.

Bjork, R. A. (1998). Assessing our own competence: Heuristics and biases. In D. Gopher & A. Koriat (Eds.), *Attention and performance* (Vol. 17). Orlando: Academic Press.

Bjork, R. A. (1999). Assessing our own competence: Heuristics and illusions. In D. Gopher & A. Koriat (Eds.), *Attention and performance XVII. Cognitive regulation of performance: Interaction of theory and application* (pp. 435–459). Cambridge: MIT Press.

Bjork, R. A. (2001, March). How to succeed in college: Learn how to learn. *American Psychological Society Observer, 14,* 9.

Bjork, R. A., & Linn, M. C. (2006). The science of learning and the learning of science. *APS Observer, 19,* 29, 39.

Bjorklund, D. F., & Green, B. L. (1992). The adaptive nature of cognitive immaturity. *American Psychologist, 47,* 46–54.

Blackwell, B. (1973). Psychotropic drugs in use today. *Journal of the American Medical Association, 225,* 1637–1641.

Blackwood, D. H. R., Visscher, P. M., & Muir, W. J. (2001). Genetic studies of bipolar affective disorder in large families. *British Journal of Psychiatry, 178*(Suppl. 14), 134–136.

Blagrove, M. (1996). Problems with the cognitive psychological modeling of dreaming. *Journal of Mind and Behavior, 17,* 99–134.

Blair, I. V., Judd, C. M., & Fallman, J. L. (2004). The automaticity of race and Afrocentric facial features in social judgments. *Journal of Personality and Social Psychology, 87,* 763–778.

Blake, J., & de Boysson-Bardies, B. (1992). Patterns in babbling: A cross-linguistic study. *Journal of Child Language, 19,* 51–74.

Blake, R. (1998). What can be "perceived" in the absence of visual awareness? *Current Directions in Psychological Science, 6,* 157–162.

Blakeslee, S. (2000, January 4). A decade of discovery yields a shock about the brain. *New York Times.*

Blakeslee, S. (2001, August 28). Therapies push injured brains and spinal cords into new paths. *New York Times.* Retrieved July 28, 2003, from http://www.nytimes.com/2001/08/28/health/anatomy/28REHA.html

Blascovich, J., Spencer, S. J., Quinn, D., & Steele, C. (2001). African Americans and high blood pressure: The role of stereotype threat. *Psychological Science, 12,* 225–229.

Blass, T. (2000). The Milgram paradigm 35 years later: Some things we know about obedience to authority. In T. Blass (Ed.), *Current perspectives on the Milgram paradigm* (pp. 35–59). Mahwah, N.J: Erlbaum.

Blass, T. (2004). *The man who shocked the world: The life and legacy of Stanley Milgram.* New York: Basic Books.

Blass, T., & Schmitt, C. (2001). The nature of perceived authority in the Milgram paradigm: Two replications. *Current Psychology: Developmental, Learning, Personality, Social, 20,* 115–121.

Bleck, T. P., & Klawans, H. L. (1986). Neurologic emergencies. *Medical Clinics of North America, 70*(5), 1167–1184.

Bleil, M. E., McCaffery, J. M., Muldoon, M. F., Sutton-Tyrrell, K., & Manuck, S. B. (2004). Anger-related personality traits and carotid artery atherosclerosis in untreated hypertensive men. *Psychosomatic Medicine, 66,* 633–639.

Block, J. (2001). Millennial contrarianism: The Five-Factor approach to personality description 5 years later. *Journal of Research in Personality, 35,* 98–107.

Block, J. A. (1971). *Lives through time.* Berkeley: Bancroft Books.

Block, R. I., & Ghoneim, M. M. (1993). Effects of chronic marijuana use on human cognition. *Psychopharmacology, 110*(1–2), 219–228.

Blood, A. J., & Zatorre, R. J. (2001). Intensely pleasurable responses to music correlate with activity in brain regions implicated in reward and emotion. *Proceedings of the National Academy of Science, 98,* 11818–11823.

Bloom, L. (1995). *The transition from infancy to language: Acquiring the power of expression.* New York: Cambridge University Press.

Blow, A. J., & Timm, T. M. (2002). Promoting community through family therapy: Helping clients develop a network of significant social relationships. *Journal of Systematic Therapies, 21,* 67–89.

Blum, R. W., Beuhring, T., & Rinehart, P. M. (2000). *Protecting teens: Beyond race, income and family structure.* Minneapolis, MN: Center for Adolescent Health, University of Minnesota.

Blumberg, H. P., Leung, H.-C., Skudlarski, P., Lacadie, C. M., Fredericks, C. A., Harris, B. C., et al. (2003). A functional magnetic resonance imaging study of bipolar disorder: State- and trait-related dysfunction in ventral prefrontal cortices. *Archives of General Psychiatry, 60,* 601–609.

Blumberg, M. S., & Lucas, D. E. (1994). Dual mechanisms of twitching during sleep in neonatal rats. *Behavioral Neuroscience, 108*(6), 1196–1202.

Blume, E. S. (1998). *Secret survivors: Uncovering incest and its aftereffects in women.* New York: Ballantine.

Blumenthal, J. A., Babyak, M., Wei., J., O'Conner, C., Waugh, R., Eisenstein, E., et al. (2002). Usefulness of psychosocial treatment of mental stress-induced myocardial ischemia in men. *American Journal of Cardiology, 89,* 164–168.

Blundell, J. E., & Cooling, J. (2000). Routes to obesity: Phenotypes, food choices, and activity. *British Journal of Nutrition, 83,* S33–S38.

Boake, C., Yeates, K. O., & Donders, J. (2002). Association of postdoctoral programs in clinical neuropsychology: Update and new directions. *Clinical Neuropsychology, 16*(1), 1–6.

Boardman, A. P., & Healy, D. (2001). Modeling suicide risk in affective disorders. *European Psychiatry, 16,* 400–405.

Boden-Albala, B., Litwak, E., Elkind, M. S., Rundek, T., & Sacco, R. L. (2005). Social isolation and outcomes post stroke. *Neurology, 64,* 1888–1892.

Bodian, S. (1999). *Meditation for dummies.* Indianapolis: IDG Books Worldwide.

Boehning, D., & Snyder, S. H. (2003). Novel neural modulators. *Annual Review of Neuroscience, 26,* 105–131.

Bogaert, A. F. (2003). Number of older brothers and social orientation: New tests and the attraction/behavior distinction in two national probability samples. *Journal of Personality and Social Psychology, 84,* 644–652.

Bogaert, A. F. (2006). Biological versus nonbiological older brothers and men's sexual orientation. *Proceedings of the National Academy of Sciences, 103,* 10771–10774.

Bogartz, R. S., Shinskey, J. L., & Speaker, C. J. (1997). Interpreting infant looking: The event set x event set design. *Developmental Psychology, 33,* 408–422.

Bohner, G., & Schwarz, N. (2001). Attitudes persuasion and behavior. In A. Tesser & N. Schwarz (Eds.), *Blackwell handbook of social psychology: Intraindividual processes* (pp. 413–435). Oxford, UK: Blackwell.

Bolla, K. I., Brown, K., Eldreth, D., Tate, K. & Cadet, J. L. (2002). Dose-related neurocognitive effects of marijuana use. *Neurology, 59,* 1337–1343.

Bomze, H. M., Bulsara, K. R., Iskandar, B. J., Caroni, P., & Skene, J. H. (2001). Spinal axon regeneration evoked by replacing two growth cone proteins in adult neurons. *Nature Neuroscience, 4,* 38–43.

Bonanno, G. A. (2004). Loss, trauma, and human resilience: Have we underestimated the human capacity to thrive after extremely aversive events? *American Psychologist, 59,* 20–28.

Bonanno, G. A. (2005). Resilience in the face of potential trauma. *Current Directions in Psychological Science, 14,* 135–138.

Bonci, A., Bernardi, G., Grillner, P., & Mercuri, N. B. (2003). The dopamine-containing neuron: Maestro or simple musician in the orchestra of addiction? *Trends in Pharmacological Science, 24,* 172–177.

Bond, F. W., & Bunce, D. (2003). The role of acceptance and job control in mental health, job satisfaction, and work performance. *Journal of Applied Psychology, 88,* 1057–1067.

Bond, G., Aiken, L., & Somerville, S. (1992). The Health Beliefs Model and adolescents with insulin-dependent diabetes mellitus. *Health Psychology, 11,* 190–198.

Bond, L. A., & Hauf, A. M. C. (2004). Taking stock and putting stock in primary prevention: Characteristics of effective programs. *Journal of Primary Prevention, 24,* 199–221.

Bonner, R. (2001, August 24). Death row inmate is freed after DNA test clears him. *The New York Times.*

Bonwell, C. C., & Eison, J. A. (1991). *Active learning: Creating excitement in the classroom.* Washington, DC: George Washington University.

Booth, P. B., & Lindaman, S. (2000). Theraplay for enhancing attachment in adopted children. In H. G. Kaduson & C. Schaefer (Eds.), *Short-term play therapy for children.* New York: Guilford.

Bordnick, P. S., Elkins, R. L., Orr, T. E., Walters, P., & Thyer, B. A. (2004). Evaluating the relative effectiveness of three aversion therapies designed to reduce craving among cocaine abusers. *Behavioral Interventions, 19,* 1–24.

Borg, M. B., Jr. (2002). The Avalon Garden men's association: A community health psychology case study. *Journal of Health Psychology, 7,* 345–357.

Borgida, E., Conner, C., & Monteufel, L. (1992). Understanding living kidney donors: A behavioral decision-making perspective. In S. Spacapan & S. Oskamp (Eds.), *Helping and being helped* (pp. 183–212). Newbury Park, CA: Sage.

Borkenau, P., Riemann, R., Angleitner, A., & Spinath, F. M. (2002). Similarity of childhood experiences and personality resemblance in monozygotic and dizygotic twins: A test of the equal environments assumption. *Personality & Individual Differences, 33,* 261–269.

Borkovec, T. C., & Costello, E. (1993). Efficacy of applied relaxation and cognitive behavioral therapy in the treatment of generalized anxiety disorder. *Journal of Consulting and Clinical Psychology, 61,* 611–619.

Borman, W. C., Hanson, M. A., & Hedge, J. W. (1997). Personnel selection. *Annual Review of Psychology, 48,* 299–337.

Borman, W. C., Penner, L. A., Allen T. D. & Motowidlo, S. (2001). Personality predictors of citizenship performance. *International Journal of Selection and Assessment, 9,* 52–69.

Borry, P., Schotsmans, P., & Dierickx, K. (2006). Evidence-based medicine and its role in ethical decision-making. *Journal of Evaluation in Clinical Practice, 12,* 306–311.

Bosma, H., Marmot, M. G., Hemingway, H., Nicholson, A. C., Brunner, E., & Stansfeld, S. A. (1997). Low job control and risk of coronary heart disease in Whitehall II (prospective cohort) study. *British Medical Journal, 314,* 558–565.

Bosompra, K., Ashikaga, T., Worden, J. K., & Flynn, B. S. (2001). Is more optimism associated with better health? Findings from a population-based survey. *International Quarterly of Community Health Education, 20,* 29–58.

Botwinick, J. (1961). Husband and father-in-law: A reversible figure. *American Journal of Psychology, 74,* 312–313.

Bouchard, T. J. (1999). Genes, environment, and personality. In S. J. Ceci & W. M. Williams (Eds.), *The nature-nurture debate: The essential readings* (pp.97–103). Malden, MA: Blackwell.

Bouchard, T. J., Jr. (2004). Genetic influence on human psychological traits: A survey. *Current Directions in Psychological Science, 13,* 148–151.

Bouchard, T. J., & McGue, M. (1981). Familial studies of intelligence: A review. *Science, 212*(4498), 1055–1059.

Bourassa, M., & Vaugeois, P. (2001). Effects of marijuana use on divergent thinking. *Creativity Research Journal, 13,* 411–416.

Bouret, S. G., Draper, S. J., & Simerly, R. B. (2004). Trophic action of leptin on hypothalamic neurons that regulate feeding. *Science, 304,* 108–110.

Bouton, M. E. (1993). Context, time, and memory retrieval in the interference paradigms of Pavlovian learning. *Psychological Bulletin, 114,* 80–99.

Bouton, M. E. (2000). A learning theory perspective on lapse, relapse, and the maintenance of behavior change. *Health Psychology, 19,* 57–63.

Bouton, M. E. (2002). Context, ambiguity, and unlearning: Sources of relapse after behavioral extinction. *Biological Psychiatry, 52,* 976–986.

Bouton, M., Mineka, S., & Barlow, D. (2001). A modern learning theory perspective on the etiology of panic disorder. *Psychological Review, 107,* 4–32.

Bowden, C. L. (2000). Efficacy of lithium in mania and maintenance therapy of bipolar disorder. *Journal of Clinical Psychiatry, 61,* 35–40.

Bowden, C. L., Calabrese, J. R., Sachs, G., Yatham, L. N., Asghar, S. A., Hompland, M., et al. (2003). A placebo-controlled 18-month trial of lamotrigine and lithium maintenance treatment in recently manic or hypomanic patients with bipolar I disorder. *Archives of General Psychiatry, 60,* 392–400.

Bower, G. H. (1981). Mood and memory. *American Psychologist, 36,* 129–148.

Bower, J. M., & Parsons, L. M. (2003). Rethinking the "lesser brain". *Scientific American, 289,* 50–57.

Bowlby, J. (1973). *Attachment and loss: Vol. 2. Separation.* New York: Basic Books.

Bowman, E. S., & Nurnberger, J. I. (1993). Genetics of psychiatry diagnosis and treatment. In D. L. Dummer (Ed.), *Current psychiatric therapy* (pp. 46–56). Philadelphia: Saunders.

Boxer, A. L., & Miller, B. L. (2005). Clinical features of frontotemporal dementia. *Alzheimer Disease and Associated Disorders, 19* (Suppl. 1), S3–S6.

Boyer, J. L., Harrison, S., & Ro, T. (2005). Unconscious processing of orientation and color without primary visual cortex. *Proceedings of the National Academy of Sciences of the USA, 102,* 16875–16879.

Boyle, S. H., Williams, R. B., Mark, D. B., Brummett, B. H., Siegler, I. C., Helms, M. J., & Barefoot, J. C. (2004).Hostility as a predictor of survival in patients with coronary artery disease. *Psychosomatic Medicine, 66,* 629–632.

Bozarth, M. A., & Wise, R. A. (1984). Anatomically distinct opiate receptor fields mediate reward and physical dependence. *Science, 224,* 516–518.

Brach, J. S., FitzGerald, S., Newman, A. B., Kelsey, S., Kuller, L., VanSwearingen, J. M., & Kriska, A. M. (2003). Physical activity and functional status in community-dwelling older women. *Archives of Internal Medicine, 163,* 2565–2571.

Bradley, R., Greene, J., Russ, E., Dutra, L., & Westen, D. (2005). A multidimensional meta-analysis of psychotherapy for PTSD. *American Journal of Psychiatry, 162,* 214–227.

Bradley-Johnson, S., Graham, D. P., & Johnson, C. M. (1986). Token reinforcement on WISC-R performance for white, low-socioeconomic, upper and lower elementary-school-age students. *Journal of School Psychology, 24,* 73–79.

Bradshaw, G. L. (1993a). Why did the Wright brothers get there first? Part 1. *Chemtech, 23*(6), 8–13.

Bradshaw, G. L. (1993b). Why did the Wright brothers get there first? Part 2. *Chemtech, 23*(7), 16–22.

Brainerd, C. J., & Reyna, V. F. (2005). *The science of false memory.* New York: Oxford University Press.

Brainerd, C. J., Reyna, V. F., Wright, R., & Mojardin, A. H. (2003). Recollection rejection: False memory editing in children and adults. *Psychological Review, 110,* 762–784.

Brambilla, P., Cipriani, A., Hotopf, M., & Barbul, C. (2005). Side-effect profile of fluoxentine in comparison with other SSRIs, tricyclic, and newer antidepressants: A meta-analysis of clinical trial data. *Pharmacopsychiatry, 38,* 69–77.

Brandimonte, M. A., Hitch, G. J., & Bishop, D. V. M. (1992). Influence of short-term memory codes on visual image processing: Evidence from image transformation tasks. *Journal of Experimental Psychology: Learning, Memory, and Cognition, 18,* 157–165.

Brandtstadter, J., & Renner, G. (1990). Tenacious goal pursuit and flexible goal adjustment: Explication and age-related analysis of assimilative and accommodative strategies of coping. *Psychology and Aging, 5,* 58–67.

Brannick, M., & Levine, E. (2002). *Job analysis.* Thousand Oaks: CA: Sage.

Bransford, J. D., & Stein, B. S. (1993). *The ideal problem solver* (2nd ed.). New York: Freeman.

Brasher, E. E., & Chen, P. Y. (1999). Evaluation of success criteria in job search: A process perspective. *Journal of Occupational and Organizational Psychology, 72,* 57–70.

Braun, A. E., Balkin, T. J., & Wesensten, N. J. (1998). Dissociated pattern of activity in visual cortices and their projections during human rapid eye movement sleep. *Science, 279,* 91–95.

Braunstein, G. D., Sundwall, D. A., Katz, M., Shifren, J. L., Buster, J. E., Simon, J. A., et al. (2005). Safety and efficacy of a testosterone patch for the treatment of hypoactive sexual desire disorder in surgically menopausal women: A randomized, placebo-controlled trial. *Archives of Internal Medicine, 165,* 1582–1589.

Braver, T. S., Reynolds, J. R., & Donaldson, D. I. (2003). Neural mechanisms of transient and sustained cognitive control during task switching. *Neuron, 39,* 713–726.

Bray, G. A., & Tartaglia, L. A. (2000). Medicinal strategies in the treatment of obesity. *Nature, 404,* 672–677.

Bredt, D. S., & Nicoll, R. A. (2003). AMPA receptor trafficking at excitatory synapses. *Neuron, 40,* 361–379.

Breed, A. G. (2006, January 28). Stress from Katrina is called "recipe for suicide." *Naples Daily News,* p. 4A.

Breggin, P. R. (1997). *Brain-disabling treatments in psychiatry: Drugs, electroshock, and the role of the FDA.* New York: Springer.

Breggin, P. R. (2005). Recent U.S., Canadian, and British regulatory agency actions concerning antidepressant-induced harm to self and others: A review and analysis. *Ethical Human Psychology and Psychiatry, 7,* 7–22.

Brehm, S. (1992). *Intimate relationships.* New York: McGraw-Hill.

Brehm, S., Kassin, S., & Fein, S. (1999). *Social psychology* (4th ed., Table 6.4). Boston: Houghton Mifflin.

Brehm, S., Kassin, S., & Fein, S. (2005). *Social psychology* (6th ed.). Boston, MA: Houghton-Mifflin.

Breier, J. I., Adair, J. C., Gold, M., Fennell, E. B., Gilmore, R. L., & Heilman, K. M. (1995). Dissociation of anosognosia for hemiplegia and aphasia during left-hemisphere anesthesia. *Neurology, 45,* 65–67.

Brelsford, J. W. (1993). Physics education in a virtual environment. In *Proceedings of the 37th Annual Meeting of the Human Factors and Ergonomics Society.* Santa Monica, CA: Human Factors.

Bremner, J. D., Shobe, K. K., & Kihlstrom, J. F. (2000). False memories in women with self-reported childhood sexual abuse. *Psychological Science, 11,* 333–337.

Brems, C., & Namyniuk, L. (2002). The relationship of childhood abuse history and substance use in an Alaska Sample. *Substance Use and Misuse, 37,* 473–494.

Brener, N. D., Hassan, S. S., & Barrios, L. C. (1999). Suicidal ideation among college students in the United States. *Journal of Consulting and Clinical Psychology, 67,* 1004–1008.

Brenes, G. A., Rapp, S. R., Rejeski, W. J., & Miller, M. E. (2002). Do optimism and pessimism predict physical functioning? *Journal of Behavioral Medicine, 25,* 219–231.

Brennan, F. X. & Charnetski, C. J. (2000). Explanatory style and Immunoglobulin A (IgA). *Integrative Physiological & Behavioral Science, 35,* 251–255.

Brennen, T., Baguley, T., Bright, J., & Bruce, V. (1990). Resolving semantically induced tip-of-the-tongue states for proper nouns. *Memory & Cognition, 18,* 339–347.

Brenner, R. A., Trumble, A. C., Smith, G. S., Kessler, E. P., & Overpeck, M. D. (2001). Where children drown, United States, 1995. *Pediatrics, 108,* 85–89.

Brenner, R. P. (2005). The interpretation of the EEG in stupor and coma. *Neurologist, 11*(5), 271–284.

Breslau, N., Reboussin, B. A., Anthony, J. C., & Storr, C. L. (2005). The structure of posttraumatic stress disorder: Latent class analysis in 2 community samples. *Archives of General Psychiatry, 62,* 1343–1351.

Breteler, M. H., Hilberink, S. R., Zeeman, G., & Lammers, S. M. (2004). Compulsive smoking: The development of a Rasch homogeneous scale of nicotine dependence. *Addiction and Behavior, 29,* 199–205.

Brewer, J. B., Zhao, Z., Desmond, J. E., Glover, G. H., & Gabriel, J. D. E. (1998). Making memories: Brain activity that predicts how well visual experience will be remembered. *Science, 281,* 1185–1187.

Brewer, M. B., & Pierce, K. P. (2005). Social identity complexity and outgroup tolerance. *Personality and Social Psychology Bulletin, 31,* 428–437.

Brewer, W. F. (1977). Memory for the pragmatic implications of sentences. *Memory & Cognition, 5,* 673–678.

Brewer, W. F., & Treyens, J. C. (1981). Role of schemata in memory for places. *Cognitive Psychology, 13,* 207–230.

Brigham, C. C. (1923). *A study of American intelligence.* Princeton, NJ: Princeton University Press.

Bright, J. I., Baker, K. D., & Neimeyer, R. A. (1999). Professional and paraprofessional group treatments for depression: A comparison of cognitive-behavioral and mutual support interventions. *Journal of Consulting and Clinical Psychology, 67,* 491–501.

Brinkhaus, B., Witt, C. M., Jena, S., Linde, K., Streng, A., Wagenpfeil, S., et al. (2006). Acupuncture in patients with chronic low back pain: A randomized controlled trial. *Archives of Internal Medicine, 166,* 450–457.

Brislin, R. (1993). *Understanding culture's influence on behavior.* Fort Worth: Harcourt, Brace, Jovanovich.

British Medical Association. (2000). *Acupuncture: Efficacy, safety, and practice.* London: Harwood Academic.

Broadbent, E., Petrie, K. J., Alley, P. G., & Booth, R. J. (2003). Psychological stress impairs early wound repair following surgery. *Psychosomatic Medicine, 65,* 865–869.

Broca, P. (1861). Remargues sur le siege de la faculte de la porle articulee, suives d'une observation d'aphemie (perte de parole). *Bulletin Societie Anatomie, 36,* 330–357.

Broca, P. (1865). Sur la faculté du langage articulé. *Bulletin Societe Anthropologie Paris, 6,* 337–393.

Brock, J. W., Farooqui, S. M., Ross, K. D., & Payne, S. (1994). Stress-related behavior and central norepinephrine concentrations in the REM sleep-deprived rat. *Physiology and Behavior, 55*(6), 997–1003.

Broderick, J. E., Junghaenel, D. U., & Schwartz, J. E. (2005). Written emotional expression produces health benefits in fibromyalgia patients. *Psychosomatic Medicine, 67,* 326–34.

Brody, N. (2003). Construct validation of the Sternberg Triarchic Abilities Test: Comment and reanalysis. *Intelligence, 31,* 319–330.

Brody, N., & Ehrlichman, H. (1998). *Personality psychology: The science of individuality.* Upper Saddle River, NJ: Prentice-Hall.

Brondolo, E., Rieppi, R., Erickson, S. A., Bagiella, E., Shapiro, P. A., McKinley, P., & Sloan, R. P. (2003). Hostility, interpersonal interactions, and ambulatory blood pressure. *Psychosomatic Medicine, 65,* 1003–1011.

Brooks-Gunn, J., & Chase-Lansdale, P. L. (2002). Adolescent parenthood. In M. H. Bornstein (Ed.), *Handbook of parenting* (2nd ed). Mahwah, NJ: Erlbaum.

Brooks-Gunn, J., Klebanov, P. K., & Duncan, G. J. (1996). Ethnic differences in children's intelligence test scores: Role of economic deprivation, home environment, and maternal characteristics. *Child Development, 67,* 396–408.

Brown, A. L., Campione, J. C., Webber, L. S., & McGilly, K. (1992). Interactive learning environments: A new look at assessment and instruction. In B. Gifford & M. C. O'Connor (Eds.), *Changing assessments: Alternative views of aptitude, achievement, and instruction* (pp. 121–212). Boston: Kluever.

Brown, A. S. (1991). A review of the tip-of-the-tongue experience. *Psychological Bulletin, 109,* 204–233.

Brown, A. S. (2004). *The déjà vu experience.* New York: Psychology Press.

Brown, A. S., Begg, M. D., Gravenstein, S., Schaefer, C. A., Wyatt, R. J., Bresnahan, M., et al. (2004). Serologic evidence of prenatal influenza in the etiology of schizophrenia [Electronic version]. *Archives of General Psychiatry, 61,* 774–780.

Brown, A. S., Begg, M. D., Gravenstein, S., Schaefer, C. A., Wyatt, R. J., Bresnahan, M., et al. (2005). Serologic evidence of prenatal influenza in the etiology of schizophrenia. *Obstetrical and Gynecological Survey, 60,* 77–78.

Brown, A. S., & Nix, L. A. (1996). Age-related changes in the tip-of-the-tongue experience. *American Journal of Psychology, 109,* 79–91.

Brown, A. S., Schaefer, C. A., Quesenberry, C. P., Jr., Liu, L., Babulas, V. P., & Susser, E. S. (2005). Maternal exposure to toxoplasmosis and risk of schizophrenia in adult offspring. *American Journal of Psychiatry, 162,* 767–773.

Brown, C. (2003, January 31). The man who mistook his wife for a deer. *New York Times Magazine.* Retrieved December 13, 2004, from http://query.nytimes.com/gst/abstract.html?res=F10614FB395D0C718CDDAB0894DB404482

Brown, G. K., Beck, A. T., Steer, R. A., & Grisham, J. R. (2000). Risk factors for suicide in psychiatric outpatients: A 20-year prospective study. *Journal of Consulting and Clinical Psychology, 68,* 371–377.

Brown, G. W., & Moran, P. M. (1997). Single mothers, poverty and depression. *Psychological Medicine, 27,* 21–33.

Brown, J. (1958). Some tests of the decay theory of immediate memory. *Quarterly Journal of Experimental Psychology, 10,* 12–21.

Brown, L. M., Bongar, B., & Cleary, K. M. (2004). A profile of psychologists' views of critical risk factors for completed suicide in older adults. *Professional Psychology: Research and Practice, 35,* 90–96.

Brown, N. (2000). *Creating high performance classroom groups.* New York: Falmer.

Brown, P. D., & O'Leary, K. D. (2000). Therapeutic alliance: Predicting continuance and success in group treatment for spouse abuse. *Journal of Consulting and Clinical Psychology, 68,* 340–345.

Brown, P. J. (1991). Culture and the evolution of obesity. *Human Nature, 2,* 31–57.

Brown, R. A. (1973). *First language.* Cambridge: Harvard University Press.

Brown, R., & Kulik, J. (1977). Flashbulb memories. *Cognition, 5,* 73–99.

Brown, R., & McNeill, D. (1966). The "tip-of-the-tongue" phenomenon. *Journal of Verbal Learning and Verbal Behavior, 5,* 325–337.

Brown, S. L., Nesse, R. M., Vinokur, A. D., & Smith, D. M. (2003). Providing social support may be more beneficial than receiving it: Results from a prospective study of mortality. *Psychological Science, 14,* 320–327.

Brown, T., DiNardo, P. A., Lehman, C, & Campbell, L. A. (2001). Reliability of DSM-IV anxiety and mood disorders: Implications for classification of emotional disorders. *Journal of Abnormal Psychology, 110,* 49–58.

Browne, K. D., & Hamilton-Giachritsis, C. (2005). The influence of violent media on children and adolescents: A public health approach. *Lancet, 365,* 702–710.

Brownell, K. D., & Rodin, J. (1994). The dieting maelstrom: Is it possible and advisable to lose weight? *American Psychologist, 49*(9), 781–791.

Bruce, D., Dolan, A., & Phillips-Grant, K. (2000). On the transition from childhood amnesia to the recall of personal memories. *Psychological Science, 11,* 360–364.

Bruce, T. J., Spiegel, D. A., & Hegel, M. T. (1999). Cognitive-behavioral therapy helps prevent relapse and recurrence of panic disorder following Alpazolam discontinuation: A long-term follow-up of the Peoria and Dartmouth studies. *Journal of Consulting and Clinical Psychology, 67,* 151–156.

Bruck, M., Cavanagh, P., & Ceci, S. J. (1991). Fortysomething: Recognizing faces at one's 25th reunion. *Memory and Cognition, 19,* 221–228.

Brummett, B. H., Mark, D. B., Siegler, I. C., Williams, R. B., Babyak, M. A., Clapp-Channing, N. E., & Barefoot, J. C. (2005). Perceived social support as a predictor of mortality in coronary patients: Effects of smoking, sedentary behavior, and depressive symptoms. *Psychosomatic Medicine, 67,* 40–45.

Brüning, J. C., Gautam, D., Burks, D. J., Gillette, J., Schubert, M., Orban, P. C., et al. (2000). Role of brain insulin receptor in control of body weight and reproduction. *Science, 289,* 2122–2125.

Brunvald, J. H. (1989). *Curses! Broiled again! The hottest urban legends going.* New York: Norton.

Brush, D. H., Moch, M. K., & Pooyan, A. (1987). Individual demographic differences and job satisfaction. *Journal of Occupational Behaviour, 8,* 139–155.

Bryant, R. A., & Guthrie, R. M. (2005). Maladaptive appraisals as a risk factor for posttraumatic stress. *Psychological Science, 16,* 749–752.

Bryant, R. A., & Mallard, D. (2003). Seeing is believing: The reality of hypnotic hallucinations. *Consciousness and Cognition, 12,* 219–230.

Bryant, R. A., & McConkey, K. M. (1989). Hypnotic blindness: A behavioral and experiential analysis. *Journal of Abnormal Psychology, 98,* 71–77.

Bryson, S. E., & Smith, I. M. (1998). Autism. *Mental Retardation and Developmental Disabilities Research Reviews, 4,* 97–103.

Buccino, G., Vogt, S., Ritzl, A., Fink, G. R., Zilles, K., Freund, H. J., et al. (2004). Neural circuits underlying imitation learning of hand actions: An event-related fMRI study. *Neuron, 42,* 323–334.

Buckner, R. L., & Wheeler, M. E. (2001). The cognitive neuroscience of remembering. *Nature Reviews Neuroscience, 2,* 1–12.

Budney, A. J., Hughes, J. R., Moore, B. A., & Novy, P. L. (2001). Marijuana abstinence effects in marijuana smokers maintained in their home environment. *Archives of General Psychiatry, 58,* 917–924.

Budney, A. J., Moore, B. A., Vandrey, R. G., & Hughes, J. R. (2003). The time course and significance of cannabis withdrawal. *Journal of Abnormal Psychology, 112,* 393–402.

Bugental, D. B., & Grusec, J. E. (2006). Socialization processes. In W. Damon & R. M. Lerner (Series Eds.) & N. Eisenberg (Vol. Ed.), *Handbook of child psychology: Vol. 3. Social, emotional, and personality development* (6th ed.). New York: Wiley.

Bui, K.-V. T., Peplau, L. A., & Hill, C. T. (1996). Testing the Rusbult model of relationship commitment and stability in a 15-year study of heterosexual couples. *Personality and Social Psychology Bulletin, 22,* 1244–1257.

Buka, S. L., Shenassa, E. D., & Niaura, R. (2003). Elevated risk of tobacco dependence among offspring of mothers who smoked during pregnancy: A 30-year prospective study. *American Journal of Psychiatry, 160,* 1978–1984.

Bulevich, J. B., Roediger, H. L., Balota, D. A., & Butler, A. C. (2006). Failures to find suppression of episodic memories in the think/no-think paradigm. *Memory and Cognition.*

Bulik, C. M., Sullivan, P. F., Tozzi, F., Furberg, H., Lichtenstein, P., & Pedersen, N. L. (2006). Prevalence, heritability, and prospective risk factors for anorexia nervosa. *Archives of General Psychiatry, 63,* 305–312.

Bulik, C. M., Sullivan, P. F., Wade, T. D., & Kendler, K. S. (2000). Twin studies of eating disorders: A review. *International Journal of Eating Disorders, 27,* 1–20.

Bulik, C. M., Tozzi, F., Anderson, C., Mazzeo, S. E., Aggen, S., & Sullivan, P. F. (2003). The relation between eating disorders and components of perfectionism. *American Journal of Psychiatry, 160,* 366–368.

Buller, D. B., Buller, M. K., & Kane, I. (2005). Web-based strategies to disseminate a sun safety curriculum to public elementary schools and state-licensed child-care facilities. *Health Psychology, 24,* 470–476.

Buller, D. J. (2005). *Adapting minds: Evolutionary psychology and the persistent quest for human nature.* Cambridge, MA: MIT Press.

Bullough, V. L. (1995, August). Sex matters. *Scientific American,* pp. 105–106.

Bunde, J., & Suls, J. (2006). A quantitative analysis of the relationship between the Cook-Medley hostility scale and traditional coronary artery disease risk factors. *Health Psychology, 25,* 493–500.

Burchard, R. E. (1992). Coca chewing and diet. *Current Anthropology, 33*(1), 1–24.

Burger, J. M., & Cornelius, T. (2003). Raising the price of agreement: Public commitment and the lowball compliance procedure. *Journal of Applied Social Psychology, 33,* 923–934.

Burger, J. M., & Guadagno, R. E. (2003). Self-concept clarity and the foot-in-the-door procedure. *Basic and Applied Social Psychology, 25,* 79–86. Burish, T., & Jenkins, R. (1992). Effectiveness of biofeedback and relaxation training in reducing the side effects of cancer chemotherapy. *Health Psychology, 11,* 17–23.

Burleson, B. R., Albrecht, T. L., & Sarason, I. G. (Eds.). (1994). *Communication of social support: Messages, interactions, relationships, and community.* Thousand Oaks, CA: Sage.

Burleson, M. H., Gregory, W. L., & Trevarthen, W. R. (1995). Heterosexual activity: Relationship with ovarian function. *Psychoneuroendocrinology, 20*(4), 405–421.

Burr, D. C., Morrone, C., & Fiorentini, A. (1996). Spatial and temporal properties of infant colour vision. In F. Vital-Durand, J. Atkinson, & O. J. Braddick (Eds.), *Infant vision* (pp. 63–77). Oxford: Oxford University Press.

Burris, C. T., Branscombe, N. R., & Klar, Y. (1997). Maladjustment implications of self and group gender-role discrepancies: An ordered-discrepancy model. *European Journal of Social Psychology, 27,* 75–95.

Burton, A. M., Wilson, S., Cowan, M., & Bruce, V. (1999). Face recognition in poor-quality video: Evidence from security surveillance. *Psychological Science, 10,* 243–248.

Bushman, B. J. (1998). Priming effects of media violence on the accessibility of aggressive constructs in memory. *Personality and Social Psychology Bulletin, 24,* 537–545.

Bushman, B. J., & Anderson, C. A. (2001). Media violence and the American public: Scientific facts versus media misinformation. *American Psychologist, 56,* 477–489.

Bushman, B. J., Bonacci, A. M., Pedersen, W. C., Vasquez, E. A., & Miller, N. (2005). Chewing on it can chew you up: Effects of rumination on triggered displaced aggression. *Journal of Personality and Social Psychology, 88,* 969–983.

Bushman, B. J., & Huesmann, L. R. (2000). Effects of televised violence on aggression. In D. Singer & J. Singer (Eds.), *Handbook of children and the media* (pp. 223–254). Thousand Oaks, CA: Sage.

Buss, A. H. (1997). Evolutionary perspectives on personality traits. In R. Hogan, J. Johnson, & S. Briggs (Eds.), *Handbook of personality psychology* (pp. 345–366). San Diego: Academic Press.

Buss, D. M. (2004). *Evolutionary psychology: The new science of the mind* (2nd ed.). Boston: Allyn & Bacon.

Büssing, A., & Höge, A. (2004). Aggression and violence against home care workers. *Journal of Occupational Health Psychology, 9,* 206–219.

Bustillo, J. R., Lauriello, J., Horan, W. P., & Keith, S. J. (2001) The psychosocial treatment of schizophrenia: An update. *American Journal of Psychiatry, 158,* 163–175.

Buston, P. M., & Emlen, S. T. (2003). Cognitive processes underlying human mate choice: The relationship between self-perception and mate preference in Western society. Proceedings of the National Academy of Sciences, 100, 8805–8810.

Butcher, J. N. (2004). Personality assessment without borders: Adaptation of the MMPI-2 across cultures. *Journal of Personality Assessment, 83,* 90–104.

Butcher, J. N., & Rouse, S. V. (1996). Personality: Individual differences and clinical assessment. *Annual Review of Psychology, 47,* 87–111.

Butler, R. (1998). Information seeking and achievement motivation in middle childhood and adolescence: The role of conceptions of ability. *Developmental Psychology, 35,* 146–163.

Butters, N. (1981). The Wernicke-Korsakoff syndrome: A review of psychological, neuropathological and etiological factors. *Currents in Alcohol, 8,* 205–232.

Buunk, B., & Oldersma, F. L. (2001). Social comparisons and close relationships. In G. Fletcher & M. Clark (Eds.), *Blackwell handbook of social psychology: Interpersonal processes* (pp. 388–408). Oxford, UK: Blackwell.

Buunk, B. P., Zurriaga, R., Peiró, J. M., Nauta, A., & Gonsalvez, I. (2005). Social comparisons at work as related to a cooperative social climate and to individual differences in social comparison orientation. *Applied Psychology: An International Review, 54,* 61–80.

Buxhoeveden, D. P., Switala, A. E., Roy, E., Litaker, M., & Casanova, M. F. (2001). Morphological differences between minicolumns in human and nonhuman primate cortex. *American Journal of Physical Anthropology, 115,* 361–371.

Buxton, R. B., Uludag, K., Dubowitz, D. J., & Liu, T. T. (2004). Modeling the hemodynamic response to brain activation. *Neuroimage, 23*(Suppl. 1), S220–233.

C

Cabanac, M., & Morrissette, J. (1992). Acute, but not chronic, exercise lowers the body weight set-point in male rats. *Physiology and Behavior, 52*(6) 1173–1177.

Cabeza, R., Rao, S. M., Wagner, A. D., Mayer, A. R., & Schacter, D. L. (2001). Can medial temporal lobe regions distinguish true from false? An event-related functional MRI study of veridical and illusory recognition memory. *Proceedings of the National Academy of Science, 98,* 4805–4810.

Cabot, P. J. (2001). Immune-derived opioids and peripheral antinociception. *Clinical and Experimental Pharmacology and Physiology, 28,* 230–232.

Cacioppo, J. T., Berntson, G. G., & Petty, R. E. (1997). *Persuasion. Encyclopedia of human biology* (Vol. 6, pp. 679–690). San Diego: Academic Press.

Cacioppo, J. T., Berntson, G. G., Sheridan, J. F., & McClintock, M. K. (2000). Multilevel integrative analyses of human behavior: Social neuroscience and the complementing nature of social and biological approaches. *Psychological Bulletin, 126,* 829–843.

Cacioppo, J. T., Malarkey, W. B., Kiecolt-Glaser, J. K., Uchino, B. N., Sgoutas-Emch, S. A., Sheridan, J. F., et al. (1995). Heterogeneity in neuroendocrine and immune responses to brief psychological stressors as a function of autonomic cardiac activation. *Psychosomatic Medicine, 57,* 154–164.

Cacioppo, J. T., Petty, R. E., & Crites, S. L. (1993). Attitude change. In V. S. Ramachandran (Ed.), *Encyclopedia of human behavior* (pp. 261–270). San Diego: Academic Press.

Cacioppo, J. T., Poehlmann, K. M., Kiecolt-Glaser, J. K., Malarkey, W. B., Burleson, M. H., Berntson, G. G., & Glaser, R. (1998). Cellular immune responses to acute stress in female caregivers of dementia patients and matched controls. *Health Psychology, 17,* 182–189.

Cadinu, M., Maass, A., Rosabianca, A., & Kiesner, J. (2005). Why do women underperform under stereotype threat? *Psychological Science, 16,* 572–578.

Cadoret, R. J., Yates, W. R., Troughton, E., Woodworth, G., & Stewart, M. A. (1995). Adoption study demonstrating two genetic pathways to drug abuse. *Archives of General Psychiatry, 52,* 42–52.

Cahill, L., & McGaugh, J. L. (1998). Mechanisms of emotional arousal and lasting declarative memory. *Trends in Neuroscience, 21,* 294–299.

Cahill, S. P., Carrigan, M. H., & Frueh, B. C. (1999). Does EMDR work? And if so, why?: A critical review of controlled outcome and dismantling research. *Journal of Anxiety Disorders, 13,* 5–33.

Cahn, B. R., & Polich, J. (2006). Meditation states and traits, EEG, ERP, and neuroimaging studies. *Psychological Bulletin, 132,* 180–211.

Cain, D. J., & Seeman, J. (Eds.). (2002). *Humanistic psychotherapies: Handbook of research and practice.* Washington, DC: APA Books.

Cairns, R. B., Gariepy, J., & Hood, K. E. (1990). Development, microevolution, and social behavior. *Psychological Review, 97,* 49–65.

Campbell, F. A., Pungello, E. P., Miller-Johnson, S., Burchinal, M., & Ramey, C. T. (2001). The development of cognitive and academic abilities: Growth curves from an early childhood educational experiment. *Developmental Psychology, 37,* 231–242.

Campbell, F. A., Tramer, M. R., Carroll, D., Reynolds, D. J., Moore, R. A., & McQuay, H. J. (2001). Are cannabinoids an effective and safe treatment option in the management of pain? A qualitative systematic review. *British Medical Journal, 323,* 13–16.

Campbell, L., Simpson, J. A., Boldry, J., & Kashy, D. A. (2005). Perceptions of conflict and support in romantic relationships: The role of attachment anxiety. *Journal of Personality and Social Psychology, 88,* 510–531.

Campbell, R. S., & Pennebaker, J. W. (2003). The secret life of pronouns: Flexibility in writing style and physical health. *Psychological Science, 14,* 60–65.

Campion, M. A., & Campion, J. E. (1987). Evaluation of an interviewee skills training program in a natural field experiment. *Personnel Psychology, 40,* 676–691.

Campion, M. A., Palmer, D. K., & Campion, J. E. (1997). A review of structure in the selection interview. *Personnel Psychology, 50,* 655–702.

Campione, J. C., Brown, A. L., & Ferrara, R. A. (1982). Mental retardation and intelligence. In R. J. Sternberg (Ed.), *Handbook of human intelligence* (pp. 392–490). Cambridge: Cambridge University Press.

Campos, J. J. (1980). Human emotions: Their new importance and their role in social referencing. *Research and Clinical Center for Child Development, 1980–81 Annual Report,* 1–7.

Candia, V., Weinbruch, C., Elbert, T., Rockstroh, B., & Ray, W. (2003). Effective behavioral treatment of focal hand dystonia in musicians alters somatosensory cortical organization. *Proceedings of the National Academy of Sciences, 100,* 7942–7946.

Cann, A., & Ross, D. A. (1989). Olfactory stimuli as context cues in human memory. *American Journal of Psychology, 102,* 91–102.

Cannon, T. D., Zorrilla, L. E., Shtasel, D., Gur, R. E., Gur, R. C., Marco, E. J., Moberg, P., & Price, A. (1994). Neuropsychological functioning in siblings discordant for schizophrenia and healthy volunteers. *Archives of General Psychiatry, 51,* 651–661.

Cannon, W. B. (1987). The James-Lange theory of emotions: A critical examination and an alternative theory. Special issue: 100 years of the American Journal of Psychology. *American Journal of Psychology, 100*(3–4), 567–586. (Original work published 1927)

Cannon, W. B., & Washburn, A. L. (1912). An explanation of hunger. *American Journal of Physiology, 29,* 444–454.

Cantor-Graae, E., & Selten, J.-P. (2005). Schizophrenia and migration: A meta-analysis and review. *American Journal of Psychiatry, 162,* 2–24.

Caplan, D. (2003a). Aphasic syndromes. In K. M. Heilman & E. Valenstein (Eds.), *Clinical neuropsychology* (4th ed.). New York: Oxford.

Caplan, D. (2003b). Syntactic aspects of language disorders. In K. M. Heilman & E. Valenstein (Eds.), *Clinical neuropsychology* (4th ed.). New York: Oxford University Press.

Caplan, L. R. (2004). Clinical diagnosis of patients with cerebrovascular disease. *Primary Care, 31*(1), 95–109.

Caplan, L. R. (2005). Stroke. *Review of Neurological Disorders, 2,* 223–225.

Caplan, P. J. (1995). *They say you're crazy. How the world's most powerful psychiatrists decide who's normal.* Reading, MA: Addison-Wesley.

Capron, C., & Duyme, M. (1989). Assessment of effects of socio-economic status on IQ in a full cross-fostering study. *Nature, 340,* 552–553.

Capron, C., & Duyme, M. (1996). Effect of socioeconomic status of biological and adoptive parents on WISC-R subtest scores of their French adopted children. *Intelligence, 22,* 259–276.

Caramazza, A., & Hillis, A. E. (1991). Lexical organization of nouns and verbs in the brain. *Nature, 349,* 788–790.

Cardinali, D. P., Bortman, G. P., Liotta, G., Perez Lloret, S., Albornoz, L.E., Cutrera, R.A., et al. (2002). A multifactorial approach employing melatonin to accelerate resynchronization of sleep-wake cycle after a 12 time-zone westerly transmeridian flight in elite soccer athletes. *Journal of Pineal Research, 32,* 41–46.

Cardon, L. R., & Fulker, D. W. (1993). Genetics of specific cognitive abilities. In R. Plomin, & G. McClearn (Eds.), *Nature, nurture, and psychology* (pp. 99–120). Washington, DC: American Psychological Association.

Cardon, L. R., Fulker, D. W., DeFries, J. C., & Plomin, R. (1992). Multivariate genetic analysis of specific cognitive abilities in the Colorado Adoption Project at age 7. *Intelligence, 16,* 383–400.

Carey, M. P., Carey, K. B., Maisto, S. A., Gordon, C. M., Schroeder, K. E. E., & Vanable, P. A. (2004). Reducing HIV-risk behavior among adults receiving outpatient psychiatric treatment: Results from a randomized controlled trial. *Journal of Consulting and Clinical Psychology, 72,* 252–268.

Carli, L. L. (1999). Cognitive reconstruction, hindsight, and reactions to victims and perpetrators. *Personality and Social Psychology Bulletin, 25,* 966–979.

Carli, L. L., Ganley, R., & Pierce-Otay, A. (1991). Similarity and satisfaction in romantic relationships. *Personality and Social Psychology Bulletin, 17,* 419–426.

Carlson, E. A., Sroufe, L. A., & Egeland, B. (2004). The construction of experience: A longitudinal study of representation and behavior. *Child Development, 75,* 66–83.

Carlson, L. E., Speca, M., Patel, K. D., & Goodey, E. (2003). Mindfulness-based stress reduction in relation to quality of life, mood, symptoms of stress, and immune parameters in breast and prostate cancer outpatients. *Psychosomatic Medicine, 65,* 571–581.

Carlson, N. R. (2001). *Physiology of behavior* (7th ed.). Boston: Allyn & Bacon.

Carmichael, L. L., Hogan, H. P., & Walter, A. A. (1932). An experimental study of the effect of language on the reproduction of visually perceived form. *Journal of Experimental Psychology, 15,* 73–86.

Carnegie Task Force on Learning in the Primary Grades. (1996). *Years of promise: A comprehensive learning strategy for America's children.* New York: Carnegie Corporation.

Carney, S. M., & Goodwin, G. M. (2005). Lithium—A continuing story in the treatment of bipolar disorder. *Acta Psychiatricia Scandinavica, 111,* 7–12.

Carpenter, J. T. (2004). EMDR as an integrative psychotherapy approach: Experts explore the paradigm prism. *Psychotherapy Research, 14,* 135–136.

Carper, R. A., & Courchesne, E. (2000). Inverse correlation between frontal lobe and cerebellum sizes in children with autism. *Brain, 123,* 836–844.

Carr, G. D., Moretti, M. M., & Cue, B. J. H. (2005). Evaluating parenting capacity: Validity problems with the MMPI-2, PAI, CAPI, and ratings of child adjustment. *Professional Psychology: Research and Practice, 36,* 188–196.

Carraher, T. N., Carraher, D., & Schliemann, A. D. (1985). Mathematics in the streets and in the schools. *British Journal of Developmental Psychology, 3,* 21–29.

Carrillo, E., & Lopez, A. (Eds.). (2001). *The Latino psychiatric patient: Assessment and treatment.* Washington, DC: American Psychiatric Press.

Carroll, J., Neitz, M., Hofer, H., Neitz, J., & Williams, D. R. (2004). Functional photoreceptor loss revealed with adaptive optics: An alternate cause of color blindness. *Proceedings of the National Academy of Sciences, 101,* 8461–8466.

Carstensen, L. (1997, August). *Psychology and the aging revolution: Changes in social needs and social goals across the lifespan.* Paper presented at the annual convention of the American Psychological Association.

Carter, M. M., & Barlow, D. H. (1995). Learned alarms: The origins of panic. In W. T. O'Donohue & L. Krasner (Eds.), *Theories of behavior therapy: Exploring behavior change* (pp. 209–228). Washington, DC: American Psychological Association.

Carter, M. M., Hollon, S. D., Carson, R., & Shelton, R. C. (1995). Effects of a safe person on induced distress following a biological challenge in panic disorder with agoraphobia. *Journal of Abnormal Psychology, 104,* 156–163.

Cartwright, R. D. (1978). *A primer on sleep and dreaming.* Reading, MA: Addison-Wesley.

Cartwright, R. D. (1993). Who needs their dreams? The usefulness of dreams in psychotherapy. *Journal of the American Academy of Psychoanalysis, 21*(4), 539–547.

Carver, C. S., & Scheier, M. F. (2002). The hopeful optimist. *Psychological Inquiry, 13,* 288–290.

Carver, C., & Scheier, M. (2004). *Perspectives on personality* (5th ed.). Boston, MA: Pearson.

Carver, K., Joyner, K., & Udry, J. R. (2003). National estimates of adolescent romantic relationships. In P. Florsheim (Ed.), *Adolescent romantic relations and sexual behavior: Theory, research, and practical implications* (pp. 23–56). Mahwah, NJ: Erlbaum.

Casacalenda, N., Perry, J. C., & Looper, K. (2002). Remission in major depressive disorder: A comparison of pharmacotherapy, psychotherapy, and control conditions. *American Journal of Psychiatry, 159,* 1354–1360.

Casagrande, M., Violani, C., Lucidi, F., Buttinelli, E., & Bertini, M. (1996). Variations in sleep mentation as a function of time of night. *International Journal of Neuroscience, 85,* 19–30.

Casbon, T. S., Curtin, J. J., Lang, A. R., & Patrick, C. J. (2003). Deleterious effects of alcohol intoxication: Diminished cognitive control and its behavioral consequences. *Journal of Abnormal Psychology, 112,* 476–487.

Case, L., & Smith, T. B. (2000). Ethnic representation in a sample of the literature of applied psychology. *Journal of Consulting and Clinical Psychology, 68,* 1107–1110.

Casey, B. J., Galvan, A., & Hare, T. A. (2005). Changes in cerebral functional organization during cognitive development. *Current Opinion in Neurobiology, 15,* 239–244.

Caspi, A. (2000). The child is the father of man: Personality continuities from childhood to adulthood. *Journal of Personality and Social Psychology, 78,* 158–172.

Caspi, A., Begg, D., Dickson, N., Harrington, H., Langley, J., Moffitt, T. E., & Silva, P. A. (1997). Personality differences predict health-risk behaviors in young adulthood: Evidence from a longitudinal study. *Journal of Personality and Social Psychology, 73,* 1052–1063.

Caspi, A., Bem, D. J., & Elder, G. H., Jr. (1989). Continuities and consequences of interactional styles across the life course. *Journal of Personality, 57,* 375–406.

Caspi, A., Harrington, H., Milne, B., Amell, J. W., Theodore, R. F., & Moffitt, T. E. (2003). Children's behavioral styles at age 3 are linked to their adult personality traits at age 26. *Journal of Personality, 71,* 495–513.

Caspi, A., Henry, B., McGee, R. O., Moffitt, T. E., & Silva, P. A. (1995). Temperamental origins of child and adolescent behavior problems: From age 3 to Age 15. *Child Development, 66,* 55–68.

Caspi, A., McClay, J., Moffitt, T. E., Mill, J., Martin, J., Craig, I. W., et al. (2002). Role of genotype in the cycle of violence in maltreated children. *Science, 297,* 851–854.

Caspi, A., Moffitt, T. E., Morgan, J., Rutter, M., Taylor, A., Arseneault, L., et al. (2004). Maternal expressed emotion predicts children's antisocial behavior problems: Using monozygotic-twin differences to identify environmental effects on behavioral development. *Developmental Psychology, 40,* 149–161.

Caspi, A., Roberts, B. W., & Shiner, R. L. (2005). Personality development: Stability and change. *Annual Review of Psychology, 56,* 453–484.

Caspi, A., & Shiner, R. L. (2006). Personality development. In W. Damon & R. M. Lerner (Series Eds.) & N. Eisenberg (Vol. Ed.), *Handbook of child psychology: Vol. 3, Social, emotional, and personality development* (6th ed., pp. 300–365). New York: Wiley.

Caspi, A., & Silva, P. A. (1995). Temperamental qualities at age 3 predict personality traits in young adulthood: Longitudinal evidence from a birth cohort. *Child Development, 66,* 468–498.

Caspi, A., Sugden, K., Moffitt, T. E., Taylor, A., Craig, I.W., Harrington, H., et al. (2003). Influence of life stress on depression: Moderation by a polymorphism in the 5-HTT gene. *Science, 301,* 386–389.

Cassel, E., & Bernstein, D. A. (2001). *Criminal behavior.* Boston: Allyn & Bacon.

Cassel, E., & Bernstein, D. A. (2007). *Criminal behavior* (2nd ed.). Mahwah, NJ: Erlbaum.

Cattell, R. B., Eber, H. W., & Tatsuoka, M. (1970). *Handbook for the sixteen personality factor questionnaire (16PF).* Champaign, IL: Institute for Personality Testing.

Cavaiola, A. A., & Desordi, E. G. (2000). Locus of control in drinking driving offenders and nonoffenders. *Alcoholism Treatment Quarterly, 18,* 63–73.

Ceci, S. J., Huffman, M. L. C., Smith, E., & Loftus, E. F. (1994). Repeatedly thinking about a non-event: Source misattributions among preschoolers. *Consciousness and Cognition, 3,* 388–407.

Centers for Disease Control and Prevention. (2001). Deaths: Preliminary data for 2000. *National Vital Statistics Reports, 49,* 1–40.

Centers for Disease Control and Prevention. (2002a). *National Center for Health Statistics faststats, A to Z: Suicide.*

Centers for Disease Control and Prevention. (2002b). *Table 47: Death rates for suicide, according to sex, race, Hispanic origin, and age: United States, selected years 1950–1999.* Retrieved September 25, 2002 from http://www.cdc.gov/nchs/faststats/pdf/nvsr49_11tb1/pds.

Centers for Disease Control and Prevention. (2004). Web-based injury statistics query and reporting system (WISQARS). Retrieved December 7, 2004, from http://www.cdc.gov/ncipc/wisquars. Centerwall, L. (1990). Controlled TV viewing and suicide in countries: Young adult suicide and exposure to television. *Social Psychiatry and Social Epidemiology, 25,* 149–153.

Centerwall, L. (1990). Controlled TV viewing and suicide in countries: Young adult suicide and exposure to television. *Social Psychiatry and Social Epidemiology, 25,* 149–153.

Centonze, D., Picconi, B., Baunez, C., Borrelli, E., Pisani, A., Bernardi, G., & Calabresi, P. (2002). Cocaine and amphetamine depress striatal GABAergic synaptic transmission through D2 dopamine receptors. *Neuropsychopharmacology, 26,* 164–175.

Çeponien, R., Lepisto, T., Shesakova, A., Vanhala, R., Alku, P., Naatanen, R., & Yaguchi, K. (2003). Speech-sound-selective auditory impairment in children with autism: They can perceive but do not attend. *Proceedings of the National Academy of Sciences, 100,* 5567–5572.

Cervone, D. (2005). Personality architecture: Within-person structures and processes. *Annual Review of Psychology, 56,* 423–452.

Cervone, D., & Shoda, Y. (1999). *The coherence of personality: social cognitive bases of consistency, variability, and organization.* New York: Guilford.

Cha, J. H., Farrell, L. A., Ahmed, S. F., Frey, A., Hsiao-Ashe, K. K., Young, A. B., et al. (2001). Glutamate receptor dysregulation in the hippocampus of transgenic mice carrying mutated human amyloid precursor protein. *Neurobiological Disorders, 8,* 90–102.

Chakrabarti, S., & Fombonne, E. (2001). Pervasive developmental disorders in preschool children. *Journal of the American Medical Association, 285,* 3093–3099.

Chamberlin, J. (2000). Easing children's psychological distress in the emergency room. *Monitor on Psychology, 31,* 40–42.

Chambless, D. L., & Hollon, S. D. (1998). Defining empirically supported therapies. *Journal of Consulting and Clinical Psychology, 66,* 7–18.

Chambless, D. L., & Ollendick, T. H. (2001). Empirically supported psychological treatments. *Annual Review of Psychology, 52,* 685–716.

Champion, V., & Huster, G. (1995). Effect of interventions on stage of mammography adoption. *Journal of Behavioral Medicine, 18,* 159–188.

Chan, A., Asbjørn, H., Haahr, M. T., Gøtzsche, P. C., & Altman, D. G. (2004). Empirical evidence for selective reporting of outcomes in randomized trials. *Journal of the American Medical Association, 291,* 2457–2465.

Chan, D. (2005). Current directions in personnel selection research. *Current Directions in Psychological Science, 14,* 220–223.

Chandola, T., Brunner, E., & Marmot, M. (2006). Chronic stress at work and the metabolic syndrome: Prospective study. *British Medical Journal, 332,* 521–525.

Chang, E. F., & Merzenich, M. M. (2003). Environmental noise retards auditory cortical development. *Science, 300,* 498–502.

Chanoine, J. P., Hampl, S., Jensen, C., Boldrin, M., & Hauptman, J. (2005). Effect of orlistat on weight and body composition in obese adolescents: A randomized controlled trial. *Journal of the American Medical Association, 293,* 2873–2883.

Chao, R. K. (1994). Beyond parental control and authoritarian parenting style: Understanding Chinese parenting through the cultural notion of training. *Child Development, 65,* 1111–1119.

Chapman, D. Z., & Zweig, D. I. (2005). Developing a nomological network for interview structure: Antecedents and consequences of the structured selection interview. *Personnel Psychology, 58,* 673–702.

Chapman, S., & Morrell, S. (2000). Barking mad? Another lunatic hypothesis bites the dust. *British Medical Journal, 321,* 1561–1563.

Charles, S. T., Mather, M., & Carstensen, L. L. (2003). Aging and emotional memory: The forgettable nature of negative images for older adults. *Journal of Experimental Psychology: General, 132,* 310–324.

Charleton, T., Gunter, B., & Coles, D. (1998). Broadcast television as a cause of aggression? Recent findings from a naturalistic study. *Emotional and Behavioral Difficulties, 3,* 5–13.

Chase, T. N. (1998). The significance of continuous dopaminergic stimulation in the treatment of Parkinson's disease. *Drugs, 55*(Suppl. 1), 1–9.

Chassin, L., Pitts, S. C., & Prost, J. (2002). Binge drinking trajectories from adolescence to emerging adulthood in a high-risk sample: Predictors and substance abuse outcomes. *Journal of Consulting and Clinical Psychology, 70,* 67–78.

Chemers, M. M. (2000). Leadership research and theory: A functional integration. *Group Dynamics, 4,* 27–43.

Chemers, M. M., Watson, C. B., & May, S. T. (2000). Dispositional affect and leadership effectiveness: A comparison of self-esteem, optimism, and efficacy. *Personality and Social Psychology Bulletin, 26,* 267–277.

Chen, D., Magavi, S. S. P., & Macklis, J. D. (2004). Neurogenesis of corticospinal motor neurons extending spinal projections in adult mice. *Proceedings of the National Academy of Sciences of the USA, 101,* 16357–16362.

Chen, X. Y., Chen, L., & Wolpaw, J. R. (2003). Conditioned H-reflex increase persists after transection of the main corticospinal tract in rats. *Journal of Neurophysiology, 90,* 3572–3578.

Cheng, A. T. A., Gau, S.-F., Chen, T. H. H., Chang, J.-C., & Chang, Y.-T. (2004). A 4-year longitudinal study on risk factors for alcoholism. *Archives of General Psychiatry, 61,* 184–191.

Cheng, L.-C., Tavazoie, M., & Doetsch, F. (2005). Stem cells: From epigenetics to microRNAs. *Neuron, 46,* 363–367.

Cheng, R., Juo, S. H., Loth, J. E., Nee, J., Iossifov, I., Blumenthal, R., et al. (2006). Genome-wide linkage scan in a large bipolar disorder sample from the National Institute of Mental Health genetics initiative suggests putative loci for bipolar disorder, psychosis, suicide, and panic disorder. *Molecular Psychiatry, 11,* 252–260.

Cheng, Y., Kawachi, I., Coakley, E. H., Schwartz, J., & Colditz, G. (2000). Association between psychosocial work characteristics and health functioning in American women: Prospective study. *British Medical Journal, 320,* 1432–1436.

Chesney, M. A., Chambers, D. B., Taylor, J. M., Johnson, L. M., & Folkman, S. (2003). Coping effectiveness training for men living with HIV: Results from a randomized clinical trial testing a group-based intervention. *Psychosomatic Medicine, 65,* 1038–1046.

Chisholm, K. (1997, June). Trauma at an early age inhibits ability to bond. *APA Monitor,* p. 11.

Chivers, M. L., Rieger, G., Latty, E., & Bailey, J. M. (2004). A sex difference in the specificity of sexual arousal. *Psychological Science, 15,* 736–744.

Cho, H. J., Meira-Lima, I., Cordeiro, Q., Michelon, L., Sham, P., Vallada, H., et al. (2005). Population-based and family-based studies on the serotonin transporter gene polymorphisms and bipolar disorder: A systematic review and meta-analysis. *Molecular Psychiatry, 10,* 771–781.

Chodosh, J., Reuben, D. B., Albert, M. S., & Seeman, T. E. (2002). Predicting cognitive impairment in high-functioning community-dwelling older persons: MacArthur studies of successful aging. *Journal of the American Geriatrics Society, 50*(6), 1051–1060.

Choi, J., & Silverman, I. (2003). Processes underlying sex differences in route-learning strategies in children and adolescents. *Personality and Individual Differences, 34,* 1153–1166.

Choi, Y. H., Jang, D. P., Ku, J. H., Shin, M. B., Kim, S. I. (2001). Short-term treatment of acrophobia with virtual reality therapy (VRT): A case report. *CyberPsychology and Behavior, 4,* 349–354.

Chomsky, N. (1965). *Aspects of the theory of syntax.* Cambridge, MA: MIT Press.

Chomsky, N. (1986). *Knowledge of language: Its nature, origin, and use.* New York: Praeger.

Chorney, M. L., Chorney, K., Sense, N., Owen, M. J., Daniels, J., McGuffin, P., et al. (1998). A quantitative trait locus (QTL) associated with cognitive ability in children. *Psychological Science, 9,* 159–166.

Chouinard, G. (2004). Issues in the clinical use of benzodiazepines: Potency, withdrawal, and rebound. *Journal of Clinical Psychiatry, 65*(Suppl. 5), 7–21.

Christensen, A., Atkins, D. C., Berns, S., Wheeler, J., Baucom, D. H., & Simpson, L. E. (2004). Traditional versus integrative behavioral couple therapy for significantly and chronically distressed married couples. *Journal of Consulting and Clinical Psychology, 72,* 176–191.

Christensen, H., Griffiths, K. M., & Jorm, A. F. (2004). Delivering interventions for depression by using the Internet: Randomized controlled trial. *British Medical Journal, 328,* 265.

Christensen, H. C., Schüz, J., Kosteljanetz, M., Poulsen, H. S., Boice, J. D., Jr., McLaughlin, J. K., & Johansen, C. (2005). Cellular telephones and risk for brain tumors: A population-based, incident case-control study. *Neurology, 64,* 1189–1195.

Christopher, K. (2003). Autistic boy killed during exorcism. *Skeptical Inquirer, 27,* 11.

Chu, J. (1994). Active learning in epidemiology and biostatistics. *Teaching and Learning in Medicine, 6,* 191–193.

Chua, H. F., Boland, J. E., & Nisbett, R. E. (2005). Cultural variation in eye movements during scene perception. *Proceedings of the National Academy of Sciences of the USA, 102,* 12629–12633.

Chugani, H. T., & Phelps, M. E. (1986). Maturational changes in cerebral function in infants determined by 18FDG positron emission tomography. *Science, 231,* 840–843.

Chumakov, I., Blumenfeld, M., Guerassimenko, O., Cavarec, L., Palicio, M., Abderrahim, H., et al. (2002). Genetic and physiological data implicating the new human gene G72 and the gene for D-amino acid oxidase in schizophrenia. *Proceedings of the National Academies of Science, 99,* 13675–13680.

Churchland, P. M. (1989). *A neurocomputational perspective: The nature of mind and the structure of science.* Cambridge, MA: MIT Press.

Cialdini, R. B. (1995). Principles and techniques of social influence. In A. Tesser (Ed.), *Advanced social psychology* (pp. 257–282). New York: McGraw-Hill.

Cialdini, R. B. (2001). *Influence: Science and practice* (4th ed.). Boston: Allyn & Bacon.

Cialdini, R. B., & Goldstein, N. J. (2004). Social influence: Compliance and conformity. *Annual Review of Psychology, 55,* 591–621.

Cialdini, R. B., Wosinska, W. B., Barrett, D. W., Butner, J., & Gornik-Durose, M. (2001). The differential impact of two social influence principles on individualists and collectivists in Poland and the United States. In W. Wosinska, R. B. Cialdini, D.W. Barrett, & J. Reykowski (Eds.), *The practice of social influence in multiple cultures: Applied social research* (pp. 33–50). Mahwah, NJ: Erlbaum.

Ciccocioppo, R., Martin-Fardon, R., & Weiss, F. (2004). Stimuli associated with a single cocaine experience elicit long-lasting cocaine-seeking. *Nature Neuroscience, 7,* 495– 496.

Ciccocioppo, R., Sanna, P. P., & Weiss, F. (2001). Cocaine-predictive stimulus induces drug-seeking behavior and neural activation in limbic brain regions after multiple months of abstinence: Reversal by D1 antagonists. *Proceedings of the National Academy of Sciences, 98,* 1976–1981.

Clancy, S. A., McNally, R. J., Schacter, D. L., Lenzenweger, M. F., & Pitman, R. K. (2002). Memory distortion in people reporting abduction by aliens. *Journal of Abnormal Psychology, 111,* 455–461.

Clancy, S. A., Schacter, D. L., McNally, R. J., & Pittman, R. K. (2000). False recognition in women reporting recovered memories of sexual abuse. *Psychological Science, 11,* 26–31.

Clark, A., Oswald, A., & Warr, P. (1996). Is job satisfaction U-shaped in age? *Journal of Occupational and Organizational Psychology, 69,* 57–81.

Clark, D. C., & Fawcett, J. (1992). Review of empirical risk factors for evaluation of the suicidal patient. In B. Bongar (Ed.), *Suicide: Guidelines for assessment, management, and treatment* (pp. 16–48). New York: Oxford University Press.

Clark, D. M., Ehlers, A., McManus, F., Hackmann, A., Fennell, M., Campbell, H., et al. (2003). Cognitive therapy versus fluoxetine in generalized social phobia: A randomized placebo-controlled trial. *Journal of Consulting and Clinical Psychology, 71,* 1058–1067.

Clark, E. V. (1983). Meanings and concepts. In P. H. Mussen, J. H. Flavell, & E. M. Markman (Eds.), *Handbook of child psychology: Vol. 3. Cognitive development* (4th ed., pp. 787–840). New York: Wiley.

Clark, E. V. (1993). *The lexicon in acquisition.* Cambridge: Cambridge University Press.

Clark, L. A., Watson, D., & Reynolds, S. (1995). Diagnosis and classification of psychopathology: Challenges to the current system and future directions. *Annual Review of Psychology, 46,* 121–153.

Clark, M. S., & Pataki, S. P. (1995). Interpersonal processes influencing attraction and relationships. In A. Tesser (Ed.), *Advanced social psychology* (pp. 283–332). New York: McGraw-Hill.

Clarke, L., Ungerer, J., Chahoud, K., Johnson, S., Stiefel, I. (2002). Attention deficit hyperactivity disorder is associated with attachment insecurity. *Clinical Child Psychology and Psychiatry, 7,* 179–198.

Clarke-Stewart, A., & Allhusen, V. (2005). *What we know about childcare.* Cambridge, MA: Harvard University Press.

Clarke-Stewart, A., & Brentano, C. (2006). *'Til divorce do us part: Causes and consequences of marital separation for children and adults.* New Haven, CT: Yale University Press.

Clarke-Stewart, K. A. (1989). Infant day care: Maligned or malignant? *American Psychologist, 44,* 266–273.

Clausen, J., Sersen, E., & Lidsky, A. (1974). Variability of sleep measures in normal subjects. *Psychophysiology, 11,* 509–516.

Clay, R. A. (2000). Often, the bells and whistles backfire. *Monitor on Psychology, 31,* 64–65.

Clendenen, V. I., Herman, C. P., & Polivy, J. (1995). Social facilitation of eating among friends and strangers. *Appetite, 23,* 1–13.

Clifton, R. K. (1992). The development of spatial hearing in human infants. In L. A. Werner & E. W. Rubel (Eds.), *Developmental psychoacoustics* (pp. 135–157). Washington, DC: American Psychological Association.

Clifton, R. K., Rochat, P., Litovsky, R., & Perris, E. (1991). Object representation guides infants' reaching in the dark. *Journal of Experimental Psychology: Human Perception and Performance, 17,* 323–329.

Cloutier, J., Mason, M. F., & Macrae, C. N. (2005). The perceptual determinants of person construal: Reopening the social-cognitive toolbox. *Journal of Personality and Social Psychology, 88,* 885–894.

Clower, C. E., & Bothwell, R. K. (2001). An exploratory study of the relationship between the Big Five and inmate recidivism. *Journal of Research in Personality, 35,* 231–237.

CNN/Time. (1997). Poll: U.S. hiding knowledge of aliens. *CNN/Time*. Retrieved December 13, 2004, from http://www-cgi.cnn.com/US/9706/15/ufo.poll/index.html

Coccaro, E. F. (1989). Central serotonin and impulsive aggression. *British Journal of Psychiatry, 155,* 52–62.

Cofer, L. F., Grice, J., Palmer, D., Sethre-Hofstad, L., & Zimmermann, K. (1992, June 20–22). *Evidence for developmental continuity of individual differences in morningness-eveningness.* Paper presented at the annual meeting of the American Psychological Society, San Diego, CA.

Cohen, C. E. (1981). Person categories and social perception: Testing some boundaries of the processing effects of prior knowledge. *Journal of Personality and Social Psychology, 40,* 441–452.

Cohen, D. (1998). Culture, social organization, and patterns of violence. *Journal of Personality and Social Psychology, 75,* 408–419.

Cohen, D. A., Farley, T. A., Taylor, S. N., Martin, D. H., & Schuster, M. A. (2002). When and where do youths have sex? The potential role of adult supervision. *Pediatrics, 110,* e66.

Cohen, J., & Servan-Schreiber, D. (1992). Context, cortex, and dopamine: A connectionist approach to behavior and biology in schizophrenia. *Psychological Review, 99,* 45–77.

Cohen, N. J., & Corkin, S. (1981). The amnesic patient H. M.: Learning and retention of a cognitive skill. *Neuroscience Abstracts, 7,* 235.

Cohen, P., Kasen, S., Chen, H., Hartmark, C., & Gordon, K. (2003). Variations in patterns of developmental transitions in the emerging adulthood period. *Developmental Psychology, 39,* 657–669.

Cohen, S., Doyle, W. J., Turner, R. B., Alper, C. M., & Skoner, D. P. (2003a). Emotional style and susceptibility to the common cold. *Psychosomatic Medicine, 65,* 652–657.

Cohen, S., Doyle, W. J., Turner, R., Alper, C. M., & Skoner, D. P. (2003b). Sociability and susceptibility to the common cold. *Psychological Science, 14,* 389–395.

Cohen, S., & Herbert, T. B. (1996). Health psychology: Psychological factors and physical disease from the perspective of human psychoneuroimmunology. *Annual Review of Psychology, 47,* 113–142.

Cohen, S., & Pressman, S. D. (2006). Positive affect and health. *Current Directions in Psychological Science, 15,* 122–125.

Cohen-Cory, S. (2002). The developing synapse: Construction and modulation of synaptic structures and circuits. *Science, 298,* 770–776.

Colak, A., Soy, O., Uzun, H., Aslan, O., Barut, S., Belce, A., et al. (2003). Neuroprotective effects of GYKI 52466 on experimental spinal cord injury in rats. *Journal of Neurosurgery, 98,* 275–281.

Cole, K. N., Mills, P. E., Dale, P. S., & Jenkins, J. R. (1991). Effects of preschool integration for children with disabilities. *Exceptional Children, 58,* 36–45.

Coleman, D. (1992). Why do I feel so tired? Too little, too late. *American Health, 11*(4), 43–46.

Collacott, E. A., Zimmerman, J. T., White, D. W., & Rindone, J. P. (2000). Bipolar permanent magnets for the treatment of chronic low back pain: A pilot study. *Journal of the American Medical Association, 283,* 1322–1325.

Collins, R. L., Elliott, M. N., Berry, S. H., Kanouse, D. E., Kunkel, D., Hunter, S. B., et al. (2004). Watching sex on television predicts initiation of sexual behavior. *Pediatrics, 114,* e280–e289.

Collins, W. A., Maccoby, E. E., Steinberg, L., Hetherington, E. M., & Bornstein, M. H. (2000). Contemporary research on parenting: The case for nature and nurture. *American Psychologist, 55,* 218–232.

Colloca, L., & Benedetti, F. (2005). Placebos and painkillers: Is mind as real as matter? *Nature Reviews Neuroscience, 6,* 545–552.

Colombo, M., D'Amato, M. R., Rodman, H. R., & Gross, C. G. (1990). Auditory association cortex lesions impair auditory short-term memory in monkeys. *Science, 247,* 336–338.

Committee to Review the Scientific Evidence on the Polygraph. (2003). *The polygraph and lie detection.* Washington, DC: National Academies Press.

Compas, B. E., Haaga, D. A. F., Keefe, F. J., Leitenberg, H., & Williams, D. A. (1998). Sampling of empirically supported psychological treatments from health psychology: Smoking, chronic pain, cancer, and bulimia nervosa. *Journal of Consulting and Clinical Psychology, 66,* 89–112.

Compton, W. M., Conway, K. P., Stinson, F. S., Colliver, J. D., & Grant, B. F. (2005). Prevalence, correlates, and comorbidity of DSM-IV antisocial personality syndromes and alcohol and specific drug use disorders in the United States: Results from the national epidemiologic survey on alcohol and related conditions. *Journal of Clinical Psychiatry, 66,* 677–685.

Condic, M. L. (2001). Adult neuronal regeneration induced by transgenic integrin expression. *Journal of Neuroscience, 21,* 4782–4788.

Condon, J. W., & Crano, W. D. (1988). Inferred evaluation and the relationship between attitude similarity and interpersonal attraction. *Journal of Personality and Social Psychology, 54,* 789–797.

Cone, E. J., Fant, R. V., Rohay, J. M., Caplan, Y. H., Ballina, M., Reder, R. F., et al. (2004). Oxycodone involvement in drug abuse deaths: II. Evidence for toxic multiple drug-drug interactions. *Journal of Analytical Toxicology, 28,* 616–624.

Conel, J. L. (1939/1967). *The postnatal development of the human cerebral cortex* (Vols. 1, 8). Cambridge, MA: Harvard University Press.

Conger, R. D., Cui, M., Bryant, C. M., & Elder, G. H. (2000). Competence in early adult romantic relationships: A developmental perspective on family influences. *Journal of Personality and Social Psychology, 79*(2), 224–237.

Conklin, H. M., & Iacono, W. G. (2002). Schizophrenia: A neurodevelopmental perspective. *Current Directions in Psychological Science, 11,* 33–37.

Connor, L. T., Balota, D. A., & Neely, J. H. (1992). On the relation between feeling of knowing and lexical decision: Persistent subthreshold activation of topic familiarity? *Journal of Experimental Psychology: Learning, Memory, and Cognition, 18,* 544–554.

Conrad, R. (1964). Acoustic confusions in immediate memory. *British Journal of Psychology, 55,* 75–84.

Consedine, N. S., & Magai, C. (2003) Attachment and emotion experience in later life: The view from emotions theory. *Attachment and Human Development, 5,* 165–187.Constantino, J. N., & Todd, R. D. (2003). Autistic traits in the general population: A twin study. *Archives General Psychiatry, 60,* 524–530.

Constantine, M. G. (2002). Predictors of satisfaction with counseling: Racial and ethnic minority clients' attitudes toward counseling and ratings of their counselors' general and multicultural competence. *Journal of Counseling Psychology, 49,* 255–263.

Constantino, J. N., & Todd, R. D. (2003). Autistic traits in the general population: A twin study. *Archives General Psychiatry, 60,* 524–530.

Constantino, M. J., Arnow, B. A., Blasey, C., & Agras, W. S. (2005). The association between patient characteristics and the therapeutic alliance in cognitive-behavioral and interpersonal therapy for bulimia nervosa. *Journal of Consulting and Clinical Psychology, 73,* 203–211.

Consumer Reports. (1995, November). Mental health: Does therapy help? *Consumer Reports,* pp. 734–739.

Cook, J. A., Leff, H. S., Blyler, C. R., Gold, P. B., Goldberg, R. W., Mueser, K. T., et al. (2005). Results of a multisite randomized trial of supported employment interventions for individuals with severe mental illness. *Archives of General Psychiatry, 62,* 505–512.

Cookson, J., & Duffett, R. (1998). Fluoxetine: Therapeutic and undesirable effects. *Hospital Medicine, 59,* 622–626.

Cooper, A. (2004). *The inmates are running the asylum: Why high tech products drive us crazy and how to restore the sanity* (2nd ed.). New York: Pearson.

Cooper, M. L., Russell, M., Skinner, J. B., Frone, M. R., & Mudar, P. (1992). Stress and alcohol use: The moderating effects of gender, coping, and alcohol expectancies. *Journal of Abnormal Psychology, 101,* 139–152.

Corbetta, M., Miezin, F. M., Dobmeyer, S., Shulman, G. L., & Petersen, S. E. (1991). Selective and divided attention during visual discriminations of shape, color, and speed: Functional anatomy by positron emission tomography. *Journal of Neuroscience, 11,* 2383–2402.

Cordery, J. L., Mueller, W. S., & Smith, L. M. (1991). Attitudinal and behavioral effects of autonomous group working: A longitudinal field study. *Academy of Management Journal, 34,* 464–476.

Coren, S. (1999). Psychology applied to animal training. In A. Stec & D. Bernstein (Eds.), *Psychology: Fields of application.* Boston: Houghton Mifflin.

Coren, S., & Girgus, J. S. (1978). *Seeing is deceiving: The psychology of visual illusions.* Hillsdale, NJ: Erlbaum.

Cork, R. C., Kihlstrom, J. F., & Hameroff, S. R. (1992). Explicit and implicit memory dissociated by anesthetic technique. *Society for Neuroscience Abstracts, 22,* 523.

Corkin, S. (2002). What's new with the amnesic patient H.M.? *Nature Reviews. Neuroscience, 3*(2), 153–160.

Cornblatt, B., & Erlenmeyer-Kimling, L. E. (1985). Global attentional deviance in children at risk for schizophrenia: Specificity and predictive validity. *Journal of Abnormal Psychology, 94,* 470–486.

Cornelius, R. R. (1996). *The science of emotion.* Upper Saddle River, NJ: Prentice-Hall.

Cornelius-White, J. H. D. (2002). The phoenix of empirically supported therapy relationships: The overlooked person-centered bias. *Psychotherapy: Theory, Research, Practice, Training, 39,* 219–222.

Correll, C. U., Leucht, S., & Kane, J. M. (2004). Lower risk for tardive dyskinesia associated with second-generation antipsychotics: A systematic review of 1-year studies. *American Journal of Psychiatry, 161,* 414–425.

Correll, J., Park, B., Judd, C. M., & Wittenbrink, B. (2002). The police officer's dilemma: Using ethnicity to disambiguate potentially threatening individuals. *Journal of Personality and Social Psychology, 83,* 1314–1329.

Corruble, E., Damy, C. & Guelfi, J. D., (1999). Impulsivity: A relevant dimension in depression regarding suicide attempts. *Journal of Affective Disorders, 53,* 211–215.

Corsini, R. J., & Wedding, D. (2001). *Current psychotherapies* (6th ed.). Itasca, IL: Peacock.

Corwin, M. J., Lesko, S. M., Heeren, T., Vezina, R. M., Hunt, C. E., Mandell, F., et al. (2003). Secular changes in sleep position during infancy: 1995–1998. *Pediatrics, 111,* 52–60.

Coryell, W., Scheftner, W., Keller, M., Endicott, J., Maser, J., & Klerman, G. (1993). The enduring consequences of mania and depression. *American Journal of Psychiatry, 150,* 720–727.

Coslett, H. B., & Saffran, E. (1991). Simultanagnosia. To see but not two see. *Brain, 114* (Pt. 4), 1523–1545.

Costa, P. (2001, June). *New insights on personality and leadership provided by the five-factor model.* Paper presented at Annual Convention of American Psychological Society, Toronto, Canada.

Costa, P. T., & McCrae, R. R. (2002). Looking backwards: Changes in mean levels of personality traits from 80 to 12. In D. Cervone, & W. Mischel (Eds.), *Advances in personality science* (pp. 196–217). New York: Guilford Press.

Costa, P. T., Jr., & McCrae, R. (1992). *Revised NEO Personality Inventory: NEO PI and NEO Five-Factor Inventory (NEO FFI: Professional Manual).* Odessa, FL: Psychological Assessment Resources.

Costello, E. J., Mustillo, S., Erkanli, A., Keeler, G., & Angold, A. (2003). Prevalence and development of psychiatric disorders in childhood and adolescence. *Archives of General Psychiatry, 60,* 837–844.

Cota, D., Marsicano, G., Lutz, B., Vicennati, V., Stalla, G.K., Pasquali, R., & Pagotto, U. (2003). Endogenous cannabinoid system as a modulator of food intake. *International Journal of Obesity, 27,* 289–301.

Cota, D., Proulx, K., Smith, K. A. B., Kozma, S. C., Thomas, G., Woods, S. C., et al. (2006). Hypothalamic mTOR signaling regulates food intake. *Science, 312,* 927–930.

Cotanche, D. A. (1997). Hair cell regeneration in the avian cochlea. *Annals of Otology, Rhinology,and Laryngology Supplement, 168,* 9–15.

Cote, J. K., & Pepler, C. (2002). A randomized trial of a cognitive coping intervention for acutely ill HIV-positive men. *Nursing Research, 51,* 237–244.

Cottrell, C. A., & Neuberg, S. L. (2005). Different emotional reactions to different groups: A sociofunctional threat-based approach to prejudice. *Journal of Personality and Social Psychology, 88,* 770–789.

Courchesne, E., Karns, C. M., Davis, H. R., Ziccardi, R., Carper, R. A., Tigue, Z. D., et al. (2001). Unusual brain growth patterns in early life in patients with autistic disorder: An MRI study. *Neurology, 57,* 245–254.

Couturier, J. L. (2005). Efficacy of rapid-rate repetitive transcranial magnetic stimulation in the treatment of depression: A systematic review and meta-analysis. *Journal of Psychiatry and Neuroscience, 30,* 83–90.

Cowan, C. A., Atienza, J., Melton, D. A., & Eggan, K. (2005). Nuclear reprogramming of somatic cells after fusion with human embryonic stem cells. *Science, 309,* 1369–1373.

Cowan, D. T., Allan, L. G., Libretto, S. E., & Griffiths, P. (2001). Opiod drugs: A comparative survey of therapeutic and "street" use. *Pain, 2,* 193–203.

Cowan, N. (1988). Evolving concepts of memory storage, selective attention, and their mutual constraints within the human information-processing system. *Psychological Bulletin, 104,* 163–191.

Cowey, A. (1994). Cortical visual areas and the neurobiology of higher visual processes. In M. J. Farah & G. Ratcliff (Eds.), *The neurophysiology of high-level vision: Collected tutorial essays* (pp. 3–31). Hillsdale, NJ: Erlbaum.

Crabbe, J. C. (2002). Alcohol and genetics: new models. *American Journal of Medical Genetics, 114,* 969–974.

Craig, A. D., & Bushnell, M. C. (1994). The thermal grill illusion: Unmasking the burn of cold pain. *Science, 265,* 252–254.

Craik, F. I. M., Moroz, T. M., Moscovitch, M., Stuss, D. T., Winocur, G., Tulving, E., & Kapur, S. (1999). In search of the self: A positron emission topography study. *Psychological Science, 10,* 26–34.

Craik, F. I. M., & Rabinowitz, J. C. (1984). Age differences in the acquisition and use of verbal information. In H. Bouma & D. G. Bouwhuis (Eds.), *Attention and performance* (Vol. 10, pp. 471–499). Hillsdale, NJ: Erlbaum.

Cramer, P. (2003). Personality change in later adulthood is predicted by defense mechanism use in early adulthood. *Journal of Research in Personality, 37,* 76–104.

Crandall, C. S., Preisler, J. J., & Aussprung, J. (1992). Measuring life event stress in the lives of college students: The Undergraduate Stress Questionnaire (USQ). *Journal of Behavioral Medicine, 15,* 627–662.

Crano, W. D., & Chen, X. (1998). The leniency contract and persistence of majority and minority influence. *Journal of Personality and Social Psychology, 74,* 1437–1450.

Craske, M. G. (1999). *Anxiety disorders: Psychological approaches to theory and treatment.* Boulder, CO: Westview Press.

Crawford, H. J., Brown, A. M., & Moon, C. E. (1993). Sustained attentional and disattentional abilities: Differences between low and highly hypnotizable persons. *Journal of Abnormal Psychology, 102*(4), 534–543.

Crawford, T. N., Cohen, P., & Brooks, J. S. (2001). Dramatic-erratic personality disorder symptoms: II. Developmental pathways from early adolescence to adulthood. *Journal of Personality Disorders, 15,* 336–350.

Creed, T. A., & Kendall, P. C. (2005). Therapist alliance-building behavior within a cognitive-behavioral treatment for anxiety in youth. *Journal of Counseling and Clinical Psychology, 73,* 498–505.

Creery, D., & Mikrogianakis, A. (2004). Sudden infant death syndrome. *Clinical Evidence, 12,* 545–555.

Crick, F., & Koch, C. (1998). Consciousness and neuroscience. *Cerebral Cortex, 8,* 97–107.

Crick, N. R., Ostrov, J. M., Appleyard, K., Jansen, E. A., & Casas, J. F. (2004). Relational aggression in early childhood: "You can't come to my birthday party unless. . . ." In M. Putallaz & K. L. Bierman (Eds.), *Aggression, antisocial behavior, and violence among girls: A developmental perspective.* (pp. 71–89). New York: Guilford Press.

Critchley, E. M. (1991). Speech and the right hemisphere. *Behavioural Neurology, 4*(3), 143–151.

Crocker, J., & Wolfe, T. (2001). Contingencies of self-worth. *Psychological Review, 108,* 593–623.

Croen, L. A., Grether, J. K., & Selvin, S. (2001). The epidemiology of mental retardation of unknown cause. *Pediatrics, 107,* 86.

Cronbach, L. J. (1990). *Essentials of psychological testing* (5th ed.). New York: Harper & Row.

Cronbach, L. J. (1996). Acceleration among the Terman males: Correlates in midlife and after. In C. P. Benbow & D. J. Lubinski (Eds.), *Intellectual talent: Psychometric and social issues* (pp. 179–191). Baltimore: Johns Hopkins University Press.

Cross, S. E., & Madson, L. (1997). Models of the self: Self-construals and gender. *Psychological Bulletin, 122,* 5–37.

Cross, S. E., & Markus, H. R. (1999). The cultural constitution of personality. In L. Pervin & O. John (Eds.), *Handbook of personality research* (2nd ed., pp. 378–398). New York: Guilford.

Cross-National Collaborative Group. (2002). The changing rate of major depression: Cross-national comparisons. *Journal of the American Medical Association, 268,* 3098–3105.

Crowther, J. H., Sanftner, J., Bonifazi, D. Z., & Shepherd, K. L. (2001). The role of daily hassles in binge eating. *International Journal of Eating Disorders, 29,* 449–454.

Cruz, A., & Green, B. G. (2000). Thermal stimulation of taste. *Nature, 403,* 889–892.

Csernansky, J. G., Schindler, M. K., Splinter, N. R., Wang, L., Gado, M., Selemon, L. D., et al. (2004). Abnormalities of thalamic volume and shape in schizophrenia. *American Journal of Psychiatry, 161,* 896–902.

Culbertson, F. M. (1997). Depression and gender. An international review. *American Psychologist, 52,* 25–31.

Cullen, M. J., Hardison, C. M., & Sackett, P. R. (2004). Using SAT–grade and ability–job performance relationships to test predictions derived from stereo-type threat theory. *Journal of Applied Psychology, 89,* 220–230.

Culp, R. E., Cook, A. S., & Housley, P. C. (1983). A comparison of observed and reported adult-infant interactions: Effects of perceived sex. *Sex Roles, 9,* 475–479.

Cummings, B. J., Uchida, N., Tamaki, S. J., Salazar, D. L., Hooshmand, M., Summers, R., et al. (2005). Human neural stem cells differentiate and promote locomotor recovery in spinal cord-injured mice. *Proceedings of the National Academy of Sciences of the USA, 102,* 14069–14074.

Cummings, J. L. (2003). Toward a molecular neuropsychiatry of neurodegenerative diseases. *Annals of Neurology, 54*(2), 147–154.

Cummings, J. L. (2004). Alzheimer's disease. *New England Journal of Medicine, 351,* 56–67.

Cumsille, P. E., Sayer, A. G., & Graham, J. W. (2000). Perceived exposure to peer and adult drinking as predictors of growth in positive alcohol expectancies during adolescence. *Journal of Consulting and Clinical Psychology, 68,* 531–536.

Cunningham, W. A., Johnson, M. K., Raye, C. L., Gatenby, J. C., Gore, J. C., & Banaji, M. R. (2004). Separable neural components in the processing of black and white faces. *Psychological Science, 15,* 806–813.

Curioni, C. C., & Lourenço, P. M. (2005). Long-term weight loss after diet and exercise: A systematic review. *International Journal of Obesity, 29,* 1168–1174.

Curran, H. V., & Monaghan, L. (2001). In and out of the K-hole: A comparison of the acute and residual effects of ketamine in frequent and infrequent ketamine users. *Addiction, 96,* 749–760.

Curtis, T., Miller, B. C., & Berry, E. H. (2000). Changes in reports and incidence of child abuse following natural disasters. *Child Abuse & Neglect, 24,* 1151–1162.

Cusack, K., & Spates, C. R. (1999). The cognitive dismantling of eye movement desensitization and reprocessing (EMDR) treatment of posttraumatic stress disorder (PTSD). *Journal of Anxiety Disorders, 13,* 87–99.

Cutrona, C. E., Russell, D. W., Brown, P. A., Clark, L. A., Hessling, R. M., & Gardner, K. A. (2005). Neighborhood context, personality, and stressful life events as predictors of depression among African American women. *Journal of Abnormal Psychology, 114,* 3–15.

Czeisler, C. A., Duffy, J. F., Shanahan, T. L., Brown, E. N., Mitchell, J. F., Rimmer, D. W., et al. (1999). Stability, precision, and near 24-hour period of the human circadian pacemaker. *Science, 284,* 2177–2181.

Czeisler, C. A., Walsh, J. K., Roth, T., Hughes, R. J., Wright, K. P., Kingsbury, L., et al. (2005). Modafinil for excessive sleepiness associated with shift-work sleep disorder. *New England Journal of Medicine, 353,* 476–486.

D

Dabbs, J., & Dabbs, M. G. (2001). *Heroes, rogues, and lovers: Testosterone and behavior.* New York: McGraw-Hill.

Dabbs, J. M., Jr., Riad, J. K., & Chance, S. E. (2001). Testosterone and ruthless homicide. *Personality and Individual Differences, 31,* 599–603.

Dadds, M. R., Holland, D. E., Laurens, K. R., Mullins, M., Barrett, P. M., & Spence, S. H. (1999). Early intervention and prevention of anxiety disorders in children: Results at 2-year follow-up. *Journal of Consulting & Clinical Psychology, 67,* 145–150.

Daglish, M. R., & Nutt, D. J. (2003). Brain imaging studies in human addicts. *European Neuropsychopharmacology, 13,* 453–458.

D'Agostino, R. B., Sr., Grundy, S., Sullivan, L. M., & Wilson, P. (2001). Validation of the Framingham coronary heart disease prediction scores: Results of a multiple ethnic groups investigation. *Journal of the American Medical Association, 286,* 180–187.

Dale, P. S. (1976). *Language and the development of structure and function.* New York: Holt, Rinehart & Winston.

Daley, K. C. (2004). Update on sudden infant death syndrome. *Current Opinion in Pediatrics, 16,* 227–232.

Dallman, M. F., Pecoraro, N., Akana, S. F., La Fleur, S. E., Gomez, F., Houshyar, H., et al. (2003). Chronic stress and obesity: A new view of "comfort food." *Proceedings of the National Academies of Science, 100,* 11696–11701.

Dalton, D. R., & Mesch, D. J. (1991). On the extent and reduction of avoidable absenteeism: An assessment of absence policy provisions. *Journal of Applied Psychology, 76,* 810–817.

Daly, J. J., Prudic, J., Devanand, D. P., Nobler, M. S., Mitchell, S., Lisanby, S. H., et al. (2001). ECT in bipolar and unipolar depression: Differences in speed of response. *Bipolar Disorders, 3,* 95–104.

Damasio, A. R. (1994). *Descartes' error.* New York: Putnam.

Damasio, A. R., Grabowski, T. J., Bechara, A., Damasio, H., Ponto, L. L. B., Parvizi, J., & Hichwa, R. D. (2000). Subcortical and cortical brain activity during the feeling of self-generated emotions. *Nature Neuroscience, 3,* 1049–1056.

Damos, D. (1992). *Multiple task performance.* London: Taylor & Francis.

Dannenberg, A. L., Burton, D. C., & Jackson, R. J. (2004). Economic and environmental costs of obesity: The impact on airlines. *American Journal of Preventive Medicine, 27,* 264–264.

Dansereau, F., Jr., Graen, G., & Haga, W. J. (1975). A vertical dyad linkage approach to leadership with formal organizations. *Organizational Behavior and Human Performance, 13,* 46–78.

Dapretto, M., Davies, M. S., Pfeifer, J. H., Scott, A. A., Sigman, M., Bookheimer, S. Y., et al. (2006). Understanding emotions in others: Mirror neuron dysfunction in children with autism spectrum disorders. *Nature Neuroscience, 9,* 28–30.

Dark, V. J., & Benbow, C. P. (1993). Cognitive differences among the gifted: A review and new data. In D. K. Detterman (Ed.), *Current topics in human intelligence* (Vol. 3, pp. 85–120). Norwood, NJ: Ablex.

Darkes, J., & Goldman, M. S. (1993). Expectancy challenge and drinking reduction. *Journal of Clinical and Consulting Psychology, 61,* 344–353.

Darwin, C. E. (1965). *The expression of emotions in man and animals.* Chicago: University of Chicago Press. (Original work published 1872)

Dasgupta, A. M., Juza, D. M., White, G. M., & Maloney, J. F. (1995). Memory and hypnosis: A comparative analysis of guided memory, cognitive interview, and hypnotic hypermnesia. *Imagination, Cognition, and Personality, 14*(2), 117–130.

Daus, C. S., Sanders, D. N., & Campbell, D. P. (1998). Consequences of alternative work schedules. In C. L. Cooper & I. T. Robertson (Eds.), *International review of industrial and organizational psychology 1998* (pp. 185–223). Chichester, UK: Wiley.

Davachi, L., Mitchell, J. P., & Wagner, A. D. (2003). Multiple routes to memory: Distinct medial temporal lobe processes build item and source memories. *Proceedings of the National Academy of Sciences, 100,* 2157–2162.

Davanloo, H. (1999). Intensive short-term dynamic psychotherapy-central dynamic sequence: Phase of challenge. *International Journal of Short-Term Dynamic Psychotherapy, 13,* 237–262.

Davidson, J. K., & Moore, N. B. (1994). Guilt and lack of orgasm during sexual intercourse: Myth versus reality in college women. *Journal of Sex Education and Therapy, 20*(3), 153–174.

Davidson, J. M., Camargo, C. A., & Smith, E. R. (1979). Effects of androgen on sexual behavior in hypogonadal men. *Journal of Clinical Endocrinological Metabolism, 48,* 955–958.

Davidson, J. R., Foa, E. B., Huppert, J. D., Keefe, F. J., Franklin, M. E., Compton, J. S., et al. (2004). Fluoxetine, comprehensive cognitive behavioral therapy, and placebo in generalized social phobia. *Archives of General Psychiatry, 61,* 1005–1013.

Davidson, K., Hall, P., & MacGregor, M. (1996). Gender differences in the relation between interview-derived hostility scores and resting blood pressure. *Journal of Behavioral Medicine, 19,* 185–201.

Davidson, P. R., & Parker, K. C. (2001). Eye movement desensitization and reprocessing (EMDR): A meta-analysis. *Journal of Consulting and Clinical Psychology, 69,* 305–316.

Davidson, R. J. (2000). Affective style, psychopathology, and resilience: Brain mechanisms and plasticity. *American Psychologist, 55,* 1196–1214.

Davidson, R. J., Ekman, P., Saron, C., Senulis, J., & Friesen, W. V. (1990). Approach-withdrawal and cerebral asymmetry: Emotional expression and brain physiology: I. *Journal of Personality and Social Psychology, 58,* 330–341.

Davidson, R. J., Kabat-Zinn, J., Schumacher, J., Rosenkranz, M., Muller, D., Santorelli, S. F., et al. (2003). Alterations in brain and immune function produced by mindfulness meditation. *Psychosomatic Medicine, 65,* 564–570.

Davidson, R. J., Shackman, A. J., & Maxwell, J. S. (2004). Asymmetries in face and brain related to emotion. *Trends in Cognitive Science, 8,* 389–391.

Davies, C. (1999, April 21). Junior doctor is cleared in baby overdose death. *London Daily Telegraph,* p. 2.

Davis, J. A., & Smith, T. W. (1990). *General social surveys, 1972–1990: Cumulative codebook.* Chicago: National Opinion Research Center.

Davis, J. D., Gallagher, R. J., Ladove, R. F., & Turansky, A. J. (1969). Inhibition of food intake by a humoral factor. *Journal of Comparative and Physiological Psychology, 67,* 407–414.

Davis, J. L., & Rusbult, C. (2001). Attitude alignment in close relationships. *Journal of Personality and Social Psychology, 81,* 65–84.

Davis, J. M., Chen, N., & Glick, I. D. (2003). A meta-analysis of the efficacy of second-generation antipsychotics. *Archives of General Psychiatry, 60,* 553–564.

Davis, M., Falls, W. A., Campeau, S., & Kim, M. (1993). Fear-potentiated startle: A neural and pharmacological analysis. *Behavioural Brain Research, 58*(1–2), 175–198.

Davis, M., Myers, K. M., Ressler, K. J., & Rothbaum, B. O. (2005). Facilitation of extinction of conditioned fear by D-cycloserine. *Current Directions in Psychological Science, 14,* 214–219.

Davis, M. H. (1994). *Empathy: A social psychological approach.* Madison, WI: Brown and Benchmark.

Davis, M. H., Luce, C., & Kraus, S. J. (1994). The heritability of characteristics associated with dispositional empathy. *Journal of Personality, 60,* 369–391.

Davis, R. A., & Moore, C. C. (1935). Methods of measuring retention. *Journal of General Psychology, 12,* 144–155.

Davison, G. C., & Neale, J. M. (1990). *Abnormal psychology* (5th ed.). New York: Wiley.

Dawes, R. M. (1994). *House of cards: Psychology and psychotherapy built on myth.* New York: Free Press.

Dawes, R. M. (1998). Behavioral decision making and judgment. In D. Gilbert, S. T. Fiske, & G. Lindzey (Eds.), *Handbook of social psychology* (Vol. 1, 4th ed., pp. 497–549). Boston: McGraw-Hill.

Dawes, R. M., & Messick, D. M. (2000). Social dilemmas. *International Journal of Psychology, 35,* 111–116.

Dawkins, K., & Potter, W. (1991). Gender differences in pharmacokinetics and pharmacodynamics of psychotropics: Focus on women. *Psychopharmacology Bulletin, 27,* 417–426.

Dawson, M., Schell, A. M., & Filion, D. L. (2000). The electodermal system. In J. Cacioppo, L. Tassinary, & G. Bernston (Eds.), *Handbook of psychophysiology* (2nd ed., pp. 200–222). New York: Cambridge University Press.

Dawson-Basoa, M., & Gintzler, A. R. (1997). Involvement of spinal cord delta opiate receptors in the antinociception of gestation and its hormonal simulation. *Brain Research, 757,* 37–42.

Day, A. L., & Jreige, S. (2002). Examining Type A behavior pattern to explain the relationship between job stressors and psychosocial outcomes. *Journal of Occupational Health Psychology, 7,* 109–120.

Dayan, K., Kasten, R., & Fox, S. (2002). Entry-level police candidate assessment center: An efficient tool or a hammer to kill a fly? *Personnel Psychology, 55,* 827–849.

de Araujo, I. E., Rolls, E. T., Kringelbach, M. L., McGlone, F., & Phillips, N. (2003). Taste-olfactory convergence, and the representation of the pleasantness of flavour, in the human brain. *European Journal of Neuroscience, 18,* 2059–2068.

de Castro, J. M., & Goldstein, S. J. (1995). Eating attitudes and behaviors pre- and postpubertal females: Clues to the etiology of eating disorders. *Physiology and Behavior, 58*(1), 15–23.

de Charms, R., Levy, J., & Wertheimer, M. (1954). A note on attempted evaluations of psychotherapy. *Journal of Clinical Psychology, 10,* 233–235.

de Gelder, B., Snyder, J., Greve, D., Gerard, G., & Hadjikhani, N. (2004). Fear fosters flight: A mechanism for fear contagion when perceiving emotion expressed by a whole body. *Proceedings of the National Academy of Sciences of the USA, 101,* 16701–16706.

de Houwer, A. (1995). Bilingual language acquisition. In P. Fletcher & B. MacWhinney (Eds.), *The handbook of child language* (pp. 219–250). Cambridge, MA: Blackwell.

De Los Reyes, A., & Kazdin, A. E. (2006). Conceptualizing changes in behavior in intervention research: The range of possible changes model. *Psychological Review, 113,* 554–583.

De Macedo-Soares, M. B., Moreno, R. A., Rigonatti, S. P., & Lafer, B. (2005). Efficacy of electroconvulsive therapy in treatment-resistant bipolar disorder: A case series. *Journal of ECT, 21,* 31–34.

de Moor, J. S., de Moor, C. A., Basen-Engquist, K., Kudelka, A., Bevers, M. W., & Cohen, L. (2006). Optimism, distress, health-related quality of life, and change in cancer antigen 125 among patients with ovarian cancer undergoing chemotherapy. *Psychosomatic Medicine, 68,* 555–562.

de Rios, M. D. (1989). Power and hallucinogenic states of consciousness among the Moche: An ancient Peruvian society. In C. A. Ward (Ed.), *Altered states of consciousness and mental health: A cross-cultural perspective* (pp. 285–299). Newbury Park, CA: Sage.

de Silva, P. (1994). Psychological treatment of sexual problems. *International Review of Psychiatry, 6*(2–3), 163–173.

DeAngelis, T. (2001). APA has lead role in revising classification system. *Monitor on Psychology, 32,* 54–56.

Deary, I. J., & Der, G. (2005). Reaction time explains IQ's association with death. *Psychological Science, 16*(1), 64–69.

Deary, I. J., Whiteman, M. C., Starr, J. M., Whalley, L. J., & Fox., H. C. (2004). The impact of childhood intelligence on later life: Following up the Scottish mental surveys of 1932 and 1947. *Journal of Personality and Social Psychology, 86,* 130–147.

Death Penalty Information Center. (2006). *Innocence and the death penalty.* Washington, DC: Death Penalty Information Center. Retrieved September 26, 2006, from http://www.deathpenaltyinfo.org/article.php?did=412&scid=6.

deBeurs, E., van Balkom, A. J. L. M., Lange, A., Koele, P., & van Dyck, R. (1995). Treatment of panic disorder with agoraphobia: Comparison of fluvoxamine, placebo, and psychological panic management combined with exposure and of exposure in vivo alone. *American Journal of Psychiatry, 152*(5), 683–691.

deCharms, R. C., Maeda, F., Glover, G. H., Ludlow, D., Pauly, J. M., Soneji, D., et al. (2005). Control over brain activation and pain learned by using real-time functional MRI. *Proceedings of the National Academy of Sciences of the USA, 102,* 18626–18631.

Deci, E. L, Koestner, R., & Ryan, R. M. (1999). The undermining effect is a reality after all—Extrinsic rewards, task interest, and self-determination: Reply to Eisenberger, Pierce, and Cameron (1999) and Lepper, Henderlong, and Gingras (1999). *Psychological Bulletin, 125,* 692–700.

Deci, E. L., Koestner, R., & Ryan, R. M. (2001). A meta-analytic review of experiments examining the effects of extrinsic rewards on intrinsic motivation. *Psychological Bulletin, 125,* 627–668.

Deeprose, C., & Andrade, J. (2006). Is priming during anesthesia unconscious? *Consciousness and Cognition, 15,* 1–23.

DeJonghe, F., Hendriksen, M., Van Aalst, S. K., Peen, V., Van, R., van den Eijnden, E., et al. (2004). Psychotherapy alone and combined with pharmacotherapy in the treatment of depression. *British Journal of Psychiatry, 185,* 37–45.

Delamater, A. R. (2004). Experimental extinction in Pavlovian conditioning: Behavioural and neuroscience perspectives. *Quarterly Journal of Experimental Psychology, 57B,* 97–132.

DeLisi, L. E., Maurizio, A., Yost, M., Papparozzi, C. F., Fulchino, C., Katz, C. L., et al. (2003). A survey of New Yorkers after the Sept. 11, 2001, terrorist attacks. *American Journal of Psychiatry, 160,* 780–783.

Demaray, M. K., & Malecki, C. K. (2002). Critical levels of perceived social support associated with student adjustment. *School Psychology Quarterly, 17,* 213–241.

Dement, W. (1960). The effect of dream deprivation. *Science, 131,* 1705–1707.

Dement, W., & Kleitman, N. (1957). Cyclic variations in EEG during sleep and their relation to eye movements, body motility and dreaming. *Electroencephalography and Clinical Neurophysiology, 9,* 673–690.

Demerouti, E., Geurts, S. A. E., Bakker, A. B., & Euwema, M. (2004). The impact of shiftwork on work-home conflict, job attitudes, and health. *Ergonomics, 47,* 987–1002.

Demo, D. H., Allen, K. R., & Fine, M. A. (Eds.). (2000). *Handbook of family diversity.* New York: Oxford University Press.

DeNeve, K. M. (1999). Happy as an extraverted clam? The role of personality for subjective well-being. *Current Directions in Psychological Science, 8,* 141–144.

Denrell, J. (2005). Why most people disapprove of me: Experience sampling in impression formation. *Psychological Review, 112,* 951–978.

DePaulo, B. M. (1994). Spotting lies: Can humans learn to do better? *Current Directions in Psychological Science, 3,* 83–86.

DePrince, A. P., & Freyd, J. J. (2004). Forgetting trauma stimuli. *Psychological Science, 15,* 488–492.

Derogowski, J. B. (1989). Real space and represented space: Cross-cultural perspectives. *Behavior and Brain Sciences, 12,* 51–73.

Derryberry, D., & Tucker, D. M. (1992). Neural mechanisms of emotion. *Journal of Consulting and Clinical Psychology, 60,* 329–338.

DeRubeis, R. J., & Crits-Christoph, P. (1998). Empirically supported individual and group psychological treatments for adult mental disorders. *Journal of Consulting and Clinical Psychology, 66,* 37–52.

DeRubeis, R. J., Hollon, S. D., Amsterdam, J. D., Shelton, R. C., Young, P. R., Salomon, R. M., et al. (2005). Cognitive therapy vs medications in the treatment of moderate to severe depression. *Archives of General Psychiatry, 62,* 409–416.

Deschaumes, M. C., Dittmar, A., Sicard, G., & Vernet, M. E. (1991). Results from six autonomic nervous system responses confirm "autonomic response specificity" hypothesis. *Homeostasis in Health and Disease, 33*(5–6), 225–234.

Deutsch, M., & Gerard, H. B. (1955). A study of normative and informative social influences on individual judgments. *Journal of Abnormal and Social Psychology, 51,* 629–636.

Devenport, L. D. (1998). Spontaneous recovery without interference: Why remembering is adaptive. *Animal Learning and Behavior, 26,* 172–181.

Devi, G., & Quitschke, W. (1999). Alois Alzheimer, neuroscientist (1864–1915). *Alzheimer Disease and Associated Disorders, 13*(3), 132–137.

DeVries, R. (1969). Constancy of generic identity in the years three to six. *Monographs of the Society for Research in Child Development, 34* (3, Serial No. 127).

DeWitt, L. A., & Samuel, A. G. (1990). The role of knowledge-based function in music perception. *Journal of Experimental Psychology: General, 119,* 123–144.

DeWolff, M. S., & van IJzendoorn, M. H. (1997). Sensitivity and attachment: A meta-analysis on parental antecedents of infant attachment. *Child Development, 68,* 571–591.

Dhurandhar, N. V., Israel, B. A., Kolesar, J. M., Mayhew, G. F., Cook, M. E., & Atkinson, R. L. (2000). Increased adiposity in animals due to a human virus. *International Journal of Obesity, 24,* 989–996.

Di Marzo, V., Goparaju, S. K., Wang, L., Liu, J., Batkai, S., Jarai, Z., et al. (2001). Leptin-regulated endocannabinoids are involved in maintaining food intake. *Nature, 410,* 822–825.

Di Milia, L. (2006). Shift work, sleepiness, and long distance driving. *Transportation Research, 9,* 278–285.

Diakidoy, I. N., & Spanoudis, G. (2002). Domain specificity in creativity testing: A comparison of performance on a general divergent-thinking test and a parallel, content-specific test. *Journal of Creative Behavior, 36,* 41–61.

Diamond, L. M. (2004). Emerging perspectives on distinctions between romantic love and sexual desire. *Current Directions in Psychological Science, 13,* 116–119.

Dickinson, A. (2001). Causal learning: Association versus computation. *Current Directions in Psychological Science, 10,* 127–132.

Diener, E. (2000). Subjective well-being: The science of happiness and a proposal for a national index. *American Psychologist, 55,* 34–43.

Diener, E. (2003). What is positive about positive psychology: The curmudgeon and Pollyanna. *Psychological Inquiry, 14,* 115–120.

Diener, E., & Biswas-Diener, R. (2002). Will money increase subjective well-being? *Social Indicators Research, 57,* 119–169.

Diener, E., & Diener, C. (1995). Most people are happy. *Psychological Science, 7,* 181–185.

Diener, E., & Seligman, M. E. P. (2004). Beyond money: Towards an economy of well-being. *Psychological Science in the Public Interest, 5,* 1–31.

Dijksterhuis, A., Bos, M. W., Nordgren, L. F., & van Baaren, R. B. (2006). On making the right choice: The deliberation-without-attention effect. *Science, 311,* 1005–1007.

Dijksterhuis, A., & Nordgren, L. F. (2006). A theory of unconscious thought. *Perspectives on Psychological Science, 1,* 95–109.

Dijkstra, A., DeVries, H., & Bakker, M. (1996). Pros and cons of quitting, self-efficacy, and the stages of change in smoking cessation. *Journal of Consulting and Clinical Psychology, 64,* 758–763.

Dimidjian, S., Hollon, S. D., Dobson, K. S., Schmaling, K. B., Kohlenberg, R. J., Addis, M. E., et al. (2006). Randomized trial of behavioral activation, cognitive therapy, and antidepressant medication in the acute treatment of adults with major depression. *Journal of Consulting and Clinical Psychology, 74,* 658–670.

Dinan, T. G. (2001). Novel approaches to the treatment of depression by modulating the hypothalamic-pituitary-adrenal axis. *Human Psychopharmacology: Clinical and Experimental, 16,* 89–93.

Dingfelder, S. F. (2005, January). Closing the gap for Latino patients. *Monitor on Psychology,* 58–61.

Dion, K. (2003). Prejudice, racism and discrimination. In T. Millon & M. Lerner (Eds.) *Handbook of psychology: Volume 5: Personality and social psychology* (pp. 507–536). Hoboken, NJ: Wiley.

Dionne, V. E., & Dubin, A. E. (1994). Transduction diversity in olfaction. *Journal of Experimental Biology, 194,* 1–21.

Dittmann, M. (2003). Psychology's first prescribers. *Monitor on Psychology, 34,* 36–39.

Dittmann, M. (2004, June). Alternative health care gains steam. *Monitor on Psychology,* 42–44.

Dittmann, M. (2005, July/August). When health fears hurt health. *Monitor on Psychology,* 100–103.

Dittmar, H., Halliwell, E., & Ive, S. (2006). Does Barbie make girls want to be thin?: The effect of experimental exposure to images of dolls on the body image of 5- to 8-year-old girls. *Developmental Psychology, 42,* 283–292.

Dixon, J., Durrheim, K., & Tredoux, C. (2005). Beyond the optimal contact strategy: A reality check for the contact hypothesis. *American Psychologist, 60,* 697–711.

Dixon, J. B., Schachter, L. M., & O"Brien, P. E. (2005). Polysomnography before and after weight loss in obese patients with severe sleep apnea. *International Journal of Obesity, 29,* 1048–1054.

Dixon, M., Brunet, A., & Laurence, J.-R. (1990). Hypnotizability and automaticity: Toward a parallel distributed processing model of hypnotic responding. *Journal of Abnormal Psychology, 99,* 336–343.

Dobson, K. S. (Ed.). (2001). *Handbook of cognitive-behavioral therapies* (2nd ed.). New York: The Guilford Press.

Dodd, M. L., Klos, K. J., Bower, J. H., Geda, Y. E., Josephs, K. A., & Ahlskog, J. E. (2005). Pathological gambling caused by drugs used to treat Parkinson disease. *Archives of Neurology, 62,* 1377–1381.

Dodge, K. A. (2004). The nature-nurture debate and public policy. *Merrill-Palmer Quarterly, 50,* 418–427.

Dohrenwend, B. P., Raphael, K. G., Schwartz, S., Stueve, A., & Skodol, A. (1993). The structured event probe and narrative rating method for measuring stressful life events. In L. Goldenberger & S. Breznitz (Eds.), *Handbook of stress: Theoretical and clinical aspects* (2nd ed.). New York: The Free Press.

Dolan, M., & Park, I. (2002). The neuropsychology of antisocial personaity disorder. *Psychological Medicine, 32,* 417–427.

Dollard, J., Doob, L., Miller, N., Mowrer, O. H., & Sears, R. R. (1939). *Frustration and aggression.* New Haven, CT: Yale University Press.

Dollinger, S. J. (2000). Locus of control and incidental learning: An application to college students. *College Student Journal, 34,* 537–540.

Domhoff, G. W. (1996). *Finding meaning in dreams: A quantitative approach.* New York: Plenum.

Domhoff, G. W. (1999). Drawing theoretical implications from descriptive empirical findings on dream content. *Dreaming, 9,* 201–210.

Domhoff, G. W. (2001). A new neurocognitive theory of dreams. *Dreaming: Journal of the Association for the Study of Dreams, 11,* 13–33.

Domino, E. F. (2003). Effects of tobacco smoking on electroencephalographic, auditory evoked and event related potentials. *Brain and Cognition, 53,* 66–74.

Domjan, M. (2005). Pavlovian conditioning: A functional perspective. *Annual Review of Psychology, 56,* 179–206.

Donnerstein, E. (1984). Pornography: Its effects on violence against women. In N. M. Malamuth & E. Donnerstein (Eds.), *Pornography and sexual aggression.* New York: Academic Press.

Donnerstein, E., & Linz, D. (1995). The mass media: A role in injury causation and prevention. *Adolescent Medicine: State of the Art Reviews, 6,* 271–284.

Donnerstein, E., Slaby, R. G., & Eron, L. D. (1995). The mass media and youth aggression. In L. Eron, J. Gentry, & P. Schlegel (Eds.), *Reason to hope: A psychosocial perspective on violence and youth* (pp. 219–250). Washington, DC: American Psychological Association.

Donovan, J. J., & Radosevich, D. J. (1999). A meta-analytic review of the distribution of practice effect: Now you see it, now you don't. *Journal of Applied Psychology, 84,* 795–805.

Dordain, G., & Deffond, D. (1994). Pyridoxine neuropathies: Review of the literature. *Therapie, 49(4),* 333–337.

Dovidio, J. F., & Penner, L. A. (2001). Helping and altruism. In G. Fletcher & M. Clark (Eds.), *Blackwell handbook of social psychology: Interpersonal processes* (pp. 162–195). Boston: Blackwell.

Dovidio, J. F., Kawakami, K., & Gaertner, S. L. (2000). Reducing contemporary prejudice: Combating explicit and implicit bias ai the individual and intergroup level. In S. Oskamp (Ed.), *Reducing prejudice and discrimination* (pp. 137–163). Hillsdale, NJ: Erlbaum.

Dovidio, J. F., Piliavin, J. A., Gaertner, S. L., Schroeder, D. A., & Clark, R. D., III. (1991). The arousal: cost-reward model and the process of intervention: A review of the evidence. In M. Clark (Ed.), *Review of personality and social psychology: Vol. 12. Prosocial behavior* (pp. 86–118). Newbury Park, CA: Sage.

Dowson, D. I., Lewith, G. T., & Machin, D. (1985). The effects of acupuncture versus placebo in the treatment of headache. *Pain, 21,* 35–42.

Doyle, J. (2005). *True witness: Cops, courts, science, and the battle against misidentification.* New York: Palgrave Macmillan.

Dresner, R., & Grolnick, W. S. (1996). Constructions of early parenting, intimacy and autonomy in young women. *Journal of Social and Personal Relationships, 13,* 25–40.

Dreyfus, H. L., & Dreyfus, S. E. (1988). Making a mind versus modeling the brain: Intelligence back at a branchpoint. In S. R. Graubard (Ed.), *The artificial intelligence debate.* Cambridge: MIT Press.

Drinkwater, J., & Stewart, A. (2002). Cognitive behavior therapy for young people. *Current Opinion in Psychiatry, 15,* 377–381.

Driskell, J. E., Willis, R., & Copper, C. (1992). Effect of overlearning on retention. *Journal of Applied Psychology, 77,* 615–622.

Driver, J., Tabares, A., Shapiro, A., Nahm, E. Y., & Gottman, J. M. (2003). Interactional patterns in marital success and failure: Gottman laboratory studies. In F. Walsh (Ed.), *Normal family processes: Growing diversity and complexity* (3rd ed., pp. 493–513). New York: Guilford.

Driver, J. L., & Gottman, J. M. (2004). Daily marital interactions and positive affect during marital conflict among newlywed couples. *Family Process, 43,* 301–314.

Drucker-Colin, R., & Verdugo-Diaz, L. (2004). Cell transplantation for Parkinson's disease: Present status. *Cellular and Molecular Neurobiology, 24,* 301–316.

Druckman, D., & Bjork, R. A. (1994). *Learning, remembering, believing: Enhancing human performance.* Washington, DC: National Academy Press.

Drummond, S. P., Brown, G. G., Gillin, J. C., Stricker, J. L., Wong, E. C., & Buxton, R. B. (2000). Altered brain response to verbal learning following sleep deprivation. *Nature, 403,* 655–657.

Druss, B. G., Rosenheck, R. A., & Sledge, W. H. (2000). Health and disability costs of depressive illness in a major U.S. Corporation. *American Journal of Psychiatry, 157,* 1274–1278.

Duarte, N. T., Goodson, J. R., & Klich, N. R. (1993). How do I like thee? Let me appraise the ways. *Journal of Organizational Behavior, 14,* 239–249.

Dube, S. R., Felitti, V. J., Dong, M., Chapman, D. P., Giles, W. H., & Anda, R. F. (2003). Childhood abuse, neglect, and household dysfunction and the risk of illicit drug use: the adverse childhood experiences study. *Pediatrics, 111,* 564–572.

Dubois, B. (2004). Amnestic MCI or prodromal Alzheimer's disease? *Lancet Neurology, 3*(4), 246–248.

DuBois, D. L., Felner, R. D., Brand, S., Adan, A. M., & Evans, E. G. (1992). A prospective study of life stress, social support, and adaptation in early adolescence. *Child Development, 63,* 542–557.

DuBois, G. E. (2004). Unraveling the biochemistry of sweet and umami tastes. *Proceedings of the National Academy of Sciences, 101,* 13972–13973.

DuBreuil, S. C., Garry, M., & Loftus, E. F. (1998). Tales from the crib: Memories of infancy. In S. J. Lynn, & K. M. McConkey (Eds.), *Truth in memory* (pp. 137–160). New York: Guilford.

Dubrovsky, B. O. (2005). Steroids, neuroactive steroids and neurosteroids in psychopathology. *Progress in Neuropsychopharmacology and Biological Psychiatry, 29,* 169–192.

Duclos, S. E., & Laird, J. D. (2001). The deliberate control of emotional experience through control of expressions. *Cognition and Emotion, 15,* 27–56.

Dudai, Y. (2004). The neurobiology of consolidations, or, how stable is the engram? *Annual Review of Psychology, 55,* 51–86.

Dudley, N. M., Orvis, K. A., Lebeicki, J. E., & Cortina, J. M. (2006). A meta-analytic investigation of conscientiousness in the prediction of job performance: Examining the intercorrelations and the incremental validity of narrow traits. *Journal of Applied Psychology, 91,* 40–57.

Duggan, A., Fuddy, L., Burrell, L., Higman, S. M., McFarlane, E., Windham, A., et al.. (2004). Randomized trial of a statewide home visiting program to prevent child abuse: Impact in reducing parental risk factors. *Child Abuse and Neglect, 28,* 623–643.

Dujovne, V., & Houston, B. (1991). Hostility-related variables and plasma lipid levels. *Journal of Behavioral Medicine, 14,* 555–564.

Dumont, F., & Corsini, R. J. (2000). *Six therapists and one client.* New York: Springer.

Duncan, B. L. (2002). The legacy of Saul Rosenweig: The profundity of the dodo bird. *Journal of Psychotherapy Integration, 12*(1), 32–57.

Duncan, G. J., Brooks-Gunn, J., & Klebanov, P. K. (1994). Economic deprivation and early childhood development. *Child Development, 65,* 296–318.

Dunn, J., Brown, H., Slomkowski, C., Tesla, C., & Youngblade, L. (1991). Young children's understanding of other people's feelings and beliefs: Individual differences and their antecedents. *Child Development, 62,* 1352–1366.

Dunn, J., & Hughes, C. (2001). "I got some swords and you're dead!": Violent fantasy, antisocial behavior, friendship, and moral sensibility in young children. *Child Development, 72,* 491–505.

Dunne, E., & Fitzpatrick, A. C. (1999). The views of professionals on the role of self-help groups in the mental health area. *Irish Journal of Psychological Medicine, 16,* 84–89.

Dunning, D., Johnson, K., Ehrlinger, J., & Kruger, J. (2003). Why people fail to recognize their own incompetence. *Current Directions in Psychological Science, 12,* 83–87.

Durantini, M. R., Albarracin, D., Mitchell, A. L., Earl, A. N.,& Gillette, J. C. (2006). Conceptualizing the influence of social agents of behavior change: A meta-analysis of the effectiveness of HIV-prevention interventionists for different groups. *Psychological Bulletin, 132,* 212–248.

Durka, P. J., Malinowska, U., Szelenberger, W., Wakarow, A., & Blinowska, K. J. (2005). High resolution parametric description of slow wave sleep. *Journal of Neuroscience Methods, 147,* 15–21.

Durose, M. R., Harlow, C. W., Langan, P. A., Motivans, M., Rantala, R. R., & Smith, E. L. (2005). *Family violence statistics.* Washington, DC: Bureau of Justice Statistics.

Dutton, D. G., & Aron, A. P. (1974). Some evidence for heightened sexual attraction under conditions of high anxiety. *Journal of Personality and Social Psychology, 30,* 510–517.

Dweck, C. S. (1998). The development of early self-conceptions: Their relevance for motivational processes. In J. Heckhausen & C. S. Dweck (Eds.), *Motivation and self-regulation across the life span.* New York: Cambridge University Press.

Dwork, A. J., Arango, V., Underwood, M., Iievski, B., Rosoklija, G., Sackeim, H. A., et al. (2004). Absence of histological lesions in primate models of ECT and magnetic seizure therapy. *American Journal of Psychiatry, 161,* 576–578.

Dyche, L., & Zayas, L. H. (2001). Cross-cultural empathy and training the contemporary psychotherapist. *Clinical Social Work Journal, 29,* 245–258.

d'Ydewalle, G., & Rosselle, H. (1978). Text expectations in text learning. In M. M. Gruneberg, P. E. Morris, & R. N. Sykes (Eds.), *Practical aspects of memory.* Orlando, FL: Academic Press.

Dyken, M. E., & Yamada, T. (2005). Narcolepsy and disorders of excessive somnolence. *Primary Care, 32,* 389–413.

E

Eagly, A. H. (1987). *Sex differences in social behavior: A social-role interpretation.* Hillsdale, NJ: Erlbaum.

Eagly, A. H., Johannesen-Schmidt, M. C., & van Engen, M. L. (2003). Transformational, transactional, and laissez-faire leadership styles: A meta-analysis comparing women and men. *Psychological Bulletin, 129,* 569–591.

Eagly, A. H., & Karau, S. J. (1991). Gender and the emergence of leaders: A meta-analysis. *Journal of Personality and Social Psychology, 60,* 685–710.

Eagly, A. H., Karau, S. J., & Makhijani, M. G. (1995). Gender and the effectiveness of leaders: A meta-analysis. *Psychological Bulletin, 117,* 125–145.

Eagly, A. H., Makhijani, M. G., & Klonsky, B. G. (1992). Gender and evaluation of leaders: A meta-analysis. *Psychological Bulletin, 111,* 3–22.

Eagly, A. H., & Wood, W. (1999). The orgins of sex diffrences in human behavior: Evolved dispositions versus social roles. *American Psychologist, 54,* 408–423.

Eberhardt, J. L. (2005). Imaging race. *American Psychologist, 60,* 181–190.

Ebert, S. A., Tucker, D. C., & Roth, D. L. (2002). Psychological resistance factors as predictors of general health status and physical symptom reporting. *Psychology Health & Medicine, 7,* 363–375.

Ebstein, R. B. (2006). The molecular genetic architecture of human personality: Beyond self-report questionnaires. *Molecular Psychiatry, 11,* 427–445.

Eby, L. T., Casper, W. J., Lockwood, A., Bordeaux, C., & Brinley, A. (2005). Work and family research in IO/OB: Content analysis and review of the literature (1980–2002). *Journal of Vocational Behavior, 66,* 124–197.

Eccleston, C., & Crombez, G. (1999). Pain demands attention: A cognitive-affective model of the interruptive function of pain. *Psychological Bulletin, 125,* 356–366.

Echeburua, E., de Corral, P., Garcia Bajos, E., & Borda, M. (1993). Interactions between self-exposure and alprazolam in the treatment of agoraphobia without current panic: An exploratory study. *Behavioural and Cognitive Psychotherapy, 21,* 219–238.

Eddy, K. T., Dutra, L., Bradley, R., & Westen, D. (2004). A multidimensional meta-analysis of psychotherapy and pharmacotherapy for obsessive-compulsive disorder. *Clinical Psychology Review, 24,* 1011–1030.

Edelman, G. M. (2003). Naturalizing consciousness: A theoretical framework. *Proceedings of the National Academy of Sciences, 100,* 5520–5524.

Edinger, J. D., Wohlgemuth, W. K., Radtke, R. A., Marsh, G. R., & Quillian, R. E. (2001). Cognitive behavioral therapy for treatment of chronic primary insomnia. *American Medical Association, 285,* 1856–1864.

Edmond, T., & Rubin, A. (2004). Assessing the long-term effects of EMDR: Results from an 18-month follow-up study with adult female survivors of CSA. *Journal of Child Sexual Abuse, 13,* 69–86.

Egeland, J. A., Gerhard, D. S., Pauls, D. L., Sussex, J. N., Kidd, K. K., Allen, C. R., et al. (1987). Bipolar affective disorders linked to DNA markers on chromosome 11. *Nature, 325,* 783–787.

Egner, T., Jamieson, G., & Gruzelier, J. (2005). Hypnosis decouples cognitive control from conflict monitoring processes of the frontal lobe. *Neuroimage, 27,* 969–978.

Ehlers, A. (1995). A 1-year prospective study of panic attacks: Clinical course and factors associated with maintenance. *Journal of Abnormal Psychology, 104,* 164–172.

Ehrlichman, H., & Halpern, J. N. (1988). Affect and memory: Effects of pleasant and unpleasant odors on retrieval of happy and unhappy memories. *Journal of Personality and Social Psychology, 55,* 769–779.

Eich, E. (1989). Theoretical issues in state dependent memory. In H. L. Roediger & F. I. M. Craik (Eds.), *Varieties of memory and consciousness.* Hillsdale, NJ: Erlbaum.

Eich, E., & Macaulay, D. (2000). Are real moods required to reveal mood-congruent and mood-dependent memory? *Psychological Science, 11,* 244–248.

Eich, E., & Metcalfe, J. (1989). Mood dependent memory for internal versus external events. *Experimental Psychology: Learning, Memory, and Cognition, 15,* 443–455.

Eich, J. E., Weingartner, H., Stillman, R. C., & Gillin, J. C. (1975). State dependent accessibility of retrieval cues in the retention of a categorized list. *Journal of Verbal Learning and Verbal Behavior, 14,* 408–417.

Eichelman, B. (1983). The limbic system and aggression in humans. *Neuroscience and Biobehavioral Reviews, 7,* 391–394.

Einhorn, H., & Hogarth, R. (1982). Prediction, diagnosis and causal thinking in forecasting. *Journal of Forecasting, 1,* 23–36.

Eisen, J. A., Mancebo, M. A., Pinto, A., Coles, M. E., Pagano, M. E., Stout, R., et al. (2006). Impact of obsessive-compulsive disorder on quality of life. *Comprehensive Psychiatry, 47,* 270–275.

Eisenberg, M., Kobilo, T., Berman, D. E., & Dudai, Y. (2003). Stability of retrieved memory: Inverse correlation with trace dominance. *Science, 301,* 1102–1104.

Eisenberg, N., & Fabes, R. A. (1998). Prosocial development. In W. Damon & N. Eisenberg (Eds.), *Handbook of child psychology: Vol. 3. Social, emotional, and personality development* (5th ed., pp. 701–778). New York: Wiley.

Eisenberg, N., Fabes, R. A., & Murphy, B. C. (1995). Relations of shyness and low sociability to regulation and emotionality. *Journal of Personality and Social Psychology, 68,* 505–518.

Eisenberg, N., Fabes, R. A.., & Spinrad, T. L. (2006). Prosocial development. In W. Damon & R. M. Lerner (Series Eds.) & N. Eisenberg (Vol. Ed.), *Handbook of child psychology: Vol. 3. Social, emotional, and personality development* (6th ed.). New York: Wiley.

Eiser, A. S. (2005). Physiology and psychology of dreams. *Seminars in Neurology, 25,* 97–105.

Ekman, A., Lindholm, M. L., Lennmarken, C., & Sandin, R. (2004). Reduction in the incidence of awareness using BIS monitoring. *Acta Anaesthesiology Scandinavia, 48,* 20–26.

Ekman, P. (1993). Facial expression and emotion. *American Psychologist, 48,* 384–392.

Ekman, P. (1994). Strong evidence for universals in facial expressions: A reply to Russell's mistaken critique. *Psychological Bulletin, 115*(2), 268–287.

Ekman, P., & Davidson, R. J. (1993). Voluntary smiling changes regional brain activity. *Psychological Science, 4*(5), 342–345.

Ekman, P., Davidson, R. J., Ricard, M., & Alan, W. B. (2005). Buddhist and psychological perspectives on emotions and well-being. *Current Directions in Psychological Science, 14,* 59–63.

Ekman, P., Friesen, W. V., & Ellsworth, P. (1972). *Emotion in the human face: Guidelines for research and a review of findings.* New York: Pergamon Press.

Ekman, P., Levenson, R. W., & Friesen, W. V. (1983). Autonomic nervous system activity distinguishes among emotions. *Science, 221,* 1208–1210.

El Yacoubi, M., Bouali, S., Popa, D., Naudon, L., Leroux-Nicollet, I., Hamon, M., et al. (2003). Behavioral, neurochemical, and electrophysiological characterization of a genetic mouse model of depression. *Proceedings of the National Academy of Sciences, 100,* 6227–6232.

Eliot, A. J., Chirkov, V. I., Kim, Y., & Shelldon, K. M. (2001). A cross-cultural analysis of avoidance (relative to approach) personal goals. *Psychological Science, 12,* 505–510.

Elkin, I. (1994). The NIMH treatment of depression collaborative research program: Where we began and where we are. In A. E. Bergin & S. L. Garfield (Eds.), *Handbook of psychotherapy and behavior change* (pp. 114–139). New York: Wiley.

Elkin, I. (1999). A major dilemma in psychotherapy outcome research: Disentangling therapists from therapies. *Clinical Psychology: Science and Practice, 6,* 10–32.

Elkins, I. J., King, S. M., McGue, M., & Iacono, W. G. (2006). Personality traits and the development of nicotine, alchohol, and illicit drug disorders: Prospective links from adolescence to young adulthood. *Journal of Abnormal Psychology, 115,* 26–39.

Elliot, A. J., & Devine, P. G. (1994). On the motivational nature of cognitive dissonance: Dissonance as psychological discomfort. *Journal of Personality and Social Psychology, 67,* 382–394.

Elliot, S. N., Reynolds, C. R., & Kratochwill, T. R. (2006). *School psychology: Essentials of theory and practice.* Hoboken, NJ: Wiley.

Elliott, R., Watson, J. C., & Goldman, R. N. (2004a). Empty chair work for unfinished interpersonal issues. In R. Elliott & J. Watson (Eds.), *Learning emotion-focused therapy: The process-experiential approach to change* (pp. 243–265). Washington, DC: American Psychological Association.

Elliott, R., Watson, J. C., & Goldman, R. N. (2004b). Two-chair work for conflict splits. In R. Elliott & J. Watson (Eds.), *Learning emotion-focused therapy: The process-experiential approach to change* (pp. 219–241). Washington, DC: American Psychological Association.

Ellis, A. (1962). *Reason and emotion in psychotherapy.* New York: Lyle Stuart.

Ellis, A. (1993). Reflections on rational-emotive therapy. *Journal of Consulting and Clinical Psychology, 61,* 199–201.

Ellis, A. (1995). Rational emotive behavior therapy. In R. J. Corsini & D. Wedding (Eds.), *Current psychotherapies* (5th ed., pp. 162–196). Itasca, IL: Peacock.

Ellis, A. (2004a). Why I (really) became a therapist. *Journal of Rational-Emotive and Cognitive Behavior Therapy, 22*(2), 73–77.

Ellis, A. (2004b). Why rational emotive behavior therapy is the most comprehensive and effective form of behavior therapy. *Journal of Rational-Emotive and Cognitive Behavior Therapy, 22*(2), 85–92.

Ellis, A. L., & Mitchell, R. W. (2000). Sexual orientation. In L. T. Szuchman & F. Muscarella (Eds.), *Psychological perspectives on human sexuality* (pp. 196–231). New York: Wiley.

Ellis, N. R. (1991). Automatic and effortful processes in memory for spatial location. *Bulletin of the Psychonomic Society, 29,* 28–30.

Elovainio, M., Kivimäki, M., & Vahtera, J. (2002). Organizational justice: Evidence on a new psychosocial predictor of health. *American Journal of Public Health, 92,* 105–108.

Else-Quest, N. M., Hyde, J. S., Goldsmith, H. H., & Van Hulle, C. A. (2006). Gender differences in temperament: A meta-analysis. *Psychological Bulletin, 132,* 33–72.

Emanuele, E., Politi, P., Bianchi, M., Minoretti, P., Bertona, M., & Geroldi, D. (2006). Raised plasma nerve growth factor levels associated with early-stage romantic love. *Psychoneuroendocrinology, 31,* 288–294.

Emery, C. E. (2002). Death, taxes, and failed psychic predictions: Tabloid psychics fail again in 2002. Skeptical Inquirer, 27, 6–7.

Engebretson, T. O., & Stoney, C. M. (1995). Anger expression and lipid concentrations. *International Journal of Behavioral Medicine, 2,* 281–298.

Engeland, H. V. (1993). Pharmacotherapy and behaviour therapy: Competition or cooperation? *Acta Paedopsychiatrica International Journal of Child and Adolescent Psychiatry, 56*(2), 123–127.

Engen, T., Gilmore, M. M., & Mair, R. G. (1991). Odor memory. In T. V. Getchell et al. (Eds.), *Taste and smell in health and disease.* New York: Raven Press.

Engle, R. W., & Oransky, N. (1999). The evolution from short-term to working memory: Multi-store to dynamic models of temporary storage. In R. Sternberg (Ed.), *The nature of human cognition* (pp. 514–555). Cambridge: MIT Press.

Engler, B. (2003). *Personality theories: An introduction* (6th ed.). Boston: Houghton Mifflin.

Enoch, M. A.(2003). Pharmacogenomics of alcohol response and addiction. *American Journal of Pharmacogenomics, 3,* 217–232.

Epping-Jordan, M. P., Watkins, S. S., Koob, G. F., & Markou, A. (1998). Dramatic decreases in brain reward function during nicotine withdrawal. *Nature, 393,* 76–79.

Epstein, E. M., Sloan, D. M., & Marx, B. P. (2005). Getting to the heart of the matter: Written disclosure, gender, and heart rate. *Psychosomatic Medicine, 67,* 413–419.

Epstein, L. H., Valoski, A., Wing., R. R., & McCurley, J. (1994). Ten-year outcomes of behavioral family-based treatment for childhood obesity. *Health Psychology, 13,* 373–383.

Epstein, R., Kirshit, C. E., Lanza, R. P., & Rubin, C. L. (1984). "Insight" in the pigeon: Antecedents and determinants of an intelligent performance. *Nature, 308,* 61–62.

Erdelyi, M. H. (1985). *Psychoanalysis: Freud's cognitive psychology.* San Francisco: Freeman.

Erickson, R. J., Nichols, L., & Ritter, C. (2000). Family influences on absenteeism: Testing an expanded process model. *Journal of Vocational Behavior, 57,* 246–272.

Ericsson, K. A., & Charness, N. (1994). Expert performance: Its structure and acquisition. *American Psychologist, 49,* 725–747.

Ericsson, K. A., & Simon, H. A. (1994). *Protocol analysis: Verbal reports as data* (Rev. ed.). Cambridge, MA: MIT Press.

Ericsson, K. A., & Staszewski, J. (1989). Skilled memory and expertise: Mechanisms of exceptional performance. In D. Klahr & K. Kotovsky (Eds.), *Complex information processing: The impact of Herbert A. Simon.* Hillsdale, NJ: Erlbaum.

Erikson, E. H. (1968). *Identity: Youth and crisis.* New York: Norton.

Erikson, R., Goldthorpe, J. H., Jackson, M., Yaish, M., & Cox, D. R. (2005). On class differentials in educational attainment. *Proceedings of the National Academy of Sciences of the USA, 102,* 9730–9733.

Eriksson, P. S., Perfilieva, E., Bjork-Eriksson, T., Alborn, A. M., Nordborg, C., Peterson, D. A., & Gage, F. H. (1998). Neurogenesis in the adult human hippocampus. *Nature Medicine, 4,* 1313–1317.

Ernst, M., Matochik, J. A., Heishman, S. J., Van Horn, J. D., Jons, P. H., Henningfield, J. E., & London, E. D. (2001). Effect of nicotine on brain activation during performance of a working memory task. *Proceedings of the National Academy of Science, 98,* 4728–4733.

Eron, L. D., Huesmann, L. R., Lefkowitz, M. M., & Walder, L. O. (1996). Does television violence cause aggression? In D. F. Greenberg (Ed.), *Criminal careers: Vol. 2. The international library of criminology, criminal justice and penology* (pp. 311–321). Aldershot, UK: Dartmouth.

Esel, E., Ozsay, S., Tutus, A., Sofiuoglu, S., Kartaici, S., Bayram, F., et al. (2005). Effects of antidepressant treatment and of gender on serum leptin levels in patients with major depression. *Progress in Neuro-Psychopharmacology and Biological Psychiatry, 29,* 565–570.

Esterson, A. (2001). The mythologizing of psychoanalytic history: Deception and self-deception in Freud's account of the seduction theory episode. *History of Psychiatry, 12,* 329–352.

Ettlin, T. M., Beckson, M., Benson, D. F., Langfitt, J. T., Amos, E. C., & Pineda, G. S. (1992). Prosopagnosia: A bihemispheric disorder. *Cortex, 28*(1), 129–134.

Evans, G. W. (2004). The environment of childhood poverty. *American Psychologist, 59,* 77–92.

Evans, G. W., & Johnson, D. (2000). Stress and open-office noise. *Journal of Applied Psychology, 85,* 779–783.

Evans, G. W., Wells, N. M., Chan, H.-Y. E., & Saltzman, H. (2000). Housing quality and mental health. *Journal of Consulting and Clinical Psychology, 68,* 526–530.

Evans, G. W., & Wener, R. E. (2006). Rail commuting duration and passenger stress. *Health Psychology, 25,* 408–412.

Everaerd, W., & Laan, E. (1994). Cognitive aspects of sexual functioning and dysfunctioning. *Sexual and Marital Therapy, 9,* 225–230.

Everitt, B. J., & Robbins, T. W. (2005). Neural systems of reinforcement for drug addiction: From actions to habits to compulsion. *Nature Neuroscience, 8,* 1481–1489.

Eysenck, H. J. (1952). The effects of psychotherapy: An evaluation. *Journal of Consulting Psychology, 16,* 319–324.

Eysenck, H. J. (1978). An exercise in mega-silliness. *American Psychologist, 33,* 517.

Eysenck, H. J. (1986). What is intelligence? In R. J. Sternberg & D. K. Detterman (Eds.), *What is intelligence? Contemporary viewpoints on its nature and definition.* Norwood, NJ: Ablex.

Eysenck, H. J. (1990a). Biological dimensions of personality. In L. A. Pervin (Ed.), *Handbook of personality: Theory and research* (pp. 244–276). New York: Guilford.

Eysenck, H. J. (1990b). Genetic and environmental contributions to individual differences: The three major dimensions of personality. *Journal of Personality, 58,* 245–261.

Eysenck, H. J., & Rachman, S. (1965). *The causes and cures of neurosis: An introduction to modern behavior therapy based on learning theory and the principle of conditioning.* San Diego: Knapp.

Eysenck, M. W., & Keane, M. T. (2005). *Cognitive psychology: A student's handbook* (5th ed.). East Sussex, UK: Psychology Press.

F

Fabes, R. A., Martin, C. L., & Hanish, L. D. (2003). Young children's qualities in same-, other-, and mixed-sex peer groups. *Child Development, 74,* 921–932.

Fabrigar, L. R., MacDonald, T. K., & Wegener, D. T. (2005). The structure of attitudes. In D. Albarracín, B. T. Johnson, & M. P. Zanna (Eds.), *Handbook of attitudes* (pp. 79–124). Mahwah, NJ: Erlbaum.

Faedda, G., Tondo, L., Teicher, M., Baldessarini, R., Gelbard, H., & Floris, G. (1993). Seasonal mood disorders: Patterns of seasonal recurrence in mania and depression. *Archives of General Psychiatry, 50,* 17–23.

Fagan, J. F. (2000). A theory of intelligence as processing. *Psychology, Public Policy, and Law, 26,* 168–179.

Fagot, B. I. (1997). Attachment, parenting, and peer interactions of toddler children. *Developmental Psychology, 33,* 489–499.

Farah, M. J. (1996). Is face recognition "special"? Evidence from neuropsychology. *Behavioral Brain Research, 76*(1–2), 181–189.

Farah, M. J., McMullen, P. A., & Meyer, M. M. (1991). Can recognition of living things be selectively impaired? *Neuropsychologia, 29*(2), 185–193.

Farley, F (1986). The big T in personality. *Psychology Today, 20,* 44–52.

Farmer, J. D., Patelli, P., & Zovko, I. I. (2005). The predictive power of zero intelligence in financial markets. *Proceedings of the National Academy of Sciences of the USA, 102,* 2254–2259.

Farooqi, I. S., Jebb, S. A., Langmack, G., Lawrence, E., Cheetham, C. H., Prentice, A. M., et al. (1999). Effects of recombinant leptin therapy in a child with congenital leptin deficiency. *New England Journal of Medicine, 341,* 879–884.

Farooqi, I. S., Keogh, J. M., Kamath, S., Jones, S., Gibson, W. T., Trussel, R., et al. (2001). Metabolism: Partial leptin deficiency and human adiposity. *Nature, 414,* 34–35.

Farooqi, I. S., & O'Rahilly, S. (2004). Monogenic human obesity syndromes. *Recent Progress in Hormone Research, 59,* 409–424.

Farrell, D., & Stamm, C. L. (1988). Meta-analysis of the correlates of employee absence. *Human Relations, 41,* 211–227.

Farroni, T., Csibra, G., Simion, F., & Johnson, M. H. (2002). Eye contact detection in humans from birth. *Proceedings of the National Academy of Science, 99,* 9602–9605.

Farroni, T., Johnson, M. H., Menon, E., Zulian, L., Faraguna, D., & Csibra, G. (2005). Newborns' preference for face-relevant stimuli: Effects of contrast polarity. *Proceedings of the National Academy of Sciences of the USA, 102,* 17245–17250.

Fassler, D. G., & Dumas, L. S. (1997). *Help me, I'm sad: Recognizing, treating, and preventing childhood depression.* New York: Viking Press.

Faulkner, M. (2001). The onset and alleviation of learned helplessness in older hospitalized people. *Aging & Mental Health, 5,* 379–386.

Faust, J., Olson, R., & Rodriguez, H. (1991). Same-day surgery preparation: Reduction of pediatric patient arousal and distress through participant modeling. *Journal of Consulting and Clinical Psychology, 59,* 475–478.

Fava, G. A., Grandi, S. Rafanelli, C., Ruini, C., Conti, S., & Bellurado, P. (2001). Long-term outcome of social phobia treated by exposure. *Psychological Medicine, 31,* 899–905.

Faymonville, M. E., Laureys, S., Degueldre, C., DelFiore, G., Luxen, A., Franck, G., et al. (2000). Neural mechanisms of antinociceptive effects of hypnosis. *Anesthesiology, 92,* 1257–1267.

Feder, B. J. (2004, May 31). Technology strains to find menace in the crowd. *The New York Times,* p. C1.

Federal Bureau of Investigation. (2004). *Crime in the United States, 2003: Uniform crime reports.* Washington, DC: U.S. Department of Justice.

Feigin, V. L. (2003), Stroke epidemiology: A review of population based studies of incidence, prevalence, and case-fatality in the late 20th century. *Lancet Neurology, 2*(1), 43–53.

Feinberg, L., & Campbell, I. G. (1993). Total sleep deprivation in the rat transiently abolishes the delta amplitude response to darkness: Implications for the mechanism of the "negative delta rebound." *Journal of Neurophysiology, 70*(6) 2695–2699.

Feingold, A., & Mazzella, R. (1998). Gender differences in body image are increasing. *Psychological Science, 9,* 190–195.

Feingold, L., & Flamm, B. L. (2006). Magnet therapy: Extraordinary claims, but no proved benefits. *British Medical Journal, 332,* 4.

Feist, J., & Feist, G. J. (2002). *Theories of personality* (5th ed.) New York: McGraw-Hill.

Felder, R. M. & Brent, R. (2001). Effective strategies for cooperative learning. *Journal of Cooperation & Collaboration in College Teaching, 10,* 69–75.

Feldman, D. C., & Turnley, W. H. (2004). Contingent employment in academic careers: Relative deprivation among adjunct faculty. *Journal of Vocational Behavior, 64,* 284–307.

Fellin, T., Pascual, O., Gobbo, S., Pozzan, T., Haydon, P. G., & Carmignoto, G. (2004). Neuronal synchrony mediated by astrocytic glutamate through activation of extrasynaptic NMDA receptors. *Neuron, 43,* 729–743.

Felten, D. L., Cohen, N., Ader, R., Felten, S. Y., Carlson, S. L., & Roszman, T. L. (1991). Central neural circuits involved in neural-immune interactions. In R. Ader (Ed.), *Psychoneuroimmunology* (2nd ed.). New York: Academic Press.

Feltham, C. (2000). What are counselling and psychotherapy? In C. Feltham and I. Horton (Eds.), *Handbook of counselling and psychotherapy.* London: Sage.

Fenson, L., Dale, P. S., Reznick, J. S., & Bates, E. (1994). Variability in early communicative development. *Monographs of the Society for Research in Child Development, 59,* 173.

Ferguson, C. J. (2002). Media violence: Miscast causality. *American Psychologist, 57,* 446–447.

Ferguson, M. J., & Bargh, J. A. (2004). How social perception can automatically influence behavior. *Trends in Cognitive Sciences, 8,* 33–39.

Fernald, A. (1990, December). Cited by T. Adler, "Melody is the message" of infant-directed speech. *APA Monitor,* p. 9.

Fernández-Dols, J.-M. & Ruiz-Belda, M.-A. (1995). Are smiles a sign of happiness?: Gold medal winners at the Olympic Games. *Journal of Personality and Social Psychology, 69,* 1113–1119.

Ferris, G. R., Judge, T. A., Rowland, K. M., & Fitzgibbons, D. E. (1994). Subordinate influence and the performance evaluation process: Test of a model. *Organizational and Human Decision Processes, 58,* 101–135.

Ferro, J. M. (2001). Hyperacute cognitive stroke syndromes. *Journal of Neurology, 248*(10), 841–849.

Festinger, L. (1954). A theory of social comparison processes. *Human Relations, 7,* 117–140.

Festinger, L. (1957). *A theory of cognitive dissonance.* Evanston, IL: Row, Petersen.

Festinger, L., & Carlsmith, J. M. (1959). Cognitive consequences of forced compliance. *Journal of Abnormal and Social Psychology, 58,* 203–210.

Fields, R. D. (2005). Making memories stick. *Scientific American, 292,* 74–81.

Filipek, P. A., Accardo, P. J., Baranek, G. T., Cook, E. H., Jr., Dawson, G., Gordon, B., et al. (1999). The screening and diagnosis of autistic spectrum disorders. *Journal of Autism and Developmental Disorders, 29,* 439–484.

Fine, I., Wade, A. R., Brewer, A. A., May, M. G., Goodman, D. F., Boynton, G. M., et al. (2003). Long-term deprivation affects visual perception and cortex. *Nature Neuroscience, 6,* 915–916.

Finer, N., James, W. P., Kopelman, P. G., Lean, M. E., & Williams, G. (2000). One-year treatment of obesity: A randomized, double-blind, placebo-controlled, multicentre study of orlistat, a gastrointestinal lipase inhibitor. *International Journal of Obesity and Related Metabolic Disorders, 24,* 306–313.

Fink, J. N., & Caplan, L. R. (2003). Cerebrovascular cases. *Medical Clinics of North America, 87*(4), 755–770.

Fink, M. (1999). *Electroshock: Restoring the mind.* New York: Oxford University Press.

Finkel, D., Reynolds, C. A., McArle, J. J., Gatz, M., & Pedersen, N. L. (2003). Latent growth curve analyses of accelerating decline in cognitive abilities in late adulthood. *Developmental Psychology, 39,* 535–550.

First, M. B., Pincus, H. A., Levine, J. B., Williams, J. B. W., Ustun, B., & Peele, R. (2004). Clinical utility as a criterion for revising psychiatric diagnoses. *American Journal of Psychiatry, 161,* 946–954.

Fischer, K. W., & Bidell, T. (1991). Constraining nativist inferences about cognitive capacities. In S. Carey & R. Gelman (Eds.), *The epigenesis of mind: Essays on biology and cognition* (pp. 199–235). Hillsdale, NJ: Erlbaum.

Fischer, K. W., & Hencke, R. W. (1996). Infants' construction of actions in context: Piaget's contribution to research on early development. *Psychological Science, 7,* 204–209.

Fischer, M. E., Vitek, M. E., Hedeker, D., Henderson, W. G., Jacobsen, S. J., & Goldberg, J. (2004). A twin study of erectile dysfunction. *Archives of Internal Medicine, 164,* 165–168.

Fischer, P. J., & Breakey, W. R. (1991). The epidemiology of alcohol, drug, and mental disorders among homeless persons. *American Psychologist, 46,* 1115–1128.

Fischer, S., Hallschmid, M., Elsner, A. L., & Born, J. (2002). Sleep forms memory for finger skills. *Proceedings of the National Academy of Sciences, 99,* 11987–11991.

Fischoff, B., & MacGregor, D. (1982). Subjective confidence in forecasts. *Journal of Forecasting, 1,* 155–172.

Fisher, C. B., & Fried, A. L. (2003). Internet-mediated psychological services and the American Psychological Association ethics code. *Psychotherapy: Theory, Research, Practice, and Training, 40,* 103–111.

Fisher, C. D. (2000). Mood and emotion while working: Missing pieces of job satisfaction? *Journal of Organizational Behavior, 21,* 185–202.

Fisher, C. D. (2003). Why do lay people believe that satisfaction and performance are correlated? Possible sources of a commonsense theory. *Journal of Organizational Behavior, 24,* 753–777.

Fisher, C. M. (1982). Lacunar strokes and infarcts: A review. *Neurology, 32*(8), 871–876.

Fisher, C. M. (1989). Binswanger's encephalopathy: A review. *Journal of Neurology, 236*(2), 65–79.

Fisher, S. E. (2005). Dissection of molecular mechanisms underlying speech and language disorders. *Applied Psycholinguistics, 26,* 111–128.

Fisher, W. A., Fisher, J. D., & Rye, B. J. (1995). Understanding and promoting AIDS-preventive behavior: Insights from the theory of reasoned action. *Health Psychology, 14,* 255–264.

Fiske, A. P., Kitayama, S., Markus, H. R., & Nisbett, R. E. (1998). The cultural matrix of social psychology. In D. T. Gilbert, S. T. Fiske, & G. Lindzey (Eds.), *Handbook of social psychology* (Vol. 2, 4th ed., pp. 915–981). Boston: McGraw-Hill.

Fiske, S. T. (1998). Stereotyping, prejudice, and discrimination. In D. Gilbert, S. T. Fiske, & G. Lindzey (Eds.), *Handbook of social psychology* (Vol.2, 4th ed., pp. 357–414). Boston: McGraw-Hill.

Fiske, S. T. (2000). Interdependence and the reduction of prejudice. In S. Oskamp (Ed.), *Reducing prejudice and discrimination* (pp. 115–135). Mahwah, NJ: Erlbaum.

Fitch, W. T., & Hauser, M. D. (2004). Computational constraints on syntactic processing in a nonhuman primate. *Science, 303,* 377–380.

Fitzgerald, T. E., Tennen, H., Affleck, G. S., & Pransky, G. (1993). The relative importance of dispositional optimism and control appraisals in quality of life after coronary artery bypass surgery. *Journal of Behavioral Medicine, 16,* 25–43.

Flanagan, J. C. (1954). The critical incident technique. *Psychological Bulletin, 51,* 327–358.

Flavell, J. E., Azrin, N., Baumeister, A., Carr, E., Dorsey, M., Forehand, R., et al. (1982). The treatment of self-injurious behavior. *Behavior Therapy, 13,* 529–554.

Flavell, J. H. (1996). Piaget's legacy. *Psychological Science, 7,* 200–203.

Fleeson, W. (2004). Moving personality beyond the person-situation debate: The challenge and the opportunity of within-person variability. *Current Directions in Psychological Science, 13,* 83–87.

Fleeson, W., Malanos, A. B., & Achille, N. M. (2002). An intraindividual process approach to the relationship between extraversion and positive affect: Is acting extraverted as "good" as being extraverted? *Journal of Personality & Social Psychology, 83,* 1409–1422.

Flegal, K. M., Carroll, M. D., Ogden, C. L., & Johnson, C. L. (2002). Prevalence and trends in obesity among US adults, 1999–2000. *Journal of the American Medical Association, 288,* 1723–1727.

Flegal, K. M., Graubard, B. I., Williamson, D. F., & Gail, M. H. (2005). Excess deaths associated with underweight, overweight, and obesity. *Journal of the American Medical Association, 293,* 1861–1867.

Fleishman, E. A., & Harris, E. F. (1962). Patterns of leadership behavior related to employee grievances and turnover. *Personnel Psychology, 15,* 43–56.

Flor, H., Birbaumer, N., Herman, C., Ziegler, S., & Patrick, C. J. (2002). Aversive Pavlovian conditioning in psychopaths: Peripheral and central correlates. *Psychophysiology, 39,* 505–518.

Flores, E., Cicchetti, D., & Rogosch, F. A. (2005). Predictors of resilience in maltreated and nonmaltreated Latino children. *Developmental Psychology, 41,* 338–351.

Floyd, J. A. (2002). Sleep and aging. *Nursing Clinics of North America, 37,* 719–731.

Flynn, J. T. (1999). Searching for justice: The discovery of IQ gains over time. *American Psychologist, 54,* 5–20.

Foa, E. B., Cahill, S. P., Boscarino, J. A., Hobfoll, S. E., Lahad, M., McNally, R. J., et al. (2005). Social, psychological, and psychiatric interventions following terrorist attacks: Recommendations for practice and research. *Neuropsychopharmacology, 30,* 1806–1817.

Foa, E. B., Dancu, C. V., Hembree, E. A., Jaycox, L. H., Meadows, E. A., & Street, G. P. (1999). A comparison of exposure therapy, stress-inoculation training, and their combination for reducing posttraumatic stress disorder in female assault victims. *Journal of Consulting and Clinical Psychology, 67,* 194–200.

Foa, E. B., & Kozak, M. J. (1995). DSM-IV field trial: Obsessive-compulsive disorder. *American Journal of Psychiatry, 152,* 90–96.

Fodor, J. A. (1983). *Modularity of mind: An essay on faculty psychology.* Cambridge, MA: MIT Press.

Fogg, N. P., Harrington, P., & Harrington, T. (2005). *College majors handbook with real career paths and payoffs* (2nd ed.). Indianapolis, IN: Jist.

Foley, J. M. (2004). Empirically supported treatment endeavour: A successful future or inevitable debacle? *Clinical Psychologist, 8,* 29–38.

Folk, C. L., Remington, R. W., & Wright, J. H. (1994). The structure of attentional control: Contingent attentional capture by apparent motion, abrupt onset, and color. *Journal of Experimental Psychology: Human Perception and Performance, 20,* 317–329.

Folkman, S., & Lazarus, R. (1988). *Manual for the ways of coping questionnaire.* Palo Alto, CA: Consulting Psychologists Press.

Folkman, S., Lazarus, R., Dunkel-Shetter, C., DeLongis, A., & Gruen, R. (1986). Dynamics of a stressful encounter: Cognitive appraisal, coping, and encounter outcomes. *Journal of Personality and Social Psychology, 50,* 992–1003.

Folkman, S., Lazarus, R. S., Dunkel-Schetter, C., DeLongis, A., & Gruen, R. J. (2000). The dynamics of a stressful encounter. In E. T. Higgins & A. W. Kruglanski (Eds.), *Motivational science: Social and personality perspectives* (pp. 111–127). Hove, UK: Psychology Press.

Folkman, S., Lazarus, R. S., Gruen, R. J., & DeLongis, A. (1986). Appraisal, coping, health status, and psychological symptoms. *Journal of Personality and Social Psychology, 50,* 571–579.

Folkman, S., & Moskowitz, J. T. (2000). Stress, positive emotion, and coping. *Current Directions in Psychological Science, 9*, 115–118.

Forbes, S., Bui, S., Robinson, B. R., Hochgeschwender, U., & Brennan, M. B. (2001). Integrated control of appetite and fat metabolism by the leptin-proopiommelanocortin pathway. *Proceedings of the National Academy of Science, 98*, 4233–4237.

Ford, D. E., & Kamerow, D. B. (1989). Epidemiological study of sleep disturbances and psychiatric disorders: An opportunity for prevention? *Journal of the American Medical Association, 262*, 1479–1484.

Fossati, P., Hevenor, S. J., Graham, S. J., Grady, C., Keightley, M. L., Craik, F., & Mayberg, H. (2003). In search of the emotional self: An FMRI study using positive and negative emotional words. *American Journal of Psychiatry, 160*, 1938–1945.

Fosse, R., Stickgold, R., & Hobson, J. A. (2001). Brain-mind states: Reciprocal variation in thoughts and hallucinations. *Psychological Science, 12*, 30–36.

Foster, M. D. (2000). Positive and negative responses to personal discrimination: Does coping make a difference? *Journal of Social Psychology, 140*, 93–106.

Fotinatos-Ventouratos, R., & Cooper, C. (2005). The role of gender and social class in work stress. *Journal of Managerial Psychology, 20*, 14–23.

Foulkes, D. (1985). *Dreaming: A cognitive-psychological analysis.* Hillsdale, NJ: Erlbaum.

Fountain, J. W. (2000, November 28). Exorcists and exorcisms proliferate across U.S. *The New York Times.*

Fowler, R. D. (2000). A lesson in taking our own advice. *Monitor on Psychology, 31*, 9.

Fox, A. S., & Olster, D. H. (2000). Effects of intracerebroventricular leptin administration on feeding and sexual behaviors in lean and obese female zucker rats. *Hormones and Behavior, 37*, 377–387.

Fox, P., Bain, P. G., Glickman, S., Carroll, C., & Zajicek, J. (2004). The effect of cannabis on tremor in patients with multiple sclerosis. *Neurology, 62*, 1105–1109.

Fox, S., Spector, P. E., & Miles, D. (2001). Counterproductive work behavior (CWB) in response to job stressors and organizational justice: Some mediator and moderator tests for autonomy and emotions. *Journal of Vocational Behavior, 59*, 291–309.

Fozard, J., Wolf, E., Bell, B., Farland, R., & Podolsky, S. (1977). Visual perception and communication. In J. Birren & K. Schaie (Eds.), *Handbook of the psychology of aging.* New York: Van Nostrand Reinhold.

Francis, L. A., & Birch, L. L. (2005). Maternal influences on daughters' restrained eating behavior. *Health Psychology, 24*, 548–554.

Frank, D. A., Augustyn, M., Knight, W. G., Pell, T., & Zuckerman, B. (2001). Growth, development, and behavior in early childhood following prenatal cocaine exposure: A systematic review. *Journal of the American Medical Association, 285*, 1613–1625.

Frank, J. D., & Frank, J. B. (1991). *Persuasion and healing: A comparative study of psychotherapy* (3rd ed.). Baltimore, MD: Johns Hopkins University Press.

Frank, J. S. (1978). *Psychotherapy and the human predicament.* New York: Schocken Books.

Frank, M. G., Ekman, P., & Friesen, W. V. (1993). Behavioral markers and recognizability of the smile of enjoyment. *Journal of Personality and Social Psychology, 64*(1), 83–93.

Franken, I. H. A., Muris, P., & Georgieva, I. (2006). Gray's model of personality and addiction. *Addictive Behaviors, 31*, 399–403.

Frankenberg, W. K., & Dodds, J. B. (1967). The Denver developmental screening test. *Journal of Pediatrics, 71*, 181–191.

Franko, D. L., Mintz, L. B., Villapiano, M., Green, T. C., Mainelli, D., Folensbee, L., et al. (2005). Food, mood, and attitude: Reducing risk for eating disorders in college women. *Health Psychology, 24*, 567–578.

Franzoi, S. (2003). *Social psychology* (3rd ed.). New York: McGraw-Hill.

Frasure-Smith, N., & Lespérance, F. (2005). Depression and coronary heart disease. *Current Directions in Psychological Science, 14*, 39–43.

Frederickson, B. L., & Losada, M. F. (2005). Positive affect and the complex dynamics of human flourishing. *American Psychologist, 60*, 678–686.

Freed, C. R., Greene, P. E., Breeze, R. E., Tsai, W. Y., DuMouchel, W., Kao, R., et al. (2001). Transplantation of embryonic dopamine neurons for severe Parkinson's disease. *New England Journal of Medicine, 344*, 710–719.

Freedland, R. L., & Bertenthal, B. I. (1994). Developmental changes in interlimb coordination: Transition to hands-and-knees crawling. *Psychological Science, 5*, 26–32.

Freedman, D. M., Ron, E., Ballard-Barbash, R., Doody, M. M., & Linet, M. S. (2006). Body mass index and all-cause mortality in a nationwide U.S. cohort. *International Journal of Obesity, 30*, 822–829.

Freedman, J. L. (1992). Television violence and aggression: What psychologists should tell the public. In P. Suedfeld & P. E. Tetlock (Eds.), *Psychology and social policy.* New York: Hemisphere.

Freedman, J. L. (2002). *Media violence and its effect on aggression: Assessing the scientific evidence.* Toronto, Ontario, Canada: University of Toronto Press.

Freedman, J. L., & Fraser, S. C. (1966). Compliance without pressure: The foot-in-the-door technique. *Journal of Personality and Social Psychology, 4*, 195–202.

Freedman, R. (2003). Schizophrenia. *New England Journal of Medicine, 349*, 1738–1749.

Freedman, V. A., Aykan, H., & Martin, L. G. (2001). Aggregate changes in severe cognitive impairment among older Americans: 1993 and 1998. *Journal of Gerontology, 56B*, S100–S111.

Freeman, M. P., Freeman, S. A., & McElroy, S. L. (2002). The comorbidity of bipolar and anxiety disorders: Prevalence, psychobiology, and treatment issues. *Journal of Affective Disorders, 68*, 1–23.

Fremgen, A., & Fay, D. (1980). Overextensions in production and comprehension: A methodological clarification. *Journal of Child Language, 7*, 205–211.

French, S. E., Seidman, E., Allen, L., & Aber, J. L. (2006). The development of ethnic identity during adolescence. *Developmental Psychology, 42*, 1–10.

Freres, D. R., Gillham, J. E., Reivich, K., & Shatte, A. J. (2002). Preventing depressive symptoms in middle school students: The Penn Resiliency Program. *International Journal of Emergency Mental Health, 4*, 31–40.

Frese, M., Beimel, S., & Schoenborn, S. (2003). Action training for charismatic leadership: Two evaluations of studies of a commercial training module on inspirational communication of a vision. *Personnel Psychology, 56*, 671–697.

Freud, S. (1900). The interpretation of dreams. In J. Strachey (Ed.), *The standard edition of the complete psychological works of Sigmund Freud* (Vol. 8). London: Hogarth Press.

Frey, K. S., Hirschstein, M. K., Snell, J. L., Edstrom, L. V. S., MacKenzie, E. P., & Broderick, C. J. (2005). Reducing playground bullying and supporting beliefs: An experimental trial of the steps to respect program. *Developmental Psychology, 41*, 479–491.

Fridlund, A., Sabini, J. P., Hedlund, L. E., Schaut, J. A., Shenker, J. I., & Knauer, M. J. (1990). Audience effects on solitary faces during imagery: Displaying to the people in your head. *Journal of Nonverbal Behavior, 14*(2), 113–137.

Fried, I., Wilson, C. L., MacDonald, K. A., & Behnke, E. J. (1998). Electric current stimulates laughter. *Nature, 391*, 650.

Fried, P. A., Watkinson, B., & Gray, R. (1992). A follow-up study of attentional behavior in 6-year-old children exposed prenatally to marijuana, cigarettes, and alcohol. *Neurotoxicity and Teratology, 14*(5), 299–311.

Fried, Y., & Ferris, G. R. (1987). The validity of the job characteristics model: A review and meta-analysis. *Personnel Psychology, 40*, 287–322.

Fried, Y., & Tiegs, R. B. (1995). Supervisors' role conflict and role ambiguity differential relations with performance ratings of subordinates and the moderating effect of screening ability. *Journal of Applied Psychology, 80*, 282–291.

Friedman, E., Clark, D., & Gershon, S. (1992). Stress, anxiety, and depression: Review of biological, diagnostic, and nosologic issues. *Journal of Anxiety Disorders, 6*, 337–363.

Friedman, H. S. (2000). Long-term relations of personality and health: Dynamisms, mechanisms, tropisms. *Journal of Personality, 68*, 1089–1107.

Friedman, H. S., & Schustack, M. W. (2003). *Personality: Classic theories and modern research.* Boston: Allyn & Bacon.

Friedman, H. S., Tucker, J. S., Schwartz, J. E., Martin, L. R., Tomlinson-Keasey, C., Wingard, D. L., & Criqui, M. H. (1995a). Childhood conscientiousness and longevity: Health behaviors and cause of death. *Journal of Personality and Social Psychology, 68*, 696–703.

Friedman, H. S., Tucker, J. S., Schwartz, J. E., Tomlinson-Keasey, C., Martin, L. R., Wingard, D. L., & Criqui, M. H. (1995b). Psychosocial and behavioral predictors of longevity: The aging and death of the "Termites." *American Psychologist, 50*, 69–78.

Friedman, M. A., & Brownell, K. D. (1995). Psychological correlates of obesity: Moving to the next research generation. *Psychological Bulletin, 117*(1), 3–20.

Friedman, M., Ibrahim, H., Lee, G., & Joseph, N. J. (2003). Combined uvulopalatopharyngoplasty and radiofrequency tongue base reduction for treatment of obstructive sleep apnea/hypopnea syndrome. *Otolaryngological Head and Neck Surgery, 129*, 611–621.

Friedman, M., & Rosenman, R. H. (1974). *Type A behavior and your heart.* New York: Knopf.

Frieswijk, N., Buunk, B. P., Steverink, N., & Slaets, J. P. J. (2004). The effect of social comparison information on the life satisfaction of frail older persons. *Psychology and Aging, 19,* 183–190.

Fritzler, B. K., Hecker, J. E., & Losee, M. C. (1997). Self-directed treatment with minimal therapist contact: Preliminary findings for obsessive-compulsive disorder. *Behaviour Research and Therapy, 35,* 627–631.

Frizzell, J. P. (2005). Acute stroke: Pathophysiology, diagnosis, and treatment. *AACN Clinical Issues, 16*(4), 421–440.

Fujita, F., & Diener, E. (2005). Life satisfaction set point: Stability and change. *Journal of Personality and Social Psychology, 88,* 158–164.

Fuligni, A. J., & Pedersen, S. (2002). Family obligation and the transition to young adulthood. *Developmental Psychology, 38*(5), 856–868.

Fullerton, C. S., Ursano, R. J., & Wang, L. (2004). Acute stress disorder, posttraumatic stress disorder, and depression in disaster or rescue workers. *American Journal of Psychiatry, 161,* 1370–1376.

Funder, D. (2001). Personality. *Annual Review of Psychology, 52,* 197–222.

Funder, D. C. (2004). *The personality puzzle* (3rd ed.). New York: Norton.

Fung, M. T., Raine, A., Loeber, R., Lynam, D. R., Steinhauer, S. R., Venables, P. H., et al. (2005). Reduced electrodermal activity in psychopathy-prone adolescents. *Journal of Abnormal Psychology, 114,* 187–196.

Funtowicz, M. N., & Widiger, T. A. (1999). Sex bias in the diagnosis of personality disorders: An evaluation of DSM-IV criteria. *Journal of Abnormal Psychology, 108,* 195–201.

Furey, M. L., Pietrini, P., & Haxby, J. V. (2000). Cholinergic enhancement and increased selectivity of perceptual processing during working memory. *Science, 290,* 2315–2319.

Furnham, A. (2001). Personality and individual differences in the workplace: Person-organization-outcome fit. In R. Hogan & B. Roberts (Eds.), *Personality psychology in the workplace* (pp. 223–251). Washington, DC: American Psychological Association.

G

Gabbard, G. O. (2004). *Long-term psychodynamic psychotherapy: A basic text.* Washington DC: American Psychiatric Association.

Gaillard, R., Del Cul, A., Naccache, L., Vinckier, F., Cohen, L., & Dehaene, S. (2006). Nonconscious semantic processing of emotional words modulates conscious access. *Proceedings of the National Academy of Sciences of the USA, 103,* 7524–7529.

Gais, S., & Born, J. (2004). Low acetylcholine during slow-wave sleep is critical for declarative memory consolidation. *Proceedings of the National Academy of Sciences, 101,* 2140–2144.

Galanter, E. (1962). Contemporary psychophysics. In R. Brown (Ed.), *New directions in psychology* (Vol. 1). New York: Holt, Rinehart, Winston.

Galatzer-Levy, R. M., Bachrach, H., Skolnikoff, A., & Waldron, S., Jr. (2000). *Does psychoanalysis work?* New Haven, CT: Yale University Press.

Galea, S., Ahern, J., Resnick H., Kilpatrick D., Bucuvalas M., Gold, J., & Vlahov, D. (2002). Psychological sequelae of the September 11 terrorist attacks in New York City. *New England Journal of Medicine, 346,* 982–987.

Galea, S., Resnick, H., Ahern, J., Gold, J., Bucuvalas, M., Kilpatrick, D., et al. (2002). Posttraumatic stress disorder in Manhattan, New York City, after the September 11th terrorist attacks. *Journal of Urban Health, 79,* 340–353.

Galinsky, A. D., & Kray, L. J. (2004). From thinking about what might have been to sharing what we know: The effects of counterfactual mind-sets on information sharing in groups. *Journal of Experimental Social Psychology, 40,* 606–618.

Gallagher, M. (1998, January 26). Day careless. *National Review,* pp. 37–41.

Gallagher, M., & Chiba, A. A. (1996). The amygdala and emotion. *Current Opinions in Neurobiology, 6*(2), 221–227.

Galloway, A. T., Addessi, E., Fragaszy, D. M., & Visalberghi, E. (2005). Social facilitation of eating familiar food in tufted capuchins (*Cebus appella*): Does it involve behavioral coordination? *International Journal of Primatology, 26,* 181–189.

Gallup. (1999, August 29). *American workers generally satisfied, but indicate their jobs leave much to be desired.* Princeton, NJ: Gallup Organization.

Galotti, K. M. (1999). *Cognitive psychology in and out of the laboratory* (2nd ed.). Belmont, CA: Brooks/Cole.

Gan, T. J., Jiao, K. R., Zenn, M., & Georgiade, G. (2004). A randomized controlled comparison of electro-acupoint stimulation or ondansetron versus placebo for the prevention of postoperative nausea and vomiting. *Anesthesia and Analgesia, 99,* 1070–1075.

Ganchrow, J. R., Steiner, J. E., & Daher, M. (1983). Neonatal facial expressions in response to different qualities and intensities of gustatory stimuli. *Infant Behavior and Development, 6,* 189–200.

Garb, H. N. (1997). Race bias, social class bias, and gender bias in clinical judgment. *Clinical Psychology: Science and Practice, 4,* 99–120.

Garb, H. N., Wood, J. M., Lilienfeld, S. O., & Nezworski, M. T. (2005). Roots of the Rorschach controversy. *Clinical Psychology Review, 25,* 97–118.

Garbarino, S., Nobili, L., Beelke, M., De Carli, F., & Ferrillo, F. (2001). The contributing role of sleepiness in highway vehicle accidents. *Sleep: Journal of Sleep Research and Sleep Medicine, 24,* 203–206.

Garber, J., Keiley, M. K., & Martin, N. C. (2002). Developmental trajectories of adolescents' depressive symptoms: Predictors of change. *Journal of Consulting and Clinical Psychology, 70,* 9–95.

Garbutt, J. C., Kranzler, H. R., O'Malley, S. S., Gastfriend, D. R., Pettinati, H. M., Silverman, B. L., et al. (2005). Efficacy and tolerability of long-acting injectable naltrexone for alcohol dependence: A randomized controlled trial. *Journal of the American Medical Association, 293,* 1617–1625.

Garcia, J., & Koelling, R. A. (1966). Relation of cue to consequences in avoidance learning. *Psychonomic Science, 4,* 123–124.

Garcia, S. M., Weaver, K., Moskowitz, G. B., & Darley, J. M. (2002). Crowded minds: The implicit bystander effect. *Journal of Personality and Social Psychology, 83,* 843–853.

Gardiner, H. W., & Kosmitzki, C. (2005). *Lives across cultures: Cross-cultural human development* (3rd ed.). Needham Heights, MA: Allyn & Bacon.

Gardner, H. (1993). *Multiple intelligences: The theory in practice.* New York: Basic Books.

Gardner, H. (1999). Are there additional intelligences? The case for naturalist, spiritual, and existential intelligences. In J. Kane (Ed.), *Education, information and transformation: Essays on learning and thinking* (pp. 111–131). Englewood Cliffs, NJ: Prentice Hall.

Gardner, H. (2002). *Learning from extraordinary minds.* Mahwah, NJ: Erlbaum.

Gardner, M. (1988). *The second Scientific American book of mathematical puzzles and diversions.* Chicago: University of Chicago Press.

Gardner, R., Heward, W. L., & Grossi, T. A. (1994). Effects of response cards on student participation and academic achievement: A systematic replication with inner-city students during whole-class science instruction. *Journal of Applied Behavior Analysis, 27,* 63–71.

Garfield, S. L. (1998). Some comments on empirically supported treatments. *Journal of Consulting and Clinical Psychology, 66,* 121–125.

Garlick, D. (2003). Integrating brain science research with intelligence research. *Current Directions in Psychological Science, 12,* 185–188.

Garry, M., & Gerrie, M. P. (2005). When photographs create false memories. *Current Directions in Psychological Science, 14,* 321–325.

Garry, M., & Loftus, E. (1994). Pseudomemories without hypnosis. *International Journal of Clinical and Experimental Hypnosis, 42*(4), 363–373.

Garry, M., & Polaschek, D. L. L. (2000). Imagination and memory. *Current Directions in Psychological Science, 9,* 6–10.

Gatewood, R. D., & Feild, H. S. (2001). *Human resource selection* (5th ed.). Fort Worth, TX: Harcourt.

Gaudiano, B. A., & Dalrymple, K. L. (2005). EMDR variants, pseudoscience, and the demise of empirically supported treatments? *PsycCRITIQUES, 50,* 8.

Gauvain, M. (2001). *The social context of cognitive development.* New York: Guilford.

Gazzaniga, M. S., & LeDoux, J. E. (1978). *The integrated mind.* New York: Plenum.

Ge, X., Conger, R., & Elder, G. H. (2001) Pubertal transition, stressful life events, and the emergence of gender differences in adolescent depressive symptoms. *Developmental Psychology, 37,* 404–417.

Geary, D. C. (1999). Evolution and developmental sex differences. *Current Directions in Psychological Science, 8,* 115–120.

Geary, D. C. (2000). Evolution and proximate expression of human paternal investment. *Psychological Bulletin, 126,* 55–77.

Geddes, J. R., Burgess, S., Hawton, K., Jamison, K., & Goodwin, G. M. (2004). Long-term lithium therapy for bipolar disorder: Systematic review and meta-analysis of randomized controlled trials. *American Journal of Psychiatry, 161,* 217–222.

Geen, R. G. (1998). Aggression and antisocial behavior. In D. Gilbert, S. T. Fiske, & G. Lindzey (Eds.), *Handbook of social psychology* (Vol. 2, 4th ed., pp. 317–356). Boston: McGraw-Hill.

Gelabert-Gonzalez, M., & Fernandez-Villa, J. (2001). Mutism after posterior fossa surgery: Review of the literature. *Clinical Neurology & Neurosurgery, 103,* 111–114.

Geldmacher, D. S., Provenzano, G., McRae, T., Mastey, V., & Ieni, J. R. (2003). Donepezil is associated with delayed nursing home placement in patients with Alzheimer's disease. *Journal of the American Geriatric Society, 51*(7), 937–944.

Gellhorn, E., & Loofbourrow, G. N. (1963). *Emotions and emotional disorders.* New York: Harper & Row.

Gelman, R., & Baillargeon, R. (1983). A review of some Piagetian concepts. In P. H. Mussen (Ed.), *Handbook of child psychology* (Vol. 3, pp. 167–230). New York: Wiley.

Gendle, M. H., White, T. L., Strawderman, M., Mactutus, C. F., Booze, R. M., Levitsky, D. A., & Strupp, B. J. (2004). Enduring effects of prenatal cocaine exposure on selective attention and reactivity to errors: Evidence from an animal model. *Behavioral Neuroscience, 118,* 290–297.

George, M. S., Anton, R. F., Bloomer, C., Teneback, C., Drobes, D. J., Lorberbaum, J. P., et al. (2001). Activation of prefrontal cortex and anterior thalamus in alcoholic subjects on exposure to alcohol-specific cues. *Archives of General Psychiatry, 58,* 345–352.

George, W. H., & Marlatt, G. A. (1986). The effects of alcohol and anger on interest in violence, erotica, and deviance. *Journal of Abnormal Psychology, 95,* 150–158.

Geraerts, E., Smeets, E., Jelicic, M., Merckelbach, H., & van Heerden, J. (2006). Retrieval inhibition of trauma-related words in women reporting repressed or recovered memories of childhood sexual abuse. *Behaviour Research and Therapy, 44,* 1129–1136.

Gerbner, G., Morgan, M., & Signorielli, N. (1994). *Television violence profile No. 16: The turning point.* Philadelphia: Annenberg School for Communication.

Gerhart, B. (2005). The (affective) dispositional approach to job satisfaction: Sorting out the policy implications. *Journal of Organizational Behavior, 26,* 79–97.

Gerin, W., Davidson, K. W., Christenfeld, N. J. S., Goyal, T., & Schwartz, J. E. (2006). The role of angry rumination and distraction in blood pressure recovery from emotional arousal. *Psychosomatic Medicine, 68,* 64–72.

German, T. P., & Barrett, H. C. (2005). Functional fixedness in a technologically sparse culture. *Psychological Science, 16*(1), 1–5.

Gernsbacher, M. A., Dawson, M., & Goldsmith, H. H. (2005). Three reasons not to believe in an autism epidemic. *Current Directions in Psychological Science, 14,* 55–58.

Gerschman, J. A., Reade, P. C., & Burrows, G. D. (1980). Hypnosis and dentistry. In G. D. Burrows & L. Dennerstein (Eds.), *Handbook of hypnosis and psychosomatic medicine.* Amsterdam: Elsevier.

Gershoff, E. T. (2002). Corporal punishment by parents and associated child behaviors and experiences: A meta-analytic and theoretical review. *Psychological Bulletin, 128,* 539–579.

Gershon, J., Anderson, P., Graap, K., Zimand, E., Hodges, L., & Rothbaum, B. O. (2002). Virtual reality exposure therapy in the treatment of anxiety disorders. *The Scientific Review of Mental Health Practice, 1.* Retrieved October 12, 2002 from http://www.scientificmentalhealth.org/SRMHP/current.html

Gerstner, C. R., & Day, D. V. (1997). Meta-analytic review of leader–member exchange theory: Correlates and construct issues. *Journal of Applied Psychology, 82,* 827–844.

Geschwind, N. (1968). Disconnexion syndromes in animals and man. *Brain, 88,* 237–294.

Geuze, E., Vermetten, E., & Bremner, J. D. (2005). MR-based in vivo hippocampal volumetrics: 2. Findings in neuropsychiatric disorders. *Molecular Psychiatry, 10,* 160–184.

Gfeller, J. D. (1994). Hypnotizability enhancement: Clinical implications of empirical findings. *American Journal of Clinical Hypnosis, 37*(2), 107–116.

Gianaros, P. J., May, J. C., Siegle, G. J., & Jennings, J. R. (2005). Is there a functional neural correlate of individual differences in cardiovascular reactivity? *Psychosomatic Medicine, 67,* 31–39.

Gibb, B. E., Alloy, L. B., Abramson, L. Y., Beevers, C. G., & Miller, I. W. (2004). Cognitive vulnerability to depression: A taxometric analysis. *Journal of Abnormal Psychology, 113,* 81–89.

Gibbons, R. D., Hur, K., Bhaumik, D. K., & Mann, J. J. (2005). The relationship between antidepressant use and rate of suicide. *Archives of General Psychiatry, 62,* 165–172.

Gibson, E. J., & Walk, R. D. (1960). The visual cliff. *Scientific American, 202,* 64–71.

Gifford-Smith, M., Dodge, K. A., Dishion, T. J., & McCord, J. (2005). Peer influence in children and adolescents: Crossing the bridge between developmental and intervention science. *Journal of Abnormal Child Psychology, 33,* 255–265.

Gigerenzer, G. (2004). Dread risk, September 11, and fatal traffic accidents. *Psychological Science, 15,* 286–287.

Gilbert, A. R., Rosenberg, D. R., Harenski, K., Spencer, S., Sweeney, J. A., & Keshavan, M. S. (2001). Thalamic volumes in patients with first-episode schizophrenia. *American Journal of Psychiatry, 158,* 618–624.

Gilbert, D. T. (1998). Ordinary personology. In D. Gilbert, S. T. Fiske, & G. Lindzey (Eds.), *Handbook of social psychology* (Vol.2, 4th ed., pp. 89–150). Boston: McGraw-Hill.

Gilbert, D. T., Morewedge, C. K., Risen, J. L., & Wilson, T. D. (2004). Looking forward to looking backward: The misprediction of regret. *Psychological Science, 15,* 346–350.

Gilbert, D. T., & Wilson, T. D. (1998). Miswanting: Some problems in the forecasting of future affective states. In J. P. Forgas (Ed.), *Feeling and thinking: The role of affect in social cognition* (pp. 178–197). New York: Cambridge University Press.

Gilbert, R., Salanti, G., Harden, M., & See, S. (2005). Infant sleeping position and the sudden infant death syndrome: A systematic review of observational studies and historical review of recommendations from 1940 to 2002. *International Journal of Epidemiology, 34,* 874–887.

Gilbert, S. (1997, August 20). Two spanking studies indicate parents should be cautious. *New York Times Magazine.*

Gilboa-Schechtman, E., & Foa, E. B. (2001). Patterns of recovery from trauma: The use of intraindividual analysis. *Journal of Abnormal Psychology, 110,* 392–400.

Giles, T. R. (1990). Bias against behavior therapy in outcome reviews: Who speaks for the patient? *The Behavior Therapist, 13,* 86–90.

Gilligan, C. (1982). *In a different voice: Psychological theory and women's development.* Cambridge, MA: Harvard University Press.

Gilligan, C. (1993). Adolescent development reconsidered. In A. Garrod (Ed.), *Approaches to moral development: New research and emerging themes.* New York: Teachers College Press.

Gilliland, F. D., Li, Y.-F., & Peters, J. M. (2001). Effects of maternal smoking during pregnancy and environmental tobacco smoke on asthma and wheezing in children. *American Journal of Respiratory and Critical Care Medicine, 163,* 429–436.

Gilmore, R. L., Heilman, K. M., Schmidt, R. P., Fennell, E. M., & Quisling, R. (1992). Anosognosia during Wada testing. *Neurology, 42*(4), 925–927.

Giltay, E. J., Geleijnse, J. M., Zitman, F. G., Hoekstra, T., & Schouten, E. G. (2004). Dispositional optimism and all-cause and cardiovascular mortality in a prospective cohort of elderly Dutch men and women. *Archives of General Psychiatry, 61,* 1126–1135.

Giltay, E. J., Kamphuis, M. H., Kalmijn, S., Zitman, F. G., & Kromhout, D. (2006). Dispositional optimism and the risk of cardiovascular death: The Zutphen elderly study. *Archives of Internal Medicine, 166,* 431–436.

Giorgi-Guarnieri, D., Janofsky, J., Keram, E., Lawsky, S., Merideth, P., Mossman, D., et al.(2002). AAPL practice guideline for forensic psychiatric evaluation of defendants raising the insanity defense. *Journal of the American Academy of Psychiatry and the Law, 30*(Suppl. 2), S1–S40.

Giosan, C., Glovsky, V., & Haslam, N. (2001). The lay conception of "mental disorder": A cross-cultural study. *Transcultural Psychiatry, 38,* 317–332.

Givens, B. (1995). Low doses of ethanol impair spatial working memory and reduce hippocampal theta activity. *Alcoholism Clinical and Experimental Research, 19*(3), 763–767.

Gladwell, M. (2004, January 12). Big and bad. *New Yorker,* 28–33.

Gladwell, M. (2005). *Blink: The power of thinking without thinking.* New York: Little, Brown.

Glantz, K., Rizzo, A., & Graap, K. (2003). Virtual reality for psychotherapy: Current reality and future possibilities. *Psychotherapy: Theory, Research, Practice, and Training, 40,* 55–67.

Glanzer, M., & Cunitz, A. (1966). Two storage mechanisms in free recall. *Journal of Verbal Learning and Verbal Behavior, 5,* 351–360.

Glassop, L. I. (2002). The organizational benefits of teams. *Human Relations, 55,* 225–249.

Gleaves, D. H., May, M. C., & Cardena, E. (2001). An examination of the diagnostic validity of dissociative identity disorder. *Clinical Psychology Review, 21,* 577–608.

Gleitman, L., & Landau, B. (1994). *The acquisition of the lexicon.* Cambridge: MIT Press.

Gleuckauf, R., & Quittner, A. (1992). Assertiveness training for disabled adults in wheelchairs: Self-report, role-play, and activity pattern outcomes. *Journal of Consulting and Clinical Psychology, 60,* 419–425.

Glover, J. A., Krug, D., Dietzer, M., George, B. W., & Hannon, M. (1990). "Advance" advance organizers. *Bulletin of the Psychonomic Society, 28,* 4–6.

Goenjian, A. K., Molina, L., Steinberg, A. M., Fairbanks, L. A., Alvarez, M. L., Goenjian, H. A., & Pynoos, R. S. (2001). Posttraumatic stress and depressive reactions among Nicaraguan adolescents after hurricane Mitch. *American Journal of Psychiatry, 158,* 788–794.

Goethals, G. R. (2005). Presidential leadership. *Annual Review of Psychology, 56,* 545–570.

Gogtay, N., Giedd, J. N., Lusk, L., Hayashi, K. M., Greenstein, D., Vaituzis, A. C., Nugent, T. F., III, Herman, D. H., Clasen, L. S., Toga, A. W., Rapoport, J. L., & Thompson, P. M. (2004). Dynamic mapping of human cortical development during childhood through early adulthood. *Proceedings of the National Academy of Sciences, 101,* 8174–8179.

Gold, M. S. (1994). The epidemiology, attitudes, and pharmacology of LSD use in the 1990s. *Psychiatric Annals, 24*(3), 124–126.

Goldberg, J. F., Harrow, M., & Grossman, L. S. (1995). Course and outcome in bipolar affective disorder: A longitudinal follow-up study. *American Journal of Psychiatry, 152,* 379–384.

Goldberg, J. F., & Garno, J. L. (2005). Development of posttraumatic stress disorder in adult bipolar patients with histories of severe childhood abuse. *Journal of Psychiatric Research, 39,* 595–601.

Goldblum, N. (2001). *The brain-shaped mind: A neural-network view: What the brain can tell us about the mind.* Cambridge: Cambridge University Press.

Golden, R. N., Gaynes, B. N., Ekstrom, R. D., Hamer, R. M., Jacobsen, F. M., Suppes, T., et al. (2005). The efficacy of light therapy in the treatment of mood disorders: A review and meta-analysis of the evidence. *American Journal of Psychiatry, 162,* 656–662.

Goldenberg, I., & Goldenberg, H. (1995). Family therapy. In R. J. Corsini & D. Wedding (Eds.), *Current psychotherapies* (5th ed.). Itasca, IL: Peacock.

Goldfried, M. R., & Davila, J. (2005). The role of relationship and technique in therapeutic change. *Psychotherapy: Theory, Research, Practice, Training, 42,* 421–430.

Goldman, M. S., Darkes, J., & Del Boca, F. K. (1999). Expectancy meditation of biopsychosocial risk for alcohol use and alcoholism. In I. Kirsch (Ed.), *How expectancies shape experience* (pp. 233–262). Washington, DC: American Psychological Association.

Goldstein, A. J., de Beurs, E., Chambless, D. L., & Wilson, K. A. (2000). EMDR for panic disorder with agoraphobia: Comparison with waiting list and credible attention-placebo control conditions. *Journal of Consulting and Clinical Psychology, 68,* 947–956.

Goldstein, E. B. (2002). *Sensation and perception* (6th ed.). Pacific Grove CA: Wadsworth.

Goldstein, I. L. (1993). *Training in organizations: Needs assessment, development, and evaluation* (3rd ed.). Monterey, CA: Brooks/Cole.

Goldstein, I., & Rosen, R. C. (Eds.). (2002). Guest editors' introduction: Female sexuality and sexual dysfunction. *Archives of Sexual Behavior, 31,* 391.

Goldstein, M. H., King, A. P., & West, M. J. (2003). Social interaction shapes babbling: Testing parallels between birdsong and speech. *Proceedings of the National Academy of Sciences, 100,* 8030–8035.

Goldstein, R. Z., & Volkow, N. D. (2002). Drug addiction and its underlying neurobiological basis: Neuroimaging evidence for the involvement of the frontal cortex. *American Journal of Psychiatry,159,* 1642–1652.

Goldstein, S. E., Davis-Kean, P. E., & Eccles, J. S. (2005). Parents, peers, and problem behavior: A longitudinal investigation of the impact of relationship perceptions and characteristics on the development of adolescent problem behavior. *Developmental Psychology, 41,* 401–413.

Golomb, J., Kluger, A., De Leon, M. J., Ferris, S. H., Mittelman, M., Cohen, J., & George, A. E. (1996). Hippocampal formation size predicts declining memory performance in normal aging. *Neurology, 47,* 810–813.

Goltz, H. C., DeSouza, J. F. X., Menon, R. S., Tweed, D. B., & Vilis, T. (2003). Interaction of retinal image and eye velocity in motion perception. *Neuron, 39,* 569–576.

Gone, J. (2004). Mental health services for Native Americans in the 21st century United States. *Professional Psychology: Theory and Practice, 35,* 10–18.

Gonsalves, B., & Paller, K. A. (2000). Neural events that underlie remembering something that never happened. *Nature Neuroscience, 3,* 1316–1321.

Gonsalves, B. D., Kahn, I., Curran, T., Norman, K. A., & Wagner, A. D. (2005). Memory strength and repetition suppression: Multimodal imaging of medial temporal cortical contributions to recognition. *Neuron, 47,* 751–761.

Gonzalez, J. S., Penedo, F. J., Antoni, M. H., Duran, R. E., McPherson-Baker, S., Ironson, G., et al. (2004). Social support, positive states of mind, and HIV treatment adherence in men and women living with HIV/AIDS. *Health Psychology, 23,* 413–418.

Goodenough, F. L. (1932). Expression of the emotions in a blind-deaf child. *Journal of Abnormal and Social Psychology, 27,* 328–333.

Goodglass, H., & Kaplan, E. (1982). *The assessment of aphasia and related disorders* (2nd ed.). Philadelphia: Lea & Febiger.

Goodman, G. S., Ghetti, S., Quas, J. A., Edelstein, R. S., Alexander, K. W., Redlich, A. D., et al. (2003). A prospective study of memory for child sexual abuse: New findings relevant to the repressed-memory controversy. *Psychological Science, 14,* 113–118.

Goodwin, F. K., & Jamison, K. R. (Eds.). (1990). *Manic-depressive illness.* New York: Oxford University Press.

Goodwin, G. M., Bowden, C. L., & Calabrese, J. R. (2004). A pooled analysis of 2 placebo-controlled 18-month trials of lamotrigine and lithium maintenance in bipolar I disorder. *Journal of Clinical Psychiatry, 65*(3), 432–441.

Gordon, D. B., Dahl, J. L., Miaskowski, C., McCarberg, B., Todd, K. H., Paice, J. A., et al. (2005). American Pain Society recommendations for improving the quality of acute and cancer pain management: American Pain Society Quality of Care Task Force. *Archives of Internal Medicine, 165,* 1574–1580.

Gorman, J. M. (2003). Treating generalized anxiety disorder. *Journal of Clinical Psychiatry,* 64(Suppl. 2), 24–29. Gosling, S. D. (2001). From mice to men: What can we learn about personality from animal research? *Psychological Bulletin, 127,* 45–86.

Gorman, J. M. (2005). Benzodiazepines: Taking the good with the bad and the ugly. *CNS Spectrums, 10,* 14–15.

Gorter, R. W., Butorac, M., Cobian, E. P., & van der Sluis, W. (2005). Medical use of cannabis in the Netherlands. *Neurology, 64,* 917–919.

Gosling, S. D. (2001). From mice to men: What can we learn about personality from animal research? *Psychological Bulletin, 127,* 45–86.

Gosling, S. D., Kwan, V. S. Y., & John, O. P. (2003). A dog's got personality: A cross-species comparative approach to personality judgments in dogs and humans. *Journal of Personality and Social Psychology, 85,* 1161–1169.

Gosling, S. D., Vazire, S., Srivastava, S., & John, O. P. (2004). Should we trust web-based studies? A comparative analysis of six preconceptions about Internet questionnaires. *American Psychologist, 59,* 93–104.

Goss Lucas, S., & Bernstein, D. A. (2005). *Teaching psychology: A step by step guide.* Mahwah, NJ: Erlbaum.

Gotlib, I. H., & Hammen, C. L. (1992). *Psychological aspects of depression: Toward cognitive interpersonal integration.* Chichester, England: Wiley.

Gotlib, I. H., Krasnoperova, E., Yue, D. N., & Joorman, J. (2004). Attentional biases for negative interpersonal stimuli in clinical depression. *Journal of Abnormal Psychology, 113,* 127–135.

Gottesman, I. I. (1991). *Schizophrenia genesis: The origins of madness.* New York: Freeman.

Gottfredson, L. S. (1997). Why g matters: The complexity of everyday life. *Intelligence, 24,* 79–132.

Gottfredson, L. S. (2004). Intelligence: Is it the epidemiologists' elusive "fundamental cause" of social class inequalities in health? *Journal of Personality and Social Psychology, 86,* 174–199.

Gottfredson, L. S., & Deary, I. J. (2004). Intelligence predicts health and longevity, but why? *Current Directions in Psychological Science, 13,* 1–4.

Gottfried, A. W. (1997, June). Parents' role is critical to children's learning. *APA Monitor,* p. 24.

Gottman, J. M., & Levenson, R. W. (2002). A two-factor model for predicting when a couple will divorce: Exploratory analyses using 14-year longitudinal data. *Family Process, 41,* 83–96.

Gould, E., Beylin, A., Tanapat, P., Reeves, A., & Schors, T. J. (1999). Learning enhances adult neurogenesis in the hippocampal formation. *Nature Neuroscience, 2,* 260–265.

Gould, R. A., Otto, M. W., Pollack, M. H., & Yap, L. (1997). Cognitive behavioral and pharmacological treatment of generalized anxiety disorder: A preliminary meta-analysis. *Behavior Therapy, 28,* 285–305.

Gow, A. J., Whiteman, M. C., Pattie, A., Whalley, L., Starr, J., & Deary, I. J. (2005). Lifetime intellectual function and satisfaction with life in old age: Longitudinal cohort study. *British Medical Journal, 331,* 141–142.

Graeber, M. B., & Mehraein, P. (1999). Reanalysis of the first case of Alzheimer's disease. *European Archives of Psychiatry and Clinical Neuroscience, 249*(Suppl. 3), 10–13.

Grammer, K., Fink, B., & Neave, N. (2005). Human pheromones and sexual attraction. *European Journal of Obstetrics, Gynecology, and Reproductive Biology, 118,* 135–142.

Grandin, T. (1996). *Thinking in pictures: And other reports from my life with autism.* New York: Vintage Press.

Grant, B. F., Dawson, D. A., Stinson, F. S., Chou, S. P., Dufour, M. C., & Pickering, R. P. (2004). The 12-month prevalence and trends in DSM-IV alcohol abuse and dependence: United States, 1991–1992 and 2001–2002. *Drug and Alcohol Dependence, 74,* 223–234.

Grant, H., & Dweck, C. S. (2003). Clarifying achievement goals and their impact. *Journal of Personality and Social Psychology, 85,* 541–553.

Grant, J. E., & Kim, S. W. (2002). *Stop me because I can't stop myself: Taking control of impulsive behavior.* New York: McGraw-Hill.

Grassi, L., Rasconi, G., Pedriali, A., Corridoni, A., & Bevilacqua, M. (2000). Social support and psychological distress in primary care attenders. *Psychotherapy and Psychosomatics, 69,* 95–100.

Graves, L., Pack, A., & Abel, T. (2001). Sleep and memory: A molecular perspective. *Trends in Neurosciences, 24,* 237–243.

Gray, J. A. (1991). Neural systems, emotions, and personality. In J. Madden IV (Ed.), *Neurobiology of learning, emotion, and affect* (pp. 272–306). New York: Raven Press.

Gray, J. R., Chabris, C. F., & Braver, T. S. (2003). Neural mechanisms of general fluid intelligence. *Nature Neuroscience, 6,* 316–322.

Gray, N., & Nye, P. S. (2001). American Indian and Alaska Native substance abuse: Co-morbidity and cultural issues. *American Indian and Alaska Native Mental Health Research, 10,* 67–84.

Gray, N. S., MacCulloch, M. J., Smith, J., Morris, M., & Snowden, R. J. (2003). Forensic psychology: Violence viewed by psychopathic murderers. *Nature, 423,* 497.

Gray-Little, B., & Hafdahl, A. R. (2000). Factors influencing racial comparisons of self-esteem: A quantitative review. *Psychological Bulletin, 126,* 26–54.

Graziano, M. S., Taylor, C. S., & Moore, T. (2002). Complex movements evoked by microstimulation of precentral cortex. *Neuron, 34,* 841–851.

Graziano, M. S. A., Alisharan, S. E., Hu, X., & Gross, C. G. (2002). The clothing effect: Tactile neurons in the precentral gyrus do not respond to the touch of the familiar primate chair. *Proceedings of the New York Academy of Sciences, 99,* 11930–11933.

Green, A. I., & Patel, J. K. (1996) The new pharmacology of schizophrenia. *Harvard Mental Health Letter, 13*(6), 5–7.

Green, C. S., & Bavelier, D. (2003). Action video game modifies visual selective attention. *Nature, 423,* 534–537.

Green, D. M., & Swets, J. A. (1966). *Signal detection theory and psychophysics.* New York: Wiley.

Green, R. A., Cross, A. J., & Goodwin, G. M. (1995). Review of the pharmacology and clinical pharmacology of 3,4-methylenedioxymethamphetamine (MDMA or "ecstacy"). *Psychopharmacology, 119,* 247–260.

Greenberg, J. (2002). Who stole the money and when? Individual and situational determinants of employee theft. *Organizational Behavior and Human Decision Processes, 89,* 985–1003.

Greenberg, J. R., & Mitchell, S. A. (1983). *Object relations in psychoanalytic theory.* Cambridge, MA: Harvard University Press.

Greenberg, J., Pyszczynski, T., & Solomon, S. (2003). A perilous leap from Becker's theorizing to empirical science: Terror management and research. In D. Leichty (Ed.), *Death and denial: Interdisciplinary essays: The legacy of Ernest Becker.* New York: Praeger.

Greenberg, J., Solomon, S., Pyszczynski, T., & Rosenblatt, A. (1992). Why do people need self-esteem? Converging evidence that self-esteem serves an anxiety-buffering function. *Journal of Personality and Social Psychology, 63,* 913–922.

Greenberg, M. T., Lengua, L. J., Coie, J. D., Pinderhughes, E. E., Bierman, K., Dodge, K. A., et al. (1999). Predicting developmental outcomes at school entry using a multiple-risk model: Four American communities. *Developmental Psychology, 35,* 403–417.

Greenberg, R. M., & Kellner, C. H. (2005). Electroconvulsive therapy: A selected review. *American Journal of Geriatric Psychiatry, 13,* 268–281.

Greenfield, P. M. (1994). Video games as cultural artifacts. *Journal of Applied Developmental Psychology, 15,* 3–12.

Greenfield, P. M., & Childs, C. P. (1991). Developmental continuity in biocultural context. In R. Cohen & A. W. Siegel (Eds.), *Context and development* (pp. 135–159). Hillsdale, NJ: Erlbaum.

Greenfield, P. M., Suzuki, L. K., & Rothstein-Fisch, C. (2006). Cultural pathways through human development. In W. Damon & R. M. Lerner (Series Eds.) & K. A. Renninger & I. E. Sigel (Vol. Eds.), *Handbook of child psychology: Vol. 4. Child psychology in practice* (6th ed.). New York: Wiley.

Greenhaus, J. H., Parasuraman, S., & Wormley, W. M. (1990). Effects of race on organizational experiences, job performance evaluations, and career outcomes. *Academy of Management Journal, 33,* 64–86.

Greenland, P., Knoll, M. D., Stamler, J., Neaton, J. D., Dyer, A. R., Garside, D. B., & Wilson, P. W. (2003). Major risk factors as antecedents of fatal and nonfatal coronary heart disease events. *Journal of the American Medical Association, 290,* 891–897.

Greenwald, A. G., & Banaji, M. R. (1995). Implicit social cognition: Attitudes, self-esteem, and stereotypes. *Psychological Review, 102,* 4–27.

Greenwald, A. G., Klinger, M. R., & Schuh, E. S. (1995). Activation by marginally perceptible ("subliminal") stimuli: Dissociation of unconscious from conscious cognition. *Experimental Psychology: General, 124*(1), 22–42.

Greenwood, T. A., Schork, N. J., Eskin, E., & Kelsoe, J. R. (2006). Identification of additional variants within the human dopamine transporter gene provides further evidence for an association with bipolar disorder in two independent samples. *Molecular Psychiatry, 11,* 125–133.

Greer, A. E., & Buss, D. M. (1994). Tactics for promoting sexual encounters. *Journal of Sex Research, 31*(3), 185–201.

Gregory, R. L. (2005). Seeing after blindness. *Nature Neuroscience, 6,* 909–910.

Gregory, S. W., & Webster, S. (1996). A nonverbal signal in voices of interview partners effectively predicts communication accommodation and social status perceptions. *Journal of Personality and Social Psychology, 70,* 1231–1240.

Griesinger, C. B., Richards, C. D., & Ashmore, J. F. (2005). Fast vesicle replenishment allows indefatigable signalling at the first auditory synapse. *Nature, 435,* 212–215.

Griffeth, R. W., Hom, P. W., & Gaertner, S. (2000). A meta-analysis of antecedents and correlates of employee turnover: Update, moderator tests, and research implications for the next millennium. *Journal of Management, 26,* 463–488.

Griffin, M. A., & Neal, A. (2000). Perceptions of safety at work: A framework for linking safety climate to safety performance, knowledge, and motivation. *Journal of Occupational Health Psychology, 5,* 347–358.

Griffitt, W. B., & Guay, P. (1969) "Object" evaluation and conditioned affect. *Journal of Experimental Research in Personality, 4,* 1–8.

Grigorenko, E. L. (2002). In search of the genetic engram of personality. In D. Cervone & W. Mischel (Eds.), *Advances in personality science* (pp. 29–82). New York: The Guilford Press.

Grinspoon, L. (1999). The future of medical marijuana. *Forsch Komplementarmed, 6,* 40–43.

Grinspoon, S., Thomas, E., Pitts, S., Gross, E., Mickley, D., Killer, K., et al. (2000). Prevalence and predictive factors for regional osteopenia in women with anorexia nervosa. *Annals of Internal Medicine, 133,* 790–794.

Grob, C., & Dobkin de Rios, M. (1992). Adolescent drug use in cross-cultural perspective. *Journal of Drug Issues, 22*(1), 121–138.

Gronau, N., Ben-Shakhar, G., & Cohen, A. (2005). Behavioral and physiological measures in the detection of concealed information. *Journal of Applied Psychology, 90,* 147–158.

Grønnerød, C. (2003). Temporal stability in the Rorschach method. *Journal of Personality Assessment, 80,* 272–293.

Groopman, J. (2000, January 24). Second opinion. *The New Yorker,* pp. 40–49.

Groopman, J. (2002, July 29). Hormones for men. *The New Yorker,* pp. 34–38.

Groopman, J. (2005, May 2). A model patient. *New Yorker,* 48–54.

Gross, J. J. (2001). Emotion regulation in adulthood: Timing is everything. *Current Directions in Psychological Science, 10,* 214–219.

Grossberg, S., & Seidman, D. (2006). Neural dynamics of autistic behaviors: Cognitive, emotional, and timing substrates. *Psychological Review, 113,* 483–525.

Grossman, M., & Ash, S. (2004). Primary progressive aphasia: A review. *Neurocase, 10*(1), 3–18.

Grote, N. K., & Clark, M. S. (2001). Perceiving unfairness in the family: Cause or consequence of marital distress? *Journal of Personality and Social Psychology, 80,* 281–293.

Groth-Marnat, G. (1997). *Handbook of psychological assessment* (3rd ed.). New York: Wiley.

Grubb, P. L., Roberts, R. K., Swanson, N. G., Burnfield, J. L., & Childress, J. H. (2005). Organizational factors and psychological aggression: Results from a nationally representative sample of US companies. In V. Bowie, B. S. Fisher, & C. L. Cooper (Eds.), *Workplace violence: Issues, trends, strategies* (pp. 37–59). Portland, OR: Willan Publishing.

Grunberg, N. E. (1994). Overview: Biological processes relevant to drugs of dependence. *Addiction, 89*(11), 1443–1446.

Grusec, J. E., Davidov, M., & Lundell, L. (2002). Prosocial and helping behavior. In P. K. Smith & C. H. Hart (Eds.), *Blackwell handbook of childhood social development* (pp. 457–474). Malden, MA: Blackwell.

Grusec, J. E., & Goodnow, J. J. (1994). Impact of parental discipline methods on the child's internalization of values. *Developmental Psychology, 30,* 4–19.

Guadagno, R. E., Asher, T., Demaine, L. J., & Cialdini, R. B. (2001). When saying yes leads to saying no: Preference for consistency and the reverse foot-in-the-door effect. *Personality and Social Psychology Bulletin, 27,* 859–867.

Guerin, D. W., Gottfried, A. W., & Thomas, C. W. (1997). Difficult temperament and behaviour problems: A longitudinal study from 1.5 to 12 years. *International Journal of Behavioral Development, 21,* 71–90.

Guilford, J. P. (1959). Traits of creativity. In H. H. Anderson (Ed.), *Creativity and its cultivation* (pp. 142–161). New York: Harper & Row.

Guilleminault, C., Palombini, L., Pelayo, R., & Chervin, R. D. (2003). Sleepwalking and sleep terrors in prepubertal children: What triggers them? *Pediatrics, 111,* 17–25.

Guimon, J. (2004). Evidence-based research studies on the results of group therapy: A critical review. *European Journal of Psychiatry, 18*(Suppl.), 49–60.

Gupta, V. K., & Reiter, E. R. (2004). Current treatment practices in obstructive sleep apnea and snoring. *American Journal of Otolaryngology, 25,* 18–25.

Gur, R. C., Skolnic, B. E., & Gur, R. E. (1994). Effects of emotional discrimination tasks on cerebral blood flow: Regional activation and its relation to performance. *Brain and Cognition, 25*(2), 271–286.

Gura, T. (1999). Leptin not impressive in clinical trial. *Science, 286,* 881–882.

Gurman, A. S., & Jacobson, N. S. (2002). *Clinical handbook of couple therapy* (3rd ed.). New York: Guilford Press.

Gushue, G. V. (2004). Race, color-blind attitudes, and judgments about mental health: A shifting standards perspective. *Journal of Counseling Psychology, 51,* 398–407.

Gushue, G. V. (2004). Race, color-blind racial attitudes, and judgments about mental health: A shifting standards perspective. *Journal of Counseling Psychology, 51,* 398–407.

Gustafson, D., Rothenberg, E., Blennow, K., Steen, B., & Skoog, I. (2003) An 18-year follow-up of overweight and risk of Alzheimer disease. *Archives of Internal Medicine, 163,* 1524–1528.

Guthrie, R. M., & Bryant, R. A. (2005). Auditory startle response in firefighters before and after trauma exposure. *American Journal of Psychiatry, 162,* 283–290.

Guyer, B., Freedman, M. A., Strobino, D. M., & Sondik, E. J. (2000). Annual summary of vital statistics: Trends in the health of Americans during the 20th century. *Pediatrics, 106,* 1307–1317.

Guyton, A. C. (1991). *Textbook of medical physiology* (8th ed.). Philadelphia: Saunders.

H

Ha, H., Tan, E. C., Fukunaga, H., & Aochi, O. (1981). Naloxone reversal of acupuncture analgesia in the monkey. *Experimental Neurology, 73,* 298–303.

Haaga, D. A. (2000). Introduction to the special section on stepped care models in psychotherapy. *Journal of Consulting and Clinical Psychology, 68,* 547–548.

Haber, R. N. (1979). Twenty years of haunting eidetic imagery: Where's the ghost? *The Behavioral and Brain Sciences, 2,* 583–629.

Haberlandt, K. (1999). *Human memory: Exploration and application.* Boston: Allyn & Bacon.

Haberstroh, J. (1995). *Ice cube sex: The truth about subliminal advertising.* South Bend, IN: Cross Cultural Publications/Crossroads.

Hackel, L. S., & Ruble, D. N. (1992). Changes in the marital relationship after the first baby is born: Predicting the impact of expectancy-disconfirmation. *Journal of Personality and Social Psychology, 62,* 944–957.

Hacking, I. (1995). *Rewriting the soul: Multiple personality and the sciences of memory.* Princeton, NJ: Princeton University Press.

Hackman, J. R. (1998). Why don't teams work? In R. S. Tindale, J. Edwards, & E. J. Posavac (Eds.), *Applications of theory and research on groups to social issues.* New York: Plenum.

Hackman, J. R., & Oldham, G. R. (1980). *Work redesign.* Reading, MA: Addison-Wesley.

Haddock, G., & Zanna, M. P. (1998). Affect, cognition, and the prediction of social attitudes. In W. Stroebe & M. Hewstone (Eds.), *European review of social psychology* (Vol. 10). New York: Wiley.

Hadjikhani, N., & de Gelder, B. (2003). Seeing fearful body expressions activates the fusiform cortex and amygdale. *Current Biology, 13,* 2201–2205.

Hagen, E. P. (1980). *Identification of the gifted.* New York: Teachers College Press.

Hake, R. R. (1998). Interactive-engagement vs. traditional methods: A six-thousand-student survey of mechanics test data for introductory physics courses. *American Journal of Physics, 66,* 64–74.

Hakuta, K., Bialystok, E., & Wiley, E. (2003). Critical evidence: A test of the critical-period hypothesis for second language acquisition. *Psychological Science, 14,* 31–38.

Haldeman, D. C. (1994). The practice and ethics of sexual orientation-conversion therapy. *Consulting and Clinical Psychology, 62*(2), 221–227.

Halford, G. S., Baker, R., McCredden, J. E., & Bain, J. D. (2005). How many variables can humans process? *Psychological Science, 16*(1), 70–76.

Hall, C. S., Lindzey, G., & Campbell, J. P. (1998). *Theories of personality* (4th ed.). New York: Wiley.

Hall, L. K., & Bahrick, H. P. (1998). The validity of metacognitive predictions of widespread learning and long-term retention. In G. Mazzoni & T. Nelson (Eds.), *Metacognition and cognitive neuropsychology: Monitoring and control processes* (pp. 23–36). Mahwah, NJ: Erlbaum.

Hall, W., & Degenhardt, L. (2003). Medical marijuana initiatives: Are they justified? How successful are they likely to be? *CNS Drugs, 17,* 689–697.

Halligan, P. W., & David, A. S. (Eds.). (1999). *Conversion hysteria: Towards a cognitive neuropsychological account.* Hove, UK: Psychology Press.

Halloran, M. J., & Kashima, E. S. (2004). Social identity and worldview validation: The effects of ingroup identity primes and mortality salience on value endorsement. *Personality and Social Psychology Bulletin, 30,* 915–925.

Halperin, J. M., & Schulz, K. P. (2006). Revisiting the role of the prefrontal cortex in the pathophysiology of attention-deficit/hyperactivity disorder. *Psychological Bulletin, 132,* 560–581.

Halpern, D. F. (1997). Sex differences in intelligence. *American Psychologist, 52,* 1091–1102.

Halpern, D. F. (2005). Psychology at the intersection of work and family: Recommendations for employers, working families, and policymakers. *American Psychologist, 60,* 397–409.

Halpern, D. F., & Hakel, M. D. (2003). *Applying the science of learning to university teaching and beyond: New directions for teaching and learning.* San Francisco: Jossey-Bass.

Hamad, G. G. (2004). The state of the art in bariatric surgery for weight loss in the morbidly obese patient. *Clinics in Plastic Surgery, 31,* 591–600.

Hamann, S., Herman, R. A., Nolan, C. L., & Wallen, K. (2004). Men and women differ in amygdala response to sexual stimuli. *Nature Neuroscience, 7,* 411–416.

Hamarat, E., Thompson, D., Steele, D., Matheny, K., & Simons, C. (2002). Age differences in coping resources and satisfaction with life among middle-aged, young-old, and oldest-old adults. *Journal of Genetic Psychology, 163*(3), 360–367.

Hamilton, C. E. (2000). Continuity and discontinuity of attachment from infancy through adolescence. *Child Development, 71,* 690–694.

Hamilton, D. L., & Sherman, J. (1994). Social stereotypes. In R. S. Wyer & T. K. Srull (Eds.), *Handbook of social cognition* (2nd ed.). Hillsdale, NJ: Erlbaum.

Hamilton, S. P., Fyer, A. J., Durner, M., Heiman, G. A., Baisre de Leon, A., Hodge, S. E., et al. (2003). Further genetic evidence for a panic disorder syndrome mapping to chromosome 13q. *Proceedings of the National Academy of Sciences, 100,* 2550–2255.

Hamilton, W. D. (1964). The evolution of social behavior: Parts I and II. *Journal of Theoretical Biology 7,* 1–52.

Hamm, A. O., Vaitl, D., & Lang, P. J. (1989). Fear conditioning, meaning, and belongingness: A selective association analysis. *Journal of Abnormal Psychology, 98,* 395–406.

Hammad, T. A., Laughren, T., & Racoosin, J. (2006). Suicidality in pediatric patients treated with antidepressant drugs. *Archives of General Psychiatry, 63,* 332–339.

Hammerness, P., Basch, E., & Ulbricht, C. (2003). St. John's wort: A systematic review of adverse effects and drug interactions for the consultation psychiatrist. *Journal of Consultation Liaison Psychiatry, 44*(4), 271–282.

Hampson, S. E., Goldberg, L. R., Vogt, T. M., & Dubanoski, J. P. (2006). Forty years on: Teachers' assessments of children's personality traits predict self-reported health behaviors and outcomes at midlife. *Health Psychology, 25,* 57–64.

Hamrick, N., Cohen, S., & Rodriguez, M. S. (2002). Being popular can be healthy or unhealthy: Stress, social network diversity, and incidence of upper respiratory infection. *Health Psychology, 21,* 294–298.

Han, S., & Shavitt, S. (1994). Persuasion and culture: Advertising appeals in individualist and collectivist societies. *Journal of Experimental Social Psychology, 30,* 326–350.

Hancox, R. J., & Poulton, R. (2006). Watching television is associated with childhood obesity: But is it clinically important? *International Journal of Obesity, 30,* 171–175.

Handgraaf, M. J. J., & van Raaij, W. F. (2005). Fear and loathing no more: The emergence of collaboration between economists and psychologists. *Journal of Economic Psychology, 28,* 387–391.

Haney, M., Ward, A. S., Comer, S. D., Foltin, R. W., & Fischman, M. W. (1999). Abstinence symptoms following smoked marijuana in humans. *Psychopharmacology, 141,* 395–404.

Hankin, B. L., & Abramson, L. Y. (2001). Development of gender differences in depression: An elaborated cognitive vulnerability-transactional stress theory. *Psychological Bulletin, 127,* 773–796.

Hankin, B. L., Fraley, R. C., & Abela, J. R. Z. (2005). Daily depression and cognitions about stress: Evidence for a traitlike depressogenic cognitive style and the prediction of depressive symptoms in a prospective daily diary study. *Journal of Personality and Social Psychology, 88,* 673–685.

Hankin, B. L., Fraley, R. C., Lahey, B. B., & Waldman, I. D. (2005). Is depression best viewed as a continuum or discrete category? A taxometric analysis of childhood and adolescent depression in a population-based sample. *Journal of Abnormal Psychology, 114,* 96–110.

Hanson, G., & Venturelli, P. J. (1995). *Drugs and society* (4th ed.). Boston: Jones & Bartlett.

Hanson, S. J., & Burr, D. J. (1990). What connectionist models learn: Learning and representations in connectionist networks. *Behavioral and Brain Sciences, 13,* 471–518.

Hara, K., Kubota, N., Tobe, K., Terauchi, Y., Miki, H., Komeda, K., et al. (2000). The role of PPARg as a thrifty gene both in mice and humans *British Journal of Nutrition, 84*(Suppl. 2), S235–S239.

Hare, R. D. (1993). *Without conscience: The disturbing world of the psychopaths among us.* New York: Pocket Books.

Hariri, A. R., Drabant, E. M., Munoz, K. E., Kolachana, B. S., Mattay, V. S., Egan, M. F., et al. (2005). A susceptibility gene for affective disorders and the response of the human amygdala. *Archives of General Psychiatry, 62,* 146–152.

Harlow, H. F. (1959, June). Love in infant monkeys. *Scientific American,* pp. 68–74.

Harlow, T., Greaves, C., White, A., Brown, L., Hart, A., & Ernst, E. (2004). Randomised controlled trial of magnetic bracelets for relieving pain in osteoarthritis of the hip and knee. *British Medical Journal, 329,* 1450–1454.

Harmon, A. (2004, May 9). Neurodiversity forever: The disability movement turns to brains. *The New York Times,* p.1.

Harmon-Jones, E. (2004). On the relationship of frontal brain activity and anger: Examining the role of attitude toward anger. *Cognition and Emotion, 18,* 337–361.

Harmon-Jones, E., & Sigelman, J. (2001). State anger and prefrontal brain activity: Evidence that insult-related relative left prefrontal activation is associated with experienced anger and aggression. *Journal of Personality and Social Psychology, 80,* 797–804.

Harré, N., Brandt, T., & Houkamau, C. (2004). An examination of the actor-observer effect in young drivers' attributions for their own and their friends' risky driving. *Journal of Applied Social Psychology, 34,* 806–824.

Harris, C. V., & Goetsch, V. L. (1990). Multi-component flooding treatment of adolescent phobia. In E. L. Feindler & G. R. Kalfus (Eds.), *Adolescent behavior therapy handbook* (Vol. 22). New York: Springer.

Harris, G. C., & Aston-Jones, G. (1995). Involvement of D2 dopamine receptors in the nucleus accumbens in opiate withdrawal syndrome. *Nature, 371,* 155–157.

Harris, J. R. (1995). Where is the child's environment? A group socialization theory of development. *Psychological Review, 102,* 458–489.

Harris, J. R. (1998). *The nurture assumption.* New York: Free Press.

Harris, J. R. (2000). Context-specific learning, personality, and birth order. *Current Directions in Psychological Science, 9,* 174–177.

Harrison, D. A., Newman, D. A., & Roth, P. L. (2006). How important are job attitudes? Meta-analytic comparisons of integrative behavioral outcomes and time sequences. *Academy of Management Journal, 49,* 305–325.

Harrison, K. (2003). Fitness and excitation. In J. Bryant, & D. Roskos-Ewoldsen (Eds.), *Communication and emotion: Essays in honor of Dolf Zillmann* (pp. 473–489). Mahwah, NJ: Erlbaum.

Harrison, P. J., & Law, A. J. (in press). Neuregulin 1 and schizophrenia: Genetics, gene expression, and neurobiology. *Biological Psychiatry.*

Hart, A. J., Whalen, P. J., Shin, L. M., McInerney, S. C., Fischer, H., & Rauch, S. L. (2000). Differential response in the human amygdala to racial outgroup vs. ingroup face stimuli. *Neuroreport, 11,* 2351–2355.

Hart, C. L., Taylor, M. D., Smith, G. D., Whalley, L. J., Starr, J. M., Hole, D. J., et al. (2003). Childhood IQ, social class, deprivation, and their relationships with mortality and morbidity risk in later life: Prospective observational study linking the Scottish mental survey of 1932 and the midspan studies. *Psychosomatic Medicine, 65,* 877–883.

Harter, S. (2006). The self. In W. Damon & R. M. Lerner (Series Eds.) & N. Eisenberg (Vol. Ed.), *Handbook of child psychology: Vol. 3. Social, emotional, and personality development* (6th ed.). New York: Wiley.

Hartung, C. M., & Widiger, T. A. (1998). Gender differences in the diagnosis of mental disorders: Conclusions and controversies of *DSM-IV. Psychological Bulletin, 123,* 260–278.

Hartup, W. W., & Stevens, N. (1997). Friendships and adaptation in the life course. *Psychological Bulletin, 121,* 355–370.

Harwood, H., Fountain, D., & Livermore, G. (1998). *The economic costs of alcohol and drug abuse in the United States, 1992* (Publication No. 98–4327). Bethesda, MD: National Institute on Drug Abuse and the National Institute on Alcohol Abuse and Alcoholism.

Hasin, D. S., Goodwin, R. D., Stinson, F. S., & Grant, B. F. (2005). Epidemiology of major depressive disorder: Results from the national epidemiologic survey on alcoholism and related conditions. *Archives of General Psychiatry, 62,* 1097–1106.

Hassin, R. R., Uleman, J. S., & Bargh, J. A. (2004). *The new unconscious.* New York: Oxford University Press.

Hatcher, D., Brown, T., & Gariglietti, K. P. (2001). Critical thinking and rational emotive behavior therapy. *Inquiry: Critical Thinking Across the Disciplines, 20,* 6–18.

Hatfield, J., Job, R. F. S., Hede, A. J., Carter, N. L., Peploe, P., Taylor, R., & Morrell, S. (2002). Human response to environmental noise: The role of perceived control. *International Journal of Behavioral Medicine, 9,* 341–359.

Hathaway, W. (2002, December 22). Henry M: The day one man's memory died. *Hartford Courant.*

Hattori, M., Fujiyama A., Taylor, T. D., Watanabe, H., Yada, T., Park, H. S., et al. (2000). The DNA sequence of human chromosome 21. *Nature, 405,* 311–319.

Hauck, F. R., Moore, C. M., Herman, S. M., Donovan, M., Kalelkar, M., Christoffel, K. K., et al. (2002). The contributions of prone sleeping to the racial disparity in sudden infant death syndrome: The Chicago Infant Mortality Study. *Pediatrics, 110,* 772–780.

Hauptman, J., Lucas, C., Boldrin, M. N., Collins, H., & Segal, K. R. (2000). Orlistat in the long-term treatment of obesity in primary care settings. *Archives of Family Medicine, 9,* 160–167.

Hausknecht, J. P., Day, D. V., & Thomas, S. C. (2004). Applicant reactions to selection procedures: An updated model and meta-analysis. *Personnel Psychology, 57,* 639–683.

Haw, R. M., & Fisher, R. P. (2004). Effects of administrator-witness contact on eyewitness identification accuracy. *Journal of Applied Psychology, 89,* 1106–1112.

Hawkins, H. L., Kramer, A. R., & Capaldi, D. (1993). Aging, exercise, and attention. *Psychology and Aging, 7,* 643–653.

Hayes, A. M., & Harris, M. S. (2000). The development of an integrative therapy for depression. In S. L. Johnson & A. M. Hayes (Eds.), *Stress, coping, and depression* (pp. 291–306). Mahwah, NJ: Erlbaum.

Haynes, J.-D., & Rees, G. (2005). Predicting the stream of consciousness from activity in human visual cortex. *Current Biology, 15,* 1301–1307.

Hays, W. L. (1981). *Statistics* (3rd ed) New York: Holt, Rinehart & Winston.

Hazeltine, E., & Ivry, R. B. (2002). Neuroscience: Can we teach the cerebellum new tricks? *Science, 296,* 1979–1980.

He, L. F. (1987). Involvement of endogenous opioid peptides in acupuncture analgesia. *Pain, 31,* 99–121.

Heatherton, T. F., Macrae, C. N., & Kelley, W. M. (2004). What the social brain sciences can tell us about the self. *Current Directions in Psychological Science, 13,* 190–193.

Hebb, D. O. (1955). Drives and the C. N. S. (conceptual nervous system). *Psychological Review, 62,* 243–254.

Hebert, L. E., Scherr, P. A., Bienias, J. I., Bennett, D. A., & Evans, D. A. (2003). Alzheimer disease in the U.S. population: Prevalence estimates using the 2000 Census. *Archives of Neurology, 60,* 1119–1122.

Hedge, A., & Yousif, Y. H. (1992). Effects of urban size, urgency, and cost of helpfulness: A cross-cultural comparison between the United Kingdom and the Sudan. *Journal of Cross-Cultural Psychology, 23,* 107–115.

Hedge, J. W., Borman, W. C., & Lammlein, S. E. (2006). *The aging workforce: Realities, myths, and implications for organizations.* Washington, DC: American Psychological Association.

Hedley, A. A., Ogden, C. L., Johnson, C. L., Carroll, M. D., Curtin, L. R., & Flegal, K. M. (2004). Prevalence of overweight and obesity among US children, adolescents, and adults, 1999-2002. *Journal of the American Medical Association, 291,* 2847–2850.

Hegarty, J. D., Baldessarini, R. J., Tohen, M., Waternaux, C., & Oepen, G. (1994). One hundred years of schizophrenia: A meta-analysis of the outcome literature. *American Journal of Psychiatry, 151,* 1409–1416.

Hegerl, U., Plattner, A., & Moller, H. J. (2004). Should combined pharmaco- and psychotherapy be offered to depressed patients? A qualitative review of randomized clinical trials from the 1990s. *European Archives of Psychiatry and Clinical Neuroscience, 254,* 99–107.

Heiby, E. M., DeLeon, P. H., & Anderson, T. (2004). A debate on prescription privileges for psychologists. *Professional Psychology: Research and Practice, 35,* 336–344.

Heilman, K. M., Barrett, A. M., & Adair, J. C. (1998). Possible mechanisms of anosognosia: A defect in self-awareness. *Philosophical Transactions of the Royal Society of London: Series B. Biological Sciences, 353*(1377), 1903–1909.

Heilman, K. M., & Gonzalez-Rothi, L. (2003). Apraxia. In K. M. Heilman & E. Valenstein (Eds.), *Clinical neuropsychology* (4th ed.). New York: Oxford University Press.

Heilman, K. M., & Valenstein, E. (Eds.). (2003). *Clinical neuropsychology* (4th ed.). New York: Oxford University Press.

Heilman, K. M., Valenstein, E., & Watson, R. T. (2000). Neglect and related disorders. *Seminars in Neurology, 20*(4), 463–470.

Heilman, K. M., Watson, R. T., & Valenstein, E. (2003). Neglect and related disorders. In K. M. Heilman & E. Valenstein (Eds.), *Clinical neuropsychology* (4th ed.). New York: Oxford University Press.

Heim, C., Newport, J., Heit, S., Graham, Y. P., Wilcox, M., Bonsall, R., et al. (2000). Pituitary-adrenal and autonomic responses to stress in women after sexual and physical abuse in childhood. *Journal of the American Medical Association, 284,* 592–597.

Heiman, J. R. (2002). Sexual dysfunction: Overview of prevalence, etiological factors, and treatments. *Journal of Sex Research, 39,* 73–78.

Heine, S. J. (2003). Self-enhancement in Japan? A reply to Brown & Kobayashi. *Asian Journal of Social Psychology, 6,* 75–84.

Heine, S. J., Harihara, M., & Niiya, Y. (2002). Terror management in Japan. *Asian Journal of Social Psychology, 5,* 187–196.

Heinrichs, R. W. (2005). The primacy of cognition in schizophrenia. *American Psychologist, 60,* 229–242.

Heiss, W. D., & Teasel, R. W. (2006). Brain recovery and rehabilitation. *Stroke, 37*(2), 314–316.

Hejmadi, A., Davidson, R. J., & Rozin, P. (2000). Exploring Hindu Indian emotion expressions: Evidence for accurate recognition by Americans and Indians. *Psychological Science, 11,* 183–187.

Heller, W. (1993). Neuropsychological mechanisms of individual differences in emotion, personality, and arousal. *NeuroPsychology, 7*(4), 486–489.

Heller, W., Nitschke, J. B., & Miller, G. A. (1998). Lateralization in emotion and emotional disorders. *Current Directions in Psychological Science, 7,* 26–32.

Helmers, K. F., & Krantz, D. S. (1996). Defensive hostility, gender and cardiovascular levels and responses to stress. *Annals of Behavioral Medicine, 18,* 246–254.

Helms, J. E. (1992). Why is there no study of cultural equivalence in standardized cognitive ability testing? *American Psychologist, 47,* 1083–1101.

Helms, J. E. (1997). The triple quandary of race, culture, and social class in standardized cognitive ability testing. In D. P. Flanagan, J. L. Genshaft, & P. L. Harrison (Eds.), *Contemporary intellectual assessment: Theories, tests, and issues.* New York: Guilford Press.

Helson, R., & Moane, G. (1987). Personality change in women from college to midlife. *Journal of Personality and Social Psychology, 53,* 176–186.

Helzer, J. E., Canino, G. J., Yeh, E., Bland, R. C., Lee, C. K., Hwu, H., & Newman, S. (1990). Alcoholism—North America and Asia: A comparison of population surveys with the diagnostic interview schedule. *Archives of General Psychiatry, 47,* 313–319.

Helzer, J. E., & Hudziak, J. J. (Eds.). (2002). *Defining psychopathology in the 21st century: DSM-V and beyond.* Washington DC: American Psychiatric Publishing, Inc.

Hendrick, B. (2003, May 8). Exam day rituals help students feel lucky. *Naples Daily News.*

Hendrick, C., & Hendrick, S. S. (2003). Romantic love: Measuring cupid's arrow. In S. J. Lopez & C. R. Snyder (Eds.), *Positive psychological assessment: A handbook of models and measures* (pp. 235–249). Washington, DC: American Psychological Association.

Hendricks, P. S., & Thompson, J. K. (2005). An integration of cognitive-behavioral therapy and interpersonal psychotherapy for bulimia nervosa: A case study using the case formulation method. *International Journal of Eating Disorders, 37,* 171–174.

Henig, R. (2004, April 4). The quest to forget. *The New York Times,* p. 32.

Henkel, L. A. (2004). Erroneous memories arising from repeated attempts to remember. *Journal of Memory and Language, 50,* 26–46.

Henkel, L. A., Franklin, N., & Johnson, M. K. (2000). Cross-modal source monitoring, confusion between perceived and imagined events. *Journal of Experimental Psychology: Learning, Memory and Cognition, 26,* 321–335.

Henker, F. O. (1979). Acute brain syndromes. *Journal of Clinical Psychiatry, 40*(3), 117–120.

Hennig, J., Reuter, M., Netter, P., Burk, C., & Landt, O. (2005). Two types of aggression are differentially related to serotonergic activity and the A779C TPH polymorphism. *Behavioral Neuroscience, 119,* 16–25.

Henquet, C., Murray, R., Linszen, D., & van Os, J. (2005). The environment and schizophrenia: The role of cannabis use. *Schizophrenia Bulletin, 31,* 608–612.

Heppner, P. P., Heppner, M. J., Lee, D., Wang, Y.-W., Park, H., & Wang, L. (2006). Development and validation of a collectivist coping styles inventory. *Journal of Counseling Psychology, 53,* 107–125.

Hepworth, S. J., Schoemaker, M. J., Muir, K. R., Swerdlow, A. J., van Tongeren, M. J. A., & McKinney, P. A. (2006). Mobile phone use and risk of glioma in adults: Case control study. *British Medical Journal, 332,* 883–887.

Herbert, J. D., Lilienfeld, S. O., Lohr, J. M., Montgomery, R. W., O'Donohue, W. T., Rosen, G. M., & Tolin, D. F. (2000). Science and pseudoscience in the development of eye movement desensitization and reprocessing: Implications for clinical psychology. *Clinical Psychology Review, 20,* 945–971.

Heres, S., Davis, J., Maino, K., Jetzinger, E., Kissling, W., & Leucht, S. (2006). Why olanzapine beats risperidone, risperidone beats quetiapine, and quetiapine beats olanzapine: An exploratory analysis of head-to-head comparison studies of second-generation antipsychotics. *American Journal of Psychiatry, 163,* 185–194.

Hermann, R. C., Dorwart, R. A., Hoover, C. W., & Brody, J. (1995). Variation in ECT use in the United States. *American Journal of Psychiatry, 152,* 869–875.

Hernandez, D. J. (1997). Child development and the social demography of childhood. *Child Development, 68,* 149–169.

Herrmann, D. J., & Searleman, A. (1992). Memory improvement and memory theory in historical perspective. In D. Herrmann, H. Weingartner, A. Searlman, & C. McEvoy (Eds.), *Memory improvement: Implications for memory theory.* New York: Springer-Verlag.

Herrnstein, R. J., & Murray, C. (1994). *The bell curve: Intelligence and class structure in American Life.* New York: Free Press.

Hertenstein, M. J., & Campos, J. J. (2004). The retention effects of an adult's emotional displays on infant behavior. *Child Development, 75,* 585–613.

Hertlein, K., & Ricci, R. J. (2004). A systematic research synthesis of EMDR studies: Implementation of the platinum standard. *Trauma, Violence, and Abuse, 5,* 285–300.

Herz, R. S., & Cahill, E. D. (1997). Differential use of sensory information in sexual behavior as a function of gender. *Human Nature, 8,* 275–286.

Herzog, D. B., Dorer, D. J., Keel, P. K., Selwyn, S. E., Ekeblad, E. R., Flores, A. T., et al. (1999). Recovery and relapse in anorexia and bulimia nervosa: A 7.5-year follow-up study. *Journal of the American Academy of Child and Adolescent Psychiatry, 38,* 829–837.

Herzog, D. B., Greenwood, D. N., Dorer, D. J., Flores, A. T., Ekeblad, E. R., Richards, A., et al. (2000). Mortality in eating disorders: A descriptive study. *International Journal of Eating Disorders, 28,* 20–26.

Hespos, S. J., & Baillargeon, R. (2001). Infants' knowledge about occlusion and containment events: A surprising discrepancy. *Psychological Science, 12,* 141–147.

Hesse, J., Mogelvang, B., & Simonsen, H. (1994). Acupuncture versus metropolol in migraine prophylaxis: A randomized trial of trigger point inactivation. *Journal of Internal Medicine, 235,* 451–456.

Hetherington, E. M., & Clingempeel, W. G. (1992). Coping with marital transitions. *Monographs of the Society for Research in Child Development, 57* (2–3, Serial No. 227).

Hettema, J. M., Annas, P., Neale, M. C., Kendler, K. S., & Fredrikson, M. (2003). A twin study of the genetics of fear conditioning. *Archives of General Psychiatry, 60,* 702–708.

Hettema, J. M., Neale, M. C., & Kendler, K. S. (2001). A review and meta-analysis of the genetic epidemiology of anxiety disorders. *American Journal of Psychiatry, 158,* 1568–1578.

Hettema, J. M., Prescott, C. A., Myers, J. M., Neale, M. C., & Kendler, K. S. (2005). The structure of genetic and environmental risk factors for anxiety disorders in men and women. *Archives of General Psychiatry, 62,* 182–189.

Heuer, H., Kleinsorge, T., Klein, W., & Kohlisch, O. (2004). Total sleep deprivation increases the costs of shifting between simple cognitive tasks. *Acta Psychologica (Amsterdam), 117,* 29–64.

Heward, W. L. (1997). Four validated instructional strategies. *Behavior and Social Issues, 7,* 43–51.

Heymsfield, S. B., Greenberg, A. S., Fujioa, K., Dixon, R. M., Kushner, R., Hunt, T., et al. (1999). Recombinant leptin for weight loss in obese and lean adults. *Journal of the American Medical Association, 282,* 1568–1575.

Hicks, B. M., Krueger, R. F., Iacono, W. G., McGue, M., & Patrick, C. J. (2004). Family transmission and heritability of externalizing disorders. *Archives of General Psychiatry, 61*, 922–928.

Hicks, R. A., Fernandez, C., & Pelligrini, R. J. (2001). The changing pattern of sleep habits of university students: An update. *Perceptual and Motor Skills, 93*, 648.

Highley, J. R., Walker, M. A., Crow, T. J., Esiri, M. M., & Harrison, P. J. (2003). Low medial and lateral right pulvinar volumes in schizophrenia: A postmortem study. *American Journal of Psychiatry, 160*, 1177–1179.

Hildebrandt, M. G., Steyerberg, E. W., Stage, K. B., Passchier, J., Kragh-Soerensen, P., and the Danish University Antidepressant Group. (2003). Are gender differences important for the clinical effects of antidepressants? *American Journal of Psychiatry, 160*, 1643–1650.

Hilgard, E. R. (1965). *Hypnotic susceptibility.* New York: Harcourt, Brace & World.

Hilgard, E. R. (1977). *Divided consciousness: Multiple controls in human thought and action.* New York: Wiley.

Hilgard, E. R. (1979). *Personality and hypnosis: A study of imaginative involvement.* Chicago: University of Chicago Press.

Hilgard, E. R. (1982). Hypnotic susceptibility and implications for measurement. International *Journal of Clinical and Experimental Hypnosis, 30*, 394–403.

Hilgard, E. R. (1992). Divided consciousness and dissociation. *Consciousness and Cognition, 1*, 16–31.

Hilgard, E. R., Morgan, A. H., & MacDonald, H. (1975). Pain and dissociation in the cold pressor test: A study of "hidden reports" through automatic key-pressing and automatic talking. *Journal of Abnormal Psychology, 84*, 280–289.

Hill, C. (2005). Therapist techniques, client involvement, and the therapeutic relationship: Inextricably intertwined in the therapy process. *Psychotherapy: Theory, Research, Practice, Training, 42*, 431–442.

Hill, C. T., & Peplau, L. A. (1998). Premarital predictors of relationship outcomes: A 15-year follow-up of the Boston Couples Study. In T. N. Bradbury (Ed.), *The developmental course of marital dysfunction* (pp. 237–278). New York: Cambridge University Press.

Hill, J. O., & Peters, J. C. (1998). Environmental contributions to the obesity epidemic. *Science, 280*, 1371–1374.

Hill, T., Lewicki, P., Czyzewska, M., & Boss, A. (1989). Self-perpetuating biases in person perception. *Journal of Personality and Social Psychology, 57*, 373–386.

Hilliard, R. B., Henry, W. P., & Strupp, H. H. (2000). An interpersonal model of psychotherapy: Linking patient and therapist developmental history, therapeutic process, and types of outcome. *Journal of Consulting and Clinical Psychology, 68*, 125–133.

Hilton, D. (2002). Thinking about causality: Pragmatic, social and scientific rationality. In P. E. Carruthers, S. Stich, & M. Siegal (Eds.), *The cognitive basis of science* (pp. 211–231). New York: Cambridge University Press.

Hilton, H. (1986). *The executive memory guide.* New York: Simon & Schuster.

Hinshaw, S. P., Zupan, B. A., Simmel, C., Nigg, J. T., & Melnick, S. (1997). Peer status in boys with and without attention-deficit hyperactivity disorder: Predictions from overt and covert antisocial behavior, social isolation, and authoritative parenting beliefs. *Child Development, 68*, 880–896.

Hinton, D., Um, K., & Ba, P. (2001). Kyol goeu ('wind overload') Part I: A cultural syndrome of orthostatic panic among Khmer refugees. *Transcultural Psychiatry, 38*, 403–432.

Hintzman, D. L. (1978). *The psychology of learning and memory.* Freeman: San Francisco.

Hiroto, D. S. (1974). Locus of control and learned helplessness. *Journal of Experimental Psychology, 102*, 187–193.

Hirschfeld, R. M., Allen, M. H., McEvoy, J. P., Keck, P. E., Jr, & Russell, J. M. (1999). Safety and tolerability of oral loading divalproex sodium in acutely manic bipolar patients. *Journal of Clinical Psychiatry, 60*, 815–818.

Hirschfeld, R. M. A., & Vornik, L. A. (2004). Newer antidepressants: Review of efficacy and safety of escitalopram and duloxetine. *Journal of Clinical Psychiatry, 65*(Suppl. 4), 46–52.

Hirsch-Pasek, K., Treiman, R., & Schneiderman, M. (1984). Brown and Hanlon revisited: Mothers' sensitivity to ungrammatical forms. *Journal of Child Language, 11*, 81–88.

Ho, B.-C., Andreasen, N. C., Nopoulos, P., Arndt, S., Magnotta, V., & Flaum M. (2003). Progressive structural brain abnormalities and their relationship to clinical outcome: A longitudinal magnetic resonance imaging study early in schizophrenia. *Archives of General Psychiatry, 60*, 585–594.

Ho, D. Y., & Chiu, C. (1998). Component ideas of individual, collectivism, and social organization. In U. Kim, C. Kagitcibasi, & H. C. Triandis (Eds.), *Individualism and collectivism: Theory, method, and applications.* Thousand Oaks, CA: Sage.

Ho, Y.-C., Cheung, M., & Chan, A. S. (2003). Music training improves verbal but not visual memory: Cross-sectional and longitudinal explorations in children. *Neuropsychology, 17*, 439–450.

Hobson, J. (1997). Dreaming as delirium: A mental status analysis of our nightly madness. *Seminar in Neurology, 17*, 121–128.

Hobson, J. A. (2005). Sleep is of the brain, by the brain and for the brain. *Nature, 437*, 1254–1256.

Hobson, J. A., Pace-Schott, E. F., Stickgold, R., & Kahn, D. (1998). To dream or not to dream? Relevant data from new neuroimaging and electrophysical studies. *Current Opinions in Neurobiology, 8*, 239–244.

Hobson, J. A., & Stickgold, R. (1994). Dreaming: A neurocognitive approach. *Consciousness and Cognition, 3*, 1–15.

Hoegl, M., & Parboteeah, K. P. (2006). Autonomy and teamwork in innovative projects. *Human Resource Management, 45*, 67–79.

Hoel, H., Faragher, B., & Cooper, C. L. (2004). Bullying is detrimental to health, but all bullying behaviors are not necessarily equally damaging. *British Journal of Guidance and Counseling, 32*, 367–387.

Hoffman, D. (1999, February 11). When the nuclear alarms went off, he guessed right. *International Herald Tribune*, p. 2.

Hoffmann, J. P., & Cerbone, F. G. (2002). Parental substance use disorder and the risk of adolescent drug abuse: An event history analysis. *Drug and Alcohol Dependence, 66*, 255–264.

Hofmann, S. G., Meuret, A. E., Smits, J. A., Simon, N. M., Pollack, M. H., Eisenmenger, K., et al. (2006). Augmentation of exposure therapy with D-cycloserine for social anxiety disorder. *Archives of General Psychiatry, 63*, 298–304.

Hogarth, R. M., & Einhorn, H. J. (1992). Order effects in belief updating: The belief adjustment model. *Cognitive Psychology, 24*, 1–55.

Hoglinger, G. U., Widmer, H. R., Spenger, C., Meyer, M., Seiler, R. W., Oertel, W. H., & Sautter, J. (2001). Influence of time in culture and BDNF pretreatment on survival and function of grafted embryonic rat ventral mesencephalon in the 6-OHDA rat model of Parkinson's disease. *Experimental Neurology, 167*, 148–157.

Hohman, A. A., & Shear, M. K. (2002). Community-based intervention research: Coping with the "noise" of real life in study design. *American Journal of Psychiatry, 159*, 201–207.

Holbrook, A. L., Berent, M. K., Krosnick, J. A., Visser, P. S., & Boninger, D. S. (2006). Attitude importance and the accumulation of attitude-relevant knowledge in memory. *Journal of Personality and Social Psychology, 88*, 749–769.

Holden, C. (1996). Small refugees suffer the effects of early neglect. *Science, 274*, 1076–1077.

Holden, C. (1998). New clues to alcoholism risk. *Science, 280*, 1348–1349.

Hollinger, R. C., Dabney, D. A., Lee, G., Hayes, R., Hunter, J., & Cummings, M. (1996). *1996 national retail security survey final report.* Gainesville: University of Florida.

Hollon, S. D., Jarrett, R. B., Nienberg, A. A., Thase, M. E., Trivendi, M., et al. (2005). Psychotherapy and medication in the treatment of adult and geriatric depression: Which monotherapy or combined therapy? *Journal of Clinical Psychiatry, 66*, 455–468.

Hollon, S. D., Stewart, M. O., & Strunk, D. (2006).Enduring effects for cognitive behavior therapy in the treatment of depression and anxiety. *Annual Review of Psychology, 57*, 285–315.

Hollon, S. D., Thase, M. E., & Markowitz, J. C. (2002). Treatment and prevention of depression. *Psychological Science in the Public Interest, 3*, 39–77.

Holman, B. R. (1994). Biological effects of central nervous system stimulants. *Addiction, 89*(11), 1435–1441.

Holmes, D. S. (1991). *Abnormal psychology.* New York: HarperCollins.

Holmes, T. H., & Rahe, R. H. (1967). The Social Readjustment Rating Scale. *Journal of Psychosomatic Research, 11*, 213–218.

Holtmaat, A., Wilbrecht, L., Knott, G. W., Welker, E., & Svoboda, K. (2006). Experience-dependent and cell-type-specific spine growth in the neocortex. *Nature, 441*, 979–983.

Holway, A. H., & Boring, E. G. (1941). Determinants of apparent visual size with distance variant. *American Journal of Psychology, 54*, 21–37.

Hommer, D. W., Momenan, R., Kaiser, E., & Rawlings, R. R. (2001). Evidence for a gender-related effect of alcoholism on brain volumes. *American Journal of Psychiatry, 158*, 198–204.

Hong, Y., Morris, M. W., Chiu, C., & Benet-Martinez, V. (2000). Multicultural minds: A dynamic constructivist approach to culture and cognition. *American Psychologist, 55*, 709–720.

Honts, C. R., & Quick, B. D. (1995). The polygraph in 1996: Progress in science and the law. *North Dakota Law Review, 71*, 997–1020.

Hood, B. M., Willen, J. D., & Driver, J. (1998). Adult's eyes trigger shifts of visual attention in human infants. *Psychological Science, 9,* 131–134.

Hood, M. Y., Moore, L. L., Sundarajan-Ramamurti, A., Singer, M., Cupples, L. A., & Ellison, R. C. (2000). Parental eating attitudes and the development of obesity in children: The Framingham children's study. *International Journal of Obesity, 24,* 1319–1325.

Hooker, E. (1993). Reflections of a 40-year exploration: A scientific view on homosexuality. *American Psychologist, 48,* 450–453.

Hooley, J. M. (2004). Do psychiatric patients do better clinically if they live with certain kinds of families? *Current Directions in Psychological Science, 13,* 202–205.

Hopf, H. C., Muller, F. W., & Hopf, N. J. (1992). Localization of emotional and volitional facial paresis. *Neurology, 42*(10), 1918–1923.

Hopper, K., & Wanderling, J. (2000) Revisiting the developed versus developing country distinction in course and outcome in schizophrenia: Results from ISoS, the WHO Collaborative Followup Project. *Schizophrenia Bulletin, 26,* 835–846.

Horgan, J. (1996, December). Why Freud isn't dead. *Scientific American,* pp. 106–111.

Horne, J. A. (1988). *Why we sleep: The functions of sleep in humans.* Oxford: Oxford University Press.

Horner, P. J. & Gage, F. H. (2002). Regeneration in the adult and aging brain. *Archives of Neurology, 59,* 1717–1720.

Horney, K. (1937). *Neurotic personality of our times.* New York: Norton.

Horowitz, J. L., & Garber, J. (2006). The prevention of depressive symptoms in children and adolescents: A meta-analytic review. *Journal of Consulting and Clinical Psychology, 74,* 401–415.

Horowitz, L. M., Rosenberg, S. E., & Bartholomew, K. (1993). Interpersonal problems, attachment styles, and outcome in brief dynamic psychotherapy. *Journal of Consulting and Clinical Psychology, 61,* 549–560.

Horvath, A. O. (2005). The therapeutic relationship: Research and theory: An introduction to the special issue. *Psychotherapy Research, 15,* 3–7.

Horwitz, A. V., Widom, C. S., McLaughlin, J., & White, H. R. (2001). The impact of childhood abuse and neglect on adult mental health: A prospective study. *Journal of Health and Social Behavior, 42,* 184–201.

Horwitz, P., & Christie, M. A. (2000). Computer-based manipulatives for teaching scientific reasoning: An example. In M. J. Jacobson & R. B. Kozuma (Eds.), *Innovations in science and mathematics education: Advanced designs for technologies of learning* (pp. 163–191). Mahwah, NJ: Erlbaum.

Hoshino-Browne, E., Zanna, A. S., Spencer, S. J., Zanna, M. P., Kitayama, S., & Lackenbauer, S. (2005). On the cultural guises of cognitive dissonance: The case of Easterners and Westerners. *Journal of Personality and Social Psychology, 89,* 294–310.

Houpt, T. R. (1994). Gastric pressure in pigs during eating and drinking. *Physiology and Behavior, 56*(2), 311–317.

House, J. S., Landis, K. R., & Umberson, D. (1988a). Social relationships and health. *Science, 241,* 540–545.

House, J. S., Landis, K. R., & Umberson, D. (1988b). Structures and processes of social support. *Annual Review of Sociology, 14,* 293–318.

House, R. J., Hanges, P. J., Ruiz-Quintanilla, S. A., Dorfman, P. W., Javidan, M., Dickson, M., et al. (1999). Cultural influences on leadership and organizations: Project GLOBE. In W. H. Mobley, M. J. Gessner, & V. Arnold (Eds.), *Advances in global leadership* (Vol. 1, pp. 171–233). Stamford, CT: JAI.

Hoven, C. W., Duarte, C. S., Lucas, C. P., Wu, P., Mandell, D. J., Goodwin, R. D., et al. (2005). Psychopathology among New York city public school children 6 months after September 11. *Archives of General Psychiatry, 62,* 545–552.

Howard, D. V. (1983). *Cognitive psychology.* New York: Macmillan.

Howarth, E., & Weissman, M. M. (2000). The epidemiology and cross-national presentation of obsessive-compulsive disorder. *Psychiatric Clinics of North America, 23,* 493–507.

Howe, M. J. A., Davidson, J. W., & Sloboda, J. A. (1998). Innate talent: Reality or myth? *Behavioral and Brain Sciences, 21,* 399–442.

Howe, M. L. (2003). Memories from the cradle. *Current Directions in Psychological Science, 12,* 62–65.

Hoyert, D. L., Kung, H.-C., & Smith, B. L. (2005). Deaths: Preliminary data for 2003. *National Vital Statistics Reports, 53,* 1–48.

Hoyle, R. H. (1993). Interpersonal attraction in the absence of explicit attitudinal information. *Social Cognition, 11,* 309–320.

Hoyle, R. H., Harris, M. J., & Judd, C. M. (2002). *Research methods in social relations.* Belmont, CA: Wadsworth.

Hser, Y. I., Hoffman, V., Grella, C. E., & Anglin, M. D. (2001). A 33-year follow-up of narcotics addicts. *Archives of General Psychiatry, 58,* 503–508.

Hu, S., Patatucci, A. M. L., Patterson, C., Li, L., Fulker, D. W., Cherny, S. S., et al. (1995). Linkage between sexual orientation and chromosome Xq28 in males but not females. *Nature Genetics, 11,* 248–256.

Hua, J. Y., & Smith, S. J. (2004). Neural activity and the dynamics of central nervous system development. *Nature Neuroscience, 7,* 327–332.

Huang, L., & Li, C. (2000). Leptin: A multifunctional hormone. *Cell Research, 10,* 81–92.

Hubble, M. A., Duncan, B. L., & Miller, S. D. (Eds.). (1999). *The heart and soul of change: What works in psychotherapy.* Washington, DC: American Psychological Assocation.

Hubel, D. H., & Wiesel, T. N. (1979). Brain mechanisms of vision. *Scientific American, 241,* 150–162.

Hudson, W. (1960). Pictorial depth in perception in subcultural groups in Africa. *Journal of Social Psychology, 52,* 183–208.

Hudziak, J. J., Derks, E. M., Althoff, R. R., Rettew, D. C., & Boomsma, D. I. (2005). The genetic and environmental contributions to attention deficit hyperactivity disorder as measured by the Conners' Rating Scales—Revised. *American Journal of Psychiatry, 162,* 1614–1620.

Hudziak, J. J., van Beijsterveldt, C. E. M., Bartels, M., Rietveld, M. J. H., Rettew, D. C., Derks, E. M., et al. (2003). Individual differences in aggression: Genetic analyses by age, gender, and informant in 3-, 7-, and 10-year-old Dutch twins. *Behavior Genetics, 33,* 575–589.

Huesmann, L. R. (1995). *Screen violence and real violence: Understanding the link.* Auckland, NZ: Media Aware.

Huesmann, L. R. (1998). The role of social information processing and cognitive schema in the acquisition and maintenance of habitual aggressive behavior. In R. G. Geen & E. Donnerstein (Eds.), *Human aggression.* San Diego: Academic Press.

Huesmann, L. R., & Eron, L. D. (1986). *Television and the aggressive child: A cross-national comparison.* Hillsdale, NJ: Erlbaum.

Huesmann, L. R., Moise, J., Podolski, C., & Eron, L. (1997, April). *Longitudinal relations between early exposure to television violence and young adult aggression: 1977–1992.* Paper presented at the annual meeting of the Society for Research in Child Development, Washington, DC.

Huesmann, L. R., Moise-Titus, J., Podolski, C., & Eron, L. D. (2003). Longitudinal relations between children's exposure to TV violence and their aggressive and violent behavior in young adulthood: 1977–1992. *Developmental Psychology, 39,* 201–221.

Huffcutt, A. I., & Arthur, W. (1994). Hunter and Hunter (1984) revisited: Interview validity for entry-level jobs. *Journal of Applied Psychology, 79,* 184–190.

Huffcutt, A. I., Conway, J. M., Roth, P. L., & Stone, N. J. (2001). Identification and meta-analytic assessment of psychological constructs measured in employment interviews. *Journal of Applied Psychology, 86,* 897–913.

Hughes, B. M. (2006). Lies, damned lies, and pseudoscience: The selling of eye movement desensitization and reprocessing (EMDR). *PsycCritiques, 51,* 10.

Hughes, J. R., Higgins, S. T., & Bickel, W. K. (1994). Nicotine withdrawal versus other drug withdrawal syndromes: Similarities and dissimilarities. *Addiction, 89*(11), 1461–1470.

Hui, C., Lam, S. S. K., & Law, K. K. S. (2000). Instrumental values of organizational citizenship behavior for promotion: A field quasi-experiment. *Journal of Applied Psychology, 85,* 822–828.

Huizink, A. C., Mulder, E. J. H., & Buitelaar, J. K. (2004). Prenatal stress and risk for psychopathology. *Psychological Bulletin, 130,* 115–142.

Hull, C. L. (1951). *Essentials of behavior.* New Haven, CT: Yale University Press.

Humphreys, L. G. (1984). General intelligence. In C. R. Reynolds & R. T. Brown (Eds.), *Perspectives on bias in mental testing.* New York: Plenum.

Hunsley, J., & Di Giulio, G. (2002). Dodo bird, phoenix, or urban legend? The question of psychotherapy equivalence. *Scientific Review of Mental Health Practice, 1,* 11–22.

Hunsley, J., Lee, C. M., & Wood, J. M. (2003). Controversial and questionable assessment techniques. In S. O. Lilienfeld & S. J. Lynn (Eds.), *Science and pseudoscience in clinical psychology* (pp. 39–76). New York: Guilford Press.

Hunsley, J., & Rumstein-McKean, O. (1999). Improving psychotherapeutic services via randomized trials, treatment manuals, and component analysis designs. *Journal of Clinical Psychology, 55,* 1507–1517.

Hunt, E. (1983). On the nature of intelligence. *Science, 219,* 141–146.

Hunt, M. (1982). *The universe within.* New York: Simon & Schuster.

Hunt, M., & Forand, R. (2005). Cognitive vulnerability to depression in never depressed subjects. *Cognition and Emotion, 19,* 763–770.

Hunt, R., & Rouse, W. B. (1981). Problem solving skills of maintenance trainees in diagnosing faults in simulated power plants. *Human Factors, 23,* 317–328.

Hunter, M. A., & Ames, E. W. (1988). A multifactor model of infants' preferences for novel and familiar stimuli. In C. Rovee-Collier & L. P. Lipsitt (Eds.), *Advances in infancy research* (Vol. 5, pp. 69–91). Norwood, NJ: Ablex.

Hurt, H., Brodsky, N. L., Betancourt, L., & Braitman, L. E. (1995). Cocaine-exposed children: Follow-up through 30 months. *Journal of Developmental and Behavioral Pediatrics, 16*(1), 29–35.

Huston, A. C., & Wright, J. C. (1989). The forms of television and the child viewer. In G. Comstock (Ed.), *Public communication and behavior* (Vol. 2, pp. 103–159). San Diego: Academic Press.

Huttenlocher, P. R. (1990). Morphometric study of human cerebral cortex development. *Neuropsychologia, 28,* 517–527.

Hyde, J. S. (1986). Gender differences in aggression. In J. S. Hyde & M. C. Linn (Eds.), *The psychology of gender: Advances through meta-analysis.* Baltimore: Johns Hopkins University Press.

Hyde, J. S. (2005). The gender similarities hypothesis. *American Psychologist, 60,* 581–592.

Hyde, J. S., & Durik, A. M. (2000). Gender differences in erotic plasticity–Evolutionary or sociocultural forces? Comment on Baumeister (2000). *Psychological Bulletin, 126,* 375–379.

Hygge, S., Evans, G.W., & Bullinger, M. (2002). A prospective study of some effects of aircraft noise on cognitive performance in schoolchildren. *Psychological Science, 13,* 469–474.

Hyman, I. E., Jr. (2000). The memory wars. In U. Neisser & I. E. Hyman Jr. (Eds.), *Memory observed* (2nd ed., pp. 374–379). New York: Worth.

Hyman, I. E., & Pentland, J. (1996). The role of mental imagery in the creation of false childhood memories. *Journal of Memory and Language, 35,* 101–117.

Hyman, R. (2002). Why and when are smart people stupid? In R. J. Sternberg (Ed.), *Why smart people can be so stupid* (pp. 1–23). New Haven, CT: Yale University Press.

Hypericum Depression Trial Study Group. (2002). Effect of *Hypericum perforatum* (St. John's wort) in major depressive disorder: A randomized, controlled trial. *Journal of the American Medical Association, 287,* 1807–1814.

I

Igalens, J., & Roussel, P. (1999). A study of the relationships between compensation package, work motivation, and job satisfaction. *Journal of Organizational Behavior, 20,* 1003–1025.

Ilgen, D. R., & Pulakos, E. D. (Eds.). (1999). *The changing nature of performance: Implications for staffing, motivation, and development.* San Francisco, CA: Jossey-Bass.

Ilies, R., & Judge, T. A. (2003). On the heritability of job satisfaction: The mediating role of personality. *Journal of Applied Psychology, 88,* 750–759.

Ilies, R., Scott, B. A., & Judge, T. A. (2006). The interactive effects of personal traits and experienced states on intraindividual patterns of citizenship behavior. *Academy of Management Journal, 49,* 561–575.

Imtiaz, K. E., Nirodi, G., & Khaleeli, A. A. (2001). Alexia without agraphia: A century later. *International Journal of Clinical Practice, 55*(3), 225–226.

Inciardi, J. A., Surratt, H. L., & Saum, C. A. (1997). *Cocaine-exposed infants: Social, legal, and public health issues.* Thousand Oaks, CA: Sage.

Indovina, I., & Sanes, J. N. (2001). On somatotopic representation centers for finger movements in human primary motor cortex and supplementary motor area. *Neuroimage, 13,* 1027–1034.

Inness, M., Barling, J., & Turner, N. (2005). Understanding supervisor-targeted aggression: A within-person, between-jobs design. *Journal of Applied Psychology, 90,* 731–739.

Institute of Medicine. (2006, April 5). *Sleep disorders and sleep deprivation: An unmet public health problem* [Press release]. Retrieved September 26, 2006, from http://www.iom.edu/CMS/3740/23160/33668.aspx.

International Association for the Evaluation of Education Achievement. (1999). *Trends in mathematics and science achievement around the world.* Boston: Lynch School of Education, Boston College.

International Human Genome Sequencing Consortium. (2001). Initial sequencing and analysis of the human genome. *Nature, 409,* 860–921.

Inzlicht, M., & Ben-Zeev, T. (2000). A threatening intellectual environment: Why females are susceptible to experiencing problem-solving deficits in the presence of males. *Psychological Science, 11,* 365–371.

Ironson, G., Freund, B., Strauss, J. L., & Williams J. (2002). Comparison of two treatments for traumatic stress: A community-based study of EMDR and prolonged exposure. *Journal of Clinical Psychology, 58,* 113–128.

Ironson, G., Wynings, C., Schneiderman, N., Baum, A., Rodriguez, M., Greenwood, D., et al. (1997). Posttraumatic stress symptoms, intrusive thoughts, loss, and immune function after Hurricane Andrew. *Psychosomatic Medicine, 59,* 128–141.

Ironson, G. H., Smith, P. C., Brannick, M. T., Gibson, W. M., & Paul, K. B. (1989). Constitution of a Job in General scale: A comparison of global, composite, and specific measures. *Journal of Applied Psychology, 74,* 193–200.

Irwin, M., Daniels, M., Smith, T., Bloom, E., & Weiner, H. (1987). Impaired natural killer cell activity during bereavement. *Brain, Behavior, and Immunity, 1,* 98–104.

Iversen, L. L., & Snyder, S. H. (2000). *The science of marijuana.* Oxford, England: Oxford University Press.

Iwahashi, K., Matsuo, Y., Suwaki, H., Nakamura, K., & Ichikawa, Y. (1995). CYP2E1 and ALDH2 genotypes and alcohol dependence in Japanese. *Alcoholism Clinical and Experimental Research, 19*(3), 564–566.

Iwamasa, G. Y., Sorocco, K. H., & Koonce, D. A. (2002). Ethnicity and clinical psychology: A content analysis of the literature. *Clinical Psychology Review, 22,* 932–944.

Izac, S. M., & Eeg, T. R. (2006). Basic anatomy and physiology of sleep. *American Journal of Electroneurodiagnostic Technology, 46*(1), 18–38.

Izard, C. E. (1977). *Human emotions.* New York: Plenum.

Izard, C. E. (1993). Organizational and motivational functions of discrete emotions. In M. Lewis and J. M. Haviland (Eds.), *Handbook of emotions.* New York: Guilford.

Izard, C., Fine, S., Schultz, D. Mostow, A., Ackerman, B., & Youngstrom, E. (2001). Emotion knowledge as a predictor of social behavior and academic competence in children at risk. *Psychological Science, 12,* 18–23.

Izumikawa, M., Minoda, R., Kawamoto, K., Abrashkin, K. A., Swiderski, D., L., Dolan, D. F., et al. (2005). Auditory hair cell replacement and hearing improvement by *Atoh1* gene therapy in deaf animals. *Nature, 11,* 271–276.

J

Jaccard, J., Blanton, H., & Dodge, T. (2005). Peer influences on risk behavior: An analysis of the effects of a close friend. *Developmental Psychology, 41,* 135–147.

Jackson, B., Sellers, R. M., & Peterson, C. (2002). Pessimistic explanatory style moderates the effect of stress on physical illness. *Personality & Individual Differences, 32,* 567–573.

Jackson, J. W. (2002). The relationship between group identity and intergroup prejudice is moderated by sociostructural variation. *Journal of Applied Social Psychology, 32,* 908–933.

Jacob, S., Kinnunen, L. H., Metz, J., Cooper, M., & McClintock, M. K. (2001). Sustained human chemosignal unconsciously alters brain function. *Neuroreport, 12,* 2391–2394.

Jacob, S., & McClintock, M. K. (2000). Psychological state and mood effects of steroidal chemosignals in women and men. *Hormones and Behavior, 37,* 57–78.

Jacob, T., Waterman, B., Heath, A., True, W., Bucholz, K. K., Haber, R., et al. (2003). Genetic and environmental effects on offspring alcoholism: New insights using an offspring-of-twins design. *Archives of General Psychiatry, 60,* 1265–1272.

Jacobi, C., Hayward, C., de Zwaan, M., Kraemer, H. C., & Agras, W. S. (2004). Coming to terms with risk factors for eating disorders: Application of risk terminology and suggestions for a general taxonomy. *Psychological Bulletin, 130,* 19–65.

Jacobs, B. L. (2004). Depression: The brain finally gets into the act. *Current Directions in Psychological Science, 13,* 103–106.

Jacobs, G. D., Pace-Schott, E. F., Stickgold, R., & Otto, M. W. (2004). Cognitive behavior therapy and pharmacotherapy for insomnia: A randomized controlled trial and direct comparison. *Archives of Internal Medicine, 164,* 1888–1896.

Jacobs, R., & Solomon, T. (1977). Strategies for enhancing the prediction of job performance from job satisfaction. *Journal of Applied Psychology, 62,* 417–421.

Jacobson, K. (2002). ADHD in cross-cultural perspective: Some empirical results. *American Anthropologist, 104,* 283–286.

Jacobson, N. S., Christensen, A., Prince, S. E., Cordova, J., & Eldridge, K. (2000). Integrative behavioral couples therapy: An acceptance-based, promising new treatment for couple discord. *Journal of Consulting and Clinical Psychology, 68,* 351–355.

Jaffee, S., & Hyde, J. S. (2000). Gender differences in moral orientation: A meta-analysis. *Psychological Bulletin, 126,* 703–726.

Jaffee, S. R., Caspi, A., Moffitt, T. E., & Taylor, A. (2004). Physical maltreatment to antisocial child: Evidence of an environmentally mediated process. *Journal of Abnormal Psychology, 113,* 44–55.

Jago, R., Baranowski, T., Baranowski, J. C., Thompson, D., & Greaves, K. A. (2005). BMI from 3–6 y of age is predicted by TV viewing and physical activity, not diet. *International Journal of Obesity, 29,* 557–564.

Jahnke, J. C., & Nowaczyk, R. H. (1998). *Cognition.* Upper Saddle River, NJ: Prentice-Hall.

Jain, A. (2005). Treating obesity in individuals and populations. *British Medical Journal, 331,* 1387–1390.

James, J. E. (2004). Critical review of dietary caffeine and blood pressure: A relationship that should be taken more seriously. *Psychosomatic Medicine, 66,* 63–71.

James, W. (1884). Some omissions of introspective psychology. *Mind, 9,* 1–26.

James, W. (1890). *Principles of psychology.* New York: Holt.

James, W. (1892). *Psychology: Briefer course.* New York: Holt.

Jamieson, P., Jamieson, K. H., & Romer, D. (2003). The responsible reporting of suicide in print journalism. *American Behavioral Scientist, 46,* 1643–1660.

Jancke, L., & Kaufmann, N. (1994). Facial EMG responses to odors in solitude and with an audience. *Chemical Senses, 19*(2), 99–111.

Jancke, L., & Kaufmann, N. (1994). Facial EMG responses to odors in solitude and with an audience. *Chemical Senses, 19*(2), 99–111.

Janis, I. L. (1989). *Crucial decisions: Leadership in policy making and crisis management.* New York: Free Press.

Janowiak, J. J., & Hackman, R. (1994). Meditation and college students' self-actualization and rated stress. *Psychological Reports, 75*(2), 1007–1010.

Janowitz, H. D. (1967). Role of gastrointestinal tract in the regulation of food intake. In C. F. Code (Ed.), *Handbook of physiology: Alimentary canal 1.* Washington, DC: American Physiological Society.

Jansen, P. G., & Vinkenburg, C. J. (2006). Predicting managerial career success from assessment center data: A longitudinal study. *Journal of Vocational Behavior, 68,* 253–266.

Jason, L. A., Witter, E., & Torres-Harding, S. (2003). Chronic fatigue syndrome, coping, optimism and social support. *Journal of Mental Health, 12,* 109–118.

Jefferis, B. M. J. H., Power, C., & Hertzman, C. (2002). Birth weight, childhood socioeconomic environment, and cognitive development in the 1958 British birth cohort study [Electronic version]. *British Medical Journal, 325,* 305.

Jeffries, K. J., Fritz, J. B., & Braun, A. R. (2003). Words in melody: An H(2)15O PET study of brain activation during singing and speaking. *Neuroreport, 14,* 749–754.

Jemal, A., Ward, E., Hao, Y., & Thun, M. (2005). Trends in the leading causes of death in the United States, 1970–2002. *Journal of the American Medical Association, 294,* 1255–1259.

Jenkins, M. R., & Culbertson, J. L. (1996). Prenatal exposure to alcohol. In R. L. Adams, O. A. Parsons, J. L. Culbertson, & S. J. Nixon (Eds.), *Neuropsychology for clinical practice: Etiology, assessment, and treatment of common neurological disorders* (pp. 409–452). Washington, DC: American Psychological Association.

Jenkins, R. O., & Sherbum, R. E. (2005). Growth and survival of bacteria implicated in sudden infant death syndrome on cot mattress materials. *Journal of Applied Microbiology, 99,* 573–579.

Jevtovic-Todorovic, V., Wozniak, D. F., Benshoff, N. D., & Olney, J. W. (2001). A comparative evaluation of the neurotoxic properties of ketamine and nitrous oxide. *Brain Research, 895,* 264–267.

Jex, S. M., Adams, G. A., Elacqua, T. C., & Bachrach, D. G. (2002). Type A as a moderator of stressors and job complexity: A comparison of achievement strivings and impatience-irritability. *Journal of Applied Social Psychology, 32,* 977–996.

Jhanwar, U. M., Beck, B., Jhanwar, Y. S., & Burlet, C. (1993). Neuropeptide Y projection from the arcuate nucleus to the parvocellular division of the paraventricular nucleus: Specific relation to the ingestion of carbohydrate. *Brain Research, 631*(1), 97–106.

Johansen, J. P., Fields, H. L., & Manning, B. H. (2001). The affective component of pain in rodents: Direct evidence for a contribution of the anterior cingulate cortex. *Proceedings of the National Academy of Sciences, 98,* 8077–8082.

Johnson, B. T., Maio, G. R., & Smith-McLallen, A. (2005). Communication and attitude change: Causes, processes, and effects. In D. Albarracín, B. T. Johnson, & M. P. Zanna (Eds.), *Handbook of attitudes* (pp. 617–669). Mahwah, NJ: Erlbaum.

Johnson, D. R., Westermeyer, J., Kattar, K., & Thuras, P. (2002). Daily charting of posttraumatic stress symptoms: A pilot study. *Journal of Nervous & Mental Disease, 190,* 683–692.

Johnson, J., & Vickers, Z. (1993). Effects of flavor and macronutrient composition of food servings on liking, hunger and subsequent intake. *Appetite, 21*(1), 25–39.

Johnson, J. G., Cohen, P., Dohrenwend, B. P., Link, B. G., & Brook, J. S. (1999). A longitudinal investigation of social causation and social selection processes involved in the association between socioeconomic status and psychiatric disorders. *Journal of Abnormal Psychology, 108,* 490–499.

Johnson, J. G., Cohen, P., Smailes, E. M., Kasen, S., & Brook, J. S. (2002). Television viewing and aggressive behavior during adolescence and adulthood. *Science, 295,* 2468–2471.

Johnson, J. M., & Endler, N. S. (2002). Coping with human immunodeficiency virus: Do optimists fare better? *Current Psychology: Developmental, Learning, Personality, Social, 21,* 3–16.

Johnson, J. S., & Newport, E. L. (1989). Critical period effects in second language learning. *Cognitive Psychology, 21,* 60–99.

Johnson, L. E., & Thorpe, G. L. (1994). Review of psychotherapy and counseling with minorities: A cognitive approach to individual differences, by Manuel Ramirez. *Behavioural and Cognitive Psychotherapy, 22,* 185–187.

Johnson, M. A., Dziurawiec, S., Ellis, H., & Morton, J. (1991). Newborns' preferential tracking of face-like stimuli and its subsequent decline. *Cognition, 4,* 1–19.

Johnson, M. K., & Raye, C. L. (1998). False memories and confabulation. *Trends in Cognitive Sciences, 2,* 137–145.

Johnson, S. L. (2003). *Therapist's guide to clinical intervention: The 1-2-3's of treatment planning.* San Diego, CA: Academic Press.

Johnson, S. L., & Birch, L. L. (1994).Parents' and children's adiposity and eating style. *Pediatrics, 94,* 653–656.

Johnson, S. P. (2005). Development of perceptual completion in infancy. *Psychological Science, 15,* 769–775.

Johnson, S. P., Amso, D., & Slemmer, J. A. (2003). Development of object concepts in infancy: Evidence for early learning in an eye-tracking paradigm. *Proceedings of the National Academy of Sciences of the USA, 100,* 10568–10573.

Johnson, W., & Krueger, R. F. (2005). Higher perceived life control decreases genetic variation in physical health: Evidence from a national twin study. *Journal of Personality and Social Psychology, 88,* 165–173.

Johnson, W., McGue, M., & Krueger, R. F. (2005). Personality stability in late adulthood: A behavioral genetic analysis. *Journal of Personality, 73,* 523–551.

Johnson, W., McGue, M., Krueger, R. F., & Bouchard, T. J., Jr. (2004). Marriage and personality: A genetic analysis. *Journal of Personality and Social Psychology, 86,* 285–294.

Johnson, W. R., & Neal, D. (1998). Basic skills and the black-white earnings gap. In C. Jencks & M. Phillips (Eds.), *The black-white test score gap* (pp. 480–497). Washington, DC: Brookings Institute Press.

Johnson-Laird, P. N. (1983). *Mental models: Toward a cognitive science of language, inference, and consciousness.* Cambridge: Harvard University Press.

Johnston, K. (1988). Adolescents' solutions to dilemmas in fables: Two moral orientations. In C. Gilligan, J. V. Ward, J. M. Taylor, & B. Bardige (Eds.), *Mapping the moral domain: A contribution to psychological theory and education.* Cambridge: Harvard University Press.

Jolij, J., & Lamme, V. A. (2005). Repression of unconscious information by conscious processing: Evidence from affective blindsight induced by transcranial magnetic stimulation. *Proceedings of the National Academy of Science of the USA, 102,* 10747–10751.

Jonas, E., Schimel, J., Greenberg, J., & Pyszczynski, T. (2002). The Scrooge effect: Evidence that mortality salience increases prosocial attitudes and behavior. *Personality and Social Psychology Bulletin, 28,* 1342–1353.

Jones, E. E. (1982). Psychotherapists' impressions of treatment outcome as a function of race. *Journal of Clinical Psychology, 38,* 722–731.

Jones, G. V. (1990). Misremembering a common object: When left is not right. *Memory & Cognition, 18,* 174–182.

Jones, H. E. (2006) Drug addiction during pregnancy. *Current Directions in Psychological Science, 15,* 126–130.

Jones, J. R., & Schaubroeck, J. (2004). Mediators of the relationship between race and organizational citizenship behavior. *Journal of Managerial Issues, 16,* 505–527.

Jones, M. A., Botsko, M., & Gorman, B. S. (2003) Predictors of psychotherapeutic benefit of lesbian, gay, and bisexual clients: The effects of sexual orientation matching and other factors. *Psychotherapy: Theory, Research, Practice, Training, 40,* 289–301.

Jonides, J., Lacey, S. C., & Nee, D. E. (2005). Processes of working memory in mind and brain. *Current Directions in Psychological Science,14,* 2–5.

Jordan, N. C., Huttenlocher, J., & Levine, S. C. (1992). Differential calculation abilities in young children from middle- and low-income families. *Developmental Psychology, 28,* 644–653.

Josephson, W. L. (1987). Television violence and children's aggression: Testing the priming, social script, and disinhibition predictions. *Journal of Personality and Social Psychology, 53,* 882–890.

Joy, J. E., Watson, S. J., Jr., & Benson, J. A., Jr. (1999). *Marijuana and medicine: Assessing the science base.* Washington, DC: National Academy Press.

Judd, F. K., Jackson, H. J., Komiti, A., Murray, G., Hodgins, G., Fraser, C. (2002). High prevalence disorders in urban and rural communities. *Australian and New Zealand Journal of Psychiatry, 36,* 104–113.

Judge, T. A., Colbert, A. E., & Ilies, R. (2004). Intelligence and leadership: A quantitative review and test of theoretical propositions. *Journal of Applied Psychology, 89,* 542–552.

Judge, T. A., Piccolo, R. F., & Ilies, R. (2004). The forgotten ones? The validity of consideration and initiating structure in leadership research. *Journal of Applied Psychology, 89,* 36–51.

Judge, T. A., Thoresen, C. J., Bono, J. E., & Patton, G. K. (2001). The job satisfaction-job performance relationship: A qualitative and quantitative review. *Psychological Bulletin, 127,* 376–407.

Julien, R. M. (2005). *A primer of drug action* (10th ed.). New York: Worth.

Jung, C. G. (1916). *Analytical psychology.* New York: Moffat.

Jung, C. G. (1933). *Psychological types.* New York: Harcourt, Brace and World.

Jureidini, J. N., Doecke, C. J., Mansfield, P. R., Haby, M. M., Menkes, D. B., & Tonkin, A. L. (2004). Efficacy and safety of antidepressants for children and adolescents. *British Medical Journal, 328,* 879–883.

Jussim, L., & Eccles, J. S. (1992). Teacher expectations: II. Construction and reflection of student achievement. *Journal of Personality and Social Psychology, 63,* 947–961.

Just, M. A., Carpenter, P. A., Keller, T. A., Emery, L., Zajac, H., & Thulborn, K. R. (2001). Interdependence of nonoverlapping cortical systems in dual cognitive tasks. *Neuroimage, 14,* 417–426.

Just, N., & Alloy, L. B. (1997). The response styles theory of depression: Tests and an extension of the theory. *Journal of Abnormal Psychology, 106,* 221–229.

Juul-Dam, N., Townsend, J., & Courchesne, E. (2001). Prenatal, perinatal, and neonatal factors in autism, pervasive developmental disorder–not other-wise specified, and the general population. *Pediatrics, 107,* e63.

K

Kadotani, H., Kadotani, T., Young, T., Peppard, P. E., Finn, L., Colrain, I. M., et al. (2001). Association between apolipoprotein E epsilon4 and sleep-disordered breathing in adults. *Journal of the American Medical Association, 285,* 2888–2890.

Kagan, J. R., Snidman, N., Arcus, D., & Resnick, J. S. (1994). *Galen's prophecy: Temperament in human nature.* New York: Basic Books.

Kahn, E., & Rachman, A. W. (2000). Carl Rogers and Heinz Kohut: A historical perspective. *Psychoanalytic Psychology, 17,* 294–312.

Kahneman, D., Krueger, A. B., Schkade, D., Schwarz, N., & Stone, A. A. (2006). Would you be happier if you were richer? A focusing illusion. *Science, 312,* 1908–1910.

Kahneman, D., & Tversky, A. (1973). On the psychology of prediction. *Psychological Review, 80,* 237–251.

Kahneman, D., & Tversky, A. (1984). Choices, values, and frames. *American Psychologist, 29,* 341–356.

Kaitaro, T. (2001). Biological and epistemological models of localization in the nineteenth century: From Gall to Charcot. *Journal of Historical Neuroscience, 10*(3), 262–276.

Kajantie, E. J., & Phillips, D. I. W. (2006). The effects of sex and hormonal status on the physiological response to acute psychosocial stress. *Psychoneuroendocrinology, 31,* 151–178.

Kajiya, K., Inaki, K., Tanaka, M., Haga, T., Kataoka, H., & Touhara, K. (2001). Molecular bases of odor discrimination: Reconstitution of olfactory receptors that recognize overlapping sets of odorants. *Journal of Neuroscience, 21,* 6018–6025.

Kalb, L. M., & Loeber, R. (2003). Child disobedience and noncompliance: A review. *Pediatrics, 111,* 641–652.

Kales, A., & Kales, J. (1973). Recent advances in the diagnosis and treatment of sleep disorders. In G. Usdin (Ed.), *Sleep research and clinical practice.* New York: Brunner/Mazel.

Kalivas, P. W., & Volkow, N. D. (2005). The neural basis of addiction: A pathology of motivation and choice. *American Journal of Psychiatry, 162,* 1403–1413.

Kamin, L. J. (1969). Predictability, surprise, attention, and conditioning. In B. A. Campbell & R. M. Church (Eds.), *Punishment and aversive behavior* (pp. 279–296). New York: Appleton-Century-Crofts.

Kammeyer-Mueller, J. D., Wanberg, C. R., Glomb, T. M., & Ahlburg, D. (2005). The role of temporal shifts in turnover processes: It's about time. *Journal of Applied Psychology, 90,* 644–658.

Kammrath, L. K., Mendoza-Denton, R., & Mischel, W. (2005). Incorporating if . . . then . . . personality signatures in person perception: Beyond the person situation dichotomy. *Journal of Personality and Social Psychology, 88,* 605–618.

Kamphuis, J. H., & Emmelkamp, P. M. (2001). Traumatic distress among support-seeking female victims of stalking. *American Journal of Psychiatry, 158,* 795–798.

Kancelbaum, B., Singer, B., & Wong, N. (2004). *Therapy in America, 2004.* Retrieved October 2, 2005, from http://cms.psychologytoday.com/pto/press_release_050404.html.

Kane, J. M., Eerdekens, M., Lindenmayer, J.-P., Keith, S. J., Lesem, M., & Karcher, K. (2003). Long-acting injectable risperidone: Efficacy and safety of the first long-acting atypical antipsychotic. *American Journal of Psychiatry, 160,* 1125–1132.

Kanki, B. J., & Foushee, H. C. (1990). Crew factors in the aerospace workplace. In S. Oskamp & S. Spacepan (Eds.), *People's reactions to technology* (pp. 18–31). Newbury Park, CA: Sage.

Kanner, B. (1995). *Are you normal?* New York: St. Martin's Press.

Kaplan, M. F., & Miller, C. E. (1987). Group decision making and normative vs. informational influence: Effects of type of issue and assigned decision rule. *Journal of Personality and Social Psychology, 53,* 306–313.

Kaptchuk, T. J. (2001). Methodological issues in trials of acupuncture. *Journal of the American Medical Association, 285,* 1015–1016.

Kaptchuk, T. J., Stason, W. B., Legedza, A. R. T., Schnyer, R. N., Kerr, C. E., Stone, D. A., et al. (2006). Sham device vs. inert pill: Randomised controlled trial of two placebo treatments. *British Medical Journal, 332,* 391–397.

Kapur, N. (1999). Syndromes of retrograde amnesia: A conceptual and empirical synthesis. *Psychological Bulletin, 125,* 800–825.

Kapur, S. (2003). Psychosis as a state of aberrant salience: A framework linking biology, phenomenology, and pharmacology in schizophrenia. *American Journal of Psychiatry, 160,* 13–23.

Kapur, S., Sridhar, N., & Remington, G. (2004). The newer antipsychotics: Underlying mechanisms and the new clinical realities. *Current Opinion in Psychiatry, 17*(2), 115–121.

Karni, A., Meyer, G., Adams, M., Turner, R., & Ungerleider, L. G. (1994). The acquisition and retention of a motor skill: A functional MRI study of long-term motor cortex plasticity. *Abstracts of the Society for Neuroscience, 20,* 1291.

Karon, B. P., & Widener, A. J. (1997). Repressed memories and World War II: Lest we forget. *Professional Psychology: Research and Practice, 28*(4), 338–340.

Karp, D. A. (1991). A decade of reminders: Changing age consciousness between fifty and sixty years old. In B. B. Hess & E. W. Markson (Eds.), *Growing old in America* (pp. 67–92). New Brunswick, NJ: Transaction.

Kasagi, F., Akahoshi, M., & Shimaoki, K. (1995). Relation between cold pressor test and development of hypertension based on 28-year follow-up. *Hypertension, 25,* 71–76.

Kass, S. (1999). Frequent testing means better grades, studies find. *APA Monitor, 30,* 10.

Kassin, S. M., Rigby, S., & Castillo, S. R. (1991). The accuracy-confidence correlation in eyewitness testimony: Limits and extensions of the retrospective self-awareness effect. *Journal of Personality and Social Psychology, 61,* 698–707.

Kastenbaum, R., Kastenbaum, B. K., & Morris, J. (1989). *Strengths and preferences of the terminally ill: Data from the National Hospice Demonstration Study.*

Kastin, A. J., & Pan, W. (2005). Targeting neurite growth inhibitors to induce CNS regeneration. *Current Pharmaceutical Design, 11,* 1247–1253.

Katkin, E. S., Wiens, S., & Öhman, A. (2001). Nonconscious fear conditioning, visceral perception, and the development of gut feelings. *Psychological Science, 12,* 366–370.

Kato, S., Wakasa, Y., & Yamagita, T. (1987). Relationship between minimum reinforcing doses and injection speed in cocaine and pentobarbital self-administration in crab-eating monkeys. *Pharmacology, Biochemistry, and Behavior, 28,* 407–410.

Katzell, R. A., & Thompson, D. E. (1990). Work motivation: Theory and practice. *American Psychologist, 45,* 144–153.

Kauffman, N. A., Herman, C. P., & Polivy, J. (1995). Hunger-induced finickiness in humans. *Appetite, 24,* 203–218.

Kaufman, J., & Charney, D. (2000). Comorbidity of mood and anxiety disorders. *Depression and Anxiety, 12*(Suppl. 1), 69–76.

Kaufman, L., & Kaufman, J. H. (2000). Explaining the moon illusion. *Proceedings of the National Academy of Sciences of the USA, 97,* 500–505.

Kawakami, K., Dovidio, J. F., & van Kamp, S. (2005). Kicking the habit: Effects of nonstereotypic association training and correction processes on hiring decisions. *Journal of Experimental Social Psychology, 41,* 68–75.

Kawamura, N., Kim, Y., & Asukai, N. (2001). Suppression of cellular immunity in men with a past history of posttraumatic stress disorder. *American Journal of Psychiatry, 158,* 484–486.

Kawasaki, H., Adolphs, R., Kaufman, O., Damasio, H., Damasio, A. R., Granner, M., et al. (2001). Single-neuron responses to emotional visual stimuli recorded in human ventral prefrontal cortex. *Nature Neuroscience, 4,* 15–16.

Kaye, W. H., Klump, K. L., Frank, G. K., & Strober, M. (2000). Anorexia and bulimia nervosa. *Annual Review of Medicine, 51,* 299–313.

Kazarian, S. S., & Evans, D. R. (Eds.). (2001). *Handbook of cultural health psychology.* New York: Academic Press.

Kazdin, A. E. (1994a). *Behavior modification in applied settings* (5th ed.). Pacific Grove, CA: Brooks/Cole.

Kazdin, A. E. (1994b). Methodology, design, and evaluation in psychotherapy research. In A. E. Bergin & S. L. Garfield (Eds.), *Handbook of psychotherapy and behavior change* (4th ed., pp. 19–71). New York: Wiley.

Kazdin, A. E., & Weisz, J. R. (1998). Identifying and developing empirically supported child and adolescent treatments. *Journal of Consulting and Clinical Psychology, 66,* 19–36.

Keating, D. P. (1990). Adolescent thinking. In S. S. Feldman & G. R. Elliott (Eds.), *At the threshold: The developing adolescent* (pp. 4–89). Cambridge, MA: Harvard University Press.

Kee, M., Hill, S. M., & Weist, M. D. (1999). School-based behavior management of cursing, hitting, and spitting in a girl with profound retardation. *Education and Treatment of Children, 22,* 171–178.

Keel, P. K., & Klump, K. L. (2003). Are eating disorders culture-bound syndromes?: Implications for conceptualizing their etiology. *Psychological Bulletin, 129,* 749–769.

Keeling, L. J., & Hurink, J. F. (1996). Social facilitation acts more on the consummatory phase on feeding behaviour. *Animal Behaviour, 52,* 11–15.

Keenan, K., & Wakschlag, L. S. (2004). Are oppositional defiant and conduct disorder symptoms normative behaviors in preschoolers? A comparison of referred and nonreferred children. *American Journal of Psychiatry, 161,* 356–358.

Keesey, R. E., & Powley, T. L. (1986). The regulation of body weight. *Annual Review of Psychology, 37,* 109–133.

Keinan, G., Friedland, N., & Ben-Porath, Y. (1987). Decision making under stress: Scanning of alternatives under physical threat. *Acta Psychologica, 64,* 219–228.

Keller, M. B., McCullough, J. P., Klein, D. N., Arnow, B., Dunner, D. L., Gelenberg, A. J., et al. (2000). A comparison of nefazodone, the cognitive behavioral-analysis system of psychotherapy, and their combination for the treatment of chronic depression. *New England Journal of Medicine, 342,* 1462–1470.

Keller, R. T. (2006). Transformational leadership, initiating structure, and substitutes for leadership: A longitudinal study of research and development project team performance. *Journal of Applied Psychology, 91,* 202–210.

Keller-Cohen, D., Toler, A., Miller, D., Fiori, K., & Bybee, D. (2004, August). *Social contact and communication in people over 85.* Paper presented at the convention of the American Psychological Association, Honolulu, HI.

Kelley, A. E., & Berridge, K. C. (2002). The neuroscience of natural rewards: Relevance to addictive drugs. *Journal of Neuroscience, 22,* 3306–3311.

Kelley, K. W. (1985). Immunological consequences of changing environmental stimuli. In G. P. Moberg (Ed.), *Animal stress.* Bethesda, MD: American Physiological Society.

Kellman, P. J., & Arterberry, M. E. (2006). Infant visual perception. In W. Damon & R. M. Lerner (Series Eds.) & D. Kuhn & R. Siegler (Vol. Eds.), *Handbook of child psychology: Vol. 2. Cognition, perception, and language* (6th ed.). New York: Wiley.

Kellner, C. H., Fink, M., Knapp, R., Petrides, G., Husain, M., Rummans, T., et al. (2005). Relief of expressed suicidal intent by ECT: A consortium for research in ECT study. *American Journal of Psychiatry, 162,* 977–982.

Kellum, K. K., Carr, J. E., & Dozier, C. L. (2001). Response-card instruction and student learning in a college classroom. *Teaching of Psychology, 28,* 101–104.

Kelly, G. A. (1980). A psychology of the optimal man. In A. W. Landfield & L. M. Leitner (Eds.), *Personal construct psychology: Psychotherapy and personality.* New York: Wiley.

Kelly, J. F. (2003). Self-help for substance-use disorders: History, effectiveness, knowledge gaps and research opportunities. *Clinical Psychology Review, 23*(5), 639–663.

Kelly, T. H., Foltin, R. W., Emurian, C. S., & Fischman, M. W. (1990). Multidimensional behavioral effects of marijuana. *Progress in Neuro-Psychopharmacology and Biological Psychiatry, 14,* 885–902.

Keltner, D., & Buswell, B. N. (1996). Evidence for the distinctiveness of embarrassment, shame, and guilt: A study of recalled antecedents and facial expressions of emotion. *Cognition and Emotion, 10,* 117–125.

Kemble, E. D., Filipi, T., & Gravlin, L. (1985). Some simple classroom experiments on cerebral lateralization. *Teaching of Psychology, 12,* 81–83.

Kemeny, M. E. (2003). The psychobiology of stress. *Current Directions in Psychological Science, 12,* 124–129.

Kendall, P. C. (1999). Clinical significance. *Journal of Consulting and Clinical Psychology, 67,* 283–284.

Kendall, P. C., & Chambless, D. L. (Eds.). (1998). Special section: Empirically supported psychological therapies. *Journal of Consulting and Clinical Psychology, 66,* 3–167.

Kendall, P. C., & Sheldrick, R. C. (2000). Normative data for normative comparisons. *Journal of Consulting and Clinical Psychology, 68,* 767–773.

Kendell, R., & Jablensky, A. (2003). Distinguishing between the validity and utility of psychiatric diagnoses. *American Journal of Psychiatry, 160,* 4–12.

Kendler, K. S. (2005). "A gene for…": The nature of gene action in psychiatric disorders. *American Journal of Psychiatry, 162,* 1243–1252.

Kendler, K. S., Gardner, C. O., & Prescott, C. A. (2002). Toward a comprehensive developmental model for major depression in women. *American Journal of Psychiatry, 159,* 1133–1145.

Kendler, K. S., Gardner, C. O., & Prescott, C. A. (2006). Toward a comprehensive developmental model for major depression in men. *American Journal of Psychiatry, 163,* 115–124.

Kendler, K. S., Gatz, M., Gardner, C. O., & Pedersen, N. L. (2006). A Swedish national twin study of lifetime major depression. *American Journal of Psychiatry, 163,* 109–114.

Kendler, K. S., Heath, A. C., Neale, M. C., Kessler, R. C., & Eaves, L. J (1992). A population-based twin study of alcoholism in women. *Journal of the American Medical Association, 268,* 1877–1882.

Kendler, K. S., Hettema, J. M., Butera, F., Gardner, C. O., & Prescott, C. A. (2003). Life event dimensions of loss, humiliation, entrapment, and danger in the prediction of onsets of major depression and generalized anxiety. *Archives of General Psychiatry, 60,* 789–796.

Kendler, K. S., Jacobson, K. C., Myers, J., & Prescott, C. A. (2002). Sex differences in genetic and environmental risk factors for irrational fears and phobias. *Psychological Medicine, 32,* 209–217.

Kendler, K. S., Jacobson, K. C., Prescott, C. A., & Neale, M. C. (2003). Specificity of genetic and environmental risk factors for use and abuse/dependence of cannabis, cocaine, hallucinogens, sedatives, stimulants, and opiates in male twins. *American Journal of Psychiatry, 160,* 687–695.

Kendler, K. S., Kessler, R. C., Walters, E. E., MacLean, C., Neale, M. C., Heath, A. C., & Eaves, L. J. (1995). Stressful life events, genetic liability, and onset of an episode of major depression in women. *American Journal of Psychiatry, 152,* 833–842.

Kendler, K. S., Kuhn, J., & Prescott, C. A. (2004). The interrelationship of neuroticism, sex, and stressful life events in the prediction of episodes of major depression. *American Journal of Psychiatry, 161,* 631–636.

Kendler, K. S., Kuhn, J. W., Vittum, J., Prescott, C. A., & Riley, B. (2005). The interaction of stressful life events and a serotonin transporter polymorphism in the prediction of episodes of major depression: A replication. *Archives of General Psychiatry, 62,* 529–535.

Kendler, K. S., Meyers, J., Prescott, C. A., & Neale, M. C. (2001). The genetic epidemiology of irrational fears and phobias in men. *Archives of General Psychiatry, 58,* 257–265.

Kendler, K. S., Thornton, L. M., & Gardner, C. O. (2000). Stressful life events and previous episodes in the etiology of major depression in women: An evaluation of the "kindling" hypothesis. *American Journal of Psychiatry, 157,* 1243–1251.

Kendler, K. S., Thornton, L. M., & Gardner, C. O. (2001). Genetic risk, number of previous depressive episodes, and stressful life events in predicting onset of major depression. *American Journal of Psychiatry, 158,* 582–586.

Kendler, K. S., Thornton, L. M., Gilman, S. E., & Kessler, R. C. (2000). Sexual orientation in a U.S. national sample of twin and nontwin sibling pairs. *American Journal of Psychiatry, 157,* 1843–1846.

Kendler, K. S., Thornton, L. M., & Prescott, C. A. (2001). Gender differences in the rates of exposure to stressful life events and sensitivity to their depressogenic effects. *American Journal of Psychiatry, 158,* 587–593.

Kenrick, D. T., Groth, G., Trost, M., & Sadalla, E. K. (1993). Integrating evolutionary and social exchange perspectives on relationships: Effects of gender, self-appraisal, and involvement level on mate selection. *Journal of Personality and Social Psychology, 64,* 951–969.

Kenrick, D. T., Neuberg, S., & Cialdini, R. (2005). *Social psychology: Unraveling the mystery* (3rd ed). Boston, MA: Pearson.

Kensinger, E. A., & Corkin, S. (2004). Two routes to emotional memory: Distinct neural processes for valence and arousal. *Proceedings of the National Academy of Sciences, 101,* 3310–3315.

Kent, S., Rodriguez, F., Kelley, K. W., & Dantzer, R. (1994). Reduction in food and water intake induced by microinjection of interleukin-1b in the ventromedial hypothalamus of the rat. *Physiology and Behavior, 56*(5), 1031–1036.

Kenworthy, J. B., Turner, R. N., Hewstone, M., & Voci, A. (2006). Intergroup contact: When does it work, and why. In J. Dovidio, P. Glick, & L. Rudman (Eds.), *On the nature of prejudice: Fifty years after Allport.* Boston, MA: Blackwell.

Keogh, E., Bond, F. W., & Flaxman, P. E. (2006). Improving academic performance and mental health through a stress management intervention: Outcomes and mediators of change. *Behaviour Research and Therapy, 44,* 339–357.

Kepner, J. (2001). Touch in Gestalt body process psychotherapy: Purpose, practice, and ethics. *Gestalt Review, 5,* 97–114.

Kerr, M. P., & Payne, S. J. (1994). Learning to use a spreadsheet by doing and by watching. *Interacting with Computers, 6,* 3–22.

Kerr, N. L., & Tindale, R. S. (2004). Group performance and decision making. *Annual Review of Psychology, 55,* 623–655.

Kertesz, A. (1993). Clinical forms of aphasia. *Acta Neurochirurgica. Supplementum (Wien), 56,* 52–58.

Kersting, K. (2004, September). Cross-cultural training: 30 years and going strong. *Monitor on Psychology,* 48–49.

Keselman, H. J., Othman, A. R., Wilcox, R. R., & Fradette, K. (2004). The new and improved two-sample t test. *Psychological Science, 15,* 47–51.

Kessler, R. C., Adler, L., Barkley, R., Biederman, J., Conners, C. K., Demler, O., et al. (2006). The prevalence and correlates of adult ADHD in the United States: Results from the National Comorbidity Survey Replication. *American Journal of Psychiatry, 163,* 716–723.

Kessler, R. C., Berglund, P., Borges, G., Nock, M., & Wang, P.S. (2005). Trends in suicide ideation, plans, gestures, and attempts in the United States, 1990–1992 to 2001–2003. *Journal of the American Medical Association, 293,* 2487–2495.

Kessler, R. C., Berglund, P., Demler, O., Jin, R., Koretz, D., Merikangas, K.R., et al. (2003). The epidemiology of major depressive disorder: Results from the national comorbidity survey replication (NCS-R). *Journal of the American Medical Association, 289,* 3095–3105.

Kessler, R. C., Berglund, P., Demier, O., Jin, R., & Walters, E. E. (2005). Lifetime prevalence of and age of onset distributions of DSM-IV disorders in the national comorbidity survey replication. *Archives of General Psychiatry, 62,* 593–602.

Kessler, R. C., Chiu, W. T., Demier, O., & Walters, E. E. (2005). Prevalence, severity, and comorbidity of 12-month DSM-IV disorders in the national comorbidity survey replication. *Archives of General Psychiatry, 62,* 617–627.

Kessler, R. C., Chiu, W. T., Jin, R., Ruscio, A. M., Shear, K., & Walters, E. E. (2006). The epidemiology of panic attacks, panic disorder, and agoraphobia in the National Comorbidity Survey Replication. *Archives of General Psychiatry, 63,* 415–424.

Kessler, R. C., Demler, O., Frank, R. G., Olfson, M., Pincus, H. A., et al. (2005). Prevalence and treatment of mental disorders, 1990 to 2003. *New England Journal of Medicine, 352,* 2515–2523.

Kessler, R. C., Keller, M. B., & Wittchen, H-U. (2001). The epidemiology of generalized anxiety disorder. *Psychiatric Clinics of North America, 24,* 19–39.

Kessler, R. C., McGonagle, K. A., Zhao, S., Nelson, C. B., Hughes, M., Eshleman, S., et al. (1994). Lifetime and 12-month prevalence of DSM-III-R psychiatric disorders in the United States. *Archives of General Psychiatry, 51,* 8–19.

Kest, B., Wilson, S. G., & Mogil, J. S. (1999). Sex differences in supraspinal morphine analgesia are dependent on genotype. *Journal of Pharmacology & Experimental Therapeutics, 289,* 1370–1375.

Kety, S. S., Wender, P. H., Jacobsen, B., Ingraham, L. J., Jansson, L., Faber, B., & Kinney, D. K. (1994). Mental illness in the biological and adoptive relatives of schizophrenic adoptees. *Archives of General Psychiatry, 51,* 442–455.

Khan, A., Leventhal, R. M., Khan, S., & Brown, W. A. (2002). Suicide risk in patients with anxiety disorders: A meta-analysis of the FDA database. *Journal of Affective Disorders, 69,* 183–190.

Khan, J., Wei, J. S., Ringner, M., Saal, L. H., Ladanyi, M., Westermann, F., et al. (2001). Classification and diagnostic prediction of cancers using gene expression profiling and artificial neural networks. *Nature Medicine, 7,* 673–679.

Khot, U. N., Khot, M. B., Bajzer, C. T., Sapp, S. K., Ohman, E. M., Brener, S. J., et al. (2003). Prevalence of conventional risk factors in patients with coronary heart disease. *Journal of the American Medical Association, 290,* 898–904.

Kiecolt-Glaser, J. K., & Glaser, R. (2001). Stress and immunity: Age enhances the risks. *Current Directions in Psychological Science, 10,* 18–21.

Kiecolt-Glaser, J. K., Loving, T. J., Stowell, J. R., Malarkey, W. B., Lemeshow, S., Dickinson, S. L., et al. (2005). Hostile marital interactions, proinflammatory cytokine production, and wound healing. *Archives of General Psychiatry, 62,* 1377–1384.

Kiecolt-Glaser, J. K., McGuire, L., Robles, T. F., & Glaser, R. (2002). Psychoneuroimmunology: Psychological influences on immune function and health. *Journal of Consulting & Clinical Psychology, 70,* 537–547.

Kiecolt-Glaser, J. K., & Newton, T. L. (2001). Marriage and health: His and hers. *Psychological Bulletin, 127,* 472–503.

Kiecolt-Glaser, J. K., Page, G. G., Marucha, P. T., MacCallum, R. C., & Glaser, R. (1998). Psychological influences on surgical recovery: Perspectives from psychoneuroimmunology. *American Psychologist, 11,* 1209–1218.

Kiecolt-Glaser, J. K., Preacher, K. J., MacCallum, R. C., Atkinson, C., Malarkey, W. B., & Glaser, R. (2003). Chronic stress and age-related increases in the proinflammatory cytokine IL-6. *Proceedings of the National Academy of Sciences, 100,* 9090–9095.

Kieffer, K. M., Schinka, J. A., & Curtiss, G. (2004). Person-environment congruence and personality domains in the prediction of job performance and work quality. *Journal of Counseling Psychology, 51,* 168–177.

Kiehl, K. A., Bates, A. T., Laurens, K. R., Hare, R. D., & Liddle, P. F. (2006). Brain potentials implicate temporal lobe abnormalities in criminal psychopaths. *Journal of Abnormal Psychology, 115,* 443–453.

Kieseppä, T., Partonen, T., Haukka, J., Kaprio, J., & Lönnqvist, J. (2004). High concordance of bipolar I disorder in a nationwide sample of twins. *American Journal of Psychiatry, 161,* 1814–1821.

Kiesler, D. J. (1996). *Contemporary interpersonal theory and research.* New York: Wiley.

Kiewra, K. A. (1989). A review of note-taking: The encoding storage paradigm and beyond. *Educational Psychology Review, 1,* 147–172.

Kihlstrom, J. F. (1999). The psychological unconscious. In L. Pervin & O. John (Eds.), *Handbook of personality* (pp. 424–442). New York: Guilford.

Kim, E. Y., Mahmoud, G. S., & Grover, L. M. (2005). REM sleep deprivation inhibits LTP in vivo in area CA1 of rat hippocampus. *Neuroscience Letters, 388,* 163–167.

Kim, J., & Hatfield, E. (2004). Love types and subjective well-being: A cross-cultural study. *Social Behavior and Personality, 32,* 173–182.

Kim, K., & Rohner, R. P. (2002). Parental warmth, control, and involvement in schooling: Predicting academic achievement among Korean American adolescents. *Journal of Cross-Cultural Psychology, 33*(2), 127–140.

Kim, N. S., & Ahn, W.-K. (2002). Clinical psychologists' theory-based representations of mental disorders predict their diagnostic reasoning and memory. *Journal of Experimental Psychology: General, 131,* 451–476.

Kimble, G. A. (2000). Behaviorism and unity in psychology. *Current Directions in Psychological Science, 9,* 208–212.

Kim-Cohen, J., Arseneault, L., Caspi, A., Tomás, M. P., Taylor, A., & Moffitt, T. E. (2005). Validity of DSM-IV conduct disorder in 41/2-5-year-old children: A longitudinal epidemiological study. *American Journal of Psychiatry, 162,* 1108–1117.

King, J., & Pribram, K. H. (Eds.). (1995). *The scale of conscious experience: Is the brain too important to be left to specialists to study?* Mahwah, NJ: Erlbaum.

King, J. E., Weiss, A., & Farmer, K. H. (2005). A chimpanzee (*pan troglodytes*) analogue of cross-national generalization of personality structure: Zoological parks and an African sanctuary. *Journal of Personality, 73,* 389–410.

Kingdom, F. A. (2003). Color brings relief to human vision. *Nature Neuroscience, 6,* 641–644.

Kinsbourne, M., & Cook, J. (1971). Generalized and lateralized effects of concurrent verbalization on a unimanual skill. *Quarterly Journal of Experimental Psychology, 23*, 341–345.

Kinsey, A. C., Pomeroy, W. B., & Martin, C. E. (1948). *Sexual behavior in the human male.* Philadelphia: Saunders.

Kinsey, A. C., Pomeroy, W. B., Martin, C. E., & Gebhard, P. H. (1953). *Sexual behavior in the human female.* Philadelphia: Saunders.

Kircher, J. C., Horowitz, S. W., & Raskin, D. C. (1988). Meta-analysis of mock crime studies of the control question polygraph technique. *Law and Human Behavior, 12*, 79–90.

Kirkpatrick, B., Buchanan, R. W., Ross, D. E., & Carpenter, W. T., Jr. (2001). A separate disease within the syndrome of schizophrenia. *Archives of General Psychiatry, 58*, 165–171.

Kirsch, I. (1994a). Clinical hypnosis as a nondeceptive placebo: Empirically derived techniques. *American Journal of Clinical Hypnosis, 37*(2), 95–106.

Kirsch, I. (1994b). Defining hypnosis for the public. *Contemporary Hypnosis, 11*(3), 142–143.

Kirsch, I., & Braffman, W. (2001). Imaginative suggestibility and hypnotizability. *Psychological Science, 10*, 57–61.

Kirsch, I., Moore, T. J., Scoboria, A., & Nicholls, S. S. (2002). The emperor's new drugs: An analysis of antidepressant medication data submitted to the U.S. Food and Drug Administration [Electronic version]. *Prevention and Treatment, 5*, np.

Kirsch, I., Scoboria, A., & Moore, T. J. (2002). Antidepressants and placebos: Secrets, revelations, and unanswered questions. *Prevention and Treatment, 5*, np.

Kirschenbaum, H., & Jourdan, A. (2005). The current status of Carl Rogers and the person-centered approach. *Psychotherapy: Theory, Research, Practice, Training, 42*, 37–51.

Kishi, T., & Elmquist, J. K. (2005). Body weight is regulated by the brain: A link between feeding and emotion. *Molecular Psychiatry, 10*, 132–146.

Kishioka, S., Miyamoto, Y., Fukunaga, Y., Nishida, S., & Yamamoto, H. (1994). Effects of a mixture of peptidase inhibitors (Amastatin, Captopril and Phosphoramidon) on met enkephalin, beta-endorphin, dynorphin (1–13) and electroacupuncture induced antinociception in rats. *Japanese Journal of Pharmacology, 66*, 337–345.

Kisilevsky, B. S., Hains, S. M. J., Lee, K., Xie, X., Huang, H., Ye, H. H., et al. (2003). -Effects of experience on fetal voice recognition. *Psychological Science, 14*, 220–224.

Kitano, H., Chi, I., Rhee, S., Law, C., & Lubben, J. (1992). Norms and alcohol consumption: Japanese in Japan, Hawaii, and California. *Journal of Studies on Alcohol, 53*, 33–39.

Kitayama, N., Vaccarino, V., Kutner, M., Weiss, P., & Bremner, J.D. (2005). Magnetic resonance imaging (MRI) measurement of hippocampal volume in posttraumatic stress disorder: A meta-analysis. *Journal of Affective Disorders, 88*, 79–86.

Kitayama, S., Duffy, S., Kawamura, T., & Larsen, J. T. (2003). Perceiving an object and its context in different cultures: A cultural look at new look. *Psychological Science, 14*, 201–206.

Kitayama, S., Duffy, S., & Uchida, Y. (in press). Self as cultural mode of being. In S. Kitayama & D. Cohen (Eds.), *Handbook of cultural psychology.* New York: Guilford Press

Kitayama, S., & Markus, H. R (1992, May). *Construal of self as cultural frame: Implications for internationalizing psychology.* Paper presented to the Symposium on Internationalization and Higher Education, Ann Arbor.

Kitayama, S., Snibbe, A. C., Markus, H. R., & Suzuki, T. (2004). Is there any "free" choice?: Self and dissonance in two cultures. *Psychological Science, 15*, 527–533.

Kitayama, S., & Uchida, Y. (2003). Explicit self-criticism and implicit self-regard: Evaluating self and friend in two cultures. *Journal of Experimental Social Psychology, 39*, 476–482.

Kjaer, T. W., Bertelsen, C., Piccini, P., Brooks, D., Alving, J., & Lou, H. C. (2002). Increased dopamine tone during meditation-induced change of consciousness. *Cognitive Brain Research, 13*, 255–259.

Klahr, D., & Simon, H. (1999). Studies of scientific discovery: Complementary approaches and convergent findings. *Psychological Bulletin, 125*, 524–543.

Klaus, M. H., & Kennell, J. H. (1976). *Maternal infant bonding: The impact of early separation or loss on family development.* St. Louis: Mosby.

Klausner, H. A., & Lewandowski, C. (2002). Infrequent causes of stroke. *Emergency Medicine Clinics of North America, 20*, 657–670.

Kleemola, P., Jousilahti, P., Pietinen, P., Vartiainen, E., & Tuomilehto, J. (2000). Coffee consumption and the risk of coronary heart disease and death. *Archives of Internal Medicine, 160*, 3393–3400.

Klein, D., Lewinsohn,. P. M., Seeley, J. R., & Rohde, P. (2001). A family study of major depressive disorder in a community sample of adolescents. *Archives of General Psychiatry, 58*, 13–20.

Klein, D. C., & Seligman, M. E. P. (1976). Reversal of performance deficits and perceptual deficits in learned helplessness and depression. *Journal of Abnormal Psychology, 85*, 11–26.

Klein, D. N., Santiago, N. J., Vivian, D., Blalock, J. A., Kocsis, J. H., Markowitz, J. C., et al.(2004). Cognitive-behavioral analysis system of psychotherapy as a maintenance treatment for chronic depression. *Journal of Consulting and Clinical Psychology, 72*, 681–688.

Klein, M. (1975). *The writings of Melanie Klein: Vol. 3.* London: Hogarth Press.

Kleinknecht, R. A. (1991). *Mastering anxiety: The nature and treatment of anxious conditions.* New York: Plenum.

Kleinknecht, R. A. (1994). Acquisition of blood, injury, and needle fears and phobias. *Behaviour Research and Therapy, 32*, 817–823.

Kleinknecht, R. A. (2000). Social phobia. In M. Hersen & M. K. Biaggio (Eds.), *Effective brief therapies: A clinician's guide.* New York: Academic Press.

Kleinman, A. (1991, April). *Culture and DSM-IV: Recommendations for the introduction and for the overall structure.* Paper presented at the National Institute of Mental Health-sponsored Conference on Culture and Diagnosis, Pittsburgh, PA.

Kleinman, A. (2004). Culture and depression. *New England Journal of Medicine, 351*, 951–953.

Klepp, K.-I., Kelder, S. H., & Perry, C. L. (1995). Alcohol and marijuana use among adolescents: Long-term outcomes of the class of 1989 study. *Annals of Behavioral Medicine, 17*, 19–24.

Kline, S., & Groninger, L. D. (1991). The imagery bizarreness effect as a function of sentence complexity and presentation time. *Bulletin of the Psychonomic Society, 29*, 25–27.

Klinesmith, J., Kasser, T., & McAndrew, F. T. (2006). Guns, testosterone, and aggression: An experimental test of a mediational hypothesis. *Psychological Science, 17*, 568–571.

Kling, K. C., Hyde, J. S., Showers, C. J., & Buswell, B. N. (1999). Gender differences in self-esteem: A meta-analysis. *Psychological Bulletin, 125*, 470–500.

Klintsova, A. Y., & Greenough, W. T. (1999). Synaptic plasticity in cortical systems. *Current Opinion in Neurobiology, 9*, 203–208.

Klohnen, E., & Bera, S. (1998). Behavioral and experiential patterns of avoidantly and securely attached women across adulthood: A 31-year longitudinal perspective. *Journal of Personality and Social Psychology, 74*, 211–223.

Klosko, J. S., Barlow, D. H., Tassinari, R., & Cerny, J. A. (1990). A comparison of alprazolam and behavior therapy in treatment of panic disorder. *Journal of Consulting and Clinical Psychology, 58*, 77–84.

Kluger, A. N., & DeNisi, A. (1998). Feedback interventions: Toward the understanding of a double-edged sword. *Current Directions in Psychological Science, 7*, 67–72.

Knafo, A., Iervolino, A. C., & Plomin, R. (2005). Masculine girls and feminine boys: Genetic and environmental contributions to atypical gender development in early childhood. *Journal of Personality and Social Psychology, 88*, 400–412.

Knopman, D. S. (2006). Dementia and cerebrovascular disease. *Mayo Clinic Proceedings, 81*(2), 223–230.

Knopman, D., & Selnes, O. (2003). Neuropsychology of dementia. In K. M. Heilman & E. Valenstein (Eds.), *Clinical neuropsychology* (4th ed.). New York: Oxford University Press.

Koger, S. M., Schettler, T., & Weiss, B. (2005). Environmental toxicants and developmental disabilities: A challenge for psychologists. *American Psychologist, 60*, 243–255.

Koh, P. O., Undie, A. S., Kabbani, N., Levenson, R., Goldman-Rakic, P. S., & Lidow, M. S. (2002). Up-regulation of neuronal calcium sensor-1 (NCS-1) in the prefrontal cortex of schizophrenic and bipolar patients. *Proceedings of the National Academies of Science, 100*, 313–317.

Kohlberg, L., & Gilligan, C. (1971). The adolescent as a philosopher: The discovery of the self in a postconventional world. *Daedalus, 100*, 1051–1086.

Köhler, W. (1924). *The mentality of apes.* New York: Harcourt Brace.

Köhler, W. (1976). *The mentality of apes* (E. Winter, Trans.). Oxford, UK: Liveright.

Kohnert, K. (2004). Cognitive and cognate-based treatments for bilingual aphasia: A case study. *Brain and Language, 91*, 294–302.

Kohut, H. (1984). Selected problems of self-psychological theory. In J. D. Lichtenberg & S. Kaplan (Eds.), *Reflections on self psychology* (pp. 387–416). Hillsdale, NJ: Erlbaum.

Kok, M. R., & Boon, M. E. (1996). Consequences of neural network technology for cervical screening: increase in diagnostic consistency and positive scores. *Cancer, 78*, 112–117.

Kolata, G. (2002, August 19.). Male hormone therapy popular but untested. *The New York Times.*

Kolata, G. (2003, April 22). Hormone studies: What went wrong? *The New York Times.*

Kolata, G., & Markel, H. (2001, April 29). Baby not crawling? Reason seems to be less tummy time. *New York Times.*

Kolb, B., Gibb, R., & Robinson, T. E. (2003). Brain plasticity and behavior. *Current Directions in Psychological Science, 12,* 1–5.

Kolb, B., Gorny, G., Li, Y., Samaha, A.-N., & Robinson, T. E. (2003). Amphetamine or cocaine limits the ability of later experience to promote structural plasticity in the neocortex and nucleus accumbens. *Proceedings of the National Academy of Sciences, 100,* 10523–10528.

Konrad, K., Neufang, S., Hanisch, C., Fink, G. R., & Herpertz-Dahlmann, B. (2006). Dysfunctional attentional networks in children with attention deficit/hyperactivity disorder: Evidence from an event-related functional magnetic imaging study. *Biological Psychiatry, 59,* 643–651.

Konradi, C., Eaton, M., MacDonald, M. L., Walsh, J., Benes, F. M. & Heckers, S. (2004). Molecular evidence for mitochondrial dysfunction in bipolar disorder. *Archives of General Psychiatry, 61,* 300–308.

Koob, G. F., & Bloom, F. E. (1988). Cellular and molecular mechanisms of drug dependence. *Science, 242,* 715–723.

Kop, W. J., Berman, D. S., Gransar, H., Wong, N. D., Miranda-Peats, R., White, M. D., et al. (2005). Social network and coronary artery calcification in asymptomatic individuals. *Psychosomatic Medicine, 67,* 343–352.

Koppenaal, L., & Glanzer, M. (1990). An examination of the continuous distractor task and the "long-term recency effect." *Memory & Cognition, 18,* 183–195.

Kordower, J. H., Emborg, M. E., Bloch, J., Ma, S. Y., Chu, Y., Leventhal, L., et al. (2000). Neurodegeneration prevented by lentiviral vector delivery of GDNF in primate models of Parkinson's disease. *Science, 290,* 767–773.

Korner, J., & Leibel, R. L. (2003). To eat or not to eat—How the gut talks to the brain. *The New England Journal of Medicine, 349,* 926–928.

Korochkin, L. I. (2000). New approaches in developmental genetics and gene therapy: Xenotransplantation of Drosophila embryonic nerve cells into the brain of vertebrate animals. *Genetika, 36,* 1436–1442.

Kotani, N., Hashimoto, H., Sato, Y., Sessler, D. I., Yoshioka, H., Kitayama, M., et al. (2001). Preoperative intradermal acupuncture reduces postoperative pain, nausea and vomiting, analgesic requirement, and sympathoadrenal responses. *Anesthesiology, 95,* 349–356.

Kouider, S., & Dupoux, E. (2005). Subliminal speech priming. *Psychological Science, 16,* 617.

Kouri, E. M., Pope, H. G., & Lukas, S. E. (1999). Changes in aggressive behavior during withdrawal from long-term marijuana use. *Psychopharmacology, 143,* 302–308.

Kouyoumdjian, H. (2004). Influence of unannounced quizzes and cumulative exams on attendance and study behavior. *Teaching of Psychology, 31,* 110–111.

Kozak, M. J., Liebowitz, M. R., & Foa, E. B. (2000). Cognitive behavior therapy and pharmacotherapy for obsessive-compulsive disorder: The NIMH-sponsored collaborative study. In W. K. Goodman, M. V. Rudorfer, & J. D. Maser (Eds.), *Obsessive-compulsive disorder: Contemporary issues in treatment* (pp. 501–530). Mahwah, NJ: Erlbaum.

Kozel, F. A., Padgett, T. M., & George, M. S. (2004). A replication study of the neural correlates of deception. *Behavioral Neuroscience, 118,* 852–856.

Kozorovitskiy, Y., Gross, C. G., Kopil, C., Battaglia, L., McBreen, M., Stranahan, A. M., et al. (2005). Experience induces structural and biochemical changes in the adult primate brain. *Proceedings of the National Academy of Sciences of the USA, 102,* 17478–17482.

Krain, A. L., & Castellanos, F. X. (2006). Brain development and ADHD. *Clinical Psychology Review, 26,* 433–444.

Krakauer, J. (1997). *Into thin air.* New York: Villard.

Kramer, A. F., & Willis, S. (2002). Enhancing the cognitive vitality of older adults. *Current Directions in Psychological Science, 11,* 173–177.

Krantz, D., & Durel, L. (1983). Psychobiological substrates of the Type A behavior pattern. *Health Psychology, 2,* 393–411.

Krantz, D., Contrada, R., Hill, D., & Friedler, E. (1988). Environmental stress and biobehavioral antecedents of coronary heart disease. *Journal of Consulting and Clinical Psychology, 56,* 333–341.

Krantz, D. S., & McCeney, M. K. (2002). Effects of psychological and social factors on organic disease: A critical assessment of research on coronary heart disease. *Annual Review of Psychology, 53,* 341–369.

Kraus, W. E., Houmard, J. A., Duscha, B. D., Knetzger, K. J., Wharton, M. B., McCartney, J. S., et al. (2002). Effects of the amount and intensity of exercise on plasma lipoproteins. *The New England Journal of Medicine, 347,* 1483–1492.

Krause, M. S. (2005). How the psychotherapy research community must work toward measurement and why. *Journal of Clinical Psychology, 61,* 269–283.

Krause, N., & Shaw, B. A. (2000). Role-specific feelings of control and mortality. *Psychology and Aging, 15,* 617–626.

Kraut, R., Olson, J., Banaji, M., Bruckman, A., Cohen, J., & Couper, M. (2004). Psychological research online: Report of board of scientific affairs' advisory group on the conduct of research on the Internet. *American Psychologist, 59,* 105–117.

Krauzlis, R. J. (2002). Reaching for answers. *Neuron, 34,* 673–674.

Krauzlis, R. J., & Lisberger, S. G. (1991). Visual motion commands for pursuit eye movements in the cerebellum. *Science, 253,* 568–571.

Kravitz, R. L., Epstein, R. M., Feldman, M. D., Franz, C. E., Azari, R., Wilkes, M. S., (2005). Influence of patients' requests for direct-to-consumer advertised antidepressants: A randomized controlled trial. *Journal of the American Medical Association, 293,* 1995–2002.

Kray, L. J., & Galinsky, A. D. (2003). The debiasing effect of counterfactual mindsets: Increasing the search for disconfirmatory information in group decisions. *Organizational Behavior and Human Decision Processes, 91,* 69–81.

Krebs, D. L., & Denton, K. (2005). Toward a more pragmatic approach to morality: A critical evaluation of Kohlberg's model. *Psychological Review, 112,* 629–649.

Kreek, M. J., Nielsen, D. A., Butelman, E. R., & LaForge, K. S. (2005). Genetic influences on impulsivity, risk taking, stress responsivity and vulnerability to drug abuse and addiction. *Nature Neuroscience, 8,* 1450–1457.

Kring, A. M., & Gordon, A. H. (1998). Sex differences in emotion: Expression, experience, and physiology. *Journal of Personality & Social Psychology, 74,* 686–703.

Kristof, N. D. (1997, August 17). Where children rule. *New York Times Magazine.*

Krohne, H. W., & Slangen, K. E. (2005). Influence of social support on adaptation to surgery. *Health Psychology, 24,* 101–105.

Krosnick, J. A., Betz, A. L., Jussim, L. J., & Lynn, A. R. (1992). Subliminal conditioning of attitude. *Personality and Social Psychology Bulletin, 18,* 152–162.

Krueger, R. F., & Markon, K. E. (2006). Understanding psychopathology: Melding behavior genetics, personality, and quantitative psychology to develop an empirically based model. *Current Directions in Psychological Science 15,* 113–117.

Krueger, R. F., Markon, K. E., & Bouchard, T. J., Jr. (2003). The extended genotype: The heritability of personality accounts for the heritability of recalled family environments in twins reared apart. *Journal of Personality, 71,* 809–833.

Krueger, R. F., Watson, D., & Barlow, D. H. (2005). Introduction to the special section: Toward a dimensionally based taxonomy of psychopathology. *Journal of Abnormal Psychology, 114,* 491–493.

Kruger, D. J. (2003). Evolution and altruism: Combining psychological mediators with naturally selected tendencies. *Evolution and Human Behavior, 24,* 118–125.

Kruger, J., Wirtz, D., & Miller, D. T. (2005). Counterfactual thinking and the first instinct fallacy. *Journal of Personality and Social Psychology, 88,* 725–735.

Kryger, M. H., Roth, T., & Dement, W. C. (2000). *Principles and practice of sleep medicine* (3rd ed.). Philadelphia: Saunders.

Krykouli, S. E., Stanley, B. G., Seirafi, R. D., & Leibowitz, S. F (1990). Stimulation of feeding by galanin: Anatomical localization and behavioral specificity of this peptide's effects in the brain. *Peptides, 11*(5), 995–1001.

Kubzansky, L. D., Davidson, K. W., & Rozanski, A. (2005). The clinical impact of negative psychological states: Expanding the spectrum of risk for coronary artery disease. *Psychosomatic Medicine, 67*(S1), S10–S14.

Kuhn, D., & Franklin, S. (2006). The second decade: What develops (and how)? In W. Damon & R. M. Lerner (Series Eds.) & D. Kuhn & R. Siegler (Vol. Eds.), *Handbook of child psychology: Vol. 2. Cognition, perception, and language* (6th ed.). New York: Wiley.

Kuhnen, C. M., & Knutson, B. (2005). The neural basis of financial risk taking. *Neuron, 47,* 763–770.

Kukull, W. A., Higdon, R., Bowen, J. D., McCormick, W. C., Teri, L., Schellenberg, G. D., et al. (2002). Dementia and Alzheimer disease incidence: A prospective cohort study. *Archives of Neurology, 59,* 1737–1746.

Kuncel, N. R., Hezlett, S. A., & Ones, D. (2004). Academic performance, career potential, creativity, and job performance: Can one construct predict them all? *Journal of Personality and Social Psychology, 86,* 148–161.

Kunen, S., Niederhauser, R., Smith, P. O., Morris, J. A., & Marx, B. D. (2005). Race disparities in psychiatric rates in emergency departments. *Journal of Consulting and Clinical Psychology, 73,* 116–126.

Kunkel, D., Wilson, B. J., Linz, D., Potter, J., Donnerstein, E., Smith, S. L., et al. (1996). *The national television violence study.* Studio City, CA: Mediascope.

Kurbat, M. A. (1997). Can the recognition of living things really be selectively impaired? *Neuropsychologia, 35*(6), 813–827.

Kurdek, L. A. (2005). What do we know about gay and lesbian couples? *Current Directions in Psychological Science, 14,* 251–254.

Kushner, M. G., Thuras, P., Kaminski, J., Anderson, N., Neumeyer, B., & Mackenzie, T. (2000). Expectancies for alcohol to affect tension and anxiety as a function of time. *Addictive Behaviors, 25,* 93–98.

Kutchins, H., & Kirk, S. A. (1997). *Making us crazy: The psychiatric bible and the creation of mental disorders.* New York: Free Press.

Kwan, M., Greenleaf, W. J., Mann, J., Crapo, L., & Davidson, J. M. (1983). The nature of androgen action on male sexuality: A combined laboratory-self-report study on hypogonadal men. *Journal of Clinical Endocrinology and Metabolism, 57,* 557–562.

Kwate, N. O. A. (2001). Intelligence or misorientation? *Journal of Black Psychology, 27,* 221–238.

Kyrios, M., Sanavio, E., Bhar, S., & Liguori, L. (2001). Associations between obsessive-compulsive phenomena, affect, and beliefs: Cross-cultural comparisons of Australian and Italian data. *Behavioural and Cognitive Psychotherapy, 29,* 409–422.

L

Laan, E., Everaerd, W., Van Aanhold, M. T., & Rebel, M. (1993). Performance demand and sexual arousal in woman. *Behavior Research and Therapy, 31,* 25–36.

Laboratory of Comparative Human Cognition. (1982). Culture and intelligence. In R. J. Sternberg (Ed.), *Handbook of intelligence* (pp. 642–722). New York: Cambridge University Press.

Labouvie-Vief, G. (1982). Discontinuities in development from childhood. In T. M. Field, A. Huston, H. C. Quay, L. Troll, & G. E. Finley (Eds.), *Review of human development.* New York: Wiley.

Labouvie-Vief, G. (1992). A new-Piagetian perspective on adult cognitive development. In R. J. Sternberg & C. A. Berg (Eds.), *Intellectual development.* New York: Cambridge University Press.

Lacayo, A. (1995). Neurologic and psychiatric complications of cocaine abuse. *Neuropsychiatry, Neuropsychology, and Behavioral Neurology, 8*(1), 53–60.

Ladd, G. (2005). *Peer relationships and social competence of children and youth.* New Haven, CT: Yale University Press.

LaFrance, M., Hecht, M. A., & Paluck, E. L. (2003). The contingent smile: A meta-analysis of sex differences in smiling. *Psychological Bulletin, 129,* 305–334.

Lagerspetz, K. M. J., & Lagerspetz, K. Y. H. (1983). Genes and aggression. In E. C. Simmel, M. E. Hahn, & J. K. Walters (Eds.), *Aggressive behavior: Genetic and neural approaches.* Hillsdale, NJ: Erlbaum.

LaGreca, A. M., Silverman, W. K., Vernberg, E. M., & Prinstein, M. J. (1996). Symptoms of posttraumatic stress in children after Hurricane Andrew: A prospective study. *Journal of Consulting and Clinical Psychology, 64,* 712–723.

Lahey, B. B., Applegate, B., Waldman, I. D., Loft, J. D., Hankin, B. L., & Rick, J. (2004). The structure of child and adolescent psychopathology: Generating new hypotheses. *Journal of Abnormal Psychology, 113,* 358–385.

Lahey, B. B., Loeber, R., Burke, J. D., & Applegate, B. (2005). Predicting future anti-social personality disorder in males from a clinical assessment in childhood. *Journal of Consulting and Clinical Psychology, 73,* 389–399.

Lahey, B. B., Loeber, R., Hart, E. L., Frick, P. J., & Applegate, B. (1995). Four-year longitudinal study of conduct disorder in boys: Patterns and predictors of persistence. *Journal of Abnormal Psychology, 104,* 83–93.

Lai, C. S. L., Fisher, S. E., Hurst, J. A., Vargha-Khadem, F., & Monaco, A. P. (2001). A forkhead-domain gene is mutated in severe speech and language disorder. *Nature, 413,* 519–523.

Laird, R. D., Jordan, K. Y., Dodge, K. A., Pettit, G. S., & Gates, J. E. (2001). Peer rejection in childhood, involvement with antisocial peers in early adolescence, and the development of externalizing behavior problems. *Development and Psychopathology, 13,* 337–354.

Lakdawalla, D. N., Bhattacharya, J., & Goldman, D. P. (2004). Are the young becoming more disabled? *Health Affairs, 23,* 168–176.

Lakin, J. L., & Chartrand, T. L. (2003). Using nonconscious behavioral mimicry to create affiliation and rapport. *Psychological Science, 14,* 334–339.

Lalumière, M. L., Blanchard, R., & Zucker, K. J. (2000). Sexual orientation and handedness in men and women: A meta-analysis. *Psychological Bulletin, 126,* 575–592.

Lam, D. H., Watkins, E. R., Hayward, P., Bright, J., Wright, K., Kerr, N., Parr-Davis, G., & Sham, P. (2003). A randomized controlled study of cognitive therapy for relapse prevention for bipolar affective disorder: outcome of the first year. *Archives of General Psychiatry, 60,* 145–152.

Lamar, J. (2000). Suicides in Japan reach a record high. *British Medical Journal, 321,* 528.

Lamb, M. E. (Ed.). (1997). *The role of the father in child development* (3rd ed.). New York: Wiley.

Lamb, M. E. (1998). Assessments of children's credibility in forensic contexts. *Current Directions in Psychological Science, 7,* 43–46.

Lamb, M. E., & Ahnert, L. (2006). Nonparental child care. In W. Damon & R. M. Lerner (Series Eds.) & K. A. Renninger & I. E. Sigel (Vol. Eds.), *Handbook of child psychology: Vol. 4. Child psychology in practice* (6th ed.). New York: Wiley.

Lamberg, L. (2004). Impact of long working hours explored. *Journal of the American Medical Association, 292,* 25–26.

Lambert, M. J., & Barley, D. E. (2001). Research summary on the therapeutic relationship and psychotherapy outcome. *Psychotherapy, 38,* 357–361.

Lambert, M. J., & Bergin, A. E. (1994). The effectiveness of psychotherapy. In A. E. Bergin & S. L. Garfield (Eds.), *Handbook of psychotherapy and behavior change* (4th ed.). New York: Wiley.

Lambert, M. J., & Hill, C. E. (1994). Assessing psychotherapy outcomes and processes. In A. E. Bergin & S. L. Garfield (Eds.), *Handbook of psychotherapy and behavior change* (4th ed.). New York: Wiley.

Lambert, N. M. (1999). Developmental trajectories in psychology: Applications to education and training. *American Psychologist, 54,* 991–1002.

Landrigan, C. P., Rothschild, J. M., Cronin, J. W., Kaushal, R., Burdick, E., Katz, J. T., et al. (2004). Effect of reducing interns' work hours on serious medical errors in intensive care units. *New England Journal of Medicine, 351,* 1838–1848.

Landrine, H. (1991). Revising the framework of abnormal psychology. In P. Bronstein & K. Quina (Eds.), *Teaching a psychology of people.* Washington, DC: American Psychological Association.

Landsdale, M., & Laming, D. (1995). Evaluating the fragmentation hypothesis: The analysis of errors in cued recall. *Acta Psychologica, 88,* 33–77.

Lang, A. R., Goeckner, D. J., Adesso, V. J., & Marlatt, G. A. (1975). Effects of alcohol on aggression in male social drinkers. *Journal of Abnormal Psychology, 84,* 508–518.

Lang, C., Barco, A., Zablow, L., Kandel, E. R., Siegelbaum, S. A., & Zakharenko, S. S. (2004). Transient expansion of synaptically connected dendritic spines upon induction of hippocampal long-term potentiation. *Proceedings of the National Academy of Sciences of the USA, 101,* 16665–16670.

Lang, P. J. (1995). The emotion probe: Studies of motivation and attention. *American Psychologist, 50*(5), 372–385.

Lang, P. J., & Melamed, B. G. (1969). Avoidance conditioning therapy of an infant with chronic ruminative vomiting. *Journal of Abnormal Psychology, 74,* 1–8.

Lange, C., & Byrd, M. (2002). Differences between students' estimated and attained grades in a first-year introductory psychology course as a function of identity development. *Adolescence, 37*(145), 93–108.

Langenberg, P., Ballesteros, M., Feldman, R., Damron, D., Anliker, J., Havas, S. (2000). Psychosocial factors and intervention-associated changes in those factors as correlates of change in fruit and vegetable consumption in the Maryland WIC 5 a day promotion program. *Annals of Behavioral Medicine, 22,* 307–315.

Langleben, D. D., Loughead, J. W., Bilker, W. B., Ruparel, K., Childress, A. R., Busch, S. I., & Gur, R. C. (2005). Telling truth from lie in individual subjects with fast event-related fMRI. *Human Brain Mapping, 26,* 262–272.

Langlois, J. H., Kalakanis, L., Rubenstein, A. J., Larson, A., Hallam, M., & Smoot, M. (2000). Maxims or myths of beauty: A meta-analytic and theoretical review. *Psychological Bulletin, 126,* 390–423.

Lansky, D., & Wilson, G. T. (1981). Alcohol, expectations and sexual arousal in males: An information processing analysis. *Journal of Abnormal Psychology, 89,* 528–538.

Lapierre, L. M., & Allen, T. D. (2006). Work-supportive family, family-supportive supervision, use of organizational benefits, and problem-focused coping: Implications for work-family conflict and employee well-being. *Journal of Occupational Health Psychology, 11,* 169–181.

Lapointe, L. (1990). *Aphasia and related neurogenic language disorders.* New York: Thieme Medical.

LaRoche, M. J., & Martin, J. (2005). The cultural context and the psychotherapeutic process: Toward a culturally sensitive psychotherapy. *Journal of Psychotherapy Integration, 15,* 169–185.

Larsen, J. T., McGraw, A. P., Mellers, B. A., & Cacioppo, J. T. (2004). The agony of victory and thrill of defeat: Mixed emotional reactions to disappointing wins and relieving losses. *Psychological Science, 15,* 325–330.

Larsen, R., & Buss, D. M. (2005). *Personality psychology: Domains of knowledge about human nature* (2nd ed.) New York: McGraw-Hill.

Larson, E. B., Wang, L., Bowen, J. D., McCormick, W. C., Teri, L., Crane, P., & Kukull, W. (2006). Exercise is associated with reduced risk of incident dementia among persons 65 years of age and older. *Annals of Internal Medicine, 144,* 73–81.

Larson, J. R., Jr., Christensen, C., Franz, T. M., & Abbott, A. S. (1998). Diagnosing groups: The pooling, management, and impact of shared and unshared case information in team-based medical decision making. *Journal of Personality and Social Psychology, 75,* 93–108.

Larson, R. W., & Verma, S. (1999). How children and adolescents spend time across the world: Work, play, and developmental opportunities. *Psychological Bulletin, 125,* 701–736.

Latané, B. (1981). The psychology of social impact. *American Psychologist, 36,* 343–356.

Latané, B., & Rodin, J. (1969). A lady in distress: Inhibiting effects of friends and strangers on bystander intervention. *Journal of Experimental Social Psychology, 5,* 189–202.

Latham, G. P. (2004). Motivate employee performance through goal-setting. In E. A. Locke (Ed.), *Handbook of principles of organizational behavior* (pp. 107–119). Malden, MA: Blackwell.

Latham, G. P., Skarlicki, D., Irvine, D., & Siegel, J. P. (1993). The increasing importance of performance appraisals to employee effectiveness in organizational settings in North America. In C. L. Cooper & I. T. Robertson (Eds.), *International review of industrial and organizational psychology 1993* (pp. 87–132). Chichester, UK: Wiley.

Latkin, C. A., Sherman, S., & Knowlton, A. (2003). HIV prevention among drug users: Outcome of a network-oriented peer outreach intervention. *Health Psychology, 22,* 332–339.

Lau, M. A., Pihl, R. O., & Peterson, J. B. (1995). Provocation, acute alcohol intoxication, cognitive performance, and aggression. *Journal of Abnormal Psychology, 104,* 150–155.

Laughery, K. R. (1999). Modeling human performance during system design. In E. Salas (Ed.), *Human/technology interaction in complex systems* (Vol. 9, pp. 147–174). Stamford, CT: JAI Press.

Laughlin, P. L. (1999). Collective induction: Twelve postulates. *Organizational Behavior and Human Decision Processes, 80,* 50–69.

Laumann, E. O., Gagnon, J. H., Michael, R. T., & Michaels, S. (1994). *The social organization of sexuality: Sexual practices in the United States.* Chicago: University of Chicago Press.

Laumann, E. O., & Michael, R. T. (Eds.). (2000). *Sex, love, and health in America: Private choices and public policies.* Chicago: University of Chicago Press.

Laumann, E. O., Paik, A., & Rosen, R. C. (1999). Sexual dysfunction in the United States: Prevalence and predictors. *Journal of the American Medical Association, 281,* 537–544.

Laurenceau, J.-P., Stanley, S. M., Olmos-Gallo, A., Baucom, B., & Markman, H. J. (2004). Community-based prevention of marital dysfunction: Multilevel modeling of a randomized effectiveness study. *Journal of Consulting and Clinical Psychology, 72,* 933–943.

Laureys, S. (2004). Functional neuroimaging in the vegetative state. *NeuroRehabilitation, 19*(4), 335–341.

Law, D. J., Pellegrino, J. W., & Hunt, E. B. (1993). Comparing the tortoise and the hare: Gender differences and experience in dynamic spatial reasoning tasks. *Psychological Science, 4,* 35–40.

Law, K. L., Stroud, L. R., LaGasse, L. L., Niaura, R., Liu, J., & Lester, B. M. (2003). Smoking during pregnancy and newborn neurobehavior. *Pediatrics, 111,* 1318–1323.

Lawford, B. R., Young, R. M., Rowell, J. A., Qualichefski, J., Fletcher, B. H., Syndulko, et al. (1995). Bromocriptine in the treatment of alcoholics with the D2 dopamine receptor A1 allele. *Nature Medicine, 1*(4), 337–341.

Lawless, H. T., & Engen, T. (1977). Associations to odors: Interference, memories and verbal learning. *Journal of Experimental Psychology, 3,* 52–59.

Lawson, C. A. (2004). Treating the borderline mother: Integrating EMDR with a family systems perspective. In M. M. MacFarlane (Ed.), *Family treatment of personality disorders: Advances in clinical practice* (pp. 305–334). Binghamton, NY: Haworth Clinical Practice Press.

Lazarus, A. A. (1971). *Behavior therapy and beyond.* New York: McGraw-Hill.

Lazarus, C. N., & Lazarus, A. A. (2002). EMDR: An elegantly concentrated multi-modal procedure? In F. Shapiro (Ed.), *EMDR as an integrative psychotherapy approach: Experts of diverse orientations explore the paradigm prism* (pp. 209–223). Washington, DC: American Psychological Association.

Lazarus, R. S. (1966). *Psychological stress and the coping process.* New York: McGraw-Hill.

Lazarus, R. S. (1991). *Emotion and adaptation.* New York: Oxford University Press.

Lazarus, R. S. (1999). *Stress and emotion: A new synthesis.* New York: Springer.

Lazarus, R. S., & Folkman, S. (1984). *Stress, appraisal, and coping.* New York: Springer-Verlag.

Lazarus, R. S., Opton, E. M., Nomikos, M. S., & Rankin, M. O. (1965). The principle of short-circuiting of threat: Further evidence. *Journal of Personality, 33,* 622–635.

LeBlanc, M. M., & Barling, J. (2004). Workplace aggression. *Current Directions in Psychological Science, 13,* 9–12.

LeBlanc, M. M., Dupre, K. E., & Barling, J. (2006). Public-initiated violence. In K. E. Kelloway, J. Barling, & J. J. Hurrell (Eds.), *Handbook of workplace violence* (pp. 261–280). Thousand Oaks, CA: Sage.

LeDoux, J. E. (1995). Emotion: Clues from the brain. *Annual Review of Psychology, 46,* 209–235.

Lee, H. S., Nelms, J. L., Nguyen, M., Silver, R., & Lehman, M. N. (2003). The eye is necessary for a circadian rhythm in the suprachiasmatic nucleus. *Nature Neuroscience, 6,* 111–112.

Lee, J. L. C., Everitt, B. J., & Thomas, K. L. (2004). Independent cellular processes for hippocampal memory consolidation and reconsolidation. *Science, 304,* 839–843.

Lee, R. M., & Yoo, H. C. (2004). Structure and measurement of ethnic identity for Asian American college students. *Journal of Counseling Psychology, 51,* 263–269.

Lee, S., Colditz, G., Berkman, L., & Kawachi, I. (2003). Caregiving to children and grandchildren and risk of coronary heart disease in women. *American Journal of Public Health, 93,* 1939–1944.

Legerstee, M., Anderson, D., & Schaffer, A. (1998). Five- and eight-month-old infants recognize their faces and voices as familiar and social stimuli. *Child Development, 69,* 37–50.

Lehman, D. R., Chiu, C., & Schaller, M. (2004). Psychology and culture. *Annual Review of Psychology, 55,* 689–714.

Lehman, H. E. (1967). Schizophrenia: IV. Clinical features. In A. M. Freedman, H. I. Kaplan, & H. S. Kaplan (Eds.), *Comprehensive textbook of psychiatry.* Baltimore: Williams & Wilkins.

Leibel, R. L., Rosenbaum, M., & Hirsch, J. (1995). Changes in energy expenditure resulting from altered body weight. *New England Journal of Medicine, 332*(10), 621–628.

Leibowitz, H. W., Brislin, R., Perlmutter, L., & Hennessy, R. (1969). Ponzo perspective illusion as a manifestation of space perception. *Science, 166,* 1174–1176.

Leibowitz, S. F. (1992). Neurochemical-neuroendocrine systems in the brain controlling macronutrient intake and metabolism. *TINS, 15,* 491–497.

Leigh, B. C., & Stacy, A. W. (2004). Alcohol expectancies and drinking in different age groups. *Addiction, 99,* 215–227.

Leippe, M. R., Manion, A. P., & Romanczyk, A. (1992). Eyewitness persuasion: How and how well do fact finders judge the accuracy of adults' and children's memory reports? *Journal of Personality and Social Psychology, 63,* 181–197.

Lejuez, C. W., Hopko, D. R., Levine, S., Gholkar, R., & Collins, L. (2005). The therapeutic alliance in behavior therapy. *Psychotherapy: Theory, Research, Practice, and Training, 42,* 456–468.

Lemly, B. (2000, February). Isn't she lovely? *Discover,* 43–49.

Lemmer, B., Kern, R. I., Nold, G., & Lohrer, H. (2002). Jet lag in athletes after eastward and westward time-zone transition. *Chronobiology International, 19,* 743–764.

Lenneberg, E. H. (1967). *Biological foundations of language.* New York: Wiley.

Leonard, B. E. (1992). *Fundamentals of psychopharmacology.* New York: Wiley.

Leonhardt, D. (2000, May 24). Makes sense to test for common sense. Yes? No? *New York Times.*

LePage, J. P., DelBen, K., Pollard, S., McGhee, S., Vanhorn, L., Murphy, J., et al. (2003). Reducing assaults on an acute psychiatric unit using a token economy: A 2-year follow-up. *Behavioral Interventions, 18,* 179–190.

Lepore, S. J. (1995a). Measurement of chronic stressors. In S. Cohen, R. C. Kessler, & L. U. Gordon (Eds.), *Measuring stress: A guide for health and social scientists.* New York: Oxford University Press.

Lerner, J. S., Gonzalez, R. M., Small, D. A., & Fischhoff, B. (2003). Effects of fear and anger on perceived risks of terrorism: A national field experiment. *Psychological Science, 14,* 144–150.

Levant, R. F. (2005). Evidence-based practice in psychology. *Monitor on Psychology, 36,* 5.

LeVay, S. (1991). A difference in hypothalamic structure between heterosexual and homosexual men. *Science, 253,* 1034–1037.

Levenson, H. (2003). Time-limited dynamic psychotherapy: An integrationist perspective. Journal of Psychotherapy Integration, 13, 300-333.

Levenson, R. W., Ekman, P., & Friesen, W. V. (1990). Voluntary facial action generates emotion-specific autonomic nervous system activity. *Psychophysiology, 27*(4), 363–384.

Levenson, R. W., Ekman, P., Heider, K., & Friesen, W. V. (1992). Emotion and autonomic nervous system activity in the Minangkabau of West Sumatra. *Journal of Personality and Social Psychology, 62*(6), 972–988.

Leventhal, T., & Brooks-Gunn, J. (2000). The neighborhoods they live in: The effects of neighborhood residence on child and adolescent outcomes. *Psychological Bulletin, 126,* 309–337.

Levine, M. W., & Shefner, J. M. (1981). *Fundamentals of sensation and perception.* Reading, MA: Addison-Wesley.

Levine, R. V., Martinez, T. M., Brase, G., & Sorenson, K. (1994). Helping in 36 U.S. cities. *Journal of Personality and Social Psychology, 67,* 69–82.

Levine, R., Sato, S., Hashimoto, T., & Verna, J. (1995). Love and marriage in eleven cultures. *Journal of Cross-Cultural Psychology, 26,* 554–571.

Levine, S. (1999, February 1). In a loud and noisy world, baby boomers pay the consequences. *International Herald Tribune.*

Levinson, D. F. (2006). The genetics of depression: A review. *Biological Psychiatry, 60,* 84–92.

Levinson, D. J., Darrow, C. N., Klein, E. B., Levinson, M. H., & McKee, B. (1978). *The seasons of a man's life.* New York: Knopf.

Levinthal, C. F. (2001). *Drugs, behavior, and modern society* (3rd ed.). Boston: Allyn & Bacon.

Levy, B. R., Slade, M. D., Kunkel, S. R., & Kasl, S. V. (2002). Longevity increased by positive self-perceptions of aging. *Journal of Personality & Social Psychology, 83*(2), 261–270.

Levy, D. A., Bayley, P. J., & Squire L. R. (2004). The anatomy of semantic knowledge: Medial vs. lateral temporal lobe. *Proceedings of the National Academies of Science, 101,* 6710–6715.

Levy, R. L., Cain, K. C., Jarrett, M., & Heitkemper, M. M. (1997). The relationship between daily life stress and gastrointestinal symptoms in women with irritable bowel syndrome. *Journal of Behavioral Medicine, 20,* 177–194.

Levy-Shiff, R. (1994). Individual and contextual correlates of marital change across the transition to parenthood. *Developmental Psychology, 30,* 591–601.

Lewicki, P. (1992). Nonconscious acquisition of information. *American Psychologist, 47,* 796–801.

Lewin, T. (2003, October 29). A growing number of video viewers watch from crib. *New York Times,* p. 1.

Lewinsohn, P. M., Joiner, T. E., & Rohde, P. (2001). Evaluation of cognitive diathesis-stress models in precicting Major Depressive Disorder in adolescents. *Journal of Abnormal Psychology, 110,* 203– 215.

Lewinsohn, P. M., & Rosenbaum, M. (1987). Recall of parental behavior by acute depressives, remitted depressives, and nondepressives. *Journal of Personality and Social Psychology, 52,* 611–619.

Lewis, J. W., Brefczynski, J. A., Phinney, R. E., Janik, J. J., & DeYoe, E. A. (2005). Distinct cortical pathways for processing tool versus animal sounds. *Journal of Neuroscience, 25*(21), 5148–5158.

Lewis, T. T., Everson-Rose, S. A., Powell, L. H., Matthews, K. A., Brown, C., Karavolos, K., et al. (2006). Chronic exposure to everyday discrimination and coronary artery calcification in African-American women: The SWAN heart study. *Psychosomatic Medicine, 68,* 362–368.

Lewith, G. T., White, P. J., & Pariente, J. (2005). Investigating acupuncture using brain imaging techniques: The current state of play. *Evidence Based Complementary and Alternative Medicine, 2,* 315–319.

Lewontin, R. (1976). Race and intelligence. In N. J. Block & G. Dworkin (Eds.), *The IQ controversy: Critical readings.* New York: Pantheon.

Lewy, A. J., Lefler, B. J., Emens, J. S., & Bauer, V. K. (2006). The circadian basis of winter depression. *Proceedings of the National Academy of Sciences of the USA, 103,* 7414–7419.

Lezak, M. D., Loring, D. W., & Howieson, D. B. (2004). *Neuropsychological assessment* (4th ed.). New York: Oxford University Press.

Li, D.-K., Willinger, M., Petitti, D. B., Odouli, R., Liu, L., & Hoffman, H. J. (2006). Use of a dummy (pacifier) during sleep and risk of sudden infant death syndrome (SIDS): Population based case-control study. *British Medical Journal, 332,* 18–22.

Li, F., Harmer, P., McAuley, E., Duncan, T., Duncan, S. C., Chaumeton, N., & Fisher, K. J. (2001). An evaluation of the effects of Tai Chi exercise on physical function among older persons: A randomized controlled trial. *Annals of Behavioral Medicine, 23,* 139–146.

Li, J. (2005). Mind or virtue: Western and Chinese beliefs about learning. *Current Directions in Psychological Science, 14,* 190–194.

Li, L. C., & Kim, B. S. K. (2004). Effects of counseling style and client adherence to Asian cultural values on counseling process with Asian American college students. *Journal of Counseling Psychology, 51,* 158–167.

Li, N. P., & Kenrick, D. T. (2006). Sex similarities and differences in preferences for short-term mates: What, whether, and why. *Journal of Personality and Social Psychology, 90,* 468–489.

Li, S., Cullen, W., Anwyl, R., & Rowan, M. J. (2003). Dopamine-dependent facilitation of LTP induction in hippocampal CA1 by exposure to spatial novelty. *Nature Neuroscience, 6,* 526–531.

Li, S. C., Lindenberger, U., Hommel, B., Aschersleben, G., Prinz, W., & Baltes, P. B. (2004). Transformations in the couplings among intellectual abilities and constituent cognitive processes across the life span. *Psychological Science, 15,* 155–163.

Liao, H., & Rupp, D. E. (2005). The impact of justice climate and justice orientation on work outcomes: A cross-level multifoci framework. *Journal of Applied Psychology, 90,* 242–256.

Liben, L. (1978). Perspective-taking skills in young children: Seeing the world through rose-colored glasses. *Developmental Psychology, 14,* 87–92.

Liben-Nowell, D., Novak, J., Kumar, R., Raghaven, P., & Tomkins, A. (2005). Geographic routing in social networks. *Proceedings of the National Academy of Sciences of the USA, 102,* 11623–11628.

Liberman, R. P., Wallace, C. J., Blackwell, G., Kopelowicz, A., Vaccaro, J. V., & Mintz, J. (1998). Skills training versus psychosocial occupational therapy for persons with persistent schizophrenia. *American Journal of Psychiatry, 155,* 1087–1091.

Lichtenstein, P., & Annas, P. (2000). Heritability and prevalence of specific fears and phobias in childhood. *Journal of Child Psychology and Psychiatry and Allied Disciplines, 41,* 927–937.

Lickey, M., & Gordon, B. (1991). *Medicine and mental illness: The use of drugs in psychiatry.* San Francisco: Freeman.

Liden, R. C., Wayne, S. J., Jaworski, R. A., & Bennett, N. (2004). Social loafing: A field investigation. *Journal of Management, 30,* 285–304.

Lieberman, A., & Pawl, J. (1988). Clinical applications of attachment theory. In J. Bellsky & T. Nezworski (Eds.), *Clinical applications of attachment.* Hillsdale, NJ: Erlbaum.

Lieberman, J. A., Stroup, T. S., McEvoy, J. P., Swartz, M. S., Rosenheck, R. A., Perkins, D. O., et al. (2005). Effectiveness of antipsychotic drugs in patients with chronic schizophrenia. *New England Journal of Medicine, 353,* 1209–1223.

Lieberman, J. A., Tollefson, G., Tohen, M., Green, A. I., Gur, R. E., Kahn, R., et al. (2003). Comparative efficacy and safety of atypical and conventional antipsy-chotic drugs in first-episode psychosis: A randomized, double-blind trial of olanzapine versus haloperidol. *The American Journal of Psychiatry, 160,* 1396–1404.

Lieberman, M. A., & Tobin, S. (1983). *The experience of old age.* New York: Basic Books.

Liebert, R. M., & Spiegler, M. D. (1994). *Personality: Strategies and issues.* Pacific Grove, CA: Brooks/Cole.

Liechti, M. E., Gamma, A., & Vollenweider, F. X. (2001). Gender differences in the subjective effects of MDMA. *Psychopharmacology, 154,* 161–168.

Liepert, J., Bauder, H., Miltner, W. H. R., Taub, E., & Weiller, C. (2000). Treatment-induced cortical reorganization after stroke in humans. *Stroke, 31,* 1210.

Lievens, F., Harris, M. M., Van Keer, E., & Bisqueret, C. (2003). Predicting cross-cultural training performance: The validity of personality, cognitive ability, and dimensions measured by an assessment center and a behavior description interview. *Journal of Applied Psychology, 88,* 476–489.

Light, K. C., Girdler, S. S., Sherwood, A., Bragdon, E. E., Brownley, K. A., West, S. G., & Hinderliter, A. L. (1999). High stress responsivity predicts later blood pressure only in combination with positive family history and high life stress. *Hypertension, 33,* 1458–1464.

Light, L. K., Grewen, K. M., Amico, J. A., Brownley, K. A., West, S. G., Hinderliter, A. L., et al. (2005). Oxytocinergic activity is linked to lower blood pressure and vascular resistance during stress in postmenopausal women on estrogen replacement. *Hormones and Behavior, 47,* 540–548.

Lilienfeld, S. O., Lynn, S. J., Kirsch, I., Chaves, J. F., Sarbin, T. R., Ganaway, G. K., & Powell, R. A. (1999). Dissociative identity disorder and the sociocognitive model: Recalling the lessons of the past. *Psychological Bulletin, 125,* 507–523.

Lim, B.-C., & Ployhart, R. E. (2004). Transformational leadership: Relations to the five-factor model and team performance in typical and maximum contexts. *Journal of Applied Psychology, 89,* 610–621.

Lim, S.-L., & Kim, J.-H. (2005). Cognitive processing of emotional information in depression, panic, and somatoform disorder. *Journal of Abnormal Psychology, 114,* 50–61.

Lim, V. K. G., Teo, T. S. H., & Loo, G. L. (2003). Sex, financial hardship and locus of control: An empirical study of attitudes towards money among Singaporean Chinese. *Personality and Individual Differences, 34,* 411–429.

Lin, K.-M. & Poland, R. E. (1995). Ethnicity, culture, and psychopharmacology. In F. E. Bloom & D. J. Kupfer (Eds.), *Psychopharmacology: The fourth generation of progress.* New York: Raven Press.

Lin, L., Umahara, M., York, D. A., & Bray, G. A. (1998). Beta-casomorphins stimulate and enterostatin inhibits the intake of dietary fat in rats. *Peptides, 19,* 325–331.

Lin, S., Thomas, T. C., Storlien, L. H., & Huang, X. F. (2000). Development of high fat diet-induced obesity and leptin resistance in C57Bl/6J mice. *International Journal of Obesity Related Metabolic Disorders, 24,* 639–646.

Lin, Y., & Raghubir, P. (2005). Gender differences in unrealistic optimism about marriage and divorce: Are men more optimistic and women more realistic? *Personality and Social Psychology Bulletin, 31,* 198–207.

Linde, K., Streng, A., Jurgens, S., Hoppe, A., Brinkhaus, B., Witt, C., et al. (2005). Acupuncture for patients with migraine: A randomized controlled trial. *Journal of the American Medical Association, 293,* 2118–2125.

Lindsay, D. S., Hagen, L., Read, J. D., Wade, K., & Gary, M. (2004). True photographs and false memories. *Psychological Science, 15,* 149–154.

Lindsey, K. P., & Paul, G. L. (1989). Involuntary commitments to public mental institutions: Issues involving the overrepresentation of blacks and assessment of relevant functioning. *Psychological Bulletin, 106,* 171–183.

Lindvall, O., & Hagell, P. (2001). Cell therapy and transplantation in Parkinson's disease. *Clinical Chemistry and Laboratory Medicine, 39,* 356–361.

Linnet, K. M., Dalsgaard, S., Obel, C., Wisborg, K., Henriksen, T. B., Rodriguez, A., et al. (2003). Maternal lifestyle factors in pregnancy risk of attention deficit hyperactivity disorder and associated behaviors: Review of the current evidence. *American Journal of Psychiatry, 160,* 1028–1040.

Linnet, K. M., Wisborg, K., Obel, C., Secher, N. J., Thomsen, P. H, Agerbo, E., & Henriksen, T. B. (2005). Smoking during pregnancy and the risk for hyperkinetic disorder in offspring. *Pediatrics, 116,* 462–467.

Linz, D., Donnerstein, E., & Penrod, S. (1987). The findings and recommendations of the Attorney General's Commission on Pornography: Do the psychological facts fit the political fury? *American Psychologist, 42,* 946–953.

Lippa, R. A. (2003). Are 2D:4D finger-length ratios related to sexual orientation?: Yes for men, no for women. *Journal of Personality and Social Psychology, 85,* 179–188.

Lira, A., Zhou, M., Castanon, N., Ansorge, M. S., Gordon, J. A., Francis, J. H., et al. (2003). Altered depression-related behaviors and functional changes in the dorsal raphe nucleus of serotonin transporter-deficient mice. *Biological Psychiatry, 54,* 960–971.

Lisanby, S. H. (Ed.). (2004). *Brain stimulation in psychiatric treatment.* Washington, DC: American Psychiatric Association.

Lisspers, J., Sundin, Ö., Öhman, A., Hofman-Bang, C., Rydén, L., & Nygren, Å. (2005). Long-term effects of lifestyle behavior change in coronary artery disease: Effects on recurrent coronary events after percutaneous coronary intervention. *Health Psychology, 24,* 41–48.

Littlewood, R. (1992). Psychiatric diagnosis and racial bias: Empirical and interpretative approaches. *Social Science & Medicine, 34,* 141–149.

Liu, S., Prince, M., Blizard, B., & Mann, A. (2002). The prevalence of psychiatric morbidity and its associated factors in general health care in Taiwan. *Psychological Medicine, 32,* 629–637.

Lively, W. M. (2001). Syncope and neurologic deficits in a track athlete: A case report. *Medicine and Science in Sports and Exercise, 33,* 345–347.

Locke, E. A. (2000). Motivation, cognition, and action: An analysis of studies of task goals and knowledge. *Applied Psychology: An International Review, 49,* 408–429.

Locke, E. A., & Latham G. P. (1990). *A theory of goal setting & task performance.* Englewood Cliffs, NJ: Prentice Hall.

Locke, E. A., & Latham, G. P. (2002). Building a practically useful theory of goal setting and task motivation: A 35-year odyssey. *American Psychologist, 57,* 705–717.

Lockhart, R. S., & Craik, F. I. M. (1990). Levels of processing: A retrospective commentary on a framework for memory research. *Canadian Journal of Psychology, 44,* 87–112.

Loehlin, J. C. (1989). Partitioning environmental and genetic contributions to behavioral development. *American Psychologist, 44,* 1285–1292.

Loehlin, J. C. (1992). *Genes and environment in personality development.* Newbury Park, CA: Sage.

Loehlin, J. C., Neiderhiser, J. M., & Reiss, D. (2003). The behavior genetics of personality and the NEAD study. *Journal of Research in Personality, 37,* 373–387.

Loewenstein, G. (1994). The psychology of curiosity: A review and reinterpretation. *Psychological Bulletin, 116*(1), 75–98.

Loftus, E. F. (1992). When a lie becomes memory's truth: Memory distortion after exposure to misinformation. *Psychological Science, 3,* 121–123.

Loftus, E. F. (1997a). Memory for a past that never was. *Current Directions in Psychological Science, 6,* 60–65.

Loftus, E. F. (1997b). Repressed memory accusations: Devastated families and devastated patients. *Applied Cognitive Psychology, 11,* 25–30.

Loftus, E. F. (1998). The price of bad memories. *Skeptical Inquirer, 22,* 23–24.

Loftus, E. F. (2003, January). *Illusions of memory.* Presentation at the 25th Annual National Institute on the Teaching of Psychology, St. Petersburg Beach, Florida.

Loftus, E. F. (2004). Memories of things unseen. *Current Directions in Psychological Science, 13,* 145–147.

Loftus, E. F., & Hoffman, H. G. (1989). Misinformation and memory: The creation of new memories. *Journal of Experimental Psychology: General, 118,* 100–104.

Loftus, E. F., & Ketcham, K. (1991). *Witness for the defense.* New York: St. Martin's Press.

Loftus, E. F., & Ketcham, K. (1994). *The myth of repressed memory: False memories and allegations of sexual abuse.* New York: St. Martin's Press.

Loftus, E. F., & Palmer, J. C. (1974). Reconstruction of automobile destruction: An example of the interaction between language and memory. *Journal of Verbal Learning and Verbal Behavior, 13,* 585–589.

Loftus, E. F., & Pickrell, J. E. (1995). The formation of false memories. *Psychiatric Annals, 25,* 720–725.

Loftus, E., & Guyer, M. (2002). Who abused Jane Doe? The hazards of the single case history (Part 1). *Skeptical Inquirer, 26,* 24–32.

Loftus, T. M., Jaworsky, D. E., Frehywot, G. L., Townsend, C. A., Ronnett, G. V., Lane, M. D., & Kuhajda, F. P. (2000). Reduced food intake and body weight in mice treated with fatty acid synthase inhibitors. *Science, 288,* 2379–2381.

Logue, A. W. (1985). Conditioned food aversion in humans. *Annals of the New York Academy of Sciences, 104,* 331–340.

Loher, B. T., Noe, R. A., Moeller, N. L., & Fitzgerald, M. P. (1985). A meta-analysis of the relation of job characteristics to job satisfaction. *Journal of Applied Psychology, 70,* 280–289.

Lohman, D. F. (2004). Aptitude for college: The importance of reasoning tests for minority admissions. In R. Zwick (Ed.), *Rethinking the SAT: The future of standardized testing in college admissions.* New York: RoutledgeFalmer.

Lohman, D. F. (2005). The role of non-verbal ability tests in identifying academically gifted students: An aptitude perspective. *Gifted Child Quarterly, 49,* 111–138.

Lohman, D. F., & Hagen, E. (2001). *Cognitive abilities test (Form 6): Interpretive guide for teachers and counselors.* Itasca, IL: Riverside.

Lohr, J. M., Hooke, W., Gist, R., & Tolin, D. F. (2003) Novel and controversial treatments for trauma-related stress disorders. In S. O. Lilienfeld, S. J. Lynn, & J. M. Lohr (Eds.), *Science and pseudoscience in clinical psychology* (pp. 243–272). New York: Guilford Press.

LoLordo, V. M. (2001). Learned helplessness and depression. In M. E. Carroll & J. B. Overmier (Eds.), *Animal research and human health: Advancing human welfare through behavioral science* (pp. 63–77). Washington, DC: American Psychological Association.

London Daily Telegraph. (1998, September 19). "'Cat' that turned out to be a clock." *London Daily Telegraph.*

Longo, N., Klempay, S., & Bitterman, M. E. (1964). Classical appetitive conditioning in the pigeon. *Psychonomic Science, 1,* 19–20.

Lonn, S., Ahlbom, A., Hall, P., & Feychting, M. (2004). Mobile phone use and the risk of acoustic neuroma. *Epidemiology, 15,* 653–659.

Loos, R. J. F., Rankinen, T., Chagnon, Y., Tremblay, A., Pérusse, L., & Bouchard, C. (2006). Polymorphisms in the leptin and leptin receptor genes in relation to resting metabolic rate and respiratory quotient in the Québec Family Study. *International Journal of Obesity, 30,* 183–190.

Lopes, P. N., Salovey, P., Côté, S., & Beers, M. (2005). Emotion regulation abilities and the quality of social interaction. *Emotion, 5,* 113–118.

Lopez, S. R. (1989). Patient variable biases in clinical judgment: Conceptual overview and methodological considerations. *Psychological Bulletin, 106,* 184–203.

Lord, C. G. (1997). *Social psychology.* Fort Worth: Harcourt, Brace.

Losh, S. C., Tavani, C. M., Njoroge, R., Wilke, R., & McAuley, M. (2003). What does education really do? Educational dimensions and pseudoscience support in the American general public, 1979–2001. *Skeptical Inquirer, 27,* 30–35.

Louzá, M. R., & Bassitt, D. P. (2005). Maintenance treatment of severe tardive dyskinesia with Clozapine: 5 years' follow-up. *Journal of Clinical Psychopharmacology, 25,* 180–182.

Love, J. M., Kisker, E. E., Ross, C., Raikes, H., Constantine, J., Boller, K., et al.. (2005). The effectiveness of early head start for 3-year-old children and their parents: Lessons for policy and programs. *Developmental Psychology, 41,* 885–901.

Low, C. A., Stanton, A. L., & Danoff-Burg, S. (2006). Expressive disclosure and benefit finding among breast cancer patients: Mechanisms for positive health effects. *Health Psychology, 25,* 181–189.

Löw, K., Crestani, F., Keist, R., Benke, D., Brunig, I., Benson, J. A., et al. (2000). Molecular and neuronal substrate for the selective attenuation of anxiety. *Science, 290,* 131–134.

Lubinski, D., Benbow, C. P., Webb, R. M., & Bleske-Rechek, A. (2006). Tracking exceptional human capital over two decades. *Psychological Science, 17*(3), 194–199.

Lu, J., Sherman, D., Devor, M., & Saper, C. B. (2006). A putative flip-flop switch for control of REM sleep. *Nature, 441,* 589–594.

Lubinski, D., Webb, R. M., Morelock, M. J., & Benbow, C. P. (2001). Top 1 in 10,000: A 10-year follow-up of the profoundly gifted. *Journal of Applied Psychology, 86,* 718–729.

Luborsky, L. (1972). Another reply to Eysenck. *Psychological Bulletin, 78,* 406–408.

Luborsky, L., Rosenthal, R., & Diguer, L. (2003). Are some psychotherapies much more effective than others? *Journal of Applied Psychoanalytic Studies, 5*(4), 455–460.

Luborsky, L., Rosenthal, R., Diguer, L., Andrusyna, T. P., Berman, J. S., Levitt, J. T., et al. (2002). The dodo bird verdict is alive and well–mostly. *Clinical Psychology: Science and Practice, 9,* 2–12.

Luborsky, L., Singer, B., & Luborsky, L. (1975). Comparative studies of psychotherapies: Is it true that everyone has won and all must have prizes? *Archives of General Psychiatry, 32,* 995–1008.

Lucas, J. A. (2005). Disorders of memory. *Psychiatric Clinics of North America, 28*(3), 581–597.

Lucas, R. E., Clark, A. E., Georgellis, Y., & Diener, E. (2004). Unemployment alters the set point for life satisfaction. *Psychological Science, 15,* 8–13.

Luchins, A. S. (1942). Mechanization in problem solving: The effect of Einstellung. *Psychological Monographs, 54*(6, Whole No. 248).

Luciana, M., Conklin, H. M., Hooper, C. J., & Yarger, R. S. (2005). The development of nonverbal working memory and executive control processes in adolescents. *Child Development, 76,* 697–712.

Lund, T., Labriola, M., Christensen, K. B., Bültmann, U., & Villadsen, E. (2006). Physical work environment risk factors for long-term sickness absence: Prospective findings among a cohort of 5357 employees in Denmark. *British Medical Journal, 332,* 449–452.

Luntz, B. K., & Widom, C. S. (1994). Antisocial personality disorder in abused and neglected children grown up. *American Journal of Psychiatry, 151,* 670–674.

Luria, Z. (1992, February). *Gender differences in children's play patterns.* Paper presented at University of Southern California, Los Angeles.

Lustig, R. H., Sen, S., Soberman, J. E., & Velasquez-Mieyer, P. A. (2004). Obesity, leptin resistance, and the effects of insulin reduction. *International Journal of Obesity, 28,* 1344–1348.

Luthar, S. S., & Latendresse, S. J. (2005) Children of the affluent. *Current Directions in Psychological Science, 14,* 49–53.

Lutz, D. J., & Sternberg, R. J. (1999). Cognitive development. In M. H. Bornstein & M. E. Lamb (Eds.), *Developmental psychology: An advanced textbook* (4th ed.) Mahwah, NJ: Erlbaum.

Lykken, D. T. (1998). *A tremor in the blood: Uses and abuses of the lie detector.* Cambridge, MA: Perseus Publishing.

Lykken, D. T. (1999). *Happiness: What studies on twins show us about nature, nurture, and the happiness set point.* New York: Golden Books.

Lynam, D. R. (1996). The early identification of chronic offenders: Who is the fledgling psychopath? *Psychological Bulletin, 120,* 209–234.

Lynam, D. R., & Widiger, T. A. (2001). Using the five-factor model to represent the *DSM-IV* personality disorders: An expert consensus approach. *Journal of Abnormal Psychology, 110,* 401–412.

Lynn, R. (1996). Racial and ethnic differences in intelligence in the U.S. on the Differential Ability Scale. *Personality and Individual Differences, 20,* 271–273.

Lynn, S. J., & Kirsch, I. (2006). *Essentials of clinical hypnosis: An evidence-based approach.* Washington, DC: American Psychological Association.

Lynn, S. J., Lilienfeld, S. O., & Lohr, J. M. (Eds.). (2003). *Science and pseudoscience in clinical psychology.* New York: Guilford Press.

Lynn, S. J., Myers, B., & Malinoski, P. (1997). Hypnosis, pseudomemories, and clinical guidelines: A sociocognitive perspective. In J. D. Read & D. S. Lindsay (Eds.), *Recollections of trauma: Scientific evidence and clinical practice. NATO ASI series: Series A: Life sciences* (Vol. 291, pp. 305–336). New York: Plenum Press.

Lynn, S. J., & Rhue, J. W. (1986). The fantasy-prone person: Hypnosis, imagination, and creativity. *Journal of Personality and Social Psychology, 51,* 404–408.

Lynn, S. J., Vanderhoff, H., Shindler, K., & Stafford, J. (2002). Defining hypnosis as a trance vs. cooperation: Hypnotic inductions, suggestibility, and performance standards. *American Journal of Clinical Hypnosis, 44,* 231–240.

Lynskey, M. T., Heath, A. C., Bucholz, K. K., Slutske, W. S., Madden, P. A. F., Nelson, E. C., et al. (2003). Escalation of drug use in early-onset cannabis users vs. co-twin controls. *Journal of the American Medical Association, 289,* 427–433.

Lyons, D., & McLoughlin, D. M. (2001). Clinical review: Psychiatry. *British Medical Journal, 323,* 1228–1231.

Lyubomirsky, S. (2001). Why are some people happier than others?: The role of cognitive and motivational processes in well-being. *American Psychologist, 56,* 239–249.

Lyubomirsky, S., King, L., & Diener, E. (2005). The benefits of frequent positive affect: Does happiness lead to success? *Psychological Bulletin, 131,* 803–855.

Lyubomirsky, S., & Nolen-Hoeksema, S. (1995). Effects of self-focused rumination on negative thinking and interpersonal problem solving. *Journal of Personality and Social Psychology, 69,* 176–190.

M

Ma, J., Qin, W., Wang, X. Y., Guo, T. W., Bian, L., Duan, S. W., et al. (2006). Further evidence for the association between G72/G30 genes and schizophrenia in two ethnically distinct populations. *Molecular Psychiatry, 11,* 479–487.

MacAndrew, C., & Edgerton, R. B. (1969). *Drunken comportment.* Chicago: Aldine.

MacArthur Foundation. (1999). *Research network on successful midlife development.* Vero Beach, FL: The John D. and Catherine T. MacArthur Foundation. Retrieved December 13, 2004, from http://midmac.med.harvard.edu/

MacDonald, M., & Bernstein, D. A. (1974). Treatment of a spider phobia with in vivo and imaginal desensitization. *Journal of Behavior Therapy and Experimental Psychiatry, 5,* 47–52.

Macey, P. M., Henderson, L. A., Macey, K. E., Alger, J. R., Frysinger, R. C., Woo, M. A., et al. (2002). Brain morphology associated with obstructive sleep apnea. *American Journal of Respiratory and Critical Care Medicine, 166,* 1382–1387.

Mack, A. (2003). Inattentional blindness: Looking without seeing. *Current Directions in Psychological Science, 12,* 180–184.

Mack, A., & Rock, I. (1998). *Inattentional blindness.* Cambridge, MA: MIT Press.

Mackay, D. G. (2006, March 29). Aging, memory, and language in amnesic H.M. *Hippocampus.* Retrieved Sepptember 26, 2006, from http://www3.interscience.wiley.com/cgi-bin/jissue/112597200.

MacMillan, H. L., Fleming, J. E., Steiner, D. L., Lin, E., Boyle, M. H., Jamieson, E., et al. (2001). Childhood abuse and lifetime psychopathology in a community sample. *American Journal of Psychiatry, 158,* 1878–1883.

MacMillan, N. A., & Creelman, C. D. (2004*). Detection theory: A user's guide* (2nd ed.). Hillsdale, NJ: Erlbaum.

MacQueen, G. M., Hajek, T., & Alda, M. (2005). The phenotypes of bipolar disorder: Relevance for genetic investigations. *Molecular Psychiatry, 10,* 811–826.

Maddi, S. R., & Khoshaba, D. M. (2005). *Resilence at work.* New York: American Management Association.

Maddux, J. E., & Gosselin, J. T. (2003). Self-efficacy. In M. R. Leary & J. P. Tangney (Eds.), *Handbook of self and identity* (pp. 218–238). New York: Guilford Press.

Madon, S., Guyll, M., Spoth, R. L., Cross, S. E., & Hilbert, S. J. (2003). The self-fulfilling influence of mother expectations on children's underage drinking. *Journal of Personality and Social Psychology, 84,* 1188–1205.

Madon, S., Guyll, M., Spoth, R., & Willard, J. (2004). Self-fulfilling prophecies. *Psychological Science, 15,* 837–845.

Mah, S., Nelson, M. R., Delisi, L. E., Reneland, R. H., Markward, N., James, M. R., et al. (2006). Identification of the semaphorin receptor PLXNA2 as a candidate for susceptibility to schizophrenia. *Molecular Psychiatry, 11,* 471–478.

Mahroo, O. A., & Lamb, T. D. (2004). Recovery of the human photopic electroretinogram after bleaching exposures: Estimation of pigment regeneration kinetics. *Journal of Physiology, 554,* 417–437.

Maier, S. F., & Watkins, L. R. (2000). The immune system as a sensory system: Implications for psychology. *Current Directions in Psychological Science, 9,* 98–102.

Mains, J. A., & Scogin, F. R. (2003). The effectiveness of self-administered treatments: A practice-friendly review of the research. *Journal of Clinical Psychology, 59,* 237–245.

Maj, M., Gaebal, W., Lopez-Ibor, J. J., & Sartorius, N. (Eds.). (2002). *Psychiatric diagnosis and classification.* New York: Wiley.

Major, B., Sciacchtinano, A. M., & Crocker, J. (1993). In-group versus out-group comparisons and self-esteem. *Personality and Social Psychology Bulletin, 19,* 711–721.

Makeover, R. B. (2004). *Treatment planning for psychotherapists* (2nd ed.). Washington, DC: American Psychiatric Publishing.

Malamuth, N. M. (1998). The confluence model as an organizing framework for research on sexually aggressive men: Risk moderators, imagined aggression, and pornography consumption. In R. G. Geen & E. Donnerstein (Eds.), *Human aggression* (pp. 230–247). San Diego: Academic Press.

Malamuth, N., & Addison, T. (2001). Helping and altruism. In G. Fletcher & M. Clark (Eds.), *Blackwell handbook of social psychology: Interpersonal processes* (pp. 162–195). Oxford, UK: Blackwell.

Malamuth, N. M., Addison, T., & Koss, M. (2000). Pornography and sexual aggression: Are there reliable effects and can we understand them? *Annual Review of Sex Research, 11,* 26–91.

Malamuth, N. M., & Check, J. V. P. (1983). Sexual arousal to rape depictions: Individual differences. *Journal of Abnormal Psychology, 92,* 55–67.

Malarkey, W. B., Kiecolt-Glaser, J. K., Pearl, D., & Glaser, R. (1994). Hostile behavior during marital conflict alters pituitary and adrenal hormones. *Psychosomatic Medicine, 56,* 41–51.

Malaspina, D., Goetz, R. R., Friedman, J. H., Kaufmann, C. A., Faraone, S. V., Tsuang, M., et al. (2001). Traumatic brain injury and schizophrenia in members of schizophrenia and bipolar disorder pedigrees. *American Journal of Psychiatry, 158,* 440–446.

Malenka, R. C. (1995). LTP and LTD: Dynamic and interactive processes of synaptic plasticity. *The Neuroscientist, 1,* 35–42.

Malenka, R. C., & Nicoll, R. A. (1999). Long-term potentiation—a decade of progress? *Science, 285,* 1870–1874.

Malgrange, B., Rigo, J. M., Van de Water, T. R., Staecker, H., Moonen, G., & Lefebvre, P. P. (1999). Growth factor therapy to the damaged inner ear: Clinical prospects. *International Journal of Pediatric Otorhinolaryngology, 49*(Suppl. 1), S19–S25.

Malleret, G., Haditsch, U., Genoux, D., Jones, M. W., Bliss, T. V. P., Vanhoose, A. M., et al. (2001). Inducible and reversible enhancement of learning, memory, and long-term potentiation by genetic inhibition of calcineurin. *Cell, 104,* 675–686.

Maltby, N., Kirsch, I., & Mayers, M. (2002). Virtual reality exposure therapy for the treatment of fear of flying: A controlled investigation. *Journal of Consulting and Clinical Psychology, 70*(5), 1112–1118.

Mandelid, L. J. (2003). Dodofugl-dommen og psykoterapeuters credo. [The Dodo-bird verdict and the beliefs of psychotherapists]. *Tidsskrift for Norsk Psykologforening, 40*(4), 307–312.

Manderscheid, R., & Barrett, S. (Eds.). (1987). *Mental health, United States, 1987* (DHHS Pub. No. ADM 87–1518). Bethesda, MD: National Institute of Mental Health.

Maner, J. K., Luce, C. L., Neuberg, S. L., Cialdini, R. B., Brown, S., & Sagarin, B. J. (2002). The effects of perspective taking on motivations for helping: Still no evidence for altruism. *Personality and Social Psychology Bulletin, 28,* 1601–1610.

Manfield, P., & Shapiro, F. (2004). Application of eye movement desensitization and reprocessing (EMDR) to personality disorders. In J. J. Magnavita (Ed.), *Handbook of personality disorders: Theory and practice* (pp. 304–328). New York: Wiley.

Manheimer, E., White, A., Berman, B., Forys, K., & Ernst, E. (2005). Meta-analysis: Acupuncture for low back pain. *Annals of Internal Medicine, 142,* 651–663.

Mann, J. J., Apter, A., Bertolote, J., Beautrais, A., Currier, D., Haas, A., et al. (2005). Suicide prevention strategies: A systematic review. *Journal of the American Medical Association, 294,* 2064–2074.

Mann, K., Roschke, J., Nink, M., Aldenhoff, J., Beyer, J., Benkert, O., & Lehnert, H. (1992). Effects of corticotropin-releasing hormone administration in patients suffering from sleep apnea syndrome. *Society for Neuroscience Abstracts, 22,* 196.

Manning, C. (2004). Beyond memory: Neuropsychologic features in differential diagnosis of dementia. *Clinical Geriatric Medicine, 20*(1), 45–58.

Mannuzza, M., Schneider, F. R., Chapman, T. F., Liebowitz, M. R., Klein, D. F., & Fyer, A. J. (1995). Generalized social phobia. *Archives of General Psychiatry, 52,* 230–237.

Mansfield, P. K., Voda, A., & Koch, P. B. (1995). Predictors of sexual response changes in heterosexual midlife women. *Health Values, 19*(1), 10–20.

Manson, J. E., Skerrett, P. J., Greenland, P., & VanItallie, T. B. (2004). The escalating pandemics of obesity and sedentary lifestyle: A call to action for clinicians. *Archives of Internal Medicine, 164,* 249–258.

Mantell, E. O., Ortiz, S. O., & Planthara, P. M. (2004). What price prescribing? A commentary on the effect of prescription authority on psychological practice. *Professional Psychology: Research and Practice, 35,* 164–169.

Maquet, P. (2001). The role of sleep in learning and memory. *Science, 294,* 1048–1052.

March, J., Silva, S., Petrycki, S., Curry, J., Wells, K., Fairbank, J., et al. (2004). Fluoxetine, cognitive-behavioral therapy, and their combination for adolescents with depression: Treatment for Adolescents with Depression Study (TADS) randomized controlled trial. *Journal of the American Medical Association, 292,* 807–820.

Marcotte, D. E., & Wilcox-Goek, V. (2001). Estimating the employment and earnings costs of mental illness: Recent developments in the United States. *Social Science and Medicine, 53,* 21–27.

Marcus, G. F. (1996). Why do children say "breaked"? *Current Directions in Psychological Science, 5,* 81–85.

Marenco, S., & Weinberger, D. R. (2000). The neurodevelopmental hypothesis of schizophrenia: Following a trail of evidence from cradle to grave. *Developmental Psychopathology, 12,* 501–527.

Margetic, S., Gazzola, C., Pegg, G. G., & Hill, R. A. (2002). Leptin: A review of its peripheral actions and interactions. *Obesity, 26,* 1407–1433.

Markman, E. M. (1994). Constraints children place on word meanings. In P. Bloom (Ed.), *Language acquisition: Core readings* (pp. 154–173). Cambridge, MA: MIT Press.

Markon, K. E., Krueger, R. F., & Watson, D. (2005). Delineating the structure of normal and abnormal personality: An integrative hierarchical approach. *Journal of Personality and Social Psychology, 88,* 139–157.

Marks, I. M. (2002). Reduction of fear: Towards a unifying theory. *Psicoterapia Cognitiva e Comportamentale, 8*(1), 63–66.

Markus, H. R., & Kitayama, S. (1991). Culture and the self: Implications for cognition, emotion, and motivation. *Psychological Review, 98,* 224–253.

Markus, H. R., Kitayama, S., & Heiman, R. J. (1996). Culture and "basic" psychological principles. In E. T. Higgins & A. W. Kruglanski (Eds.), *Social psychology: Handbook of basic principles* (pp. 857–913). New York: Guilford.

Marmarosh, C., Holtz, A., & Schottenbauer, M. (2005). Group cohesiveness, group-derived collective self-esteem, group-derived hope, and the well-being of group therapy members. *Group Dynamics: Theory, Research, and Practice, 9,* 32–44.

Maron, E., Nikopensius, T., Koks, S., Altmae, S., Heinaste, E., Vabrit, K., et al. (2005). Association study of 90 candidate gene polymorphisms in panic disorder. *Psychiatric Genetics, 15,* 17–24.

Marsh, A. A., Ambady, N., & Kleck, R. E. (2005). The effects of fear and anger facial expressions on approach- and avoidance-related behaviors. *Emotion, 5,* 119–124.

Marshall, S. J., Biddle, S. J., Gorely, T., Cameron, N., & Murdey, I. (2004). Relationships between media use, body fatness and physical activity in children and youth: A meta-analysis. *International Journal of Obesity, 28,* 1238–1246.

Marshall, W. L. (1989). Pornography and sex offenders. In D. Zillmann & J. Bryant (Eds.), *Pornography: Research advances and policy considerations.* Hillsdale, NJ: Erlbaum.

Marti, P. R., Singleton, C. K., & Hiller-Sturmhofel, S. (2003). The role of thiamine deficiency in alcoholic brain disease. *Alcohol Research Health, 27*(2), 134–142.

Martin, B., & Hoffman, J. (1990). Conduct disorders. In M. Lewis & S. M. Miller (Eds.), *Handbook of developmental psychopathology.* New York: Plenum.

Martin, C. L., & Fabes, R. A. (2001). The stability and consequences of young children's same-sex peer interactions. *Developmental Psychology, 37,* 431–446.

Martin, D. J., Garske, J. P., & Davis, M. K. (2000). Relation of the therapeutic alliance with outcome and other variables: A meta-analytic review. *Journal of Consulting & Clinical Psychology, 68,* 438–450.

Martin, R. A. (2001). Humor, laughter, and physical health: Methodological issues and research findings. *Psychological Bulletin, 127,* 504–519.

Martin, R., Gardikiotis, A., & Hewstone, M. (2002). Levels of consensus and majority and minority influence. *European Journal of Social Psychology, 32,* 645–665.

Martin, R., & Hewstone, M. (2003). Majority versus minority influence: When, not whether, source status instigates heuristic or systematic processing. *European Journal of Social Psychology, 33,* 313–330.

Martinez, C. R., & Forgatch, M. S. (2001). Preventing problems with boys' noncompliance: Effects of a parent training intervention for divorcing mothers. *Journal of Consulting and Clinical Psychology, 69,* 416–428.

Martinez, C., Rietbrock, S., Wise, L., Ashby, D., Chick, J., Moseley, J., Evans, S., et al. (2005). Psychogenic seizures in an Espiritismo context: The role of culturally sensitive psychotherapy. *Psychotherapy: Theory, Research, Practice, Training, 42,* 6–13.

Martinez, D., Gil, R., Slifstein, M., Hwang, D.-R., Huang, Y., Perez, A., et al. (2005). Alcohol dependence is associated with blunted dopamine transmission in the ventral striatum. *Biological Psychiatry, 58,* 779–786.

Martinez, M. (2000). *Education as the cultivation of intelligence.* Mahwah, NJ: Erlbaum.

Martinez-Taboas, A. (2005). The plural world of culturally sensitive psychotherapy: A response to Castro-Blanco's (2005) comments. *Psychotherapy: Theory, Research, Practice, Training, 42,* 17–19.

Martinot, M.-L. P., Bragulat, V., Artiges, E., Dolle, F., Hinnen, F., Jouvent, R., et al. (2001). Decreased presynaptic dopamine function in the left caudate of depressed patients with affective flattening and psychomotor retardation. *American Journal of Psychiatry, 158,* 314–316.

Marzuk, P. M., Tardiff, K., Leon, A. C., Hirsch, C. S., Stajic, M., Portera, L., et al. (1995). Fatal injuries after cocaine use as a leading cause of death among young adults in New York City. *New England Journal of Medicine, 332*(26), 1753–1757.

Masand, P., Popli, A. P., & Welburg, J. B. (1995). Sleepwalking. *American Family Physician, 51*(3), 649–653.

Maslach, C. (2003). Job burnout: New directions in research and intervention. *Current Directions in Psychological Science, 12,* 189–192.

Masland, R. H. (2001). Neuronal diversity in the retina. *Current Opinion in Neurobiology, 11,* 431–436.

Maslow, A. H. (1943). A theory of human motivation. *Psychological Review, 50,* 370–396.

Maslow, A. H. (1954). *Motivation and personality.* New York: Harper.

Maslow, A. H. (1970). *Motivation and personality* (2nd ed.). New York: Harper & Row.

Maslow, A. H. (1971a). *The farther reaches of human nature.* New York: McGraw-Hill.

Maslow, A. H. (1971b). *Toward a psychology of being.* Princeton, NJ: Van Nostrand.

Masters, J. C., Burish, T. G., Hollon, S. D., & Rimm, D. C. (1987). *Behavior therapy: Techniques and empirical findings* (3rd ed.). San Diego: Harcourt Brace Jovanovich.

Masters, W. H., & Johnson, V. E. (1966). *Human sexual response.* Boston: Little, Brown & Co.

Mathew, S. J., Amiel, J. M., & Sackeim, H. A. (2005). Electroconvulsive therapy in treatment-resistant depression. *Primary Psychiatry, 12,* 52–56.

Matlin, M. W. (1998). *Cognition* (4th ed.). Fort Worth, TX: Harcourt Brace.

Maton, K., Kohout, J. L., Wicherski, M., Leary, G. E., & Vinokurov, A. (2006). Minority students of color in the psychology graduate pipeline: Disquieting and encouraging trends, 1989–2003. *American Psychologist, 61,* 117–131.

Matson, J., Sevin, J., Fridley, D., & Love, S. (1990). Increasing spontaneous language in autistic children. *Journal of Applied Behavior Analysis, 23,* 227–223.

Matsuda, K. T., Cho, M. C., Lin, K. M., Smith, M. W., Young, A. S., & Adams, J. A. (1996). Clozapine dosage, serum levels, efficacy, and side-effect profiles: a comparison of Korean-American and Caucasian patients. *Psychopharmacol Bulletin, 32,* 253–257.

Matsumoto, D. (2000) *Culture and psychology: People around the world.* Belmont, CA: Wadsworth.

Matsumoto, D., & Ekman, P. (1989). American-Japanese cultural differences in intensity ratings of facial expressions of emotion. *Motivation and Emotion, 13,* 143–157.

Matsumoto, D., Yoo, S. H., Hirayama, S., & Petrova, G. (2005). Development and validation of a measure of display rule knowledge: The display rule assessment inventory. *Emotion, 5,* 23–40.

Mattanah, J. F., Hancock, G. R., & Brand, B. L. (2004). Parental attachment, separation-individuation, and college student adjustment: A structural equation analysis of mediational effects. *Journal of Counseling Psychology, 51,* 213–225.

Mattar, A. A. G., & Gribble, P. L. (2005). Motor learning by observing. *Neuron, 46,* 153–160.

Matthews, K. A., Katholi, C. R., McCreath, H., Whooley, M. A., Williams, D. R., Zhu, S., et al. (2004). Blood pressure reactivity to psychological stress predicts hypertension in the CARDIA study. *Circulation, 110,* 74–78.

Matthews, K. A., Salomon, K., Kenyon, K., & Zhou, F. (2005). Unfair treatment, discrimination, and ambulatory blood pressure in black and white adolescents. *Health Psychology, 24,* 258–265.

Matthies, E., Hoeger, R., & Guski, R. (2000). Living on polluted soil: Determinants of stress symptoms. *Environment and Behavior, 32,* 270–286.

Maupin, H. E., & Fisher, J. R. (1989). The effects of superior female performance and sex-role orientation in gender conformity. *Canadian Journal of Behavioral Science, 21,* 55–69.

Maviel, T., Durkin, T. P., Menzaghi, F., & Bontempi, B. (2004). Sites of neocortical reorganization critical for remote spatial memory. *Science, 305,* 96–99.

Maxwell, J. P. (2003). The imprint of childhood physical and emotional abuse: A case study on the use of EMDR to address anxiety and a lack of self-esteem. *Journal of Family Violence, 18,* 281–293.

May, E. R., & Zelikow, P. D. (Eds.). (1997). *The Kennedy tapes: Inside the White House during the Cuban Missile Crisis.* New York: Belknap Press.

May, G. L., & Kahnweiler, W. M. (2000). The effect of a mastery practice design on learning and transfer in behavior modeling training. *Personnel Psychology, 53,* 353–373.

Mayberry, R. I., & Lock, E. (2003). Age constraints on first versus second language acquisition. *Brain and Language, 87,* 369–384.

Mayberry, R. I., Lock, E., & Kazmi, H. (2002). Linguistic ability and early language exposure. *Nature, 417,* 38.

Mayer, D. J., & Price, D. D. (1982). A physiological and psychological analysis of pain: A potential model of motivation. In D. W. Pfaff (Ed.), *The physiological mechanisms of motivation.* New York: Springer-Verlag.

Mayer, F. S., & Sutton, K. (1996). *Personality: An integrative approach.* Upper Saddle River, NJ: Prentice-Hall.

Mayer, J. D. (2005). A tale of two visions: Can a new view of personality help integrate psychology? *American Psychologist, 60,* 294–307.

Mayes, L. Cicchetti, D., Acharyya, S., & Zhang, H. (2003). Developmental trajectories of cocaine-and-other-drug-exposed and non-cocaine-exposed children. *Journal of Developmental Behavioral Pediatrics, 24,* 323–335.

Mayeux, R. (2003). Epidemiology of neurodegeneration. *Annual Review of Neuroscience, 26,* 81–104.

Mazoyer, B., Tzouri-Mazoyer, N., Mazard, A., Denis, M., Mellet, E. (2002). Neural basis of image and language interactions. *International Journal of Psychology, 37,* 204–208.

Mazzoni, G. A., & Loftus, E. F. (1996). When dreams become reality. *Consciousness and Cognition, 5,* 442–462.

Mazzoni, G., & Memon, A. (2003). Imagination can create false autobiographical memories. *Psychological Science, 14,* 186–188.

McAdams, D. P., & Pals, J. L. (2006). A new big five: Fundamental principles for an integrative science of personality. *American Psychologist, 61,* 204–217.

McAuley, E. (1992). The role of efficacy cognitions in the prediction of exercise behavior in middle-aged adults. *Journal of Behavioral Medicine, 15,* 65–88.

McAuley, E., Kramer, A. F., & Colcombe, S. J. (2004). Cardiovascular fitness and neurocognitive function in older adults: A brief review. *Brain, Behavior, and Immunity, 18,* 214–220.

McCabe, K. M. (2002). Factors that predict premature termination among Mexican-American children in outpatient psychotherapy. *Journal of Child and Family Therapy, 11,* 347–359.

McCaffery, E. J., & Baron, J. (2006). Thinking about tax. *Psychology, Public Policy, and Law, 12,* 106–135.

McCarley, J. S., Kramer, A. F., Wickens, C. D., Vidoni, E. D., & Boot, W. R. (2004). Visual skills in airport-security screening. *Psychological Science, 15,* 302–306.

McCarthy, H. D., Ellis, S. M., & Cole, T. J. (2003). Central overweight and obesity in British youth aged 11–16 years: Cross sectional surveys of waist circumference. *British Medical Journal, 326,* 624.

McCaul, K. D., Hockemeyer, J. R., Johnson, R. J., Zetocha, K., Quinlan, K., & Glasgow, R. E. (2006). Motivation to quit using cigarettes: A review. *Addictive Behaviors, 31,* 42–56.

McClain, M., & Foundas, A. (2004). Apraxia. *Current Neurology and Neuroscience Reports, 4*(6), 471–476.

McClelland, D. C. (1958). Risk-taking in children with high and low need for achievement. In J. W. Atkinson (Ed.), *Motives in fantasy, action, and society* (pp. 306–321). Princeton, NJ: Van Nostrand.

McClelland, D. C. (1985). *Human motivation.* Glenview, IL: Scott, Foresman.

McCloskey, M. (1983). Naïve theories of motion. In D. Gentner & K. Stevens (Eds.), *Mental models* (pp. 299–324). Northvale, NJ: Erlbaum.

McClure, E. B. (2000). A meta-analytic review of sex differences in facial expression processing and their development in infants, children, and adolescents. *Psychological Bulletin, 126,* 424–453.

McCormick, D. A., & Thompson, R. F. (1984). Cerebellum essential involvement in the classically conditioned eyelid response. *Science, 223,* 296–299.

McCormick, E. J., Jeanneret, P. R., & Mecham, R. C. (1972). A study of job characteristics and job dimensions as based on the position analysis questionnaire (PAQ). *Journal of Applied Psychology, 56,* 347–368.

McCrae, R. R., & Costa, P. T., Jr. (2004). A contemplated revision of the NEO Five-Factor Inventory. *Personality and Individual Differences, 36,* 587–596.

McCrae, R. R., Costa, P. T., Jr., Martin, T. A., Oryol, V. E., Rukavishnikov, A. A., et al. (2004). Consensual validation of personality traits across cultures. *Journal of Research in Personality, 38,* 179–201.

McCrae, R. R., & John, O. (1992). An introduction to the five-factor model and its applications. *Journal of Personality, 60,* 175–215.

McCrae, R. R., & Terracciano, A. (2005). Universal features of personality traits from the observer's perspective: Data from 50 cultures. *Journal of Personality and Social Psychology, 88,* 547–561.

McDermott, K. B. (2002). Explicit and implicit memory. In V. S. Ramachandran (Ed.), *Encyclopedia of the human brain* (Vol. 2, pp. 773–781). New York: Academic Press.

McDermott, K. B., & Buckner, R. L. (2002). Functional neuroimaging studies of human memory retrieval. In L. R. Squire & D. L. Schacter (Eds.), *Neuropsychology of memory* (3rd ed., pp. 166–171). New York: Guilford Press.

McDermott, K. B., & Chan, J. C. K. (2006). Effects of repetition on memory for pragmatic inferences. *Memory and Cognition.*

McDermott, K. B., & Roediger, H. L. (1998). Attempting to avoid illusory memories: Robust false recognition of associates persists under conditions of explicit warnings and immediate testing. *Journal of Memory and Language, 39,* 508–520.

McDiarmid, M. A., & Condon, M. (2005). Organizational safety culture/climate and worker compliance with hazardous drug guidelines: Lessons from the blood-borne pathogen experience. *Journal of Occupational and Environmental Medicine, 47,* 740–749.

McDonald, A. J., Wang, N., & Camargo, C. A. (2004). US emergency department visits for alcohol-related diseases and injuries between 1992 and 2000. *Archives of Internal Medicine, 164,* 531–537.

McDonald, R., & Siegel, S. (2004). The potential role of drug onset cues in drug dependence and withdrawal: Reply to Bardo (2004), Bossert and Shaham (2004), Bouton (2004), and Stewart (2004). *Experimental and Clinical Psychopharmacology, 12,* 23–26.

McDougall, W. (1908). *An introduction to social psychology.* London: Methuen.

McElroy, S. L., Zarate, C. A., & Cookson, J. (2004). A 52-week, open-label continuation study of lamotrigine in the treatment of bipolar depression. *Journal of Clinical Psychiatry, 65*(2), 204–210.

McEvoy, G. M., & Beatty, R. W. (1989). Assessment centers and subordinate appraisals of managers: A seven-year examination of predictive validity. *Personnel Psychology, 42,* 37–52.

McEwen, B. S., & Seeman, T. (1999). Protective and damaging effects of mediators of stress: Elaborating and testing concepts of allostasis and allostatic load. *Annals of the New York Academy of Sciences, 896,* 30–47.

McGehee, D. S., Heath, M. J. S., Gelber, S., Devay, P., & Role, L. W. (1995). Nicotine enhancement of fast excitatory synaptic transmissions in CNS by presynaptic receptors. *Science, 269,* 1692–1696.

McGlashan, T. H., & Hoffman, R. E. (2000). Schizophrenia as a disorder of reduced synaptic connectivity. *Archives of General Psychiatry, 57,* 637–648.

McGlynn, F. D., Moore, P. M., Lawyer, S., & Karg, R. (1999). Relaxation training inhibits fear and arousal during in vivo exposure to phobia-cue stimuli. *Journal of Behavior Therapy and Experimental Psychiatry, 30,* 155–168.

McGlynn, S. M. & Schacter, D. L. (1989). Unawareness of deficits in neuropsychological syndromes. *Journal of Clinical and Experimental Neuropsychology, 11*(2), 143–205.

McGorry, P. D., Yung, A. R., Phillips, L. J., Yuen, H. P., Francey, S., Cosgrave, E. M., et al. (2002). Randomized controlled trial of interventions designed to reduce the risk of progression to first-episode psychosis in a clinical sample with subthreshold symptoms. *Archives of General Psychiatry, 59,* 921–928.

McGue, M. (1992). When assessing twin concordance, use the probandwise not the pairwise rate. *Schizophrenia Bulletin, 18,* 171–176.

McGue, M. (1999). The behavioral genetics of alcoholism. *Current Directions in Psychological Science, 8,* 109–115.

McGuffin, P., Rijsdijk, F., Andrew, M., Sham, P., Katz, R., & Cardno, A. (2003). The heritability of bipolar affective disorder and the genetic relationship to unipolar depression. *Archives of General Psychiatry, 60,* 497–502.

McHugh, P. R. (2005). Striving for coherence: Psychiatry's efforts over classification. *Journal of the American Medical Association, 293,* 2526–2528.

McLeod, J. D., Kessler, R. C., & Landis, K. R. (1992). Speed of recovery from major depressive episodes in a community sample of married men and women. *Journal of Abnormal Psychology, 101,* 277–286.

McLoyd, V. C. (1998). Socioeconomic disadvantage and child development. *American Psychologist, 53,* 185–204.

McMahon, P. (2000, January 31). Oregon man leads life without frills, leaves $9 million to charities, children. *USA Today,* p. 4A.

McNally, R. J. (2003). Recovering memories of trauma: A view from the laboratory. *Current Directions in Psychological Science, 12,* 32–35.

McNally, R. J., Clancy, S. A., Barrett, H. M., & Parker, H. A. (2005). Reality monitoring in adults reporting repressed, recovered, or continuous memories of childhood sexual abuse. *Journal of Abnormal Psychology, 114,* 147–152.

McNally, R. J., Clancy, S. A., & Schacter, D. L. (2001). Directed forgetting of trauma cues in adults reporting repressed or recovered memories of childhood sexual abuse. *Journal of Abnormal Psychology, 110,* 151–156.

McNally, R. J., Clancy, S. A., Schacter, D. L., & Pittman, R. K. (2000a). Cognitive processing of trauma cues in adults reporting repressed, recovered, or continuous memories of childhood sexual abuse. *Journal of Abnormal Psychology, 109,* 355–359.

McNally, R. J., Clancy, S. A., Schacter, D. L., & Pittman, R. K. (2000b). Personality profiles, dissociation, and absorption in women reporting repressed, recovered, or continuous memories of childhood sexual abuse. *Journal of Consulting and Clinical Psychology, 68,* 1033–1037.

McNay, E. C., McCarty, R. C., & Gold, P. E. (2001). Fluctuations in brain glucose concentration during behavioral testing: Dissociations between brain areas and between brain and blood. *Neurobiology of Learning and Memory, 75,* 325–337.

McNulty, J. K., & Karney, B. R. (2004). Positive expectations in the early years of marriage: Should couples expect the best or brace for the worst? *Journal of Personality and Social Psychology, 86,* 729–743.

McQuaid, J. R., Granholm, E., McClure, F. S., Roepke, S., Pedrelli, P., Patterson, T. L., et al. (2000). Development of an integrated cognitive-behavioral and social skills training intervention for older patients with schizophrenia. *Journal of Psychotherapy Practice and Research, 9,* 149–156.

McTigue, K. M., Harris, R., Hemphill, B., Lux, L., Sutton, S., Bunton, A. J., & Lohr, K. N. (2003). Screening and interventions for obesity in adults: Summary of the evidence for the U.S. Preventive Services Task Force. *Annals of Internal Medicine, 139,* 933–949.

Medin, D. L., & Bazerman, M. H. (1999). Broadening behavioral decision research: Multiple levels of cognitive processing. *Psychonomic Bulletin & Review, 6,* 533–546.

Medin, D. L., Ross, B. H., & Markman, A. B. (2001). *Cognitive psychology* (3rd ed.). Fort Worth, TX: Harcourt.

Mednick, S., Nakayama, K., & Stickgold, R. (2003). Sleep-dependent learning: A nap is as good as a night. *Nature Neuroscience, 6,* 697–698.

Medsker, G. J., Katkowski, D. A., & Furr, D. (2003). Income and employment survey results for the Society of Industrial and Organizational Psychology. *Industrial Psychologist, 43,* 36–54.

Mehl, M. R. & Pennebaker, J. W. (2003a). The social dynamics of a cultural upheaval: Social interactions surrounding September 11, 2001. *Psychological Science, 14,* 579–585.

Mehl, M. R. & Pennebaker, J. W. (2003b). The sounds of social life: A psychometric analysis of students' daily social environments and natural conversations. *Journal of Personality and Social Psychology, 84,* 857–870.

Mehle, T. (1982). Hypothesis generation in an automobile malfunction inference task. *Acta Psychologica, 52,* 87–116.

Meichenbaum, D. (1977). *Cognitive behavior modification: An integrative approach.* New York: Plenum.

Meichenbaum, D. H. (1995). Cognitive-behavioral therapy in historical perspective. In B. Bongar & L. E. Beutler (Eds.), *Comprehensive textbook of psychotherapy: Theory and practice* (pp. 140–158). New York: Oxford University Press.

Melamed, S., Fried, Y., & Froom, P. (2001). The interactive effect of chronic exposure to noise and job complexity on changes in blood pressure and job satisfaction: A longitudinal study of industrial employees. *Journal of Occupational Health Psychology, 6,* 182–195.

Melander, H., Ahlqvist-Rastad, J., Meijer, G., & Beerman, B. (2003). Evidence b(i)ased medicine—selective reporting from studies sponsored by pharmaceutical industry: Review of studies in new drug applications. *British Medical Journal, 326,* 1171–1173.

Melchart, D., Streng, A., Hoppe, A., Brinkhaus, B., Witt, C., Wagenpfeil, S., et al. (2005). Acupuncture in patients with tension-type headache: Randomised controlled trial. *British Medical Journal, 331,* 376–382.

Melchior, C. L. (1990). Conditioned tolerance provides protection against ethanol lethality. *Pharmacology, Biochemistry and Behavior, 37,* 205–206.

Meltzer, H. Y. (1997). Treatment-resistant schizophrenia: The role of clozapine. *Current Medical Research Opinion, 14,* 1–20.

Melzack, R., & Wall, P. D. (1965). Pain mechanisms: A new theory. *Science, 150,* 971–979.

Memon, A., Vrij, A., & Bull, R. (2004). *Psychology and law: Truthfulness, accuracy and credibility* (2nd ed.). New York: Wiley.

Menaker, M., & Vogelbaum, M. A. (1993). Mutant circadian period as a marker of suprachiasmatic nucleus function. *Journal of Biological Rhythms, 8,* 93–98.

Mendez, I., Sanchez-Pernaute, R., Cooper, O., Vinuela, A., Ferrari, D., Bjorklund, L., et al. (2005). Cell type analysis of functional fetal dopamine cell suspension transplants in the striatum and substantia nigra of patients with Parkinson's disease. *Brain, 128,* 1498–1510.

Mendl, M. (1999). Performing under pressure: Stress and cognitive function. *Applied Animal Behaviour Science, 65,* 221–244.

Meng, M., Remus, D. A., & Tong, F. (2005). Filling-in of visual phantoms in the human brain. *Nature Neuroscience, 8,* 1248–1254.

Menini, A., Picco, C., & Firestein, S. (1995, February 2). Quantal-like current fluctuations induced by odorants in olfactory receptor cell. *Nature, 373,* 435–437.

Menon, G. J., Rahman, I., Menon, S. J., & Dutton, G. N. (2003). Complex visual hallucinations in the visually impaired: The Charles Bonnet syndrome. *Survey Ophthalmology, 48,* 58–72.

Mercer, C. H., Fenton, K. A., Johnson, A. M., Wellings, K., Macdowall, W., McManus, et al. (2003). Sexual function problems and help seeking behaviour in Britain: National probability sample survey. *British Medical Journal, 327,* 426–427.

Merchant, J. A., & Lundell, J. A. (2001). *Workplace violence: A report to the nation.* Iowa City: University of Iowa.

Merckelbach, H., Devilly, G. J., & Rassin, E. (2002). Alters in dissociative identity disorder: Metaphors or genuine entities? *Clinical Psychology Review, 22,* 481–497.

Merry, T., & Brodley, B. T. (2002). The nondirective attitude in client-centered therapy: A response to Kahn. *Journal of Humanistic Psychology, 42,* 66–77.

Merzenich, M. (1998). Long-term change of mind. *Science, 282,* 1062–1063.

Mesman, J., & Koot, H. M. (2000). Common and specific correlates of preadolescent internalizing externalizing psychopathology. *Journal of Abnormal Psychology, 109,* 428–437.

Mesquita, B., & Frijda, N. H. (1992). Cultural variations in emotions: A review. *Psychological Bulletin, 112,* 179–204.

Messer, S. B. (2004). Evidence-based practice: Beyond empirically supported treatments. *Professional Psychology: Research and Practice, 35,* 580–588.

Messer, S. B., & Wampold, B. E. (2002). Let's face facts: Common factors are more potent than specific therapy ingredients. *Clinical Psychology: Science and Practice, 9,* 21–25.

Messick, S. (1989). Validity. In R. Linn (Ed.), *Educational measurement* (3rd ed., pp. 13–103). New York: American Council on Education/Macmillan.

Messinger, A., Squire, L. R., Zola, S. M., & Albright, T. D. (2001). Neuronal representations of stimulus associations develop in the temporal lobe during learning. *Proceedings of the National Academy of Science, 98,* 12239–12244.

Messinger, D. S., Bauer, C. R., Das, A., Seifer, R., Lester, B. M., Lagasse, L. L., et al. (2004). The maternal lifestyle study: Cognitive, motor, and behavioral outcomes of cocaine-exposed and opiate-exposed infants through three years of age. *Pediatrics, 113,* 1677–1685.

Mesulam, M. M. (1990). Large-scale neurocognitive networks and distributed processing for attention, language, and memory. *Annals of Neurology, 28*(5), 597–613.

Mesulam, M. M. (2001). Primary progressive aphasia. *Annals of Neurolology, 49*(4), 425–423.

Metzinger, T. (Ed.). (2000). *Neural correlates of consciousness: Empirical and conceptual questions.* Cambridge: MIT Press.

Meyer, B. H. F. L., Ehrhardt, A. A., Rosen, L. R., & Gruen, R. S. (1995). Prenatal estrogens and the development of homosexual orientation. *Developmental Psychology, 31*(1), 12–21.

Meyer, G. J., Finn, S. E., Eyde, L. D., Kay, G. G., Moreland, K. L., Dies, R. R., et al. (2001). Psychological testing and psychological assessment: A review of evidence and issues. *American Psychologist, 56,* 128–165.

Meyer, I. H. (2003). Prejudice, social stress, and mental health in lesbian, gay, and bisexual populations: Conceptual issues and research evidence. *Psychological Bulletin, 129,* 674–697.

Meyer, J. D., & Salovey, P. (1997). What is emotional intelligence? In P. Salovey & D. Sluyter (Eds.), *Emotional development and emotional intelligence* (pp. 3–31). New York: Basic Books.

Meyer, R. G. (1975). A behavioral treatment of sleepwalking associated with test anxiety. *Behavior Therapy and Experimental Psychiatry, 6,* 167–168.

Meyers, C., & Jones, T. B. (1993). *Promoting active learning: Strategies for the college classroom.* San Francisco: Jossey-Bass.

Meyre, D., Bouatia-Naji, N., Tounian, A., Samson, C., Lecoeur, C., Vatin, V., et al. (2005). Variants of ENPP1 are associated with childhood and adult obesity and increase the risk of glucose intolerance and type 2 diabetes. *Nature Genetics, 37,* 863–867.

Mezey, E., Key, S., Vogelsang, G., Szalayova, I., Lange, G. D., & Crain, B. (2003). Transplanted bone marrow generates new neurons in human brains. *Proceedings of the National Academy of Sciences, 100,* 1364–1369.

Mezulis, A. H., Abramson, L. Y., Hyde, J. S., & Hankin, B. L. (2004). Is there a universal positivity bias in attributions? A meta-analytic review of individual, developmental, and cultural differences in the self-serving attributional bias. *Psychological Bulletin, 130,* 711–747.

Mezzacappa, E. S., Katkin, E. S. & Palmer, S. N. (1999). Epinephrine, arousal and emotion: A new look at two-factor theory. *Cognition and Emotion, 13,* 181–199.

Miceli, G., Fouch, E., Capasso, R., Shelton, J. R., Tomaiuolo, F., & Caramazza, A. (2001). The dissociation of color from form and function knowledge. *Nature Neuroscience, 4,* 662–667.

Michael, R. T., Wadsworth, J., Feinleib, J., Johnson, A. M., Laumann, E. O., & Wellings, K. (1998). Private sexual behavior, public opinion, and public health policy related to sexually transmitted diseases: A US-British comparison. *American Journal of Public Health, 88,* 749–754.

Michel, C., Rossion, B., Han, J., Chung, C.-S., & Caldara, R. (2006). Holistic processing is finely tuned for faces of one's own race. *Psychological Science, 17,* 608–615.

Mick, E., Biederman, J., Prince, J., Fischer, M. J., & Faraone, S. V. (2002). Impact of low birth weight on attention-deficit hyperactivity disorder. *Journal of Developmental and Behavioral Pediatrics, 23,* 16–22.

Midlarsky, E., Jones, S., & Corley, R. (2005). Personality correlates of heroic rescue during the holocaust. *Journal of Personality, 73,* 907–934.

Miklowitz, D. J., & Alloy, L. B. (1999). Psychosocial factors in the course and treatment of bipolar disorder: Introduction to the special section. *Journal of Abnormal Psychology, 108,* 555–557.

Mikulincer, M. & Shaver, P. R. (2005). Mental representations of attachment security: Theoretical foundation for a positive social psychology. In M. W. Baldwin (Ed.), *Interpersonal cognition* (pp. 233–266). New York: Guilford Press.

Milak, M. S., Parsey, R. V., Keilp, J., Oquendo, M. A., Malone, K. M., & Mann, J. J. (2005). Neuroanatomic correlates of psychopathologic components of major depressive disorder. *Archives of General Psychiatry, 62,* 397–408.

Milev, P., Ho, B. C., Arndt, S., & Andreasen, N. C. (2005). Predictive values of neurocognition and negative symptoms on functional outcome in schizophrenia: A longitudinal first-episode study with 7-year follow-up. *American Journal of Psychiatry, 162,* 495–506.

Milgram, S. (1963). Behavioral study of obedience. *Journal of Abnormal and Social Psychology, 67,* 371–378.

Milgram, S. (1965). Some conditions of obedience and disobedience to authority. *Human Relations, 18,* 57–76.

Milgram, S. (1974). *Obedience to authority.* New York: Harper & Row.

Milgram, S. (1977, October). Subject reaction: The neglected factor in the ethics of experimentation. *Hastings Center Report* (pp. 19–23).

Milisen, K., Braes, T., Fick, D. M., & Foreman, M. D. (2006). Cognitive assessment and differentiating the 3 Ds (dementia, depression, delirium). *Nursing Clinics of North America, 41*(1), 1–22.

Millar, H. R., Wardell, F., Vyvyan, J. P., Naji, S. A., Prescott, G. J., & Eagles, J. M. (2005). Anorexia nervosa mortality in Northeast Scotland, 1965–1999. *American Journal of Psychiatry, 162,* 753–757.

Miller, G. (1956). The magical number seven, plus or minus two: Some limits on our capacity to process information. *Psychological Review, 63,* 81–97.

Miller, G. (2003). Spying on the brain, one neuron at a time. *Science, 300,* 78.

Miller, G. (2005a). Neuroscience: The dark side of glia. *Science, 308,* 778–781.

Miller, G. (2005b). Neuroscience: Reflecting on another's mind. *Science, 308,* 945–947.

Miller, G. A. (1991). *The science of words.* New York: Scientific American Library.

Miller, G. A., Heise, G. A., & Lichten, W. (1951). The intelligibility of speech as a function of the context of the test materials. *Journal of Experimental Psychology, 41,* 329–335.

Miller, J. (2001). The cultural grounding of social psychological theory. In A. Tesser & N. Schwarz (Eds.), *Blackwell handbook of social psychology: Intraindividual processes* (pp. 22–43). Oxford, UK: Blackwell.

Miller, J. D., Lynam, D., Zimmerman, R. S., Logan, T. K., Leukefeld, C., & Clayton, R. (2004). The utility of the Five Factor Model in understanding risky sexual behavior. *Personality and Individual Differences, 36,* 1611–1626.

Miller, J. G. (2002). Bringing culture to basic psychological theory—Beyond individualism and collectivism: Comment on Oyserman et al. *Psychological Bulletin, 128,* 97–109.

Miller, J. G., & Bersoff, D. M. (1994). Cultural influences on the moral status of reciprocity and the discounting of endogenous motivation. *Personality and Social Psychology Bulletin, 20,* 592–602.

Miller, K. F., Smith, C. M., Zhu, J., & Zhang, H. (1995). Preschool origins of cross-national differences in mathematical competence: The role of number-naming systems. *Psychological Science, 6,* 56–60.

Miller, L. C., Putcha-Bhagavatula, A., & Pedersen, W. C. (2002). Men's and women's mating preferences: Distinct evolutionary mechanisms? *Current Directions in Psychological Science, 11,* 88–93.

Miller, L. K. (1999). The savant syndrome: Intellectual impairment and exceptional skill. *Psychological Bulletin, 125,* 31–46.

Miller, L. T., & Vernon, P. A. (1997). Developmental changes in speed of information processing in young children. *Developmental Psychology, 33,* 549–554.

Miller, N. E. (1959). Liberalization of basic S-R concepts: Extensions to conflict behavior, motivation, and social learning. In S. Koch (Ed.), *Psychology: A study of science* (Vol. 2, pp. 196–292). New York: McGraw-Hill.

Millon, T., & Davis, R. D. (1996). *Disorders of personality.* DSM-IV *and beyond* (2nd ed.). New York: Wiley.

Mills, P. E., Cole, K. N., Jenkins, J. R., & Dale, P. S. (1998). Effects of differing levels of inclusion on preschoolers with disabilities. *Exceptional Children, 65,* 79–90.

Milner, B. (1966). Amnesia following operation on temporal lobes. In C. W. M. Whitty & O. L. Zangwill (Eds.), *Amnesia.* London: Butterworth.

Milner, B. (2005). The medial temporal-lobe amnesic syndrome. *Psychiatric Clinics of North America, 28*(3), 599–611.

Milner, D. (1983). *Children and race.* Beverly Hills, CA: Sage.

Miltenberger, R. G. (2003). *Behavior modification: Principles and procedures* (3rd ed.). Pacific Grove, CA: Wadsworth.

Mineka, S., & Zinbarg, R. (2006). A contemporary learning theory perspective on the etiology of anxiety disorders: It's not what you thought it was. *American Psychologist, 61,* 10–26.

Ming, E. E., Adler, G. K., Kessler, R. C., Fogg, L. F., Matthews, K. A., Herd, J. A., & Rose, R. M. (2004). Cardiovascular reactivity to work stress predicts subsequent onset of hypertension: The air traffic controller health change study. *Psychosomatic Medicine, 66,* 459–465.

Minsky, S., Vega, W., Miskimen, T., Gara, M., & Escobar, J. (2003). Diagnostic patterns in Latino, African American, and European American psychiatric patients. *Archives of General Psychiatry, 60,* 637–644.

Miotto, K., Darakjian, J., Basch, J., Murray, S., Zogg, J., & Rawson, R. (2001). Gamma-hydroxybutyric acid: Patterns of use, effects and withdrawal. *American Journal on Addictions, 10,* 232–241.

Miranda, J., & Green, B. L. (1999). The need for mental health services research focusing on poor young women. *Journal of Mental Health Policy and Economics, 2,* 73–89.

Mischel, W. (2004a). *Introduction to personality: Toward an integration.* Hoboken, NJ: Wiley.

Mischel, W. (2004b). Toward an integrative science of the person. *Annual Review of Psychology, 55,* 1–22.

Mischel, W., & Shoda, Y. (1999). Integrating dispositions and processing dynamics. In L. Pervin & O. John (Eds.), *Handbook of personality: Theory and research* (2nd ed., pp. 197–218). New York: Guilford.

Mischel, W., Shoda, Y., & Smith, R. (2004). *Introduction to personality: Toward an integration* (7th ed.) New York: Wiley.

Mitchell, K. J., & Zaragoza, M. S. (1996). Repeated exposure to suggestion and false memory: The role of contextual variability. *Journal of Memory and Learning, 35,* 246–260.

Mitte, K. (2005). Meta-analysis of cognitive-behavioral treatments for generalized anxiety disorder: A comparison with pharmacotherapy. *Psychological Bulletin, 131,* 785–795.

Miyamoto, S., Duncan, G. E., Marx, C. E., & Lieberman, J. A. (2005). Treatments for schizophrenia: A critical review of pharmacology and mechanisms of action of antipsychotic drugs. *Molecular Psychiatry, 10,* 79–104.

Miyamoto, Y., & Kitayama, S. (2002). Cultural variation in correspondence bias: The critical role of attitude diagnosticity of socially constrained behavior. *Journal of Personality and Social Psychology, 83,* 1239–1248.

Miyamoto, Y., Nisbett, R. E., & Masuda, T. (2006). Culture and the physical environment: Holistic versus analytic perceptual affordances. *Psychological Science, 17,* 113–119.

Moffitt, T. E. (2002). Teen-aged mothers in contemporary Britain. *Journal of Child Psychology & Psychiatry & Allied Disciplines, 43,* 727–742.

Moffitt, T. E., Caspi, A., & Rutter, M. (2005). Strategy for investigating interactions between measured genes and measured environments. *Archives of General Psychiatry, 62,* 473–481.

Mogenson, G. J. (1976). Neural mechanisms of hunger: Current status and future prospects. In D. Novin, W. Wyrwicka, & G. Bray (Eds.), *Hunger: Basic mechanisms and clinical applications.* New York: Raven.

Moghaddam, F. M. (2005). The staircase to terrorism: A psychological exploration. *American Psychologist, 60,* 161–169.

Mohr, C., Binkofski, F., Erdmann, C., Buchel, C., & Helmchen, C. (2005). The anterior cingulate cortex contains distinct areas dissociating external from self-administered painful stimulation: A parametric fMRI study. *Pain, 114,* 347–357.

Mohr, C., Rohrenbach, C. M., Landis, T., & Regard, M. (2001). Associations to smell are more pleasant than to sound. *Journal of Clinical and Experimental Neuropsychology, 23,* 484–489.

Mohr, D. C., Hart, S. L., Julian, L., Catledge, C., Honos-Webb, L., Vella, L., et al. (2005). Telephone-administered psychotherapy for depression. *Archives of General Psychiatry, 62,* 1007–1014.

Mokdad, A. H., Ford, E. S., Bowman, B. A., Dietz, W. H., Vinicor, F., Bales, V. S., et al. (2003). Prevalence of obesity, diabetes, and obesity-related health risk factors, 2001. *Journal of the American Medical Association, 289,* 76–79.

Molden, D. C., & Dweck, C. S. (2000). Meaning and motivation. In C. Sansone & J. M. Harackiewicz (Eds.), *Intrinsic and extrinsic motivation: The search for optimal motivation and performance.* San Diego: Academic Press.

Moldin, S. O., & Gottesman, I. I. (1997). At issue: Genes, experience, and chance in schizophrenia—positioning for the 21st century. *Schizophrenia Bulletin, 23,* 547–561.

Molsa, P. K., Marttila, R. J., & Rinne, U. K. (1995). Long-term survival and predictors of mortality in Alzheimer's disease and multi-infarct dementia. *Acta Neurologica Scandinavica, 91,* 159–164.

Molteni, R., Zheng, J.-Q., Ying, Z., Gómez-Pinilla, F., & Twiss, J. (2004). Voluntary exercise increases axonal regeneration from sensory neurons. *Proceedings of the National Academies of Science, 101,* 8473–8478.

Monane, M., Leichter, D., & Lewis, O. (1984). Physical abuse in psychiatrically hospitalized children and adolescents. *Journal of the American Academy of Child and Adolescent Psychiatry, 23,* 653–658.

Moncrief, W. C., Babakus, E., Cravens, D. W., & Johnston, M. W. (2000). Examining gender differences in field sales organizations. *Journal of Business Research, 49,* 245–257.

Moncrieff, J., & Kirsch, I. (2005). Efficacy of antidepressants in adults. *British Medical Journal, 331,* 155–157.

Monroe, S. M., Rohde, P., Seeley, J. R., & Lewinsohn, P. M. (1999). Life events and depression in adolescence: Relationship loss as a prospective risk factor for first onset of major depressive disorder. *Journal of Abnormal Psychology, 108,* 606–614.

Monroe, S., Thase, M., & Simons, A. (1992). Social factors and psychobiology of depression: Relations between life stress and rapid eye movement sleep latency. *Journal of Abnormal Psychology, 101,* 528–537.

Montague, P. R., Hyman, S. E., & Cohen, J. D. (2004). Computational roles for dopamine in behavioural control. *Nature, 431,* 760–767.

Monteith, M. J., Sherman, J. W., & Devine, P. G. (1998). Suppression as a stereotype control strategy. *Personality & Social Psychology Review, 2,* 63–82.

Monteith, M. J., Zuwerink, J. R., & Devine, P. G. (1994). Prejudice and prejudice reduction: Classic challenges and contemporary approaches. In P. G. Devine,

D. L. Hamilton, & T. M. Ostrom (Eds.), *Social cognition: Impact on social psychology* (pp. 324–346). San Diego: Academic Press.

Moon, R. Y., Oden, R. P., & Grady, K. C. (2004). Back to sleep: An educational intervention with women, infants, and children program clients. *Pediatrics, 113,* 542–547.

Moon, Y. (2003). Don't blame the computer: When self-disclosure moderates the self-serving bias. *Journal of Consumer Psychology, 13,* 125–137.

Moore, J. W., Tingstom, D. H., Doggett, R. A., & Carlyon, W. D. (2001). Restructuring an existing token economy in a psychiatric facility for children. *Child & Family Behavior Therapy, 23,* 53–60.

Moorman, R. H., & Byrne, Z. S. (2005). How does organizational justice affect organizational citizenship behavior? In J. Greenberg & J. A. Colquitt (Eds.), *Handbook of organizational justice* (pp. 355–380). Mahwah, NJ: Erlbaum.

Moos, R., Schaefer, J., Andrassy, J., & Moos, B. (2001). Outpatient mental health care, self-help groups, and patients' one-year treatment outcomes. *Journal of Clinical Psychology, 57,* 273–287.

Moradi, B., Dirks, D., & Matteson, A. V. (2005). Roles of sexual objectification experiences and internalization of standards of beauty in eating disorder symptomatology: A test and extension of objectification theory. *Journal of Counseling Psychology, 52,* 420–428.

Moran, C. C. (2002). Humor as a moderator of compassion fatigue. In C. R. Figley (Ed.), *Treating compassion fatigue* (pp. 139–154). New York: Brunner-Routledge.

Moran, D. R. (2000, June). *Is active learning for me?* Poster presented at APS Preconvention Teaching Institute, Denver.

Morewedge, C. K., Gilbert, D. T., & Wilson, T. D. (2005). The least likely of times: How remembering the past biases forecasts of the future. *Psychological Science, 16*(8), 626–630.

Morgan, C. D., & Murray, H. A. (1935). A method for investigating fantasy: The Thematic Apperception Test. *Archives of Neurology and Psychiatry, 34,* 289–306.

Morris, J. S., DeGelder, B., Weiskrantz, L., & Dolan, R. J. (2001). Differential extrageniculostriate and amygdala responses to presentation of emotional faces in a cortically blind field. *Brain, 124,* 1241–1252.

Morris, J. S., Friston, K. J., Buchel, C., Frith, C. D., Young, A. W., Calder, A. J., et al. (1998). A neuromodulatory role for the human amygdala in processing emotional facial expressions. *Brain, 121,* 47–57.

Morris, L. (2000, December 5). Hold the anaesthetic. I'll hypnotise myself instead. *Daily Mail,* p. 25.

Mortimer, J. A., Snowdon, D. A., & Markesbery, W. R. (2003). Head circumference, education, and risk of dementia: Findings from the nun study. *Journal of Clinical and Experimental Neuropsychology, 25,* 671–679.

Mortimer, R. G., Goldsteen, K., Armstrong, R. W., & Macrina, D. (1988). *Effects of enforcement, incentives, and publicity on seat belt use in Illinois.* University of Illinois, Dept. of Health & Safety Studies, Final Report to Illinois Dept. of Transportation (Safety Research Report 88–11).

Moscovici, S. (1985). Social influence and conformity. In G. Lindzey & E. Aronson (Eds.), *The handbook of social psychology* (Vol. 2, 3rd ed.). New York: Random House.

Moskowitz, G. B. (2005). *Social cognition: Understanding self and others.* New York: Guilford Press.

Moss, E., Bureau, J.-F., Cyr, C., Mongeau, C., & St.-Laurent, D. (2004). Correlates of attachment at age 3: Construct validity of the preschool attachment classification system. *Developmental Psychology, 40,* 323–334.

Mroczek, D. K., & Spiro, A., III. (2005). Changing life satisfaction during adulthood: Findings from the Veterans Affairs normative aging study. *Journal of Personality and Social Psychology, 88,* 189–202.

Muchinsky, P. M. (2003). *Psychology applied to work* (7th ed.). Belmont, CA: Thomson.

Mufson, L., Dorta, K. P. Moreau, D., & Weissman, M. M. (2004). *Interpersonal psychotherapy for depressed adolescents* (2nd ed.). New York: Guilford Press.

Muir, J. L. (1997). Acetylcholine, aging, and Alzheimer's disease. *Pharmacological and Biochemical Behavior, 56*(4), 687–696.

Mullen, B. (1986). Atrocity as a function of lynch mob composition: A self-attention perspective. *Personality and Social Psychology Bulletin, 12,* 187–197.

Mullin, R. E. (2000). *The new handbook of cognitive therapy techniques.* New York: Norton.

Mumford, M. D., Connelly, M. S., Helton, W. B., Strange, J. M., & Osburn, H. K. (2001). On the construct validity of integrity tests: Individual and situational factors as predictors of test performance. *International Journal of Selection and Assessment, 9,* 240–257.

Mumme, D. L., & Fernald, A. (2003). The infant as onlooker: Learning from emotional reactions observed in a television scenario. *Child Development, 74,* 221–237.

Munakata, Y. (2006). Information processing approaches to development. In W. Damon & R. M. Lerner (Series Eds.) & D. Kuhn & R. Siegler (Vol. Eds.), *Handbook of child psychology: Vol. 2. Cognition, perception, and language* (6th ed.). New York: Wiley.

Munley, P. H. (2002). Comparability of MMPI-2 scales and profiles over time. *Journal of Personality Assessment, 78,* 145–160.

Munte, T. F., Altenmuller, E., & Jancke, L. (2002). The musician's brain as a model of neuroplasticity. *Nature Reviews: Neuroscience, 3,* 473–478.

Murphy, C. M., Winters, J., O'Farrell, T. J., Fals-Stewart, W., & Murphy, M. (2005). Alcohol consumption and intimate partner violence by alcoholic men: Comparing violent and nonviolent conflicts. *Psychology of Addictive Behaviors, 19,* 35–42.

Murray, B. (2000). Learning from real life. *APA Monitor, 31,* 72–73.

Murray, E. A., & Mishkin, M. (1985). Amygdalectomy impairs crossmodal association in monkeys. *Science, 228,* 604–606.

Murray, H. A. (1938). *Explorations in personality.* New York: Oxford University Press.

Murray, H. A. (1971). *Thematic Apperception Test.* Cambridge: Harvard University Press.

Murray, J. A., & Terry, D. (1999). Parental reactions to infant death: The effects of resources and coping strategies. *Journal of Social and Clinical Psychology, 18,* 341–369.

Murrell, W., Feron, F., Wetzig, A., Cameron, N., Splatt, K., Bellette, B., et al. (2005). Multipotent stem cells from adult olfactory mucosa. *Developmental Dynamics, 233,* 496–515.

Mussweiler, T. (2003). "Everything is relative": Comparison processes in social judgment: The 2002 Jaspars Lecture. *European Journal of Social Psychology, 33,* 719–733.

Myers, B. J. (1987). Mother-infant bonding as a critical period. In M. H. Bornstein (Ed.), *Sensitive periods in development: Interdisciplinary perspectives.* Hillsdale, NJ: Erlbaum.

Myers, D. G. (2000). *The American paradox: Spiritual hunger in an age of plenty.* New Haven, CT: Yale University Press.

Myers, D. G. (2004). *Intuition: Its powers and perils.* New Haven, CT: Yale University Press.

Myers, M. G., Reeves, R. A., Oh, P. I., & Joyner, C. D. (1996). Overtreatment of hypertension in the community? *American Journal of Hypertension, 9,* 419–425.

Myers, S. L. (2001, March 12). Sub's crew may have hesitated to question a trusted captain. *New York Times.*

N

Nabeshima, T., & Yamada, K. (2000). Neurotrophic factor strategies for the treatment of Alzheimer disease. *Alzheimer Disease & Associated Disorders, 14* (Suppl. 1), S39–46.

Naccache, L., Gaillard, R., Adam, C., Hasboun, D., Clémenceau, S., Baulac, M., et al. (2005). A direct intracranial record of emotions evoked by subliminal words. *Proceedings of the National Academy of Sciences of the USA, 102,* 7713–7717.

Nadeau, S., & Crosson, B. (1995). A guide to the functional imaging of cognitive processes. *Neuropsychiatry, Neuropsychology, and Behavioral Neurology, 8,* 143–162.

Nader, K., Schafe, G. E., & Le Doux, J. E. (2000). Fear memories require protein synthesis in the amygdala for reconsolidation after retrieval. *Nature, 406,* 722–726.

Naëgelé, B., Thouvard, V., Pépin, J.-L., Lévy, P., Bonnet, C., Perret, J. E., et al. (1995). Deficits of cognitive functions in patients with sleep apnea syndrome. *Sleep, 18*(1), 43–52.

Nagy, T. F. (1999). *Ethics in plain English: An illustrative casebook for psychologists.* Washington, DC: American Psychological Association.

Naito, M., & Miura, H. (2001). Japanese children's numerical competencies: Age- and schooling-related influences on the development of number concepts and addition skills. *Developmental Psychology, 37,* 217–230.

Nakamura, J., & Csikszentmihalyi, M. (2001). Catalytic creativity. *American Psychologist, 56,* 337–341.

Nakano, K., & Kitamura, T. (2001). The relation of the anger subcomponent of Type A behavior to psychological symptoms in Japanese and foreign students. *Japanese Psychological Research, 43,* 50–54.

Nanchahal, K., Morris, J. N., Sullivan, L. M., & Wilson, P. W. (2005). Coronary heart disease risk in men and the epidemic of overweight and obesity. *International Journal of Obesity, 29*, 317–323.

Narrow, W. E., Rae, D. S., Robins, L. N., & Regier, D. A. (2002). Revised prevalence based estimates of mental disorders in the United States: Using a clinical significance criterion to reconcile two survey estimates. *Archives of General Psychiatry, 59*, 115–123.

Nash, A. J., & Fernandez, M. (1996). P300 and allocation of attention in dual-tasks. *International Journal of Psychophysiology, 23*, 171–180.

Nash, I. S., Mosca, L., Blumenthal, R. S., Davidson, M. H., Smith, S. C., Jr., & Pasternak, R. C. (2003). Contemporary awareness and understanding of cholesterol as a risk factor: Results of an American Heart Association national survey. *Archives of Internal Medicine, 163*, 1597–1600.

Nathan, P. E., & Langenbucher, J. W. (1999). Psychopathology: Description and classification. *Annual Review of Psychology, 50*, 79–107.

Nathan, P. E., Stuart, S. P., & Dolan, S. L. (2000). Research on psychotherapy efficacy and effectiveness: Between Scylla and Charybdis? *Psychological Bulletin, 126*, 964–981.

Nathanson, M., Bergman, P. S., & Gordon, G. G. (1952). Denial of illness: Its occurrence in one hundred consecutive cases of hemiplegia. *Archives of Neurology and Psychiatry, 68*, 380–397.

National Association of Anorexia Nervosa and Associated Disorders. (2002). *Facts about eating disorders.* Retrieved August 26, 2003, from http://www.altrue.net/site/anadweb/content.php?type=1&id=6982

National Center for Chronic Disease Prevention and Health Promotion. (2002). Trends in Sexual Risk Behaviors Among High School Students—United States, 1991–2001. *Morbidity and Mortality Weekly Report, 51*, 856–859.

National Center for Education Statistics. (2000). *National assessment of education progress.* Washington, DC: NCES.

National Center for Education Statistics. (2002). *Digest of education statistics, 2001.* Washington, DC: Office of Educational Research & Improvement, U.S. Dept. of Education.

National Center for Education Statistics. (2003). *Postsecondary institutions in the United States: Fall 2002 and degrees and other awards conferred: 2001–02.* Washington, DC: U.S. Department of Education.

National Center for Health Statistics. (2000). *Trends in pregnancies and pregnancy rates by outcome: Estimates for the United States, 1976–1996.* Washington, DC: Centers for Disease Control and Prevention.

National Center for Health Statistics. (2001). *Births, marriages, divorces, and deaths: Provisional data for January–December 2000.* Hyattsville, Maryland: Public Health Service.

National Center for Health Statistics. (2003). Births: Final data for 2002. *National Vital Statistics Reports, 52*(10). Washington, DC: Centers for Disease Control and Prevention.

National Center for Health Statistics. (2004). *Health, United States, 2004: With chartbook on trends in the health of Americans.* Hyattsville, MD: U.S. Department of Health and Human Services.

National Center for Injury Prevention and Control. (2002). *Ten leading causes of death, United States.* Washington, DC: Centers for Disease Control.

National Center on Addiction and Substance Abuse. (2004). *National Survey of American Attitudes on Substance Abuse: IX. Teen dating practices and sexual activity.* New York: Author.

National Computer Systems. (1992). *Catalog of assessment instruments, reports, and services.* Minneapolis: National Computer Systems.

National Highway Traffic Safety Administration. (2005). *Traffic safety facts.* Washington, DC: National Center for Statistics and Analysis.

National Institute for Clinical Excellence. (2004). *Depression: Management of depression in primary and secondary care* (Clinical Practice Guideline No. 23). Retrieved August 11, 2005, from http://www.nice.org.uk/page.aspx?o=cg023.

National Institute for Occupational Safety and Health. (1999). *Stress at work.* Washington, DC: NIOSH Publication No. 99–101.

National Institute of Mental Health. (1995). *Medications.* Washington, DC: U.S. Department of Health and Human Services.

National Institute of Mental Health. (2004, April 23). *Statement on antidepressant medications for children: Information for parents and caregivers.* Retrieved April 24, 2004, from www.nimh.nih.gov/press/StmntAntidepmeds.cfm

National Institute on Alcohol Abuse and Alcoholism. (2000). *Tenth special report to the U.S. Congress on alcohol and health* (Publication No. 00–1583). Washington, DC: National Institutes of Health.

National Institute on Alcohol Abuse and Alcoholism. (2001). *Alcoholism: Getting the facts.* Bethesda, MD: Author.

National Institute on Drug Abuse. (2000). Facts about MDMA (Ecstacy). *NIDA Notes, 14.* Retrieved December 13, 2004, from http://drugabuse.gov/NIDA_Notes/NNVol14N4/tearoff.html

National Institutes of Health Consensus Conference. (1998). Acupuncture. *Journal of the American Medical Association, 280*, 1518–1524.

National Institutes of Health. (2001). *Eating disorders: Facts about eating disorders and the search for solutions* (NIH Publication No. 01–4901). Washington, DC: U.S. Department of Health and Human Services.

National Safety Council. (2004). *Reports on injuries in America, 2003.* Itasca, IL: Author.

National Science Foundation. (2004a). *Doctoral scientists and engineers: 2001 profile tables.* Arlington, VA: Author.

National Science Foundation. (2004b). *Women, minorities, and persons with disabilities in science and engineering.* Arlington, VA: Author.

Navarrete-Palacios, E., Hudson, R., Reyes-Guerrero, G., & Guevara-Guzman, R. (2003). Lower olfactory threshold during the ovulatory phase of the menstrual cycle. *Biological Psychology, 63*, 269–279.

Neary, D., & Snowden, J. (1996). Fronto-temporal dementia: Nosology, neuropsychology, and neuropathology. *Brain and Cognition, 31*(2), 176–187.

Neary, D., Snowden, J. S., & Mann, D. M. (1993). The clinical pathological correlates of lobar atrophy. *Dementia, 4*(3–4), 154–159.

Needham, A., & Baillargeon, R. (1999). Effects of prior experience on 4.5 month-old infants' object segregation. *Infant Behavior & Development, 21*, 1–24.

Neff, L. A., & Karney, B. R. (2005). To know you is to love you: The implications of global adoration and specific accuracy for marital relationships. *Journal of Personality and Social Psychology, 88*, 480–497.

Neher, A. (1991). Maslow's theory of motivation: A critique. *Journal of Humanistic Psychology, 31*, 89–112.

Neisser, U. (1998). *The rising curve: Long-term gains in I.Q. and related measures.* Washington, DC: American Psychological Association.

Neisser, U. (2000a). Memorists. In U. Neisser & I. E. Hyman, Jr. (Eds.), *Memory observed* (2nd ed., pp. 475–478). New York: Worth.

Neisser, U. (2000b). Snapshots or benchmarks? In U. Neisser & I. E. Hyman, Jr. (Eds.), *Memory observed* (2nd ed., pp. 68–74). New York: Worth.

Neisser, U., Boodoo, G., Bouchard, T. J., Boykin, A. W., Brody, N., Ceci, S. J., et al. (1996). Intelligence: Knowns and unknowns. *American Psychologist, 51*, 77–101.

Nelson, C. A. (1999). Neural plasticity and human development. *Current Directions in Psychological Science, 8*, 42–45.

Nelson, D. L. (1999). Implicit memory. In D. E. Morris & M. Gruneberg (Eds.), *Theoretical aspects of memory.* London: Routledge.

Nelson, K., & Fivush, R. (2004). The emergence of autobiographical memory: A social cultural developmental theory. *Psychological Review, 111*, 486–511.

Nelson, T. D., & Steele, R. G. (2006). Beyond efficacy and effectiveness: A multifaceted approach to treatment evaluation. *Professional Psychology: Research and Practice, 37*, 389–397.

Nelson-LeGall, S., & Resnick, L. (1998). Help seeking, achievement motivation, and the social practice of intelligence in school. In S. A. Karabenick (Ed.), *Strategic help seeking* (pp. 39–60). Mahwah, NJ: Erlbaum.

Nemeroff, C. B., Heim, C. M., Thase, M. E., Klein, D. N., Rush, A. J., Schatzberg, A. F., et al. (2003). Differential responses to psychotherapy versus pharmacotherapy in patients with chronic forms of major depression and childhood trauma. *Proceedings of the National Academy of Science, 100*, 14293–14296.

Nestadt, G., Hsu, F.-C., Samuels, J., Bienvenu, O. J., Reti, I. Costa, P. T., Jr., et al. (2005). Latent structure of the *Diagnostic and Statistical Manual of Mental Disorders, Fourth Edition*, personality disorder criteria. *Comprehensive Psychiatry, 47*, 54–62.

Nestler, E. J. (2001). Molecular basis of long-term plasticity underlying addiction. *National Review of Neuroscience, 2*, 119–128.

Nestler, E. J. (2005). Is there a common molecular pathway for addiction? *Nature Neuroscience, 8*, 1445–1449.

Neugarten, B. L. (1977). Personality and aging. In J. E. Birren & K. W. Schaie (Eds.), *Handbook of the psychology of aging.* New York: Van Nostrand Reinhold.

Neumann, C. S., Grimes, K., Walker, E. F., & Baum, K. (1995). Developmental pathways to schizophrenia: Behavioral subtypes. *Journal of Abnormal Psychology, 104*, 558–566.

Neumeister, A., Bain, E., Nugent, A. C., Carson, R. E., Bonne, O., Luckenbaugh, D. A., et al. (2004). Reduced serotonin type 1A receptor binding in panic disorder. *Journal of Neuroscience, 24*, 589–591.

Neuwelt, E. A. (2004). Mechanisms of disease: The blood-brain barrier. *Neurosurgery, 54*, 131–140.

Neves-Pereira, M., Cheung, J. K., Pasdar, A., Zhang, F., Breen, G., Yates, P., et al. (2005). BDNF gene is a risk factor for schizophrenia in a Scottish population. *Molecular Psychiatry, 10,* 208–212.

Newberg, A., Alavi, A., Baime, M., Pourdehnad, M., Santanna, J., & d'Aquili, E. (2001). The measurement of regional cerebral blood flow during the complex cognitive task of meditation: A preliminary SPECT study. *Psychiatry Research, 106,* 113–122.

Newcombe, N., & Fox, N. A. (1994). Infantile amnesia: Through a glass darkly. *Child Development, 65,* 31–40.

Newcombe, N. S., Drummey, A. B., Fox, N. A., Lie, E., & Ottinger-Alberts, W. (2000). Remembering early childhood: How much, how, and why (or why not). *Current Directions in Psychological Science, 9,* 55–58.

Newell, A., & Simon, H. A. (1972). *Human problem solving.* Englewood Cliffs, NJ: Prentice-Hall.

Newsome, J. T. (1999). Another side to caregiving: Negative reactions to being helped. *Current Directions in Psychological Science, 8,* 183–187.

Newsome, J. T., & Schulz, R. (1998). Caregiving from the recipient's perspective: Negative reactions to being helped. *Health Psychology, 17,* 172–181.

Niaura, R., Bock, B., Lloyd, E. E., Brown, R., Lipsitt, L. P., & Buka, S. (2001). Maternal transmission of nicotine dependence: Psychiatric, neurocognitive and prenatal factors. *American Journal on Addictions, 10,* 16–29.

Nicassio, P. M., Meyerowitz, B. E., & Kerns, R. D. (2004). The future of health psychology interventions. *Health Psychology, 23,* 132–137.

NICHD Early Child Care Research Network. (2001, April). *Further explorations of the detected effects of quantity of early child care on socioemotional adjustment.* Paper presented at the biennial meetings of the Society for Research in Child Development, Minneapolis.

NICHD Early Child Care Research Network. (2005). *Child care and child development: Results from the NICHD Study of Early Child Care and Youth Development.* New York: Guilford.

NICHD Early Child Care Research Network. (2006a). Infant-mother attachment classification: Risk and protection in relation to changing maternal caregiving quality. *Developmental Psychology, 42,* 38–58.

NICHD Early Child Care Research Network. (2006b). Child-care effect sizes for the NICHD study of early child care and youth development. *American Psychologist, 61,* 99–116.

Nicholson, A., Fuhrer, R., & Marmot, M. (2005). Psychological distress as a predictor of CHD events in men: The effect of persistence and components of risk. *Psychosomatic Medicine, 67,* 522–530.

Nicholson, I. R., & Neufeld, R. W. J. (1993). Classification of the schizophrenias according to symptomatology: A two factor model. *Journal of Abnormal Psychology, 102,* 259–270.

Nickell, J. (1997, January/February). Sleuthing a psychic sleuth. *Skeptical Inquirer, 21,* 18–19.

Nickell, J. (2001). Exorcism! Driving out the nonsense. *Skeptical Inquirer, 25,* 20–24.

Nickerson, C., Schwarz, N., Diener, E., & Kahneman, D. (2003). Zeroing in on the dark side of the American dream: A closer look at the negative consequences of the goal for financial success. *Psychological Science, 14,* 531–536.

Nickerson, R. A., & Adams, M. J. (1979). Long-term memory for a common object. *Cognitive Psychology, 11,* 287–307.

Niederhoffer, K. G., & Pennebaker, J. W. (2002). Sharing one's story: On the benefits of writing or talking about emotional experience. In C. R. Snyder & S. J. Lopez (Eds.), *Handbook of positive psychology* (pp. 573–583). London: Oxford University Press.

Niederman, R., & Richards, D. (2005). Evidence-based dentistry: Concepts and implementation. *Journal of the American College of Dentistry, 72,* 37–41.

Nienhuys, J. W. (2001). Spontaneous human combustion: Requiem for Phyllis. *Skeptical Inquirer, 25,* 28–34.

Nietzel, M. T., Bernstein, D. A., Kramer, G, & Milich, R. (2003). *Introduction to clinical psychology* (6th ed.). Englewood Cliffs, NJ: Prentice-Hall.

Nigg, J. T. (2000). On inhibition/disinhibition in developmental psychopathology: Views from cognitive and personality psychology and a working inhibition taxonomy. *Psychological Bulletin, 126,* 220–246.

Nigg, J. T. (2001). Is ADHD a disinhibitory disorder? *Psychological Bulletin, 127,* 571–598.

Niiya, Y., Crocker, J., & Bartmess, E. N. (2004). From vulnerability to resilience: Learning orientations buffer contingent self-esteem from failure. *Psychological Science, 15,* 801–805.

Nijstad, B. A., Stroebe, W., & Lodewijkx, H. F. M. (2003). Production blocking and idea generation: Does blocking interfere with cognitive processes? *Journal of Experimental Social Psychology, 39,* 531–548.

Nilsson, G. (1996, November). Some forms of memory improve as people age. *APA Monitor,* p. 27.

Nisbett, R. E. (2003). *The geography of thought.* New York: The Free Press.

Nisbett, R. E., & Masuda, T. (2003). Culture and point of view. *Proceedings of the National Academy of Sciences, 100,* 11163–11170.

Nishino, S., & Kanbayashi, T. (2005). Symptomatic narcolepsy, cataplexy and hypersomnia, and their implications in the hypothalamic hypocretin/orexin system. *Sleep Medicine Reviews, 9,* 269–310.

Noble, H. B. (2000, January 25). Outgrowth of new field of tissue engineering. *New York Times.*

Noblett, K. L., & Coccaro, E. F. (2005). Molecular genetics of personality. *Current Psychiatry Reports, 7,* 73–80.

Nock, M. K., & Kessler, R. C. (2006). Prevalence of and risk factors for suicide attempts versus suicide gestures: Analysis of the National Comorbidity Survey. *Journal of Abnormal Psychology, 115,* 616–623.

Nolen-Hoeksema, S. (1990). *Sex differences in depression.* Stanford, CA: Stanford University Press.

Nolen-Hoeksema, S. (2001). Gender differences in depression. *Current Directions in Psychological Science, 10,* 173–176.

Nolen-Hoeksema, S., Larson, J., & Grayson, C. (1999). Explaining gender differences in depression. *Journal of Personality and Social Psychology, 77,* 1061–1072.

Nolen-Hoeksma, S., Morrow, J., & Fredrickson, N. (1993). Response styles and the duration of episodes of depressed mood. *Journal of Abnormal Psychology, 102,* 20–28.

Noll, R. B. (1994). Hypnotherapy for warts in children and adolescents. *Journal of Developmental and Behavioral Pediatrics, 15*(3), 170–173.

Norcross, J. C. (2002). *Psychotherapy relationships that work: Therapist contributions and responsiveness to patients.* London: Oxford University Press.

Norcross, J. C., Beutler, L. E., & Levant, R. F. (2005). *Evidence-based practices in mental health: Debate and dialogue on the fundamental questions.* Washington, DC: American Psychological Association.

Norcross, J. C., Hedges, M., & Castle, P. H. (2002). Psychologists conducting psychotherapy in 2001: A study of Division 29 membership. *Psychotherapy: Theory, Research, Practice, Training, 39,* 97–102.

Norcross, J. C., Hedges, M., & Prochaska, J. O. (2002). The face of 2010: A Delphi poll on the future of psychotherapy. *Professional Psychology: Research and practice, 33,* 316–322.

Norcross, J. C., Santrock, J. W., Campbell, L. F., Smith, T. P., Sommer, R., & Zuckerman, E. L. (2000). *Authoritative guide to self-help resources in mental health.* New York: Guilford.

Nosek, B. A., Banaji, M., & Greenwald, A. G. (2002). Harvesting implicit group attitudes and beliefs from a demonstration web site. *Group Dynamics: Theory, Research, and Practice, 6,* 101–115.

Nott, K. H., & Vedhara, K. (2000). Psychoneuroimmunology and HIV infection. In K. H. Nott & K. Vedhara (Eds.), *Psychosocial and biomedical interactions in HIV infection: Biobehavioural perspectives on health and disease prevention* (pp. 197–227). UK: Harwood Academic Publishers.

Nourkova, V. V., Bernstein, D. M., & Loftus, E. F. (2004) Biography becomes autobiography: Distorting the subjective past. *American Journal of Psychology, 117,* 65–80.

Nowak, M. A., Komarova, N. L., & Niyogi, P. (2001). Evolution of universal grammar. *Science, 291,* 114–118.

Nurnberger, J. I., Jr., Foroud, T., Flury, L., Su, J., Meyer, E. T., Hu, K., et al. (2001). Evidence for a locus on chromosome 1 that influences vulnerability to alcoholism and affective disorder. *American Journal of Psychiatry, 158,* 718–724.

Nutt, D. J. (2005a). Death by tricyclic: The real antidepressant scandal? *Journal of Psychopharmacology, 19,* 123–124.

Nutt, D. J. (2005b). Overview of diagnosis and drug treatments of anxiety disorders. *CNS Spectrums, 10,* 49–56.

Nyberg, L., Petersson, K. M., Nilsson, L. G., Sandblom, J., Aberg, C., & Ingvar, M. (2001). Reactivation of motor brain areas during explicit memory for actions. *Neuroimage, 14,* 521–528.

O

Oatley, K. (1993). Those to whom evil is done. In R. S. Wyer & T. K. Srull (Eds.), *Toward a general theory of anger and emotional aggression: Advances in social cognition* (Vol. 6). Hillsdale, NJ: Erlbaum.

O'Brien, T. L. (1991, September 2). Computers help thwart "groupthink" that plagues meetings. *Chicago Sun Times.*

Ochsner, K. N. (2004). Current directions in social cognitive neuroscience. *Current Opinion in Neurobiology, 14,* 254–258.

Oden, M. H. (1968). The fulfillment of promise: 40-year follow-up of the Terman gifted group. *Genetic Psychology Monographs, 17,* 3–93.

O'Donohue, W., Fisher, J. E., & Hayes, S. C. (Eds.). (2003). *Cognitive behavior therapy: Applying empirically supported techniques in your practice.* New York: Wiley.

O'Driscoll, M., Brough, P., & Kalliath, T. (2006). Work-family conflict and facilitation. In F. Jones, R. J. Burke, & M. Westman (Eds.), *Work-life balance: A psychological perspective* (pp. 117–142). New York: Psychology Press.

Ogden, C. L., Carroll, M. D., Curtin, L. R., McDowell, M. A., Tabak, C. J., & Flegal, K. M. (2006). Prevalence of overweight and obesity in the United States, 1999–2004. *Journal of the American Medical Association, 295,* 1549–1555.

Ogrondniczuk, J. S., & Piper, W. E. (2003). The effect of group climate on outcome in two forms of short-term group therapy. *Group Dynamics: Theory, Research, and Practice, 7,* 64–76.

Ohayon, M. M., & Roth, T. (2003). Place of chronic insomnia in the course of depressive and anxiety disorders. *Journal of Psychiatric Research, 37,* 9–15.

Öhman, A., Dimberg, U., & Öst, L. G. (1985). Animal and social phobias: A laboratory model. In S. Reiss & R. R. Bootzin (Eds.), *Theoretical issues in behavior therapy.* Orlando, FL: Academic Press.

Öhman, A., & Mineka, S. (2001). Fears, phobias, and preparedness: Toward an evolved module of fear and fear learning. *Psychological Review, 108,* 483–522.

Öhman, A., & Mineka, S. (2003). The malicious serpent: Snakes as a prototypical stimulus for an evolved module of fear. *Current Directions in Psychological Science, 12,* 5–9.

Öhman, A., & Soares, J. F. (1994). "Unconscious anxiety": Phobic responses to masked stimuli. *Journal of Abnormal Psychology, 103*(2), 231–240.

Ohring, R., Graber, J. A., & Brooks-Gunn, J. (2002). Girls' recurrent and concurrent body dissatisfaction: Correlates and consequences over 8 years. *International Journal of Eating Disorders, 31*(4), 404–415.

Ohta, H., Yamazaki, S., & McMahon, D. G. (2005). Constant light desynchronizes mammalian clock neurons. *Nature Neuroscience, 8,* 267–269.

Oishi, S., Diener, E., Lucas, R. E., & Suh, E. M. (1999). Cross-cultural variations in predictors of life-satisfaction: Perspectives from needs and values. *Personality and Social Psychology Bulletin, 25,* 980–990.

Okie, S. (2005). Medical marijuana and the Supreme Court. *New England Journal of Medicine, 353,* 648–651.

Okonkwo, D. O. (2003). Basic science of closed head injuries and spinal cord injuries. *Clinics of Sports Medicine, 22*(3), 467–481.

Oldenberg, P.-A., Zheleznyak, A., Fang, Y.-F., Lagenaur, C. F., Gresham, H. D., & Lindberg, F. P. (2000). Role of CD47 as a marker of self on red blood cells. *Science, 288,* 2051–2054.

Olds, J. (1973). Commentary on positive reinforcement produced by electrical stimulation of septal areas and other regions of rat brain. In E. S. Valenstein (Ed.), *Brain stimulation and motivation: Research and commentary.* Glenview, IL: Scott, Foresman.

Olds, J., & Milner, P. (1954). Positive reinforcement produced by electrical stimulation of septal areas and other regions of the rat brain. *Journal of Comparative and Physiological Psychology, 47,* 419–427.

O'Leary, D. S., Block, R. I., Koeppel, J. A., Flaum, M., Schulz, S. K., Andreason, N. C., et al. (2002). Effects of smoking marijuana on brain perfusion and cognition. *Neuropsychopharmacology, 26,* 802–816.

Olfson, M., Marcus, S. C., Druss, B., Elinson, L., Tanielian, T., & Pincus, H. A. (2002). National trends in the outpatient treatment of depression. *Journal of the American Medical Association, 287,* 203–209.

Olfson, M., Mechanic, D., Hansell, S., Boyer, C. A., & Walkup, J. (1999). Prediction of homelessness within three months of discharge among inpatients with schizophrenia. *Psychiatric Services, 50,* 667–673.

Oliner, S. P., & Oliner, P. M. (1988). *The altruistic personality: Rescuers of Jews in Nazi Europe.* New York: Free Press.

Olio, K. A. (1994). Truth in memory. *American Psychologist, 49,* 442–443.

Ollendick, T. H., & Prinz, R. J. (2002). Editors' comment: International consensus statement on attention deficit hyperactivity disorder (ADHD). *Clinical Child and Family Psychology Review, 5,* 87.

Olshansky, S. J., Passaro, D. J., Hershow, R. C., Layden, J., Carnes, B. A., Brody, J., et al. (2005). A potential decline in life expectancy in the United States in the 21st century. *New England Journal of Medicine, 352,* 1138–1145.

Olson, I. R., Rao, H., Moore, K. S., Wang, J., Detre, J. A., & Aguirre, G. K. (2006). Using perfusion fMRI to measure continuous changes in neural activity with learning. *Brain and Cognition, 60,* 262–271.

Olson, J. M., & Stone, J. (2005). The influence of behavior on attitudes. In D. Albarracín, B. T. Johnson, & M. P. Zanna (Eds.), *Handbook of attitudes* (pp. 223–271). Mahwah, NJ: Erlbaum.

Olson, J. M., Vernon, P. A., Harris, J. A., & Jang, K. L. (2001). The heritability of attitudes: A study of twins. *Journal of Personality and Social Psychology, 80,* 845–860.

Olson, L. (1997). Regeneration in the adult central nervous system. *Nature Medicine, 3,* 1329–1335.

Olson, M. B., Krantz, D. S., Kelsey, S. F., Pepine, C. J., Sopko, G., Handberg, E., et al. (2005). Hostility scores are associated with increased risk of cardiovascular events in women undergoing coronary angiography: A report from the NHLBI-sponsored WISE study. *Psychosomatic Medicine, 67,* 546–552.

Ölveczky, B. P., Baccus, S. A., & Meister, M. (2003). Segregation of object and background motion in the retina. *Nature, 423,* 401–408.

Omaha, J. (2004). *Psychotherapeutic interventions for emotion regulation: EMDR and bilateral stimulation for affect management.* New York: Norton.

O'Neill, H. (2000, September 24). After rape, jail—a friendship forms. *St. Petersburg Times,* pp. 1A, 14A.

Ones, D., & Viswesvaran, C. (1996). Bandwidth-fidelity dilemma in personality measurement for personnel selection. *Journal of Organizational Behavior, 17,* 609–626.

Ones, D., & Viswesvaran, C. (2001). Personality at work: Criterion focused occupational personality scales used in personnel selection. In R. Hogan & B. Roberts (Eds.), *Personality psychology in the workplace* (pp. 63–92). Washington, DC: American Psychological Association.

Ones, D. S., Viswesvaran, C., & Schmidt, F. L. (2003). Personality and absenteeism: A meta-analysis of integrity tests. *European Journal of Personality, 17,* S19–S38.

Onishi, K. H., & Baillargeon, R. (2005). Do 15-month-old infants understand false beliefs? *Science, 308,* 255–258.

Operario, D., & Fiske, S. T. (2001). Stereotypes: Processes, structures, content, and context. In R. Brown & S. Gaertner (Eds.), *Blackwell handbook in social psychology: Intergroup processes* (pp. 22–44). Oxford, UK: Blackwell.

Oppel, S. (2000, March 5). Managing ABCs like a CEO. *St. Petersburg Times,* 1A, 12–13A.

Oquendo, M. A., Ellis, S. P., Greenwald, S., Malone, K. M., Weissman, M. M., & Mann, J. J. (2001). Ethnic and sex differences in suicide rates relative to major depression in the United States. *American Journal of Psychiatry, 158,* 1652–1658.

Oquendo, M. A., & Mann, J. J. (2000). The biology of impulsivity and suicidality. *Psychiatric Clinics of North America, 23,* 11–25.

Oquendo, M. A., & Mann, J. J. (2001). Identifying and managing suicide risk in bipolar patients. *Journal of Clinical Psychiatry, 62,* 31–34.

Orban, P., Rauchs, G., Balteau, E., Degueldre, C., Luxen, A., Maquet, P., et al. (2006). Sleep after spatial learning promotes covert reorganization of brain activity. *Proceedings of the National Academy of Sciences of the USA, 103,* 7124–7129.

Organ, D. W., & Ryan, K. (1995). A meta-analytic review of attitudinal and dispositional predictors of organizational citizenship behavior. *Personnel Psychology, 48,* 775–802.

Orne, M. T., & Evans, F. J. (1965). Social control in the psychological experiment: Antisocial behavior and hypnosis. *Journal of Personality and Social Psychology, 1,* 189–200.

Orne, M. T., Sheehan, P. W., & Evans, F. J. (1968). Occurrence of posthypnotic behavior outside the experimental setting. *Journal of Personality and Social Psychology, 9,* 189–196.

Oskamp, S., & Schultz, P. W. (1998). *Applied social psychology* (2nd ed.). Upper Saddle River, NJ: Prentice-Hall.

Öst, L.-G. (1978). Behavioral treatment of thunder and lightning phobia. *Behavior Research and Therapy, 16,* 197–207.

Öst, L.-G. (1992). Blood and injection phobia: Background and cognitive, physiological and behavioral variables. *Journal of Abnormal Psychology, 101,* 68–74.

Öst, L.-G., Hellström, K., & Kåver, A. (1992). One- versus five-session exposure in the treatment of needle phobia. *Behavior Therapy, 23,* 263–282.

Öst, L.-G., Svensson, L., Hellström, K., & Lindwall, R. (2001). One-session treatment of specific phobias in youths: A randomized clinical trial. *Journal of Consulting and Clinical Psychology, 69,* 814–824.

Otto, M. W., Bruce, S. E., & Deckersbach, T. (2005). Benzodiazepine use, cognitive impairment, and cognitive-behavioral therapy for anxiety disorders: Issues in the treatment of a patient in need. *Journal of Clinical Psychiatry, 66*(Suppl. 2), 34–38.

Otto, M. W., Pollack, M. H., Gould, R. A., Worthington, J. J., III, McArdle, E. T., Rosenbaum, J. F., & Heimberg, R. G. (2000). A comparison of the efficacy of clonazepam and cognitive-behavioral group therapy for the treatment of social phobia. *Journal of Anxiety Disorders, 14,* 345–358.

Ottosson, H., Ekselius, L., Grann, M., & Kullgren, G. (2002). Cross-system concordance of personality disorder diagnoses of *DSM-IV* and Diagnostic Criteria for Research of ICD-10. *Journal of Personality Disorders, 16,* 283–292.

Overmier, J. B. (2002). On learned helplessness. *Integrative Physiological & Behavioral Science, 37,* 4–8.

Overmier, J. B., & Seligman, M. E. P. (1967). Effects of inescapable shock upon subsequent escape and avoidance learning. *Journal of Comparative and Physiological Psychology, 63,* 23–33.

Overton, D. A. (1984). State dependent learning and drug discriminations. In L. L. Iverson, S. D. Iverson, & S. H. Snyder (Eds.), *Handbook of psychopharmacology* (Vol. 18). New York: Plenum.

Overton, P. G., Richards, C. D., Berry, M. S. & Clark, D. (1999). Long-term potentiation at excitatory amino acid synapses on midbrain dopamine neurons. *Neuroreport, 10,* 221–226.

Oyama, H., Koida, J., Sakashita, T., & Kudo, K. (2004). Community-based prevention for suicide in elderly by depression screening and follow-up. *Community Mental Health Journal, 40,* 249–263.

Oyserman, D., Coon, H. M., & Kemmelmeier, M. (2002). Rethinking individualism and collectivism: Evaluation of theoretical assumptions and meta-analyses. *Psychological Bulletin, 128,* 3–72.

P

Pachankis, J. E., & Goldfried, M. R. (2004). Clinical issues in working with lesbian, gay, and bisexual clients. *Psychotherapy: Theory, Research, Practice, Training, 41,* 227–246.

Paik, H., & Comstock, G. (1994). The effects of television violence on antisocial behavior: A meta-analysis. *Communication Research, 21,* 516–546.

Paivio, S. C., & Greenberg, L. S. (1995). Resolving "unfinished business": Efficacy of experiential therapy using empty-chair dialogue. *Journal of Consulting and Clinical Psychology, 63,* 419–425.

Palkovitz, R., Copes, M. A., & Woolfolk, T. N. (2001). It's like … you discover a new sense of being: Involved fathering as an evoker of adult development. *Men & Masculinities, 4*(1), 49–69.

Palmer, S. E. (1999). *Vision science: Photons to phenomenology.* Cambridge, MA: MIT Press.

Palmisano, M., & Herrmann, D. (1991). The facilitation of memory performance. *Bulletin of the Psychonomic Society, 29,* 557–559.

Paluszynska, D. A., Harris, K. A., & Thach, B. T. (2004). Influence of sleep position experience on ability of prone-sleeping infants to escape from asphyxiating microenvironments by changing head position. *Pediatrics, 114,* 1634–1639.

Paul-Labrador, M., Polk, D., Dwyer, J. H., Velasquez, I., Nidich, S., Rainforth, M., et al. (2006). Effects of a randomized controlled trial of transcendental meditation on components on the metabolic syndrome in subjects with coronary heart disease. *Archives of Internal Medicine, 166,* 1218–1224.

Pandharipande, P., Jackson, J., & Ely, E. W. (2005). Delirium: Acute cognitive dysfunction in the critically ill. *Current Opinion in Critical Care, 11*(4), 360–368.

Paoletti, M. G. (1995). Biodiversity, traditional landscapes and agroecosystem management. *Landscape and Urban Planning, 31*(1–3), 117–128.

Pardini, D. A., & Lochman, J. E. (2003). Treatment of oppositional defiant disorder. In M. A. Reinecke, F. M. Dattilio, & A. Freeman (Eds.), *Cognitive therapy with children and adolescents.* New York: Guilford Press.

Parents Television Council. (2006). *TV bloodbath: Violence on primetime broadcast TV: A PTC state of the television industry report, March.* Retrieved May 24, 2006, from http://www.parentstv.org/PTC/publications/reports/stateindustryviolence/main.asp#_ftn8.

Pariente, J., White, P., Frackowiak, R. S., & Lewith, G. (2005). Expectancy and belief modulate the neuronal substrates of pain treated by acupuncture. *NeuroImage, 25,* 1161–1167.

Park, D., & Gutchess, A. (2006). The cognitive neuroscience of aging and culture. *Current Directions in Psychological Science, 15,* 105–108.

Park, D. C. (2001, August). *The aging mind.* Paper presented at the annual convention of the American Psychological Association, San Francisco.

Park, D. C., Lautenschlager, G., Hedden, T., Davidson, N. S., Smith, A. D., & Smith, P. (2002). Models of visuospatial and verbal memory across the adult life span. *Psychology & Aging, 17*(2), 299–320.

Park, J., White, A. R., & Ernst, E. (2001). New sham method in auricular acupuncture. *Archives of Internal Medicine, 161,* 894.

Park, W.-W. (2000). A comprehensive empirical investigation of the relationships among variables of the groupthink model. *Journal of Organizational Behavior, 21,* 873–887.

Parke, R. D. (2002). Fathers and families. In M. H. Bornstein (Ed.), *Handbook of parenting* (2nd ed., pp. 27–63). Mahwah, NJ: Erlbaum.

Parke, R. D., & Buriel, R. (2006). Child development and the family. In W. Damon & R. M. Lerner (Series Eds.) & N. Eisenberg (Vol. Ed.), *Handbook of child psychology: Vol. 3. Social, emotional, and personality development* (6th ed.). New York: Wiley.

Parker, G., Gladstone, G., & Chee, K. T. (2001). Depression in the planet's largest ethnic group: The Chinese. *American Journal of Psychiatry, 158,* 857–864.

Parker, J. G., Saxon, J. L., Asher, S. R., & Kovacs, D. M. (2001). Dimensions of children's friendship adjustment: Implications for understanding loneliness. In K. J. Rotenberg & S. Hymel (Eds.), *Loneliness in childhood and adolescence.* New York: Cambridge University Press.

Parnas, J., Cannon, T., Jacobsen, B., Schulsinger, H., Schulsinger, F., & Mednick, S. (1993). Lifetime *DSM-III-R* diagnostic outcomes in the offspring of schizophrenic mothers. *Archives of General Psychiatry, 50,* 707–714.

Parolaro, D., Massi, P., Rubino, T., & Monti, E. (2002). Endocannabinoids in the immune system and cancer. *Prostaglandins Leukotrienes & Essential Fatty Acids, 66,* 319–332.

Parsons, T. J., Power, C., & Manor, O. (2005). Physical activity, television viewing and body mass index: A cross-sectional analysis from childhood to adulthood in the 1958 British cohort. *International Journal of Obesity, 29,* 1212–1221.

Pascual, A., & Guéguen, N. (2005). Foot-in-the-door and door-in-the-face: A comparative meta-analytic study. *Psychological Reports, 96,* 122–128.

Pascual-Leone, A. (2001). The brain that plays music and is changed by it. *Annals of the New York Academy of Science, 930,* 315–329.

Pascual-Leone, A., & Torres, F. (1993). Plasticity of the sensorimotor cortex representation of the reading finger in Braille readers. *Brain, 116,* 39–52.

Pashler, H., Rohrer, D., & Cepeda, N. J. (2006). Temporal spacing and learning. *APS Observer, 19,* 30, 38.

Patel, S. R., White, D. P., Malhotra, A., Stanchina, M. L., & Ayas, N. T. (2003). Continuous positive airway pressure therapy for treating sleepiness in a diverse population with obstructive sleep apnea: Results of a meta-analysis. *Archives of Internal Medicine, 163,* 565–571.

Patkowski, M. (1994). The critical age hypothesis and interlanguage phonology. In M. Yavas (Ed.), *First and second language phonology* (pp. 205–221). San Diego: Singular Publishing Group.

Patten, S. B., Williams, J. V. A., Wang, J., Adair, C. E., Brant, C. E., Casebeer, A., et al. (2005). Antidepressant pharmacoepidemiology in a general population sample. *Journal of Clinical Psychopharmacology, 25,* 285–287.

Patterson, C. H. (2000). *Understanding psychotherapy: Fifty years of client-centered theory and practice.* Ross-on-Wye, UK: PCCS Books.

Patterson, C. J. (2004). *Lesbian and gay parents and their children: Summary of research findings.* Washington, DC: American Psychological Association. Retrieved September 26, 2006, from http://www.apa.org/pi/parent.html.

Patterson, D. R. (2004). Treating pain with hypnosis. *Current Directions in Psychological Science, 13,* 252–255.

Patterson, D. R., & Jensen, M. P. (2003). Hypnosis and clinical pain. *Psychological Bulletin, 129,* 495–521.

Patton, G. C., Coffey, C., Carlin, J. B., Degenhardt, L., Lynskey, M., & Hall, W. (2002). Cannabis use and mental health in young people: Cohort study. *British Medical Journal, 325,* 1195–1198.

Patton, G. C., McMorris, B. J., Toumbourou, J. W., Hemphill, S. A., Donath, S., & Catalano, R. F. (2004). Puberty and the onset of substance use and abuse [Electronic version]. *Pediatrics, 114*(3), e300-6.

Pauk, W. (2005). *How to study in college* (8th ed.). Boston: Houghton Mifflin.

Paul, G. L. (1969). Behavior modification research: Design and tactics. In C. M. Franks (Ed.), *Behavior therapy: Appraisal and status* (pp. 29–62). New York: McGraw-Hill.

Paul, G. L. (2000). Milieu therapy. In A. E. Kazdin (Ed.), *The encyclopedia of psychology.* Washington, DC: American Psychological Association.

Paul, G. L., & Lentz, R. J. (1977). *Psychosocial treatment of chronic mental patients: Milieu versus social learning programs.* Cambridge: Harvard University Press.

Paul, G. L., Stuve, P., & Cross, J. V. (1997). Real-world inpatient programs: Shedding some light—A critique. *Applied and Preventive Psychology, 6,* 193–204.

Paulhus, D. L., Trapnell, P., & Chen, D. (1999). Birth order effects on personality and achievement within families. *Psychological Science, 10,* 482–488.

Pauls, D. L., Alsobrook, J. P., II, Goodman, W., Rasmussen, S., & Leckman, J. F. (1995). A family study of obsessive-compulsive disorder. *American Journal of Psychiatry, 152,* 76–84.

Paus, T., Zijdenbos, A., Worsley, K., Collins, D. L., Blumenthal, J., Giedd, J. N., et al. (1999). Structural maturation of neural pathways in children and adolescents: In vivo study. *Science, 283,* 1908–1911.

Pavkov, T., Lewis, D., & Lyons, J. (1989). Psychiatric diagnosis and racial bias: An empirical investigation. *Professional Psychology: Research and Practice, 20,* 364–368.

Payne, J. D., & Nadel, L. (2004). Sleep, dreams, and memory consolidation: The role of the stress hormone cortisol. *Learning and Memory, 11,* 671–678.

Pear, J., & Martin, G. L. (2002). *Behavior modification: What it is and how to do it* (7th ed.). Englewood Cliffs, NJ: Prentice Hall.

Pearson, G. (2000, July 2). Rite-minded: Sports fans find rituals help them get through the game. *Milwaukee Journal-Sentinal.*

Pedersen, P. B., & Draguns, J. G. (2002). *Counseling across cultures.* Thousand Oaks, CA: Sage.

Peigneux, P., Laureys, S., Delbeuck, X., & Maquet, P. (2001). Sleeping brain, learning brain: The role of sleep for memory systems. *Neuroreport, 12,* A111–A124.

Peirce, T. R., Bray, N. J., Williams, N. M., Norton, N., Moskvina, V., Preece, A., et al. (2006). Convergent evidence for 2′,3′-cyclic nucleotide 3′-phosphodiesterase as a possible susceptibility gene for schizophrenia. *Archives of General Psychiatry, 63,* 18–24.

Peña, M., Maki, A., Kovaci, D., Dehaene-Lambertz, G., Koizumi, H., Bouquet, F., & Mehler, J. (2003). Sounds and silence: An optical topography study of language recognition at birth. *Proceedings of the National Academy of Sciences,100,* 11702–11705.

Penedo, F. J., & Dahn, J. (2004). Psychoneuroimmunology and aging. In M. Irwin & K. Vedhara (Eds.), *Psychoneuroimmunology.* New York: Kluwer.

Penfield, W., & Rasmussen, T. (1968). *The cerebral cortex of man: A clinical study of localization of function.* New York: Hafner.

Pennebaker, J. W. (1995). *Emotion, disclosure, and health.* Washington, DC: American Psychological Association.

Pennebaker, J. W. (2000). The effects of traumatic disclosure on physical and mental health: The values of writing and talking about upsetting events. In J. M. Violanti, D. Paton, & C. Dunning (Eds.), *Posttraumatic stress intervention: Challenges, issues, and perspectives* (pp. 97–114). Chicago: Charles C. Thomas.

Pennebaker, J. W., & Chew, C. H. (1985). Deception, electrodermal activity, and inhibition of behavior. *Journal of Personality and Social Psychology, 49,* 1427–1433.

Pennebaker, J. W., & O'Heeron, R. C. (1984). Confiding in others and illness rate among spouses of suicide and accidental death victims. *Journal of Abnormal Psychology, 93,* 473–476.

Penner, L. A. (2002). Dispositional and organizational influences on sustained volunteerism: An interactionist perspective. *Journal of Social Issues, 58,* 447–467.

Penner, L. A., Brannick, M., Connell, P., & Webb, S. (2005). The effects of the September 11 attacks on volunteering: An archival analysis. *Journal of Applied Social Psychology, 35,* 1333–1360.

Penner, L. A., & Craiger, J. P. (1992). The weakest link: The performance of individual group members. In R. W. Swezey & E. Salas (Eds.), *Teams: Their training and performance* (pp. 57–74). Norwood, NJ: Ablex.

Penner, L. A., Dovidio, J., & Albrecht, T. L. (2001). Helping victims of loss and trauma: A social psychological perspective. In J. Harvey & E. Miller (Eds.), *Loss and trauma: General and close relationship perspectives* (pp. 62–85). Philadelphia: Brunner Routledge.

Penner, L. A., Dovidio, J. F., Piliavin, J. A., & Schroeder, D. A. (2005). Prosocial behavior: Multilevel perspectives. *Annual Review of Psychology, 56,* 365–392.

Penner, L. A., & Finkelstein, M. A. (1998). Dispositional and structural determinants of volunteerism. *Journal of Personality and Social Psychology, 74,* 525–537.

Penner, L. A., Fritzsche, B. A., Craiger, J. P., & Friefeld, T. R. (1995). Measuring the prosocial personality. In J. Butcher & C. D. Spielberger (Eds.), *Advances in personality assessment* (Vol. 10, pp. 147–163). Hillsdale, NJ: Erlbaum.

Penner, L. A., Knoff, H., Batchshe, G., Nelson, D. L., & Spielberger, C. D. (Eds.). (1994). *Contributions of psychology to science and math education.* Washington, DC: American Psychological Association.

Penney, L. M., & Spector, P. E. (2005). Job stress, incivility, and counterproductive work behavior (CWB): The moderating role of negative affectivity. *Journal of Organizational Behavior, 26,* 777–796.

Penninx, B. W., Beekman, A. T., Honig, A., Deeg, D. J., Schoevers, R. A., van Eijk, J. T., van Tilburg, W. (2001). Depression and cardiac mortality: Results from a community-based longitudinal study. *Archives of General Psychiatry, 58,* 221–227.

Peplau, L. A. (2003). Human sexuality: How do men and women differ? *Current Directions in Psychological Science, 12,* 37–40.

Perkonigg, A., Pfister, H., Stein, M. B., Hofler, M., Lieb, R., Maercker, A., et al. (2005). Longitudinal course of posttraumatic stress disorder and posttraumatic stress disorder symptoms in a community sample of adolescents and young adults. *American Journal of Psychiatry, 162,* 1320–1327.

Perlis, M. L., Sharpe, M., Smith, M. T., Greenblatt, D., & Giles, D. (2001). Behavioral treatment of insomnia: Treatment outcomes and the relevance of medical and psychiatric morbidity. *Journal of Behavioral Medicine, 24,* 281–296.

Perls, F. S. (1969). *Ego, hunger and aggression: The beginning of Gestalt therapy.* New York: Random House.

Perls, F. S., Hefferline, R. F., & Goodman, P. (1951). *Gestalt therapy.* New York: Julian Press.

Peroutka, S. J., Newman, H., & Harris, H. (1988). The subjective effects of 3, 4-methylenedioxymethamphetamine in recreational users. *Neuropharmacology, 1(4),* 273–277.

Perry, E. K. (1980). The cholinergic system in old age and Alzheimer's disease. *Age and Ageing, 9(1),* 1–8.

Persons, J. B., Davidson, J., & Tompkins, M. A. (2001). *Essential components of cognitive-behavior therapy for depression.* Washington, DC: American Psychological Association.

Pervin, L. A., Cervone, D., & John, O. P. (2005). *Personality: Theory and research.* New York: Wiley.

Petersen, R. C., & Morris, J. C. (2005). Mild cognitive impairment as a clinical entity and treatment target. *Archives of Neurology, 62(7),* 1160–1163.

Petersen, R. C., Smith, G. E., Waring, S. C., Ivnik, R. J., Tangalos, E., & Kokmen, E. (1999). Mild cognitive impairment: Clinical characterization and outcome. *Archives of Neurology, 56,* 303–308.

Petersen, R. C., Thomas, R. G., Grundman, M., Bennett, D., Doody, R., Ferris, S., et al. (2005). Vitamin E and donepezil for the treatment of mild cognitive impairment. *New England Journal of Medicine, 352,* 2379–2388.

Peterson, A., Compas, B., Brooks-Gunn, J., Stemmler, M., Ey, S., & Brant, K. (1993). Depression in adolescence. *American Psychologist, 48,* 155–168.

Peterson, C. (1995, April). *The preschool child witness: Errors in accounts of traumatic injury.* Paper presented at the biennial meeting of the Society for Research in Child Development, Indianapolis.

Peterson, C., Maier, S. F., & Seligman, M. E. (1993). *Learned helplessness: A theory for the age of personal control.* New York: Oxford University Press.

Peterson, C., & Seligman, M. E. P. (1984). Causal explanations as a risk factor for depression: Theory and evidence. *Psychological Review, 91,* 347–374.

Peterson, C., Seligman, M. E. P., Yurko, K. H., Martin, L. R., & Friedman, H. S. (1998). Catastrophizing and untimely death. *Psychological Science, 9,* 127–130.

Peterson, L. R., & Peterson, M. J. (1959). Short-term retention of individual verbal items. *Journal of Experimental Psychology, 58,* 193–198.

Peterson, N. G., Mumford, M. D., Borman, W. C., Jeanneret, P. R., Fleishman, E. A., Levin, K. Y., et al. (2001). Understanding work using the Occupational Information Network (O*NET): Implications for practice and research. *Personnel Psychology, 54,* 451–492.

Petrakis, I. L., Limoncelli, D., Gueorguieva, R., Jatlow, P., Boutros, N. N., Trevisan, L., et al. (2004). Altered NMDA glutamate receptor antagonist response in individuals with a family vulnerability to alcoholism. *American Journal of Psychiatry, 161,* 1776–1782.

Petrill, S. A., Plomin, R., Berg, S., Johansson, B., Pederson, N. L., Ahern, F., & McClearn, G. E. (1998). The genetic and environmental relationship between general and specific cognitive abilities in twins age 80 and older. *Psychological Science, 9,* 183–189.

Petrocelli, J. V. (2002). Effectiveness of group cognitive-behavioral therapy for general symptomatology: A meta-analysis. *Journal of Specialists in Group Work, 27,* 92–115.

Petrovic, P., Dietrich, T., Fransson, P., Andersson, J., Carlsson, K., & Ingvar, M. (2005). Placebo in emotional processing: Induced expectations of anxiety relief activate a generalized modulatory network. *Neuron, 46,* 957–969.

Petry, N. M. (2001). Substance abuse, pathological gambling and impulsivity. *Drug and Alcohol Dependence, 63,* 29–38.

Pettigrew, T. F. (1979). The ultimate attribution error: Extending Allport's cognitive analysis of prejudice. *Personality and Social Psychology Bulletin, 5,* 461–476.

Pettigrew, T. & Tropp, L. R. (2006). Allport's intergroup contact hypothesis: Its history and influence: In J. Dovidio, P. Glick, & L. Rudman (Eds.), *On the nature of prejudice: Fifty years after Allport.* Boston, MA: Blackwell.

Pettit, D. L., Shao, Z, & Yakel, J. L. (2001). Beta-amyloid(1–42) peptide directly modulates nicotinic receptors in the rat hippocampal slice. *Journal of Neuroscience, 21,* RC120.

Pfefferbaum, A., Rosenbloom, M., Deshmukkh, A., & Sullivan, E., (2001). Sex differences in the effects of alcohol on brain structure. *American Journal of Psychiatry, 158,* 188–197.

Pfister, J. A., Stegelmeier, B. L., Gardner, D. R., & James, L. F. (2003). Grazing of spotted locoweed (*Astragalus lentiginosus*) by cattle and horses in Arizona. *Journal of Animal Science, 81,* 2285–2293.

Pham, L. B., Taylor, S. E., & Seeman, T. E. (2001) Effects of environmental predictability and personal mastery on self-regulatory and physiological processes. *Personality & Social Psychology Bulletin, 27,* 611–620.

Phares, E. J. (1976). *Locus of control in personality.* Morristown, NJ: General Learning Press.

Phelan, J. C., Link, B. G., Stueve, A., & Pescosolido, B. A. (2000). Public conceptions of mental illness in 1950 and 1996: What is mental illness and is it to be feared? *Journal of Health and Social Behavior, 41,* 188–207.

Phelps, E. A., & LeDoux, J. E. (2005). Contributions of the amygdala to emotion processing: From animal models to human behavior. *Neuron, 48,* 175–187.

Phelps, E. A., O'Connor, K. J., Cunningham, W. A., Funayama, E. S., Gatenby, J. C., Gore, J. C., & Banaji, M. R. (2000). Performance on indirect measures of race evaluation predicts amygdala activation. *Journal of Cognitive Neuroscience, 12,* 729–738.

Philip, P., Vervialle, F., Le Breton, P., Taillard, J., & Horne, J. A. (2001). Fatigue, alcohol, and serious road crashes in France: Factorial study of national data. *British Medical Journal, 322,* 829–830.

Phillips, M. R., Li, X., & Zhang, Y. (2002). Suicide rates in China, 1995–99. *Lancet 359,* 835–840.

Phillips, N. A. (2000). Female sexual dysfunction: Evaluation and treatment. *American Family Physician, 62,* 127–136, 141–142.

Phillips, P. E., Stuber, G. D., Heien, M. L., Wightman, R. M., & Carelli, R. M. (2003). Subsecond dopamine release promotes cocaine seeking. *Nature, 422,* 614–618.

Phinney, J. S., Ferguson, D. L., & Tate, J. D. (1997). Intergroup attitudes among ethnic minority adolescents: A causal model. *Child Development, 68,* 955–969.

Piaget, J. (1952). *The origins of intelligence in children.* New York: International Universities Press.

Piasecki, T. M. (2006). Relapse to smoking. *Clinical Psychology Review, 26,* 196–215.

Pickering, A. D., & Gray, J. A. (1999). The neuroscience of personality. In L. Pervin & O. John (Eds.), *Handbook of personality: Theory and research* (2nd ed., pp. 277–299). New York: Guilford.

Pickler, N. (2002, November 19). *NTSB cites fatigue, sleep apnea in fatal train wreck.* Associated Press. Retrieved August 25, 2003, from http://newsobserver.com/24hour/nation/v-print/story/626769p-4807167c.html

Pietro, P., Guazzeli, M., Basso, G., Jaffe, K., & Grafman, J. (2000). Neural correlates of imaginal aggressive behavior assessed by positron emission tomography in healthy subjects. *American Journal of Psychiatry, 157,* 1772–1781.

Pike, K. M., Walsh, B. T., Vitousek, K., Wilson, G. T., & Bauer, J. (2003). Cognitive behavior therapy in the posthospitalization treatment of anorexia nervosa. *American Journal of Psychiatry, 160,* 2046–2049.

Piliavin, J. A., Dovidio, J. F., Gaertner, S. L., & Clark, R. D., III. (1981). *Emergency intervention.* New York: Academic Press.

Pillard, R. C., & Bailey, J. M. (1998). Human sexual orientation has a heritable component. *Human Biology, 70,* 347–365.

Pillemer, K., & Suitor, J. J. (2002). Explaining mothers' ambivalence towards their adult children. *Journal of Marriage and Family, 64,* 602–613.

Pilling, S., Bebbington, P., Kuipers, E., Garety, P., Geddes, J., Orbach, G., & Morgan, C. (2002). Psychological treatments in schizophrenia: I. Meta-analysis of family intervention and cognitive behavior therapy. *Psychological Medicine, 32,* 763–782.

Pinker, S. (1994). *The language instinct: How the mind creates language.* New York: Morrow.

Pipes, R. B., Holstein, J. E., & Aguirre, M. G. (2005). Examining the personal-professional distinction: Ethics codes and the difficulty of drawing a boundary. *American Psychologist, 60,* 325–334.

Pitman, R. K., Shin, L. M., & Rauch, S. L. (2001). Investigating the pathogenesis of posttraumatic stress disorder with neuroimaging. *Journal of Clinical Psychiatry, 62,* 47–54.

Pittler, M. H., Verster, J. C., & Ernst, E. (2005). Interventions for preventing or treating alcohol hangover: Systematic review of randomised controlled trials. *British Medical Journal, 331,* 1515–1518.

Plant, E. A., & Peruche, B. M. (2005). The consequences of race for police officers' responses to criminal suspects. *Psychological Science, 16,* 180–183.

Plant, E. A., & Sachs-Ericsson, N. (2004). Racial and ethnic differences in depression: The roles of social support and meeting basic needs. *Journal of Consulting and Clinical Psychology, 72,* 41–52.

Plaud, J. J. (2003). Pavlov and the foundation of behavior therapy. *Spanish Journal of Psychology, 6,* 147–154.

Plomin, R. (1994). *Genetics and experience: The developmental interplay between nature and nurture.* Newbury Park, CA: Sage.

Plomin, R. (2004). *Two views about the nurture assumption.* Retrieved June 15, 2005, from PsycCRITIQUES database.

Plomin, R., Corley, R., Caspi, A., Fulker, D. W., & DeFries, J. C. (1998). Adoption results for self-reported personality: Not much nature or nurture? *Journal of Personality and Social Psychology, 75,* 211–218.

Plomin, R., & Crabbe, J. C. (2000). DNA. *Psychological Bulletin, 126,* 806–828.

Plomin, R., DeFries, J. C., Craig, I. W., & McGuffin, P. (2002). *Behavioral genetics in the postgenomic era.* Washington, DC: American Psychological Association.

Plomin, R., DeFries, J. C., McClearn, G. E., & McGuffin, P. (2001). *Behavioral genetics* (4th ed.). New York: Worth.

Plomin, R., & McGuffin, P. (2003). Psychopathology in the postgenomic era. *Annual Review of Psychology, 54,* 205–228.

Plomin, R., & Spinath, F. M. (2004). Intelligence: Genetics, genes, and genomics. *Journal of Personality and Social Psychology, 86,* 112–129.

Ploner, M., Gross, J., Timmermann, L., & Schnitzler, A. (2002). Cortical representation of first and second pain sensation in humans. *Proceedings of the National Academy of Sciences, 99,* 12444–12448.

Plous, S. (1996). Attitudes toward the use of animals in psychological research and education: Results from a national survey of psychologists. *American Psychologist, 51,* 1167–1180.

Plum, F., & Posner, J. B. (2000). *Diagnosis of stupor and coma.* New York: Oxford University Press.

Plutchik, R., & Conte, H. R. (Eds.). (1997). *Circumplex models of personality and emotions.* Washington, DC: American Psychological Association.

Poczwardowski, A., & Conroy, D. E. (2002). Coping responses to failure and success among elite athletes and performing artists. *Journal of Applied Sport Psychology, 14,* 313–329.

Pol, H. E. H., Schnack, H. G., Bertens, M. G. B. C., van Haren, N. E. M., van der Tweel, I., Staal, W. G., et al. (2002). Volume changes in gray matter in patients with schizophrenia. *American Journal of Psychiatry, 159,* 244–250.

Poldrack, R. A., & Wagner, A. D. (2004). What can neuroimaging tell us about the mind? *Current Directions in Psychological Science, 13,* 177–181.

Polivy, J., & Herman, C. P. (2002). If at first you don't succeed: False hopes of self-change. *American Psychologist, 57,* 677–689.

Pollack, I. (1953). The assimilation of sequentially coded information. *American Journal of Psychology, 66,* 421–435.

Pollack, V. (1992). Meta-analysis of subjective sensitivity to alcohol in sons of alcoholics. *American Journal of Psychiatry, 149,* 1534–1538.

Polusny, M. A., & Follette, V. M. (1995). Long-term correlates of child sexual abuse: Theory and review of the empirical literature. *Applied and Preventive Psychology, 4,* 143–166.

Polusny, M. A., & Follette, V. M. (1996). Remembering childhood abuse: A national survey of psychologists' clinical practices, beliefs, and personal experiences. *Professional Psychology: Research and Practice, 27,* 41–52.

Poole, D. A., Lindsay, D. S., Memon, A., & Bull, R. (1995). Psychotherapy and the recovery of memories of childhood sexual abuse: U.S. and British practitioners' opinions, practices, and experiences. *Journal of Consulting and Clinical Psychology, 63,* 426–437.

Pope, H. G., Jr., Hudson, J. I., Bodkin, J. A., & Oliva, P. (1998). Questionable validity of "dissociative amnesia" in trauma victims: Evidence from prospective studies. *British Journal of Psychiatry, 172,* 210–215.

Pope, H. G., Jr., Kouri, E. M., & Hudson, J. I. (2000). Effects of supraphysiologic doses of testosterone on mood and aggression in normal men: A randomized controlled trial. *Archives of General Psychiatry, 57*(2), 133–140.

Pope, H. G., & Yurgelun-Todd, D. (1996). The residual cognitive effects of heavy marijuana use in college students. *Journal of the American Medical Association, 275,* 521–527.

Pope, K. S. (1998). Pseudoscience, cross-examination, and scientific evidence in the recovered memory controversy. *Psychology, Public Policy, and Law, 4,* 1160–1181.

Pope-Davis, D. B., Reynolds, A. L., Dings, J. G., & Nielson, D. (1995). Examining multicultural counseling competencies of graduate students in psychology. *Professional Psychology: Research and Practice, 26,* 322–329.

Porcerelli, J. H., Cogan, R., Kamoo, R., & Leitman, S. (2004). Defense mechanisms and self-reported violence toward partners and strangers. *Journal of Personality Assessment, 82,* 317–320.

Porges, S. W., Doussard, R. J. A., & Maita, A. K. (1995). Vagal tone and the physiological regulation of emotion. *Monographs of the Society for Research on Child Development, 59*(2–3), 167–186, 250–283.

Porrino, L. J., Daunais, J. B., Rogers, G. A., Hampson, R. E., & Deadwyler, S. A. (2005). Facilitation of task performance and removal of the effects of sleep deprivation by an ampakine (CX717) in nonhuman primates. *Public Library of Science Biology, 3,* e299.

Port, C. L., Engdahl, B., & Frazier, P. (2001). A longitudinal and retrospective study of PTSD among older prisoners of war. *American Journal of Psychiatry, 158,* 1474–1479.

Porte, H. S., & Hobson, J. A. (1996). Physical motion in dreams: One measure of three theories. *Journal of Abnormal Psychology, 105,* 329–335.

Porter, J., Anand, T., Johnson, B., Khan, R. M., & Sobell, N. (2005). Brain mechanisms for extracting spatial information from smell. *Neuron, 47,* 581–592.

Porter, R. H. (1991). Human reproduction and the mother-infant relationship. In T. V. Getchell et al. (Eds.), *Taste and smell in health and disease.* New York: Raven Press.

Porter, R. H., Cernich, J. M., & McLaughlin, F. J. (1983). Maternal recognition of neonates through olfactory cues. *Physiology and Behavior, 30,* 151–154.

Porter, R. H., Makin, J. W., Davis, L. B., & Christensen, K. M. (1992). Breast-fed infants respond to olfactory cues from their own mother and unfamiliar lactating females. *Infant Behavior and Development, 15,* 85–93.

Porter, S., Birt, A. R., Yuille, J. C., & Lehman, D. R. (2000). Negotiating false memories: Interviewer and rememberer characteristics relate to memory distortion. *Psychological Science, 11,* 507–510.

Porter, S., Yuille, J. C., & Lehman, D. R. (1999). The nature of real, implanted, and fabricated memories for emotional childhood events: Implications for the recovered memory debate. *Law & Human Behavior, 23,* 517–537.

Posener, J. A., DeBattista, C., Williams, G. H., Kraemer, H. C., Kalehzan, B. M., & Schatzberg, A. F. (2000). 24-hour monitoring of cortisol and corticotropin secretion in psychotic and nonpsychotic major depression. *Archives of General Psychiatry, 57,* 755–760.

Posner, M. I., & Peterson, S. E. (1990). The attention system of the human brain. *Annual Review of Neurosciences, 13,* 24–42.

Posner, M. I., & Raichle, M. E. (1994). *Images of mind.* New York: Scientific American Books.

Potkin, S. G., Saha, A. R., Kujawa, M. J., Carson, W. H., Ali, M., Stock, E., et al. (2003). Aripiprazole, an antipsychotic with a novel mechanism of action, and risperidone vs placebo in patients with schizophrenia and schizoaffective disorder. *Archives of General Psychiatry, 60,* 681–690.

Potter, P. T., & Zautra, A. J. (1997). Stressful life events' effects on rheumatoid arthritis disease activity. *Journal of Consulting and Clinical Psychology, 65,* 319–323.

Povinelli, D. J., & Bering, J. M. (2002). The mentality of apes revisited. *Current Directions in Psychological Science, 11,* 115–119.

Powch, I. G., & Houston, B. K. (1996). Hostility, anger-in, and cardiovascular activity in White women. *Health Psychology, 15,* 200–208.

Powell, K. B., & Voeller, K. K. (2004). Prefrontal executive function syndromes in children. *Journal of Child Neurology, 19,* 785–797.

Powell, L. H., Shahabi, L., & Thoresen, C. E. (2003). Religion and spirituality: Linkages to physical health. *American Psychologist, 58,* 36–52.

Powell, R. A., & Boer, D. P. (1995). Did Freud misinterpret reported memories of sexual abuse as fantasies? *Psychological Reports, 77,* 563–570.

Powley, T. L., & Keesey, R. E. (1970). Relationship of body weight to the lateral hypothalamic feeding syndrome. *Journal of Comparative & Physiological Psychology, 70,* 25–36.

Poyares, D., Guilleminault, C., Ohayon, M. M., & Tufik, S. (2004). Chronic benzodiazepine usage and withdrawal in insomnia patients. *Journal of Psychiatric Research, 38,* 327–334.

Pratkanis, A., & Aronson, E. (2001). *The age of propaganda: The everyday use and abuse of propaganda.* New York: W. H. Freeman.

Pratkanis, A. R. (1992). The cargo-cult science of subliminal persuasion. *Skeptical Inquirer, 16,* 260–273.

Pratkanis, A. R., Eskenazi, J., & Greenwald, A. G. (1994). What you expect is what you believe (but not necessarily what you get): A test of the effectiveness of self-help audiotapes. *Basic and Applied Social Psychology, 15,* 251–276.

Preciado, J. (1994). The empirical basis of behavior therapy applications with Hispanics. *Behavior Therapist, 17,* 63–65.

Prescott, J. W. (1996). The origins of human love and violence. *Pre- and Peri-Natal Psychology Journal, 10,* 143–188.

President's New Freedom Commission on Mental Health. (2003). *Achieving the promise: Transforming mental health care in America.* Rockville, Maryland: U.S. Department of Health and Human Services.

Pressman, S. D., & Cohen, S. (2005). Does positive affect influence health? *Psychological Bulletin, 131,* 925–971.

Pressman, S. D., Cohen, S., Miller, G. E., Barkin, A., Rabin, B., & Treanor, J. J. (2005). Loneliness, social network size, and immune response to influenza vaccination in college freshman. *Health Psychology, 24,* 297–306.

Prinstein, M. J., & La Greca, A. M. (2002). Peer crowd affiliation and intrenalizing distress in childhood and adolescence: A longitudinal follow-back study. *Journal of Research on Adolescence, 12,* 35–351.

Prochaska, J. O. (1994). Strong and weak principles for progressing from precontemplation to action on the basis of twelve problem behaviors. *Health Psychology, 13,* 47–51.

Prochaska, J. O., DiClemente, C., & Norcross, J. (1992). In search of how people change: Application to addictive behaviors. *American Psychologist, 47,* 1102–1114.

Program for International Student Assessment. (2004). *Learning for tomorrow's world: First results from PISA 2003.* Paris: OECD.

Program for International Student Assessment. (2005). *Learning for tomorrow's world: First results from PISA 2004.* Paris: OECD.

Pryor, T. (1995). Diagnostic criteria for eating disorders: *DSM-IV* revisions. *Psychiatric Annals, 25*(1), 40–45.

Pulakos, E. D., Schmitt, N., Dorsey, D. W., Arad, S., Hedge, J. W., & Borman, W. C. (2002). Predicting adaptive performance: Further tests of a model of adaptability. *Human Performance, 15,* 299–324.

Putnam, F. W. (2003). Ten-year research update review: Child sexual abuse. *Journal of the American Academy of Child & Adolescent Psychiatry, 42,* 269–278.

Pyszczynski, T., Greenberg, J., Solomon, S., Arndt, J., & Schimel, J. (2004). Why do people need self-esteem? A theoretical and empirical review. *Psychological Bulletin, 130,* 435–468.

Q

Quinn, G. E., Shin, C. H., Maguire, M. G., & Stone, R. A. (1999). Myopia and ambient lighting at night. *Nature, 399,* 113–114.

Quinn, P. C., & Bhatt, R. S. (2005). Learning perceptual organization in infancy. *Psychological Science, 16,* 511–515.

Quintana, S. M. (1998). Children's developmental understanding of ethnicity and race. *Applied and Preventive Psychology, 7,* 27–45.

Quintana, S. M., & Bernal, M. E. (1995). Ethnic minority training in counseling psychology: Comparisons with clinical psychology and proposed standards. *The Counseling Psychologist, 23*(1), 102–121.

R

Rabasca, L. (1999, July/August). Behavioral interventions can cut the use of restraints. *APA Monitor,* p. 27.

Rabinowitz, J., De Smedt, G., Harvey, P. D., & Davidson, M. (2002). Relationship between premorbid functioning and symptom severity as assessed at first episode of psychosis. *American Journal of Psychiatry, 159,* 2021–2026.

Rabinowitz, J., Lichtenberg, P., Kaplan, Z., Mark, M., Nahon, D., & Davidson, M. (2001). Rehospitalization rates of chronically ill schizophrenic patients discharged on a regimen of risperidone, olanzapine, or conventional antipsychotics. *American Journal of Psychiatry, 158,* 266–269.

Racenstein, J. M., Harrow, M., Reed, R., Martin, E., Herbener, E., & Penn, D. L. (2002). The relationship between positive symptoms and instrumental work functioning in schizophrenai: A 10-year follow-up study. *Schizophrenia Research, 56,* 95–103.

Rachlin, H. (2000). *The science of self-control.* Cambridge, MA: Harvard University Press.

Rachman, S. J. (1990). *Fear and courage* (2nd ed.). San Francisco: Freeman.

Rada, J. B., & Rogers, R. W. (1973). *Obedience to authority: Presence of authority and command strength.* Paper presented at the annual convention of the Southeastern Psychological Association.

Radcliffe, N. M., & Klein, W. M. (2002). Dispositional, unrealistic and comparative optimism: Differential relations with the knowledge and processing of risk information and beliefs about personal risk. *Personality & Social Psychology Bulletin, 28,* 836–846.

Radford, B. (2005). Voice of reason: Exorcisms, fictional and fatal. *Skeptical Inquirer.* Retrieved August 1, 2005, from http://www.csicop.org/specialarticles/exorcist-rituals.html.

Radvansky, G. A. (1999). Aging, memory, and comprehension. *Current Directions in Psychological Science, 8,* 49–53.

Rae, C., Harasty, J. A., Dzendrowskyj, T. E., Talcott, J. B., Simpson, J. M., Blamire, A. M., et al. (2002). Cerebellar morphology in developmental dyslexia. *Neuropsychologia, 40,* 1285–1292.

Raffaelli, M., & Crockett, L. J. (2003). Sexual risk taking in adolescence: The role of self- regulation and attraction to risk. *Developmental Psychology, 39,* 1036–1046.

Raggatt, P. T. (1991). Work stress among long-distance coach drivers: A survey and correlational study. *Journal of Organizational Behavior, 12,* 565–579.

Raguram, R., & Bhide, A. (1985). Patterns of phobic neurosis: A retrospective study. *British Journal of Psychiatry, 147,* 557–560.

Raij, T. T., Numminen, J., Narvanen, S., Hiltunen, J., & Hari, R. (2005). Brain correlates of subjective reality of physically and psychologically induced pain. *Proceedings of the National Academy of Sciences of the USA, 102,* 2147–2151.

Raine, A., Brennan, P., & Mednick, S. (1994). Birth complications combined with early maternal rejection at age 1 year predispose to violent crime at age 18 years. *Archives of General Psychiatry, 51,* 984–988.

Raine, A., Lencz, T., Bihrle, S., LaCasse, L., & Colletti, P. (2000). Reduced prefrontal gray matter volume and reduced autonomic activity in antisocial personality disorder. *Archives of General Psychiatry, 57,* 119–127.

Raine, A., Moffitt, T. E., Caspi, A., Loeber, R., Stouthamer-Loeber, M., & Lynam, D. (2005). Neurocognitive impairments in boys on the life-course persistent antisocial path. *Journal of Abnormal Psychology, 114,* 38–49.

Rains, G. C., Utley, S. L., & Lewis, W. J. (2006). Behavioral monitoring of trained insects for chemical detection. *Biotechnology Progress, 22,* 2–8.

Rakic, P. (2002). Neurogenesis in adult primate neocortex: An evaluation of the evidence. *Nature Reviews Neuroscience, 3,* 65–71.

Ramachandran, V. S. (1988, August). Perceiving shape from shading. *Scientific American,* pp. 76–83.

Ramey, C. T., Ramey, S. L., & Lanzi, R. G. (2006). Children's health and education. In W. Damon & R. M. Lerner (Series Eds.) & K. A. Renninger & I. E. Sigel (Vol. Eds.), *Handbook of child psychology: Vol. 4. Child psychology in practice* (6th ed.). New York: Wiley.

Ramirez, S. Z., Wassef, A., Paniagua, F. A., & Linskey, A. O. (1996). Mental health providers' perceptions of cultural variables in evaluating ethnically diverse clients. *Professional Psychology: Research and Practice, 27,* 284–288.

Rapaport, M. H., Clary, C., Fayyad, R., & Endicott, J. (2005). Quality-of-life impairment in depressive and anxiety disorders. *American Journal of Psychiatry, 162,* 1171–1178.

Rapee, R., Brown, T., Antony, M., & Barlow, D. (1992). Response to hyperventilation and inhalation of 5.5% carbon dioxide-enriched air across *DSM-III* anxiety disorders. *Journal of Abnormal Psychology, 101,* 538–552.

Rapee, R., Kennedy, S., Ingram, M., Edwards, S., & Sweeney, L. (2005). Prevention and early intervention of anxiety disorders in inhibited preschool children. *Journal of Consulting and Clinical Psychology, 73,* 488–497.

Rapoport, J. L., Addington, A. M., & Frangou, S. (2005). The neurodevelopmental model of schizophrenia: Update 2005. *Molecular Psychiatry, 10,* 434–449.

Rapp, S. R., Brenes, G., & Marsh, A. P. (2002). Memory enhancement training for older adults with mild cognitive impairment: A preliminary study. *Aging & Mental Health, 6*(1), 5–11.

Rasch, V. (2003). Cigarette, alcohol, and caffeine consumption: Risk factors for spontaneous abortion. *Acta Obstetric Gynecology Scandivia, 82,* 182–188.

Rasinski, K. A., Kuby, A., Bzdusek, S. A., Silvestri, J. M., & Weese-Mayer, D. E. (2003). Effect of a sudden infant death syndrome risk reduction education program on risk factor compliance and information sources in primarily black urban communities. *Pediatrics, 111,* 347–354.

Raskin, D. C. (1986). The polygraph in 1986: Scientific, professional and legal issues surrounding applications and acceptance of polygraph evidence. *Utah Law Review, 1,* 29–74.

Raskin, N. J., & Rogers, C. R. (2001). Person-centered therapy. In R. J. Corsini & D. Wedding (Eds.), *Current psychotherapies* (6th ed.) Itasca, IL: Peacock.

Rasmussen, K. G. (2003). Clinical applications of recent research on electroconvulsive therapy. *Bulletin of the Menninger Clinic, 67*(1), 18–31.

Ratcliff, R., & McKoon, G. (1989). Memory models, text processing, and cue-dependent retrieval. In H. L. Roediger & F. I. M. Craik (Eds.), *Varieties of memory and consciousness.* Hillsdale, NJ: Erlbaum.

Rathbone, D. B., & Huckabee, J. C. (1999). *Controlling road rage: A literature review and pilot study.* Washington, DC: American Automobile Association.

Ratner, C. (1994). The unconscious: A perspective from sociohistorical psychology. *Journal of Mind and Behavior, 15*(4), 323–342.

Rattenborg, N., Lima, S. L., & Amlaner, C. J. (1999). Half-awake to the risk of predation. *Nature, 397,* 397–398.

Raudenbush, B., & Meyer, B. (2002). Effect of nasal dilators on pleasantness, intensity and sampling behaviors of foods in the oral cavity. *Rhinology, 39,* 80–83.

Rauscher, F. H., Shaw, G. L., Levine, L. J., Wright, E. L., Dennis, W. R., & Newcomb, R. L. (1997). Music training causes long-term enhancement of preschool children's spatial-temporal reasoning. *Neurological Research, 19,* 2–8.

Rawson, P. (2003). *Short-term psychodynamic psychotherapy: An analysis of the key principles.* London: Karnac Books.

Rawson, P. (2006). *Handbook of short-term psychodynamic psychotherapy.* London: Karnac Books.

Ray, D. W., Wandersman, A., Ellisor, J., & Huntington, D. E. (1982). The effects of high density in a juvenile correctional institution. *Basic and Applied Social Psychology, 3,* 95–108.

Raynor, H. A., & Epstein, L. H. (2001). Dietary variety, energy regulation, and obesity. *Psychological Bulletin, 127,* 325–341.

Raz, A., Fan, J., & Posner, M. I. (2005). Hypnotic suggestion reduces conflict in the brain. *Proceedings of the National Academy of Sciences of the USA, 102,* 9978–9983.

Razali, S. M., Aminah, K., & Umeed, A. (2002). Religious-cultural psychotherapy in the management of anxiety patients. *Transcultural Psychiatry, 39,* 130–136.

Reber, A. S. (1992). The cognitive unconscious: An evolutionary perspective. *Consciousness and Cognition: An International Journal, 1*(2), 93–133.

Redd, W. H. (1984). Psychological intervention to control cancer chemotherapy side effects. *Postgraduate Medicine, 75,* 105–113.

Reed, S. K. (2000). *Cognition* (5th ed.). Belmont, CA: Wadsworth.

Reedy, M. N. (1983). Personality and aging. In D. S. Woodruff & J. E. Birren (Eds.), *Aging: Scientific perspectives and social issues* (2nd ed.). Monterey, CA: Brooks/Cole.

Reeve, J. M. (1996). *Understanding motivation and emotion.* New York: Harcourt, Brace, Jovanovich.

Reeves, M. J., & Rafferty, A. P. (2005). Healthy lifestyle characteristics among adults in the United States, 2000. *Archives of Internal Medicine, 165,* 854–857.

Regan, P. C., & Berscheid, E. (1999). *Lust: What we know about human sexual desire.* Thousand Oaks, CA: Sage.

Reger, M. A., Welsh, R. K., Watson, G. S., Cholerton, B., Baker, L. D., & Craft, S. (2004). The relationship between neuropsychological functioning and driving ability in dementia: A meta-analysis. *Neuropsychology, 18,* 85–93.

Reich, D. A. (2004). What you expect is not always what you get: The roles of extremity, optimism, and pessimism in the behavioral confirmation process. *Journal of Experimental Social Psychology, 40,* 199–215.

Reif, A., & Lesch, K. P. (2003). Toward a molecular architecture of personality. *Behavioural Brain Research, 139,* 1–20.

Reinisch, J. M., Ziemba-Davis, M., & Sanders, S. A. (1991). Hormonal contributions to sexually dimorphic behavioral development in humans. *Psychoneuroendocrinology, 16,* 213–278.

Reis, B. F., & Brown, L. G. (2006). Preventing therapy dropout in the real world: The clinical utility of videotape preparation and client estimate of treatment duration. *Professional Psychology: Research and Practice, 37,* 311–316.

Reisenzein, R. (1983). The Schachter theory of emotion: Two decades later. *Psychological Bulletin, 94,* 239–264.

Reiss, A. J., & Roth, J. A. (1993). *Understanding and preventing violence.* Washington, DC: National Academy Press.

Reiss, D., Neiderhiser, J. M., Hetherington, E. M., & Plomin, R. (2000). *The relationship code: Deciphering genetic and social influences on adolescent development.* Cambridge, MA: Harvard University Press.

Reitman, D., & Drabman, R. S. (1999). Multifaceted uses of a simple timeout record in the treatment of a noncompliant 8-year-old boy. *Education and Treatment of Children, 22,* 136–145.

Ren, T. (2002). Longitudinal pattern of basilar membrane vibration in the sensitive cochlea. *Proceedings of the National Academy of Sciences, 99,* 17101–17106.

Rendall, D., Cheney, D. L., & Seyfarth, R. M. (2000). Proximate factors mediating "contact" calls in adult female baboons (*Papio cynocephalus ursinus*) and their infants. *Journal of Comparative Psychology, 114,* 36–46.

Reneman, L., Lavalaye, J., Schmand, B., de Wolff, F. A., van den Brink, W., den Heeten, G. J., & Booij, J. (2001). Cortical serotonin transporter density and verbal memory in individuals who stopped using 3, 4-methylenedioxymethamphetamine (MDMA or "ecstasy"). *Archives of General Psychiatry, 58,* 901–906.

Rentz, D. M., Huh, T. J., Faust, R. R., Budson, A. E., Scinto, L. F. M., Sperling, R. A., & Daffner, K. R. (2004). Use of IQ-adjusted norms to predict progressive cognitive decline in highly intelligent older individuals. *Neuropsychology, 18*, 38–49.

Rescorla, L. A. (1981). Category development in early language. *Journal of Child Language, 8*, 225–238.

Rescorla, R. A. (1968). Probability of shock in the presence and absence of CS in fear conditioning. *Journal of Comparative and Physiological Psychology, 66*, 1–5.

Rescorla, R. A. (2004). Spontaneous recovery varies inversely with the training-extinction interval. *Learning and Behavior, 32*, 401–408.

Rescorla, R. A., & Wagner, A. R. (1972). A theory of Pavlovian conditioning: Variations in the effectiveness of reinforcement and nonreinforcement. In A. H. Black & W. F. Prokasy (Eds.), *Classical conditioning II*. New York: Appleton Century Crofts.

Ressler, K. J., Rothbaum, B. O., Tannenbaum, L., Anderson, P., Graap, K., Zimand, E., et al. (2004). Cognitive enhancers as adjuncts to psychotherapy: Use of D-cycloserine in phobic individuals to facilitate extinction of fear. *Archives of General Psychiatry, 61*, 1136–1144.

Reuter, J., Raedler, T., Rose, M., Hand, I., Glascher, J., & Buchel, C. (2005). Pathological gambling is linked to reduced activation of the mesolimbic reward system. *Nature Neuroscience, 8*, 147–148.

Revell, V. L., & Eastman, C. I. (2005). How to trick mother nature into letting you fly around or stay up all night. *Journal of Biological Rhythms, 20*, 353–365.

Reynolds, C. A., Finkel, D., McArdle, J. J., Gatz, M., Berg, S., & Pederson, N. L. (2005). Quantitative genetic analysis of latent growth curve models of cognitive abilities in adulthood. *Developmental Psychology, 41*, 3–16.

Reynolds, J. S., & Perrin, N. A. (2004). Mismatches in social support and psychosocial adjustment to breast cancer. *Health Psychology, 23*, 425–430.

Rhee, S. H., Hewitt, J. K., Young, S. E., Corley, R. P., Crowley, T. J., & Stallings, M. C. (2003). Genetic and environmental influences on substance initiation, use, and problem use in adolescents. *Archives of General Psychiatry, 60*, 1256–1264.

Ribases, M., Gratacos, M., Badia, A., Jimenez, L., Solano, R., Vallejo, J., et al. (2005). Contribution of NTRK2 to the genetic susceptibility to anorexia nervosa, harm avoidance and minimum body mass index. *Molecular Psychiatry, 10*, 851–860.

Ricciardelli, L. A., & McCabe, M. P. (2004). A biopsychosocial model of disordered eating and the pursuit of muscularity in adolescent boys. *Psychological Bulletin, 130*, 179–205.

Riccio, D. C., Millin, P. M., & Gisquet-Verrier, P. (2003). Retrograde amnesia: Forgetting back. *Current Directions in Psychological Science, 12*, 41–44.

Rice, G., Anderson, C., Risch, H., & Ebers, G. (1999). Male homosexuality: Absence of linkage to microsatellite markers at Xq28. *Science, 284*, 665–667.

Rice, M. E. (1997). Violent offender research and implications for the criminal justice system. *American Psychologist, 52*, 414–423.

Richards, J. M., & Gross, J. J. (2000). Emotion regulation and memory: The cognitive costs of keeping one's cool. *Journal of Personality and Social Psychology, 79*, 410–424.

Richards, K. C., Anderson, W. M., Chesson, A. L. Jr., & Nagel, C. L. (2002). Sleep-related breathing disorders in patients who are critically ill. *Journal of Cardiovascular Nursing, 17*, 42–55.

Richards, P. S., & Bergin, A. E. (Eds.). (2000). *Handbook of psychotherapy and religious diversity* (pp. 105–129). Washington, DC: American Psychological Association Press.

Richardson-Klavehn, A., & Bjork, R. A. (1988). Measures of memory. *Annual Review of Psychology, 39*, 475–543.

Rickels, K., & Rynn, M. (2002). Pharmacotherapy of generalized anxiety disorder. *Journal of Clinical Psychiatry, 63*(Suppl. 14), 9–16.

Rickels, K., Schweizer, E., Weiss, S., & Zavodnick, S. (1993) Maintenance drug treatment of panic disorder: II. Short- and long-term outcome after drug taper. *Archives of General Psychiatry, 50*, 61–68.

Rickels, K., Zaninelli, R., McCafferty, J., Bellew, K., Iyengar, M., & Sheehan, D. (2003). Paroxetine treatment of generalized anxiety disorder: A double-blind, placebo-controlled study. *American Journal of Psychiatry, 160*, 749–756.

Ridley, M. (2000). *Genome: The autobiography of a species in 23 chapters*. New York: HarperCollins.

Riggio, R. E. (1989). *Introduction to industrial/organizational psychology*. Glenview, IL: Scott, Foresman.

Rihmer, Z. (2001). Can better recognition and treatment of depression reduce suicide rates? A brief review. *European Psychiatry, 16*, 406–409.

Riis, J., Loewenstein, G., Baron, J., Jepson, C., Fagerlin, A., & Ubel, P. A. (2005). Ignorance of hedonic adaptation to hemodialysis: A study using ecological momentary assessment. *Journal of Experimental Psychology: General, 134*, 3–9.

Rind, B., & Tromovitch, P. (1997). A meta-analytic review of findings from national samples on psychological correlates of child sexual abuse. *Journal of Sex Research, 34*, 237–255.

Rind, B., Tromovitch, P., & Bauserman, R. (1998). A meta-analytic examination of assumed properties of child sexual abuse using college samples. *Psychological Bulletin, 124*, 22–53.

Rinn, W. E. (1984). The neuropsychology of facial expressions: A review of the neurological and psychological mechanisms for producing facial expressions. *Psychological Bulletin, 95*, 52–77.

Rioult-Pedotti, M.-S., Friedman, D., & Donoghue, J. P. (2000). Learning-induced LTP in neocortex. *Science, 290*, 533–536.

Ripple, C. H., Gilliam, W. S., Chanana, N., & Zigler, E. (1999). Will fifty cooks spoil the broth? The debate over entrusting Head Start to the states. *American Psychologist, 54*, 327–343.

Rips, L. J. (1994). *The psychology of proof: Deductive reasoning in human thinking*. Cambridge, MA: MIT Press.

Risen, J. (1998, July 7). CIA seeks "curmudgeon" to signal its mistakes. *New York Times*.

Rittenhouse, C. D., Stickgold, R., & Hobson, J. A. (1994). Constraint on the transformation of characters, objects, and settings in dream reports. *Consciousness and Cognition, 3*(1), 100–113.

Rizzolatti, G., & Arbib, M. A. (1998). Language within our grasp. *Trends in Neuroscience, 21*, 188–194.

Rizzolatti, G., Fadiga, L., Gallese, V., & Fogassi, L. (1996). Premotor cortex and the recognition of motor actions. *Brain Research: Cognitive Brain Research, 3*, 131–141.

Ro, T., Shelton, D., Lee, O. L., & Chang, E. (2004). Extrageniculate mediation of unconscious vision in transcranial magnetic stimulation-induced blindsight. *Proceedings of the National Academy of Sciences, 101*, 9933–9935.

Robbins, T. W., & Everitt, B. J. (1999). Interaction of the dopaminergic system with mechanisms of associative learning and cognition: Implications for drug abuse. *Psychological Science, 10*, 199–202.

Roberts, B. W., & Bogg, T. (2004). A longitudinal study of the relationships between conscientiousness and the social-environmental factors and substance-use behaviors that influence health. *Journal of Personality, 72*, 325–353.

Roberts, B. W., & DelVecchio, W. F. (2000). The rank-order consistency of traits from childhood to old-age: A quantitative review of longitudinal studies. *Psychological Bulletin, 126*, 3–25.

Roberts, B. W., Caspi, A., & Moffitt, T. E. (2001). The kids are alright: Growth and stability in personality development from adolescence to adulthood. *Journal of Personality & Social Psychology, 81*(4), 670–683.

Roberts, B. W., Helson, R., & Klohnen, E. C. (2002). Personality development and growth in women across 30 years: Three perspectives. *Journal of Personality, 70*, 79–102.

Roberts, B. W., Walton, K. E., & Viechtbauer, W. (2006). Patterns of mean-level change in personality traits across the life course: A meta-analysis of longitudinal studies. *Psychological Bulletin, 132*, 1–25.

Roberts, M. C. (2002). The process and product of the Felix decree review of empirically supported treatments: Prospects for change. *Clinical Psychology: Science and Practice, 9*, 217–219.

Robertson, I. H., & Murre, J. M. J. (1999). Rehabilitation of brain damage: Brain plasticity and principles of guided recovery. *Psychological Bulletin, 125*, 544–575.

Robertson, J., & Robertson, J. (1971). Young children in brief separation: A fresh look. *Psychoanalytic Study of the Child, 26*, 264–315.

Robins, L. N., & Regier, D. A. (Eds.). (1991). *Psychiatric disorders in America: The Epidemiologic Catchment Area study*. New York: Free Press.

Robinson, J. H., & Pritchard, W. S. (1995). "The scientific case that nicotine is addictive": Reply. *Psychopharmacology, 117*(1), 16–17.

Robinson, N. M., Zigler, E., & Gallagher, J. J. (2000). Two tails of the normal curve: Similarities and differences in the study of mental retardation and giftedness. *American Psychologist, 55*, 1413–1424.

Robinson, S., Sandstrom, S. M., Denenberg, V. H., & Palmiter, R. D. (2005). Distinguishing whether dopamine regulates liking, wanting, and/or learning about rewards. *Behavioral Neuroscience, 119*, 5–15.

Robinson, T. N., Wilde, M. L., Navracruz, L. C., Haydel, K. F., & Varady, A. (2001). Effects of reducing children's television and video game use on aggressive behavior: A randomized controlled trial. *Archives of Pediatrics and Adolescent Medicine, 155*, 17–23.

Robles, T. F., Glaser, R., & Kiecolt-Glaser, J. K. (2005) Out of balance: A new look at chronic stress, depression, and immunity. *Current Directions in Psychological Science, 14,* 111–115.

Robles, T. F., & Kiecolt-Glaser, J. K. (2003). The physiology of marriage: Pathways to health. *Physiology and Behavior, 79,* 409–416.

Rochon, P. A., Stukel, T. A., Sykora, K., Gill, S., Garfinkel, S., Anderson, G. M., et al. (2005). Atypical antipsychotics and Parkinsonism. *Archives of Internal Medicine, 165,* 1882–1888.

Rock, I. (1978). *An introduction to perception.* New York: Macmillan.

Rock, I. (1983). *The logic of perception.* Cambridge, MA: MIT Press.

Rodgers, J. (2000). Cognitive performance amongst recreational users of "ecstasy". *Psychopharmacology, 151,* 19–24.

Rodier, P. M. (2000). The early origins of autism. *Scientific American, 282,* 56–63.

Rodrigo, M. F., & Ato, M. (2002). Testing the group polarization hypothesis by using logit models. *European Journal of Social Psychology, 32,* 3–18.

Rodriguez de Fonseca, F., Carrera, M. R. A., Navarro, M., Koob, G. F., & Weiss, F. (1997). Activation of corticotropin-releasing factor in the limbic system during cannabinoid withdrawal. *Science, 276,* 2050–2054.

Rodriguez, I., Greer, C. A., Mok, M. Y., & Mombaerts, P. (2000). A putative pheromone receptor gene expressed in human olfactory mucosa. *Nature Genetics, 26,* 18–19.

Roe, K. V. (2001). Relationship between male infants' vocal responses to mother and stranger at three months and self-reported academic attainment and adjustment measures in adulthood. *Psychological Reports, 89*(2), 255–258.

Roediger, H. L., & Gallo, D. A. (2001). Levels of processing: Some unanswered questions. In M. Naveh-Benjamin, M. Moscovitch, & H.L. Roediger (Eds.), *Perspectives on human memory and cognitive aging: Essays in hounour of Fergus Craik* (pp. 28–47). New York: Psychology Press.

Roediger, H. L., III, Guynn, M. J., & Jones, T. C. (1995). Implicit memory: A tutorial review. In G. d'Ydewalle, P. Eelen, & P. Bertelson (Eds.), *International perspectives on psychological science: Vol. 2. The state of the art* (pp. 67–94). Hove, UK: Erlbaum.

Roediger, H. L., III, Jacoby, D., & McDermott, K. B. (1996). Misinformation effects in recall: Creating false memories through repeated retrieval. *Journal of Memory and Learning, 35,* 300–318.

Roediger, H. L., Marsh, E. J., & Lee, C. J. (2002). Varieties of memory. In H. Pashler (Ed.), *Stevens' handbook of experimental psychology* (Vol. 2, pp. 1–41). New York: Wiley.

Roediger, H. L., III, McDaniel, M., & McDermott, K. (2006). Test enhanced learning. *APS Observer, 19,* 28.

Roediger, H. L., III, & McDermott, K. B. (1995). Creating false memories: Remembering words not presented in lists. *Journal of Experimental Psychology: Learning, Memory, and Cognition, 21,* 803–814.

Roediger, H. L., & McDermott, K. B. (2000). Tricks of memory. *Current Directions in Psychological Science, 9,* 123–127.

Roediger, H. L., Meade, M. L., & Bergman, E. T. (2001). Social contagion of memory. *Psychonomic Bulletin and Review, 8,* 365–371.

Roehrich, L., & Goldman, M. S. (1995). Implicit priming of alcohol expectancy memory processes and subsequent drinking behavior. *Experimental and Clincial Psychopharmocology, 3,* 402–410.

Roffwarg, H. P., Hermann, J. H., & Bowe-Anders, C. (1978). The effects of sustained alterations of waking visual input on dream content. In A. M. Arkin, J. S. Antrobus, & S. J. Ellman (Eds.), *The mind in sleep.* Hillsdale, NJ: Erlbaum.

Roffwarg, H. P., Muzio, J. N., & Dement, W. C. (1966). Ontogenetic development of the human sleep-dream cycle. *Science, 152,* 604–619.

Rog, D. J., Nurmikko, T. J., Friede, T., & Young, C.A. (2005). Randomized, controlled trial of cannabis-based medicine in central pain in multiple sclerosis. *Neurology, 65,* 812–819.

Rogers, A. A., Aldrich, M. S., & Lin, A. (2001). A comparison of three different sleep schedules for reducing daytime sleepiness in narcolepsy. *Journal of Sleep and Sleep Disorders Research, 24,* 385–391.

Rogers, C. R. (1961). *On becoming a person.* Boston: Houghton Mifflin.

Rogers, C. R. (1970). *Carl Rogers on encounter groups.* New York: Harper & Row.

Rogers, C. R. (1980) *A way of being.* Boston: Houghton Mifflin.

Rogers, J., Madamba, S. G., Staunton, D. A., & Siggins, G. R. (1986). Ethanol increases single unit activity in the inferior olivary nucleus. *Brain Research, 385,* 253–262.

Rogers, M. R., & Molina, L. E. (2006). Exemplary efforts in psychology to recruit and retain graduate students of color. *American Psychologist, 61,* 143–156.

Rogers, R. (1995). *Diagnostic and structured interviewing: A handbook for psychologists.* Odessa, FL: Psychological Assessment Resources.

Rogers, R. (2001). *Handbook of structured clinical interviewing* (2nd ed.). New York: Guilford.

Rogoff, B., & Waddell, K. J. (1982). Memory for information organized in a scene by children from two cultures. *Child Development, 53,* 1224–1228.

Rohan, M. J., & Zanna, M. P. (1996). Value transmission in families. In C. Seligman, J. M. Olson, & M. P. Zanna (Eds.), *The psychology of values: The Ontario symposium* (Vol. 8, pp. 253–276). Mahwah, NJ: Erlbaum.

Roid, G. H. (2003). *Stanford-Binet Intelligence Scale* (5th ed.). Itasca, IL: Riverside.

Roisman, G. I., Masten, A. S, Coatsworth, J. D., & Tellegen, A. (2004). Salient and emerging developmental tasks in the transition to adulthood. *Child Development, 75,* 123–133.

Rolland-Cachera, M.-F., Castetbon, K., Arnault, N., Bellisle, F., Romano, M.-C., Lehingue, Y., et al. (2002). Body mass index in 7-9-y-old French children: frequency of obesity, overweight and thinness. *International Journal of Obesity, 26,* 1610–1616.

Rolls, E. T. (1997). Taste and olfactory processing in the brain and its relation to the control of eating. *Critical Review of Neurobiology, 11,* 263–287.

Rome, E. S., Ammerman, S., Rosen, D. S., Keller, R. J., Lock, J., Mammel, K. A., et al. (2003). Children and adolescents with eating disorders: The state of the art. *Pediatrics, 111,* e98–e108.

Romeo, R. D., Richardson, H. N., & Sisk, C. L. (2002). Puberty and the maturation of the male brain and sexual behavior: Recasting a behavioral potential. *Neuroscience and Biobehavioral Review, 26,* 381–391.

Romer, D., Jamieson, K. H., & deCoteau, N. J. (1998). The treatment of persons of color in local television news: Ethnic blame discourse or realistic group conflict? *Communication Research, 25,* 286–305.

Roorda, A., & Williams, D. R. (1999). The arrangement of the three cone classes in the living human eye. *Nature, 397,* 520–522.

Rooy, D. L. V., Dilchert, S., Viswesvaran, C., & Ones, D. (2006). Multiplying intelligences: Are general, emotional, and practical intelligences equal? In K. R. Murphy (Ed.), *A critique of emotional intelligence: What are the problems and how can they be fixed?* (pp. 235–262). Mahwah, NJ: Erlbaum.

Rosch, E., Mervis, C. B., Gray, W. D., Johnson, D. M., & Boyes-Braem, P. (1976). Basic objects in natural categories. *Cognitive Psychology, 8,* 382–439.

Rosen, B. C., & D'Andrade, R. (1959). The psychosocial origins of achievement motivation. *Sociometry, 22,* 188–218.

Rosen, D., Stukenberg, K. W., & Saeks, S. (2001). The group-as-a-whole-object relations model of group psychotherapy. *Bulletin of the Menninger Clinic, 65,* 471–488.

Rosen, G. M. (1999). Treatment fidelity and research on eye movement desinsitization and reprocessing (EMDR). *Journal of Anxiety Disorders, 13,* 173–184.

Rosen, R. (1991). *The healthy company.* Los Angeles: Tarcher.

Rosenbaum, M., & Bennett, B. (1986). Homicide and depression. *American Journal of Psychiatry, 143,* 367–370.

Rosenbaum, R. S., Priselac, S. K., Black, S. E., Gao, F., Nadel, L., & Moscovitch, M. (2000). Remote spatial memory in an amnesiac person with extensive bilateral hippocampal lesions. *Nature Neuroscience, 3,* 1044–1048.

Rosenfarb, I. S., Goldstein, M. J., Mintz, J., & Nuechterlein, K. H. (1995). Expressed emotion and subclinical psychopathology observable within the transactions between schizophrenic patients and their family members. *Journal of Abnormal Psychology, 104,* 259–267.

Rosenfarb, I. S., Nuechterlein, K. H., Goldstein, M. J., & Subotnik, K. L. (2000). Neurocognitive vulnerability, interpersonal criticism, and the emergence of unusual thinking by schizophrenic patients during family transactions. *Archives of General Psychiatry, 57,* 1174–1179.

Rosenfeld, J. P. (1995). Alternative views of Bashore and Rapp's (1993) alternatives to traditional polygraphy: A critique. *Psychological Bulletin, 117*(1), 159–166.

Rosenkranz, M. A., Jackson, D. C., Dalton, K. M., Dolski, I., Ryff,C. D., Singer, B. H., et al. (2003). Affective style and in vivo immune response: Neurobehavioral mechanisms. *Proceedings of the National Academy of Sciences, 100,* 11148–11152.

Rosenstock, I. M. (1974). Historical origins of the health belief model. *Health Education Monographs, 2,* 328–335.

Rosenthal, R. R. (1966). *Experimenter effects in behavioral research.* New York: Appleton-Century-Crofts.

Rosenzweig, M. R., & Bennett, E. L. (1996). Psychobiology of plasticity: Effects of training and experience on brain and behavior. *Behavioural Brain Research, 78,* 57–65.

Ross, C. A. (1997). *Dissociative identity disorder: Diagnosis, clinical features, and treatment of multiple personality.* New York: Wiley.

Ross, C. A., Anderson, G., Fleisher, W. P., & Norton, G. R. (1991). The frequency of multiple personality disorder among psychiatric inpatients. *American Journal of Psychiatry, 148,* 1717–1720.

Ross, E. D. (1981). The aprosodias: Functional-anatomic organization of the affective components of language in the right hemisphere. *Archives of Neurology, 38(9),* 561–569.

Ross, M. W. (2002). Sexuality and health challenges: Responding to a public health imperative. *Journal of Sex Research, 39,* 7–9.

Ross, S. M., & Ross, L. E. (1971). Comparison of trace and delay classical eyelid conditioning as a function of interstimulus interval. *Journal of Experimental Psychology, 91,* 165–167.

Roth, H. L., Lora, A. N., & Heilman, K. M. (2002). Effects of monocular viewing and eye dominance on spatial attention. *Brain, 125,* 2023–2035.

Roth, P. L., Huffcutt, A. I., & Bobko, P. (2003). Ethnic group differences in measures of job performance: A new meta-analysis. *Journal of Applied Psychology, 88,* 694–706.

Rothbart, M. K., & Derryberry, D. (2002). Temperament in children. In C. von Hofsten & L. Baeckman (Eds.), *Psychology at the turn of the millennium: Vol. 2. Social, developmental, and clinical perspectives* (pp. 17–35). Florence, KY: Taylor & Frances/Routledge.

Rothbart, M. R., & Bates, J. E. (2006). Temperament. In W. Damon & R. M. Lerner (Series Eds.) & N. Eisenberg (Vol. Ed.), *Handbook of child psychology: Vol. 3. Social, emotional, and personality development* (6th ed.). New York: Wiley.

Rothbaum, B. O., Hodges, L. F., Alarcon, R., Ready, D., Shahar, F., Graap, K., et al. (1999). Virtual reality exposure therapy for PTSD Vietnam veterans: A case study. *Journal of Traumatic Stress, 12,* 263–271.

Rothbaum, B. O., Hodges, L., Anderson, P. L., Price, L., & Smith, S. (2002). Twelve-month follow-up of virtual reality and standard exposure therapies for fear of flying. *Journal of Consulting and Clinical Psychology, 70,* 428–432.

Rothbaum, B. O., Hodges, L. F., Kooper, R., & Opdyke, D. (1995). Effectiveness of computer-generated virtual reality graded exposure in the treatment of acrophobia. *American Journal of Psychiatry, 152,* 626–628.

Rothbaum, B. O., Hodges, L., Smith, S., Lee, J. H., & Price, L. (2000). A controlled study of virtual reality exposure therapy for the fear of flying. *Journal of Consulting and Clinical Psychology, 68,* 1020–1026.

Rothbaum, F., Pott, M., Azuma, H., Miyake, K., & Weisz, J. (2000). The development of close relationships in Japan and the United States: Paths of symbiotic harmony and generative tension. *Child Development, 71,* 1121–1142.

Rothwell, P. M. (2003). Incidence, risk factors and prognosis of stroke and TIA: The need for high-quality, large-scale epidemiological studies and meta-analyses. *Cerebrovascular Disease, 16*(Suppl. 3), 2–10.

Rottenstreich, Y., & Tversky, A. (1997). Unpacking, repacking, and anchoring: Advances in support theory. *Psychological Review, 104,* 406–415.

Rotter, J. B. (1954). *Social learning and clinical psychology.* New York: Prentice Hall.

Rotter, J. B. (1982). *The development and application of social learning theory.* New York: Praeger.

Rotton, J. (1990). Individuals under stress. In C. E. Kimble (Ed.), *Social psychology: Living with people.* New York: Brown.

Rotton, J., & Kelly, I. W. (1985). Much ado about the full moon: A meta-analysis of lunar-lunacy research. *Psychological Bulletin, 97,* 286–306.

Rouch, I., Wild, P., Ansiau, D., & Marquie, J-C. (2005). Shiftwork experience, age, and cognitive performance. *Ergonomics, 48,* 1282–1293.

Rouéché, B. (1986, December 8). Cinnabar. *New Yorker.*

Rounsaville, B. J., & Carroll, K. M. (2002). Commentary on dodo bird revisited: Why aren't we dodos yet? *Clinical Psychology: Science & Practice, 9(1),* 17–20.

Rovee-Collier, C. (1999). The development of infant memory. *Current Directions in Psychological Science, 8,* 80–85.

Rowe, D. C. (1997). Genetics, temperament, and personality. In R. Hogan, J. Johnson, & S. Briggs (Eds.), *Handbook of personality psychology* (pp. 367–386). San Diego: Academic Press.

Rowe, D. C. (2005). Under the skin: On the impartial treatment of genetic and environmental hypotheses of racial differences. *American Psychologist, 60,* 60–70.

Rowe, D. C., Jacobson, K. C., & Van den Oord, E. J. C. G. (1999). Genetic and environmental influences on vocabulary IQ: Parental education level as moderator. *Child Development, 70,* 1151–1162.

Roy, D. K., & Pentland, A. P. (2002). Learning words from sights and sounds: A computational model. *Cognitive Science, 26,* 113–146.

Roy-Byrne, P. P., Craske, M. G., Stein, M. B., Sullivan, G., Bystritsky, A., Katon, W., et al. (2005). A randomized effectiveness trial of cognitive-behavioral therapy and medication for primary care panic disorder. *Archives of General Psychiatry, 62,* 290–298.

Roy-Byrne, P., Stang, P., Wittchen, H.-U., Ustun, B., Walters, E. E., & Kessler, R. (2000). Lifetime Panic-Depression comorbidity in the National Comorbidity Survey. *British Journal of Psychiatry, 176,* 229–235.

Rozin, P. (1982). "Taste-smell confusions" and the duality of the olfactory sense. *Perception and Psychophysics, 31,* 397–401.

Rozin, P. (1996). Sociocultural influences on human food selection. In E. D. Capaldi (Ed.), *Why we eat what we eat: The psychology of eating* (pp. 233–263). Washington DC: American Psychological Association.

Rubens, A. B., & Benson, D. F. (1971). Associative visual agnosia. *Archives of Neurology, 24,* 304–316.

Rubin, E. (1915). *Synsoplevede figure.* Copenhagen: Gyldendalske.

Rubin, K. H., Bukowski, W., & Parker, J. G. (2006). Peer interactions, relationships, and groups. In W. Damon & R. M. Lerner (Series Eds.) & N. Eisenberg (Vol. Ed.), *Handbook of child psychology: Vol. 3. Social, emotional, and personality development* (6th ed.). New York: Wiley.

Rubinstein, S., & Caballero, B. (2000). Is Miss America an undernourished role model? *Journal of the American Medical Association, 283,* 1569.

Ruble, D. N., Martin, C. L., & Berenbaum, S. A. (2006). Gender development. In W. Damon & R. M. Lerner (Series Eds.) & N. Eisenberg (Vol. Ed.), *Handbook of child psychology: Vol. 3, Social, emotional, and personality development* (6th ed., pp. 858–932). New York: Wiley.

Rudman, L. A., Greenwald, A. G., Mellott, D. S., & Schwartz, J. L. K. (1999). Measuring the automatic components of prejudice: Flexibility and generality of the Implicit Association Test. *Social Cognition, 17,* 437–465.

Rudolph, K. D., Lambert, S. F., Clark, A. G., & Kurlakowsky, K. D. (2001). Negotiating the transition to middle school: The role of self-regulatory processes. *Child Development, 72,* 929–946.

Rudorfer, M. V., Henry, M. E., & Sackheim, H. A. (1997). Electroconvulsive therapy. In A. Tasman, J. Kay, & J. A. Lieberman (Eds.), *Psychiatry* (pp. 1535–1556). Philadelphia: Saunders.

Rueckert, L., Baboorian, D., Stavropoulos, K., & Yasutake, C. (1999). Individual differences in callosal efficiency: Correlation with attention. *Brain and Cognition, 41,* 390–410.

Rugg, M. D., & Wilding, E. L. (2000). Retrieval processing and episodic memory. *Trends in Cognitive Sciences, 4,* 108–115.

Ruiz, P., Varner, R. V., Small, D. R, & Johnson, B. A. (1999). Ethnic differences in the neuroleptic treatment of schizophrenia. *Psychiatric Quarterly, 70,* 163–172.

Rumelhart, D. E., & McClelland, J. L. (1986). *Parallel distributed processing: Explorations in the microstructure of cognition: Vol. 1. Foundations.* Cambridge, MA: Bradford.

Runyon, M., & Kenny, M. C. (2002). Relationship of attributional style, depression, and posttrauma distress among children who suffered physical or sexual abuse. *Child Maltreatment, 7,* 254–264.

Rusbult, C. E., Arriagi, X. B., & Agnew, C. R (2001). Interdependence in close relationships. In G. Fletcher & M. Clark (Eds.), *Blackwell handbook of social psychology: Interpersonal processes* (pp. 359–387). Oxford, England: Blackwell.

Rusbult, C. E., & Van Lange, P. A. M. (1996). Interdependence processes. In E. T. Higgins & A. W. Kruglanski (Eds.), *Social psychology: Handbook of basic principles* (pp. 564–596). New York: Guilford.

Ruscio, J. (2005). Exploring controversies in the art and science of polygraph testing. *Skeptical Inquirer, 29,* 34–39.

Rushton, J. P., & Bons, T. A. (2005). Mate choice and friendship in twins. *Psychological Science 16,* 555–559.

Rushton, J. P., & Jensen, A. R. (2005). Thirty years of research on race differences in cognitive ability. *Psychology, Public Policy, and Law, 11,* 235–294.

Ruskin, P. E., Silver-Aylaian, M., Kling, M. A., Reed, S. A., Bradham, D. D., Hebel, J. R., et al. (2004). Treatment outcomes in depression: Comparison of remote treatment through telepsychiatry to in-person treatment. *American Journal of Psychiatry, 161,* 1471–1476.

Russell, J. A. (1991). Culture and the categorization of emotions. *Psychological Bulletin, 110,* 426–450.

Russell, J. A. (1994). Is there universal recognition of emotion from facial expression? A review of the cross-cultural studies. *Psychological Bulletin, 155(2),* 102–141.

Russell, J. A. (1995). Facial expressions of emotion: What lies beyond minimal universality? *Psychological Bulletin, 118,* 379–391.

Russell, M. C. (2006). Treating combat-related stress disorders: A multiple case study utilizing eye movement desensitization and reprocessing (EMDR) with battlefield casualties from the Iraqi War. *Military Psychology, 18,* 1–18.

Rutkowski, G. K., Gruder, C. L., & Romer, D. (1983). Group cohesiveness, social norms, and bystander intervention. *Journal of Personality and Social Psychology, 44,* 545–552.

Rutledge, T., Reis, S. E., Olson, M., Owens, J., Kelsey, S. F., Pepine, C. J., et al. (2004). Social networks are associated with lower mortality rates among women with suspected coronary disease: The National Heart, Lung, and Blood Institute-Sponsored Women's Ischemia Syndrome Evaluation study. *Psychosomatic Medicine, 66,* 882–888.

Rutter, M., O'Connor, T. G., & ERA Study Team. (2004). Are there biological programming effects for psychological development? Findings from a study of Romanian adoptees. *Developmental Psychology, 40,* 81–94.

Rutter, M., Pickles, A., Murray, R., & Eaves, L. (2001). Testing hypotheses on specific environmental causal effects on behavior. *Psychological Bulletin, 127,* 291–324.

Rutter, M., & Schopler, E. (1992). Classification of pervasive developmental disorders: Some concepts and practical considerations. *Journal of Autism and Developmental Disorders, 22,* 459–482.

Ryan, R. H., & Geiselman, R. E. (1991). Effects of biased information on the relationship between eyewitness confidence and accuracy. *Bulletin of the Psychonomic Society, 29,* 7–9.

Rymer, R. (1993). *Genie: A scientific tragedy.* New York: HarperCollins.

Rynders, J., & Horrobin, J. (1980). Educational provisions for young children with Down's syndrome. In J. Gottlieb (Ed.), *Educating mentally retarded persons in the mainstream* (pp. 109–147). Baltimore: University Park Press.

Rynes, S. L., Gerhart, B., & Parks, L. (2005). Performance evaluation and pay for performance. *Annual Review of Psychology, 56,* 571–600.

S

Saarni, C. (2006). Emotion regulation and personality development in childhood. In D. K. Mroczek & T. D. Little (Eds.), *Handbook of personality development* (pp. 245–262). Mahwah, NJ: Erlbaum.

Sachs, J. (1967). Recognition memory for syntactic and semantic aspects of connected discourse. *Perception and Psychophysics, 2,* 437–442.

Sackeim, H. A. (1994). Central issues regarding the mechanisms of action of electroconvulsive therapy: Directions for future research. *Psychopharmacology Bulletin, 30,* 281–308.

Sackeim, H. A., Haskett, R. F., Mulsant, B. H., Thase, M. E., Mann, J. J., Pettinati, H. M., et al. (2001). Continuation pharmacotherapy in the prevention of relapse following electroconvulsive therapy: A randomized controlled trial. *Journal of the American Medical Association, 285,* 1299–1307.

Sackeim, H. A., Prudic, J., Devanand, D. P., Nobler, M. S., Lisanby, S. H., Peyser, S., et al. (2000). A prospective, randomized, double-blind comparison of bilateral and right unilateral electroconvulsive therapy at different stimulus intensities. *Archives of General Psychiatry, 57,* 425–434.

Sackett, P. R., Hardison, C. M., & Cullen, M. J. (2004). On interpreting stereotype threat as accounting for African American-White differences on cognitive tests. *American Psychologist, 59,* 7–13.

Sackett, P. R., Schmitt, N., Ellington, J. E., & Kabin, M. B. (2001). High-stakes testing in employment, credentialing, and higher education: Prospects in a post-affirmative action world. *American Psychologist, 56,* 302–318.

Sacks, O. (1985). *The man who mistook his wife for a hat.* New York: Summit Books.

Sacks, O. (1992, July 27). The landscape of his dreams. *New Yorker.*

Sacks, O. (2002, October 7). The case of Anna H. *New Yorker,* pp. 62–73.

Saffran, J. R., Senghas, A., & Trueswell, J. C. (2001). The acquisition of language by children. *Proceedings of the National Academy of Science, 98,* 12874–12875.

Safren, S. A., Gershuny, B. S., Marzol, P., Otto, M. W., Pollack, M. H. (2002). History of childhood abuse in panic disorder, social phobia, and generalized anxiety disorder. *Journal of Nervous and Mental Disease, 190,* 453–456.

Sagan, C. (1996). *The demon-haunted world.* New York: Ballantine.

Sakairi, Y. (1992). Studies on meditation using questionnaires. *Japanese Psychological Review, 35*(1), 94–112.

Salgado, J. F., Anderson, N., Moscoso, S., Bertua, C., de Fruyt, F., & Rolland, J. P. (2003). A meta-analytic study of general mental ability validity for different occupations in the European community. *Journal of Applied Psychology, 88,* 1068–1081.

Salin-Pascual, R., Gerashchenko, D., Greco, M., Blanco-Centurion, C., & Shiromani, P. J. (2001). Hypothalamic regulation of sleep. *Neuropsychopharmacology, 25* (Suppl. 5), S21.

Salokangas, R. K. R. (2004). Gender and the use of neuroleptics in schizophrenia. *Schizophrenia Research, 66,* 41–49.

Salovey, P., & Grewal, D. (2005). The science of emotional intelligence. *Current Directions in Psychological Science, 14,* 281–285.

Salovey, P., Mayer, J. D., & Rosenhan, D. L. (1991). Mood and helping: Mood as a motivator of helping and helping as a regulator of mood. In M. S. Clark (Ed.), *Review of personality and social psychology: Vol. 12. Prosocial behavior* (pp. 215–237). Newbury Park, CA: Sage.

Salzer, M. S., Rappaport, J., & Segre, L. (1999). Professional appraisal of professionally led and self-help groups. *American Journal of Ortho-Psychiatry, 69,* 536–540.

Sambunaris, A., & Hyde, T. M. (1994). Stroke-related aphasias mistaken for psychotic speech: Two case reports. *Journal of Geriatric Psychiatry and Neurology, 7*(3), 144–147.

Sammons, M. T., Paige, R. U., & Levant, R. F. (Eds.). (2003). *Prescriptive authority for psychologists: A history and guide.* Washington, DC: APA Books.

Sanai, N., Tramontin, A. D., Quinones-Hinojosa, A., Barbaro, N. M., Gupta, N., Kunwar, S., et al. (2004). Unique astrocyte ribbon in adult human brain contains neural stem cells but lacks chain migration. *Nature, 427,* 740–744.

Sanders, M. R., Markie-Dadds, C., Tully, L. A., & Bor, W. (2000). The triple p-positive parenting program: A comparison of enhanced, standard, and self-directed behavioral family intervention for parents of children with early onset conduct problems. *Journal of Consulting and Clinical Psychology, 68,* 624–640.

Sanders Thompson, V. L., Bazile, A., & Akbar, M. (2004). African Americans' perceptions of psychotherapy and psychotherapists. *Professional Psychology: Research and Practice, 35,* 19–26.

Sanderson, W. C., Rapee, R. M., & Barlow, D. H. (1989). The influence of an illusion of control on panic attacks induced via inhalation of 5.5% carbon dioxide-enriched air. *Archives of General Psychiatry, 46,* 157–162.

Santry, H. P., Gillen, D. L., & Lauderdale, D. S. (2005). Trends in bariatric surgical procedures. *Journal of the American Medical Association, 294,* 1909–1917.

Saper, C. B., Chou, T. C., & Scammell, T. E. (2001). The sleep switch: Hypothalamic control of sleep and wakefulness. *Trends in Neurosciences, 24,* 726–731.

Saper, C. B., Scammell, T. E., & Lu, J. (2005). Hypothalamic regulation of sleep and circadian rhythms. *Nature, 437,* 1257–1263.

Sarafino, E. P., & Goehring, P. (2000). Age comparisons in acquiring biofeedback control and success in reducing headache pain. *Annals of Behavioral Medicine, 22,* 1–9.

Sarason, B. R., Sarason, I. G., & Gurung, R. A. R. (1997). Close personal relationships and health outcomes: A key to the role of social support. In S. Duck (Ed.), *Handbook of personal relationships* (pp. 547–573). New York: Wiley.

Sarason, I. G., Johnson, J., & Siegel, J. (1978). Assessing impact of life changes: Development of the life experiences survey. *Journal of Clinical and Consulting Psychology, 46,* 932–946.

Sarin, S., Abela, J. R. Z., & Auerbach, R. P. (2005). The response styles theory of depression: A test of specificity and causal mediation. *Cognition and Emotion, 19,* 751–761.

Sasaki, Y., Jadjikhani, N., Fischl, B., Liu, A. K., Marret, S., Dale, A. M., & Tootell, R. B. H. (2001). Local and global attention are mapped retinotopically in human occipital cortex. *Proceedings of the National Academy of Sciences, 98,* 2077.

Sass, D. A., Twohig, M. P., & Davies, W. H. (2004). Defining the independent variables and ensuring treatment integrity: A comparison across journals of different theoretical orientations. *Behavior Therapist, 27,* 172–174.

Satterfield, J. M., Folkman, S., & Acree, M. (2002). Explanatory style predicts depressive symptoms following AIDS-related bereavement. *Cognitive Therapy and Research, 26,* 393–403.

Sattler, D. N., Kaiser, C. F., & Hittner, J. B. (2000). Disaster preparedness: Relationships among prior experience, personal characteristics, and distress. *Journal of Applied Social Psychology, 30,* 1396–1420.

Saucier, G., Georgiades, S., Tsaousis, I., & Goldberg, L. R. (2005). The factor structure of Greek personality adjectives. *Journal of Personality and Social Psychology, 88,* 856–875.

Saudino, K. J., Ronald, A., & Plomin, R. (2005). The etiology of behavior problems in 7-year-old twins: Substantial genetic influence and negligible shared environmental influence for parent ratings and ratings by same and different teachers. *Journal of Abnormal Child Psychology, 33,* 113–130.

Sauter, S., Murphy, L., Colligan, M., Swanson, N., Hurrell, J., Jr., Scharf, F., Jr., et al. (1999). *Stress at work* (DHHS [NIOSH] Publication No. 99–101). Washington, DC: National Institute on Occupational Health and Safety.

Saveliev, S. V., Lebedev, V. V., Evgeniev, M. B., & Korochkin, L. I. (1997). Chimeric brain: Theoretical and clinical aspects. *International Journal of Developmental Biology, 41,* 801–808.

Savelkoul, M., Post, M. W. M., de Witte, L. P., & van den Borne, H. B. (2000). Social support, coping, and subjective well-being in patients with rheumatic diseases. *Patient Education and Counseling, 39,* 205–218.

Savic, I., Berglund, H., Gulyas, B., & Roland, P. (2001). Smelling of odorous sex hormone-like compounds causes sex-differentiated hypothalamic activations in humans. *Neuron, 31,* 661–668.

Savic, I., Berglund, H., & Lindström, P. (2005). Brain response to putative pheromones in homosexual men. *Proceedings of the National Academy of Sciences of the USA, 102,* 7356–7361.

Savin-Williams, R. C. (2006). Who's gay? Does it matter? *Current Directions in Psychological Science, 15,* 40–44.

Savin-Williams, R. C., & Demo, D. H. (1984). Developmental change and stability in adolescent self-concept. *Developmental Psychology, 20,* 1100–1110.

Saxe, L., & Ben-Shakhar, G. (1999). Admissibility of polygraph tests: The application of scientific standards post-Daubert. *Psychology, Public Policy, and Law, 5,* 203–223.

Sayers, J. (1991). *Mother of psychoanalysis.* New York: Norton.

Scandura, T. A., & Lankau, M. J. (1997). Relationships of gender, family responsibility and flexible work hours to organizational commitment and job satisfaction. *Journal of Organizational Behavior, 18,* 377–391.

Scandura, T. A., & Schriesheim, C. A. (1994). Leader-member exchange and supervisor career mentoring as complementary constructs in leadership research. *Academy of Management Journal, 37,* 1588–1602.

Scarr, S. (1998). How do families affect intelligence? Social environmental and behavior genetic prediction. In J. J. McArdle & R. W. Woodcock (Eds.), *Human cognitive abilities in theory and practice* (pp. 113–136). Mahwah, NJ: Erlbaum.

Scarr, S., & Carter-Saltzman, L. (1982). Genetics and intelligence. In R. Sternberg (Ed.), *Handbook of human intelligence* (pp. 792–896). Cambridge, UK: Cambridge University Press.

Schabracq, M. J. (2003). Organizational culture, stress, and change. In M. J. Schabracq, J. A. M. Winnubst, & C. L. Cooper (Eds.), *Handbook of work and health psychology* (pp.37–62). West Sussex, UK: Wiley.

Schachter, S., & Singer, J. (1962). Cognitive, social and physiological determinants of emotional state. *Psychological Review, 69,* 379–399.

Schacter, D. L. (1999). The seven sins of memory: Insights from psychology and cognitive neuroscience. *American Psychologist, 54,* 182–203.

Schacter, D. L. (2001). *The seven sins of memory.* Boston: Houghton Mifflin.

Schacter, D. L., Chiu, C.-Y. P., & Ochsner, K. N. (1993). Implicit memory: A selective review. *Annual Review of Neuroscience, 16,* 159–182.

Schacter, D. L., Cooper, L. A., Delaney, S. M., Peterson, M. A., & Tharan, M. (1991). Implicit memory for possible and impossible objects: Constraints on the construction of structural descriptions. *Journal of Experimental Psychology: Learning, Memory, and Cognition, 17,* 3–19.

Schacter, D. L., Norman, K. A., & Koutstaal, W. (1998). The cognitive neuroscience of constructive memory. *Annual Review of Psychology, 49,* 289–318.

Schaefer, J., Sykes, R., Rowley, R., & Baek, S. (1988, November). *Slow country music and drinking.* Paper presented at the 87th annual meeting of the American Anthropological Association, Phoenix, AZ.

Schafer, J., & Brown, S. A. (1991). Marijuana and cocaine effect expectancies and drug use patterns. *Journal of Consulting and Clinical Psychology, 59,* 558–565.

Scharf, M., Mayseless, O., & Kivenson-Baron, I. (2004). Adolescents' attachment representations and developmental tasks in emerging adulthood. *Developmental Psychology, 40,* 430–444.

Scharff, J. S., & Scharff, D. E. (2004). Guest editorial, special issue: Object relations couple and family therapy. *International Journal of Applied Psychoanalytic Studies, 1,* 211–213.

Schatzberg, A. F., Rush, A. J., Arnow, B. A., Banks, P. L., Blalock, J. A., Borian, F. E., et al. (2005). Chronic depression: Medication (nefazodone) or psychotherapy (CBASP) is effective when the other is not. *Archives of General Psychiatry, 62,* 513–520.

Schaubroeck, J., Jones, J. R., & Xie, J. J. (2001). Individual differences in utilizing control to cope with job demands: Effects on susceptibility to infectious disease. *Journal of Applied Psychology, 86,* 265–278.

Schaufeli, W. B., & Buunk, B. P. (2003). Burnout: An overview of 25 years of research and theorizing. In M. J. Schabracq, J. A. M. Winnubst, & C. L. Cooper (Eds.), *Handbook of work and health psychology* (pp.383–428). West Sussex, UK: Wiley.

Scheck, B., Neufeld, P., & Dwyer, J. (2000). *Actual innocence: Five days to execution and other dispatches from the wrongly convicted.* New York: Doubleday.

Scheerer, M., Rothmann, R., & Goldstein, K. (1945). A case of "idiot savant": An experimental study of personality organization. *Psychology Monograph, 58*(4), 1–63.

Scheidinger, S. (2004). Group psychotherapy and related helping groups today: An overview. *American Journal of Psychotherapy, 58,* 265–280.

Scheier, M. F., Matthews, K. A., Owens, J. F., Magovern, G. J., Lefebvre, R. C., Abbott, R. A., et al. (1989). Dispositional optimism and recovery from coronary artery bypass surgery: The beneficial effects on physical and psychological well-being. *Journal of Personality and Social Psychology, 57,* 1024–1040.

Scheier, M. F., Matthews, K. A., Owens, J. F., Schulz, R., Bridges, M. W., Magovern, G. J., et al. (1999). Optimism and rehospitalization after coronary artery bypass graft surgery. *Archives of Internal Medicine, 159,* 829–835.

Schell, T. L., Martino, S. C., Ellickson, P. L., Collins, R. L., & McCaffrey, D. (2005). Measuring developmental changes in alcohol expectancies. *Psychology of Addictive Behaviors, 19,* 217–220.

Schellenberg, E. G. (2004). Music lessons enhance IQ. *Psychological Science, 15,* 511–514.

Schenck, C. H., & Mahowald, M. W. (1992). Motor dyscontrol in narcolepsy: Rapid eye movement (REM) sleep without atonia and REM sleep behavior disorder. *Annals of Neurology, 32*(1), 3–10.

Scheufele, P. M. (2000). Effects of progressive relaxation and classical music on measurements of attention, relaxation, and stress responses. *Journal of Behavioral Medicine, 23,* 207–228.

Schiff, N. D., Rodriguez-Moreno, D., Kamal, A., Kim, K. H., Giacino, J. T., Plum, F., et al. (2005). fMRI reveals large-scale network activation in minimally conscious patients. *Neurology, 64*(3), 514–523.

Schiffman, S. S., Graham, B. G., Sattely-Miller, E. A., & Warwick, Z. (1999). Orosensory perception of dietary fat. *Current Directions in Psychological Science, 7,* 137–143.

Schleicher, D. J., Watt, J. D., & Greguras, G. J. (2004). Reexamining the job satisfaction–performance relationship: The complexity of attitudes. *Journal of Applied Psychology, 89,* 165–177.

Schloss, P., & Williams, D. C. (1998) The serotonin transporter: A primary target for antidepressant drugs. *Journal of Psychopharmacology, 12,* 115–121.

Schmidt, N. B., Lerew, D. R., & Jackson, R. J. (1999). Prospective evaluation of anxiety sensitivity in the pathogenesis of panic: Replication and extension. *Journal of Abnormal Psychology, 108,* 532–537.

Schmidt, N. B., Storey, J., Greenberg, B. D., Santiago, H. T., Li, Q., & Murphy, D. L. (2000). Evaluating gene x psychological risk factor effects in the pathogenesis of anxiety: A new model approach. *Journal of Abnormal Psychology, 109,* 308–320.

Schmidtke, A., & Hafner, H. (1988). The Werther effect after television films: New evidence for an old hypothesis. *Psychological Medicine, 18,* 665–676.

Schmitt, D. P. (2003). Universal sex differences in the desire for sexual variety: Tests from 52 nations, 6 continents, and 13 islands. *Journal of Personality and Social Psychology, 85,* 85–104.

Schmolck, H., Buffalo, E. A., & Squire, L. R. (2000). Memory distortions over time: Recollections of the O. J. Simpson trial verdict after 15 and 32 months. *Psychological Science, 11,* 39–47.

Schnall, S., & Laird, J. D. (2003). Keep smiling: Enduring effects of facial expressions and postures on emotional experience and memory. *Cognition & Emotion, 17,* 787–797.

Schnee, M. E., Lawton, D. M., Furness, D. N., Benke, T. A., & Ricci, A. J. (2005). Auditory hair cell-afferent fiber synapses are specialized to operate at their best frequencies. *Neuron, 47,* 243–254.

Schneider, B. (1985). Organizational behavior. *Annual Review of Psychology, 36,* 573–611.

Schneider, B. H., Atkinson, L., & Tardif, C. (2001). Child-parent attachment and children's peer relations: A quantitative review. *Developmental Psychology, 37,* 86–100.

Schneider, K. T., Hitlan, R. T., & Radhakrishnan, P. (2000). The nature and correlates of ethnic harassment experiences in multiple contexts. *Journal of Applied Psychology, 85,* 3–12.

Schneider, K. T., Swan, S., & Fitzgerald, L. F. (1997). Job-related and psychological effects of sexual harassment in the workplace: Empirical evidence from two organizations. *Journal of Applied Psychology, 82,* 401–415.

Schneider, R. H., Alexander, C. N., Staggers, F., Rainforth, M., Salerno, J. W., Hartz, A., et al. (2005). Long-term effects of stress reduction on mortality in persons > or = 55 years of age with systemic hypertension. *American Journal of Cardiology, 95,* 1060–1064.

Schneider, T. R., Ring, C., & Katkin, E. S. (1998). A test of the validity of the method of constant stimuli as an index of heartbeat detection. *Psychophysiology, 35,* 86–89.

Schneider, W., & Bjorklund, D. F. (1998). Memory. In W. Damon, D. Kuhn, & R. Siegler (Eds.), *Handbook of child psychology: Vol. 2. Cognition, language and perception* (5th ed., pp. 467–521). New York: Wiley.

Schneiderman, N. (2004). Psychosocial, behavioral, and biological aspects of chronic diseases. *Current Directions in Psychological Science, 13,* 247–251.

Schneiderman, N., Antoni, M. H., Saab, P. G., & Ironson,G. (2001). Health psychology: Psychosocial and biobehavioral aspects of chronic disease management. *Annual Review of Psychology, 52,* 555–580.

Schoemaker, M. J., Swerdlow, A. J., Ahlbom, A., Auvinen, A., Blaasaas, K. G., Cardis, E., et al. (2005). Mobile phone use and risk of acoustic neuroma: Results of the Interphone case-control study in five North European countries. *British Journal of Cancer, 93,* 842–848.

Schoenbaum, M., Sherbourne, C., & Wells, K. (2005). Gender patterns in cost effectiveness of quality improvement for depression: Results of a randomized controlled trial. *Journal of Affective Disorders, 87,* 319.

Scholz, H., Franz, M., & Heberlein, U. (2005). The *hangover* gene defines a stress pathway required for ethanol tolerance development. *Nature, 436,* 845–847.

Schott, B. H., Henson, R. N., Richardson-Klavehn, A., Becker, C., Thoma, V., Heinze, H. J., & Duzel, E. (2005). Redefining implicit and explicit memory: The functional neuroanatomy of priming, remembering, and control of retrieval. *Proceedings of the National Academy of Sciences of the USA, 102,* 1257–1262.

Schreiber, G. B., Robins, M., Striegel-Moore, R., Obarzanek, E., Morrison, J. A., & Wright, D. J. (1996). Weight modification efforts reported by black and white preadolescent girls: National Heart, Lung, and Blood Institute Growth and Health Study. *Pediatrics, 98,* 63–70.

Schroeder, D. A. (1995). An introduction to social dilemmas. In D. Schroeder (Ed.), *Social dilemmas: Perspectives on individuals and groups* (pp. 1–13). Westport, CT: Praeger.

Schroeder, D. A., Penner, L. A., Dovidio, J. F., & Piliavin, J. A. (1995). *The psychology of helping and altruism: Problems and puzzles.* New York: McGraw-Hill.

Schuckit, M. A. (1998). Biological, psychological, and environmental predictors of alcoholism risk: A longitudinal study. *Journal of Studies in Alcoholism, 59,* 485–494.

Schultheiss, O. C., & Rohde, W. (2002). Implicit power motivation predicts men's testosterone changes and implicit learning in a contest situation. *Hormones and Behavior, 41,* 195–202.

Schultz, D., & Schultz, S. E. (2002). *Psychology and work today: An introduction to industrial and organizational psychology* (8th ed.). Upper Saddle River, NJ: Prentice Hall.

Schultz, D. P., & Schultz, S. E. (2000). *A history of modern psychology* (7th ed.). Fort Worth, TX: Harcourt Brace.

Schultz, D. P., & Schultz, S. E. (2002). *A history of modern psychology* (8th ed.). Fort Worth, TX: Harcourt Brace.

Schultz, D. P., & Schultz, S. E. (2005). *Theories of personality* (8th ed.) Belmont, CA: Wadsworth.

Schulz, R. (1978). *The psychology of death, dying, and bereavement.* Reading, MA: Addison-Wesley.

Schulz, R., Beach, S. R., Lind, B., Martire, L. M., Zdaniuk, B., Hirsch, C., et al. (2001). Involvement in caregiving and adjustment to death of a spouse: Findings from the caregiver health effects study. *Journal of the American Medical Association, 285,* 3123–3129.

Schulz-Hardt, S., Frey, D., Luthgens, C., & Moscovici, S. (2000). Biased information search in group decision making. *Journal of Personality and Social Psychology, 78,* 665–669.

Schumann, A., Meyer, C., Rumpf, H. J., Hannover, W., Hapke, U., & John, U. (2005). Stage of change transitions and processes of change, decisional balance, and self–efficacy in smokers: A transtheoretical model validation using longitudinal data. *Psychology of Addictive Behaviors, 19,* 3–9.

Schutter, D. J. L. G. (2005). A framework for targeting alternative brain regions with repetitive transcranial magnetic stimulation in the treatment of depression. *Journal of Psychiatry and Neuroscience, 30,* 91–97.

Schwartz, C. E., Wright, C. I., Shin, L. M., Kagan, J., & Rauch, S. L. (2003). Inhibited and uninhibited infants "grown up": Adult amygdala response to novelty. *Science, 300,* 1952–1953.

Schwartz, J. (2004, September 5). Always on the job, employees pay with health. *The New York Times,* p. 1.

Schwartz, J. R. (2005). Modafinil: New indications for wake promotion. *Expert Opinion in Pharmacotherapy, 6,* 115–129.

Schwartz, M. W., Woods, S. C., Porte Jr., D., Seeley, R. J., & Baskin, D. G. (2000). Central nervous system control of food intake. *Nature, 404,* 661–671.

Schwarz, N., & Bohner, G. (2001). The construction of attitudes. In A. Tesser & N. Schwarz (Eds.), *Blackwell handbook of social psychology: Intraindividual processes* (pp. 436–457). Oxford, UK: Blackwell.

Schwarz, N., & Scheuring, B. (1992). Frequency reports of psychosomatic symptoms: What respondents learn from response alternatives. *Zeutschrift fur Klinische Psychologie, 22,* 197–208.

Schwarzer, R. (2001). Social-cognitive factors in changing health-related behaviors. *Current Directions in Psychological Science, 10,* 47–51.

Schwender, D., Klasing, D., Daunderer, M., Maddler, C., Poppel, E., & Peter, K. (1995). Awareness during general anesthetic: Definition, incidence, clinical relevance, causes, avoidance, and medicolegal aspects. *Anaesthetist, 44,* 743–754.

Schyns, B. (2006). Are group consensus in leader-member exchange (LMX) and shared work values related to organizational outcomes? *Small Group Research, 37,* 20–35.

Scott, S., Knapp, M., Henderson, J., & Maughan, B. (2001). Financial cost of social exclusion: Follow up study of antisocial children into adulthood. *British Medical Journal, 323,* 191.

Scourfield, J., Van den Bree, M., Martin, N., & McGuffin, P. (2004). Conduct problems in children and adolescents: A twin study. *Archives of General Psychiatry, 61,* 489–496.

Scoville, W. B., & Milner, B. (1957). Loss of recent memory after bilateral hippocampal lesions. *Journal of Neurology, Neurosurgery, and Psychiatry, 20,* 11–21.

Sears, R. (1977). Sources of satisfaction of the Terman gifted men. *American Psychologist, 32,* 119–128.

Seegert, C. R. (2003). Token economies and incentive programs: Behavioral improvement in mental health inmates housed in state prisons. *Behavior Therapist, 26*(1), 208, 210–211.

Seeman, M. V. (2004). Gender differences in the prescribing of antipsychotic drugs. *American Journal of Psychiatry, 161,* 1324–1333.

Seeman, P., Weinshenker, D., Quirion, R., Srivastava, L. K., Bhardwaj, S. K., Grandy, D. K., (2005). Dopamine supersensitivity correlates with D2^{High} states, implying many paths to psychosis. *Proceedings of the National Academy of Sciences of the USA, 102,* 3513–3518.

Seeman, T., & Chen, X. (2002). Risk and protective factors for physical functioning in older adults with and without chronic conditions: MacArthur studies of successful aging. *Journals of Gerontology: Series B. Psychological Sciences & Social Sciences, 57*(3), S135–S144.

Segal, Z. V., Gemar, M., & Williams, S. (2000). Differential cognitive response to a mood challenge following successful cognitive therapy or pharmacotherapy for unipolar depression. *Journal of Abnormal Psychology, 108,* 3–10.

Segall, M. H., Dasen, P. R., Berry, J. W., & Poortinga, Y. H. (1990). *Human behavior in global perspective: An introduction to cross-cultural psychology.* Elmwood, NY: Pergamon Press.

Segerstrom, S. C., Taylor, S. E., Kemeny, M. E., & Fahey, J. L. (1998). Optimism is associated with mood, coping, and immune change in response to stress. *Journal of Personality and Social Psychology, 74,* 1646–1655.

Seghier, M. L., Boex, C., Lazeyras, F., Sigrist, A., & Pelizzone, M. (2005). FMRI evidence for activation of multiple cortical regions in the primary auditory cortex of deaf subjects users of multichannel cochlear implants. *Cerebral Cortex, 15,* 40–48.

Segurado, R., Conroy, J., Meally, E., Fitzgerald, M., Gill, M., & Gallagher, L. (2005). Confirmation of association between autism and the mitochondrial aspartate/glutamate carrier SLC25A12 gene on chromosome 2q31. *American Journal of Psychiatry, 162,* 2182–2184.

Seiger, A., Nordberg, A., Vonholst, H., Backman, L., Ebendal, T., Alafuzoff, I., et al. (1993). Intracranial infusion of purified nerve growth factor to an Alzheimer patient: The 1st attempt of a possible future treatment strategy. *Behavioral Brain Research, 57,* 255–261.

Sejnowski, T. J., & Destexhe, A. (2000). Why do we sleep? *Brain Research, 886,* 208–223.

Selemon, L. D., Mrzljak, J., Kleinman, J. E., Herman, M. M., & Goldman-Rakic, P. S. (2003). Regional specificity in the neuropathologic substrates of schizophrenia: A morphometric analysis of Broca's area 44 and area 9. *Archives of General Psychiatry, 60,* 69–77.

Seligman, M. E. P. (1975). *Helplessness: On depression, development, and death.* San Francisco: Freeman.

Seligman, M. E. P. (1991). *Learned optimism.* New York: Knopf.

Seligman, M. E. P. (1995). The effectiveness of psychotherapy: The *Consumer Reports* study. *American Psychologist, 50,* 965–974.

Seligman, M. E. P., Castellon, C., Cacciola, J., Shulman, P., Luborsky, L., Ollove, M., & Downing, R. (1988). Explanatory style change during cognitive therapy for unipolar depression. *Journal of Abnormal Psychology, 97,* 13–18.

Seligman, M. E. P., & Schulman, P. (1986). Explanatory style as a predictor of productivity and quitting among life insurance agents. *Journal of Personality and Social Psychology, 50,* 832–838.

Seligman, M. E. P., Steen, T. A., Park, N., & Peterson, C. (2005). Positive psychology progress: Empirical validation of interventions. *American Psychologist, 60,* 410–421.

Sell, R. L., Wells, J. A., & Wypij, D. (1995). The prevalence of homosexual behavior and attraction in the United States, the United Kingdom, and France: Results of national population-based samples. *Archives of Sexual Behavior, 24*(3), 235–248.

Selye, H. (1956). *The stress of life.* New York: McGraw-Hill.

Selye, H. (1974). The general adaptation syndrome. In H. Selye, *Stress without distress.* New York: HarperCollins.

Selye, H. (1976). *The stress of life* (2nd ed.). New York: McGraw-Hill.

Semmler, C., Brewer, N., & Wells, G. L. (2004). Effects of postidentification feedback on eyewitness identification and nonidentification confidence. *Journal of Applied Psychology, 89,* 334–346.

Senghas, A., & Coppola, M. (2001). Children creating language: How Nicaraguan sign language acquired a spatial grammar. *Psychological Science, 12,* 323–328.

Sergeant, J. A., Geurts, H., & Oosterlaan, J. (2002). How specific is a deficit of executive functioning for attention deficit/hyperactivity disorder? *Behavioural Brain Research, 130,* 3–28.

Serpell, R. (1994). The cultural construction of intelligence. In W. J. Lonner & R. S. Malpass (Eds.), *Psychology and culture.* Boston: Allyn & Bacon.

Servan-Schreiber, E., & Anderson, J. R. (1990). Learning artificial grammars with competitive chunking. *Journal of Experimental Psychology: Learning, Memory, and Cognition, 16,* 592–608.

Seto, M. C., Maric, A., & Barbaree, H. E. (2001). The role of pornography in the etiology of sexual aggression. *Aggression and Violent Behavior, 6,* 35–53.

Sewell, M. C., Goggin, K. J., Rabkin, J. G., Ferrando, S. J., McElhiney, M. C., & Evans, S. (2000). Anxiety syndromes and symptoms among men with AIDS: A longitudinal controlled study. *Psychosomatics, 41,* 294–300.

Shadish, W. R., & Baldwin, S. A. (2005). Effects of behavioral marital therapy: A meta-analysis of randomized controlled trials. *Journal of Counseling and Clinical Psychology, 73,* 6–14.

Shadish, W. R., Cook, T. D., & Campbell, D. T. (2002). *Experimental and quasi-experimental designs for generalized causal inference.* Boston: Houghton Mifflin.

Shadish, W. R., Matt, G. E., Navarro, A. M., & Phillips, G. (2000). The effects of psychological therapies under clinically representative conditions: A meta-analysis. *Psychological Bulletin, 126,* 512–529.

Shaffer, D. R. (1973). *Social and personality development* (Box 4–2). Pacific Grove, CA: Brooks/Cole.

Shaffer, D. R. (1999). *Developmental psychology: Childhood and adolescence.* Pacific Grove, CA: Brooks/Cole.

Shah, J. (2003). Automatic for the people: How representations of significant others implicitly affect goal pursuit. *Journal of Personality and Social Psychology, 84,* 661–681.

Shalev, A. Y., & Freedman, S. (2005). PTSD following terrorist attacks: A prospective evaluation. *American Journal of Psychiatry, 162,* 1188–1191.

Shalev, A. Y., Tuval, R., Frenkiel-Fishman, S., Hadar, H., & Eth, S. (2006). Psychological responses to continuous terror: A study of two communities in Israel. *American Journal of Psychiatry, 163,* 667–673.

Shamay-Tsoory, S. G., & Tomer, R. (2005). The neuroanatomical basis of understanding sarcasm and its relationship to social cognition. *Neuropsychology, 19,* 288–300.

Shand, M. A. (1982). Sign-based short-term memory coding of American Sign Language and printed English words by congenitally deaf signers. *Cognitive Psychology, 14,* 1–12.

Shanks, D. R. (1995). *The psychology of associative learning.* New York: Cambridge University Press.

Shapiro, A. F., Gottman, J. M., & Carrere, S. (2000). The baby and the marriage: Identifying factors that buffer against decline in marital satisfaction after the first baby arrives. *Journal of Family Psychology, 14,* 59–70.

Shapiro, D. H., & Walsh, R. N. (Eds.). (1984). *Meditation: Classical and contemporary perspectives.* New York: Aldine.

Shapiro, F. (1989a). Efficacy of the eye movement desensitization procedure in the treatment of traumatic memories. *Journal of Traumatic Stress, 2,* 199–223.

Shapiro, F. (1989b). Eye movement desensitization: A new treatment for post-traumatic stress disorder. *Journal of Behavior Therapy and Experimental Psychiatry, 20,* 211–217.

Shapiro, F. (1991). Eye movement desensitization and reprocessing procedure: From EMD to EMD/R—A new treatment model for anxiety and related traumata. *Behavior Therapist, 15,* 133–135.

Shapiro, F., & Forrest, M. S. (2004). *EMDR: The breakthrough therapy for overcoming anxiety, stress, and trauma.* New York: Basic Books.

Shapiro, K. A., Moo, L. R., & Caramazza, A. (2006). Cortical signatures of noun and verb production. *Proceedings of the National Academy of Sciences of the USA, 103,* 1644–1649.

Shaver, P. R., & Mikulincer, M. (2005). Attachment theory and research: Resurrection of the psychodynamic approach to personality. *Journal of Research in Personality, 39,* 22–45.

Shaw, D. S., Dishion, T. J., Supplee, L., Gardner, F., & Arnds, K. (2006). Randomized trial of a family-centered approach to the prevention of early conduct problems: 2-year effects of the family check-up in early childhood. *Journal of Consulting and Clinical Psychology, 74,* 1–9.

Shaw, D. S., Owens, E. B., Giovannelli, J., Winslow, E. B. (2001). Infant and toddler pathways leading to early externalizing disorders. *Journal of the American Academy of Child and Adolescent Psychiatry, 40,* 36–43.

Shaw, J. S., III. (1996). Increases in eyewitness confidence resulting from persistent questioning. *Journal of Experimental Psychology: Applied, 2,* 126–146.

Shaywitz, B. A., Shaywitz, S. E., Pugh, K. R., Constable, R. T., Skudlarski, P., Fulbright, R. K., et al. (1995). Sex differences in the functional organization of the brain for language. *Nature, 373,* 607–609.

Shea, M. T., Stout, R., Gunderson, J., Morey, L. C., Grilo, C. M., McGlashan, T., et al. (2002). Short-term diagnostic stability of schizotypal, borderline, avoidant, and obsessive-compulsive personality disorders. *American Journal of Psychiatry, 159,* 2036–2041.

Shechtman, Z. (1992). A group assessment procedure as a predictor of on-the-job performance of teachers. *Journal of Applied Psychology, 77,* 383–387.

Shedler, J., & Westen, D. (2004). Refining personality disorder diagnoses: Integrating science and practice. *American Journal of Psychiatry, 161,* 1350–1365.

Sheehy, R., & Horan, J. J. (2004). Effects of stress inoculation training for 1st-year law students. *International Journal of Stress Management, 11*(1), 41–55.

Sheldon, K. M., & Kasser, T. (2001). Getting older, getting better? Personal striving and psychological maturity across the life span. *Developmental Psychology, 37,* 491–501.

Sheldon, K. M., & King, L. (2001). Why positive psychology is necessary. *American Psychologist, 56,* 216–217.

Shenker, J. I. (2005, April). *When you only see trees, is there still a forest?* Paper presented at the American Academy of Neurology Annual Meeting, Miami Beach, FL.

Shenker, J. I., Wylie, S. A., Fuchs, K., Manning, C. A., & Heilman, K. M. (2004). On-line anosognosia: Unawareness for chorea in real time but not on videotape delay. *Neurology, 63*(1), 159–160.

Shepard, R. N., & Metzler, J. (1971). Mental rotation of three-dimensional objects. *Science, 171,* 701–703.

Shepherd, C., Kohut, J. J., & Sweet, R. (1989). *News of the weird.* New York: New American Library.

Shepherd, G. M. (2005). Perception without a thalamus: How does olfaction do it? *Neuron, 46,* 166–168.

Shepherd, R. K., Coco, A., Epp, S. B., & Crook, J. M. (2005). Chronic depolarization enhances the trophic effects of brain-derived neurotrophic factor in rescuing auditory neurons following a sensorineural hearing loss. *Journal of Comparative Neurology, 486,* 145–158.

Sher, K. J., Walitzer, K., Wood, P., & Brent, E. (1991). Characteristics of children of alcoholics: Putative risk factors, substance use and abuse, and psychopathology. *Journal of Abnormal Psychology, 100,* 427–448.

Sher, K. J., Wood, M. D., Wood, P. K., & Raskin, G. (1996). Alcohol outcome expectancies and alcohol use: A latent variable cross-lagged panel study. *Journal of Abnormal Psychology, 105,* 561–574.

Shera, C. A., Guinan, J. J., & Oxenham, A. J. (2002). Revised estimates of human cochlear tuning from otoacoustic and behavioral measurements. *Proceedings of the National Academy of Sciences, 99*(5), 3318–3323.

Sherer, M. R., & Schreibman, L. (2005). Individual behavioral profiles and predictors of treatment effectiveness for children with autism. *Journal of Consulting and Clinical Psychology, 73,* 525–538.

Sherif, M. (1937). An experimental approach to the study of attitudes. *Sociometry, 1,* 90–98.

Sherman, J. W., & Bessenoff, G. R. (1999). Stereotypes as source-monitoring cues: On the interaction between episodic and semantic memory. *Psychological Science, 10,* 106–110.

Sherman, R. T., & Thompson, R. A. (2004). The female athlete triad. *Journal of School Nursing, 20,* 197–202.

Sherman, S. J. (1980). On the self-erasing nature of errors of prediction. *Journal of Personality and Social Psychology, 39,* 211–221.

Sherwin, B. B., & Gelfand, M. M. (1987). The role of androgen in the maintenance of sexual functioning in oophorectomized women. *Psychosomatic Medicine, 49,* 397–409.

Sherwin, B. B., Gelfand, M. M., & Brender, W. (1985). Androgen enhances sexual motivation in females: A prospective crossover study of sex steroid administration in the surgical menopause. *Psychosomatic Medicine, 47,* 339–351.

Shields, L. B. E., Hunsaker, D. M., Muldoon, S., Corey, T. S., & Spivack, B. S. (2005). Risk factors associated with sudden unexplained infant death: A prospective study of infant care practices in Kentucky. *Pediatrics, 116,* e13–e20.

Shiffman, S., Engberg, J. B., Paty, J. A., & Perz, W. G. (1997). A day at a time: Predicting smoking lapse from daily urge. *Journal of Abnormal Psychology, 106,* 104–116.

Shiller, R. J. (2001). *Irrational exuberance.* Princeton, NJ: Princeton University Press.

Shimamura, A. P., Berry, J. M., Mangels, J. A., Rusting, C. L., & Jurica, P. J. (1995). Memory and cognitive abilities in university professors: Evidence for successful aging. *Psychological Science, 6,* 271–277.

Shin, S.-M., Chow, C., Camacho-Gonzalves, T., Levy, R. J., Allen, I. E., & Leff, H. S. (2005). A meta-analytic review of racial-ethnic matching for African American and Caucasian American clients and clinicians. *Journal of Counseling Psychology, 52,* 45–56.

Shinskey, J. L., & Munakata, Y. (2005) Familiarity breeds searching. *Psychological Science, 16,* 596–600.

Shiraev, E., & Levy, D. (2004). *Cross-cultural psychology: Critical thinking and contemporary applications* (2nd ed.). Boston: Allyn & Bacon.

Shiwach, R. S., Reid, W. H., & Carmody, T. J. (2001). An analysis of reported deaths following electroconvulsive therapy in Texas, 1993–1998. *Psychiatric Services, 52,* 1095–1097.

Shneidman, E. S. (1987). A psychological approach to suicide. In G. VandenBos & B. K. Bryant (Eds.), *Cataclysms, crises, and catastrophes: Psychology in action. The master lectures* (Vol. 6, pp. 147–183). Washington, DC: American Psychological Association.

Shoda, Y., & LeeTiernan, S. (2002). What remains invariant? Finding order within a person's thoughts, feelings, and behavior across situations. In D. Cervone & W. Mischel (Eds.), *Advances in personality science* (pp. 241–270). New York: Guilford Press.

Shreeve, J. (1993, June). Touching the phantom. *Discover,* pp. 35–42.

Shu, S. Y., Wu, Y. M., Bao, X. M., Wen, Z. B., Huang, F. H., Li, S. X., et al. (2002). A new area in the human brain associated with learning and memory: Immunohistochemical and functional MRI analysis. *Molecular Psychiatry, 7,* 1018–1022.

Shweder, R. A., Much, N. C., Mahapatra, M., & Park, L. (1994). The "big three" of morality (autonomy, community, and divinity), and the "big three" explanations of suffering, as well. In A. Brandt & P. Rozin (Eds.), *Morality and health.* Stanford, CA: Stanford University Press.

Siebert, S. E., & Kraimer, M. L. (2001). The five-factor model of personality and career success. *Journal of Vocational Behavior, 58,* 1–21.

Siegal, M. (1997). *Knowing children: Experiments in conversation and cognition* (2nd ed.). Hove, UK: Psychology Press/Erlbaum/Taylor & Francis.

Siegel, J. M. (2005). Clues to the functions of mammalian sleep. *Nature, 437,* 1264–1271.

Siegel, J. M., & Rogawski, M. A. (1988). A function for REM sleep: Regulation of noradrenergic receptor sensitivity. *Brain Research Review, 13,* 213–233.

Siegel, S. (2005). Drug tolerance, drug addiction, and drug anticipation. *Current Directions in Psychological Science, 14,* 296–300.

Siegel, S., Hirson, R. E., Krank, M. D., & McCully, J. (1982). Heroin "overdose" death: The contribution of drug associated environmental cues. *Science, 216,* 430–437.

Siegler, R. S. (1994). Cognitive variability: A key to understanding cognitive development. *Current Directions in Psychological Science, 3,* 1–4.

Siegler, R. S. (2006). Microgenetic analysis of learning. In W. Damon & R. M. Lerner (Series Eds.) & D. Kuhn & R. Siegler (Vol. Eds.), *Handbook of child psychology: Vol. 2. Cognition, perception, and language* (6th ed.). New York: Wiley.

Sigalovsky, N. (2003) Awareness under general anesthesia. *American Association of Nurse Anesthetists Journal, 71,* 373–379.

Sigmundsson, T., Suckling, J., Maier, M., Bullmore, E., Greenwood, K., Ron, M., et al. (2001). Structural abnormalities in frontal, temporal, and limbic regions and interconnecting white matter tracts in schizophrenic patients with prominent negative symptoms. *American Journal of Psychiatry, 158,* 234–243.

Silber, M. H. (2001). Sleep disorders. *Neurology Clinics, 19,* 173–186.

Silbert, M. H., & Pines, A. M. (1984). Pornography and sexual abuse of women. *Sex Roles, 10,* 857–868.

Silver, E. (1995). Punishment or treatment? Comparing the lengths of confinement of successful and unsuccessful insanity defendants. *Law and Human Behavior, 19,* 375–388.

Silver, E., Cirincione, C., & Steadman, H. J. (1994). Demythologizing inaccurate perceptions of the insanity defense. *Law and Human Behavior, 18,* 63–70.

Silver, S. M., Rogers, S., Knipe, J., & Colelli, G. (2005). EMDR therapy following the 9/11 terrorist attacks: A community-based intervention project in New York City. *International Journal of Stress Management, 12,* 29–42.

Silverman, K., Evans, A. M., Strain, E. C., & Griffiths, R. R. (1992). Withdrawal syndrome after the double-blind cessation of caffeine consumption. *New England Journal of Medicine, 327,* 1109–1114.

Silverthorne, C. (2001) Leadership effectiveness and personality: A cross cultural evaluation. *Personality & Individual Differences, 30,* 303–309.

Silvotti, L., Montanu, G., & Tirindelli, R. (2003). How mammals detect pheromones. *Journal of Endocrinological Investigation, 26,* 49–53.

Simcock, G., & Hayne, H. (2002). Breaking the barrier? Children fail to translate their preverbal memories into language. *Psychological Science, 13,* 225–231.

Simeon, D., Greenberg, J., Knutelska, M., Schmeidler, J., & Hollander, E. (2003). Peritraumatic reactions associated with the World Trade Center disaster. *The American Journal of Psychiatry, 160,* 1702–1705.

Simion, F., Cassia, V. M., Turati, C., & Valenza, E. (2003). Non-specific perceptual biases at the origins of face processing. In O. Pascalis & A. Slater (Eds.), *The development of face processing in infancy and early childhood* (pp. 13–25). Hauppauge, NY: Nova Science.

Simons, D. J., & Ambinder, M. S. (2005). Change blindness: Theory and consequences. *Current Directions in Psychological Science, 14,* 44–48.

Simons, T., & Roberson, Q. (2003). Why managers should care about fairness: The effects of aggregate justice perceptions on organizational outcomes. *Journal of Applied Psychology, 88,* 432–443.

Simonton, D. K. (1984). *Genius, creativity and leadership.* Cambridge: Harvard University Press.

Simonton, D. K. (1999). Creativity and genius. In L. Pervin & O. John (Eds.), *Handbook of personality research* (2nd ed., pp. 629–652). New York: Guilford.

Simonton, D. K. (2002). In C. R. Snyder & J. Shane (Eds.), *Handbook of positive psychology* (pp. 189–201). London: Oxford University Press.

Simpson, J. A., & Kenrick, D. T. (1997). *Evolutionary social psychology.* Mahwah, NJ: Erlbaum.

Simpson, S., Hurtley, S. M., & Marx, J. (2000). Immune cell networks. *Science, 290,* 79.

Simpson, S. H., Eurich, D. T., Majumdar, S. R., Padwal, R. S., Tsuyuki, R. T., et al. (2006). A meta-analysis of the association between adherence to drug therapy and mortality. *British Medical Journal, 333.*

Simpson, S. G., McMahon, F. J., McInnis, M. G., MacKinnon, D. F., Edwin, D., Folstein, S. E., et al. (2002). Diagnostic reliability of bipolar II disorder. *Archives of General Psychiatry, 59,* 736–740.

Sinclair, R. C., Hoffman, C., Mark, M. M., Martin, L. L., & Pickering, T. L. (1994). Construct accessibility and the misattribution of arousal. *Psychological Science, 5*(1), 15–19.

Singer, L. T., Arendt, R., Minnes, S., Farkas, K., Salvator, A., Kirchner, L., & Kliegman, R. (2002). Cognitive and motor outcomes o f cocaine-exposed infants. *Journal of the American Medical Association, 287*(15), 1952–1960.

Singer, L. T., Arendt, R., Minnes, S., Salvator, A., Siegel, C., & Lewis, B. A. (2001). Developing language skills of cocaine-exposed infants. *Pediatrics, 107,* 1057–1064.

Singer, L. T., Minnes, S., Short, E., Arendt, R., Farkas, K., Lewis, B., et al. (2004). Cognitive outcomes of preschool children with prenatal cocaine exposure. *Journal of the American Medical Association, 291,* 2448–2456.

Singh, H., & O'Boyle, M. W. (2004). Interhemispheric interaction during global-local processing in mathematically gifted adolescents, average-ability youth, and college students. *Neuropsychology, 18,* 371–377.

Sinha, R., & Parsons, O. A. (1996). Multivariate response patterning of fear and anger. *Cognition and Emotion, 10,* 173–198.

Sirvio, J. (1999). Strategies that support declining cholinergic neurotransmission in Alzheimer's disease patients. *Gerontology, 45,* 3–14.

Skaar, D. A., Shao, Y., Haines, J. L., Stenger, J. E., Jaworski, J., Martin, E. R., et al. (2005). Analysis of the RELN gene as a genetic risk factor for autism. *Molecular Psychiatry, 10,* 563–571.

Skinner, B. F. (1961). *Cumulative record* (3rd ed.). Englewood Cliffs, NJ: Prentice-Hall.

Skitka, L. J., Bauman, C. W., & Sargis, E. G. (2005). Moral conviction: Another contributor to attitude strength or something more? *Journal of Personality and Social Psychology, 88,* 895–917.

Skre, I., Onstad, S., Toregersen, S., Lyngren, S., & Kringlin, E. (2000). The heritability of common phobic fear: A twin study of a clinical sample. *Journal of Anxiety Disorders, 14,* 549–562.

Slade, E. P., & Wissow, L. S. (2004). Spanking in early childhood and later behavior problems: A prospective study of infants and young toddlers. *Pediatrics, 113,* 1321–1330.

Slamecka, N. J., & McElree, B. (1983). Normal forgetting of verbal lists as a function of their degree of learning. *Journal of Experimental Psychology: Learning, Memory, and Cognition, 9,* 384–397.

Slater, A., Mattock, A., Brown, E., & Bremmer, J. G. (1991). Form perception at birth. *Journal of Experimental Child Psychology, 51,* 395–406.

Slife, B. D., & Reber, J. S. (2001). Eclecticism in psychotherapy: Is it really the best substitute for traditional theories? In B. D. Slife, R. N. Williams, & S. H. Barlow (Eds.), *Critical issues in psychotherapy* (pp. 213–234). Thousand Oaks, CA: Sage.

Sloan, D. M., Marx, B. P., & Epstein, E. M. (2005). Further examination of the exposure model underlying the efficacy of written emotional disclosure. *Journal of Consulting and Clinical Psychology, 73,* 549–554.

Sloan, D. M., Strauss, M. E., & Wisner, K. L. (2001). Diminished response to pleasant stimuli by depressed women. *Journal of Abnormal Psychology, 110,* 488–493.

Slocombe, K. E., & Zuberbühler, K. (2005). Functionally referential communication in a chimpanzee. *Current Biology, 15,* 1779–1784.

Slomkowski, C., & Dunn, J. (1996). Young children's understanding of other people's beliefs and feelings and their connected communication with friends. *Developmental Psychology, 32,* 442–447.

Slotnick, S. D., & Schacter, D. L. (2004). A sensory signature that distinguishes true from fales memories. *Nature Neuroscience, 7,* 664–672.

Slovic, P., Peters, E., Finucane, M. L., & MacGregor, D. G. (2005). Affect, risk, and decision making. *Health Psychology, 24,* S35–S40.

Slutske, W., Eisen, S., Xian, H., True, W., Lyons, M. J., Goldberg, J., et al. (2001). A twin study of the association between pathological gambling and antisocial personality disorder. *Journal of Abnormal Psychology, 110,* 297–308.

Slutske, W. S., Heath, A. C., Dinwiddie, S. H., Madden, P. A., Bucholz, K. K., Dunne, M. P., et al. (1998). Common genetic risk factors for conduct disorder and alcohol dependence. *Journal of Abnormal Psychology, 107,* 363–374.

Small, B. J., & Bäckman, L. (1999). Time to death and cognitive performance. *Current Directions in Psychological Science, 8,* 168–172.

Small, D. M., Gregory, M. D., Mak, Y. E., Mesulam, M. M., & Parrish, T. (2003). Dissociation of neural representation of intensity and valuation in human gustation. *Neuron, 39,* 701–711.

Smeets, G., de Jong, P. J., & Mayer, B. (2000). If you suffer from a headache, then you have a brain tumor: Domain-specific reasoning 'bias' and hypochondriasis. *Behaviour Research and Therapy, 38,* 763–776.

Smith, A. M., Malo, S. A., Laskowski, E. R., Sabick, M., Cooney, W. P., III, Finnie, S. B., et al. (2000). A multidisciplinary study of the 'yips' phenomenon in golf: An exploratory analysis. *Sports Medicine, 30,* 423–437.

Smith, A. P., & Maben, A. (1993). Effects of sleep deprivation, lunch, and personality on performance, mood, and cardiovascular function. *Physiology and Behavior, 54*(5), 967–972.

Smith, D. (2003). Angry thoughts, at-risk hearts. *Monitor on Psychology, 34,* 46.

Smith, E. E., Geva, A., Jonides, J., Miller, A., Reuter-Lorenz, P., & Koeppe, R. A. (2001). The neural basis of task-switching in working memory: Effects of performance and aging. *Proceedings of the National Academy of Sciences, 98,* 2095–2100.

Smith, E., & Mackie, D. (2000). *Social psychology* (2nd ed.). Philadelphia: Taylor & Francis.

Smith, E., & Quellar, S. (2001). Mental representations. In A. Tesser & N. Schwarz (Eds.), *Blackwell handbook of social psychology: Intraindividual processes* (pp. 499–517). Oxford, UK: Blackwell.

Smith, G. C. S., & White, I. R. (2006). Predicting the risk for sudden infant death syndrome from obstetric characteristics: A retrospective cohort study of 505,011 live births. *Pediatrics, 117,* 60–66.

Smith, K. M., Larive, L. L., & Romanelli, F. (2002). Club drugs: Methylenedioxymethamphetamine, flunitrazepam, ketamine hydrochloride, and gamma-hydroxybutyrate. *American Journal of Health Systems Pharmacology, 59,* 1067–1076.

Smith, L. B., & Sera, M. D. (1992). A developmental analysis of the polar structure of dimensions. *Cognitive Psychology, 24,* 99–142.

Smith, M. L., Glass, G. V., & Miller, T. I. (1980). *The benefits of psychotherapy.* Baltimore: Johns Hopkins University Press.

Smith, N. T. (2002). A review of the published literature into cannabis withdrawal symptoms in human users. *Addiction, 97,* 621–632.

Smith, P. B., & Bond, M. H. (1999). *Social psychology across cultures: Analysis and perspectives* (2nd ed.). Boston: Allyn & Bacon.

Smith, P. C., & Kendall, L. M. (1963). Retranslation of expectations: An approach to the construction of unambiguous anchors for rating scales. *Journal of Applied Psychology, 47,* 149–155.

Smith, P. K., & Drew, L. M. (2002). Grandparenthood. In M. H. Bornstein (Ed.), *Handbook of parenting* (2nd ed.). Mahwah, NJ: Erlbaum.

Smith, S. L., & Donnerstein, E. (1998). Harmful effects of exposure to media violence: Learning of aggression, emotional desensitization, and fear. In R. G. Geen & E. Donnerstein (Eds.), *Human aggression* (pp. 230–247) San Diego: Academic Press.

Smith, S. M., Glenberg, A. M., & Bjork, R. A. (1978). Environmental context and human memory. *Memory & Cognition, 6,* 342–355.

Smith, S. M., Vela, E., & Williamson, J. E. (1988). Shallow input processing does not induce environmental context-dependent recognition. *Bulletin of the Psychonomic Society, 26,* 537–540.

Smith, S., & Freedman, D. G. (1983, April). *Mother-toddler interaction and maternal perception of child temperament in two ethnic groups: Chinese-American and European-American.* Paper presented at the meeting of the Society for Research in Child Development, Detroit, MI.

Smith, S. S., O'Hara, B. F., Persico, A. M., Gorelick, D. A., Newlin, D. B., Vlahov, D., et al. (1992). Genetic vulnerability to drug abuse: The D2 dopamine receptor Taq i B1 restriction fragment length polymorphism appears more frequently in polysubstance abusers. *Archives of General Psychiatry, 49,* 723–727.

Smith, T. B., Constantine, M. G., Dunn, T. W., Dinehart, J. M., & Montoya, J. A. (2006). Multicultural education in the mental health professions: A meta-analytic review. *Journal of Counseling Psychology, 53,* 132–145.

Smith, T. W., Orleans, C. T., & Jenkins, C. D. (2004). Prevention and health promotion: Decades of progress, new challenges, and an emerging agenda. *Health Psychology, 23,* 126–131.

Smith, T. W., & Ruiz, J. M. (2002). Psychosocial influences on the development and course of coronary heart disease: Current status and implications for research and practice. *Journal of Consulting & Clinical Psychology, 70,* 548–568.

Smith, V. L. (1991). Prototypes in the courtroom: Lay representations of legal concepts. *Journal of Personality and Social Psychology, 44,* 787–797.

Smith-Crowe, K., Burke, M. J., & Landis, R. S. (2003). Organizational climate as a moderator of safety knowledge–safety performance relationships. *Journal of Organizational Behavior, 24,* 861–876.

Smither, J. W., London, M., & Reilly, R. R. (2005). Does performance improve following multisource feedback? A theoretical model, meta-analysis, and review of empirical findings. *Personnel Psychology, 58,* 33–66.

Snarey, J. (1987). A question of morality. *Psychological Bulletin, 97,* 202–232.

Snellingen, T., Evans, J. R., Ravilla, T., & Foster, A. (2002). Surgical interventions for age-related cataract. *Cochrane Database System Review, 2,* CD001323.

Snowden, L. R., & Cheung, F. (1990). Use of inpatient mental health services by members of ethnic minority groups. *American Psychologist, 45,* 347–355.

Snyder, C. R., & Lopez, S. J. (2006). *Handbook of positive psychology*. New York: Oxford University Press.

Snyder, C. R., & Lopez, S. J. (2007). *Positive psychology: The scientific and practical explorations of human strengths*. New York: Sage.

Sohlberg, S., & Jansson, B. (2002). Unconscious responses to "mommy and I are one": Does gender matter? In R. F. Bornstein & J. M. Masling (Eds.), *The psychodynamics of gender and gender role. Vol. 10: Empirical studies in psychoanalytic theories* (pp. 165–201). Washington, DC, US: American Psychological Association.

Soken, N. H., & Pick, A. D. (1992). Intermodal perception of happy and angry expressive behaviors by seven-month-old infants. *Child Development, 63,* 787–795.

Sokolowska, M., Siegel, S., & Kim, J. A. (2002). Intraadministration associations: Conditional hyperalgesia elicited by morphine onset cues. *Journal of Experimental Psychology: Animal Behavior Processes, 28,* 309–20.

Solomon, A. (1998, January 12). Anatomy of melancholy. *New Yorker,* pp. 46–61.

Solomon, R. L. (1980). The opponent-process theory of acquired motivation: The costs of pleasure and the benefits of pain. *American Psychologist, 35,* 691–712.

Solomon, R. L., Kamin, L. J., & Wynne, L. C. (1953). Traumatic avoidance learning: The outcomes of several extinction procedures with dogs. *Journal of Abnormal and Social Psychology, 48,* 291–302.

Solomonson, A. L., & Lance, C. E. (1997). Examination of the relationship between true halo and halo error in performance ratings. *Journal of Applied Psychology, 82,* 665–674.

Solowij, N., Stephens, R. S., Roffman, R. A., Babor, T., Kadden, R., Miller, M., et al. (2002). Cognitive functioning of long-term heavy cannabis users seeking treatment. *Journal of American Medical Association, 287,* 1123–1131.

Sorce, J., Emde, R., Campos, J., & Klinnert, M. (1981, April). *Maternal emotional signaling: Its effect on the visual cliff behavior of one-year-olds.* Paper presented at the meeting of the Society for Research in Child Development, Boston, MA.

Sørensen, H. J., Mortensen, E. L., Reinisch, J. M., & Mednick, S. A. (2003). Do hypertension and diuretic treatment in pregnancy increase the risk of schizophrenia in offspring? *American Journal of Psychiatry, 160,* 464–468.

Sorrentino, R. M., & Roney, C. J. R. (2000). *The uncertain mind: Individual differences in facing the unknown.* Philadelphia: Psychology Press.

Sowdon, J. (2001). Is depression more prevalent in old age? *Australian & New Zealand Journal of Psychiatry, 35,* 782–787.

Sowell, E. R., Delis, D., Stiles, J., & Jernigan, T. L. (2001). Improved memory functioning and frontal lobe maturation between childhood and adolescence: A structural MRI study. *Journal of the International Neuropsychological Society, 7,* 312–322.

Sowell, E. R., Peterson, B. S., Thompson, P. M., Welcome, S. E., Henkenius, A. L., & Toga, A. W. (2003). Mapping cortical change across the human life span. *Nature Neuroscience, 6,* 309–315.

Sowell, T. (2005). *Black rednecks and white liberals.* San Francisco: Encounter Books.

Spanagel, R., & Weiss, F. (1999). The dopamine hypothesis of reward: Past and current status. *Trends in Neuroscience, 22,* 521–527.

Spangler, G., Fremmer-Bombik, E., & Grossman, K. (1996). Social and individual determinants of infant attachment security and disorganization. *Infant Mental Health Journal, 17,* 127–139.

Spanier, C., Frank, E., McEachran, A. B., Grochocinski, V. J., & Kupfer, D. J. (1996). The prophylaxis of depressive episodes in recurrent depression following discontinuation of drug therapy: Integrating psychological and biological factors. *Psychological Medicine, 26,* 461–475.

Spanos, N. P. (1994). Multiple identity enactments and multiple personality disorder: A sociocognitive perspective. *Psychological Bulletin, 116,* 143–165.

Spanos, N. P. (1996). *Multiple identities and false memories: A sociocognitive perspective.* Washington, DC: American Psychological Association.

Spanos, N. P., Burnley, M. C. E., & Cross, P. A. (1993). Response expectancies and interpretations as determinants of hypnotic responding. *Journal of Personality and Social Psychology, 65*(6), 1237–1242.

Sparks, K., Cooper, C., Fried, Y., & Shirom, A. (1997). The effects of hours of work on health: A meta-analytic review. *Journal of Occupational and Organizational Psychology, 70,* 391–408.

Sparks, K., Faragher, B., & Cooper, C. L. (2001). Well-being and occupational health in the 21st century workplace. *Journal of Occupational and Organizational Psychology, 74,* 489–509.

Spears, R., Postmes, T., Lea, M., & Watt, S. E. (2001). A SIDE view of social influence. In J. P. Forgas & K. D. Williams (Eds.), *Social influence: Direct and indirect processes. The Sydney symposium of social psychology* (pp. 331–350). Philadelphia, PA: Psychology Press.

Speckhard, A. (2002). Voices from the inside: Psychological responses to toxic disasters. In J. M. Havenaar & J. G. Cwikel (Eds.), *Toxic turmoil: Psychological and societal consequences of ecological disasters* (pp. 217–236). New York: Plenum.

Specter, M. (2004, February 2). Miracle in a bottle. *New Yorker,* 64–75.

Specter, M. (2005, May 23). Higher risk. *New Yorker,* 38–45.

Spector, P. E. (1985). Measurement of human service staff satisfaction: Development of the Job Satisfaction Survey. *American Journal of Community Psychology, 13,* 693–713.

Spector, P. E. (2002). Employee control and occupational stress. *Current Directions in Psychological Science, 11,* 133–136.

Spector, P. E. (2003). *Industrial & organizational psychology: Research and practice* (3rd ed.). New York: Wiley.

Spector, P. E., Fox, S., & Domalgaski, T. (2006). Emotions, violence, and counter-productive work behavior. In E. K. Kelloway, J. Barling, & J. J. Hurrell (Eds.), *Handbook of workplace violence* (pp. 29–46). Thousand Oaks, CA: Sage.

Spelke, E. S., Breinlinger, K., Macomber, J., & Jacobson, K. (1992). Origins of knowledge. *Psychological Review, 99,* 605–632.

Spence, S. H. (2003). Social skills training with children and young people: Theory, evidence, and practice. *Child and Adolescent Mental Health, 8,* 84–96.

Spence, S. H., Donovan, C., Brechman-Toussaint, M. (2000). The treatment of childhood social phobia: The effectiveness of a social skills training-based, cognitive-behavioral intervention, with and without parental involvement. *Journal of Child Psychology and Psychiatry and Allied Disciplines, 41,* 713–726.

Spence, S. H., Sheffield, J. K., & Donovan, C. L. (2005). Long-term outcome of a school-based, universal approach to prevention of depression in adolescents. *Journal of Consulting and Clinical Psychology, 73,* 160–167.

Spencer, T. J. (2002). Attention-deficit/hyperactivity disorder. *Archives of Neurology, 59,* 314–316.

Sperry, R. W. (1968). Hemisphere deconnection and unity in conscious awareness. *American Psychologist, 23,* 723–733.

Spiegel, D. (Ed.). (1994). *Dissociation: Culture, mind, and body.* Washington, DC: American Psychiatric Press.

Spiegel, D. A., & Bruce, T. J. (1997). Benzodiazepines and exposure-based cognitive behavior therapies for panic disorder: Conclusions from combined treatment trials. *American Journal of Psychiatry, 151,* 876–881.

Spinath, F. M., Harlaar, N., Ronald, A., & Plomin, R. (2004). Substantial genetic influence on mild mental impairment in early childhood. *American Journal of Mental Retardation, 109,* 34–43.

Spinath, F. M., Price, T. S., Dale, P. S., & Plomin, R. (2004). Genetic and environmental origins of language disability and ability. *Child Development, 75,* 445–454.

Spinhoven, P., Kuile, M., Kole-Snijders, A. M., Mansfeld, H. M., Ouden, D. L., & Vlaeyen, J. W. (2005). Catastrophizing and internal pain control as mediators of outcome in the multidisciplinary treatment of chronic low back pain. *European Journal of Pain, 8,* 211–219.

Spira, J. L. (2001). Study design casts doubt on value of St. John's wort in treating depression. *British Medical Journal, 322,* 493.

Spitzer, R. L., Gibbon, M., Skodol, A. E., & Williams, J. B. W., & First, M. B. (Eds.). (1994). *DSM-IV casebook: A learning companion to the Diagnostic and Statistical Manual of Mental Disorders* (4th ed.). Washington, DC: American Psychiatric Association.

Springer, K., & Belk, A. (1994). The role of physical contact and association in early contamination sensitivity. *Developmental Psychology, 30*(6), 864–868.

Spychalski, A. C., Quinones, M. A., Gaugler, B. B., & Pohley, K. (1997). A survey of assessment center practices in organizations in the U.S. *Personnel Psychology, 50,* 71–90.

Squire, L. R. (1986). Mechanisms of memory. *Science, 232,* 1612–1619.

Squire, L. R. (1992). Memory and the hippocampus: A synthesis from findings with rats, monkeys, and humans. *Psychological Review, 99,* 195–231.

Srivastava, A., Locke, E. A., & Bartol, K. M. (2001). Money and subjective well-being: It's not the money, it's the motives. *Journal of Personality and Social Psychology, 80,* 959–971.

Srivastava, S., John, O. P., Gosling, S. D., & Potter, J. (2003). Development of personality in early and middle adulthood: Set like plaster or persistent change? *Journal of Personality and Social Psychology, 84,* 1041–1053.

Sroka, J. J., & Braida, L. D. (2005). Human and machine consonant recognition. *Speech Communication, 45,* 401–423.

St. Clair, M. (1999). *Object relations and self-psychology: An introduction.* Pacific Grove, CA: Brooks/Cole.

St. John, W. (2003, September 28). In U.S. funeral industry, triple-wide isn't a trailer. *The New York Times,* p. 1.

Stacey, J., & Biblarz, T. J. (2001). (How) Does the sexual orientation of parents matter? *American Sociological Review, 66,* 159–183.

Staddon, J. E. R., & Ettinger, R. H. (1989). *Learning: An introduction to the principles of adaptive behavior.* San Diego: Harcourt Brace Jovanovich.

Stafford, R. S., & Radley, D. C. (2003). National trends in antiobesity medication use. *Archives of Internal Medicine, 163,* 1046–1050.

Stahl, S. M. (2002). Selective actions on sleep or anxiety by exploiting GABA-A/benzodiazepine receptor subtypes. *Journal of Clinical Psychiatry, 63,* 179–180.

Staley, J. K., Sanacora, G., Tamagnan, G., Maciejewski, P. K., Malison, R. T., Berman, R. M., et al. (2006). Sex differences in diencephalon serotonin transporter availability in major depression. *Biological Psychiatry, 59,* 40–47.

Stanley, B. G., Willett, V. L., Donias, H. W., & Ha-Lyen, H. (1993). The lateral hypothalamus: A primary site mediating excitatory aminoacid-elicited eating. *Brain Research, 63*(1–2), 41–49.

Stansfeld, S. A., & Marmot, M.G. (Eds.). (2002). *Stress and the heart: Psychosocial pathways to coronary heart disease.* London: BMJ Books.

Stanton-Hicks, M., & Salamon, J. (1997). Stimulation of the central and peripheral nervous system for the control of pain. *Journal of Clinical Neurophysiology, 14,* 46–62.

Stapleton, S. (2001, February 19). Miles to go before I sleep: America is becoming a culture of sleeplessness. *Amednews.* Retrieved December 7, 2004, from http://www.ama-assn.org/sci-pubs/amnews/pick_01/hlsa0219.htm

Starkman, N., & Rajani, N. (2002). The case for comprehensive sex education. *AIDS Patient Care & STDs, 16,* 313–318.

Starkstein, S. E., Fedoroff, J. P., Price, T. R., Leigguarda, R., & Robinson, R. G. (1992). Anosognosia in patients with cerebrovascular lesions: A study of causative factors. *Stroke, 23,* 1446–1453.

Stasser, G. (1991). Pooling of unshared information during group discussion. In S. Worchel, W. Wood, & J. Simpson (Eds.), *Group processes and productivity.* Beverly Hills, CA: Sage.

Stasser, G., Stewart, D., & Wittenbaum, G. M. (1995). Expert roles and information exchange during discussion: The importance of knowing who knows what. *Journal of Experimental Social Psychology, 31,* 244–265.

Staudt, M., Grodd, W., Niemann, G., Wildgruber, D., Erb, M., & Krageloh-Mann, I. (2001). Early left periventricular brain lesions induce right hemispheric organization of speech. *Neurology 2001, 57,* 122–125.

Stauffer, J. M., & Buckley, M. R. (2005). The existence and nature of racial bias in supervisory ratings. *Journal of Applied Psychology, 90,* 586–591.

Staw, B. M., Bell, N. E., & Clausen, J. A. (1986). The dispositional approach to job attitudes: A lifetime longitudinal test. *Administrative Science Quarterly, 31,* 56–77.

Staw, B. M., & Cohen-Charash, Y. (2005). The dispositional approach to job satisfaction: More than a mirage, but not yet an oasis. *Journal of Organizational Behavior, 26,* 59–78.

Steadman, H. J. (1993). *Reforming the insanity defense: An evaluation of pre- and post- Hinckley reforms.* New York: Guilford.

Steele, C. M. (1997). A threat in the air: How stereotypes shape intellectual identity and performance. *American Psychologist, 52,* 613–629.

Steele, C. M., & Aronson, J. (2000). Stereotype threat and the intellectual test performance of African Americans. In C. Stangor (Ed.), *Stereotypes and prejudice: Essential readings* (pp. 369–389). Philadelphia: Psychology Press/Taylor & Francis.

Steele, T. D., McCann, U. D., & Ricaurte, G. A. (1994). 3,4-methylenedioxy-methamphetamine (MDMA, ecstasy): Pharmacology and toxicology in animals and humans. *Addiction, 89*(5), 539–551.

Stefanacci, L., Buffalo, E. A., Schmolck, H., & Squire, L. R. (2000). Profound amnesia after damage to the medial temporal lobe: A neuroanatomical and neuropsychological profile of patient E. P. *Journal of Neuroscience, 20*(18), 7024–7036.

Steffen, P. R., McNeilly, M., Anderson, N., & Sherwood, A. (2003). Effects of perceived racism and anger inhibition on ambulatory blood pressure in African Americans. *Psychosomatic Medicine, 65,* 746–750.

Steiger, H., Young, S. N., Ng Ying Kin, N. M. K., Koerner, N., Israel, M., Lageix, P., & Paris, J. (2001). Implications of impulsive and affective symptoms for serotonin function in bulimia nervosa. *Psychological Medicine, 31,* 85–95.

Stein, D. M., & Lambert, M. J. (1995). Graduate training in psychotherapy: Are therapy outcomes enhanced? *Journal of Consulting and Clinical Psychology, 63,* 182–196.

Stein, E. (1999). *The mismeasure of desire: The science, theory and ethics of sexual orientation.* New York: Oxford University Press.

Stein, K. D., Goldman, M. S., & Del Boca, F. K. (2000). The influence of alcohol expectancy priming and mood manipulation on subsequent alcohol consumption. *Journal of Abnormal Psychology, 109,* 106–115.

Stein, M. A. (1993, November 30). Spacewalking repair team to work on Hubble flaws; shower head inspires a device to improve focusing ability. *Los Angeles Times,* A1, A5.

Stein, M. B., Chavira, D. A., & Jang, K. L. (2001). Bringing up bashful baby: Developmental pathways to social phobia. *Psychiatric Clinics of North America, 24,* 661–675.

Steinberg, L., Dornbusch, S. M., & Brown, B. B. (1992). Ethnic differences in adolescent achievement: An ecological perspective. *American Psychologist, 47,* 723–729.

Steinberg, L., Lamborn, S. D., Darling, N., Mounts, N. S., & Dornbusch, S. M. (1994). Over-time changes in adjustment and competence among adolescents from authoritative, authoritarian, indulgent, and neglectful families. *Child Development, 65,* 754–770.

Steindler, D. A. & Pincus, D. W. (2002). Stem cells and neuropoiesis in the adult human brain. *Lancet, 359,* 1047–1054.

Steiner, J. E., Glaser, D., Hawilo, M. E., & Berridge, K. C. (2001). Comparative expression of hedonic impact: Affective reactions to taste by human infants and other primates. *Neuroscience and Biobehavioral Reviews, 25,* 53–74.

Steiner, J. M., & Fahrenberg, J. (2000). Authoritarianism and social status of former members of the Waffen-SS and SS and of the Wehrmacht: An extension and reanalysis of the study published in 1970. *Koelner Zeitschrift fuer Soziologie und Sozialpsychologie, 52,* 329–348.

Stepanski, E. J., & Perlis, M. L. (2000). Behavioral sleep medicine. An emerging subspecialty in health psychology and sleep medicine. *Journal of Psychosomatic Research, 49,* 343–347.

Stephan, K. E., Marshall, J. C., Friston, K. J., Rowe, J. B., Ritzl, A., Zilles, K., & Fink, G. R. (2003). Lateralized cognitive processes and lateralized task control in the human brain. *Science, 301,* 384–386.

Stephens, R. S., Roffman, R. A., & Simpson, E. E. (1994). Treating adult marijuana dependence: A test of the relapse prevention model. *Journal of Consulting and Clinical Psychology, 62*(1), 92–99.

Steptoe, A., Wardle, J., & Marmot, M. (2005). Positive affect and health-related neuroendocrine, cardiovascular, and inflammatory processes. *Proceedings of the National Academy of Sciences of the USA, 102,* 6508–6512.

Steriade, M., & McCarley, R. W. (1990). *Brainstem control of wakefulness and sleep.* New York: Plenum.

Stern, K., & McClintock, M. K. (1998). Regulation of ovulation by human pheromones. *Nature, 392,* 177–179.

Sternberg, R. J. (1985). *Beyond IQ: A triarchic theory of human intelligence.* Cambridge, England: Cambridge University Press.

Sternberg, R. J. (1988a). Triangulating love. In R. J. Sternberg & M. L. Barnes (Eds.), *The psychology of love* (pp. 500–520). New Haven: Yale University Press.

Sternberg, R. J. (1988b). *The triarchic mind.* New York: Cambridge Press.

Sternberg, R. J. (1996). *Successful intelligence.* New York: Simon & Schuster.

Sternberg, R. J. (1997a). Construct validation of a triangular love scale. *European Journal of Social Psychology, 27,* 313–335.

Sternberg, R. J. (1997b). *Thinking styles.* Cambridge, England: Cambridge University Press.

Sternberg, R. J. (1999). Ability and expertise: It's time to replace the current model of intelligence. *American Educator Spring 1999,* pp. 10–51.

Sternberg, R. J. (2001). What is the common thread of creativity?: Its dialectical relation to intelligence and wisdom. *American Psychologist, 56,* 360–362.

Sternberg, R. J. (2004). Culture and intelligence. *American Psychologist, 59,* 325–338.

Sternberg, R. J., & Dess, N. K. (2001). Creativity for the new millennium. *American Psychologist, 56,* 332.

Sternberg, R. J., & Grigorenko, E. L. (Eds.). (2004a). *Creativity: From potential to realization.* Washington, DC: APA Books.

Sternberg, R. J., & Grigorenko, E. L. (Eds.). (2004b). *Culture and competence: Contexts of life success.* Washington, DC: APA Books.

Sternberg, R. J., Hojjat, M., & Barnes, M. L. (2001). Empirical tests of aspects of a theory of love as a story. *European Journal of Personality, 15,* 199–218.

Sternberg, R. J., & Kaufman, J. C. (1998). Human abilities. *Annual Review of Psychology, 49,* 479–502.

Sternberg, R. J., Lautrey, J., & Lubart, T. I. (2003). Where are we in the field of intelligence, how did we get here, and where are we going? In R. J. Sternberg, J. Lautrey, et al. (Eds.), *Models of intelligence: International perspectives* (pp. 3–25). Washington, DC: American Psychological Association.

Sternberg, R. J., & Lubart, T. I. (1992). Buy low and sell high: An investment approach to creativity. *Current Directions in Psychological Science, 1*(1), 1–5.

Sternberg, R. J., & O'Hara, L. A. (1999). Creativity and intelligence. In R. J. Sternberg, et al. (Eds.), *Handbook of creativity* (pp. 251–272). New York: Cambridge University Press.

Sternberg, R. J., Wagner, R. K., Williams, W. M., & Horvath, J. A. (1995). Testing common sense. *American Psychologist, 50*, 912–927.

Sternberg, R. J., & Williams, W. M. (1997). Does the graduate record examination predict meaningful success of graduate training of psychologists? A Case Study. *American Psychologist, 52*, 630–641.

Stevens, A. (1996). *Private myths: Dreams and dreaming.* Cambridge, MA: Harvard University Press.

Stevens, J. C., & Pollack, M. H. (2005). Benzodiazepines in clinical practice: Consideration of their long-term use and alternative agents. *Journal of Clinical Psychiatry, 66*(Suppl. 2), 21–27.

Stevens, R. D., & Bhardwaj, A. (2006). Approach to the comatose patient. *Critical Care Medicine, 34*(1), 31–41.

Stevenson, H. (1992). *A long way from being number one: What we can learn from East Asia.* Washington, DC: Federation of Behavior, Psychological and Cognitive Sciences.

Stevenson, R. J., & Boakes, R. A. (2003). A mnemonic theory of odor perception. *Psychological Review, 110*, 340–364.

Stewart, G. L. (2006). A meta-analytic review of relationships between team design features and team performance. *Journal of Management, 32*, 29–55.

Stewart, J. H. (2005). Hypnosis in contemporary medicine. *Mayo Clinic Proceedings, 80*, 511–524.

Stewart, W. F., Ricci, J. A., Chee, E., Hahn, S. R., & Morganstein, D. (2003). Cost of lost productive work time among US workers with depression. *Journal of the American Medical Association, 289*, 3135–3144.

Stewart-Williams, S. (2004). The placebo puzzle: Putting together the pieces. *Health Psychology, 23*, 198–206.

Stewart-Williams, S., & Podd, J. (2004). The placebo effect: Dissolving the expectancy versus conditioning debate. *Psychological Bulletin, 130*, 324–340.

Stice, E. (2001). A prospective test of the dual-pathway model of bulimic pathology: Mediating effects of dieting and negative affect. *Journal of Abnormal Psychology, 110*, 124–135.

Stice, E., & Fairburn, C. G. (2003). Dietary and dietary-depressive subtypes of bulimia nervosa show differential symptom presentation, social impairment, comorbidity, and course of illness. *Journal of Consulting and Clinical Psychology, 71*, 1090–1094.

Stice, E., Ragan, J., & Randall, P. (2004). Prospective relations between social support and depression: Differential direction of effects for parent and peer support? *Journal of Abnormal Psychology, 113*, 155–159.

Stice, E., & Shaw, H. (2004). Eating disorder prevention programs: A meta-analytic review. *Psychological Bulletin, 130*, 206–227.

Stickgold, R. (2005). Sleep-dependent memory consolidation. *Nature, 437*, 1272–1278.

Stickgold, R., James, L., & Hobson, J. A. (2000). Visual discrimination learning requires sleep after training. *Nature Neuroscience, 3*, 1237–1238.

Stickgold, R., Malia, A., Maguire, D., Roddenberry, D., & O'Connor, M. (2000). Replaying the game: Hypnagogic images in normals and amnesics. *Science, 290*, 350–353.

Stickgold, R., Rittenhouse, C. D., & Hobson, J. A. (1994). Dream splicing: A new technique for assessing thematic coherence in subjective reports of mental activity. *Consciousness and Cognition, 3*(1), 114–128.

Stillman, J. A. (2002). Gustation: Intersensory experience par excellence. *Perception, 31*, 1491–1500.

Stillwell, M. E. (2002). Drug-facilitated sexual assault involving gamma-hydroxybutyric acid. *Journal of Forensic Science, 47*, 1133–1134.

Stoff, D. M., Breiling, J., & Maser, J. D. (Eds.). (1997). *Handbook of antisocial behavior.* New York: Wiley.

Stone, J. (2003). Self-consistency for low self-esteem in dissonance processes: The role of self-standards. *Personality and Social Psychology Bulletin, 29*, 846–858.

Stone, J., & Cooper, J. (2001). A self-standards model of cognitive dissonance. *Journal of Experimental Social Psychology, 37*, 228–243.

Stone, L. D., & Pennebaker, J. W. (2002). Trauma in real time: Talking and avoiding online conversations about the death of Princess Diana. *Basic and Applied Social Psychology, 24*, 173–183.

Stone, S. P., Halligan, P. W., & Greenwood, R. J. (1993). The incidence of neglect phenomena and related disorders in patients with acute left or right hemisphere stroke. *Age and Ageing, 22*, 46–52.

Stoney, C. M., Bausserman, L., Niaura, R., Marcus, B., & Flynn, M. (1999). Lipid reactivity to stress: II. Biological and behavioral influences. *Health Psychology, 18*, 251–261.

Stoney, C. M., & Finney, M. L. (2000). Social support and stress: Influences on lipid reactivity. *International Journal of Behavioral Medicine, 7*, 111–126.

Stoney, C. M., & Hughes, J. W. (1999). Lipid reactivity among men with a parental history of myocardial infarction. *Psychophysiology, 36*, 484–490.

Stoney, C. M., & Matthews, K. A. (1988). Parental history of hypertension and myocardial infarction predicts cardiovascular responses to behavioral stressors in middle-aged men and women. *Psychophysiology, 25*, 269–277.

Stoney, C. M., Niaura, R., Bausserman, L., & Matacin, M. (1999). Lipid reactivity to stress: I. Comparison of chronic and acute stress responses in middle-aged airline pilots. *Health Psychology, 18*, 241–250.

Strain, E. C., Mumford, G. K., Silverman, K., & Griffiths, R. R. (1994). Caffeine dependence syndrome: Evidence from case histories and experimental evaluations. *Journal of the American Medical Association, 272*(13), 1043–1048.

Strakowski, S. M., DelBello, M. P., & Adler, C. M. (2005). The functional neuroanatomy of bipolar disorder: A review of neuroimaging findings. *Molecular Psychiatry, 10*, 105–116.

Strang, J., Witten, J., & Hall, W. (2000). Improving the quality of the cannibis debate: Defining the different domains. *British Medical Journal, 320*, 108–110.

Strauss, E., & Wada, J. (1983). Lateral preferences and cerebral speech dominance. *Cortex, 19*(2), 165–177.

Strauss, R. S., & Pollack, H. A. (2001). Epidemic increases in childhood overweight: 1986–1998. *Journal of the American Medical Association, 286*, 2845–2848.

Streissguth, A. P., Barr, H. M., Bookstein, F. L., Sampson, P. D., & Olson, H. C. (1999). The long-term neurocognitive consequences of prenatal alcohol exposure: A 14-year study. *Psychological Science, 10*, 186–190.

Strickland, T., Ranganath, V., Lin, K.-M., Poland, R., Mendoza, R., & Smith, M. (1991). Psychopharmacologic considerations in the treatment of Black American populations. *Psychopharmacology Bulletin, 27*, 441–448.

Strohmetz, D. B., Rind, B., Fisher, R., & Lynn, M. (2002). Sweetening the till: The use of candy to increase restaurant tipping. *Journal of Applied Social Psychology, 32*, 300–309. Stromberg, C. D., Haggarty, D. J., Leibenluft, R. F., McMillian, M. H., Mishkin, B., et al. (1988). *The psychologist's legal handbook.* Washington, DC: Council for the National Register of Health Service Providers in Psychology.

Strongman, K. T., & Kemp, S. (1991). Autobiographical memory for emotion. *Bulletin of the Psychonomic Society, 29*, 195–198.

Stroop, J. R. (1935). Studies of interference in serial verbal reactions. *Journal of Experimental Psychology, 18*, 643–662.

Strote, J., Lee, J. E., & Wechsler, H. (2002). Increasing MDMA use among college students: Results of a national survey. *Journal of Adolescent Health, 30*, 64–72.

Strunk, D. R., Lopez, H., & DeRubeis, R. J. (2006). Depressive symptoms are associated with unrealistic negative predictions of future life events. *Behaviour Research and Therapy, 44*, 875–896.

Stuart, R. B. (2004). Twelve practical suggestions for achieving multicultural competence. *Professional Psychology: Theory and Practice, 35*, 3–9.

Sturm, R. (2003). Increases in clinically severe obesity in the United States, 1986–2000. *Archives of Internal Medicine, 163*, 2146–2148.

Stürmer, T., Hasselbach, P., & Amelang, M. (2006). Personality, lifestyle, and risk of cardiovascular disease and cancer: Follow-up of population based cohort. *British Medical Journal, 332*, 1359.

Sue, S. (1998). In search of cultural competence in psychotherapy and counseling. *American Psychologist, 53*, 440–448.

Sue, S., & Okazaki, S. (1990). Asian-American educational achievements: A phenomenon in search of an explanation. *American Psychologist, 45*, 913–920.

Sue, S., Zane, N., & Young, K. (1994). Research on psychotherapy with culturally diverse populations. In A. E. Bergin & S. L. Garfield (Eds.), *Handbook of psychotherapy and behavior change.* New York: Wiley.

Sufka, K. J. & Price, D. D. (2002). Gate control theory reconsidered. *Brain and Mind, 3*, 277–290.

Suh, E., Diener, E., & Fujita, F. (1996). Events and subjective well-being: Only recent events matter. *Journal of Personality and Social Psychology, 70,* 1091–1102.

Suinn, R. M. (2001). The terrible twos: Anger and anxiety. *American Psychologist, 56,* 27–36.

Sullivan, H. S. (1954). *The psychiatric interview.* New York: Norton.

Sullivan, J. W., & Horowitz, F. D. (1983). The effects of intonation on infant attention: The role of the rising intonation contour. *Journal of Child Language, 10,* 521–534.

Sullivan, P. F., Kendler, K. S., & Neale, M. C. (2003). Schizophrenia as a complex trait: Evidence from a meta-analysis of twin studies. *Archives of General Psychiatry, 60,* 1187–1192.

Suls, J., & Bunde, J. (2005). Anger, anxiety, and depression as risk factors for cardiovascular disease: The problems and implications of overlapping affective dispositions. *Psychological Bulletin, 131,* 260–300.

Suls, J., & Rothman, A. (2004). Evolution of the biopsychosocial model: Prospects and challenges for health psychology. *Health Psychology, 23,* 119–125.

Suls, J., & Wan, C. K. (1993). The relationship between trait hostility and cardiovascular reactivity: A quantitative review and analysis. *Psychophysiology, 30,* 1–12.

Sundberg, N., & Sue, D. (1989). Research and research hypotheses about effectiveness in intercultural counseling. In P. Pederson, J. Draguns, W. Lonner, & J. Trimble (Eds.), *Counseling across cultures* (3rd ed.). Honolulu: University of Hawaii Press.

Suomi, S. (1999). Attachment in rhesus monkeys. In J. Cassidy & P. Shaver (Eds.), *Handbook of attachment* (pp. 181–197). New York: Guilford.

Suomi, S. (2004). Aggression, serotonin, and gene-environment interactions in rhesus monkeys. In J. T. Cacioppo & G. G. Berntson (Eds.), *Essays in social neuroscience* (pp. 15–27). Cambridge, MA: MIT Press.

Suslow, T., Ohrmann, P., Bauer, J., Rauch, A. V., Schwindt, W., Arolt, V., et al. (2006). Amygdala activation during masked presentation of emotional faces predicts conscious detection of threat-related faces. *Brain and Cognition, 61,* 243–248.

Suzdak, P. D., Glowa, J. R., Crawley, J. N., Schwartz, R. D., Skolnick, P., & Paul, S. M. (1986). A selective imidazobenzodiazepine antagonist of ethanol in the rat. *Science, 234,* 1243–1247.

Svartberg, M., Stiles, T. C., & Seltzer, M. H. (2004). Randomized, controlled trial of the effectiveness of short-term dynamic psychotherapy and cognitive therapy for cluster C personality disorders. *American Journal of Psychiatry, 161,* 810–817.

Swaab, D. E., & Hofman, M. A. (1995). Sexual differentiation of the human hypothalamus in relation to gender and sexual orientation. *Trends in Neuroscience, 18*(6) 264–270.

Swaab, D. F., Chung, W. C., Kruijver, F. P., Hofman, M. A., & Ishunina, T. A. (2001). Structural and functional sex differences in the human hypothalamus. *Hormones and Behavior, 40,* 93–98.

Swan, G. E. (1996, December). Some elders thrive on working into late life. *APA Monitor,* p. 35.

Swan, G. E., & Carmelli, D. (1996). Curiosity and mortality in aging adults: A 5-year follow-up of the Western Collaborative Group Study. *Psychology and Aging, 11,* 449–453.

Swann, W. B., Jr., De La Ronde, C., & Hixon, J. G. (1994). Authenticity and positivity strivings in marriage and courtship. *Journal of Personality and Social Psychology, 66,* 857–869.

Swarte, N. B., van der Lee, M. L., van der Bom, J. G., van den Bout, J., & Heintz, A. P. M. (2003). Effects of euthanasia on the bereaved family and friends: A cross sectional study. *British Medical Journal, 327,* 189.

Sweller, J., & Gee, W. (1978). Einstellung: The sequence effect and hypothesis theory. *Journal of Experimental Psychology: Human Learning and Memory, 4,* 513–526.

Swets, J. A. (1992). The science of choosing the right decision threshold in high-stakes diagnostics. *American Psychologist, 47,* 522–532.

Swets, J. A. (1996). *Signal detection theory and ROC analysis in psychology and diagnostics.* New Jersey: Erlbaum.

Swets, J. A., Dawes, R. M., & Monahan, J. (2000). Psychological science can improve diagnostic decisions. *Psychological Science in the Public Interest, 1,* 1–26.

Swindle, R., Jr., Heller, K., Pescosolido, B., & Kikuzawa, S. (2000). Responses to nervous breakdowns in America over a 40-year period: Mental health policy implications. *American Psychologist, 55,* 740–749.

Swithers, S. E., & Hall, W. G. (1994). Does oral experience terminate ingestion? *Appetite, 23*(2), 113–138.

Symons, D. (1979). *The evolution of human sexuality.* Oxford, UK: Oxford University Press.

Szasz, T. (2003). The psychiatric protection order for the "battered mental patient." *British Medical Journal, 327,* 1449–1451.

Szatmari, P., Jones, M. B., Zwaigenbaum, L., & MacLean, J. E. (1998). Genetics of autism: Overview and new directions. *Journal of Autism and Developmental Disorders, 28,* 351–368.

Szegedi, A., Kohnen, R., Dienel, A., & Kieser, M. (2005). Acute treatment of moderate to severe depression with hypericum extract WS 5570 (St John's wort): Randomised controlled double blind non-inferiority trial versus paroxetine. *British Medical Journal, 330,* 503.

Szeszko, P. R., Ardekani, B. A., Ashtari, M., Malhotra, A. K., Robinson, D. G., Bilder, R. M., et al. (2005). White matter abnormalities in obsessive-compulsive disorder: A diffusion tensor imaging study. *Archives of General Psychiatry, 62,* 782–790.

Szymanski, K., Garczynski, J., & Harkins, S. (2000). The contribution of the potential for evaluation to coaction effects. *Group Processes and Intergroup Relations, 3,* 269–283.

T

Tabert, M. H., Manly, J. J., Liu, X., Pelton, G. H., Rosenbaum, S., Jacobs, M., et al. (2006). Neuropsychological prediction of conversion to Alzheimer disease in patients with mild cognitive impairment. *Archives of General Psychiatry, 63,* 916–924.

Taggar, S., Hackett, R., & Saha, S. (1999). Leadership emergence in autonomous work teams: Antecedents and outcomes. *Personnel Psychology, 52,* 899–926.

Tagliabue, J. (1999, January 28). Devil gets his due, but Catholic church updates exorcism rites. *International Herald Tribune,* p. 6.

Tailby, C., Wright, L. L., Metha, A. B., & Calford, M. B. (2005). Activity-dependent maintenance and growth of dendrites in adult cortex. *Proceedings of the National Academy of Sciences of the USA, 102,* 4631–4636.

Takashima, A., Petersson, K.M., Rutters, F., Tendolkar, I., Jensen, O., Zwarts, M. J., et al. (2006). Declarative memory consolidation in humans: A prospective functional magnetic resonance imaging study. *Proceedings of the National Academy of Sciences of the USA, 103,* 756–761.

Takeuchi, N., Uchimura, N., Hashizume, Y., Mukai, M., Etoh, Y., Yamamoto, K., et al. (2001). Melatonin therapy for REM behavior disorder. *Psychiatry and Clinical Neurosciences, 55,* 267–269.

Takkouche, B., Etminan, M., & Montes-Martinez, A. (2005). Personal use of hair dyes and risk of cancer. *Journal of the American Medical Association, 293,* 2516–2525.

Talarico, J. F., & Rubin, D. C. (2003). Confidence, not consistency, characterizes flashbulb memories. *Psychological Science, 14,* 455–461.

Talbott, J. A. (2004). Deinstitutionalization: Avoiding the disasters of the past. *Psychiatric Services, 55,* 1112–1115.

Talmi, D., Grady, C. L., Goshen-Gottstein, Y., & Moscovitch, M. (2005). Neuroimaging the serial position curve: A test of single-store versus dual-store models. *Psychological Science, 16,* 716–723.

Tamminga, C. A., & Holcomb, H. H. (2005). Phenotype of schizophrenia: A review and formulation. *Molecular Psychiatry, 10,* 27–39.

Tan, G., Hammond, D. C., & Joseph, G. (2005). Hypnosis and irritable bowel syndrome: A review of efficacy and mechanism of action. *American Journal of Clinical Hypnosis, 47,* 161–178.

Tanaka, H., Taira, K., Arakawa, M., Toguti, H., Urasaki, C., Yamamoto, Y., et al. (2001). Effects of short nap and exercise on elderly people having difficulty sleeping. *Psychiatry and Clinical Neurosciences, 55,* 173–174.

Tanaka-Matsumi, J., & Higginbotham, H. N. (1994). Clinical application of behavior therapy across ethnic and cultural boundaries. *Behavior Therapist, 17,* 123–126.

Tanda, G., Pontieri, F. E., & Di Chiara, G. (1997). Cannabinoid and heroin activation of mesolimbic dopamine transmission by a common mu1 opioid receptor mechanism. *Science, 276,* 2048–2050.

Tan-Laxa, M. A., Sison-Switala, C., Rintelman, W., & Ostrea, E. M. (2004). Abnormal auditory brainstem response among infants with prenatal cocaine exposure. *Pediatrics, 113,* 357–360.

Tannen, D. (2001). *You just don't understand: Women and men in conversation.* New York: HarperCollins.

Tanner, J. M. (1978). *Foetus into man: Physical growth from conception to maturity.* London: Open Books.

Tarabar, A. F. & Nelson, L. S. (2004). The gamma-hydroxybutyrate withdrawal syndrome. *Toxicological Reviews, 23,* 45–49.

Tarr, S. J., & Pyfer, J. L. (1996). Physical and motor development of neonates/infants prenatally exposed to drugs in utero: A meta-analysis. *Adapted Physical Activity Quarterly, 13,* 269–287.

Task Force on Promotion and Dissemination of Psychological Procedures. (1995). Training in and dissemination of empirically validated psychological treatments: Report and recommendations. *Clinical Psychologist, 48,* 3–23.

Tasker, F., & Golombok, S. (1995). Adults raised as children in lesbian families. *American Journal of Orthopsychiatry, 65*(2), 203–215.

Tassi, P., & Muzet, A. (2001). Defining states of consciousness. *Neuroscience and Biobehavioral Reviews, 25,* 175–191.

Taub, A. (1998). Thumbs down on acupuncture. *Science, 279,* 159.

Taub, E. (2004). Harnessing brain plasticity through behavioral techniques to produce new treatments in neurorehabilitation. *American Psychologist, 59,* 692–704.

Tavris, C. (2003). Mind games: Psychological warfare between therapists and scientists. *The Chronicle of Higher Education, 49,* B7–B9.

Tavris, C. (2004, January 3). *From Dora to Jane Doe: The use and abuse of case studies.* Paper presented at the 26th Annual National Institute on the Teaching of Psychology, St. Petersburg, Florida.

Taylor, H. A., & Tversky, B. (1992). Spatial mental models derived from survey and route descriptions. *Journal of Memory and Language, 31,* 261–292.

Taylor, J. G. (2002). Paying attention to consciousness. *Trends in Cognitive Science, 6,* 206–210.

Taylor, R. L., & Richards, S. B. (1991). Patterns of intellectual differences of Black, Hispanic, and White children. *Psychology in the Schools, 28,* 5–8.

Taylor, S. (2004). Efficacy and outcome predictors for three PTSD treatments: Exposure therapy, EMDR, and relaxation training. In S. Taylor (Ed.), *Advances in the treatment of posttraumatic stress disorder: Cognitive-behavioral perspectives* (pp. 13–37). New York: Springer.

Taylor, S., Peplau, A., & Sears, D. (2003). *Social psychology* (11th ed.). Upper Saddle River, NJ: Prentice-Hall.

Taylor, S., Thordarson, D. S., Maxfield, L., Fedoroff, I. C., Lovell, K., & Ogrodniczuk, J. (2003). Comparative efficacy, speed, and adverse effects of three PTSD treatments: Exposure therapy, EMDR, and relaxation training. *Journal of Consulting and Clinical Psychology, 71,* 330–338.

Taylor, S. E. (1995). *Health psychology* (3rd ed.). New York: McGraw-Hill.

Taylor, S. E. (1999). *Health psychology* (4th ed.). New York: McGraw-Hill.

Taylor, S. E. (2002). *Health psychology* (5th ed.). New York: McGraw-Hill.

Taylor, S. E., & Aspinwall, L. G. (1996). Mediating processes in psychosocial stress: Appraisal, coping, resistance, and vulnerability. In H. B. Kaplan (Ed.), *Psychosocial stress: Perspectives on structure, theory, life course, and methods* (pp. 71–110). New York: Academic Press.

Taylor, S. E., Dickerson, S. S., & Klein, L. C. (2002). Toward a biology of social support. In C. R. Snyder & S. L. Lopez (Eds.), *Handbook of positive psychology* (pp. 556–569). London: Oxford University Press.

Taylor, S. E., Gonzaga, G. C., Klein, L. C., Hu, P., Greendale, G. A., & Seeman, T. E. (2006). Relation of oxytocin to psychological stress responses and hypothalamic-pituitary-adrenocortical axis activity in older women. *Psychosomatic Medicine, 68,* 238–245.

Taylor, S. E., Kemeny, M. E., Aspinwall, L. G., Schneider, S. G., Rodriguez, R., & Herbert, M. (1992). Optimism, coping, psychological distress, and high-risk sexual behavior among men at risk for acquired immunodeficiency syndrome (AIDS). *Journal of Personality and Social Psychology, 63,* 460–473.

Taylor, S. E., Kemeny, M. E., Reed, G. M., Bower, J. E., & Gruenewald, T. L. (2000). Psychological resources, positive illusions, and health. *American Psychologist, 55,* 99–109.

Taylor, S. E., Klein, L. C., Lewis, B. P., Gruenewald, T. L., Gurung, R. A. R., & Updegraff, J. A. (2000). Biobehavioral responses to stress in females: Tend-and-befriend, not fight-or-flight. *Psychological Review, 107,* 411–429.

Taylor, S. E., Lerner, J. S., Sherman, K. D., Sage, R. M., & McDowell, N. K. (2003). Are self-enhancing cognitions associated with health or unhealthy biological profiles? *Journal of Personality and Social Psychology, 85,* 605–615.

Taylor, S. E., Lewis, B. P., Gruenewald, T. L., Gurung, R. A. R., Updegraff, J. A., & Klein, L. C. (2002). Sex differences in biobehavioral responses to threat: Reply to Geary and Flinn (2002). *Psychological Review, 109,* 751–753.

Taylor, S. E., & Lobel, M. (1989). Social comparison activity under threat: Downward evaluation and upward contacts. *Psychological Review, 96,* 569–575.

Teigen, K. H. (1994). Yerkes-Dodson: A law for all seasons. *Theory and Psychology, 4*(4), 525–547.

Telegraph Correspondent. (2005, April 18). Scratching your cars was art, says vandal. *Daily Telegraph,* p. 5.

Tellegen, A., Lykken, D. T., Bouchard, T. J., Wilcox, K. J., Segal, N. L., & Rich, S. (1988). Personality similarity in twins reared apart and together. *Journal of Personality and Social Psychology, 54,* 1031–1039.

Teng, Y. D., Lavik, E. B., Qu, X., Park, K. I., Ourednik, J., Zurakowski, D., et al. (2002). Functional recovery following traumatic spinal cord injury mediated by a unique polymer scaffold seeded with neural stem cells. *Proceedings of the National Academy of Science, 99,* 3024–3029.

Teplin, L. A., McClelland, G. M., Abram, K. M., & Weiner, D. A. (2005). Crime victimization in adults with severe mental illness. *Archives of General Psychiatry, 62,* 911–921.

Ter Riet, G., Kleijnen, J., & Knipschild, P. (1990). Acupuncture and chronic pain: A criteria-based meta-analysis. *Journal of Clinical Epidemiology, 43,* 1191–1199.

Terman, J. S., Terman, M., Lo, E. S., & Cooper, T. B. (2001). Circadian time of morning light administration and therapeutic response in winter depression. *Archives of General Psychiatry, 58,* 69–75.

Terman, L. M. (1906). Genius and stupidity: A study of the intellectual process of seven "bright" and seven "stupid" boys. *Pedagogical Seminary, 13,* 307–373.

Terman, L. M. (1916). *The measurement of intelligence.* Boston: Houghton Mifflin.

Terman, L. M., & Oden, M. H. (1947). *The gifted child grows up: Vol. 4. Genetic studies of genius.* Stanford, CA: Stanford University Press.

Terman, L. M., & Oden, M. H. (1959). *The gifted group at midlife.* Stanford, CA: Stanford University Press.

Terman, M., & Terman, J. S. (2005). Light therapy for seasonal and nonseasonal depression: Efficacy, protocol, safety, and side effects. *CNS Spectrums, 10,* 647–663.

Tesser, A. (2001). Self-esteem: The frequency of temporal-self and social comparisons in people's personal appraisals. In A. Tesser & N. Schwarz (Eds.), *Blackwell handbook of social psychology: Intraindividual processes* (pp. 479–498). Oxford, UK: Blackwell.

Thaker, G. K., & Carpenter, W. T., Jr. (2001). Advances in schizophrenia. *Nature Medicine, 7,* 667–671.

Thaler, E. R., Kennedy, D. W., & Hanson, C.W. (2001). Medical applications of electronic nose technology: Review of current status. *American Journal of Rhinology, 15,* 291–295.

Thanos, P. K., Volkow, N. D., Freimuth, P., Umegaki, H., Ikari, H., Roth, G., et al. (2001). Overexpression of dopamine D2 receptors reduces alcohol self-administration. *Journal of Neurochemistry, 78,* 1094–1103.

Thase, M. E. (2002). Antidepressant effects: The suit may be small, but the fabric is real. *Prevention & Treatment, 5,* Article 32. Retrieved December 13, 2004, from http://www.journals.apa.org/prevention/volume5/pre0050032c.html

Thelen, E. (1995). Motor development: A new synthesis. *American Psychologist, 50,* 79–95.

Theofilopoulos, S., Goggi, J., Riaz, S. S., Jauniaux, E., Stern, G. M., & Bradford, H. F. (2001). Parallel induction of the formation of dopamine and its metabolites with induction of tyrosine hydroxylase expression in foetal rat and human cerebral cortical cells by brain-derived neurotrophic factor and glial-cell derived neurotrophic factor. *Brain Research: Developmental Brain Research, 127,* 111–122.

Thiessen, E. D., Hill, E. A., & Saffran, J. R. (2005). Infant-directed speech facilitates word segmentation. *Infancy, 7,* 53–71.

Thom, A., Sartory, G., & Jöhren, P. (2000). Comparison between one-session psychological treatment and benzodiazepine in dental phobia. *Journal of Consulting and Clinical Psychology, 68,* 378–387.

Thomas, A., & Chess, S. (1977). *Temperament and development.* New York: Brunner/Mazel.

Thomas, E. L., & Robinson, H. A. (1972). *Improving reading in every class: A sourcebook for teachers.* Boston: Allyn & Bacon.

Thompson, C., Koon, E., Woodwell, W., Jr., & Beauvais, J. (2002). *Training for the next economy: An ASTD state of the industry report on trend in employer-provided training in the United States.* Washington, DC: American Society for Training and Development.

Thompson, D. S., & Pollack, B. G. (2001, August 26). Psychotropic metabolism: Gender-related issues. *Psychiatric Times, 14.* Available: http://www.mhsource.com/pt/p010147.html

Thompson, J. K. (1996). Introduction: Assessment and treatment of binge eating disorder. In J. K. Thompson (Ed.), *Body image, eating disorders, and obesity* (pp. 1–22). Washington, DC: American Psychological Association.

Thompson, P. M., Giedd, J. N., Woods, R. P., Macdonald, D., Evans, A. C., & Toga, A. W. (2000). Growth patterns in the developing brain detected by using continuum mechanical tensor maps. *Nature, 404,* 190–193.

Thompson, P. M., Hayashi, K. M., Simon, S. L., Geaga, J. A., Hong, M. S., Sui, Y., et al. (2004). Structural abnormalities in the brains of human subjects who use methamphetamine. *Journal of Neuroscience, 24,* 6028–6036.

Thompson, R. A. (2006). The development of the person: Social understanding, relationships, self, conscience. In W. Damon & R. M. Lerner (Series Eds.) & N. Eisenberg (Vol. Ed.), *Handbook of child psychology: Vol. 3. Social, emotional, and personality development* (6th ed.). New York: Wiley.

Thompson, R. R., George, K., Walton, J. C., Orr, S. P., & Benson, J. (2006). Sex-specific influences of vasopressin on human social communication. *Proceedings of the National Academy of Sciences of the USA, 103,* 7889–7894.

Thompson-Brenner, H., Glass, S., & Westen, D. (2003). A multidimensional meta-analysis of psychotherapy for bulimia nervosa. *Clinical Psychology: Science and Practice, 10,* 269–287.

Thomson, C. P. (1982). Memory for unique personal events: The roommate study. *Memory & Cognition, 10,* 324–332.

Thoresen, C. J., Kaplan, S. A., Barsky, A. P., Warren, C. R., & deChermont, K. (2003). The affective underpinnings of job perceptions and attitudes: A meta-analytic review and integration. *Psychological Bulletin, 129,* 914–945.

Thorndike, E. L. (1898). Animal intelligence: An experienced study of the associative process in animals. *Psychological Monographs, 2*(Whole No. 8).

Thorndike, E. L. (1905). *The elements of psychology.* New York: Seiler.

Thorndike, R. L., & Hagen, E. P. (1996). *Form 5 CogAT interpretive guide of school administrators: All levels.* Chicago: Riverside.

Thorngren, J. M., & Kleist, D. M. (2002). Multiple family group therapy: An interpersonal/postmodern approach. *Family Journal–Counseling and Therapy for Couples and Families, 10,* 167–176.

Tiihonen, J., Kuikka, J., Bergstrom, K., Hakola, P., Karhu, J., Ryynänen, O.-P., & Föhr, J. (1995). Altered striatal dopamine re-uptake site densities in habitually violent and non-violent alcoholics. Nature Medicine, 1(7), 654–657.

Tinbergen, N. (1989). *The study of instinct.* Oxford, UK: Clarendon.

Tindale, R. S., & Kameda, T. (2000). "Social sharedness" as a unifying theme for information processing in groups. *Group Processes and Intergroup Relations, 3,* 123–140.

Tobler, P. N., Fiorillo, C. D., & Schultz, W. (2005). Adaptive coding of reward value by dopamine neurons. *Science, 307,* 1642–1645.

Tohen, M., Zarate, C. A., Jr., Hennen, J., Khalsa, H.-M. K., Strakowski, S. M., Gebre-Medhin, P., et al. (2003). The McLean-Harvard first-episode mania study: Prediction of recovery and first recurrence. *American Journal of Psychiatry, 160,* 2099–2107.

Tolman, E. C., & Honzik, C. H. (1930). Introduction and removal of reward and maze performance in rats. *University of California Publication in Psychology, 4,* 257–265.

Tomasello, M. (2000). Culture and cognitive development. Current Directions in Psychological Science, 9, 37–40.

Tomes, H. (1999, April). The need for cultural competence. *APA Monitor,* p. 31.

Toni, N., Buchs, P. A., Nikonenko, I., Bron, C. R., & Muller, D. (1999). LTP promotes formation of multiple spine synapses between a single axon terminal and a dendrite. *Nature, 402,* 421–425.

Torasdotter, M., Metsis, M., Henriksson, B. G., Winblad, B., & Mohammed, A. H. (1998). Environmental enrichment results in higher levels of nerve growth factor mRNA in the rat visual cortex and hippocampus. *Behavior and Brain Research, 93,* 83–90.

Trabasso, T. R., & Bower, G. H. (1968). *Attention in learning.* New York: Wiley.

Tramer, M. R., Carroll, D., Campbell, F. A., Reynolds, D. J., Moore, R. A., & McQuay, H. J. (2001). Cannabinoids for control of chemotherapy induced nausea and vomiting: quantitative systematic review. *British Medical Journal, 323,* 16–21.

Treboux, D., Crowell, J. A., & Waters, E. (2004). When "new" meets "old": Configurations of adult attachment representations and their implications for marital functioning. *Developmental Psychology, 40,* 295–314.

Treiber, F. A., Musante, L., Kapuku, G., Davis, C., Litaker, M., & Davis, H. (2001). Cardiovascular (CV) responsivity and recovery to acute stress and future CV functioning in youth with family histories of CV disease: A 4-year longitudinal study. *International Journal of Psychophysiology, 41,* 65–74.

Treisman, A. (1999). Feature binding, attention, and object perception. In G. W. Humphreys, J. Duncan., & A. Treisman (Eds.), *Attention, space, and action* (pp. 91–111). New York: Oxford University Press.

Tremblay, R. E., Pagani-Kurtz, L., Mâsse, L., Vitaro, F., & Pihl, R. O. (1995). A bimodal preventive intervention for disruptive kindergarten boys: Its impact through mid-adolescence. *Journal of Consulting and Clinical Psychology, 63,* 560–568.

Tremblay, R. E., Pihl, R. O., Vitaro, F., & Dobkin, P. (1994). Predicting early onset of male antisocial behavior from preschool behavior. *Archives of General Psychiatry, 51,* 732–739.

Trevor, C. O. (2001). Interactions among actual ease-of-movement determinants and job satisfaction in the prediction of voluntary turnover. *Academy of Management Journal, 44,* 621–638.

Triandis, H. C. (1998). Vertical and horizontal individualism and collectivism: Theory and research implications for international management. In J. L. C. Cheng, R. B. Peterson, et al. (Eds.), *Advances in international comparative management* (Vol. 12, pp. 7–35). Stamford, CT: JAI Press.

Triandis, H. C., & Trafimow, D. (2001). Cross-national prevalence of collectivism. In C. Sedikides & M. B. Brewer (Eds.), *Individual self, relational self, collective self* (pp. 259–276). New York: Psychology Press.

Trierweiler, S. J., Neighbors, H. W., Munday, C., Thompson, E. E., Binion, V. J., & Gomez, J. P. (2000). Clinician attributions associated with the diagnosis of schizophrenia in African American and non-African American patients. *Journal of Consulting and Clinical Psychology, 68,* 171–175.

Trifiletti, L. B., Shields, W., McDonald, E., Reynaud, F., & Gielen, A. (2006). Tipping the scales: Obese children and child safety seats. *Pediatrics, 117,* 1197–1202.

Trillin, A. S. (2001, January 29). Betting your life. *New Yorker,* pp. 38–41.

Trope, Y., Cohen, O., & Alfieri, T. (1991). Behavior identification as a mediator of dispositional inference. *Journal of Personality and Social Psychology, 61,* 873–883.

Tropp, L. R., & Pettigrew, T. F. (2005). Relationships between intergroup contact and prejudice among minority and majority status groups. *Psychological Science, 16,* 951–957.

Tropp, L. R., & Wright, S. (2001). In group identification as the inclusion of ingroup in the self. *Personality and Social Psychology Bulletin, 27,* 585–600.

Trower, P. (1995). Adult social skills: State of the art and future directions. In W. O'Donohue & L. Krasner (Eds.), *Handbook of psychological skills training: Clinical techniques and applications* (pp. 54–80). Boston: Allyn & Bacon.

Truelsen, T., & Bonita, R. (2003). Advances in ischemic stroke epidemiology. *Advances in Neurology, 92,* 1–12.

Trull, T. J., & Sher, K. J. (1994). Relationship between the five-factor model of personality and Axis I disorders in a nonclinical sample. *Journal of Personality and Social Psychology, 103,* 350–360.

Trunzo, J. J., & Pinto, B. M. (2003). Social support as a mediator of optimisim and distress in breast cancer survivors. *Journal of Consulting and Clinical Psychology, 71,* 805–811.

Tryon, W. W. (2005). Possible mechanisms for why desensitization and exposure therapy work. *Clinical Psychology Review, 25,* 67–95.

Tsai, J. L., Knutson, B., & Fung, H. H. (2006). Cultural variation in affect evaluation. *Journal of Personality and Social Psychology, 90,* 288–307.

Tseng, W., Kan-Ming, M., Li-Shuen, L., Guo-Qian, C., Li-Wah, O., & Hong-Bo, Z. (1992). Koro epidemics in Guangdong China. *Journal of Nervous and Mental Disease, 180,* 117–123.

Tsuang, M. T., Stone, W. S., & Faraone, S. V. (2000). Toward reformulating the diagnosis of schizophrenia. *American Journal of Psychiatry, 157,* 1041–1950.

Tuch, S. A., & Martin, J. K. (1991). Race in the workplace: Black/white differences in the sources of job satisfaction. *The Sociological Quarterly, 32,* 103–116.

Tucker, C. M., & Herman, K. C. (2002). Using culturally sensitive theories and research to meet the academic needs of low-income African American children. *American Psychologist, 57,* 762–773.

Tuller, D. (2004, January 27). Britain poised to approve medicine derived from marijuana. *The New York Times,* p. F5.

Tulving, E. (1983). *Elements of episodic memory.* New York: Oxford University Press.

Tulving, E. (2000). Introduction to memory. In M. S. Gazzaniga (Ed.), *The new cognitive neurosciences* (pp. 727–732). Cambridge, MA: MIT Press.

Tulving, E. (2002). Episodic memory: From mind to brain. *Annual Review of Psychology, 53,* 1–25.

Tulving, E., & Psotka, J. (1971). Retroactive inhibition in free recall: Inaccessibility of information available in the memory store. *Journal of Experimental Psychology, 87,* 1–8.

Tuomilehto, J., Lindstrom, J., Eriksson, J. G., Valle, T. T., Hamalainen, H., Ilanne-Parikka, P., et al. (2001). Prevention of type 2 diabetes mellitus by changes in lifestyle among subjects with impaired glucose tolerance. *New England Journal of Medicine, 344,* 1343–1350.

Turati, C. (2004). Why faces are not special to newborns: An alternative account of the face preference. *Current Directions in Psychological Science, 13,* 5–8.

Turiel, E. (2006). The development of morality. In W. Damon & R. M. Lerner (Series Eds.) & N. Eisenberg (Vol. Ed.), *Handbook of child psychology: Vol. 3. Social, emotional, and personality development* (6th ed.). New York: Wiley.

Turkheimer, E., Haley, A., Waldron, M., D'Onofrio, B., & Gottesman, I. I. (2003). Socioeconomic status modifies heritability of IQ in young children. *Psychological Science, 14,* 623–628.

Turkheimer, E., & Waldron M. (2000). Nonshared environment: A theoretical, methodological, and quantitative review. *Psychological Bulletin, 126,* 78–108.

Turkington, C. (1987). Special talents. *Psychology Today,* pp. 42–46.

Turkington, D., Kingdon, D., & Weiden, P. J. (2006). Cognitive therapy for schizophrenia. *American Journal of Psychiatry, 163,* 365–373.

Turnbull, C. (1961). Some observations regarding the experiences and behavior of the Bambuti Pygmies. *American Journal of Psychology, 74,* 304–308.

Turner, J. C. (1991). *Social influence.* Pacific Grove, CA: Brooks/Cole.

Turner, R. J., & Lloyd, D. A. (2004). Stress burden and the lifetime incidence of psychiatric disorder in young adults: Racial and ethnic contrasts. *Archives of General Psychiatry, 61,* 481–488.

Turner, S. M., DeMers, S. T., Fox, H. R., & Reed, G. M. (2001). APA's guidelines for test user qualifications: An executive summary. *American Psychologist, 56,* 1099–1113.

Tuszynski, M. H., Grill, R., Jones, L. L., McKay, H. M., & Blesch, A. (2002). Spontaneous and augmented growth of axons in the primate spinal cord: Effects of local injury and nerve growth factor-secreting cell grafts. *Journal of Comparative Neurology, 449,* 88–101.

Tuszynski, M. H., Thal, L., Pay, M., Salmon, D. P., U, H. S., Bakay, R., et al. (2005). A phase 1 clinical trial of nerve growth factor gene therapy for Alzheimer disease. *Nature Medicine, 11,* 551–555.

Tversky, A., & Kahneman, D. (1974). Judgment under uncertainty: Heuristics and biases. *Science, 185,* 1124–1131.

Tversky, A., & Kahneman, D. (1981). The framing of decisions and the psychology of choice. *Science, 211,* 453–458.

Tversky, A., & Kahneman, D. (1991). Loss aversion in riskless choice: A reference dependent model. *Quarterly Journal of Economics, 106,* 1039–1061.

Tversky, A., & Kahneman, D. (1993). Probabilistic reasoning. In A. Goldman (Ed.), *Readings in philosophy and cognitive science* (pp. 43–68). Cambridge: MIT Press.

Tversky, B., & Tuchin, M. (1989). A reconciliation of the evidence on eyewitness testimony: Comments on McCloskey and Zaragoza. *Journal of Experimental Psychology: General, 118,* 86–91.

Tyler, K. L., & Malessa, R. (2000). The Goltz-Ferrier debates and the triumph of cerebral localizationalist theory. *Neurology, 55*(7), 1015–1024.

Tziner, A., Murphy, K. R., & Cleveland, J. N. (2005). Contextual and rater factors affecting rating behavior. *Group and Organization Management, 30,* 89–98.

U

U.K. Statistical Bulletin. (1999). *Electro convulsive therapy: Survey covering the period from January 1999 to March 1999, England.* London: Department of Health.

U.S. Census Bureau. (2004). *Current population survey, 2003 and 2004 annual social and economic supplements.* Washington, DC: U.S. Bureau of the Census.

U.S. Department of Health and Human Services. (2001a). *Alzheimer's disease fact sheet.* Washington, DC: U.S. Public Health Service (NIH Publication No. 01–3431).

U.S. Department of Health and Human Services. (2001b). *Mental health: Culture, race, and ethnicity. A supplement to mental health: A report of the Surgeon General.* Washington, DC: United States Public Health Service.

U.S. Department of Health and Human Services. (2001c). *Women and smoking: A report of the Surgeon General.* Atlanta: Centers for Disease Control and Prevention.

U.S. Department of Justice. (1999). *Eyewitness evidence: A guide for law enforcement.* Washington, DC: National Institute of Justice.

U.S. Department of Justice. (2002). *Recidivism of prisoners released in 1994.* Washington, DC: U.S. Department of Justice, Bureau of Justice Statistics.

U.S. Department of Labor. (2001–2002). *Occupational Outlook Quarterly Winter 2001–2002, 45*(4). Washington, DC: U.S. Government Printing Office.

U.S. Drug Enforcement Administration. (2002). Drug intelligence brief: OxyContin. Retrieved September 12, 2004, from http://www.usdoj.gov/dea/pubs/intel/02017/02017.html.

U.S. Department of Justice. (2005). *Crime characteristics.* Retrieved July 9, 2005, from http://www.ojp.usdoj.gov/bjs/cvict_c.htm#relate.

U.S. Surgeon General. (1999). *Mental health: A report of the surgeon general.* Rockville, MD: U.S. Department of Health and Human Services.

Uchida, Y., Kitayama, S., Mesquita, B., & Reyes, J. A. (2001, June). *Interpersonal sources of happiness: The relative significance in Japan, the Philippines, and the United States.* Paper presented at Annual Convention of American Psychological Society, Toronto, Canada.

Uchino, B. N., Cacioppo, J. T. & Kiecolt-Glaser, J. K. (1996). The relationship between social support and physiological process: A review with emphasis on underlying mechanisms and implications for health. *Psychological Bulletin, 119,* 488–531.

Udry, J. R., & Chantala, K. (2003). Masculinity-femininity guides sexual union formation in adolescents. *Personality and Social Psychology Bulletin, 30,* 44–55.

Ugajin, T., Hozawa, A., Ohkubo, T., Asayama, K., Kikuya, M., Obara, T., et al. (2005). White-coat hypertension as a risk factor for the development of home hypertension: The Ohasama study. *Archives of Internal Medicine, 165,* 1541–1546.

Uhl, G. R., Sora, I., & Wang, Z. (1999). The mu opiate receptor as a candidate gene for pain: polymorphisms, variations in expression, nociception, and opiate responses. *Proceedings of the National Academy of Sciences, 96,* 7752–7755.

Uleman, J. S., Blader, S. L., & Todorov, A. (2005). Implicit impressions In R. Hassin, J. Uleman, & J. Bargh (Eds.), *The new unconscious* (pp. 362– 392). New York: Oxford University Press.

Ulett, G. A. (2003). Acupuncture, magic, and make-believe. *The Skeptical Inquirer, 27*(2), 47–50.

Ullmann, L. P., & Krasner, L. (1965). *Case studies in behavior modification.* New York: Holt, Rinehart & Winston.

Ulrich, W. L., Richards, P. S., & Bergin, A. E. (2000). Psychotherapy with Latter-Day Saints. In P. S. Richards & A. E. Bergin (Eds.), *Handbook of psychotherapy and religious diversity* (pp. 185–209). Washington DC: American Psychological Association.

Ungerleider, L. G., & Mishkin, M. (1982). Two cortical visual systems. In D. J. Ingle, M. A. Goodale & R. J. W. Mansfield (Eds.), *Analysis of visual behavior.* Cambridge, MA: MIT Press.

Ungless, M. A., Whistler, J. L., Malenka, R. C., & Bonci, A. (2001). Single cocaine exposure in vivo induces long-term potentiation in dopamine neurons. *Nature, 411,* 583–587.

Urbach, T. P., Windmann, S. S., Payne, D. G., & Kutas, M. (2005). Mismaking memories. *Psychological Science, 16,* 19–24.

Urry, H. L., Nitschke, J. B., Dolski, I., Jackson, D. C., Dalton, K. M., Mueller, C. J., et al. (2004). Making a life worth living: Neural correlates of well-being. *Psychological Science, 15,* 367–372.

Uttal, W. R. (2003). *The new phrenology: The limits of localizing cognitive processes in the brain.* Cambridge, MA: MIT Press.

Uvnas-Moberg, K., Arn, I., & Magnusson, D. (2005). The psychobiology of emotion: The role of the oxytocinergic system. *International Journal of Behavioral Medicine, 12,* 59–65.

Uwe, H. (2005). Therapeutic alliance: The best synthesizer of social influences on the therapeutic situation? On links to other constructs, determinants of its effectiveness, and its role for research in psychotherapy in general. *Psychotherapy Research, 15,* 9–23.

V

Vaitl, D., Birbaumer, N., Gruzelier, J., Jamieson, G. A., Kotchoubey, B., Kubler, A., et al. (2005). Psychobiology of altered states of consciousness. *Psychological Bulletin, 131,* 98–127.

Valent, F., Brusaferro, S., & Barbone, F. (2001). A case-crossover study of sleep and childhood injury. *Pediatrics, 107,* e23.

Valenza, E., Simion, F., Assia, V. M., & Umilta, C. (1996). Face preference at birth. *Journal of Experimental Psychology: Human Perception and Performance, 22,* 892–903.

Van Bezooijen, R., Otto, S. A., & Heenan, T. A (1983). Recognition of vocal expression of emotion: A three-nation study to identify universal characteristics. *Journal of Cross-Cultural Psychology, 14,* 387–406.

Van den Bergh, B. R., & Marcoen, A. (2004). High antenatal maternal anxiety is related to ADHD symptoms, externalizing problems, and anxiety in 8- and 9-year-olds. *Child Development, 75,* 1085–1097.

Van der Molen, J. H. W. (2004). Violence and suffering in television news: Toward a broader conception of harmful television content for children. *Pediatrics, 113,* 1771–1775.

Van Deusen, K. M. (2004). Bilateral stimulation in EMDR: A replicated single-subject component analysis. *Behavior Therapist, 27,* 79–86.

Van Eerde, W., & Thierry, H. (1996). Vrooms's expectancy models and work-related criteria: A meta-analysis. *Journal of Applied Psychology, 81,* 575–586.

van Griensven, F., Chakkradband, S., Thienkrua, W., Pengjuntr, W., Cardozo, B. L., Tantipiwatanaskul, P., et al. (2006). Mental health problems among adults in tsunami-affected areas in southern Thailand. *Journal of the American Medical Association, 296,* 537–548.

Van Hiel, A., & Mervielde, I. (2004). Openness to experience and boundaries in the mind: Relationships with cultural and economic conservative beliefs. *Journal of Personality, 72,* 659–686.

Van Hoesen, G. W., Hyman, B. T., & Damasio, A. R. (1991). Entorhinal cortex pathology in Alzheimer's disease. *Hippocampus, 1*(1), 1–8.

van IJzendoom, M. H., & Juffer, F. (2005). Adoption as a successful natural intervention enhancing adopted children's IQ and school performance. *Current Directions in Psychological Science, 14,* 326–330.

van IJzendoorn, M. H. (1995). Adult attachment representations, parental responsiveness, and infant attachment: A meta-analysis on the predictive validity of the Adult Attachment Interview. *Psychological Bulletin, 117,* 387–403.

Van Sickel, A. D. (1992). Clinical hypnosis in the practice of anesthesia. *Nurse Anesthesiologist, 3,* 67–74.

van Wassenhove, V., Grant, K. W., & Poeppel, D. (2005). Visual speech speeds up the neural processing of auditory speech. *Proceedings of the National Academy of Sciences of the USA, 102,* 1181–1186.

van Wel, F., ter Bogt, T., & Raaijmakers, Q. (2002). Changes in the parental bond and the well-being of adolescents and young adults. *Adolescence, 37*(146), 317–333.

VandeCreek, L., Janus, M.-D., Pennebaker, J. W., & Binau, B. (2002). Praying about difficult experiences as self-disclosure to God. *International Journal for the Psychology of Religion, 12,* 29–39.

Vandello, J. A., & Cohen, D. (1999). Patterns of individualism and collectivism across the United States. *Journal of Personality and Social Psychology, 77,* 279–292.

Vanman, E. J., Saltz, J. L., Nathan, L. R., & Warren, J. A. (2004). Racial discrimination by low-prejudiced whites. *Psychological Science, 15,* 711–714.

Vasan, R. S., Pencina, M. J., Cobain, M., Freiberg, M. S., & D'Agostino, R. B. (2005). Estimated risks for developing obesity in the Framingham heart study. *Annals of Internal Medicine, 143,* 473–480.

Vattano, F. (2000). *The mind: Video teaching modules* (2nd ed.). Fort Collins, CO: Colorado State University and Annenberg/CPB.

Vecera, S. P., Vogel, E. K., & Woodman, G. F. (2002). Lower region: A new cue for figure-ground assignment. *Journal of Experimental Psychology: General, 131,* 194–205.

Velakoulis, D., Wood, S. J., Wong, M. T., McGorry, P. D., Yung, A., Phillips, L., et al. (2006). Hippocampal and amygdala volumes according to psychosis stage and diagnosis: A magnetic resonance imaging study of chronic schizophrenia, first-episode psychosis, and ultra-high-risk individuals. *Archives of General Psychiatry, 63,* 139–149.

Velicer, C. M, Heckbert, S. R., Lampe, J. W., Potter, J. D., Robertson, C. A., & Taplin, S. H. (2004). Antibiotic use in relation to the risk of breast cancer. *Journal of the American Medical Association, 291,* 827–835.

Velligan, D. I., Bow-Thomas, C. C., Huntzinger, C., Ritch, J., Ledbetter, N., Prihoda, T. J., & Miller, A. L. (2000). Randomized controlled trial of the use of compensatory strategies to enhance adaptive functioning in outpatients with schizophrenia. *American Journal of Psychiatry, 157,* 1317–1328.

Venter, J. C., et al. (2001). The sequence of the human genome. *Science, 291,* 1304–1351.

Verghese, J., LeValley, A., Derby, C., Kuslansky, G., Katz, M., Buschke, H., et al. (2006). Leisure activities and the risk of amnestic mild cognitive impairment in the elderly. *Neurology, 66,* 821–827.

Verghese, J., Lipton, R. B., Katz, M. J., Hall, C. B., Derby, C. A., Kuslansky, G., et al. (2003). Leisure activities and the risk of dementia in the elderly. *New England Journal of Medicine, 348,* 2508–2516.

Vernacchio, L., Corwin, M. J., Lesko, S. M., Vezina, R. M., Hunt, C. E., Hoffman, H. J., et al. (2003). Sleep position of low birth weight infants. *Pediatrics, 111,* 633–640.

Vernet, M. E., Robin, O., & Dittmar, A. (1995). The ohmic perturbation duration, an original temporal index to quantify electrodermal responses. *Behavioural Brain Research, 67*(1), 103–107.

Verona, E., Patrick, C. J., Curtin, J. J., Bradley, M. M., & Lang, P. J. (2004). Psychopathy and physiological response to emotionally evocative sounds. *Journal of Abnormal Psychology, 113,* 99–108.

Verster, J. C., & Volkerts, E. R. (2004). Clinical pharmacology, clinical efficacy, and behavioral toxicity of alprazolam: A review of the literature. *CNS Drug Reviews, 10,* 45–76.

Vidal, C. N., Nicolson, R., DeVito, T. J., Hayashi, K. M., Geaga, J. A., Drost, D. J., et al. (2006). Mapping corpus callosum deficits in autism: An index of aberrant cortical connectivity. *Biological Psychiatry, 60,* 218–225.

Vignoles, V. L., Regalia, C., Manzi, C., Golledge, J., & Scabini, E. (2006). Beyond self-esteem: Influence of multiple motives on identity construction. *Journal of Personality and Social Psychology, 90,* 308–333.

Villalta-Gil, V., Vilaplana, M., Ochoa, S., Dolz, M., Usall, J., Haro, J. M., et al. (2006). Four symptom dimensions in outpatients with schizophrenia. *Comprehensive Psychiatry, 47,* 384–388.

Vincent, C. A., & Richardson, P. H. (1986). The evaluation of therapeutic acupuncture: Concepts and methods. *Pain, 24,* 1–13.

Vingerhoets, G., Berckmoes, C., & Stroobant, N. (2003). Cerebral hemodynamics during discrimination of prosodic and semantic emotion in speech studied by transcranial Doppler ultrasonography. *Neuropsychology, 17,* 93–99.

Vink, T., Hinney, A., van Elburg, A. A., van Goozen, S. H. M., Sandkuijl, L. A., Sinke, R. J., et al. (2001). Association between an agouti-related protein gene polymorphism and anorexia nervosa. *Molecular Psychiatry, 6,* 325–328.

Visser, P. J., Krabbendam, L., Verhey, F. R., Hofman, P. A., Verhoeven, W. M., Tuinier, S., et al. (1999). Brain correlates of memory dysfunction in alcoholic Korsakoff's syndrome. *Journal of Neurology, Neurosurgery, and Psychiatry, 67*(6), 774–778.

Visser, P. S., Krosnick, J. A., & Lavrakas, P. J. (2000). Survey research. In H. T. Reis & C. Judd (Eds.), *Handbook of research methods in social and personality psychology* (pp. 223–252) Cambridge, UK: Cambridge University Press.

Viswesvaran, C., & Ones, D. S. (2000). Measurement error in "Big Five factors" personality assessment: Reliability generalization across studies and measures. *Educational and Psychological Measurement, 60,* 224–235.

Vitaliano, P. P., Zhang, J. M., & Scanlan, J. M. (2003). Is caregiving hazardous to one's physical health? A meta-analysis. *Psychological Bulletin, 129,* 946–972.

Vitiello, B., & Swedo, S. (2004). Antidepressant medications in children. *New England Journal of Medicine, 350,* 1489–1491.

Vocisano, C., Klein, D. N., Arnow, B., Rivera, C., Blalock, J. A., Rothbaum, B., et al.. (2004). Therapist variables that predict symptom change in psychotherapy with chronically depressed outpatients. *Psychotherapy: Theory, Research, Training, Practice, 41,* 255–265.

Vokey, J. R. (2002). Subliminal messages. In J. R. Vokey & S. W. Allen (Eds.), *Psychological sketches* (6th ed., pp. 223–246). Lethbridge, Alberta, Canada: Psyence Ink.

Vokey, J. R., & Read, J. D. (1985). Subliminal messages: Between the devil and the media. *American Psychologist, 40,* 1231–1239.

Volkow, N. D., Chang, L., Wang, G. J., Fowler, J. S., Franceschi, D., Sedler, M. J., et al. (2001). Higher cortical and lower subcortical metabolism in detoxified methamphetamine abusers. *American Journal of Psychiatry, 158,* 383–389.

Vollebergh, W. A. M., Iedema, J., Bijl, R. V., de Graaf, R., Smit, F., & Ormel, J. (2001). The structure and stability of common mental disorders: The NEMESIS study. *Archives of General Psychiatry, 58,* 597–603.

Vollset, S. E., Tverdal, A., & Gjessing, H. K. (2006). Smoking and deaths between 40 and 70 years of age in women and men. *Annals of Internal Medicine, 144,* 381–389.

Volz, J. (2000). Successful aging. The second 50. *APA Monitor, 31,* 24–28.

Von Wright, J. M., Anderson, K., & Stenman, U. (1975). Generalization of conditioned GSRs in dichotic listening. In P. M. A. Rabbitt & S. Dornic (Eds.), *Attention and performance V.* New York: Academic Press.

Voracek, M., & Fisher, M. L. (2002). Shapely centrefolds? Temporal change in body measures: trend analysis. *British Medical Journal, 325,* 1447–1448.

Vorstman, J. A. S., Staal, W. G., van Daalen, E., van Engeland, H., Hochstenbach, P. F. R., & Franke, L. (2006). Identification of novel autism candidate regions through analysis of reported cytogenetic abnormalities associated with autism. *Molecular Psychiatry, 11,* 18–28.

Vroom, V. (1964). *Work and motivation.* New York: Wiley.

Vygotsky, L. S. (1991). Genesis of the higher mental functions. In P. Light, S. Sheldon, & M. Woodhead (Eds.), *Learning to think: Child development in social context* (Vol. 2, pp. 32–41). London: Routledge.

Vyse, S. A. (2000). *Believing in magic: The psychology of superstition* (reprint ed.). New York: Oxford University Press.

W

Waagenaar, W. (1986). My memory: A study of autobiographical memory over six years. *Cognitive Psychology, 18,* 225–252.

Wacker, J., Chavanon, M.-L., & Stemmler, G. (2006). Investigating the dopaminergic basis of extraversion in humans: A multilevel approach. *Journal of Personality and Social Psychology, 91,* 171–187.

Wadden, T. A., Berkowitz, R. I., Sarwer, D. B., Prus-Wisniewski, R., & Steinberg, C. (2001). Benefits of lifestyle modification in the pharmacologic treatment of obesity: A randomized trial. *Archives of Internal Medicine, 161,* 218–227.

Wadden, T. A., Berkowitz, R. I., Womble, L. G., Sarwer, D. B., Phelan, S., Cato, R. K., et al. (2005). Randomized trial of lifestyle modification and pharmacotherapy for obesity. *New England Journal of Medicine, 353,* 2111–2120.

Wade, C. (1988, April). *Thinking critically about critical thinking in psychology.* Paper presented at the annual meeting of the Western Psychological Association, San Francisco, CA.

Wade, J. B. (2004). Neuropsychologists diagnose traumatic brain injury. *Brain Injury, 18*(7), 629–643.

Wade, W. A., Treat, T. A., & Stuart, G. L. (1998). Transporting an empirically supported treatment for panic disorder to a service clinic setting: A benchmarking strategy. *Journal of Consulting and Clinical Psychology, 66,* 231–239.

Wager, T. D. (2005). The neural bases of placebo effects in pain. *Current Directions in Psychological Science, 14,* 175–179.

Wager, T. D., Rilling, J. K., Smith, E. E., Sokolik, A., Casey, K. L., Davidson, R. J., et al. (2004). Placebo-induced changes in fMRI in the anticipation and experience of pain. *Science, 303,* 1162–1167.

Wagner, K. D., Ambrosini, P., Rynn, M., Wohlberg, C., Yang, R., Greenbaum, M.S., et al. (2003). Efficacy of sertraline in the treatment of children and adolescents with major depressive disorder: Two randomized controlled trials. *Journal of the American Medical Association, 290,* 1033–1041.

Wagner, U., Gais, S., & Born, J. (2001). Emotional memory formation is enhanced across sleep intervals with high amounts of rapid eye movement sleep. *Learning and Memory, 8,* 112–119.

Wagner, U., Gais, S., Haider, H., Verleger, R., & Born, J. (2004). Sleep inspires insight. *Nature, 427,* 352–355.

Wai, J., Lubinski, D., & Benbow, C. P. (2005). Creativity and occupational accomplishments among intellectually precocious youths: An age 13 to age 33 longitudinal study. *Journal of Educational Psychology, 97,* 484–492.

Wakefield, J. C. (1999). Evolutionary versus prototype analyses of the concept of disorder. *Journal of Abnormal Psychology, 108,* 374–399.

Walberg, H. J. (1987). Studies show curricula efficiency can be attained. *NASSP Bulletin, 71,* 15–21.

Waldman, I. D., & Gizer, I. R. (2006). The genetics of attention deficit hyperactivity disorder. *Clinical Psychology Review, 26,* 396–432.

Walker, E. F., & Diforio, D. (1998). Schizophrenia: A neural diathesis-stress model. *Psychological Review, 104,* 667–685.

Walker, L. (1991). The feminization of psychology. *Psychology of Women Newsletter of Division, 35,* 1, 4.

Walker, L. J. (1995). Sexism in Kohlberg's moral psychology? In W. M. Kurtines & J. L. Gewirtz (Eds.), *Moral development: An introduction* (pp. 83–107). Boston: Allyn & Bacon.

Walker, M. P., Brakefield, T., Hobson, J. A., & Stickgold, R. (2003). Dissociable stages of human memory consolidation and reconsolidation. *Nature, 425,* 616–620.

Wall, T. L., Shea, S. H., Chan, K. K., & Carr, L. G. (2001). A genetic association with the development of alcohol and other substance use behavior in Asian Americans. *Journal of Abnormal Psychology, 110,* 173–178.

Wall, T. L., Shea, S. H., Luczak, S. E., Cook, T. A., & Carr, L. G. (2005). Genetic associations of alcohol dehydrogenase with alcohol use disorders and endophenotypes in white college students. *Journal of Abnormal Psychology, 114,* 456–465.

Wallace, J. C., Popp, E., & Mondore, S. (2006). Safety climate as a mediator between foundation climates and occupational accidents: A group-level investigation. *Journal of Applied Psychology, 91,* 681–688.

Wallace, R. K., & Benson, H. (1972). The physiology of meditation. *Scientific American, 226,* 84–90.

Wallen, K., & Lovejoy, J. (1993). Sexual behavior: Endocrine function and therapy. In J. Shulkin (Ed.), *Hormonal pathways to mind and brain.* New York: Academic Press.

Wallerstein, R. S. (2002). The growth and transformation of American ego psychology. *Journal of the American Psychoanalytic Association, 50,* 135–169.

Walsh, R., & Shapiro, S. L. (2006). The meeting of meditative disciplines and Western psychology: A mutually enriching dialogue. *American Psychologist, 61,* 227–239.

Walton, G. E., Bower, N. J. A., & Bower, T. G. R. (1992). Recognition of familiar faces by newborns. *Infant Behavior and Development, 15,* 265–269.

Wampold, B. E., Ahn, H. & Coleman, H. L. K. (2001). Medical model as metaphor: Old habits die hard. *Journal of Counseling Psychology, 48,* 263–273.

Wanek, J. E., Sackett, P. R., & Ones, D. S. (2003). Towards an understanding of integrity test similarities and differences: An item-level analysis of seven tests. *Personnel Psychology, 56,* 873–894.

Wang, C., Collet, J. P., & Lau, J. (2004). The effect of Tai Chi on health outcomes in patients with chronic conditions: A systematic review. *Archives of Internal Medicine, 164,* 493–501.

Wang, P. S., Lane, M., Olfson, M., Pincus, H. A., Wells, K. B., & Kessler, R. C. (2005). Twelve-month use of mental health services in the United States: Results from the National Comorbidity Survey Replication. *Archives of General Psychiatry, 62,* 629–640.

Wang, S.-H., & Baillargeon, R. (2005). Inducing infants to detect a physical violation in a single trial. *Psychological Science, 16,* 542–549.

Wang, X., Merzenich, M. M., Sameshima, K., & Jenkins, W. M. (1995). Remodelling of hand representation in adult cortex determined by timing of tactile stimulation. *Nature, 378,* 71–75.

Wang, Y., & Lobstein, T. (2006). Worldwide trends in childhood overweight and obesity. *International Journal of Pediatric Obesity, 1,* 11–25.

Warburton, D. M. (1995). Effects of caffeine on cognition and mood without caffeine abstinence. *Psychopharmacology, 119,* 66–70.

Ward, C. (1994). Culture and altered states of consciousness. In W. J. Lonner & R. S. Malpass (Eds.), *Psychology and culture.* Boston: Allyn & Bacon.

Warneken, F., & Tomasello, M. (2006). Altruistic helping in human infants and young chimpanzees. *Science, 311,* 1301–1303.

Warner, L., Kessler, R., Hughes, M., Anthony, J., & Nelson, C. (1995). Prevalence and correlates of drug use and dependence in the United States. *Archives of General Psychiatry, 52,* 219–229.

Watanabe, S., Sakamoto, J., & Wakita, M. (1995). Pigeons' discrimination of paintings by Monet and Picasso. *Journal of Experimental Analysis of Behavior, 63,* 165–174.

Watanabe, T., Náñez, J. E., & Sasaki, Y. (2001). Perceptual learning without perception. *Nature, 413,* 844–848.

Waterman, A. S. (1982). Identity development from adolescence to adulthood: An extension of theory and a review of research. *Developmental Psychology, 18,* 341–358.

Waters, E., Merrick, S., Treboux, D., Crowell, J., & Albersheim, L. (2000). Attachment security in infancy and early adulthood: A twenty-year longitudinal study. *Child Development, 71,* 684–689.

Watson, J. B. (1913). Psychology as the behaviorist views it. *Psychological Review, 20,* 158–177.

Watson, J. B. (1919). *Psychology from the standpoint of a behaviorist.* Philadelphia: Lippincott.

Watson, J. B. (1925). *Behaviorism.* London: Kegan Paul, Trench, Trubner.

Watson, R. T., & Heilman, K. M. (1979). Thalamic neglect. *Neurology, 29*(5), 690–694.

Watt, N. F., & Saiz, C. (1991). Longitudinal studies of premorbid development of adult schizophrenics. In E. F. Walker (Ed.), *Schizophrenia: A life-course in developmental perspective* (pp. 157–192). San Diego: Academic Press.

Wearden, A. J., Tarrier, N., Barrowclough, C., Zastowny, T. R., & Rahill, A. A. (2000). A review of expressed emotion research in health care. *Clinical Psychology Review, 20,* 633–666.

Webb, T. L., & Sheeran, P. (2006). Does changing behavioral intentions engender behavior change? A meta-analysis of the experimental evidence. *Psychological Bulletin, 132,* 249–268.

Weber, J. M., Kopelman, S., & Messick, D. M. (2004). A conceptual review of decision making in social dilemmas: Applying a logic of appropriateness. *Personality and Social Psychology Review, 8,* 281–307.

Weber, R. J. (1992). *Forks, phonographs, and hot air balloons: A field guide to inventive thinking.* New York: Oxford University Press.

Wechsler, D. (1939). *The measurement of adult intelligence.* Baltimore: Williams & Wilkins.

Wechsler, D. (1949). *The Wechsler Intelligence Scale for Children.* New York: Psychological Corporation.

Wechsler, D. (2003). *Wechsler Intelligence Scale for Children* (4th ed.). San Antonio, TX: Psychological Corporation.

Wecker, N. S., Kramer, J. H., Hallam, B. J., & Delis, D. C. (2005). Mental flexibility: Age effects on switching. *Neuropsychology, 19,* 345–352.

Weekes, J. R., Lynn, S. J., Green, J. P., & Brentar, J. T. (1992). Pseudomemory in hypnotized and task-motivated subjects. *Journal of Abnormal Psychology, 101,* 356–360.

Wegge, J., & Haslam, S. A. (2005). Improving work motivation and performance in brainstorming groups: The effects of three group goal-setting strategies. *European Journal of Work and Organizational Psychology, 14,* 400–430.

Wegner, D. M., Wenzlaff, R. M., & Kozak, M. (2004). Dream rebound: The return of suppressed thoughts in dreams. *Psychological Science, 15,* 232–236.

Weiler, B. L., & Widom, C. S. (1996). Psychopathy and violent behavior in abused and neglected young adults. *Criminal Behaviour and Mental Health, 6,* 253–271.

Weinberg, R. A., Scarr, S., & Waldman, I. D. (1992). The Minnesota transracial adoption study: A follow-up of IQ test performance at adolescence. *Intelligence, 16,* 117–135.

Weiner, B. (1980). *Human motivation.* New York: Holt, Rinehart & Winston.

Weiner, B. (1993). On sin versus sickness: A theory of perceived responsibility and social motivation. *American Psychologist, 48*(9), 957–965.

Weinfield, N. S., Sroufe, L. A., & Egeland, B. (2000). Attachment from infancy to early adulthood in a high-risk sample: continuity, discontinuity, and their correlates. *Child Development, 71,* 695–702.

Weingarten, H. P. (1983). Conditioned cues elicit feeding in sated rats: A role for learning in meal initiation. *Science, 220,* 431–433.

Weinraub, M., Horvath, D. L., & Gringlas, M. B. (2002). Single parenthood. In M. H. Bornstein (Ed.), *Handbook of parenting: Vol. 3. Being and becoming a parent* (2nd ed., pp. 109–140). Mahwah, NJ: Erlbaum.

Weinstein, D. (1999, July 24). Who are you? *Sunday Telegraph Magazine,* pp. 24–26.

Weinstein, E. A., & Kahn, R. L. (1955). *Denial of illness: Symbolic and physiological aspects.* Springfield, IL: Thomas.

Weiskrantz, L. (2004). Roots of blindsight. *Progress in Brain Research, 144,* 229–241.

Weisman, A. (2005). Integrating culturally based approaches with existing interventions for Hispanic/Latino families coping with schizophrenia. *Psychotherapy: Theory, Research, Practice, Training, 42,* 178–197.

Weiss, A., King, J. E., & Perkins, L. (2006). Personality and subjective well-being in orangutans (*pongo pygmaeus and pongo abelii*). *Journal of Personality and Social Psychology, 90,* 501–511.

Weiss, B., & Weisz, J. R. (1995). Relative effectiveness of behavioral versus non-behavioral child psychotherapy. *Journal of Consulting and Clinical Psychology, 63,* 317–320.

Weiss, S., & Moore, M. (1990). Cultural differences in the perception of magazine alcohol advertisements by Israeli Jewish, Moslem, Druze, and Christian high school students. *Drug and Alcohol Dependence, 26,* 209–215.

Weissberg, R. P., Kumpfer, K. L., & Seligman, M. E. P. (2003). Prevention that works for children and youth. *American Psychologist, 58,* 425–432.

Weissman, M. M., Bland, R., Joyce, P. R., Newman, S., Wells, J. E., & Wittchen, H. U. (1993). Sex differences in rates of depression: Cross-national perspectives. *Journal of Affective Disorders, 29,* 77–84.

Weissman, M. M., Markowitz, J. C., & Klerman, G. L. (2000). *Comprehensive guide to interpersonal psychotherapy.* New York: Basic Books.

Weissman, M. M., Wickramaratne, P., Nomura, Y., Warner, V., Verdeli, H., Pilowsky, D. J., et al. (2005). Families at high and low risk for depression: A 3-generation study. *Archives of General Psychiatry, 62,* 29–36.

Weisz, J. R., & Jensen, P. S. (1999). Efficacy and effectiveness of psychotherapy and pharmacotherapy with children and adolescents. *Mental Health Services Research, 1,* 125–157.

Weisz, J. R., McCarty, C. A., & Valeri, S. M. (2006). Effects of psychotherapy for depression in children and adolescents: A meta-analysis. *Psychological Bulletin, 132,* 132–149.

Weisz, J. R., Weersing, V. R., & Henggeler, S. W. (2005). Jousting at straw men: Comment on Westen, Novotry, and Thompson-Brenner (2004). *Psychological Bulletin, 131,* 418–426.

Weisz, J. R., Weiss, B., Han, S. S., Granger, D. A., & Morton, T. (1995). Effects of psychotherapy with children and adolescents revisited: A meta-analysis of treatment outcome studies. *Psychological Bulletin, 117,* 450–468.

Wells, G. L., & Bradfield, A. L. (1999). Distortions in eyewitness' recollections: Can the postidentification-feedback effect be moderated? *Psychological Science, 10,* 138–144.

Wells, G. L., Malpass, R. S., Lindsay, R. C. L., Fisher, R. P., Turtle, J. W., & Fulero, S. M. (2000). From the lab to the police station: A successful application of eyewitness research. *American Psychologist, 55,* 581–598.

Wells, G. L., & Olson, E. A. (2003). Eyewitness testimony. *Annual Review of Psychology, 54,* 277–295.

Wells, G. L., Olson, E. A., & Charman, S. D. (2002). The confidence of eyewitnesses in their identifications from lineups. *Current Directions in Psychological Science, 11,* 151–154.

Wells, G. L., Olson, E. A., & Charman, S. D. (2003). Distorted retrospective eyewitness reports as functions of feedback and delay. *Journal of Experimental Psychology: Applied, 9,* 42–52.

Wells, S., Graham, K., & West, P. (2000). Alcohol-related aggression in the general population. *Journal of Studies on Alcohol, 61,* 626–632.

Weltzin, T. E., Bulik, C. M., McConaha, C. W., & Kaye, W. H. (1995). Laxative withdrawal and anxiety in bulimia nervosa. *International Journal of Eating Disorders, 17*(2), 141–146.

Wenzel, A., Sharp, I. R., Brown, G. K., Greenberg, R. L., & Beck, A. T. (2006). Dysfunctional beliefs in panic disorder: The Panic Belief Inventory. *Behaviour Research and Therapy, 44,* 819–833.

Werner, E. (2003, January 28). Police: Sons kill mom, dismember her after seeing it done on "The Sopranos." *Naples Daily News.*

Wertheimer, M. (2000). *A brief history of psychology* (4th ed.). Belmont, CA: Wadsworth.

West, M. A., Borrill, C. S., & Unsworth, K. L. (1998). Team effectiveness in organizations. In C. L. Cooper & I. T. Robertson (Eds.), *International review of industrial and organizational psychology 1998* (pp. 1–48). Chichester, UK: Wiley.

West, R., & Sohal, T. (2006). "Catastrophic" pathways to smoking cessation: Findings from national survey. *British Medical Journal, 332,* 458–460.

Westen, D. (1998). The scientific legacy of Sigmund Freud: Toward a psychodynamically informed psychological science. *Psychological Bulletin, 124,* 333–371.

Westen, D., & Bradley, R. (2005). Empirically supported complexity. *Current Directions in Psychological Science, 14,* 266–271.

Westen, D., & Gabbard, G. O. (1999). Psychoanalytic approaches to personality. In L. Pervin & O. John (Eds), *Handbook of personality: Theory and research* (2nd ed., pp. 57–101). New York: Guilford.

Westen, D., Novotny, C. M., & Thompson-Brenner, H. (2004). The empirical status of empirically supported psychotherapies: Assumptions, findings, and reporting in controlled clinical trials. *Psychological Bulletin, 130,* 631–663.

Westen, D., Shedler, J., & Bradley, R. (2006). A prototype approach to personality disorder diagnosis. *American Journal of Psychiatry, 163,* 846–856.

Weston, C., & Went, F. (1999). Speaking up for yourself: Description and evaluation of an assertiveness training program for people with learning disabilities. *Mental Handicap, 27,* 110–115.

Weuve, J., Kang, J. H., Manson, J. E., Breteler, M. M. B., Ware, J. H., & Grodstein, F. (2004). Physical activity, including walking, and cognitive function in older women. *Journal of the American Medical Association, 292,* 1454–1461.

Wexler, M. (2005). Anticipating the three-dimensional consequences of eye movements. *Proceedings of the National Academy of Sciences of the USA, 102,* 1246–1251.

Whalen, P. J. (1998). Fear, vigilance, and ambiguity: Initial neuroimaging studies of the human amygdala. *Current Directions in Psychological Science, 7,* 177–188.

Whalen, P. J., Kagan, J., Cook, R. G., Davis, F. C., Kim, H., Polis, S., et al. (2004). Human amygdala responsivity to masked fearful eye whites. *Science, 306,* 2061.

Whaley, A. L. (2001). Cultural mistrust: An important psychological construct for diagnosis and treatment of African-Americans. *Professional Psychology: Research and Practice, 32,* 555–562.

Whalley, L. J., & Deary, I. J. (2001). Longitudinal cohort study of childhood IQ up to age 76. *British Medical Journal, 322,* 819.

Wharton, C. M., Grafman, J., Flitman, S. S., Hansen, E. K., Brauner, J., Marks, A., & Honda, M. (2000). Toward neuroanatomical models of analogy: A positron emission tomography study of analogical mapping. *Cognitive Psychology, 40*, 173–197.

Wheeler, M. E., & Fiske, S. T. (2005). Controlling racial prejudice. *Psychological Science, 16*, 56–63.

Whimbey, A. (1976). *Intelligence can be taught.* New York: Bantam.

Whisman, M. A. (1999). Marital dissatisfaction and psychiatric disorders: Results from a national comorbidity study. *Journal of Abnormal Psychology, 108*, 701–706.

Whitaker, D. J., Morrison, S., Lindquist, C., Hawkins, S. R., O'Neil, J. A., Nesius, A. M., et al. (2006). A critical review of interventions for the primary prevention of perpetration of partner violence. *Aggression and Violent Behavior, 11*, 151–166.

Whitam, F. L., Diamond, M., & Martin, J. (1993). Homosexual orientation in twins: A report on 61 pairs and three triplet sets. *Archives of Sexual Behavior, 22*(3), 187–206.

White, A. T., & Spector, P. E. (1987). An investigation of age-related factors in the age-job satisfaction relationship. *Psychology and Aging, 2*, 261–265.

White, F. J. (1998). Nicotine addiction and the lure of reward. *Nature Medicine, 4*, 659–660.

Whitney, P. (2001). Schemas, frames, and scripts in cognitive psychology. In N. J. Smelser & P. B. Baltes (Eds.), *International encyclopedia of the social and behavioral sciences.* The Netherlands: Elsevier.

Whittington, C. J., Kendall, T., & Pilling, S. (2005). Are SSRIs and atypical antidepressants safe and effective for children and adolescents? *Current Opinion in Psychiatry, 18*, 21–25.

Wickens, C. D. (1989). Attention and skilled performance. In D. Holding (Ed.), *Human skills* (pp. 71–105). New York: Wiley.

Wickens, C. D. (1992). *Engineering psychology and human performance* (2nd ed.) New York: HarperCollins.

Wickens, C. D. (2002). Situation awareness and workload in aviation. *Current Directions in Psychological Science, 11*, 128–133.

Wickens, C. D., & Carswell, C. M. (2006). Information processing. In G. Salvendy (Ed.), *Handbook of human factors and ergonomics* (3rd ed.). Hoboken, NJ: Wiley Interscience.

Wickens, C. D., Stokes, A., Barnett, B., & Hyman, F. (1992). The effects of stress on pilot judgment in a MIDIS simulator. In O. Svenson & J. Maule (Eds.), *Time pressure and stress in human judgment and decision making* (pp. 271–292). New York: Plenum.

Wicker, B., Keysers, C., Plailly, J., Royet, J. P., Gallese, V., & Rizzolatti, G. (2003). Both of us disgusted in My insula: The common neural basis of seeing and feeling disgust. *Neuron, 40*, 655–664.

Wickham, D. (2001, September 3). Castration often fails to halt offenders. *USA Today.*

Wicks, S., Hjern, A., Gunnell, D., Lewis, G., & Dalman, C. (2005). Social adversity in childhood and the risk of developing psychosis: A national cohort study. *American Journal of Psychiatry, 162*, 1652–1657.

Widiger, T. A. (1997). The construct of mental disorder. *Clinical Psychology: Science and Practice, 4*, 262–266.

Widiger, T. A., & Clark, L. A. (2000). Toward *DSM-V* and the classification of psychopathology. *Psychological Bulletin, 126*, 946–963.

Widiger, T. A., & Samuel, D., B. (2005). Diagnostic categories or dimensions? A question for the *Diagnostic and Statistical Manual of Mental Disorders—Fifth Edition. Journal of Abnormal Psychology. 114*, 494–504.

Widiger, T. A., & Sanderson, C. J. (1995). Assessing personality disorders. In J. N. Butcher (Ed.), *Clinical personality assessment: Practical approaches* (pp. 380–394). New York: Oxford University Press.

Widom, C. S. (1989). The cycle of violence. *Science, 244*, 160–166.

Widom, C. S. (2000). Childhood victimization: Early adversity, later psychopathology. *National Insitute of Justice Journal, 19*, 2–9.

Wiens, S., Mezzacappa, E. S., & Katkin, E. S. (2000). Heartbeat detection and the experience of emotions. *Cognition & Emotion, 14*, 417–427.

Wiesner, W. H., & Cronshaw, S. F. (1988). A meta-analytic investigation of the impact of interview format and degree of structure on the validity of the employment interview. *Journal of Occupational Psychology, 61*, 275–290.

Wigfield, A., & Eccles, J. S. (2000). Expectancy-value theory of achievement motivation. *Contemporary Educational Psychology, 25*, 68–81.

Willams, R. B. (2001). Hostility and heart disease: Williams et al. (1980). *Advances in Mind-Body Medicine, 17*, 52–55.

Williams, J. E., & Best, D. L. (1990). *Measuring stereotypes: A multination study* (Rev. ed.). Newbury Park, CA: Sage.

Williams, K. D., & Sommer, K. L. (1997). Social ostracism by coworkers: Does rejection lead to loafing or compensation? *Personality and Social Psychology Bulletin, 23*, 693–706.

Williams, L. M. (1994). What does it mean to forget child sexual abuse? A reply to Loftus, Garry, and Feldman (1994). *Journal of Consulting and Clinical Psychology, 62*, 1182–1186.

Williams, R. A. (2005). A short course in family therapy: Translating research into practice. *Family Journal: Counseling and Therapy for Couples and Families 13*, 188–194.

Williams, R. J., & Connolly, D. (2006). Does learning about the mathematics of gambling change gambling behavior? *Psychology of Addictive Behavior, 20*, 62–68.

Williams, T. J., Pepitone, M. E., Christensen, S. E., Cooke, B. M., Huberman, A. D., Breedlove, N. J., et al. (2000). Finger-length ratios and sexual orientation. *Nature, 404*, 455–456.

Williams-Piehota, P., Pizarro, J., Schneider, T. R., Mowad, L., & Salovey, P. (2005) Matching health messages to monitor-blunter coping styles to motivate screening mammography. *Health Psychology, 24*, 58–67.

Willis, J., & Todorov, A. (2006). First impressions: Making up your mind after a 100-ms exposure to a face. *Psychological Science, 17*, 592–598.

Willis, S. L., & Schaie, K. W. (1999). Intellectual functioning in midlife. In S. L. Willis & J. D. Reid (Eds.), *Life in the middle: Psychological and social development in middle age* (pp. 233–247). San Diego: Academic Press.

Wilson, E. J., MacLeod, C., Matthews, A., & Rutherford, E. M. (2006). The causal role of interpretive bias in anxiety reactivity. *Journal of Abnormal Psychology, 115*, 103–111.

Wilson, G. T. (1985). Limitations of meta-analysis in the evaluation of the effects of psychological therapy. *Clinical Psychology Review, 5*, 35–47.

Wilson, G. T. (1995). Behavior therapy. In R. J. Corsini & D. Wedding (Eds.), *Current psychotherapies* (5th ed., pp. 197–228). Itasca, IL: Peacock.

Wilson, G. T. (1997). Dissemination of cognitive behavioral treatments: Commentary. *Behavior Therapy, 28*, 473–475.

Wilson, G. T., Loeb, K. L., Walsh, B. T., Labouvie, E., Petkova, E., Liu, X., & Waternaux, C. (1999). Psychological versus pharmacological treatments of bulimia nervosa: Predictors and processes of change. *Journal of Consulting and Clinical Psychology, 67*, 451–459.

Wilson, G. T., Nathan, P. E., O'Leary, K. D., & Clark, L. A. (1996). *Abnormal psychology.* Boston: Allyn & Bacon.

Wilson, R. S., Beckett, L. A., Barnes, L. L., Schneider, J. A., et al. (2002). Individual differences in rates of change in cognitive abilities of older persons. *Psychology & Aging, 17*(2), 179–193.

Wimo, A., & Winblad, B. (2001). Health economical aspects of Alzheimer disease and its treatment. *Psychogeriatrics, 1*, 189–193.

Winemiller, M. H., Billow, R. G., Laskowski, E. R., & Harmsen, W. S. (2003). Effect of magnetic vs sham-magnetic insoles on plantar heel pain: A randomized controlled trial. *Journal of the American Medical Association, 290*, 1474–1478.

Winer, G. A., Cottrell, J. E., Gregg, V., Fournier, J. S., & Bica, L. A. (2002). Fundamentally misunderstanding visual perception: Adults' belief in visual emissions. *American Psychologist, 57*, 417–424.

Winerman, L. (2005, July/August). A virtual cure. *Monitor on Psychology*, 87–89.

Winkelmayer, W. C., Stampfer, M. J., Willett, W. C., & Curhan, G. C. (2005). Habitual caffeine intake and the risk of hypertension in women. *Journal of the American Medical Association, 294*, 2330–2335.

Winkielman, P., Bernston, G. G., & Cacioppo, J. T. (2001). The psychophysiological perspective on the social mind. In A. Tesser & N. Schwarz (Eds.), *Blackwell handbook of social psychology: Intraindividual processes* (pp. 89–109). Oxford, UK: Blackwell.

Winkielman, P., & Berridge, K. C. (2004). Unconscious emotion. *Current Directions in Psychological Science, 13*, 120–123.

Winn, P. (1995). The lateral hypothalamus and motivated behavior: An old syndrome reassessed and a new perspective gained. *Current Directions in Psychological Science, 4*, 182–187.

Winner, E. (2000). Giftedness: Current theory and research. *Current Directions in Psychological Science, 9*, 153–156.

Winson, J. (1990, November). The meaning of dreams. *Scientific American*, pp. 86–96.

Winston, A., Been, H., & Serby, M. (2005). Psychotherapy and psychopharmacology: Different universes or an integrated future? *Journal of Psychotherapy Integration, 15*, 213–223.

Winter, D. G. (1996). *Personality: Analysis and interpretation of lives.* New York: McGraw-Hill.

Wisborg, K., Kesmodel, U., Bech, B. H., Hedegaard, M., & Henriksen, T. B. (2003). Maternal consumption of coffee during pregnancy and stillbirth and infant death in first year of life: Prospective study. *British Medical Journal, 326*, 420.

Wiseman, R., West, D., & Stemman, R. (1996, January/February). Psychic crime detectives: A new test for measuring their successes and failures. *Skeptical Inquirer, 21*, 38–58.

Wismer Fries, A. B., Ziegler, T. E., Kurian, J. R., Jacoris, S., & Pollak, S. D. (2005). Early experience in humans is associated with changes in neuropeptides critical for regulating social behavior. *Proceedings of the National Academy of Sciences of the USA, 102*, 17237–17240.

Witt, C., Brinkhaus, B., Jena, S., Linde, K., Streng, A., Wagenpfeil, S., et al.(2005). Acupuncture in patients with osteoarthritis of the knee: A randomised trial. *Lancet, 366*, 136–143.

Wittchen, H. U., & Hoyer, J. (2001). Generalized anxiety disorder: Nature and course. *Journal of Clinical Psychiatry, 62*, 15–19.

Wittchen, H. U., Zhao, S., Kessler, R. C., & Eaton, W. W. (1994). *DSM-III-R:* Generalized anxiety disorder in the national comorbidity survey. *Archives of General Psychiatry, 51*, 355–364.

Wixted, J. T. (2004). The psychology and neuroscience of forgetting. *Annual Review of Psychology, 55*, 235–269.

Wixted, J. T. (2005). A theory about why we forget what we once knew. *Current Directions in Psychological Science, 14*, 6–9.

Woehr, D. J., & Arthur, W., Jr. (2003). The construct-related validity of assessment center ratings: A review and meta-analysis of the role of methodological factors. *Journal of Management, 29*, 231–258.

Wohl, J. (1995). Traditional individual psychotherapy and ethnic minorities. In J. F. Aponte, R. Y. Rivers, & J. Wohl (Eds.), *Psychological interventions and cultural diversity* (pp. 74–91). Boston: Allyn & Bacon.

Wohlfarth, T., Storosum, J. G., Elferink, A. J. A., van Zweiten, B. J., Fouwels, A., & van den Brink, W. (2004). Response to tricyclic antidepressants: Independent of gender? *American Journal of Psychiatry, 161*, 370–372.

Woldt, A. L., & Toman, S. M. (Eds.). (2005). *Gestalt therapy: History, theory, and practice.* Newbury Park, CA: Sage.

Wolf, H., Angleitner, A., Spinath, F., Reimann, R., & Strelau, J. (2004). Genetic and environmental influences on the EPQ-RS scales: A twin study using self- and peer reports *Personality and Individual Differences. 37*, 579-590.

Wolf, P. A. (2003). Fifty years at Framingham: Contributions to stroke epidemiology. *Advances in Neurology, 92*, 165–172.

Wolpe, J. (1958). *Psychotherapy by reciprocal inhibition.* Stanford, CA: Stanford University Press.

Wolpert, I. (1924). Die Simultanagnosie: Störung der Gesamtauffassung. *Archiv für Psychiatrie und Nervenkrankheiten, vereinigt mit Zeitschrift für die gesamte Neurologie und Psychiatrie, 93*, 397–413.

Wolraich, M. L., Wibbelsman, C. J., Brown, T. E., Evans, S. W., Gotlieb, E. M., Knight, J. R., et al. (2005). Attention-deficit/hyperactivity disorder among adolescents: A review of the diagnosis, treatment, and clinical implications. *Pediatrics, 115*, 1734–1746.

Wong, C. G., Gibson, K. M., & Snead, O. C. (2004). From the street to the brain: Neurobiology of the recreational drug gamma-hydroxybutyric acid. *Trends in Pharmacological Science, 25*, 29–34.

Wong, K. F. E., & Kwong, J. Y. Y. (2005). Between-individual comparisons in performance evaluation: A perspective from prospect theory. *Journal of Applied Psychology, 90*, 284–294.

Wong, S. E., Martinez-Diaz, J. A., Massel, H. K., Edelstein, B. A., Wiegand, W., Bowen, L., & Liberman, R. P. (1993). Conversational skills training with schizophrenic inpatients: A study of generalization across settings and conversants. *Behavior Therapy, 24*, 285–304.

Wood, J. (2006). Effect of anxiety reduction on children's school performance and social adjustment. *Developmental Psychology, 42*, 345–349.

Wood, J. M., Nezworski, M. T., Lilienfeld, S. O., & Garb, H. N. (2003). *What's wrong with the Rorschach? Science confronts the controversial inkblot test.* San Francisco, CA: Jossey-Bass.

Wood, N. D., Crane, D. R., Shaalje, G. B, & Law, D. D. (2005). What works for whom: A meta-analytic review of marital and couples therapy in reference to marital distress. *American Journal of Family Therapy, 33*, 273–287.

Wood, W. (2000). Attitude change: Persuasion and social influence. *Annual Review of Psychology, 51*, 539–570.

Wood, W., & Eagly, A. H. (2002). A cross-cultural analysis of the behavior of women and men: Implications for the origins of sex differences. *Psychological Bulletin, 128*, 699–727.

Wood, W., Wong, F. Y., & Chachere, G. (1991). Effects of media violence on viewers' aggression in unconstrained social interaction. *Psychological Bulletin, 109*, 371–383.

Woods, B. T., Schoene, W., & Kneisley, L. (1982). Are hippocampal lesions sufficient to cause lasting amnesia? *Journal of Neurology, Neurosurgery, and Psychiatry, 45*(3), 243–247.

Woods, S. C., Schwartz, M. W., Baskin, D. G., & Seeley, R. J. (2000). Food intake and the regulation of body weight. *Annual Review of Psychology, 51*, 255–277.

Woods, S. C., Seeley, R. J., Porte, D., Jr., & Schwartz, M. W. (1998). Signals that regulate food intake and energy homeostasis. *Science, 280*, 1378–1383.

Woodworth, R. S., & Schlosberg, H. (1954). *Experimental psychology.* New York: Holt.

Woolfolk-Hoy, A. (1999). Psychology applied to education. In A. Stec & D. Bernstein (Eds.), *Psychology: Fields of application* (pp. 61–81). Boston: Houghton Mifflin.

Woolley, J. D. (1997). Thinking about fantasy: Are children fundamentally different thinkers and believers from adults? *Child Development, 68*, 991–1011.

Worchel, S., Cooper, J., Goethals, G. R., & Olson, J. (2000). *Social psychology.* Belmont, CA: Wadsworth.

Workman, M. (2004). Expert decision support system use, disuse, and misuse: A study using the theory of planned behavior. *Computers in Human Behavior, 21*, 211–231.

World Health Organization. (1998). *Communicable disease surveillance and response.* Geneva, Switzerland: Author.

World Health Organization. (2002a). *Nutrition: Controlling the global obesity epidemic.* Retrieved December 13, 2004, from http:www.who.int/nut/obs.htm

World Health Organization. (2002b). *WHO collaborative project on psychological problems in general health care.* Retrieved August 27, 2003, from http://www.who.int/msa/mnh/ems/primacare/ppghc/ppghc.htm

World Health Organization Mental Health Survey Consortium. (2004). Prevalence, severity, and unmet need for treatment of mental disorders in the World Health Organization World Mental Health Surveys. *Journal of the American Medical Association, 291*, 2581–2590.

Wren, C. S. (1998, September 22). For crack babies, a future less bleak. *New York Times.* Retrieved December 13, 2004, from http://query.nytimes.com/gst/abstract.html?res=F40715FA3B540C718EDDA00894D0494D81

Wren, C. S. (1999, February 24). U.N. drug board urges research on marijuana as medicine. *New York Times.* Retrieved December 13, 2004, from http://query.nytimes.com/gst/abstract.html?res=F10A13F83A590C778ED-DAB0894D1494D81

Wright, E. F., Voyer, D., Wright, R. D., & Roney, C. (1995). Supporting audiences and performance under pressure: The home-ice disadvantage in hockey championships. *Journal of Sport Behavior, 18*, 21–28.

Wurtman, R. J., & Wurtman, J. J. (1995). Brain serotonin, carbohydrate-craving, obesity and depression. *Obesity Research, 3*(Suppl. 4), 477S–480S.

Wynne, C. L. (2004). *Do animals think?* Princeton, NJ: Princeton University Press.

Wynne, K., Park, A. J., Small, C. J., Patterson, M., Ellis, S. M., Murphy, K. G., et al. (2005). Subcutaneous oxyntomodulin reduces body weight in overweight and obese subjects: A double-blind, randomized, controlled trial. *Diabetes, 54*, 2390–2395.

X

Xue, Y., Leventhal, T., Brooks-Gunn, J., & Earls, F. J. (2005). Neighborhood residence and mental health problems of 5- to 11-year-olds. *Archives of General Psychiatry, 62*, 554–563.

Y

Yaffe, K., Barnes, D., Nevitt, M., Lui, L.-Y., & Covinsky, K. (2001). A prospective study of physical activity and cognitive decline in elderly women. *Archives of Internal Medicine, 161*, 1703–1708.

Yakimovich, D., & Saltz, E. (1971). Helping behavior: The cry for help. *Psychonomic Science, 23*, 427–428.

Yalom, I. D. (1995). Stimulus-driven attentional capture. *Current Directions in Psychological Science, 2*, 156–161.

Yan, B., Li, K., Xu, J., Wang, W., Li, K., Liu, H., et al. (2005). Acupoint-specific fMRI patterns in human brain. *Neuroscience Letters, 383*, 236–240.

Yang, C.-M. & Spielman, A. J. (2001). The effect of delayed weekend sleep pattern on sleep and morning functioning. *Psychology and Health, 16*, 715–725.

Yang, T., & Kubovy, M. (1999). Weakening the robustness of perspective: Evidence for a modified theory of compensation in picture perception. *Perception and Psychophysics, 61*, 456–467.

Yantis, S. (1993). Stimulus-driven attentional capture. *Current Directions in Psychological Science, 2,* 156–161.

Yates, W. R. (2000). Testosterone in psychiatry. *Archives of General Psychiatry, 57,* 155–156.

Yearta, S. K., Maitlis, S., & Briner, R. B. (1995). An exploratory study of goal setting in theory and practice: A motivational technique that works? *Journal of Occupational and Organizational Psychology, 68,* 237–252.

Yehuda, R., Bryant, R., Marmar, C., & Zohar, J. (2005). Pathological responses to terrorism. *Neuropsychopharmacology, 30,* 1793–1805.

Yela, C., & Sangrador, J. L. (2001). Perception of physical attractiveness throughout loving relationships. *Current Research in Social Psychology, 6,* 57–75.

Yerkes, R. M. (Ed.). (1921). Psychological examining in the U.S. Army. *Memoirs of the National Academy of Sciences,* No. 15.

Yeung, L. M., Linver, M. R., & Brooks-Gunn, J. (2002). How money matters for young children's development: Parental investment and family processes. *Child Development, 73,* 1861–1879.

Yi, H., Williams, G. D., & Smothers, B. A. (2004, August). *Surveillance report #69: Trends in alcohol-related fatal traffic crashes, United States, 1977–2002.* Bethesda, MD: National Institute on Alcohol Abuse and Alcoholism, Division of Epidemiology and Prevention Research.

Yonkers, K., Kando, J., Cole, J., & Blumenthal, S. (1992). Gender differences in pharmacokinetics and pharmacodynamics of psychotropic medication. *American Journal of Psychiatry, 149,* 587–595.

York, J. L., & Welte, J. W. (1994). Gender comparisons of alcohol consumption in alcoholic and nonalcoholic populations. *Journal of Studies on Alcohol, 55*(6), 743–750.

Yoshimasu, K., Washio, M., Tokunaga, S., Tanaka, K., Liu, Y., Kodama, H., et al. (2002). Relation between Type A behavior pattern and the extent of coronary atherosclerosis in Japanese women. *International Journal of Behavioral Medicine, 9,* 77–93.

Youm, Y., & Laumann, E. O. (2002). Social network effects on the transmission of sexually transmitted diseases. *Sexually Transmitted Diseases, 29,* 689–697.

Young, M. E. (1995). On the origin of causal theories. *Psychonomic Bulletin & Review, 2,* 83–104.

Young, T., Skatrud, J., & Peppard, P. E. (2004). Risk factors for obstructive sleep apnea in adults. *Journal of the American Medical Association, 291,* 2013–2016.

Yousif, Y., & Korte, C. (1995). Urbanization, culture, and helpfulness: Cross-cultural studies in England and the Sudan. *Journal of Cross-Cultural Psychology, 26,* 474–489.

Yovel, I., & Mineka, S. (2005). Emotion-congruent attentional biases: The perspective of hierarchical models of emotional disorders. *Personality and Individual Differences, 38,* 785–795.

Yukl, G., & Van Fleet, D. D. (1992). Theory and research on leadership in organizations. In M. D. Dunnette & L. M. Hough (Eds.), *Handbook of industrial and organizational psychology* (Vol. 3, 2nd ed., pp. 147–198). Palo Alto, CA: Consulting Psychologists Press.

Yun, S., Faraj, S., & Sims, H. P. (2005). Contingent leadership and effectiveness of trauma resuscitation teams. *Journal of Applied Psychology, 90,* 1288–1296.

Z

Zadnik, K. (2001). Association between night lights and myopia: True blue or a red herring? *Archives of Ophthalmology, 119,* 146.

Zadra, A., Desjardins, S., & Marcotte, E. (2006). Evolutionary function of dreams: A test of the threat simulation theory in recurrent dreams. *Consciousness and Cognition, 15,* 450–463.

Zadra, A., & Donderi, D. C. (2000). Nightmares and bad dreams: Their prevalence and relationship to well-being. *Journal of Abnormal Psychology, 109,* 273–281.

Zahn-Waxler, C., Radke-Yarrow, M., Wagner, E., & Chapman, M. (1992). Development of concern for others. *Developmental Psychology, 28,* 1038–1047.

Zahrani, S. S., & Kaplowitz, S. A. (1993). Attributional biases in individualistic and collectivist cultures: A comparison of Americans with Saudis. *Social Psychology Quarterly, 56*(3), 223–233.

Zajonc, R. B. (1965). Social facilitation. *Science, 149,* 269–274.

Zajonc, R. B. (1998). Emotions. In D. Gilbert, S. T. Fiske, & G. Lindzey (Eds.), *Handbook of social psychology* (Vol. 1, 4th ed., pp. 591–634). Boston: McGraw-Hill.

Zajonc, R. B. (2001). Mere exposure: A gateway to the subliminal. *Current Directions in Psychological Science, 10,* 224–228.

Zakriski, A. L., Wright, J. C., & Underwood, M. K. (2005). Gender similarities and differences in children's social behavior: Finding personality in

contextualized patterns of adaptation. *Journal of Personality and Social Psychology, 88,* 844–855.

Zakzanis, K. K., & Young, D. A. (2001). Memory impairment in abstinent MDMA ("Ecstasy") users: A longitudinal investigation. *Neurology, 56,* 966–969.

Zald, D. H., & Pardo, J. V. (1997). Emotion, olfaction, and the human amygdala: Amygdala activation during aversive olfactory stimulation. *Proceedings of the National Academy of Sciences of the United States of America, 94*(8), 4119–4124.

Zalta, A. K., & Keel, P. K. (2006). Peer influence on bulimic symptoms in college students. *Journal of Abnormal Psychology, 115,* 185–189.

Zambelis, T., Paparrigopoulos, T., & Soldatos, C. R. (2002). REM sleep behaviour disorder associated with a neurinoma of the left pontocerebral angle. *Journal of Neurology, Neurosurgery, and Psychiatry, 72,* 821–822.

Zammit, S., Allebeck, P., Andreasson, S., Lundberg, I., & Lewis, G. (2002). Self reported cannabis use as a risk factor for schizophrenia in Swedish conscripts of 1969: Historical cohort study. *British Medical Journal, 325,* 1199.

Zanarini, M. C., Skodol, A. E., Bender, D., Dolan, R., Sanislow, C., Schaefer, E., et al. (2000). The collaborative longitudinal personality disorders study: Reliability of axis I and II diagnoses. *Journal of Personality Disorders, 14,* 291–299.

Zaragoza, M. S., Payment, K. E., Ackil, J. K., Drivdahl, S. B., & Beck, M. (2001). Interviewing witnesses: Forced confabulation and confirmatory feedback increase false memories. *Psychological Science, 12,* 473–477.

Zatorre, R. J. (2003). Music and the brain. *Annals of the New York Academy of Sciences, 999,* 4–14.

Zeman, A. (2001). Consciousness. *Brain, 124,* 1263–1289.

Zeman, A., Britton, T., Douglas, N., Hansen, A., Hicks, J., Howard, R., et al. (2004). Narcolepsy and excessive daytime sleepiness. *British Medical Journal, 329,* 724–728.

Zeng, F. G. (2005). Trends in cochlear implants. *Trends in Amplification, 8,* 1–34.

Zhang, Y., Hoon, M. A., Chandrashekar, J., Mueller, K. L., Cook, B., Wu, D., et al. (2003). Coding of sweet, bitter, and umami tastes: Different receptor cells sharing similar signaling pathways. *Cell, 112,* 293–301.

Zhao, M., Momma, S., Delfani, K., Carlen, M., Cassidy, R. M., Johansson, C. B., et al. (2003). Evidence for neurogenesis in the adult mammalian substantia nigra. *Proceedings of the National Academy of Sciences, 100,* 7925–7930.

Zhou, J.-N., Hofman, M. A., Gooren, L. J. G., & Swaab, D. F. (1995). A sex difference in the human brain and its relation to transsexuality. *Nature, 378,* 68–70.

Zhou, Q., Eisenberg, N., Wang, Y., & Reiser, M. (2004). Chinese children's effortful control and dispositional anger/frustration relations to parenting styles and children's social functioning. *Developmental Psychology, 40,* 352–366.

Zigler, E., & Seitz, V. (1982). Social policy and intelligence. In R. J. Sternberg (Ed.), *Handbook of human intelligence* (pp. 586–641). Cambridge, UK: Cambridge University Press.

Zillmann, D. (1984). *Connections between sexuality and aggression.* Hillsdale, NJ: Erlbaum.

Zillmann, D. (1988). Cognition-excitation interdependencies in aggressive behavior. *Aggressive Behavior, 14,* 51–64.

Zillmann, D. (2003). Theory of affective dynamics: Emotions and moods. In J. Bryant & D. Roskos-Ewoldsen (Eds.), *Communication and emotion: Essays in honor of Dolf Zillmann* (pp. 533–567). Mahwah, NJ: Erlbaum.

Zillmann, D., Katcher, A. H., & Milavsky, B. (1972). Excitation transfer from physical exercise to subsequent aggressive behavior. *Journal of Experimental Social Psychology, 8,* 247–259.

Zimbardo, P. G. (1973). The psychological power and pathology of imprisonment. In E. Aronson & R. Helmreich (Eds.), *Social psychology.* New York: Van Nostrand.

Zimbardo, P. G. (2004). Does psychology make a significant difference in our lives? *American Psychologist, 59,* 339–351.

Zimmerman, B. J., & Schunk, D. H. (2003). Albert Bandura: The scholar and his contributions to educational psychology. In B. J. Zimmerman (Ed.), *Educational psychology: A century of contributions* (pp. 431–457). Mahwah, NJ: Erlbaum.

Zimmerman, M., McDermut, W., & Mattia, J. I. (2000). Frequency of anxiety disorders in psychiatric outpatients with major depressive disorder. *American Journal of Psychiatry, 157,* 1337–1340.

Zimmerman, M., Posternak, M. A., Attiullah, N., Freidman, M., Michael, R. J., et al. (2005). Why isn't bupropion the most frequently prescribed antidepressant? *Journal of Clinical Psychiatry, 66,* 603–610.

Zinbarg, R. E., & Barlow, D. H. (1996). Structure of anxiety and the anxiety disorders: A hierarchical model. *Journal of Abnormal Psychology, 105,* 181–193.

Zoellner, L. A., Foa, E. B., Brigidi, B. D., & Przeworski, A. (2000). Are trauma victims susceptible to "false memories"? *Journal of Abnormal Psychology, 109,* 517–524.

Zola-Morgan, S. (1995). Localization of brain function: The legacy of Franz Joseph Gall (1758–1828). *Annual Review of Neuroscience, 18,* 359–383.

Zorumski, C., & Isenberg, K. (1991). Insights into the structure and function of GABA-benzodiazepine receptors: Ion channels and psychiatry. *American Journal of Psychiatry, 148,* 162–173.

Zou, Z., & Buck, L. B. (2006). Combinatorial effects of odorant mixes in olfactory cortex. *Science, 311,* 1477–1481.

Zou, Z., Li, F., & Buck, L. B. (2005). Odor maps in the olfactory cortex. *Proceedings of the National Academy of Sciences of the USA, 102,* 7724–7729.

Zsambok, C. E., & Klein, G. (1997). *Naturalistic decision making.* Hillsdale, NJ: Erlbaum.

Zuberbühler, K. (2005). The phylogenetic roots of language. *Current Directions in Psychological Science, 14,* 126–130.

Zubieta, J.-K., Bueller, J. A., Jackson, L. R., Scott, D. J., Xu, Y., Koeppe, R. A., et al. (2005). Placebo effects mediated by endogenous opioid activity on μ-opioid receptors. *Journal of Neuroscience, 25,* 7754–7762.

Zubin, J., & Spring, B. (1977). Vulnerability—A new view of schizophrenia. *Journal of Abnormal Psychology, 86,* 103–126.

Zucker, A. N., Ostrove, J. M., & Stewart, A. J. (2002). College-educated women's personality development in adulthood: Perceptions and age differences. *Psychology & Aging, 17*(2), 236–244.

Zuckerman, E. (2003). Finding, evaluating, and incorporating Internet self-help resources into psychotherapy practice. *Journal of Clinical Psychology: In Session, 59,* 217–227.

Zuckerman, M. (1984). Sensation seeking: A comparative approach to a human approach. *Behavioral and Brain Sciences, 7,* 413–471.

Zuckerman, M. (1990). Some dubious premises in research and theory on racial differences. *American Psychologist, 45,* 1297–1303.

Zuckerman, M. (1993). Out of sensory deprivation and into sensation seeking: A personal and scientific journey. In G. G. Brannigan & M. R. Merrens (Eds.), *The undaunted psychologist: Adventures in research* (pp. 45–57). Philadelphia: Temple University Press.

Zuckerman, M. (1996). "Conceptual clarification" or confusion in "The study of sensation seeking" by J. S. H. Jackson and M. Maraun. *Personality and Individual Differences, 21,* 111–114.

Zuckerman, M. (2004). The shaping of personality: Genes, environments, and chance encounters. *Journal of Personality Assessment, 82,* 11–22.

Zuvekas, S. H. (2005). Prescription drugs and the changing patterns of treatment for mental disorders, 1996-2001. *Health Affairs, 24,* 195–205.

Credits

TABLES AND ILLUSTRATIONS

Chapter 1 **p. 4** *Figure 1.1* From American Journal of Psychology. Copyright © 1961 by the Board and Trustees of the University of Illinois. Used with permission of the University of Illinois Press. **p. 5** *Figure 1.2* From *Developmental Psychology: Theory, Research and Application* 1st edition by Shaffer, 1985. Reprinted with permission of Wadsworth, a division of Thomson Learning: www.thomsonrights.com Fax 800 730-2215.

Chapter 2 **p. 67** *Figure 2.11* From *The Cerebral Cortex of Man: A Clinical Study of Localization Function by Penfield & Rasmussen*, © 1968 Gale Group. Reprinted by permission of The Gale Group. **p. 74** *Figure 2.14* Reprinted by permission of the publisher from *The Postnatal Development of the Human Cerebral Cortex*, Volume I–VIII by Jesse LeRoy Conel, Cambridge, Mass.: Harvard University Press, Copyright © 1939, 1975 by the President and Fellows of Harvard College.

Chapter 3 **p. 112** *Figure 3.18* From *Perplexing Puzzles and Tantalizing Teasers* (p. 75), by Martin Gardner, 1988, New York: Dover. Reprinted by permission of the author. **p. 124** *Figure 3.28* From *Journal of Social Psychology, 52*, 183–208. Reprinted with permission of the Helen Dwight Reid Educational Foundation. Published Heldref Publications, 1319 Eighteenth St., NW., Washington, DC 20036-1802. http://heldref.org. Copyright © 1960. **p. 125** *Figure 3.29* From *Physiology and Behavior* by Johnson et al, Vol. 50, pp. 1245–1251. Copyright © 1991 with permission from Elsevier.

Chapter 4 **p. 139** *Figure 4.2* From D. L. Schacter et al. (1991). "Implicit memory for possible and impossible objects: Constraints on the construction of structural descriptions." *Journal of Experimental Psychology: Learning, Memory, and Cognition, 17*, 3–19. Copyright © 1991 by the American Psychological Association. Adapted with permission. **p. 145** *Figure 4.3* Horne, J. A., *Why We Sleep: The Functions of Sleep in Human and Other Mammals*. Copyright © 1988 James Horne. Reprinted by permission of Oxford University Press. **p. 146** *Figure 4.4* Adapted by permission of the author from *A Primer of Sleep and Dreaming* by Rosalind Cartwright **p. 153** *Figure 4.6* Reprinted by permission of the author from *Hypnotic Age Susceptibility* by Ernest R. Hilgard. Copyright © 1965. Published by Harcourt, Brace, Jovanovich, Inc. **p. 154** *Figure 4.7* From Hilgard, E. R., *Divided Consciousness: Multiple Controls in Human Thought and Action*, (John Wiley, 1977). Reprinted by permission of Henry Hilgard.

Chapter 5 **p. 181** *Figure 5.8* From *Divided Consciousness: Multiple Controls in Human Thought and Action* by Douglas L. Hintzman. Reprinted by permission of the author. **p. 186** *Figure 5.10* Adapted with permission from *Teaching Machines*, by B. F. Skinner. Copyright © 1961. **p. 197** *Figure 5.16* From Bandura, A., Ross, et al. (1963) "Imitation of film-mediated aggressive models." *Journal of Abnormal and Social Psychology, 66*, 3–11. Reprinted with permission of the author.

Chapter 6 **p. 215** *Figure 6.3* From *Cognitive Psychology: Memory, Language, and Thought* by Darlene V. Howard. © 1983 by Darlene V. Howard. Reprinted by permission of the author. **p. 217** *Figure 6.5* Figure from "Long-Term Memory for a Common Object," by R. S. Nickerson and M. J. Adams from *Cognitive Psychology*, Volume 11, 287–307, copyright © 1979 by Academic Press, reproduced by permission of the publisher. **p. 230** *Figure 6.12* Tulvin and Psotka, "Retroactive Inhibition in Free Recall: Inaccessibility of Information Available in the Memory Store," *Journal of Experimental Psychology, 87*, pp. 1–8, 1971. Copyright © 1971 by the American Psychological Association. Adapted with permission.

Chapter 7 **p. 253** *Figure 7.4* Shepard, R. N., & Metzler, J. (1971). "Mental rotation of three-dimensional objects." *Science, 171*, 701–703. Reprinted with permission from American Association for the Advancement of Science. **p. 287** *Figure 7.14* Reprinted with permission from Robert J. Sternberg, "Testing for Practical and Creative Intelligence," *New York Times*, November 8, 1997.

Chapter 8 **p. 303** *Figure 8.2* Adapted with permission from Schwartz, M. W., Woods, S. C., Porte Jr., D., Seeley, R. J. & Baskin, D. G. (2000). Central nervous system control of food intake. *Nature, 404*, 661–671. **p. 311** *Figure 8.3* Adapted from W. H. Masters and V. E. Johnson, *Human Sexual Response*, p. 5 (Boston: Little, Brown & Company, 1966). Reprinted by permission from Masters and Johnson Institute. **p. 328** *Figure 8.9* From "Voluntary Facial Action Generates Emotion-Specific Autonomic Nervous System Activity," by R. W. Levenson, P. Ekman, and W. V. Friesen, *Psychophysiology*, 1990, 24, 363–384. Copyright © 1990 the Society for Psychophysiological Research. Reprinted with permission.

Chapter 9 **p. 353** *Figure 9.5* Baillargeon, R., "A model of physical reasoning in infancy." From C. Rovee-Collier & L. P. Lipsitt (Eds.), *Advances in Infancy Research*. Copyright © 1992. Reproduced with permission of Greenwood Publishing Group, Inc. Westport, CT. **p. 378** *Figure 9.8* Adapted from Baltes (1994). *Life-span developmental psychology: On the overall landscape of human development*. Copyright © 1994 by Blackwell Publishing. Reprinted with permission.

Chapter 10 **p. 394** *Table 10.2* C. S. Crandall, J. J. Preisler, and J. Aussprung, "Measuring life event stress in the lives of college students: The Undergraduate Stress Questionnaire (USQ)" from the *Journal of Behavioral Medicine, 15*, 627–662. Copyright © 1992 by Plenum Publishing Corp. Reprinted with kind permission from Springer Science and Business Media. **p. 395** *Figure 10.2* The General Adaptation Syndrome, from *Stress without Distress* by Hans Selye, M.D. Copyright © 1974 by Han Selye, M.D. Reprinted by permission of HarperCollins Publishers, Inc. **p. 400** *Figure 10.4* Adapted from Lazarus, Opton, Nornikos, and Rankin, *Journal of Personality, 33*:4. Copyright © Blackwell Publishers. Reprinted with permission.

Chapter 11 **p. 421** *Figure 11.1* From *Personality Strategies and Issues* by R. M. Liebert and M. D. Spiegler, 1990. Reprinted with permission of Wadsworth, a division of Thomson Learning: www.thomsonrights.com. Fax 800 730-2215. **p. 427** *Figure 11.2* Reprinted by special permission of the publisher, Psychological Assessment Resource, Inc., Odessa, Florida 33556, from the *Structured Interview of Reported Symptoms* by Richard Rogers, Ph.D., Copyright © 1986, 1992 by PAR, Inc. Further reproduction is prohibited. **p. 428** *Table 11.2* From "An Introduction to the five-factor model and its applications." *Journal of Personality, 60*, 175–215. Reprinted with permission of Blackwell Publishing. **p. 430** *Figure 11.3* From "The Causes and Cures of Neurosis: An Introduction to Modern Behavior Therapy Based on Learning Theory and the Principle of Conditioning" by H. J. Eysenck and S. Rachman. © 1965 by Edits. **p. 434** *Figure 11.4* Reprinted from *Journal of Behavior Therapy and Experimental Psychiatry, 13*, A. Bandura, "The Assessment and Predictive Generality of Self-Precepts of Efficacy," pp. 195–199. Copyright © 1982 with permission from Elsevier. **p. 445** *Figure 11.5* Form for use with the MMPI-2™ test as published and copyrighted by the Regents of the University of Minnesota. All rights reserved. "MMPI-2" and "Minnesota Multiphasic Personality Inventory-2" are trademarks owned by the Regents of the University of Minnesota.

Chapter 12 **p. 462** *Table 12.2* Reprinted with permission from the *Diagnostic and Statistical Manual of Mental Disorders*, Text Revision, Copyright 2000. American Psychiatric Association.

Chapter 13 **p. 511** *Figure 13.1* Reprinted with permission of the author from Matson, J., Sevin, J., Fridley, and Love, S. (1990). "Increasing Spontaneous Language in Autistic Children," *Journal of Applied Behavior Analysis, 23*, pp. 227–233.

Chapter 14 **p. 557** *Figure 14.6* From Kenrick, D. T., Groth, G., Trost, M., & Sadalla, E. K. (1993), "Integrating Evolutionary and Social Exchange Perspectives on Relationships: Effects of Gender, Self-Appraisal, and Involvement Level on Mate Selection," *Journal of Personality and Social Psychology*. Copyright © 1993 by Blackwell Publishing. Reprinted with permission. **p. 558** *Figure 14.7* R. J. Sternberg & M. L. Barnes, "Triangulating Love," in *The Psychology of Love* (New Haven: Yale University Press). Copyright Yale University Press. Reprinted with permission. **p. 565** *Figure 14.10* Adapted with permission from S. Milgram, "Behavioral Study of Obedience," from *Journal of Abnormal and Social Psychology, 67*, No. 4, pg. 376. Copyright © 1963. **p. 574** *Figure 14.13* Reprinted from, "Temperature and Aggression: Paradox, Controversy, and a (Fairly) Clear Picture," by C. A. Anderson, and K. P. Anderson, in *Human Aggression*, edited by R. G. Green and E. Donnerstein. Copyright © 1998 with permission from Elsevier.

Chapter 15 **p. 607** *Figure 15.2* Job Satisfaction Survey, Copyright Paul E. Spector, 1994, All rights reserved. Reprinted by permission.

Chapter 16 **p. 629** *Figure 16.2* Strub, Richard L., and F. William Black, *The Mental Status Examination in Neurology*, Third Edition. Copyright © 1993 by F. A. Davis. Reprinted with permission. **p. 632** *Figure 16.3* Freberg, Laura, *Discovering Biological Psychology*. Copyright © 2006 by Houghton Mifflin Company. Reprinted with permission. **p. 636** *Figure 16.5* Copyright © 1990 by the American Psychological Association. Reproduced with permission. The official citation that should be used in referencing this material is *Journal of Experimental Psychology: General, 119*, p. 280. **p. 637** *Figure 16.6* Freberg, Laura, *Discov-*

PHOTO CREDITS

Chapter 1 **p. 1** © David Job/Stone/Getty Images **p. 7** *(top)* © Tom Stewart/CORBIS *(bottom)* Photograph courtesy of www.baddesigns.com **p. 8** © Michael Hewes/Getty Images **p. 9** Photofest **p. 11** Archives of the History of American Psychology—The University of Akron **p. 12** Courtesy of the Harvard University Archives **p. 14** *Figure 1.5* B.A. Shaywitz et al., 1995, NMR/Yale Medical School **p. 15** *(right)* Image courtesy of Robert Levenson, Ph.D., Director, Institute of Personality and Social Research, University of California *(left)* © Jose Luis Pelaez, Inc./CORBIS **p. 17** © Mary Kate Denny/PhotoEdit **p. 18** Courtesy of Wellesley College Archives, photo by Partridge **p. 19** *(top)* Courtesy of Wilberforce University, Archives and Special Collections *(bottom)* © Francis Dean/The Image Works **p. 24** © Jack Hollingsworth/Getty Images **p. 26** © Eric Bean/Getty Images **p. 27** © David Young-Wolff/PhotoEdit **p. 28** © Everett Collection **p. 29b** © Mark Richards/PhotoEdit **p. 34** © 2005 Photodisc Inc./Getty Images **p. 36** © 1998 Joel Gordon **p. 38** © George Shelley/CORBIS **p. 41** © A. Ramey/ PhotoEdit

Chapter 2 **p. 47** © Mary Kate Denny/PhotoEdit **p. 52** *Figure 2.4* Micrograph produced by John E. Heuser of Washington University School of Medicine **p. 55** © AP WideWorld Photo **p. 58** *Figure 2.7* D. N. Levin, H. Xiaoping, K. K. Tan, S. Galhotra, C. A. Palizzare, G. T. Y. Chen, R. N. Beck, C. T. Chen, M. D. Cooper, J. F., Mullan, J. Hekmatpanah, & J. P. Spire (1989). The Brain: Integrated three-dimensional display of MR and PET images. *Radiology, 172:* 783–789. **p. 60** Image courtesy Brand Sutton, Beckman Institute Biomedical Imaging Center, Univ. of Illinois at Urbana-Champaign **p. 63** © Bachmann/ The Image Works **p. 69** © Jose Luis Pelaez, Inc./Getty **p. 72** AP Wide World Photos **p. 75** © Markel/Getty Images

Chapter 3 **p. 84** Manchan/RF/Getty Images **p. 89** © Bill Aron/Photo Edit **p. 93** © Omikron/Photo Researchers **p. 95** © Michael Simpson/Index Stock Imagery **p. 96** *Figure 3.10* Reprinted by permission from *Nature.* Roorda, A. & Williams, D. R. (1999). The arrangement of the three cone classes in the living human eye. *Nature, 397,* 520–522. Copyright 1999 Macmillan Magazines Ltd. **p. 97** *Figure 3.12* Vienot, Brettel, Mollon—MNHN, CNRS **p. 101** Yellow Dog Productions/Getty Images **p. 105** *Figure 3.17* L. M. Bartoshk and V. B. Duffy **p. 106** © Billy Hustace/ Stone/Getty Images **p. 107** AP Wide World Photos **p. 108** AP Wide World Photos **p. 115** *Figure 3.21 Dies Irae, 1987, Italy.* Photo and design are © Kurt Wenner—www.KurtWenner.com Reproduction of this image is a violation of the law. **p. 117** AP Wide World Photos **p. 118** © PictureNet/CORBIS **p. 119** Phillip Kent/www.anamorphosis.com **p. 123** © 2001 Stellerimages.com/Mark D. Phillips **p. 126** *Figure 3.30* © Mark Richards/Photo Edit

Chapter 4 **p. 135** © Trinette Reed/Getty Images **p. 136** © David Welling/Animals Animals **p. 142** AP Wide World Photos **p. 143** *(top)* Jacques Jangoux/Photo Researchers, Inc. *(bottom)* Nathan Benning/National Geographic Image Collection **p. 146** Bob Daemmrich/The Image Works **p. 147** © David Young-Wolff/PhotoEdit **p. 152** © David Parker/Photo Researchers **p. 155** © Grant Mason/Manni Mason's Pictures **p. 157** *Figure 4.9* The William H. Helfand Collection, New York **p. 159** © Jeff Greenberg/PhotoEdit **p. 160** © Kraig Geiger/CORBIS **p. 162** © 1994 Joel Gordon

Chapter 5 **p. 169** © Jim Bastardo/Getty Images **p. 175** © Steven Needham/ Envision **p. 176** © Herb Lingl/aerialarchives.com **p. 177** © Tom Stack and Associates **p. 180** *Figure 5.6* © Nina Leen/Timeplex/Getty Images **p. 182** *Figure 5.9* Frank Lotz Miller/Black Star **p. 184** © Bob Daemmrich/The Image Works **p. 185** Courtesy of the Lincoln Electric Company **p. 187** AP Wide World Photos **p. 188** *Figure 5.12* Lang and Melamed, 1969 **p. 189** *(left)* © Michael Newman/Photo Edit *(right)* © Alan Oddie/Photo Edit **p. 195** *Figure 5.15 The Mentality of Apes* by W. Kohler, 1976, courtesy of Routledge **p. 196** Paul Chesley/Getty Images **p. 197** *Figure 5.16* Albert Bandura, Stanford University **p. 200** Charles Gupton/Stock, Boston, LLC **p. 201** © Hank Morgan/Rainbow

Chapter 6 **p. 207** © Lawrence Migdale/Stock Boston **p. 210** Mary Kate Denny/Getty Images **p. 212** © Frank Siteman/Stock Boston **p. 217** *(left)* Franko Magnani, 1700 El Camino Real, Rue 21 Sp. 16, San Francisco, CA 94080-1281 *(right)* Photo by Susan Schwartzenberg, © Exploratorium, www.exploratorium.com **p. 219** Mary Kate Denny/PhotoEdit **p. 222** Courtesy Professor William F. Brewer. From Brewer, W. F., & Treyens, J. C. (1981). Role of schemata in memory for places. *Cognitive Psychology, 13,* 207–230. **p. 224** AP Wide World Photo **p. 228** © Laurence Monneret/Stone/Getty Images **p. 232** Courtesy of Elizabeth Loftus **p. 234** *Figure 6.13* Courtesy of Professor Dominique Muller **p. 236** Paul Gilham/Getty Images **p. 239** © Robert Burke/Getty Images

Chapter 7 **p. 246** © Michael Newman/Photo Edit **p. 249** AP Wide World Photo **p. 251** Jeff Greenberg/PhotoEdit **p. 254** © Paul Howell/Getty Images **p. 258** AP Wide World Photo **p. 264** © Barbara L. Johnston/Reuters **p. 267** AP Wide World Photo **p. 270** © Joe McNally **p. 272** © Michael Grecco/Stock Boston **p. 273** Dr. Ronald H. Cohn/The Gorilla Foundation/koko.org **p. 289** Fraser Hale/St. Petersburg Times

Chapter 8 **p. 296** AP Wide World Photos **p. 298** © Shawn Thew/Getty Images **p. 300** © Andrew Shennan/Getty Images **p. 304** © Richard Howard **p. 305** Peter Menzel/Stock, Boston, LLC **p. 307** © Petre Buzoianu/CORBIS **p. 314** AP Wide World Photo **p. 316** *Figure 8.4* Reprinted with permission of the publisher from Henry A. Murray, *Thematic Apperception Test,* Plate 12F, Cambridge, Mass.: Harvard University Press, Copyright © 1943 by the President and Fellows of Harvard College. © 1971 by Henry A. Murray. **p. 317** Mary Kate Denny/PhotoEdit **p. 319** © Ariel Skelley 2002 CORBIS/Stock Market **p. 322** © Myrleen Ferguson Cate/Photo Edit **p. 323** Joe Hoyle/The Daily Illini **p. 324** *Figure 8.6* From *The Neurological Examination,* 4th edition, by R. N. Dejong, New York: Lippincott/Harper & Row, 1979 **p. 329** © Bob Daemmrich/Stock, Boston, LLC **p. 331** © Bob Daemmrich/Stock, Boston, LLC **p. 333** *(top)* AP Wide World Photo *(bottom left)* Eastcott/Momatiuk/Woodfin Camp *(bottom right)* Rick Smolan/Stock, Boston, LLC

Chapter 9 **p. 341** David Young-Wolff/Photo Edit **p. 343** © Les Stone/Corbis Sygma **p. 345** © C. Salvador/Corbis Sygma **p. 346** Lennart Nilsson/Albert Bonniers Forlag AB, *Behold Man,* Little Brown and Company **p. 348** Nelson, C. A. (1987). The recognition of facial expressions in the first two years of life: Mechanisms of development. *Child Development, 58,* 889–909 **p. 349** *Figure 9.2* © Petit Format/J. DaCunha/Photo Researchers, Inc. **p. 351** *Figure 9.3* © George S. Zimbel 2004 **p. 352** *Figure 9.4* Courtesy of Carolyn Rovee-Collier **p. 355** © Pedrick/ The Image Works **p. 359** © Jose Polleross/The Image Works **p. 360** © Jim Craigmyler/CORBIS **p. 361** © Peter Correz/Getty Images **p. 362** *Figure 9.6* Martin Rogers/Stock, Boston, LLC **p. 365** Lawrence Migdale/Getty Images **p. 368** © David Grossman/Photo Researchers **p. 369** © Michelle D. Bridwell/Photo Edit **p. 374** © Mary Kate Denny/PhotoEdit **p. 379** Steve Liss/Timepix/Getty Images **p. 380** © Bob Daemmrich/Stock Boston **p. 381** *(top)* © Michael Newman/Photo Edit *(bottom)* © Reuters/Corbis

Chapter 10 **p. 389** © Chuck Savage/CORBIS **p. 393** AP Wide World Photo **p. 397** Photofest **p. 399** © Reuters New Media Inc./Corbis **p. 403** © 2005 Lauren Greenfield, All Rights Reserved **p. 408** Boehringer Ingelheim, International GmbH/photo Lennart Nilsson, *The Incredible Machine,* National Geographic Society **p. 409** © Esbin-Anderson/The Image Works **p. 411** © Gustavo Gilabert/CORBIS **p. 413** Courtesy of American Psychological Association **p. 414** BSIP/Custom Medical Stock Photo

Chapter 11 **p. 419** © Royalty-Free/Corbis **p. 421** Mary Evans Picture Library **p. 423** Bob Daemmrich/Stock, Boston, LLC **p. 427** © John Neubauer/Photo Edit **p. 429** © Robert Caputo/AURORA **p. 431** © Bruce Plotkin/Getty Images **p. 435** *(left)* © Michael Childers/Corbis Sygma *(right)* AP Wide World Photo **p. 438** *(top)* AP Wide World Photo *(bottom)* Steve Kagan/Getty Images **p. 441** AP Wide World Photo **p. 446** Charlotte Miller

Chapter 12 **p. 543** © Marcus Mok/Getty Images **p. 546** © Jim Cornfield/Corbis **p. 547** *(top)* © Grox-J.M. News/Sipa Press *(bottom)* © J.L. Dugast/Peter Arnold **p. 458** © Culver **p. 464** © Michael Banks/Getty Images **p. 468** © Abe Rezny/The Image Works **p. 470** Photo reproduced with permission of Susan Mineka **p. 478** © Dan McCoy/Rainbow **p. 483** © Grunnitus/Photo Researchers **p. 486** Hillsboro County Sheriff, Tampa, Florida **p. 489** © Juan Silva/Getty Images **p. 493** AP Wide World Photo

Chapter 13 **p. 500** © David Buffington/RF Getty Images **p. 503** Stock Montage **p. 504** Photograph © Edmund Engelman **p. 505** © Charles Gupton/Stone/Getty Images **p. 507** Michael Rougier/Timepix/Getty Images **p. 510** Georgia Tech Photo by Gary Meek **p. 512** Rick Friedman/Black Star **p. 513** Courtesy, Albert Ellis, Institute for Rational-Emotive Therapy **p. 523** © Spencer Grant/PhotoEdit **p. 524** The Medical History Museum of the University of Zurich **p. 525** Will & Deni McIntyre/Photo Researchers, Inc. **p. 526** Mario Tama/Getty Images **p. 532** © Andrew Holbrooke/Corbis

Chapter 14 **p. 538** Reuters/Corbis **p. 544** © Michael Newman/Photo Edit **p. 545** © Tom McCarthy/ Rainbow **p. 547** © Peter Ginter/Material World **p. 549** © David Woo/Stock Boston **p. 552** *Figure 14.4* © Joshua Correll **p. 553** © Bonnie Kamin/-PhotoEdit **p. 554** © Robert Brenner/PhotoEdit **p. 555** © Michelle D. Bridwell/Photo Edit **p. 560** © David Leeson/The Image Works **p. 562** *(left)* Nabeel Turner/Getty Images *(right)* © Corbis-Bettmann **p. 564** © Jonathan Nourok/Photo Edit **p. 565** *Figure 14.9* From the film *Obedience* © 1965 by Stanley Milgram and distributed by Penn State Media Sales. Permission granted by Alexandra Milgram. **p. 566** © John Chiasson/Getty Images **p. 567** © Mark Ludak/The Image Works **p. 571** Mario Tama/Getty Images **p. 575** © Ellen Sensisi/The Image Works **p. 576** © Benali/Getty Images **p. 580** AP Wide World Photo

Chapter 15 **p. 589** Digital Vision/RF/Getty Images **p. 591** © David Young-Wolff/-PhotoEdit **p. 594** © Norbert von der Groeben/The Image Works **p. 601** © Paul Conklin/Photo Edit **p. 602** © John Neubauer/Photo Edit **p. 608** © Esbin-Anderson/The Image Works **p. 613** © Mark Richards/PhotoEdit **p. 614** © Ralf-Finn Hestoft/Corbis Saba **p. 616** © Lester Lefkowitz/Corbis **p. 618** © UPPA/Topham/The Image Works

Chapter 16 **p. 624** CRNI/Photo Researchers, Inc. **p. 628** *Figure 16.1* From Corsi, P., ed. *The Enchanted Loom.* New York: Oxford University Press, 1991. **p. 635** *Figure 16.4* Courtesy Dr. Suzanne Corkin, Massachusetts Institute of Technology. **p. 644** *Figure 16.11* Photo Researchers, Inc. **p. 649** *Figure 16.15* Zephyr/Photo Researchers, Inc.

Glossary/Index

Key terms, which appear in **boldface,** are followed by their definitions. Entries that appear in blue refer to the optional Industrial/Organizational Psychology or Neuropsychology chapters.

Avoidance conditioning *The process of learning particular responses that avoid an aversive stimulus,* 180–182, 190

Avoidant personality disorder, 485, 486

Avoidant relationship, 363, 364

Awareness, absence of, 138–142, 171

AWTs. *See* **Autonomous work teams**

Axes, 461–463

Axon(s) *A fiber that carries signals away from the cell body,* 50, 51, 52, 53, 55, 56, 72, 100, 103, 104, 105, 107, 234, 325

Axtell, R., 21

Ayache, D., 100

Ayas, N. T., 147

Aykan, H., 378

Ayllon, T., 511

Ayton, P., 266, 268

Ayuso-Mateos, J. L., 475

Azar, B., 381

Azrin, N. H., 511

Ba, P., 459

Babblings *Repetitions of syllables; the first sounds infants make that resemble speech,* 270

Babinski, J., 638

Baby talk, 348, 361

Baccus, S. A., 117

Bacharach, V. R., 281

Back, S. E., 512

Backman, L., 225, 226, 382

Baddeley, A., 214, 236

Badia, P., 401

Baer, J. S., 347

Baethge, C., 527

Bagley, C., 312

Bahrick, H. P., 217, 228, 358

Bahrick, P. O., 358

Bailey, J. M., 313, 314, 315

Baillargeon, R., 352–354

Baker, D., 5, 58, 627

Baker, K. D., 532

Baker, L. A., 549

Baker, M. C., 272

Bakker, M., 412

Balaban, M. T., 333

Balance, sense of, 111–112

Balanced bilinguals, 273

Balat, O., 160

Baldessarini, R. J., 527

Baldwin, J. M., 12

Baldwin, S. A., 515

Baldwin, T. T., 602

Balfour, D. J., 160

Balkin, T. J., 152

Balleine, B., 301

Ballou, M., 510

Balota, D. A., 221

Baltes, B. B., 608, 614

Baltes, P. B., 377

Balzer, W. K., 597

Banaji, M. 35, 224, 552, 554, 555

Bancroft, J., 308, 315

Bandura, A., 196–197, 412, 433, 434, 443, 510, 570

Banich, M. T., 27, 71

Banker, R. D., 616

Banks, M. S., 348

Bantick, S. J., 107

Bar, M., 139

Barbaree, H. E., 573

Barber, J. P., 518

Barbiturates, 158, 159, 163, 490

Barbone, F., 149

Barclay, A. M., 333

Barclay, G., 569

Barclay, J. R., 219

Bard, P., 329

Bardo, M. T., 301, 330

Barger, L. K., 149

Bargh, J. A., 139, 425

Bargones, J. Y., 348

Bar-Hillel, M., 328

Bariatric surgery, 306

Barker, G. J., 56

Barley, D. E., 517

Barling, J., 612, 614, 618

Barlow, D. H., 401, 463, 467, 468, 469, 470, 530, 533

Barlow, D., 177

Barnes, L. L., 402

Barnes, M. L., 558

Barnett, J. E., 524

Barnier, A. J., 152, 153

Baron, A. S., 554

Baron, J. C., 570, 633

Baron, J., 268

Baron, R. A., 549, 558

Baron-Cohen, S., 490

Barrett, A. M., 638

Barrett, H. C., 261

Barrett, L. F., 332

Barrett, S., 464

Barrick, M. R., 443

Barrios, L. C., 476

Barron, K. E., 317

Barrowclough, C., 522

Barsalou, L. W., 251

Barsky, A. J., 471

Bartels, A., 59

Bartholomew, K., 379

Bartholow, B. D., 157

Bartlett, J. A., 411

Bartlett, P. L., 191

Bartmess, E. N., 317

Bartol, K. M., 320

Barton, J., 614

Barton, J. J., 641

Barton, R., 438

Bartoshuk, L. M., 86, 102–103, 105

BAS. *See* **Behavioral approach system**

Basal ganglia, 646

Basch, E., 526

Bashore, T. R., 378

Basic features, in recognition, 121

Basilar membrane *The floor of the fluid-filled duct that runs through the cochlea,* 99–100, 101, 102

Baskin, D., 465

Basoglu, M., 511

Bass, B. M., 581, 617, 618

Bass, E., 232

Bassett, A. S., 484

Bassitt, D. P., 526

Batal, H. A., 147

Bates, E., 272

Bates, J. E., 361

Batson, C. D., 577

Battaglia, G., 161

Batterham, R. L., 304

Baucom, D. H., 519

Bauer, P. J., 358

Bauer, R. M., 627, 640–641

Bauer, T. N., 617

Bauman, C. W., 548

Baumeister, A. A., 281

Baumeister, R. F., 298, 310, 311, 321, 440, 540, 546

Baumrind, D., 188, 367

Bauserman, R., 488

Bausserman, L., 409

Bavelier, D., 360

Bayley, P. J., 237

Bazerman, M. H., 255

Bazile, A., 523

Bazzano, L. A., 391

B-cells, 408

Beals, J., 455

Beardslee, W. R., 532

Beatty, J., 122

Beatty, R. W., 595, 597

Beauchamp-Turner, D. L., 155

Beaulieu, D., 23

Beaumont, M., 148, 160

Bech, B. H., 160

Bechara, A., 327

Beck, A. T., 469, 475, 479, 513–514

Beck, J. S., 479, 514

Beck, M., 380

Bedwetting, 462

Beels, C. C., 515

Been, H., 530

Begley, S., 347

Behavioral approach *A view based on the assumption that human behavior is determined mainly by what a person has learned in life, especially by rewards and punishments,* 16, 18
to treatment, 508–512, 516, 518, 522

Behavioral approach system (BAS), 430

Behavioral coping strategies, 414

Behavioral genetics *The study of how genes and environments combine to affect behavior and mental processes,* 37–39, 279, 313, 314, 344–345, 431, 483

Behavioral inhibition system (BIS), 430

Behavioral signatures, 435

Behavioral stress responses, 397–398

Behavior-focused rating forms, 597

Behaviorism, 12–13, 14, 16, 19, 343, 433

Behavior modification *Treatments that use operant conditioning methods to change behavior,* 189–190, 509

Behavior therapy *Treatments that use classical conditioning principles to change behavior,* 508–512, 530
techniques of, 509–512

Beilock, S. L., 397

Beimel, S., 618

Beirne, R. O., 92

Bekinschtein, T., 637

Belin, P., 101

Belk, A., 305

Bell, B. E., 226

Bell, N. E., 609

Bell, P. A., 574

Bellaby, P., 256

Belli, R. F., 225

Belmonte, M. K., 490

Belongingness, need for, 320

Belsky, J., 380

Bem, D. J., 314

Ben-Ari, A., 403

Benbow, C. P., 288

Benecke, M., 22

Benedetti, F., 108–109

Benfante, M., 574

Benight, C. C., 401

Benishay, D. S., 313

Benjamin, L. T., 5, 10, 58, 627

Bennett, B., 487

Cognition(s)   (*cont.*)
emotions and, 327, 330–332
learning and, 171, 182
motivation and, 298
personality and, 433–435
social, 433
stress and, 396, 397, 399–400
See also Thought(s)
Cognitive ability, 274. *See also* **Intelligence**
Cognitive/affective theory, 434–435
Cognitive appraisal, 392, 400, 406
Cognitive approach   *A view that emphasizes research on how the brain takes in information, creates perceptions, forms and retrieves memories, processes information, and generates integrated patterns of action,* 14, 16–17, 18
to learning, 192
to health psychology, 411–412
Cognitive-behavioral approach, 16
to personality, 436
to treatment, 512–514
Cognitive-behavior therapy   *Behavioral treatment methods that help clients change the way they think, as well as the way they behave,* 146, 508, 512–514, 522, 530
Cognitive coping strategies, 413
Cognitive development, 349–361
cultural factors in, 358–359
individual variations in, 359–360
information processing and, 356–357
language and, 272, 359
memory and, 358
moral reasoning and, 374–376, 382
stages (periods) of, 349–352, 354–356
Cognitive dissonance theory   *A theory that attitude change is driven by efforts to reduce tension caused by inconsistencies between attitudes and behaviors,* 550–552
Cognitive distortions, 513
Cognitive map(s)   *A mental model that represents familiar parts of the environment,* 195, 250, 252–253
Cognitive neuroscientists, 237
Cognitive person variables, 434–435
Cognitive psychologists   *Psychologists whose research focus is analysis of the mental processes underlying judgment, decision making, problem solving, imagining, and other aspects of human thought or cognition,* 4, 9–10, 28, 192, 255, 433
Cognitive psychology, 201
Cognitive restructuring, 413, 513, 514, 516
Cognitive science, 17
Cognitive stress responses, 397
Cognitive theories, of emotion, 330–332
Cognitive theory, of depression, 479
Cognitive therapy   *An organized problem-solving approach in which the therapist actively collaborates with clients to help them notice how certain negative thoughts precede anxiety and depression,* 513–514, 530
Cognitive unconscious, 138
Cohen, A., 329
Cohen, C. E., 543
Cohen, D., 546, 570
Cohen, D. A., 372
Cohen, J., 483
Cohen, J. D., 187
Cohen, N. J., 236
Cohen, O., 546
Cohen, P., 379, 380, 486
Cohen, S., 383, 402, 403, 404, 407
Cohen-Cory, S., 71

Cohn, J. F., 333
Colak, A., 76
Colbert, A. E., 616
Colcombe, S. J., 378
Cole, K. N., 289
Cole, T. J., 305
Coleman, D., 148
Coleman, H. L. K., 464
Coles, D., 199
Collacott, E. A., 34
Collectivist cultures, 20, 184, 268, 317, 367, 375–376, 425, 439, 440–441, 540, 546, 547, 551, 552, 561, 570, 578, 580
Collet, J. P., 155
Collins, R. L., 31
Collins, W. A., 368
Colloca, L., 108, 109
Colombo, M., 237
Color circle, 94, 95
Color vision, 94–96, 97
opponent-process theory of, 96
trichromatic theory of, 94–96
wavelengths and, 90, 94, 95, 96, 97
Colorado Adoption Project, 280
Colorblindness, 96, 97
Coma(s), 636, 637
Combat, military, 147, 399
Commitment, in intimate relationships, 557
Committee to Review the Scientific Evidence on the Polygraph, 329
Common factors, 518, 522
Common fate, in perceptual organization, 114, 120
Common region, in perceptual organization, 114, 120
Community mental health movement, 531–532
Community psychologists, 5
Community psychology   *A mental health approach whose goal is to minimize or prevent psychological disorders by promoting social change and making treatment methods more accessible to those who normally have little or no access to psychological services,* 531–533
Companionate love, 557, 558
Comparative case studies, 258–259
Compas, B. E., 519
Compensation, 422
Competition   *Any type of behavior in which individuals try to attain a goal for themselves while denying that goal to others,* 578
Complementarity, in cognitive development, 354
Compliance   *Adjusting one's behavior because of a direct request,* 560–561, 563–564, 568
Compton, W. M., 486, 492
Compulsions, 468, 469–470, 492
Compulsive sexual behavior, 530
Computer(s)
modeling of brain by, 67
problem solving by, 262–264
Comstock, G., 198
Concepts   *Categories of objects, events, or ideas that have common properties,* 250–251, 253, 269
Concrete operations   *According to Piaget, the third stage of cognitive development, during which children can learn to count, measure, add, and subtract,* 355, 357
Condic, M. L., 73
Conditioned reinforcers, 184
Conditioned response (CR)   *The response triggered by the conditioned stimulus,* 172, 173, 174, 175, 176, 177, 178, 180, 182, 192, 304, 511
Conditioned stimulus (CS)   *An originally neutral stimulus that now triggers a conditioned*

response, 172, 173, 174, 175, 176, 177, 178, 182, 184, 190, 191, 470
Conditions of worth   *According to Rogers, circumstances in which an individual experiences positive regard from others only when displaying certain behaviors or attitudes,* 437, 438, 439
Condon, J. W., 556
Condon, M., 613
Conduct disorders, 489, 513
Conduction deafness, 100
Cones   *Photoreceptors in the retina that are less light-sensitive than rods but that can distinguish colors,* 92, 93, 96, 97
Confabulation, 636
Confidence, measure of, in statistics, A4
Confidentiality, 524
Confirmation bias   *The tendency to pay more attention to evidence in support of one's hypothesis about a problem than to evidence that refutes that hypothesis,* 33, 262, 263, 268
Conflict(s)   *What occurs when a person or group believes that another person or group interferes with the attainment of a goal*
interpersonal, 578
motivational, 321–322
psychodynamic, 11, 16, 422, 423, 424, 458, 503, 504
Conformity   *Changing one's behavior or beliefs to match those of others, generally as a result of real or imagined, though unspoken, group pressure,* 540, 560, 561–563, 566, 568, 582
Confounding variable   *Any factor that affects the dependent variable along with, or instead of, the independent variable,* 33
Conger, R., 371, 380
Congruence   *In client-centered therapy, a consistency between the way therapists feel and the way they act toward clients,* 506–507, 516
Conklin, H. M., 483
Connectedness, in perceptual organization, 114, 120
Connectionist models, 191, 262–264
Conner, C., 578
Connolly, D., 266
Connor, L. T., 221
Conrad, R., 214
Conroy, D. E., 401
Conscientiousness, 383, 405, 406, 407, 428, 581, 594, 616
Conscious level   *The level of consciousness at which mental activities accessible to awareness occur,* 137, 421
Consciousness   *The awareness of external stimuli and our own mental activity,* 10, 11, 12, 14, 136–163
absence of awareness and, 138–142, 171
altered states of, 142–144
disorders of, 636–640
dreaming and, 150–152
early research on, 10, 11, 12
hypnosis and, 152–154
levels of, 137–138
meditation and, 154–155
psychoactive drugs and, 136, 155–163
sleep and, 144–150, 151
states of, 137
Consedine, N. S., 425
Consequences Test, 264
Conservation   *The ability to recognize that the important properties of a substance, such as number, volume, or weight, remain constant despite changes in shape, length, or position,* 354, 355, 356, 357, 359
Consideration, as leadership trait, 617
Constantine, M. G., 523

Shields, L. B. E., 147

Shiffman, S., 161

Shiller, R. J., 266

Shimamura, A. P., 378

Shimaoki, K., 409

Shin, L. M., 64

Shin, S.-M., 523

Shiner, R. L., 379, 431

Shinskey, J. L., 352, 353

Shiraev, E., 19

Shiwach, R. S., 525

Shneidman, E. S., 476

Shobe, K. K., 231

Shoda, Y., 433, 434, 435

Short-term dynamic psychotherapy, 504

Short-term memory (STM) *A stage of memory in which information normally lasts less than twenty seconds; a component of working memory,* 212, 214–216, 218, 238, 249, 289

    chunking and, 215

    duration of, 215–216, 218

    encoding in, 214–215

    forgetting in, 215, 216, 228–229

    long-term memory and, 218, 235, 237

    sensory memory and, 212

    storage capacity of, 212, 214, 215, 218, 260

    See also Working memory

Short-wavelength cones, 95

Shreeve, J., 85

Shu, S. Y., 56

Shunk, D. H., 434

Shuttle box, 181, 192

Shweder, R. A., 376

Shyness, 432, 469, 489

SIDS. *See* **Sudden infant death syndrome**

Siebert, S. E., 443

Siegal, M., 356

Siegel, J., 394

Siegel, J. M., 148, 149

Siegel, S., 156, 157, 178

Siegler, R. S., 356

Sigalovsky, N., 136

Sigelman, J., 324

Sigmundsson, T., 483

Signal-detection theory *A mathematical model of what determines a person's report of a near-threshold stimulus,* 88, 89

Signals, in classical conditioning, 174–176, 178, 182

Sign language, 215, 273

Signorielli, N., 198

Silber, M. H., 146, 572

Silva, P. A., 442

Silver, E., 493

Silver, S. M., 23

Silverman, I., 369

Silverman, K., 160

Silverthorne, C., 447, 581, 616

Silvotti, L., 104

Simcock, G., 358

Simeon, D., 399

Simerly, R. B., 302

Similarity

    of attitudes, attraction and, 555–556

    in perceptual organization, 113, 114, 120

Simion, F., 125

Simon, H. A., 14, 257, 258, 264

Simon, T., 274

Simons, A., 394

Simons, D. J., 127

Simonsen, H., 109

Simonton, D. K., 264, 265

Simplicity, in perceptual organization, 114, 120

Simpson, E. E., 162

Simpson, J. A., 369

Simpson, O. J., 217

Simpson, S. G., 463

Simpson, S., 408

Sims, H. P., 581

Simultanagnosia, 641–642

Sinclair, R. C., 330

Singer, B., 501

Singer, B., 518

Singer, J., 330

Singer, L. T., 160, 347

Singh, H., 288

Single-photon emission computed tomography (SPECT), 57

Singleton, C. K., 636

Sinha, R., 326

Sirvio, J., 235

Sisk, C. L., 78

Sister Alcantara, 379

Sister Claverine, 379

Sister Nicolette, 379

Situational factors

    in abnormality, 456, 457

    in aggression, 571–572

    in attraction, 555–556

    in personality, 433, 435–436, 443

Situational tests, 443

Size constancy, 118, 120, 123

Size illusions, 119–120

Skaar, D. A., 490

Skill learning, 201–202

Skinner, B. F., 13, 16, 179–180, 185, 186, 508

Skinner box, 179, 185

Skitka, L. J., 548

Skolnic, B. E., 324

Skre, I., 468, 470

Slaby, R. G., 573

Slade, E. P., 368

Slamecka, N. J., 228

Slangen, K. E., 402

Slater, A., 125

Sledge, W. H., 455

Sleep, 63, 144–152, 155, 376, 614, 636

    chemistry of, 74, 75, 77

    deprivation of, 148–149

    dreaming and, 149, 150–152

    functions of, 148–150

    mood disorders and, 478

    posttraumatic stress disorder and, 398

    rhythms of, 148

    stages of, 144–146

    wakefulness and, 148

Sleep apnea *A sleep disorder in which people briefly but repeatedly stop breathing during the night,* 147, 151

Sleep disorders, 146–147, 462, 488

Sleeping pills, 146, 159, 637

Sleepwalking *A phenomenon that starts primarily in non-REM sleep, especially in stage 4, and involves walking while asleep,* 147

Slemmer, J. A., 353

Slife, B. D., 503

Sloan, D. M., 403, 474

Sloboda, J. A., 201

Slocombe, K. E., 269

Slomkowski, C., 368

Slotnick, S. D., 233, 237

Slovic, P., 10

Slow-to-warm-up babies, 361

Slow-wave sleep *Sleep stages 3 and 4, which are accompanied by slow, deep breathing; a calm, regular heartbeat; and reduced blood pressure,* 144, 145, 151

Slutske, W. S., 486, 491

Small, B. J., 382

Small, D. M., 105

Small molecules, as class of neurotransmitters, 74–76, 77

Smeets, G., 472

Smell. *See* **Sense of smell**

Smile, 19, 324, 328, 333, 334, 342

Smith, A. M., 300

Smith, A. P., 148

Smith, B. L., 405

Smith, D., 409

Smith, E., 544

Smith, E. E., 378

Smith, E. R., 311

Smith, F. L., 227

Smith, G. C. S., 147

Smith, I. M., 490

Smith, J., 209

Smith, K. M., 161, 162

Smith, L. B., 271

Smith, L. M., 616

Smith, M. L., 517, 518, 521

Smith, N. T., 162

Smith, P. B., 567, 578

Smith, P. C., 597

Smith, P. K., 381

Smith, R., 433

Smith, S., 362

Smith, S. J., 74

Smith, S. L., 198, 199

Smith, S. M., 219, 220

Smith, S. S., 157

Smith, T. B., 35, 523

Smith, T. W., 309, 409, 411

Smith, V. L., 256

Smith-Crowe, K., 613

Smith-McLallen, A., 549

Smoking, 147, 190, 347, 383, 391, 403, 411–412, 413

Smothers, B. A., 491

Snarey, J., 375

Snead, O. C., 159

Snellingen, T., 91

Snowden, J., 644

Snowden, L. R., 465

Snowdon, D. A., 378

Snyder, C. R., 2, 4, 439, 464

Snyder, D. J., 86

Snyder, R., 2

Snyder, S. H., 76, 162

Soares, J. F., 140

Social anxiety, 469

Social categories, 553

Social cognition *Mental processes associated with people's perceptions of and reactions to other people,* 540, 548, 555, 559

Social-cognitive approach *An approach that views personality as a label summarizing the unique patterns of thinking and behavior that a person learns,* 16

    to personality, 421, 433–436, 439, 443, 508

    to psychological disorders, 459, 461, 470, 473, 479–480, 508

Social cognitive neuroscience, 582–583

Social comparison *Using other people as a basis of comparison for evaluating oneself,* 540–541

Recent Research Citations (2006) in *Essentials of Psychology,* Fourth Edition

Following is a brief tabbing guide for Recent Research Citations. Please visit the *Online Teaching Center* for this text at **college.hmco.com/pic/bernsteinessentials4e** to access the full-length tabbing guide.

*Indicates material in Chapter 15 on Industrial/Organizational Psychology or Chapter 16 on Neuropsychology—available for inclusion in your textbook upon request. Please consult your sales representative for details.

Bandura, A. (2006). Toward a psychology of human agency. *Perspectives on Psychological Science, 1,* 164–180. (Ch. 11)

Brinkhaus, B., Witt, C. M., Jena, S., Linde, K., Streng, A., Wagenpfeil, S., et al. (2006). Acupuncture in patients with chronic low back pain: A randomized controlled trial. *Archives of Internal Medicine, 166,* 450–457. (Ch. 3)

Deeprose, C., & Andrade, J. (2006). Is priming during anesthesia unconscious? *Consciousness and Cognition, 15,* 1–23. (Ch. 4)

Dijksterhuis, A., & Nordgren, L. F. (2006). A theory of unconscious thought. *Perspectives on Psychological Science, 1,* 95–109. (Ch. 4)

Eisenberg, N., Fabes, R. A.., & Spinrad, T. L. (2006). Prosocial development. In W. Damon & R. M. Lerner (Series Eds.) & N. Eisenberg (Vol. Ed.), *Handbook of child psychology: Vol. 3. Social, emotional, and personality development* (6th ed.). New York: Wiley. (Ch. 9)

*Heiss, W. D., & Teasel, R. W. (2006). Brain recovery and rehabilitation. *Stroke, 37*(2), 314–316. (Ch. 16)

Holtmaat, A., Wilbrecht, L., Knott, G. W., Welker, E., & Svoboda, K. (2006). Experience-dependent and cell-type-specific spine growth in the neocortex. *Nature, 441,* 979–983. (Ch. 2)

Kahneman, D., Krueger, A. B., Schkade, D., Schwarz, N., & Stone, A. A. (2006). Would you be happier if you were richer? A focusing illusion. *Science, 312,* 1908–1910. (Ch. 8)

Kaptchuk, T. J., Stason, W. B., Legedza, A. R. T., Schnyer, R. N., Kerr, C. E., Stone, D. A., et al. (2006). Sham device vs. inert pill: Randomised controlled trial of two placebo treatments. *British Medical Journal, 332,* 391–397. (Ch. 3)

Keogh, E., Bond, F.W., & Flaxman, P. E. (2006). Improving academic performance and mental health through a stress management intervention: Outcomes and mediators of change. *Behaviour Research and Therapy, 44,* 339–357. (Ch. 10)

Kessler, R. C., Adler, L., Barkley, R., Biederman, J., Conners, C. K., Demler, O., et al. (2006). The prevalence and correlates of adult ADHD in the United States: Results from the National Comorbidity Survey Replication. *American Journal of Psychiatry, 163,* 716–723. (Ch. 12)

*Lapierre, L. M., & Allen, T. D. (2006).Work-supportive family, family-supportive supervision, use of organizational benefits, and problem-focused coping: Implications for work-family conflict and employee well-being. *Journal of Occupational Health Psychology, 11,* 169–181. (Ch. 15)

Loos, R. J. F., Rankinen, T., Chagnon, Y., Tremblay, A., Pérusse, L., & Bouchard, C. (2006). Polymorphisms in the leptin and leptin receptor genes in relation to resting metabolic rate and respiratory quotient in the Québec Family Study. *International Journal of Obesity, 30,* 183–190. (Ch. 8)

Lubinski, D., Benbow, C. P., Webb, R. M., & Bleske-Rechek, A. (2006). Tracking exceptional human capital over two decades. *Psychological Science, 17*(3), 194–199. (Ch. 7)

McDermott, K. B., & Chan, J. C. K. (2006). Effects of repetition on memory for pragmatic inferences. *Memory and Cognition.* (Ch. 6)

Mineka, S., & Zinbarg, R. (2006). A contemporary learning theory perspective on the etiology of anxiety disorders: It's not what you thought it was. *American Psychologist, 61,* 10–26. (Ch. 12)

Miyamoto, Y., Nisbett, R. E., & Masuda, T. (2006). Culture and the physical environment: Holistic versus analytic perceptual affordances. *Psychological Science, 17,* 113–119. (Ch. 1)

Pashler, H., Rohrer, D., & Cepeda, N. J. (2006). Temporal spacing and learning. *APS Observer, 19,* 30, 38. (Ch. 5)

Roediger, H. L., III, McDaniel, M., & McDermott, K. (2006). Test enhanced learning. *APS Observer, 19,* 28. (Ch. 5)

Rogers, M. R., & Molina, L. E. (2006). Exemplary efforts in psychology to recruit and retain graduate students of color. *American Psychologist, 61,* 143–156. (Ch. 13)

Russell, M. C. (2006). Treating combat-related stress disorders: A multiple case study utilizing eye movement desensitization and reprocessing (EMDR) with battlefield casualties from the Iraqi War. *Military Psychology, 18,* 1–18. (Ch. 1)

Shapiro, K. A., Moo, L. R., & Caramazza, A. (2006). Cortical signatures of noun and verb production. *Proceedings of the National Academy of Sciences of the USA, 103,* 1644–1649. (Ch. 2)

Siegler, R. S. (2006). Microgenetic analysis of learning. In W. Damon & R. M. Lerner (Series Eds.) & D. Kuhn & R. Siegler (Vol. Eds.), *Handbook of child psychology: Vol. 2. Cognition, perception, and language* (6th ed.). New York: Wiley. (Ch. 9)

Snyder, C. R., & Lopez, S. J. (2006). *Handbook of positive psychology.* New York: Oxford University Press. (Ch. 1)

Suslow, T., Ohrmann, P., Bauer, J., Rauch, A. V., Schwindt, W., Arolt, V., et al. (2006). Amygdala activation during masked presentation of emotional faces predicts conscious detection of threat-related faces. *Brain and Cognition, 61,* 243–248. (Ch. 8)

*Tabert, M. H., Manly, J. J., Liu, X., Pelton, G. H., Rosenbaum, S., Jacobs, M., et al. (2006). Neuropsychological prediction of conversion to Alzheimer disease in patients with mild cognitive impairment. *Archives of General Psychiatry, 63,* 916–924. (Ch. 16)

Takashima, A., Petersson, K. M., Rutters, F., Tendolkar, I., Jensen, O., Zwarts, M. J., et al. (2006). Declarative memory consolidation in humans: A prospective functional magnetic resonance imaging study. *Proceedings of the National Academy of Sciences of the USA, 103,* 756–761. (Ch. 6)

Turkington, D., Kingdon, D., & Weiden, P. J. (2006). Cognitive therapy for schizophrenia. *American Journal of Psychiatry, 163,* 365–373. (Ch. 13)

Vignoles, V. L., Regalia, C., Manzi, C., Golledge, J., & Scabini, E. (2006). Beyond self-esteem: Influence of multiple motives on identity construction. *Journal of Personality and Social Psychology, 90,* 308–333. (Ch. 14)

Weiss, A., King, J. E., & Perkins, L. (2006). Personality and subjective well-being in orangutans (*pongo pygmaeus and pongo abelii*). *Journal of Personality and Social Psychology, 90,* 501–511. (Ch. 11)

Williams, R. J., & Connolly, D. (2006). Does learning about the mathematics of gambling change gambling behavior? *Psychology of Addictive Behavior, 20,* 62–68. (Ch. 7)

ESSENTIALS *of* PSYCHOL...

Essentials of Psychology challenges you to "learn by doing"—to *actively participate* using materials from the text and to *think about* what you are doing as opposed to passively receiving written information.

So that you succeed in your introductory psychology course, each chapter of the text provides lots of ways to help you learn:

- Chapter Outlines
- Preview Questions
- Margin Glossaries
- Instructional Captions

- In Review Charts
- Diagrams
- Multiple-Choice Self-Tests
- Chapter Summaries

- Recommendations for Further Reading
- Thinking Critically Sections
- Focus on Research Sections
- Linkages Sections

AND THERE'S MORE...

The Online Study Center at **college.hmco.com/pic/ bernsteinessentials4e** contains additional study aids designed to help you get a better grade:

- **Active Learning and Critical Thinking** booklets provide fun and interesting exercises that help you apply key concepts to your own experiences and develop important, critical thinking skills.

- **Interactive Tutorials** walk you through some of the more difficult concepts in the text by bringing them to life through creative scenarios, simulated research, and video. Accompanying quizzes test your understanding of the material.

- **Online Concept Maps** provide a visual way to see how topics are interrelated.

- **Study Skills Video Modules** combine video clips featuring discussions with students, instructors, and experts designed to give you a fully engaging learning experience.

A passkey may be required to access some of the content at the Online Study Center.

The **Study Guide** (ISBN-10: 0-618-82431-6, ISBN-13: 978-0-618-82431-1), written by Kelly Bouas Henry (Missouri Western State College) and Douglas A. Bernstein, augments the Active Review study materials built into every chapter of the textbook. It provides tips on developing critical thinking skills, reading a textbook, and developing writing skills. For each chapter of the text, the guide includes learning objectives, key term hints and examples, a Concepts and Exercises section that shows you how to apply your knowledge of psychology to everyday issues and concerns, a Critical Thinking exercise, and several Personal Learning Activities. A section of each chapter, called "What Should I Write About?," provides advice on how to choose an appropriate term paper topic related to the chapter. Finally, each chapter concludes with two multiple-choice quizzes and a self-diagnostic quiz analysis to pinpoint which topics you may need to review.

ABOUT THE AUTHORS

Doug Bernstein is Professor Emeritus at the University of Illinois, Urbana-Champaign, where he served for many years as director of the introductory psychology program. He is currently Courtesy Professor of psychology at the University of South Florida, and a visiting professor of psychology at the University of Southampton. He also chairs the program committee of the National Institute on the Teaching of Psychology (NITOP), and is the Founder of the American Psychological Society's preconference Institute on the Teaching of Psychology. In 2002 he received the American Psychological Foundation's award for Distinguished Teaching in Psychology. He is the lead author of *Psychology*, Seventh Edition (Houghton Mifflin, © 2006).

Peggy Nash is an award-winning community college professor at Broward Community College.

We welcome feedback about Bernstein/Nash, Essentials of Psychology, *Fourth Edition. Please contact College Marketing, Houghton Mifflin Company, 222 Berkeley Street, Boston, MA 02116-3764.*

HOUGHTON MIFFLIN

New Ways to Know ®

ISBN-13: 978-0-618-71312-7
ISBN-10: 0-618-71312-3

9 780618 713127

90000

3-0444